THE ENCYCLOPEDIA OF
JEWISH LIFE
Before and During the Holocaust

Editor in Chief **Shmuel Spector**

Consulting Editor **Geoffrey Wigoder**

Foreword by **Elie Wiesel**

Volume II
K – Sered

YAD VASHEM
Jerusalem

NEW YORK UNIVERSITY PRESS

Washington Square, New York

These three volumes are an abridgment of the multi-volume Encyclopedia of Jewish Communities published in Hebrew by Yad Vashem.

The publication was supported by a grant of the Memorial Foundation for Jewish Culture.

Foreword by Elie Wiesel translated from the French by Fred Skolnik

First pubished in the U.S.A. in 2001 by
NEW YORK UNIVERSITY PRESS
Washington Square
New York, NY 10003
www.nyupress.nyu.edu

Library of Congress Cataloging-in-Publication Data
The Encyclopedia of Jewish life before and during the Holocaust / edited by Shmuel Spector, consulting editor: Geoffrey Wigoder; foreword by Elie Wiesel
p.cm.
Three-volume set: ISBN 0-8147-9356-8 (cloth)
Volume I: ISBN 0-8147-9376-2 (cloth)
Volume II: ISBN 0-8147-9377-0 (cloth)
Volume III: ISBN 0-8147-9378-9 (cloth)
1. Jews–Europe–History–Encyclopedias. 2. Jews–Africa, North–Encyclopedias.
3. Holocaust, Jewish (1939–1945)–Encyclopedias. 4. Europe–History, Local.
5. Africa, North–History, Local. I. Spector, Shmuel. II. Wigoder, Geoffrey, 1922–1999
DS135.E8 E45 2001
940'.04924–dc21 2001030071

Prepared, edited and produced by The Jerusalem Publishing House,
39 Tchernichovski Street, Jerusalem, Israel.

Printed in China

KABA Hajdu dist., Hungary. Jews settled in the early 19th cent., numbering 195 in 1880 and 314 in 1930. A cemetery was opened in 1865, a synagogue in 1886, and a J. school in 1906. The Jews were brought to Nadudvar in May 1944 and after a month sent to the Debrecen ghetto, from where they were deported to Auschwitz in the beginning of July 1944.

Some were sent to Bergen-Belsen concentration camp via Austria. Twenty-five survivors reestablished the community but gradually most left.

KADAN Bohemia (Sudetenland), Czechoslovakia. Jews are mentioned in the first half of the 14th cent. On the death of the local ruler and their protector, Jo-

Members of tennis team, Kaba, Hungary, 1927

hann von Lobkowitz-Hassenstein, in 1517, the Jews were expelled, returning only in 1624. They were again expelled in 1650 following a blood libel. A new community was constituted in 1874 and a synagogue consecrated in 1890, the J. pop. reaching a peak of 219 in 1921 and then dropping to 116 (total 8,641) in 1930. The Jews left the city in 1938 after the annexation of the Sudetenland to the German Reich. Some managed to emigrate while most of those remaining in the Protectorate were deported to the Theresienstadt ghetto and then to the death camps of Poland. Few survived.

KADARKUT Somogy dist., Hungary. Jews arrived in the late 18th cent, trading mainly in grain. In 1830 they numbered 69. Good relations prevailed with their Protestant neighbors during the White Terror (1918–21) and even after the German occupation in 1944. In May, the Jews were sent to Kaposvar and in early July they were deported to Auschwitz.

KADINO Smolensk dist., Russia. J. settlement probably commenced in the 17th cent. In 1766, the J. pop. included 60 poll tax payers. The J. pop. increased to 466 in 1847 and 603 (total 1,148) in 1897. In the 1920s, there was a J. rural council (soviet) and about 40 J. families earned their livelihoods in agriculture. The few Jews who had neither been evacuated nor fled were murdered after the arrival of the Germans in late summer 1941.

KADIYEVKA see SERGO

KADZIDLO Bialystok dist., Poland. The J. settlement began in the early 19th cent. when seven J. artisans and their families were brought to the village by its proprietor. In 1921 the J. pop. was 133 (of a total 915). The fate of the Jews under the German occupation of Sept. 1939 is unknown.

KAGANOVICHI-KHABNOYE Kiev dist., Ukraine. Jews numbered 80 in 1765 and 1,721 in 1897. In March 1918, they were attacked by Anton Denikin's White Army troops and on 30 July 1919 by the Petlyura gangs. In the Soviet period, two Yiddish-language schools were opened and all artisans in the needle trade were Jews. In 1939 the J. pop. was 999. The Germans occupied K. on 22 Aug. 1941. On 13–15 Sept. they murdered 398 Jews in the local stadium.

In two additional *Aktions*, on 19 and 20 Nov., they murdered all the rest, together with those in mixed marriages.

KAGAROLIK Kiev dist., Ukraine. Jews numbered 21 in 1765 and 1,414 in 1897. In fall 1917, local villagers destroyed the J. cemetery and in Aug. 1919, Anton Denikin's White Army troops beat and robbed Jews. J. farmers in the settlement subsequently fled to Boguslav and Kiev. In the Soviet period, many Jews worked in a sugar refinery. In 1939, the J. pop. was 325. The Germans occupied K. on 3 Aug. 1941. In Sept. they murdered 72 Jews and by the end of the year nearly all were dead.

KAHOVKA Nikolaiev dist., Ukraine. Jews probably settled in the first half of the 19th cent. and numbered 3,003 (total 7,499) in 1897. In the early 20th cent., a *talmud torah*, a government J. school, and a private J. school were operating. The J. pop. dropped during the Soviet period, reaching 1,072 in 1939. A J. school including vocational training and boarding facilities was still in existence in the late 1920s. The Germans occupied K. on 1 Sept. 1939 and murdered about 100 Jews in the first week. On 16 Sept., 1,700 from K. and its environs were executed near the Dimitrov kolkhoz. A total of 2,000 Jews from the area were murdered during the German occupation.

KAIROUAN Kairouan dist., Tunisia. Jews are believed to have arrived from Egypt with the founding of the city in 670, invited there by the Umayyad caliph 'Abd al-Malik to give the new settlement a productive urban base. In the 9th–11th cents. the community was the most illustrious in the J. world, attracting J. merchants and scholars from the east and the west, including Eretz Israel, Babylonia, Persia, Moslem Spain (Andalusia), and southern Italy. In 919, the former exilarch Mar Ukba settled there. Jews lived in a separate quarter and engaged in extensive international trade as well as in land transactions and industrial production. Among J. artisans, jewelers and metalworkers were prominent. The community had an autonomous status, running its own rabbinical court. While its rabbis were in close contact with the academies of Sura and Pumbedita in Babylonia they exercised considerable independence in spiritual matters. The academy, or *beit midrash*, of K. was founded in the early ninth cent. and headed by a *resh kalla*. In the 10th cent., R.

Ukba and R. Yaakov bar Nissim ibn Shahin served in this capacity. In the 11th cent. the leadership of the Italian-born R. Hushi'el bar Elhanan and his son R. Hananel marked a transition from reliance on Babylonian scholars to a Palestinian orientation based more on the Jerusalem Talmud. In the mid-11th cent., R. Nissim, the son of R. Yaakov bar Nissim ibn Shahin, became prominent at the academy and was a teacher of Ibn Gabirol, the great J. Spanish poet. The secular head of the community bore the title of *nagid*. Other prominent figures were the physician R. Yitzhak bar Shelomo Yisraeli, born in Egypt in 850, and his student the philosopher and physician Dunash ibn Tamim. In addition to the *beit midrash* and rabbinical court, the community maintained an arbitration court for business disputes and various charitable institutions, including one for ransoming the many J. prisoners brought to the commercial city in the ongoing Moslem conquest. The community ended in the mid-11th cent. when Bedouin invaders destroyed the city. Surviving Jews fled to Mahdia, Tunis, Gabes, and Djerba. The fanatical Almohads subsequently declared K. a holy city and banned J. settlement. The modern J. community was founded in the late 19th cent. By 1895, 56 families were present. Some inhabited a J. quarter inside the walls of the city but the majority preferred to live in the new European quarter. For the most part they lived in straitened economic circumstances. A synagogue consecrated in 1916 became the center of community life. The status of K. as a holy city attracted fanatical Moslem groups and encouraged hostility to the Jews. On 27–28 Aug. 1917, Arab soldiers in the French army went on a rampage, attacking and robbing Jews. The frequency of anti-J. incidents caused many Jews to leave. The J. pop. thus dropped from 483 in 1909 to 226 (total 22,991) in 1936. Zionist activity commenced in 1919 with the formation of a Herut Zion group, which devoted itself to raising funds for Palestine. Later the Revisionists became prominent. In WWII, the period of Vichy rule passed in relative quiet. After the arrival of the Germans in Nov. 1942, J. property was confiscated (cars, furniture, jewelry, etc.) and the community was forced to provide the Axis forces with various supplies. Jews were also mobilized for forced labor. The city was liberated on 12 April 1943. After the war, Betar and the J. scout movement (UUJJ) operated branches, though fear of Arab reactions restrained Zionist activity. J. families began leaving for Tunis to improve their economic cir-

cumstances or prepare for emigration. Most Jews left for Israel, either after the establishment of the state or after Tunisia gained its independence in 1956.

KAISERSESCH Rhineland, Germany. According to the first available demographic evidence 13 Jews were living in K. in 1856, and by 1895, at its peak, the J. pop. numbered 52 (4% of the total). The community maintained a prayer room and a cemetery (1921). In 1925 there were 39 Jews in J. After the Nazi rise to power in 1933, many left for the U. S. On *Kristallnacht* (9–10 Nov. 1938), the prayer room was destroyed, J. homes were vandalized, and Jews were mistreated. The 16 remaining Jews were moved to a "J. house" and deported in 1942 to Nazi concentration camps.

KAISERSLAUTERN Palatinate, Germany. Jews are first mentioned in 1293. They were attacked and expelled from the city in the disturbances of 1349 and 1383 and in 1395 were permanently banned by the Palatinate elector, the future Rupert II. Only in 1798, under French aegis, were the Jews again allowed to settle with full civil rights. In the mid-19th cent., most Jews belonged to the middle class and were active in local life, joining the civil guard and serving on the municipal council. A synagogue was consecrated in 1848 and a J. school existed from 1837 to 1875, when all the city's parochial schools were consolidated into a single public school system. With the onset of industrial development in the 1860s, the J. pop. began to grow, rising from 108 in 1835 to 716 (total 26,323) in 1880. Jews opened a number of factories (cigars, soap, sewing machines, gaiters, leather, etc.). A bank and two department stores were also owned by Jews. By 1913, J. breadwinners included 88 merchants, 11 industrialists, three doctors, and seven lawyers and notary publics. Organized antisemitic incitement became prevalent in the 1880s. Antisemitic incidents, such as the desecration of the J. cemetery, also occurred during the late Weimar period (1925–33). In 1933, when the Nazis came to power, the J. pop. was 648. Jews were dismissed from jobs in the civil service. By 1937, as a result of Nazi boycott and other discriminatory measures, 21% of the Jews in K. became dependent on J. Winter Aid. In 1938, the community was forced to sell the synagogue to the municipality and the building was pulled down in Sept. 1938. In its place, the community received a room in a disused prison. By Oct. 1938, more than half the

Jews had left, the majority to the U.S. and Palestine. On *Kristallnacht* (9–10 Nov. 1938), 110 of 160 J. homes were vandalized as well as many stores; Torah scrolls were burned. About 50 J. men were sent to the Dachau concentration camp. Subsequently about 250 Jews left the city. In 1939, 90 remained. On 22 Oct. 1940, 48 were deported to the Gurs concentration camp. Others were deported through March 1945. In all, 76 perished in the Holocaust, including 36 in France and 20 in Auschwitz. A postwar community grew to 150 in the 1950s.

KAISIADORYS (Yid. Koshedar) Troki dist., Lithuania. Jews settled in K. shortly after it was founded in the second half of the 19th cent. The J. pop. in 1897 stood at 317 (38% of the total). By WWI the J. community had a synagogue, a modern *heder*, and a library. The Zionist movement won widespread support and children learned at a Tarbut school. The worsening economic situation caused many to emigrate to America, South Africa, Uruguay, and some to Palestine. By 1940, about 60 families remained in K. After the German invasion in June 1941, Lithuanian nationalists concentrated all J. men in a warehouse, sending the fit to forced labor. On 26 Aug. 1941 all were taken to nearby Vladikiskis and shot. The women and children were murdered later in a forest near K.

KAL Heves dist., Hungary. The J. pop. was 130 in 1930. The Jews were deported to Auschwitz via Egercsehi and Bagolyuk at the end of June 1944.

KALDENKIRCHEN Rhineland, Germany. The first Jew is mentioned in 1721–22. About 25 were present in the first half of the 19th cent. and 56 in 1868. A synagogue was consecrated in 1873. In the 1920s, two Jews were engaged in manufacturing cigars; the rest were mostly tradesmen. The community was affiliated to the Kempen congregation. On the eve of the Nazi rise to power in 1933, the J. pop. was 44. The synagogue was burned on *Kristallnacht* (9–10 Nov. 1938). By Feb. 1939, only 23 Jews were still living in the town. Six were deported to the Riga ghetto on 11 Dec. 1941 and three to the Theresienstadt ghetto on 25 July 1942, all but one perishing.

KALININ (until 1931, Tver) Kalinin dist., Russia. Jews settled in the mid-19th cent and numbered 454 in 1872 despite the official residence ban in the region.

In 1876, they built a synagogue. In 1897, the J. pop. was 711 (total 54,000), growing in the Soviet period to 1,443 in 1926 and 2,345 in 1939. The Germans captured K. on 17 Oct. 1941, murdering about 400 Jews. The rest apparently succeeded in escaping to Moscow before the Germans completed their occupation.

KALININDORF (I) Crimea, Russia, today Ukraine. Emigres from the interior of the Soviet Union founded K. in the 1920s as a J. agricultural settlement. In 1932, its J. pop. was 120. At first part of the J. county of Fraydorf, K. was attached to Larindorf in 1935. The Germans occupied K. in late Oct. 1941 and murdered the 36 Jews there in June 1942.

KALININDORF (II) Nikolaiev dist., Ukraine. K. was founded in 1790 as the first J. colony in the Ukraine. (Its original Hebrew name was Sede Menuha, i.e., "field of rest.") In 1897, the J. pop. was 1,786 (total 2,090). Most Jews were farmers with a few engaged in crafts. Under the Soviets, the J. pop. was 2,400 in 1926 and 1,879 (total 3,126) in 1939. On 22 March 1927, K. became the capital of the first J. Autonomous Region in the USSR. The region included 11 councils (soviets), eight of them J., and 49 settlements, 39 of them J. The J. pop. in the region was 15,833 (87% of the total) in 1927 and 7,717 (40%) in 1939. In the 1920s, K. had a J. elementary school (expanded to include the junior high school grades in the mid-1930s), a regional agricultural school, and a teachers' college. In the early 1930s, almost all J. children in K. and the region attended J. schools (about 2,000 students in 1932). A J. newspaper (*Kolvirt Emes*) was published in K. in the first half of the 1930s. The Germans captured K. on 27 Aug. 1941. On 17 Sept., 1,423 Jews were murdered. A few days later, Jews from other settlements in the region, such as Shterndorf and Judendorf, were murdered. More than 4,100 Jews were killed during the Nazi occupation.

KALINKOVICHI Polesie dist., Belorussia. The J. pop. was 108 in 1811 and 1,341 in 1897 in the all-J. town. A large number of Jews dealt in flour or worked as artisans. In March 1920, when the Polish army captured the town, the Jews were beaten and robbed. On 10 Nov. 1920, Balakhovich's troops staged a pogrom and murdered 32 Jews from K. and its environs. A J. elementary school opened in 1923 had 397 children

Two Jewish kolkhoz farmers examining seed, Kalinindorf, Ukraine

in 1930. Adult education classes were also available in a J. framework. In 1930, the authorities stripped 369 Jews of their rights, including the right to vote. In 1939, the J. pop. reached a figure of 3,386 (total 9,799). The Germans occupied the town on 22 Aug. 1941. On 22 Sept., the 700 Jews remaining there were murdered.

KALINOVKA Vinnitsa dist., Ukraine. Four Jews were present in 1765. In 1897, they numbered 1,052 (total 2,558). Jews were attacked in a pogrom in March 1919. In the Soviet period, a J. school operated until the early 1930s and a J. kolkhoz employing dozens of Jews was founded in 1924. In 1939, the J. pop. was 979. The Germans captured K. on 22 July 1941, concentrating the Jews in a ghetto. On 30 May (or July) 1942, 510 Jews were murdered outside the

town. The few dozen skilled workers kept alive were executed in late Aug.

KALINY (Hung. Alsokalinfalva) Carpatho-Russia, Czechoslovakia, today Ukraine. Jews probably settled in the first half of the 18th cent., numbering 25 in 1768 and 191 in 1880. At the end of WWI, Jews were attacked in a pogrom. One was murdered and there was extensive looting. The J. pop. rose to 394 in 1930 and 497 (total 2,851) in 1941. A few J. families farmed. The Zionist and religious parties were active. The Hungarians arrived in March 1939 and in 1941 drafted dozens of Jews into labor battalions, sending them to forced labor camps. In late July, many were expelled to the Stanislawow ghetto in Galicia and in the second half of May 1944 those left behind were deported to Auschwitz.

KALISZ   Lodz dist., Poland. Jews persecuted by the Crusaders in Germany settled in K. in 1139 and in 1264, Boleslav the Pious granted them rights to settle and engage in moneylending and commerce. This "Statute of K.," endorsed and expanded by King Casimir the Great in 1364, served as the legal basis for J. rights in Poland over many generations. In the mid-14th cent., permission was granted for the construction of a synagogue. During the 15th to 17th cents. Jews were persecuted, murdered (600 in 1655–59), and the community almost annihilated, but J. families continued to live there. In 1793 a fire burned down all the 100 houses (of a total of 423) owned by Jews. During the Polish revolt in 1830–31, Jews were conscripted into the National Guard and were heavily taxed. In summer 1878, peasants attacked the Jews, killing 13 and injuring many more. Jews who did not hold Russian citizenship were expelled in 1881, and at the beginning of WWI, 33 Jews were murdered by German troops. The J. pop. in 1897 was 7,580 (32% of the total). Jews made a major contribution to the economy of K. and in the time of Prince Mieshko the Elder (1173–1209) coins were minted with Hebrew inscriptions. They engaged in trade with foreign markets, importing perfumes and spices from the Orient and exporting farm crops, wool, furs, and wax. The majority of the community were craftsmen. K. became famous for its lace and in 1904, 25 factories and 400 workshops with 3,886 employees (2,038 Jews) were producing lace products. The Jews also played a leading role in the establishment of factories, especially in textiles. In 1893, two great synagogues and 38 prayer houses existed. Prior to WWI, Zionist and Mizrachi synagogues were built, and in 1911 a synagogue was built in a West. European style by members of the German J. community. The K. community was served by a number of famous rabbis and the first yeshiva was opened in the late 17th cent. by R. Yisrael Shapira, known as "the preacher." During the late 19th cent. the Gur Hasidim were the strongest sect in K. In 1898, Zionist activity began, and in 1900 a branch of the Bund was founded. Prior to WWI, 1,800 J. children were receiving

Pharmacy in Skalmierzyce Nowe (near Kalisz), Poland, c. 1912

an Orthodox education. In 1913, a J. bilingual high school was founded, closed during WWI and reopened in 1920. In two schools the language of instruction was Yiddish. After the war, Jews constituted 45% of the salaried workers in K. and in 1921 Jews owned 547 factories and workshops—including 34 brick kilns. K. still led in the lace industry, even though the Russian market had been closed to it. Between the World Wars, Agudat Israel controlled the community council. The community's rabbi over a period of 25 years, R.Yehezkiel Lifshitz, died in 1932. He served as president of the Polish Rabbinical Association, was an ardent supporter of Zionism, and represented unaffiliated Orthodox Jewry on the J. Agency presidium. The community's last rabbi, R. Yehuda Ayeh Levin of Gur, also served as president of the Rabbinical Association. Economic difficulties and the rise of antisemitism in this period caused 345 Jews to emigrate in 1929, and the community continued to decline up to the outbreak of WWII. The J. pop. in 1931 was 15,300 (28% of the total). Zionist youth groups were active and members trained for pioneer life in Palestine and eventually joined settlements there. Yiddish daily newspapers, weeklies, and periodicals were published up to the outbreak of WWII. Among the literary personalities in K. was the Yiddish poet Rosa Jacobson, who died in the Warsaw ghetto in 1942. The novels of Shimon Horonski described community life under German occupation in WWI, especially of the J. working class. A wind instrument ensemble was established in 1921 and a symphony orchestra in the 1930s. In the 1920s, the Yiddish poet Moshe Broderson organized a small theater troupe which presented his plays. A branch of YIVO was opened by a group of youth interested in J. folklore. A non-affiliated organization with 250 members ran sports competitions. Between the World Wars K. became a center of the antisemitic press, and antisemites attacked Jews transporting their goods to fairs. In 1937 the Jews were forced to sell their wares in a separate section of the marketplace, and their stalls were boycotted by Poles. The J. community opened many welfare institutions to aid the needy. Eleven Jews were elected to the municipal council in 1939.

The majority of the inhabitants of K. fled the city when war broke out. About 20% of the J. pop. did not return; those who did were rounded up, tortured, and humiliated. A *Judenrat* was set up on 15 Oct. 1939 and the census it was ordered to hold revealed that the J. pop. numbered 18,000. In Nov. refugees from the Poznan area reached K. on their way east, and the local community assisted them. On 20 Nov. 1939, 10,000 Jews were rounded up and forced to live under appalling conditions in the halls of the marketplace. After being imprisoned for a few weeks, they were deported to various towns in the General Gouvernement area. The Germans continued to round up the Jews of K. and deport them; by the end of 1939 only 600 remained in a ghetto. Workshops were organized and they produced goods for the Germans. On 27–30 Oct. 1940, 250 of the sick and handicapped and those defined as unfit for labor were deported to an unknown destination. On 18 Nov. another 127 suffered the same fate. The last 140 Jews were transported to the Lodz ghetto. A few survivors returned after the war and in 1946 numbered 290, but gradually all left.

KALKAR Rhineland, Germany. Jews were living in K. in the 14th cent., while the origins of the modern community date back to 1620. The small community's J. pop. peaked in 1909 at 98. It maintained a synagogue from 1826, a school closed in 1927, and a cemetery dating from the 18th cent. In June 1933, some four months after the Nazi assumption of power, there were 62 Jews in K. On *Kristallnacht* (9–10 Nov. 1938), the synagogue was burned down and J. businesses were wrecked. Forty Jews emigrated, 34 to Holland. Seven died in K. and eight went to old age homes in Essen and Rheydt. Seven Jews were deported directly from K. Altogether, at least 22 K. Jews perished in the camps, including those who had emigrated to Holland and those who went to the old age homes.

KALL Rhineland, Germany. The community, one of the oldest in the Schleiden region, maintained a synagogue and cemetery. The J. pop. was about two dozen from the mid-19th cent. and on the eve of the Nazi rise to power it reached 34. Some emigrated and 15 were deported in 1942.

KALLIES (Pol. Kalisz Pomorski) Pomerania, Germany, today Poland. Three J. families were living in K. in 1770. The J. pop. was 164 individuals in 1843 and 43 in 1898 after migration to larger towns. The community maintained a synagogue and a cemetery which was desecrated in 1926. When the Nazis came to power in 1933, there were 26 Jews in K. No further information is available about their fate during Nazi rule.

KALLOSEMJEN   Szabolcs dist., Hungary. Jews arrived in the mid-18th cent., at the invitation of estate owners to market local produce. In time, many Jews became farmers. They numbered 167 in 1880 and 112 in 1931. The community supported a synagogue, *heder*, and *talmud torah*. Jews were attacked in the aftermath of WWI and at the outset of WWII sent on forced labor to the Ukraine, where many perished. The last 100 Jews were deported to Auschwitz in late May 1944 after being detained at Nyiregyhaza and Nyirjespuszta.

KALNIBOLOTA   Kirovograd dist., Ukraine. Jews probably settled in the first half of the 19th cent., numbering 588 (total 4,992) in 1897 and 191 in 1926, with many possibly leaving because of economic conditions. After their arrival around the end of July 1941, the Germans murdered those Jews who had neither fled nor been evacuated.

KALNIK   (Hung. Beregsarret) Carpatho-Russia, Czechoslovakia, today Ukraine. J. settlement commenced in the early 19th cent. The J. pop. was 17 in 1830 and 212 (total 879) in 1880, rising to 255 in 1921 under the Czechoslovakians and 285 in 1941 A number of J. families were employed on a local farm. The Hungarians occupied K. in March 1939 and in 1941 drafted a few dozen J. men into labor battalions for forced labor on the eastern front. The last 190 or so Jews were deported to Auschwitz in May 1944.

KALOCSA   Pest–Pilis–Solt–Kiskun dist., Hungary. Due to Catholic Church opposition, an organized community only existed from 1853, forming a Neologist congregation in 1869 and reaching a peak pop. of 973 (6% of the total) in 1900. A. J. school was founded in 1842 and a synagogue in 1861. Five Jews were murdered in the White Terror (1919–21) and others perished under forced labor from 1942. In 1941, 360 Jews remained. In late May 1944, they were confined in a ghetto with Jews from nearby settlements. All were deported to Auschwitz at the end of June.

KALTINENAI   (Yid. Kaltinan) Taurage dist., Lithuania. Jews first settled in the middle of the 19th cent. There were 15–20 J. families in 1940. After the German invasion in June 1941, the J. men were taken to the Heydekrug labor camp. On 2 July 1943, they were transferred to Auschwitz. After a selection in which 100 men were killed, the rest were sent to work in the Warsaw ghetto and then transferred in summer 1944 to the Dachau concentration camp. There were no survivors. The women and children were killed at the Tubiniai forest on 16 Sept. 1941.

KALUGA   Tula dist., Russia. Jews probably settled toward the mid-19th cent. In 1858, most of the 658 Jews in the region lived in K. Many were demobilized soldiers or artisans. In 1902, the government authorized the erection of a synagogue. The J. pop. was 763 in 1897 and 833 in 1926 under the Soviets. The Germans captured K. in Oct. 1941, occupying it until it was liberated by the Red Army two months later. The Germans transferred the 150 J. families there to a ghetto in the neighboring settlement, instituting a regime of forced labor. J. hostages were held and 13 of them murdered. On 22 Dec. 1941, the houses in the settlement were put to the torch and 500 Jews from K. and its environs executed.

KALUS   Kamenets-Podolski dist., Ukraine. Jews numbered 30 in 1765 and 1,897 (62% of the total) in 1897. A J. printing press was founded in the early 19th cent. In April 1920 Cossacks attacked the Jews. In the Soviet period a J. council (soviet) was active and the J. pop. dropped to 1,192 in 1926. The Germans arrived in mid-July 1941, executing 240 Jews on 19–21 Aug. 1942. By Sept., a total of 540 had been killed.

KALUSKA WOLA   Warsaw dist., Poland. The J. pop. in 1921 was 299 (total 604). All the Jews were deported by the Germans to the Treblinka death camp in fall 1942.

KALUSZ   Stanislawow dist., Poland, today Ukraine. J. settlement dates from the mid-16th cent. with leased salt mines a primary source of livelihood up through the 19th cent. The Jews also controlled the trade in grain, hides, fur, clothing, and lumber. A fire destroyed 200 J. homes in 1905 and economic prosperity was curtailed by the failure of J. banks in 1912 and 1913 and the devastation of WWI, which left the Jews with 200 widows, 400 orphans, and nearly 250 destroyed homes. The J. pop. dropped from the prewar high of 4,363 (half the total) to 3,121 in 1921. Many illustrious rabbis served the town and Zionists and assimilationists contended with one another from the turn of the cent. In 1938, some 200 pupils were studying Hebrew.

The arrival of the Germans in July 1941 brought persecution and forced labor. A group of intellectuals was executed in the forest in Aug.; hundreds more were murdered in Oct.; and by March 1942, starvation was taking a toll of 20 a day. Killings continued through the spring, when the Jews were enclosed in a ghetto. More were murdered in the streets during a three-day *Aktion* commencing on 26 Aug., when hundreds were taken to Stanislawow for deportation to Belzec. The remainder were expelled or murdered over the next two months.

KALUSZYN   Warsaw dist., Poland. A J. community is known from the early 18th cent., becoming independent in the 1760s when the J. pop. reached 566. Jews traded in forest products, manufactured and marketed alcoholic beverages, and practiced crafts. A few wealthy merchants dealt in metals. In the first half of the 19th cent., many artisans operated big shops and later in the cent. a flourishing prayer shawl industry developed, with three factories employing 400 workers. Jews were also army suppliers and many worked in the building trades. The J. pop. grew from 1,455 in 1827 to 6,419 (total 8,428) in 1897. Of the numerous hasidic sects active in the town, Warka Hasidism was prominent from the early 19th cent. In the late 19th cent., R. Moshe David of Kozienice maintained a hasidic court and K. was the seat of the Mogelnitza dynasty until WWII. In the early 20th cent., the Bund was highly influential among J. workers and artisans and its members participated in the revolutionary events of 1905. In the years preceeding WWI, a trend of emigration to the west set in, especially among the young. During WWI the Germans instituted heavy taxes and impounded J. property. In 1916 the Zionists opened a modern Hebrew school that later joined the Tarbut network. In the aftermath of WWI, Jews were murdered by General Haller's troops and Polish mobs. In 1921, the J. pop. was 5,033. Jews were able to maintain their hold on most of K.'s factories and workshops, organizing trade unions and mutual aid societies. The Zionists were represented by many groups but in the 1930s, as economic conditions deteriorated, the non-Zionist left-wing parties grew stronger. The Germans entered K. on 11 Sept. 1939 after a heavy bombardment, and proceeded to burn down most of the town. About 1,000 Jews died. Some joined in an unsuccccessful Polish counterattack. About 4,000 Jews were then crowded into the small section of the town left standing, sometimes 15–20 to a

room. In Nov. 1939 a *Judenrat* was appointed. A typhoid epidemic broke out in the winter when the Jews were subjected to persecution, looting, and forced labor. Many attempted to flee to Soviet-held territory. In late 1939, 1,000 J. refugees were brought in from Pabianice and Kalisz. A ghetto was established in summer 1940. All J. men were put to work repairing roads and bridges, using stone from the synagogue and J. cemetery. On 25 Nov 1942, about 3,000 Jews were deported to the Treblinka death camp. The ghetto was refilled with Jews from the labor camps in the vicinity. On 9 Dec. the 2,500 Jews there were also sent to Treblinka.

KALVARIJA   (Yid. Kalvarye), Marijampole dist., Lithuania. Jews first settled by the 17th cent., when K. was still the village of Trabi. Poverty led many to emigrate in the 1880s to the U.S. and South Africa. In addition to the *hadarim*, the community's educational system included a *talmud torah*, a general school, and a "national" school for needy children which taught Hebrew and J. history. The community also maintained several synagogues. The J. pop. in 1897 was 3,581 (38% of the total), dropping to 1,233 in 1923. During WWI most Jews left for Russia, many returning after the war. Between the World Wars, a J. community council ran the affairs of the community. Four Jews served on the municipal council, one becoming deputy mayor. Poor economic conditions, coupled with a boycott of J. businesses, led many to leave for the U.S., South Africa, and the larger Lithuanian cities. The Zionist movement enjoyed widespread support. On the eve of WWII, the J. pop. was 1,000. After the German invasion in June 1941, antisemitic decrees were issued and Jews were taken to forced labor. On 30 Aug. 1941, the Jews were brought to the Marijampole barracks and on 1 Sept. murdered together with Jews from surrounding villages, making about 8,600 killed in all.

KALWARIA ZEBRZYDOWSKA   Cracow dist., Poland. J. settlement was long discouraged by the existence of a Cistercian church and monastery deemed a holy site and attracting yearly pilgrimages. Jews numbered 486 in 1921 (of a total 1,692) and were active as contractors in the town's flourishing furniture industry, employing hundreds of non-J. carpenters and other workers. Many Jews also worked as carpenters. Growth was stymied by disturbances in 1898, when

Hebrew elementary school, Kalvarija, Lithuania

500 windows of J. homes were shattered by rioting peasants and all J. stores looted. There was further rioting in 1918 and 1919. Most of the Jews identified with Bobow and Zanz Hasidism. Zionist activity commenced between the World Wars. Jews fleeing the advancing Germans in Sept. 1939 returned shortly thereafter to find their homes destroyed and stores confiscated. Forced labor and restrictions ensued, reducing the Jews to bartering personal effects for food. About 100 young Jews were sent to the Plaszow concentration camp through summer 1942. Up to 1,000 Jews including refugees were expelled on 12 Aug. to Skawina, where they were murdered or deported to the Belzec death camp on 30 Aug. Some of the youth were active in the J. underground movement. In all, about 550 of the town's Jews died in the Holocaust.

KAMAJAI (Yid. Kamai) Rokiskis dist., Lithuania. Jews first settled in the 17th cent. During the 19th cent., although the Jews controlled commerce in the town and were its artisans, they remained poor. The J. pop. in 1897 was 944 (85% of the total). The community maintained a yeshiva and two synagogues.

During WWI, the ten families who remained in K. were sent to forced labor. Between the World Wars, the Jews' economic situation deteriorated. In addition to a *heder*, a Tarbut Hebrew school was established. The Zionist movement won widespread support and Hashomer Hatzair opened a branch. By 1939, the J. pop. had dropped to 60 families. After the German invasion in June 1941, the J. men were transferred to Rokiskis and the women and children to Obeliai. Between 15–27 Aug., all were killed near Obeliai together with the rest of the Jews from the district.

KAMEN (I) Vitebsk dist., Belorussia. Jews numbered 38 in 1811 and 826 (77.5% of the total) in 1897. In 1926, under the Soviets, the J. pop. dropped to 426. Sixteen J. families were employed at a nearby kolkhoz in 1930. The Germans occupied K. in July 1941. Though forced to wear the yellow badge, the Jews continued to live in their own homes and work at the kolkhoz. On 17 Sept. the remaining 177 Jews who had not fled or been evacuated were murdered near the village of Borki.

KAMEN (II) Westphalia, Germany. Jews are mentioned in 1348 and 1403. The modern community began in the 18th century. It maintained a synagogue (mentioned in 1767 and replaced by a new building in 1901) and a cemetery (opened in 1800). The J. pop. reached 130 (total 3,728) in 1871 and dropped from 120 in 1928 to 62 (total 12,390) in 1933. On *Kristallnacht* (9–10 Nov. 1938), the synagogue was burned and the J. cemetery vandalized. Fourteen local Jews perished in the Holocaust.

KAMENETS-PODOLSKI Kamenets-Podolski dist., Ukraine. Jews are first mentioned in 1447. About 10,000 Jews sought refuge in the local fortress during the Chmielnicki massacres of 1648–49. In 1725, the Council of the Four Lands met in K. and in 1750 the Jews were expelled at the demand of local residents. During the 17th and 18th cents., Shabbateanism and the Frankist movement made inroads and in 1757 a public disputation was held between rabbis and anti-talmudic Frankists. Subsequently, the bishop ordered 1,000 copies of the Talmud burned. In 1789, the J. pop. was 286, growing to 16,211 (40% of the total) in 1897. Jews earned their livelihoods in light industry, petty trade, and crafts. A credit society provided assistance. Most Jews were Hasidim (Sadagora, Boyan, Chortkov). Among the rabbis of K. were Pinhas of Koretz and David Wahrmann, a student of R. Levi Yitzhak of Berdichev and author of halakhic works. Mendele Mokher Seforim was active in the city at the turn of the 19th cent, as were Menahem Poznansky and the poets Aharon Ashman, Shelomo Sheffen, and Avraham Rosen. Baron de Ginzburg, son of Baron Naftali Hertz Ginzburg, was born in K. in 1857, as was Prof. Fishel Schneersohn. In 1910, the J. pop. reached 22,279. Four private schools and two modernized *hadarim* were opened in the early 20th cent. The Bund, Tze'irei Tziyyon, and Po'alei Zion all became active and two Hebrew schools and a library were founded. Hehalutz started operating in 1920. In 1919, during the Russian civil war, the Petlyura gangs murdered 200 Jews. In 1922, ORT opened a number of vocational schools for J. youth. Eighty J. families left the city to settle in Birobidzhan and 76 to settle in the Crimea. The synagogue and most prayer houses operated until 1936, but Zionist activity was halted completely in 1928 and the Hebrew schools were closed down. Three Yiddish schools were opened along with two teachers' colleges. Only one Yiddish school remained active in 1938. In 1939, the J. pop. was 13,796. The Germans

captured the city on 11 July 1941. A ghetto was established on 20 July with 11,000 Jews from Hungary as well Jews from Czechoslovakia and Poland brought there at the end of the month. On 25–28 Aug., 23,600 Jews were murdered, including the refugees. Skilled workers were concentrated in a labor camp inside the ghetto, joined by others from neighboring towns. In Jan. 1942, 4,000 were executed and in late 1942, the Nazis murdered 500 children aged 4–8. Another 2,500 Jews were executed in Jan. 1943 and 2,000 in Feb. Few escaped. A community of 1,800 Jews was present in 1979.

KAMENKA (I) Moldavia, today Republic of Moldova. The J. pop. was 2,902 (total 6,746) in 1897, declining in the Soviet period to 1,864 in 1926 and 1,283 in 1939. A J. kolkhoz for 100 families existed in the 1930s. German and Rumanian forces captured K. in July 1941. On 23–25 July, 329 Jews were murdered. Under Rumanian administration, the remaining Jews in the area were confined in a ghetto. Each night during the winter of 1941–42, Rumanian gendarmes drowned groups of 20–30 Jews in the Dniester River, thus murdering over 1,000.

KAMENKA (II) Kirovograd dist., Ukraine. Jews settled in the first half of the 18th cent. or slightly thereafter and numbered 16 in 1764. In 1897, the J. pop. was 2,193 (total 6,267). In a pogrom on 6 Nov. 1917, two Jews were killed and seven injured. Denikin's White Army staged another pogrom in 1919. In the early 1920s, under the Soviets, many Jews grew and marketed tobacco. In 1922, there was a J. school with an enrollment of 60 children. The J. pop. declined to 618 in 1939. The Germans captured K. on 9 Aug. 1941 and in Dec. confined the Jews to a ghetto. In March 1942, 160 Jews were murdered. Another 150 were murdered in late 1942 at a site under local police control.

KAMENKA (III) Zaporozhe dist., Ukraine. The Germans murdered 31 Jews here in fall 1941.

KAMENNI-BROD Zhitomir dist., Ukraine. Small numbers of Jews resided in K. in the 18th cent., their pop. growing to 1,147 (of a total 1,773) in 1897. About 250 were murdered in a pogrom on 10 July 1919. In 1939, 857 remained. They were murdered by the Germans after their arrival on 8 July 1941.

KAMENSK-SHAKHTYNSKI Rostov dist., Russia. Jews probably settled in the early 20th cent. and numbered 197 (total 42,711) in 1939. After their arrival on 18 July 1942, the Germans murdered the few Jews who had neither fled nor been evacuated.

KAMIEN Lwow dist., Poland. The J. pop. in 1921 was 201 (total 4,703). The Jews were expelled by the Germans in Sept. 1939 to Soviet-held territory and were subsequently killed by the Germans in 1941–42.

KAMIENCZYK Warsaw dist., Poland. Small numbers of Jews lived in K. from the 16th cent. In 1921 there were 124 Jews (total 1,205). The Zionists and Agudat Israel were active after WWI. The Germans entered the town in Sept. 1939. The J. community was liquidated possibly in fall 1941.

KAMIENICA Silesia dist., Poland. The J. pop. in 1921 was 118. Most of the Jews died at Auschwitz in summer 1942.

KAMIENIEC LITEWSKI Polesie dist., Poland, today Belarus. Jews were present from the early 16th cent. and an organized community existed a century later. The J. pop. reached 2,722 (total 3,569) in 1897. In WWI, Russian and Hungarian soldiers successively pillaged the J. pop. and the Germans imposed forced labor from 1915, with many dying in a cholera epidemic. In 1921, the J. pop. stood at 1,902 (total 2,348). A yeshiva, Knesset Beit Yitzhak, which was transferred from Vilna in 1926, served hundreds of students from throughout Europe, but it dispersed in Sept. 1939 owing to the Soviet annexation. A few days after the German occupation of 22 June 1941, 100 Jews were murdered as alleged Communists. A third of the J. pop. was transferred to the Pruzhana ghetto in late 1941 and deported from there to Auschwitz in Feb. 1943. The others (450 families including refugees) were confined to a local ghetto and deported to the Treblinka death camp on 9 Nov. 1942.

KAMIEN KOSZYRSKI Volhynia dist., Poland, today Ukraine. Jews are first mentioned in 1569 and numbered 1,189 in 1897 (total 1,220). Most of their homes were destroyed by fire in 1904. Despite organized self-defense, 120 Jews were murdered by a roving gang in early 1921 and many left, leaving 617. Between the World Wars, petty trade and crafts prevailed,

most Jews peddling their wares and services in the villages. The Zionists and their youth movements were active and a Tarbut school was opened with an adjacent library becoming the center of J. cultural life. Antisemitism intensified in the 1930s and in 1937 local hooligans destroyed J. stores and broke windows in J. homes. The Soviet annexation of Sept. 1939 affected educational, communal, and economic life. On the Soviet departure in June 1941, the Ukrainians staged a pogrom. The Germans arrived on 2 Aug. 1941 and soon murdered 78 Jews. In June 1942, over 3,000 Jews including refugees were packed into a ghetto. On 10 Aug., all but 600 classified as skilled workers were executed. On 2 Nov. the ghetto was liquidated; 400 managed to escape. Half were killed later and 100 joined the partisans as had three smaller, organized groups that had escaped earlier.

KAMIENSK Lodz dist., Poland. Jews settled here in late 18th cent. The J. pop. was 781 in 1897 and 856 in 1921 (42% of the total). There were antisemitic outbursts, especially in July 1937. The town was destroyed almost completely in Sept. 1939, and half the 834 Jews escaped to neighboring villages. In Oct. 1942, about 500 Jews, including refugees, were deported to the Treblinka death camp.

KAMIONKA (I) Tarnopol dist., Poland, today Ukraine. The J. pop. in 1921 was 103. Many Jews were possibly murdered or fled in the Ukrainian pogroms of July 1941 with the rest sent to labor camps or expelled to Zbaraz or Skalat in Sept.–Oct. 1942.

KAMIONKA (II) Bialystok dist., Poland, today Belarus. Jews formed a majority in the late 19th cent. and numbered 326 (total 569) in 1921. Until the Polish government canceled their concession in 1929, Jews dominated the local tobacco industry. ORT helped 31 J. families develop vegetable farms instead. On 2 Nov. 1942, the Germans expelled the Jews to the Kelbasin transit camp near Grodno and from there to the Treblinka death camp.

KAMIONKA (III) Lublin dist., Poland. A few Jews were present in the late 15th cent. The growth of the community was curtailed by the Swedish invasion of the mid-17th cent., with most J. homes being burned and many Jews dying in an epidemic. Heavy taxes and local efforts to restrict J. commerce prevented recovery. Religious and public institutions developed towards the end of the 18th cent. A new synagogue was completed in 1855 as J. trade expanded into the neighboring villages. In 1921, the J. pop. was 556 (total 2,260). J. tailors were prominent, making cheap clothing which they peddled themselves. In 1939, the J. pop. was 434. The German occupation initiated a regime of persecution. A ghetto was established in 1942, its pop. swelled by deportees from Mlawa and Slovakia. Sources are unclear as to whether the Jews were deported to the Treblinka death camp on 8 Sept. or in Oct. 1942. A group of 12 escaped to join the Armia Ludowa partisans.

KAMIONKA STRUMILOWA Tarnopol dist., Poland, today Ukraine. Jews are first mentioned in 1456 and in the late 16th cent. received unrestricted residence and commercial rights. Jews dealt in cattle, salt, grain, lumber, and fish. They also worked as distillers. A devastating fire in 1913 and flight in WWI,

with many Jews never returning, brought the community's prosperity to an end as the pop. dropped from a prewar figure of 3,549 to 2,685 (total 6,518) in 1921. Zionist activity was extensive between the World Wars but all public life ended with the Soviet annexation in fall 1939. The Germans arrived on 28 June 1941, murdering 200 Jews the next day and encouraging a Ukrainian pogrom on 2 July that claimed hundreds more. On 10 Nov., 500 Jews were executed in the nearby forest. Many died from disease and starvation in the winter. In a mass *Aktion* on 15 Sept. 1942, 1,500 were deported to the Belzec death camp and on 21 Sept. another 600 were executed. The remaining Jews were deported on 28 Oct. and the local labor camp was liquidated by 10 July 1943.

KAMPEN Overijssel dist., Holland. Jews were present in the 14th cent. (until 1349–50) and again in the mid-17th cent. when Portuguese Jews received equal civil rights. This community soon disappeared

Elementary school class, Kamionka Strumilowa, Poland, c. 1930

and Jews were not found in K. until the early 18th cent. Ashkenazi Jews then settled and built a synagogue in 1771. The community developed significantly in the first half of the 19th cent. A J. school was opened in 1822, a larger synagogue was built in 1847, and a number of social welfare organizations were established. The J. pop. in 1876 was 499. The community dwindled from the early 20th cent. and in 1941 the J. pop. was 43 (total 20,935). In 1942, 39 Jews were deported and perished; four survived in hiding.

KAMYANKA Dnepropetrovsk dist., Ukraine. K. was founded as a J. colony in 1809 and numbered 75 families in 1815. The J. pop. was 767 (total 843) in 1897 and 767 in 1926. K. was attached to the Stalindorf J. Autonomous Region in 1930 and had a rural council (soviet) and J. elementary school. The Germans captured K. in mid-Aug. 1941. In late May 1942, the Jews of K. were murdered together with the Jews of the other J. settlements in the area, near the village of Zlatoustovka.

KAMYK Kielce dist., Poland. There were 27 J. families here in the early 19th cent. A synagogue was erected in 1882. In 1939 the J. pop. was 230. Some fled to Czenstochowa under the German occupation; others were seized for forced labor. The rest, primarily older people, women, and children, were deported to Auschwitz-Birkenau on 22 June 1942.

KANCZUGA Lwow dist., Poland. Jews were present from 1597 and maintained a community averaging 900–1,000 (40% of the total) from the second half of the 19th cent. Economic conditions deteriorated after WWI, but social and cultural life went on unabated with the Zionists and Agudat Israel prominent. The J. pop. in 1940 was 810 (including 80 refugees) The Germans expelled the community to the Pelkinia transit camp on 1 Aug. 1942 for selection: the old and weak were murdered in the forest, 150 of the young sent to labor camps, and the rest deported to the Belzec death camp. Thirteen survivors were murdered in spring 1945 (during Passover) by Polish nationalists.

KANDAVA (Ger. Kandau) Courland dist., Latvia. Jews settled shortly after the Russian annexation in 1795 and numbered around 1,000 (45% of the total) on the eve of WWI. Only a few dozen returned after ex-pulsion by the Russians in 1915, and had to be supported by the Joint Distribution Committee. The Germans arrived in July 1941 and murdered the J. pop. soon after. Probably some were taken to Tukums and burned to death inside the synagogue and others were killed at the cemetery in K.

KANIEW Kiev dist., Ukraine. Jews numbered 98 in 1765. In 1768, following attacks by the Haidamaks, not a single Jew remained in the town. In 1897, the J. pop. was 2,683. A few days after the outbreak of the Oct. 1917 Revolution, J. homes and stores were heavily damaged in anti-J. riots. In 1939, in the Soviet period, the J. pop. was 487. The Germans occupied K. on 16 Aug. 1941. All the Jews were concentrated in a single building under unbearable conditions while their property was pillaged. After two months they were brought to Korsun and executed.

KANTAKUZOVKA (after WWII, Pribuzhany) Odessa dist., Ukraine. Jews numbered 912 (total 2,132) in 1897 and 167 in 1926. A pogrom was staged on 14–16 April 1897. The Germans arrived in early Aug. 1941 and, probably in the fall, murdered the remaining Jews together with the Jews of the Voznesensk region.

KANTORJANOSI Szatmar dist., Hungary. Jews settled in the late 18th cent., mostly engaging in trade (groceries, woven goods, grain). They numbered 233 in 1880 and 213 in 1930. In WWII, 50 perished at forced labor. The rest were expelled to Mataszalka at the end of April 1944 and from there deported to Auschwitz on 15–16 May. Survivors reestablished the community, but by 1956 most had left.

KAPCIAMIESTIS (Yid. Koptsheve) Sejny dist., Lithuania. Jews probably first settled at the beginning of the 19th. The J. pop. in 1897 was 528 (40% of the total), dropping to about 45 families on the eve of WWII. Between the World Wars, the Gordonia movement enjoyed widespread support. After the German invasion in June 1941, all the Jews were transferred to the Katkiskes ghetto and were murdered on 3 Nov. 1941.

KAPLAVA Courland dist., Latvia. The J. pop. in 1935 was ten (total 155). Those remaining were murdered by the Germans after their arrival in July 1941.

KAPOLNASNYEK Fejer dist., Hungary. Jews from Buda settled in the early 19th cent., dealing in grain. They opened a school in 1820 and a synagogue in 1825, defining themselves as Neologist in 1869. In 1880, they numbered 92 and in 1930, 100. On 18 June 1944, they were deported to Auschwitz via Szekesfehervar.

KAPOSVAR Somogy dist., Hungary. The J. settlement began to develop in the mid-19th cent. Adolph Freistidler employed many fellow Jews on his estate and built a synagogue in 1862 and an orphanage at his own expense. The J. pop. numbered 1,078 in 1869 and 3,505 (9.2% of the total) in 1920. Jews owned five banks, 200 stores, numerous factories, and two newspapers. A. J. public school was opened in 1840 with a Neologist congregation formed in 1869. In 1941, 2,346 Jews remained. The men were seized for forced labor and, after the arrival of the Germans in March 1944, a ghetto was set up in May where 6,000 Jews, including those from surrounding settlements, were kept. All were deported to Auschwitz on 4 July.

KAPUVAR Sopron dist., Hungary. Jews arrived in K. to serve as customs agents on the Esterhazy estates in the early 18th cent. In the mid-19th cent., they marketed farm produce, mostly tobacco, to Austria. In 1869, the congregation became Status Quo, becoming Orthodox in 1897. The community maintained a synagogue, yeshiva, and J. public school. The J. pop. was 503 (6% of the total) in 1900 and 438 in 1941. On 5 July 1944, the Jews were deported to Auschwitz via Sopron. About 100 survivors reestablished the community, which gradually dispersed, with most coming to Israel after 1956.

KARACHEV Oriol dist., Russia. Jews probably arrived in the late 19th cent., numbering 306 (total 15,000) in 1897. In 1926, under the Soviets, their pop. rose to 552 and then dropped to 443 in 1939. The Germans occupied K. on 6 Oct. 1941. The few Jews who had neither fled nor been evacuated probably constituted the majority of the 245 residents from K. and its environs whom the Germans murdered.

KARAD Somogy dist., Hungary. A few Jews settled in the first half of the 18th cent. to market produce from Church-owned lands. They numbered 145 in 1880 and 83 in 1930. In late April 1944, they were brought to the Tab ghetto and on 3 July to Kaposvar. On 10 July, they were deported to Auschwitz.

KARASUBAZAR (from 1945, Belogorsk) Crimea, Russia, today Ukraine. A J. community existed in the 14th cent. The modern community was founded in the late 18th cent. and grew to 3,144 Ashkenazi and Krimchak Jews (total 13,000) in 1897. In 1939, under the Soviets, the J. pop. dropped to 429 with another few hundred Krimchak Jews. In 1932, three J. farm settlements in the county had a pop. of 149 J. families. The Germans arrived on 1 Nov. 1941. On 10 Dec. they murdered 76 Jews. On 17 Jan. 1942, 468 Krimchak Jews from K. and its environs were gassed in vans. The few remaining Jews were later shot.

KARBACH Lower Franconia, Germany. Jews are mentioned in 1726, with an organized community existing in the early 19th cent. and a synagogue dating from 1844. The J. pop. was 98 in 1867 (total 1,275) and 45 in 1933. Owing to generally good relations with the local pop., no Jews left until 1936. On *Kristallnacht* (9–10 Nov. 1938), the synagogue and J. homes were vandalized. Eleven Jews left in 1936–39 and 27 were deported to Izbica in the Lublin dist. (Poland) via Wuerzburg on 25 April 1942.

KARCAG Jasz–Nagykun–Szolnok dist., Hungary. Jews settled c. 1820 and reached a peak pop. of 1,077 (5% of the total) in 1910, with another 200 families from five surrounding settlements affiliated to the congregation. A J. school was opened in 1870 and a synagogue built in 1898. Po'alei Zion became active on the eve of WWI. In 1940, community leaders, including the rabbi, were accused of spying and tried. In 1941, the J. pop. was 778. In June 1944, Jews from K. and surrounding villages, all together 1300, were confined to a ghetto They were then brought to Szolnok and on 29 June deported to the Auschwitz and Bergen-Belsen concentration camps and to the Theresienstadt ghetto.

KARCZEW Warsaw dist., Poland. Jews settled in the early 16th cent. and engaged in the lumber trade, innkeeping, and crafts, including the manufacture of prayer shawls. The community grew rapidly

Main street of Karczew, Poland

in the 19th cent., reaching a peak pop. of 1,025 (total 2,861) in 1897. Many left for Warsaw in WWI. At the close of the war Jews were attacked by Polish mobs and General Haller's soldiers, their number dropping to 830 in 1921. Between the World Wars, Jews supplied kosher meat to Warsaw and J. shoemakers supplied boots to the Polish army. Many emigrated to Palestine and the west as antisemitism increased and economic conditions worsened. The Germans arrived in mid-Sept. 1939. A *Judenrat* was appointed under a regime of forced labor. A ghetto was established in Dec. 1940. A month later, when the Jews were transferred to Warsaw, a forced labor camp for 400 Jews, including some from K., was set up instead. Few survived it.

KARDITSA   Cardisas dist., Greece. In 1928, 49 Jews lived in K. (total pop. 13,883) but they had no community institutions. In WWII many refugees, primarily from Athens and Trikala, arrived in Italian-occupied K. bringing the J. pop. in 1940 up to 150. In Sept. 1943, the Germans took over. All the Jews

went into hiding with the assistance of Greek families and survived. Some returned after the war. The J. pop. of 51 in 1959 dwindled over the years.

KARLOVAC   (Ger. Karlstadt) Croatia, Yugoslavia, today Republic of Croatia. A J. community was established in 1852, although Jews had settled in K. prior to that date. Its jurisdiction covered many villages and towns in the region. In 1871 a synagogue was founded and in 1880 the number of Jews peaked at 905. During that period, the Jews were among the pioneers of industry in K. In the late 19th and early 20th cents., various social and cultural groups were instituted and continued to function until WWII. In 1911 a Zionist youth movement was established and Zionist activity increased from 1918, when a branch of the Zionist Organization was founded. Although J. life was vibrant at the end of the 1920s, many left for other towns; 21 converted to Christianity and half intermarried. In 1940 there were 198 Jews (total 22,153). Between May and Dec. 1941, the Nazis and Ustase arrested 171 Jews and murdered them in the Jadovno and Jasenovac death camps. Remaining Jews were deported to Stara Gradiska and elsewhere in 1943.

KARLOVY VARY   (Karlsbad) Bohemia (Sudetenland), Czechoslovakia. Despite a 350-year residence ban, there were 71 Jews present in K. in 1839. In 1857, a J. philanthropic organization in Prague established a sanatorium for needy Jews in K., the first of its kind. A community was officially formed in 1868, reaching a pop. of 1,069 (7.5% of the total) in 1890 and 2,115 in 1921. A Great Synagogue was consecrated in 1877. Dr. Ignatz Ziegler served as rabbi from 1888 to 1938 and was decorated by Francis Joseph. Many prominent Jews, including the Rothschilds, Hayyim Nahman Bialik, and contingents of Hasidim visited the local spa, which provided many Jews with a livelihood. The Zionists became active before WWI, making K. a center of their activity. During WWI, about 50 East European families formed an Orthodox congregation. All but four of the Jews left the city during the Sudetenland crisis of fall 1938. The Nazis razed the synagogue and destroyed J. stores and in 1942–45 deported 166 Jews from K. and the surrounding area to the Theresienstadt ghetto; 82 survived. The postwar community, including Marianske Lazne, numbered 971 in 1948, mostly refugees from Carpatho-Russia.

KARLSBAD   see KARLOVY VARY.

KARLSRUHE   Baden, Germany. Jews arrived with a promise of equal rights when the city was founded in 1715 as the new capital of Baden-Durlach. Among the settlers was Yosef Yaakov of Ettlingen, founder of the well-known Ettlingen family, and the Court Jew Immanuel Roettlinger. Under the count's

*Building where 13th Zionist Congress convened, Karlovy Vary (Karlsbad), Czechoslovakia, 1923. (*Top right: *emblem of Congress)*

Synagogue in Karlsruhe, Germany

general and personal letters of protection the community grew rapidly to 282 members in 1733. In 1724, Salomon Meier Wessel (d. 1774), son-in-law of the prominent Court Jew Marx Model of Pforzheim, was appointed community head (*parnas*), subsequently founding a yeshiva. With the publication of the edicts of Baden in 1807–09, most Jews were granted full civil rights and a Central Council (*Oberrat*) for Baden Jews was established in K. In 1806 a new synagogue was consecrated and in 1827 the city became the seat of the district rabbinate. A J. elementary school was opened in 1816, enrolling 100 children within a few years as the J. pop. grew steadily through the cent., rising from 893 in 1825 to 2,577 in 1900 (total 107,765). In addition to being the seat of J. institutions serving all of Baden, the community maintained a broad range of social and cultural activities, with the Central Union (C.V.) and B'nai B'rith imbuing the spirit of Liberalism. The Reform movement made its first in-

roads in 1819 when ten families formed a Temple Society on the Hamburg model and instituted Reform prayer. In 1869, after an organ was introduced into the synagogue, 24 Orthodox families founded an Adass Jeshurun congregation, with its own elementary school and the only J. kindergarten in Baden. After the split in the congregation, Dr. Meir Appel (1851–1919) became chief rabbi, serving also as chairman of the Association of Liberal German Rabbis from 1899. Among J. public figures the most prominent was Moritz Ellstaetter, Baden's minister of finance in 1878–93. In 1900, Dr. Nathan Stern was appointed to the Baden Supreme Court and in 1914 became president of the Mannheim District Court (the first Jew in Germany to hold such a position). The Seligmann factories employed 800 workers and other J. factories produced paper, synthetic wool, and malt and processed leather and metals. Jews were also leading wholesalers (felt, books) and from the 18th cent. operated Hebrew printing presses. They were also active in the professions and the arts. Hermann Levi was named Court Conductor in 1864. Prof. Richard Willstaetter won the Nobel Prize for Chemistry in 1915. Though Jews participated fully in public life, it was often in the face of antisemitism, with particular outbursts in the Hep! Hep! riots of 1819 and the revolutionary disturbances of 1848. After WWI the East European component of the community grew to 22%, constituting a lower economic class aided by the rest of the community. Many national conferences of J. organizations took place in K., including Zionist youth in 1932. The focus of the community's cultural life was the Bialik Lehrhaus for adult education, where lectures, courses, concerts, and exhibitions were held. In the Weimar period the Jews maintained their leading economic position. The Knopf chain of department stores had its main branch in K.; Jews owned four banks and 26% of the city's doctors and 40% of its lawyers were Jews. Dr. Ludwig Marum was Baden's minister of justice and K.'s representative in the Reichstag in 1928–32. In 1925 the community reached a peak pop. of 3,386, but from that point on the birthrate declined steeply and a trend of negative natural increase set in. Antisemitism intensified after WWI, with anti-J. food riots in 1920 and a swastika-painting outburst in 1926.

In 1933, there were 3,199 Jews in the city. The Liberals controlled the community council with 16 of 28 seats. The community maintained two old age homes and a hospital and operated numerous welfare services (societies for the distribution of food and fuel, for the support of widows, for assistance to the sick, etc.). With the onset of Nazi rule, judges, teachers, doctors, and officials were fired from the public service and J. businessmen were forced to liquidate. The last J. bank was sold in 1939. The community continued its social and educational services and rendered assistance towards emigration. In 1936, 500 Jews were enrolled in courses at the Bialik Lehrhaus, with such lecturers as Martin Buber making appearances. The community also published a biweekly newspaper, the *Israelitisches Gemeindeblatt*, and operated an elementary school enrolling 225 children in 1938–39. Both the Zionists and the Hilfsverein had offices promoting emigration, with the ICA and J. Agency offering active assistance. In Sept. 1936 a group of 680 youngsters from K. and other places in Germany left for Palestine within the framework of Youth Aliya. In all, at least 2,000 of K.'s Jews emigrated in 1933–39. On 28 Oct. 1938, all J. men of Polish extraction were expelled to the Polish border, their families joining them later and most ultimately perishing in the ghettoes and concentration camps. On *Kristallnacht* (9–10 Nov. 1938), the Adass Jeshurun synagogue was burned to the ground, the main synagogue was damaged, and J. men were taken to the Dachau concentration camp after being beaten and tormented. Deportations commenced on 22 Oct. 1940, when 893 Jews were loaded onto trains for the three-day journey to the Gurs concentration camp in France. Another 387 were deported in 1942–45 to Izbica in the Lublin dist. (Poland), Theresienstadt, and Auschwitz. Of the 1,280 Jews deported directly from K., 1,175 perished. Another 138 perished after deportation from other German cities or occupied Europe. In all, 1,421 of K.'s Jews died during the Holocaust. A new community was formed after the war by surviving former residents, with a new synagogue erected in 1971. It numbered 359 in 1980.

KARLSTADT Lower Franconia, Germany. Jews were victims of the Rindfleisch massacres of 1298. The modern settlement commenced in the late 19th cent., numbering 72 in 1910 (total 3,225) and 35 in 1933. On *Kristallnacht* (9–10 Nov. 1938), SS and SA troops together with Hitler Youth vandalized the community's prayer hall and J. homes. Thirty-one Jews left K. in 1936–40; 12 are known to have reached the U.S.

KARPILOVKA Polesie dist., Belorussia. Jews numbered 25 in 1789 and 1,027 (of a total 2,174) in 1897. Their number presumably dropped during the Soviet period. The Germans occupied K. in July 1941. Some Jews were murdered before the end of the year. In March 1942, Jews from Bobruisk, Ozarichi, and Parichi were brought to K. All were executed in early April.

KARPILOWKA Volhynia dist., Poland, today Ukraine. The J. pop. in 1921 was 92 (total 1,410). The Jews were brought to the Sarny ghetto for liquidation in the Holocaust.

KARSAVA Latgale dist., Latvia. The J. community was founded in the late 1820s but when the Jews reached a pop. of around 700, they were expelled in 1843 by the proprietor of the town's lands. The Jews began to return 20 years later, building a new synagogue in 1875. They numbered 609 in 1897 and 2,400 (total approx. 4,000) on the eve of WWI. Many left during the war and the J. pop. stood at around 900 in the 1920s (nearly 50% of the total). It dropped further in the 1930s as many left for Palestine under the growing influence of the Zionists with their pioneer training farm. All the community's children were enrolled at the J. public school. Jews dominated the town's trade and owned 180 of its 214 business establishments. They also maintained a majority on the municipal council and served as mayors in the 1920–34 period. Under the Ulmanis regime from 1934, antisemitic incidents increased. The arrival of the Soviets in 1940 brought J. community life to an end along with the nationalization of J. businesses. Half the town's Jews left for the Soviet Union on the approach of the Germans. The Germans took K. in early July 1941, murdering 25 Jews under a regime of severe persecution. Those remaining were herded into a ghetto with refugees from nearby towns and subjected to forced labor. On 23 Aug. 1941 the Jews were led to a hill outside the town in four groups, ordered to undress, and shot beside an open ditch by a Latvian firing squad. The death toll was around 450.

KARVINA Silesia, Czechoslovakia. Jews settled in this mining and industrial town in the 19th cent. as part of the Frystat community. They numbered about 2,000 in 1921 and 1,155 (total 52,284) in 1930. In Sept. 1938, K. was annexed to Poland. In fall 1939, the Jews were deported, mainly to the Lodz ghetto, where most died.

KASEJOVICE   Bohemia, Czechoslovakia. Jews were present in 1570 and lived in a ghetto from c. 1727 to the mid-19th cent., maintaining a synagogue and J. school. Most left for larger settlements in the late 19th cent. and only 28 (2% of the total) remained in 1930. In Jan. 1942, the remaining Jews were deported to the Theresienstadt ghetto via Pilsen and a few weeks later most were sent to the death camps of the east. Few survived.

KASSEL   Hesse–Nassau, Germany. K. already had a J. quarter (*Judengasse*) in 1262. Most of the Jews perished in the Black Death persecutions of 1348–49. Until the early 17th cent., no J. community existed, although financiers such as Jud Michel were occasional residents. Jews had to worship privately in the Goldschmidt family home from 1650 to 1716, when a synagogue was opened. A larger synagogue was dedicated in 1755 and K. replaced Witzenhausen as the seat of Hesse-Kassel's rabbinate in 1772. Mayer Amschel Rothschild, founder of the banking dynasty, was the landgrave's trusted advisor and helped to protect his interests during the short-lived Kingdom of Westphalia (1807–13). Most other Jews welcomed the arrival of Jerome Bonaparte, who granted them full civil rights, and the number of J. families grew from 55 to 203 (1806–12). Established in K., with Israel Jacobson and R. Loeb Mayer Berliner at its head, the Westphalian J. consistory (1808–13) "modernized" religious education, published the first German J. periodical (*Sulamith*), and introduced changes in synagogue worship anticipating those of Reform Judaism. Once the landgrave returned (as Elector William I), J. emancipation was annulled and the consistory abolished. Religious radicals who objected to Samuel Levi Josaphat's election as communal rabbi in 1818 nevertheless chose a Reform rabbi as his successor in 1836. Lazarus Levi Adler held office for over 30 years (1852–83) and presided at the rabbinical conference held in K. (1868). When he agreed to the installation of an organ in the synagogue in 1860, Orthodox Jews formed a separate congregation and eventually dedicated a synagogue of their own in 1898, without seceding from the main community. To safeguard its educational and economic progress, the community opened new J. schools and developed technical and vocational training

schemes. By 1850 most Jews were self-supporting. After K. became part of Prussia (1866), the civil liberties of the Jews were restored, enabling them to play a major role in commerce and industry. Numbering 827 (3% of the total) in 1827, the community grew to 2,675 (2%) in 1910. Eminent Jews born there included the playwright Salomon Hermann Mosenthal (1821–77), whose three older brothers created the South African mohair industry. Israel Beer Josaphat, the rabbi's converted son, moved to London and, as Baron Paul Julius von Reuter (1816–99), founded the great Reuters news agency. The chemist Ludwig Mond (1839–1909) also emigrated to Britain, establishing the firm which his son, Alfred Mond (Lord Melchett), transformed into ICI (Imperial Chemical Industries). Franz Rosenzweig (1886–1929), whose father was likewise an industrialist, gained renown as a Bible translator, theologian (*The Star of Redemption*, 1921), and organizer of the Freies Juedisches Lehrhaus ("Free J. House of Learning") in Frankfurt (1920). Rebuilt and enlarged (1890–1907), the main synagogue accommodated 730 worshipers. After WWI, J. refugees from the east (*Ostjuden*) augmented the community, which unified its welfare organizations in 1925 in order to assist the victims of inflation. A local J. weekly appeared (1924–33) and branches of the Central Union (C.V.), J. War Veterans Association, Zionist Organization, Agudat Israel, and various youth (including sports) movements were established. The German Zionist Organization's 18th conference took place in K. in 1922, and the Union of German Rabbis also assembled there under the chairmanship of R. Leo Baeck (1873–1956). Rudolf Hallo (1896–1933), the art historian, was curator of the State Museum's J. art department from 1927.

Although Philipp Scheidemann, the Social-Democratic burgomaster (1920–25), endeavored to curb antisemitism, the Nazis gained support in K. Their leader, Roland Freisler, became notorious as head of the "People's Court" in Berlin and two J. lawyers who had clashed with him were tortured by the SA after Hitler came to power in 1933. Of the 2,301 Jews registered in 1933, 1,207 had left (372 emigrating) by 1936. On 7 Nov. 1938 Nazis set fire to the main synagogue, but firemen extinguished the blaze. Two days later, the Liberal synagogue was burned down and the Orthodox synagogue's interior was largely destroyed on *Kristallnacht* (9–10 Nov. 1938). Communal records (such as a *Memorbuch* dating from 1720) escaped damage, but valuable books and hundreds of homes were looted; 300 Jews (including the rabbi, Robert Geiss) were sent to the Buchenwald concentration camp and over 560 left (mostly emigrating to the U.S.) in 1939. The rest were eventually deported: 470 to the Riga ghetto in 1941, 99 to the Majdanek concentration camp in 1942, and 323 to the Theresienstadt ghetto in 1942. Most of them perished there. The postwar J. community of (East European) Holocaust survivors opened a modern synagogue center and numbered 106 in 1970.

KASSERINE Kasserine dist., Tunisia. A community of about 15 J. families (1% of the total), mostly from Gabes, was established in the 1920s. A synagogue, the donation of a rich Jew, Eli Nazer, was built in 1930; R. Ezer Maimon served the community for most of its existence. Children attended a French public school and a *talmud torah*. Their parents were petty tradesmen and tailors. There were 65 Jews in K. in 1926. In WWII, after the German occupation of Nov. 1942, the Jews were evacuated for a few months to Algeria by the French. When they returned they found their homes looted. Emigration to Israel commenced in the late 1940s, the last Jews leaving in 1958.

KASTELLAUN IM HUNSRUECK Rhineland, Germany. Jews were present in the 14th cent. and apparently expelled in the 1380s. In the modern period, they are first mentioned in 1862. A cemetery was opened in 1879 and a synagogue was consecrated c. 1892. Jews dominated the cattle trade, the town's economic mainstay, and were also prominent in the farm produce trade. They were well integrated in local life. In 1892, they numbered 12 families. In June 1933, about four months after the Nazi rise to power, the J. pop. numbered 66. In that year, a Jew was elected to the municipal council but anti-J. measures were strictly enforced, undermining the economic and social position of the Jews. On *Kristallnacht* (9–10 Nov. 1938), the synagogue was destroyed and J. men were sent to the Dachau concentration camp. Most of the Jews left before the onset of deportations, about 20 making it to the U.S. The last nine were deported to Auschwitz in April and Aug. 1942.

KASTORIA (Kesriye, Castoria, Kezrye) Macedonia, Greece. J. settlement in K. dates back to the sixth cent. C.E. In 1453, the Ottomans transferred most of the Romaniot community to Istanbul, where

Members of the Maccabi youth movement prior to WWII, Kastoria, Greece

the Jews formed their own congregation. After the expulsions in the late 15th cent. from Portugal, Spain, Sicily, and Italy, Sephardi Jews arrived in K. and constituted a predominant community. In the mid-17th cent., Nathan of Gaza settled there and spread the messianic faith of Shabbetai Zvi. Many leaders of the community were Shabbateans (some remained so even after the death of Shabbetai Zvi). Most Jews worked in the tanning industry and in trade. In the early 18th cent. there were four synagogues: Romaniot, Italian, Spanish, and Portuguese. In 1719–20, three synagogues were destroyed in a fire and 62 Jews died in an epidemic. In 1750, a new synagogue was built, but was destroyed in 1828; another was built in 1830. A J. school was established in 1873. In the 19th cent., the community was subject to a number of blood libels. In 1887, 70 Jews were taken captive by bandits and the community was active in redeeming them. The community was not organized, however, and there was rivalry between members. The level of J. education was low but in 1903 funds from a bequest and assistance from the Alliance Israelite helped raise the educational level. The J. pop. in 1906 was 1,600. Another blood libel took place in 1908. Following the Balkan wars (1912–13), K. was annexed to Greece. In the 1920s, the organized community maintained two synagogues, a school and kindergarten, two social welfare organizations, and a burial society. Zionist activity began in 1928 with the establishment of a highly motivated Zionist association that led to a group of youths settling in Palestine. Prior to WWII there were 900 Jews in K., In April 1941, the Germans took over the Greek mainland and K. was included in the Italian occupation zone. In Sept. 1943, when the Germans entered K., some J. families escaped to a neighboring village and a few men joined the partisans. On 23 March 1944, all the inhabitants of the J. quarter (763 Jews) were arrested and held in a school (only 50 had managed to go into hiding). The next day 30–40 were released with the assistance of the Archbishop of the Greek Orthodox Church and the rest were transferred to Salonika. From there they were taken to the death camps. After the war, there was a small community (35 Jews in 1945), but it declined over the years.

KASZOWKA Volhynia dist., Poland, today Ukraine. Jews were present before the Chmielnicki massacres of 1648–49 and numbered fewer than 500 in the late 19th cent. and 15 after most fled in WWI.

The Ukrainian police murdered the last 20 in Jan. 1943.

KATERBURG Volhynia dist., Poland, today Ukraine. Jews numbered 693 in 1897 and 408 in 1921 (total 892). They were brought to the Lanowce ghetto in Feb. 1942 and murdered by the Germans on 13–14 Aug. together with the local Jews.

KATERINI (Katerina, Ecaterin, Caterina) Pierias dist., Greece. The J. pop. in 1904 was 80. In 1943 the mayor of K. assisted K.'s 40 Jews to hide in surrounding villages. A few families were caught and sent to death camps, but the rest were saved. In 1983, five Jews remained in K.

KATERYNYPOL (Yekaterynopol) Kiev dist., Ukraine. Jews numbered 1,980 (total 7,197) in 1897, declining to 395 in 1939. In 1928, in the Soviet period, J. artisans founded two cooperatives, one for shoemakers and the other for tailors and furriers. A Yiddish elementary school was opened along with a J. kindergarten in 1928. The local council (soviet) undertook to propagate Yiddish culture. The Germans captured the town on 29 July 1941 and on 6 Sept. executed 34 people. On 17 May 1942, the Jews were expelled to the Zwenigorodka ghetto. On 14 June, the Jews of K., together with others from the ghetto, were executed in the Oforny forest.

KATHERINOVKA Zaporozhe dist., Ukraine. A neighboring J. kolkhoz, Fray Lebn, provided employment for some of the Jews of K., who were apparently among the 92 Jews murdered in the kolkhoz by the Germans in WWII.

KATOWICE (Kattowitz) Silesia dist., Poland. Jews are first mentioned in the city's future suburb of Bogoczyce in 1733 and in K. itself in 1825. The community became independent in 1866, building its first synagogue in 1862 and inaugurating the J. cemetery in 1868. A new synagogue with 1,000 seats was dedicated in 1900, when the J. pop. stood at 2,264 (total 31,738). While the Prussian-ruled city was known for its steel and coal industries, most Jews were tradesmen living in straitened economic circumstances. Nonetheless, in addition to caring for its own, the community extended assistance to J. refugees from the Russian pogroms of 1881–82 passing through K. on their way

Jewish residents of Katowice, Poland, 1933

to the west. The first signs of modern political and cultural activity were seen in 1880 with the founding of a B'nai B'rith chapter with Zionist connections. In Sept. 1884 the international conference of Hovevei Zion was organized in K. With the institution of Polish rule in 1922, the city underwent considerable demographic change owing to the influx of Poles. By 1931 both the general and J. pop. had doubled, the former to 126,158 and the latter to 5,716, with 60% of the Jews new residents from Congress Poland, Galicia, and the city of Cieszyn. Despite cultural differences, great efforts were made to unite the newcomers with the original German-J. pop. In the following decade (until 1938), the J. pop. rose to 8,587 as the Jews continued to arrive in the area hoping to find work. Despite depressed economic conditions affecting the steel and coal industries and leading to widespread unemployment, the Jews were able to maintain a measure of economic stability. About 250 J. families were among the wealthiest in the city, including bankers, industrialists, grain and lumber merchants, and operators of luxurious stores. However, among the smaller tradesmen, embracing around 1,000 families, circumstances were less satisfactory and with the effects of antisemitic agitation increasingly being felt economically through the 1930s, the need for ramified welfare services grew. An employment agency was opened in 1936 and the community operated a soup kitchen, clinic, and summer camps for needy children. Throughout the period, Zionist activity was extensive, particularly among the youth. The local Maccabi club was one of the most active in Poland and WIZO numbered 340 members. The local Nazi organization was already persecuting Jews in 1933 and in 1936 ritual kosher slaughter was banned in the city while anti-J. agitation intensified in the municipal council and local press. The Germans captured the city on 3 Sept. 1939, when the J. pop. had been swelled by refugees to 11,000–12,000. Within days, J. homes and stores were pillaged, Jews were beaten, and the synagogue was set on fire (the undamaged part being converted into Gestapo headquarters). With large numbers escaping to Soviet-held territory and neighboring villages, 3,500 Jews remained in K. at the end of Oct. Men aged 18–50 (around 800 to 1,100) were expelled across the Soviet border via Nisko; other families were able to emigrate to the west, leaving 900 Jews in the city at the end of 1939. In May–June 1940, 600 were expelled to Chrzanow, 150 to Szczakowa, and the rest to Sosnowiec and Bendzin, sharing the fate of the local Jews. In 1943–44, a number of labor camps were set up in the area, mainly for West European Jews, including 900 from France. After the war, a regional J. committee operated in the city with extensive services for the thousands of J. refugees gathering in the area or passing through on the way to the west. By 1969, only a few J. families remained.

KATSCHER (Pol. Kietrz) Upper Silesia, Germany, today Poland. The J. pop. was 36 in 1787. The community established a synagogue in 1825 and a private J. school in 1845. It maintained a cemetery. In 1840, the J. pop. was 108, rising to a peak of 186 in 1871. Early in the 20th cent., many emigrated to the big cities, mostly to Breslau and Berlin, reducing the J. pop. to 52 in 1910. In 1933, the J. pop. was 42. The Nazi racial laws were not put into force in K. until July 1937 owing to the protection of the League of Nations' minority rights convention. J. children were subsequently expelled from public schools and forced to travel to the J. school in Ratibor. On *Kristallnacht* (9–10 Nov. 1938), the synagogue was set on fire and J. stores and warehouses were destroyed. Five Jews remained on 19 Nov. 1942. Presumably the rest either emigrated or perished following deportation.

KAUKEHMEN (Rus. Yasnoye) East Prussia, Germany, today Russia. K. was a part of the Tilsit community. It had 73 members in 1925 and maintained a prayer room. No information is available about the fate of the community under Nazi rule.

KAUNAS (Yid. Kovno) Kaunas dist., Lithuania. Jews first settled in the late 14th cent., though official permission was granted only in the early 18th cent. Among the first Jews were war captives from the Crimea. Non-J. residents opposed efforts by noblemen wishing to encourage J. settlement as a means of stimulating economic growth. When persecuted or expelled, the Jews fled to the suburb of Slobodka, across the Viliya River from K. and controlled by the Radziwill family. Over time, Slobodka, referred to in Lithua-

Jewish store in Kaunas (Kovno), Lithuania

nian as Vilijampole, became part of K., but its history as a J. settlement, with a synagogue from the 16th cent., predates K.'s. Jews played a key role in K. as customs agents and tax collectors. At the end of the 15th cent., Avraham Yosefovitch, a J. customs agent, converted to Christianity and eventually became Lithuania's finance minister. Despite his conversion, he fought a 1495 edict expelling Jews. Eventually, in the beginning of the 18th cent., the Jews won the right to live in K. by agreeing to pay a special tax. Two rabbis served the community at this time, but left after a conflagration in 1731. The wars with Sweden in 1700–15 left part of K. in ruins, which enterprising Jews bought and rebuilt. In 1753, the mayor expelled the Jews but the crown's representative in K. allowed the Jews to settle on his property, which was under the king's authority. Twenty years later, after the Jews fled a pogrom in 1761, a royal court ordered their return to K., restoration of their property with compensation for damages and two weeks' imprisonment for the mayor. These events were recorded in a "K. Scroll," and read annually on Shushan Purim. Prominent in fighting the expulsion were Avraham and Moshe Soloveitchik, brothers who immigrated to K. from Brisk (Brest-Litovsk) in the mid-18th cent. They were among those who bought ruined property for rehabilitation. Moshe was the progenitor of the famous rabbinical family. The J. pop. in 1797 was 1,508 (18% of the total). By 1798, K. had become part of Russia and although Czar Pavel I ruled that Jews could conduct business throughout the city, this was only accomplished with bribes. In 1839, they won the right to participate in city elections and in 1861 they finally overcame years of opposition from K. residents and obtained a ruling enabling them to leave the ghetto. K.'s first synagogue was established by R. Moshe Soloveitchik in 1772. For many years the K. community was dependent legally on Slobodka for most of its religious functionaries and services. By 1790 the nucleus of an educational and social welfare

organization had developed in K. By 1860 it had 39 employees. The Ohel Yaakov Synagogue, constructed in 1871, enjoyed a reputation among Christians and Jews for the high level of its cantorial music. R. Yitzhak Elhanan Spektor (1864–98), highly respected in K. as well as outside of Lithuania, supported the Hovevei Zion and Haskala movements and displayed a degree of leniency in regard to various halakhic matters. He also led the struggle against antisemitic Czarist decrees by smuggling out news about them to Western countries and requesting their intervention. The community's extensive social welfare system included a hospital. First established in 1807, it was later expanded and facilities developed for hospitalizing between 70–80 patients. In the latter half of the 19th cent., the economic growth of Lithuania provided many opportunities for Jews to advance themselves. Many were merchants, trading in agricultural produce, wood, linen, grain, eggs, and cattle. Most of the larger factories were Christian-owned and refused to employ Jews. The economic situation of J. workers and artisans was not good and in the 1880s and the beginning of the 20th cent. many emigrated. Located near the German

Hebrew teachers' college, Kaunas (Kovno), Lithuania

Jewish street in the Old City of Kaunas (Kovno), Lithuania, 1936 (Budesarchive/photo courtesy of Yad Vashem, The Holocaust Martyrs' and Heroes' Remembrance Authority, Jerusalem)

border, 19th cent. K. was influenced by the cultural struggle taking place among German Jewry between the ultra-Orthodox and Haskala adherents. One of the first Haskala writers, Avraham Mapu (1808–67), was born in K. and lived most of his life there. Slobodka became the center of traditional J. education, centered primarily around the Or Hayyim yeshiva, founded in 1863, and the Hefetz Hayyim yeshiva. The excessively strict demands of Musar adherents led to the establishment of the Knesset Israel yeshiva by Musar adherents followers while opponents of the movement established the Beit Yitzhak yeshiva named after R. Spektor. The Zionist movement began to organize in K. in the early 1880s. In 1908 the Zionists established the Avraham Mapu Library, one of the more important libraries in Lithuania, which existed until WWII. (After the Holocaust hundreds of books from this library came into the possession of the National Library in Jerusalem

and the Dimona municipal library.) K. was also an important center of Bund activity after movement leaders in Vilna were arrested in 1895. The J. pop. in 1897 was 25,448 (36%), rising to 40,000 in 1914. In May 1915, during WWI, when Lithuania was under Russian rule, the Jews were expelled from K. to the Russian interior, some going to Vilna. When the German army captured K. in Sept. 1915, those who returned from Vilna found their homes, stores, and communal buildings ransacked. From the war's end in 1918 and the establishment of independent Lithuania, until 1923, many returned from Russia. In 1918, following German withdrawal, elections were held in Dec. and a 71-member city council was elected, which inclueded 22 Jews. Jews continued to play a prominent role in public life in K. until 1926, when non-Jews resorted to several measures to limit J. influence. Though Jews succeeded in many professions, they were very successful in commerce, particularly in textiles, building materials, lumber, and imports of industrial products. By the 1930s, their economic situation was beginning to deteriorate as a consequence of rising antisemitism and such measures, encouraged by the authorities, as a business boycott, the banning of ritual kosher slaughter and Hebrew signs, segregation of J. students at the university, and, in the mid-1930s, the introduction of quotas for J. university students and faculty. Emigration to Palestine, South Africa, and other countries as well as a low birthrate accounted for a declining J. pop. The educational system included kindergartens, elementary and high schools, and teachers' seminaries. Beginning in the 1920s, the Tarbut network initiated the establishment of several Hebrew schools, including two high schools and a teachers' college. Some of the teachers and directors were later to become prominent in Palestine (Dr. Schwabe, Dr. Charne, Dr. Berman, and others). Yavne elementary and high schools followed afterwards. A Shalom Aleichem Yiddish school contained a kindergarten, elementary school, high school, and library. ORT operated a vocational school. There was a rich cultural life in K. and several newspapers and journals, primarily in Yiddish, appeared regularly, including the *Yidishe Shtime*, a Zionist daily founded in 1919, and from 1933, *Unzer Moment*, published by the Revisionists. Two theaters operated in K. and groups from abroad, such as Habima and Ida Kaminska's, also played in K. K. and the surrounding suburbs maintained about 40 synagogues and *yeshivot*. In 1924, the Knesset Israel yeshiva transferred 100 students to Hebron in Palestine because of the Lithuanian government's refusal to exempt yeshiva students from the army. Social welfare services in K. included the Bikkur Holim Hospital. Serving Jews and non-Jews alike, it was one of the largest in Lithuania. In 1927, Dr. S. Lehman, director of a children's institution in K., led the emigration of about 100 children to Ben Shemen, Palestine, which became the forerunner of the Youth Aliya village there. The Zionist movement enjoyed widespread support and all the parties maintained branches in K. Many leading Zionist figures from Palestine visited K., including Jabotinsky, Ben-Gurion, Bialik, Shneur, Tchernichowsky, etc. With the Soviet Union's annexation of Lithuania in 1940, businesses were nationalized, a step which hurt the mostly J. middle class. Zionist and J. activities and Hebrew education were banned; some organizagtions and activities were continued underground. Many J.

"enemies of the people" were arrested and some were exiled.

After the German invasion in June 1941, many Jews fled to Vilna and Russia. Lithuanian nationalists staged a pogrom in Slobodka, killing 800 Jews. Another 57 were butchered at the Lietukis garage. In the Seventh Fort (one of nine forts built around K. by the czars), 6,000–8,000 Jews were incarcerated without food or water in July. All the men and 36 women were subsequently killed. On 7 Aug., the Lithuanians seized 1,200 Jews. Most were sent to the Pravienikes labor camp and shot. About 250 Jews were executed on 4 Sept. 1941 following a failed attempt to escape the camp. All the Jews were given until 15 Aug. to move into the K. ghetto which was established in Slobodka. A committee was chosen to facilitate the orderly transfer of all the Jews to the ghetto. This was followed by the election of an *Aeltestenrat* (a so-called "Committee of Community Elders" which functioned as a *Judenrat*) and the appointment of an internal, unarmed police force. In 1941, the ghetto pop. numbered 29,760. The ghetto consisted of two parts, referred to as the "little ghetto" and the "big ghetto." On 14 Aug. 1941, the Germans carried out an *Aktion*, rounding up 34 young men who were then taken to the Fourth Fort and shot. On the eve of Rosh Hashanah, the German officer in charge of the ghetto, Fritz Jordan, randomly shot ten Jews returning from work. On 26 Sept., 1,845 men, women, and children were sent to the Ninth Fort and murdered. On 4 Oct., the Germans eliminated the "little ghetto" by shooting 1,608 residents. Those with "Jordan notes" – permits issued by the ghetto commander – were transferred to the large ghetto. From Sept. 1941, thousands of J. men and women were taken to forced labor at the military air field in a K. suburb. Others worked in brigades for the German army or in factories in town. In Oct. 1941, the Germans carried out what came to be called the "Big *Aktion*." Following a selection of all ghetto residents, including the elderly and sick, approximately 9,200 men, women, and children were taken to the Ninth Fort and shot on 29 Oct. From 16 Nov. to mid-Dec. 1941, approximately 20,000 Jews from other parts of Europe were killed at the Ninth Fort. A total of 30,000 Jews from K., Austria, Germany, and Czechoslovakia and from among J. Red Army soldiers and officers were eventually killed at the Ninth Fort, the largest killing ground in Lithuania. From Aug. 1941 to 31 Dec., 13,421 ghetto residents were murdered. This left a ghetto pop. of

The Ninth Fort near Kaunas (Kovno), also known as "The Death Fort," where 80,000 Jews from Lithuania and other countries in Western Europe were murdered

17,400. Although the period from 1 Nov. 1941 to fall 1943, was referred to as the "Quiet Period" the murders continued. In May 1942, J. doctors performed hundreds of abortions following an order forbidding J. women to give birth or face execution. In fall 1942, the Germans seized approximately 750 Jews, primarily men, and sent them to the Riga ghetto. About 4,600 craftsmen worked in 44 workshops established to serve the German army. Conditions were relatively good and those in the workshops did not have to face the hardships their brethren encountered working outside the ghetto where they were abused and at times murdered. In Sept. 1943, the ghetto became the Kauen concentration camp under SS jurisdiction. In Oct., 2,700 J. men, women, and children were rounded up, ostensibly to be sent to work in Ezereclai. Instead, trains were prepared to take them to Estonia; the elderly and children were sent to Auschwitz. Most sent to Estonia were eventually sent to death camps in Germany or shot. Many succeeded in avoiding the deportations to Estonia by

hiding in underground bunkers. On 27 March 1944, the Germans mounted a Children's *Aktion*, entering the ghetto in the daytime when parents were at work and taking about 2,000 of the children and elderly to be killed. Prior to the *Aktion*, dozens of children were handed over to the custody of Lithuanian families, often with large payments, following reports on 5 Nov. 1943 of the slaughter of children, the elderly, and the sick in the Siauliai ghetto. There were four underground organizations in the ghetto from its inception. Organized under a roof organization called the Vilijampole-Kovno Zionist Center, they acted in tandem with "official" J. ghetto bodies to obtain food and supplies and to arrange for people to enter the bunkers. They also established contact with partisan fighters outside the ghetto and with other ghettoes. On Christmas Eve 1943, all 64 prisoners including partisans escaped from the Ninth Fort. Nineteen reached the ghetto 2.5 miles away; 11 joined the partisans. Between Dec. 1943 and March 1944, eight groups succeeded with underground help in escaping from the ghetto and making their way to partisan groups in the Rudnicka forest southeast of Vilna. The ninth attempt failed, when the driver of the vehicle carrying a group of Jews betrayed them to the Nazis. Of the 600 underground members, 350 succeeded in reaching the partisans; about 220 were killed in action. On 27 March 1944, the same day that the Children's *Aktion* took place, the entire J. ghetto police force was taken to the Ninth Fort where its three head officers were tortured and 40 of the 130 policemen were shot. Seven, under torture, revealed the locations of the underground ghetto bunkers. The police force and the "Committee of Community Elders" were disbanded. By 8 July, the J. pop. of the K. ghetto and work camps was 7,000–8,000 and their transfer to Germany began. When the German commandant realized that thousands were missing, having gone into hiding, every house was fire-bombed, killing at least 1,500 within the bunkers. Ninety managed to escape. On 1 Aug. 1944, K. was liberated by the Red Army. About 3,000 K. Jews survived the war: 2,500 were liberated in Germany and 500 had joined the partisans or hid out with Lithuanians. After the war, some Jews returned to K., establishing an orphanage, a school, and a synagogue, which were shut down by the Soviets in 1950. Other survivors went to Israel and other countries.

KAUNATA (Yid. Kovnat) Latgale dist., Latvia. Jews were probably among the town's original settlers in the early 20th cent., numbering 60–70 (a third of the total) between the World Wars, when they owned 12 of K.'s 15 stores and maintained a synagogue. The Germans arrived in June 1941. Through mid-Sept., Latvian auxiliary police executed 40 Jews in groups of ten, and another 126 from neighboring settlements through July 1942.

KAVALA (Cavala, Neapolis, Christoupolis) Macedonia, Greece. J. settlement began in the 16th cent., when the ruling Ottomans transferred Jews from Budapest to K. In the 1540s there were more than 500 Jews in K. The Ashkenazi community flourished in the first half of the cent., but then refugees from the Spanish and Portuguese expulsions arrived and a Sephardi community predominated. By the late 17th cent., there were four synagogues in K. In 1740, the community had dwindled to only a few families; the community remained at this level throughout the 19th cent.

After the mid-19th cent., however, K.'s trade in tobacco and other products improved, causing more Jews to settle there, primarily from Salonika, Monastir (Bitola), Seres, and Istanbul. Between 1880 and 1900, the community grew from 24 to 230 J. families (over 1,000 individuals). In the following years, the community organized and operated a school and social welfare organizations. During this period there were two blood libels (1894, 1900), but both were halted quickly by the authorities and physical harm was avoided. In 1905, a new school for boys and girls was built with the assistance of the Alliance Israelite. Bulgaria took over K. in Nov. 1912 and instituted a reign of terror. The Jews numbered 2,350 at this time. Most inhabitants suffered from poverty and food shortages. European Jews supplied funds and food to assist the J. community. In July 1913, the Greeks occupied K. A highly active Zionist organization was established that year. In WWI, however, the Bulgarians returned (1916) and the inhabitants suffered hunger once again. In Oct. 1918, the Greeks returned to K. At first 120 Jews were mobilized for six days of forced labor to restore the war-stricken city; subsequently the community was able to rehabilitate itself. In 1921, the J. community peaked at 2,500 members, the majority of whom worked in the successful tobacco industry. According to the 1928 census, K. was the third largest J. community in Greece (2,135 Jews), after Salonika and Athens. In the early 1930s, antisemitism rose while the Jews suffered the consequences of the economic depression. Their numbers increasing, distressed families received assistance from the community's welfare organizations. The J. pop. in 1940 was 2,100. On 6 April 1941 the Germans entered Greece. Within days, K. was taken over and occupied by the Bulgarians. J. movement in K. was restricted. In 1941–42, hundreds of youths and men were taken to forced labor in Bulgaria. A lack of food, clothing, and medical supplies led to epidemics in the harsh winter of 1942–43. On 3–4 March 1943, 1,484 Jews of K. were deported to the Treblinka death camp via Drama and Bulgaria. Only a few Jews who fled K. before the deportation and 40 youths who were in Bulgarian forced labor battalions survived the Holocaust. A few survivors returned to K. and in 1945 there were 42 Jews. A community was reestablished, but was dismantled in 1970. The last J. family left in 1979.

KAVARSKAS (Yid. Kovarsk) Ukmerge dist., Lithuania. Jews first settled at the end of the 18th cent., forming an organized community by the second half of the 19th cent. During WWI, the Russian army ransacked, murdered and raped, before expelling the Jews to Russia. Half returned after the war. A 1919 boycott and antisemitic riots contributed to emigration, mainly to South Africa, with some going to Palestine. The Zionist movement won widespread support. The J. pop., which in 1897 stood at 979 (63% of the total), dropped to 436 in 1923 (42%). Shortly after the German invasion, Lithuanian nationalists took control of K., and murdered a group of 30 J. men and women on 26 June 1941. The remaining Jews were transferred to Ukmerge and shot on 5 Sept. 1941.

KAWECZYN SEDZISZOWSKI   Cracow dist., Poland. The J. pop. in 1921 was 190 (total 1,520). The Jews were probably murdered or deported to the Belzec death camp in July 1942 after expulsion to Sedziszow Malopolski.

KAYDANOVO   (Hung. Kajdano) Carpatho-Russia, Czechoslovakia, today Ukraine. J. settlement probably began in the early 19th cent. The J. pop. was 11 in 1830 and 113 (total 1,043) in 1880 with an organized community at mid-cent. A few Jews were farmers. In 1921 the J. pop. was 126, dropping to 94 in 1941. The Hungarians occupied the town in March 1939 and in summer 1941 drafted a number of J. men into labor battalions for forced labor on the eastern front. In Aug. about ten J. families without Hungarian citizenship were expelled to Kamenets-Podolski and murdered. The rest were deported to Auschwitz in the second half of May 1944.

KAZANOW   Kielce dist., Poland. Jews numbered 469 in 1857 and 336 (total 814) in 1921. Reliable information is unavailable, but according to one source, 180 were murdered by the Germans when they took the town in Sept. 1939. The rest perished in Oct.–Dec. 1942 when the remaining communities in the area were liquidated.

KAZATIN   Vinnitsa dist., Ukraine. Four Jews were present in 1765, their pop. growing to 1,731 (total 8,614) in 1897. In the Soviet period, most J. children attended a J. elementary school. In the late 1920s, many Jews were employed at a sugar refinery, the railroad, and two J. kolkhozes. The J. pop. in 1939 was

2,648. The Germans captured the city on 14 July 1941 and set up a ghetto. On 4 June 1942, they murdered 508 Jews; in early July, another 250 at the village of Talimonovka; in Aug., 183; and in Dec., the last 30.

KAZIMIERZA WIELKA   Kielce dist., Poland. A community of 293 Jews (total 2,264) existed in 1921, maintaining a J. school and Zionist youth movements. The Germans captured K. in Sept. 1939. Under General Gouvernement administration, the Jews were subjected to forced labor and Gestapo killings. A *Judenrat* was established and deportees arrived from eastern Upper Silesia. On 8 Nov. 1942, 210 Jews trying to escape the impending *Aktion* were lured out of hiding and executed in the forest. Betrayed by a Polish informer, 22 were found and murdered in a bunker. Another 27 were caught and murdered after escaping to the village of Buzanka.

KAZIMIERZ DOLNY   (Yid. Kuzmir) Lublin dist., Poland. Jews may have been present by the early 11th cent. and maintained an organized community during the reign of King Casimir the Great (1333–70), who expanded J. rights. Jews were active as moneylenders, as tax agents, and as lumber and grain merchants doing business in Danzig. Under local and Church pressure, J. trade and residence were somewhat restricted in the early 15th cent. The community suffered grievously in the Swedish invasions of 1655–59. In the 18th cent., full rights were restored and Jews played a major role in the economic development of the city in the 19th cent., with Jews importing perfumes and spices and establishing paper, porcelain, and glass factories, hide-processing plants, beer breweries, and flour mills. At the turn of the 18th cent., K. became famous as a hasidic center when R. Yehezkel Taub (d. 1856) founded a dynasty there. R. Mordekhai Twersky, son of Avraham, the *Maggid* of Trisk, maintained a hasidic court there from the 1880s until 1905. The J. pop. was 1,555 in 1857 and 1,382 (total 3,407) in 1921. The Zionists became active in the early 20th cent. and operated intensively between the World Wars, founding a Hebrew school in 1927 and dominating the community council until Agudat Israel prevailed in 1932. The largest Zionist party was Po'alei Zion. The German occupation of 19 Sept. 1939 was followed by the establishment of a *Judenrat* charged with furnishing forced labor and tributes. In spring 1940, a ghetto was sealed off where 2,000 Jews, in-

Market day near the church in Kazimierz, Poland

cluding many refugees from Pulawy, were concentrated. On 25 March 1942, they were deported to the Belzec death camp via Opole after the able-bodied were sent to the Nalenczow labor camp.

KAZLU-RUDA (Yid. Kazlove-Rude) Marijampole dist., Lithuania. A J. community existed by the second half of the 19th cent. and maintained a synagogue. Many were engaged in the lumber industry. The Zionist movement won widespread support. The J. pop. in 1940 amounted to several hundred. All the Jews were killed by Aug. 1941. At the labor camp the Germans built near K. for digging peat, there were 400 Jews from Kovno (Kaunas) and Vilna.

KCYNIA Poznan dist., Poland. Jews settled in the 16th cent. The community was destroyed by the troops of Stefan Czarniecki, the Polish irregular leader fighting against the Swedish invaders in the mid-17th cent.. It revived only after Prussian annexation in 1793. A yeshiva built in 1811 attracted students from

all over Poland. The J. pop. rose to 477 (total 2,618) in 1871 and then declined steadily to 87 in Sept. 1939. Twenty Jews were immediately murdered by the Germans and the rest expelled to General Gouvernement territory.

KEBILI Southern Tunisia dist., Tunisia. French development of K. led to J. settlement in the early 20th cent., the first Jews coming from Gabes. By 1909, the J. community numbered 90 (18% of the total) and 325 (17%) in 1936. Though mainly tailors or dealers in textiles, some Jews were moneylenders to Arabs. For an isolated settlement, K.'s community was well developed, with great emphasis on helping the needy. The community maintained a synagogue, *talmud torah*, cemetery, and *mikve*. A committee governed the community, while the rabbi served in a variety of communal capacities. Relations with the Arabs were workable until after WWII and the rise of the Neo-Dustur. The Vichy regime's anti-J. decrees had little impact on K.'s Jews but the closure of borders affected trade and undermined their livelihood. In Nov. 1942, the German-Italian army captured K. To escape Allied bombing all Jews fled to the periphery, primarily settling in Burj al-Ka'bi, where community life continued and trade with the Italian soldiers, mainly in textiles, developed. K. Arabs looted J. property and assisted the Germans, but in an unorganized fashion. After WWII, the American Joint Distribution Committee helped reestablish the community. Following the creation of Israel in 1948, relations with the Arabs worsened. Although modern Hebrew was taught from the late 1940s, there were never any Zionist youth groups in K. After 1952, K.'s Jews left for Israel by way of Gabes, Tunis, and Marseille.

KECEL Pest–Pilis–Solt–Kiskun dist., Hungary. Jews are mentioned in the late 18th cent. and were prominent as wool merchants. The community organized in 1868, establishing a synagogue in 1882 and a J. school in 1878. Its pop. was 130 (2% of the total) in 1880 and 110 in 1941. On 17 June 1944, the Jews were brought to Szeged and from there deported at the end of June to Auschwitz and other camps. Most of those reaching Strasshof in Austria survived the war.

KECEROVSKE PEKLANY Slovakia, Czechoslovakia, today Republic of Slovakia. The J. pop. was about 150 in the mid-19th cent., dropping to 50 in 1929. Most of the Jews were sent to the death camps in 1942

KECSKEMET Pest–Pilis–Solt–Kiskun dist., Hungary. Jews were present under the Turks in the 16th cent. In 1746, Jews were given exclusive rights to buy up hides from local farmers, but only gained residence rights in 1840. A synagogue was consecrated in 1823 and a J. school opened in 1844. In 1869, the community founded a Neologist congregation. Among its rabbis was Dr. Armin Perls (serving in 1853–1914), one of the great orators among Hungary's rabbis. The J. pop. was 2,022 (3% of the total) in 1910 and 1,346 in 1941. Jews were severely victimized in the White Terror (1919–21) following WWI and subsequently subjected to continuing antisemitism. Zionism increased and cultural life, embracing neighboring settlements, flourished in the community. The German occupation of 19 March 1944 was accompanied by the arrival of a Gestapo unit that seized leading figures for deportation to Auschwitz. The 940 remaining Jews were crowded into a ghetto and the men put to

Kindergarten children at a Purim party, Kedainiai, Lithuania

forced labor. On 26 June, they were deported to Auschwitz. The Zionists managed to save 13 by providing them with counterfeit certificates. The postwar community numbered 81 in 1955.

KEDAINIAI (Yid. Keidan) Kedainiai dist., Lithuania. Jews first settled at the late 15th cent. They were expelled for a short time and then allowed to return. In the 17th cent. Prince Radziwill granted all citizens, including Jews, the right to vote while his son, Yanush, provided Jews with military training in case of emergency. Boguslav, the heir of Yanush, restricted the Jews to a ghetto, but leased his palace to a Jew, to whom he gave authority to judge and impose fines upon fellow Jews. The K. J. community was one of the original members of the J. self-governing Council of the Land of Lithuania (1623–1764). After the Council's demise, K. was the site of two more meetings of the Lithuanian J. communities. The Vilna Gaon (1720–97) was educated in K. and married a K. native. A large and beautiful synagogue was completed in 1807. A yeshiva was founded in the beginning of the 18th cent. which existed until the Holocaust. In 1884, with the help of K. natives in New York, the Ohel Moshe *talmud torah*, named for Moses Montefiore, was founded; in 1888 it became a modern school, teaching both secular and religious subjects. K. had many adherents of the Haskala movement. In the 1880s and 1890s, the economic situation and antisemitism led many to emigrate to England, the U.S., and South Africa. By 1898 there were seven synagogues. Even prior to the Hovevei Zion movement of the 1880s, some immigrated to Eretz Israel. In 1811, Shelomo Zalman Tzoref went to Palestine with other followers of the Vilna Gaon. He was the grandfather of Yoel Moshe Solomon, one of the founders of Petah Tikva. In the 1880s and 1890s, several Zionist organizations were established and many contributed to settlement funds for Eretz Israel. The J. pop. in 1897 was 3,733 (61% of the total). During WWI, the Russian army expelled the Jews to Russia; some went to Vilna. After the war most returned. Relations with the Lithuanians were good and Jews actively supported Lithuanian independence. Between the World Wars, a J. council ran the community's affairs. In 1926, two competing organizations took over its functions. Five of the 12 city councilors elected in 1931 were Jews. In the 1930s, relations with the Lithuanians worsened and J. businesses were boycotted. The community maintained

a Hebrew school, a Yiddish school, a *heder*, and a Hebrew junior high school. The Zionist movement won widespread support. Many of the youth emigrated to Palestine, the U.S., and South Africa. On the eve of the German invasion in 1941, the J. pop. was about 2,500. The Germans issued a variety of antisemitic decrees and Lithuanian nationalists introduced a regime of terror and mass arrests which led to the immediate murder of 125 J. men and women in the Babenai forest. In July, 200 Jews were killed in the Tevciunai forest. The remaining Jews were put in a ghetto, together with 1,000 Jews from surrounding towns. On 28 Aug. 1941, after 13 days without food, all were brought to Smilaga Creek, forced into pits, and shot.

KEFALONIA (Kephallinia, Cephallonia, Kefallinia) Ionian Islands, Greece. The first Jews to settle on the island of K. lived in Achelous in the 12th–13th cents. Jews were brought to K. in the 17th cent. by its governor, who was interested in developing the bookbinding industry. Most lived in the capital, Argostoli. After 1821, when the Greek revolt broke out, many Jews escaping anti-J. ferment settled in K. But antisemitism also occurred in K., such as a blood libel in 1822. The J. pop. in 1823 was 130 (total 53,090). Jews did not enjoy equal civil rights until K. was annexed to Greece in 1864. In the 1890s, the community's financial position was undermined and its members became indifferent to the problems related to J. community life. The community was soon dismantled. The J. pop. in 1907 was 18. Only one Jew lived there in 1940.

KEHL AM RHEIN Baden, Germany. Jews first settled in 1862 after emancipation accorded them freedom of residence in Baden. A community was officially formed in 1881 and a synagogue was consecrated in 1889. The community maintained a pop. of around 150 in the early 20th cent. (2% of the total), with the majority trading in cattle. Despite anti-J. agitation, the Jews participated fully in local life. After WWI, the J. pop. dropped through emigration and a declining birthrate, numbering 109 in 1933. Under the Nazis, persecution commenced immediately in 1933 and most J. businesses were soon liquidated. In 1934–39, 49 emigrated, 12 to Palestine and 26 to nearby France. On *Kristallnacht* (9–10 Nov. 1938), the synagogue was vandalized and J. men were sent to the Dachau concentration camp after being beaten and tormented. Eight more Jews subsequently emigrated, while in the whole period 39 left for other German cities. On 22 Oct. 1940, 18 were deported to the Gurs concentration camp. Another 21 were deported to the camps in Eastern Europe from their places of refuge in France and other German cities. Only seven survived the Holocaust.

KELME (Yid. Kelm) Raseiniai dist., Lithuania. Jews first settled in the 16th cent. Until the end of the 19th cent., the Jews were a majority and dominated K.'s commerce in grain, lumber, leather, textiles, pig bristles, and, to a great extent, the leather-processing and bristle industries. In the second half of the 19th cent., S.Z. Broide, a student of the Musar movement's founder, R. Yisrael Salanter, founded a yeshiva, dedicated not to training rabbis but to educating ordinary people to be good and moral Jews, an approach which attracted many Jews from around the world. The community maintained four synagogues, the first built in the mid-18th cent. The J. pop. in 1897 was 2,710 (69% of the total). Between the World Wars, relations with non-Jews were good, until the 1930s when boycotts and other antisemitic activities occurred. In 1919, K. became one of the first communities in Lithuania to establish a Hebrew elementary school. Both the Yavne and Tarbut movements maintained schools in K. The Zionist movement, which began to take root in the late 19th cent., enjoyed widespread support. The J. pop. in 1939 was about 2,000 (54%). When the Soviets annexed Lithuania in 1940, J. and Zionist organizations were disbanded and factories and businesses were nationalized, adversely affecting the livelihood of many Jews. On 29 July 1941, following the German invasion in June, 125 J. men were shot. On 22 Aug., the women and children were murdered. Several dozen managed to escape but were handed over to the authorities. Only 15 Jews survived the war.

KELSTERBACH Hesse, Germany. Affiliated with the Orthodox rabbinate of Darmstadt, the community numbered 82 (7% of the total) in 1861, but economic factors led to its decline and by *Kristallnacht* (9–10 Nov. 1938) it had ceased to exist. Of the 47 Jews living there in 1933, 20 emigrated and 27 perished in the Holocaust.

KEMECSE Szabolcs dist., Hungary. Jews settled in the mid-18th cent. at the encouragement of estate owners. Jews played a leading role in the economic, social, and cultural life of the city. A J. group from Budapest set up a kosher wine industry which marketed its goods throughout Hungary. The community organized in 1810 and a synagogue was built in 1824. Most Jews were followers of R. Yeshayahu Steiner (the *Tzaddik* of Bodrogkeresztur). The J. pop. was 297 in 1880 and 367 in 1930. Mizrachi was active in the 1930s and sent pioneers to Palestine. In 1941, the local rabbi saved J. refugees from Poland by issuing them counterfeit certificates of residence. In 1942, Jews were mobilized for forced labor, some perishing in the Ukraine. In April 1944, the rest were sent to Nyiregyhaza and from there to Nyirjespuszta before deportation to Auschwitz from 17 May. Thirty-six survivors reestablished the community but by 1960 most had left.

KEMPEN Rhineland, Germany. A J. community existed there before 1288. In that year, 20 local Jews were murdered in the wake of the Oberwesel blood libel of 1287. They were attacked again during the Black Death persecutions of 1348-49. Finally, in 1385, J. settlement came to an end, to be renewed only in the early 19th cent. under French rule. In the first half of the 19th cent., most Jews were butchers or dealt in cattle and horses. Isaak Konen, a prosperous landowner, opened a silk-weaving mill in 1837. He also served as a city councilor. A synagogue and schoolhouse were built in the mid-19th cent. In 1847, K. became the seat of a regional congregation with a number of affiliated communities. The J. pop. of K. grew to a peak of 132 (total 4,906) in 1871 and then declined steadily to 61 in 1933. Under the Nazis, J. businesses were boycotted. On *Kristallnacht* (9–10 Nov. 1938), the synagogue was set on fire and J. homes and stores were vandalized. Thirty-one Jews emigrated, including about ten each to England and the U.S. Of those remaining, 11 were deported to the Riga ghetto on 11 Dec. 1941 and 18 to the Theresienstadt ghetto on 25 July 1942.

KEMPNO Poznan, Poland. Jews settled in 1674 with liberal building rights and tax exemptions on communal property. The synagogue erected in 1689 became famous throughout Poland for its original design and especially its interior woodwork. In 1691, many Jews lost their homes in a fire. In the 18th cent. many of the city's tailors, furriers, and tanners were Jews though most engaged in the retail trade. Trade expanded after the annexation to Prussia in

1793 as J. merchants made K. the biggest sheepwool market on the European continent. J. artisans also entered new areas like the building trades. With the J. pop. growing to 4,000 in 1840 (total 6,000), K. became known as a J. city (*Judenstadt*), with immigrants from Congress Poland, Lithuania, and Galicia (Brody). A second synagogue was completed in 1815 and later a J. elementary school was opened. The community was also famous for its musicians, with many later appearing in German orchestras. With education expanding and Jews entering the professions a process of emigration set in, reducing the J. pop. to 739 in 1910 and 250 in 1939. All were deported by the Germans to General Gouvernement territory in Jan. 1940 and from there to the death camps.

KEMPTEN (Allgaeu) Swabia, Germany. Jews are mentioned in the late 14th and early 15th cents. The modern community was founded in the 1870s, numbering 91 in 1910 (total 21,001) and 50 in 1933, when it was under the authority of the Ichenhausen district rabbinate. Twenty-six Jews left in 1933–40, 14 of them emigrating from Germany; ten were deported to Piaski (Poland) via Munich on 3 April 1942 and another seven were sent to the Theresienstadt ghetto in Sept. 1942 and Feb. 1945.

KERCH Crimea, Russia, today Ukraine. Jews settled in the 1830s and numbered 91 in 1847. Their number then grew to 4,774 (total 33,347) in 1897. A *talmud torah* was founded in the mid-19th cent. and later on, two private J. schools, one for girls and a Hebrew-Russian one for boys. A pogrom on 31 July–1 Aug. 1905 claimed several J. lives. Most Jews engaged in trade and crafts. There were a few professional people and service personnel. The Soviet authorities closed down the Great Synagogue and a J. hospital (founded in the 19th cent.) in the 1920s. Presumably a number of Yiddish-language schools were in operation as in other J. settlements with a substantial J. pop. In 1939, the J. pop. rose to 5,573 (total 104,443). The Germans captured the city on 16 Nov. 1941. On 1–3 Dec. they murdered about 2,500 Jews. The rest were murdered at the end of the month. When the Germans reoccupied the city on 23 May 1942 (after being driven out by the Red Army on 30 Dec. 1941) they murdered the few Jews, including Krimchaks, still there. In all, the Germans murdered about 7,000 Jews from K. and its environs.

KERECKY (Hung. Kerecke) Carpatho-Russia, Czechoslovakia. Jews probably settled in the first half of the 19th cent., numbering nine in 1840 and 75 (total 1,561) in 1880. In 1921 their pop. rose to 252 and in 1941 (after the Hungarian occupation of 1939) to 327. Most died in the gas chambers of Auschwitz after their deportation in the second half of May 1944.

KERPEN Rhineland, Germany. During the First Crusade massacres of 1096, K. served as a place of refuge for Jews under the protection of Archbishop Hermann III. The J. community was destroyed in the Black Death persecutions of 1348–49. Jews are again mentioned in the second half of the 17th cent. In the 1720s, a few Jews living there under letters of protection engaged in trade, beer brewing, and moneylending. A cemetery was opened in 1823 and a synagogue was erected in 1853. A J. school operated from 1828, averaging 10–20 pupils until WWII. The J. pop. was 128 (total 2,977) in 1871, declining to 95 in 1933. Under the Nazis, many left. Eight of those who emigrated were later deported to concentration camps from occupied Europe. On *Kristallnacht* (9–10 Nov. 1938), the synagogue was wrecked, J. homes were vandalized, and Jews were beaten. The last 31 Jews were deported in 1942; 29 perished.

KESTRICH Hesse, Germany. The community, numbering 100 (25% of the total) in 1861, disbanded in 1936 and within a year most of the Jews had left. Three were deported in 1942.

KESZTHELY Zala dist., Hungary. J. merchants from Rohonc arrived in the early 18th cent. Jews dominated the trade in hides, cloth, porcelain, and glass and owned the city's four banks, its printing house, and the local weekly newspaper. The community organized in 1766, building a synagogue in 1780 and opening a J. school in 1849. In 1869, the congregation became Neologist. The J. pop. rose to 1,034 (15% of the total) in 1890 but declined after WWI as antisemitism intensified, dropping to 755 in 1941. The young were seized for forced labor in 1941, most perishing. In June 1944, the Jews were taken to Zalaegerszeg and on 4 July deported to Auschwitz, where 829 died. After the deportations, J. workers from six forced labor units were brought to K. and executed. The postwar community numbered 80 in 1958.

KETHELY Somogy dist., Hungary. Jews are mentioned in the census of 1746 and numbered 94 in 1880 and 50 in 1930. The community was Neologist and maintained a synagogue. The J. pop. was deported to Auschwitz via Maracali at the beginning of July 1944.

KETTENBACH (now part of Aarbergen) Hesse-Nassau, Germany. The community built a synagogue in 1760, numbered 54 (12% of the total) in 1895, and also drew members from other villages. By Dec. 1938 all the Jews had left.

KETTWIG Rhineland, Germany. Jews settled in the late 18th cent. A synagogue was erected in 1807 and a J. elementary school was started in 1873-74. The J. pop. was 23 (total 3,069) in 1871 and 53 in 1933 (total 10,239). Under the Nazis, eight Jews emigrated between 1933 and Oct. 1938. On *Kristallnacht* (9-10 Nov. 1938), the synagogue was burned and J. homes were vandalized. By 1941, another 16 Jews had left. Of those who emigrated, ten reached the U.S and four Palestine. Fifteen Jews who were deported to the east perished.

KETY Cracow dist., Poland. Permanent settlement commenced after the lifting of the residence ban in 1860, with the J. pop averaging 350-400 from the late 19th cent. (about 6% of the total). Though a traditional-hasidic milieu prevailed, the Zionists were active from 1905. Under the German occupation the young were sent to local labor camps from late 1940 through 1941. The community was expelled to Wadowice in June 1942 and caught up in the *Aktions* there between July and Aug. Most were sent to Auschwitz.

KEZMAROK Slovakia, Czechoslovakia, today Republic of Slovakia. Jews settled in the mid-19th cent. after long-standing opposition by German residents. A synagogue was constructed in the 1870s. The community's first rabbi, Avraham Greenburg, served from 1874 to 1918, founding a yeshiva in the mid-1880s. The J. pop. rose from 659 in 1890 to 1,145 (total 6,166) in 1919 with refugees from Galicia arriving in WWI and opening a *shtibl*, mostly as followers of Zanz Hasidism. A Zionist society was founded in 1899 and Zionist activity expanded after WWI with Mizrachi and WIZO playing a leading role and the Zionist youth movements opening branches. Jews served on the mu-

nicipal council and owned about 100 stores and 25 workshops. With the creation of the Slovakian state in March 1939, local Germans began persecuting the Jews and vandalizing their property, including the synagogue. The authorities expelled J. children from the public schools and closed down J. businesses. Hundreds of J. men were also mobilized for forced labor. In late March 1942, 229 young J. women were rounded up for deportation to Auschwitz and in early April about 80 young men were sent to Majdanek. On 30 April, 159 local Jews were dispatched to Zilina and on 1 June another 800 were sent to the Lublin dist., able-bodied men to Majdanek, the others to Sobibor. Dozens more were sent to Auschwitz via Zilina on 21 Sept. Altogether, 75% of the area's Jews were deported in 1942. The Germans murdered hundreds more after arriving in the city in fall 1944. Of those who escaped, 48 joined the partisans or the Czechoslovakian army. In 1949, the J. pop. was 142,

KHARKOV Kharkov dist., Ukraine. J. residence was still officially banned in the early 19th cent. but somewhat later, J. Cantonists released from the Czar's army were allowed to settle. In the 1850s, Jews arriving for the annual fairs were permitted temporary residence. The city and district, however, remained outside the Pale of Settlement and Jews without residence permits were periodically rounded up and expelled in police raids. By 1863, the J. pop. was 775 and the community maintained two synagogues. In 1867, the J. pop. included 12 merchants, 23 artisans, 26 students, and 63 demobilized soldiers. In the early 1880s, Jews owned two banks and 16 wholesale warehouses. A hospital and soup kitchen were also opened. In 1880, Avraham Goldfaden's Yiddish theater group played a full month in K. By 1897, the J. pop. was 11,013 (total 175,000). On the eve of WWI, the police were still hounding "illegal" J. residents. Thousands of J. refugees arrived in 1915 and were taken in by the community. The Feb. 1917 Revolution brought on a great Zionist awakening, with thousands participating in rallies. After the Oct. 1917 Revolution and during the civil war (1918-21), pogroms were continually on the verge of breaking out, but violence was limited to breaking windows in J. homes and stores. When K. became the capital of the Ukrainian SSR (until its transfer to Kiev in 1934), the J. pop. grew substantially, reaching 130,250 in 1939. J. life was gradually thwarted. The Great Synagogue was expropriated and

Group of Jewish authors at the Kharkov Museum of Culture, Ukraine, 1933 (seated third from left: Itzik Pfeffer) (State Central Photo and Film Archives, Kiev/photo courtesy of Yad Vashem, The Holocaust Martyrs' and Heroes' Remembrance Authority, Jerusalem)

made over into a theater and club; the J. political parties were shut down; and the Zionist youth groups were forced to go underground until the arrests of 1925 ended their existence. The community's last rabbi, Eliyahu Aharon Mileykowski, emigrated to Palestine in 1928 and was appointed to the Tel Aviv Chief Rabbinate. As a substitute, J. life took on Soviet garb, adopting Yiddish as its only means of expression. In 1925, a J. newspaper, *Der Shtern*, appeared under the auspices of the Ukrainian Communist Party and the All-Ukrainian J. National Theater opened, operating in K. until it moved to Kiev when the capital was transferred there. In its place, a traveling chamber theater founded in 1929 became the J. National Theater of K. in 1938. In the late 1920s, one of the city's courts and police stations transacted business in Yiddish. Yiddish was also the language of instruction in

four elementary schools (two of them included vocational training), a high school, machinists' school, teachers' college, and J. dept. at the university. However, only a fifth of the Jews studied at J. institutes. Thousands of Jews were enrolled at the university and other institutes of higher education. Occupational changes were seen already in the first half of the 1920s as Jews moved from light industry to factory work. While in 1923, 52% were employed in home industries, by 1926 the figure had dropped to 29%. The number of construction workers increased while J. merchants dropped to 10% of all breadwinners in 1923 and 6% in 1926. The complete numerical breakdown for 1926 was: white-collar workers 17,215; blue-collar workers 6,394; artisans 3,255; merchants 2,276; professionals 1,570; unemployed 5,807; and misc. 2,748. Following the increase in industrial employment, 1,000 Jews could be found in the local tractor plant in 1931; 2,500 in a plant for railway engines and cars; and 1,200 in a shoe factory.

On 24 Oct. 1941, the Germans captured K., which remained under military government with a Ukrainian municipal council throughout the occupation. Thousands of hostages were taken from the outset of the occupation, most of them Jews, and shot or hanged in the city center. In early Nov., the municipal council was ordered to select a *Judenrat*. Food rations for the Jews were cut to 40% and 10,271 Jews were registered in an operation which many Jews evaded. On 22 Nov., the municipal council requested from the German authorities that Jews be made to wear the yellow badge and be concentrated in a single quarter. Paul Blobel, commander of the *Sonderkommando 4a*, ordered the Jews into a makeshift ghetto behind the tractor plant, about 7 miles from the center of the city, where they were housed in shack-like structures. The transfer began on 15 Dec., with Jews beaten, robbed, and murdered along the way. In the ghetto, 700–800 Jews were packed into a building without doors or windows. They no longer received food and were prevented from obtaining any by themselves or from leaving their quarters after dark. Many died of starvation, exposure, or disease. On 26 Dec., 500 Jews were made to volunteer for work in Poltava, Romny, and Kremenchug and brought instead to nearby Drobitzky Yar and executed. On 2 Jan. 1942, the liquidation of the ghetto commenced, taking a number of days as the Jews were again brought to Drobitzky Yar and murdered. Gas trucks were also used in the executions. Soviet sources place the number of victims at 15,000 while German sources give an overall figure of 21,685. After the liberation, Jews began returning to K., numbering 81,500 in 1959. However, their number declined in the 1970s and 1980s.

KHARTSIZK Stalino dist., Ukraine. Jews settled in the early 20th cent. following the development of the local metal industry. In 1939, the J. pop. was 127 (total 13,622). The Germans arrived on 25 Oct. 1941. Presumably most of their 56 victims were Jews.

KHASHCHEVATOYE Odessa dist., Ukraine. Jews settled in the late 18th cent. Their pop. reached 125 in the 1790s and 3,266 (total 4,850) in 1897. In a pogrom on 22 April 1918, nine Jews were injured. In the Soviet period, many (260 Jews in a total J. pop. of 3,170 in

1926) were employed in the three J. kolkhozes in the area. The town had a J. council (soviet) and a J. elementary school with an enrollment of 250 in 1924. The Germans captured K. on 29 July 1941 and on 16 Feb. 1942, they murdered 960 Jews, including 376 children, near the South Bug River.

KHERSON Nikolaiev dist., Ukraine. About 220 Jews settled here in the late 18th cent. Their numbers subsequently grew from 3,822 in 1847 to 17,755 (total 59,000) in 1897. A synagogue was probably built in the 1780s. In the late 19th cent., a *talmud torah* using the "Hebrew through Hebrew" method of instruction was in operation. In the early 20th cent., the community maintained a hospital and there were a number of private schools for boys and girls. A pogrom causing serious damage to J. property erupted in Oct. 1905. In April 1919, Denikin's White Army troops attacked the Jews. At various times in the Soviet period, a J. court, J. schools, an industrial college, and a J. dept. in the local university were operating. In the early 1930s, many Jews were employed in factories like the Petrovski plant, where 1,500 of the 4,500 workers were Jews. The J. pop. was 16,145 (total 96,987) in 1939. The Germans captured the city on 19 Aug. 1941. On 29 Aug. they murdered 100 Jews and 110 in early Sept. On 7 Sept., the Jews were moved to a ghetto. A *Judenrat* and J. police force were organized. On 24–25 Sept., a *Einsatzkommando 11a* unit murdered about 8,000 Jews. Afterwards they rounded up and murdered Jews in hiding. In Feb. 1942, they killed about 400 children of mixed marriages. A total of about 8,780 Jews were murdered.

KHISLAVICHI Smolensk dist., Russia. An organized community was already in existence in the mid-18th cent., with a pop. of 237 in 1766. The J. pop. rose to 2,205 in 1847. A fire in 1880 left 100 J. families homeless. In 1897, the J. pop. reached 3,901 (total 5,066), while in the Soviet period it dropped to 2,101 in 1926 and 1,427 in 1939. A J. school operated in the 1920s along with a number of clandestine *hadarim*. Jews were prominently represented in the local artisan cooperative. The Germans captured the town on 16 July 1941. In early Sept., the Jews were transferred to a ghetto and in late Sept., 150–200 were murdered. The remaining 800 from K. and its environs were murdered on 20 March 1942.

Sawing logs at a Joint Distribution Committee sawmill, Kherson, Ukraine, 1923 (YIVO Archive, New York/photo courtesy of Yad Vashem, The Holocaust Martyrs' and Heroes' Remembrance Authority, Jerusalem)

KHMELEVOE Kirovograd dist., Ukraine. Jews probably settled in the late 19th cent. The J. pop. dropped from 305 (total 3,507) in 1897 to 112 in 1926. The Germans captured the town in late July 1941, murdering about 100 Jews in Oct.–Nov.

KHMELNIK Vinnitsa dist., Ukraine. J. settlement commenced in 1565. The J. pop. was 1,417 in 1765 and 5,977 (total 11,657) in 1897. A number of J. lives were lost in a pogrom in July 1919. Under the Soviets, the J. pop. grew in the 1920s but dropped to 4,793 in 1939. In the late 1930s, about 250 J. breadwinners earned their livelihoods as factory workers; 300 as white-collar workers; 630 as artisans; and 70 as farmers. A J. council (soviet) was active in the mid-1920s and a J. elementary school was open until the late 1930s, with an enrollment of 600 in 1934. The Germans captured K. on 24 July 1941 and murdered 400 Jews in their first *Aktion* on 12 Aug. A ghetto and *Judenrat* were established in late Dec. In the *Aktion* of 9–16 Jan. 1942, 7,000 Jews were executed. Another 360 were killed on 12 June 1942; 1,650 on

3 March 1943; and 120 families of skilled workers in late June 1943. According to a Soviet source, 11,750 Jews were murdered in K., including thousands expelled to the ghetto from numerous settlements in the area.

KHODAKI Zhitomir dist., Ukraine. A few Jews were present in the first half of the 18th cent. The J. pop. was 270 (total 1,280) in 1897. During the civil war (1918–21) Jews were robbed. Their number probably declined between the World Wars. Those who did not flee the Germans in July 1941 were murdered.

KHODORKOV Zhitomir dist., Ukraine. Jews appeared after the settlement destroyed by Chmielnecki in the mid-17th cent. was rebuilt in 1720. Their pop. was 372 in 1765 and 3,672 (total 6,910) in 1897. On 15 July 1919, during the civil war, Jews were attacked in a pogrom. As a result of pogroms and internal migration the J. pop. declined to 361 in 1923. The Germans captured K. on 14 July 1941 and murdered the remaining Jews.

KHOINIKI Polesie dist., Belorussia. Jews probably settled in the early 18th cent. Their pop. was 89 in 1811 and 1,668 (total 2,685) in 1897. In 1920, the Balakhovich brigade staged a pogrom in which 42 Jews were murdered and most J. homes looted. A J. kolkhoz was founded in the same year and in 1930 supported 19 J. families. A J. council (soviet) was established in 1927 and a J. elementary school was open until 1938. A Hehalutz group was still very active in the mid-1920s. In the early 1930s, about half the J. breadwinners were artisans. In 1939, the J. pop. was 1,645. The Germans occupied K. in early Aug. 1941. Some Jews managed to flee. The rest were murdered near the town in two *Aktions* in Sept. and Oct. 1941.

KHOLM Kalinin dist., Russia. Jews settled in the mid-19th cent. and numbered 204 (of a total 5,894) in 1897. A synagogue was in use in the early 20th cent. By 1939, under the Soviets, only 32 Jews remained. Following the German occupation of 3 Aug. 1941, those who had neither fled nor been evacuated were murdered.

KHOLMI Chernigov dist., Ukraine. A few Jews were present in the late 19th cent. In 1939, they numbered 95 (total 4,838). The few who had neither fled nor been evacuated when the Germans arrived on 23 Aug. 1941 were murdered.

KHOLMICH Gomel dist., Belorussia. Jews probably settled in the late 17th cent. In 1897, their pop. was 1,380 (total 2,315). Two J. schools, for boys and for girls, were opened in 1910. The Germans occupied K. in Aug. 1941. Four days later they murdered 35 Jews on the banks of the Dnieper River. The remaining Jews were murdered later.

KHOLOPENICHI Minsk dist., Belorussia. Jews began arriving after the town received economic privileges in 1783 and numbered 1,343 (total 2,254) in 1897. In 1929, under Soviet rule, nearly half the 188 J. families in K. worked in artisan cooperatives while 23% had no defined means of support or were unemployed and only two families engaged in agriculture. In 1931, a four-year J. elementary school was still in operation. By 1939, the J. pop. had dropped to 500. The Germans occupied the town on 5 July 1941 and in Sept. murdered about 900 Jews from K. and the surrounding area along with another 700 from the Shamki area.

KHOMS (Homs) Tripolitania dist., Libya. Jews were present in the Roman period during the reigns of Septimius Severus (193–211 C. E.) and his son Caracalla (211–17). A large community apparently existed under the Fatimids and Zeirids in the 11th–12th cents., prospering from the trans-Sahara trade. The Almohad persecutions of the 12th–13th cents. probably caused the end of the medieval community. The trade in the *alafa* plant revived the community in the 19th cent. Most Jews in 19th cent. K. came from Tripoli. In 1902, the J. pop. was 300 and in 1911 it rose to 525 (total 10,813). A splendid fortress-like synagogue with marble floors and columns was built in 1905. Most children went to Italian schools, attending a *talmud torah* in the afternoons. From 1928, R. Ferija Zouartz officiated as rabbi, promoting Hebrew study and Zionist activity. In 1934, he founded a local branch of the Ben-Yehuda Association. In addition to trading in *alafa*, Jews engaged in traditional crafts and peddling, also benefiting economically from the city's position as a seaside vacation site. Relations with local Arabs and the Italian authorities were generally satisfactory. In Aug. 1942, 3,000 Jews from Tripoli were brought to the Sidi Azaz forced labor camp 6 miles (10 km) south of the city. Most were soon sent back home. Three hundred, however, were transferred to the Buqbuq camp and up to 1,000 remained, including a few dozen Jews from K. Under the British occupation, the camp was dismantled. Local Jews and J. soldiers serving in the British army forged close relations. The Ben-Yehuda Association again began to operate and Jews were now able to join the local police force. In 1944, the J. pop. was 930. The riots of 1945 left the community untouched, but relations with the Arab pop. deteriorated with the arrival of the British. In 1950–51 most of the Jews left for Israel.

KHOROL Poltava dist., Ukraine. Jews settled in the early 19th cent. and numbered 2,056 (total 8,997) in 1897. The community operated elementary schools for boys and girls as well as a *heder* system. Benzion Dinur (Dinaburg), historian of the Jews and Israel's first education minister, was born in K. in 1884. There was a pogrom against the Jews in Oct. 1905 and by General Denikin's White Army troops in 1919 during the civil war. In 1939, the J. pop. was 701. The Germans arrived on 13 Sept. 1941, murdering 460 Jews in a valley outside the town in Oct.

KHOTIMSK Mogilev dist., Belorussia. The J. pop. was 549 in 1847 and 2,178 (of a total 3,154) in 1897. A synagogue was erected in the late 18th cent. and three *battei midrash* and various charitable institutions were in operation in the 19th cent. In the Soviet period, the J. pop. dropped to 1,792 in 1926 and 786 in 1939 as many of the young left for the big cities to study or work. In 1930, 34 J. families worked on two nearby kolkhozes. Many Jews worked at a linen plant. A J. elementary school with an enrollment of 270 was opened in 1927 and operated until June 1941. A synagogue and three prayer houses were active until 1929. The Germans captured K. in July 1941, ordering the Jews to register and wear the yellow badge. On 12 July 1942, they were brought to the J. school and held there almost a month under conditions of hunger and overcrowding. On 5 Aug. they were executed at the linen plant on the outskirts of the town. A few escaped.

KHOTOVIZH Mogilev dist., Belorussia. The J. pop. was 122 (total 584) in 1880 and 490 (100% of the total) in 1897. Until the Oct. 1917 Revolution, most Jews engaged in petty trade and crafts. In 1929, under the Soviets, all 37 J. families in K. worked the land. It is believed that the Germans arrived in Aug. 1941 and presumably executed the Jews in the fall.

KHUTOR MIKHAILOVSKII Sumy dist., Ukraine. The J. pop. in 1939 was 205. After their occupation of K. on 1 Oct. 1941, the Germans murdered the remaining Jews who had neither fled nor been evacuated.

KIBLITCH Vinnitsa dist., Ukraine. The J. pop. in 1897 was 1,067 (of a total 3,096). A pogrom was staged in May 1919 and only 24 Jews remained in 1926. Those still there after the German occupation of July 1941 were murdered with the rest of the Jews of the region, probably in Nov. 1942.

KIEL Schleswig–Holstein, Germany. Numbering 37 in 1766, this Baltic port's J. community did not attain importance until Prussia annexed Schleswig–Holstein 100 years later. After dedicating a synagogue in 1869, the community affiliated itself with Altona's chief rabbinate and grew from 192 to 430 in three decades (1875–1905). A religious school with 64 pupils was headed by the first rabbi, Moritz Stern (1891–98), and a mixed choir was introduced in 1907. By the time of Emil Cohn (1908–12), one of the few strong-minded Zionists in Germany's Liberal rabbinate, the community was the second largest in Schleswig–Holstein, its new synagogue, built in 1910, accommodating 650 worshipers. A J. historical and cultural society as well as branches of the German Zionist Organization, Agudat Israel, and the Central Union (C.V.), were established before 1914. Several Jews gained distinction at the University of K. Prof. Otto Meyerhof was awarded the Nobel Prize for Medicine in 1923 and Max Pappenheim, a law professor of J. origin, became rector in 1900. Zionism gained support after WWI. Two Zionist youth movements, Habonim and Torah va-Avodah, were likewise active, along with Mizrachi. After the Nazis came to power, two J. lawyers were murdered and the university dismissed most of its "non-Aryan" teachers. In response to Nazi boycott measures, the community organized relief work and promoted J. cultural and social life (1934–37). Members attended Hebrew courses and 95% of the younger generation belonged to a Zionist youth movement. An urban pioneer training facility provided vocational training. All children were removed from "J. classes" in public schools and taught at a school founded by the community in 1938. Most of the 200 Jews from the east (*Ostjuden*) were deported from K. on 29 Oct. 1938. On *Kristallnacht* (9–10 Nov. 1938), SA and SS units destroyed the synagogue and communal archives, looted J. property, and dispatched 29 J. men to the Sachsenhausen concentration camp. A total of 586 Jews left during the Nazi era: 305 emigrated and 281 moved or were transported to other German cities. Of those who remained, 12 committed suicide and 85 were deported; 112 Jews from K. perished in Nazi camps and ghettoes. Fewer than a dozen Holocaust survivors returned after WWII.

KIELCE Kielce dist., Poland. Despite a residence ban dating from the 16th cent., Jews began settling in 1819. When the ban was lifted by the Russians in 1831, after the failure of the Polish rebellion, Polish merchants backed by the Church engaged in protracted agitation against J. residence. The Jews were expelled in 1845, although 101 were present by 1857. After the ban was officially lifted in 1863, the J. pop. grew to 6,173 in 1897 and 11,351 (total 31,171) in 1910. A small class of wealthy J. merchants, dealing in building materials and cloth, initiated fundraising campaigns to endow a J. hospital, completed in 1897, and a new synagogue, consecrated in 1903. In 1899, a J. vocational school was opened. The existence of a modern J. school and Hebrew school was short-lived. A Zionist society became active in 1900. K. was known as a center of Hasidism. R. Hayyim Shemuel Horowitz, a scion of the Seer of Lublin, was the first of the Hasidim to settle there. Later, R. Mordekhai Twersky of the Chernobyl dynasty (the Rabbi of Kuzmir; d. 1917) established a court. In 1918, a pogrom was staged by the local rabble and demobilized Polish soldiers, killing ten Jews and injuring 400. The J. pop. rose to 15,530 in 1921 and 18,083 (of a total 58,236) in 1931. In 1921, Jews owned 633 workshops, including 422 in the garment industry employing 568 Jews. In the mid-1920s, 4,659 J. merchants were registered in the city (82% of the total). Two J. banks were founded in the 1920s. Zionist activity was renewed during WWI. A Hashomer Hatzair branch was started in 1916 and Mizrachi became active in 1917. In 1926, Hehalutz started a pioneer training facility, which had a peak membership of 130 in 1933. Throughout the period, the Bund was involved in the city's labor struggle. Agudat Israel was active in education. The community maintained a number of libraries and a small theater. A J. weekly, the *Kieltzer Zeitung*, with a circulation of 500, was published in 1932–39. In 1925 an association was founded to raise money for the Hebrew University of Jerusalem. K. was one of the antisemitic Endecja Party's strongholds in Poland and a hotbed of anti-J. agitation throughout the 1930s. The Germans entered the city on 4 Sept. 1939. A *Judenrat* was established on 21 Sept. under a regime of forced labor and property confiscation. With the influx of refugees, the J. pop. grew to 25,400 by March 1940, including 3,000 from Cracow and others from Lodz and Kalisz. In Feb.–March 1941, 7,500 Jews arrived from Vienna. Two ghettoes were set up in early April 1941. Jews were employed in local shops and labor camps. Mass *Aktions* commenced on 20 Aug. 1942, lasting three days. About 21,000 Jews were deported to the Treblinka death camp while another 3,000 were murdered in the city. The 1,600 remaining Jews were confined in a "small ghetto." *Judenrat* members were murdered on 20 Nov. 1942 and 12 of the ghetto's 13 doctors and their families were executed on 21 March 1943. Many others were put to work in Hassag munitions factories and other labor camps. An underground group in Ludwikow was uncovered by the Germans and its members were executed. A group of 20 Jews

working in Pionki managed to escape to the forest and a few joined the Russian partisans while others were murdered by antisemitic partisans. After the war, around 250 Jews returned, mostly from places of refuge in the Soviet Union. About 200 of them resided in the 7 Planty St. apartment house where the community's offices were also located. On 4 July 1946, thousands of local residents attacked the building, provoked by the alleged kidnapping of a Polish child. During the rioting, 60–70 Jews were murdered, including children and pregnant women. About 100 were injured. Only at the end of the day did Polish soldiers arrive and in the aftermath few in authority condemned the rioting. Its effect upon the Jews of Poland was very traumatic and accelerated flight from Poland to Palestine.

KIELCZYGLOW   Lodz dist., Poland. Jews were living here in the 1840s. The J. pop. in 1921 was 241 (42% of the total). In July 1942 the 500 Jews were expelled to Osiakow and then deported to Chelmno.

KIEMIELISZKI   Vilna dist., Poland, today Belarus. Jews settled in the late 19th cent., growing to a pop. of 101 (total 507) in 1897 and dominating trade. The economic situation during WWI impoverished the community, which subsequently recovered with the aid of the J. Relief Committee for War Victims (YEKOPO) and an American relief committee. A Yiddish public school was founded in 1921. In 1931, there were 36 J. families (total 140). Most owned stores but faced competition and heavy taxes. Many Zionist youth movement graduates emigrated to Palestine. The Germans arrived in late June 1941 and in Oct. confined the Jews to a ghetto where many died. The young were sent out to work at forced labor. All who remained were murdered in late Oct. 1942.

KIERNOZIA   Warsaw dist., Poland. Jews are mentioned in the early 19th cent. and numbered 284 (total 726) in 1921. The Germans arrived on 16 Sept. 1939, confining the Jews to a ghetto in March 1940. In March 1941 all 650 Jews including refugees were expelled to the Warsaw ghetto.

KIEV   capital of Ukraine. A Khazar community with a garrison, carrying on trade with the Khazar kingdom, existed in the first half of the ninth cent. In 986 the famous disputation described in Yehuda Halevi's *Kuzari* took place between J., Christian, and Moslem representatives in the presence of Prince Vladimir. In the same period a J. community was present in K. and is mentioned in ancient Russian chronicles. J. merchants from Europe, the Crimea, and Caucasia frequented the city on their travels. They are mentioned in the sources as "Radhanites." There are also references to Jews in the 11th cent. biographies of Church metropolitans. During this period, Jews were living in two quarters, Khazar and Zhidovi. In the first half of the 12th cent. there were uprisings and local mobs attacked Jews, burning and pillaging their homes. The well-known rabbi, Moshe of Kiev, lived there at the time but in the wake of the pogrom left for France with his students. The Mongols destroyed the city in the 13th cent. The Grand Prince subsequently invited the Jews to return. In 1320, the city was annexed to the principality of Lithuania. The local princes granted charters of rights to Jews and the community was able to grow. Many were employed as tax agents. In 1482, the Tartars attacked K. and some Jews were taken prisoner and brought to the Crimea. The rest were expelled in 1495 together with all the Jews of Lithuania. They returned in 1503, receiving a new charter of rights from King Sigismund I. The local pop. habitually complained to the king about J. commercial activity and occasionally received privileges restricting J. trade, but their demand to expel the Jews was rejected. At the end of the 15th cent., Moshe ben Yaakov wrote commentaries which are still extant. In 1648, Chmielnicki's Cossack troops massacred the Jews. The city, along with those parts of the Ukraine across the Dnieper River, was then annexed to Russia and J. settlement banned. In 1794, K. was included in the J. Pale of Settlement and Jews once again were permitted to live there and engage in trade

Jewish market in Kiev, Ukraine, 1905 (The Central Archive for the History of the Jewish People, Jerusalem/photo courtesy of Yad Vashem, The Holocaust Martyrs' and Heroes' Remembrance Authority, Jerusalem)

and crafts. By 1815, they numbered 1,500, with the community maintaining two synagogues and other institutions. Once more the local pop. agitated against their presence and in 1835, permanent J. residence was again banned under Czar Nicholas I. In the 1850s, during the Crimean War, Jews connected with the army were allowed to live in the city and in 1859, certain merchants were permitted to reside there. Subsequently the categories were expanded to include the educated class, army veterans, and employees of residents. The Jews were permitted to reside in two suburbs: Podol and Lebed. Residence restrictions were officially lifted only in Feb. 1917. Despite the existing restrictions, there were over 20 synagogues, two *talmudei torah*, an orphanage, and a J. public school in K. in the early 20th cent. The Society for the Promotion of Culture among the Jews of Russia had one of its most active branches in K. and in 1909 supported 21 schools, including two kindergartens and a modernized *heder*. From the late 19th cent., numerous charity and welfare agencies were operating, including a free hospital, a surgical clinic, and a tuberculosis sanatorium for the needy. Two J. sugar magnates, Zaitsev and Brodsky, contributed generously to community institutions. The latter endowed a magnificent synagogue in 1898 which was converted into a theater under the Soviets. (Today, the building serves as the central place of worship for the Jews of K.) Socialist groups became active in the 1890s, including the Bund and the Zionists. In 1897, the J. pop. was 31,800 (13% of the total). Pogroms were a common aspect of life at the end of the 19th cent. and the beginning of the 20th in K. The first one occurred in May 1881. A number of Jews were killed, about 20 women raped, and property worth millions of rubles was destroyed. The authorities only intervened on the second day of the rioting. On 18–21 Oct. 1905, a second pogrom was staged, with the police and army preventing J. self-defense groups from intervening. This pogrom also led to loss of lives and property. On 1 Sept. 1911, when the head of the Russian Council of Ministers, Stolipin, was assassinated by an anarchist, Jews were blamed. Only the presence of Czar Nicholas II in the city prevented another pogrom. The notorious Beilis trial opened in K. in the same year, one of the last blood libels of modern times. Oscar Grusenberg, the well-known J. attorney and activist, defended him. Public figures throughout Russia condemned the trial and in the end Beilis was acquitted, but throughout the two-year period of the trial,

anti-J. feelings ran high and government action was necessary to prevent new pogroms. The J. pop. reached a pre-WWI figure of 81,256. The J. hospital (founded in 1862) served Jews throughout the entire Ukraine. The surgical clinic became a hospital and an eye clinic was opened under the well-known Dr. M. Mandelstamm. In 1911, 888 Jews attended K. University, representing 17% of the student body. Among the Hebrew writers active in the city were J. Kaminer, J. L. Levin (Yehalel), I. J. Weissberg, and E. Schulman. Shalom Aleichem also lived in K. for a time, calling it "Yehupets" in his descriptions of life there. During WWI, the city filled with J. refugees from the war zone and the authorities were forced to relax residence restrictions. The Oct. 1917 Revolution produced a great public awakening, leading to the organization of the community along democratic lines with the Zionist activist Moshe Nahum Syrkin (1878–1919) as its head. Various congresses were held in the city and Hebrew and Yiddish newspapers were published with the support of Tarbut and the Kultur Lige, respectively. Hebrew elementary and secondary schools were also opened. All this activity virtually ceased after the outbreak of the civil war (1918–21). After the withdrawal of the Red Army, the Petlyura gangs executed 36 members of J. self-defense units and in 1919 General Denikin and his White Army thugs went on a rampage of murder, rape, and looting. In 1920, Jews constituted a third of the city's pop. At the outset of Soviet rule, they suffered from hunger and a typhoid epidemic. Zionist organizations and institutions were shut down and those that continued to operate clandestinely saw their members arrested and sent to the camps. A similar fate befell religious institutions, including a yeshiva that operated clandestinely until 1925. On the other hand, K. became a government-supported center of Yiddish culture in the 1920s. A J. school system was created along with a school for the arts and Yiddish departments in a number of institutes of higher learning, including a department of Yiddish culture within the Ukrainian Academy of Sciences. In 1920, the Kunst Vinkel troupe was founded, evolving into K.'s municipal J. theater in 1928. A children's theater and a youth theater were also in operation from the late 1920s and when Ukraine's capital was transferred from Kharkov to K., the national J. theater also moved to the city, amalgamating with the municipal theater. It continued to operated until 1941, when it was evacuated to Uzbekistan. After WWII, the theater was not permitted to return to K., but housed in Chernovitz until closed down with the liquidation of J. culture in 1948. Yiddish institutions began to cease operations in the early 1930s, mainly under government pressure. The J. section in the Department of Education was eliminated; a number of schools were closed; and the J. department in the Academy of Sciences became the Institute of Proletarian J. Culture. K. was the home of the national Yiddish writers' association and David Hofstein and Itzik Feffer were active there. In 1939, the J. pop. was 224,236 (25% of the total).

The Germans entered the city on 19 Sept. 1941 after a prolonged siege. Many Jews managed to flee beforehand. Mass arrests commenced after Soviet sappers blew up German headquarters in the center of the city and thousands, including many Jews, were executed. Some from among the local pop. displayed hostility toward the Jews and acted as informers. On 28 Sept.

1941, all Jews were ordered to report the next day with their valuables, clothes, and other items to a location near the J. and Christian cemeteries in the Babi Yar area. The proximity of a train station allowed the Germans to spread the rumor that the Jews were to be transported out of the city. On 29 Sept., the day before Yom Kippur, Jews commenced arriving from the morning hours. They were led through the gates of the J. cemetery, ordered to undress and leave their belongings behind. They were then marched to the edge of the Babi Yar ravine, where they were machine-gunned down by *Einsatzkommando 4a* troops. Afterwards their bodies were pushed down into the ravine and covered with earth by a bulldozer. According to German reports, 33,771 Jews were executed by the next day. At the end of Sept., 300 J. mental patients from the Pavlov Psychiatric Hospital were murdered. On 9 Nov. 1941, another 15,000 Jews were executed in the ravine. Jews

Brodsky Synagogue in Kiev, Ukraine, 1917 (The Central Archive for the History of the Jewish People, Jerusalem/photo courtesy of Yad Vashem, The Holocaust Martyrs' and Heroes' Remembrance Authority, Jerusalem)

Pogrom in a Kiev synagogue, Ukraine, 1920 (The Central Archive for the History of the Jewish People, Jerusalem/photo courtesy of Yad Vashem, The Holocaust Martyrs' and Heroes' Remembrance Authority, Jerusalem)

were seized for execution at Babi Yar throughout the German occupation. Others were confined in labor camps inside the city. A large number were held in the Syretsk area under the harshest of conditions, with many perishing. In Aug. 1943, with the fighting drawing near, the Germans attempted to obliterate all traces of their crimes by burning the bodies buried in Babi Yar. A crew of 327 prisoners, including 100 Jews, was brought over from Syretsk and charged with opening the mass graves and burning the bodies over huge bonfires. Nine of the Jews escaped and lived to tell the story of Babi Yar. The Soviet commission that investigated Nazi war crimes in K. failed to find any of the graves but estimated that over 100,000 had perished there. The Jews who escaped estimated that over 50,000 of those who perished were Jews. Jews participated in the urban underground operating against the Nazis. Shimon Bruz, who headed the underground for a time, fell

in battle against Gestapo agents, while Tanya Marcus, who acted as its liaison officer, was caught and executed. After the liberation, Jews began returning to K. but were received with hostility and even physically attacked in Sept. 1945. Antisemitic material was disseminated in early 1953. For many years the Soviet authorities refused to authorize a monument for the victims of the massacres. In the 1970s, pressure increased, with protests from such non-J. writers as Yevgenii Yevtushenko (author of the poem *Babi Yar*), Viktor Nekrasov, and Anatoly Kuznitzov. In 1976, the monument was erected, but without mentioning the Jews. In 1979 the J. pop. of K. was 132,000 (6% of the total).

KIKINDA (Hung. Nagy-Kikinda) Vojvodina dist., Yugoslavia. Jews arrived from the mid-18th cent. By 1900 there were 777 Jews (total 24,843) and in 1940 they numbered 512. In Aug. 1941 the Jews were deported with great cruelty to the Sajmiste death camp (Beograd) and murdered there.

KIKOL   Warsaw dist., Poland. An organized community existed from the first half of the 19th cent. The J. pop. in 1921 was 350. Details of the fate of the community between the World Wars and in the Holocaust are unknown.

KILIKIEV   Kamenets-Podolski dist., Ukraine. The J. pop. was 267 in 1847 and 576 (total 1,928) in 1897, growing to 653 in 1923 under the Soviets. The Germans captured the town on 9 or 10 July 1941. On 28 July 1941, 200 Jews from K. were killed at Annopol. The rest were executed at Slavuta on 26 June 1942.

KINGISEPP   (until 1922, Yamburg) Leningrad dist., Russia. Jews probably settled in the early 20th cent., numbering 65 in 1926 and 84 in 1939. When the Germans arrived in Aug. 1941, they murdered the remaining few who had not fled or been evacuated. In Oct. 1943, the Nazis also murdered 11 Jews from the nearby village of Dubrovka.

KIPPENHEIM   Baden, Germany. Jews are first mentioned in 1654, abandoning the village in 1689 on the approach of the French in the Nine Years War. New families, expelled from neighboring Ettenheim, were present in 1716. The Weil family played a leading role in the community up to the 20th cent. In the 18th cent. Immanuel Weil held the iron and hide monopolies for the whole principality. A modest synagogue was erected in 1793 and a J. elementary school was opened in the 1830s. The J. pop. reached a peak of 323 in 1871, but then commenced to drop steadily through emigration and the declining J. birthrate. In 1933, 144 remained, subjected to increasing anti-J. agitation. By 1938, all J. businesses had been liquidated and 93 Jews had emigrated (58 to the U.S.). On *Kristallnacht* (9–10 Nov. 1938), the synagogue was vandalized and J. men were detained in the Dachau concentration camp. On 22 Oct. 1940, 31 Jews were deported to the Gurs concentration camp; another 12 were deported from their places of refuge after leaving K. In all, 29 Jews perished in the camps, 17 of them in Auschwitz in 1942–44.

KIRCHBERG I. HUNSRUECK   Rhineland, Germany. A J. settlement existed in the 13th cent. and local Jews were subjected to several persecutions in 1287, 1340, and 1348–49. Jews began to settle again toward the end of the 18th cent. In 1843, the J. pop. was 92, remaining fairly stable until WWI. A synagogue was erected in 1817 and a new one in 1882. A J. elementary school was opened in 1842. In June 1933, four months after the Nazi rise to power, there were 67 Jews in K. From the outset of the Nazi period, J. store windows were smashed and J. merchants kept out of the local cattle market. On *Kristallnacht* (9–10 Nov. 1938), the synagogue was destroyed. By Sept. 1939, all Jews had left the town, 46 for other German cities (including 31 for Cologne) and 15 for the U.S. It may be assumed that all those who did not reach safe havens perished in the Holocaust.

KIRCHEN   Baden, Germany. The first J. families arrived in 1736 after being expelled from Switzerland and were subjected to numerous disabilities and restrictions. The community began to grow toward the end of the cent. and its economic situation improved with inclusion in the Duchy of Baden in the early 19th cent. A synagogue was built in 1831 and a cemetery was opened in 1865, with the J. pop. reaching a peak of 192 in 1873, characterized by its exceptionally low mean age and high natural increase. Thereafter emigration was stepped up and the birthrate declined. A measure of prosperity was achieved in the early 20th cent. but the community was hard hit in the post-WWI economic crisis. In 1933, 60 Jews remained (including seven in neighboring Efringen). On *Kristallnacht* (9–10 Nov. 1938), the synagogue was burned and men were detained in the Dachau concentration camp. With the outbreak of war in Sept. 1939, the entire pop. was evacuated, the Jews mostly to Konstanz. Ultimately, 21 emigrated, nine left for other German cities, and 26 were deported (five surviving).

KIRCHHAIN   Hesse–Nassau, Germany. Jews lived there from the 17th cent., trading in livestock and agricultural produce. Elhanan Hendel Kirchhan, the first rabbi (1744–54), published a work on traditional life, customs, and music in Hesse (*Simhat ha–Hayyim*, 1727) which ran to numerous editions. The J. community grew to 221 (9% of the total) in 1910, maintaining an elementary school (1835–1924) where children from nearby Amoeneburg were also taught. A large synagogue in the Romanesque style was opened in 1904 together with a communal center. Two eminent Jews born in K. were the pioneer neurologist Benedikt Stilling (1810–79) and the political philosopher Leo Strauss (1899–1973). Branches of the Central Union (C.V.) and J. War Veterans Association were established during the Weimar Republic. Affiliated with Marburg's rabbinate, the community still numbered 189 (7%) in 1925, but Nazi boycott measures and violence reduced it to 77 in July 1938. SS men organized a pogrom shortly before *Kristallnacht* (9–10 Nov. 1938), destroying the synagogue's interior. By Jan. 1939, 157 Jews had left (59 emigrating); a further 29 emigrated by March 1941 and 20 were deported in 1941–42.

KIRCHHEIM A. D. ECK   Palatinate, Germany. A J. community of 25 families existed at the outset of the 19th cent., maintaining a prayer house and a cemetery. In 1848, it numbered 22 families (93 Jews), with trade as the primary livelihood. The J. pop. dropped to 70 (total 903) in 1871. A religious teacher was employed in 1830, teaching children from neighboring communities as well. A synagogue was erected c. 1885 and a women's society was started in 1900. In 1928, the J. cemetery was desecrated. In 1932, the community included eight Jews from Grosskarlbach, eight from Weissenheim a. Brg., and two from Kleinkarlbach. In the Nazi era, the local J. pop. dropped from 22 in mid-1933 to 14 in May 1939. The synagogue was seriously damaged on *Kristallnacht* (9–10 Nov. 1938), and sold off to the local authorities in 1939. The few Jews who remained were deported to the Gurs concentration camp in Oct. 1940. At least 12 perished in the Holocaust. During the war, the synagogue was desecrated and the tombstones used to build pig sties.

KIRCHHEIMBOLANDEN   Palatinate, Germany. An ancient settlement apparently existed here. In the early 18th cent., three J. families were permitted to reside in the town. The community maintained a synagogue, which was damaged by fire in 1833, and a cemetery. The congregation was Liberal in its religious orientation. The J. pop. reached a peak of 188 in 1830 and then declined steadily. In June 1933, about four months after the Nazi rise to power, there were 65 Jews in K. Local residents strictly adhered to the general boycott of April 1933. In Oct. 1938, 28 Jews remained in K. and in late 1939 just 11. Of those who emigrated in

1935–39, 37–39 reached the U.S. On *Kristallnacht* (9–10 Nov. 1938), the synagogue was burned, J. homes and stores were vandalized, and J. men were sent to the Dachau concentration camp. Ten Jews were deported to the Gurs concentration camp on 22 Oct. 1940.

KIRF   Rhineland, Germany. The Jews of K. belonged to the Freudenburg community in the first half of the 19th cent. By mid-cent., an independent community was established. The J. pop. grew from 32 in 1808 to a peak of 117 (total 659) in 1905. In June 1933, about four months after the Nazi rise to power, there were 78 Jews in K. From early in the Nazi period, J. property was repeatedly vandalized. In 1933–39, 30 Jews emigrated, including 11 to France and 11 to the U.S.; 44 left for other German cities, including 27 for Trier. The synagogue was destroyed on *Kristallnacht* (9–10 Nov. 1938). At the outbreak of WWII, the village with all its inhabitants, including the remaining Jews, was evacuated to central Germany. It may be assumed that all those who did not make it in time to safe havens perished in the Holocaust.

KIRN   Rhineland, Germany. J. settlement already existed in the 13th cent. but the Jews left after six were killed in riots in 1287, apparently in the wake of the Oberwesel blood libel. Jews began to settle again in the first half of the 19th cent., their number rising from five in 1843 to 59 in 1871 and a peak of 109 in 1905 (total 6,588). A synagogue was consecrated in 1888. In June 1933, about four months after the Nazi rise to power, the J. pop. in K. numbered 78. By 1938, 45 Jews remained in K., most of them elderly people. On *Kristallnacht* (9–10 Nov. 1938), 12 J. homes and the synagogue were destroyed. Of the 27 Jews who emigrated from June 1933, 13 reached the U.S.; another 38 moved to other German cities. Eleven Jews were deported in July 1942.

KIROV   (until 1936, Pesochnaya) Smolensk dist., Russia. Jews probably settled at the turn of the 19th cent., numbering 145 in 1926 and 182 (total 15,313) in 1939. The few Jews who had not fled or been evacuated were murdered during the short German occupation of 4 Oct. 1941–11 Jan. 1942.

KIROVOGRAD   (until 1924, Yelyzavetgrad; in 1924–36, Zinovyevsk; in 1936–39, Kirovo) Kirovo-

Елисаветградъ. Большая Синагога. Изд. Ф. М. Сановича.

Great Synagogue of Kirovograd, Ukraine

grad dist., Ukraine. Jews settled in the early 18th cent., numbering 574 in 1803 and growing to 23,967 (total 61,488) in 1897. In an April 1881 pogrom, one Jew was killed and J. property suffered considerable damage. Jews were active as wine producers and tobacco manufacturers. In the early 20th cent., the community maintained 17 J. schools, numerous *hadarim*, a vocational school, and a *talmud torah*. One of the worst pogroms of the civil war (1918–21) occurred in mid-May 1919 when Ataman Grigoryev gangs massacred up to 3,000 Jews. In the first two years of Soviet rule, J. political parties and newspapers appeared. In May 1918, community council elections were held with the Zionists obtaining a majority. The council was disbanded after Soviet rule stabilized. During the 1920s, a few J. schools remained in operation, including a vocational school founded in 1925. In the 1930s, a special department for J. students was maintained in the local institute of arts and crafts. Most Jews were employed in artisans' cooperatives as tailors (90% of the total), leather workers (70–

75%), printers (70–75%), etc. Hundreds were employed in industry, including 300–400 in a farm machinery plant. Many left the city to work in agriculture, including 142 families in summer 1927 alone. By 1939, the J. pop. had declined to 14,641. The Germans captured the city on 14 Aug. 1943 and on 23 Aug. a *Sonderkommando 4b* unit murdered several hundred Jews. A similar massacre occurred in mid-Sept., and again on 19 Sept. when hundreds of J. males were taken to the Kustchevka camp and shortly afterwards executed in the antitank ditches near K. Another few hundred Jews were murdered at the end of the month. In all, about 5,000 Jews were murdered by the end of Sept. In Nov., 150 J. prisoners of war were executed.

KIRTORF Hesse, Germany. Numbering 66 (7% of the total) in 1880, the Jews were mainly livestock traders. From 1933 the Nazi boycott hastened their departure. Over one-third (12) emigrated and the last seven were deported in 1942.

KISBER Kamarom dist., Hungary. J. settlement commenced in the mid-19th cent. The community organized in 1851 and maintained a synagogue and school. The J. pop. stood at 220 in 1938. In 1941, J. males were sent to the Ukraine for forced labor, most perishing. In June 1944, the remaining Jews were brought to Kamarom, from where they were deported to Auschwitz on 13 June.

KISHINEV see CHISINAU.

KISIELIN Volhynia dist., Poland, today Ukraine. Jews numbered 873 in 1897 (total 889) and 94 (total 458) after the rigors of WWI. The Germans expelled them to Torczyn in Jan. 1942 and executed them together with the local Jews on 23 Aug. 1942.

KISKOROS Pest–Pilis–Solt–Kiskun dist., Hungary. Jews arrived from Maramaros in Transylvania in the late 18th cent., mainly trading in wine and grain. The J. pop. was 350 (5% of the total) in 1869 and 509 in 1941. Originally Status Quo, the congregation became Orthodox in 1912. A school was opened in 1880 and a yeshiva was founded by R. David Lelovics, who served the community in 1899–1942. At the end of June 1944, the remaining Jews, about 580 including those from the surrounding area, were deported to Auschwitz via Kecskemet. Survivors reestablished the community, but it gradually dispersed.

KISKUNFELEGYHAZA Pest–Pilis–Solt–Kiskun dist., Hungary. The first Jews arrived from Albertirsa in the mid-19th cent. Most traded in farm produce (mainly poultry) and Jews operated factories producing bricks, vinegar, cement, and ceramics. A school was opened in 1853 and a synagogue erected in 1860. In 1890, the J. pop. was 830 (3% of the total). Jews were murdered in the White Terror of 1919–21 and in 1941 families of doubtful citizenship were deported to Kamenets-Podolski and also murdered. Others perished under forced labor on the eastern front. On 25 June 1944, the Jews were deported to Auschwitz via Kecskemet. The 1946 community of 227 gradually dispersed.

KISKUNHALAS Pest–Pilis–Solt–Kiskun dist., Hungary. J. settlement began in the early 18th cent. and the community organized in 1826, building a synagogue in 1858 and defining itself first as Orthodox and then, toward the end of the 19th cent., as Neologist. R. Eliezer

Zussman, who served in 1856–86, founded an important yeshiva. Dr. Yoel Hayyim Dohany, who was rabbi in 1915–49, was an influential Zionist whose activities militated against assimilationist tendencies. The J. pop. rose from 499 in 1880 to 1,018 (3% of the total) in 1900, maintaining that level until WWII. With the arrival of the Germans at the end of May 1944, the Jews were expelled to Szeged and at the end of June they were deported to Auschwitz and later to camps in Austria. A group of 208 Jews transported from Ujvidek for forced labor in Oct. 1944 was murdered at the train station by SS men. After the war, 450 Jews returned but most left, many for Israel.

KISKUNLACHAZA Pest dist., Hungary. The community was founded in 1860 and numbered 100 in 1930. No other details are available.

KISKUNMAJSA Pest–Pilis–Solt–Kiskun dist., Hungary. Jews arrived in 1840. A synagogue was built in 1870 and a school opened in 1903. The J. pop. was 152 in 1869 (2% of the total) and 138 in 1941. In the White Terror of 1919–21 and during the first years of WWII, the Jews were severely persecuted. Sixteen perished at forced labor in the Ukraine and the rest were deported to Auschwitz via Szeged on 24–26 June 1944.

KISLETA Szabolcs dist., Hungary. Jews are mentioned in 1747 and numbered 68 in 1930. The community maintained a synagogue. The Jews were deported on 12 May 1944 to Auschwitz via Nyiregyhaza.

KISLOVODSK Stavropol territory, Russia. Jews probably settled at the turn of the 19th cent., numbering 417 (360 Ashkenazi and 57 Mountain Jews [Tats]) in 1926. The Germans occupied K. toward mid-Aug. 1942. Many J. refugees from the western parts of the Soviet Union were present. The Germans set up a *Judenrat* under a regime of forced labor and extortion. They murdered most of the Jews at Minaralnyie Vody on 9 Sept.

KISPEST suburb of Budapest, Hungary. Jews settled in the late 19th cent. The municipal council was headed by a Jew in 1888. The community, defining itself as Neologist, maintained a cemetery, synagogue, and school. Most of the young became members of the Betar youth movement. The J. pop. reached

3,456 in 1931 and 4,000 in 1943. A ghetto was set up in May 1944. On 30 June 1944, the Jews were brought to Monor and held ten days without food or water and then deported to Auschwitz on 8 July. A few hundred returned after the war, but most left for Israel.

KISSINGEN, BAD see BAD KISSINGEN.

KISTARCSA Pest–Pilis–Solt–Kiskun dist., Hungary. Jews settled in the late 19th cent. and numbered 88 in 1930. In 1942, the men were sent to forced labor. In April 1944, some managed to flee to Pest; the rest were deported to Auschwitz in late May. A concentration camp existing since 1937 became a Gestapo facility which by summer 1944 held some 15,000 Budapest Jews. The deportation of these Jews to Auschwitz, which commenced in April under Eichmann's orders, was stopped through international pressure. The remaining 1,000 Jews at the camp were sent to labor camps on 27 Sept. 1944.

KISTELEK Csongrad dist., Hungary. Jews were present in the 18th cent. and numbered 141 in 1880 and 218 in 1930. The community was affiliated with Szeged. The Jews were probably deported via Szeged to Auschwitz at the end of June 1944.

KISTERENYE Nograd dist., Hungary. The J. pop. stood at 87 in 1930. The Jews were deported to Auschwitz on 4 June 1944.

KISUJSZALLAS Jasz–Nagykun–Szolnok dist., Hungary. Jews were allowed to settle in K. in the late 19th cent. and numbered 525 in 1900 (4% of the total) and 210 in 1941. The Schuck family provided all the community's rabbis. A synagogue was established in 1869 and a school in 1883. The Jews were brought to Szolnok on 16 June 1944 and from there deported to Auschwitz and Austria on 26–29 June. More than 100 survivors reestablished the community but most left by 1956.

KISVARDA Szabolcs dist., Hungary. Jews are first mentioned in 1730. They traded in farm produce and were prominent in the food-processing industry. They also founded a number of banks. The community organized in 1796, erecting a synagogue in 1801 and a hospital in 1896. R. Avraham Yitzhak Weinberger, who served in 1844–84, founded a yeshiva. The J.

pop. grew from 1,238 in 1869 to 2,614 in 1900 and 3,770 (25.5% of the total) in 1941. The Zionists became active after WWI and the J. educational system had an enrollment of 370 by 1940. Dov Gruner (1912–46), who was hanged in Palestine by the British for underground activities, was born in K. In 1942, the young were sent to the Ukraine under forced labor, most perishing. A regional ghetto confining 7,000 Jews was established in mid-April 1944. On 25 and 27 May, all were deported to Auschwitz. The reestablished community numbered 804 in 1946, but most left over the next decade.

KISVARSANY Szabolcs dist., Hungary. Jews settled in the late 18th cent., numbering 118 in 1880 and 54 in 1930. On 25–27 June 1944, they were deported to Auschwitz via Kisvarda.

KITAIGOROD (I) Vinnitsa dist., Ukraine. The J. pop. was 469 in 1765 and 735 (total 2,794) in 1897. In 1926, the J. pop. grew to 1,571. After the German occupation of 25 July 1941, 180 Jews were expelled to Dashev, probably towards the end of the year, and executed there.

KITAIGOROD (II) Kamenets-Podolski dist., Ukraine. Jews settled in the 17th cent., forming an organized community. In 1765, the J. pop. included 489 tax payers. In 1897, the J. pop. stood at 642. The community maintained a synagogue and *beit midrash*. In 1905, peasants from a neighboring village drove off Cossacks seeking to attack the Jews. In 1919, the Petlyura gangs staged a pogrom and killed 84 Jews. The Germans occupied the town in July 1941. The Jews were expelled to a labor camp in Kamenets-Podolski. In Jan 1942, they were murdered together with other Jews in the area.

KITTSEE Burgenland, Austria. The community was one of the Seven Communities (*Sheva Kehillot*). Jews first settled in K. in 1600, when a synagogue and a J. cemetery were consecrated. Jews earned their living as tailors, shoemakers, hairdressers, and goldsmiths. They were represented in the professional class as doctors. In 1934, there were 58 Jews in K. In April 1938, the Jews were thrown out of their houses at night and their property was confiscated. They were brought to the border and sent out on a boat on the Danube. They were saved by the Czechoslovakian authorities.

KITZINGEN Lower Franconia, Germany. An organized J. community existed in the mid-12th cent. under the auspices of the rabbi of Wuerzburg. It suffered grievously over the next two centuries: 11 Jews were tortured and killed in a blood libel in 1242, 15 were murdered in the Rindfleisch massacres of 1298. Many were again slaughtered in the Armleder massacres of 1336–39 and the community was totally destroyed in the Black Death persecutions of 1348–49. Jews resettled in the late 14th cent. under letters of protection and were fairly prosperous but lived under the constant threat of expulsion. In 1771, Jews were attacked in food riots and in 1789 they were expelled, only resettling in the 1830s and 1840s and forming an officially recognized community in 1864. In 1871, K. became the seat of the district rabbinate with 26 communities attached to it and R. Immanuel Adler serving as chief rabbi until 1911. The J. pop. rose to 337 in 1880 and 478 (total 9,113) in 1910. Jews dominated the very important wine industry, with 69 wine merchants in 1908. Dr. Josef Wohlgemuth served as district rabbi in 1914–35. In 1933, Jews numbered 360, augmented by newcomers in the Nazi era. The prevailing atmosphere of tolerance in previous years soon gave way to persecution as Jews were isolated economically and socially. On *Kristallnacht* (9–10 Nov. 1938), the synagogue was partially burned and all its contents were destroyed, J. homes were wrecked, and 23 J. men were sent to the Dachau concentration camp. Large numbers left in 1938–39. In all, 192 Jews emigrated, including 84 to the U.S. and 52 to Palestine, and 111 left for other German cities. Of those remaining in 1942, 76 were deported to Izbica in the Lublin dist. (Poland) on 24 April and 19 to the Theresienstadt ghetto on 23 Sept. 1942.

KIWERCE Volhynia dist., Poland, today Ukraine. Jews settled with the coming of the railroad in the early 20th cent., reaching a pop. of around 500 in 1910 and dropping to 175 (total 552) after much suffering in WWI. The Germans murdered 270 Jews in May 1942 and the few J. doctors who had been left alive were killed by the end of 1942.

KLADNO Bohemia, Czechoslovakia. Jews settled in the early 19th cent., consecrating a synagogue in 1889. Numbering 430 in 1900, they played an active role in the mining industry. In 1930, 210 remained (total 20,751). In Feb. 1942, they were among the 1,623 Jews transported from the county to the Theresienstadt ghetto, all but 120 perishing.

KLAGENFURT Carinthia, Austria. A J. quarter (*Judendorf*) within the city boundaries of K. is first mentioned in 1162 and in 1279 there was a J. quarter outside the city gate. In 1335, there were 36 J. taxpayers. They were engaged in moneylending. In 1496, Maximilian I expelled all Jews from the region. In 1783, Jews were permitted to attend the fairs in K. They resettled in the city in the second half of the 19th cent. With the support of Adolf Fischhof, a J. physician and one of the leaders of the 1848 revolution in Austria, a religious association (*Kultusverein*) was founded in 1886. Jews were engaged in trade and entered the professional class as doctors and dentists. In 1905, the community bought an existing building and converted it into a synagogue. In 1922, the Jews were finally allowed to constitute their own community, having been until then under the jurisdiction of the bigger Graz community. In 1869, the J. pop. stood at 16, increasing to 126 in 1899 (total 21,630), 180 in 1934, and a peak of 200 in 1938. In the 1930s, the Zionists were active. Immediately after the *Anschluss* (13 March 1938), the synagogue was closed and several J. officials were arrested. By the end of March 1938, the local Zionist group was dissolved and bank accounts belonging to Jews and the community were confiscated. In the following months, several J. homes were destroyed and J. shops were "Aryanized." On *Kristallnacht* (9–10 Nov. 1938), the synagogue was vandalized and community archives were seized and brought to Gestapo headquarters. Most Jews managed to emigrate; some left for Vienna. In May 1939, there were 14 Jews in K. A few managed to escape to Italy. The others were sent to Vienna and from there to the death camps in the east where all perished.

KLATOVY Bohemia, Czechoslovakia. Jews are mentioned in the 14th cent. and may have formed a community by the 16th cent. but subsequently their residence was banned until the mid-19th cent. A synagogue was consecrated in 1873 and the J. pop. grew to 724 in 1893, with Jews owning most of the city's factories. In WWI, 1,100 East European Jews found refuge with the community. In 1930, the J. pop. was 344 (2% of the total). In July 1941, Czech Fascists pillaged the synagogue and on 26 Nov. 1942, the Jews were deported to the Theresienstadt ghetto. Most were sent to Auschwitz in Jan. and Sept. 1943. Few survived.

KLECK   Nowogrodek dist., Poland, today Belarus. Jews are first mentioned in 1529. In 1796, the Radziwills erected a synagogue for the community. R. Meir Berlin (Bar-Ilan), the Mizrachi leader, was born in K. in 1880. In 1897, the J. pop. reached 3,415 (total 4,684). Jews earned a living marketing farm produce and also owned flour mills, oil presses, wool-processing plants, and tanneries. The J. pop. in 1921 was 4,190. In 1921 the Etz Hayyim yeshiva of Slutsk was transferred to the town, reaching an enrollment of 260 in 1939. A Hebrew elementary school was also started and Zionist activity was widespread. In 1937 a fire destroyed 280 J. homes. On 24 Oct. 1941, four months after arriving in K., the Germans murdered 3,880 Jews at the Catholic cemetery. The remaining 1,400 were confined to a ghetto. As the final *Aktion* commenced on 21 July 1942, the J. underground set the ghetto on fire and 400 attempted to escape in the resulting pandemonium. Only a few dozen reached the forest and about 25 survived the war fighting with the partisans.

KLECZEW   Lodz dist., Poland. J. settlement began in the mid-18th cent. and in 1897 numbered 734 (31% of the total). Jews exported agricultural produce and wool, mainly to Prussia. The Germans entered K. on 15 Sept. 1939, and a *Judenrat* was set up. On 17–18 Aug. 1940, the Jews were expelled to Belkhatow, Zagorow, Grodziec, and Zhgow and were murdered in the Kazimierz Biskupi forests.

KLEINBARDORF   Lower Franconia, Germany. Jews are first mentioned in 1574. The ancient cemetery served 37 communities. A new synagogue was built in 1896. The J. pop. was 80 in 1837 (total 260) and declined steadily thereafter to 11 in 1933. Three emigrated in 1939–40 and the last five were expelled in 1942: three to Izbica in the Lublin dist. (Poland) on 25 April and two to the Theresienstadt ghetto on 23 Sept.

KLEINBOCKENHEIM   Palatinate, Germany. Ten J. families (41 Jews) were present in 1848, forming a united congregation with Grossbockenheim (86 Jews) and Kindenheim (123). In 1875, the first two communities broke away and formed their own independent congregation. In that year, the J. pop. of K. was 50.

Main street, Kleck, Poland

The number dropped to 38 in 1900 and 27 in 1933. At that time, the synagogue in use was located in Grossbockenheim and the cemetery in Kindenheim while the 11 remaining Jews there were attached to the K. congregation. During the Nazi era, 18 Jews emigrated and three perished after deportation to the Gurs concentration camp in Oct. 1933.

KLEINEIBSTADT   Lower Franconia, Germany. A J. community existed in the mid-18th cent. A synagogue was erected in 1828 and a J. public school opened in the early 1870s. The J. pop. was 114 (of a total 522) in 1880 and seven in 1933. The synagogue building was sold in 1937. Six Jews were brought to K. from Koenigshofen in 1941 and of the total of 11 present in 1942, six were deported to Izbica in the Lublin dist. (Poland) on 25 April and three elderly women to the Theresienstadt ghetto on 10 Sept. 1942 via Schweinfurt.

KLEINEICHHOLZHEIM   (in J. sources, Ikoldsheim) Baden, Germany. Jews were present from the first quarter of the 18th cent. and constituted a community of 35 in 1825, purchasing a few sections of the local castle in 1843 to set up a synagogue and community facilities. They numbered 93 in 1875 (total 284). In 1933, 28 remained, operating two department stores, two hotels, and a farm that also served for pioneer training; all these operations were liquidated by 1938 under the Nazi economic boycott. Seven Jews emigrated to the U.S. in 1933–1938 and seven more after *Kristallnacht* (9–10 Nov. 1938), when the synagogue and J. homes were vandalized. Fifteen were deported to the Gurs concentration camp on 22 Oct. 1940; four survived.

KLEINHEUBACH   Lower Franconia, Germany. Jews are first known from 1349, when one was killed in the Black Death persecutions. An organized community existed in the second half of the 17th cent. A synagogue was built in 1728 and a cemetery was consecrated in 1730. The J. pop. stood at 145 (total 1,570) in 1837, with 40 emigrating to the U.S. in 1844–54. In 1933, 36 Jews remained. Fourteen emigrated and 11 left for other German cities in 1933–41. The last three Jews were deported to Izbica in the Lublin dist. (Poland) and the Theresienstadt ghetto in 1942.

KLEIN-KROTZENBURG   Hesse, Germany. At its height, in 1880, the community numbered 37 (2% of the total). On *Kristallnacht* (9–10 Nov. 1938), the synagogue was vandalized and within a year all the Jews had left, most emigrating.

KLEINLANGHEIM   Lower Franconia, Germany. Jews are first mentioned in 1415 and subsequently formed a single community with Grosslangheim (until the late 18th cent.). The J. pop. numbered 118 (total 1,210) in 1837 and 38 in 1933. From the 1920s, the Jews suffered from anti-J. agitation and occasional violence. On *Kristallnacht* (9–10 Nov. 1938), the synagogue was vandalized and J. homes were looted. In 1937–39, 13 Jews emigrated and 22 left for other German cities. The last three were deported to the Theresienstadt ghetto on 23 Sept. 1942.

KLEINSTEINACH   Lower Franconia, Germany. Jews are first mentioned in 1453. From the late 16th cent., the J. cemetery there served numerous communities and in the 17th cent. K. was the seat of the Grabfeld district rabbinate. The J. pop. was 159 in 1814 and 129 in 1900 (total 488). In 1933, 33 Jews were left, mainly trading in cattle and farming. On *Kristallnacht* (9–10 Nov. 1938), J. homes were vandalized and the synagogue's contents destroyed. Nineteen Jews left K. in 1936–40, including 12 for the U.S. In 1942, four were deported to Izbica in the Lublin dist. (Poland) on 25 April and five to the Theresienstadt ghetto on 10 Sept.

KLEINWALLSTADT   Lower Franconia, Germany. A J. community existed in the early 18th cent. A new synagogue was built in 1900, when the J. pop. stood at 81 (total 1,477). In 1933, 45 Jews remained. Windows in the synagogue and J. homes were smashed in 1933–34 and in 1936 rioters broke up prayer services. All the Jews left in 1934–38, including 16 to the U.S. and 11 to Frankfurt.

KLENOVEC   Slovakia, Czechoslovakia, today Republic of Slovakia. The J. pop. was 72 in 1900 and 33 in 1940. The community maintained a synagogue and cemetery. Most Jews were deported to the death camps in 1942.

KLESOW   Volhynia dist., Poland, today Ukraine. Jews settled near the new railroad station in the late 19th cent. and numbered 142 in 1921. J.-owned quarries served as a nationwide Hehalutz training facility in 1924–37, with 8,000 pioneers passing through on their way to Palestine. The Jews were deported by the Germans to the Poleska camp in Sarny and murdered there together with the local Jews on 28 Aug. 1942.

KLESZCZELE Bialystok dist., Poland. Jews first arrived in the 16th cent., continuing to live there in small numbers even after the *de non tolerandis Judaeis* privilege granted to the town in 1688. By 1807, at the beginning of Russian rule, they numbered 75, increasing to 710 (total 2,013) in 1897, when an organized community existed. After WWI a Yiddish school and a Hebrew school were founded along with branches of Hehalutz and Hashomer Hatzair which almost all the young joined. The J. pop. in 1939 was 750. Under Soviet rule in 1939–41, the Jews accommodated themselves to the new system. The Germans arrived on 23 June 1941, instituting a regime of forced labor. In Sept. a ghetto was established, crowding together over 600 Jews despoiled of their possessions by frequent "contributions" and suffering from hunger and disease. On 5 Nov. 1942, 1,000 Jews from Milejczyce were taken to the ghetto and the next day all were brought to the old Polish cavalry barracks near Bialystok and from there deported to the Treblinka death camp.

KLESZCZOW Lodz dist., Poland. Jews lived here from the mid-18th cent. and in 1897 numbered 226 (44% of the total). They were expelled by the Russians during WWI and by the Germans to the Treblinka death camp during WWII.

KLETNYIA (until the mid-1930s, Ludinka) Oriol dist., Russia. Jews settled in 1881, two years after the town was founded. In 1897, their pop. was 42, increasing to a few dozen families on the eve of WWI. A synagogue and cemetery were consecrated in this period. Under the Soviets, the J. pop. rose to 386 in 1926 and then dropped to 286 (total 6,456) in 1939. A J. class at the local school was eliminated in 1928. The synagogue remained open until the late 1920s. A few Jews were employed at a local multinational kolkhoz from 1928 until it disbanded in the early 1930s. A J. reading room was closed in 1937. Many Jews succeeded in fleeing before the arrival of the Germans on 10 Aug. 1941. The remaining 110–120 were murdered in two groups: in Aug. 1941 and in late April

1942. In May 1969, a monument was dedicated to the J. victims of the Nazis.

KLEVE (Cleves) Rhineland, Germany. The Jews were expelled from the city in 1349 during the Black Death persecutions. J. settlement was renewed in the 17th cent. A member of the local Gompertz family was a banker and Court Jew under the patronage of the Duke of Brandenburg. The family endowed a synagogue and *beit midrash* in 1671 and for many years paid the salaries of those providing religious services. The J. pop. grew to 111 in 1790 and a new synagogue was consecrated in 1821. Two Jews sat on the municipal council in 1843. In 1880, the J. pop. reached a peak of 185. In 1901, a Jew was the victim of a blood libel. In June 1933, the J. pop. was 158. On *Kristallnacht* (9–10 Nov. 1938), SS and SA troops burned the synagogue after vandalizing its contents. The single remaining J. store in K. was wrecked and looted and J. men were dispatched to concentration camps. By May 1939, 50 Jews were living in K. About 30 were deported to the Riga, Lodz, and Theresienstadt ghettoes in 1941–43. Two Jews remained in the city in 1944. In all, about 50 perished, including some deported from occupied Europe.

KLEWAN Volhynia dist., Poland, today Ukraine. Jews settled in the 16th cent. Under Russian rule from the late 18th cent., they engaged in the lumber and summer tourist trade, the marketing of farm produce, and crafts. The Zionists became active in the early 20th cent. The J. pop. dropped from 2,432 in 1897 to 1,545 (total 3,287) in 1921. A day after the German occupation of 3 July 1941, 645 Jews were executed outside the town. The rest were ghettoized and put to forced labor. About 2,000, including refugees, were murdered beside open pits on 11 July 1942; the remaining 280 were murdered on 14 July.

KLICANOVO (Hung. Klacsano; Yid. Klitshanif) Carpatho-Russia, Czechoslovakia, today Ukraine. Three J. families were present in 1768. The J. pop. then grew to 55 in 1830 and 187 (total 704) in 1880. A few families earned their livelihoods in agriculture and Jews owned two quarries. In 1921, the J. pop. was 215, remaining stable until WWII. Following the Hungarian occupation in March 1939, dozens of Jews were drafted into forced labor battalions and dispatched to the eastern front, where most died. In Aug.

1941, a number of J. families without Hungarian citizenship were expelled to the German-occupied Ukraine and murdered. The rest were deported to Auschwitz in the second half of May 1944.

KLICHEV Mogilev dist., Belorussia. The J. pop. was 97 in 1794 and 115 in 1819. Most Jews were artisans and the community maintained a prayer house. In 1931, under the Soviets, a four-year J. elementary school was opened. In 1939, the J. pop. was 433 (18% of the total). The Germans arrived in early July 1941, subsequently murdering 450 people, almost all of them Jews.

KLIMONTOW Kielce dist., Poland. Jews may have been present by the 16th cent. They suffered grievously in the Swedish invasion of 1655, particularly from the depredations of Stefan Czarniecki's irregular Polish troops. In the mid-19th cent., the community possessed considerable property, including a new synagogue, as the J. pop. grew to 1,514. Jews owned stores and restaurants while others were peddlers and artisans. The Jews suffered from the economic crisis in the aftermath of WWI, necessitating the mobilization of relief and welfare agencies within the community. Popular and institutional antisemitism was also a constant factor. Nonetheless, J. public life flourished. The Zionists became active and Mizrachi founded a modern Hebrew *heder*. Agudat Israel ran a Beth Jacob school for girls and dominated the community council until 1936. The J. pop. rose to 2,652 in 1921 and 3,100 (total 4,000) in 1939. Versions differ as to whether the Germans captured K. on 11 or 13 Sept. 1939. They established a *Judenrat* in Oct. and instituted a regime of forced labor and extortion. Many Jews died under the overcrowded conditions as refugees from Lodz and Vienna arrived. In summer 1942, 300 Jews were sent to the Skarzysko-Kamienna labor camp. A family of 14 was executed along with 22 additional Jews from K. when one of its members escaped from the camp. On 30 Oct. 1942, after a selection of 150 Jews for forced labor in the Belzec death camp, 4,000 were deported to the Treblinka death camp with many murdered on the way. Another 265 left behind were also sent to labor camps.

KLIMOVICHI Mogilev dist., Belorussia. J. settlement probably began in the 18th cent. The J. pop. was 528 in 1847 and 2,263 in 1897, increasing to 2,587 in 1926 under the Soviets. Many Jews worked in an alcohol factory and a brickyard. Five prayer houses were in operation in 1917. One was converted into a vocational school and another into a cultural center. A J. school was also opened while a *heder* operated clandestinely. In 1919 a J. agricultural cooperative, one of the first in Belorussia, was started near the town, becoming a kolkhoz in the late 1920s and maintaining its own four-year J. elementary school. Before WWII, it supported 30 J. families. A multinational kolkhoz founded in 1929 had 29 J. families in 1930. In 1928, artisans organized themselves into cooperatives. In 1939, the J. pop. was 1,693. The Germans occupied the town on 10 Aug. 1941. A number of J. families managed to flee to the east. The Jews were subjected to forced labor and made to wear the yellow badge. On 7 Nov., Nazis and local police massacred over 800. Sixty J. men were murdered shortly afterwards. The remaining Jews were murdered in winter 1942 together with Jews from the neighboring settlements. Children of mixed marriages were murdered in 1943.

KLIMOVO Oriol dist., Russia. Jews were present in the late 18th cent. Their pop. was 541 (total 5,023) in 1897 and then dropped under the Soviets to 431 in 1926 and 224 in 1939. The Germans occupied K. in Aug. 1941, murdering 21 J. men in a nearby forest on 21 Aug. Another 112, apparently from K. and its environs, were subsequently murdered. Four hundred Jews from the area were executed in Feb. 1942.

KLIN Moscow dist., Russia. Jews probably settled in the early 20th cent., numbering 94 in 1926 and 300 (total 27,778) in 1939. The few remaining Jews who had not fled or been evacuated were murdered during the short German occupation of 23 Nov.–mid-Dec. 1941.

KLINGENMUENSTER Palatinate, Germany. Jews were present in the early 14th cent. Eleven J. families were living there in 1848. Two Jews were deported by the Nazis to southern France on 22 Oct. 1940.

KLINTSY Oriol dist., Russia. Jews probably settled at the turn of the 18th cent. In 1897 their pop. was 2,605 (total 12,166). Many refugees from central Poland (Warsaw, Lodz, etc.) arrived during WWI. During the Soviet period, the J. pop. grew to 5,248 in 1926 and

6,505 in 1939. In the 1920s, there was a J. elementary school and an evening school for adults. The Germans moved the Jews to a ghetto after occupying the city on 20 Aug. 1941. About 150 skilled workers were removed to an unknown destination and never returned. In an *Aktion* in early Dec., the Germans executed about 3,000 Jews.

KLOBUCKO Kielce dist., Poland. Jews, first mentioned in the second half of the 18th cent., formed an organized community in 1821. Most were employed in petty trade and crafts but some engaged in the lumber and grain trade on a large scale and in the late 19th cent. Jews opened a beer brewery, flour mill, and vinegar factory. Others supplied units of the Russian army in the area. The J. pop. grew from 255 in 1827 to 1,027 in 1897 and 1,647 (total 5,222) in 1921. The Bund became active in the early 20th cent. Before WWI, most children studied in the traditional *heder* and *talmud torah*, some continuing their studies in the local yeshiva. After WWI, J. economic recovery was assisted by the Joint Distribution Committee but many emigrated in the face of ongoing economic hardship. Zionist activity expanded, with Mizrachi particularly influential and such youth movements as Hashomer Hatzair, Hehalutz, and Betar organizing extensive cultural activity. Agudat Israel had 200 members and ran a Beth Jacob school for 100 girls. The official recognition by the Polish Ministry of Education of a Tarbut school established in 1929 was a rare event at the time. Jews were well represented on the municipal council, generally winning six of the 15 seats in elections. Anti-J. riots and economic boycotts marked the 1930s. The Germans captured K. on 1 Sept. 1939, murdering 15 Jews in the first few days and instituting a reign of terror. The synagogue was converted into a stable and J. property confiscated. A *Judenrat* was appointed in late Oct. All able-bodied Jews were placed at the disposal of the Schmelt Organization, which set up 145 forced labor camps in Upper Silesia, to which K. was annexed in Nov. 1939. In Sept. 1941, the Germans destroyed 150 J. houses and a month later confined the 1,500 or so Jews still residing in the city to a ghetto. On 22 June 1942, the Jews were gathered at the local firehouse as the Germans unleashed dogs and fired into the crowd to hasten their movement. Many were murdered and the rest were deported to Auschwitz after a selection for the labor camps. About 100 Jews survived the war.

KLODAWA Lodz dist., Poland. Jews settled here in 1487, but a community was first organized in the 1820s. The J. pop. in 1897 was 874 (30% of the total) and 1,148 in 1921. Between 9–12 Jan. 1942, 1,100 Jews were deported by the Germans to Chelmno.

KLOSTERNEUBURG-TULLN Lower Austria, Austria. Jews were first mentioned in K. in 1187 and in T. in the 1230s. They operated as moneylenders and established a splendid synagogue in K. During the Wiener Gesera persecutions (1421), Jews were expelled from both cities and the synagogue handed over to the church. The Jews resettled in K. in the second half of the 18th cent. and there are records of a synagogue in 1757. A J. cemetery in K. was consecrated in 1874 and expanded in 1906. The community gained recognition as a religious corporation (*Kultusgemeinde*) in 1890. In 1892, the J. communities of K. and T. were united. A new synagogue was inaugurated in K. in 1914. In 1934 the J. pop. for both cities stood at 700, declining to 300 in May 1938. In Nov. 1938, the K. community was incorporated into the Vienna community. On *Kristallnacht* (9–10 Nov. 1938), the interior of the synagogue in K. was destroyed. In T., the SS plundered J. homes, vandalized the cemetery, and arrested the men. Shortly after, all the Jews of K. were sent to Vienna and from there to the east.

KLUCZNIKOWICE Cracow dist., Poland. The J. pop. in 1921 was 121. The Jews were expelled to Sosnowiec and Bendzin for liquidation in April 1941.

KLWOW Lodz dist., Poland. Jews lived here from the 19th cent. The J. pop. in 1897 was 467 (43.5% of the total). On 22 Oct. 1942, the 500 Jews were expelled to Dzhewica and then deported to the Treblinka death camp.

KNIAZDWOR Stanislawow dist., Poland, today Ukraine. The J. pop. in 1921 was 126. The Jews were possibly expelled to Kolomyja for liquidation in April or Sept. 1942.

KNIAZE Stanislawow dist., Poland, today Ukraine. The J. pop. in 1921 was 126. The Jews were probably executed locally by the Germans between Sept. and Dec. 1941.

KNIHYNICZE Stanislawow dist., Poland, today

Ukraine. The J. settlement dating from the 18th cent. developed in the 19th, reaching a pop. of 648 (40% of the total) in 1880, but emigration during WWI subsequently reduced it by a third. The community was expelled by the Germans to Bukaczowce in April 1942 and in the fall to the Belzec death camp.

KNYAZHITSY Mogilev dist., Belorussia. The J. pop. was 473 in 1847 and 668 (total 731) in 1897, dropping to 277 in 1923 under the Soviets. An artisan cooperative was organized in 1928. In late July 1941, the Germans occupied the town. They murdered 32 Jews on 25 Sept. and on an unknown date locked 380 Jews into a lumber warehouse and burned them alive.

KNYSZYN Bialystok dist., Poland. Jews are first mentioned in 1568 and continued to maintain a presence despite the *de non tolerandis Judaeis* privilege granted to the town in 1672. They built a synagogue in 1705. Jews traded in glass, grain, cattle, and salt from the king's overseas mines. In 1857, the Russian senate reversed an 1845 ban to keep Jews from acquiring new real estate holdings and entering the developing spinning and weaving industries. Jews opened 14 textile plants, most of whose 308 workers were also Jews. In 1897, the J. pop. was 3,542 (total 5,487). Most Jews were strictly Orthodox but Zionism and revolutionary ideas made inroads at the turn of the 19th cent. In 1915 the Jews were forced to evacuate their factories and workers to the interior of Russia as the German armies advanced. Many remained and others emigrated overseas after WWI, leaving a J. pop. of 1,235 in 1921. In their short-lived occupation in Sept. 1939, the Germans seized 80 Jews for forced labor in Dzialdowo, murdering 77 of them instead of exchanging them for Germans as agreed upon with the Soviets, who subsequently took possession of the town. The Germans returned on 27 June 1941, murdering Jews as alleged Communists and setting up a ghetto at the end of the year. On 2 Nov. 1942, after murdering 74 Jews in the town, the Germans sent the remaining 1,500 to the old Polish cavalry barracks near Bialystok en route to the Treblinka death camp. Eighty escaped, some reaching the partisans.

KOBANYA industrial suburb of Budapest, Hungary. Jews are mentioned in 1851. In 1930 they numbered 5,000. The community defined itself as Neologist, es-

tablishing a synagogue in 1911 and opening a private school in 1928. In late Nov. 1944, the Jews were transferred to the Pest ghetto and shared the fate of the Budapest community. The postwar community of 1,000 was amalgamated with the Budapest community in 1950.

KOBERSDORF Burgenland, Austria. K. was one of the Seven Communities (*Sheva Kehillot*). Jews first settled in K. in 1529 and were under the protection of the house of Esterhazy from the beginning of the 17th cent. until the 1850s. In 1860, a synagogue was inaugurated. In 1829, the J. pop. was 746 (total 1,519), declining sharply to 395 in 1880 and 170 in 1934. Jews were engaged in trade, many dealing in cattle. In May 1938, there were only 95 Jews in K. Their property was confiscated and most left for Vienna. Some were able to emigrate from there; the others were deported to the east.

KOBIERZYN Cracow dist., Poland. The J. pop. in 1921 was 155 (total 1,814). In 1942, the Germans probably killed the Jews along with other Jews from the region.

KOBLENZ Rhineland, Germany. Jews are first mentioned in 1100. A sizable J. community began to develop with Jews from K. playing an important role as moneylenders to the nobility and the Church from the end of the 13th cent. Among the prominent J. scholars were R. Hayyim ben Yehiel, a follower of R. Meir of Rothenburg, and his brother Asher. In 1344, R. Eliezer ben Shemuel ha-Levi produced a surviving parchment Bible with commentaries. The medieval community fell victim to recurring persecutions (in 1265, 1281, 1287–88, 1337) and was totally destroyed in the Black Death disturbances of 1348–49. Jews resettled but were expelled definitively in 1418. They were allowed to return in 1518. A renewed J. community began to develop, establishing a synagogue in 1702. The community was served by several notable rabbis, amongst them the kabbalist and Talmud scholar Yair Hayyim Bacharach (1666–69). Under French rule in the early 19th cent., the Jews were accorded equal rights but community autonomy was curtailed under the consistory system. Although Napoleon's "Infamous Decree," which remained in effect until 1847, limited their freedom of movement and trade, Jews nonetheless began to achieve prominence in the city. The first Jew was elected to the municipal council in 1842 and a Jew became a district judge in 1879. The J. pop. increased from 342 in 1808 to 634 (total 45,147) in 1900. In the latter half of the 19th cent., the economic circumstances of the Jews improved considerably. Most were merchants in the food and textile trade and a number of clothing stores like Tietz and Jacobi were court suppliers. Antisemitic outbreaks also occurred, during the Hep! Hep! riots of 1819 and again in 1848. Anti-J. feeling was also manifest in the last decade of the 19th cent. with the spread of antisemitic incitement. The community was in the forefront of the movement for religious reform. A new synagogue with an organ and mixed choir was consecrated in 1851. However, from 1878 Neo-Orthodoxy made a comeback when Dr. Adolf Levin became rabbi. A branch of the Central Union (C.V.) was founded in 1893 and the Zionists were active by 1913. The J. pop. grew to 800 in 1929. In June 1933, about four months after the Nazi takeover, 669 Jews were counted in K. The J. pop. suffered from the economic boycott and mounting persecution. The Tietz establishment was sold off in 1933 and Jews were gradually pushed out of the grain and cattle trade. Forced to sell their stores, homes, and land, they began to emigrate. J. cultural life nonetheless continued under the auspices of the J. Cultural Association (350 members in 1935), the Zionists, and B'nai B'rith. A Zionist Habonim youth group was founded in 1935. On *Kristallnacht* (9–10 Nov. 1938), the synagogue, over 40 J. homes, and at least 19 J. stores were destroyed. About 100 J. men were sent to the Dachau concentration camp, two dying of heart attacks. In May 1939 only 308 Jews remained. Deportations commenced in 1942, with K. serving as a regional concentration point. The first transport for the east left on 22 March, with 120 Jews and another 100 from the Sayn psychiatric hospital. Additional transports left on 15 June, 27 July, and 28 Feb. 1943 and in July 1943. A few dozen survivors returned after the war. In 1987, the J. pop. was 100.

KOBRYN   Polesie dist., Poland, today Belarus. Jews were present before the expulsion from Lithuania in 1503. Many were killed by the Cossacks in the Chmielnicki massacres of 1648–49 and the community suffered further in subsequent wars, epidemics, and fires. The town began to develop under Russian rule, with the J. pop. rising to 6,738 in 1897 and constituting two-thirds of the total pop. until the 1930s, when it fell

to 50% after an influx of Polish administrative workers. In the early 19th cent. R. Moshe Rabinowitz established a hasidic dynasty, alongside the Slonim Hasidim, that endured until WWII. The Zionists and the Bund became active at the turn of the cent., the latter organizing strikes that won reduced hours for workers. In WWI, Cossacks burned and pillaged J. homes and murdered 18 Jews during the Russian withdrawal. Between the World Wars, economic conditions improved with support from the Joint Distribution Committee and American relatives as Jews engaged in light industry and owned around 400 of the town's stores. Through the 1920s they maintained a majority on the municipal council. The arrival of the Red Army on 20 Sept. 1939 resulted in the Sovietization of economic life and the school system. The Germans entered on 23 June 1941, establishing a *Judenrat* and instituting a regime of forced labor and extortion with periodic killings. A ghetto crowding together 8,000 Jews including refugees was set up in Nov. 1941, with skilled workers and their families separated into a special section in early 1942. The unskilled, about 3,000, were brought to Brona Gora on 27 July 1942 and murdered. Most of the others were executed 3 miles (5 km) outside the town on 14 Oct. 1942. About 500 escaped in the midst of an armed uprising by the local J. underground, but only 100 made it to the forest; many of these were later caught and killed.

KOBYLECKA POLANA   (Hung. Gyertyanliget) Carpatho-Russia, Czechoslovakia. Jews probably settled in the mid-19th cent and numbered 98 (total 1,171) in 1880. Their number rose to 265 in 1921 and 427 in 1941. About 14 were engaged in trade and four or five were artisans. The Hungarians occupied the town in March 1939, drafting a few dozen Jews into forced labor battalions. In Aug. 1941, about 130 Jews without Hungarian citizenship were expelled to the German-occupied Ukraine and murdered. The rest were deported to Auschwitz in the second half of May 1944.

KOBYLIN   Poznan dist., Poland. An organized community is mentioned in 1827. A J. elementary school was in operation and a new synagogue was completed in 1854. The J. pop. reached a peak of 452 (total 2,000) in 1857. Afterwards Jews began to emigrate from K. The Zionists became active in 1908. Thirty Jews remained on the outbreak of WWII. All were expelled by the Germans to General Gouvernement territory in Nov. 1939.

KOBYLNIK Vilna dist., Poland, today Belarus. Jews from the neighboring villages arrived in 1807–20 after Czar Alexander I prohibited them from leasing estate lands or dealing in alcoholic beverages. The coming of the railroad promoted J. trade at the twice-yearly local fair and opened new vistas in the fields of hostelry and brokerage in an era of prosperity that lasted until WWI. In 1897, the J. pop. reached 591 (of a total 1,055). Economic conditions deteriorated between the World Wars in the face of local competition and heavy taxes, necessitating assistance from the Joint Distribution Committee. A devastating fire depressed the condition of the community still further. Many emigrated, leaving a J. pop. of 300 in 1931. A CYSHO Yiddish school was opened in the 1930s. After two years of Soviet rule, the Germans arrived on 27 June 1941. On 12 July, all religious books in the synagogue were burned in the market. In Oct. 1941, 48 Jews were executed as alleged Communists and on 21 Sept. 1942 over 150 were executed at the Catholic cemetery. Many of those escaping were killed by Polish partisans in the forest; others were killed in Wilejka, Postawy, and the Ponary woods.

KOCBOROWO Pomerania dist., Poland. A number of Jews were present in the early 18th cent., engaging in farming, crafts, leaseholding, and brokerage. In 1921, there were 126 after many arrived from Starogard. The Germans executed all the remaining Jews in the forest near the village of Skurcze in Sept. 1939.

KOCK (Kotsk) Lublin dist., Poland. Jews settled in the late 17th cent. K. became the most important hasidic center in Poland after R. Menahem Mendel Morgenstern (1787–1859), known as "the Rabbi of Kock" and one of the movement's most original thinkers, established his court there in 1829. Most of his followers left after his death. In 1809, Berek Joselewicz, head of the J. cavalry battalion in the Kosciuszko uprising, was killed outside the town in a battle between Warsaw Duchy soldiers and Hungarian forces of the Austrian army. He was buried in K. The J. pop. was 1,612 in 1856 and 3,014 (total 7,738) in 1897. In 1927, 400 J. families lost their homes in a great fire. With the town rebuilt in brick and stone and new roads boosting commerce, the circumstances of J. life improved. In

1928, Jews owned 124 stores, 13 bakeries, and ten butcher shops. A few conducted large-scale trade in lumber and grain. Tarbut and Beth Jacob schools were also opened. In the late 1930s, antisemitic persecution intensified. Fifteen Jews were killed in German bombardments on 8 Sept. 1939. The Germans set up a *Judenrat* in early 1940. With the arrival of 1,100 refugees, the J. pop. rose to over 3,000, subjected to a regime of forced labor. In summer 1942, the Gestapo murdered 17 Jews and soon after another 220 were executed. On 19–25 Aug., 100 families, mostly refugees, were deported to Treblinka via Parczew. More were sent to Lukow in the same month, as were the last 120 Jews on 27 Sept., all to be deported to the Treblinka death camp in early Oct. 1942.

KOCSORD Szatmar dist., Hungary. Jews settled in the late 18th cent. and numbered 65 in 1930. They were deported to Auschwitz via Mateszalka in May 1944.

KODEN Lublin dist., Poland. Jews settled in the late 18th cent. The J. pop. was 748 in 1857 (total 2,190) and 541 in 1921. Between the World Wars, economic conditions deteriorated. The Zionists, the Bund, and Agudat Israel were all active. Only 100 Jews remained when the Germans arrived in late Sept. 1939. Their numbers increased with the arrival of 105 refugees from Cracow in spring 1940. All were confined to a ghetto. In Sept. 1942, the Jews were expelled to Miendzyrzec Podlaski and in Oct. deported to the Treblinka death camp.

KODNIA Zhitomir dist., Ukraine. Jews are first mentioned in 1593. They were attacked in the Chmielnicki massacres of 1648-49. The community apparently revived in the 18th cent. In 1897, the J. pop. was 688 (total 1,820). Between the World Wars, with the J. pop. declining, 72 breadwinners were artisans and 51 were in trade. The Germans captured K on 8 July 1941, murdering its 185 Jews outside the town in Aug.

KODRY Kiev dist., Ukraine. A few dozen Jews lived in K. during the 19th cent. On 13 July 1919, the Petlyura gangs attacked the Jews here. In 1939, under the Soviets, their pop. was 109 (total 2,867). The Germans arrived on 20 July 1941 and soon afterwards murdered all the Jews.

KODYMA   Moldavia, today Ukraine. A J. community existed by the early 19th cent. It numbered 2,241 (90% of the total) in 1897 and 1,641 (total 6,418) in 1939. R. Nisan Titivsky was rabbi before the Oct. 1917 Revolution and continued to serve the community in a semi-official capacity in the Soviet period. German and Rumanian forces captured K. on 22 July 1941. In early Aug., an *Aktion* was carried out against nonresident Jews and on 12 Aug. the Germans murdered 120 Jews aged 17–20 in the nearby forest. With K. under Rumanian administrative control from early Sept., a ghetto was established. When an epidemic broke out there two months later, the Rumanians expelled the Jews to the German zone of occupation, but 300 returned when the Germans blocked the way. The Rumanian police murdered the 195 surviving Jews in Jan. 1942.

KOENEN   Rhineland, Germany. Jews are first mentioned in 1808. Their pop. rose to a peak of 120 (of a total 599) in 1871 and then declined steadily to 67 in 1925. A new synagogue and a cemetery were opened in 1905. In June 1933, about four months after the Nazi takeover, there were 54 Jews in K. On *Kristallnacht* (9–10 Nov. 1938), the interior of the synagogue was destroyed and the J. cemetery desecrated. By May 1939, all Jews had left for other towns in Germany as well as abroad. It may be assumed that all those who did not make it in time to safe havens perished in the Holocaust.

KOENIG, BAD   see BAD KOENIG.

KOENIGHEIM   Baden, Germany. The 13th cent. community was destroyed in the Rindfleisch massacres of 1298. Jews settled again in the early 15th cent. but a community was only formed after the Thirty Years War (1618–48). A synagogue was built in 1831 and a cemetery was consecrated in 1875. In the 1830s, a J. elementary school began operating. The J. pop. grew to 121 in 1875 (total 1,838) and then declined steadily to 37 in 1933. By the end of 1938, 20 had emigrated and seven moved to other German cities. On *Kristallnacht* (9–10 Nov. 1938), the synagogue was vandalized and in Sept. 1939 the 13 remaining Jews were confined to a single house under virtual arrest until the deportations to the Gurs concentration camp on 22 Oct. 1940. In all, 15 Jews were deported; three survived.

KOENIGSBACH   Baden, Germany. The first three J. families settled in 1699, joined by another dozen or so in the early 18th cent. An elementary school was started in 1835 and the J. pop. grew to 220 in 1875 (of a total 2,033). By the turn of the cent., the J. pop. had dropped to 167, a level it remained at for 25 years, subsequently falling to 102 in 1933. By 1938 all J. stores had been closed down under the economic boycott. On *Kristallnacht* (9–10 Nov. 1938), the synagogue was vandalized and other J. property damaged. In the Nazi era, 88 Jews left K., most emigrating from Germany. Ten were deported to the Gurs concentration camp on 22 Oct. 1940 and another 17 were deported after leaving K. (14 from Pforzheim); four of those deported survived; 17 were sent to Auschwitz and perished there.

KOENIGSBERG   (Rus. Kaliningrad) East Prussia, Germany, today Russia. Despite opposition from local merchants, J. settlement, backed by the government of the principality, began in the middle of the 17th cent. Settlement was limited to a small number of well-to-do Jews, who had to pay exorbitant taxes and were subjected to numerous restrictions. In 1680, they were allowed to dedicate a prayer room and in 1703 they established a J. cemetery, serving a community which numbered about 30 Jews with their families. In 1756, the community dedicated its first synagogue and by the end of the cent. the J. pop. was 856. The growing fame of the city's university, the Albertina — the university of Immanuel Kant — had a significant impact on Haskala. The J. disciples of Kant became passionate adherents of Moses Mendelssohn, who himself stayed in K. in 1777. From 1784, Isaac Euchel (1756–1804) edited the Hebrew-language journal *Ha-Me'assef*, the most important organ of early German-J. Haskala. Some of the more important exponents of Haskala in K. later moved to Berlin, including Euchel himself and above all David Friedlaender (1750–1834), the most prominent. The community's Orthodox rabbis, such as the renowned rabbinical scholar Levin Marcus Epstein, who taught in K. between 1744 and 1775, or the kabbalist Zwi Mecklenburg, who was active between 1830 and 1865, championed the traditional way. Until the 1870s, the Orthodox dominated religious life. In 1896, the community dedicated a new Reform-style synagogue and in 1911 a synagogue was privately erected in a nearby seaside resort frequented by many wealthy Jews from abroad.

The older synagogue established in 1815 was given to the Orthodox, who reinstituted the traditional religious service. A J. religious school was only established in the wake of the Prussian Law of 1847, which introduced compulsory religious education. In the course of the 19th cent., the J. pop. of K. rose from 956 (2% of the total) in 1816 to 3,836 in 1871 and a peak of 5,324 (4%) in 1880. The growth of the J. community was fostered by the improved economic oppor-

Central synagogue of Koenigsberg, Germany (Beth Hatefutsoth Photo Archive, Tel Aviv/courtesy of Max Perls, Israel)

tunities afforded in part by the Edict of Emancipation (1812) and in part by the flourishing commerce with Russia, signaled by the construction of the Eastern Railway in 1853. Up to two-thirds of the J. breadwinners in K. were engaged in trade, most earning enough to ensure their economic survival and, at times, even prospering. For the Jews the university's role was ambivalent. It opened its gates to J. students from Eastern Europe, who flocked to it in the hundreds, but practiced a policy of institutional discrimination with regard to the employment of J. lecturers on their academic staff. Nevertheless, there were ten J. professors, most of them in the faculty of medicine. The East European students were the core of a large East European J. colony. On the eve of WWI, J. students at the

Albertina constituted up to 10% of the student body while in the medical faculty they made up 40%. At the same time, as in other German cities, the student associations were a hotbed of virulent antisemitism, prompting the K. J. students to establish their own Zionist and non-Zionist associations. One prominent student Zionist activist was Shmarya Levin (1867–1935), a future Zionist leader. The occupational pattern of the J. pop. was based on trade, the free professions, and public service. J. participation in local politics had a long tradition in K., going back to 1809, when Samuel Wulff Friedlaender was elected – for the first time in Prussia – city councilor. In 1838-40 at least five Jews were elected city councilors and in 1895 there were no fewer than 15 J. members on the city council. Jews also played a vital role in the social and cultural life of the city. Of the German J. organizations, a branch of the Central Union (C.V.) was opened in K. only in 1903 and the Union for Liberal Judaism in 1908. Zionism found its first supporters in K. among the emigrants from Russia. The shift to rabid nationalism after WWI was a death blow to the spirit of tolerance which had characterized the city in the past. The liberal camp lost ground to the German People's Party and to the national-racist antisemitic parties. From 1924, the Social Democratic Party of Germany (SPD) was the only party which had J. representatives on the city council. The situation of the Jews in the town became even worse because of the chronic economic crisis, which had severe repercussions on the well-being of less affluent Jews. In the latter years of the Weimar Republic, physical assaults on community institutions and J. citizens became frequent. The expulsion of foreign Jews was a major factor in reducing the size of the J. pop. From 1925 to 1930 it dropped from 4,049 to 3,619. There was also a high intermarriage rate which in 1915 peaked at 47%, remaining as high as 33% in 1933, when the Nazis came to power.

In June 1933, the J. pop. of K. was 3,170. By Oct. 1938 it had declined by 35% to 2,036. About 300 Jews already left in the first months before June 1933. Nazi terror made itself felt almost immediately. The old synagogue and several J. shops were the target of arson attacks on 7 March and 9 March, respectively. A few days later, a J. movie theater manager died following interrogation at SA headquarters while a J. Communist and member of the Reichstag was brutally murdered. Other J. left-wing political activists were placed under "protective" custody, one dying later in a concentration camp. The discriminatory boycott legislation after 1 April 1933 hit the J. community in K. hard because so many of its members were academics, medical doctors, lawyers, and technical experts. At least 16 J. university lecturers were forced into early retirement in April 1933 and the number of J. students, which had already dropped during the Weimar years, was restricted by a countrywide *numerus clausus*. J. schoolchildren, who were exposed to daily harassment from teachers and classmates, enrolled at the new J. school which opened in 1935. J. inner life intensified under Nazi pressure. There was a revival of interest in all facets of J. religious education and the J. Cultural Association (Juedischer Kulturbund) organized musical performances and cultural programs. The Zionist branch doubled its membership by Dec. 1933, although many Zionist activists had left for Palestine in the previous months. On *Kristallnacht* (9–10 Nov. 1938), SS troops burned down the new synagogue. The buildings adjacent to the synagogue, occupied by the J. orphanage, the improvised J. school, and apartments of community officials, were likewise demolished, together with the mortuary at the J. cemetery. J. shops and private homes were wrecked and looted. In the morning hours, 450 Jews were rounded up and brought to police headquarters, where they were maltreated. Since East Prussia itself had no concentration camps, the arrested Jews were incarcerated in the city jail and in the old fire station. They were kept there for about a month, watched over by older, relatively humane prison guards. By May 1939, 500 more Jews had left K., reducing the J. pop. to 1,586. As of 1939, the remaining Jews were forced to move into a few, inhumanly crowded "J. houses." Deportations from K. started in June 1942. In the first transport, on 24 June, about 465 persons were moved to the Minsk ghetto in Belorussia. Other transports to Minsk followed on 25–26 June and on 7 Aug. On 25 Aug. 1942, there was a transport to the Theresienstadt ghetto and in Sept. a transport to the Riga ghetto. Only about 45 families in mixed marriages remained in K. in the wake of the mass deportations of 1942. In all, probably over 1,100 Jews from K. were deported to the death camps and ghettoes in Eastern Europe. From 1943, numerous Polish Jews were moved to K. from the Stutthof and Soldau concentration camps to do forced labor in the town and in other parts of East Prussia. At the end of Jan. 1945, about 3,700 took part in the horrendous death march from K. to Palmnicken, near the Baltic. Few survived.

KOENIGSBERG IN DER NEUMARK (Pol. Chojna) Brandenburg, Germany, today Poland. Jews were living in K. before 1351, but in that year fell victim to persecution. The 15th cent. settlement came to an end with the expulsion of the Jews of Brandenburg in 1510. Evidence from 1690 indicates the presence of five J. families in K. In 1880, the J. pop. was 158. The community maintained a synagogue with a new building constructed in 1907 and a cemetery. When the Nazis came to power in 1933, there were 31 Jews in K. No further information about their fate is available.

KOENIGSHOFEN-IM-GRABFELD   Lower Franconia, Germany. Jews were victims of the Rindfleisch massacres of 1298 and the Black Death disturbances of 1348–49. The modern community grew to 101 in 1910 (total 1,802), with a synagogue built in 1904 and a cemetery opened in 1921. Both were desecrated in 1925. In 1933, 94 Jews remained; 69 left the town by the end of 1938, including 27 for the U.S. and 37 for other German cities. On *Kristallnacht* (9–10 Nov. 1938), the synagogue was wrecked, all the tombstones in the J. cemetery were smashed, and eight J. men were sent to the Dachau concentration camp. Another 13 Jews left in 1939. The last six were expelled to Kleineibstadt in Aug. 1941 and from there to Izbica in the Lublin dist. (Poland) via Wuerzburg on 25 April 1942.

KOENIGSTEIN   Hesse–Nassau, Germany. In 1301, ten J. families are mentioned in K. Jews lived in the town in the 15th cent. but ultimately left for Frankfurt. Centuries later, Jews again came to live in K. and contributed to its development as a health resort. Numbering 60 (4% of the total) in 1871, they opened a sanatorium and dedicated a synagogue in 1906. Baron Wilhelm Karl von Rothschild (1828–1901) maintained a palatial residence on 100 acres of land to which the crowned heads of Europe were invited. Of the 73 Jews living in K. in 1933, 50 had emigrated by Nov. 1938. On *Kristallnacht* (9–10 Nov. 1938), the synagogue was burned down and J. homes were also vandalized in neighboring Kronberg. At least 24 members of the community were deported in 1942.

KOENIGSWINTER   Rhineland, Germany. Jews are

first mentioned in 1146. The first synagogue was built in 1754. In 1828 the Jews numbered 104 but because of the decline in their pop. the community was attached first to Oberdollendorf and later to Bad Honnef. Most Jews emigrated in the Nazi era. Six perished.

KOERDORF Hesse–Nassau, Germany. Established in 1842, the community renovated its old synagogue in 1844–45 and numbered 34 (6% of the total) in 1885. Affiliated with the Wiesbaden rabbinate, it had a district membership but ceased to exist after *Kristallnacht* (9–10 Nov. 1938).

KOESLIN (Pol. Koszalin) Pomerania, Germany, today Poland. The first J. family was living in K. in 1699 and played an important role in the local textile industry. There was a prayer room in 1755. In 1880, the J. pop. was 361. By the end of the 19th cent., several Jews had important businesses, with one Jew becoming director of the local savings bank and another head of the commercial school. Jews also served as members of the city council. The antisemitic riots which broke out in Pomerania when the Neustettin synagogue was burned down in 1881 spread to K. An attempt in 1846 to establish services on Sundays under Reform rabbi Dr. Heymann Jolowicz was short-lived. After the consecration of a synagogue in 1886, the community became Reform, introducing an organ. A new cemetery was set up about 1900. When the Nazis came to power in 1933, the community numbered 140. By 1935 the boycott measures had nearly ruined J. businessmen. On *Kristallnacht* (9–10 Nov. 1938), the synagogue and the mortuary at the new cemetery were burned down; the old cemetery was desecrated and J. business premises were wrecked. By May 1939, there were 37 Jews and 20 persons of partial J. origin (*Mischlinge*) still living in the town. The remaining Jews were deported to the east in July and Aug. 1942 with the exception of five Jews who were probably protected by marriage to non-Jews.

KOETHEN Anhalt, Germany. The first evidence of a modern J. settlement with five families dates from 1620–21. In 1777, when there were 22 J. families living in K., an officially recognized community was set up. There was a cemetery and in 1802 a synagogue was dedicated. With a pop. of 270 individuals in 1884, the community established a new cemetery in 1885 and a new and larger synagogue in 1891. By

1933, the J. pop. numbered 156 individuals. On *Kristallnacht* (9-10 Nov. 1938), the synagogue was burned down and the two cemeteries were desecrated. By 1939, there were only 56 Jews in K. Those who failed to emigrate were deported in May 1942 to Poland or in Dec. 1942 to the Theresienstadt ghetto. Six Jews managed to survive in K., probably protected by marriage to non-Jews.

KOJETIN Moravia, Czechoslovakia. According to tradition, Jews arrived in the 12th cent. By the mid-16th cent., a community of several hundred was in existence. Refugees fleeing the Chmielnicki massacres of 1648–49 introduced Polish usages into the community's prayer service. Refugees from Vienna arrived in 1670. In the late 17th cent., Jews were peddlers and cattle growers. After J. houses were destroyed in a 1714 fire, the Archbishop of Prague authorized the construction of new ones and the J. pop. reached 470 in 1727. In the first half of the 19th cent., Jews traded mainly in hides, wax, feathers, and wool. Their pop. reached 506 in 1857 and then, with many leaving for Vienna and Brno, declined steadily to 72 (total 6,214) in 1930. On the eve of WWII, a few Jews managed to emigrate to Palestine or the U.S. The rest were deported to the Theresienstadt ghetto via Olomouc on 26 June 1942. Shortly thereafter, they were sent on to Maly Trostinec and the Treblinka death camp. A few others were sent from the Theresienstadt ghetto to Auschwitz in 1943–44. Few returned.

KOKA Pest–Pilis–Solt–Kiskun dist., Hungary. Jews arrived in the early 19th cent. and numbered 69 in 1930. The Neologist community established a synagogue in the beginning of the 20th cent. The Jews were deported to Auschwitz via Nagykata and Kecskemet at the end of June 1944.

KOKAVA Slovakia, Czechoslovakia, today Republic of Slovakia. Jews numbered 111 in 1900, maintaining a synagogue, cemetery, and school. In 1940, 64 remained. Most were deported to the death camps in 1942.

KOKHANOVO Vitebsk dist. Belorussia. The J. pop. was 637 (total 984) in 1897, dropping to 480 in 1926 under the Soviets. In the mid-1920s, 29 of the 100 J. families in the town worked in agriculture and 25 in crafts. A four-year J. elementary school was

opened. The Germans occupied K. in July 1941, setting up a ghetto in Sept. which also held Jews from
nearby Galoshnevo. In Jan. 1942, all 300 Jews in the
ghetto were murdered near the J. cemetery.

KOKNESE (Ger. Kokenhausen) Livonia dist., Latvia. The J. pop. in 1935 was 16 (total 647). Those
not escaping to the Soviet Union were murdered by
the Germans with Latvian assistance after the occupation of July 1941.

KOLACZYCE (Yid. Koloshitz) Cracow dist., Poland. Jews were present from the second half of the
19th cent., numbering 247 (total 1,792) in 1900.
Anti-J. riots shook the community in 1892 and 1898
and antisemitism intensified in the 1930s. All 260
Jews of K. and the surrounding villages were executed
by the Germans in a nearby forest on 12 Aug. 1942.

KOLAY (from 1944, Azovskoye) Crimea, Russia,
today Ukraine. Jews were only accorded temporary
residence rights in the late 19th cent. for the purpose
of buying grain. In 1903, they were allowed to settle
permanently but without the right to buy land outside
the town. The large train station there encouraged the
establishment of numerous J. farm settlements in the
1920s. A J. high school served the region. In 1939,
the J. pop. was 80. The Germans arrived on 1 Nov.
1941, murdering the Jews near Mayfeld in late Jan.
1942.

KOLBERG (Pol. Kolobrzeg) Pomerania, Germany,
today Poland. Jews are first mentioned in 1261, probably making K. the oldest J. settlement in Pomerania.
The 15th cent. community came to an end when
Jews were expelled from Pomerania in 1491–93. A settlement was once again established in the 19th cent.
and in 1893 the J. pop. was 600. The community established a synagogue in 1845 and a cemetery in 1812.
Many Jews worked at K.'s health resorts and spas.
Dr. Salomon Goldschmidt, who served as rabbi from
the 1860s until 1925, helped found in 1874 a J. convalescent home for needy resort clientele. In 1919, antisemitic posters appeared at spa facilities. When the
Nazis came to power in 1933, the community numbered about 200 members. J. patients at the health resort were soon exposed to antisemitic attacks. On *Kristallnacht* (9–10 Nov. 1938), the synagogue was destroyed and the J. convalescent home was closed. By

May 1939, there were only 85 Jews and 33 persons
of partial J. origin (*Mischlinge*) in K. Those Jews
who did not manage to move away were deported to
the Lublin dist. (Poland) on 11–12 Feb. 1940 together
with the Jews of Stettin. By Oct. 1942, there were only
seven Jews in K., probably protected by marriage to
non-Jews.

KOLBIEL Warsaw dist., Poland. Jews probably settled in the late 18th cent. Their pop. grew from 125 in
1820 to 2,077 (total 2,322) in 1909 but subsequently
dropped sharply through emigration in the face of
WWI depredations and economic hardship. Agudat Israel was the dominant force in the community but in the
course of time Zionist influence increased. The Germans entered the town on 15 Sept. 1939. In Nov. a *Judenrat* was appointed, charged with supplying forced
labor and meeting extortionate demands. Refugees
brought the J. pop. up to 1,100 in Sept. 1941, all confined to a ghetto. On 27 Sept. 1942 they were deported
to the Treblinka death camp. Another 100 who returned
after escaping the *Aktion* were ultimately expelled,
mostly to the Warsaw ghetto.

KOLBUSZOWA (Yid. Kolbsow) Lwow dist., Poland. Jews were present from the beginning of the settlement in the early 16th cent., becoming an important
factor in its economic development as exporters of the
locally made furniture. They were also prominent as
carpenters as well as being employed as tailors, shoemakers, bakers, and butchers. Economic conditions deteriorated under the heavy taxation of the Austrians,
but the J. pop. continued to grow, maintaining a level
of nearly 2,000 (two-thirds of the total) from the early
19th cent. through WWI. Most of the community identified with Ropshits Hasidism. The Zionists became active in the late 19th cent. The renewal of Polish rule
after WWI was accompanied by a pogrom in which
20 Jews were injured and 100 families reduced to penury after the pillaging. The depressed economic conditions of the 1930s worsened the situation still further,
but social and communal life continued unabated,
with the Zionists expanding their activity. The J. pop.
in 1939 was 1,756. With the advance of the Germans
in Sept. 1939, hundreds of J. refugees settled in K.
Forty Jews were killed fighting the Germans, who entered the town in the second week of Sept. Many of the
young escaped to Soviet-held territory as Jews were
seized for forced labor under a reign of terror. Homes

and stores were pillaged and large-scale property confiscations were carried out on 15 Nov., including food items. Through Jan.–Feb. 1940, 150–250 Jews a day were required to work for the Germans without pay or a food allotment. A *Judenrat* was set up in March and periodically visited by Gestapo units from Rzeszow for purposes of extortion. On Passover, the Joint Distribution Committee was able to supply the community with a ton of *matzot* for its 1,800 residents; it also provided medicines for the clinic set up by the *Judenrat*. In the following months, Jews were sent to the quarries near Nowy Soncz and to the Pustkow labor camp. In June 1941 the Jews were confined to a ghetto. Hunger and poverty increased with the influx of refugees in the fall. Execution awaited those caught smuggling food or engaging in "illegal" trade. The *Judenrat* organized a soup kitchen and set up workshops for vital services to the Germans as a hedge against deportation. However, all were expelled to Rzeszow on 24 June 1942 and most met their end in the deportations to the Belzec death camp in July. A hundred Jews were sent back to K. to dismantle the ghetto and for other tasks; 37 escaped after Rosh Hashanah when the murder of 210 Jews in a nearby forest forewarned them of their intended fate and some tried to escape to Hungary. On 14 Nov., those remaining were sent back to Rzeszow to join the next day's consignment to the Belzec death camp. Only nine of those in hiding in or near the town survived.

KOLIN   Bohemia, Czechoslovakia. In the Middle Ages K. was one of the four J. communities (together with Roudnice, Bumsla (Mlada Boleslav), and Nachod) referred to by the Hebrew acronym "Karban." It was second in size and importance only to the Prague community. The Jews were expelled by King Ferdinand in 1541 and again in 1561. In the course of time they developed from moneylenders into merchants dealing in a wide variety of products, from arms and musical instruments to grain, salt, and tobacco. A new synagogue was consecrated in 1696 and a famous yeshiva operated for hundreds of years. In 1839, the Beth Hamidrash Anstalt was opened, endowed by Moses Montefiore after a visit in 1855. The J. pop. reached a peak of 1,347 (15% of the total) in 1857. Jews opened a major chemical factory, joined the professional class, and served on the municipal council (four members in 1867). Subsequently the J. pop. dropped to 806 in 1900 and 430 in 1930. Dr.

Richard Feder was rabbi in 1917–42 and chief rabbi of Czechoslovakia in 1960–70. Between the World Wars, K. was a center of the Czecho-J. movement (*Svaz Cechu-zidu*) but the Zionists were active as well. In 1940, J. stores were confiscated and in 1940–41 J. students were expelled from the schools. Most of the city's Jews were deported to the Theresienstadt ghetto on 13 June 1942 in the third and final transport from the dist. From there they were sent to the death camps in Poland. After the war, there were 64 survivors in K..

KOLKI   Volhynia dist., Poland, today Ukraine. Jews settled in the mid-16th cent. The community was destroyed in the Chmielnicki massacres of 1648–1649 but grew to 2,537 in 1897 (total 4,394). The Jews exported timber and agricultural products. The hasidic sects worshiped in four synagogues. The Jews fled in WWI as the town was burned, with 724 returning (total 2,145). The Germans arrived on 3 July 1941, crowding 2,500 Jews including refugees into a ghetto in Oct. Most were executed beside open pits in Sept. 1942; the rest a month later.

KOLNO   Bialystok dist., Poland, today Belarus. A few J. families were present in the mid-18th cent. An organized community existed in the 1820s. J. tradesmen ran shops and stalls. In 1892, 36 of the town's 41 artisans were Jews. A yeshiva was in operation from the 1880s. Until WWI, most children studied in the *heder* system, with a reformed *heder* opened a few years before the war. The J. pop. rose from 784 in 1827 to 2,763 (total 4,876) in 1897. In the aftermath

Hayyim Kadesz beside his coach on the Kolno–Stawiski line, Poland

of WWI, Jews suffered from the depredations of General Haller's Polish troops. Between the World Wars, most struggled economically, living in one or two rooms in wooden structures without running water. Almost all the J. political parties were active. Many of the young underwent pioneer training and some emigrated to Palestine. Half the members of the municipal council were Jews, including the deputy mayor, but already in 1927 antisemitic incidents occurred in the town, intensifying in the 1930s. Under Soviet rule in 1939–41 Jews labeled "hostile" or "unproductive" were expelled or exiled. The Germans entered K. on 22 June 1941, instituting a reign of terror with Polish participation. On 4 July 1941, a Polish mob murdered 37 Jews, raping women and looting J. property. On 15 July, all young J. males were executed beside trenches near the border. On 18 July, their families were murdered at the village of Msciwoje. At the end of the month the rest of the Jews were taken out of the town and murdered after the infants were killed in the streets with their heads smashed against the pavement. Over 2,000 Jews were murdered during the two weeks.

KOLO (Yid. Koyl) Lodz dist., Poland. Jews first settled in the 16th cent. They traded in agricultural produce and worked in the textile and food industries. The J. pop. in 1897 was 9,359 (43% of the total). A self-defense unit protected the J. pop. during the antisemitic riots in 1919 and again in 1936. Zionist activity began in 1898. The Zionist parties dominated the community council and set up nursery schools, an elementary school, a high school, two libraries, and a popular university. Ten J. representatives were elected in 1929 to the 24-member municipal council. The Bund was active in the field of education and culture. The Germans captured K. on 18 Sept. 1939 and from Oct. all males aged 14 and over were sent to forced labor. On 10 Dec. 1939, 1,139 Jews were transferred to Izbica Kujawska; many died of starvation and disease. On 2 Oct. 1940, 150 families were transferred to Bugaj and Nowiny Brdowskie. In Jan. 1942 they were deported to Chelmno. The J. pop. was ghettoized in Dec. 1940. In June 1941, 500 males were sent to labor camps near Poznan and in Aug., 100 females to a labor camp in Breslau. On 7–11 Dec. 1941, all remaining Jews were deported to Chelmno. A few dozen survivors returned after the war but in view of the antisemitic atmosphere, soon left.

Advertisement for a Jewish theater performance in Kolo, Poland, 1928 (Photo courtesy of Arie Butzker)

KOLOCAVA (Hung. Alsokalocsa) Carpatho-Russia, Czechoslovakia, today Ukraine. J. settlement probably began in the mid-18th cent. Six Jews were present in 1768. The J. pop. rose to 81 in 1830 and 147 (of a total 1,590) in 1880. Jews engaged in trade (12), crafts (nine), and agriculture (three) and also owned three flour mills. In 1921, under the Czechoslovakians, the J. pop. reached 285, increasing to 358 in 1941. The Hungarians occupied the town in March 1939, drafting Jews into forced labor battalions. In Aug. 1941, they expelled eight families without Hungarian citizenship to Kamenets-Podolski, where they were murdered. The rest were deported to Auschwitz in May 1944.

KOLODNIYA Smolensk dist., Russia. Jews probably arrived in the early 20th cent., numbering 11 in

1926 and 125 (total 12,500) in 1939. The Germans occupied K. in early fall 1941, murdering the few Jews who had not fled or been evacuated.

KOLOMYJA Stanislawow dist., Poland, today Ukraine. The J. community began to develop in the 16th cent. as J. merchants gathered in the city under various privileges in recognition of their commercial importance. In the Chmielnicki massacres of 1648–49, 300 Jews were killed. The community revived towards the end of the 17th cent. and regained its leading economic position. From its beginnings it dominated the wholsesale trade in farm produce and a few J. families controlled the trade in grain and cattle with Moldavia and Walachia. Jews also imported wine from Hungary. By 1715, Jews were paying three-quarters of the city's taxes. In the early 18th cent., Shabbateanism gained a foothold in the community. K. also became an important center of Hasidism. A widespread legend that its founder, the Ba'al Shem Tov, was born in the area contributed to its growth. In the second half of the 18th cent., as K. came under Austrian rule, the Jews comprised the majority of the pop. and were concentrated in the center of the city. After a number of fires, J. residential areas were rebuilt in stone in the late 1780s. Despite severe anti-J. fiscal and administrative measures, the Jews expanded their economic activity, becoming leaders in the tobacco industry and entering the hide and lumber trade as well as the candle industry. After 1860 Jews were also allowed to purchase land and toward the end of the 19th cent. became active in the textile and petrochemical industries. In 1883 a factory for manufacturing prayer shawls was set up that grew into a home industry marketing its products throughout the Austrian Empire and beyond. A three-month strike in 1892, organized with the help of J. activists in the Social Democratic Party, gave rise to a trade union and cooperative organization but many weavers left for the U.S. In the early 20th cent., Jews also became active in preparing and marketing pig bristles for brushmaking and J. carters handled all the hauling work in the city and its environs. Most Jews lived

The marketplace in Kolomyja, Poland

in straitened economic circumstances, with an upper class of around 100 wealthy families in a J. pop. of 16,568 in 1900 (total 34,188). To improve the situation, loan funds and vocational training were organized. Throughout the period the community was controlled by Orthodox circles. R. Hillel Lichtenstein, who served the community in 1867–91, was a staunch opponent of modernism. A *talmud torah* for 120 children was set up in the 1860s. In 1886, a J. elementary school was opened by the Alliance Israelite, reaching an enrollment of 691 in 1905. Most of the 30 or so synagogues in the city were built after a fire in 1865 that left nearly 1,000 J. families homeless. In 1878, the Jews won a majority of the seats in the city council and Dr. Maximilian Trachtenberg was elected mayor. Jews were also elected regularly to the Austrian parliament. In 1891 Jews were attacked in peasant riots connected with the parliamentary election campaign. During WWI, the J. economy was hard hit, with many J. factories destroyed in the fighting and recovery slow in the face of economic crisis and discriminatory government measures. In 1921 there were 499 J. factories (mostly small) and workshops, over half in the clothing industry and employing over 1,000 Jews. About 200 young J. women were employed in a modern lacework factory and another 200 Jews from K. worked as lace salesmen throughout Poland. With increasing economic difficulties in the 1930s, the community expanded its welfare services, operating soup kitchens and providing schoolchildren with assistance. Between the World Wars a number of Yiddish newspapers and periodicals were published. The Zionists were particularly active in pioneer training, as K. was an important way station for the illegal *aliya* to Palestine via Rumania. Agudat Israel dominated community institutions.

With the arrival of the Soviets in Sept. 1939, J. communal and commercial life was curtailed, with just a few kiosks left in J. hands by 1941. The Hungarian army entered the city at the beginning of July 1941, instituting a regime of forced labor and property confiscations but restraining the Ukrainians from violence. The Germans took over the administration of the city on 1 Aug. when it was incorporated into the General Gouvernement. A *Judenrat* was set up, headed by Mordekhai Horowitz. In additions to managing the local community, it was burdened with housing and feeding 2,000 refugees arriving from Hungary. In a mass *Aktion* commencing on 12 Oct. 1941, 2,850 Jews were murdered in the Szeparowce forest 5 miles (8 km) from

The Ba'al Shem Tov, from an 18th cent. painting, Kolomyja, Poland

the city. The Germans also burned down the main synagogue and other prayer houses. Hundreds more were executed in the forest on 6 Nov. During the winter, starvation and disease claimed 50 lives a day. On 23 Dec., 1,200 Jews of foreign nationality, including the refugees from Hungary and also from Germany, were executed and on 24 Jan. 1942, 400 from among the J. intelligentsia. A ghetto was sealed off on 25 March, crowding together over 18,000 Jews. In early April, 5,000 Jews were deported to the Belzec death camp, with 250 murdered inside the ghetto and 86 burned alive in buildings set on fire by the Germans. On 7 Sept. another 7,000 were sent to Belzec and 1,000 among the sick and those caught hiding were killed on the spot. Sporadic killing continued until another 4,000 were shipped to Belzec on 11 Oct., including the children in the J. orphanage. After the last *Aktion* suicides multiplied, including Mordekhai Horowitz. On 4 Nov., the Germans and Ukrainians set the ghetto on fire and murdered all those not consumed by the flames – 5,000 Jews that same night and another 1,000 in the Szeparowce forest two days later. Jews clustering in the ghetto brought its pop. back up to 2,000 in Jan. 1943. On 1 Feb., 1,500 were taken to Szeparowce for execution and the rest were killed subsequently. In 1942–1943 there were attempts to escape to Hungary and Rumania but few succeeded.

KOLONIA IZAAKA   Bialystok dist., Poland, today Belarus. K. was settled as a J. colony by 26 J. families in 1849 on 1,000 acres of land. The Jews grew cereal crops and peas and despite difficult conditions the pop. stabilized by the end of the cent., numbering 221. By then, most used hired labor and worked in Bialystok in the weaving industry or in other trades. However, the outbreak of WWI forced the Jews to work their land themselves again. Between the World Wars, the J. pop. dropped to 140 (total 217). Farm produce was marketed 10 miles (16 km) away in Sokolka and during the winter season many worked as artisans. ORT and the ICA provided financial assistance to the settlement, which was unique in the region for its picturesque appearance and healthy environment. All the Jews of K. were expelled by the Germans to the Kelbasin transit camp near Grodno in Nov. 1942 and perished in Auschwitz.

KOLONJA SYNAJSKA   Nowogrodek dist., Poland, today Belarus. K. was founded in 1849 by eight J. families as a farm settlement, growing to 25 families on 500 acres of land in the late 19th cent. Twelve or 13 left for Palestine in 1934, settling in Rishon le-Zion and Petah Tikva. The remaining 60–80 Jews were expelled by the Germans to the Dereczyn ghetto and murdered there on 23 July 1942.

KOLTA   Slovakia, Czechoslovakia, today Republic of Slovakia. Jews probably settled in the early 18th cent., and possibly earlier, reaching a peak pop. of 362 (of a total 1,432) in 1828. A synagogue was erected in the early 19th cent. Jews traded in livestock and farm produce and some farmed or managed estates. Following the exodus of the young to the big cities, mainly Nove Zamky, the J. pop. declined to 236 in 1840; 136 in 1880; and 75 in 1941. After the annexation to Hungary in Nov. 1938, Jews were seized for forced labor. On 5 June 1944, they were ghettoized in Nove Zamky and on 13 June deported to Auschwitz.

KOLTYNIANY   Vilna dist., Poland, today Belarus. Jews were leased land to build homes by the town's proprietor and numbered 23 families by the late 19th cent. With the coming of the railroad, their economic situation remained satisfactory until WWI, when economic activity came to a standstill and the Germans subjected the inhabitants to forced labor. During the war, R. Yosef Kahaneman, head of the Ponevezh yeshiva, lived in K. After the war the Jews recovered with the assistance of the YEKOPO relief organization. In the 1920s, a Tarbut Hebrew school was founded along with a branch of Hehalutz. The economic crisis of 1929 caused many Jews to emigrate to Argentina, France, and other countries. The J. pop. in 1931 was 30 families. The German *Wehrmacht* entered the town in late June 1941, murdering a number of Jews as alleged Communists. The rest were sent to the Poligany camp in late Sept. 1941 and murdered there with 8,000 Jews from Swienciany province.

KOLUMNA   Lodz dist., Poland. In the 1930s, the Radoshits hasidic rabbi had his court at this vacation resort. In WWII, the Jews either fled or were deported. A J. labor camp that existed in K. from Oct. 1942 was liquidated on 30 Aug. 1943.

KOLUSZKI   Lodz dist., Poland. Jews lived here from the 18th cent. The J. pop. in 1921 was 387 (29% of the total). In Sept. 1939, the J. pop. was 475, rising with the influx of refugees to 3,000 by Dec. 1941. All were deported to the Treblinka death camp in Oct. 1942.

KOLYSHKI   Vitebsk dist., Belorussia. J. settlement dates back to the mid-18th cent. The J. pop. was 1,127 (total 1,568) in 1897 and 1,006 in 1926 under the Soviets. A J. council (soviet) was established in 1926 and a J. elementary school was open until 1939. The Germans occupied K. in early July 1941. A Red Army unit took the town in Feb. 1942 and some Jews were able to flee east. On 17 March, the Germans rounded up the remaining Jews and took them to the village of Adamenki for execution. Some were also murdered with local Jews at Liozno.

KOMADI   Bihar dist., Hungary. Jews were only allowed to settle in the early 19th cent. The community organized in 1855, soon building a synagogue. Its pop. was 166 in 1880 and 224 (2% of the total) in 1941. In 1941, the men were sent to forced labor. In early May 1944 the remaining Jews were brought to Nagyvarad and in early June deported to Auschwitz.

KOMARGOROD   Vinnitsa dist., Ukraine. Jews numbered 86 in 1765 and 481 (total 1,909) in 1897. After the Oct. 1917 Revolution, the J. pop. dropped, reaching 294 in 1926. The Germans captured the town on 22 July 1941. On 25 July, they murdered eight Jews and later on, apparently, the rest.

KOMARICHI Oriol dist., Russia. Jews probably settled in the mid-19th cent. Their pop. was 172 (total 1,469) in 1921 and 81 in 1939. The few Jews who had neither fled nor been evacuated were murdered after the German occupation of Aug. 1941.

KOMARIN Polesie dist., Belorussia. The J. pop. was 547 (total 550) in 1897. A J. elementary school (four grades) was opened in 1925. In the late 1920s, 50% of the Jews were artisans and 15% merchants, with 20 families working at a kolkhoz set up near the town in 1929. In 1933, the J. pop. was 500 (29% of the total). The Germans occupied K. on 28 Aug. 1941. In Sept. and early Oct., they murdered the 89 Jews who had not managed to flee.

KOMARNO (I) Lwow dist., Poland, today Ukraine. Jews apparently settled in the 1530s and were among the town's defenders during the unsuccessful siege of 1648 by Chmielnicki's Cossack forces. A decline set in under Austrian rule, with cutbacks in the major weaving industry. In the 19th cent., Jews traded in agricultural produce (fruit and honey as well as fish) and from the 1880s a professional class emerged, with the J. pop. reaching 2,161 (40% of the total) in 1890 and continuing to grow up to WWI. A local hasidic dynasty founded by R. Alexander Sender Safrin was prominent until the Holocaust. At the end of the 19th cent., a Jew served as mayor of K. and the Zionists were active from the early 20th cent. The Jews suffered severe hardship in WWI at the hands of the Russian army, which murdered 17 of the 50 Jews taken hostage by their retreating forces. The J. pop. at this time dropped by nearly 25% to stand at 2,004 in 1921. The Germans arrived on 30 June 1941 and immediately set up a *Judenrat* to supply forced labor. Hundreds of leading figures were rounded up and murdered in the nearby forest on 24 Oct. 1941. Through the winter of 1941–42 the streets filled with corpses as starvation took its toll. On 6 Nov. 1942 around a thousand Jews were deported to the Belzec death camp. The remaining few hundred were crowded into a ghetto containing about a dozen small houses until expelled in Dec. to the Rudki ghetto where they met their death on 9 April 1943.

KOMARNO (II) (Hung. Komarom) Slovakia, Czechoslovakia, today Republic of Slovakia. Jews were apparently present in the Middle Ages, though not uninterruptedly. Settlement in the modern era commenced around the turn of the 17th cent. The community grew rapidly in the 1840s and numbered 849 in 1850. Following the repression by the Austrians of the Hungarian uprising of 1848–49, heavy fines undermined the J. economy but recovery was rapid and the J. pop. grew to 2,296 (total 16,816) in 1900. A J. elementary school was opened in the 1850s and a new, 400-seat synagogue was erected in 1863. After the split of 1869, the community formed a Neologist congregation. About 20 Orthodox families formed a separate congregation, building their own synagogue in 1904. The city's location on the banks of the Danube encouraged exports and Jews were prominent as lumber exporters. The Zionists were active from the late 19th cent. With the city divided after WWI, most Jews found themselves in the Czechoslovakian sector, faced with the necessity of reorganizing the community, now cut off from the Neologist center in Budapest. An Orthodox yeshiva reached an enrollment of 100 in the 1930s. The Orthodox community also maintained a *talmud torah* and a Beth Jacob school for girls but shared the elementary school with the Neologists. Jews served on the municipal council and dominated the city's trade. Zionist activity expanded and Agudat Israel also became active. The J. pop. in 1941 was 2,734. After the annexation to Hungary in Nov. 1938, the Jews were subjected to a regime of persecution and forced labor. Jews were murdered by members of the fascist Arrow Cross Party as well as after expulsion to the Ukraine. By 1944, about 2,170 remained. In May, most were forced into a ghetto, to be joined in June by over 2,000 additional Jews from the area. All were deported to Auschwitz on 13 and 16 June. In all, 1,884 local Jews perished in the death camps, 23 at forced labor, and 15 in Hungarian concentration camps. About 250 survivors reestablished the community after the war, which grew to 500 in 1948. In 1949, 306 left for Israel.

KOMAROM Komarom dist., Hungary. The J. settlement was one of the earliest in the Danube region, dating from the Magyar conquest of the ninth cent. After the destruction of the country by Genghis Khan in the 13th cent., King Bela IV invited wealthy Jews from Austria to help resettle the land. An organized community was formed in the 18th cent. and the first synagogue was built in 1803. In 1880, the J. pop. was 109, reaching a peak of 294 (3% of the total) in 1910. The community was Neologist. Between the World Wars, assimilationist tendencies prevailed and there was hardly any interest in Zionism. The J. pop. fell to 110 in 1941. Hungary's 1938 racial laws undermined J. livelihoods. A harsh regime of forced labor was subsequently instituted and on 13 June 1944 the Jews were deported to Auschwitz.

KOMAROW Lublin dist., Poland. An organized community with a synagogue and cemetery existed by the first half of the 19th cent. The J. pop. was 943 in 1856 and 1,752 (total 2,895) in 1921. On 28 Aug. 1920, Bulak-Balakhovich soldiers murdered 16 Jews, severely injured 60, and raped 47 women. On the approach of the Germans in Sept. 1939, many fled with the Red Army. In summer 1941, a ghetto was established, swelled by 1,300 refugees, including 700 from Czechoslovakia. On 23 May 1942, most of the refugee pop. was sent to the Belzec death camp. In Oct.–Nov., those still remaining in K. were shot or sent to Belzec.

KOMAROWKA Lublin dist., Poland. Fifteen Jews were present in 1883 and 412 in 1921 (of a total 1,038). In summer 1941, three years after the Germans captured K., the Jews were expelled to Miendzyrzec Podlaski and from there deported to the Treblinka death camp six weeks later. The few dozen who remained as workers were deported to the Majdanek concentration camp in April 1943.

KOMJATICE Slovakia, Czechoslovakia, today Republic of Slovakia. One J. family was present in 1738, joined in the 1740s by refugees from Moravia. A cemetery was opened c. 1879 and the community grew slowly to a peak of about 130 in the 1890s. Jews engaged in petty trade, dealt in livestock and farm produce, and farmed. After WWI, they owned various businesses, including a few grocery stores and a distillery. The J. pop. was 73 (of a total 3,958) in 1941. After the annexation to Hungary, Jews were seized for forced labor. After the German occupation, the 50 who remained were deported to Auschwitz via Nove Zamky on 12 June 1944.

KOMOTINI (Gumulgina, Comotini, Komotene,

Gumulcine, Gumuldjina) Thrace, Greece. J. settlement in K. began in the early 16th cent. when Jews from Adrianople (Edirne) and Salonika arrived there. Down through the centuries, the community was predominantly Sephardi. Nathan of Gaza brought renown to K. in the 17th cent., when he stayed there for awhile and spread the beliefs of Shabbetai Zvi (even after the latter had converted to Islam). Nathan of Gaza was eventually ostracized and left K. for Salonika. J. settlement was significantly increased in the 1860s. By 1904, the J. pop. numbered 1,200. There were two J. schools (one for boys, the other for girls), which were combined in 1910. During this period, four social welfare organizations were active. During the Balkan wars, Bulgaria occupied K. at the end of 1912 and many families suffered the financial consequences of war. In 1913 there were 1,290 Jews (total 381,159). A J. Bulgarian association that encouraged Hebrew language and culture opened a branch in K. during Bulgarian rule; it had 120 members in 1919. K. was annexed to Greece in WWI. The J. school was closed temporarily after the war, when the building was needed for refugees. Zionist activity was particularly enthusiastic in the 1920s. The J. pop. in 1928 came to 1,159. The global economic depression of the 1930s affected the Jews of K. too, most of whom were tradesmen. Community funding dropped and many families fell into financial distress. Nevertheless, communal welfare and social activity continued and flourished during the period. Prior to WWII there were 850 Jews in K. In April 1941, K. came under Bulgarian occupation. Anti-J. decrees were implemented, including restricted movement, and Jews were forced to mark their clothing and homes. In early 1942, young Jews were taken to forced labor camps, where they were held under harsh conditions. In the winter of that year, the inhabitants suffered from starvation, epidemics, and a high death rate. In March 1943, the Bulgarians arrested the Jews. Different lists recording their numbers vary from 864 to 878. Only 28 managed to evade the arrests. The Jews were held in detention camps, treated brutally, and their possessions confiscated. They were then transferred to Bulgaria along with Jews from Alexandropoulis and Ksanthi. All the 4,055 Jews were then boarded on four ships. One ship sank with evidence indicating that it may have been sunk intentionally. The other three reached Vienna on 25–28 March 1943. The Jews were then sent to the Treblinka death camp; none survived. A few Jews returned to K. after the war but the community numbered only 22 in 1948. Over the years all left for Athens, Israel, or the U. S.

KOMSOMOLSKOYE (until 1935, Makhnovka) Vinnitsa dist., Ukraine. Jews are first mentioned in 1648 when Chmielnicki's Cossacks attacked the local fortress and murdered a number of Poles and Jews. Six Jews were present in 1765 and 2,435 (total 5,343) in 1897. In the mid-1920s, under the Soviets, a J. rural council (soviet) was set up. Jews were employed in a sugar refinery, brickyard, asphalt plant, and kolkhoz. A. J. elementary school was opened in 1925, operating up to the 1930s. A few dozen children attended a *heder* set up in the late 1920s. In 1939, the J. pop. was 843. The Germans captured the town on 14 July 1941 and on 9 Sept. executed 835 Jews in the Zhezhlevsk forest 3 miles (5 km) from K. A ghetto (or camp) was then set up for the few hundred Jews still in the area. They were murdered in a number of *Aktions* in 1942. On 13 Dec. 1942, the last seven J. artisans were murdered.

KOMZETOVKA Odessa dist., Ukraine. K. was founded in the early 1920s as a J. colony and included 70 farm units and 345 J. inhabitants in 1929. In 1929 it became the seat of a J. rural council (soviet) for three J. settlements: K., Kotovskoye, and Grinfeld (the last with 150 inhabitants on 28 farm units). A coeducational J. school was operating from the early 1930s. Presumably the Jews in all three settlements were murdered during the Nazi occupation.

KONETSPOL Odessa dist., Ukraine. Nine Jews were present in 1784. A stone synagogue was built in 1853. The J. pop. increased to 456 (total 1,514) in 1897 and 590 in 1926. The Germans captured K. on 4 Aug. 1941 and in the fall murdered the few Jews who had neither escaped nor been evacuated.

KONIECPOL Lodz dist., Poland. In 1764, 110 J. families inhabited 70 houses. The J. pop. in 1897 was 656 (43% of the total). Between the World Wars, a sizable group of J. factory owners assisted Jews requiring relief (20% of the community). The community had a large stone synagogue as well as prayer houses of the Gur, Radomsk, and Aleksandrow Hasidim. Zionist activity began in 1924 and the Zionists dominated the community council. At the outbreak

of WWII, the Germans set up a *Judenrat*, but the Jews were not ghettoized. The J. pop. in May 1941 was 1,182, including 518 refugees. In Sept. 1942, the Jews from the neighboring villages and from towns in Radomsk county were brought to K. On 6 Oct. 1942, 1,600 Jews were deported to the Treblinka death camp.

KONIN Lodz dist., Poland. About 180 Jews settled in the 15th cent. and were involved later in the export of grain, establishment of factories, transport of goods and people, and building. A yeshiva was established in the early 18th cent. The J. pop. in 1897 was 2,482 (32% of the total). The Bund was active in the 1905–06 strikes and demonstrations. In 1914, 200 Zionists established a group. In 1916, a Jew was head of the city council, while between the World Wars Agudat Israel dominated the community council. On 30 Nov. 1939, 1,000 Jews were expelled to Ostrowiec Kielecki in the General Gouvernement. In July 1940, 1,500 Jews were expelled to Grodziec and Zhgow. Those in Grodziec were murdered in the Jozefow (Bilgorajski) forest in March 1941. In Oct. 1941 the remaining Jews of the area were murdered in the Kazimierz Biskupi forests. In March 1942, the Germans brought 800 Jews from Gostynin and Gambin to a labor camp in K. and in 1943 they were deported to Chelmo.

KONOTOP Sumy dist., Ukraine. About 80 Jews were present in the early 19th cent., their number growing to 4,426 (total 18,770) in 1897. In a pogrom occurring on 29 April 1881, one Jew was killed and much J. property destroyed. General Denikin's White Army troops initiated another pogrom on 19 Sept. 1919, in which six Jews were killed and ten injured. Women were raped and J. stores and homes robbed. In the 1920s, 500 J. artisans organized themselves into cooperatives and started a savings and loan fund. A branch of the Society for the Promotion of J. Settlement (OZET) was active in K., directing 83 J. families from the area to J. colonies in the Kherson dist. In 1939, the J. pop. was 3,941. The Germans captured the city on 9 Sept. 1941, killing 123 Jews in the first days of the occupation. Over 1,000 Jews were later registered, made to wear the yellow badge, and ordered to report for forced labor. In early Nov. 1941, all the Jews were concentrated at the local jail and prisoner-of-war camp and within a few days executed. In 1959, 1,900 Jews were living in K.

KONSKIE Lodz dist., Poland. Jews first settled in the 16th cent. and by the 19th cent. K. became one of the largest J. communities in the district. In the late 18th cent. a synagogue was built that served as a model for such wooden constructions. R. Pinhas Rabinowitz established a hasidic center in the late 19th cent. The J. pop. in 1857 was 6,521 (66% of the total). Zionist activity began in the late 19th cent. The local Bund was founded in 1905–06. In the 1920s, Jews constituted 93% of the hired workers in local factories. Between the World Wars, all the Zionist parties and their youth movements active in Poland had branches in K. Zionists controlled the community council until the 1930s and after that Agudat Israel. The majority of J. representatives on the municipal council were members of the Bund (five out of six in 1936). A yeshiva was founded in 1928 with 100 students. There were several J. schools at this time. Antisemitism was rife. Germans attacked Jews in Sept. 1939 and burned the synagogue. A *Judenrat* was set up and established a public kitchen for the needy. In spring 1940, the J. pop. of 7,500 (including 2,000 refugees) was ghettoized. In 1942, over 400 Jews worked in German factories; others were sent to forced labor. On 3–9 Nov. 1942, the 9,000 inhabitants and refugees were transferred to Szydlowiec and then deported to their deaths in Treblinka. The remaining K. Jews were deported to Treblinka on 13 Jan. 1943. After the war approx. 300 survivors returned, but soon left.

KONSKOWOLA Lublin dist., Poland. Jews were present in the 17th cent. and in 1718 received a privilege allowing them to live and work in K. without restrictions. By the late 18th cent., they had formed an organized community with a synagogue and cemetery. Most were tradesmen; some supplied the local Russian garrison. In the late 19th cent., Jews opened a number of small factories manufacturing porcelain wall and floor tiles. The J. pop. was 872 in 1827 and 1,453 in 1897, dropping to 876 in 1921 A fire in 1911 left 100 J. families homeless and in 1918 Austrian bombardments also destroyed many homes. Between the World Wars, the Jews suffered from the general economic crisis in Poland. Most Zionist groups were represented along with Agudat Israel and the Bund. Anti-J. riots broke out throughout the 1930s. The Germans established a ghetto in K. in late 1940. On 8 May 1942, 1,600 of the town's 2,000 Jews (including refugees) were deported to the Sobibor death camp. Imme-

diately afterwards over 3,000 Jews were brought to K. from Czechoslovakia and K. was declared a J. city with Jews arriving from various cities in the Lublin area. With the influx of additional refugees, the J. pop. rose to 5,000, with 3,000 consigned to local labor camps. In Oct. 1942, 1,100 women, children, and other "unproductive" Jews were executed outside the town. In May 1943, the labor camps were liquidated and the remaining Jews transferred to other camps.

KONSTADT (Pol. Wolczyn) Upper Silesia, Germany, today Poland. The J. pop. was 86 in 1787 and 216 in 1867. The community maintained a synagogue and cemetery. In 1925, the J. pop. was 103, dropping to 80 in 1932. In the same year a handgrenade was thrown into a J. store. The Nazi racial laws instituted from 1933 were not applied to the Jews of K. until 16 July 1937 owing to the protection of the League of Nations' minority rights convention. Nevertheless, local Jews still suffered from persecution in this period. In 1933, a list of J. businesses was posted at the municipality building with a warning not to deal with them. The introduction of the racial laws was accompanied by antisemitic disturbances. On *Kristallnacht* (9–10 Nov. 1938), rioters destroyed the J. prayer house and a number of J. homes and stores. Many of the 76 Jews in the city subsequently emigrated. Presumably those who remained were deported and perished. By 19 Nov. 1942, just seven were still living in K. Their fate is unknown.

KONSTANCINEK Warsaw dist., Poland. The J. pop. in 1921 was 399 (total 1,455). All were presumably expelled to the Warsaw ghetto after the German occupation in WWII.

KONSTANTYNOW Lodz dist., Poland. Jews were granted permission to settle from 1830. They entered the textile industry in the second half of the 19th cent. The J. pop. in 1897 was 1,091 (19.5% of the total). Up to the end of WWI, the J. community was dominated by Hasidim with 80 young men enrolled at the yeshiva. The first Zionist groups were organized during WWI. Agudat Israel controlled the community council between the World Wars. During the 1930s, there were numerous manifestations of antisemitism, mostly by local German Hitler Youth. The Germans occupied K. on 7 Sept. 1939 and took possession of

J. factories and property. On 22 Dec. 1939, they expelled all the J. inhabitants to Glowno. Many escaped to Lodz and Warsaw, where they shared the fate of the local Jews.

KONSTANTYNOWO (I) Polesie dist., Poland, today Ukraine. This J. farm settlement founded in 1848 had a pop. of 217 in 1923. In the Holocaust, the Jews were expelled to the Rozhana ghetto for liquidation.

KONSTANTYNOWO (II) Lublin dist., Poland. An established community appears to have existed in the second half of the 18th cent., growing to 517 in 1827 and 783 (total 957) in 1921. The Zionists and Agudat Israel were active between the World Wars. In Sept. 1939, 1,200 Jews were present. Under German rule, a *Judenrat* was appointed in summer 1940 and a ghetto was set up in late 1940. Starvation, disease, and the cold claimed many victims in winter 1942. In Sept. 1942, the Jews were expelled to the Biala Podlaska ghetto, where the old were murdered. The able-bodied were selected for labor camps. The rest were dispatched to Miendzyrzec Podlaski for deportation to the Treblinka death camp on 17 Oct.

KONSTANZ (in J. sources, Kashnitz) Baden, Germany. Jews apparently settled in the first half of the 13th cent. and earned their livelihood as moneylenders. In 1312 and again a few years later they were massacred in Host desecration libels and in March 1349, 330 were burned alive after a well-poisoning libel. Others were burned to death half a year later. Jews settled again later in the cent. at the invitation of the town council but in 1385 they were arrested and the promissory notes in their possession confiscated. In 1390 many were massacred in a blood libel. Despite such violence and numerous disabilities, the Jews rehabilitated the community and by 1418 comprised 25 households concentrated in a special quarter with a new synagogue. In 1430, rioting townsmen imprisoned the Jews in the local tower for 20 weeks and pillaged their homes. In 1443, following another blood libel, they were again confined to the tower, this time for five years. The community did not recover and only in the mid-19th cent. was J. settlement permitted again. A community with a Liberal orientation was organized in 1863 and a synagogue was consecrated in 1893, with the J. pop. reaching

565 in 1900 (total 22,478). The first Jew to sit on the city council (1904–12) was Immanuel Rothschild, head of the community and owner of a large cigarette factory. The Zionists were active from early in the cent. In 1925, K. became the seat of the district rabbinate, with jurisdiction over 16 communities. By 1933, the J. pop. of K. stood at 443. Many were industrialists, merchants, and operators of big business establishments, while others were sales representatives for German and Swiss firms or members of the professional class. Because of K.'s position as a tourist center and border town, local Nazis exercised a measure of restraint in their anti-J. activities and J. economic life was at first affected less than elsewhere. Soon, however, persecution intensified. In 1936 the synagogue was partially burned and in 1938 the community opened an elementary school after J. children were forced out of the public schools. A number of Jews transferred their businesses and domiciles across the Swiss border to Kreuzlingen, where a community of 130, mostly from K., was formed. On 28 Oct. 1938, Jews of Polish origin were deported to Poland. On *Kristallnacht* (9–10 Nov. 1938), the synagogue was blown up and Jews were beaten mercilessly at Gestapo headquarters before being sent to the Dachau concentration camp. During the Nazi era, 338 Jews emigrated from K. and 251 left for other German cities. On 22 Oct 1940, 110 were deported to the Gurs concentration camp; 52 were able to find refuge in the U.S., France, and Switzerland; most of the others perished in Auschwitz. The 44 Jews in the attached community of Singen all left by 1939. A small community was formed in K. after the war, attached to Freiburg.

KONYAR Bihar dist., Hungary. The Jews were only allowed to settle here in the mid-19th cent. The community organized in 1840, building a synagogue in c. 1900. They numbered 80 in 1930. Being very observant, they opposed Zionism. In 1941, the men were sent for forced labor to the Ukraine, where most perished. At the end of May 1944, the remaining Jews were sent to Nagyvarad and at the end of June deported to Auschwitz.

KOPACZEWKA Volhynia dist., Poland, today Ukraine. The J. pop. in 1921 was 274. In the Holocaust, the Jews were brought to the Rozyszcze ghetto for liquidation.

KOPASNOVO (Hung. Gyernyes; Yid. Kapashne) Carpatho-Russia, Czechoslovakia. Jews apparently settled in the late 18th cent. Eight were present in 1768, the J. pop. then growing to 115 (total 1,292) in 1880. A few Jews farmed. In 1921, the J. pop. was 190, increasing to 247 in 1941. Following the Hungarian occupation in March 1939, dozens of Jews were drafted into forced labor battalions and sent to the eastern front. In Aug. 1941, a number of J. families were expelled to the German-occupied Ukraine and murdered. The rest were deported to Auschwitz in the second half of May 1944.

KOPATKEVICHI Polesie dist., Belorussia. The J. pop. was 54 in 1811 and 1,310 (total 1,768) in 1897. There was a J. school in the late 19th cent. In 1920–21, 144 Jews were murdered and many J. homes looted in two pogroms staged by the Balakhovich brigades. A J. council (soviet) was established in 1926 and a J. elementary school was attended by 140 children in the same year. Both were closed down in the late 1930s. In the late 1920s, half the Jews were artisans. A J. kolkhoz was founded near the town in 1929 with 50 J. families working there. In 1939, the J. pop. was 881. The Germans occupied K. on 1 Aug 1941. In early 1942, all the Jews who had failed to flee the town were murdered. Another 12 Jews were apprehended in March 1942 and burned alive at the J. cemetery.

KOPAYGOROD Vinnitsa dist., Ukraine. The J. pop. was 337 in 1765 and 1,720 (total 2,950) in 1897. In the Soviet period, a J. council (soviet) from 1929 and J. elementary school were in operation. In the early 1930s, most Jews were unemployed; others worked in cooperatives or a J. kolkhoz. In 1939, the J. pop. was 1,075. The Germans captured the town on 20 July 1941. Local residents and other civilians seized 200 Jews and held them for ransom. Of the approximately 4,500 Jews from Bessarabia and Bukovina whom the Rumanians expelled to K. after it was annexed to Transnistria in early Sept., 2,808 perished. A *Judenrat* and J. police force were established along with a ghetto. In late July 1942, most Jews were transferred from the ghetto to an open camp outside the town where many died. Skilled workers remained in the ghetto. In all, 5,197 J. refugees and hundreds from K. perished in the region.

KOPRIVNICA (Hung. Kaproncza) Croatia, Yugo-

slavia, today Republic of Croatia. J. settlement in K. began at the end of the 17th cent. The number of Jews increased towards the mid-19th cent. and a community was established. By 1896 there were 398 Jews (total 5,710) and 358 in 1940. A synagogue was founded in 1875. Zionist activity began in 1918. From April 1941 the Ustase, rounded up the Jews and sent them to death camps, including Auschwitz and Jasenovac.

KOPRZYWNICA Kielce dist., Poland. Jews settled under Austrian rule in the late 18th cent. after a long-standing residence ban. Many died in an 1893 cholera epidemic and others lost their homes soon after in a devastating fire. Homes were rebuilt in brick and Jews opened 60 new stores. In 1921, the J. pop. was 812 (total 2,349). Between the World Wars, the Zionists were active, while the influence of Agudat Israel in community institutions grew in the 1930s. Anti-J. government policy and boycotts undermined J. livelihoods. The German occupation of Sept. 1939 introduced a regime of random killings and extortionate tributes. A *Judenrat* was established in Oct. 1939 and a ghetto in Dec. 1941, where hundreds of refugees from Radom, Vienna, and other places were crowded together. On 30 Oct. 1942, about 1,600 Jews were deported to the Treblinka death camp.

KOPTSEVICHI Polesie dist., Belorussia. The J. pop. was 279 (total 1,056) in 1926 and 504 in 1939. The Germans captured K. in early Aug. 1941, instituting a regime of forced labor. In late Sept., the 100 or so Jews who had failed to flee were murdered outside the town.

KOPYCZYNCE Tarnopol dist., Poland, today Ukraine. Jews apparently settled in the late 17th cent., the J. pop. growing to 2,467 (total 6,967) by 1890, then declining through emigration before rising again to its previous level as WWI refugees joined the community. The hasidic court established by R. Avraham Yehoshua Heschel in 1894 generated jobs catering to visitors and also served to retard the spread of Zionism. Pinhas Lavon (Lubianiker), Israel's minister of defense in 1953–54 and a native of K., founded a Gordonia den there in the 1920s. In the 1930s, economic conditions deteriorated in the face of competition from the Polish and Ukrainian cooperatives and anti-J. measures. The Soviet regime of 1939–41 ended J. community and

Children in Kopyczynce, Poland

commercial life. The Germans arrived on 7 July 1941. Forced labor and sporadic killing followed and the synagogue was burned in Aug. On 30 Sept. 1942, 1,000 Jews were deported to the Belzec death camp after a selection and the murder of 50 of the sick. Refugees arrived in Oct. and were crowded into a ghetto together with the local Jews. Four hundred were murdered on 15 April 1943 with most managing to hide out. On 23 June, in an *Aktion* lasting a week, 4,000 Jews were rounded up and murdered in the forest near the J. cemetery. The remaining 1,000 Jews were killed over the next month.

KOPYL (Yid. Kopulia) Minsk dist., Belorussia. Jews are first mentioned in 1720. In 1897, their pop. was 2,671 (total 4,463). Of the many fires in K. the one in April 1886 destroyed hundreds of homes, the Great Synagogue (probably dating back to the 17th cent.), and a number of *battei midrash*. K. was the birthplace of the writer Mendele Mokher Seforim (Shalom Yaakov Abramowitsch; 1835–1917) and of Yaakov Avraham Paperna (1840–1919), the literary critic,

educator, and writer. In the late 1920s and early 1930s, a few dozen J. families worked in kolkhozes. A J. elementary school was active through the early 1930s. In 1939, the J. pop. was 1,435. The Germans occupied the town a few days after their attack on the Soviet Union. In late June 1941, they established a *Judenrat*, J. police force, and ghetto in which thousands of Jews from K. and its environs were held. Within several months, the Germans and the local police murdered several thousand Jews. The rest were executed on 23 July 1942. A number of Jews escaped and some fought with the Zhukov partisans in the Czapayev brigade of General Kapustin's division.

KOPYS Vitebsk dist., Belorussia. Jews settled in the mid-17th cent. In 1766, the J. pop. included 304 poll tax payers. A very active J. printing press was founded in 1818. Most Jews were Hasidim. In 1897 the J. pop. was 1,399 (total 3,384). A pogrom was staged in April 1905. There were two J. private schools for boys in the town in the early 20th cent. Most Jews earned their livelihoods manufacturing and exporting tiles. In

1924, under the Soviets, a J. elementary school (four grades) was opened. The Germans occupied K. in July 1941. In Dec., a ghetto for 250 Jews was set up in the yard of the local linen plant. The Jews were murdered in Jan. 1942.

KORBACH Hesse–Nassau, Germany. Numbering 65 in 1782, the J. community grew to 151 (over 5% of the total) in 1880. It was affiliated with the rabbinate of Kassel. An organ was installed in the new synagogue built in 1895. The Nazis imposed a strict boycott against the Jews and the nondenominational old age home was "Aryanized" in 1935. Of the 127 Jews living in K. in 1933, 89 left (51 emigrating) before *Kristallnacht* (9–10 Nov. 1938), when the synagogue was burned down. The others were mostly deported to the Lublin dist. (Poland) in 1942 and perished in the Holocaust.

KORCZYNA Lwow dist., Poland. Jews settled in the first half of the 17th cent. The development of neighboring Krosno overshadowed the community, causing a drop in the pop. from a 1900 peak of 1,026 (total 5,422) to 746 in 1921. Market and fair days in K. and in Krosno were an important source of livelihood as was the home industry for the manufacture of cloth. The Rubin family, scions of the hasidic Ropshits and Lyzhansk dynasties, provided the town with rabbis from the first half of the 19th cent. up to the Holocaust. The Zionists were active from the early 20th cent., renewing their activity after WWI despite the vehement opposition of traditional circles. The German occupation from Sept. 1939 was marked by increasingly severe measures, including sporadic killing, forced labor, and wide-ranging restrictions. The community of 1,500 including refugees was liquidated on 12 Aug. 1942 when the old and sick were murdered and the rest, excluding 120 earmarked for labor, deported to the Belzec death camp via Krosno.

KORELICZE Nowogrodek dist., Poland, today Belarus. J. settlement probably commenced in the 17th cent., under the aegis of the Radziwill family, which leased flour mills and inns to the Jews. Their pop. grew to 1,840 (total 2,259) in 1897. A 1911 fire destroyed half the houses in K. and during WWI the Jews were evacuated to Nowogrodek and environs. They recovered slowly in the aftermath of the war. An-

other fire set back the community in 1929. Economic conditions deteriorated in the mid-1930s. Children attended a Tarbut Hebrew school and the Zionists were active. The J. pop. in 1931 was 1,300. After the arrival of the Germans on 27 June 1941, a *Judenrat* was appointed and the Jews placed under a regime of forced labor. In Aug., 105 young J. men were murdered. In Feb. 1942, the Jews were confined to a ghetto. Most were sent to the Nowogrodek ghetto in May and June 1942 and murdered in the *Aktions* there.

KORENOVSKAYA Krasnodar territory, Russia. The Germans murdered about 40 J. families from the village near the local airport after telling them they were being resettled.

KORIUKOVKA Chernigov dist., Ukraine. Jews settled in the 19th cent., numbering 381 in 1897 and 745 (total 9,744) in 1939. The Germans captured K. on 5 Sept. 1941 and murdered 246 Jews from the area, including those from K.

KORMA Gomel dist., Belorussia. The J. pop. was 1,175 in 1847 and 1,328 (total 1,534) in 1897. Jews earned their livelihoods from petty trade, crafts, and export of grain and lumber to Germany. Most Jews were Hasidim. K. was the birthplace of the writer Hillel Zeitlin (1871–1942). In 1924, under the Soviets, a J. council (soviet) was established. In 1930, eight J. families worked at a kolkhoz. In the same year, 64 of the 125 J. artisans in the town were members of a cooperative. Despite the existence of a J. elementary school (attended by 108 children), illegal *hadarim* were still operating in 1926–27. In 1939, the J. pop. was 981. The Germans arrived on 15 Aug. 1941. The remaining 700 Jews who had not fled or been evacuated were herded into a ghetto where they suffered from hunger, overcrowding, and the cold. In Nov. they were executed outside the town.

KORMEND Vas dist., Hungary. Jews enjoying equal rights were present by 1300 and others of Spanish origin may have settled in the late 16th cent. In 1799, the J. pop. was 237 and 740 in 1869, when a Neologist congregation was formed. A J. school was founded in 1860 and a new synagogue was consecrated in 1922. The Zionists became active in 1935 and increased their influence after the publication of Hungary's 1938 racial laws. On 5 May 1944, K.'s

300 remaining Jews were confined to a ghetto and in early June transferred to the Szombathely ghetto, from where most were deported to Auschwitz on 5 July 1944. Some of the men were taken to forced labor at Muhldorf near Munich, where most perished. Survivors reestablished the community but by 1950 they dispersed.

KORNIK Poznan dist., Poland. Jews are first mentioned in the late 17th cent. Many were artisans (60% of breadwinners in 1793), primarily tailors, who set up their own guild. In the 19th cent., artisans enlarged their workshops and the growing merchant class dealt in wool, clothing, grain, and lumber. The J. pop. reached a peak of 1,170 (total 2,635) in 1840 but thereafter declined sharply (to 399 in 1871 and 92 in 1910) through emigration to the big German cities. The 36 Jews remaining in Sept. 1939 were expelled by the Germans to Lodz and Kalisz on 12 Dec. 1939 to share the fate of the Jews there.

KORNIN Zhitomir dist., Ukraine. Jews are mentioned in 1618. All were murdered in the Chmielnicki massacres of 1648–49. In 1897, the J. pop. was 807 (total 3,103). In an Aug. 1919 pogrom, Petlyura's soldiers and local gangs murdered dozens of Jews, raped women, and pillaged property. The town was subsequently abandoned, with Jews later returning in small numbers. The Germans arrived on 14 July 1941 and murdered 380 people in the region, most of them Jews.

KORNITSA Kamenets-Podolski dist., Ukraine. Jews settled in the 17th cent. In 1649, Tartars massacred the Jews of K. in a raid. In 1765, the J. pop. included 49 poll tax payers and in 1897 it reached 515 (total 1,251). In 1923, under the Soviets, the J. pop. fell to 322. The Germans arrived on 4 July 1941. The Jews were presumably murdered at Lakhovtsy in the second half of 1942.

KOROLIVKA Vinnitsa dist., Ukraine. This J. colony was founded in 1848 by 235 settlers, growing mainly sugar beet. In 1897, the J. pop. was 402 (total 589). Many were murdered in a pogrom in April 1919. There were only 100 left in 1926. The Germans occupied the village in mid-July 1941, murdering the few Jews who had neither fled nor been evacuated.

KOROLOWKA Tarnopol dist., Poland, today Ukraine. The J. settlement dates from the late 17th cent. The town was the birthplace of Jakob Frank (1726–91), founder of the Frankist movement. The Russians destroyed the town in WWI, with the J. pop. dropping from a 1900 figure of 1,596 to 1,161 (over a third of the total). The Germans arrived in July 1941 and on 26 Sept. 1942 expelled 700–900 Jews to Borszczow for deportation to the Belzec death camp with some murdered on the spot. Most of the rest met a similar fate a month later.

KORONOWO Poznan dist., Poland. Jews apparently settled only after the Prussian annexation in 1772, forming an organized community by the 1830s. In 1871 it reached a peak pop. of 620 (total 3,592) and late in the cent. was operating an elementary school. A synagogue was built in the 1870s. The Zionists were active from 1913. Emigration reduced the J. pop. to 40 in 1933. Those remaining in Sept. 1938 were expelled by the Germans to General Gouvernement territory and from there to the labor and death camps.

KOROP Chernigov dist., Ukraine. The J. pop. was 673 (total 6,262) in 1897 and 350 in 1939. A pogrom was staged in 1917. The Germans arrived on 28 Aug. 1941, with most of the Jews fleeing. On 9 Feb. 1942, 111 were murdered.

KOROPIEC Tarnopol dist., Poland, today Ukraine. Jews are first mentioned in 1635, with an organized community in the late 19th cent. and a pop. of 176 (total 4,775) in 1921. Most were expelled by the Germans on 24 March 1942 to nearby Monasterzyska and from there in the fall to the Belzec death camp.

KOROSLADANY Bekes dist., Hungary. Jews settled in the late 19th cent., numbering 156 in 1880 and 119 in 1930. They maintained a school and synagogue. They were brought to the Szeghalom ghetto in mid-May 1944 and then sent to Szolnok on 26 June before deportation to Auschwitz on 29 June.

KOROSTEN (Iskorost) Zhitomir dist., Ukraine. In 1618, a Jew is mentioned as the leaseholder of the village but no J. community is known until the 19th cent. In 1897, the J. pop. was 1,299, increasing rapidly with the coming of the railroad. During the civil war (1918–

21), the Jews were attacked by the Petlyura gangs in Feb. 1919 and by the Red Army on 13 March and 20 July 1919. A conference chaired by R. Shelomo Yosef Zevin, later one of the outstanding rabbis of Jerusalem, and attended by 90 Ukrainian rabbis and 1,500 guests was held in K. in Oct. 1926. J. workers were employed in a local iron foundry, a furniture factory, porcelain factory, and brickyard. Jews also worked for the railroad and J. artisans were organized in nine cooperatives. Attempts were made to settle Jews, particularly those designated "classless," on south Ukrainian farms. Two Yiddish-language schools, one including ten grades, were founded. Enrollment was 1,000 in 1934 and 700 in 1937. In 1939, the J. pop. was 10,991. The Germans captured the city on 8 Aug. 1941. Most of the Jews were evacuated or fled. In Sept., the Germans murdered 770 and another 1,000 in March 1942. A few thousand returned at the end of the war.

KOROSTISHEV Zhitomir dist., Ukraine. Jews settled in the late 16th cent. In the 18th cent. the community was the third largest in the Zhitomir dist. after Berdichev and Chudnov, reaching a pop. of 4,160 (total 7,863) in 1897. The poet David Hofstein was born there in 1889. In the late 1920s, there were 478 J. laborers, most working in a large paper factory; 475 artisans; 82 engaged in trade; and 120 unemployed. The pogroms of the civil war (1918–21) and internal migration in the Soviet period caused the J. pop. to drop to 2,170 in 1939. The Germans captured K. on 12 July 1941 and in Aug. executed 2,138 Jews, including 198 children, in retaliation for the alleged murder of two German officers. Another 906 Jews, including 102 children, were murdered in May 1942. Included among the victims were dozens of Jews from the neighboring villages.

KORSCHENBROICH Rhineland, Germany. Jews are first mentioned as moneylenders in 1761. In 1808, four received a license to work as butchers and horse traders. The J. pop. was 37 in 1822; 63 (total 3,161) in 1885; and 52 in 1905. A synagogue was consecrated in 1829 and a cemetery was opened in 1885. In 1932, 20 Jews remained, dwindling to 11 in 1939 following emigration under the Nazis. The synagogue was destroyed on *Kristallnacht* (9–10 Nov. 1938).

KORSHEVATA Kiev dist., Ukraine. Jews were present by 1763 and numbered 1,265 (total 5,663) in 1897. Their number presumably dropped in the Soviet period. In Sept. 1941, shortly after the Germans arrived, 48 Jews were murdered. The rest were apparently murdered later on.

KORSUN Kiev dist., Ukraine. Jews settled in the 17th cent. About a quarter of the community escaped a Cossack massacre in 1702. In 1734, Haidamaks murdered 27 and pillaged J. property. The J. pop. was 187 in 1785 and 3,797 in 1897. A yeshiva was opened in 1881 where Russian and arithmetic were also taught. On 1 March 1918, Bolshevik rioters murdered several community leaders, including the rabbi, and burned down J. stores. Shortly afterwards, General Denikin's White Army troops attacked the Jews and murdered 16. In the Soviet period, the J. pop. fell from 2,449 in 1926 to 1,329 in 1939. A J. council was active in K. The Germans arrived on 30 July 1941 and in Sept. murdered 228 Jews. The rest were apparently murdered in a second *Aktion* in Nov. 1942.

KORTELISY Volhynia dist., Poland, today Ukraine. In the Holocaust, K.'s 60 J. families were brought to the Ratno ghetto for liquidation.

KORYCIN Bialystok dist., Poland, today Belarus. Jews were living in K. by the early 17th cent. When the town passed from Prussian to Russian rule in 1807, Jews numbered 149. Their pop. stood at 411 (total 683) in 1897. Most children attended a modernized *heder* and after WWI, with the J. pop. dropping to 265 in 1921, Zionist influence dominated among the young despite the activities of the rival Bund youth group. Under Soviet rule in 1939–41, most Jews accommodated themselves to the new system and some of the many J. refugees passing through the town remained there. The Germans took K. in late June 1941, allowing local Poles to unleash a reign of terror against the Jews. On 2 Nov. 1942 all were brought to the notorious Kelbasin transit camp near Grodno and shortly thereafter deported to Auschwitz.

KORYTNICA Volhynia dist., Poland, today Ukraine. Jews settled in the 16th cent. and suffered greatly in the Chmielnicki massacres of 1648–49. Their pop. grew to nearly 500 in 1897 but many fled in WWI. The 60 remaining families, living in straitened economic circumstances, were dispersed after the Soviet

Entrance to cemetery in Korzec, Poland (The Central Archive for the History of the Jewish People, Jerusalem/photo courtesy of Yad Vashem, The Holocaust Martyrs' and Heroes' Remembrance Authority, Jerusalem)

annexation of 1939; 40 returned and were executed by the Germans on 9 May 1942.

KORZEC (Yid. Korets) Volhynia dist., Poland, today Ukraine. Jews settled in the 16th cent. and suffered severely in the Chmielnicki massacres of 1648–1649. The town developed in the late 18th cent. as J. factories began to operate (cloth, porcelain, printing). Prominent Hasidim like Dov Baer (the *Maggid* of Mezhirech; d. 1772) and Pinhas (Shapiro) of Korets (1726–91) resided in K. for a time. By the end of the 18th cent., two printing housess operated; in one of them the first hasidic book, *Toledot Yaakov Yosef*, was published. In 1881, a great fire destroyed most of the town's houses and 13 synagogues. During this period the outstanding public figure was R. Nehemia Hirschenhorn, who founded a hospital, old age home, library, and modern *talmud torah* as well as being among the town's first Zionist activists. In 1897 the J. pop. reached 4,608 (total 6,060) with tanning and

sugar factories opening and Jews engaged in the grain and lumber trade. With much of the town's agricultural hinterland included in the Soviet Union after WWI, an economic decline set in and the J. pop. dropped to 3,888 in 1921. A Tarbut school and the Zwihil yeshiva headed by R. Yoel Shurin operated there. Hundreds were active in the Zionist youth movements. The Germans arrived on 2 July 1941. In two *Aktions* in Aug., they executed over 450 Jews. Over 1,000 were put to forced labor while confined to a ghetto. A *Judenrat* and J. police force were established. On 21 May 1942, over 2,200 Jews, including 1,600 women and children, were brought outside the town and murdered. Many of the remaining 1,000 fled in panic as a new *Aktion* commenced on 25 Sept.; most were caught and murdered. A group of 11 young men under the command of Misha Gildenman escaped to the forest and formed an effective partisan unit.

KOS (Istankeuy, Cos, Coo) Dodecanese Islands,

Greece. Jews are mentioned as residing in K. in the second cent. B.C.E. In the 14th cent. Romaniot Jews lived there, but were expelled in 1502. A small J. community existed from the beginning of Ottoman rule (1522). A synagogue was built in 1747. In 1850, there were about 40 J. families, but their numbers dwindled thereafter. Occasionally the Jews suffered from Greek anti-J. disturbances, including a blood libel in 1850. At the beginning of the 20th cent., there were only four J. families in K., but following WWI Jews returned to the island and in 1934 the community built a new synagogue after an earthquake destroyed the old one. K. was under Italian rule from 1912. The Jews numbered 166 in 1938, dropping to 85–100 in 1943. On 3 Oct. 1943, the Germans occupied K. In July 1944, the Jews were arrested and transported by ship, along with the Jews of Rhodes (2,000 in all), to Piraeus, arriving there on 31 July. They were held under brutal conditions at an SS prison camp outside Athens prior to deportation to Auschwitz-Birkenau and other death camps on 3 Aug. 1944. The Turkish consul saved 13 Jews from K. and was named one of the Righteous among the Nations in 1989. None of the 12 Jews of K. who survived the Holocaust returned there.

KOSELOVO (Hung. Keselymezo; Yid. Kasheli) Carpatho-Russia, Czechoslovakia, today Ukraine. J. settlement probably began in the late 18th cent. The J. pop. was 54 in 1830 and 243 in 1880. In 1930, under the Czechoslovakians, it reached 423, dropping to 410 in 1941. Jews engaged in trade, crafts, and agriculture and owned three flour mills. The Hungarians arrived in March 1939 and in 1940–41 drafted a few dozen Jews into forced labor battalions. In Aug. 1941, they expelled about half the town's Jews, who lacked Hungarian citizenship, to Kamenets-Podolski, where they were murdered. The rest were deported to Auschwitz on 27 May 1944.

KOSHNYTSHA WIELIKAYA Vinnitsa dist., Ukraine. Four Jews were present in 1765 and 781 (total 5,861) in 1897. In 1939, under the Soviets, the J. pop. dropped to 164. Those who remained after the German occupation in July 1941 were murdered with the other Jews of the region in the fall.

KOSICE (Yid. Kashoi; Hung. Kassa) Slovakia, Czechoslovakia, today Republic of Slovakia. Jews were present in the 15th cent. The 24 who lived in K. in 1833 were members of the Rozhanovce congregation. After the abrogation of residence restrictions in 1840, the J. pop. grew steadily, to 729 in 1857; 2,178 in 1869; and 5,627 (total 40,102) in 1900. In 1848 riots, 198 J. homes and stores were looted and the prayer house was desecrated. The Jews prospered in the late 19th cent., enjoying equal rights from 1867. Most were tradesmen but some joined the professional class or opened factories, mainly processing farm produce. Many Jews were proponents of Haskala, agitating for religious reform under the leadership of R. Dr. Aharon (Siegfried) Bettelheim, editor of the Reform periodical *Der Jude*, the first of its kind in Slovakia. A progressive synagogue, with 500 seats, was opened in 1866 and the majority of the congregation joined the Neologists after the 1869 split. Orthodox worshipers consecrated a new synagogue in 1882 and the new cemetery consecrated in 1888 had separate sections for the two congregations. The Orthodox community maintained its own yeshiva, *talmud torah, beit midrash, mikve,* and poultry slaughterhouse. A Status Quo congregation, one of the first in Hungary, broke away from the Orthodox one in 1871, calling itself Adath Shalom. The first J. elementary school, the Israelische Volksschule, was opened in 1859–60. A new one was opened in 1868–69 and was attended by 326 children in 1872–73. In this period, Jews identified with Hungarian culture and adopted the spoken language. They also controlled the city's trade and were prominent in its industry and financial institutions. The Zionists became active c. 1900, making the city one of Hungary's Zionist centers. Galician and other Hasidim, including R. Shemuel Angel of Radomysl and R. Avraham Shalom Halberstam of Stropkov, also established their courts in the city. The J. pop. rose to 8,792 in 1921 and 11,504 (total 70,117) in 1930. The Neologists built a splendid new synagogue with 1,100 seats in 1927 while the Orthodox yeshiva under R. Shaul Brukh reached an enrollment of 250–300. The Orthodox also consecrated a new synagogue in 1927. Jews served on the municipal council and held various public positions. WIZO had 670 members and youth movements like Hashomer Hatzair, Bnei Akiva, and Betar were active as was Agudat Israel with a few hundred children in its youth movement. J. professionals numbered 30 doctors, 54 lawyers, 15 engineers, and seven pharmacists. J. factories produced machinery and wood, chemical, and cement products. Under Hungarian rule from Nov. 1938, hundreds of

Jews were expelled to the Slovakian border or sent to the Garany concentration camp. They were also abused by the Iron Guard and had their business licenses revoked. Hundreds more were seized for forced labor from summer 1940. In July 1941, about 300 Jews lacking Hungarian citizenship were expelled to the German-occupied Ukraine (Kamenets-Podolski) and murdered there in the fall. In late 1941, there were 10,000 Jews remaining in K. In April 1944, 7,883 Jews from K. and 4,006 from the surrounding area were confined in a ghetto. Another 1,000 essential workers and privileged Jews were held separately. Deportations commenced on 15 May, when two transports with 6,680 Jews left for Auschwitz. On 19 May, another 6,524 Jews were sent to Auschwitz in two transports and followed by a fifth and final transport with 2,439 Jews on 3 June. The postwar community numbered about 4,000 in 1948. Most left for Israel or other countries in 1948–49 with a few hundred still remaining in the 1990s.

KOSINO (Hung. Mezokaszony; Yid. Kasan) Carpatho-Russia, Czechoslovakia, today Ukraine. Jews from Galicia settled in the first half of the 18th cent. In 1746 three J. distillers were living in the town The J. pop. grew to 110 in 1830 and 314 (total 1,454) in 1880. The community maintained a J. school and a *talmud torah* in addition to a broad network of welfare and charity organizations. Its first rabbi, Yosef Halevi Rotenberg, also ran the local Ateret Tzevi yeshiva. The J. pop. reached 601 in 1921 and then fell to 479 in 1941. Some Jews earned their livelihood from farming and from producing high-quality wine. The Zionist and religious parties were mostly active among the young. The Hungarians occupied the town in Nov. 1938. Of the more than 100 Jews drafted into forced labor battalions in 1941, some were murdered. In Aug. 1941, a few J. families were expelled to Kamenets-Podolski and executed. The rest were deported to Auschwitz by the Hungarian gendarmerie in the second half of May 1944.

KOSOVSKAYA POLYANA (Hung. Kaszomezo; Yid. Polien Kossovitski) Carpatho-Russia, Czechoslovakia, today Ukraine. Jews probably settled in the mid-19th cent., numbering 33 (total 1,348) in 1880; 139 in 1921; and 178 in 1941. Following the Hungarian occupation in March 1939, dozens of Jews were drafted into forced labor battalions. In Aug. 1941, a number of J. families without Hungarian citizenship were expelled

to Kamenets-Podolski and murdered. The rest were deported to Auschwitz in the second half of May 1944.

KOSOW (I) Stanislawow dist., Poland, today Ukraine. Jews are first mentioned in 1635. An independent community existed from the early 18th cent. Under the Austrians, rumors in 1850 of a minimum marital age for men led to a spate of early marriages down to the age of ten. The institution of equal rights for Galician Jews in 1868 improved their situation. The carpet industry became a major employer, with the Hilman factory becoming the first in the town to introduce an electric motor. The manufacture of hairnets occupied about 100 girls aged 12–20. Most of K.'s tailors, locksmiths, blacksmiths, watchmakers, and jewelers were also Jews. The Hager family established a long-lived hasidic dynasty, preserving a traditional way of life into the 20th cent. In 1900 the J. pop. reached 2,563 (over 80% of the total). The Zionists were active from the early 20th cent. During WWI many fled as K. changed hands time and again. Between the World Wars, when a railroad line was laid, tourism became an additional source of income owing to the proximity of the Carpathian foothills. The early days of WWII brought many refugees. The Soviet regime, from Sept. 1939, incorporated the carpet industry into a cooperative framework with J. experts maintaining key positions. Religious life endured as well. The arrival of the Hungarian army in early July 1941 forestalled a Ukrainian pogrom but at the same time led to a regime of forced labor, extortion, and disabilities which the Germans stepped up on entering the town in Sept. On 16–17 Oct. they executed 2,200 Jews on a hill near the Moskalowka bridge with the active participation of the Ukrainians. Pious Jews went to their deaths wrapped in their prayer shawls and wearing phylacteries. The synagogue was also burned down. A further 700 Jews were expelled to Kolomyja on 24 April 1942. On 1 May the remainder were confined to a ghetto where sporadic killings and a large-scale *Aktion* on 28 Sept., claiming 150 lives and deporting 600, were followed by final liquidation on 4 Nov.

KOSOW (II) Lublin dist., Poland. A. J. settlement existed in the late 18th cent., numbering 315 in 1827 and 1,316 in 1921. There were only a few dozen Christians living in K. throughout this period. At the turn of the 19th cent., Jews manufactured clothing and footwear in numerous shops and operated two tanneries.

The community was very observant but Zionist influence increased between the World Wars. The Germans arrived in late Sept. 1939, establishing a *Judenrat* and ghetto and sending Jews from Kalisz there in early 1941. On 10 Oct. 1942, all were deported to the Treblinka death camp. The few who managed to escape from the transport were handed over to the Germans by the Poles.

KOSOW POLESKI   Polesie dist., Poland, today Belarus. J. settlement began in the late 16th cent. and numbered 2,028 in 1897 and 1,473 in 1921 (total 2,433). A Hebrew school existed. The Germans arrived on 1 July 1941 and instituted a regime of forced labor and periodic killings. Refugees swelled the J. pop. to 2,250 by Oct. In June 1942, three ghettoes were set up, for skilled workers, the unproductive, and families of labor camp inmates. Those in the latter two camps (1,200 people) were executed on 25 July. All J. hospital patients were murdered previously. On 2 Aug., partisans temporarily captured the town and a few dozen young Jews were selected to join them; most of the rest were murdered when the Germans returned.

KOSSEWO   Bialystok dist., Poland. The J. pop. in 1921 was 143 (total 503). The Jews were apparently expelled by the Germans to Sniadowo and in Jan. 1943 deported to Auschwitz.

KOSTELEC NAD ORLICI   Bohemia, Czechoslovakia. The Jews were expelled in 1841 and returned in 1860. In 1893, they numbered about 150, most engaged in farming, and 26 (total 5,394) in 1930. In Dec. 1942, the Jews were deported to the Theresienstadt ghetto and from there to Auschwitz in 1943.

KOSTOPOL   Volhynia dist., Poland, today Ukraine. The J. settlement began to grow with the opening of a railroad station and the growth of industry in the town in the late 19th cent. The J. pop. was 1,101 in 1897 (total 1,706). After a great fire in 1906, most houses were rebuilt in brick and a new synagogue was constructed. The pop. remained stable through WWI, with a J. self-defense group protecting the community. The Zionists became active after the Feb. 1917 Revolution, sending 209 young people to Palestine up to the eve of WWII. Between the World Wars the local economy flourished as industry continued to expand. Jews

Betar members throwing a party, Kosow Poleski, Poland

Dedication of the Tarbut Hebrew school in Kostopol, Poland, 1928–1929

owned the third largest plywood factory in Poland as well as 180 of the town's 260 stores as their pop. grew to 3,920 (total 9,800). In 1937 a Hebrew school, kindergarten, and library flourished. The Germans arrived on 1 July 1941 and on 16 Aug. executed 470 J. men, mostly leading figures in the community. On 1 Oct., 1,400 members of their families were killed. A *Judenrat* was established and a ghetto was set up on 5 Oct. On 25 Aug. 1942, all were executed beside open pits near a neighboring village. Inmates of the local labor camp organized a mass escape but only a few survived.

KOSTYUKOVICHI Mogilev dist., Belorussia. Jews settled in the 18th cent. with an organized community in existence by 1759. The J. pop. was 1,057 in 1847 and 2,186 in 1897. Three prayer houses were active in the community and in 1910, J. schools were opened for boys and girls, respectively, and attended by many. In 1924–25, under the Soviets, 30 J. families were employed in agriculture. A multinational kolkhoz was founded near the town in 1928 and supported 19 J. families in 1930. A five-year J. elementary school was also in operation. The J. pop. fell to 1,608 in 1926 and to 1,134 in 1939. The Germans occupied K. on 14 Aug. 1941. Some Jews managed to escape to the east. In Sept. 1942, the Nazis murdered 382 Jews near the local railway station. Another 161 Jews from the area were executed near the town's rope factory in March 1943.

KOSZEG Vas dist., Hungary. Jews were present in the Middle Ages under a privilege granting religious liberty, subsequently extended as a reward for fighting off the Turks in 1532. The community began to grow in the 19th cent., reaching a peak pop. 266 (3% of the total) in 1910 as Jews opened factories and became wealthy as merchants. Zionist activity commenced in the 1920s. In 1941, 109 Jews remained. On 4 July 1944, they were deported to Auschwitz after being detained in a ghetto. A labor camp for over 5,000 Jews was established in K. in Nov. 1944. About 2,000 perished under the inhuman conditions.

KOSZYCE Kielce dist., Poland. Despite a residence ban officially in force until 1862, 24 J. merchants settled in 1827. By 1897, the J. pop. of 366 had established a community. The J. pop. rose to 678 (total 1,478) in 1921. In 1927, the synagogue burned down and was never rebuilt. Between the World Wars, economic conditions deteriorated, exacerbated by the anti-J. agitation of the Endecja Party. The Zionists were the leading force in community life. With the German occupation of 5 Sept. 1939, a *Judenrat* was appointed under a regime of forced labor and property expropriations. Towards the end of Aug. 1942, the Jews were transferred to the Slomniki transit camp. After a selection for the labor camps, the rest were deported to the Belzec death camp. The few dozen remaining in K. were brought to the Miechow ghetto on 6 Nov. 1942 and a day later executed in the Choduw forest.

KOTAJ Szabolcs dist., Hungary. Jews settled in 1800, some entering light industry. The community organized in 1820 and established a synagogue in 1867. The community was highly observant and no Zionist activities were allowed. Jews numbered 216 in 1880 and 136 in 1944. At the end of April 1944, they were detained at Nyirjespuszta and then deported to Auschwitz on 17 May.

KOTEKHBALSKI (county) Krasnodar territory, Russia. The Germans murdered about 50 Jews in the area in Sept. 1942.

KOTELNIA Zhitomir dist., Ukraine. Jews were present from the early 18th cent., numbering 157 in 1756 and 1,345 (total 3,183) in 1897. On several occasions in fall 1917, local peasants looted J. property. Consequently, and as a result of internal migration, the J. pop. dropped to 896 in 1926 and probably continued to dwindle until WWII. The Germans captured K. on 16 July 1941 and presumably murdered the Jews who had not fled or been evacuated.

KOTESOVA Slovakia, Czechoslovakia, today Republic of Slovakia. The J. pop. was 108 in 1835 and 128 in 1880, with a synagogue and cemetery in use. In 1940, 21 Jews remained.

KOTOVSK (until 1935, Birzula) Moldavia, today Ukraine. Jews settled in the early 19th cent. and numbered 95 (total 913) in 1897. In 1905, they were attacked in a pogrom. The J. pop. was 2,375 (total 16,795) in 1939. German and Rumanian forces captured the city on 6 Aug. 1941 and a sub-unit of *Einsatzgruppe D* killed 115 Jews. J. refugees from Bessarabia and Bukovina arrived in Oct. 1941. In summer 1942, the Rumanian authorities set up workshops for 100 of the artisans among them. A ghetto was also established and in May 1943, K. became the main center of Balta Labor Brigade 120, where 1,200 Jews from the Regat and Transylvania were put to work constructing military loading ramps along the Odessa railroad line.

KOTOVSKOYE (Yid. Kotovsk) Odessa dist., Ukraine. K. was founded in the 1920s as a J. colony and included about 100 farm units and 485 inhabitants in 1929. It operated a J. school and was attached to the Komzetovka J. council (soviet) from 1929. The few Jews who had neither fled nor been evacuated presumably perished under the German occupation instituted in Aug. 1941.

KOTUN Lublin dist., Poland. The J. pop. was 138 in 1921 (total 712). During WWII, some Jews made their way to Soviet-held territory, while others fled to Siedlce, where they shared the fate of local Jews.

KOVCHITSY Polesie dist., Belorussia. K. was founded in 1847 as a J. farming colony and had a pop. of 528 (97% of the total) in 1897. Most had second jobs (as carters, lumberjacks, building workers), with farming becoming a sideline. On 15 July 1921, the Balakhovich brigade with the help of the local pop. staged a pogrom in which it murdered 84 Jews and robbed many others. In the Soviet period a J. elementary school of four grades was in operation with an enrollment of 90 children in 1924. In 1930, a J. kolkhoz for 49 families was set up near the town. Eighty J. families were living in K. before WWII. The Germans arrived in early July 1941. In winter 1942 they executed the remaining 318 Jews outside the settlement.

KOWAL Warsaw dist., Poland. Jews probably settled in the first half of the 16th cent. The J. pop. rose to 1,402 (total 3,993) in 1897. After WWI, J. tradesmen did their business on market days and by peddling their wares in the surrounding villages. The Zionists were influential among the young and Agudat Israel derived its strength from the Gur Hasidim. The Germans captured the town on 15 Sept. 1939. In Dec. 1940 Jews living near the marketplace were expelled from K., ultimately arriving in Warsaw. On 23 June 1941, 350 J. men were transferred to a labor camp in the Poznan dist., most dying there from starvation and disease. The remnant were sent to Auschwitz. In Oct., 400 women and children were deported to the Lodz ghetto and from there to the Chelmno death camp.

KOWALE PANSKIE Lodz dist., Poland. Few Jews lived in this agricultural area before WWII. On 20 Oct. 1941, 4,000 Jews from the Turk dist. were ghettoized in 16 villages surrounding K. On 8 Nov. 1941, 1,000 Jews were sent to Dobra and on 13–14 Nov. they were deported to Chelmno, the remainder following on 20 July 1942.

KOWEL Volhynia dist., Poland, today Ukraine. J. settlement commenced after K. was accorded urban status in 1518. The Jews received various privileges but lived in constant friction with the local pop. over taxation and other obligations. The community suffered severely in the Chmielnicki massacres of 1648–49. The wealthy succeed in fleeing but the poor were drowned in the river. The community recovered quickly and soon had other settlements under its aegis. K. came under Russian rule in 1795 and developed rapidly as an important railway junction. The community was able to recover from a fire in 1857 that destroyed many homes and most of the synagogues. The construction of Russian army barracks in the city further boosted the economy. J. industrialists operated flour mills, distilleries, breweries, and oil- and hide-processing plants. In 1897 the J. pop. reached 8,521 (total 17,697). The community supported a J. hospital and a pharmacy dispensing free medicine. Among the Hasidim, the Trisk, Neskhizh, and Ruzhin sects were represented. The Hovevei Zion became active in the 1890s and in 1905–06 the Bund organized strikes and demonstrations among workers. The occupation of K. by Austro-German forces in 1915 brought much hardship to the Jews, who suffered from severe food shortages and epidemics and were subjected to forced labor. Under Polish rule after WWI, the J. majority of 12,758 (total 1921 pop. 20,818) was underrepresented on the municipal council and discriminated against in the allocation of public funds. Among J. educational institutions were two Hebrew schools, a Hebrew high school for 250 students, and a J. high school teaching in Polish. The Tarbut organization operated the biggest library in the city (5,000 volumes in Polish and Hebrew) and two Yiddish weeklies were published. Among the J. welfare institutions was an orphanage and old age home. The export trade included cattle, flour, and cherries. Among the craftsmen, most shoemakers, tailors, and carpenters were Jews, as well as 80% of those engaged in petty trade. J. banks supported the community's economic activity. Among the Zionists, the Revisionists had considerable support. In the 1930s, Betar numbered 400 members while Hashomer Hatzair reached 700. The Soviet annexation

(1939–41) put an end to J. public and commercial life. On 28 June 1941, the Germans captured the city and immediately executed 60–80 Jews belonging to the intelligentsia. Executions continued over the next month, claiming around 1,000 J. victims. Under a Ukrainian municipal administration, Jews then had their water and electricity supplies cut off. At the end of July, Torah scrolls were publicly burned, valuables were impounded, and a large fine was extorted from the community. A *Judenrat* was established. Jews were put to forced labor on a ration of 4 ounces of bread per day. On 21 May 1942, the Jews were packed into two ghettoes, for workers and their families (8,000 individuals) and for the "nonproductive" (6,000). The latter were brought by rail on 2 June to quarries near the village of Bichawa, where they were executed. The other ghetto was liquidated on 19 Aug. 1942, with the majority also brought to Bichawa for execution. Most of the 1,000 or so who were in hiding were caught and executed at the J. cemetery.

KOZANGRODEK Polesie dist., Poland, today Belarus. The J. settlement dates from the 17th cent., numbering 1,597 in 1897 and 783 in 1921 (total 2,706). The Germans executed all the Jews outside the town on 18 Aug. 1942.

KOZELETS Chernigov dist., Ukraine. J. settlement probably commenced in the late 18th cent. In 1897, the J. pop. was 1,634 (total 5,141). In a pogrom on 22 Oct. 1905, J. stores were looted. The J. pop. was 394 in 1939. The Germans captured the town on 11 Sept. 1941 and 125 Jews were murdered on 22 Oct.

KOZELSK Smolensk dist., Russia. Jews probably settled in the early 20th cent. Their pop. was 115 in 1926 and 56 (total 8,182) in 1939. The Germans arrived on 8 Oct. 1941, murdering the few Jews still there.

KOZIANY Vilna dist., Poland, today Belarus. In the 19th cent. the community supported itself mainly in trade and between the World Wars numbered 50 families. With the help of relief organizations, 17 J. stores were opened, but Jews were pushed out of the lumber trade by the Polish government. Most Jews had auxiliary farms and most children attended a CYSHO Yiddish school. Hehalutz was active from the 1920s. With the arrival of the Germans in July 1941, a regime of persecution and forced labor was instituted. In July 1942 the Jews were transferred to the Glembokie ghetto. Many fled to the forest, setting up a family camp under the aegis of the Spartacus partisan group, which withstood German manhunts in 1942 and 1943 with the result that a relatively large number of K.'s Jews survived the war. Those in Glembokie were murdered in the massacre of 20 Aug. 1943.

KOZIEGLOWY Kielce dist., Poland. Jews settled after 1862 and numbered 343 (total 2,476) in 1921. The community ran two *battei midrash*, a *talmud torah*, and a yeshiva. In 1940, under the German occupation, the Jews numbered 229. In May 1942 they were expelled to Zawiercie and from there deported to Auschwitz in Aug. 1942.

KOZIENICE (Yid. Kozienitz) Kielce dist., Poland. Jews settled in the early 17th cent. under a royal privilege. In the late 18th cent., K. became an important hasidic center when R. Yisrael Hofstein (died 1814), known as "the *Maggid* of Kozienitz," established a dynasty there. The J. pop. was 1,185 in 1827 and 3,764 (total 6,391) in 1897. After WWI, Jews owned 165 sew-

Jews from Ozierany on sleigh ride near the house of Yisrael Leib Grosser, Kozienice, Poland, 1936

ing shops, 24 bakeries, and 224 workshops and small factories, employing 497 Jews. In 1932, 108 of the city's 132 stores and market stalls were in J. hands. The needleworkers' union was controlled by Po'alei Zion while the Bund dominated the J. shoemakers' union. The first Zionist group was founded in 1917 and Agudat Israel was also active, opening a Beth Jacob school for girls. Between the World Wars, K. remained an im-

portant hasidic center. Antisemitic incidents multiplied in the late 1930s. The city was captured by the Germans on 9 Sept. 1939. A *Judenrat* was soon established and a regime of forced labor instituted. In Oct., the Germans burned down the synagogue and shot several trying to save Torah scrolls. The J. pop. was 4,208 in Jan. 1940. In fall 1940, a ghetto was sealed off. The Joint Distribution Committee in Warsaw helped set up a soup kitchen, daily feeding 1,000 Jews. A school was opened for 70 children. In the winter of 1941–42, many died in a typhoid epidemic. In Aug. 1942, refugees doubled the ghetto pop. and on 2 Sept. 1942, 8,000 Jews were deported to the Treblinka death camp.

KOZIN Volhynia dist., Poland, today Ukraine. The J. settlement dates from the mid-16th cent. It was destroyed in the Chmielnicki massacres of 1648–49 but grew to a pop. of 972 in 1897 (half the total) before dropping to 525 in 1921. The Germans took the town on 25 June 1941, murdering a number of Jews and burning down the synagogue. Another 372 (half the J. pop) was taken from the ghetto and executed on 30 May 1942; the rest on 6 Oct.

KOZLOVICHI VTORYE Polesie dist., Belorussia. K. was founded in 1844 as a J. colony and had a pop. of 301. Most earned their living as lumberjacks and from fattening beef calves. The settlement had many prosperous farms whose owners worked exclusively in agriculture. In the mid-1920s, under the Soviets, about 30 families farmed and many Jews worked as artisans. The Germans occupied K. in early July 1941, murdering the Jews who had not fled or been evacuated.

KOZLOW Tarnopol dist., Poland, today Ukraine. The J. community began to develop in the late 18th cent. and prospered as K. served as a center for 20 surrounding settlements and hosted seven annual trade fairs. In 1880, the J. pop. reached 1,247 (total 4,072). WWI brought destruction and economic decline, the J. pop. falling to 715 in 1921 as young people emigrated, mainly to Argentina and the U.S. The end came in Sept. 1942 when the remaining Jews were expelled by the Germans to Tarnopol for deportation to the Belzec death camp.

KOZLOWSZCZYZNA Nowogrodek dist., Poland,

today Belarus. Jews settled around the turn of the 19th cent., many as farmers, and numbered 328 (total 467) in 1921. The Germans arrived in late June 1941. On 24 Nov. 1941 about 300 Jews were brought to freshly dug pits outside the town and executed.

KOZMIN Poznan dist., Poland. The J. settlement dates from the 15th cent. when most of the Jews were engaged in the grain trade. They suffered greatly during the Swedish invasion of 1655 and in the epidemics that followed it, with many survivors leaving the city. The J. pop. grew after Prussian annexation in 1793, reaching a peak of 722 (total 3,429) in 1840. In 1836, 120 of the community's 180 young children studied in a J. elementary school and in 1864, all were enrolled there. In the same period, welfare and charity organizations were set up. Emigration accelerated in the late 19th cent, mostly to Berlin and Breslau. The J. pop. in 1932 was 135. Only a few Jews remained when the Germans captured the city in Sept. 1939. They were soon deported to General Gouvernement ghettoes and camps.

KOZMINEK Lodz dist., Poland. Jews were living here in the late 18th cent. The J. pop. in 1897 was 473 (27.5% of the total). Of the 1,800 inhabitants of the ghetto set up by the Germans in 1940, 600 were deported to Chelmno on 29 Nov. 1941 and 900 in Jan.–March 1942. On 18 May 1942, 100 were sent to forced labor in Poznan and the remainder to the Lodz ghetto in Aug. 1942.

KOZOWA Tarnopol dist., Poland, today Ukraine. Jews arrived in the late 17th cent. and by 1880 numbered 1,510 in a total pop. of 4,070. A great fire in 1906 left 300 J. families homeless. Between the World Wars there was intense communal and Zionist activity. The German occupation on 3 July 1941 was followed by the massacre of 300 Jews two days later. A refugee-swelled ghetto was set up in 1942. On 21 Sept., 800–1,000 Jews were rounded up and sent to Brzezany for deportation to the Belzec death camp. Over 1,000 were dragged from their homes and murdered just before Passover in April 1943. The rest were executed at the J. cemetery on 12 June.

End of school year in Kozowa, Poland, June 1939

KRAISK Minsk dist., Belorussia. Jews probably settled at the turn of the 18th cent., numbering 152 in 1847 and 549 (total 629) in 1897. In 1923, under the Soviets, a J. school (probably four grades) was opened. In the mid-1920s, 20 J. families were engaged in agriculture, increasing to 30 in 1930, when all were employed at a multinational kolkhoz. The Jews who remained in the town after the German occupation of 25 or 26 June 1941 were murdered.

KRAJNO Kielce dist., Poland. The J. pop. was 108 in 1921 (total 1,893). The five remaining J. families were deported by the Germans to the Treblinka death camp via Bodzentyn in fall 1942.

KRAKES (Yid. Krok) Keidani dist., Lithuania. Jews first settled in the mid-17th cent. The community maintained three synagogues. The J. pop. in 1897 was 1,090 (59% of the total). The pre-WWI period, saw an increase of Haskala adherents and clashes with the community establishment over Zionism. Many began immigrating at this time, mainly to South Africa. Between the World Wars, a Hebrew school was established. The J. pop. in 1941 was 470. After the German invasion in June 1941, Lithuanian nationalists shot J. Communists and communal leaders. On 2 Sept. 1941, the remaining Jews were taken to Pestinukai, outside K., and murdered.

KRAKOW see CRACOW.

KRAKOWIEC Lwow dist., Poland, today Ukraine. The 17th cent. community grew to 1,003 in 1880 (total pop. 1,891) but large-scale emigration reduced it by two-thirds over the next 50 years. The community was liquidated by the Germans in Nov. 1942.

KRALOVO (Hung. Kiralyhaza) Carpatho-Russia, Czechoslovakia, today Ukraine. Jews probably began to settle in the 1840s and numbered 202 in 1880, 513 (total 3,450) in 1921, and 713 in 1941. The community's rabbi, Yosef Levi, ran a yeshiva for 50 students and a new synagogue was erected in 1929. The Zionist and religious organizations were active among the young. A few families farmed and others belonged to the professional class. The Hungarians occupied the town in March 1939, drafting dozens of Jews into forced labor battalions and dispatching them to the eastern front, where most died. In Aug.

1941, they expelled a number of Jews without Hungarian citizenship to the German-occupied Ukraine, where they were murdered. The rest (678 in March 1944) were deported to Auschwitz in early June 1944.

KRALOVSKY CHLUMEC (Hung. Kiralyhelmec) Slovakia, Czechoslovakia, today Republic of Slovakia. Jews are first mentioned in 1746. In the late 18th cent., Jews arrived from Galicia and Carpatho-Russia. Under R. Mordekhai Menahem Wald (1840–75) a synagogue and yeshiva were opened. Jews traded in farm produce and some owned farms as well. Their pop. grew to 311 in 1880 and 691 (total 2,795) in 1919. The Zionists became active after WWI with the young joining Betar and many receiving pioneer training prior to *aliya*. Agudat Israel was also influential, organizing Orthodox girls in the Beth Jacob movement. Jews served on the local council and owned 44 of the town's 50 business establishments, 19 workshops, and a flour mill. In 1941, after the annexation to Hungary, the J. pop. of 886 was subjected to persecution and forced labor. On 16 April 1944, the Jews were moved to a ghetto and in early May they were sent to Satoraljaujhely for deportation to Auschwitz. A postwar community numbered 490 in 1948, most emigrating to Israel and other places by 1949.

KRALUPY NAD VLTAVOU Bohemia, Czechoslovakia. The J. community was founded in 1870, maintaining a small synagogue in neighboring Mikovice. With the paving of a road between the two towns and with economic prosperity, most Jews in the area moved to K. and the J. pop. reached 264 in 1893. In 1930, 140 Jews remained (total 9,587). Most were deported to the Theresienstadt ghetto in 1942 together with the Jews of Prague. From there they were sent to the death camps of Poland.

KRAMATORSK Stalino dist., Ukraine. The influx of Jews commenced in the Soviet period when K. became an industrial center. In 1939, the J. pop. was 1,849 (total 94,114). The Germans captured the city on 20 Oct. 1941. A closed ghetto was set up in the Melovaya Gora area. From there hundreds were brought to the local quarries for execution. Other killing sites were Chervoni Yar near the town of Krasnogorovka and the quarry at the village of Ivanovka. In all, 6,000 women, children, and elderly people were murdered in these places, including 4,000 Jews in the *Aktion* of 25 Jan. 1942.

KRANOARMIEYSK (Pulin) Zhitomir dist., Ukraine. The J. pop. was 1,168 (total 2,736) in 1897, dropping by 50% between the World Wars. In 1929, 124 Jews were engaged in trade (changing their occupations in the 1930s) and 92 in crafts while 54 were defined as "classless." In 1939, the J. pop. was 523. The Germans captured the town on 10 July 1941. The Jews were crowded into a ghetto (20 to a room) surrounded by barbed wire and made to wear the yellow star. In Sept. 1941, 274 were executed at the local "Ice Mountain." The remaining Jews were murdered there in Nov. 1941.

KRASILOV Kamenets-Podolski dist., Ukraine. An organized community existed from the 18th cent., reaching a pop. of 273 in 1765 and 2,563 (total 6,994) in 1897. Fifteen Jews were murdered in pogroms during the civil war (1918–21). In 1939, under the Soviets, the J. pop. dropped to 1,250. The Germans occupied the town on 8 July 1941, setting up a ghetto for 2,000 Jews. All were brought to Manevtsy in July 1942 and shot there.

KRASLAVA Latgale dist., Latvia. The community was founded in 1764 when a few dozen families arrived from Vilna and numbered 733 (half the total) when the Russians annexed the town in 1772. The J. pop. grew rapidly in the late 19th cent., reaching 4,051 in 1897. Many were employed as artisans and factory workers, including most of the 200 workers in a J.-owned bristle factory and another 300 in the home bristlemaking industry. J. bakeries were famous for their *matzot* (unleavened bread), supplying many communities. A bristlemakers union began agitating for better working conditions in the 1890s, ultimately winning an eight-hour day. Together with the Bund, the union was in the forefront of the local labor movement and the revolutionary struggle of the early 20th cent. After the Kishinev pogrom in 1903, the Bund and Po'alei Zion formed a self-defense group with 250 members. After WWI, as part of independent Latvia, the town was cut off from its agricultural hinterland in Russia and Poland and the bristle factory and most other manufacturing establishments failed to reopen. Returning refugees brought the J. pop. to a level of 1,716 in 1925 (total 4,485), receiving substantial assistance from the Joint Distribution Committee. The Bund remained the community's leading political party, gradually giving way to the Zionists, and many

of the young were active in illegal Komsomol cells. For most of the period, up to the Ulmanis revolt in 1934, Jews served as mayors of the town. The J. economy picked up somewhat in the 1930s, when Jews owned 183 of the town's 372 business establishments. With continuing emigration, including 200 to Palestine, the J. pop. dropped to 1,444 in 1935. Under Soviet rule in 1940–41, J. community institutions were closed down. Many Zionist youth left for Riga. About 200 Jews left with the Soviets in the face of the German advance in June 1941. Under the Germans, the Jews suffered from extreme Latvian brutality, which claimed dozens of J. lives. On 29, July the Jews were brought to the Daugavpils (Dvinsk) ghetto, with many murdered on the way. They were executed shortly after in the Pogulianka forest with Jews from other provincial towns. The 30 families remaining in K. were killed by Sept. After the war a community of 40 families reestablished itself; most left for Riga in the 1950s and reached Israel in the 1970s.

KRASNAYA GORA (until Oct. 1917, Popova Gora) Oriol dist., Russia. Jews settled in the mid-19th cent. and numbered 276 (total 2,729) in 1897. In the Soviet period, their number dropped to 270 in 1926 and 64 in 1939. After their arrival on 17 Aug. 1941, the Germans murdered the few Jews who had neither fled nor been evacuated.

KRASNAYA SLOBODA (until Oct. 1917, Vizhnia) Minsk dist., Belorussia. J. settlement probably began in the first half of the 19th cent. In 1897 the J. pop. was 532 (total 1,593). In 1921, under the Soviets, a four-year J. school was opened. Many Jews worked in agriculture. A J. kolkhoz was founded near the town in the mid-1920s, accommodating 35 families, and in 1924–25 a total of 245 Jews were engaged in farming (in 1930, over 40 families). In 1939, the J. pop. was 648. The Germans occupied K. in July 1941. Most of the remaining Jews were murdered shortly afterwards.

KRASNE (I) Volhynia dist., Poland, today Ukraine. The J. pop. in 1921 was 312 in the farm settlement and 92 in the village. As a suburb of Luck, it suffered the same fate in the Holocaust.

KRASNE (II) Vilna dist., Poland, today Lithuania. Jews probably settled in the first half of the 19th cent. J. wholesalers dealt in lumber, grain, and brush bristles. In 1897, the J. pop. was 573. Nearly all fled in WWI and 319 Jews were living there in 1921. Most had lost all their property and were helped by the YEKOPO relief organization and relatives abroad. In the 1920s, some Jews emigrated to South Africa and Palestine. The Zionists, active from the early 20th cent., continued to operate between the World Wars and many children attended a Tarbut school. Agudat Israel received the support of most of the Orthodox. The Germans arrived in late June 1941 and soon established a *Judenrat* and ghetto under a regime of forced labor, which included Jews from neighboring towns confined to a separate labor camp. In early March 1943, the Jews in the ghetto were brought to a barn and burned alive. The 4,000 Jews in the labor camp were murdered on 19–21 March at a nearby brickyard.

KRASNICZYN Lublin dist., Poland. Jews are first mentioned in 1618. They numbered around 480 between the World Wars. Jews operated all of K's 30 stores and a small furniture factory. Under the German occupation (from Sept. 1939) the J. pop. rose to 2,000 with the arrival of refugees from Czechoslovakia and western Poland, all crowded into a ghetto in early 1942. In June 1942, the Jews were deported to the Belzec death camp.

KRASNIK Lublin dist., Poland. J. settlement was banned until 1580 and the community that developed afterwards was destroyed in the Chmielnicki massacres of 1648–49. J. life in K. revived in the late 17th cent as Jews came to dominate the grain and cattle trade. In 1740, they were granted a charter by the town's proprietor according them unrestricted trade and residence rights. In the 19th cent., they traded in foodstuffs, textiles, and lumber and manufactured and sold alcoholic beverages. In the early 20th cent., with the construction of railway lines and army camps in the area, Jews became active as building contractors. The J. pop. grew from 1,961 in 1827 to 3,261 in 1897 and 4,200 (total 8,289) in 1921. Not until the late 1920s, with assistance from the Joint Distribution Committee, did the community recover economically from the ordeals of WWI. Both the Zionists and Agudat Israel were influential between the World Wars and the Bund operated from the early 1930s, promoting Yiddish culture. The Germans captured the city in mid-Sept. 1939, setting up a *Judenrat* in Oct. and transferring large numbers

of Jews to K. from Lodz, Cracow, and other places. A ghetto was established in Aug. 1940, accommodating about 800 refugees in addition to 4,700 local Jews. Hundreds were subsequently sent to labor camps (in Biala Podlaska, Radom, Chelm, etc.). On 11–12 April 1942, 2,000 Jews were deported to the Belzec death camp. Another 2,700 were sent there on 1 Nov. 1942. The remaining 300 were employed in local labor camps where the J. pop. rose to about 550 in late 1943. Of these, 295 were sent to the Plaszow concentration camp in June 1944. Other Jews worked in the Budzin labor camp 4 miles (6 km) away, where the Heinkel aircraft company ran a factory and workshops. The number of Jews there reached 3,000 in late 1943, including 800 from the Warsaw ghetto. Many died of disease or were executed. The rest were dispersed among other labor camps on the approach of the Red Army in summer 1944.

KRASNI LIMAN (until 1938, Liman) Stalino dist., Ukraine. The J. pop. in 1939 was 148 (total 25,201). The Germans captured K. in July 1942. Those Jews who had neither fled nor been evacuated perished during the occupation.

KRASNIYE OKNA Moldavia, Ukraine, today Republic of Moldova. J. settlement began in the early 19th cent. In 1882, the Jews were attacked in a pogrom. The J. pop. was 1,530 (total 2,430) in 1897, growing in the Soviet period to 1,972 in 1926 but then dropping to 1,258 (27% of the total) in 1939. During the 1930s, 88 J. families joined the five kokhozes in the city and another 264 J. families worked in a commune. German and Rumanian troops entered the city on 7 Aug. 1941. By Oct. 1941, 290 local Jews had been murdered. In a Sept. 1941 *Aktion*, 2,000 Jews from the area, including 800 children, were expelled to Dubossary, where they were executed.

KRASNOARMEISK (until 1934, Grishino; in 1934–38, Postishevo; until 1964, Krasnoarmeyskoye) Stalino dist., Ukraine. Jews settled in the latter half of the 19th cent. following the development of the town's metal industry. In 1897, they numbered 227. R. Yehuda Leib Levin (who became rabbi of Moscow in 1957) officiated in 1914–16. The poet and Zionist activist Hanania Reichman (Ben-Shelomo, Avi-Avshalom) was active in K. in the early 1920s. A J. school opened in 1926. In 1939, the J. pop. was 1,366 (total

29,617). The Germans captured K. on 21 Oct. 1941. About 50 Jews were murdered in 1942, the rest having fled before the occupation.

KRASNOBROD Lublin dist., Poland. Jews settled in the late 16th cent. The community grew from 424 in 1827 to 1,378 (total 1,817) in 1897. In the first half of the 19th cent., Ruzhin, Trisk, Gur, and Belz Hasidim were prominent. In the aftermath of WWI, Polish hooligans and Balakhovich's soldiers attacked the community, the latter in a rampage of rape and murder on 29 Aug. 1920. After WWI and the ensuing economic crisis, the J. pop. dropped to 1,148 in 1921 with many emigrating, to South America. In the 1930s, anti-J. agitation and boycotts further increased the hardships of the Jews. Zionist activity was extensive throughout the period. In the Sept. 1939 fighting between the Poles and Germans, 198 Jews were killed. The Germans appointed a *Judenrat* in Feb. 1940 and instituted a regime of forced labor under ghetto conditions, with the addition of refugees from Lodz and Wloclawek. In late May 1942, the Jews were deported to the Belzec death camp. Some who escaped the deportation returned to K., believing that the danger had passed. In July 1942, the Germans returned and set fire to J. homes. The dozens in hiding were flushed out and executed in the following months. In 1943, the Germans destroyed the synagogue and leveled the cemetery.

KRASNODAR Krasnodar territory, Russia. Jews probably settled in the late 19th cent. They included demobilized soldiers, professionals, well-to-do merchants, and highly skilled artisans, In 1897, the J. pop. was 562, rising to 1,746 (total 162,520) around 1926. The Germans captured the city on 12 Aug. 1942 and on 21–22 Aug. murdered about 500 Jews at a kolkhoz outside the city.

KRASNODON (until 1938, Sorokino) Voroshilovgrad dist., Ukraine. Jews probably settled in the early Soviet period and numbered 107 (total 22,287) in 1939. The Germans captured the city on 20 July 1942. In Sept., they brought about 60 Jews to Voroshilovgrad for execution. An underground called the Young Guard, which included Jews among its number, was active during the Nazi occupation.

KRASNOGOROVKA Stalino dist., Ukraine. The J. pop. in 1939 was 121 (total 13,562). The Germans cap-

tured the city on 19 March 1941. On 22 Feb. 1942 they murdered 70 Jews, including 25 children.

KRASNOGRAD (Konstantingrad) Kharkov dist., Ukraine. Jews settled in the early 19th cent. and numbered 1,099 (total 6,455) in 1897. In the early 20th cent., the community had a *talmud torah*, modernized *heder*, and private schools for boys and girls. The Jews also operated a savings and loan fund with 661 members. A pogrom occurred in spring 1918. In the Soviet period, the J. pop. dropped sharply to 237 in 1939. The Germans captured K. on 20 Sept. 1941. In June 1942, about 90 Jews were murdered at the village of Natalino.

KRASNOGVARDEYSK (until 1923 and from 1944, Gatchina; in 1923–29, Trock) Leningrad dist., Russia. Jews probably settled in the late 19th cent. Their pop. was 184 in 1926 and 780 (total 38,235) in 1939. The Germans captured the city on 13 Sept. 1941, murdering the few Jews who had neither fled nor been evacuated.

KRASNOLUKI Minsk dist., Belorussia. Jews probably settled in the late 18th cent., numbering 94 in 1811 and 519 (total 787) in 1897. In 1905, Jews were attacked in a pogrom. In the Soviet period, a J. school was in operation, with 25 children attending in 1926. The Germans occupied K. in early July 1941 and in March 1942 murdered around 300 local Jews and another 50 refugees.

KRASNOPEREKOPSK Crimea, Russia, today Ukraine. J. settlement commenced in 1930, apparently with the founding of the settlement. In 1939, the J. pop. was 116 (total 11,098). The Germans occupied K. in late Oct. 1941, murdering 14 Jews on 26 Nov. In March 1942, they murdered 21 J. families. *Sonderkommando 10b* forces executed the other Jews in the region at the village of Voyenka on 25 Feb. 1942.

KRASNOPOLE Mogilev dist., Belorussia. Jews arrived in the early 18th cent. as lessees. Their pop. was 1,458 in 1847 and 2,692 (83% of the total) in 1897. Many Jews engaged in petty trade and some operated as lumber and cloth wholesalers. Twenty-seven Jews had farms. In Oct. 1920, during the civil war, anti-government peasant gangs rioted against the Jews, looting and damaging 100 stores. In 1924–25, under the Soviets, 151 families (882 Jews) earned their livelihoods in agriculture. A J. kolkhoz founded nearby in 1928 employed 50 J. families in 1930. A J. elementary school was opened in the 1920s. In 1939, the J. pop. was 1,181. The Germans occupied K. on 15 Aug. 1941. In late Oct. they murdered about 250 Jews in a nearby forest. The rest were moved to an open ghetto and then murdered on the outskirts of the town in late Nov.

KRASNOSELKA   Zaporozhe dist., Ukraine. Jews from the Vitebsk and Mogilev regions founded K. as a J. colony in 1845. Its pop. was 623 in 1858, mostly Jews. During the May 1881 pogroms, peasants from the neighboring village of Fedorovka protected the Jews of K. In an Aug. 1920 pogrom, a number of Jews were killed and much J. property was put to the torch. The J. pop. fell to 515 in 1897 and 442 in 1926. In the mid-1920s, two J. kolkhozes were set up on the colony's land. The few Jews remaining after the German occupation of Oct. 1941 were murdered.

KRASNOSIELC   Warsaw dist., Poland. Fifty J. families were present by the 19th cent., selling cloth in the neighborhood and buying up farm produce for sale in the cities. Zionist groups began to form in the early 20th cent. In 1921 the J. pop. was 926 (total 1,942). The Germans occupied the town on 2 Sept. 1939. On 8 Sept., a few dozen Jews were pulled out of the forced labor gangs and murdered. On 28 Sept. all the rest were expelled, many reaching Soviet-held territory.

KRASNOSTAV   Kamenets-Podolski dist., Ukraine. The J. pop. was 246 in 1847 and 1,222 (total 2,194) in 1897. Thirty-one Jews were injured in the civil war (1918–21). In the Soviet period, a J. rural council (soviet) was active, with the J. pop. standing at 1,204 in 1926. The Germans occupied K. in 1941. On 7 Aug., they executed 47 Jews in a forest near the village of Senigov and on 29 Aug. over 700 were murdered in the forest near the village of Gut. On 4 March 1942, 175 Jews were brought to Slavuta for execution.

KRASNOYE (I)   Vinnitsa dist., Ukraine. Jews are first mentioned in 1648 when they fled to Bar during the Chmielnicki massacres. In 1765, the J. pop. was 466 and in 1897 it was 2,590 (total 2,844). Nearly all the town's stores were in J. hands and most of its artisans were Jews. In 1926, under the Soviets, the J. pop. was 2,002 (total 3,183). A J. council (soviet) was ac-

tive in the late 1920s and a J. elementary school was in operation. The Germans occupied the town in the second half of July 1941. After K. was annexed to Transnistria, 300 Jews from Bessarabia and Bukovina were expelled to the ghetto established there. In fall 1942, Jews from the Skazinets camp and other places were also expelled to K. Many of K.'s Jews perished in the Holocaust.

KRASNOYE (II)   Smolensk dist., Russia. Jews settled in the 19th cent. Their pop. was 298 (total 2,803) in 1926 and 100 in 1939. The Germans occupied the town on 13 July 1941, confining the Jews in a ghetto together with Jews from the neighboring town of Rudniya. Several dozen were murdered on 24 Oct. and the rest on 8 April 1942.

KRASNOYE SELO   Leningrad dist., Russia. Jews probably settled in the early 20th cent. Their pop. was 58 in 1926 and 125 (total 12,654) in 1939. The Germans occupied K. in mid-Jan. 1941 and murdered the few Jews who had neither fled nor been evacuated.

KRASNY LUCH   (until 1920, Krindachevka) Voroshilovgrad dist., Ukraine. Jews probably settled in the early 20th cent. as the city developed into a coal mining center. In 1939, their pop. was 918 (total 50,601). The Germans captured K. on 18 July 1942, building a concentration camp in the city where Communists, partisans, and Jews were held. All the Jews were murdered in Oct.

KRASNYSTAW   Lublin dist., Poland. Though J. merchants visited the town from at least the late 15th cent, a *de non tolerandis Judaeis* privilege virtually excluded J. settlement until the advent of Prussian rule in 1795 and again in Congress Poland until 1862. The J. pop. grew to 1,763 in 1899 and 2,254 (total 9,637) in 1913. Jews were expert craftsmen in the garment and metalworking industries and opened a number of factories. Under Austrian rule in WWI, public life flourished, with the Bund and the Zionists active. After WWI, Jews operated 191 workshops employing 373 Jews. Most work was seasonal, leaving many without income for many months. Discriminatory government measures added further hardship and many required assistance from the Joint Distribution Committee and relatives abroad. In 1921, the J. pop. was 1,754. The Zionists were the dominant force on the community council.

Agudat Israel ran a Beth Jacob school for 150 girls. The Germans entered K. on 14 Sept. 1939, immediately hanging seven Jews. They returned in Oct. after a short Soviet occupation with Jews leaving with the retreating Red Army. A *Judenrat* was established in early 1940 and a ghetto in Aug. 1940, its pop. rising from 1,200 to 2,000 with the arrival of refugees. On 12 April 1942, all were expelled to Izbica in the Lublin dist. (Poland) and from there most were deported to the Belzec death camp.

KRAUTHEIM Baden, Germany. The 13th cent. community was wiped out in the Rindfleisch massacres of 1298 when 19 Jews were murdered. The revived community was then destroyed in the Armleder massacres of 1336–39. The J. settlement was reestablished in the late 14th cent. and existed continuously until the Nazi era. It reached a pop. of 85 in 1875 (total 764), dropping to 28 in 1933. By 1938 all J. businesses had been liquidated. By 1940, 19 had left for the U.S. and five for other German cities. In Jan. 1941, the J. inmates of the local mental institution were put to death.

KRAZIAI (Yid. Krozh) Raseiniai dist., Lithuania. Jews first settled in the 17th cent. A large fire in 1848 and the construction of a railway that bypassed K. caused the economic situation in 1880 to deteriorate and many emigrated to South Africa, the U.S., and Australia. K. had an ancient *beit midrash*, containing two small synagogues. A beautiful domed synagogue was built in the mid-19th cent. Zionist activity began in the 1880s and some of K.'s rabbis were active Zionists. The J. pop. in 1897 was 906 (51% of the total), dropping after WWI to half of what it had been before the war. A Hebrew school was established in 1921. A blood libel in 1929, the Lithuanian boycott of J. businesses, and other antisemitic acts during the 1930s led many Jews to emigrate. The Zionist movement won widespread support, particularly among the young, some of whom joined a kibbutz training camp. The J. pop. in 1941 stood at 525. After the German invasion in June 1941, the Jews were confined to a "Jews' Camp" on the outskirts of K. From there, on 16 July 1941, most were taken in groups to the Kupris forest, herded into pits, and shot. The remaining Jews, mainly children, were shot in the Medziokalnis forest on 2 Sept. 1941.

KRECHOWICE Stanislawow dist., Poland, today Ukraine. The Jews numbered 175 in 1921 (total 2,189), many employed in the local sawmill. The community was liquidated by the Germans in the summer of 1942.

KREFELD Rhineland, Germany. First mention of a Jew receiving residence rights dates from 1617. Others followed in small numbers, earning their living as butchers and small-scale moneylenders. In the late 18th cent., 10–11 J. families were present, expanding into the horse and cattle trade and bettering their economic circumstances. Isaak Meyer Fuld, a relative of Heinrich Heine, operated the mint in K. and became the wealthiest member of the community. A synagogue was erected in 1764. Under French rule, Jews from smaller settlements settled in K. and the J. pop. grew to 196 in 1812. Three J. family banks, including Fuld's, became prominent, gaining control of local credit, while the new settlers, comprising over half the total, generally eked out a living in petty trade and peddling. In 1809, K. became capital of a district consistory embracing 20 communities and 5,484 Jews. R. Yehuda Loeb Carlburg became chief rabbi. Under Napoleon's "Infamous Decree" (1808) and later under Prussian rule, the Jews lost their control of credit facilities. However, they entered new commercial and industrial fields, becoming prominent as manufacturers and merchants of silk. The economic development of the city continued to attract Jews throughout the 19th cent., their pop. rising to 1,085 in 1871 and a peak of 2,000 (total 107,245) in 1895. A Jew was first elected to the municipal council in 1846 with others following. At the same time, antisemitic groups also became vocal. Under Prussian community reorganization law, K. was reduced to a center for three attached communities in 1854 (Anrath, Uerdingen, Fischeln). Reform tendencies were reflected in the new synagogue charter of 1876, which aroused Orthodox opposition in the community. A J. elementary school was opened in 1840, reaching an enrollment of 140 in 1865 and 200 at the turn of the cent. The community sponsored vocational education for needy children. In 1903, an additional 129 J. children attended public secondary schools, representing, in the Weimar period, twice the percentage of Jews in the overall pop. Over half the Jews at the time (about 350) were independent merchants (most owning stores) and 150 were salaried workers. J. factories and workshops produced silk ties, cigarettes, hats, and shoes.

Fifteen J. doctors and ten J. lawyers (total 47 in 1930–34) practiced in the city. Moritz Beterthal was one of the most substantial grain merchants in western Germany. Eighty East European Jews maintained an Orthodox prayer house and the J. school was now attended by 70 children with another 65 public school children receiving religious instruction in the afternoons. Antisemitic incidents, such as the desecration of the cemetery, the smashing of the synagogue windows, and the throwing of tear gas bombs at J. department stores, became rampant in the late Weimar period (1927–32).

In June 1933, about four months after the Nazi takeover, there were 1,481 Jews in K. Economic boycott, extortion, and harassment caused 585 Jews to leave the city up to 1938, 300 emigrating directly abroad. Many arrived from the provincial towns, so that the J. pop. maintained its 1933 level. On the initiative of Kurt Alexander, a leading Central Union (C.V.) activist and from 1936 chairman of the community, a branch of the J. Cultural Association (Juedischer Kulturbund) opened in K. (300 members in 1937). Needy members of the community received assistance from J. Winter Aid and from traditional welfare organizations. On *Kristallnacht* (9–10 Nov. 1938), the synagogue was burned and J. homes and stores were vandalized. About 50 J. men were sent to the Dachau concentration camp. In May 1939, 800 Jews still remained. Deportations commenced in late 1941: 50 were deported to the Lodz ghetto on 26 Oct.; 144 to the Riga ghetto on 11 Dec.; 149 directly to the death camps on 22 April and 15 June 1942; and 223 to the Theresienstadt ghetto on 25 July. The postwar J. community reached a pop. of 111 in 1964, when a community center and synagogue were opened.

KREKENAVA (Yid. Krakinove) Panevezys dist., Lithuania. Jews first settled at the end of the 17th cent. The community supported three synagogues, a yeshiva, and a *talmud torah*. The J. pop. in 1897 was 1,505 (69% of the total). In WWI, the Russian government expelled all Jews to Russia and burned the town down. A third of the Jews returned. Between the World Wars, the Zionist movement won widespread support and all the Zionist parties were represented. There were about 60 J. families in K. in 1940. After the German invasion in June 1941, young Jews and others who had attempted to flee were shot. Most of the men were murdered on the road to Panevezys towards the end of June; on 27 July, the women and children were taken to the Pajuoste airport and murdered.

KREMENCHUG Poltava dist., Ukraine. Jews are first mentioned in 1782. Their pop. was 3,475 in 1847 and 29,869 (total 63,997) in 1897. A J. hospital was founded in the first half of the 19th cent. R. Yosef Tomarkin opened a Habad yeshiva in 1844. In the late 19th cent., two *talmudei torah* were operating, one with carpentry and metalworking classes. There were also a number of private schools for boys and girls. In 1897, Jews owned ten sawmills and a number of tobacco factories. Among the city's illustrious native sons were the Zionist leader Yehiel Tschlenow (1863–1918), the painter Mane-Katz (1894–1962), the poet Avraham Shlonsky (1900–73), and the Red Army officer Alexander Pechersky (b. 1919), who led the uprising at the Sobibor death camp. In 1915, the Slobodka yeshiva of Kovno (Kaunas) in Lithuania and the Habad yeshiva of Lubavich were transferred here. They continued to operate clandestinely in the Soviet period until they were liquidated in the early 1930s. Three pogroms were staged in K.: in Oct. 1905; in early April 1918; and in Aug. 1919 by General Denikin's White Army troops. In 1925, a J. kolkhoz was founded with a pop. of 32 J. families. In the late 1920s, Jews constituted 70–80% of the workers in the tobacco (mainly women), shoe, and carpentry industries. In all, Jews comprised about 50% of factory workers, including those in railway engine shops. In the 1930s, there were two J. schools with an enrollment of 932 as well as a technical college (electro-mechanics) founded in 1896. There was also a J. public library and theater. In 1939, the J. pop. was 19,880. The Germans captured K. on 9 Sept. 1941. In the first days of the occupation, the Germans and Ukrainian police robbed the Jews. After a week they were required to wear the Star of David on their sleeves and barred from buying food in stores. On 27 Sept., they were ordered to register and move to shacks in the suburb of Novo-Ivanovka, where all their possessions were taken from them. Between 27 Sept. and 7 Nov. 1941, 8,000 were executed. The few dozen professional people left alive (such as doctors and nurses) were murdered in Jan. 1942. Hundreds of Jews in a large prisoner-of-war camp for Russian soldiers were also murdered. In 1970, the J. pop. of K. was about 1,000.

KREMNICA (Hung. Kormocbanya) Slovakia, Czechoslovakia, today Republic of Slovakia. A number of J. mintmasters were present in the 14th cent. From the 16th cent. until the mid-19th cent., J. residence was banned. In 1869, when the community founded a Neologist congregation, the J. pop. was 105, subsequently rising to 229 (total 4,978) in 1880 and maintaining a level of about 300 in 1900–30. A synagogue was erected in 1890. After WWI, 21 neighboring settlements came under the local rabbi's jurisdiction. Jews held public positions and owned 40 business establishments, four workshops, and two factories. The Zionists were active, with Hashomer Hatzair, WIZO, and the Maccabi sports club operating branches. In 1940, there were 215 Jews remaining in K., augmented by J. villagers driven out of their homes by the German minority, who also burned down the synagogue and community center in 1940. By order of the Slovakian authorities, most J. businesses were liquidated in 1941. Young Jews were deported in late March 1942 and another 140 were sent to the Sobibor death camp on 7 June over the protests of dozens of local Slovakian residents led by clergymen.

KREMS Lower Austria, Austria. Jews were present in K. from the 13th to the 15th cents. but were expelled several times. Nevertheless K. is known for the many J. scholars residing there, especially in the 15th cent. Jews settled permanently in K. at the beginning of the 19th cent. They engaged in trade. A J. cemetery was consecrated in 1853 and another in 1880. A synagogue was inaugurated in 1893. The J. pop. stood at 595 In 1880; 400 in 1925 (total 13,940); and 200 in 1934. During the 1920s, the Blau-Weiss and Zionist youth organizations were active. A Zionist home, serving youth from all over Austria, was founded. Antisemitic agitation intensified and in May 1938 there were only 116 Jews remaining in K. Most J. property had been confiscated by this time. In Sept. 1938, the interior of the synagogue was destroyed. About 80 Jews fled to Vienna and succeeded in emigrating from there. The others were deported to the east where all perished.

KRETINGA (Yid. Kretinge) Kretinga dist., Lithuania. Jews first settled in the early 17th cent. After receiving privileges from the Polish king, large-scale settlement occurred in the mid-18th cent. The community maintained three synagogues. Between 1870

and 1880 many emigrated to England. In 1860, a school teaching secular and J. subjects was established. Similarly, a modern *heder* was established in 1902. Prior to the First Zionist Congress, many contributed money for settlement in Eretz Israel. The J. pop. in 1897 was 1,202 (35% of the total). At the end of WWI, a joint J.–Lithuanian committee administered the town. Between the World Wars, Jews won five out of 15 municipal council seats. In 1928–35, a community center included a Hebrew school. In the 1930s, the economic situation and a boycott led many to emigrate. Antisemitic incidents increased in 1939 under the influence of Nazi Germany and Lithuanian nationalism. The Zionist movement won widespread support and all the Zionist parties were represented in the city. The J. pop. in 1940 was about 1,000. After the German invasion in June 1941, the Nazis shot about 200 men at the Prismantai farm outside the town on 26 June. This was followed by subsequent massacres in July and Aug. of the remaining men, women, and children.

KREUZBURG (Pol. Kluczbork) Upper Silesia, Germany, today Poland. Jews are first mentioned in 1414, but permanent settlement dates only from the mid-18th cent. The J. pop. was 24 in 1772 and 48 in 1830. The first J. prayer house was built in 1840. The community grew rapidly in the following decades, reaching a peak of 406 in about 1869. J. educational facilities were maintained and a synagogue was consecrated in 1885. In 1926, the J. pop. was 174. A new cemetery was opened in 1928 and in the 1920s the Zionists and a branch of the J. War Veterans Association were active. K. was a hotbed of antisemitism from the late 19th cent. and in the years preceding the Nazi rise to power the racist right initiated violent antisemitic activity. The antisemitic periodical *Kreuzberger Nachrichten* was published there. The J. pop. was 160 in 1933. The Nazi racial laws were not put into force until 16 July 1937 owing to the application of the League of Nations' minority rights convention to the area. Nonetheless, Jews suffered from discrimination throughout the period, including violent incidents. The J. pop. dropped to 102 in 1935 and 81 in 1937. On *Kristallnacht* (9–10 Nov. 1938), the synagogue and J. stores were set on fire. Subsequently most Jews emigrated, with just one reported remaining in Nov. 1942. There is no information on the fate of the rest of the community.

KREUZNACH, BAD see BAD KREUZNACH.

KREWO Vilna dist., Poland, today Belarus. In 1847, 438 Jews were registered in the town, leasing estate facilities and trading in grain and flax as well as peddling. In 1897 they numbered 809 (total 2,201). The town was completely destroyed in WWI. With the aid of the YEKOPO relief agency, 115 homes were rebuilt. Yiddish and Hebrew schools were set up and the Zionist youth movements became active. The Germans arrived in late June 1941 and established a ghetto at the end of the year. In Oct. 1942 the Jews were expelled to the Oszmiana ghetto, where the sick and old were murdered on 24–25 Oct. The rest were dispersed to the Vilna and Kovno ghettoes to share the fate of the Jews there.

KRICHEV Mogilev dist., Belorussia. Jews are first mentioned in 1494. A J. lessee named Eliash Isakovich was active c. 1667 and contributed much to the town's economic development. In 1744, rioting peasants pillaged and damaged J. homes and property. The J. pop. was 1,225 in 1847 and 2,566 in 1897. Under the Soviets, a J. kolkhoz was started nearby in 1928. It employed 18 families in 1930. A J. elementary school operated in the town and many Jews worked at a cement factory. The J. pop. was 1,362 in 1939. The Germans occupied K. on 17 July 1941. Some Jews succeeded in fleeing. In Oct. 1941, those who remained were confined in a ghetto under a regime of forced labor. Two months later, all 130 were murdered near the cement factory.

KRICHOVO (Hung. Kricsfalva; Yid. Kritshif) Carpatho-Russia, Czechoslovakia, today Ukraine. Jews are first mentioned in 1746. After abandoning the town, they returned in the early 19th cent., numbering 25 in 1830 and 98 (total 1,115) in 1880. The J. pop. then grew to 116 in 1921 and 134 in 1941. The Hungarians arrived in March 1939 and in summer 1941 drafted a number of young Jews into forced labor battalions. In Aug., they expelled a few J. families without Hungarian citizenship to Kamenets-Podolski, where they were murdered. The rest were deported to Auschwitz in the second half of May 1944.

KRIEGSHABER Swabia, Germany. The community was probably founded in the 14th cent. by Augsburg Jews fleeing the Black Death persecutions of 1348–49; others expelled from Augsburg arrived in 1438–40. The community grew further with the arrival of Jews expelled from the Burgau margravate in 1617. Jews numbered 402 in 1737, with such well-known Court Jews as the Maendle family active there. The community dwindled in the first half of the 19th cent. with the growth of the new Augsburg community, to which it was attached in 1916.

KRILOV Kirovograd dist., Ukraine. A few Jews were probably present in the 17th cent. Residence was officially permitted in 1792. The J. pop. was 240 (total 1,943) in 1897 and 19 in 1926. After their arrival in Aug. 1941, the Germans murdered the few remaining Jews.

KRIUKAI (Yid. Kruk) Sakiai dist., Lithuania. Jews were here at the beginning of the 19th cent. and by the end of the cent. had organized a community. As WWII approached and the economic situation worsened, many Jews emigrated. The Jews in 1940 numbered about 80. The Lithuanians murdered all following the German conquest of 1941.

KRIUKIAI Siauliai dist., Lithuania. Jews first settled in the early 19th cent. In the late 19th cent., following a large fire and a declining economic situation, many emigrated to the U.S. and South Africa. Between the World Wars, emigration continued, in some cases to Palestine. The J. pop. in 1897 was 450 (66% of the total), dropping to 184 in 1923 (40%). After the German invasion in June 1941, all the Jews were taken to Zagare and murdered on Yom Kippur in fall 1941.

KRIUKOV Poltava dist., Ukraine. Jews probably settled in the late 19th cent. and numbered 714 in 1847. They were expelled in the wake of the May Laws of the 1880s restricting J. residence and trade. They were only permitted to return in 1903. In 1926, their pop. was 1,166 (total 5,204). A. J. school with 300 students in 1927 operated in the Soviet period. The Germans occupied the town on 8 Aug. 1941 and murdered the Jews soon after concentrating them for disposition in early Nov.

KRIVE (Hung. Nagykirva) Carpatho-Russia, Czechoslovakia, today Ukraine. Jews settled in the latter half of the 18th cent., numbering 29 in 1830 and 117 in 1880. In 1930, their pop. was 365, dropping to 299 (total 1,449) in 1941. The Hungarians occupied the town in March 1939 and in 1941 drafted a few dozen J. men into forced labor battalions, sending them to the eastern front. In Aug. 1941, they expelled a few J. families without Hungarian citizenship to Kamenets-Podolski, where they were murdered. The 230 remaining Jews fled to the forests in March 1944, when it became known that they were to be deported to the east. The Hungarian gendarmerie hunted them down and after severe torture deported them to Auschwitz in the second half of May 1944.

KRIVOY ROG Dnepropetrovsk dist., Ukraine. Jews settled in the late 19th cent. A pogrom was staged in 1883. In 1897, the J. pop. was 2,672 (total 14,397). Another two pogroms occurred in 1905. In the early 20th cent., a number of private J. school for boys and girls were operating along with a *talmud torah*. In the Soviet period, the J. pop. grew rapidly to a 1939 figure of 12,745 (total 197,546). A J. school was attended by over 220 children in ten grades, though it was probably closed in the mid-1930s. Many Jews were employed in the numerous factories started up in the 1930s. The Germans captured the city on 14 Aug. 1941 and murdered 105 Jews at the end of the month. In mid-Oct. 1941, the Germans murdered 4,000–5,000 Jews at the local mines, having murdered the directors of the J. farm settlements in the area there the previous month.

KRIZEVCI (Hung. Koros; Ger. Kreuz), Croatia, Yugoslavia, today Republic of Croatia. Jews first settled in the 18th cent. and a community was established in 1844 (which included a large number of Jews from neighboring villages). By 1900 there were 365 Jews, who were very active in the economy, culture, and social life of K. The first Zionist group was founded in 1907 and Zionist activity increased after WWI. Following the war the number of Jews decreased. In 1931 they numbered 183 (total 1,035). A few days after the German invasion in 1941, the synagogue (built in 1895) was wrecked. In June–Dec. 1941, the Jews were publicly humiliated and their property confiscated. They were put to forced labor and deported to death camps by the Ustase. Only a few who escaped to Italian areas survived the Holocaust.

KRNOV Silesia, Czechoslovakia. Jews are men-

tioned in the late 14th cent and were expelled in the 16th cent., returning only in the mid-19th cent. A synagogue was consecrated in 1871 and a cemetery in 1873. Most Jews spoke German and over half belonged to the professional class as the J. pop. rose to a peak of 534 in 1900. In 1930, 318 remained (total 21,925). Most were forced to leave after the Sudetenland crisis of Sept. 1938 and many emigrated.

KROJANKE (Pol. Krajenka) Posen–West Prussia, Germany, today Poland. Jews are first mentioned in 1557. In the second half of the 17th cent., there is evidence of a synagogue and a cemetery, with the presence of a rabbi from 1682 on. When K. came under Prussian rule in 1772, the J. pop. numbered 200. In 1799, the J. pop. was 693 and in 1851 it was 648. The Jews constituted 44% of the total pop. in 1804 and 23% in 1846. On the eve of the Nazi assumption of power, about 250 Jews were living in K. By Aug. 1933, ten families had moved away. In 1936, there were only 146 Jews in K. By 1935, there was only one business still in J. hands. Zionist activities intensified under Nazi rule; the Central Union (C.V.) barely had any supporters by 1935. On *Kristallnacht* (9–10 Nov. 1938), the synagogue was destroyed and J. men were taken to the Sachsenhausen concentration camp. The remaining Jews were interned in March 1940 in the Buergergarten camp near Schneidemuehl and afterwards deported to the east where they perished.

KROLEVIETS Sumy dist., Ukraine. Jews were present in small numbers during the 18th cent. In 1897, the J. pop. was 1,815 (17.5% of the total). In 1939, 619 remained. The Germans captured K. on 3 Nov. 1941, subjecting the Jews to a regime of forced labor. On 26 Nov. 1941, 73 were brought outside the town and murdered.

KROLEWSZCZYZNE Vilna dist., Poland today Belarus. Jews arrived in the early 20th cent. and numbered 32 (total 246) in 1921 and were active in the lumber industry as well as carting and the building trades, which centered around the local railroad station. The 85 families present when the Germans occupied K. in late June 1941 were subjected to severe persecution and expelled to the Glembokie ghetto in April 1942; most were murdered in the *Aktion* of 20 Aug 1943.

KROMERIZ Moravia, Czechoslovakia. Jews lived

under the protection of the Church from 1322 to 1848 against heavy tax payments. In 1643, during the Thirty Years War (1618–48), the Swedish General Torstenson's soldiers massacred most of the town's Jews (over 70) but the community recovered quickly and was able to shelter refugees from the Chmielnicki massacres of 1648–49. In 1742, during the War of the Austrian Succession, rioting peasants killed six Jews and looted homes and stores in the J. ghetto. The Familiants Laws of 1797, which restricted the number of J. families to 106, remained in force until 1848, when the city tore down the ghetto walls. In 1880, the J. pop. was 783. A new synagogue was consecrated in 1910. Most Jews supported the German Liberal Party as traditional values eroded after the emancipation but the emergence of the Zionists after WWI served as a counterweight. The J. pop. was 382 (total 18,546) in 1930. In summer 1939, the Nazis vandalized the J. cemetery and antisemitic laws were enacted and implemented. On 26 June 1942, the Jews were deported to the Theresienstadt ghetto; 268 perished in the Holocaust.

KROMOLOW   Kielce dist., Poland. Jews settled in the 16th cent. The community suffered periodically from natural disasters. R. Natan Nahum Rabinowicz of Radomsk established a hasidic court in K. in the early 20th cent. In WWI, the J. pop. dropped radically, from 517 in 1857 to 275 (total 2,476) in 1921, and between the World Wars economic conditions remained difficult. There were 200 Jews present when the Germans took the town in Sept. 1939. Jews were persecuted; the synagogue and *beit midrash* were burned; and in March 1941 the community was expelled to Zawiercie for deportation to Auschwitz, probably in early 1942.

KROMPACHY   (Hung. Korompa) Slovakia, Czechoslovakia, today Republic of Slovakia. Jews first settled in the 1850s, opening a synagogue and elementary school in the early 20th cent. as their pop. grew from 67 in 1869 to 321 (total 4,723) in 1900 and then to a peak of about 400 on the eve of WWI. Shemuel David Unger of Piestany served as rabbi in 1910–18, founding a yeshiva and later becoming one of the leaders of Orthodox Jewry in Slovakia. In 1940, 302 Jews remained, subjected to persecution and attack in the Slovakian state while being forced out of their businesses. In March–April 1942, the young were deported to Majdanek and Auschwitz

and dozens of others were sent to the death camps of the east in the following months.

KRONACH   Upper Franconia, Germany. Ten Jews were murdered during the Rindfleisch massacres of 1298. Jews are again mentioned in 1636 and 1644 under letters of protection. In 1760 Jews were allotted a street outside the city walls and in 1824 the *Matrikel* law limited J. residence to three families. The community revived with the arrival of Jews from Friesen in the 1870s, the J. pop. increasing to 101 in 1890 (total 4,140). Thereafter it declined to 35 in 1933. The synagogue was sold in 1938 and by 1939, seven Jews emigrated and eight left for other German cities; eight were expelled on 25 April 1942 to Izbica in the Lublin dist. (Poland) via Bamberg.

KROSCIENKO (I)   Lwow dist., Poland, today Ukraine. The Jews numbered 241 in 1921 (total 1,486), engaging in farming, the lumber trade, and tourism centering on the hasidic Belazow rabbi's summer court. The community was liquidated by the Germans in July 1942.

KROSCIENKO (II)   Cracow dist., Poland. Jews were present in the second half of the 18th cent. and numbered 239 (total 1,955) in 1900 in a traditional-hasidic milieu. Jews were beaten and pillaged in the peasant riots of Nov. 1918. The Germans took the town in Sept. 1939 and instituted a regime of forced labor and extortion, with the Gestapo murdering 22 Jews in March and April 1942. On 30 Aug. the Jews were expelled to Nowy Targ, with many murdered in the town and along the way. From there, most were sent to the Belzec death camp; some to labor camps.

KROSNIEWICE   Lodz dist., Poland. Jews were living here in 1568. The J. pop. in 1897 was 5,054 (43% of the total). After WWI the economic situation of the J. community declined. Jews were persecuted by Polish soldiers in 1920 and many died during the typhus epidemic at that time. By 1925 most of the Zionist groups were functioning, and the Bund was active. The Germans entered K. on 15 Sept. 1939, persecuted the Jews, desecrated the synagogue, and plundered their property. A *Judenrat* was set up and the 1,500–1,600 Jews, including refugees, were ghettoized in 1940. The first of four transports of Jews to forced labor camps took place on Rosh Hashanah (22 Sept. 1941).

In March 1942 (Purim) the 900 remaining Jews were deported to Chelmno.

KROSNO Lwow dist., Poland. The organized J. community dates from the early 20th cent., growing with the development of the local oil industry from 327 in 1880 to 1,725 (total 6,287) in 1921. In WWI, rampaging Russian troops and severe epidemics caused many to flee, subsequently returning to find their homes and possessions gone. Assistance from the Joint Distribution Committee and former residents in the U.S. along with the continued development of the town led to gradual recovery. The Depression years and the competition of the Polish cooperatives again eroded economic conditions, with antisemitism intensifying in the 1930s. The Germans entered on 9 Sept. 1939 and around the end of 1939 set up a *Judenrat* responsible for supplying forced labor. In 1941 Jews were sent to the Frysztak labor camp to work on the preparation of Hitler's local headquarter complex. By the end of 1941, refugees brought the local J. pop. up to 2,072. In Aug. 1942, the sick and old were murdered after a selection and over 1,000 were deported to the Belzec death camp. Between 300 and 600 of the able-bodied remained in a closed ghetto for work at the nearby airfield and the Dukla quarries. On 4 Dec. 1942, all but 25 were sent to Rzeszow, to share the fate of its Jews.

KROTOSZYN Poznan dist., Poland. Jews were present in the 14th cent. The community was decimated in the Swedish wars. Massacres by the troops of the Polish irregular leader Stefan Czarniecki and other depredations reduced its pop. from 400 to 50 families. The community recovered in the 18th cent., reaching a pop. of 1,749 in 1764. In the second half of the 18th cent., J. merchants expanded commercial ties with Breslau, Leipzig, and Frankfurt. Economic prosperity continued after the annexation to Prussia in 1793. A *matza* (unleavened bread) factory marketed throughout the Poznan district; J. woodworking shops proliferated; and two Hebrew printing presses were in operation, one of which printed the standard version of the Jerusalem Talmud. The town was a center of J. scholarship: the bibliographer Shabbetai Bass was active there and in the 19th cent. the scholars David Joel and Edward Baneth were rabbis in K. Jews also became active in public life. Friction between Orthodox and Liberal circles led to the erection of a second synagogue

which was probably the first in the Poznan dist. to introduce an organ and choir. A J. elementary school enrolled 192 children in 1896. The Zionists became active in 1907. Emigration reduced the J. pop. from 2,213 in 1837 to 1,149 in 1871 and 527 (total 12,675) in 1907. After WWI, 119 remained and 50 on the eve of WWII. The 17 still there in Sept. 1939 were deported by the Germans to the Lodz ghetto on 21 Nov.

KRUCHA Mogilev dist., Belorussia. Jews numbered 186 in 1880 and 713 in 1897. In 1910, a modern *heder* teaching secular subjects was set up. In 1923, under the Soviets, the J. pop. was 379, dropping to 297 in 1926. In 1924–25, 30 J. families earned their livelihoods in agriculture and in 1930 a multinational kolkhoz was founded where 11 J. families were employed. The Germans arrived in early July 1941. In Oct. 1941, with the assistance of local police, they murdered 156 Jews.

KRUGLOYE Mogilev dist., Belorussia. The J. pop. was 381 in 1847 and 553 (total 1,442) in 1897, dropping to 428 in 1926 under the Soviets. In 1925, 125 Jews signed up to receive allocations of farmland. Jews also worked in cooperatives as carters and shoemakers and in a linen-processing plant opened in 1935. The town's J. elementary school (four grades) was closed in 1935. In 1939 the J. pop. was 238. The Germans captured K. on 8 July 1941. Among the Jews were refugees from Poland. On 15 Sept., 100 Jews were shot in a nearby forest and in Oct., 28 J. women were murdered. The remaining 200 Jews in the area were executed in May 1942.

KRUKIENICE Lwow dist., Poland, today Ukraine. The Jews numbered 231 in 1921 (total 1,619). They were expelled by the Germans to Mosciska in the summer or fall of 1942 and shared the fate of the local Jews.

KRUMBACH-HUERBEN (in J. sources, Hiche, Hirbe) Swabia, Germany. Jews are first mentioned in 1504, with newcomers arriving from Donauwoerth in 1518 and Neuburg in 1540 after the expulsions there. A cemetery was consecrated in 1608 and a synagogue in 1675. The Huerben community (consolidated with K. in 1902) grew rapidly in the 18th cent. into one of the largest in Bavaria, with a J. pop. of 576 in 1839. A J. public school was opened in 1790. The Semitic scholar Samuel Landauer was born in K. in 1846. In 1933, 65 Jews remained, most merchants. The synagogue was vandalized on *Kristallnacht* (9–10 Nov. 1938), and Jews were forced to liquidate their businesses shortly thereafter. Forty-five left in 1933–41, 17 emigrating to the U.S. and 18 to other German cities. Fifteen were deported to Piaski (Poland) via Munich on 3 April 1942.

KRUONIS (Yid. Kron) Troki dist., Lithuania. Jews first settled in the 16th cent. A large Karaite community was present until the mid-18th cent. An 1882 order expelling K.'s Jews was canceled. The community failed to develop and at the end of the 19th cent. Jews began emigrating to England and the U.S. During WWI, K. was occupied by the Germans and the Jews were sent to forced labor in 1915–18. Emigration continued between the World Wars. Most J. youth were active in Zionist organizations. The J. pop. in 1940 was 120 (14% of the total). Under the German occupation, the Jews were transferred to Darsuniskis and forced to live in a virtual ghetto with other Jews from the area. On 15 Aug., Lithuanians murdered the men in the Komenduliai forest. Only two sisters survived the war.

KRUPIEC Volhynia dist., Poland, today Ukraine. K. was abandoned by its 100 J. families before WWI owing to restrictions applying to it as a Russian border town near Austrian Galicia.

KRUPINA (Hung. Korpona), Slovakia, Czechoslovakia, today Republic of Slovakia. Jews probably first settled in the 1840s. The community maintained a synagogue, cemetery, and school. In 1869, a Status Quo congregation was formed and at the turn of the cent. the community's pop. was about 100 (total 4,000). Zionist activity commenced in 1920 with most of the young joining Maccabi Hatzair. Jews owned 11 business establishments and three workshops. In 1940, the J. pop. reached a peak of 163. In the Slovakian state, J. children were expelled from the public schools and the authorities liquidated or "Aryanized" J. businesses. Most Jews were deported to the death camps in spring 1942. A concentration camp was set up in the town in March 1944 where Jews fleeing German-occupied Hungary were confined. During the Slovakian national uprising of fall 1944, several dozen Jews gathered here and succeeded in escaping before the Germans arrived.

KRUPKI Minsk dist., Belorussia. Individual Jews are mentioned in 1678. An organized community was in existence in the mid-18th cent., its pop. reaching 1,080 (total 1,523) in 1897. In 1930, about 15 J. families worked in kolkhozes and in 1931 a J. elementary school was still open. In 1939 the J. pop. was 870. The Germans captured the town in early July 1941, concentrating the Jews in a ghetto. On 18 Sept. (5 Oct. according to another source) the Germans murdered 1,000–1,800 Jews from K. and its environs. In 1943 they opened the graves and burned the bodies.

KRUSTPILS (Yid. Kreizburg) Latgale dist., Latvia. The J. community was one of the first in Latgale, apparently formed by Jews from nearby Courland in the late 17th cent. At the end of the 19th cent., when the J. pop. reached 3,164 (total 4,142), it was living in relative material and spiritual poverty, stricken by an epidemic that killed 300 of the town's younger children in 1888 and by a fire in 1900 that destroyed mainly J. homes and stores. The town was virtually destroyed in WWI. With the J. pop. down to 1,331 in 1925 the Jews lost their majority on the municipal council but retained the position of mayor until 1930. Their number declined further (1,043 in 1935) through emigration to Riga. Jews owned 86 of the town's 117 stores in 1935 and in 1928, 206 children attended the J. public school. The Zionists were active throughout the period. J. institutions were closed down under the Soviets in 1940–41 while J. businesses were nationalized. A few hundred Jews escaped to the Soviet Union as the Germans approached in June 1941. The Jews of K. were murdered by the Germans in summer and fall 1941, most in the Koksene forest.

KRYCZYLSK Volhynia dist., Poland, today Ukraine. The J. pop. in 1921 was 100. The Jews were brought to the Stepan ghetto for liquidation during the Holocaust.

KRYLOW Lublin dist., Poland. Jews are first mentioned in 1550 but the community only began to grow in the late 19th cent., reaching a pop. of 1,512 (total 3,314) in 1897. Many left in WWI, leaving 750 Jews in 1921. In Sept. 1939, some managed to flee east to Soviet-controlled territory. The Germans confined those remaining behind to a ghetto and in summer 1942 deported them to the Belzec death camp.

KRYMNO Volhynia dist., Poland, today Ukraine. The 70 or so J. families were murdered by Ukrainian police in fall 1942.

KRYNICA ZDROJ (Yid. Krenitz) Cracow dist., Poland. Jews first settled in the early 19th cent. The development of the town as a health resort in the 1860s, attracting a well-to-do J. clientele, provided comfortable livings for around a quarter of the J. pop. in the hotel and restaurant trades and stimulated its growth from 280 in 1880 to 1,023 (total 2,341) in 1921. The WWI years passed quietly and tourist-related economic prosperity continued unabated, with cordial relations with the non-J. pop. prevailing until the late 1930s. The Zionists organized early in the 20th cent. and were also active among the J. vacationers. The arrival of the Germans in Sept. 1939 initiated a regime of forced labor, extortion, and restricted movement. The

Jews in Krynica Zdroj, Poland

Jews were expelled in Nov. 1940, mainly to Nowy Soncz and Grybow, where they shared the fate of the local Jews.

KRYNKI Bialystok dist., Poland. Jews are first mentioned in 1639. In 1662 they were granted a wide-ranging charter of rights by King John Casimir which remained in force despite local opposition and was reaffirmed by King Augustus III in 1745. K. was under the jurisdiction of Grodno until the late 18th cent. The Lithuanian Council convened there in 1687. In the 1860s a local textile industry began to develop but declined in the 1890s in the face of competition from Bialystok. Three great fires in 1879, 1882, and 1887 further shook the community. Subsequently the tanning industry grew, with 20 tanneries in 1896 employing hundreds of Jews. The J. pop. was 2,823 in 1878 and 3,495 (total 5,206) in 1921. The *maggid* R. Tzevi Hirsch Orlansky settled in K. in 1886 and inspired many of the young to join Hovevei Zion. During WWI the economy collapsed under the German occupation with its forced labor and heavy taxes but public life continued and most children were enrolled in a Hebrew school. With the loss of the Russian market after WWI and the shortage of raw materials, the leather industry, once employing over half the town, failed to recover until the late 1930s, causing the Jews much economic distress. The Zionists expanded their activities, founding a Tarbut school, and Hehalutz Hatzair was the largest youth movement. In 1939 the J. pop. was about 4,000. The Soviets occupied K. in 1939–41, instituting their regime. The Germans captured the city on 28 June 1941 after 50 Jews were killed in bombardments. Others were murdered as the Germans subjected the Jews to forced labor and extortionate "contributions." In Dec. 1941, the Jews were confined to a ghetto, where many died from a typhoid epidemic; rape and murder were widespread. In spring 1942, 1,200 Jews arrived from Brzostowica Wielka, causing another typhoid epidemic in the overcrowded conditions. On 2 Nov. 1942, all but the J. leather workers and a few others were transferred to the notorious Kelbasin transit camp and from there deported to the Treblinka death camp. The workers were sent to Sokolka on 17 Jan. 1943 and subsequently deported to Auschwitz. A group of 20–30 youngsters escaping to the forest formed a partisan unit and engaged in effective action until wiped out by the Germans.

KRYSTYNOPOL   (Yid. Krasnipali) Lwow dist., Poland, today Ukraine. Jews settled soon after the town was founded in 1692, establishing themselves as a preponderant majority of the pop. (78% in 1880 when they numbered 2,747) as well as controlling trade, particularly in grain. Belz Hasidism dominated the community, suppressing all efforts at modernization until after WWI, when the Zionists came to the fore. In WWI, Cossack violence, mass expulsions, and the continuing economic decline marked by the cessation of the grain trade caused the J. pop. to drop to 2,086. Most Jews crossed the Bug River with Soviet forces in 1939 to remain in Soviet-controlled Sokal and Witkow Nowy under the Soviet regime. In summer 1940 many were exiled to distant parts of the USSR.

KRYVOYE OZERO   Odessa dist., Ukraine. Nine Jews were present in 1765. A stone synagogue was built in 1853. In the 1880s, most of the town's 90 stores belonged to Jews and two J. colonies were located nearby. In 1897, the J. pop. was 5,478 (total 7,836). In 1919, General Denikin's White Army troops staged two pogroms, killing 280 Jews in the first and hundreds more in the second (late Dec. 1919). In early 1920, they struck again, this time with far fewer casualties. During the Soviet period, a J. elementary school was in operation, with 300 J. children attending in 1938. The J. Kotovsky kolkhoz was still active in the late 1930s, with 60 J. families (180 people) and a J. elementary school (four grades) and nursery. In the late 1930s, many Jews worked in cooperatives and in a butter factory. The local library housed a large Yiddish collection. In 1939, the J. pop. of K. was 1,447. The Germans captured the town on 2 Sept. 1941. On 5 Sept., 52 Jews were murdered. The Jews were confined to a ghetto around Dec. 1941. After K. was annexed to Transnistria in the fall, the Rumanians expelled hundreds of Jews from Bukovina to K. and the neighboring villages. A total of 184 Jews were murdered in Berezki (on 11 Oct.); 59 in Trudovy; and 37 in Velikaya Mechetnya. On 1 Jan. 1942, 184 local Jews were executed at the J. cemetery and the next day another 44 were shot in Chausove. In late 1943, 624 Jews still remained in K.

KRYZHOPOL   Vinnitsa dist., Ukraine. Three Jews were present in 1765, their number growing to 668 (total 1,126) in 1897. In the Soviet period, Jews worked mainly in the cooperatives as tailors and shoe-makers and at a J. kolkhoz established in 1928. A J. elementary school was attended by 185 children (half from K.) in 1931. In 1939, the J. pop. was 1,400. The Germans arrived on 22 July 1941, shooting 14 Jews on the same day. After a month, the town was annexed to Transnistria and numerous Jews from Bukovina and Bessarabia were expelled to the ghetto established there (74 remaining in 1943). About 1,700 Jews from the region were murdered.

KRZEMIENIEC   (Kremenets) Volhynia dist., Poland, today Ukraine. The J. settlement began to develop after 1503. Jews were prominent in the salt trade and the importation of bulls from Walachia. Many Jews fled under the Cossack siege of 1648 but others were murdered. Subsequent development of the community was stemmed by further Cossack incursions, the Swedish wars in the early 18th cent., a blood libel in 1753, and sharp competition in trade from Christian townsmen. Under Russian rule from 1793, after the Second Partition of Poland, the Jews lived under the constant threat of expulsion because of smuggling as K. became a border town. The J. pop. rose rapidly in the 19th cent., reaching 6,339 (total 17,704) in 1897, when most factories (soap, candles, paper, bricks, metal casting) were in J. hands as well as most petty trade, carting, and porterage. A great synagogue was built in the 1830s and by the 1860s there were eight others. R. Yitzhak Baer Levinsohn (Ribal), one of the founders of the J. Haskala in Russia, was born in K. in 1788 and returned to spend the last 40 years of his life there (d. 1860). Hovevei Zion became active in the 1890s. The Feb. 1917 Revolution awakened J. public life, with the Zionists and the Bund intensifying their activities. The Leftist groups organized J. self-defense in the face of a threatened pogrom in Dec. 1917. After recovering from the rigors of WWI, the J. economy flourished through the 1920s, but with the Depression a decline set in as heavy taxes and government support of the Polish cooperatives undermined J. trade. The Hehalutz youth movement ran a pioneer training center with 300 participants in 1933, sending youngsters to Palestine throughout the period between the World Wars. A Tarbut school had 200 students. Soviet rule (1939–41) put an end to J. public and commercial life. Factories were nationalized and artisans organized into cooperatives, while the Tarbut school went over to Yiddish instruction and a Soviet curriculum. The Germans entered the city on 1

Market day in Krzemieniec, Poland, 1925

July 1941. The next day the Ukrainian militia rounded up 800 Jews and in the largest pogrom staged in Volhynia murdered them all in retaliation for allegedly killing Ukrainian prisoners who were in fact executed by the Russian NKVD. In Aug. the Germans murdered a group of educated Jews supposedly chosen for work outside the city. They established a *Judenrat*. Shortly thereafter the Great Synagogue was blown up and on 1 March 1942, 9,340 Jews were sealed into an overcrowded ghetto and forced to live on a daily ration of 3.5 ounces of bread. Hunger and disease claimed 10–12 lives a day. On 10–11 Aug. 1942, after a selection transferred 1,500 able-bodied Jews to Bialokrynica, all the others were executed beside trenches outside the city. Those taken to Bialokrynica were murdered on 18 Aug.

KRZEPICE Kielce dist., Poland. The date when the first Jews appeared in K. is unknown, but an organized community existed by the mid-17th cent. In the late 19th cent., Jews set up a number of small hide-process-ing plants while others supplied the town's textile factories with raw materials. The J. pop. rose from 846 in 1827 to 1,395 in 1897 and 1,772 (total 4,168) in 1921. The first Zionist and Bund groups were organized in the early 20th cent. During WWI, J. economic life came to a virtual standstill but community life flourished as a Zamir society for drama and sports was founded along with a J. library. Economic conditions remained difficult between the World Wars, further exacerbated by stiff Polish competition. The Zionists contended with Agudat Israel, supported by the large number of Gur Hasidim in K., for dominance on the community council, with the latter gaining the upper hand in the 1931 elections. Most J. children studied in a *talmud torah* and a Beth Jacob school for girls. Jews were also well represented on the municipal council. The Germans captured K. on 1 Sept. 1939. About 200 Jews were expelled to Czenstochowa, leaving 1,500 in K. and neighboring Koznicka, both annexed to the Reich. A *Judenrat* was established under a regime of forced labor and extortion, but the Germans refrained from setting up a ghetto. On 22 June 1942, the Jews were deported to Auschwitz-Birkenau and apparently murdered on their arrival.

KRZESZOW   Lublin dist., Poland. A small J. settlement in the late 16th cent was wiped out in the Chmielnicki massacres of 1648–49 and only renewed in the 18th cent. The J. pop. grew to 650 (total 1,093) in 1867, then dropped to 281 in 1921. Zionist influence spread between the World Wars and the Zionists eventually took control of community institutions from the Orthodox. With the arrival of J. refugees after the German occupation of Sept. 1939, the J. pop. rose to 600. On 2 Nov. 1942, all were deported to the Belzec death camp after the sick and the old were murdered along with young children.

KRZESZOWICE   Cracow dist., Poland. The J. settlement started growing in the late 19th cent. with the town's economic development based on sawmills, ceramics factories, and mineral springs. The J. pop. increased from 118 in 1880 to 506 in 1921 (total 2,933). In 1918–19 J. stalls and stores in the town's marketplace were looted three times by rioting villagers and local thugs. The arrival of the Germans in Sept. 1939 brought unrelenting persecution and a series of expulsions until the community was liquidated in fall 1942.

KRZYWCZA   (Yid. Kriptsh) Lwow dist., Poland, today Ukraine. An organized community developed in the late 18th cent., never exceeding 250 Jews (around 25% of the total). They were dispersed among other settlements by the Germans toward the end of July 1942 for deportation to the Belzec death camp.

KRZYWCZE GORNE   (Yid. Krivtsch) Tarnopol dist., Poland, today Ukraine. A J. settlement apparently existed from the mid-18th cent., growing to a peak pop. of 719 (a third of the total) in 1880 but subsequently declining to 362 in the wake of emigration and the tribulations of WWI. With the German occupation on 3 July 1941, one able-bodied person per family was demanded for forced labor camps. Those remaining were expelled on 25 Sept. 1942, ultimately reaching the Borszczow ghetto to await their end.

KRZYWICZE   Vilna dist., Poland, today Belarus.

Jews may have been present in the 17th cent. and numbered 457 (total 520) in 1897. Many of those arriving from neighboring villages after the expulsion of 1881 raised vegetables and fruit trees and Jews soon opened stores in the market. Most of the Jews were Habad Hasidim, with a minority of Koidanov Hasidim. In the face of difficult economic circumstances, many of the young emigrated in the late 19th cent. The upheaval of WWI left many homeless, with the J. relief organizations coming to their assistance. In 1925, the J. pop. was 1,200 (total 1,800). A government cooperative created in 1926 all but destroyed J. petty trade and the situation was further exacerbated by the exclusion of Jews from the tobacco industry and anti-J. boycotts. A Hebrew school was established in 1923, its teachers promoting Zionist activity. The Germans entered the town on 1 July 1941, instituting a regime of forced labor and persecution while murdering alleged Communists at the instigation of local Nazi collaborators. A *Judenrat* was set up in Oct. 1941. On 28 April 1942, the Jews of K. were burned alive in an abandoned barn. Some of the 80 left behind were later executed at a flour mill; others were blown up in Sept. 1942 in a handgrenade attack. Of those escaping, some joined Mikhail Kalinin's partisan unit.

KSANTHI   (Xanthi, Xanthie, Eskedje) Ksanthi dist., Greece. In the early 20th cent., Sephardi Jews from Adrianople (Edirne), Didimoticho, and Salonika settled in K. and in 1913 established a community there. A J. Bulgarian association that encouraged Hebrew language and culture opened a branch in K. during Bulgarian rule (1913–18). In the early 1920s, the community founded and maintained a J. school for girls and boys. A synagogue was built in 1926, when there were five social welfare organizations. Zionist activity also began in the 1920s. Zionist organizations and clubs were founded and funds were raised to assist settlement in Palestine. The community was financially stable until the depression of the late 1920s and early 1930s, when K.'s acclaimed tobacco industry declined. About half the community then left for other towns, leaving about 130 J. families in K. In the 1930s immigration to Palestine also began. Numbering 718 Jews in 1928, the community was reduced to 500 by 1934. In 1940, there were about 600 Jews in K. (total 26,500). On 6 April 1940, Germany invaded Greece, took over Thrace, and handed the K. region over to Bulgaria. The Bulgarians extended the Nuremberg Laws to K. and J.

movement and business were restricted; shops and homes were plundered; and all movable possessions were confiscated. With no income to pay for food, the Jews starved. On 4 March 1943, all the Jews were arrested and held in a tobacco warehouse. On the following day, Jews from the surrounding villages were brought to the warehouse and together they were transferred to Bulgaria via Drama. They were held in Bulgaria for ten days and then, on 19 March, transported to Vienna and to the Treblinka death camp. After the war, in 1945, only six Jews remained in K. By 1960, the last J. family had emigrated to Israel.

KSIONZ WIELKI Kielce dist., Poland. Jews probably settled at the turn of the 16th cent. By the 1840s, the community maintained a synagogue, hospital, and school. The J. pop. reached 723 in 1897 and 852 (total 1,715) in 1921. The Zionists became active before WWI and most of the Zionist parties and youth movements were represented after the war. The Germans captured K. on 6 Sept. 1939, appointing a *Judenrat* to supply forced labor. Refugees increased the J. pop. from 850 in 1939 to about 1,230 in 1942. The first *Aktion* occurred on 5 Sept. 1942. After Polish police murdered 16 Jews, most were dispatched to Slomniki to join the thousands there awaiting deportation. After a selection for the labor camps, the rest were deported to the Belzec death camp. Most of the 200–300 left behind in K. were executed around the end of Nov. 1942.

KUBLICHI Vitebsk dist., Belorussia. The J. pop. was 181 in 1847 and 935 (total 1,291) in 1897, dropping to 546 in 1926 under the Soviets. A J. elementary school (four grades) was opened in 1926 and a J. council operated from 1930. The Germans occupied K. on 3 Aug. 1941, setting up a ghetto. In Dec. all but 15 artisan families were transferred to the empty ghetto of Ushachi along with Jews from the neighboring villages, making a total of 500 confined there. Jews set the ghetto on fire, with some attempting to escape, but the Germans rounded them up and murdered them.

KUDIRKOS-NAUMIESTIS (Yid. Naishtot-Shaki) Sakiai dist., Lithuania. Jews first settled in the beginning of the 18th cent. In the 19th cent. there was a *talmud torah*. The J. pop. in 1835 was 3,348 (76% of the total). Zionist activity began in 1884 with the establishment of a Hovevei Zion branch. The J. pop. in 1897 was 2,091 (45%). Many emigrated to the U.S. and South Africa. During WWI, K. changed hands several times and the city was damaged, causing many to flee. When Germany captured the city in 1915, 70% of the Jews returned. In three municipal council elections, Jews won four of nine seats twice and three seats once. With a deteriorating economy, many Jews emigrated to the west. The community maintained a Yiddish kindergarten and school, a Hebrew elementary school, a Hebrew high school, a *heder*, a small yeshiva, a Yiddish library, and a Hebrew library. Zionist youth groups and parties were active. The vast majority of K.'s Jews voted for the Zionist list in elections to the Lithuanian Sejm. The American Zionist leader Rabbi Abba Hillel Silver (1893–1963) was from K. J. economic and communal life suffered during the Soviet annexation of 1940–41. After the Germans took the town on 22 June 1941, the Jews were taken to forced labor. In July, all J. males aged 14 and up were shot at the J. cemetery, in the presence of the dist. governor and mayor. On 16 Sept. 1941, the women and children were murdered in the Parazniai forest.

KUELSHEIM Baden, Germany. The medieval J. community was decimated in the Rindfleisch massacres of 1298 and completely wiped out in the Black Death massacres of 1348–49. It was renewed in 1378 and Jews maintained a presence over the following centuries. In the 19th cent., disabilities and social distance persisted despite liberalizing laws. The J. pop. grew to 196 in 1871 (total 1,833), with nearly half the Jews operating as cattle traders at the turn of the cent. From the 1880s, the J. pop. began to drop through emigration and the exodus to the big cities, numbering 106 in 1910 and 36 in 1933. Under the Weimar Republic, Jews were active in public life but with the rise of the Nazis they were subjected to increasing social and economic isolation. Sixteen Jews emigrated through 1940 while ten left for other German cities. The last 13 were deported to the Gurs concentration camp on 22 Oct. 1940 and six were deported after leaving K.; 15 perished in the camps.

KUENZELSAU Wuerttemberg, Germany. Jews fell victim to the Rindfleisch massacres of 1298 and further disturbances in 1304 and were forced to leave K. in the late 16th cent. after being allowed to resettle in 1580. The community was reestablished after 1850 and numbered 114 in 1900 (total 3,067), living off the cattle trade, moneylending, peddling, and brokerage. In

Synagogue in Kuenzelsau, Germany

1907, a synagogue was dedicated and the Nagelsberg community (dwindling from 167 Jews in 1854 to seven in 1910) was attached to K. In 1933, 60 remained, subjected to increasing persecution. The synagogue was burned on *Kristallnacht* (9–10 Nov. 1938), and at least ten men were taken to the Dachau concentration camp. By 1941, 36 had emigrated while 19 were expelled to their deaths to the Riga, Izbica (Lublin dist. of Poland), and Theresienstadt ghettoes in Dec.

KUESTRIN (Pol. Kostrzyn) Brandenburg, Germany, today Poland. A J. settlement developed in 1815. By 1849, the J. pop. was 105. It was 222 in 1880 and 132 in 1895. The community maintained a synagogue (1884–1930) and a cemetery (expanded in 1899). In 1902, the Jews of Sonnenburg, whose small community was dissolved, joined the K. community. By June 1933, about four months after the

Nazis came to power, there were 96 Jews in K. They succeeded in overcoming the resistance of the authorities and in 1934 dedicated a new synagogue. By May 1939, only 24 Jews and nine persons of partial J. origin (*Mischlinge*) remained in the town. It may be assumed that those Jews who did not manage to emigrate were deported to the east. In Nov. 1944, one J., probably married to a non-Jew, was living in K.

KUKTISKES (Yid. Kuktishok) Utena dist., Lithuania. The J. pop. of 172 in 1923 included Jews from the surrounding villages. On 29 Aug. 1941, following the German arrival in June, the Lithuanians murdered all the Jews of K. together with those from nearby Utena.

KULA Vojvodina dist., Yugoslavia. Jews settled in the 17th cent. and a community was established in the mid-19th cent. The J. pop. in 1931 was 112 (total 10,314). All the Jews perished in the Holocaust.

KULACZKOWCE Stanislawow dist., Poland, today Ukraine. Jews are mentioned from 1637. The J. pop. declined from 266 in 1880 (total 2,303) to 124 in 1921. The Jews were probably expelled by the Germans to the neighboring Gwozdziec ghetto in early 1942.

KULAUTUVA (Yid. Kalatove) Kaunas dist., Lithuania. In the beginning of the 1930s there were 16 J. families here, most engaged in providing services to vacationers. During the Holocaust, local Lithuanian nationalists killed some and the rest were sent to the Kovno (Kaunas) ghetto.

KULCHIN Kamenets-Podolski dist., Ukraine. Jews numbered 177 in 1765 and 2,031 (47% of the total) in 1897. In the Soviet period, a J. rural council (soviet), elementary school, and literary and drama circles were active. In 1926, the J. pop. was 1,266. The Germans occupied K. in early July 1941. All the town's Jews were executed at the nearby village of Manevtsy in June 1942.

KULDIGA Kurzeme (Courland) dist., Latvia. Despite a residence ban, Jews from Poland and Lithuania settled in the area in the late 17th cent. and traded in the town with the blessing of the local nobility. A permanent settlement was only formed after the annexation to Russia in 1795. In 1840, 171 Jews (7.5% of the total) left for the Kherson province to settle as farmers. The J. pop. grew, reaching 2,713 in 1881 (total 8,072), including an expansion of the merchant class which gave the Jews control of commerce. Jews also owned a match factory. A synagogue and *talmud torah* operated from the early 19th cent. Ze'ev Wolf Lipkin, father of Musar founder Yisrael Salanter, was the community's rabbi from around 1830. The Zionists became active in 1902 and the Bund took part in the revolutionary events of 1905. The Jews were expelled to Russia in 1915, with around a third returning after WWI, 70% of them on relief. With assistance from the Joint Distribution Committee the community slowly recovered. Despite its declining pop. (646 in 1935) it maintained a strong economic position, operating 95 of the town's 205 larger business establishments. Most J. children studied at a German school,

with a third at the J. school. Zionist influence reached its peak in the mid-1930s. Under Russian rule (1940–41), J. public life was terminated. The Germans arrived on 1 July 1941. Local Latvians immediately commenced a reign of terror claiming J. lives. Jews were evicted from their homes and confined in the synagogue. Shortly afterwards a group of J. men was murdered in the nearby forest. The rest of the Jews were subsequently executed in the Padura forest and other sites by Latvian firing squads. After the war a small J. community reestablished itself in K. until the 1950s.

KULESZCZE KOSCIELNE Bialystok dist., Poland. The J. pop. in 1921 was 185 (total 278). The Jews were expelled by the Germans to the Wysokie Mazowieckie ghetto in Aug. 1941 and from there to the Treblinka and Auschwitz death camps in Nov. 1942.

KULIAI Kretinga dist., Lithuania. Jews first settled in the 18th cent., establishing a community in the early 20th cent. R. Yosef Shelomo Kahaneman (1888–1969), who founded the Ponevezh yeshiva in Benai Berak, came from K. The J. pop. in 1897 was 181 (29% of the total). In 1940 there were about 20 families. After the German invasion in June 1941, Lithuanian nationalists incarcerated the Jews. On 29 June 1941 they were tricked into believing that they were to help extinguish a fire and killed outside of town

KULIKOW Lwow dist., Poland, today Ukraine. Jews are first mentioned in 1544. In the 18th and 19th cents. they controlled the manufacture and sale of mead. In 1910 the J. pop. numbered 1,211 (a third of the total). In the 20th cent. the baking of a specialty bread marketed in Lwow provided a livelihood for dozens of J. families. The attractions of the latter town and the trials of WWI served to reduce the J. pop. to 509 by 1921. The Germans arrived on 29 June 1941. Two farm labor camps were set up in Sept. 1941. All the workers were deported to the Belzec death camp a year later and those remaining were expelled at the end of Nov. 1942 to the Zolkiew ghetto where they shared the fate of the local Jews.

KULMBACH Upper Franconia, Germany. Jews were present in the second half of the 14th cent. under a letter of protection giving them freedom of movement. In 1584 they were expelled by the local count. The modern community dates from the late 19th cent. and numbered 41 (total 12,476) in 1933. By 1939, 14 emigrated and 15 left for other German cities. Of the remaining Jews, seven were brought to Bamberg on 24 April 1942 and deported from there to Izbica in the Lublin dist. (Poland).

KUNAGOTA   Csanad dist., Hungary. Jews settled in the mid-19th cent., numbering 43 in 1880 and 92 in 1930. On 26 June 1944, they were deported to Auschwitz via Magyarbanhegyes.

KUNEV   Kamenets-Podolski dist., Ukraine. The J. pop. was 173 in 1765 and 1,661 (57% of the total) in 1897, dropping to 1,314 in 1926 under the Soviets. The Germans occupied the town on 3 July 1941. In Aug. 1941, SS units murdered 159 Jews. In June and July 1942 nearly 700 more Jews were executed.

KUNHEGYES   Jasz–Nagykun–Szolnok dist., Hungary. Jews settled after 1848. They founded a synagogue and school in 1893. The J. pop. was 162 in 1880 and 356 (3% of the total) in 1920. In 1941, 224 remained. They were deported via Szolnok to Austria on 25–27 June 1944 and to Auschwitz on 29 June. The 126 survivors, mainly from Austria, reestablished the community, but it gradually declined.

KUNMADARAS   Jasz–Nagykun–Szolnok dist., Hungary. Jews arrived c. 1840. The community organized in 1850, building a synagogue around 1880 and maintaining a school. The J. pop. reached 215 in 1885 and 302 in 1930. Jews were brutally attacked in the White Terror in 1919. On 24 April 1944, they were brought to the Karcag ghetto, then to Szolnok on 10 June prior to deportation to Auschwitz on 25–27 June. In 1946, three Jews in the reestablished community of 51 were murdered in a pogrom.

KUNOW   Kielce dist., Poland. A community of 115 in 1827 grew to 510 in 1921 (total 2,145). The Joint Distribution Committee helped the Jews rehabilitate their ruined economy after WWI. On the eve of WWII, the J. pop. was 495 (100 families). Many of the young fled eastward on the approach of the Germans in Sept. 1939. In 1940, the Germans impounded J. businesses and exacted large tributes from the community. In March 1941, 100 refugees arrived from Vienna. In Oct. 1942, SS forces and Ukrainian auxilia-

ries surrounded the J. quarter and after executing the sick and old outside the town deported the rest, about 500, to the Treblinka death camp

KUNSZENTMARTON   Jasz–Nagykun–Szolnok dist., Hungary. The Jews were only allowed to settle after 1848. They operated a flour mill, wood-processing plant, and printing press. In 1880–1920, the community maintained a J. school and a synagogue. The J. pop. was 260 (2.5% of the total) in 1890 and 202 in 1941. In late May 1944, the Jews were brought to Kecskemet and on 23 June deported to Auschwitz. Survivors reestablished the community but only two Jews remained in 1965.

KUNSZENTMIKLOS   Pest–Pilis–Solt–Kiskun dist., Hungary. Jews settled in the early 19th cent. The J. pop. was 633 in 1880. A synagogue, built in 1898, was desecrated in the White Terror of 1919–21. In 1930, 155 Jews remained. The young were mobilized for forced labor in 1941, most perishing. The rest were deported to Auschwitz on 23 June 1944 after being detained in Kiskoros and Kecskemet.

KUPEL   Kamenets-Podolski dist., Ukraine. J. settlement commenced in the 18th cent. A J. printing press was in operation in 1796. In 1897, the J. pop. was 2,727 (63% of the total). After the Oct. 1917 Revolution, pogroms were staged against the Jews, especially on 5–10 Dec. 1917. In 1926, under the Soviets, the J. pop. was 1,828. A J. rural council (soviet) was active and in 1929 a J. kolkhoz was founded. The Germans occupied the town on 5 July 1941, murdering 89 Jews the same day. In July 1942, 600 were executed at the village of Volochisk. In Aug., another 261 were murdered and in Jan. 1943, 172.

KUPIANSK   Kharkov dist., Ukraine. Jews settled in small numbers in the early 19th cent. and numbered 71 in 1897 and 124 (total 20,961) in 1939. The few remaining Jews perished after the German occupation of 23 June 1942.

KUPICZOW   Volhynia dist., Poland, today Ukraine. In the Holocaust, K.'s 30 J. families were brought from K. to Kowel for liquidation.

KUPIN   Kamenets-Podolski dist., Ukraine. The J. pop. was 405 in 1765 and 1,351 in 1897. Most Jews earned their livelihoods as lessees, petty traders, and artisans. A few exploited the proximity to the Austrian border to trade in farm produce. Most Jews were Hasidim. A Hovevei Zion group and Bund cell were founded in the late 19th cent. Two modernized *hadarim* were opened and eventually evolved into a Tarbut school. Tze'irei Tziyyon became active in 1917 and later Hehalutz started to operate. In the Soviet period, the Tarbut school was closed down and Zionist activity prohibited. A J. kolkhoz was started. The Germans captured K. in July 1941. Ukrainian police murdered 300 Jews in early Oct. 1941. Another 500 Jews were executed in late 1942.

KUPISKIS (Yid. Kupishok) Panevezys dist., Lithuania. The origins of the J. community are not known; the earliest graves date from the beginning of the 18th cent. The community was divided between Hasidim and *Mitnaggedim*, each group with its own rabbi. Disputes between the two groups continued until the *Mitnagged* rabbi founded a yeshiva, gaining hasidic support. At the end of the 19th cent., many emigrated to the U.S. and South Africa. The J. pop. in 1897 stood at 2,661 (71% of the total). Between the World Wars, the strife between the Hasidim and *Mitnaggedim* continued, as did emigration. The town maintained three synagogues, a *talmud torah*, two Hebrew schools, a Yiddish school, a library, and social welfare and cultural organizations. The world economic situation coupled with foreign and local competition and an anti-J. boycott all contributed to the difficult economic conditions of the Jews. Most Zionist parties were represented in K. The J. pop. in 1938 was 1,200 (42%). When Lithuania was annexed to the Soviet Union in 1940, some J.-owned businesses were nationalized. After the Germans arrived in June 1941, they ordered the Jews into a crowded ghetto, with little food and difficult conditions. A German teacher who had posed previously as a Communist but was a planted Nazi agent prepared lists of Jews, according to which they were taken from the ghetto and murdered by Lithuanians between July and Sept. 1941. The numbers of victims, including those from the surrounding area, exceeded 3,000.

KUPPENHEIM Baden, Germany. The 16th cent. community was expelled in 1584 together with most of the Jews of the principality. The J. settlement was renewed after the Thirty Years War (1618–1648) and was still subject to numerous disabilities in the early

19th cent. The cemetery consecrated in 1692 was one of the most beautiful in the region and served many communities until the end of the 19th cent. A synagogue was erected in 1825. In 1865 the J. pop. reached a peak of 142 (total 1,829). In 1933, 51 Jews remained. Nineteen emigrated by Nov. 1938 (17 to the U.S.) and six left for other German cities. On *Kristallnacht* (9–10 Nov. 1938), the synagogue was burned and Jews were detained in Dachau. Another four left for the U.S. and on 22 Oct. 1940 the remaining 16 were deported to the Gurs concentration camp; five survived the Holocaust.

KURESSAARE (also Kingsepp) Estonia. Jews settled in the mid-19th cent. in this island port city, numbering 110 in 1881 and, after continued emigration, 22 in 1934 (total 4,478). Some escaped by sea to the Soviet Union on the approach of the Germans in fall 1941; the rest were murdered.

KURGANSKAYA Krasnodar territory, Russia. A few Jews were among the 750 people murdered in the village by the Germans in summer 1942.

KURIMA Slovakia, Czechoslovakia, today Republic of Slovakia. Jews settled in the early 18th cent. and formed an organized community by the late 18th cent. A wooden synagogue was consecrated in 1810. Galician newcomers in the 1820s reinforced the prevailing hasidic atmosphere in the community, which grew to a peak of 414 (total 1,146) in 1880 with 40 other settlements under the jurisdiction of its regional rabbinate. Most Jews were shopkeepers and peddlers at first; later they traded in farm produce as well. The existing *talmud torah* was converted into an elementary school. From the late 19th cent., the J. pop. declined steadily, reaching 188 in 1940. Mizrachi, Bnei Akiva, and Betar were active between the World Wars. In the Slovakian state, the authorities closed down J. businesses and dozens of Jews were seized for forced labor. in March 1942 young men and women were deported to the Majdanek and Auschwitz death camps, respectively, and J. families were sent to the Lublin dist. of Poland in May–June. The last few dozen Jews were evacuated to western Slovakia in May 1944. In all, about 180 perished in the Holocaust.

KURKLIAI (Yid. Kurkle) Ukmerge dist., Lithuania. Jews first settled at the end of the 18th cent. The J. pop. in 1897 was 257 (32% of the total). Between the World

Wars, many emigrated because of the difficult economic situation to South Africa, the U. S., Cuba, and Brazil. The Zionist movement enjoyed widespread support. By 1940 there were only about 50 families. After the German occupation of 1941, all the Jews were murdered in the Pivonija forest on 5 Sept.

KURMAN (from 1944, Krasnogvardeyskoye) Crimea, Russia, today Ukraine. A few J. grain merchants lived with their families near the local train station in the 1880s. They were expelled in 1895 on the basis of the 1882 May Laws restricting J. residence and trade but returned clandestinely. After the Feb. 1917 Revolution, a few dozen J. families were present. In 1939, the J. pop. was 211 (total 2,878) with 1,910 in the entire region. The Germans arrived in late Oct. or early Nov. 1941. In late Jan. 1942, with the help of local Germans, they murdered some of the remaining 1,300 Jews of K. and the surrounding area. The rest (probably the majority) were brought to Dzhankoy for execution. Another 42 were murdered on 17 Feb.

KUROW Lublin dist., Poland. A few J. families were present in the late 16th cent. In the early 17th cent., the community consecrated a synagogue and cemetery but later on the Chmielnicki massacres of 1648–49 decimated the community, which did not reestablish itself until the late 18th cent., when K. became a hasidic center. By 1857, the J. pop. was 1,564 (total 2,665). Jews traded in hides, lumber, grain, and eggs, produced and marketed alcoholic beverages, and operated a number of small factories for producing candles, prayer shawl fringes, etc. The first Zionist group was organized in the early 20th cent. In 1921, the J. pop. was 2,230. Although economic circumstances were difficult, political and cultural life flourished. Agudat Israel controlled the community council in the 1920s and the late 1930s and founded a Beth Jacob school for girls. The Zionists opened Yavne (Mizrachi) and Tarbut schools. In the wake of German bombardments in Sept. 1939, 300 J. families fled to Lublin and its environs. The Germans arrived on 15 Sept., setting up a *Judenrat* in early 1940 and instituting a regime of forced labor and property confiscation. A ghetto was established in Feb. 1942. On 8 April 1942 the Jews were marched to Konskowola and from there deported to the Sobibor death camp. Prior to the deportation, a group of young people managed to escape to the forest where some joined up with partisans. In spring 1943,

Polish peasants informed on the K. group to the Germans and most were killed.

KUROZWENKI Kielce dist., Poland. Jews settled in the mid-16th cent. In 1921, they numbered 224 (total 1,033). No exact information about the community between the World Wars is available, but it is believed that in WWII the few Jews present may have been transferred to a nearby ghetto by the Germans and that in Oct.–Nov. 1942 all the Jews in the area were deported to the Treblinka death camp.

KURSENAI (Yid. Kurshan) Siauliai dist., Lithuania. Jews first settled in the 19th cent. The J. pop. in 1897 was 1,542 (48% of the total). Prior to WWI, many Jews emigrated to South Africa and the U.S. Some of the Jews expelled by the Russian army during WWI to the Russian interior returned after the war. In the 1930s, many emigrated because of the economic situation and an anti-J. boycott. The Zionist movement won widespread support and a Tarbut school was established. Among K.'s natives was Aryeh Kubowitzki (Kubovy; 1896–1966), who served as Israel's ambassador to Czechoslovakia and Argentina and as chairman of Yad Vashem (1959). The J. pop. in 1939 stood at about 900 (30%). After the German invasion in June 1941, 150 men were taken to Siauliai, forced into pits, and shot. The remaining men were killed on 16 July 1941. Women and children were transferred to Zagare and murdered together with the Jews of Zagare.

KURSK Kursk dist., Russia. A small number of Jews was apparently living in K. in the late 18th cent. In 1858, their pop. was 465, rising to 1,800 in 1880. The community was accorded the right to erect a synagogue in the late 19th cent. A pogrom was staged on 20 Oct. 1905. During the Soviet period, the J. pop. rose to 4,154 in 1926 and 4,914 (total 119,977) in 1939. A J. elementary school was opened in the early 1920s. The Germans captured the city on 2 Nov. 1941, murdering nine Jews a week later and another 150 by Feb. 1942. An additional 100 Jews were murdered at the village of Solyanki in early June or July 1942.

KURYLOWKA Lwow dist., Poland. The J. pop. in 1921 was 101 (total 1,561). The Jews were expelled to Soviet-held territory and murdered there by the Germans in 1941–42; or deported to the Belzec death camp via Lezajsk in Sept. 1942.

KURZELOW Kielce dist., Poland. Jews are first mentioned in the early 19th cent. and numbered 191 (total 1,516) in 1921. Under the German occupation, 275 refugees from Wloszczowa were added to the town's 119 Jews in Feb. 1940. In Sept. 1942, 13 Jews were murdered and the entire J. pop. sent back to Wloszczowa for deportation to the Treblinka death camp.

KURZENIEC Vilna dist., Poland, today Belarus. By the 1860s, K. was a center of Lubavich Hasidism. In 1897 the J. pop. was 1,613 (total 1,774). J. shops were located in a big wooden building on the market square and J. artisans circulated through the neighboring villages to sell their wares. Mutual aid and social welfare services were highly developed in the community. After WWI, economic conditions deteriorated and the J. relief organizations became active. Most J. homes and stores were destroyed in a 1924 fire and recovery was slow. Zionist activity intensified after the publication of the Balfour Declaration in 1917 and a Tarbut Hebrew school was in operation from 1921. The Germans arrived in late June 1941, appointing a *Judenrat* and instituting a regime of forced labor. SS troops and Lithuanian police murdered 54 Jews on 14 Oct. 1941. In a final *Aktion* on 9 Sept. 1942, 1,052 Jews were burned alive in a barn or shot trying to escape. The 200–300 who reached the partisans were seen safely to Soviet territory.

KUSEL Palatinate, Germany. Jews lived in K. from the 14th cent. on. They suffered in the Black Death persecutions of 1348–49 and were finally expelled in 1543 with all the Jews of the Duchy of Zweibruecken. Settlement was apparently renewed only in the mid-18th cent. Numbering 13 individuals in 1827, the J. pop. grew to 55 (total 3,122) in 1900 and 66 in 1930. The community maintained a prayer room and buried its dead at the J. cemetery of Thallichtenberg. In June 1933, about four months after the Nazi assumption of power, 56 Jews were living in K. Their prayer room as well as stores and homes was vandalized on *Kristall-nacht* (9–10 Nov. 1938). J. men were sent to the Dachau concentration camp. About 15 Jews from K. managed to emigrate to safe havens, and about 30 moved to other German cities and neighboring countries. It may

be assumed that of the latter group several were deported and perished, as was the case also for the Jews remaining in K.

KUSNICE (Hung. Kovacsret) Carpatho-Russia, Czechoslovakia, today Ukraine. Three J. families were living in the town in 1768. The number of Jews then rose to 49 in 1830; 121 (total 1,083) in 1880; 294 in 1921; and 434 in 1941. A few Jews farmed their own land. The Hungarians occupied K. in March 1939 and in 1940–41 drafted dozens of Jews into labor battalions for forced labor or service on the eastern front, where many were killed. The rest, 445 in March 1944, were deported to Auschwitz in the second half of May.

KUTINA Croatia, Yugoslavia, today Republic of Crotia. In the 17th cent., Jews settled in K. but no details are known about the community until the 20th cent. The synagogue was dedicated in 1848. There were 148 Jews in 1914; almost all perished in the Holocaust.

KUTNA HORA Bohemia, Czechoslovakia. Jews were not accorded residence rights until the late 19th cent. They erected a synagogue in 1902 and their pop. grew to 205 (total 15,542) in 1910. In 1930, only three of the community's 140 Jews defined themselves as being of J. nationality; the rest saw themselves as Czechs. Between April and June 1942, the Jews were deported to the Theresienstadt ghetto and from there to the death camps, mainly Treblinka.

KUTNO Lodz dist., Poland. A J. community existed in the mid-15th cent. A synagogue was built in 1766 and survived until 1939. The J. pop. in 1897 was 10,356 (50% of the total). K. was a center of rabbinical learning, and prominent personalities such as Nahum Sokolow and Sholem Asch studied at the yeshiva. Asch (1880–1957) was born in K. and immortalized the town in his works. The Haskala movement was active and in the 1820s a secular school was opened. Zionist activity began in 1898 and most of the Zionist political parties and youth movements were founded prior to WWI. A Yiddish school was founded in 1916, and existed until 1935. The majority of the community was employed as salaried workers during the 19th cent., and they increased proportionally during the 20th cent., mainly in the textile and food industries.

The income of J. shopowners and artisans was adversely effected by the boycott imposed by the Endecja Party between the World Wars. Shortly after WWI, a trade union was set up by the Bund and a J. labor union was organized while a J. merchants' association was established in 1932. In the 1924 community council elections, the Zionists won 50% of the seats. J. representatives were elected to the municipal council. A J. government elementary school opened in 1926 and in 1928 a school with Yiddish instruction was established. A popular university was opened in 1925 as well as a branch of YIVO. During the 1930s membership in Zionist organizations was doubled. After the Germans entered K. on 15 Sept. 1939, J. males were sent to forced labor in Piatek and a group of 70 to a prison camp at Leczyca. Jews were persecuted daily and J. property was plundered. The synagogue was burned, only the walls remaining. A *Judenrat* was established in Nov. 1939 and 7,000 Jews were ghettoized on 16 June 1940 in extremely overcrowded conditions. Jews were sent to work at the railway yards and air base, enabling them to smuggle food into the ghetto. Although the *Judenrat* tried to organize food supplies to the ghetto, the situation deteriorated, and disease and starvation claimed 663 victims between Dec. 1940 and March 1941. In July 1941, the J. pop. numbered 6,015 (including refugees) and in March 1942 all were deported to Chelmno. In Oct. 1945, 50 survivors returned, but they soon left.

KUTY   (Yid. Kitev) Stanislawow dist., Poland, today Ukraine. Jews settled with full rights on the founding of K. in 1715. Under Austrian rule with its heavy taxation their situation declined, but improved when equality was granted throughout Galicia in 1868. The best known of K.'s rabbis was Avraham Gershon Kit-

Family celebration at Zaida Mendel's house, Kuty, Poland, 1938

over, the Ba'al Shem Tov's brother-in-law (according to hasidic legend the Ba'al Shem Tov lived here for a time). The local synagogue was the town's largest and most luxurious building. By 1880 the J. pop. had leveled off at around 3,000 (almost half the total), though emigration to the U.S. increased from the turn of the cent. Between the World Wars, two new sources of livelihood were opened: tourism and carpet manufacturing as a home industry. The Soviets took over K. on 17 Sept. 1939. On 1 July 1941, the Rumanians and Hungarians occupied K. and persecuted the Jews. The Germans took over in Sept. and instituted a regime of forced labor and extortion. Starvation and disease claimed many J. lives in the winter of 1941–42. On 10 April 1942, SS and Gestapo units joined by the Ukrainian police went on a killing spree, murdering around 950 Jews. Two weeks later, about 500 without work permits were expelled to the Kolomyja ghetto. The community was liquidated on 7 Sept. when another 800 Jews were sent to Kolomyja for deportation to the Belzec death camp while a group of the young and fit were transferred to the Janowska Road Camp in Lwow.

KUZMIN (I) Kamenets-Podolski dist. (Gorodok prov.), Ukraine. Jews numbered 208 in 1765 and 890 (total 2,940) in 1897. The Germans occupied K. in late July 1941 and murdered Jews in small groups. The last group was sent to the Krasilov ghetto and was murdered at Manivtsy in July 1942.

KUZMIN (II) Kamenets-Podolski dist. (Krasilov prov.), Ukraine. Jews numbered 641 in 1847 and 830 (total 3,368) in 1897. A pogrom was staged on 7 July 1918, during the civil war. In 1923, under the Soviets, the J. pop. dropped to 453. The Germans captured K. on 8 July 1941. On 17 Feb. 1942, all the Jews were crowded into a sealed structure and gassed to death.

KUZMINO (Hung. Beregszilvas) Carpatho-Russia, Czechoslovakia, today Ukraine. Jews probably settled in the early 19th cent. Six were living there in 1830, growing to 152 (total 411) in 1880 with a similar level maintained until WWII. A few J. families farmed. The Hungarians occupied the town in March 1939, deporting the Jews to Auschwitz in mid-May 1944.

KUZNICA Bialystok dist., Poland, today Belarus. A small J. community attached to Grodno existed from 1623. It grew to 780 residents (total 1,343) by 1897, most living near the market where they had their stores, with some circulating through the neighboring villages to conduct petty trade. In 1931, the J. pop. was 556 as many left because of economic hardship. Children studied at Yiddish and Hebrew (Horev) schools as well as the local public school. The Zionist youth movements were active. The Germans captured K. in late June 1941, establishing a *Judenrat* and ghetto under a regime of forced labor. On 2 Nov. 1942 all were sent to the Kelbasin transit camp near Grodno and from there deported to Auschwitz.

KVASY (Hung. Tiszaborkut) Carpatho-Russia, Czechoslovakia, today Ukraine. Jews probably arrived in the mid-19th cent, numbering 23 (total 721) in 1880. Many earned their livelihoods operating or supplying the local boarding houses catering to vacationers. The J. pop. rose to 143 in 1921 and 156 in 1941. Zionist activity among the young was extensive in the 1920s and 1930s. The Hungarians occupied the town in March 1939, drafting a group of J. men into forced labor battalions. In Aug. 1941, they expelled a number of J. families without Hungarian citizenship to Kamenets-Podolski, where they were murdered. The rest were deported to Auschwitz in the second half of May 1944.

KVEDARNA (Yid. Khveidan) Taurage dist., Lithuania. Jews first settled here in the 17th cent. In the 19th cent. R. Avraham Karelitz (1878-1963), known as Hazon Ish, studied there for many years. The J. pop. in 1897 was 671 (56% of the total). In 1938 it was 350 (32%). After the German invasion in June 1941, the SS and Lithuanian nationalists arrested all J. males aged 15 and over and sent them to the Silute (Heydekrug) work camp. Periodically a selection was made and those not fit to work were executed. The rest died at Auschwitz or in the Warsaw ghetto after clearing the debris of the ghetto. The women and children were detained in July 1941, abused, raped, and murdered.

KVIETISKIS (Yid. Kvetishok) Marijampole dist., Lithuania. The J. pop. in 1923 was 97. All the Jews were murdered after the German occupation of June 1941.

KYBARTAI (Yid. Kibart) Vilkaviskis dist., Lithuania. The town was located on the border with Germany. Jews first settled in the 1860s and profited from the trade between the two countries. There were several modernized *hadarim*. Because of the proximity to Germany, the more affluent sent their children to study in German schools. An elementary school was founded by the Haskala movement. The community maintained two synagogues, although most were not religious. The J. pop. in 1897 was 533 (45% of the total). Zionist activity began around the turn of the cent. with many contributing money to the community in Eretz Israel. Between the World Wars, economic activity shifted to Memel and Kaunas, with many Jews moving to the latter. Jews were active in city politics, winning six of 25 seats in the 1924 city council elections. The Zionists were active and a Hebrew school existed in 1925–40. Many bought shares in the fledgling Bank Hapoalim. Lithuania's largest training farm for those planning to leave for Palestine was located next to K. and an urban preparatory kibbutz was established in 1932. Most young Jews left for Kaunas and Palestine in the 1930s because of reduced economic contact with Nazi Germany and an anti-J. boycott. During the 1940–41 Soviet occupation, J. factories and stores were nationalized and border police officers were housed in J. homes. The. J. pop. in 1941 was about 350. After the German invasion in June 1941, Lithuanian nationalists introduced various antisemitic measures. On 6 July 1941, outside the village of Gutkaimis, all men aged 16 and up were herded into the pits they had been made to dig and shot. The remaining Jews, primarily women, children, and the elderly, were held in military barracks for a month and then murdered by Germans and Lithuanians at the Verbalis ghetto on 11 Sept. 1941.

KYJOV (Yid., Gaya) Moravia, Czechoslovakia. The J. community was most probably established in 1603 though individual Jews were present before then. Throughout the 17th cent. and into the 18th cent., the Jews faced local hostility. In 1722, 20 families were expelled for exceeding the residence quota. In 1848–1918, the community enjoyed political autonomy and had its own mayor. A new synagogue was erected in 1852. The J. pop. grew to a peak of 884 in 1869 and then declined steadily to 319 (total 4,505) in 1930. The Zionists were active from the late 19th cent. During WWI, the community extended aid to 6,000 J. refugees in a nearby camp. Another 670 J. refugees from the Sudetenland and Vienna were held in the camp in 1938. The camp was again used as an assembly point for the 2,852 Jews from K. and the surrounding area before their deportation to the Theresienstadt ghetto in three transports in early 1943. Later in the year, nearly all were sent to Auschwitz. The Nazis destroyed the two J. cemeteries, the remains of the J. ghetto, and the synagogue.

KYLLBURG Rhineland, Germany. Jews first settled in the 19th cent., numbering 22 (total 1,139) in 1905 and rising to 40 in 1925. A synagogue was consecrated in 1911. In June 1933, four months after the Nazi rise to power, there were 43 Jews in K. On *Kristallnacht* (9–10 Nov. 1938), the synagogue was destroyed. In all, 31 Jews emigrated to the U.S. and South America; another six left for other German cities and six were deported in 1942.

KYSUCKE NOVE MESTO (Hung. Kiszuczaujhely) Slovakia, Czechoslovakia, today Republic of Slovakia. Jews probably settled at the turn of the 18th cent., forming a Neologist congregation after the split in 1869 and reaching a peak pop. of 159 (total 1,954) in 1880. A synagogue in the Renaissance style was built in 1906. The Zionists were active after WWI and Jews served on the local council. They owned taverns, restaurants, and groceries and were active as lumber, hide, and livestock merchants. In spring 1942, most of the prewar pop. of 50 was deported to the east where it perished.

L

LAASPHE Westphalia, Germany. J. merchants were probably trading in L. by the 13th cent. but Jews only seem to have been allowed to settle there permanently from the mid-17th cent. A synagogue was constructed in 1824. Most Jews were cattle traders or butchers. After 1847, L. became the seat of a regional congregation with the communities of Banfe and Erndtebrueck attached to it. A J. school was opened in 1869. The J. pop. rose from 80 in 1819 to a peak of 151 (total 2,184) in 1880. In the 1890s, against a background of economic hardship, antisemitism intensified in the heretofore liberal town as Adolf Stoecker's antisemitic party received 43% of the vote in the 1892 elections. In the Weimar period, Jews were active in public, social, and economic life though antisemitism continued to make itself felt. In 1930, 121 Jews remained in L. In 1934, a year after the Nazi takeover, J. children were expelled from public schools, years before such a step was taken in Nazi Germany as a whole. A Zionist "work group" was formed in 1935. Persecution continued until just 16 Jews remained in 1938, with nine escaping before deportations commenced. On *Kristallnacht* (9-10 Nov. 1938), J. homes and workshops were vandalized, the J. cemetery was desecrated, and the synagogue seriously damaged. Ten Jews were sent to the Sachsenhausen concentration camp. About 60 Jews are known to have left the city from 1933, 26 for the U.S. Another 62 were deported: 43 apparently to Zamosc (Lublin dist., Poland) on 28 April 1942 and 19 to the Theresienstadt ghetto on 27 July 1942. All but two perished.

LABES (Pol. Lobez) Pomerania, Germany, today Poland. The first Jews are mentioned in 1705. A J. community developed slowly and numbered 167 individuals in 1861, shrinking to 87 in 1909. It maintained a synagogue and a cemetery. When the Nazis came to power in 1933, there were only 38 Jews. By 1935, J.

businessmen were facing financial ruin. Since the synagogue was located close to other buildings, it was not burned down on *Kristallnacht* (9-10 Nov. 1938). Later, however, it was turned into a carpentry workshop and finally burned down in 1945 when the Soviet Army entered the town. No further information about the fate of the Jews under Nazi rule is available.

LABIAU (Pol. Polessk) East Prussia, Germany, today Russia. The J. pop. was 131 in 1880; 150 in 1895; and 42 in 1905. The community established a synagogue in the beginning of the 1870s and two cemeteries, the second c. 1863. On the eve of the Nazi assumption of power in 1933, there were 23 Jews in L. By May 1939, the J. pop. of L. and the neighboring localities was 13. It may be assumed that those who did not emigrate or were not protected by marriage to non-Jews were deported to the east. By Oct. 1942, only one Jew remained in L.

LABINSKAYA Krasnodar territory, Russia. Jews settled in the late 19th cent., among them converts. During the civil war (1918-21), they were robbed and beaten by White Russian gangs. The Germans occupied L. on 7 Aug. 1942. In two *Aktions* in late Aug. and early Sept., the Germans herded Jews into the local school building and murdered 300, including many refugees from the western parts of the Soviet Union. In all, 540 Jews were murdered in the area, mostly refugees.

LABISZYN Poznan dist., Poland. The first Jews settled in 1564. Many died in the Swedish war of the mid-17th cent. and the plague of 1707-11, with most of the others leaving. The J. settlement was renewed in 1816, reaching a pop. of 900 (total 2,200) in 1850, with most engaged in petty trade and shopkeeping. Emigration to the big cities reduced the J. pop. to 376 in 1898, 119 in 1920, and just ten in 1933. Their fate is unknown.

LABOWA   Cracow dist., Poland. The Jews numbered 221 (total 876) in 1921. Under the German occupation from Sept. 1939, they were subjected to persecution and forced labor before being expelled in the first half of 1942 to the Nowy Soncz ghetto for subsequent deportation.

LABUN   Kamenets-Podolski dist., Ukraine. Jews are first mentioned in 1705. In the early 17th cent. they were attacked by Cossacks and Polish soldiers. The J. pop. was 432 in 1765, rising to 1,192 in 1847 and dropping to 952 in 1923. A J. rural council (soviet) and kolkhoz were active in the Soviet period. The Germans occupied L. on 5 July 1941. Most of the Jews were murdered in June–July 1942.

LA CHEBBA   Sfax dist., Tunisia. Jews arrived from Sfax and Sousse and numbered 85 in 1926, most leaving after WWII.

LACHEN   Palatinate, Germany. The J. pop. was 46 (of a total 2,184) in 1875 and 25 in 1900. Two Jews were deported to the Gurs concentration camp in 1940, perishing in the Holocaust.

LACHOWICZE   Nowogrodek dist., Poland, today Belarus. A J. community is first mentioned in 1623, growing to a peak pop. of 3,846 (total 5,016) in 1897. In the mid-19th cent. most of L.'s Jews were Stolin Hasidim but the local dynasty founded by R. Mordekhai ben Noah in the late 18th cent. as an offshoot of Karlin Hasidism gradually got the upper hand, though diminishing in influence after the 1880s. Despite staunch hasidic opposition, the Zionists became active in the 1890s. Economic crisis and the trials of WWI leading to emigration overseas reduced the J. pop. to 1,656 in 1921. Between the World Wars, the Zionists expanded their activities among the young. A Tarbut Hebrew school operated until WWII and 50 students attended a local yeshiva. The Germans captured L. on 26 June 1941. A number of community leaders were murdered on 28 June and a few days later 82 Jews were killed in a local pogrom. On 28 Oct. 1941, 2,000 of the town's 3,500 Jews deemed "unproductive" were executed near the rail-

road station. The rest were confined to a small ghetto together with refugees. Escapes and underground activity were organized but on 10 June 1942 about 1,200 were slaughtered amidst armed resistance. The rest were killed on 25 June despite further fighting.

LACHWA   Polesie dist., Poland, today Belarus. An organized community existed from 1655 and developed with the coming of the railroad, reaching a pop. of 1,057 in 1897 (total 2,426). About a quarter of the J. pop. were Karlin-Stolin Hasidim. The Zionists were active from the late 19th cent. A Hebrew religious school and library existed. The Germans arrived on 8 July 1941 and instituted forced labor, extortion, and property confiscations. A ghetto was set up on 1 April 1942, crowding together 2,350 Jews soon joined by refugees. In anticipation of an *Aktion*, a revolt, one of the first in Poland, was organized. On 3 Sept. 1942 houses were set ablaze and police were attacked as 1,000 Jews burst out of the ghetto. About 600 made it to the forest, where most, along with those who remained behind, were murdered; others fought as partisans; 90 survived the war.

LACKENBACH   Burgenland, Austria. L. was one of the Seven Communities (*Sheva Kehillot*). J. settlement began in 1527. In 1582 a synagogue and a J. cemetery were consecrated. From about 1630 until 1800, Jews were under the protection of the House of Esterhazy. Jews earned their living as shoemakers, hairdressers, tailors, and butchers. They were represented in the professional class as doctors. In 1829 and 1902, fires severely damaged J. houses and the synagogue. About 1910, a splendid synagogue was inaugurated. In 1934, there were approximately 430 Jews in L. Shortly after the *Anschluss* (13 March 1938), J. property was confiscated. In April 1938, the expulsion of Jews from L. began. By Oct. of that year, when the community was officially closed down, some succeeded in emigrating or escaping. Most, however, were sent to Vienna and from there to the east.

LACKIE SZLACHECKIE   Stanislawow dist., Poland, today Ukraine. The J. pop. in 1921 was 133. The Jews were probably expelled to Tlumacz or Stanislawow for liquidation in April–May 1942.

LACKO   Cracow dist., Poland. The J. community numbered 232 (total 2,001) in 1921. After enduring a regime of forced labor and persecution under the Germans, the Jews were expelled to the Nowy Soncz ghetto in early 1942 and subsequently deported to the death camps.

LADENBURG Baden, Germany. Jews are first mentioned in 1291. The community was destroyed in the Black Death persecutions of 1348–49 and new settlers were expelled in 1391. The community was renewed in the mid-17th cent. The well-known Ladenburger family of Court Jews and bankers had its origins there. L. was the seat of the district rabbinate. A J. elementary school was opened in the mid-1830s. The J. pop. reached 114 in 1871, dropping to 88 in 1933 (total 5,111). At the outset of the Nazi era, many Jews were employed as traveling salesmen for foreign companies or as workers in the cigarette factories. Newcomers increased the J. pop. to 136. Forty-six emigrated and 54 left for other German cities in the period. On *Kristallnacht* (9–10 Nov. 1938), the synagogue was vandalized. The last 27 Jews were deported to the Gurs concentration camp on 22 Oct. 1940; another ten were deported after leaving L. Of the 37 deportees, 11 survived the Holocaust.

LADOMIROVA Slovakia, Czechoslovakia, today Republic of Slovakia. Jews from Poland settled in the early 18th cent. and Jews from Galicia in the 1780s. The J. pop. rose from 153 in 1828 to a peak of 309 (total 816) in 1880. After WWI, the Zionists were active. In 1940, the J. pop. was 193. A J. school was opened in the same year. In 1941, the Slovakian authorities forced Jews out of their businesses and young men were seized for forced labor. Young men and women were deported to Majdanek and Auschwitz, respectively, in late March 1942. A few dozen J. families were sent to the Pulawy ghetto in the Lublin dist. of Poland on 17 May. Another 97 Jews were sent to the Rejowiec ghetto in Poland on 24 May.

LADOSHKAYA Krasnodar territory, Russia. Immediately after their arrival in summer 1942, the Germans murdered about 3,000 Jews from the village and county of L., most of them refugees.

LADYZHENKA Kiev dist., Ukraine. Jews numbered 35 in 1790 and 1,173 in 1897. On 14 May 1919, gangs murdered 100 Jews, raped J. women, and looted J. property. In 1939, under the Soviets,

101 Jews remained. The Germans arrived on 29 July 1941 and murdered the Jews soon afterwards.

LADYZHYN Vinnitsa dist., Ukraine. Jews settled in the mid-17th cent. and numbered 303 in 1765 and 3,212 (total 6,589) in 1897. In the Soviet period, the J. pop. declined, to 720 in 1939. In the mid-1920s, about half the Jews were without rights and unemployed. J. artisans, too, were living in straitened economic circumstances. A J. council (soviet) was established in 1925 and a J. elementary school was also in operation in the mid-1920s. The Germans occupied L. on 24 July 1941. *Einsatzgruppe D* units murdered 504 Jews in an *Aktion* on 12 Sept. 1941. After the town was attached to Transnistria, the Rumanians expelled hundreds of Jews there from Trostyanets, Bukovina, and Bessarabia. Some were deported in early 1942 to the Pechera camp on the German side of the Bug River. In mid-Sept. 1942, 550 were sent to the Krasnopole camp. As the fighting drew near, the Germans murdered the last Jews in these camps in Dec. 1943.

LA GOULETTE Tunis dist., Tunisia. The permanent J. settlement was probably founded in the 19th cent. The J. pop. grew after the Bey's constitutional reform of 1857 granted equal rights and residence was officially permitted. The influx of Jews to the city increased still further under the French Protectorate instituted in 1881. After WWI, many arrived from Tunis from among the Touansa (native) J. pop. as opposed to the Jews of Leghorn (Italy) origin. The J. pop. grew from 825 in 1909 to 2,057 (including neighboring Carthage) in 1926 (total 3,426, excluding Europeans). Most Jews lived in the new quarter in the Bratel area, where a central synagogue and three smaller ones were built. R. Rahmine Chemila was the chief rabbi and unofficial head of the community. Many vacationers, including Jews, from Tunis and such distant places as Sfax and Sousse, visited the seaside resort in the summer. Most commerce in the city was in J. hands. The community depended upon Tunis for various services, such as the rabbinical court, a J. secondary school, and specialized medical care. Four *talmudei torah*, attached to the synagogues, operated in L. between the World Wars, supplementing morning classes in the French public school. Zionist activity commenced in 1921 with a Hovevei Zion group of 50 members. Betar operated in the 1930s. Young Jews were particularly active in sports and Jews also dominated the man-

The kutab *(school) in La Goulette, Tunisia (Beth Hatefutsoth Photo Archive, Tel Aviv/courtesy of Roland Fellous, Sarcelles)*

agement of the local athletic clubs. Under the Vichy laws of WWII, Jews in the civil service were dismissed from their jobs. Restrictions were imposed on J. property holders and schoolchildren. With the restraining hand of the French removed, relations with the Arabs also deteriorated. The arrival of the Germans marked the beginning of Allied bombardments. Many Jews fled to Tunis and La Marsa. The Germans set up a labor camp on the coast where Jews from the surrounding area, including Tunis, worked on fortifications and unloaded German ships. The Jews returned when the Allies liberated the city. In 1946, their pop. was 2,577 and in 1956, 3,313 (total 26,323). The renewal of Zionist activity encouraged Hebrew education and led to the founding of a modern J. elementary school in 1952 in place of the outdated *talmudei torah*. Zionist activity was now geared to *aliya*. Among the first to leave for Israel were the leaders of Betar. Tze'irei Tziyyon–Deror then became the leading youth movement. Emigration increased through the 1950s, reaching a peak after Tunisian independence in 1956. The last Jews left during the Bizerte crisis in 1961.

LAGOW   Kielce dist., Poland. Sixty Jews were present in 1827, increasing to 1,269 (total 2,527) in 1921. Difficult economic circumstances both before and after WWI led many to leave in the 1920s. Between the World Wars, the Zionists with their youth movements were active while Gur and Aleksandrow Hasidim gathered around their *shtiblekh*. With the German occupation of Sept. 1939, many of the young fled to Soviet-occupied territory. A regime of forced labor was instituted and a *Judenrat* established. Refugees from Vienna and Radom arrived in 1941 and in March 1942 the J. quarter was sealed off as a ghetto. In July 1942, 460 young Jews were led away to an unknown destination and on 27 Oct., after the sick and old were murdered in their beds along with children, 2,000 were transported to Kielce, from where they were soon deported to the Treblinka death camp.

LAHR   (in J. sources, Lara) Baden, Germany. The small 14th cent. community, inhabiting a special quarter with a synagogue, was destroyed in the Black Death persecutions of 1348–49 and only renewed in the late

19th cent. after emancipation. The J. pop. grew to 141 by 1900 (of a total 13,557). Jews operated large wholesale establishments (shoes, clothing, metal products) and factories, including one of the largest steel plants in Europe. In 1933 the J. pop. stood at 96. Community life expanded, including Zionist activity, with the Habonim youth movement operating from 1935. By 1938, 58 Jews had left, 31 emigrating from Germany (including 14 to the U.S.). Another eight emigrated in 1939–40 after *Kristallnacht* (9–10 Nov. 1938), when J. homes and businesses were vandalized and J. men detained at the Dachau concentration camp. Twenty Jews were deported to the Gurs concentration camp on 22 Oct. 1940; another four were deported to the camps from Holland and seven from other German cities after leaving L. Of all these, only four survived the Holocaust.

LAIZUVA Mazeikiai dist., Lithuania. Jews first settled here in the early 18th cent. A synagogue was built in the 19th cent. after the old one collapsed. After a fire in 1884, Jews and non-Jews responded to an appeal for aid. Many emigrated to South Africa, the U.S., and England; a few went to Eretz Israel. The J. pop. was 434 in 1897 (46% of the total) and 50 in 1940. Most Jews were killed after the German occupation of summer 1941.

LAJOSMIZSE Pest–Pilis–Solt–Kiskun dist., Hungary. Jews settled in the late 19th cent. and were terrorized by the gangs of Ivan Hejjas after WWI. Their pop. declined from a peak of 154 (2% of the total) in 1900 to 52 in 1941. The men were sent to forced labor in 1942 and on 8 July 1944, the 48 remaining Jews in L. were deported to Auschwitz via Monor. There were 18 survivors.

LAKHOVTSY (from 1944, Belogorye) Kamenets-Podolski dist., Ukraine. In 1629 the town numbered 37 J.-owned houses (of a total 318). In 1705–07 (the Swedish wars), the town was completely destroyed in anti-J. pogroms. In 1765, the J. pop. was 589, increasing to 1,384 (26% of the total) in 1897. Pogroms were also staged against the Jews in fall 1917 and early Jan. 1919. In 1939, the J. pop. was 908. The Germans captured the town on 5 July 1941. In early 1942 they starved 160 Jews to death and in June–July they executed 2,300 from L. and its environs at the village of Trostyanka.

LA MARSA Tunis dist., Tunisia. Traces of J. settlement exist from the first cent. C.E. The settlement presumably declined in the Byzantine period and is not heard from again until the late 19th cent, under the French Protectorate. Between the World Wars, the J. pop. declined steadily from 360 in 1921 to 131 in 1936 (total 5,669). Those from Tunis came under French influence and underwent a process of Europeanization. The first synagogue was consecrated in 1927 and a J. summer school was opened to occupy the children of lower middle class J. vacationers at the seaside resort. The location of the Bey's summer palace in the city encouraged Arab nationalism and led to Arab-J. tension but in WWII many Jews from Tunis fled there hoping its existence would prevent Allied bombing. In early 1942, over 400 Jews of French and Tunisian nationality, expelled from Tripolitania by the Italians, arrived in the city and were housed in rickety shacks along the beach. On 10 March 1943, 100 Jews, mainly refugees, and 300 Arabs were killed in an Allied air attack. After the war the community was absorbed by Tunis.

LAMBSHEIM Palatinate, Germany. A few J. families were present in 1343, all burned at the stake following a blood libel. The community was again destroyed in 1349 during the Black Death persecutions. A permanent J. settlement only emerged again in the mid-17th cent. In 1658, there was one family; three in 1703; and seven (43 Jews) in 1743. The J. pop. then grew to 81 in 1803; 152 in 1833; and a peak of 184 in 1848. Most were engaged in petty trade. A cemetery was opened in 1822 and a synagogue was consecrated in 1829 with a *mikve* attached. With the founding of a J. elementary school in 1842, a classroom and an apartment for the teacher-*hazzan* (who also served as the *shohet* from 1845) were set up in the synagogue. The municipality partially financed the school, which reached an enrollment of 23–37 in the 1842–58 period. Declining attendance caused it to close down in 1874. A society to aid the sick was founded in 1856. The J. pop. dropped to 95 in 1876 and 65 in 1900. In 1933 the J. pop. was 31 with 18 Jews from Weisenheim a. Sand and one from Eppstein belonging to the congregation. In 1938, 11 Jews remained. On *Kristallnacht* (9–10 Nov. 1938), Hitler Youth burned the contents of the synagogue and J. homes and stores were wrecked. In all, 25 Jews left L. in the 1933–40 period: 11 for the U.S., two for England, one for France, and 11 for other cities in Germany. The eight remaining Jews were deported to the Gurs concentration camp in Oct. 1940, five perishing along with another Jew originally from L.

LAMPERTHEIM   Hesse, Germany. There are references to Jews living in L. from 1615. The community, numbering 160 (3% of the pop.) in 1861, was affiliated with Darmstadt's Liberal rabbinate. After the synagogue was burned down on *Kristallnacht* (9–10 Nov. 1938), SS men tortured a Jew to death and some townsfolk helped to destroy J. property. Most of the 85 Jews living there in 1933 had left by 1939; three were deported to Auschwitz in 1942. Several thousand Displaced Persons from Eastern Europe established a new community in L. after WWII, but almost all of them emigrated to Israel.

LANCUT   Lwow dist., Poland. A J. community with a wooden synagogue and cemetery existed in the late 16th cent. With Austrian rule from 1772, 11 smaller settlements came under its aegis. Its magnificent synagogue, built in 1761, was damaged in WWII but has been restored as a museum. Yaakov Yitzhak Horowitz, "the Seer of Lublin" (1745–1818), was active in L. in the late 18th cent. and the burial in the town of Naftali Tzevi of Ropshits attracted thousands of hasidic pilgrims every year. The hasidic character of the J. community was strengthened by the residence of Elimelekh of Lyzhansk in the nearby town of that name. Despite hasidic opposition, Haskala began to make modest inroads in the 1870s and the first Zionist group was formed in 1894. The J. pop. stood at 1,940 in 1900 (total 4,850). During WWI, the Jews suffered looting and arson as the town changed hands between the Russians and Austrians. In its aftermath a J. militia was organized for self-defense. Despite J. ownership of 71 factories in 1921 (mainly food and clothing, but for the most part employing only family members), economic decline marked the period between the World Wars as depressed conditions, economic boycotts, and Polish competition eroded J. livelihoods. Support from the Joint Distribution Committee became extensive. Nonetheless, Zionist activity expanded, with almost all the Zionist parties represented. Agudat Israel was also active, founding a Beth Jacob school for 100 girls. The Germans entered L. on 9 Sept. 1939 and on 22–23 Sept. expelled all but 300 of the town's 2,750 Jews to Soviet-held territory. Refugees and re-

turning residents brought the J. pop. up to 1,300 in late 1940, barely staying alive by selling off personal effects. The *Judenrat* organized a soup kitchen, bakery, and clinic. With the outbreak of war between Germany and the Soviet Union, more of the previously expelled Jews began to return, starting in Nov. 1941. Some were murdered by the Germans and sporadic killing continued through 1942. Final expulsion came on 3 Aug. 1942 when the Jews were transported to a transit camp in Jaroslaw, robbed of their possessions, and deported to the Belzec death camp after the old and sick were murdered along with the children. Nine hundred of L.'s Jews survived the war, mostly in the Soviet Union. They settled in other cities in Poland but before long emigrated.

LANCZYN   Stanislawow dist., Poland, today Ukraine. The small community numbered 383 (total 4,152) in 1921 and was presumably expelled to Nadworna in the summer of 1942 if not liquidated earlier.

LANDAU   Palatinate, Germany. First mention of a Jew dates from 1273 and a small J. community existed by 1292. The Jews abandoned the town in the Black Death persecutions of 1348–49, returning in 1353. Their number was restricted to ten families in 1517. They engaged in moneylending and traded in spices and medicinal herbs. In 1541, the city council required them to wear a yellow badge and in the following years their trading rights were subject to severe restrictions. A synagogue was opened in 1648 and a new one was built after it burned down in 1691. In the early 18th cent., Jews monopolized the salt, textile, and wine trade, supplied nearby army camps with food, and dealt in cattle and grain. Dr. Elias Gruenebaum became regional rabbi in 1837 and served for 57 years, advocating both religious reform and equal rights for Jews. A new and luxurious synagogue was consecrated in 1884. A private J. school was opened in 1837 but closed in 1869 when the town's parochial schools were amalgamated. In 1864–67, two Jews served on the municipal council. Simon Levi became community chairman in 1870, serving in the Landrat and sitting on the municipal council from 1868 to 1900. Jews continued to be elected to the municipal council until the Nazi era. The J. pop. rose from 237 in 1810 to a peak of 821 (of a total 15,824) in 1900. In the 1890s and through the Weimar period, over 60% of the wine merchants in the city were Jews. In June

1933, about four months after the Nazi rise to power, there were 596 Jews in L. Already in March 1933, a J. state attorney was severely beaten. Similar physical assaults became a recurring pattern in the following years. In 1935, Jews were banned from using public facilities. In early 1938, "Jews Not Welcome Here" signs were hung in stores, banks, the post office, and the train station. Gas stations were forbidden to serve Jews and the Nazified municipality even considered banning Jews from obtaining heating materials, gas, electricity, and water. On *Kristallnacht* (9–10 Nov. 1938), axe-wielding SA troops destroyed J. homes and set the synagogue on fire. J. men were sent to the Dachau concentration camp and women were dispatched to Mannheim with their children. Between 1933 and late 1939, 226 Jews left L. for other German cities. Five were deported to Poland in Oct. 1938 and 260 emigrated, including 115 to the U.S. On 22 Oct. 1940, 35 Jews were deported to the Gurs concentration camp. In all, at least 158 of the J. inhabitants of L. in 1933 were deported to Nazi concentration camps.

LANDECK (I)   (Pol. Ladek Zdroj) Lower Silesia, Germany, today Poland. Though Jews visited the local mineral baths, they only settled in 1843. Their number rose from eight in 1850 to 34 in 1906. The community maintained a prayer house and a cemetery from 1926. On the eve of the Nazi rise to power in 1933, the J. pop. was 25. After the promulgation of the Nuremberg Laws in 1935, Jews were banned from bathing together with "Aryans" and were sent to a separate room at the public baths. In 1937, seven Jews remained. On *Kristallnacht* (9–10 Nov. 1938), rioters destroyed a J.-owned store. No information is available on the fate of the Jews in WWII. Presumably those who were unable to emigrate were deported and perished.

LANDECK (II)   (Pol. Ledyczek) Posen-West Prussia, Germany, today Poland. Jews are first mentioned in 1724. The J. pop. grew from 25 in 1799 to 143 in 1831 (24% of the total) and a peak of 193 in 1880. The community established a cemetery and in the beginning of the 1920s a synagogue. On the eve of the Nazi assumption of power in 1933, 45 Jews were living in L. On *Kristallnacht* (9–10 Nov. 1938), the synagogue was destroyed and J. businesses were demolished. The remaining Jews were interned in March 1940 in the Buergergarten camp near Schneidemuehl and deported to the east shortly afterwards.

LANDESHUT   (Pol. Kamienna Gora) Lower Silesia, Germany. Jews were granted residence rights in 1812 and numbered 53 in 1840. They maintained a prayer house and two cemeteries (from 1824 and 1880). A synagogue was consecrated in 1858. The J. pop. reached a peak of 177 in 1884 but dropped to 74 by the start of the Nazi era. Most Jews left in the face of Nazi persecution, with just 14 remaining in 1939. On *Kristallnacht* (9–10 Nov. 1938), four J. business establishments were destroyed. No information is available as to the fate of the community during WWII. Presumably those Jews who were unable to leave were deported and died.

LANDSBERG   (Pol. Gorowo Ilaweckie) East Prussia, Germany, today Poland. The J. pop. stood at 211 in 1858, dropping to 77 in 1884. The community consecrated a synagogue in 1865 and maintained a cemetery. Windows of J. businesses were broken in 1932. Of the 22 Jews there when the Nazis assumed power, only two were still living in L. by Oct. 1942, probably protected by marriage to non-Jews. It may be assumed that the other J. residents, if they did not emigrate, were deported.

LANDSBERG AN DER WARTHE   (Pol. Gorzow Wielkopolski) Brandenburg, Germany, today Poland. Jews were probably living in L. in the middle of the 14th cent. and possibly until the expulsion of all Jewry from Brandenburg in 1573. From 1655, as a result of the Swedish invasion of Poland, J. refugees from Greater Poland found shelter in the town. In 1671, they were joined by Jews who had been expelled from Vienna. By 1690, the J. community numbered 21 families and had a rabbi. In 1765, there were 45 families. The J. pop. was 304 in 1817 and 730 in 1871. A synagogue was dedicated in 1755 and a combined poorhouse-hospital in 1766. The community was Liberal and in 1910 the J. pop. was 449. At the beginning of the 20th cent., there were branches of the Central Union (C.V.), the Union for Liberal Judaism, and a B'nei B'rith lodge. Zionist influence was felt at the latest in the early Weimar days. In 1927, a J. old age home serving Brandenburg and the Grenzmark was established. In 1932, Nazis attacked and seriously injured a Jew and the house of a senior J. district-court official was damaged in a bomb attack. By June 1933, about four months after the Nazis assumed power, there were 435 Jews in L. The local branch of the German Zionist Organization and a Hehalutz group, founded at the beginning of 1934, were active in helping community members to emigrate. By 1934, the J. pop. was 285 and in 1939 it was 95. It may be assumed that those who failed to emigrate were deported to the east. In Nov. 1944, there were four Jews in L., probably protected by marriage to non-Jews.

LANDSHUT   Lower Bavaria, Germany. The 13th cent. J. community was destroyed in 1338 in the wake of the massacre of the Jews in nearby Deggendorf. The renewed community was expelled in 1452. The modern community, attached to Straubing, was organized in the late 19th cent. and numbered 48 in 1933 (total 30,858). Seventeen managed to emigrate until 1939, mostly to England and the U.S. Another 14 left for other German cities, mainly Munich. Of those remaining, six committed suicide and 11 were expelled to Piaski in the Lublin dist. (Poland) on 2 April 1942.

LANDSTUHL   Palatinate, Germany. Jews were present in the Middle Ages but were expelled in the 16th cent. From 1868, they again lived in the town, reaching a peak pop. of 81 in 1925. Most were cattle traders with some dealing in clothing. The community maintained a prayer room and a cemetery (established in 1895). In June 1933, about four months after the Nazi takeover, there were 61 Jews (total 5,539) in L. In 1936, with emigration mounting, 12 belonged to the Zionist movement. Twenty-six Jews remained in 1938. On *Kristallnacht* (9–10 Nov. 1938), the synagogue was set on fire and J. homes and stores were destroyed. The last seven able-bodied Jews were deported to the Gurs concentration camp on 21–22 Oct. 1940.

LANGEN   Hesse, Germany. Founded by petty traders in the late 17th cent., the community grew from 60 (2% of the total) in 1861 to 102 in 1910. After WWI, its allegiance changed from the Orthodox to the Liberal rabbinate of Darmstadt. In May 1935, after the synagogue was desecrated by hooligans, the community proclaimed a fast day. On *Kristallnacht* (9–10 Nov. 1938), local Nazis burned down the synagogue and a courageous Social Democrat rescued the 19 remaining Jews from the mob. Of the 53 Jews living

there in 1933, 25 emigrated and the rest left before 1939. A memorial to the synagogue was erected by L.'s town council in 1947.

LANGENDIEBACH   (now part of Erlensee) Hesse–Nassau, Germany. Jews lived there from the 17th cent. and the J. community numbered 100 (7% of the total) in 1861. On *Kristallnacht* (9–10 Nov. 1938), the synagogue was destroyed; 21 Jews emigrated by 1939 and 11 were deported in 1942.

LANGENDORF   (Pol. Wielowies) Upper Silesia, Germany, today Poland. The J. pop. was 75 in 1900, dropping to 35 in 1906. The community maintained a prayer house but used the nearby Gleiwitz J. cemetery. In 1933, the J. pop. was 30. Nazi racial laws were not enforced in L. until July 1937 since the Jews came under the protection of the League of Nations' minority rights convention. On *Kristallnacht* (9–10 Nov. 1938), the prayer house was set on fire. A number of Jews managed to emigrate. All the rest were deported to General Gouvernement territory in May and June 1942 and presumably did not survive the war.

LANGENLONSHEIM   Rhineland, Germany. Jews are first mentioned in the late 17th cent. Their pop. reached ten families (32 Jews) in the early 19th cent. and in 1848 they numbered 141. In 1848, 23 engaged in trade, three were artisans, and 11 were day laborers or beggars. A cemetery was opened in the first half of the 18th cent. and a synagogue was erected in 1856. The J. pop. subsequently dropped to 91 (total 1,433) in 1871 and 40 in 1932. Under the Nazis, a number of Jews were sent early on to the camps in 1933. A few emigrated but most left for other localities in Germany, from where they were later deported to their deaths in the camps. Including the last five Jews deported directly from L., the number of Jews who perished in the Holocaust reached 34. The synagogue was seriously damaged on *Kristallnacht* (9–10 Nov. 1938), and razed in 1958.

LANGENSELBOLD   Hesse–Nassau, Germany. Established in the late 17th cent., the community dedicated a synagogue in 1714 (enlarged in 1849), maintained a J. elementary school from 1824 to 1934, and was strictly Orthodox. Affiliated with the rabbinate of Hanau, its members engaged in the livestock trade. They numbered 178 (over 6% of the total) in

1861 and 226 (4%) in 1933. The synagogue's interior and its Torah scrolls were burned immediately after *Kristallnacht* (9–10 Nov. 1938). By 1940, 172 Jews had left (97 emigrating); at least 41 died in the Holocaust.

LANGERWEHE Rhineland, Germany. Jews are mentioned in the second half of the 17th cent. and numbered 45 in 1871 and 38 in 1925. A synagogue was dedicated in 1899 and the community also maintained a cemetery. The community was affiliated to Dueren. At least 22 were deported and perished in the Holocaust.

LANG-GOENS Hesse, Germany. Jews lived there from the late 18th cent., numbering 64 (4% of the total) in 1861. The community dwindled to ten in 1933, when the synagogue was demolished. Three Jews emigrated, one committed suicide, and six were eventually deported.

LANGHADA (Langadas, Langaza) Salonika dist., Greece. A small J. community was established in L. in the late 19th cent. The J. pop. in 1928 numbered 161 (of a total 47,276), dropping to 50 by 1940. All were sent on the first transport to Auschwitz from Salonika on 15 March 1943.

LANGSDORF Hesse, Germany. Numbering 65 (7% of the pop.) in 1880, this Orthodox community faced recurrent waves of antisemitism. One Jew was murdered in a Nazi pogrom in 1934. By Oct. 1938 the remaining 20 Jews had emigrated or moved elsewhere.

LANOWCE Volhynia dist., Poland, today Ukraine. Jews probably settled after 1569 when municipal charters were granted under the Polish king. The J. pop. numbered 1,174 in 1897 (total 2,525) and 640 in 1921 after a series of pogroms and disturbances. A Tarbut school operated alongside a small yeshiva and the Zionists with their youth movements were active. Sporadic killing and forced labor under brutal Ukrainian guards accompanied the German occupation from 3 July 1941. In the *Aktion* liquidating the ghetto on 13–14 Aug. 1942, 1,833 Jews including refugees were murdered beside open pits.

LAPANOW Cracow dist., Poland. The Jews numbered 230 in 1880 and 114 in 1921 (total 468). They were expelled by the Germans to Bochnia on 23 Aug. 1942 and suffered the fate of the local Jews.

LAPICHI Mogilev dist., Belorussia. Jews numbered 24 in 1811 and 736 (98% of the total) in 1897. In 1925, under the Soviets, the J. pop. of 143 families consisted of 72 artisans, 24 blue-collar workers, 22 white-collar workers, and 22 engaged in petty trade. Three owned small factories. A J. school was active. The Germans captured L. in early July 1941. On 25 July, the Jews attempted to flee but were cut off by the rapid German advance and forced to return. On 27 Aug., 107 Jews were shot. The rest were murdered in a second *Aktion*, on 12 March 1942.

LAPY Bialystok dist., Poland. A small community was formed in the 19th cent., trading in farm produce and engaging in crafts. In 1921, the J. pop. was 623 (total 3,495). Almost all the Zionist groups were active between the World Wars. The Germans took the city in Sept. 1939, immediately executing 13 of the community's leading figures. On 2 Nov. 1942, the 400 remaining Jews were murdered in the Kossaki forest.

L'ARIANA (also al-Ariana) Tunis dist., Tunisia. Jews from Andalusia reached A. in the 17th cent. When Jews from Algeria settled there in the 18th cent. the al-Ghariba synagogue was built in A.'s northwest section and a J. community nucleus coalesced around it. Tunis, 2.5 miles (4 km) away, supplied A.'s religious needs and schooling. In 1909, A. had 153 Jews (15.3% of the total); 2,619 (47.4%) in 1936; and 3,128 (32.4%) in 1946. From 1857, J. residence in A. became legal and the community developed. Under the French Protectorate (from the end of the 19th cent.). A. became a resort town with many Jews earning their livelihood from tourists. By 1909, there were two Jews serving on the city council. In the 1920s, many Jews moved there from Tunis seeking an improved quality of life. A J. school called Kutab Kisrawi was opened, the first modern *talmud torah* in Tunisia and a hub of communal and religious activity. The school committee in fact ran community affairs. R. Avraham Smaja served as principal in 1923–67. Other synagogues opened in A.'s new quarter, mostly inhabited by Jews. In 1920, the Tunis J. community sponsored an old age home in A. Zionist activities blossomed during the 1920s and 1930s and Betar and Hashomer Hatzair branches were opened. At about the same time, violent anti-J. acts, carried out by the Muslim pop., also increased. French soldiers instigated an antisemitic fracas during Passover 1924. The riots damaged the Soraya synagogue, J.-owned cafes, and other property. In WWII, the Germans occupied A. shortly after invading Tunisia (Nov. 1942). J. men served as forced laborers, some at the Bizerta camp, others at a camp established locally. Three Jews from A. assumed responsibility for organizing the workers. An 18-year-old yeshiva student, Victor-Haim Nataf, was arrested by the Germans during the first Allied bombing (13 Dec. 1942) and executed for signaling to the Allied planes. He became a symbol, his name synonymous with the maltreatment of Tunisian Jews by the Nazis. After the war, a street was named after him in A. The second Allied bombing, on 6 Jan. 1943, hit the J. labor camp. After the war, J. life returned to normal, with the Kisrawi school reopening. An ORT school for boys was established. Several of A.'s Jews left for Israel in 1948. After Tunisian independence (1956), most Jews emigrated to France.

LARINDORF Crimea, Russia, today Ukraine. L. was probably founded in the 1920s as a farm settlement within the framework of J. agricultural settlement in the Crimea. It had a J. pop. of 125 families in 1932. In 1935, when the Fraydorf dist. was divided, L. became the center of a new J. region. L. was the seat of a J. rural council (soviet) and had a J. school. Of the 18 councils in the county, eight were J., as were 21 of the 53 kolkhozes under their jurisdiction. A J. high school (probably regional) was still open in the settlement in the late 1930s and a J. cultural center was completed in 1937. In 1939 the J. regional pop. was 3,492. A number of Jews fled to Simferopol before the German occupation of late Oct. 1941, sharing the fate of the local Jews. The rest were probably murdered in Nov. or Dec. 1941 after finishing the seasonal farm work. About 400 Jews from the area were murdered during the occupation, including 61 in the village of Kamenka in Jan. 1942 and 119 in such J. kolkhozes as Yudendorf, Der Emes, and Lekert in June 1942.

LARINO Dnepropetrovsk dist., Ukraine. L. was a J. farm settlement founded in 1923 during the Soviet period by emigrants, "classless" Ukrainian Jews, and particularly by Jews from Tagancha, who were dispersed when General Denikin and his White Army attacked

the town. The L. council (soviet) was attached to the Stalindorf J. Autonomous Region and included within its bounds 2,639 Jews in 1930 (total 3,795). In 1933, the three J. settlements (of a total of six) belonging to the council numbered 1,345 residents, most of them living in L., where the only farm machine shop in the region was located. Most Jews in the area were farmers or craftsmen, with some employed in the sock factory at the nearby Kolektivizator kolkhoz, where about 30 J. families were living in 1931. The J. pop. of the council settlements was 748 in 1939. The Germans arrived in mid-Aug. 1941 and in May 1942 probably murdered the few Jews who had neither fled nor been evacuated.

LARISSA (Larisa, Yenisehir) Thessaly, Greece. Jews first settled in L. in the fifth cent. The small Romaniot community (dating from the Byzantine period) flourished under Ottoman rule (from the late 14th cent.). In the 16th and 17th cents., a small Sephardi congregation also existed. Many Jews dealt in moneylending, the textile trade, and peddling. During the 17th–19th cents., a number of emissaries from Eretz Israel visited and became involved in settling community disputes. In 1685, many Jews, especially from Patras and Lamia, fleeing the Venetian conquerors settled in L. In the 18th cent., an umbrella organization of the various congregations was established and some wealthy members founded charitable institutions. Following the Greek revolt of 1821, many Jews left for Salonika. The J. pop. in 1848 was 1,500 (total 6,000). With the Greek nationalist ferment of the 1850s, the Jews encountered financial difficulties. In 1857, a severe fire destroyed two synagogues and left 250 J. families without means. The Alliance Israelite ran a J. school from 1868 to 1874, alongside the existing school for religious studies. Anti-J. agitation found expression in the 1870s; emigration to Salonika increased and the community declined. The J. pop. in 1880 was about 2,000. L. was annexed to Greece in 1881. There was a blood libel in 1893. In 1896, an organization to assist the poor was established. In 1897 the Greek-Turkish war left the Jews in financial distress; many J. homes and shops were plundered. The Greeks accused the Jews of being Turkish sympathizers and persecuted them. Once the Turks were defeated hundreds of Jews emigrated to Turkey. Emigration to Greek towns ensued over the following decades and the J. pop. dropped to 1,069 in 1907. Zionist organizations were established in the early 20th cent, the Alliance Israelite school was reopened, and cultural movements were founded. In the Balkan wars (1912–13), 72 L. Jews joined the fighting ranks. In the 1920s, there were seven synagogues in L., serving a pop. of 1,175 in 1940. In spring 1941, bombing and an earthquake forced the inhabitants of L. to escape to neighboring villages. Under Italian rule, the Jews were not persecuted and J. refugees from Salonika escaping to Athens passed through L. Many received false identification cards and passports and were assisted by the Italian military to reach Athens. Because of the severe hunger in Greece at this time, many Jews had no alternative but to return to L. from late 1941 until 1943. The Germans then arrived and many fled again to the villages in the surrounding mountains, assisted by the partisan movement. Some Jews remained and in March 1944, 235 were arrested by the Germans; 225 were deported

to the Auschwitz death camp, only six of whom survived. After the war, survivors returned to L. and the community was revived. It grew to be one of the largest in Greece, after Athens and Salonika.

LASK   Lodz dist., Poland. In the 16th cent., Jews were granted permission by the lord of the town to practice their religion, engage in trade and crafts, and build houses. During the 17th and 18th cents., the J. community was the largest in the region and many surrounding communities were subordinate to it. L. was a center of J. learning and several famous rabbis served the community. Restrictions were imposed on the Jews by the Prussian conquerors in 1793 and the community's fortunes waned. The situation worsened in the first half of the 19th cent., when the satellite communities ceased to pay levies. A yeshiva was opened at the beginning of the 19th cent., headed by

Commerce in Lask, Poland, 1937

R. Yehuda Leib Zilberberg and later by R. David Dov Meisels. During this period, the hasidic movement became strong. The J. pop. in 1897 was 2,862 (68% of the total). Between the World Wars, the Jews supplied services to nearby summer vacation resorts. During the economic slump over 500 persons requested assistance from J. welfare institutions. In this period the Zionist movements flourished and Ha-No'ar ha-Tziyyoni had a training farm which functioned until 1938. At first the community was run by representatives of the Zionists, but in the mid-1920s Agudat Israel gained control. When the Germans entered the city in Sept. 1939, they turned the synagogue into a stable and a slaughterhouse. They pillaged J. property and demanded huge sums of money from the community's coffers. A *Judenrat* was set up and the Germans and Poles forced the Jews to work in restoring the bridges leading to the town. The ghetto was established in March 1940 and in Nov. the remaining Jews were brutally transferred there. A hospital and private teachers operated in the ghetto. From fall 1940, a few hundred Jews were sent to various labor camps. In Sept. 1939 L.'s J. pop. numbered 3,864 and in Oct. 1940 there were 2,837 in the ghetto, including 630 refugees. On 24 Aug. 1942, 3,500 Jews were held in a church outside the city for several days. Some 900 able-bodied men were taken to work in the Lodz ghetto and the remainder were deported to Chelmno.

LASKARZEW Lublin dist., Poland. Jews settled in the late 18th cent. and grew in number from 157 in 1857 to 1,258 (total 2,821) in 1897 as J. tailors made L. a center for readymade wear. Nine small villages were attached to the community and a synagogue was completed in 1893. After WWI, the Zionists renewed prewar activity, joined by the Bund and Agudat Israel. With the loss of the Russian market, the clothing trade collapsed and most Jews lost their sources of income. On the eve of WWII, there were 1,476 Jews in L. After capturing L. on 17 Sept. 1939, the Germans executed 38 of the town's J. defenders. Another 27 were murdered on 21 Nov. A *Judenrat* was established in late 1939, charged with supplying forced labor, and a ghetto was set up in Oct. 1940. In an *Aktion* begun on 30 Sept. 1942, 400 Jews were deported to the Treblinka death camp after hundreds escaped to the forests. In the next month, another 800 were hunted down in the forests and executed. In Nov. 1943, five Poles were killed for hiding two Jews. After liberation

by the Red Army in Oct. 1944, 17 survivors returned to L. but when three were murdered by the Polish underground in 1945, all left.

LASKOD Szabolcs dist., Hungary. Jews settled in the late 18th cent. They numbered 43 in 1880 and 59 in 1930. In April 1944, they were sent to Kisvarda and on 25–27 May deported to Auschwitz.

LASKOWCE Tarnopol dist., Poland. The J. pop. in 1921 was 126. The Jews were expelled to Trembowla for liquidation in Oct. 1942.

LASOCIN Kielce dist., Poland. Jews were present by the first half of the 19th cent. and numbered about 100 on the eve of WWII. They were expelled by the Germans to the Ozarow ghetto in summer 1942 and deported from there to the Treblinka death camp in Oct. 1942.

LASZCZOW Lublin dist., Poland. Jews were present by the first half of the 17th cent., reaching a peak pop. of 1,626 (total 1,806) in 1897. In Sept. 1920, rampaging Cossacks staged a violent pogrom, raping 100 J. women. Many left the city and by 1921 the J. pop. had dropped to 1,041, with Jews barely eking out a living between the World Wars. The Germans arrived in late Sept. 1939 and after maintaining a regime of forced labor and extortion deported the Jews to the Belzec death camp on 17 May 1942.

LATHEN Hanover, Germany. After settling there in 1822, Jews from Soegel acquired their own burial ground and prayer house, maintaining links with the Soegel community but enjoying congregational independence under the law of secession (1876). By 1913, this Orthodox community had grown to 47 and a new synagogue was dedicated in 1932. Stormtroopers burned the synagogue on *Kristallnacht* (9–10 Nov. 1938) and the assembled male worshipers were dispatched to the Sachsenhausen concentration camp. Ten Jews emigrated (nine to Holland) and the others were eventually deported. At least 17 perished in the Riga ghetto and in the Auschwitz and Dachau concentration camps. Only a handful survived.

LATOWICZ Warsaw dist., Poland. A J. settlement existed from the late 16th cent., with few remaining after an expulsion order in 1599. The community was reestablished in the first half of the 19th cent., numbering 172 after WWI and spread over 18 neighboring villages. All were deported to the Treblinka death camp on 14 Oct. 1942.

LAUBACH-RUPPERTSBURG Hesse, Germany. The community, dating from the early 18th cent., numbered 115 (5% of the total) in 1861, but dwindled to 50 in 1910 and 35 in 1933. On *Kristallnacht* (9–10 Nov. 1938), the synagogue was vandalized and most of the remaining Jews then left; eight were deported in 1942.

LAUBAN (Pol. Luban) Lower Silesia, Germany, today Poland. J. settlement began no earlier than the mid-19th cent. The J. pop. was 36 in 1925 and 26 on the eve of the Nazi era, when the community was attached to the Goerlitz congregation. In 1939, 19 Jews remained and in 1942, four Jews were sent to the nearby Tormersdorf camp. Other than these details, nothing is known about the fate of the Jews under Nazi rule. Presumably those unable to emigrate were deported and died.

LAUDENBACH (I) Wuerttemberg, Germany. The community suffered in the Armleder massacres of 1336–39 and in the Thirty Years War (1618–1648) and grew from 74 in 1807 to 155 in 1854 before members began emigrating. A J. elementary school was opened in the 1840s but closed in 1911 for lack of students. The synagogue was vandalized on *Kristallnacht* (9–10 Nov. 1938) and partially blown up in Dec. 1938. Of the 13 Jews in L. in 1933, four may have survived the Holocaust.

LAUDENBACH (II) (in J. sources, Ladboch, Loytibach) Lower Franconia, Germany. The J. community was founded in the first half of the 17th cent. With many other communities in the Wuerzburg region it was under the aegis of the chief rabbinate at Heidingsfeld until the early 19th cent. A synagogue was in existence in 1736 and a cemetery known from the 17th cent. served numerous other communities. The J. pop. was 179 in 1816 (total 892) and 79 in 1933. In 1933–40, 21 Jews emigrated (12 to Palestine and nine to the U.S.) and 40 left for other German cities (half to Wuerzburg). J. homes were vandalized during the Sudetenland crisis (Sept. 1938) and on *Kristallnacht* (9–10 Nov. 1938), when the synagogue was also wrecked. Eleven Jews were deported to Izb-

Community center and Jewish school, Laudenbach, Lower Franconia, Germany

ica in the Lublin dist. (Poland) on 25 April 1942 and the last two to the Theresienstadt ghetto on 10 Sept. 1942.

LAUDONA Livonia dist., Latvia. The J. pop. in 1930 was 47. Under the German occupation, the Jews were murdered by Latvian police in fall 1941.

LAUENBURG (Pol. Lebork) Pomerania, Germany, today Poland. In 1752, there were 15 Jews living in L. In 1812, the J. community numbered 15 families and by 1871 it had grown to 381 members. A synagogue was established in 1845, followed by two cemeteries. The antisemitic riots which broke out in Pomerania when the Neustettin synagogue was burned down in 1881 spread to L. When the Nazis came to power in 1933, the community numbered 239 Jews. By 1935, numbers had shrunk to 184 and severe boycott measures were in force. On *Kristallnacht* (9–10 Nov. 1938), the synagogue and the mortuary at the cemetery were set on fire. By May 1939, 104 Jews and 12 individuals of partial J. origin (*Mischlinge*) remained in the town. No further information is available about their fate.

LAUFENSELDEN (now part of Heidenroth) Hesse–Nassau, Germany. Established around 1712, the community opened a synagogue in 1861. There were 90 Jews (8% of the total) in 1895. Affiliated with the Wiesbaden rabbinate, the community dwindled to 34 in 1933. The synagogue was destroyed on *Kristallnacht* (9–10 Nov. 1938), and by April 1939 all the Jews had left.

LAUFERSWEILER Rhineland, Germany. Individual Jews were probably present in the 17th cent. The J. pop. was 36 in 1808 and reached a peak of 156 (total 799) in 1895. Jews were cattle traders and butchers. A new synagogue was built after a fire in 1839 destroyed the old one along with ten J. homes. In 1911 a third synagogue was built. A J. school enrolled 48 children in 1903. On the eve of the Nazi rise to power in 1933, about 80 Jews lived in L. In 1936, 56 remained, many leaving before 1940. The synagogue was destroyed on *Kristallnacht* (9–10 Nov. 1938). In 1942, seven were deported to the east and ten to the Theresienstadt ghetto. It may be assumed that all those who did not make it in time to safe havens perished in the Holocaust.

LAUKUVA Taurage dist., Lithuania. Jews first settled in the 18th cent. The J. pop. in 1897 was 418 (55% of the total). Between the World Wars many emigrated to the west, South Africa, and Palestine. A *talmud torah*, Hebrew school, and social welfare and Zionist organizations were in operation. The J. pop. in 1940 was about 300 (37% of the total). After the German invasion in June 1941, 70 men were taken to the Silute (Heydekrug) labor camp. In July 1943 they were sent to the gas chambers of Auschwitz. The women and children were murdered in July 1941 at the Giruliai camp and in Dec. 1941 at Rainiai.

LAUPHEIM Wuerttemberg, Germany. An early J. settlement apparently ended in the Black Death persecutions of 1348–49. The settlement was renewed in 1742 under various disabilities and grew to be the largest in Wuerttemberg in 1856 with a J. pop. of 796 despite large-scale emigration to the U.S. (balanced by an influx from other communities). Jews were a dominant factor in the trade in hops and leather

and in the course of the 19th cent. became active in banking and industry, owning textile, wood-processing, and wig factories. The town's first printing press was set up by a Jew in 1844 and a disproportionate number of Jews were university graduates, mainly in medicine and law. Relations with the local pop. were generally satisfactory, with Jews serving on the municipal council after receiving civil rights in 1869. The first synagogue was founded in 1822 and a year later a J. elementary school was opened, reaching an enrollment of 162 in 1874. A girls' vocational school was also operated by the community. After 1869, when the J. pop. reached a peak of 852 (of a total 3,800), the number of Jews declined steadily. In 1933 it stood at 231, suffering severe persecution and economic boycott throughout the Nazi era. On *Kristallnacht* (9–10 Nov. 1938), the synagogue was set on fire and nearly 40 Jews were interned in the Dachau concentration camp. By 1938 most J. businesses had been closed or "Aryanized." Many were able to emigrate through the efforts of former townsman Carl Laemmle (1867–1939), founder of Universal Studios in Hollywood. In all, at least 134 left Germany; another 74 were expelled to their deaths in the Riga ghetto in late 1941 and to the Theresienstadt ghetto in Aug. 1942. A refugee camp was set up in the town after the war, accommodating 2,000 Jews by 1948 when it was dismantled and the Jews emigrated to Israel.

LAUTERBACH Hesse, Germany. Jews were forbidden to settle here until the mid-19th cent. and only established a community in 1898. Affiliated with Giessen's Orthodox rabbinate, it numbered 121 (3% of the total) in 1905 and—unlike most in Hesse—continued to grow after WWI, numbering 139 in 1925. After 1933, however, the Nazi boycott forced Jews to leave. On *Kristallnacht* (9–10 Nov. 1938), townsfolk destroyed the synagogue's interior before SA and SS troops arrived to set the building on fire; Hitler Youth also vandalized J. property. The 132 Jews who lived there in 1933 had all left by 1940, more than half settling elsewhere in Germany.

LAUTERBOURG (Ger. Lauterburg) Bas-Rhin dist., France. The Jews of L. are first mentioned in the 13th cent. They suffered during the Black Death persecutions of 1348–49. In 1760, a synagogue was constructed. The community numbered 89 members by

1784 and 293 in 1865. After the Franco-Prussian War of 1870–71, the J. pop. declined. In 1900 there were only 64 Jews in L., dropping to 43 in 1936. During WWII, the Germans expelled all to the south of France. In 1956, only ten Jews remained in L.

LAWOCZNE   Stanislawow dist., Poland, today Ukraine. The J. pop. in 1921 was 140. The Germans arrived on 15 Aug. 1941 and instituted a reign of terror. The men were put to forced labor and after a series of killings, 160 Jews remained in Aug. 1942. They were deported to the Belzec death camp via Skole on 4 Sept. 1942.

LAZDIJAI   (Yid. Lazdai) Saini dist., Lithuania. Jews first settled in 1689. Despite several devastating fires in the 19th cent. the J. community was well organized. The J. pop. in 1897 was 1,439 (57% of the total). During WWI the Jews were expelled, most returning later. In the 1930s, Lithuanians boycotted J. businesses. Many young Jews moved to Kovno or emigrated to the west. There were several synagogues, a religious Hebrew school, a yeshiva, library, social welfare organizations, and cultural activities. All Zionist parties were represented in L. and two training kibbutzim were in operation. The J. pop. in 1939 was 1,212 (40%). After the Germans entered on 22 June 1941, the Jews were concentrated in one or two shacks. Suspected J. Communists were taken to Marijampole and murdered. In Sept., all the Jews were moved to ghetto barracks in Katkiskes. The men were sent to forced labor. On 3 Nov. 1941, the Jews were shot and buried in previously prepared mass graves.

LAZY   Kielce dist., Poland. The J. pop. in 1921 was 234 (total 1,579). Most of the 363 wartime Jews, including refugees who had arrived from Silesia in 1940–41, were deported by the Germans to Auschwitz on 16 June 1942. Some were sent to labor camps at Sosnowiec and Bendzin.

LEBEDIN   Sumy dist., Ukraine. Jews numbered about 250 in the early 20th cent. and 179 (less than 1%) in 1939. In 1919, they were attacked in a pogrom. The Germans captured L. on 10 Oct. 1941 and ordered the Jews to wear the yellow badge. The remaining eight J. families were confined to the dormitory of the local teachers' college and all 40 members were executed outside the town in early March 1942.

LEBEDZIOW   Vilna dist., Poland, today Belarus. A community of 470 Jews existed by 1847, growing to 1,232 (total 2,275) in 1897. Most left during WWI, when many were killed. Those who returned found their homes destroyed. The J. pop. in 1921 was 740. Between the World Wars, most Jews barely earned a living because of local competition. About 100 children attended a Tarbut Hebrew school, which encouraged the Zionist youth movements. The Germans entered the town in late June 1941. In late Oct. a ghetto was set up. Fifteen young Jews were murdered by the SS in late 1941 and on 24 June 1942, 650–800 were executed near the village of Markowo and their 138 homes burned to the ground.

LECHENICH   Rhineland, Germany. Jews lived in L. from the 13th cent. on, with several interruptions. They suffered persecution in the riots following the Oberwesel blood libel of 1287 and in the Black Death disturbances of 1348–49. The modern community began to develop in the 17th cent. and by 1806 it numbered 39 Jews, reaching a peak in 1890 with 171. The community maintained a prayer room and a cemetery (both dating from the 17th century). A new synagogue was consecrated in 1886 and a new cemetery in 1892. Jews served in the municipal council from 1846. In 1894, Gerson von Bleichroeder, Bismarck's personal banker and one of the outstanding J. figures in Germany, purchased the local castle and retired there. A branch of the Central Union (C.V.) opened in 1893 and the Zionists became active in 1902. In 1933, when the Nazis came to power, 74 Jews (total 4,020) lived in the town. On *Kristallnacht* (9–10 Nov. 1938), J. homes were destroyed and the synagogue was burned. Nine J. men were sent to the Dachau concentration camp. Those who did not make it to safe havens in time were deported during the war.

LECHNITA   (Hung. Szaszlekence; Ger. Lechnitz) N. Transylvania dist., Rumania. Jews settled in the 1850s despite the objections of the German majority. The J. pop. in 1920 was 206 (10% of the total). The community's rabbi, Shimon Lichtenstein (1879–1944), was one of the leading scholars in Transylvania. In May 1944 the community was transferred to the Bistrita ghetto and in June deported to Auschwitz.

LEEHEIM   Hesse, Germany. Established around

1780, the community numbered 45 (4% of the total) in 1861. All the Jews left by May 1939, some emigrating to the U.S.

LEEK Groningen dist., Holland. A J. community was organized in the late 18th cent. and numbered 164 in 1892. The J. pop. in 1941 was 72 (total 8,271). Only eight Jews from L. and its surroundings survived the Holocaust.

LEER Hanover, Germany. L. became the chief marketing center for cattle in East Friesland and by 1637 Jews had established a community there. They built a synagogue in 1793 and by 1828 they numbered 173. An elementary school opened in 1846 continued to function until 1941. Thanks to the economic boom after the Franco-Prussian War (1870–71), the community grew to 306 (over 2% of the total) in 1885, when a larger and more elegant synagogue was dedicated. As Jews played a vital role in the cattle trade, the Wednesday market did not open on J. festivals and Yiddish expressions crept into local speech. A branch of the Central Union (C.V.) was active during the Weimar Republic and the new J. Youth Association had 100 members in 1920. In 1928 Jews found guilty of attacking Nazis in the old cattle market had their sentences remitted on appeal. In response to Nazi boycott measures, J. community life intensified. The Youth Association organized sports events and lectures about Palestine. By 9 Nov. 1938, 166 Jews had left the town (87 emigrating). On *Kristallnacht* (9–10 Nov. 1938), Nazis burned the synagogue to the ground, looted and vandalized J. property, arrested Jews, and dispatched the men to the Sachsenhausen concentration camp. All J. business enterprises in L. ceased to exist by Dec. Of the 331 Jews listed as residents from 1933, a total of 115 emigrated, including 58 to Holland, ten to Belgium, 15 to England, and 17 to Latin America. A much larger number (192) left for—or were eventually moved to—cities within the Reich. At least 74 Jews are known to have perished in the Holocaust and only four remaining in Europe to have survived.

LEEUWARDEN (Ljouwert) Friesland dist., Holland. J. settlement in L. started in the 17th cent. and community activity began by 1700. The J. presence was not well tolerated in the 18th cent., especially of poor Jews, and J. trade was restricted. Nevertheless, the community continued to grow and develop from

mid-cent. The chief rabbinate of the region was seated in L. In the 19th cent., Jews lived concentrated around the synagogue and L. became a center of J. culture. The community ran a number of social welfare organizations, a branch of the Alliance Israelite, and an old age home (established in 1859). A J. school was founded in 1842. The J. pop. in 1883 was 1,120. From the beginning of the 20th cent. the community's pop. dwindled, but branches of Agudat Israel, the Zionist Organization, and Zionist youth movements were established. The J. pop. in 1941 was 677 (total 55,763). During the Holocaust, L.'s rabbi, Abraham Levisson, was active in assisting German refugees in Holland while strengthening the L. community. Some 80 refugees arrived in L. in 1940 from the coastal regions of Holland. Deportations began in Aug. 1942 and ended in March 1943. In all, 115 Jews survived in hiding, two returned from the camps, and two survived by escaping to Indonesia. A small community was reestablished after the war.

LEGHORN (Livorno) Tuscany, Italy. The J. community of L. was constituted after 1500 following an official invitation issued in 1593 by Ferdinand I to settle in this port city as well as in Pisa., Addressed to "Levantines, Spaniards, Portuguese, Germans, and Italians," the invitation was directed to the Jews of these countries and offered extensive privileges in order to make the two cities centers of trade. Most Jews who arrived were of Spanish origin or Marranos from Portugal. Few Italian and German Jews joined the community. In 1595, Abram Israel opened a loan bank in L. He was followed by the brothers Mose and Daniel Cordovero and Abramo Sullema. Spanish and Portuguese became the primary languages in L. and the Sephardi religious rite predeominated. The local J. community, referred to as the "J. nation" until 1860, began constructing a very impressive synagogue in 1602. It was enlarged in 1789. In 1675, L. received the status of a free port and became the most important center for the transit of goods between the Atlantic and North Sea ports and those of the Mediterranean and the Near East. Jews enjoyed extensive freedom and prospered economically, dominating at the port and becoming major ship outfitters. The Jews were also involved in manufacturing soap and paper as well as the processing of coral, which they exported. Referred to as the "little Jerusalem of Italy," the community maintained numerous charitable institutions, *yeshivot*, and Hebrew printing presses. Jedidiah Gabbai, who established the first press in 1650, was followed by Abraham ben Raphael Meldola and his son Raphael and by the house of Solomon Belforte. The J. pop. grew rapidly, from 114 in 1601 (total pop. 4,362) to 1,175 in 1642, 3,476 in 1738, and 4,327 in 1784. Sir Moses Montefiore was born in L. in 1784 at the home of his great-uncle Moses Haim Racah. In the second half of the 18th cent., the community reached its greatest splendor under the enlightened reforms of Leopold I. The J. community began to decline when the British blockaded the port during the Napoleonic wars. In 1859, when Tuscany was annexed to the Kingdom of Italy, Jews lost the special privileges they had enjoyed and other ports began to compete with L. In the second half of the 19th cent., a dominant figure in L. was the famous mystic writer Eliyahu Benamozegh. The community, numbering 4,870 in 1873, dropped to 4,050 in 1886 and 4,200 in 1910. According to the 1930 law reforming the J. communities in Italy, L. was declared one of 26 legally recognized communities. Its district comprised Elba, Grosseto, and Pitigliano. In 1936, the community numbered 2,000 Jews. Its rabbi was Elio Toaff. During the Holocaust, from 12 Nov. 1943, 35 Jews were arrested in L. and deported to death camps. The synagogue was completely destroyed by bombing. After the war, the community consisted of 1,000 Jews, reduced to 600 in 1965. In 1975, the community numbered 850 members.

LEGYESBENYE Zemplen dist., Hungary. Jews arrived in the late 18th cent. They numbered 78 in 1880 and 60 in 1930. In late April 1944, they were concentrated in the Satoraljaujhely ghetto and in late May deported to Auschwitz.

LEHRBERG Middle Franconia, Germany. The community was founded in the late 16th cent. and numbered 140 in 1837 (total 1,090). Ten remained in 1933, attached to the Ansbach community. All left by Jan. 1939.

LEHRENSTEINSFELD Wuerttemberg, Germany. Jews settled in the 17th cent. In the 19th cent. they were mainly engaged in the cattle trade, their pop. growing to 124 in 1843 and thereafter declining through emigration. In 1832–62, L. was the seat of the district rabbinate, serving ten other communities. Relations with the local pop. were close, the latter

even helping clean the streets before the J. Sabbath and later resisting Nazi anti-J. measures. The four J. families in the town in 1933 emigrated.

LEIDEN Zuid-Holland dist., Holland. A J. presence in L. is recorded in the 16th cent. J. students lived there temporarily from the 17th cent. A community was instituted in the early 18th cent. and grew rapidly from 1723. In 1733 restrictions were imposed on new J. settlement. The community continued to grow from the end of the 18th cent. until the 1830s, and again towards the end of the 19th cent. In 1807 the synagogue and school were heavily damaged when an ammunition ship exploded, with a number of Jews, including schoolchildren, killed. Social welfare organizations were founded in the 19th cent., including an orphanage in 1891. The J. pop. in 1896 was 461 (total 53,368). The Zionist movement was active from 1903. In the 1930s, 30 J. refugees arrived from Germany. The J. pop. in 1941 was 375, with 133 in nearby Wassenaar, 68 in Valkenburg, and 42 in Oegsgeest. A number of J. professors at L. University became well known, particularly in the field of law. In 1940, the university was closed temporarily by the Germans following a students strike in support of the dismissed J. professors. In June 1941, the Jews were forced out of their homes to live elsewhere in L. Restrictions on movement were imposed from Jan. 1942. By March 1943, all the Jews were deported; 113 survived the Holocaust, most in hiding. J. life was renewed after the war.

LEIHGESTERN Hesse, Germany. Jews were living there by the mid-18th cent. and numbered 44 (4% of the total) in 1861. On *Kristallnacht* (9–10 Nov. 1938), the synagogue and J. homes were wrecked. About 20 Jews emigrated after 1933 and 13 were eventually deported.

LEIMEN Baden, Germany. Jews settled in the early 18th cent. and numbered 82 in 1780, with the community ceasing to exist in 1905. The Seligman family of Court Jews lived there in the 18th cent. The five Jews in L. in 1933 were affiliated with the Nussloch congregation.

LEIMERSHEIM Palatinate, Germany. Two J. families were present in the early 18th cent. and ten in the early 19th cent. In 1880, the J. pop. reached a peak of 118, then dropped to 26 in 1932. In Oct. 1938, German soldiers vandalized the synagogue, which was erected in the mid-19th cent. On *Kristallnacht* (9–10 Nov. 1938), the work of destruction was completed. J. men were dispatched to the Dachau concentration camp; women, children, and the elderly to Karlsruhe and other places. Four Jews perished in the Holocaust.

LEIPALINGIS (Yid. Leipun) Saini dist., Lithuania. Jews first settled in the 19th cent. A J. colony was built on land granted to the J. community by the Russian authorities in 1847. A beautiful synagogue was erected. The J. pop. in 1897 was 134 (10% of the total). Between the World Wars many were affiliated with the Zionists. The J. pop. in 1940 was about 30 families. All the Jews were killed by Lithuanians after the German conquest of 1941.

LEIPZIG Saxony, Germany. In the first half of the 13th cent., there was a community in L. with a synagogue and a religious school. There is no evidence of persecutions during the Black Death period (1348–49), but in 1352 the synagogue was transferred to Christian ownership, indicating that the community no longer existed. Jews are again mentioned from 1364 and Abraham of L. served as Court Jew at the Meissen-Saxon court from 1418 to 1446. After 1446, only individual Jews lived in L. Jews took part in the L. fairs and in 1268 the fair days of the three annual fairs were moved from Saturday to Friday. Although there was a ban on J. residence in L., Jews were present in the city because of the fairs, and between 1490 and 1710 even played a central role in the city's economic life. From 1675 to 1764, the fair was attended by 82,000 Jews, mainly from Germany but also from Bohemia, Moravia, Austria, Silesia, Hungary, and later from Russia. They dealt in textiles; wool, leather, and silk goods; tobacco products; and books. Later, primarily Russian Jews traded in furs on a grand scale. Until its demolition in the 17th cent., the medieval J. quarter was used to provide accommodations to those coming to the fair. The fair also served as an important forum for exchanging information of all kinds. It also attracted large numbers of J. beggars, traveling entertainers, and artists. Since the city profited from J. attendance at the fairs, J. participation was encouraged. On the other hand, a number of restrictions were imposed upon the Jews, such as a ban on burial in L. Special customs duties and conditions were imposed on the "fair Jews." These restrictions referred to entry, regis-

tration, and above all trading, and laid down the purchase and sales volumes as well as the kind of goods that could be traded. In 1687, Jews were banned from selling goods in archways opening onto the street. Instead they were relegated to out-of-the-way side streets. In 1737, a ban on holding religious services was issued. At the beginning of the 18th cent., a J. community began to emerge from among the "fair Jews." In 1710, a Hamburg Jew was permitted to settle in L. and to buy silver and gold for the Saxony Mint. Requests by other Jews to move to Leipzig were rejected but in 1767 the city allowed the first Jew to register at the university and in 1769, another J. businessman was allowed to settle in order to make preparations for the arrival of the "fair Jews." It was, however, the "fair Jews" who propagated J. life in the city. The restrictions were slowly eased. In 1763, the ban on holding J. services was revoked and it became possible for prayer rooms to operate once again, though only during fair time. In 1813, the "fair Jews" received an area in which to bury their dead, and in 1818, hav-

Interior of Leipzig synagogue, Germany (sketch)

ing threatened a boycott, they managed to reverse the ban on trading in open archways. In 1831, all restrictions on "fair Jews" were revoked. In 1834 a community is mentioned for the first time. Its membership consisted of 74 Jews living in L. plus two J. university students. Four years later, there were 162 Jews living in L. Gradually restrictions imposed on Jews living in Leipzig were revoked. In 1838, the first Jew received a doctorate from L. University, and three Jews were for the first time allowed to become master craftsmen. In 1839, the first Jew received civil rights and a Jew was appointed to the university faculty, initially being refused the title of professor. The community managed to consecrate its first synagogue in 1855. In addition, there were various prayer rooms. In 1864, when the "fair Jews'" cemetery was closed, the community consecrated a new cemetery. A *mikve* existed from 1870. In 1858, the community appointed its first rabbi, Dr. Abraham Meyer Goldschmidt (1812–89), who served the community until his death. His wife, Henriette, was a nationally known proponent of women's education and a cofounder of the German Women's League. In 1871, the J. pop. was 1,739. Numbers rose steadily as a result of the influx of Jews from Eastern Europe. By the turn of the cent., the J. pop. was 6,200 and in the pre-WWI period about 10,000, with East European Jews comprising 75% of the community's pop. Since they had no voting rights in the community, serious conflicts ensued, up to the Weimar period, when foreign Jews were allowed to seat at least 25% of all representatives in communal institutions. Although there was a J. proletariat, which constituted a third of community members, the socio-economic structure was shaped by middle-class businessmen, skilled craftsmen, and white-collar workers, as well as intellectuals, physicians, and lawyers. Prior to WWI, of the 400 furriers in L., 200 were J., and at the fair a mixture of Yiddish and German was still spoken in certain branches of trade. In 1925, the community reached a peak of 13,030 members (about 2% of the total pop.). It was the largest community in Saxony (50% of Saxony's J. pop lived in the city) and the sixth largest in Germany. In 1923, a new synagogue with 1,300 seats was consecrated. In 1928, another cemetery was opened. Although the L. community was known for its distinct Liberal tendencies and lack of consideration for its Orthodox members, there were both Orthodox and Liberal rabbis, including Dr. Ephraim Carlebach, who took office in 1901 and emigrated in 1936. The

Jewish Fur Center in Bruehl, Leipzig, 1925. Top: Scheiner Brothers fur store around the corner (Photo courtesy of Alex Scheiner)

community established a number of educational institutions: a religious school in 1877; a J. elementary school in 1912; a Hebrew high school; and a school for Hebrew language and literature. It ran a library from 1900; an old age home from 1895; a day nursery and a children's home from 1905; a kindergarten from 1915; a J. hospital from 1928 (financed by the Chaim Eitingon Foundation); and a youth center from 1929. From 1925 the community issued a newsletter. In the Weimar period, there were as many as 79 associations in L., including 17 youth and sports clubs, the

Central Union (C.V.), Agudat Israel from 1914, and various Zionist organizations from Mizrachi to Ha-Po'el ha-Tza'ir. Jews were active in the arts, culture, science, and economic life. Dr. Max Abraham (1831–1900), proprietor of the C.F. Peter music publishing house, was internationally famous. J. academics taught at L. University, including Victor Ehrenberg (1851–1929) and Dr. Paul Ehrlich (1854–1915), Nobel Prize laureate and founder of modern immunology. Abraham Adler (1850–1922) established the Leipzig Commercial College and Max Eitingon was a key figure in the development of psychiatry. In 1880–90, as in the whole of Saxony, increasing antisemitism became noticeable in L., where several antisemitic newspapers were published. Attacks were constantly directed against East European Jews. In 1924 and 1925, there were attacks against the synagogue, and in 1926 meetings of the Central Union were carried out under police protection because of threats by nationalistic circles. In 1927, "ethnogenics" (racial studies) became a subject at the university.

In 1933, the J. pop. was 11,564, of whom 3,847 were of German background and 7,126 of East European descent. Following the boycott of J. stores on 1 April 1933, Jews were dismissed en masse from public positions, including 12 professors from the university. A number of Jews who had been active in Communist circles were arrested. In addition to other isolated arrests during the early years of the Nazi regime, 45 Jews were summarily arrested in June 1938; 31 were taken to the Sachsenhausen concentration camp. Raids and confiscations were frequently carried out at the various community institutions. In 1936, all the members of the community's board of directors, whom the Nazis defined as "assimilationists," were forced to resign. In 1935, earlier than elsewhere in the Reich, Jews living in L. were excluded from cultural events. By the middle of 1938, 1,600 J. stores and businesses had been "Aryanized." Despite this state of affairs, the community managed to inject new vitality into its inner life in the early years of Nazi rule. The Central Union and the Zionist groups organized a wide range of events. Vocational retraining courses for youngsters were offered and an orchestra was set up. In 1937, 651 children attended the J. elementary school and 399 the J. junior high school. According to estimates, between 1933 and Nov. 1938, 3,000 Jews managed to emigrate. In Oct. 1938, 1,652 Jews of non-German citizenship living in L. were deported to Poland. On

Kristallnacht (9–10 Nov. 1938), two synagogues, the main one in L. and another, were set on fire; six prayer rooms were destroyed; and two school institutions and the old age home were wrecked. All three J. cemeteries were desecrated. At one the mortuary was burned down. An arson attack was carried out against a J. department store and 200 J. stores and 34 apartments were looted and vandalized. Organizational offices were either sealed up or destroyed. At least 553 Jews were arrested and maltreated; 270 were taken to the Buchenwald concentration camp, where eight perished. After the pogrom, the community was stripped of its property. There was no place to carry out religious services, organizational offices could no longer be used, and the oldest cemetery was leveled and turned into a playground. The Zionist Organization, whose membership had grown to 1,200 compared with 500 in 1935, attracted large numbers of Jews to its events. At the beginning of 1939, another 1,000 individuals were deported to Poland, and according to the May 1939 census, the J. community had shrunk to 4,284 members. From this time on, the Jews were used for forced labor. In 1941, the city had 43 "J. houses," where practically all of the then remaining 2,500 Jews were forced to live. The Nazis closed down the community's schools in 1942. In Jan. 1942, the deportations to the east began. Up to Feb. 1945, 2,580 Jews and persons of partial J. origin (*Mischlinge*) were dispatched to the east and perished in nine deportations. Twenty people committed suicide before their scheduled deportation. According to estimates, several thousand Jews from L. fell into Nazi hands at other locations in the Reich or in occupied neighboring countries, including the majority of the Jews deported to Poland in Oct. 1938 and at the beginning of 1939. In 1945, the 15 Jews remaining in L. formed a community, which soon had 300 members with the return of inmates liberated from Buchenwald. Despite dwindling membership figures (195 in 1955 and 99 in 1969), the L. community was counted among the largest in the former German Democratic Republic, together with those in East Berlin and Erfurt. The building formerly housing the *talmud torah* school became a community center. In the course of the 1990s, the community grew once again as a result of the immigration of Jews from the former USSR.

LEIWEN Rhineland, Germany. Jews apparently lived in L. before 1592, at which time they were among those expelled from the principality of Trier. The modern community began to develop in the 17th century, growing to 29 individuals in 1808 and 61 at its peak in 1930. In 1852, a small synagogue was opened and in 1913 a new one was consecrated. In June 1933, 45 Jews were present (total pop. 1,230). Most Jews left before Nov. 1938, either to German cities or to other countries (including Holland, the U.S., and Argentina). On *Kristallnacht* (9–10 Nov. 1938), the synagogue was wrecked and subsequently the last 11 Jews left for Trier. It may be assumed that most perished in the Holocaust along with those, who did not emigrate to safety.

LEJASCIEMS (Ger. Neuhof, Aahof) Livonia dist., Latvia. A community with its own synagogue and cemetery was founded in 1867 and abandoned a few years later.

LE KEF Le Kef dist., Tunisia. A J. settlement may have existed before the seventh cent. Moslem conquest. The composition of the J. pop. of L. is believed to have included so-called desert Jews (conceivably descendants of Judaized Berbers). Others arrived from Tunis and Bizerte. The J. pop. was about 200 in 1830. Between the World Wars it was 800–900 (10% of the total). The arrival of Europeans after WWI, along with the existence of a French military base and the development of intensive agriculture, gave J. trade a big boost. A dozen leading J. merchants traded in farm produce (grain, hides, and wool). In 1931, 107 Jews were in trade, 75 were artisans, and 36 were day laborers. The Western influence led the Jews to send their children to the French public school (supplemented by a *talmud torah* in the afternoons) and some to adopt European dress, creating a growing cultural gap between the traditional and modern segments of the community. One synagogue served all the Jews in L. Named al-Ghariba like the one in Djerba, it too had legends and miraculous properties associated with it. The J. Relief Fund (Casse de Secours et de Bienfaisance) ran the community's social welfare and religious activities. In the 1920s, the chief rabbi was Eliyahu Kohen, who did much to promote Zionism. A small Betar group was founded in the late 1930s. Events in Palestine provoked anti-J. outbursts by the Arabs. French and Arab antisemitism reached its peak under the Vichy regime as J. civil servants were dismissed from their jobs and J. school-

children abused. Many Jews left the city, though it was spared occupation by the Germans. Despite economic growth in L. after the war, the Jews began leaving, unable to adapt to the increased industrialization. In 1946, 357 Jews remained. Most left for Israel and France after Tunisian independence in 1956.

LEKERT (from 1944, Trudolubovka) Dnepropetrovsk dist., Ukraine. L. was a J. colony attached to the Stalindorf J. Autonomous Region. The L. rural council (soviet) had jurisdiction over 2,383 Jews in 1932. A J. elementary school was apparently in operation from the mid-1920s and boasted a large library and boarding facilities. Two J. kolkhozes—Novaya Zorya and Budyony—were nearby. The Germans arrived in Aug. 1941 and in May 1942 murdered the few Jews who had neither fled nor been evacuated.

LELCHITSY Polesie dist., Belorussia. Jews probably settled in the late 18th cent. and numbered 180 (total 890) in 1897. In a 1919 pogrom, the Balakhovich brigade murdered one Jew and looted many J. homes. A J. elementary school (four grades) was opened in 1925 and attended by 67 children in 1927. In 1939, the J. pop. was 746. The Germans occupied L. on 10 July 1941. On 4 Sept., 700 Jews were executed not far from the town. Two days later, another 300 were murdered in the same place. A group of J. skilled workers, spared by the Nazis and subsequently liberated by the Kovpak division on its sweep west in Dec. 1942, joined the partisans.

LELES Slovakia, Czechoslovakia, today Republic of Slovakia. Permanent J. settlement probably commenced in the 1830s. The J. pop. was 192 (total 2,169) in 1869 and 220 in 1919, subsequently dropping to 135 in 1941 as the young left for the big cities. The community maintained a synagogue and cemetery and Jews owned a few stores and workshops. After the annexation to Hungary in Nov. 1938, their livelihoods were undermined and they were seized for forced labor. On 15 April 1944, they were rounded up for deportation via Satoraljaujhely, leaving on the transport to Auschwitz in mid-May.

LELIUNAI (Yid. Lelion) Utena dist., Lithuania. The J. pop. was 140 in 1897 and 63 in 1940 (26% of the total). All the Jews were killed after the German occupation of 1941.

LELOW Lublin dist., Poland. Jews are first mentioned in the late 18th cent., forming an organized community in the mid-19th cent. After R. David Biderman (d. 1814) established a dynasty there, L. became an important hasidic center, creating new sources of income as followers flooded the town. In the early 20th cent., Jews started a glass factory, two hide-processing plants, and a sawmill. The J. pop. rose from 339 in 1827 to 638 (total 1,227) in 1921. Zionist influence, retarded by Hasidism, began to spread after WWI. In the 1930s, the economic boycott undermined J. livelihoods, particularly among artisans, market stallowners, and shopkeepers. The Germans burned down most of the town on their arrival on 2 Sept. 1939 and executed 20. Many Jews fled, leaving behind just 350 of the 600 present before the war. The young were subjected to forced labor. In Sept. 1942, 382 Jews were deported to the Treblinka death camp. Those who escaped the *Aktion* arrived at the Radomsko or Czenstochowa ghettoes and were subsequently deported.

LEMESANY Slovakia, Czechoslovakia, today Republic of Slovakia. The community was apparently founded in the early 19th cent., becoming the seat of the regional rabbinate with about 30 attached settlements at mid-cent. The J. pop. rose to a peak of 133 (total 633) in 1880 and then dropped through emigration to the cities, reaching 54 in 1940. Jews owned a few stores and workshops as well as a flour mill and sawmill. Under the Slovakians, Jews were forced out of their businesses and put to forced labor. In mid-April 1942, most were deported to Auschwitz. Some were sent in May to the Demblin ghetto in the Lublin dist. of Poland.

LEMFOERDE Hanover, Germany. Dating from 1700, the community had a synagogue or prayer house, a burial ground, and an elementary school with 21 pupils in 1894. Numbering over 60 (7-8% of the pop.) between 1848 and 1895, the community declined to 22 in 1933. Ritual objects survived a *Kristallnacht* attack on the synagogue (9–10 Nov. 1938), but at least eight L. Jews perished during the Nazi era.

LEMGO Lippe, Germany. Jews living there established one of the nine J. communities in Westphalia in the 14th cent. From 1676, members of the Goldschmidt family served as court agents. The community had two burial grounds, maintained a J. school that had

28 pupils in 1872, and dedicated a synagogue in 1883. Numbering 105 in 1884, the J. pop. declined to 68 after WWI. Jews were mostly engaged in the livestock, grain, and clothing trade. Some owned factories or imported fruit. The Jews were prominent in local affairs. On *Kristallnacht* (9–10 Nov. 1938), Nazis burned the synagogue and desecrated the J. cemeteries. Four of the 53 Jews registered in 1933 emigrated; 36 were deported to Auschwitz, the Theresienstadt ghetto, and other camps, where they perished. Only three survived the Holocaust.

LENCZNA Lublin dist., Poland. Present in the late 16th cent., Jews numbered 500 by 1765. The Council of the Four Lands regularly held its meetings there during the fairs. A beautiful synagogue erected in the early 18th cent. remained standing until WWII. In 1711, two Jews were executed as the result of a blood libel. In the 19th cent., Jews were prominent as carters and at the turn of the cent. they opened small knitting mills, a sawmill, and a flour mill. By 1897, the J. pop. was 2,446 (of a total 3,766). Community life flourished under Zionist influence, which had began to develop in 1898. The Germans arrived in Sept. 1939 and burned down the synagogue, appointing a *Judenrat* in Jan. 1940 and subjecting the Jews to severe persecution and tributes. In 1941, 30 Jews were taken off the street and shot outside the city. In May 1942, 1,500 Jews were transferred to L. from other towns in the dist. and in Oct., 3,000 were deported to the Treblinka death camp. Of the remaining Jews, 1,260 were executed in L. in Nov. 1942 and 330 kept in a labor camp were deported to the Sobibor death camp and the Trawniki camp on 23 April 1943. All the Jews in Trawniki were murdered on 3 Nov. 1943.

LENCZYCA Lodz dist., Poland. L. was one of the oldest communities in the Lodz region. Jews are first mentioned in 1453. In 1564, their pop. was 460 (30% of the total). In 1639, two Jews were accused of murdering a Christian boy, and in 1652 the majority of the J. houses and the synagogue went up in flames. In 1656 the entire J. pop. was annihilated by the Polish army for siding with the invading Swedes. The community was revived in the 18th cent. The establishment of industry in the town provided a source of income for the Jews and by 1820 they constituted a majority. Competition from Lodz and Ozorkow forced many factories to close. In 1897 the J. pop. was 3,444 (41%).

The majority made their living from peddling their wares at fairs and in the nearby villages. Some well-known J. spiritual leaders and scholars came from this ancient community or served there such as R. Shelomo Efrayyim of L. and R. Meir Leibush ben Yitzhak Michael (the "Malbin"). There was an active Bund group and a Hovevei Zion society, both established in the early 20th cent. Between the World Wars the economic situation of the Jews declined due to the impoverishment of the rural pop. as well as the boycott of J. shops and stalls. During this period Agudat Israel was the dominant community organization, followed by the Zionists. When the Germans invaded L. on 7 Sept. 1939, they imprisoned the Jews in the synagogue and took hostages. A *Judenrat* was set up in 1940 and ordered to pay a million zlotys as a fine for the alleged wounding of a German officer. A ghetto was set up between Dec. 1940 and Feb. 1941. In early 1941, some 1,000 Jews were expelled to Poddembice, Grabow, and other towns. On 1 Jan. 1941, there were 3,400 Jews in the ghetto; in April 1942, after more deportations, only 1,750 remained. In March 1942, ten Jews charged with smuggling were hanged publicly and on 10–12 April the remaining Jews were deported to Chelmno.

LENDERSHAUSEN Lower Franconia, Germany. Jews are first mentioned in the mid-18th cent. as visitors to the Leipzig fair. Jews numbered 136 in 1837 (total 460) and seven in 1933; five left after 1938 and two were deported to Izbica in the Lublin dist. (Poland) in April 1942.

LENGERICH Westphalia, Germany. Jews are first mentioned in 1576. During the Thirty Years War (1618–48), Jews helped finance the cloth industry developed by the Count of Tecklenburg. In the 18th cent., the J. pop. averaged about eight families. In 1849, the Jews reached a peak pop. of 105, making the community the largest in the dist. A new synagogue was consecrated in 1821 and a J. school was opened in 1829. From the mid-19th cent., the J. pop. dropped steadily as many of the young left for the U.S. or the big cities of northern Germany. Jews remained active in local life, joining gymnastics and marksmen's clubs, but antisemitism was also apparent. In June 1933, about four months after the Nazi rise to power, 43 Jews remained (total 13,181). The anti-J. boycott under the Nazis succeeded in isolating the Jews economically; social isolation soon followed. In March 1938, 23 Jews remained in the city and another 13 were confined in the local mental institution. On *Kristallnacht* (9–10 Nov. 1938), the synagogue was wrecked along with J. homes. Of the 36 Jews who left L. in 1933–42, 32 moved to other German cities. Four were deported to the Riga ghetto on 9 Dec. 1941, all perishing. The last seven inmates of the mental institution were moved to Brandenburg on 27 Sept. 1940 and put to death.

LENGFELD Hesse, Germany. The community, numbering 57 (6% of the total) in 1861, disposed of its synagogue around 1932 and the last Jews fled after *Kristallnacht* (9–10 Nov. 1938). A Holocaust memorial was erected there in 1988.

LENIN Polesie dist., Poland, today Belorus. Jews from Slutsk and Lachwa settled in the early 18th cent. and engaged in the burgeoning lumber industry in the 19th cent. as the J. pop. grew to 753 in 1897 and 928 (total 1,520) in 1921. Ninety percent of J. children attended the Hebrew school. The Germans arrived on 18 July 1941, introducing a regime of forced labor and sporadic killing. A ghetto was set up on 10 May 1942. On 13 Aug. 1,100 Jews were taken outside the town and murdered; 28 artisan families who were spared were liberated in a partisan attack in Sept. 1942. About 150 of L.'s Jews fought in partisan units, half of them falling in battle.

LENINDORF (until the 1920s, Karabulat; from 1944, Leninskoye) Nikolaiev dist., Ukraine. In the Soviet period, J. settlement began here with so-called "classless" Jews cultivating vineyards, tobacco, and fruit trees. In the late 1930s, the area under the jurisdiction of the L. rural council (soviet) included about 1,000 Jews. L. was a regional center for a number of J. kolkhozes. A J. elementary school was in existence. The Germans captured L. in mid-Sept. 1941 and on 4 Oct. murdered up to 1,000 Jews in the area.

LENINGRAD (until 1914 and from 1992, St. Petersburg; in 1914–24, Petrograd) Leningrad dist., Russia. The first Jews (possibly converts of Portuguese-J. origin, including doctors and financiers) arrived not long after Peter the Great founded the city in 1703. A J. cemetery was probably consecrated in the early 19th cent., next to the Lutheran cemetery. In the mid-1820s, the J.

Jewish farmers, Lenindorf, Crimea

pop. was 370. Despite restrictions, especially under Nicholas I, the J. pop. continued to grow throughout most of the 19th cent., reaching a figure of 6,654 in 1869 and 16,649 (of a total 1.2 million) in 1897. In 1869, few of the city's Jews regarded Yiddish as their mother tongue; the percentage increased to 83% in 1883 with the growth of the J. pop. but fell to 67% in 1891. Jews were accorded the right to erect permanent synagogues in 1869 and six were already functioning by the 1880s. The community was legally established in 1870. A new J. cemetery was laid out in the early 1870s and a Great Synagogue seating 1,200 was inaugurated in 1893. Following official recognition, the community was served by a number of well-known, government-appointed rabbis, such as M. Eisenstadt, A. Neumann, and A. Drabkin. Yitzhak Blaser was prominent among the rabbis the community chose in the 1860s and 1870s. L. was an important center of J. culture in the latter half of the 19th cent. Hebrew periodicals such as *Ha-Melitz* and *Ha-Yom* began appearing in the 1870s and 1880s along with such Russian-language

J. publications as *Vestnik Russkikh Evreev.* With the emergence of the Zionist movement, a number of Zionist periodicals appeared: *Yevreyskaya Zhizn, Kronika Yevreyskoy Zhizni,* and *Razsvet.* The number of J. publications increased in the late 19th and early 20th cent. to include *Der Fraynd* (Russia's first Yiddish newspaper), *Di Yiddishe Velt, Dos Yiddishe Folksblat,* the Hebrew *Ha-Zeman,* and the Russian *Voskhod.* Non-Zionist parties such as the Bund were also active. In 1881, the socio-occupational profile of the community showed a high proportion of professional people (doctors, lawyers, journalists, actors, scientists, and hundreds of students) and a well-to-do class of about 2,000 breadwinners (40% of the total); about 1,500 (30%) of the Jews were artisans and another 1,000 engaged in trade. The number of J. entrepreneurs was particularly large and Jews were prominent in banking and business, the leading families including the Vavelbergs, Ginzburgs, Polyakovs, Varshavskis, Frydlands, and Rosenthals. The city's most important loan bank was in J. hands. The importance of L. as a J. cultural center extended into the early 20th cent. Among the important publications was the 16-volume *Yevreyskaya Entsiklopediya*. L. was also the center of the Society for the Promotion of Culture among the Jews of Russia (founded in 1863) and the home of the Hovevei Sefat Ever Society. (Called Tarbut after 1917, the organization founded a Hebrew school system that continued to operate in independent Poland between the World Wars.) A number of additional organizations were founded and operated in L., such as the ICA (for land settlement), the OZE (public health), and ORT (vocational education). In WWI, the J. Committee for the Relief of War Victims (YEKOPO) became active. Following the Feb. 1917 Revolution, all restrictions forbidding J. residence were removed. On the eve of the Oct. 1917 Revolution, a J. self-defense battalion was formed, later commanded by Yosef Trumpeldor. Following the Revolution, the J. pop. dropped to 25,000 in 1920. With the stabilization of the Soviet regime, it rose quickly, to 52,374 in 1923 and to 84,503 in 1926. In 1939, the J. pop. reached a peak of 201,542 (total 3,188,956). Tens of thousands of the new J. settlers came from the Ukraine and Belorussia. With the waves of emigration that accompanied

the changes in Soviet society in the late 1920s, the social composition of the local J. pop. changed as well. J. civil servants (including the intelligentsia) increased from 40% in 1926 to 60% in 1939 and J. workers from 7% in 1923 to 14% in 1939. Toward the end of the period, two classes vanished entirely: merchants and artisans (15% in 1929) and the unemployed (20% in 1926). After a short period of intense cultural and political activity, nearly all party newspapers, mainly Zionist, were closed down in 1919–20 along with all the political parties other than the Communist Party. A few J. journals (in Russian) kept publishing until the late 1920s, among them *Yevreyskaya Mysl* and *Yevreyskaya Letopis*, both until 1926, and *Yevreyskaya Starina*, the quarterly of the J. Historical-Ethnographic Society, until 1930. The Lubavich Rebbe, Yosef Yitzhak Schneersohn, lived in the city in 1924–27. The special character of the city, particularly after the Oct. Revolution, produced a constant growth in the number of Jews who considered Russian their mother tongue, from 42% before WWI to over 68% in 1926 and nearly 79% in 1939 (and 92% in 1959). Russian-Yiddish culture also flourished. The only Russian-language J.

Museum of Jewish Ethnography, Leningrad (St. Petersburg), Russia, 1925 (Israel Museum, Jerusalem/photo courtesy of Yad Vashem, The Holocaust Martyrs' and Heroes' Remembrance Authority, Jerusalem)

newspaper of the period, *Yevreyskaya Trybuna*, was published here from 1919. A J. university, later becoming an institute of J. studies, was open until 1925; a J. historical-ethnographic museum functioned until 1930; and a society for the promotion of culture among J. laborers (OPE) operated until 1929. An educational unit for Yiddish stagecraft, founded in 1919, led to the establishment of a number of Yiddish theater groups until the early 1930s (the last group disbanding in 1937). The percentage of J. high school and college graduates was much higher than among the general pop. (402 per 1,000 Jews as opposed to 286 per 1,000 in the non-J. pop.). The percentage of academicians among the Jews was also high (123 vs. 31 per 1,000 in 1939). The rabbinate continued to exist in L. until the late 1920s; the Soviets ended it a short while before the death of the community's last rabbi, David Tevel Katzenellbogen, in Feb. 1931.

With the approach of the German army, tens of thousands of residents were drafted into the army and auxiliary forces, including thousands of Jews. On 10 July 1941, the air defense of the city commenced and on 8 Sept. 1941, the 900-day German siege of L. began (with liberation coming in late Jan. 1944). In the course of the fighting and bombardments during this period, 800,000–900,000 Russians died, most from starvation. Among them were tens of thousands of Jews whose suffering was no different from that of the rest of the city's residents. Among the J. writers (writing in Russian) who remained in the city and documented its tribulations were A. Chakovski and the poetess Vera Inber. In the late 1940s, the J. intellectual class was decimated by the war waged by the Stalinist regime against what were termed "cosmopolitans." The census of 1959 gave the first postwar pop. figure for the Jews of L., placing their number at 162,344, but the actual number was much higher, probably around 200,000. Nearly 14,000 Jews declared Yiddish to be their mother tongue. The Great Synagogue maintained some activity despite the arrest of its rabbi and his confinement in a forced labor camp during the Stalinist period. He was released only after Stalin's death. The limited J. cultural activity within the Soviet framework of the 1930s was curtailed entirely.

LENINGRADSKAYA   Krasnodar territory, Russia. After they arrived in summer 1942, the Germans murdered the few Jews who had not fled or been evacuated.

LENINO (I)   (until Oct. 1917, Romanovo) Minsk dist., Belorussia. Jews probably settled in the early 19th cent., numbering 31 in 1811 and 494 (total 1,535) in 1897. In 1923, their pop. was 222. Many worked as farmers. A J. school was apparently opened in the mid-1920s. The Germans occupied L. in late June 1941. On 12 June 1942, they murdered about 70 Jews (140 according to a Soviet source).

LENINO (II)   (until 1918, Romanovo) Mogilev dist., Belorussia. The J. pop. was 634 (64% of the total) in 1897. Most Jews engaged in petty trade and crafts. In 1923, under the Soviets, the J. pop. was 498 and in 1925, 80 J. families engaged in agriculture and 41 Jews were artisans. A J. school opened in 1925 had 42 students in 1927. In 1930, 42 J. families worked at a nearby multinational kolkhoz. Within a few days of occupying L. in early July 1941, the Germans shot 77 Jews. In the fall, the remaining 60 were expelled to the Gorki ghetto, where they perished.

LENS   Pas-de-Calais dist., France. Immigrants from Poland, most very religious, established a J. community after WWI. They followed the Polish gentiles who had came to the area to work in the mines and in agriculture. A synagogue was inaugurated in 1931 and the cornerstone of a *mikve* was laid in 1934. On 11 Sept. 1942, the arrests of the Jews of L. started. They were taken during the night by train to Lille and from there deported to Auschwitz via Malines (Mechelen).

LEOBSCHUETZ   (Pol. Glubczyce) Upper Silesia, Germany, today Poland. J. settlement is known from 1360 and the existence of a J.-owned beer brewery from the mid-15th cent. In 1539, the Jews were expelled following a blood libel. Only in 1812 were they again accorded residence rights. Their pop. reached 62 in 1818 and a peak of 301 in 1862. The community maintained a synagogue from 1865 and opened a new cemetery in 1896. By 1910 the J. pop. dropped to 174 and in 1933 to 111. The Nazi racial laws were not enforced in L. until July 1937 since the Jews were under the protection of the League of Nations' minority rights convention. In 1936, the J. pop. was 92. On *Kristallnacht* (9–10 Nov. 1938), the synagogue was burned, J. stores and warehouses were destroyed, and ten Jews were arrested. Forty-four remained in 1939; 15 were expelled to General Gouvernement territory in July 1942 and 13 were deported to the Theresienstadt ghetto in Dec. 1942. Most probably perished.

LEONCIN Warsaw dist., Poland. The J. pop. in 1921 was 149 (total 288). Those remaining after accelerated emigration between the World Wars were expelled by the Germans to nearby ghettoes toward the end of 1940 and shared the fate of the Jews there.

LEONOPOL Vilna dist., Poland, today Belarus. Jews settled in the first half of the 19th cent., numbering 65 (total 109) in 1866. They traded in lumber, flax, grain, and mushrooms. A few had stores in the market and some rented rooms to vacationers during the summer resort season. The Germans arrived in June

1941. The 125 Jews in L. were sent to the Druja ghetto in late June 1942 and murdered there on 2 July.

LEORDINA (Yid. Lerdene) N. Transylvania dist., Rumania. An organized J. community existed in 1850. The majority were members of the Sighet hasidic sect. Jews engaged in the lumber industry. The J. pop. in 1920 was 356 (19% of the total). The community was represented on the village committee and Jews were even senior officials. In April 1944 the community was transferred to the Viseul de Sus ghetto and then deported to Auschwitz.

LEOVA Bessarabia, Rumania, today Republic of Moldova. The J. pop. in 1930 was 2,326. In June

Class of 1922, Tarbut Hebrew high school, Leova, Bessarabia, Rumania (Beth Hatefutsoth Photo Archive, Tel Aviv/photo courtesy of Yad Vashem, The Holocaust Martyrs' and Heroes' Remembrance Authority, Jerusalem)

1941 the majority of the Jews attempted to flee with the help of retreating Russians, but were murdered by Rumanian soldiers and gendarmes in other villages and towns, as were those who remained in L. About 30 families returned after the war.

LEPEL Vitebsk dist., Belorussia. The J. pop. was 1,509 in 1847 and 3,379 (total 6,284) in 1897. In the early 20th cent., state J. schools for boys (emphasizing vocational training) and for girls were in operation. A J. elementary school was in operation during the Soviet period. By 1939, internal immigration had reduced the J. pop. to 1,919. The Germans captured the town on 3 July 1941, setting up a ghetto. On 28 Feb. 1942, all 1,000 Jews there were murdered near the village of Chernoruchie.

LEPJUNY Vilna dist., Poland, today Belarus. L. was founded as a J. farming settlement in 1847 and numbered 99 Jews in 1919. The Germans expelled the Jews to Ejszyszki via Olkeniki on 25 Sept. 1941 and murdered them there.

LEROS (Leryos) Dodecanese Islands, Greece. No more than a dozen Jews lived in L. in the late 19th cent. In WWII two or three families were deported.

LESBOS (Lesvos, Metelin, Mytilini, Metelin, Mytilene, Midilli) North Aegean Islands, Greece. Benjamin of Tudela, the 12th cent. J. traveler, recorded a J. community on the island. During the 19th cent., there were 20–30 J. families, but by 1941 only one Jew remained.

LESHCHIN Zhitomir dist., Ukraine. Jews probably settled in the first half of the 18th cent. Their pop. grew from 192 in 1775 to 572 in 1847 but then dropped to 337 (total 1,666) in 1897. Under Soviet rule, the J. pop. dropped to 157 in 1926. Most Jews were employed in petty trade with many transferring to farming in the 1920s. The Germans occupied the town in the first half of July 1941, murdering the remaining Jews in late Aug. or early Sept.

LESKO (Yid. Linsk) Lwow dist., Poland, today Ukraine. Jews are first reported in the 16th cent. and engaged in the wine trade as well as dealing in cattle and horses and imported goods and leasing inns and salt deposits. The community prospered and grew until the Swedish invasion of 1704 destroyed the town,

with 303 Jews dying in an epidemic as well. Recovery was slow, impeded by a great fire in 1886 which destroyed almost all J. homes. During WWI, Russians troops pillaged the town and epidemics decimated the pop. In 1890, the J. pop. reached 2,425 (40% of the total), subsequently rising and then dropping back to that level in the aftermath of WWI. From 1782 to 1939, R. Menahem-Mendel Horowitz-Rubin and his descendants served as rabbis in the town while the Zanz dynasty claimed the majority of followers among the Hasidim. The Soviets closed down J. commerce and public life on their arrival in 1939. With the German conquest in 1941, a regime of restrictions, extortion, and forced labor was instituted with periodic executions until the entire pop. was expelled to the Zaslawie labor camp in Sept. 1942. Before leaving, the Jews made a mass pilgrimage to the local cemetery. The Zaslawie camp was finally liquidated on 15 Jan. 1943. Around 30 survived the war.

LESKOVAC Serbia, Yugoslavia. A Sephardi community existed by the 19th cent. and a spacious synagogue was built in the center of the city in 1863. The J. pop. reached a peak of 120 in 1921 (total 13,702) but by 1940–41 there were only 59 Jews there. The community was totally destroyed in the Holocaust, most dying in the Nis concentration camp.

LESZNIOW Tarnopol dist., Poland, today Ukraine. Jews were present from the early 17th cent., linked economically to nearby Brody and prospering until the latter's decline in the late 19th cent. Emigration subsequently reduced the J. pop. from 696 (a third of the total) in 1890 to 179 in 1921. Under the German occupation (end of June 1941) a ghetto was set up on 2 Nov. 1942 and the Jews were expelled to Brody on 17 April 1943.

LESZNO (I) (Yid. Lissa) Poznan dist., Poland. Jews may have settled as early as 1534. Many more, apparently refugees from Silesia, arrived in 1595. In the Chmielnicki massacres of 1648–49 and the Swedish invasion of 1655 the community suffered greatly, with 100 of its 400 families leaving the city. Nonetheless, recovery was rapid and J. trade expanded as merchants dealing in woven goods, furs, and hides reached Moscow and the Turkish border. Close commercial ties were maintained with Breslau, Frankfurt, and Leipzig. In 1767–90 the community

Synagogue in Leszno, Poland, 1939

Small synagogue in Letichev, Ukraine (today a tavern)

reached the peak of its development under Polish rule with a pop. of nearly 5,000. A great fire in 1790 ushered in a period of decline which was only reversed after the city was re-annexed to Prussia in 1815. Jews again captured the German market and were prominent in banking and industry and entered the professional class. Among the community's well-known rabbis were Mordekhai ben Tzevi Hirsch (1721–53), who was invited to mediate in the dispute between Yaakov Emden and Yonatan Eybeschuetz, and his brother Avraham Abusch, who served as chief rabbi of Frankfurt in 1753–59. R. Akiva Eger founded a yeshiva in L. which burned down in 1791. R Yaakov Lorbeerbaum officiated in 1809–1821 and R. Shemuel Baeck, the father of Leo Baeck, in 1864–1912. Leo Baeck (1873–1956), outstanding religious thinker and leader of German Jewry in the Nazi era, was born in L. Despite relative prosperity the J. pop. declined from 3,446 (of a total 8,667) in 1840 to 1,206 in 1895 and 299 in 1921, most leaving for Berlin and Breslau. The 170 Jews remaining on the eve of WWII were expelled from the city by the Germans on 17 Oct. 1939, either to the Lodz ghetto or to General Gouvernement territory.

LESZNO (II) Warsaw dist., Poland. The J. pop. was 146 in 1930 (total 728) and 258 in 1921 (total 1,858). The town's 300 Jews were expelled by the Germans to the Warsaw ghetto in Feb. 1940 and suffered the fate of the other J. refugees there.

LETICHEV Kamenets-Podolski dist., Ukraine. J. settlement commenced in 1581. In 1765, the J. pop. reached 652 and in 1897 it was 4,108 (57% of the total). In 1881–82, Jews were attacked in pogroms. In

1939, under the Soviets, the J. pop. was 1,946. The Germans entered the town on 17 July 1941. In Sept. 1942, they murdered 3,000 Jews from L. and its environs. In Nov., they murdered 4,000 from the provinces of Volkovinets and Derazhnya. The Jews in the local labor camp were probably murdered in early 1943.

LEUTERSHAUSEN (I) Middle Franconia, Germany. Jews were present with full civil rights in the mid-15th cent. They lived there again in 1520–40 and from 1612. In 1890 they numbered 81 and in 1933, 32 (total 1,400), mostly engaged in the cattle trade. In Oct. 1938, the synagogue was twice vandalized and J. homes were wrecked. By Feb. 1939 all the Jews had left the town.

LEUTERSHAUSEN (II) Baden, Germany. Jews are mentioned in the mid-16th and early 18th cent. The community grew to 150 in 1871 (of a total 1,411), with an elementary school opened in 1858 and a synagogue in 1862. Jews sat on the village council and participated in local social life. Toward mid-cent. some were artisans and successful farmers. In 1933, 32 remained. All left by March 1939. Of the 13 Jews (in 1933) in the attached community of Luetzelsachsen, where nearly 100 Jews had lived in the early 19th cent., seven were deported to the Gurs concentration camp on 22 Oct. 1940, five perishing.

LEVELEK Szabolcs dist., Hungary. Jews were present in the mid-18th cent. and numbered 114 in 1880 and 103 in 1930. J. merchants traded in grain, feathers, and hides and Jews owned a distillery, a flour mill, and a factory for processing medicinal herbs. They suffered in the White Terror after WWI and from a generally antisemitic atmosphere afterwards. The Jews were sent to Kisvarda in spring 1944 and on 17 May deported to Auschwitz.

LEVERKUSEN Rhineland, Germany. The J. community only developed in the Weimar period. It included the Jews of Wiesdorf and the surrounding area. Those from Opladen joined later. The first J. family settled in Wiesdorf in 1753. By 1824 there were 16 families there. There were 23 Jews in Opladen in 1843 and they maintained a cemetery from 1853 and established a synagogue in 1879. When the Nazis came to power in 1933, about 150 Jews from the area were affiliated with the L. community. On *Kristallnacht* (9–10 Nov. 1938), the synagogue in Opladen was burned down while in L., J. businesses and homes were wrecked. The community members, including women and children, were arrested and the men were deported for a certain period to the Dachau concentration camp. Most Jews left between 1933 and 1939, 65 moving to other locations within the Reich and 37 emigrating abroad. In Oct. 1941, 27 Jews – 13 from L. and 14 from Opladen – were deported to the east. Yad Vashem honored Elfriede Stichnoth from L. as one of the Righteous among the Nations for hiding a J. woman in her home.

LEVICE (Hung. Leva) Slovakia, Czechoslovakia, today Republic of Slovakia. Jews settled in the early 18th cent. The community founded an elementary school in 1854 and erected a synagogue in 1857. In 1869, the community became Neologist and in 1874 an Orthodox faction formed a separate congregation. The two were reunited ten years later under the Status Quo banner and the local rabbinate extended its jurisdiction to over 30 smaller communities. The J. pop. grew to 1,259 (total 8,325) in 1900 and a peak of 1,448 in 1930. In the Czechoslovakian Republic, six Jews served on the municipal council and in 1921, Jews owned 163 business establishments, 39 workshops, and three factories. Eight were doctors (of a total 11 in the city) and ten (of 14) were lawyers. The Zionists were very active with dozens leaving for kibbutzim in Palestine. After the annexation to Hungary in Nov. 1938, a few dozen J. families were expelled and in 1940 Jews were thrown out of work and seized for forced labor. In March 1944, when the Germans occupied L., 1,005 Jews remained. In May, they were herded into a ghetto, joined by another

572 Jews from neighboring settlements. On 14 June, 1,695 were transported to Auschwitz. Most of the postwar community of 300 emigrated to Israel in 1949.

LEVOCA (Hung. Locse) Slovakia, Czechoslovakia, today Republic of Slovakia. Jews settled in the mid-19th cent. and in 1869 formed a Status Quo congregation. A synagogue was consecrated in 1899 with a school attached as the J. pop. rose from 299 in 1880 to 709 (total 6,845) in 1900. A separate Orthodox congregation was constituted in 1922. Under Czechoslovakian rule between the World Wars, Jews were active in public and economic life with two serving on the municipal council. Jews owned 40 stores, 18 workshops, and a distillery and brewery. The Zionists and their youth movements were active. In 1940, the J. pop. was 484. After the establishment of the Slovakian state in March 1939, the German minority immediately attacked J. homes and stores. In March 1942, 40 young J. women were deported to Auschwitz while young men were sent to the Majdanek concentration camp. On 27 May, 190 Jews were deported to ghettoes and camps in the Lublin dist. in Poland. Of the few dozen Jews spared as essential workers, some escaped and the rest were deported to concentration camps or executed locally by the Germans in Sept. 1944.

LEZAJSK (Yid. Lyzhansk) Lwow dist., Poland, today Ukraine. Jews lived permanently in L. from at least 1521, enjoying wide-ranging residence and trade privileges under the Polish kings. There was an organized community in the early 17th cent., which gained its independence from the auspices of the Przemysl community in 1718. In 1772, R. Elimelekh Lippmann (Elimelekh of Lyzhansk), a disciple of Dov Baer, the *Maggid* of Mezhirech, established his seat there, making L. a center of Hasidism and after his death in 1787 a place of pilgrimage for thousands of followers. Austrian rule from 1772, with its heavy taxation, impoverished much of the community. In 1880 the J. pop. stood at 1,868 (total 4,945). A few wealthy merchants dealt in lumber and grain as leaseholders of the local count's estates; tradesmen received a yearly boost from the arrival of the pilgrims. The hasidic character of the community discouraged Zionist activity until after WWI, when the two camps contended for control of the community council. Destruction during the war was extensive. The community was looted in Nov. 1918 and the Joint Distribution Committee provided relief. A German bombardment preceded the occupation of the town in Sept. 1939. On 14 Sept. (Rosh Hashanah) the synagogue was burned down and widespread persecution ensued. A couple of weeks later (Sukkot) the Jews were expelled to Soviet-held territory, some remaining in E. Galicia, others being exiled to the interior of Russia. The 40 J. families remaining in L. were joined by refugees; all werre confined to a single street, which became a closed ghetto in 1941. In Sept. 1942 they were expelled to the Tarnogrod ghetto and from there mainly to the Belzec death camp.

LGOV Kursk dist., Russia. Jews probably settled in the late 19th cent., mainly after the town was linked to the railroad. In 1926, under the Soviets, their pop. was 183. The few who had neither fled nor been evacuated were murdered after the arrival of the Germans in late Oct. 1941.

LIBEREC Bohemia (Sudetenland), Czechoslovakia. Jews were present in small numbers in the 14th or 15th cent. and numbered 63 in 1810. J. merchants helped develop the wool and cloth industry in the city. Few were present in 1848 after decades of anti-J. measures but subsequently a community was officially organized and the J. pop. grew to 957 in 1890. During WWI, the community cared for 1,600 J. refugees from Eastern Europe and 1,000 J. prisoners of war from the Russian army. After the war, in the Czechoslovakian Republic, most Jews identified with German culture, but the Zionists were also active. In 1930, the J. pop. was 1,392 (total 38,568). The Jews left in fall 1938 during the Sudetenland crisis. The remaining 30 were deported to concentration camps in Germany. The city's Great Synagogue was burned on *Kristallnacht* (9–10 Nov. 1938). The postwar J. community numbered 1,211 in 1946.

LIBUCHORA Lwow dist., Poland, today Ukraine. The J. pop. in 1921 was 210. The Jews were probably deported to the Belzec death camp in the second half of 1942, directly or via Turka.

LICH Hesse, Germany. Jews are mentioned from 1622 and numbered 71 (3% of the total) in 1828. The J. pop. changed little up to 1933. A new synagogue was established in 1922. On *Kristallnacht* (9–10 Nov. 1938), the synagogue's interior was destroyed, but the building survived. Most of the Jews

had already left, with 29 emigrating; ten others were deported in 1942.

LICHENROTH (now part of Birstein) Hesse-Nassau, Germany. The community established a synagogue in 1833 and maintained an elementary school from 1853 to 1924. The J. pop. dwindled from 114 (22% of the total) in 1885 to 51 in 1925. By Jan. 1937 the community disbanded.

LICHTENAU Baden, Germany. Jews are mentioned as temporary residents in the 17th cent., forming a permanent settlement only from the early 18th. Local pressure confined the Jews to moneylending and the used clothing trade. J. homes were vandalized in the revolutionary disturbances of 1848 and Jews were again victimized by antisemitism in the 1880s and 1890s. In the early 20th cent., most Jews were cattle traders or shopkeepers and ran auxiliary farms. The J. pop. reached 244 in 1871 and then declined steadily to 84 (total 1,060) in 1933. Forty-six Jews left at this time, 20 emigrating. On *Kristallnacht* (9–10 Nov. 1938), the remaining men were taken to the Dachau concentration camp, where two were shot. The last 24 Jews were deported to the Gurs concentration camp on 22 Oct. 1940; eight others were deported after leaving L. Of the 32 deportees, 11 died in Auschwitz and seven survived the Holocaust.

LICHTENFELS Upper Franconia, Germany. The 13th cent. community was expelled during the Rindfleisch massacres of 1298 and again in 1499 after reestablishing itself in 1447. The community was renewed in 1667 under the protection of the Bishop of Bamberg. A synagogue was built in the J. quarter in 1757. The J. pop. reached 155 in 1812 (total 1,564) and thereafter declined steadily to 69 in 1933 (total 6,970). On *Kristallnacht* (9–10 Nov. 1938), the synagogue was vandalized, ten Torah scrolls were burned, J. homes and stores were looted, and 22 Jews were arrested. Fifty-three Jews left the city in the Nazi era, including 15 to England and 13 to the U.S. On 25 April 1942, six of the remaining Jews were deported to Izbica in the Lublin dist. (Poland) and another eight were sent to the Theresienstadt ghetto.

LIDA Nowogrodek dist., Poland, today Belarus. Jews may have settled in the mid-16th cent. In 1579, King Stephen Bathory authorized the erection of a synagogue. In the early 18th cent. most Jews ran inns or traded in farm produce. In the late 19th cent. most of the town's shopkeepers and artisans were Jews and J.-owned factories proliferated. The J. pop. grew from 1,980 in 1847 to 5,294 (total 9,323) in 1897. In 1886, Yitzhak Yaakov Reines (b. 1839), one of the outstanding leaders of religious Zionism and principal founder of Mizrachi, became rabbi, officiating until his death in 1918 and founding a yeshiva in 1905 that was famous throughout the country. After WWI a J. factory producing rubber galoshes, with 1,000 workers, was the second largest in Poland and J. artisans ran 302 workshops. A Tarbut Hebrew school was founded in the 1920s, joining the CYSHO Yiddish school founded in 1919. The community also had a hospital, orphanage, and old age home. Four Yiddish weeklies appeared for short periods. Hehalutz and Hashomer Hatzair were the leading Zionist movements. The J. pop. in 1931 was 6,335. After two years under the Soviet regime in 1939–41, L. was captured by the Germans on 27 June 1941 after a heavy bombardment killed about 500 Jews (of a total 2,000 dead). About 8,500 Jews were then living in L. An *Einsatzgruppe B* unit immediately executed 92 Jews belonging to the professional class. A *Judenrat* was set up and the Jews were put to forced labor. On 1 March 1942, 200 of the sick and old were murdered in their homes when they failed to report for an identity parade. On 8 May 1942, 5,670 Jews, adults and children as well as refugees from Vilna and Bielica, were murdered outside the city. The 1,500 Jews left in the ghetto as skilled workers were joined by another 2,500 refugees On 18 Sept. 1943 they were all deported to the Majdanek concentration camp. A Zionist underground with 120 members operated in L. Numerous groups of Jews escaped to the forests, many joining the partisans. About 150 Jews survived the war but did not remain in L.

LIDZBARK Pomerania dist., Poland. Jews probably settled after the annexation to Prussia in 1772, reaching a peak pop. of 489 in 1885, with wide-ranging cultural and social activity in the second half of the 19th cent. Emigration depleted the community to 60 after WWI. Those remaining were either murdered on the spot by the Germans or expelled to the General Gouvernement shortly after the occupation in Sept. 1939.

LIEBLOS (now part of Gruendau) Hesse–Nassau, Germany. Numbering 29 in 1835, the J. community

also had members in Gettenbach (44), Niedergruendau (16), and Mittelgruendau (eight). After *Kristallnacht* (9–10 Nov. 1938), the seven remaining Jews fled.

LIEBSTADT (Pol. Milakowo) East Prussia, Germany, today Poland. The J. pop. numbered 110 in 1880; 86 in 1905; and 32 in 1925. The community maintained a synagogue and a cemetery, but in the Weimar period, religious services were held only on holidays. No information on the fate of the J. residents under Nazi rule is available.

LIEGE (Flem. Luik) Liege prov., Belgium. There was a J. community in the 19th cent. which in 1808, under French rule, belonged to the consistory of Krefeld, and in 1815, under Dutch rule, to the Maastricht district. There were 24 Jews living in L. in 1811 and 45 in 1846. By the second half of the 19th cent. 20–30 J. families lived in L. After 1917, Jews from Eastern and Central Europe began to settle. In 1925, the J. community in the province of L. numbered 600, most of Dutch origin. In 1940, the number increased to 2,000 after the arrival of East and Central European Jews. The Zionist organizations, Deror and Hashomer Hatzair, were active in L. in the 1930s. According to the German census of 1 Oct. 1941, there were 1,808 Jews in L. The city was one of four in Belgium where Jews were allowed to live after Sept. 1941. By Oct. 1942, numerous deportations had occurred. In all, 600 Jews were deported from L. On liberation, there were 1,200 Jews there. In 1962, the community numbered about 1,000 members.

LIEGNITZ (Pol. Legnica) Lower Silesia, Germany, today Poland. Jews are first mentioned in 1301 and at mid-cent they lived in a Street of the Jews and maintained a synagogue and cemetery. In 1559, J. settlement was banned, only to be renewed in 1812, at which time a prayer house was opened. A cemetery was established in 1815. The community founded an old age home in 1828 and reached a pop. of 236 in 1838 and a peak of 877 in 1900. New synagogues were consecrated in 1847 and 1879 and additional cemeteries were opened in 1838 and 1923. The community also maintained a building housing a religious school and library. Among the organizations operating in the community were the Middle Class Society, a B'nai B'rith lodge, the Zionist movement with a youth group, the J. Artisans Association, and the

Moses Mendelssohn Youth League. On the eve of the Nazi era, the J. pop. was about 850. The community subsequently organized courses in farming and gardening for potential emigrants; the Zionists provided Hebrew classes. A branch of Hehalutz was opened as late as 1938. On *Kristallnacht* (9–10 Nov. 1938), the synagogue and a number of J. stores were set on fire. In Oct. 1942, 22 Jews married to non-Jews remained in the city. There is no additional information about the fate of the community in WWII. Presumably those unable to emigrate met their deaths after deportation.

LIEPAJA Kurzeme (Courland) dist., Latvia. After a long residence ban, some Jews were allowed to live in L. from 1799 and by 1850 the pop. numbered 1,348. The J. community developed rapidly in the second half of the 19th cent., as this Baltic port city with its German majority became the second largest in Courland with direct links to the Russian grainlands. Most of the new J. settlers came from the Pale of Settlement (Russia, Poland, Lithuania) and were permitted to live in the city, forming a lower economic stratum vis-a-vis the original J. settlers, who dominated the grain trade. Jews also owned 11 of the city's 43 factories. In 1881 the J. pop. reached 6,651 and in 1911 a peak of 10,308 (total 83,650). In 1890, 400 of the new J. families were expelled and many lost their livelihoods in the 1892 grain crisis. New jobs were created in hotels, restaurants, and travel agencies as tens of thousands of Jews emigrating from Russia clustered around the port (approximately 40,000 a year in 1906–10). At the outset of settlement under Russian rule, a cemetery was established in 1803 and a prayer house in 1814. A second synagogue was built in 1828 and in the 1830s a *talmud torah* was opened. The original settlers, who dominated the community, underwent a process of Germanization during the first two-thirds of the 19th cent. while the new settlers remained loyal to traditional Orthodoxy and the Yiddish language as well as constituting a more strongly na-

Jewish wedding, Liepaja, Latvia, 1928

tionalistic element. The community boasted many loan societies and welfare agencies and extended substantial aid to the J. emigrants passing through. With the growth of the J. pop., the educational system expanded significantly, with a modern Hebrew school operating from 1885, a private girls' high school enrolling 200 before WWI, and over 500 public school children receiving supplementary Hebrew education in the afternoons. In 1885 a Hovevei Zion society became active with the community's rabbi, Dr. Hillel ha-Kohen Klein, as its chairman. In 1890–1904, Yehuda Leib Kantor, founder in 1886 of the first daily Hebrew newspaper, *Ha-Yom*, was official rabbi and from 1907 until after WWI the community was served by R. Aharon Ber Nurock, one of the leaders of religious Zionism in Latvia. Many Jews left L. at the beginning of WWI and the J. pop. fell to 7,379 in 1935 (total 57,098). Between the World Wars, the economic position of the Jews remained strong despite Latvia's loss of the Russian agricultural hinterland after independence and the decline of the city's importance. Jews owned 40% of L.'s larger business establishments and maintained their leading position in industry and the crafts while providing the city with all 24 of its doctors and 27 of its 35 dentists (in 1931). Until the advent of the repressive Ulmanis regime in 1934, the community functioned as an efficient and modern democratic organization under R. Nurock's leadership. It operated a day care center, summer camp, orphanage, old age home, clinic, and 16-bed tuberculosis sanatorium. A. J. public school with Yiddish as the language of instruction served 350 children. At a rival J. public school Hebrew replaced German in the 1920s as the language of instruction for its 400 pupils while another 140 studied at a Tarbut Hebrew school founded in 1928. A J. vocational school operated under the auspices of ORT. J. political activity was intense, with the Bund, Agudat Israel, and the Zionists with their youth movements active. The Maccabi sports club had 150–180 members. J. communal and commercial life came to an end under Soviet rule (1940–41). Only the Yiddish school was allowed to operate with a Soviet curriculum and some 50 J. property-owning families were exiled to the Soviet Union, where most died under harsh living conditions.

The Germans entered L. on 29 June 1941 after a few hundred Jews managed to escape to the Soviet Union. Around 7,000 remained. Political arrests and executions followed with the assistance of the Latvian "self-defense" organization, including a group of 33 J. men in early July and hundreds more on 8–9 July. On 5 July, the Nazi authorities published a long list of measures directed against the Jews: forced labor for males aged 16–60, curfews, bans in public places, confiscations of radios, typewriters, cars, bicycles, etc. In addition, Jews were fired from their jobs, robbed of property, and thrown out of their homes. At the end of July, another 1,000 J. men were rounded up and executed along with a few dozen J. mental patients. From Aug. to early Dec. 1941, in a period of relative quiet when the Jews were forced to work mainly for the German military establishment, another 658 were executed. On the night of 13 Dec., a mass *Aktion* commenced. All the Jews except for 1,000 or so with special work permits and their families, were brought to the environs of Skeden on the Baltic shore in sub-freezing weather and ordered to undress. They were then executed by German and Latvian firing squads. The killing continued for three days (15–17 Dec) and claimed 2,700–2,800 lives. Further *Aktions* through the spring brought the J. pop. down to 800, confined to a ghetto in July 1942. A council of elders (*Aeltestenrat*), appointed in early 1942 to regulate J. life, now operated to ensure a semblance of normalcy. The council organized a library and drama circle as well as a *minyan* and soup kitchen. The ghetto also accommodated for awhile a group of 160 Jews transferred from the Riga ghetto. The entire ghetto was liquidated on Oct. 1943 when all the remaining Jews were transported to the Kaiserwald concentration camp near Riga. From there the "unfit" – about half the Jews – were dispatched to the Latvian section of the Riga ghetto to share the fate of its inhabitants. The others remained at Kaiserwald. A few small groups of Jews survived the war in hiding and a few hundred returned to L. after the war, all leaving in the course of time.

LIGATNE Yidzeme Livonia dist., Latvia. The J. pop. in 1935 was 11 (total 249). Under the German occupation the Jews were murdered in a nearby forest by a Latvian "self-defense" unit in Aug. 1941.

LILLE (formerly L'Isle, Lisle) Nord dist., France. The J. community was founded in the 19th cent. In 1810, there were 136 Jews in L., most originating from Alsace-Lorraine. The synagogue was inaugurated in 1891. From 1872, L. was the seat of a chief rabbinate. The first chief rabbi, Binyamin Lippmann, formerly chief rabbi of Colmar, left Alsace after its annexation by Germany. Rabbi Shelomo Poliakoff, former rabbi of Luneville, served as chief rabbi in L. from 1921. He was greatly renowned for his assistance to the hundreds of J. immigrants from Poland who arrived in L. in 1923. In 1942, there were 1,259 Jews living in L., but only 247 were native-born. The Commisariat Generale aux Questions Juives (CGQJ) had an office in L. The Germans executed five Jews in L. in March-April 1942 in reprisal for a partisan raid. In Oct. 1943, the chief rabbi of L., Leon Berman, and his family were arrested, interned in Drancy, and deported to Auschwitz together with 336 other Jews. After the war, the community reorganized, numbering 3,200 Jews in 1964.

LIMANOWA Cracow dist., Poland. The community became organized in the 19th cent., growing to a pop. of 571 in 1880 and 905 (total 2,143) in 1921. Anti-J. riots erupted in 1898 and 1918 and between the World Wars economic conditions declined in the face of boycotts and competition from the Polish cooperatives. A flood in 1935 added to the distress. The Germans arrived on 10 Sept. 1939 and two days later murdered 12 well-to-do Jews for allegedly contributing to the Polish defense fund. In April 1942 all members of the *Judenrat* were murdered for not supplying a list of the old and sick. In June 1942, 1,500 Jews, including 600 refugees, were packed into a ghetto and on 18 Aug., after 160 of the old and sick were murdered, all were marched to Nowy Soncz for subsequent deportation to the Belzec death camp.

LIMBAZI Vidzeme (Livonia) dist., Latvia. Jews began settling in the 1860s, reaching a peak pop. of 254 in 1881 and thereafter declining steadily to a level of around 100 (3% of the total) between the World Wars. Their children were enrolled in the Latvian school and no community institutions functioned. The Germans arrived in early July 1941 and by Sept. had murdered off the J. pop. with active Latvian participation.

LIMBURG Hesse–Nassau, Germany. Jews living in L. founded a community but fell victim to the Black Death persecutions of 1348–49. The community which was established later worshiped in a disused church from 1867 until 1903 – when it dedicated a big new synagogue – and numbered 281 (3% of the total) in 1910. Under the Weimar Republic, branches of the Central Union (C.V.) and J. War Veterans Association were active. From 244 in 1933, the community dwindled to 67 in Nov. 1938. SS troops organized a pogrom shortly before *Kristallnacht* (9–10 Nov. 1938), and burned down the synagogue. Men, women, and children, were imprisoned. Altogether, 79 Jews emigrated and 117 moved to other German cities; at least 20 perished in the Holocaust.

LIMOGES Haute-Vienne dist., France. The J. presence dates back to the tenth cent. In the middle of the 11th cent., R. Yosef Tov Elem-Bonfils, a student of Rashi, headed the community. The modern J. community started in 1775. The regional rabbinate was located in L. During WWII, prior to the armistice signed between France and Germany in 1940, L. was the site of a camp in which 75% of the interned refugees were foreign Jews. L. became the primary haven for J. refugees from Alsace. About 1,500 families and many institutions were transferred to L. According to the 1941 census, the community comprised 2,500 Jews. After the war, in 1949, a new community was formed which numbered 560 members in 1964.

LINDHEIM Hesse, Germany. In 1910 the community numbered 44 (7% of the total). On *Kristallnacht* (9–10 Nov. 1938), the synagogue (which had probably been sold) was not damaged. All the Jews left (mostly emigrating) by 1939.

LINGEN Hanover, Germany. Jews arrived in the late 17th cent. but only a few J. families lived there until the last third of the 19th cent. Until 1869, when the community became independent, its members formed part of the neighboring Freren congregation. A synagogue was consecrated in 1878. The cemetery was opened in the mid-18th cent. In 1880, the J. pop. was 104, dropping to 40 under the Nazis. The synagogue was burned on *Kristallnacht* (9–10 Nov. 1938), and the next day the last J. business establishment in the town was looted. About 20 Jews were arrested; six were sent to the Buchenwald concentration camp. Two-thirds of the local Jews left Germany before 1939, most to Holland and Belgium, but many of these were subsequently deported following the German occupation. On the outbreak of war, 15 Jews remained in L. Two managed to emigrate to the U.S. in 1941; the rest were sent to the east.

LINGOLSHEIM Bas-Rhin dist., France. The J. community in L., today a suburb of Strasbourg, dates from the 18th cent. In 1766, there were 15 families in L. In 1784 the community comprised 18 families (84 persons). The synagogue was inaugurated in 1864. In 1936, there were 66 Jews listed in L. During WWII they were expelled by the Germans to the south of France, along with the rest of Alsace-Lorraine Jews. Twenty were deported. The local synagogue was vandalized and looted.

LINKMENYS (Yid. Lingmian) Utena dist., Lithuania. Jews first settled in the mid-19th cent. A Jew, Akiva Itzkovich, served with distinction as county governor. Between the World Wars, the ceasefire line between Lithuania and Poland divided the town. The J. pop. in 1940 was about 40. All the Jews were killed after the German conquest of 1941.

LINKUVA Siauliai dist., Lithuania. Jews first settled in the beginning of the 18th cent. The J. pop. in 1897 was 1,213 (61% of the total). At the end of the 19th cent., the Zionist movement was active. The J. pop. in 1923 was 625 (34%). Among L.'s natives was R. Bernard Revel (1885-1940), founder and president of Yeshiva College, New York (the precursor of Yeshiva U.). Under Soviet rule (1940-41) businesses were nationalized and Zionist activities forbidden. When the Nazis entered L. on 28 June 1941, there were about 1,000 Jews in the town, including refugees from Siauliai and surrounding communities. All were killed in the following month.

LINNICH Rhineland, Germany. Jews were probably expelled during the Black Death persecutions of 1348–49 along with the rest of the Jews in the bishopric of Cologne. They are mentioned again late in the cent. and in the mid-16th cent. None were present in the 1580–1624 period but subsequently a J. moneylender was accorded a letter of protection and the community proceeded to develop, its pop. rising from 46 in 1806 to a peak of 149 (total 1,928) in 1871. A private J. elementary school was opened in 1804. In 1865, L. became the seat of a regional congregation including the communities of Roerdorf, Setterich, and Gereonsweiler. A synagogue was consecrated in 1913 and a new building constructed for the J. elementary school next door in 1914. Over half the Jews engaged in trade, mostly as livestock dealers and butchers. Their

economic situation worsened considerably after WWI. One Jew was a member of the municipal council in 1927-33. In 1933, the J. pop. was 124. Under the Nazis, Jews were persistently subjected to harassment and economic boycott. On *Kristallnacht* (9-10 Nov. 1938), the synagogue was burned down, the J. cemetery was desecrated, and J. men under the age of 60 were sent to the Oranienburg concentration camp. The last 40 Jews were deported to the east via Kirchberg in early 1941. A total of 90 Jews perished in the Holocaust, 27 of them in Auschwitz.

LINOWA Polesie dist., Poland, today Belarus. Jews were present from the early 20th cent. and numbered 125 in 1921 (total 377). Around 150 were executed by the Germans in July 1942.

LINTFORT Rhineland, Germany. The J. pop. in 1933 was 41. Thirteen Jews remained in May 1939. Six or seven were deported to the Riga ghetto on 10 Dec. 1941, all perishing.

LINZ (I) Rhineland, Germany. Jews are first mentioned in 1218-1222. The community was destroyed in the Black Death persecutions of 1348-49. Small numbers of Jews were present in the 15th and 16th cents. and a permanent community was formed in the late 16th cent. In late 1819, Jews were attacked in the Hep! Hep! riots. A J. elementary school was started in 1844; a new synagogue was consecrated in 1851; and a cemetery was opened in 1854. The J. pop. reached a peak of about 130 in the last quarter of the 19th cent. (4% of the total). In the aftermath of WWI, a number of antisemitic incidents occurred and in the postwar economic crisis, a number of J. businesses closed down. In June 1933, about four months after the Nazi rise to power, there were 64 Jews in L. Under Nazi persecution, most left in 1933-38. On *Kristallnacht* (9-10 Nov. 1938), the synagogue and seven J. homes were wrecked and J. men arrested. The last 19 were moved to "J. houses" on 15 Sept. 1941; 12 were deported to the east on 30 March 1942 and seven to the Theresienstadt ghetto on 25 July. At least 23 perished in the Holocaust.

LINZ (II) Upper Austria, Austria. Jews were present in the 13th cent. and engaged in moneylending. In 1420, following Host desecration libels, many Jews were expelled or arrested. Others were beaten to

Dressing up as Jews in the antisemitic city of Linz, Austria (Archiv der Stadt Linz/photo courtesy of Yad Vashem, The Holocaust Martyrs' and Heroes' Remembrance Authority, Jerusalem)

death or forcibly baptized. In the beginning of the 16th cent., Jews resettled in L., but were expelled again in 1669. The modern community dates from 1789. Jews were engaged in the tobacco and salt trade. In 1856, the community was acknowledged as a religious corporation (*Kultusgemeinde*). In 1877 a splendid synagogue was inaugurated. During this time Adolf Kurrein served as rabbi and historian of the community. In 1911, a Blau-Weiss youth group was founded, which later obtained a hostel that served as a haven for young Austrian Jews after the *Anschluss* (13 March 1938). There were several Zionist groups active in L., including Keren Kayemet. The community maintained its own newspaper. A high percentage of Jews was represented in the professional class as doctors, lawyers, and teachers. In 1933, antisemitism became intense and often violent. In 1934, the community numbered 1,200 (total 200,000), dropping to 650 in 1938. Immediately after the *Anschluss* several Jews, including community leaders, were arrested and deported to the Dachau concentration camp. In May 1938, a J. school was closed down. On *Kristallnacht*

(9–10 Nov. 1938), the synagogue was completely burned down. Of those who managed to emigrate, 145 went to Palestine, 92 to the U.S., 45 to England, and 23 to South America. The others were deported to Vienna and from there to the east. In June 1939, the management of the L. community was transferred to the Vienna community. After the war, a small community was reestablished.

LIOZNO Vitebsk dist., Belorussia. Jews numbered 82 in 1766 and 1,665 (total 2,474) in 1897. A private J. school for boys and girls was in operation in 1910. In the Soviet period, the J. pop. dropped to 1,204 in 1926 and 711 in 1939. A J. elementary school was active. Many Jews worked in cooperatives and 20 families earned their livelihoods at a kolkhoz founded near the town in 1930. The Germans occupied L. on 16 July 1941. The 600 Jews who had not fled or been evacuated were joined by refugees from Vitebsk, Minsk, Bobruisk, and Warsaw. On 23 Feb. 1942, they were all brought to the village of Adamenky and murdered there in the course of three days, together with Jews from Kolyshki, Dobromysl, and Babinovichi making a total of nearly 1,500 dead.

LIPCA (Hung. Lipcse; Yid. Lipsha) Carpatho-Russia, Czechoslovakia, today Ukraine. Jews probably settled in the mid-18th cent., with 12 present in 1768. The J. pop. grew to 86 in 1830 and 260 (total 1,948) in 1880. In 1921, in the Czechoslovakian Republic, it was 515 and in 1941, 542. Seventeen J. families engaged in trade, 12 in crafts, and a few farmed. Jews also owned the local flour mill. The Zionists and Agudat Israel comprised the main J. political parties. After the Hungarian occupation of March 1939, a few dozen Jews were drafted into forced labor battalions, with some sent to the eastern front. In July–Aug. 1941, the Hungarian authorities undertook to expel a few J. families without Hungarian citizenship to the Ukraine, but when the operation was canceled, they returned home. The last 500 or so Jews were deported to Auschwitz in the second half of May 1944. Thirty Jews returned after the war but most left.

LIPCANI (Targ) Bessarabia, Rumania, today Republic of Moldova. Jews settled in the mid-17th cent. and became the main exporters of produce from northern Bessarabia to Austria, Germany, and other countries. Twenty synagogues functioned with every artisan union having its own prayer house. The J. pop. in 1930 was 4,693 (80% of the total). Zionist activity flourished between the World Wars. The young trained for the pioneer life and the first group of immigrants left for Palestine in 1921. In May 1936, swastikas appeared on walls during the convention of the Cuza Fascist Party in L. but a J. self-defense group prevented attacks. On 22 June 1941, German bombardments devastated the city and the Soviet authorities ordered the inhabitants to evacuate it. They fled to Bricena and some tried to escape with Soviet forces in July, only to be shot by German soldiers at Iampol. On 18 July, the Jews were marched toward Edineti, over 80% dying on the way. Throughout 1941–42 the J. pop. was moved from place to place, even back to L. and then on again to Transnistria where most died from starvation and disease or were killed by the local gendarmes. The few surviving families returned in 1944 to find their houses destroyed. The majority emigrated to Palestine.

LIPECKA POLANA (Hung. Lipcsemezo; Yid.

Palyien-Lipsha) Carpatho-Russia, Czechoslovakia, today Ukraine. J. settlement probably began at the turn of the 19th cent. Jews numbered 43 in 1830 and 119 (of a total 1,127) in 1880. Eight Jews engaged in trade, eight in crafts, and two operated flour mills. A few Jews were also farmers. The J. pop. rose to 238 in 1921 and 280 in 1941. The Hungarians occupied the town in March 1939 and in 1940–41 drafted dozens of Jews into forced labor battalions. In mid-May 1944, the remaining 260 or so Jews were deported to Auschwitz.

LIPEN (until the Soviet period, Kholui) Mogilev dist., Belorussia. Jews settled in the late 18th cent. Their pop. was 461 (of a total 532) in 1897 and 441 in 1926. In the mid-1920s, 56 J. families engaged in agriculture. In the first years of Soviet rule the Zionist movement maintained a foothold in the community. The Kadima youth movement and the Zionist Socialists were prominent. Zionist activity was curtailed by government decree in 1928. The Germans captured L. in early July 1941. In Oct., the Nazis and the local police executed the town's 300 Jews on the shores of Lake Svisloch. A few escaped to the forests.

LIPIANY (Hung. Hethars) Slovakia, Czechoslovakia, today Republic of Slovakia. Jews probably arrived in the early 18th cent. In 1848, they numbered about 130 and in 1859 they erected a wooden synagogue. In the early 20th cent., a *beit midrash* with a *talmud torah* was opened and a yeshiva operated intermittently as the J. pop. maintained a level of about 300 (20% of the total) until WWII. Hermann Kopp initiated Zionist activity in 1900 and was one of the founders of Mizrachi. Zionist activity expanded after WWI, with WIZO, Hashomer Hatzair, and Betar all active. A new synagogue was consecrated in 1929. Jews owned 38 commercial establishments, a sawmill, distillery, and dairy. In 1941, the Slovakian authorities closed down J.-owned businesses and seized their owners for forced labor. About 55 young J. men and women were deported to Majdanek and Auschwitz, respectively, in late March 1942. About 300 Jews from L. and its environs were deported to the Rejowiec ghetto in the Lublin dist. of Poland on 22 May.

LIPNIK NAD BECVOU Moravia, Czechoslovakia. J. refugees arrived from Olomouc and Znojmo in 1454. The community's synagogue, dating, at least, to the first half of the 16th cent. and in use until the Nazi era, was the oldest in Moravia and one of the oldest in Central Europe. In the 16th cent., Jews engaged in the cloth and livestock trade. They suffered under the Swedish occupation in 1643. In the mid-19th cent., the J. pop. rose to about 1,680, making L. the third largest community in Moravia, then dropped steadily to 154 (total 7,306) in 1930. The pianist Arthur Schnabel (1882–1951) was born in L. The Jews were deported to the Theresienstadt ghetto via Olomouc in late June–early July 1942. A few weeks later they were sent to Maly Trostinec and the Treblinka death camp where they perished.

LIPNISZKI Nowogrodek dist., Poland, today Belarus. J. settlement apparently commenced at the turn of the 17th cent. The community reached a peak pop. of 612 (total 1,377) in 1897, thereafter declining through emigration. Of the 100 J. families present in 1931, 30 owned stores, 40 earned their livelihood from crafts, 20 farmed, and a few were lumber merchants. However, under prevailing economic circumstances, 75% of the community required support from the Joint Distribution Committee and American relatives in the 1930s. The Zionist parties and youth movements were active between the World Wars and a J. elementary school was in operation. Under Soviet rule in 1939–41, the Jews were forced into the cooperative system. The Germans entered the town on 26 June 1941. In fall 1941 they expelled all the Jews to the Iwje ghetto. Most were murdered in the *Aktion* there on 12 May 1942. The rest were murdered after being transferred to Borisov around the end of the year. Underground resistance attempts were made prior to the final massacre.

LIPNO Warsaw dist., Poland. A J. settlement apparently existed in the 18th cent., confined to a special quarter by an 1824 edict. A new synagogue seating hundreds was built in the second half of the 19th cent. while a number of *shtiblekh* served the Hasidim. By 1897 the J. pop. stood at 2,079 (total 6,214). At the end of WWI, the Jews suffered from the depredations of Polish soldiers and were aided by the Joint Distribution Committee in rebuilding the community. Between the World Wars almost all the Zionist groups were active, as were the Bund and Agudat Israel. Antisemitism intensified in the late 1930s, with boycotts striking at J. shopkeepers. Many Jews fled east on the approach of the Germans at the outset of WWII. The rest were ex-

pelled in Nov. 1939, mostly to Warsaw, and shared the fate of local Jews.

LIPOVA (Hung. Lippa) S. Transylvania dist., Rumania. A J. community was founded in 1860 and in 1868 joined the Neologist association. The J. pop. was 255 in 1930 (4% of the total). On 10 July 1941, the J. pop was transferred to Timisoara. The property of those deported was confiscated and the synagogue was turned into a stable.

LIPOVETS Vinnitsa dist., Ukraine. Jews in L. are first mentioned in 1747. There were over 1,000 in the area in the early 18th cent. In 1897, the J. pop of L. was 4,135 (of a total 8,658). Two state J. schools were operating in the early 20th cent. In the Soviet period a J. elementary school was opened and a J. council (soviet) was active. Dozens of J. families earned their livelihoods in agriculture. In 1939, the J. pop. was 1,353. The Germans arrived on 24 July 1941. On 12 Sept. they murdered 183 Jews and in Oct. another 60–70 in a nearby forest.

LIPPEHNE (Pol. Lipiany) Brandenburg, Germany, today Poland. The community maintained a synagogue and a cemetery. The J. pop. was 70–85 throughout the 19th cent., dropping to 60 in the first decades of the 20th cent. When the Nazis came to power in 1933, there were 46 Jews in the town. The community's cemetery was desecrated in 1935. By Oct. 1942, only one Jew was living in L., probably protected by marriage to a non-Jew. No further information about the fate of the other Jews is available, but it is assumed that those who did not manage to emigrate to safe countries were deported to the east.

LIPPSTADT Westphalia, Germany. Jews may have been present before the Black Death persecutions of 1348–49. David Gans, one of the first J. scholars to engage in secular studies, and a disciple of the Maharal of Prague, was born in L. in 1541. Between 1738 and 1779, the Herz family held the only two letters of protection in L. They were also made citizens of the town, the earliest known case in Prussia. Economic competition in the 18th cent. produced friction between J. and Christian tradesmen, leading occasionally to violence. During the 19th cent., the J. pop. rose from 37 in 1817 to 152 in 1861 and a peak of 270 (total 10,406) in 1890. A synagogue was already in use by 1748 and a new one with room for an elementary school was completed in 1852. Most Jews were independent merchants. Some opened factories, including two flour mills and Westphalia Metal Industries for tin, the city's largest plant in the early 20th cent. Jews served as town councilors but antisemitic incidents and anti-J. incitement were conspicuous. In the Weimar Republic, Jews continued to engage mainly in trade (79.1% of 43 breadwinners in 1923, including 13 cattle dealers). The only remaining J. factory manufactured brooms and brushes. In 1933, the J. pop. was 115. In Oct. 1935, Jews were banned from entering all local restaurants, a rare measure in Germany at the time. By June 1938, only ten J. business establishments were still operating in the city. On *Kristallnacht* (9–10 Nov. 1938), the synagogue was set on fire, all J. stores were destroyed, and 25 J. men were sent to the Oranienburg concentration camp. Thirty Jews were moved to two "J. houses." Between Nov. 1938 and Jan. 1942, 26 Jews emigrated and 13 or 14 moved to other German cities. In all, 51 or 53 succeeded in emigrating, including 19 to Holland and 22 to South America. Twenty-two Jews remained in the city in early April 1942. On 28 April, five were deported to Zamosc in the Lublin dist. (Poland) via Dortmund together with other Jews from the area. Others were sent to "J. houses" in different cities and on 29 July 1942 they were deported to the Theresienstadt ghetto together with the four Jews still living in L. and all the other Jews remaining in the area. All 18 Jews deported from L. perished as did 16 local Jews deported from other cities in Germany and nine from Holland. Towards the end of the war, industrial forced labor camps for J. women, mainly from Hungary, Slovakia, and Poland, were set up in the city as an adjunct of Buchenwald. On 31 July and 23 Nov. 1944, 833 women were brought in from Auschwitz; 250 were moved from the Ravensbrueck concentration camp on 20 Nov. and a few dozen were later moved from the Bergen-Belsen concentration camp. All survivors were marched toward Bergen-Belsen and Leipzig in April 1945.

LIPSKO (I)   Lwow dist., Poland, today Ukraine. Jews settled in the 17th cent. and constituted a majority of the pop. by the late 18th, trading in grain, hides, and lumber. By 1921 the J. pop. had declined to 248. Most escaped to the Soviet Union in Sept.–Oct. 1939.

LIPSKO (II)   Kielce dist., Poland. Jews were present by the first half of the 18th cent., numbering 766 in 1827 and 1,376 (total 2,472) in 1921. The Germans arrived on 9 Sept. 1939 and immediately killed 12 Jews trying to flee their burning houses. A labor camp was established in 1940 and a ghetto in Dec. 1941 for 3,000 Jews including refugees. All were transferred to the Tarlow ghetto on 17 Oct. 1942 and from there deported to the Treblinka death camp. In Dec. 1942, the Germans killed a Polish family of three for hiding Jews.

LIPTOVSKY HRADOK   (Hung. Liptoujvar) Slovakia, Czechoslovakia, today Republic of Slovakia. Jews were present in the first half of the 18th cent. Their pop. was 83 (total 692) in 1900 and 63 in 1940. On 2 June 1942, most were deported to death camps in the Lublin dist. (Poland).

LIPTOVSKY SVATY MIKULAS   (Hung. Liptoszentmiklos) Slovakia, Czechoslovakia, today Republic of Slovakia. Jews settled under the protection of Count Pongrac in the early 18th cent. Local fairs and market days attracted J. merchants and peddlers and promoted the rapid growth of the J. community, which erected a synagogue in 1731. Its first rabbi was apparently Moshe ha-Kohen, who founded a *talmud torah*. He was followed by R. Loeb Kunitz in 1772–1813, who opened one of the first *yeshivot* in Slovakia in 1776. Under R. Eliazar Loew (1820–30), the yeshiva had over 100 students and L. became one of the most important centers of learning in Hungary. The community formed a Neologist congregation after the 1869 split and was reunited with Orthodox elements under the banner of Status Quo in 1875. The J. pop. grew from 801 in 1828 to 1,115 (total 2,811) in 1880. A J. hospital was opened in 1860. A ramified J. educational system developed, with its progressive elementary school attracting children from distant settlements, including non-Jews. It had an enrollment of 351 in 1855. Down through WWI, Jews were active in public life with a number serving as mayor. Jews were also among the pioneers of local industry. Among the town's native sons was Samuel Fischer (1859–1934), founder of Berlin's S. Fischer-Verlag publishing house. Jews included 12 industrialists, 81 merchants, and 25 artisans. The Zionist organization in L. was one of the largest and most active in Slovakia. WIZO, Hashomer Hatzair, Bnei Akiva, and the Maccabi sports club all had branches. In 1940, 957 Jews remained. In the Slovakian state, J. businesses were closed down and J. children

Jewish schoolchildren in a performance of Popelka *("Cinderella"), Liptovsky Sv. Mikulas, Slovakia, 1934 (Beth Hatefutsoth Photo Archive, Tel Aviv)*

expelled from public schools. Dozens of Jews were also seized for forced labor and in Nov. 1941, the synagogue and J. homes were vandalized. In fall 1941, 540 J. refugees from Bratislava arrived. In late March–early April 1942, 120 young Jews were deported, the men to the Majdanek concentration camp and the women to Auschwitz. On 2 June, 596 Jews from L. and its environs were transported to the Lublin dist. (Poland), the able-bodied men for labor at Majdanek and the rest for extermination in Sobibor. About 300 Jews were able to flee to the forests and neighboring villages before the Germans arrived in 1944. The postwar community (242 in 1949) continued into the 1980s.

LISBERG   Upper Franconia, Germany. The community numbered 95 in 1810 (total 562) and ended officially in 1904 when it was attached to Trabelsdorf.

LISIATYCZE   Stanislawow dist., Poland, today Ukraine. The J. pop. in 1921 was 119. The Jews were probably expelled to Stryj for liquidation in Sept. 1942.

LISICHANSK   (also Lisichya Balka, Lisichi Buyer-

ak) Voroshilovgrad dist., Ukraine. Jews probably settled in this coal mining town in the late 19th cent. In 1902, 40–50 J. breadwinners were engaged in petty trade and crafts. A Zionist society was organized in 1901 along with a library and J. educational facilities. In 1939, the J. pop. was 333 (of a total 26,181). After their arrival on 10 July 1942, the Germans murdered those Jews who had neither escaped nor been evacuated.

LISNIAKI   Poltava dist., Ukraine. The J. pop. in 1939 was 111. The Germans captured the town on 15 Sept. 1941 and murdered the few Jews who had neither escaped nor been evacuated.

LITENE   Livonia dist., Latvia. The J. pop. in 1930 was 16. The Jews were murdered by the Germans in fall 1941.

LITENI   Moldavia dist., Rumania. Jews settled in the mid-19th cent. The J. pop. in 1930 was 191 (6% of the total). Jews were persecuted after the rise to power of Goga-Cuza in 1937. On 22 June 1941, the J. community was expelled to Falticeni.

18th cent. inn, Litin, Ukraine

LITIN   Vinnitsa dist., Ukraine. Jews are first mentioned in 1578 and numbered 481 in 1765. In 1897, their pop. was 3,874 (total 9,420). A school for boys and a school for girls were operating in 1910. On 14 May 1919, 110 Jews were murdered in a pogrom. Additional riots, without loss of life, occurred in late May and July. A J. elementary school was opened in the early 1920s under the Soviets. A savings and loan fund helped needy J. artisans. A J. woman headed the local council (soviet) for many years. The J. pop. was 1,410 in 1939. The Germans captured L. on 17 July 1941, murdering 56 young Jews on 20 Aug. In an *Aktion* on 19 Dec., about 1,800 Jews were executed at a nearby army base. The few hundred skilled workers held in a camp in L. were killed off in a number of small *Aktions* in mid-1942. The last few dozen Jews were murdered in fall 1942. Over 1,000 Jews expelled from Bukovina were also executed in L. According to Soviet sources, 3,353 perished in all.

LITOMERICE   Bohemia (Sudetenland), Czechoslovakia. J. wine and salt merchants are mentioned in the mid-11th cent., the earliest reference to Jews in Bohemia other than to those in Prague. They were attacked and expelled in 1541 and in 1546 a *de non tolerandis Judaeis* privilege was accorded to the city, preventing the Jews from settling there for 300 years. From the late 19th cent. to 1930, the J. pop. averaged around 450 (total 18,498 in the latter year). A synagogue was consecrated in 1883. The Zionists were active after WWI. Nearly all Jews left during the Sudetenland crisis in fall 1938. The few J. men remaining were sent to concentration camps. Up to 1942, the Nazis operated a detention camp for J. families from the Sudetenland in nearby Dlazkovice. They also operated branches of the Flossenbuerg concentration camp in L. and its environs.

LIUBAN (I)   Minsk dist., Belorussia. Jews probably settled in the early 19th cent. after the settlement was accorded municipal status in 1808. By the late 1820s, they already numbered 561. In 1897, their pop. was 732 (total 766). A few dozen Jews were killed in a pogrom in late May 1921. In the Soviet period, a four-year J. school was still active in the early 1930s. A number of Jews worked in nearby kolkhozes. L. was the birthplace of the poet Zalman Epstein (1860–1936). In 1939, the J. pop. was 1,077. The Germans occupied the town in mid-July 1941. On 4 Aug., they murdered 150 J. men beside a pit 3 miles (5 km) outside the city. Somewhat later, another 700 from L. and its environs were also murdered. In 1943, the Germans opened the graves of the victims and burned their bodies

LIUBAN (II)   Leningrad dist., Russia. Jews probably

settled around the turn of the 19th cent. and numbered 121 in 1926 and 63 in 1939. The few who had not escaped or been evacuated when the Germans arrived on 25 Aug. 1941 were murdered.

LIUDINOVO   Oriol dist., Russia. Jews probably settled in the late 19th cent. and numbered 380 in 1926 and 232 (of a total 17,581) in 1939. A J. school was opened in 1926. After their arrival on 4 Oct. 1941, the Germans murdered the few Jews who had neither fled nor been evacuated.

LIUDVINAVAS   (Yid. Ludvinove) Marijampole dist., Lithuania. Jews began settling here in 1742. The J. pop. in 1897 was 369 (34% of the total). Fires and WWI caused many Jews to leave. The J. pop. in 1940 was about 20 families. After the German occupation of 1941, all the Jews were taken to Marijampole and murdered.

LIVADA   (Hung. Sarkoz) N. Transylvania dist., Rumania. Jews settled in the late 18th cent. The J. pop. in 1920 was 205 (5% of the total). In May 1944 the community was transferred to the Satu Mare ghetto and in June deported to Auschwitz.

LIVANI   Latgale dist., Latvia. A small community existed in the first half of the 19th cent., growing to 1,406 (total 2,658) in 1897. The Bund was active in the early 20th cent., joining local Latvian revolutionaries in their struggle against the Russian czar. In 1915, the Russian army expelled the Jews. Between the World Wars the returning J. pop. leveled off at around 1,000 (nearly a third of the total). They lived in straitened economic circumstances. The Zionist youth movements sent pioneers to Palestine while in 1925 Agudat Israel received most of the J. votes in the elections to the Latvian Sejm. A J. public school operated from 1921 and in a precedent-setting Latvian Supreme Court decision in 1929, it was determined that Hebrew would be the language of instruction as requested by the majority of parents. In the early 1930s the school enrolled 210 students while the new Yiddish school had 170. A Habad yeshiva also operated. J. communal life ended with the Soviet annexation in 1940. The Germans took the town on 29 June 1941. Local Latvians herded the Jews into the community's four synagogues and systematically killed them off in the forests in the following two months.

LIVNY   Oriol dist., Russia. J. settlement dates from the late 19th cent. The J. pop. was 302 (total 19,873) in 1926 and 140 in 1939. After their arrival on 26 Nov. 1941, the Germans murdered those Jews who had neither fled nor been evacuated.

LIW   Lublin dist., Poland. Jews were present by the early 17th cent. and numbered 125 in 1921. They were presumably deported to the Treblinka death camp.

LJUBLJANA   (Ger. Laibach) Slovenia, Yugoslavia, today Republic of Slovenia. A J. community existed at the end of the 12th cent. Under Austro-Hungarian rule the Jews were expelled in 1515. J. settlement was renewed in 1855 and by the end of the 19th cent. the Jews numbered nearly 100. From 1894 they were attached to the Graz community and from 1918 (with the founding of Yugoslavia) to Murska Sobota. On 16 April 1941, the German army penetrated Yugoslavia and L. was handed over to Italy. Only one J. family (five households) was left in L. at that point; some escaped to Italy and survived. A J. community was established in L. after the Holocaust.

LJUTA   (Hung. Havaskoz; Yid. Lita) Carpatho-Russia, Czechoslovakia, today Ukraine. Jews probably settled in the early 19th cent. Their pop. was 16 in 1830 and 80 (of a total 1,915) in 1880. In 1921, under the Czechoslovakians, the J. pop. rose to 121 and in 1941 to 317. The Zionists were active, particularly among the young. Nineteen Jews earned their livelihoods from trade and seven from crafts. The Hungarians occupied the town in March 1939 and in 1940–41 drafted dozens of young Jews into forced labor battalions, some being sent to the eastern front, where many were killed. The rest of the Jews were deported to Auschwitz in the second half of May 1944.

LOBZENICA   Poznan dist., Poland. Jews apparently settled in the late 15th cent. They suffered greatly in the Swedish war of the mid-17th cent. and particularly from the depredations of Stefan Czarniecki's Polish irregular troops in the aftermath. Their situation improved under Prussian rule from 1772, with a burgeoning cloth trade developing. A new synagogue was built in 1850 after the J. pop. reached a peak of 790 (of a total 2,384) in 1831. Emigration reduced the J. pop. to 77 in 1921. Some were murdered by the Germans in Sept. 1939 as they tried to flee the city; the others were presumably expelled to General Gouvernement territory.

LOCHEM Gelderland dist., Holland. A J. presence is recorded in the 14th cent. and again in 1665. Uninterrupted settlement began in the 18th cent. A community was organized in the last quarter of the cent. and numbered 152 in 1902. The J. pop. in 1941 was 125 (total 5,680). Most were deported in 1942–43; 14 survived the Holocaust in the camps or in hiding.

LODZ Lodz dist., Poland. Jews first settled at the end of the 18th cent. Within a relatively short time they constituted a third of the pop. and dominated economic life, mainly in trade and crafts. The first synagogue was built in 1809. Community council elections took place in 1810. The J. pop. increased rapidly, and from 1822 was confined to a J. quarter around the market square. The quarter was built up rapidly but was soon overcrowded through the influx of Jews from the surrounding villages attracted by the city's industrial development. In 1861 permission was granted to expand the quarter. About half the Jews of L. were involved in purchasing raw materials for the flourishing textile industry and the sale of the manufactured goods within Poland and, after 1850, to Russia. They also opened warehouses for storing yarn sold to the weavers. J. tailors, furriers, and hatmakers joined the local guilds and set up their own organizations with their own synagogues. During the early 19th cent., Jews entered professional life as lawyers and doctors and entered nursing. J. schools were opened in the 1860s. Religious life was dominated by the Hasidim, the majority from the court of the Rabbi of Kotsk and others from the Przysucha and Gur courts. During the second half of the 19th cent., L. became the second largest J. community in Poland (after Warsaw) and one of the largest in the world. The J. pop. in 1897 was 98,671 (32% of the total). The decline in the J. pop. in the late 19th and early 20th cent. was due to economic crises, Russian administrative restrictions on the import of Polish goods, and the migration of Jews to the U.S. During the last two decades of the 19th cent., Jews established factories in L. (105 of 261), most of which were small enterprises with fewer employees than in non-J.-owned industry with its modern equipment. The J. contribution, especially in the J.-owned textile factories, was the variety of goods manufactured. On the eve of WWI, 7,000 of the 17,000 weavers working on their own looms in their homes – usually the entire family – were Jews. They worked up to 16 hours a day under difficult conditions, in most cases earning less than factory employees. Jews constituted only a small proportion of factory employees because they preferred to retain their independent status, mainly for religious reasons, i.e. the fact that they were unable to work on the Sabbath, and because of the refusal of non-J. craftsmen (mainly Germans) to train Jews. The Bund in 1897 began to organize J. workers clandestinely. Their members joined in mass demonstrations and published underground periodicals. In 1903, a Zionist socialist group was organized which in 1905 became the Po'alei Zion party. The Russians exiled many of the leaders to Siberia after the 1905–07 revolution. In 1903 the Polish Socialist Party (PPS) organized a J. section in L. In the first decade of the 20th cent., Christian religious preachers incited workers to carry out pogroms against the Jews. Zionist activity began in 1897 and as their numbers increased, the Zionists took over some synagogues and prayer houses and opened a Zionist *talmud torah* with 800 pupils. An old age home, a hospital, an orphanage, and a school were opened in the early 20th cent. by J. philanthropists. A yeshiva was founded in 1912 and was soon attended by hundreds of students. Other *yeshivot* were established during WWI or between the World Wars. Modern J. schools were opened in L. at the end of the 19th cent. and a vocational school was established in 1907. The first J. high school in the Russian Empire was opened by R. Dr. Mordekhai (Markus) Braude in 1912, serving as a model for J. high schools throughout Poland during the interwar period. These were bilingual (Hebrew-Polish) schools with national Zionist educational trends. The Zamir society founded by Zionists in 1899 had its own choir and concert hall and in 1905 established a theater troupe. The Bund created its own cultural society (the Arpeh) in 1908. The first J. sports association in Poland, Bar Kokhba, was established in L. in 1912. In 1908, J. newspapers began to appear. R. Eliyahu Hayyim Meisel, who served the community from 1873 to 1912, repudiated Zionism and all political organization, but was popular among the members of the community, especially the Hasidim. A Reform congregation established its own synagogue in 1888 and from 1908 its rabbi was Dr. Braude. He was also secretary of the J. faction in the Austrian parliament, chairman of the J. Elementary and Secondary School Association of Poland, and an ardent Zion-

The Lodz Symphony Orchestra, Poland, 1916

ist. In 1908, the periodical *Lodzer Tagblat* began to appear, and in 1912 *Lodzer Morgenblat* was published.

From the outbreak of WWI to the German invasion on 6 Dec. 1914, the J. pop. declined from 200,000 to less than 150,000 as a result of evacuation, conscription into the army, and restrictions imposed by the Russians. The Jews moved eastwards or took refuge in surrounding villages to wait out the war. The Germans confiscated all raw materials, manufactured goods, and machinery, and cut off trade with Russia. The situation of the Jews declined radically and at times ended in starvation, sickness, and death. The community and the J. political parties provided financial aid, set up soup kitchens, and took steps to relieve the suffering. The Zionist organizations flourished during the war years and some of the synagogues permitted Zionist activities on their premises. The J. education system expanded and in 1919 the network of *szabasowki* elementary schools were attended by 7,694 pupils studying in 184 classes. A number of elementary and high schools were opened where the language of instruction was Hebrew or Yiddish. In 1915, the Zamir society founded an orchestra that per-

formed with its choir under the baton of leading J. conductors. After the war, Jews returned from other towns and villages and the J. pop. increased, to 202,497 (30% of the total) in 1931. Seventy-one percent of J. workers were employed in small businesses, mainly workshops and cottage industries, earning minimum wages. Manifestations of antisemitism were rife immediately after the war and increased considerably during the 1930s. Students organized anti-J. riots; youths belonging to the Endecja Party boycotted J. shops and destroyed J.-owned stalls; and the local press spread Nazi antisemitic propaganda. On 17 Feb. 1936, the Jews held a mass rally protesting manifestations of antisemitism, boycotts, and riots. Agudat Israel controlled the community council from 1931 until the outbreak of WWII. Zionist parties played a leading role in the community and a Zionist representative was elected to the Sejm. Many Jews were supporters of the illegal Communist Party and the Bund was quite strong. Between the World Wars, the majority of the pupils in government high schools were Jews. Three J. high schools existed where the language of instruction was Hebrew, the larg-

Two sisters, Gutta and Hela Berliner, taking a stroll on the Sabbath in Lodz, Poland, 1939

est (600 pupils) directed by the poet Itzhak Katzenelson (1886–1944), a native of L. Agudat Israel ran a network of Yesodei Torah schools for boys and Beth Jacob school for girls. The Beth Jacob national teachers' training seminary was located in L. The Tarbut organization ran adult education classes in Hebrew language and literature and Bible. The Beit Yisrael yeshiva had an enrollment of 400 students. At the local branch of the YIVO Institute for J. Research 200 persons were engaged in the study of J. topics. The Friends of the Hebrew University founded in Lodz in 1925 had 500 members. The J. press flourished, and hundreds of books on rabbinic and general J. subjects were published in Yiddish and Hebrew. J. theaters thrived between the World Wars with actors famous in the J. world appearing on their stages. The L. community was proud of the large number of authors who made an important contribution to Yiddish and Hebrew letters. The Polish poet Julian Tuvim was born in L. as were the painters Samuel Hirszenberg, Jankel Adler, and Arthur Szyk.

During the first days of WWII, 60,000 Jews fled the city. When the German army entered L. on 8–9 Sept. 1939, persecution of Jews began immediately. In addition to physical attacks, J. bank accounts were blocked; Jews were forbidden to have more than 2,000 zloty in their possession; and Jews were banned from dealing in textiles. German officials raided J. homes and robbed their possessions, stole goods from J.-owned shops, and rounded up Jews for menial tasks. Intellectuals and community functionaries were arrested and interned in the Radogoszcz camp. Many were murdered in the nearby forests. Some were transferred to other internment camps and the remainder deported to the General Gouvernement. On 15–17 Nov., the Germans set fire to the synagogues or blew them up. The Nazis continued to attack and degrade the Jews in L., especially the rabbis and religious leaders. Jews were forced out of their homes to provide accommodations for German officials. On 12–13 Dec. 1939, thousands of Jews were deported to the General Gouvernement. On 24 Jan. 1940, the J. pop. was ghettoized in the Old City area, the process continuing until 1 March, when the several thousand Jews living in the city were attacked, beaten, and herded into the ghetto. Others were taken to internment camps and some were shot in the nearby forest. On 1 May 1940, there were 163,777 Jews (including 6,471 refugees) within the confines of the ghetto. The Germans set up a *Judenrat* on 13–14 Oct. 1939 and appointed Mordekhai Hayyim Rumkowski chairman with a 31-member council, all of whom were arrested on 11 Nov. 1939 and taken to the Radogoszcz interment camp; only eight returned. A new *Judenrat* was appointed in Jan. 1940. A J. police force was set up under the control of the *Judenrat*. The overcrowding, lack of drinking water, and primitive sanitary conditions in the ghetto were so acute that a typhus epidemic broke out in March 1940. By Sept. 1940, over 100,000 of the ghetto inhabitants were completely dependent on the *Judenrat* for their sustenance, as little work was available and the meager food supplies were rationed. By July 1941, to alleviate the situation, 45 workshops for tailoring, shoemaking, woodwork, metalwork, weaving, upholstery, and tanning were set up to fill orders from the German army as well as from private firms and institutions which supplied the raw materials and machinery. This became the main source of income of the ghetto and provided employment for 53,000 workers by March 1942. As soon as the Jews entered the ghetto, they were made to exchange all their foreign currency for special currency

Selling books in Lodz Ghetto, Poland

valid in the ghetto only. The Germans also confiscated all jewelry and monies brought in or received from outside. The ghetto committee also expropriated all tools, raw materials, and personal belongings. All these items were registered with the promise to return them after the war. Food was rationed, but many were unable to pay for their entire allotment and the surplus was sold on the black market. Public soup kitchens were opened in summer 1940. Some operated for specific groups: political groups such as the Zionists and the Bund; the intelligentsia; the ultra-Orthodox (kosher kitchens), officials of certain institutions (e.g., the J. police, the fire brigade); schoolchildren; and closed welfare institutions. Persons holding public positions or engaged in manual labor were given extra rations. The mortality rate increased throughout the ghetto period, reaching its peak in summer 1942. The main causes of death were heart disease, tuberculosis, and undernourishment. In 1940, 45 religious and secular educational institutions were functioning in the ghetto. These included schools for the deaf and dumb, the retarded, and institutionalized juvenile delinquents, a high school for boys and a high school for girls, and a vocational school. All subjects were taught in Yiddish. The schools were closed down at the end of 1941 when their premises were allocated to refugees. The orphanage in the ghetto (the Kolonia) provided for children aged 7-15 and at its peak housed 1,500 children. Within the ghetto, the political groups—especially the Bund—organized lectures, choir performances and symphony concerts, plays and literary evenings; these events were attended by hundreds of adults and young people. Art exhibits were organized. The artists were augmented at the end of 1941 by an influx of refugee artists from Western Europe. An official archives containing documentation on life in the ghetto was set up and from Jan. 1941 to July 1944 published a daily bulletin. Sections of the archives survived the Holocaust and serve as source material for research on the L. community. Archive workers gathered an impressive library of rabbinical and religious works. The Sonnenberg library had some 7,500 books with a readership of 4,000. In 1940, religious services were permitted on the high holidays, but after that none was permitted, although services were held clandestinely. A rabbinical council, functioning alongside the *Judenrat*, attended to the religious requirements of the ghetto community. The Zionist parties continued to function within the ghetto and their youth groups (950 pioneers) trained in agriculture in over 30 cooperatives. Members of these groups also served as counselors in the Kolonia orphanage and were conscripted for work in the ghetto. These cooperatives operated for about one year. They were disbanded in spring 1941. Youth work was then restricted to organizing functions and teaching. The conscription of Jews for labor battalions began in Dec. 1940 and by Nov. 1941, 3,859 J. males were sent mainly to camps in the Poznan area to build the highway to Frankfurt. In March 1940 and again on 27 July, the Germans took several hundred inmates of mental hospitals, as well as the chronically ill in the J. hospitals, to the Zgierz forest and shot them. From 16 Jan. 1942, 10,000 Jews were deported to the Chelmno extermination camp. Another 3,074 followed on 2 Apr. 1942. In Oct.–Nov. 1941, 20,000 Jews from Germany, mainly the elderly and ill, were brought to L. and accommodated under the worst conditions, with many starving to death. In May 1942 over half were deported to Chelmno. A further 15,500 Jews from other towns and villages were brought to L. The last stage of the deportations took place at the beginning of Sept. 1942, when 16,000 Jews were sent to their death in Chelmno. Some 90,000 Jews still remained in L., mainly to man the workshops providing goods to the Germans. This labor camp was the last surviving J. community in Nazi-occupied Poland. As the destruction of the ghetto progressed, groups of youth organized to carry out underground activities and sabotage. The final deportation of the 76,000 remaining Jews began in June 1944 and continued up to 29 Aug. The majority were sent to Auschwitz. Rumkowski, who had ruled the ghetto with a high hand, was deported with his family to Auschwitz, where they died. There are differing and conflicting assessments among survivors and researchers of Rumkowski's behavior in the ghetto. The 900 survivors were liberated by Soviet forces in Jan. 1945. Another 10,000–20,000 survived the war in Nazi camps or in the USSR. After the war, L. became the largest J. center in Poland and the head offices of J. organizations were established there. In fall 1945, 20,000 Jews were registered with the J. Community Council. Another 40,000 were registered temporarily. The Council provided accommodation, clothing, medical attention, and employment. The community was given financial assistance by the Joint Distribution Committee. A J. elementary school teaching in Yiddish was opened in 1945 and in the course of time it expanded to include a high school. It was closed in 1969 due to lack of pupils. The Zionist movement opened a school in 1945 in which the language of instruction was Hebrew. In the 1947–48 school year it was attended by up to 200 pupils. Writers and artists were attracted to L. and an association of writers and journalists was founded whose members organized literary evenings, plays, and concerts. J. artists also set up their own organization and organized exhibits. The Central Committee for J. History opened its offices in L. and up to the end of 1946 published 26 works on the history of the Jews in Poland. Zionist parties renewed their activities in L. immediately after the war, as did the youth movements. A branch of the Bund was opened, but all these organizations were disbanded in 1949 with the Soviet domination of Poland. A J. congregation whose activities were confined to religious affairs was organized. From 1949 to the 1970s, Jews left L. in three waves of emigration to Israel, Western Europe, and the U.S. Only a few hundred remained.

LOERRACH   Baden, Germany. Jews first settled after the Thirty Years War (1618–48), enjoying freedom of trade and worship. There were none present in the late 17th cent. A permanent J. settlement developed during the 18th cent. with the arrival of Swiss refugees. In 1808 a synagogue was erected, with the community continuing to maintain a conservative posture in the era of religious reform. The J. pop. grew to 248 in 1875 (total 8,455). Thereafter it declined steadily with the exodus of the young. The Zionists became active in the 1920s. In 1933, 162 Jews remained, operating numerous business establishments. Emigration was stepped up as the process of "Aryanization" took hold. About two-thirds left by 1940. Community life was nonetheless maintained. On *Kristallnacht* (9–10 Nov. 1938), the synagogue was burned, the two J. cemeteries were desecrated, and J. men were detained at the Dachau concentration camp. On 22 Oct. 1940, 50 Jews were deported to the Gurs concentration camp; another 18 local Jews were sent to the camps from other places. In all, 30 were murdered in Auschwitz while 19 survived the Holocaust.

LOETZEN (Pol. Gizycko) East Prussia, Germany, today Poland. Jews probably stayed occasionally in L. from the Middle Ages. A small group of Jews from Flatow established a permanent settlement in 1813. The J. pop. was 46 in 1843; 172 in 1873; and 96 in 1925. A J. cemetery dated back to 1807 at the latest and a synagogue was dedicated in 1880. J. businesses were attacked in summer 1932. On the eve of the Nazi assumption of power in 1933, there were 73 Jews in L. As early as March 1933, J. residents were arrested, charged with engaging in Communist activities or possession of firearms. On *Kristallnacht* (9–10 Nov. 1938), the synagogue was burned down. Many Jews emigrated and by May 1939 only 20 were left in the town. It may be assumed that those who did not manage to flee abroad were deported.

LOEV Gomel dist., Belorussia. Jews probably settled in the 16th cent. In 1766, 194 were registered as paying a poll tax. A synagogue and four prayer houses were erected in the late 19th cent. and in 1897 the J. pop. rose to 2,150 (total 4,667). J. property was destroyed in anti-J. riots in 1905 but no lives were lost. In the early 1920s, under the Soviets, many Jews moved to the big cities and the J. pop. dropped to 1,064 in 1926. A kolkhoz was founded nearby in 1928 and in 1930 nine J. families were employed there. A J. elementary school was in operation. In 1939 the J. pop. was 535. The Germans occupied L. on 27 Aug. 1941 and within a short period of time, four Jews were shot on the banks of the Dnieper River. In late Oct., SS men took over 150 Jews to a camp in Gomel; the rest of the Jews were executed shortly thereafter at the Dnieper.

LOEWEN (Pol. Lewin Brzeski) Lower Silesia, Germany, today Poland. The J. pop. was 28 (total 1,600) in 1849 and 80 in 1880. The community maintained a cemetery from 1882 and a synagogue was established in 1901. In 1932, the J. pop. was 39 and in 1937 it was 30. On *Kristallnacht* (9–10 Nov. 1938), rioters burned the prayer house and destroyed three J. stores. Two Jews married to non-Jews remained in Nov. 1942. No additional information is available about the fate of the community in WWII. Presumably those Jews who failed to leave perished after deportation.

LOEWENBERG (Pol. Lwowek Slaski) Lower Silesia, Germany, today Poland. Jews inhabited a Street of the Jews by the mid-14th cent. In 1453, the Jews of L. were imprisoned and then expelled from the city with the king distributing their land and houses to local residents. J. settlement was only renewed in the early 19th cent. A synagogue was consecrated in 1808. The J. pop. was 52 in 1840, 38 in 1913, and 22 in 1925. In 1926, Nazis desecrated the J. cemetery (opened in 1871), smashing tombstones and painting swastikas on graves. The J. pop. dropped to 20 on the eve of the Nazi rise to power in 1933 and to 12 (total 6,334) in 1937. One Jew married to a non-Jew remained in Nov. 1942. No additional information is available about the fate of the community under the Nazis. Presumably those Jews who did not emigrate were deported and perished.

LOGOYSK Minsk dist., Belorussia. Jews probably settled in the first half of the 18th cent. In 1766, the J. pop. was 223, rising to 1,442 (of a total 2,296) in 1897. In the Soviet period, the J. pop. dropped to 864. Some Jews worked in agriculture – ten families in a J. kolkhoz in 1925 and 60 families in a number of mixed kolkhozes in 1930. A J. school was still active in 1931. The Germans captured L. in late June 1941 and on 30 Aug. murdered 1,200 Jews from L. and the surrounding area beside pits prepared outside the town, in the direction of Gayna.

LOHISZYN Polesie dist., Poland, today Belarus. The J. pop. numbered 1,587 in 1897 (total 3,336) and declined to a few hundred in the 1920s. The Jews were executed by an SS cavalry unit on 10 Aug. 1941.

LOHRA Hesse dist., Germany. Previously united with the Jews of Fronhausen and Roth, the L. community numbered 35 (3% of the total) in 1933 and worshiped in rented premises until 1937. Most of the Jews left, eight emigrating, but four were deported in 1942.

LOHR-AM-MAIN Lower Franconia, Germany. Jews were victims of the Rindfleisch massacres of 1298. Few Jews lived there from the mid-16th cent. until Bavarian Jews attained equal rights in 1861. The modern community, which was founded by Jews from Steinbach, was well integrated into the city's social and cultural life. There was organized J. education for the children. The J. pop. was 91 in 1900 and 70 in 1933 (total 6,133). From the outset of Nazi rule in 1933 the Jews suffered from anti-J. agitation and the economic boycott, with anti-J. rioting after the *Anschluss* (13 March 1938). The synagogue and J. homes were vandalized on *Kristallnacht* (9–10 Nov. 1938). Fifty Jews subsequently left for other German cities and 19 emigrated.

LOHRHAUPTEN (now part of Floersbachtal) Hesse–Nassau, Germany. Dating from the 18th cent., the J. community numbered 59 (7% of the total) in 1861 and built a synagogue in 1889. Reduced to 21 in 1933, the community disbanded four years later and the nine remaining Jews left.

LOKACZE Volhynia dist., Poland, today Ukraine. Jews are first recorded in 1569, fleeing during the Chmielnicki massacres of 1648–49 and subsequently enjoying favorable economic conditions. Dov Baer, the *Maggid* of Mezhirech, was born there c. 1704 and in the 19th cent. Olyka, Turzysk (Trisk), and Ruzhin Hasidism were represented in the community. In 1897, the J. pop. reached a peak of 1,730 (of a total 2,309), falling to 1,270 in 1921. Between the World Wars, the Zionist youth movements became active. Jews engaged in the lumber and farm produce trade. The Germans took the town on 23 June 1941, instituting a regime of forced labor and extortion and appointing a *Judenrat*. In Oct., the Jews were confined to a closed ghetto and on 13 Sept. 1942, 1,350, including refugees, were executed beside open pits.

LOKHVITSA Poltava dist., Ukraine. Jews settled in the first half of the 17th cent. when the town was under the proprietorship of Prince Vishnieviecki. Many were killed in a Cossack raid in 1636. The Jews fled in 1648 from the Chmielnicki threat but returned by the

late 18th cent. They numbered 2,465 (total 8,911) in 1897. The community maintained a *talmud torah* and elementary school (three grades). The Oct. 1917 Revolution inspired a public awakening and new J. schools opened and Zionist activity was organized. All this came to an end in the 1920s under Soviet rule. In 1939, the J. pop. was 614. The Germans occupied L. on 12 Sept. 1941 and murdered 287 Jews on 12 May 1942.

LOKNYA Kalinin dist., Russia. Jews probably settled at the turn of the 19th cent. In 1939 their pop. was 193 (total 2,193). After the Germans occupied the town in fall 1941, they transferred the Jews to a single building. From there, 50 were brought to the nearby village of Danilovka in early Feb. 1942 and executed.

LOLLAR Hesse, Germany. Numbering 62 in 1871, the community dwindled to eight in 1933. Its synagogue was destroyed on *Kristallnacht* (9–10 Nov. 1938) and the last four Jews were deported in 1942.

LOMAZY Lublin dist., Poland. Jews probably settled in the late 16th cent., establishing an organized community in the early 17th cent. The community grew to a pop. of 725 in 1827 and 1,793 (total 3,183) in 1897. In the late 19th cent., Jews opened a hide-processing plant, a soap and candle factory, and an oil factory. Economic and wartime conditions reduced the J. pop. to 829 in 1921 and in 1933 nearly half the J. pop. required assistance to get through the Passover holidays. In 1934, the community was victimized by a pogrom. The Germans occupied the town permanently in early Oct. 1939 and in early 1940 confined the Jews to a ghetto under a regime of forced labor. In May 1942, the ghetto pop. stood at 1,700. On 17 Aug. 1942, over 1,000 Jews including refugees were executed in the nearby forest.

LOMIANKI GORNE Warsaw dist., Poland. The J. pop. in 1921 was 130 (total 215). Most of the town's 300 Jews (including refugees) were expelled by the Germans to the Warsaw ghetto in early 1941.

LOMNA Lwow dist., Poland, today Ukraine. The small 19th cent. community was reduced to a pop. of 235 (total 2,010) after the turn of the cent. owing to emigration and WWI flight. The Germans entered in July 1941 and expelled the Jews to the Turka ghetto in July 1942 where they were killed off in separate *Aktions* over the next few months.

LOMZHA Bialystok dist., Poland. An organized community with a synagogue and cemetery already existed by 1494, with Jews dominating the lumber trade. Local efforts to undermine J. tradesmen led to the granting of a *de non tolerandis Judaeis* decree by King Sigismund Augustus II in 1556, which was definitively enforced in 1598. Many of the Jews settled nearby, in Piatnica and in the fishing village of Rybaki, in order to continue doing business in L. Only in the first half of the 18th cent. did Jews begin settling in L. again. Their status improved somewhat after Napoleon passed through the town on his way to Russia in 1812 (quartering in a Jew's home, the largest in L.). Although the old restrictions remained officially in force under the Polish Kingdom founded in 1815, the J. pop. grew and commerce flourished. After the Polish rebellion of 1830, the Jews were allowed to live in all parts of the city and within 30 years their pop. doubled, reaching 2,608 (total 5,881) in 1857 as Jews renewed the Danzig–Kaunas (Kovno) transit trade via the Augustine Canal. The J. pop. again rose after residence restrictions were officially ended by imperial edict in 1862, reaching a level of 8,752 in 1897 (total 19,223) which remained stable until WWII. In the late 19th cent., the Poles again attempted to undermine J. trade, initiating boycotts and founding cooperatives. A monopoly law excluding Jews from the trade in alcoholic beverages also severely affected J. livelihoods. Nonetheless, the Jews adapted themselves to changing conditions, setting up factories (sugar, soap, chicory, bricks and shingles), seven windmills, and carpentry and metalworking shops, one of the latter developing into a vocational school and another becoming a big machine-casting plant. They also benefited as contractors in the construction of army barracks in the city and continued to constitute the majority of craftsmen. Jews participated in the revolutionary events of 1905, organizing strikes and joining demonstrations. In WWI hundreds were drafted into the Russian army and thousands left the city. Those remaining suffered from severe food shortages under the German occupation. Among the community's rabbis, R. Yehuda Leib Gordin encouraged Zionist circles and his Russian-language pamphlet on the Talmud was cited by the defense in the Beilis trial in 1913. R. Yitzhak Halevi Herzog (1888–1959), future chief rabbi of Israel, was born in L.; his father,

R. Yoel, subsequently served as rabbi in Leeds, England, and Paris. A splendid *beit midrash* was built in 1841 and a new synagogue was completed in 1881. Among the community's institutions were an orphanage founded in 1893, an old age home for 300 residents set up in 1894, and a new J. hospital established in 1897. A *talmud torah* founded in 1831 was gradually converted into a J. elementary school with secular and Hebrew-language studies. In the 1890s, Zionist groups proliferated, but in the 1920s the Bund and Agudat Israel still outweighed them in the municipal and community councils, respectively. The Po'alei Zion group only came to dominate the latter in 1932. Also prominent were Mizrachi, which promoted modern Orthodox education, and the Ha-Tehiyya youth movement (founded in 1909), whose clubhouse was the focus of Zionist activity for many years. The Hehalutz organization, with 800 members, sent numerous pioneers to Palestine (30 in 1921–22 alone). The community also maintained theater and sports groups and nine newspapers and journals appeared between the World Wars. Throughout the period discriminatory measures continued against J. tradesmen. Bakers and butchers were closed down in the late 1930s and J. merchants were physically attacked on market days. In 1937, Polish children attacked students in the J. school with knives and in 1938, 1,000 windows were smashed in J. homes. The Germans entered the city on 22 June 1941 after a two-year Soviet occupation. Throughout July, Jews were loaded onto trucks and transported to the Galczyn forest, where 2,000 were machinegunned down. A *Judenrat* was set up in the same month and on 12 Aug. over 10,000 Jews including refugees were packed into a ghetto. Over 200 Jews "suspected" of Communism were executed on 16 Aug. Two thousand more without work permits were murdered in the forest on 17 Sept. In the ghetto, efforts were made to sustain the community. A soup kitchen, hospital, old age home, and orphanage were set up as well as clandestine classrooms. Nonetheless, thousands died from starvation and disease. On 1 Nov. 1942, the 8,000 or so Jews who remained were sent to the Zambrow barracks and other transit points and from there mostly deported to Auschwitz on 14–18 Jan. 1943.

LONDORF Hesse, Germany. Jews first settled in 1650 and numbered 103 (13% of the total) in 1828. The community was affiliated with Giessen's Liberal rabbinate. Of the 40 Jews living there in 1933, 21 emigrated before 1939. On *Kristallnacht* (9–10 Nov. 1938) the synagogue was burned down and the remaining 15 Jews perished in the Holocaust.

LONKA RUSTYKALNA Lwow dist., Poland, today Ukraine. The J. pop. in 1921 was 150. The Jews were expelled to Sambor for extermination in Aug. 1942.

LOPATYN Tarnopol dist., Poland, today Ukraine. Jews arrived around the beginning of the 19th cent., their numbers leveling off at 500 or so (15% of the total) toward the end of the cent. The rival Belz and Husyatin-Ruzhin hasidic courts dominated the community's religious life. Russian soldiers pillaged and burned J. homes in WWI and economic conditions worsened between the World Wars with many Jews leaving the town. Under Soviet rule (1939–41), J. public and commercial life was shut down. The Germans arrived on 24 June 1941 and immediately instituted a regime of extortion and forced labor. In a mass *Aktion* in fall 1942, Jews were rounded up and deported to the Belzec death camp. Shortly afterwards, the rest were ordered to Radziechow, though many made their way to Stanislawczyk. In either case they shared the same fate.

LOPIANKA Lublin dist., Poland. The J. pop. was 224 (total 421) in 1921. Most worked in the Perlis factories in Baczki and Ostrow. In Sept. 1942, the Jews were deported by the Germans to the Treblinka death camp via Baczki.

LOPUSZNO Kielce dist., Poland. Jews formed a majority of the pop. in the 19th cent. – 587 of a total 828. Many left for larger cities and in 1921 they numbered 397. On the eve of the German occupation in Sept. 1939, there were 100–150 Jews in L. All were deported to the Treblinka death camp via the Chencini ghetto in Sept. 1942 after 30 were murdered locally.

LORINCI Nograd dist., Hungary. Jews settled in the early 19th cent. A J. sugar refinery, one of the largest in Hungary, employed 78 in 1930. Jews also owned a cement factory and flour mill. Because of the J. economic contribution to L., relations with townsmen were good until the racial laws of 1938 when J. factories were confiscated and Jews fired. Twenty young men were sent to forced labor. The J. pop. was 254 in 1930. In

spring 1944, about 200 Jews were brought to Salgotarjan and from there deported to Auschwitz on 15 June.

LORSCH Hesse, Germany. Established before 1750, the community drew members from nearby Kleinhausen and numbered 110 (about 3% of the total) in 1871. Affiliated with the Orthodox rabbinate of Darmstadt, it maintained good relations with the largely Catholic pop. Of the 66 Jews living there in 1933, 26 left before *Kristallnacht* (9–10 Nov. 1938) when the synagogue was burned down. By 1939 most had emigrated to the U.S.

LOSHA Minsk dist., Belorussia. The J. pop. was 16 in 1808 and 302 in 1924. In the Soviet period, about 25 J. families received material assistance from the U.S. until the late 1920s. From the early 1930s, about ten J. families worked in a kolkhoz. After the German occupation of late June 1941, the Jews were apparently expelled to the Uzda ghetto, sharing the fate of the Jews there, most of whom were murdered on 16–17 Oct. 1941.

LOSIACZ Tarnopol dist., Poland, today Ukraine. The J. pop. in 1921 was 104. The Jews were possibly deported to the Belzec death camp in Sept.–Oct. 1942, directly or via Borszczow.

LOSICE Lublin dist., Poland. Jews were present by the early 16th cent., receiving privileges to deal in alcoholic beverages. There was continuing tension between J. and local Polish merchants. In the early 20th cent., hundreds of Jews were employed in the shoe industry with shoes being sold to Russian J. merchants supplying the Russian army. J. workers began to organize themselves into modern trade unions under the influence of the Bund. The J. pop. grew from 654 in 1827 to 1,487 in 1884 and 2,708 (total 3,888) in 1921. During WWI, economic life came to a standstill and many Jews were reduced to penury. In Aug. 1920, the Polish army staged a violent four-day pogrom marked by looting and rape. Between the World Wars, the major source of J. income was tailoring. Zionist activity commenced after the publication of the Balfour Declaration in 1917. Because of differences between religious groups, three rabbis presided in the late 1920s, while Kotsk and Sokolow Hasidim maintained their own *shtiblekh*. Economic conditions deteriorated in the 1930s in the face of Polish competition and economic boycotts. German bombardments in Sept. 1939 destroyed the synagogue and many J. homes. In early Oct., the Germans occupied the town permanently. A *Judenrat* was established in early 1940 and hundreds of Jews were sent to the Siedlce labor camp. In Dec. 1940, a ghetto was set up, with the influx of refugees increasing the J. pop. from a pre-war total of about 2,900 to nearly 6,000 in May 1942. On 22 Aug., about 5,500 Jews were marched to Siedlce and immediately deported to the Treblinka death camp while another 1,000 were shot along the way. The last 300 Jews were deported to Treblinka via Siedlce on 30 Nov. 1942.

LOSTICE Moravia, Czechoslovakia. Seven J. families are mentioned in 1544. A synagogue was erected in 1651 and 80 families were present in 1727. A new synagogue was completed in 1805, serving the community until the Holocaust. The J. pop. reached a peak of 438 (17% of the total) in 1848 and then declined steadily to 55 in 1930. Six families remained in 1938. All were deported to the Theresienstadt ghetto together with the Jews of Brno and from there sent to the death camps of Poland; 11 survived.

LOTOWA Polesie dist., Poland, today Belarus. This J. farm community, founded in 1847, numbered 41 in 1898. In 1941 the Jews were brought to the Kamieniec Litewski ghetto by the Germans for liquidation.

LOUNY Bohemia, Czechoslovakia. By the 14th cent., Jews inhabited their own quarter and maintained a synagogue and cemetery. They earned their livelihoods as moneylenders and land dealers and belonged to the Prague congregation. Their pop. grew steadily in the period between the 1541 expulsion in Bohemia and a devastating fire in 1655. As a consequence of the Familiants Laws (1726–27), curtailing J. settlement, only one J. family was legally present up to the mid-19th cent. A synagogue was consecrated in 1871, a cemetery in 1874, and 30–40 children were enrolled in the community's J. school (founded in the late 18th cent.). The J. pop. was 567 in 1890 and 205 (total 11,896) in 1930, with most Jews assimilated. The Germans closed the synagogue in Oct. 1941 and in 1942 deported the remaining Jews to the Theresienstadt ghetto and from there to the death camps.

LOVASBERENY Fejer dist., Hungary. Jews were probably present under the Turks in the 17th cent. and others arrived from Moravia and Austria in the early 18th cent. Under the patronage of estate owners, in particular the Cziraky family, the Jews gained freedom of worship and extensive trade rights over the years. A synagogue was built in 1720 and a J. school was opened in 1845. The J. pop. rose to 1,240 in 1840 but afterwards declined sharply as many of the young left for other cities. After WWI, the community declined socially and economically and many converted. In 1930, 53 Jews remained. On 5 June 1944, they were deported to Auschwitz via Szekesfehervar.

LOVIN Chernigov dist., Ukraine. L. was founded in 1837 as a J. farm settlement on purchased land. In 1898, the J. pop. was 151 but for lack of resources few farmed, the majority working as laborers. In 1939, the J. pop. was 231. The Germans arrived on 28 Aug. 1941. The fate of the Jews is unknown.

LOVOSICE Sudetenland, Czechoslovakia. The J. community is believed to have been founded by Jews expelled from Litomerice in 1541. It numbered 320 in 1933. The Jews left during the Sudetenland crisis of fall 1938; most were eventually admitted to the Czechoslovakian Republic. The Nazis destroyed the synagogue erected in 1762.

LOWICZ Lodz dist., Poland. Permission for Jews to live in L. was granted only at the end of the 18th cent. Their numbers increased in the mid-19th cent. (2,061 in 1862), many of them engaged in the sale of liquor and the supply of provisions to the armed forces bivouacked in the city. In the late 19th and early 20th cents., J. industrialists set up factories and Jews produced textile goods in home workshops. The synagogue, completed in 1897, was one of the largest and most ornate in the region. The first Zionist groups became active at the end of the 19th cent. and were followed by the Bund. The J. pop. in 1897 was 3,552 (35% of the total). The Jews suffered economically after the capture of the city by the Germans in Dec. 1914 and J. soup kitchens were providing up to 700 meals a day. In 1916, the J. tailors union led a strike. Jews won six of 12 mandates in the 1916 municipal elections. Between the World Wars the percentage of Jews in the city's pop. declined to 25% (4,339 Jews in 1931) as many left for the big cities or went overseas in search of employment. Various sects of Hasidim (Gur being the largest) were active during this period. There were numerous manifestations of antisemitism during the 1930s, especially boycotts of J. businesses. When the Germans captured L. on 13 Sept. 1939 they immediately began to abuse the Jews. The synagogue and many of the surrounding houses were burned down, forced labor was instituted, and J. property was plundered. A *Judenrat* was set up in Oct. or Nov. 1939. Overcrowding in the J. quarters led to an outbreak of cholera and a number of deaths at the beginning of 1940. In April 1940, the "large" and "small" ghettoes were created on either side of the marketplace. The situation of the inhabitants worsened; a soup kitchen was providing over 1,000 meals daily and death from starvation increased. From summer 1940 Jews were sent to the Jozefow forced labor camp in the Lublin dist. (Poland). By the beginning of 1941, there were over 7,000 Jews living in L. including refugees. From Feb. 1941, 300 Jews were expelled daily to Warsaw, where large numbers starved to death. The remaining 150 Jews were put to work by the Germans until they too were expelled to Warsaw in Sept. 1941. In Oct. 1945, there were 35 survivors in L. but following attacks by the local pop. they soon left.

LOZA (Hung. Fuzesmezo) Carpatho-Russia, Czechoslovakia, today Ukraine. J. settlement probably began in the mid-18th cent. Three J. families were present in 1768 and in 1880 the J. pop. was 119 (total 637). A few Jews were farmers. In 1921, under the Czechoslovakians, the J. pop. rose to 181 and in 1941 to 200. The Hungarians occupied the town in March 1939 and in 1941 drafted dozens of young Jews into forced labor battalions. In late July 1941, a number of J. families without Hungarian citizenship were expelled to Kamenets-Podolski and murdered. The rest were deported to Auschwitz in mid-May 1944.

LOZOVAYA Kharkov dist., Ukraine. Jews numbered 813 (total 3,717) in 1897 and 528 in 1939. Presumably, the Jews fled or were evacuated before the German occupation of 11 Oct. 1941.

LUBACZOW Lwow dist., Poland, today Ukraine. Jews are mentioned from 1498. The community suffered grievously in the Chmielnicki massacres of 1648–49. It recovered and grew to around 2,000 (a third of the pop.) by the beginning of the 20th cent. despite a fire in 1899 that left half the Jews homeless.

There was considerable Zionist activity between the World Wars. Under the German occupation, the typhoid-stricken ghetto pop., swelling after the arrival of refugees to three times its prewar size, was liquidated on 6–8 Jan. 1943; 1,200 Jews were murdered at the local cemetery and the rest deported to the Belzec death camp.

LUBANA Vidzeme (Livonia) dist., Latvia. The J. pop. in 1935 was 53. The Germans arrived at the beginning of July 1941 and in the following months murdered the Jews who had not fled.

LUBAR Zhitomir dist., Ukraine. J. settlement commenced in the early 17th cent. The community suffered in the Chmielnicki massacres of 1648–49. The Jews returned afterwards in small numbers. In the 18th cent., Jews numbered 408 and in 1897 their pop. reached 6,111 (total 12,507). A Hebrew elementary school and a loan fund operated until WWI. In May 1920, during the civil war, Red Army units staged a pogrom against the Jews. A J. local council (soviet) with deliberations in Yiddish operated in the 1920s along with a Yiddish-language elementary school and kindergarten and a savings and loan fund for J. artisans. The J. pop. dropped to 1,857 in 1939. The Germans captured L. on 8 July 1941. On 13 Sept., 1,199 Jews were murdered at a sandlot outside the town. Another 200 skilled workers who had been spared were executed in the same place in Oct. 1941. Among those murdered were dozens of Jews from neighboring towns.

LUBARTOW Lublin dist., Poland. Jews were present by the late 16th cent. but the community was destroyed in the Chmielnicki massacres of 1648–49 and was only reestablished in the 18th cent. A synagogue built by the community at this time survived until the Holocaust. R. Levi Yitzhak of Berdichev lived here. At the turn of the 19th cent. Jews contributed to the town's industrial development, opening a sawmill, flour mill, and factory for steel products. The J. pop grew to 2,623 in 1897 and 3,269 (total 6,102) in 1921. The Zionists became active in the early 20th cent. and after WWI their influence increased. In 1923, Jews operated 306 workshops and small factories, mostly in the garment industry, but the J. economy never recovered from its wartime stagnation. The Germans captured L. on 17 Sept. 1939, dismantling the synagogue and J. cemetery for building materials and systematically looting J. stores. In fall 1939, a *Judenrat* was appointed. In Nov. 1939, although 2,500 Jews were expelled to Ostrow, Parczew, and Kock, leaving 800 behind for forced labor, most were able to return within a year by bribing officials. Other groups were sent to distant labor camps in 1940–41 while about 450 refugees arrived from Mlawa and Lublin. On 9 April 1942, 800 Jews were deported to the Belzec death camp; some were sent to labor camps. On 15 April 1942, about 1,500 Jews arrived from Slovakia. The able-bodied among the refugees were sent to help erect the Majdanek death camp, many perishing there. By June the J. pop. was 3,134, including 2,000 refugees, all packed into a ghetto and joined in early Oct. by refugees from Kamionka, Ostrow, and Czemierniki. On 9 Oct. 1942, during the second *Aktion*, another 3,000 Jews were deported, most to Belzec and some to the Sobibor death camp with 500 more executed in the J. cemetery. The last 300 or so were sent to Piaski Luterskie on 24 Oct. for deportation. In Feb. 1943, the Germans delcared L. "free of Jews" (*judenrein*). A number of J. partisan groups in the area engaged in effective action against the Germans and saved many J. families, necessitating the establishment of a special camp in the forest for them.

LUBCZA Nowogrodek dist., Poland, today Belarus. A J. community apparently existed by the 17th cent. under a charter of privileges allowing the Jews freedom of trade and the right to practice crafts. J. merchants dealt primarily in grain, flax, and livestock. In 1897 the J. pop. reached 2,463 (total 3,374) but fell considerably during WWI when the town was sharply contested on the Nieman River line. By 1925 the J. pop. stood at around 1,000. In 1924–29 the YEKOPO relief agency helped refurbish 235 J. homes. The Tarbut Hebrew school founded in 1924 was a focus of Zionist activity. A Yiddish school was also set up at the same time. Under Soviet rule in 1939–41, most Jews worked in the new cooperatives. The J. pop. in 1940 was 1,500. The Germans arrived on 23 June 1941, murdering 40–50 Jews within two weeks and establishing a ghetto. In April 1942, 125 Jews were sent to Nowogrodek, about 550 to the forced labor camp in Worobjewicze Wielkie and 300 to the forced labor camp in Dworzec. Those in Nowogrodek, joined by another 450 from L., including children, were murdered on 7 Aug. 1942, as

were the 550 at Worobjewicze. Those at Dworzec were also executed in the summer and another 150 remaining in L. on 24 Aug.

LUBELLA Lwow dist., Poland, today Ukraine. The J. pop. in 1921 was 112. The Jews were possibly deported to the Belzec death camp in Nov. 1942, directly or via Zolkiew.

LUBIANKA Odessa dist., Ukraine. The Germans captured L. in early Aug. 1941. On 6 March 1942, they murdered 150 Jews at the nearby village of Orsulovo. The same German unit entered L. and murdered 330 people there, most of them apparently Jews. Afterwards they burned the bodies. Another 365 Jews were murdered in the village of Petrovka and its environs. A total of 845 Jews were murdered in the territory of the local rural council (soviet), almost all refugees from Odessa and a small number from L.

LUBICZ Warsaw dist., Poland. A J. community existed in the 19th cent., numbering 362 (total 865) in 1921. The community was liquidated by the Germans in fall 1939 when the Jews were expelled to the Warsaw area, most perishing in the Holocaust. A labor camp was set up in the area in Aug. 1943 as a branch of the Stutthof concentration camp. The 1,000 J. women from the Kaunas ghetto confined there in Nov. 1944 were liberated by the Red Army in Jan. 1945.

LUBIEN Warsaw dist., Poland. Jews probably settled in the second half of the 18th cent. and reached a pop. of 797 (total 2,120) in 1921. In WWII they were expelled by the Germans to the Warsaw area and shared the fate of the local Jews.

LUBIEN WIELKI Lwow dist., Poland, today Ukraine. A small J. community of 197 residents in 1921 (total 2,672) benefited from the development of the town as a health resort and engaged in ancillary occupations. The Ukrainians murdered most of the Jews in a violent rampage shortly after the Germans occupied the town on 29 June 1941.

LUBIESZOW Volhynia dist., Poland, today Ukraine. The Jews of L. fled in the Chmielnicki massacres of 1648–49. The community numbered 500 in the mid-18th cent. and grew to 2,000 before WWI (two-thirds of the total). The Cossacks burned down the town on the Russian withdrawal in 1915 and the German occupation force expelled all but one J. family. The Jews only begin to return in 1924, numbering 1,500 in 1936. In July 1941, an attempted pogrom by Ukrainians was repulsed by a J. self-defense group. Forced labor, extortion, and executions marked the German occupation from 26 July 1941 and a *Judenrat* was established. A ghetto was set up in May 1942 and on 10 Aug., 1,200 Jews were murdered beside open pits; the remaining 80 artisans and their families were murdered in Nov.

LUBLIN (I)   Bessarabia, Rumania, today Republic of Moldova. This J. settlement was first established in 1842 and the settlers engaged in agriculture. Toward the end of the 19th cent., J. artisans sold their products in the neighboring villages. L. was almost totally destroyed during WWI and the Jews rebuilt it with the aid of ICA and the Joint Distribution Committee. The J. pop. in 1930 was 274. During WWII, the J. pop. suffered the same fate as other J. communities; there were no survivors.

LUBLIN (II)   Lublin dist., Poland. First mentioned in the 15th cent., Jews were confined to a J. quarter until residence restrictions were removed in 1862 in Congress Poland. In 1566 the Maharshal synagogue was built and in the following years additional synagogues and prayer houses were consecrated. By the late 16th cent., the J. quarter had expanded to include 100 houses. As a center of religion and culture, L. was considered the most important community in Poland, constituting the focal point of what would become the Council of the Four Lands and serving as its seat until 1680. Among its illustrious rabbis was Shalom Shakna ben Yosef, appointed rabbi of Lesser Poland by the king in 1541 and founder of a yeshiva in L. where the great halakhists of Poland studied, including Moshe Isserles (the "Rema"). Other rabbis were Shelomo ben Yehiel Luria ("Maharshal"; d. 1574), considered with Isserles the greatest halakhist of the age, Mordekhai ben Avraham Yaffe (d. 1612), and Meir ben Gedalya ("Maharam of L."; d. 1616). Later 17th cent. rabbis were Shemuel Eliezer Edels ("Maharsha") and Yoel Sirkes. Although L. was a great center of commerce, attracting J. merchants from all over Poland

R. Avraham Lifschitz and the Hakhmei Lublin Yeshiva, Lublin, Poland

to its fairs, the Jews of L. continually had to struggle against numerous restrictions and heavy taxes to solidify their commercial position. Occasionally they met with violence at the hands of local looters. In 1598, a blood libel led to the deaths of three Jews and in 1646, riots led by Catholic college students left eight dead. Many houses in the J. quarter were also pillaged. J. craftsmen also encountered considerable opposition from Christian craftsmen with restrictions imposed at their urging. By the late 18th cent., however, Jews constituted a majority in many trades (as tailors, glaziers, furriers, jewelers, etc.). Jews also engaged in money-lending and tax farming and won renown as Hebrew printers. The Shahor (Schwarz) family set up shop in 1547 while in 1578, Kalonymus ben Mordekhai Yaffe founded a printing establishment that published 103 books in 1550–1690 and continued to operate until the 19th cent. A number of prominent physicians also resided in L., such as Shelomo Luria, who published a medical treatise, Shemuel ben Mattityahu, Moshe Montalto, and the 17th cent. court physician Hayyim (Felix) Vitalis. In 1655, the city was captured by the Cossacks and despite the payment of a large

tribute, 10,000 Jews were massacred, including a considerable number of refugees. The J. pop. only succeeded in attaining its previous level in the early 19th cent. and in reversing the economic decline at mid-cent. During this period, Jews again had to contend with bans and restrictions stemming from the Catholic opposition. Hasidism began to spread in the second half of the 18th cent., particularly after Yaakov Yitzhak Horwitz (the Seer of L.; 1745–1815) settled there, crowning the dynastic heads of Dinow and Belz Hasidism and many others from among his students. Opposition to the Hasidim was led by R. Azriel Horovitz (d. 1819). In the mid-19th cent., a hasidic dynasty was founded by Yehuda Leib Eiger, persevering until WWII. The J. pop. rose from 2,973 in 1806 and 8,747 in 1857 to 23,586 (total 46,301) in 1897. In the second half of the 19th cent., as Poles moved outside the city walls, Jews began settling in the Old City, which took on the nature of a new ghetto. Many Jews earned their livelihoods in the grain trade, buying at the fairs or from the estates and selling in Warsaw and Danzig (Gdansk). Other important items of J. trade were hides, brush bristles, and lumber. However,

Advertisements for Yiddish theater performances, Lublin, Poland

most J. tradesmen were shopkeepers and peddlers. The Jews were prominent as artisans in a variety of professions. The community operated a 90-bed hospital (founded in 1886), an old age home, and an orphanage as well as numerous charitable organizations and mutual aid societies. In the late 19th cent., 800 boys and 100 girls studied in 43 private *hadarim* and a *talmud torah* served the needy. In 1897–98, two Hebrew schools were opened and in 1913 a Yavne school began operating. Another important cultural institution was the Zamir society, which promoted Hebrew literature and song and ran a library and drama circle. Hovevei Zion became active at the turn of the cent. and the first Bund office was opened in 1904. At the outbreak of WWI, the Russians gave the Cossacks license to pillage J. property. With the arrival of the Austrians in 1915, community life was renewed, but again in 1919 the Jews were victimized by rampaging mobs, which left three dead and caused considerable damage to J. property. In 1921 the J. pop. was 37,337. Recovering from the war, Jews operated 1,714 workshops and business establishments. Small J. factories manufactured mostly clothing and food products. In the leather industry, Jews maintained a virtual monopoly. They also ran a distillery, beer brewery, brickyards, flour mills, and a plant for tobacco products founded in 1860 and at one time employing 400 workers but impounded after the war by the government when it took over the tobacco monopoly. J. trade unions embraced most J. workers. With expanding social welfare services, the TOZ organized infirmaries staffed by 22 doctors and sponsored summer camps which reached a peak in 1939 with 1,200 children. Zionist activity intensified after the publication of the Balfour Declaration in 1917. Among the youth movements, Hashomer Hatzair was the most prominent and among the community's educational institutes the Tarbut Hebrew school had a central position, joining Mizrachi's Yavne school and a Beth Jacob school for 200 girls set up by Agudat Israel. The most famous yeshiva was Hakhmei Lublin. A building housing the yeshiva was completed in 1930 and resembled a modern university in its conditions. The Yiddish daily *Lubliner Togblat* expressed views similar to those of the Bund, whose main strength was in the trade unions. Antisemitism intensified in the 1930s as J. businesses were boycotted and tradesmen attacked. As war approached, more and more Jews lost their livelihoods and even the once prosperous had to turn to the community for assistance.

The Germans entered L. on 18 Sept. 1939 after two weeks of heavy fighting left thousands dead, wounded, and homeless. The J. pop. at the time was around 40,000 (total 120,000). Jews were immediately seized for forced labor and a heavy tribute was exacted from the community. On 26 Oct. 1939, L. was incorporated into General Gouvernement territory and on 9 Nov., Odilo Globocnik, a Himmler intimate and responsible for building the Majdanek, Belzec, Sobibor, and Treblinka death camps, became head of the district police and SS, signaling the start of a reign of terror directed against the local pop. and the Jews. A *Judenrat* of 24 members was set up in Jan. 1940. Its moving spirit was Dr. Mark Alten, a lawyer and former officer in the Austrian army. Numerous departments were created to sustain the community as a series of extortionate demands for goods and money was made by the Germans. Forced labor was institutionalized to cover everyone from children to 60-year-olds. A total of 28,806 Jews were classified as "fit to work." Groups were sent out to construct a labor camp on Lipowa Street, to local factories, and to farms. Late in Aug. 1940, a camp was opened in the former airport and in mid-Jan. 1942, a camp for women was established. A total of 117 labor camps would be constructed for Jews throughout General Gouvernement territory in the 1940–44 period. Within the city, Jews were forbidden to engage in trade, visit doctors, use public transportation, or appear in places of entertainment. All J. business establishments were impounded. The winter of 1939–40 was especially severe, with temperatures dropping to –30° F. and serious shortages of food, clothing, coal, and firewood. About 10,000 Jews required community assistance in addition to the 5,000 refugees from Lodz, Sieradz, Kalisz, and other places (2,400 of them being housed in 43 public shelters). Hundreds of operations were performed each day on frozen limbs. The CENTOS organization provided 309,587 free meals to 2,000 children in April–Aug. 1940 and the TOZ inoculated 32,000 Jews against typhoid fever and cholera. In Feb. 1940, the Nazis scrapped their plan to create a J. reservation in the L. dist and in March 1941, they removed around 10,000 Jews from L., dispersing them among 100 small settlements in the area. The rest were ordered into a ghetto, which was fenced off with barbed wire the following winter. In the course of 1940, beginning in the spring, the Germans allowed 3,200 J. prisoners of war, mainly former soldiers in the Polish army, to return to their

Lubartowska St., Lublin, Poland

homes scattered throughout the General Gouvernement. In Dec. 1941, all furs were confiscated. In
Nov.–Dec., 500 died in a typhoid epidemic. In Feb
1942, Jews working in German facilities were separated into a second ghetto. In mid-March 1942, Operation Reinhardt for the extermination of Polish Jewry
commenced. Each day 1,400 Jews were loaded onto
trains and deported to the Belzec death camp. The
old, the sick, the weak, and 80–100 children from the
orphanage were murdered. In all, 30,000 were exterminated at Belzec by mid-April while 2,500 were killed
in L. and its environs. The remaining Jews were sent
to the Majdan Tatarski suburb of L., which was being
billed as a model ghetto. On 21 April 1,200 "illegals"
were weeded out and sent running to the nearby Majdanek death camp. Here they were held without food
or water for five days while a daily truckload of Jews
was taken out to be executed. On 2 Sept., another 500
women, children, and old people were sent to Majda-

nek from the ghetto and on 25 Oct., still another
1,000 Jews. The ghetto was liquidated on 9 Nov.
1942 when the last 2,350 Jews were taken to Majdanek, with only the fit spared for labor. Most of the Jews
still in the labor camps were executed at Majdanek in
May 1943. The 18,400 remaining Jews of the L. district were murdered at Majdanek, Trawniki, and Ponia-
towa on 3 Nov. 1943. The Majdanek death camp had
commenced operating in early 1942 and witnessed
the execution of about 360,000 "enemies of the Third
Reich," among them an estimated 130,000–200,000
Jews, 85% of them from Poland, some by firing squad
beside mass graves, some in the camp's seven gas
chambers. In early 1940, groups of J. prisoners of
war from the Polish army were brought to the Lipowa
Street camp built by J. forced labor. In Feb. 1942, the
Germans took a group of prisoners (630 or 880, according to different sources) and forcibly marched
them, naked and barefoot, to Biala Podlaska. Those

who faltered were killed. A hundred were shot when the group stopped for the night. Many froze to death from the cold. When they reached Paraczew, only 300 remained alive. Although the Jews there bribed the guards with gold to release the prisoners, they were still sent to Biala Podlaska. To ease their journey, they hired horse-drawn carriages. Though not recognized by the Germans as prisoners of war, since most were from eastern Poland, those at the Lipowa Street camp refused to remove their uniforms and maintained a military regimen. A total of 2,000–3,000 were confined there. Dozens were able to escape to the forests, forming several partisan groups, the largest commanded by Shemuel Jaeger, but most joined the Yehiel Grynszpan unit in the Parczew forest. All the rest were murdered at Majdanek, most of them on 3 Nov. 1943. Hundreds of J. artisans being held in L. Fortress were executed in July 1944, just before the German withdrawal from the city. Just 230 of L.'s Jews survived within German-occupied territory, some helped by Poles at the risk of their lives. By 1946, 6,662 Jews had gathered in the city, including 824 who returned from the Soviet Union. By 1970, few remained.

LUBLINIEC Silesia dist., Poland. Jews arrived in the 18th cent., numbering 432 (of a total 3,364) in 1861 under Prussian rule. Only a few families remained under Polish rule after WWI. They were expelled by the Germans in WWII.

LUBNY Poltava dist., Ukraine. Jews settled in the first half of the 17th cent. under the protection of Prince Vishnieviecki. Jews were among the town's defenders and victims in the Pavliuk revolt in 1637–38 and about 200 were killed in the Chmielnicki massacres of 1648–49. The J. community revived in the late 18th cent. and reached a pop. of 3,006 (total 10,097) in 1897. The Yiddish author and humorist Shalom Aleichem (1859–1916) served as state rabbi in 1880–82. In 1881, a number of J. homes and stores were looted. In the early 20th cent., the community supported a *talmud torah*, public library, and credit bank. Zionist activity intensified after the Oct. 1917 Revolution and of the 27 members of the community council, 12 were Zionists. In the 1920s, about 100 Jews worked in a tobacco factory; many others were employed at a flour mill and about 1,200 were artisans. A J. school was in operation. In 1939, the J. pop. was 2,833. The Germans captured L. on 13 Sept. 1941. On 16 Oct., at a site outside the city, they murdered 4,500 Jews from the area. Dozens caught in hiding or spared as skilled workers were murdered in April and May 1942.

LUBOML Volhynia dist., Poland, today Ukraine. Jews are recorded in 1370–82. In 1557 they received legal privileges but were restricted in purchasing land and houses until 1600. In the 1670s, a fortresslike synagogue was constructed to provide protection in time of need. It was the only J. building to remain standing after a fire in 1728. With annexation to the Russian Empire in the late 18th cent., when the J. pop. was about 1,000, an economic decline set in. By 1897, the J. pop. had grown to 3,247 (total 4,470). Under the Austrian occupation of 1915–18 the Jews endured hunger, disease, and a regime of forced labor. With stability returning under Polish rule, the Zionists became active. In 1921 the J. pop. was 3,141 (95% of the total). Most of the crafts and petty trade were in J. hands along with a few flour mills and the marketing of agricultural produce. There were two Hebrew schools – Tarbut and the religious Yavne – and a small yeshiva. Antisemitism intensified in the 1930s. The Germans took L. on 25 June 1941 and some of the 500 local Jews who had been drafted into the Red Army in April–May 1941 were captured and murdered. On 22 July the Germans murdered 400 J. men outside the town and on 21 Aug. another 400, mostly young women. A *Judenrat* was established. On 5 Dec. the Jews were packed into a ghetto 10–20 to a room. A regime of forced labor was introduced. In Oct. 1942, the community was liquidated in a week of killing with 1,800 executed on the first day. Of those organizing to escape, one group was cut down in a pitched battle with Ukrainian police and another, numbering 30, reached the forest to join the partisans.

LUBOTIN Kharkov dist., Ukraine. The J. pop. in 1939 was 118 (total 26,335). The Jews remaining after the German occupation of 20 Oct. 1941 perished.

LUBRANIEC Warsaw dist., Poland. Jews are known from the late 17th cent. and were permitted to open a synagogue and cemetery in 1750. The J. pop. was 1,148 in 1827 and 834 (total 2,196) in 1921. After WWI, the Zionists were especially influential among the young. The town was captured by the Germans on 10 Sept. 1939. Most of the men were sent to labor camps in the Poznan dist. in June 1941, perishing

After the wedding, Luboml, Poland, 1928

from disease and starvation or being murdered in Auschwitz. The rest were dispatched to the Lodz ghetto in July, most dying there.

LUBYCZA KROLEWSKA Lwow dist., Poland, today Ukraine. Jews comprised as much as 90% of the pop., numbering 821 in 1900. WWI left the community with 60 orphans and ruined homes, with the Joint Distribution Committee providing aid. The community was liquidated by the Germans in the course of 1942.

LUCENEC (Hung. Losonc) Slovakia, Czechoslovakia, today Republic of Slovakia. Jews settled in the 18th cent. In 1804, a few J. families lived in the Tuhar suburb, but after the mid-19th cent., most lived within the city and the two communities united. A synagogue in the Moorish style was built in 1863 and the congregation became Neologist in 1870. Opponents of innovation maintained their own prayer service. The Neologist community opened J. elementary schools in 1864 and 1881 with 130 and 242 students, respectively, as the community grew from 335 in 1848 to 1,139 in 1880 and 1,990 (total 8,952) in 1900. The Or-

thodox congregation opened its own school in 1875. Jews pioneered industry in the city, opening one of the first metalworking plants in the country in 1854 and a factory manufacturing kitchenware and cooking stoves in 1884. Jews also operated 78% of the 335 business enterprises in the city and 25 Jews were

The Lucenec syngagogue built in 1925 by Lipot Baumhorn, one of the foremost synagogue architects of his time, Slovakia (J. B. Gassner, Haifa/photo courtesy of Yad Vashem, The Holocaust Martyrs' and Heroes' Remembrance Authority, Jerusalem)

among its 35 highest taxpayers. In 1918, J. homes and stores were looted in riots. After WWI, the Neologist congregation included 480 families and the Orthodox 70. A new Neologist synagogue in the Byzantine style, the largest in Slovakia, was consecrated in 1925. Agudat Israel, the General Zionists, WIZO, and the Zionist youth movements were all active between the World Wars. Ten Jews served on the municipal council and Jews owned 147 stores, 48 workshops, and ten factories with many belonging to the professional class (18 lawyers, nine doctors, five engineers). In 1941, the J. pop. was 2,103. After the annexation to Hungary in Nov. 1938, Jews were seized for forced labor and sent to the eastern front, most perishing there. A few were also tortured and murdered in the city. In May 1944, under the Germans, the Jews were confined in a ghetto under a *Judenrat*. All were deported to Auschwitz on 12 June. About half the post-war community of 300 emigrated to Israel in 1949. There were about 50 Jews in the 1990s.

LUCHINETS   Vinnitsa dist., Ukraine. The J. pop. was 432 in 1765 and 1,050 (total 3,869) in 1897. Extreme poverty caused many to emigrate at the turn of the 19th cent. In 1919, General Denikin's White Army troops attacked the Jews here. In 1926 the J. pop. was 745. After the German occupation in July 1941, L. was annexed to Transnistria and a ghetto established where 2,700 Jews expelled from Bessarabia and Bukovina were sent. Nearly 1,700 of them perished together with the hundreds of Jews of L.

LUCK   Volhynia dist., Poland. Jews were living in L. in the early 15th cent. and probably before as L. was part of the area in which Jews had received a charter of privileges from the principality of Lithuania. In

Hospital staff, Luck, Poland, 1933

the late 16th cent. they numbered about 1,000, comprising a third of the Jews of Volhynia and monopolizing customs taxes. In 1628 they were authorized to build a fortress-synagogue to help defend the city. After the Chmielnicki massacres of 1648–49, only a quarter of their homes remained standing, but recovery was rapid. Together with Wlodzimierz Wolynski, the community represented Volhynia in the Council of the Four Lands. Among its well-known rabbis was Yaakov Schor, who headed the local yeshiva in the early 17th cent. A great fire destroyed most of the synagogues in L. in 1789. Through the 19th cent. the Jews comprised about 60% of the pop., increasing from 2,003 in 1802 to 9,468 in 1897. Many hasidic sects were active and in 1897 a Hovevei Zion society opened its offices. Before WWI a number of J. schools were in operation, including a modernized *talmud torah* teaching both Hebrew and Russian and a rival Orthodox yeshiva. Under the Austrian occupation in WWI, Jews were subjected to a regime of forced labor and restricted movement. With the Russian reoccupation in Aug. 1916 and the Feb. 1917 Revolution, J. public life revived, with the Zionists becoming prominent and a Tarbut Hebrew school for 400 children opened. The Jews suffered again on the arrival of General Haller in 1919 but with aid from U.S organizations recovered economically in the 1920s while their share in the pop. dropped to 40% (17,366 in 1931) as many Poles flocked to the city after it became the dist. capital. Jews continued to dominate commercial life, owning 82% of the city's stores and monopolizing such wholesale branches as textiles, footwear, foodstuffs, and pharmaceuticals. They also owned all the city's hotels and boarding houses. The community operated various welfare agencies, a hospital, orphanage, day care centers, and public health facilities. All the Zionist groups were represented, with the Irgun organizing military training. The arrival of the Soviets in Sept. 1939 was accompanied by the nationalization of J. businesses and the closure of J. public institutions. The Germans entered the city on 27 June 1941 after a heavy bombardment. On 30 June, 300 Jews were murdered in retaliation for Soviet executions and on 2 July, 2,000 were shot by an *Einsatzkommando 4a* unit near the ruins of the Lubart fortress. A *Judenrat* was appointed in late July and large quantities of goods and valuables were extorted from the community by the Germans. A labor camp for 500 Jews was set up in Oct. 1941 and on 11–12 Dec. 1941 the rest of the Jews were herded into a ghetto, where many died from disease, starvation, and the cold. On 20–23 Aug. 1942, about 17,500 Jews were brought to the Gorki Polanie area and executed. Another 2,000 were murdered on 3 Sept., leaving a small number in the labor camp, who offered spirited armed resistance when German and Ukrainian police entered the camp on 11 Dec. for a final *Aktion*. All were killed after an artillery barrage and a few hours of fighting. Many Jews who escaped from the city were helped by the local pop., especially Czech peasants, one of whom sheltered 34 Jews. Other Jews joined Soviet partisan groups. After the city was liberated on 5 Feb. 1944, most of the 150 surviving Jews left for Rowne.

LUCKENWALDE Brandenburg, Germany. Uninterrupted J. settlement began only in 1763. In 1812, the community numbered three families. They opened a cemetery in 1815. In 1869, when the J. pop. was 74, an independent community was constituted. A synagogue was dedicated in 1897 and the J. pop. was 155 in 1907. From the mid-19th cent., Jews played a leading role in local industry, especially in textile manufacturing and the hat industry. During WWI, J. textile workers from Lodz were brought to L. as replacements for conscripted German laborers. In 1930, a J. physician, Dr. Hermann Salomon, became mayor of the city but was compelled to resign in 1933 and was arrested. When the Nazis came to power in 1933, there were about 140 Jews in L. Two community members died under Nazi arrest and at least three were included in the Oct. 1938 deportation of Jews of Polish descent. On *Kristallnacht* (9–10 Nov. 1938), the synagogue was wrecked and J. men were interned in the Sachsenhausen concentration camp. By May 1939, 35 Jews and 43 persons of partial J. origin (*Mischlinge*), were still living in L. While a few managed to emigrate, most Jews were deported to the east. In Oct. 1942, there were ten Jews in L., probably protected by marriage to non-Jews. Between 1943 and 1944, a resistance group of Jews and non-Jews from L. and Berlin was active. Altogether, 81 Jews from L. perished under Nazi rule.

LUDBREG Croatia, Yugoslavia, today Republic of Croatia. A J. community was active from the second half of the 19th cent. In 1931 there were 74 Jews (total 12,374). The community was totally destroyed in the Holocaust.

LUDENEVICHI Polesie dist., Belorussia. The J. pop. was 167 (total 985) in 1897. Under the Soviets, some Jews ran private farms until the mid-1920s. The Germans arrived in late July 1941, murdering all 105 Jews in the village in Sept.–Dec.

LUDUS (Hung. Marosludas) S. Transylvania dist., Rumania. A J. community was founded in 1872. The Great Synagogue was considered the most beautiful of the city's building. A J. school was opened at the beginning of the 20th cent. and functioned up to the Holocaust. The *talmud torah* and yeshiva, run by R. Moshe Mendel Rosenberg, were famed throughout Transylvania. Between the World Wars, the J. community in L. was culturally and politically backward compared to other communities at this time. After WWI, the Betar Zionist movement attracted many of the young. In 1930, the J. pop. was 567 (11% of the total). In June 1941, the J. pop. was transferred to Turda, but returned in Dec. In 1942, J. men were drafted for forced labor; some were deported to Transnistria. In fall 1944, the majority returned. When Hungarian forces entered L. on 5 Sept. 1944, 90% of the Jews fled to Sibiu. Jews returned after the liberation and the community was reorganized. By 1947, most had left for the larger cities and for Palestine.

LUDWIGSBURG Wuerttemberg, Germany. The first Jews to settle in 1725 were Court Jews providing supplies to the local garrison and luxury items to the local count. The small community was attached to neighboring Aldingen until the mid-19th cent. It began to grow after emancipation in 1864, reaching a peak of 243 in 1900 (about 1% of the total). A synagogue was dedicated in 1884. The master-weaver Benedikt Elsas helped set up one of Wuerttemberg's first textile factories, which employed 70–80 workers in the 1880s and remained in the family until the Nazi era. There were 187 Jews in L. in 1933, with 57 subsequently joining the community. All were subject to

Expulsion of Jews from their homes in Ludwigshafen, Germany, to the Gurs concentration camp in France, 1940 (Deutsche Bibliothek/ photo courtesy of Yad Vashem, The Holocaust Martyrs' and Heroes' Remembrance Authority, Jerusalem)

increasing social and economic isolation. On *Kristall-nacht* (9–10 Nov. 1938), the synagogue was burned and Jews were soon forced to close or sell their businesses. Until 1941, at least 146 managed to leave Germany, half for the U.S.; 62 were deported to the camps, of whom four survived. In 1958, the Ludwigsburger Zentralstelle was established as the central office in Germany for the investigation of Nazi crimes.

LUDWIGSHAFEN Palatinate, Germany. The J. settlement developed with the growth of the city from the mid-19th cent. and its integration was facilitated by the liberal, free atmosphere characteristic of a modern town. The first Jew was already elected to the municipal council in 1860, nine years before the unrestricted franchise was granted to the Jews in Bavaria. Jews received the salt concession and opened factories manufacturing chemicals and processing wool, coffee, and vinegar. Most Jews engaged in trade. A synagogue was dedicated in 1865 in a building which had previously served both the Catholic and Protestant communities as a place of worship. A J. elementary school existed from 1856 until 1870, when the municipality established a nondenominational school. The J. pop. rose from 107 in 1855 to 608 in 1905. Jews from the east began to arrive at that time and by 1931 the J. pop. was 1,400 (with 45% foreign nationals, mostly from the east). In the Weimar Republic, 69% of the Jews continued to engage in trade; 15% were in crafts and industry; 15% in services; and 53% of the city's lawyers were Jews. There were also 13 J. doctors and six J. dentists. A quarter of the larger stores in the center of the city were J.-owned. In June 1933, about four months after the Nazi rise to power, there were 1,070 Jews (total 107,344) in L. J. businessmen were targeted for economic boycott, J. officials were fired from municipal employment, and J. doctors were banned from public employment. In 1935–36, the process of "Aryanization" of J. property intensified. In Jan. 1938, only 660 Jews remained and in Oct. 1938, all Polish nationals were expelled from the city. On *Kristallnacht* (9–10 Nov. 1938), the synagogue was set on fire, J. homes were destroyed, J. men were sent to the Dachau concentration camp, and J. women and children were rowed across the Rhine to Mannheim with a warning never to return to the city. Two weeks later they had to leave Mannheim by order of the Gestapo and most returned. From May 1939 on, the remaining Jews were moved to "J. houses." The last

183 were deported to the Gurs concentration camp on 22 Oct. 1940. A total of 239 Jews from L. perished in the Holocaust. In 1973, 60 Jews were living in the city.

LUDWIPOL Volhynia dist., Poland, today Ukraine. The Jews numbered 1,210 (of a total 1,498) in 1897 and 916 in 1921. Socialism and the Zionist movement made their appearance in the early 20th cent. Fire, disease, and rampaging gangs plagued the community during WWI. Between the World Wars, Hebrew elementary and vocational schools and a kindergarten operated. Ukrainian collaborators carried out a pogrom followed the German occupation of 6 July 1941. A *Judenrat* was established and on 13 Oct., 1,500 Jews were crowded into a ghetto and put to forced labor. On 25 Sept. 1942, they were led to the forest for execution; 300–350 escaped, crossing the Slucz River, and lived in camps under partisan protection. About 40 survived to greet the Soviet liberation forces on 10 Jan.1944.

LUDZA (Yid. Lutsin) Latgale dist., Latvia. According to tradition, a small community existed in the 16th cent., the Jews fleeing on the approach of Ivan the Terrible's soldiers in 1577. The Jews returned in 1582 but the community only began to grow in the 19th cent. after the expulsion of the Jews from villages and estates. About 60 J. families emigrated to the Kherson and Yekaterinoslav provinces, where they settled as farmers from 1835 through the 1850s. A fire in 1866 destroyed half the town's homes and further reduced the J. pop., which dropped from 2,299 in 1847 to 1,915 in 1868 before rising to 3,000 (half the total) at the end of the cent. Jews traded in lumber, grain, and flax and many farmed. Over 40% of the J. artisans were tailors. L. was known for its rabbis and Torah scholars. The Zioni and Don Yahya families, related by marriage, provided the community with an unbroken line of rabbis from the early 19th cent. up to the Holocaust. Secular J. education started with the founding of a private boys' school in 1865. In 1907, the first and only printing press in Latgale was set up by a member of the Zioni family. During WWI, hundreds of Jews fled to Russia. At the same time, there was an influx of refugees from western Latvia and Lithuania. Most homes were damaged when the town changed hands in 1918–19. At the end of the war about 2,000 Jews remained, propped up by assistance from the Joint Distribution

Committee. Poor harvests and the cessation of grain imports by the Soviet Union brought further economic hardship in the mid-1920s. By 1935, when the J. pop. stood at 1,518 (total 5,546), Jews owned 191 of the town's 302 larger business establishments. A fire in 1938 destroyed 212 homes and 117 stores, 95% of them belonging to Jews. Most of the community's children studied at the Hebrew public school founded in 1918. The community produced a large number of Hebrew teachers and most students were fluent in the language. The Zionists were active between the World Wars, with Betar and the Revisionists particularly strong. The arrival of the Soviets in 1940 brought J. communal and commercial life to an end. Hundreds fled to the Soviet Union with the approach of the Germans. The Germans took L. on 3 July and immediately instituted a regime of severe persecution. A ghetto was established on 20 July, with forced labor, murder, and rape the lot of its inhabitants. On 17 Aug. around 800 Jews were executed at Lake Zorba 4 miles (6 km) from the town. The few hundred remaining Jews were killed off in a number of *Aktions*, the last in May 1942. About 100 Jews returned to L. after the war but by the 1970s most had emigrated to Israel.

LUEBBECKE   Westphalia, Germany. The medieval J. community was destroyed in the Black Death persecutions of 1348–49. A few J. merchants were present in the 16th cent. but all Jews were apparently expelled in 1595. A permanent J. settlement numbering about eight families was established in the 18th cent. From the mid-19th cent., Jews played an important part in the town's commerce and industry as their pop. rose to a peak of 129 (total 2,825) in 1849. They were especially prominent in the textile industry. In June 1933, four months after the Nazi rise to power, 41 Jews were counted in L. On *Kristallnacht* (9–10 Nov. 1938), the synagogue was burned to the ground while two J. stores and 12 J. homes were wrecked. Most of the Jews left L. before the onset of deportations, either to other destinations in Germany itself or to other countries (U.S., England, Palestine, Chile, Holland, and South Africa). In May 1939, there were only 15 Jews in L. The last Jew was deported to Auschwitz on 2 March 1943. It may be assumed that all those who did not make it in time to safe havens perished in the Holocaust.

LUEBBEN   Brandenburg, Germany. Jews lived in L.

in the 15th and 16th cents., up to 1573. A settlement developed in 1761. In 1857 an independent community was set up and a synagogue dedicated. In 1910 there were 63 Jews in L. and 26 when the Nazis came to power in 1933. On *Kristallnacht* (9–10 Nov. 1938), the synagogue was set on fire and gutted. The cemetery was leveled in 1941 and sold to a cannery. Most Jews probably moved to Berlin and were deported from there.

LUEBECK   Free Hanseatic city, Germany. No Jews were admitted to L. while it was a bastion of the Hanseatic League (1230–1535) and for over 100 years thereafter. Of the two J. families permitted to live and trade there from 1680, only one remained in 1701. Polish Jews fleeing the Chmielnicki massacres of 1648–49 settled in the neighboring Danish-ruled village of Moisling in 1650. Here they were allowed to open a synagogue in 1686 and acquire a burial ground. Growing from 12 to 38 families in less than three decades (1709–35), the community was placed under the jurisdiction of Altona's chief rabbinate. Since J. traders and peddlers from Moisling endured constant humiliation in L., they were at loggerheads with the city's protected Jews (*Schutzjuden*), who also had a vested interest in keeping them out. After the French occupation in 1806, Jews obtained full citizenship and the community opened a new synagogue in L. in 1812. The J. pop. in L. grew to 308 while that of Moisling declined from 381 to 140 (1811–15). Carl August Buchholz (1785–1843) – a lawyer representing the Bremen, Hamburg, and L. communities – tried vainly to oppose demands at the Congress of Vienna (1814–15) for the abolition of J. civil rights following Napoleon's defeat. Ignoring similar appeals by the liberal Prussian chancellor Karl August von Hardenberg, who favored unrestricted J. emancipation, L. senators used every kind of pressure to remove Jews from their city (1814–24), even offering to build a larger synagogue in Moisling, where the J. pop. grew to 465 (57% of the total) in 1845. A more enlightened approach was fostered by Gabriel Riesser (1806–63), leader of the German J. emancipation, and Buchholz, who suggested in 1843 practical measures to alleviate J. distress. Taking its cue from legislation passed by the Frankfurt National Assembly, the L. senate abolished all discriminatory laws and granted Jews full and equal citizenship on 19 Oct. 1848. The community was now able to establish its permanent center in L. Ephraim Fischel Joel, the rigidly traditionalist communal rabbi (1825–51), unsuccessfully opposed the creation – and later attempts to modernize the curriculum – of a J. elementary school which in 1837 had an enrollment of 100 children. Only 198 of the 493 members lived in L. when a temporary synagogue was opened there in 1851. The following 20 years brought a dramatic change, with 529 Jews residing in L. and 36 in Moisling. To satisfy the demand for a place of worship clearly distinguishable from a church (in return for a municipal loan), the community built in 1880 its new synagogue in the fashionable Moorish style. R. Salomon Carlebach (1870–1919) was an admired scholar and writer, a member of the city parliament, and founder of a rabbinical dynasty. He also impressed L. patricians such as the great novelist Thomas Mann, who immortalized Carlebach in his *Doktor Faustus*, published in 1947. Numbering 670 in 1900, the community had a solid membership of businessmen and professionals.

From 629 in 1925, the J. pop. declined to 497 when the Nazis came to power in 1933. Dr. Fritz Solmitz, who edited the Social Democratic *Luebecker Volksbote*, became one of their first victims when he was murdered at the Fuhlsbuettel concentration camp in Sept. 1933. Nazi boycott measures, from the dismissal of J. lawyers and physicians to the burning of proscribed books, also resulted in the collapse and "Aryanization" of leading business firms. Enthusiastic support for this campaign was expressed by the neo-pagan German Faith movement, of which the city's new Lutheran bishop was a key representative. Foreseeing the worst, L. Zionists moved to Palestine and in 1934–40 the community operated an elementary school with vocational and agricultural training programs. Since negotiations for the municipality's purchase of the synagogue had already begun, SA units contented themselves with destroying its interior on *Kristallnacht* (9–10 Nov. 1938). Altogether, 359 Jews left L. Many emigrated between 1933 and 1940; 90 were deported to the Riga ghetto in Dec. 1941 and over 50 were sent to the Theresienstadt ghetto in 1942. Eleven of those who remained in Europe survived the Holocaust. Numbering 400 in 1946, the postwar community virtually disappeared by 1970. It was revived by J. immigrants from the former Soviet Union and in 1999 there was a J. pop. of 560.

LUEDENSCHEID Westphalia, Germany. Jews are first mentioned in 1690. The J. pop. rose from 12 in 1821 to 59 in 1880 and a peak of 169 (total 29,356) in 1905. From the late 19th cent., Jews engaged in a wide range of professions (law, medicine, architecture, photography, acting and directing, etc.). Eight were industrialists, the largest J. factory being a brass foundry. Most Jews, however, engaged in trade. In June 1933, about four months after the Nazi rise to power, there were 102 Jews in L. Two J. families of Polish origin were expelled in Sept. 1938. On *Kristallnacht* (9–10 Nov. 1938), J. men were sent to the Sachsenhausen concentration camp. From June 1933 to Sept. 1939, 54 Jews left for other German cities. Another 24 emigrated (16 in 1938–40). The last 12 Jews were deported to concentration camps between May 1940 and Sept. 1944.

LUEDINGHAUSEN Westphalia, Germany. Jews settled in the early 19th cent. and from the mid-19th cent. maintained a pop. of about 40 (about 1% of the total). A synagogue was consecrated in 1839 and a cemetery was established in 1893. A J. elementary school was in operation in the 1830s and again in 1864–73. In the Weimar period, nine of 11 J. breadwinners were merchants, about half dealing in cattle. In June 1933, about four months after the Nazi rise to power, there were 26 Jews in L. On *Kristallnacht* (9–10 Nov. 1938), the synagogue and J. homes were vandalized. In 1940, the last four J. homeowners were forced to sell their houses. After emigration, arrests, and two suicides the last ten Jews were deported: on 13 Dec. 1941 to the Riga ghetto; on 22 Jan. 1942 to the Minsk ghetto; and on 31 July 1942 to the Theresienstadt ghetto.

LUELSFELD Lower Franconia, Germany. Jews numbered 68 in 1816 and 13 in 1933 (total 410). Their fate was similar to the Frankenwinheim community, to which they were attached: some emigrated and the others were sent eastward where they were killed.

LUENEBURG Hanover, Germany. A J. community existed in the 13th cent., but it was destroyed in the Black Death persecutions of 1348–49. Although individual Jews lived in L. in the 15th and 16th cents., a J. settlement only began to develop in 1680, when the son of the Hanover Court Jew Leffmann Behrens was allowed to settle in the town. Until the beginning of the 19th cent., no more than five J. families were allowed to live in L. Following the abolition of this restriction, the J. pop. grew to 127 in 1871, peaking at 175 in 1905. The community established a cemetery in 1823 and a synagogue in 1894. During the 1890s and the Weimar years, antisemitic campaigns and incidents were a common occurrence. The synagogue was repeatedly vandalized. In 1933, there were 114 Jews in L. Under Nazi pressure, many left, mostly to Hamburg and Berlin. Some emigrated to other countries. By 1937, only five families remained. The synagogue, which had been sold in late Oct. 1938, was being demolished at the time of *Kristallnacht* (9–10 Nov. 1938). Those Jews who did not emigrate in time were deported during the war years, except for two Jews who were married to non-Jews. Altogether 42 Jews from L. perished under Nazi rule. A Displaced Persons community existed in L. for several years after 1945.

LUENEN   Westphalia, Germany. Jews are first mentioned in 1660 and two to three families continued to live there under letters of protection until the early 19th cent. Under French domination, restrictions were lifted and the J. pop. subsequently grew to 14 families by 1846, including five cattle dealers who were also butchers. A synagogue was consecrated in 1833 and a J. elementary school enrolled 25 in 1909. The J. pop. rose to 101 in 1907 and to 115 in 1927. On the eve of the Nazi rise to power in 1933, the J. pop. numbered 140. In 1936, it was 116. In 1935–38, 24 J. businesses were liquidated, with most of the owners emigrating abroad. The last two were closed in 1939. The events of *Kristallnacht* (9–10 Nov. 1938) were the most violent in Westphalia. Two Jews were shot to death, one was drowned, and another died of injuries as local Nazis celebrated the 1923 Beer Hall Putsch. The synagogue was wrecked and its contents piled up in the market square and burned. J. homes were broken into and destroyed and Jews were brutally beaten. Ninety Jews managed to emigrate, most of them to safety in England, the U.S., Argentina, and Palestine. Those who emigrated to nearby countries like Holland and Belgium were caught up again in the Nazi maelstrom after the outbreak of war, together with those who remained in L.

LUETZELSACHSEN   Baden, Germany. A J. community of nearly 100 was present in 1825. Thirteen remained in 1933, of whom four emigrated to the U.S. and seven were deported to the Gurs concentration camp on 22 Oct. 1940. Two survived.

LUGA   Leningrad dist., Russia. J. settlement probably commenced in the mid-19th cent. The J. pop. was 382 (total 5,617) in 1897 and 554 in 1939. The few Jews who had not escaped or been evacuated were murdered after the German occupation of 24 Aug. 1941.

LUGINI   Zhitomir dist., Ukraine. Jews were present before the Chmielnicki massacres of 1648–49, 20 fleeing on the approach of the Cossacks. J. settlement was renewed in the early 18th cent. In 1897, the J. pop. reached 1,599 (total 2,535). On 2 Jan. 1918, soldiers looted J. stores. They were confronted by armed J. self-defense forces when they returned a second time. In the resulting clash, a number of J. fighters were killed or wounded. In 1926, almost all the town's inhabitants were Jews as well as the majority of municipal council members. The town's 100 J. artisans worked as tailors, cobblers, hatmakers, and blacksmiths and enjoyed the use of a community loan fund. Jews were also employed as construction workers and as factory hands in the leather industry. In 1933, 321 children attended a J. elementary school (four grades). The J. pop. was 1,622 (total 4,732) in 1939. The Germans arrived on 9 Aug. 1941 and soon afterwards murdered 745 Jews.

LUGOJ   (Hung. Lugos) S. Transylvania dist., Rumania. Jews first settled in the early 18th cent. and engaged in manufacturing and running the transport system. The community joined the Neologist association. A J. school was founded in 1883. When L. came under Rumanian rule after WWI, many Jews left. Zionist activity commenced in 1919. In 1930, the J. pop. stood at 1,418 (6% of the total). During WWII, economic sanctions were imposed on the Jews and the men were sent to forced labor camps near Olt and in the vicinity of Brasov. Four youths aged 14–15, charged with Communist activities, were deported to Transnistria and died there. After the war, many Jews left the city, most emigrating to Palestine.

LUJENI   (formerly Luzan, Luschan) Bukovina, Rumania. Jews settled in the 18th cent. but maintained an independent community only from 1930. The J. pop. in 1930 was 374 (15% of the total). In June 1941, the Jews were driven across the border to Sniatyn, Poland, but were taken back to L., transferred to Secureni, and then deported to Transnistria. Few survived.

LUKASHEVKA   Vinnitsa dist., Ukraine. Jews numbered 35 in 1765 and 1,724 (total 4,326) in 1897. The J. pop. dropped to 522 in 1926 under the Soviets. Up to half the Jews worked in a J. kolkhoz while many of the young left the town. During the German occupation, 322 Jews were murdered, most in an *Aktion* on 29 May 1942.

LUKOML   Vitebsk dist., Belorussia. The J. pop. was 131 in 1766 and 813 (total 1,596) in 1897. In the Soviet period, most Jews were employed in artisan cooperatives and in trade. In 1923, their pop. was 640. A J. elementary school (four grades) was still open in the late 1930s. Fifteen Jews worked at a nearby kolkhoz founded in 1925. The Germans occupied the town on 18 July 1941. About 300 Jews were murdered on 13 Oct. on the way to Chashniki.

LUKOV   Slovakia, Czechoslovakia, today Republic of Slovakia. The community is believed to have been founded in the mid-19th cent. after 150 years of sporadic settlement. It reached a peak pop. of 115 (total 682) in 1880, mostly comprised of Galician Hasidim, and then declined to 44 in 1940. The Jews were deported to the Pulawy ghetto in the Lublin dist. (Poland) on 17 May 1942.

LUKOW   Lublin dist., Poland. Jews may have been present by the mid-13th cent. In the 15th cent. they were granted a liberal royal privilege which was renewed after most J. homes and the synagogue were razed in the Chmielnicki disturbances of 1648–49. R. Yoel Sirkes officiated in the community in 1585–87. The J. pop. rose from 2,023 in 1827 to 4,799 in 1897 and 7,792 (total 12,489) in 1910. Industrial development was slow but in 1906–07 a big Warsaw shoe factory relocated to L., becoming a major source of J. employment. Hasidism was the dominant force in

The Lukow marketplace with city bell for fire alarms and community events, Poland

the community until WWI. R. Hershele Morgensztern (d. 1920) the great-grandson of R. Menahem Mendel of Kock, lived in L. An important yeshiva headed by R. Shemuel Shelomo Braun attracted many students. In 1916, J. political parties opened branches in L. In Aug. 1920, when the Soviet army withdrew, rampaging antisemites attacked Jews and J. property, and the Polish police executed 12 Jews as alleged Bolsheviks. In 1921, the J. pop. was 6,145. Jews comprised 43% of the city's textile and garment workers and 29% of hide-processing workers. With the growth of the J. proletariat, Bund influence spread, while Zionist activity also intensified. The leading youth movements were Hashomer Hatzair, Betar, and Hehalutz. All the J. political parties contended fiercely for dominance in the community. In the 1930s, discriminatory government measures began to undermine J. livelihoods. The Germans entered the city on 19 Sept. 1939, burning 25 houses and murdering several dozen Jews in retaliation for Polish sniper fire against their troops. The Soviets captured the city a few days later and 500 Jews fled with them when the Germans returned. Another 70 Jews were soon murdered and a regime of forced labor was instituted. With the influx of refugees, the J. pop. rose in July 1940 to 7,500, all confined to a ghetto. By Oct. 1942, the J. pop. was 12,000 as refugees arrived from Slovakia and other places. On 3 Oct. 1942, the first large-scale *Aktion* commenced: 5,000 Jews were deported to the Treblinka death camp and 2,000 were murdered outside the city. On 7–8 Nov. an additional 3,000–4,000 were sent to Treblinka and 200 executed at the J. cemetery. The last 1,500 Jews were rounded up in May 1943. Some were murdered at the cemetery and the rest were dispatched to Treblinka.

LUKOWA Lublin dist., Poland. Jews were present in the 19th cent. and numbered 224 in WWII. Some were sent to Tarnogrod in summer 1942 where they were murdered in July. Others were transferred to Jozefow and deported to the Belzec death camp in Nov.

LUKY Slovakia, Czechoslovakia, today Republic of Slovakia. Jews probably settled in the early 18th cent., possibly before. Their pop. was 190 (total 953) in 1828 and 70 in 1940. In spring 1942, they were deported to Auschwitz and the Lublin dist. of Poland.

LUNCA BRADULUI (Hung. Palotailva) N. Tran-

sylvania dist., Rumania. Jews settled in the late 19th cent. The J. pop. in 1920 was 166 (11% of the total). In May 1944 the community was transferred to the Reghin ghetto and in June deported to Auschwitz.

LUNCA DE JOS (Hung. Gyimeskozeplak) N. Transylvania dist., Rumania. An organized J. community existed in the early 20th cent. The J. pop. in 1930 was 286 (6% of the total). The J. community was expelled in summer 1941 and scattered throughout Transylvania.

LUNEVILLE Meurthe-et-Moselle dist., France. Several Jews are mentioned in L. in 1470–72. From 1702, L. was the seat of the ducal court and several privileged Jews were permitted to live there. Most came from Metz or the Low Countries. By the time a synagogue was built in 1785, there were 16 J. families in L. In 1791, the community acquired a cemetery. In the latter part of the 18th cent. and the beginning of the 19th cent. a Hebrew printing press owned by Abraham Brissac was active in L. By 1855, the J. community consisted of 400 members. From 1856, several charity organizations were founded. In 1870, the community was augmented by a number of manufacturers from Alsace. Alfred Levy, chief rabbi of France in 1907–19, was rabbi of L. in 1869–80. Among the founders of the L. congregation were the ancestors of the poet Andre Spire (1868–1966). During WWI, the minister of the congregation, S. Weill, his six-year-old daughter, and several other civilians were slaughtered in L. Fourteen other Jews fell on the battlefield. Between the World Wars, the majority of L. Jews were engaged in commerce. The local Religious Association (Association Cultuelle) was established in 1905. In 1939 there were 350 Jews in L. Pop. records from 1942 vary, with some listing 214 Jews and others claiming 294. About 150 refugees arrived from Alsace. On 19 July 1942 and on 9 Oct. 1942, 69 Jews were arrested. Those who found refuge in such nearby localities as Vichy and Aigueperse (Puy-de-Dome) were caught as well. Deportations of all 63 Jews remaining in the town continued until 2 March 1944 and on 19 May 1944. In all, 194 were deported, including 129 members of the community and 65 refugees. Only nine deportees returned. The occupying German forces completely destroyed the synagogue. About 200 Jews from L. found refuge during the occupation in the southern zone, among them active members of the resistance movement. In

1945, the community consisted of 140 members, growing to 360 in 1964, half from North Africa.

LUNINIEC Polesie dist., Poland, today Belarus. J. settlement began with the coming of the railroad. The first synagogue was built in 1895 and the Zionists and the Bund were active from the early 20th cent. with a resurgence after the Feb. 1917 Revolution, when the Zionists came to dominate public life. The J. pop. stood at 2,045 (total 8,267) in 1921. A Tarbut school, visited by Hayyim Nahman Bialik in 1931, enrolled 250 children and a yeshiva for 90 was operated by the Karlin-Stolin Hasidim. The Germans arrived in early July 1941 and immediately murdered the J. doctors in the town. On 10 Aug. they murdered J. males over 14. A ghetto for 3,000 Jews, mostly women and children, was set up in March 1942. On 18 Aug, around 2,800 were executed outside the town; about 180 Jews survived the war, many in the Soviet Union.

LUNNA Bialystok dist., Poland, today Belarus. Jews may have been present by the 16th cent. A small organized community existed in the mid-19th cent., growing to 1,364 (of a total 1,835) by 1897. Many traded in lumber and some lived off the summer resort trade that developed in the late 19th cent. but most engaged in petty trade and crafts. Jews also set up three flour mills. During WWI the Jews suffered from food shortages and were subjected to forced labor under the German occupation. The J. pop. in 1921 was 1,373. Under Polish rule after the war their livelihoods were undermined by heavy taxes and other discriminatory government measures. Most children attended Hebrew and Yiddish schools and Zionist influence spread in the 1920s despite the strict Orthodoxy of most Jews. After two years of Soviet rule, the Germans took the town on 28 June 1941, initiating a regime of forced labor and "contributions." A *Judenrat* was appointed. On 2 Sept. 1942 the Jews were sent to the notorious Kelbasin transit camp near Grodno and on 6 Dec. all 1,400 were deported to Auschwitz, 1,085 to be gassed immediately at Birkenau and the rest put to forced labor there. Few survived.

LUNOCHARSKOE Vitebsk dist., Belorussia. Thirty-one J. farming families were present in the mid-1920s. In 1930, Jews founded the Nadezhda kolkhoz, which supported 18 families. The Germans arrived in July 1941 and murdered the few Jews who had not fled or been evacuated.

LUOKE (Yid. Luknik) Telsai dist., Lithuania. Jews first settled here in the 17th cent. A devastating fire in 1887, a blood libel and the resulting pogrom in

Children at Luoke Jewish school, Lithuania

1888, and the general economic situation caused many Jews to emigrate to America, South Africa, and Eretz Israel. The J. pop. in 1897 was 798 (49% of the total). Between the World Wars, a Hebrew school, two study halls, a library, and Zionist and social welfare organizations operated. The J. pop. in 1941 was about 300. After the Germans invasion in June 1941, Jews were robbed, abused, and raped. Men were seized for forced labor and then murdered at the nearby Gudiske labor camp. The women and children were murdered at the Geruliai camp.

LUPENI (Hung. Lupeny) S. Transylvania dist., Rumania. Jews first settled in 1870-80. The majority were mine workers and artisans. During WWI, most Jews fled and J. families from other areas settled. The J. pop. in 1930 was 333 (2% of the total). In July 1941, the majority were expelled to Hateg, Nalacz, and Paclisa. The J. men were drafted for forced labor. After the liberation, about half the J. pop. returned, dwindling over the years.

LUPOLOVO Mogilev dist., Belorussia. Under the Soviets, a kolkhoz was founded near L. in 1925 and employed 33 J. families in 1930. The Germans arrived in the area in late July 1941, expelling the Jews to the Mogilev ghetto, where they were murdered together with a group of local Jews in Nov.

LUTOMIERSK Lodz dist., Poland. In 1787, Pinhas Yisraelowicz opened a weaving mill in L., the first by a Jew in Poland. In the 1780s a wooden synagogue was built, one of the most attractive of its type in Poland. The J. pop. in 1857 was 999 (46% of the total). Between the World Wars, Agudat Israel was the leading party in the community. A boycott of J. businesses was imposed in 1937. When the Germans entered the town in 1939, they abused the Jews and plundered their property. In summer 1940, the 750 Jews were ghettoized. At the end of July 1942, they were transported to Chelmno.

LUTOWISKA Lwow dist., Poland, today Ukraine. Jews settled in the early 19th cent. and constituted a majority of the pop., reaching 1,570 in 1900 (total 2,442). Most fled before the Russians in WWI and while economic conditions worsened between the World Wars, community life flourished with ramified Zionist activity. Under the Soviet regime (27 Sept. 1939–22 June 1941) businesses were nationalized and J. institutions disbanded. The community was liquidated by the Germans in the summer of 1942 when 800, mostly children and the aged, were murdered in the town after a selection. The rest were subsequently deported to their deaths in the Zaslawie camp.

LUTUTOW Lodz dist., Poland. Jews settled permanently from the first part of the 19th cent. Jews were involved in trade throughout the Polish kingdom, Galicia, and Silesia. The J. pop. in 1897 was 829 (57% of the total). All the Zionist parties were active between the World Wars and Agudat Israel was for awhile the leading party in the community council. About 100 Jews were injured in a pogrom at a local fair in July 1923 and there were many more manifestations of antisemitism throughout the 1930s. When the Germans captured the town on 2 Sept. 1939, they arrested young Jews, took them to Germany, and paraded them before the pop. as criminals who had shot at German soldiers. A German film crew came to L. and filmed Jews tearing at each other's beards and burning Torah scrolls. A *Judenrat* was set up and by Dec. 1940 there were 1,370 Jews in the ghetto (including 247 refugees). On 25 Aug. 1942, the Jews were incarcerated in the church; 80 able-bodied men were sent to Wielun and Lodz and the remaining Jews were deported to Chelmno. After the war, 20 survivors returned to L. and built a memorial. They soon left.

LUXEMBOURG grand duchy and capital city. Jews are first mentioned in 1279. In 1349, during the Black Death persecutions, local Jews were massacred and the remainder expelled from the cities of L. and Echternach. Expelled again in 1391, Jews returned individually. In 1420, seven resided in Grevenmacher. By 1515, there were 15 J. families in L., Echternach and Arlon (today in Belgium). All the Jews were expelled in 1530, returning only in the Napoleonic era. In 1808, there were 75 Jews in L. Between 1815 and 1830, L. was part of the Netherlands. Under Napoleon's auspices, a religious framework was established for the Jews in the grand duchy in accordance with the French model. The imperial decree of 1808 fixed the legal status of the Jews, who were attached to the consistory of Trier until a separate body was established in 1838. The first synagogue in L. was opened in 1823. The first chief rabbi, Samuel Hirsch, was appointed in 1843. In 1880, there were 87 J. families (369 individuals) in the city of L. and an additional 63 families in the province. A new synagogue was consecrated in 1894. Another one was erected in Esch-sur-Alzette in 1899. In 1927, the J. pop. of the duchy was 1,171, increasing with the arrival of refugees from Germany. In 1935, there were 3,144 Jews in L., but only 870 were citizens. Aside from the capital with its 2,069 Jews, there were 470 Jews in Esch; 187 in Diekirch; 78 in Echternach; 79 in Grevenmacher; and 99 in Renich. The immigrants enriched the social life of the community. In the capital, many of them en route to France or Belgium rented homes in a quarter called the New Jerusalem. By 1940, there were about 3,500 Jews in L. With the German invasion of 10 May 1940, L. came under the jurisdiction of *Gauleiter* Gustav Simon. Most Jews left the country, heading for France, Belgium, Portugal, and Spain. As of 5 Sept. 1940, the remaining Jews were denied their most basic rights: intermarriage between Jews and non-Jews was prohibited; Jews were excluded from the public service; J. children were expelled from public schools; 355 J.-owned businesses were handed over to "Aryans" and 380 J.-owned farms were leased to new managers. The synagogues in L. and Esch-sur-Alzette were destroyed and Jews were banned from cafes, restaurants, sports clubs, and public transportation facilities and forced to wear the yellow badge. At the same time, the Jews were subjected to forced labor. Between Aug. 1940 and Oct. 1941, nearly 1,450 Jews were expelled to the borders of Belgium, France, and Portugal. On 15 Oct. 1941, the Germans appointed Alfred Oppenheimer chairman of the consistory, renamed the Council of J. Elders in April 1942. From Aug. 1941, the 750 Jews left in L. were concentrated in a small ghetto in the Funfbrunnen camp. From there, starting on 16 Oct. 1941, Jews were deported to the east in convoys. The first brought 331 Jews to the Lodz ghetto and on 17 June 1942 the last convey was directed to the Theresienstadt ghetto. Of the 729 Jews deported during the Holocaust, 690 perished. There were about ten Jews in L. when it was liberated on 10 Sept. 1944. By 1947, the community consisted of 870 Jews, only 487 of them natives of the city. A new synagogue was consecrated in 1953. In 1978, the J. pop. of the city of L. was nearly 865, with another 110 Jews in Esch-sur-Alzette; 12 in Mondorf-les-Bains; eight in Ettelbruck; and five in Diekirch.

LUZE Bohemia, Czechoslovakia. Jews are mentioned in 1620 but were probably there in the late 16th cent. Their pop. was about 300 in 1837, 142 in 1880, and 32 in 1930. Those remaining were deported to the Theresienstadt ghetto via Pardubice in Dec. 1942. Nearly all were sent to Auschwitz in 1943. Six returned.

LUZHKI Vilna dist., Poland. A small community existed in the mid-18th cent., growing to 761 in 1897 (total 1,672) but dropping to 442 in 1921, most living in straitened economic circumstances between the World Wars. The Germans entered the town in late June 1941, setting up a *Judenrat* and ghetto. On 1 June 1942, 528 Jews were machinegunned down by SS men in the courtyard of the *beit midrash*.

LVOVO Nikolaiev dist., Ukraine. L. was founded as a J. colony in 1841 by Jews from the Vitebsk and Mogilev regions and numbered 500–550 people on 119 farm units. The J. pop. grew to 1,060 in 1859 and 1,338 (total 1,402) in 1897. Most Jews earned their livelihoods from agriculture and from employment in a local dairy. Despite a pogrom in 1919 (with no fatalities), the J. pop. continued to grow, reaching 1,356 in 1926. A rural J. council (soviet) was active there in the 1920s and the local J. agricultural school was still accepting new students for the 1937–38 school year. A J. elementary school was also operating. The Soviet agricultural crisis of the 1930s led to a large drop in the J. pop., with about 550 (130 families) remaining c. 1931. The Germans captured L. on 24 Aug. 1941. On 11 Oct., they murdered 70 Jews. By the end of the year a total of 160 Jews had been killed.

LWOW (Lvov; Ger. Lemberg) Lwow dist., Poland, today Ukraine. The first Jews to settle in L. arrived from Byzantium and Khazaria in the tenth cent. Much later they were joined by Jews from Germany and Poland and in the 13th cent. by Karaites as well. The Jews engaged in the region's transit trade in competition with Greeks and Armenians. Throughout the 15th and 16th cents. the community suffered from foreign invasion, mostly by the Tartars. This was compounded by a series of natural disasters (earthquakes, floods, fires, epidemics). Nonetheless, after the annexation to the Polish Kingdom in 1349, the J. community expanded, particularly the German element, whose language and culture ultimately prevailed. At the same

Zionist pioneer training group, Lwow, Poland, 1934

time, the Karaite community dwindled and in effect ceased to exist by 1457. In 1550, the J. pop. included 352 families within the walled city and 559 in the suburb outside the walls. J. life was regulated by privileges granted by the kings of Poland but was often circumscribed by parallel and contradictory privileges granted to the local pop. that entailed restrictions and disabilities, particularly in the realm of trade. Jews engaged in moneylending, tax farming, and wholesale and retail trade. They were particularly active in trade with the east, marketing imported goods throughout Poland, especially after the fall of Constantinople in 1453, when Christian merchants were afraid to visit lands under Turkish rule. Jews dealt in perfumes, silk goods, and other exotic items, with Jews from Constantinople opening branches in L. In the late 15th cent. Jews expanded commercial ties with Nuremberg, Breslau, and Danzig. They also imported goods from Hungary, Italy, Holland, and England, dealing in grain, cattle, hides, wine, and other goods. Jews also earned a livelihood in various trades, always in the face of opposition and restrictions. By 1610, there were 70 J. butchers in the city. Jews were also active as tailors, tanners,

and silversmiths. In the poorer (and separate) J. community outside the city walls, many were peddlers. The community was led for a hundred years (from the second half of the 16th cent.) by Yitzhak ben Nahman and his descendants. R. Yitzhak built a Gothic-style synagogue in 1571 which remained standing until WWII after a fierce (and successful) struggle with the Jesuits over possession of the building. The synagogue was called by some *"Di Gildene Roiz."* A second magnificent synagogue, also in existence until WWII, was built for the congregation outside the walls in 1632. Another illustrious family was founded by R. Yisrael Eideles, whose son-in-law R. Yehoshua Falk (c. 1555–1614) established a famous yeshiva in L. and wrote the well-known *Shulhan Arukh* commentary *Sefer Me'irat Einayim*. Jews were constantly under the threat of attack. Most frequent was the rioting of Jesuit students, but the local garrison, nobility, and peasants also participated in periodic depredations. During the Chmielnicki massacres of 1648–49 the city was under a month-long siege. Jews participated in its defense and in the heavy tribute paid to raise the siege after the mayor refused to hand the Jews over to the

Cantor Moshe Harari in pre-WWII visit to Lwow, Poland

Cossacks. However, starvation and disease within the city and the sword and torch outside its walls claimed thousands of J. lives, particularly among refugees. Another tribute was exacted in 1656 by the prince of Transylvania and in May 1664, 400 armed Jews fought off Jesuit students reinforced by peasants and townsmen until the soldiers sent to protect the Jews went over to the other side. The result was that 102 Jews were killed and over 200 were wounded. Renewed rioting a month later left another 129 Jews dead and another 200 wounded. A Tartar invasion in 1695 and the capture of the city by the Swedes in 1704 claimed still more J. lives and the Catholic reaction of the same years produced blood libels culminating in the execution of innocent Jews. All these events left the community saddled with debts and in the throes of economic decline, contributing to the growing independence of satellite communities once under its sway. The Jews enjoyed a short respite from persecution under the sympathetic King John Sobieski, but on his death in 1696, residence and trade restrictions were again threatened and only averted at great financial sacrifice. By 1708, Jews dominated a number of trades

and the center of the city was full of J. stores. By 1764 the J. pop. numbered 6,142. In addition to the 335 tradesmen among the 834 J. breadwinners, there were 295 salaried workers, servants, carters, and porters, and an additional 109 community workers (rabbis, beadles, clerks, etc). Among the outstanding rabbis of the period were David ben Shemuel Halevi ("Taz"; d. 1667), author of the well-known halakhic commentary *Turei Zahav*. In 1714–18, Tzevi Hirsch ben Yaakov Ashkenazi, author of the responsa collection *Hakham Tzevi*, served as rabbi of the two communities. Hayyim ha-Kohen Rapoport served in 1741–71 and is best known for his staunch opposition to the sectarian Frankists, culminating in a disputation in L.'s cathedral in 1759 after their leader Jakob Frank himself was removed from the city in 1755. In 1772, L. came under Austrian rule and under its "enlightened" monarchy, Jews were earmarked for Europeanization in an attempt to turn them into "useful" and "productive" subjects while at the same crushing them under a heavy tax burden and limiting their natural growth. Despite a marriage tax and residence restrictions, the J. pop. grew to 19,277 in 1826, owing mainly to the influx of Jews from the provincial towns, leading to severe overcrowding and unhealthy living conditions. In 1829, 415 deaths were registered in the J. hospital following a typhoid epidemic. Economic conditions worsened when Jews were cut off from such market cities as Danzig and Leipzig and excluded from the grain trade as well as from traditional leaseholdings. However, Jews were soon able to dominate the wholesale trade between Russia and Austria. They also became army suppliers and played a part in the city's industrial development. In 1820 Jews owned 265 of the city's 290 stores. About 55% of L.'s merchants, 25% of its artisans, and nearly all its peddlers were Jews. The J. hospital founded in 1801 had a full J. medical staff, treating 1,304 patients in 1843, when it opened an 80-bed convalescence facility. In 1843, an orphanage for 170 children was also opened. Yaakov Meshullam ben Mordekhai Ze'ev Ornstein (1775-1839), who served as rabbi from 1805, was one of the great halakhists of his time and author of *Yeshu'ot Yaakov*.

The unpopular J. educational network founded by Naftali Herz Homberg on behalf of the Austrian government was closed down in 1806 and most J. children were absorbed into the public school system. At the same time Jews began to be accepted into L. University, giving rise to a professional class. The professionals together with the sons of wealthy merchants became the first adherents of Haskala. In 1844-45 they founded a J. elementary school which reached an enrollment of 738 within two years and they also inaugurated a Temple with *bat mitzva* exercises for girls. At the same time Hasidism, mainly of the Belz dynasty, began to spread in L.

By the time of the revolutionary events of 1848, two cultural and political factions had emerged in the J. community, the one pro-Austro-German, the other Polish in orientation. The political activities of the pro-Austrian assimilationists were channeled through the Shomer Israel organization founded in 1868 and its German-language weekly *Der Israelit*.

Ukrainian police report on the use of live ammunition against the Jews, Lwow, Poland, Aug. 1942

Pro-Polish circles founded Doresh Shalom in 1878 (re-established as Agudat Ahim in 1883). Many in the two organizations joined the Polish Socialist Party in the 1890s. The first Zionist groups were organized in the 1880s, producing numerous periodicals and founding various youth groups. Orthodox circles were organized in the Mahzikei Dat society, with Agudat Israel becoming active from 1912. Under R. Yosef Shaul Nathanson (d. 1875) dozens of new prayer houses sprang up in a resurgence of traditional forces. Enlightened circles agitated for J. equal rights within the Empire. Most special taxes were canceled in 1848 and trade restrictions were abrogated in 1859 and 1860. In the following years, Jews played a leading role in industry, banking, and commerce (already in 1848, seven of the 15 members of the local chamber of commerce were Jews). Jews controlled the wholesale trade in leather and knitted goods, foodstuffs, and agricultural machinery and J. capital was invested in the building industry. There were also 100 J. doctors and 100 J. lawyers (in each case a third of the city's total at the end of the cent.). Most J. tradesmen, however, were artisans, shopkeepers, and peddlers, whose livelihoods were undermined by the new Polish cooperatives. Industrial activity was for the most part confined to workshops employing an average of ten workers, half of them in the clothing industry, where 4,000 Jews were employed in 1914. In 1903, Jews in the needle trade went on strike, as did workers in the metal and building industries. With economic conditions for the masses worsening, 20,000 Jews were receiving welfare support in 1905. In 1873–74, 53 charitable organizations were in existence and at the end of the cent., 60 separate endowment funds served the needs of the community's members. A new J. hospital, one of the best in Poland, was built in 1884 and a new orphanage was opened in 1902. Another organization supporting the community was the Alliance Israelite, promoting vocational education and home industry. Jews continued to exploit the facilities for secondary education made available to them by the state. At times, the Jews constituted over 50% of L.'s high school students and in 1897 they comprised 315 of the 1,513 students at L. University, with 253 Jews studying Law. During this period, J. culture flourished with an outpouring of Hebrew and Yiddish literature, including such writers as Yosef Hayyim Brenner (1881–1921) and Gershon Shofman (1880–1972). In 1890, Yaakov Ber Gimpel founded the first J. theater

in Poland. Hebrew printing expanded, with the Halevi house producing a new edition of the Talmud in 1860–68 and the Herz and Balaban presses continuing to operate. In 1880, the J. pop. numbered 30,961 and in 1910, 57,387 (total 206,113). At the outbreak of WWI, L. was flooded with thousands of J. refugees fleeing the barbarities of the Cossacks. The Russians took the city on 3 Sept. 1914 after the Austrians withdrew. About 16,000 Jews succeeded in fleeing. The 40,000 who remained were subjected to severe abuse, with 40 killed over the alleged shooting of a Russian soldier and some taken hostage and exiled on the Russian withdrawal in May 1915. Dozens more were killed in the disturbances following the disintegration of Austrian rule at the end of the war. The collapse of the economy in the war further increased J. hardship, with the J. death rate increasing by over a thousand percent. In the struggle between the Poles and Ukrainians for supremacy in Eastern Galicia, the Jews tried to maintain a position of neutrality while defending themselves with a 300-man militia. On 22 Nov. 1918, the Poles captured the city and unleashed a brutal pogrom against the Jews, killing 100 and injuring hundreds more while burning and looting J. homes with the participation of the local Polish pop. After the pogrom, thousands of Jews were fired from their jobs, including 400 from the postal service, business licenses were revoked, and a regime of unrelenting anti-J. agitation was instituted. The attempt of the Jews to organize their own cooperatives to meet competition were largely unsuccessful. After the war, the Jews continued to maintain their traditional occupations. Half the J. manufacturing establishments (and factory workers) were in the clothing industry. Jews comprised 66% of the city's wholesalers and 80% of its petty traders. But the economic crisis, exacerbated by anti-J. government policy, continued to take its toll throughout the period between the World Wars. In the 1930s, when the J. pop. had risen to about 100,000, the number of J. stores dropped by 475. J. doctors (a total of 650) and lawyers now comprised 60% of the total but were excluded from the public service. By 1937, nearly half the community required assistance to get through the Passover holiday season. Various organizations dispensed free meals to the needy throughout the year and the community's public health organizations offered extensive services as the community continued to maintain its 130-bed hospital and an old age home for another 130 in addition to facilities for 880 orphans. J. representation on the city council was kept down to 20%, with the Zionists gaining increasing strength. The General Zionists with their youth movement were the leading party. Mizrachi and the Revisionists were also active. The Bund gained strength among J. workers in the 1930s and many Jews were active in the illegal Communist Party. L. remained one of the most important centers of J. education and culture in Poland. Three J. high schools were maintained with Hebrew instruction added to the state curriculum as well as a college for J. studies, a teachers' college, vocational schools, and a network of religious schools set up by Agudat Israel. The Tarbut educational association organized Hebrew courses for 1,500 students and in 1926 an open university. At the same time J. attendance in the city's institutes of higher learning shrank as they became hotbeds of antisemitism. In the late 1930s, physical attacks on Jews increased, including stabbings. The Soviets entered the city on 22 Sept. 1939. In Nov. all J. community institutions were closed down. Political activity was immediately curtailed and the J. youth movements were banned. A number of J. leaders, including Zionists, were exiled to the interior of the Soviet Union. Big businesses were nationalized and J. shopkeepers were instructed to sell out their stocks, afterwards being forced to liquidate their businesses for want of merchandise. Artisans were organized into cooperatives or employed by the government and while Jews at first occupied leading positions in local administration, they were soon pushed out in a process of "Ukrainization." Some synagogues, which remained the focus of J. community life under the Soviets, were also forced to close down under the burden of heavy taxes. The educational system, too, was Sovietized as 5,000 J. children were concentrated in 20 Yiddish-language schools with a Soviet curriculum. However, here too the Ukrainian language was gradually introduced at the expense of Yiddish. Only at the university level were the Jews unhampered. The number of J. faculty members increased and Jews constituted 30–40% of medical students. About 100,000 J. refugees from western Poland gathered in the city during the Soviet period, contributing to the widespread Yiddish cultural activity in the city during this time. Large numbers who turned down Soviet citizenship were expelled to the interior of Russia, including 70,000 on 30 June–3 July 1940.

The Germans captured L. on 30 June 1941. A large-scale pogrom was immediately carried out by the German *Einsatzgruppe C* and Ukrainian nationalists, claiming 4,000 J. lives in a four-day period (30 June–3 July). Murders continued throughout July, culminating in the massacre of 2,000 Jews on 25–27 July by rampaging Ukrainians. A J. council was appointed on 22 July, officially becoming a *Judenrat* on 1 Aug., when Eastern Galicia was absorbed by the General Gouvernement. In early Aug. the first extortionate "contribution" was exacted from the community and though paid in full, the hostages taken by the Germans all disappeared. The *Judenrat* operated numerous departments for the welfare of the community but its primary function was to supply forced labor. The thousands sent out each day to work on roads and bridges and in military camps were subjected to unrelenting abuse. The *Judenrat* was also forced to supply the Germans with coveted items from J. homes. At the same time, the Germans systematically destroyed the synagogues and cemeteries. The first head of the *Judenrat*, Dr. Yosef Parnes, was murdered when he refused to supply a list of Jews for work in a labor camp. On 8 Nov. 1941, the Germans ordered the Jews into a ghetto, weeding out the old and sick, 5,000 of whom were subsequently murdered. The ghetto remained open for a time, with Jews continuing to live outside it as well. In the winter of 1941–42, they suffered from hunger, cold, and disease. The J. medical service, with a staff of 80 doctors, managed to contain a typhoid epidemic when the well-known bacteriologist Prof. Ludwig Falk developed a vaccine under primitive conditions after the Jews were denied access to drugstores. On 4 Jan. 1942, Jews were forced to hand over furs and sweaters to the Germans. Many were sent to labor camps in the area while others were employed in workshops, organized by the *Judenrat* to supply essential services as an alternative to forced labor, or in big factories set up by German industrialists. In March 1942, about 15,000 Jews were deported to the Belzec death camp. Another 200 in the J. police who were not enthusiastic enough about rounding up Jews were sent to Belzec and the Jaktorow labor camp. On 8 July 1942, 7,000 Jews without work permits, mostly women and the old, were taken to the Janowska camp and murdered. In Aug., the German Employment Office was closed and responsibility for the Jews was transferred entirely to the German police and SS. Another selection was made and 50,000 Jews were sent to their deaths in Belzec in a mass *Aktion* that lasted from 10 to 23 Aug. There now remained about 50,000 Jews in the city out of the 160,000 present at the outset of the German occupation. The ghetto was sealed off and the killing continued, including a large group of *Judenrat* members. In Nov., another 5,000–7,000 Jews were sent to Janowska and Belzec. With the ghetto designated a labor camp, a further 10,000 "illegals" were rounded up and murdered in Jan. 1943. Under an iron hand, camp inmates were marched out to work while the sick were sent to Janowska for execution and family members were killed off as a matter of course during the day. After the Aug. 1942 *Aktion* various underground groups attempted to organize resistance but were unable to make any impact. Many hid within the ghetto as the killings continued. There were also attempts to escape to the surrounding forests and link up with the partisans in order to fight the Nazis and their Ukrainian helpers. In spring 1943, the J. work force was reduced, many were sent to Piaski and Janowska to die, and the last women and children in the ghetto were murdered. The final phase of liquidation commenced on 1 June 1943, when about 20,000 Jews remained in the ghetto. Around 7,000 J. men were taken to the Janowska camp for execution and around 3,000 Jews were killed inside the ghetto, a few in a pitched battle that lasted two hours. Children were savagely murdered, their heads smashed or thrown bodily into burning buildings. The *Aktion* continued until 20 June and the search for Jews still in hiding continued for a few weeks after that. The Ukrainian police were active participants in all the murders inside and outside the ghetto. The Janowska Road camp, originally set up in Sept. 1941 as a transit and forced labor camp and housing the German Armament Works (DAW), had soon been made over into a concentration and extermination camp where tens of thousands of Jews ultimately met their deaths, including many from L. The camp was liquidated in Nov. 1943, with a small number of Jews escaping after attacking guards. The Soviets took the city on 22 July 1944. By the end of Sept., about 3,400 Jews had gathered there from among the survivors and those returning from the Soviet Union. Many later emigrated to Israel and the West. In the 1960s, the J. pop. reached 28,000 as Russian Jews settled in the city.

LWOWEK Poznan dist., Poland. Jews settled in the late 16th cent., forming an organized community in the 17th. After a devastating fire in 1696, most left, subsequently returning under a charter granting them trade rights and internal autonomy. The growth of the community was accelerated after the annexation to Prussia in 1793, reaching a peak pop. of 540 (total 2,546) in 1871. With Jews broadening their education and entering the professions in the late 19th cent., many left for the big German cities and others for the U.S. and Eretz Israel. On the eve of WWII, 28 remained. On 7 Nov. 1939 they were expelled by the Germans to General Gouvernement territory to share the fate of the Jews there.

LYADY Vitebsk dist., Belorussia. Jews are first mentioned in the mid-18th cent., their pop. including 207 paying a poll tax in 1766. A J. printing press was founded in the town in 1805. Shneur Zalman of L., the founder of Habad Hasidism, spent the last years of his life there (1801–12). In 1897, the J. pop. was 3,763 (total 4,483). A J. council (soviet) was established in 1929 and a J. elementary school was in operation. A J. kolkhoz was also founded nearby in 1929 and employed 14 J. families. In 1939, the J. pop. was 897. The Germans occupied the town on 18 July 1941. In March 1942, 2,000 Jews were herded into a school building and held there without food until 2 April, when they were executed outside the town.

LYANTSKORUN (from 1944, Zarechanka) Kamenets-Podolski dist., Ukraine. The J. pop. was 609 in 1765 and 1,893 (50% of the total) in 1897. In 1926,

Wooden 18th cent. synagogue in Lyantskorun, Ukraine

in the Soviet period, the J. pop. was 1,638. A. J. council was active. The Germans occupied L. on 9 July 1941, transferring the Jews in summer 1942 to the Kamenets-Podolski ghetto, where they perished.

LYCK (Pol. Elk) East Prussia, Germany, today Poland. As early as 1698 there is evidence of the presence of J. traders from Poland and Lithuania at the L. fairs. By 1715 a settlement existed with 29 Jews. A cemetery was established in 1837 at the latest, a synagogue in 1859. At this time L. became a center of J. and Hebrew publishing. In 1857 Eliezer Lippman Silbermann founded the first Hebrew weekly, *Ha-Maggid*. Silbermann also founded in 1864 the Mekize Nirdamim society for the printing of Hebrew manuscripts and rare books. Among its publications were S.D. Luzzatto's edition of Yehuda Halevi's *Diwan* and parts of I. Lampronti's *Pahad Yitzhak*. In 1866 the first part of the travel book *Even Sappir* by Yaakov Saphir was published in L. By virtue of its proximity to the border, L. served in the second half of the 19th cent. as a center for smuggling prohibited Hebrew books into Russia. By 1880, the J. pop. included 250 individuals, declining to about 190 in the first decades of the 20th cent. Antisemitism reached a high level already in the late Weimar years: calls for boycotts threatened J. businessmen, the synagogue was vandalized in 1930, and J. businesses were attacked in 1932. In 1933, there were still 137 Jews living in L. Zionist activities were intensified in the first years and a local branch of the German Zionist Organization was founded. On *Kristallnacht* (9–10 Nov. 1938), the synagogue was burned by SA troops. By May 1939, only 18 Jews remained. Of those who had left L., many departed for Berlin and other places in Germany. At least 63 community members perished in the Holocaust.

LYDUVENAI (Yid. Lidevian, Lidovian) Raseiniai dist., Lithuania. There were several Jews here in 1662. Numbers grew in the 19th cent. and in 1923 about 90 Jews lived in L. In the 1922 elections for the Lithuania Sejm, most Jews supported the Zionist list. The few Jews left in L. were killed in the Holocaust.

LYGUMAI Siauliai dist., Lithuania. Jews first settled in the 18th cent., with community institutions established by the 19th cent. The J. pop. in 1897 was 482 (60% of the total). Prior to WWI, many Jews emigrated to the U.S., England, and South Africa. During

Jewish farmstead, Lygumai, Lithuania, before WWII

WWI, all of L.'s Jews were expelled, most returning later. The majority of young Jews in the 1930s were Zionists. The J. pop. in 1940 was about 120. All the Jews were killed within a month of the German occupation in 1941.

LYNGMIANY Vilna dist., Poland, today Belarus. Jews probably settled in the 1850s, helping make L. a center of commerce until WWI. Jews leased forests for lumber and lakes for fish and crabs. After WWI, when the town was divided between Poland and Lithuania, most Jews remained on the Polish side while most farmland went to Lithuania, leaving J. merchants cut off from the agricultural hinterland. Only once a year, on Tisha be-Av, were the Jews permitted to reunite on the neutral ground of the J. cemetery. In 1925, the J. pop. was 540 (total 1,000). Many Jews left for South Africa, leaving a J. pop. of 359 when the Soviets reunited the town in 1939. In late July 1941, after the Germans took over, pro-Nazi Lithuanian partisans murdered all the Jews of L. in their homes.

LYNTOPY Vilna dist., Poland, today Belarus. Jews probably settled in the first half of the 19th cent., numbering 50 (total 477) in 1866. After WWI, many worked in the J.-managed sawmill, distillery, and turpentine factories on a local estate. Children studied at a Tarbut school under Zionist influence. The J. pop. in 1930 was 70 families. The Germans took the town in June 1941. All but 100 skilled workers were expelled to the Swienciany ghetto; most were murdered in the Ponary woods near Vilna on 4 April 1943. On 19 Dec. 1942, L. was burned to the ground by Soviet partisans. Most of the 100 J. workers left in L.'s labor camp were taken into the forest by the Germans with the help of Lithuanian police and shot. Some escaped to a partisan unit in the forests. Six Jews from L. survived the war.

LYON   Rhone dist., France. There was a flourishing J. community in the beginning of the ninth cent. with the Jews living in their own quarter. The Jews were expelled in 1250 and for a century they were allowed only to visit the city. In the second half of the 14th cent., a small community emerged. Since L. was not part of the Kingdom of France, the Jews were not affected by the edict of expulsion of 1394. However, they were expelled several years later. A new community was established in the 16th cent. by Jews who came primarily from Avignon, but also from Comtat Venaissin, Alsace, and Bordeaux. In 1808, it was attached to the consistory of Marseille. By 1840, the community, headed by the industrialist Samuel Heyman de Ricqules, consisted of 400 members. By 1854, when L. became the site of a regional rabbinate, there were 1,200 members. In 1857, it formed its own consistory, including Saint-Etienne (116 Jews), Chalon-sur-Saone (125 Jews), Besancon (379 Jews), and Montbeliard (202 Jews). In the beginning of the 20th cent. with the influx of immigrants from the Mediterranean area, a Sephardi community was formed and members living in the suburb of Saint-Fons founded a synagogue in 1919. By 1928, the Sephardi community consisted of about 400 Jews, most from Morocco. About 170 earned their living as factory workers. They established a cultural society. In June 1941, the J. community of L. consisted of about 7,000 members (500–600 families). Becoming a "free" city after the Franco-German agreement (June 1940), L. became a haven for many Jews and a center of the resistance movement. In addition to the offices of the Central Consistory, various Zionist and J. philanthropic organizations transferred to L. Arrests reached their peak in Aug. 1944. On 11 Aug., 230 Jews were deported to Auschwitz. Afterwards 559 Jews from the "J. sections" in the Monluc Fort prison were shot. Other prisoners were taken to Bron airfield to clear the area of unexploded shells after the bombardment. They were executed there. Three-quarters of the community was lost through deportations. After the war, the community numbered 25,000 members (in 1964), most new immigrants from North Africa.

LYSAIA GORA   Odessa dist., Ukraine. Jews settled in the latter half of the 19th cent. and numbered 315 (total 6,588) in 1939. The Germans captured L. on 1 Aug. 1941. All the Jews, including some from neighboring villages – in all, about 320 – were executed at the local J. cemetery on 30 Sept.

LYSIANKA   Kiev dist., Ukraine. Jews settled in the late 17th cent. The Haidamaks looted J. property in 1702 and again in 1768 with a number of fatalities. In 1897, the J. pop. was 2,845 (total 7,207). On 5 June 1919, General Denikin's White Army troops and the Petlyura gangs attacked the Jews, murdering 50 and seriously injuring 40. In 1939, under the Soviets, the J. pop. was 215. The Germans captured L. on 22 July 1941, expelling all 593 Jews in the province to the Bodoshchy camp where they were forced to engage in road and farm work. All were soon murdered.

LYSIEC   Stanislawow dist., Poland, today Ukraine. The community began to grow in the 18th cent., reaching a pop. of 1,095 (40% of the total) in 1900. The town was virtually destroyed in WWI by the Russians, the J. pop. dropping to 275. Despite economic hardship, organized community life was maintained between the World Wars. The community was liquidated by the Germans in the fall of 1942.

LYSKOW   Bialystok dist., Poland, today Belarus. Jews are believed to have settled in the 16th cent. An organized community existed in the 19th cent., with the J. pop. standing at 658 in 1897 (of a total 876). Jews were active in the lumber industry and most stores in the market were J.-owned. Almost all had auxiliary farms. Haskala began to make inroads and the Zionists and the Bund began to organize groups. Many emigrated in the early 20th cent. At the outset of WWI the Jews suffered from the depredations of the Cossacks. During the German occupation (1915–18) they suffered from food shortages and a regime of forced labor. The J. pop. in 1921 was 450. Between the World Wars the J. economy was undermined by heavy taxes and Polish competition, inducing further emigration. The Germans arrived on 28 June 1941. A *Judenrat* was set up, with forced labor and "contributions" exacted from the community. On 2 Nov. 1942, all 700 Jews were transferred to the Wolkowysk transit camp and within a few days deported to the Treblinka death camp.

LYSOBYKI   Lublin dist., Poland. Jews, present from

the mid-18th cent., numbered 356 in 1862 and 438 (total 1,402) in 1921. Most were expelled to Lukow, with some to Michow, and shared the fate of the local Jews.

LYSZKOWICE (Yid. Liskewitz) Lodz dist., Poland. In 1852 a Jew established what was to become one of the largest sugar refineries in Congress Poland. The J. pop. in 1897 was 373. In the 1930s, 90% of the Jews received aid from J. welfare organizations. In 1940, the 600 Jews, half of whom were refugees, were ghettoized and in March 1941 expelled to the Warsaw ghetto.

LYTOMYSL Bohemia, Czechoslovakia. Jews apparently settled only in the late 19th cent. and numbered 182 in 1921 and 143 (total 7,205) in 1930. Most were deported to the Theresienstadt ghetto and then to the death camps of the east in 1942.

LYUBASHEVKA Odessa dist., Ukraine. In the Soviet period, in the late 1930s, a J. elementary school was active. In 1939, the J. pop. was 671 (total 3,360). The Germans captured L. on 4 Aug. 1941. In late Nov., after L. was annexed to Transnistria, the Jews were expelled to a ghetto set up in the village of Gvozdovka, where Jews from Moldavia were also held. Many died of starvation, disease, and the cold. In the fall, 395 Jews were murdered there. Another 145 from Ananev, Moldavia, were murdered in late Nov. About 2,000 Jews were murdered in the area.

LYUBAVICHI (also Lubavich) Smolensk dist., Russia. L. became famous as the center of Habad Hasidism after R. Dov Baer, son of R. Shneur Zalman (the Habad founder), transferred his seat there from Lyady in 1813.

The J. pop. of L. was 1,164 in 1847 and 1,660 (total 2,711) in 1897. A two-year state J. school was opened in 1852. In 1910, girls attended a separate session and the school also offered vocational training. The residents of L. derived their income from the flax trade and from the masses of Hasidim who flooded the town to visit the Rebbe. R. Shalom Baer founded the Tomkhei Temimim yeshiva in 1897. He left the town in 1915 but its name remained associated with Habad Hasidism. In 1926, the J. pop. was 967. With the economic decline of L. after the Oct. 1917 Revolution, some J. families (about 43 of a total 205 in 1926) went over to agriculture, mostly at a J. kolkhoz. Another 80 families earned their livelihoods in crafts and 27 in trade; the remaining 50 were unemployed. A J. school with about 175 children and an orphanage with 36 were operating in the 1920s. The Germans occupied L. on 21 or 22 July 1941. A few days later they murdered a group of Jews supposedly being taken to work. Subsequently a ghetto was established, which also accommodated J. refugees from Vitebsk and Rudniya. In early Nov. 1941, 483 Jews were murdered outside the town.

LYUBONICHI Mogilev dist., Belorussia. The J. pop. was 247 in 1819 and 506 in 1897. Jews earned their livelihoods as lumber merchants and artisans. Rioting Polish soldiers beat and robbed Jews in March 1920. In the Soviet period, most Jews worked in an artisan cooperative as tailors and shoemakers. A four-grade J. school operated until 1934. In 1939, the J. pop. comprised 60 families, including refugees from Poland. The Germans arrived in early Aug. 1941. In Nov. they murdered all the J. men beside freshly dug pits. A month later, the women and children were taken to an unknown destination, never to return.

M

MAASSLUIS Zuid-Holland dist., Holland. A J. community was established in the 18th cent. Its number reached 116 in 1892 but decreased to 19 by 1941 (total 9,210). In the Holocaust five Jews were deported and perished.

MAASTRICHT Limburg dist., Holland. A J. community – the oldest in Holland – dates back to the 13th cent., but was destroyed in the 14th cent. Settlement began again after the mid-18th cent. and a community was established by the end of the cent. Social welfare organizations were founded in the 19th cent. From 1815, M. was the seat of the chief rabbinate of the Limburg region (united with the chief rabbinate of Noord-Brabant in 1907). In 1840–41 a synagogue was built. The J. pop. in 1892 was 390 (total 32,755). The community began to dwindle in the early 20th cent., but by 1938 the community included 232 refugees. The J. pop. in 1941 was 420 (with 44 in nearby Ambij). The local police mostly protected the

Synagogue in Maastricht, Holland (Avraham Lebovitch/photo courtesy of Yad Vashem, The Holocaust Martyrs' and Heroes' Remembrance Authority, Jerusalem)

Interior of synagogue in Maciejow, Poland, 1939

Jews from Nazi measures. The main deportations were in June, Aug., and Nov. 1942 and lasted until April 1943; 219 perished in the Holocaust. The community was reestablished after the war.

MACIEJOW   Volhynia dist., Poland, today Ukraine. Jews are first recorded in 1563. The community reached a peak pop. of 2,337 in 1897 (total 3,897), living in straitened economic circumstances. Most were Turzysk (Trisk) Hasidim. The Bund and the Zionists became active after WWI. The Germans arrived on 24 June 1941, killing off the J. pop. in a series of mass executions until final liquidation in Sept. 1942.

MACIEJOWICE   Lublin dist., Poland. The J. community developed in the first half of the 19th cent. The J. pop. was 739 (total 1,992) in 1921. Between the World Wars, Jews benefited from the tourist trade but economic conditions remained difficult. The Germans

arrived on 17 or 18 Sept. 1939, establishing a *Judenrat* and exacting tributes from the community. Half the 200 J. families in M., about 400 people, were expelled to Sobolew-Place and Laskarzew on 23 Oct. 1940. The rest were confined in a ghetto in the second half of 1941 and deported to the Treblinka death camp via Sobolew-Place in Oct. 1942.

MACZULKI   Volhynia dist., Poland, today Ukraine. The J. pop. in 1921 was 103 (total 431). The Jews were probably brought to the Klewan ghetto for liquidation.

MAD   (also Hegyalja-Mad) Zemplen dist., Hungary. Jews from Moravia and Poland settled in the first half of the 18th cent. and became prominent as winegrowers and winesellers despite local opposition. In 1890, the J. pop. was 897, declining to 304 in 1941. R. Mordekhai Winkler, who officiated in 1899–1932, founded a renowned yeshiva which numbered 200 stu-

Jewish children playing in the old Maciejowice shtetl, Poland, 1928

dents on the eve of WWI. In 1941, 10–15 J. families of doubtful nationality were deported to Kamenets-Podolski, where they perished. In 1942, the young were seized for forced labor, most dying in the Ukraine. After the German occupation of spring 1944, the remaining Jews were sent to Satoraljaujhely and from there deported to Auschwitz from 12 to 15 June. In 1946, the government accorded the synagogue the status of a preserved historical building.

MADFELD Westphalia, Germany. One J. family was present in the first quarter of the 18th cent. The J. pop. rose to five families (29 Jews) in 1738 and ten by the beginning of the 19th cent. By the mid-19th cent., the community already maintained a cemetery and a synagogue, the latter damaged in a fire in 1856 and rebuilt. In 1885, the J. pop. was 82 (total 1,128), dropping to 49 in 1905 and 21 in 1932. Of the 26 Jews present in the 1933–42 period, nine emi-

grated, ten left for other places in Germany, and six were deported to the camps in spring and summer 1942. At least 11 Jews perished in the Holocaust.

MADONA Vidzeme (Livonia) dist., Latvia. The J. pop. in 1935 was 115 (total 2,357). There were no community institutions. On 7–8 Aug. 1941 the Jews were murdered in the Smerkere forest by the Germans and the Latvian police.

MAERKISCH-FRIEDLAND (Pol. Miroslawiec) Posen–West Prussia, Germany, today Poland. An organized J. community with a *beit midrash* and a synagogue existed in the mid-18th century. Since the Jews enjoyed citizen status under Polish rule, the city perpetuated these rights when it came under Prussian rule in 1772. Towards the end of the century, Jews served in the city council. The J. pop. was 550–600 in 1774 and reached a peak of 1,151 in 1817 (about 50% of the total). From 1791 to 1815, the well-known halakhist R. Akiva Eger (1761–1837) served as community rabbi. In the early 19th cent., a large synagogue was constructed and in 1819, a school was opened, the first J. public school in Prussia. A Christian acted as principal in its first years. From the 1820s, a growing number of Jews moved to central Germany with some leading community members settling in Berlin. This caused a decline in the J. pop., which numbered 832 in 1831 (39% of the total), 303 in 1880, and 161 in 1900. The school was closed in 1879. On the eve of the Nazi assumption of power in 1933, about 70 Jews were living in M. In 1935, a pogrom-like atmosphere developed after a J. girl stole something from a Christian store. By 1937, the number of Jews had dwindled to 49. On *Kristallnacht* (9–10 Nov. 1938), the synagogue was destroyed and J. businesses were demolished. The remaining Jews were interned in March 1940 in the Buergergarten camp near Schneidemuehl and later deported to the east and perished.

MAGDEBURG Saxony, Germany. Jews are first mentioned in M. in 965. This early J. community was the oldest in the eastern part of Germany and represented the northernmost point of J. settlement in the 10th–11th cents. The community suffered from several persecutions and expulsions, including the Black Death persecutions in 1348–49. Nonetheless, the community flourished. Several known rabbis took up residence in M. and there were a yeshiva and a *beit din*. From the 14th cent., most Jews lived in a quarter (*Judendorf*) in the south of the city, where they also had their synagogue. A cemetery outside the city was established in the mid-13th cent. In 1492, an argument between two Jews and two monks provoked prolonged riots, and in 1493, the Archbishop of M. decreed the expulsion of all Jews from the city and from the archbishopric. Jews were readmitted to M. in 1671, but because of the city council's hostility, a permanent settlement was only established under French rule at the beginning of the 19th cent. In 1811 the community numbered 255. As early as 1809 a Jew was elected a member of the city council. Over the next 100 years, the community grew continuously owing to the increasing industrialization of M. The J. pop. was 1,000 in 1859 and 1,935 in 1905. The community was shaped by its most famous rabbi, Dr. Ludwig Philippson (1811–89; rabbi of M., 1833–62). Dr. Philippson, a leader of Liberal Judaism in Germany, initiated the establishment of

one of the first J. religious schools in northern Germany in 1834 and the construction of a Reform synagogue with an organ and a choir in 1851. He also founded and edited the *Allgemeine Zeitung des Judentums*, the newspaper of Liberal German Judaism, which continued to appear in M. even after he left the city. M. was also the birthplace of several well-known politicians, including Georg Gradnauer (1866–1946), minister-president of Saxony (1918–20) and minister of the interior in 1921, and Otto Landsberg (1869–1957), Social Democrat member of the city council and the Reichstag (1912–18 and 1924–33) and minister of justice in 1919. In 1925, the J. pop. was 2,361 and included many immigrants from Eastern Europe. The community maintained some 20 associations and societies, including welfare organizations and youth clubs; branches of the Central Union (C.V.), the Union for Liberal Judaism, and the German Zionist Organization; a B'nai B'rith lodge; and associations of the Jews from Eastern Europe. The community school had about 250 pupils and there were a children's home and a vocational training center for carpenters. In early 1933, the J. pop. was 1,973. Jews operated 425 stores, businesses, and banks and included 50 doctors and 29 lawyers. As early as 1933, the town was blanketed with antisemitic slogans. The guests at a J. hotel were physically attacked. Very soon, Jews were economically and socially excluded from the city's life. Two Jews who were active members of the Communist Party were arrested in 1933 and 1934, respectively. In the first show trial, on charges of so-called "racial defilement" (*Rassenschande*) in 1935, a Jew from M. was sentenced to ten years' hard labor and lifetime preventive custody. He probably died in detention. In mid-1938, the religious school began to provide regular schooling. On *Kristallnacht* (9–10 Nov. 1938), the synagogue as well as other community facilities were completely destroyed; stores and homes were looted and wrecked; and 375 men were arrested, beaten up, and taken to the Buchenwald concentration camp. Of the 679 Jews who were living in M. in 1939, some 500 were deported to camps in the east where most perished. In July 1944, there were still 185 Jews living in M., most of them of partial J. origin (*Mischlinge*) or protected by marriage to non-Jews. A new community was established in 1947, numbering about 100 members. By 1987, numbers had dropped to 29, but then grew due to the immigration of Jews from the former Soviet Union.

MAGIEROW Lwow dist., Poland, today Ukraine. Jews were present from the 16th cent., reaching a peak pop. of 1,322 in 1900 (total 3,158), despite the start of emigration to the U.S. All but three J. houses were burned to the ground by the Russians in WWI. After the war many Jews worked as furriers. The Germans took the city at the end of June 1941 and liquidated the community in the spring of 1942, partly by execution, partly by deportation to the Belzec death camp via Rawa Ruska.

MAGLOD Pest–Pilis–Solt–Kiskun dist., Hungary. Jews settled in the early 18th cent., reaching a peak pop. of 225 in 1840 before beginning to leave for the big cities. In 1941, 82 remained. All were deported to Auschwitz via Nagykata and Kecskemet at the beginning of June 1944.

MAGNUSZEW Kielce dist., Poland. Jews settled in the early 19th cent., consecrating a synagogue in 1860. They numbered 731 (total 1,567) in 1921. The Germans captured M. in Sept. 1939. In Feb. 1941, they established a ghetto for 1,200 Jews including refugees. All were deported to the Treblinka death camp via Kozienice on 29 Sept. 1942.

MAGOCS Baranya dist., Hungary. In 1769, a J. family was allowed to settle in B. as compensation for the wrongful execution of the family head. A synagogue was founded in 1873. The J. pop. rose to 210 in 1910 before dropping to 120 in 1944. On 5 July 1944, the Jews were deported to Auschwitz via Mohacs and Pecs.

MAGYARBANHEGYES Csanad dist., Hungary. Jews settled in the late 19th cent., engaging in petty trade and operating small farms. A branch of the Hungarian Zionist Organization was established in 1935. The J. pop. was 74 in 1930. On 26 June 1944, 55 Jews, those who had not been sent to forced labor, were deported to Auschwitz and Austria via Bekescsaba.

MAHARES Sfax dist., Tunisia. Jews settled in the early 20th cent., mostly from Gabes and Sfax. They numbered 84 in 1921 and 46 (total 4,413) in 1936. Most left after WWII.

MAHDIA Mahdia dist., Tunisia. J. settlement com-menced soon after the founding of the town in the tenth cent., with Jews arriving from North Africa as well as from exile and imprisonment in Italy. A synagogue and important *yeshivot* were founded and the community maintained close ties with Kairouan. Jews imported cotton, flax, dyestuffs, and spices and exported oil, soap, woven goods, and particularly the silk produced in Sousse. Under the Zeirids in the 11th–12th cents., a *nagid* headed. the community. When nomads destroyed Kairouan in the mid-11th cent., M. became a center of Torah learning and the seat of a permanent rabbinical court. The Almohads destroyed the community in the mid-12th cent. Jews forced to convert continued practicing Judaism clandestinely until they could do so openly under the Hafsids in the 13th–15th cents. In the 16th cent., many fled because of pirate attacks and the Spanish siege of 1550. They returned after the Turkish conquest in 1574. In the 17th cent., Leghornian Jews – descendants of the Spanish exiles – arrived from Italy. Under the French Protectorate, most Jews continued to live in the J. quarter, with the more wealthy moving to the center of the city. Most Jews traded in the oils produced in the region. They opened numerous business establishments and contributed significantly to the development of local industry. Eugenio Lumbroso started up factories for a patented olive-oil soap in Ksiba and M., becoming a millionaire. The J. pop. was 443 in 1921 and 338 (total 8,488) in 1936. Children studied at an Alliance school established in 1883 and attended a *talmud torah* in the afternoons. The Zionists became active in 1921, founding a Benei Zion society. Relations with the Arabs were satisfactory on a day-to-day basis, with occasional outbursts of anti-J. feeling, as in the riots of 1917 when Jews were beaten and robbed. In WWII, the racial laws of the Vichy regime hardly affected the community since there were few Jews in public service. Under the German occupation, J. property was confiscated and some Jews were evicted from their homes. Most fled to the nearby Arab village of Sidi Alouan when Allied bombardments commenced. After the war, the Joint Distribution Committee and OZE assisted many families. In the postwar period, many left for the larger cities of Sousse and Tunis. Jews began to join the professional class and managed the city's three banks. Betar, Tze'irei Tziyyon–Deror, and Hashomer Hatzair became active and after 1948 many Jews emigrated to Israel. A large number, mainly among the wealthy, also left for France.

MAINBERNHEIM Lower Franconia, Germany. Jews are first mentioned in the late 14th cent. and lived there in small numbers during the next centuries. In 1837 the prosperous community numbered 140 (total 1,633), engaged mainly in the wine and cattle trade. During the 19th cent. (until 1871) M. was the seat of the district rabbinate. The J. pop. dropped to 44 in 1867 and 20 in 1933. On *Kristallnacht* (9–10 Nov. 1938), Jews were severely beaten and their homes were wrecked, as was the synagogue. In 1933–40, 20 Jews left M., 12 of them for other German cities. The last Jews were deported to Izbica in the Lublin dist. (Poland) and to the Theresienstadt ghetto in 1942.

MAINSTOCKHEIM Lower Franconia, Germany. Jews are first mentioned in 1594. In 1771 refugees from Kitzingen settled there. The J. pop. reached a peak of 212 in 1837 (total 1,374) with a synagogue built in 1836. Jews engaged mainly in the wine trade. From the late 19th cent. the J. pop. declined steadily, dropping to 74 in 1933. A local ordinance in 1933 banned nonresident Jews from entering the village and in 1934 local agitators called for the expulsion of resident Jews. On *Kristallnacht* (9–10 Nov. 1938), SA troops and local residents vandalized the synagogue. During 1938, 13 Jews left the village, 12 for the U.S; another 13 left in 1939. Of those remaining, 27 were deported to Izbica in the Lublin dist. (Poland) via Wuerzburg on 24 March 1942 and another four to the Theresienstadt ghetto.

MAINZ (Fr. Mayence; in J. sources, Magentsa) Hesse, Germany. Established by Italian immigrants in the early tenth cent., this community—one of the oldest in Germany—was temporarily banished in 1012. Its growth in importance and numbers (to over 1,000 in 1090) resulted from M.'s strategic position on trade routes. Many J. scholars were born or settled there. Amnon of M., a legendary tenth–cent. martyr, is associated with the *U-Netanneh Tokef* prayer; Yehuda ben Meir founded a great yeshiva in 980; members of the Kalonymus family became halakhic authorities, poets, and communal leaders while Yitzhak ben Judah (d. 1080) and Yaakov ben Yakar (d. 1060) taught Rashi. Gershom ben Yehuda Me'or ha-Golah (960–1028) wrote historic *takkanot* (e.g., prohibiting a wife's divorce against her will and the *Herem de-Rabbenu Gershom* enforcing monogamy) which the

Ashkenazi world accepted. Other sages of M. were Shimon bar Yitzhak the Great, Eliezer ben Natan, and Yehuda ben Kalonymus ben Moshe, whose son Eleazar ben Yehuda Roke'ah was a leading figure in the Hasidei Ashkenaz. After the proclamation of the First Crusade (1096), Emperor Henry IV ordered his nobles and bishops to defend the Jews, but Crusaders attacked the archbishop's palace in M., where the vastly outnumbered Jews fought a heroic but hopeless battle on 27 May, many preferring suicide to apostasy. The massacre claimed 1,100 victims in all and details are preserved in several Hebrew works (especially an elegiac poem by Kalonymus ben Yehuda). The community soon revived and in 1150 the rabbinates of Speyer, Worms, and M. (known thereafter as the *"Shum"* communities after the acronym of their names) were empowered to serve as a high court for the Jews of Germany. Bernard of Clairvaux prevented another tragedy in 1146 and on the eve of the Third Crusade in 1188 many Jews took refuge in the fortress of Muenzenberg. In 1281, the synagogue was burned down; Jews were slaughtered following a blood libel in 1283; and harsh taxation drove some in 1286 to join R. Meir of Rothenburg's group of would-be emigrants to the Holy Land. When the Black Death struck the region in 1349 and Jews were charged with "poisoning the wells," they defended themselves against an enraged mob and killed 200 of their assailants, but several thousand Jews perished in the burning ghetto. Survivors returned in 1357 and the community's prestige was temporarily restored when Yaakov ben Moshe Moellin ("Maharil"; 1355–1427), the era's leading talmudist, served as chief rabbi. The Jews were repeatedly expelled (1439, 1462, 1470), their synagogue being converted into a chapel in 1473. While Johannes Reuchlin, Germany's foremost Christian Hebraist, was defending the Talmud against clerical obscurantists, the enlightened archbishop prohibited a mass burning of J. books in M. in 1513. In 1579, however, Jews were banished from the Rhineland. Following its restoration in 1583, the community built a new synagogue and grew to over 100 families around 1690. The new Age of Enlightenment and improved economic conditions enabled Jews to engage in a wider range of occupations (including medicine), and by 1800 they numbered 1,156 (5% of the total). During the period of French rule (1792–1814), when Jews were first granted civil rights, they sent delegates to Napoleon's

The New Synagogue of Mainz, Germany, 1912

Assembly of J. Notables and the French Sanhedrin (1806–07) and a regional consistory was established under Herz David Scheuer, who declined the title of *Grand Rabbin* and opposed attempts to "modernize" religious life. Three distinguished Jews born in M. were Yitzhak Bernays (1792–1849), the Orthodox rabbi of Hamburg; Ludwig Bamberger (1823–99), economist and Liberal member of the Reichstag; and Michael Creizenach (1789–1842), who ran a J. boys' school on Reform lines (1814–33) and later taught in Frankfurt. After the confirmation ceremony was adopted in 1840, traditionalists opposed further changes (especially an organ in the new synagogue) and the appointment of a Reform rabbi, Joseph Aub (1852–66). Without seceding from the main community, they established an Orthodox congregation with Dr. Marcus Lehmann as its first rabbi (1854–90). Lehmann founded *Der Israelit* (an Orthodox journal) and a coeducational school, both of which survived until the Nazi era. Numbering 2,665 (6%) in 1861, the J. pop. grew to 3,500 (4.9%) by 1890. Immigrants from Eastern Europe (*Ostjuden*) formed a J. proletariat and an independent congregation. Joseph Derenbourg, the son of a Hebrew teacher, moved to Paris and became a world-famous Orientalist; Adolf Reinach was a renowned philosopher; and Dr. Siegmund

Salfeld, the Liberal rabbi (1880–1918), published an edition of the community's ancient *Memorbuch* in 1898. During the Weimar Republic, a central welfare agency was established and all the national J. organizations had active branches: B'nai B'rith, the Central Union (C.V.) and J. War Veterans Association, Agudat Israel, the Union for Liberal Judaism, the German Zionist Organization, Blau-Weiss, Mizrachi, WIZO, and various youth movements. Jews comprised a high percentage of the city's physicians and were prominent in civic affairs, commerce, the arts, law, and journalism. Anna Seghers (Netty Radvanyi) won fame as a novelist and Carl Zuckmayer (descendant of old J. families) as a playwright. After WWI, French occupation authorities curbed Nazism in the Rhineland, but rioters celebrating the French withdrawal attacked Jews and anti-Nazis in 1930. Hitler's incitement led to more violence in 1932.

The community numbered 2,609 (2%) when the Nazi regime was established in 1933. The eradication of J. influence began with the dismissal of city officials and others in the public sector. From 9 March, patrons were deterred from entering J. business premises and on 1 April, SA troops and police inaugurated a boycott of J. lawyers, physicians, and stores. A ceremonial burning of condemned books took place on 23 June. The last J. bank was forced to close in 1935, gas and electricity supplies were cut off, and Jews were barred from hotels, cafes, and places of entertainment. In its endeavor to sustain J. morale, the community organized various welfare schemes and arranged cultural programs with an increasing emphasis on life in Palestine and on *aliya*. A regional community school, opened in 1934, later amalgamated with that of the Orthodox congregation. By 1938, however, 1,074 Jews had left – 649 (mostly young people) emigrating – and the remainder (2,073) had to cope with a stream of refugees from outlying townships. The East European Jews were expelled in Oct. 1938 and on *Kristallnacht* (9–10 Nov. 1938) a wholesale pogrom was organized in M. SS troops burned down the main (Liberal) synagogue. Nazis also destroyed the community center and the Orthodox synagogue, though some ancient documents were rescued and later transferred to London. J. homes were vandalized, a Jew was trampled to death, and about 60 others were sent to the Buchenwald concentration camp. The office established by the Union of J. Communities in Hesse was transformed into a branch of the Union of Jews of Germany (Reichsvereinigung der Juden in Deutschland) (July 1939) and served as a tool of the Gestapo. Emigration was finally halted in Oct. 1941, by which time the community had virtually disintegrated, and from Sept. 1942 the remaining 1,336 Jews were mostly deported to the Theresienstadt ghetto and Poland. A small community was established after WWII, numbering 133 in 1966.

MAJDAN (I) Lwow dist., Poland. An organized J. community existed in the mid-19th cent., the pop. standing at 550–600 (almost 30% of the total). A branch of the Dzikow dynasty maintained a hasidic court there. Anti-J. riots struck the community in 1918 and 1919. All Jews were expelled by the Germans to Rzeszow in June 1942 en route to the Belzec death camp.

MAJDAN (II) (Hung. Majdanka) Carpatho-Russia, Czechoslovakia, today Ukraine. J. settlement probably began at the turn of the 19th cent. The J. pop. was 73 in 1830 and 411 (total 1,553) in 1880. In 1921, under the Czechoslovakians, the J. pop. grew to 589 and in 1941 to 831. Most Jews engaged in trade, owning 27 business establishments. They also owned two flour mills and a sawmill; 14 were artisans; five were butchers; and one was a building contractor. Many also worked

plots of land. The Hungarians occupied the town in March 1939, undermining the livelihoods of many Jews. About 100 were drafted into labor battalions, some being dispatched to the eastern front, where they were killed. In Aug. 1941, a number of J. families without Hungarian citizenship were expelled to Kamenets-Podolski and murdered. The rest were deported to Auschwitz on 19 May 1944.

MAKAROV Kiev dist., Ukraine. The J. pop. included 217 taxpayers in 1765 and reached 3,953 in 1897. Thirty-two J. families farmed 175 acres of land. In 1918, General Denikin's White Army troops attacked the Jews and in 1919, the Petlyura gangs murdered 17 elderly Jews. In the Soviet period, the J. pop. was 269. The Germans arrived on 10 July 1941 and murdered about 100 Jews soon afterwards. Another 149 were discovered in hiding and expelled to Kiev, where they perished.

MAKEYEVKA Stalino dist., Ukraine. Jews probably settled in the late 19th cent. with the development of the local coal industry. In the Soviet period, a large number of Jews worked in the mines as well as in the leather and metal industries. In 1939, the J. pop. was 3,074 (total 241,897) The Germans captured the city on 2 Oct. 1941. On 28 Dec. 1941, about 500 Jews were brought to the mines and shot. A hundred J. women found hiding were taken to Kazachyi Kazarmy, 1 mile (1.5 km) from the city center and murdered. In Feb. 1942, 369 Jews from M. and from Gorlovka were executed. Twelve prisoner-of-war camps were built on municipal grounds, where over 20,000 prisoners, including Jews, endured great suffering.

MAKO (Heb. Makava) Csanad dist., Hungary. Jews were present under Turkish rule in the 15th cent. The modern community dates from 1740. Jews dominated commerce, particularly the substantial onion export trade, and were prominent in the professional class. The first J. school dated from 1770. A J. hospital was founded in 1831 and a school for girls in 1880. A magnificent new synagogue was consecrated in 1914. The Neologist congregation was led by R. Armin Kecskemeti in 1898–1944. Joseph Pulitzer, of American journalistic fame, was born in M. in 1847. The J. pop. rose from 1,120 in 1836 to a peak of 2,388 in 1920. After the German occupation, in May 1944, a regional ghetto with a pop. of 3,000 was set up. All the Jews were brought to Szeged and at the end of June sent to Auschwitz and to Strasshof in Austria, from where about 600 returned in 1949 to form a postwar community that has since declined.

MAKOV   Kamenets-Podolski dist., Ukraine. The J. pop. in 1787 was 117 with 55 houses under J. ownership. In 1897, the J. pop. was 144, dropping to 81 in 1926 under the Soviets. The Germans occupied the town on 10 July 1941. The few Jews still there were apparently executed in the fall together with the Jews of Shatovo.

MAKOW MAZOWIECKI   Warsaw dist., Poland. A J. settlement is known from the second half of the 16th cent. The community was struck by a devastating fire in 1620 and suffered grievously in the mid-cent. Swedish war, most Jews being murdered by the irregular Polish troops of Stefan Czarniecki in its aftermath. The community recovered and grew despite the hostility of the local pop., numbering 1,258 in 1758 with another 820 in the surrounding villages. Jews dominated the major grain and wool trade. In the first half of the 19th cent., the Jews expanded into the textile industry. Among the community's bet-

ter-known rabbis were Avraham Abish Ginzburg (d. 1771) and Aryeh Leib Zunz (d. 1833). A yeshiva was founded in the late 19th cent. The Zionists became active in 1904, with Hashomer Hatzair becoming the biggest youth movement after WWI. The Bund was influential among J. laborers and craftsmen and Agudat Israel founded schools for boys and a Beth Jacob school for girls. The J. pop. fell from 4,411 in 1897 to 3,369 (total 6,198) in 1921, living in straitened economic circumstances between the World Wars. The Germans captured the city on 5 Sept. 1939, wrecking the synagogue on 23 Sept. (Yom Kippur) and instituting a regime of forced labor and severe persecution. On 1 Oct. 1941, 5,500 Jews including refugees were sealed into a ghetto. Women were ordered to shave their heads, both men and women were arbitrarily beaten, and shootings and public hangings were periodically carried out. Many were sent to labor camps in the area and forced to do road and farm work. In Nov. 1942 all were recalled to M. and on 18 Nov. about 5,000 Jews were sent to the Mlawa ghetto. A month later they were deported to Auschwitz, where most were killed within a few days. A few dozen young Jews were included in the Birkenau *Sonderkommando* delegated to burn

Street scene, Makow Mazowiecki, Poland

corpses. Some of those who survived participated in the *Sonderkommando* uprising of 7 Oct. 1944, including Warsaw-born Leib Langfus, one of its leaders and formerly *dayyan* of M., who left behind a diary describing the events of those days.

MAKOW PODHALANSKI   Cracow dist., Poland. A community of 100–200 Jews (5% of the total) existed from the late 19th cent. Antisemitism was frequent between the World Wars, when there was also intense Zionist activity. The Germans arrived in Sept. 1939 and instituted a regime of forced labor and persecution. In spring 1942, 15 Jews were murdered as "Communists." The community was deported to the Belzec death camp on 28 Aug. 1942.

MALACKY   Slovakia, Czechoslovakia, today Republic of Slovakia. Jews probably settled in the 1730s. In the 1870s, M. became the seat of a regional rabbinate with 16 settlements attached to it. A splendid modern synagogue was erected in 1886. The J. pop. grew from 97 in 1828 to a peak of 345 (total 5,048) in 1900 and leveled off at about 300 after WWI. The Zionists became active in the early 20th cent. and gained widespread support between the World Wars. Jews served on the local council and in the 1920s owned 25 business establishments with another 12 working as artisans. In the Slovakian state, J. children were expelled from the public schools and Jews forced out of their businesses. On 28 March 1942, 45 J. girls were deported to Auschwitz via Patronka. On 27 March, a few dozen young J. men were sent to the Novaky camp and from there dispatched to the the Majdanek concentration camp. Subsequently, families were deported to Auschwitz and to the Lublin dist. After their arrival in Sept. 1944, the Germans seized the last 40 or so Jews. Some managed to hide out with Slovakian peasants.

MALA DOBRON   (Hung. Kis-Dobron; Yid. Klayn Dobron) Carpatho-Russia, Czechoslovakia, today Ukraine. Jews probably arrived in the early 19th cent., numbering 15 in 1830 and 182 (total 1,100) in 1880. The J. pop. remained stable during the Czechoslovakian period and then dropped to 139 in 1941. A few Jews farmed and some worked at the town's mineral baths, also managing them. The Hungarians annexed M. in Nov. 1938 and in 1941 drafted a number of Jews into forced labor battalions. In Aug. 1941, a few families without Hungarian citizenship were expelled to Kamenets-Podolski and murdered. The remaining 140 or so were deported to Auschwitz in mid-May 1944.

MALAYA VISHERA   Leningrad dist., Russia. Jews settled in the mid-19th cent. Their pop. was 156 in 1926 and 191 (total 17,620) in 1939. When the Germans arrived on 24 Oct. 1941, they murdered the few Jews who had not fled or been evacuated.

MALAYA VISKA   Kirovograd dist., Ukraine. Jews probably settled in the late 19th cent. In 1939, the J. pop. was 207 (total 8,092). The Germans captured the town on 2 Aug. 1941. In fall 1941, the Jews were transferred, together with other Jews from the area, to a ghetto-camp at a local sugar refinery. In late Dec., 134 were murdered in a nearby forest. In all, the Germans murdered 189 Jews from K. and its environs

MALECZ   Polesie dist., Poland, today Belarus. Jews settled in the late 16th cent. and numbered 1,201 (total 2,159) in 1897. The Zionists and the Bund became active in the early 20th cent. Most J. homes were destroyed in the fighting at the start of WWI. More suffering was caused by the harsh Austro-German occupation and by typhoid and smallpox epidemics in 1920. In 1921 the J. pop. was 479 (total 893). The Germans took the town on 23 June 1941. All Jews (800 including refugees) were expelled to Bereza Kartuska on 2 Nov. 1941; from there more than half were sent to the Pruzhana ghetto to share the fate of the local Jews.

MALE LOTWA   Nowogrodek dist., Poland, today Belarus. The J. pop. was about 100 between the World Wars. The Jews were apparently expelled by the Germans to the nearby Lachowicze ghetto and murdered there in June 1942.

MALE SARLUZKY   Slovakia, Czechoslovakia, today Republic of Slovakia. The J. pop. was over 100 in the early 20th cent. and about 80 in 1944. On 15 June 1944, the Jews were deported to Auschwitz.

MALE SIEDLISZCZE   Volhynia dist., Poland, today Ukraine. M. was founded as a J. farm settlement in 1851 on 1,700 acres of land and numbered 663 Jews (total 996) in 1921. On 26 Aug. 1942 the Germans murdered all but 20 Jews who fled.

MALI IDJOS Vojvodina dist., Yugoslavia. A community existed from the 19th cent. and numbered 67 Jews in 1931 (total 6,375). It was obliterated in the Holocaust.

MALIN Zhitomir dist., Ukraine. The J. pop. was 1,064 in 1847 and 4,256 in 1897. Rahel Yanait (Ben-Zvi), Zionist activist and wife of Israel's second president, was born here, as was the sculptress Batya Lishansky (her sister) and the scholar Shemuel Abba Horodezky (hasidic studies). In 1919, Jews were attacked in a pogrom. In 1939, their pop. was 3,607 (total 11,367). Most worked in the wood and paper industry. A J. school operated between the World Wars. The Germans captured M. on 22 July 1941 after a number of Jews succeeded in fleeing. In Aug., about 1,000 were murdered. In 1959 the J. pop. was about 1,200.

MALKINIA GORNA Bialystok dist., Poland. An independent community existed from the late 19th cent., numbering 60 families in 1921. A summer camp for 500 children was run in a nearby village from 1929. Early in WWII many of M.'s Jews presumably fled east to Soviet-occupied Poland.

MALOGOSZCZ Kielce dist. Poland. J. settlement was officially banned until 1862. In 1897, 465 Jews were present (total 1,883). Between the World Wars, their economic position deteriorated. The Germans captured M. in early Sept. 1939, finding 760 Jews there. A *Judenrat* was established in late 1939 and a ghetto in early 1941. The ghetto pop. rose to 1,130 in 1942 as refugees arrived. On 28 Aug. 1942, 830 were transferred to Jendrzejow and from there deported to the Treblinka death camp in Sept. The rest, those with essential skills, were sent to the Skarzysko-Kamienna labor camp. They were subsequently deported to Auschwitz in July–Aug. 1944.

MALOIAROSLAVETS Moscow dist., Russia. Jews probably settled in the early 20th cent., numbering 120 in 1926 and 221 (total 11,775) in 1939. The few who were still there were murdered with the arrival of the Germans on 18 Oct. 1941.

MALORYTA Polesie dist., Poland, today Belarus. Jews settled in the late 19th cent. and numbered 753 in 1921 (total 1,791). A total of 883 Jews (some from neighboring villages) were executed by SD troops and Ukrainian police on 7 July 1942.

MALSCH BEI KARLSRUHE Baden, Germany. Jews first settled during the Thirty Years War (1618–48). With the lifting of residence restrictions in the early 19th cent., the community began to expand, reaching a peak pop. of 320 in 1875 (total 3,544). In the early 20th cent. nearly half the Jews were cattle traders. In 1933, 89 remained. On *Kristallnacht* (9–10 Nov. 1938), J. homes and stores were heavily damaged and the synagogue was burned. Fifty-seven Jews were able to emigrate; the last 20 were deported to the Gurs concentration camp on 22 Oct. 1940. Five who sailed on the *St. Louis* were let off in Belgium after months at sea and died in Auschwitz. Of the survivors, seven were hidden by the French underground.

MALSCH BEI WIESLOCH Baden, Germany. The first Jews settled in the late 17th cent. A synagogue was erected in the 1830s and the J. pop. grew to 103 in 1875 (total 1,380) with Jews opening textile and cigarette factories and enjoying economic stability. In 1933, 39 Jews remained. Under the Nazis, severe persecution commenced immediately and most J. businesses had to be liquidated by 1935–36. On *Kristallnacht* (9–10 Nov. 1938), the synagogue was vandalized along with J. homes and stores. Twenty-one Jews emigrated in 1937–39; five moved to other German cities. The last 15 were deported to the Gurs concentration camp on 22 Oct. 1940 while another four were sent to the camps from other places. Five of the deportees survived the Holocaust.

MALTA (from 1936, Silmala) Latgale dist., Latvia. Five J. families were present in 1873. The J. pop stood at 211 (total 377) in 1920, with the community operating a school for 45 children until the shrinking pop. (107 in 1935) caused it to close down. Most of the remaining Jews were murdered with particular brutality in Aug. 1941 by Latvian police operating under the German occupation.

MALY BEREZNY (Hung. Kisberezna; Yid. Klayn Berezna) Carpatho-Russia, Czechoslovakia, today Ukraine. Jews arrived in the mid-18th cent., numbering seven in 1768 and 112 (total 749) in 1880 and maintaining a stable pop. until WWII. The Hungarians occupied M. in March 1939. In the second half of May 1944, the Jews were deported to Auschwitz.

MANDEL Rhineland, Germany. Ten to 30 Jews lived in M. during the first half of the 19th cent. Their pop. reached a peak of 70–85 (11–12% of the total) in the second half of the cent. In 1933, the J. pop. was 23. The synagogue, erected in 1825, was vandalized on *Kristallnacht* (9–10 Nov. 1938) and torn down in 1959–60. The Nazis desecrated the J. cemetery opened in 1860. Most left for other places in Germany during the Nazi era and perished in the camps. The last four Jews were deported from M. in July 1943. A total of 14 were deported to the camps.

MANDOK Szabolcs dist., Hungary. Jews are mentioned in 1770, growing to a pop. of 358 in 1880 and 401 in 1930. Most were merchants dealing in farm produce and cattle. The community maintained a synagogue, school, and library. In 1941, the young were seized for forced labor, many never to return. On 25–27 May 1944 the rest were transferred to Kisvarda and deported from 29–30 June to Auschwitz. After the war, 40 survivors returned but soon left.

MANIEWICZE Volhynia dist., Poland, today Ukraine. The Jews numbered 462 (total 813) in 1921, engaging in the lumber and tourist industries. Berezne, Stolin-Karlin, and Stepan Hasidim worshiped at the community's three synagogues and Betar and Hashomer Hatzair represented the Zionist youth movements. With the influx of refugees, the J. pop. swelled to 1,900 under Soviet rule (1939–41). The Germans murdered 375 J. men on 26 Aug. 1941 while the Ukrainians engaged in sporadic killing. The ghetto was liquidated on 5 Sept. 1942 when 1,500 Jews were executed; 200 escaped, many to fight in partisan groups.

MANKOVKA Kiev dist., Ukraine. A small number of Jews were present in the 18th cent. In 1939, there were 105 (total 4,725). The Germans occupied M. on 28 July 1941 and on 2 May 1942 murdered the 51 Jews still there.

MANNHEIM Baden, Germany. Five J. families from Pfeddersheim near Worms settled in 1650 as the city recovered from the devastation of the Thirty Years War (1618–48). Under the letter of protection

accorded them in 1660, they were allowed to practice all crafts. In addition, Jews were active as traders in farm produce, exporters of wine, and brokers. With the approach of the French in 1689 (in the Nine Years War), many Jews fled (188 to Heidelberg and environs) while others participated in the defense effort. Most returned in 1690 and the Jews received a new letter of protection, limiting residence to 84 families but according broader rights. The leading J. figure in the community and in all of the Palatinate was the Court Jew Lemle Moshe Reinganum (d. 1724), who settled there around 1680, receiving the salt monopoly in 1699 and in 1707 founding the well-known M. *klaus* for Talmud study. Other prominent Court Jews active there were Joseph Suess Oppenheimer, who acted as army supplier and mintmaster in 1724, and Michal Mai, who also established a *klaus*. A third *klaus* was endowed in 1758 by the Court Jew Elias Hayyum and known as the Stuttgart Shul and, together with the other two, fostered numerous scholars and rabbis. The best-known rabbi in this period was Shemuel Hellman (1726–51), who waged an uncompromising war against Shabbateanism. In 1717, under a new letter of protection, the residence quota was raised to 200 J. families. The general prosperity of the community caused the city to be called the New Jerusalem, but also aroused the jealousy of local townsmen, who enacted sumptuary laws against the Jews in the same year. In 1727 a blood libel was foiled. In 1771 the community numbered 247 households and with its growing strength a tendency to tolerate its presence was seen in the municipal council. In 1807, J. students were enrolled in the municipal high school and in 1812, 25 Jews, mostly wealthy merchants, were enjoying full civil rights in the city and were accepted in the city's exclusive social clubs. The less favored Jews established their own club in 1817, the Resource. With the synagogue already holding a concert with a mixed choir in 1834, traditional circles concentrated around the Lemle Moshe *klaus* and its head, R. Jacob Ettlinger (1825–36), one of the founders of Neo-Orthodoxy in Germany. In 1819, a J. elementary school was opened where 100 boys and girls studied in separate classes and where, from 1830, confirmation exercises were held on graduation (discontinued in 1849). In the struggle for emancipation, new antisemitic outbursts came from various sectors of the local pop. In 1819 and 1830, anti-J. riots were staged and violence was

Clearing operations at the Jewish cemetery, Mannheim, Germany, summer 1938

barely avoided in the revolutionary fervor of 1848. Nonetheless a Jew was elected to the city council for the first time in 1848. In 1852 the J. pop. was 1,803 (total 24,316). To accommodate the growing pop. a new synagogue was completed in 1854, equipped with an organ and served by R. Dr. Moses Praeger, whose Reform prayerbook was highly controversial. The community maintained a broad range of charitable institutions. The J. hospital founded in 1711 was one of the earliest in Germany. In the second half of the 19th cent., J. capital played a leading role in the city's burgeoning industry. The Ladenburg bank financed the establishment of a steamship company and one of the largest paint factories in Germany, the latter coming to be numbered among the most advanced chemical plants in the world as part of the AG Farben concern. A second major bank was founded by Hirsch Levi Hohenemser. Jews controlled the tobacco trade based on village plantations and ran flour mills, distilleries, tanneries, and textile factories. In 1871, a

Jew was chosen for the first time as president of the local chamber of commerce and in 1914 a Jew was named president of the Baden Supreme Court. Dr. Alphonse Mehrmann founded a maternity ward and midwife-training facility in 1887 that was one of the first and most advanced of its kind in the world. Ludwig Frank (1874–1914) was elected to the Landtag in 1905 and the Reichstag in 1907 on the Social Democrat ticket. By 1875 the J. pop. had grown to 3,942 and by 1910 to 6,402 (total 193,902). Intermarriage and conversion grew from the late 19th cent. The J. philanthropist Bernhard Cahan, who sat on the city council for 25 years, endowed M.'s first public library (opened in 1920); the Eberle family its art museum; and Bernhard Herschel its swimming pool. J. students in the city's high schools comprised 20% of the student body when Jews were less than 5% of the pop. While the economic crisis struck at J. capital after WWI, J. commercial life remained active, with J. wholesalers operating 40 of the city's 66 textile outlets in 1930. Zionist activity revived, attracting many of the young. The Liberals controlled about two-thirds of the seats on the community council. In 1930, two women were elected for the first time. In 1929 a *beit midrash* was opened where a wide range of courses in J. subjects was offered.

In 1933 the J. pop. was 6,509. It was characterized by an exceptionally high proportion of unmarried men and women and a relatively late age of marriage. With the onset of Nazi rule, Jews were increasingly dismissed from their jobs and their businesses undermined. Socially as well the Jews were isolated. After being banned from public bathing facilities in 1933 they were attacked on a popular private beach in summer 1935 by the SA in a mass *Aktion* where J. men were beaten and stripped to ascertain their origin and women molested. Over 600 Jews were signed up at the *beit midrash*, which by 1936 included 17 Hebrew classes along with courses in Arabic, English, French, and Italian. The J. Cultural Association (Juedischer Kulturbund) also offered a wide range of activities and social welfare services expanded to support the community economically. Children were gradually transferred into a J. school system which embraced 454 students in 1936 and vocational training was offered to graduates as well as to the newly unemployed. The Zionist youth movements remained active, with 300 members as late as 1938. On *Kristallnacht* (9–10 Nov. 1938), the main synagogue was blown up, large J. business establishments were targeted for destruction, and men under the age of 60 were sent to the Dachau concentration camp, where a number died. Priceless art objects were also destroyed in J. homes. Following *Kristallnacht* the last J. businesses, still numbering well over 500, were liquidated and within half a year, 240 children in the Zionist youth movements were taken to Palestine. In the entire 1933–40 period, 3,927 M. Jews emigrated from Germany (119 of them were subsequently trapped in the German occupation). Of these, 1,451 reached the U.S.; 551 Palestine; 462 Latin America; and 1,159 various European countries. Nearly 2,000 were deported to the Gurs concentration camp in Oct. 1940 and hundreds more were deported through 1945. In all, 2,375 perished in the camps, 40 committed suicide, and 67 died or were executed in detention. Another 14 were sent to Gurs (with one surviving) from the attached community of Feudenheim, where 113 Jews had lived in the late 19th cent. After the

war a new community was formed by East European refugees and mostly intermarried local residents. It numbered 338 in 1977.

MANSBACH   (now part of Hohenroda), Hesse–Nassau, Germany. Established in the 18th cent., the J. community had a large synagogue dating from 1717 and numbered 199 (21% of the total) in 1861 but had dwindled to 50 (6%) by 1925. An annual "gift" to the Evangelical pastor remained obligatory until 1931. Most Jews left after 1935; six were deported in 1941–42.

MANTUA   Lombardy, Italy. The J. presence dates back to the 12th cent. Under the House of Gonzaga, which ruled M. for 400 years, until 1708, the J. community flourished. The Jews were bankers, merchants, and artisans. In c. 1475, a Hebrew printing press was established, subsequently becoming the largest after Venice's. The J. community, one of the most important in Renaissance Italy, established numerous mutual-aid societies and six synagogues, half practicing Italian rites, the other three the Ashkenazi rites. The province of M. included some 50 J. settlements, among them Bozzolo, Sabbioneta, Luzzara, Guastalla, Viadana, Revere, Sermide, and Ostiano. Prominent 15th cent. scholars from the area included Messer David ben Yehuda Leon, rabbi, physician, and philosopher; Yosef Colon, regarded as one of the greatest rabbinical authorities in Italy; Mordekhai Finzi, mathematician, astronomer, doctor, and banker; and Barukh da Peschiera, scholar and merchant. At the end of the 15th cent., Jews were forced to wear the J. badge. There were riots against Jews in 1495. In the 16th cent., prominent Jews in M. included such scholars as Azariah de Rossi, Shelomo Norsa, and Yehuda Provenzali; Avraham Colorni, engineer and inventor; Salamone de Rossi, the first composer of modern J. music, Yehuda Leone Sommo, playwright and poet. In 1612, the Jews were confined to a ghetto. In 1630, the community was decimated by the plague and by an attack by German troops. Avraham Massarani wrote up the chronicles of this war. In 1708, M. came under Austrian rule. In 1770, there were 2,218 Jews living in M. (total 26,000). When the French troops entered M. in 1797, the ghetto was abolished. Under Austrian rule from 1814 to 1866, when M. was incorporated into the Kingdom of Italy, Jews were subjected to a blood libel in 1824 and anti-J. riots in 1842. In 1873, the community numbered 1,980, reduced to 1,430 in 1886. On the eve of WWI, there were 70 families (160 individuals) in M. Most were poor. By 1925, the communit, headed by Prof. Levi Isaia, numbered 600 Jews. In accordance with the 1930 law reforming the J. communities of Italy, M. was classified as a district community legally recognized by the Italian government. The district included Bergamo (25 Jews in 1936); Bozzolo (119 Jews in 1873; 20 Jews in 1936); Casalmaggiore, Sermide (13 Jews in 1909); Viadana (20 Jews in 1909); Brescia (50 Jews in 1936); Cremona (15 Jews in 1936); and Ostiano (40 Jews in 1873; ten in 1936). In 1936, Prof. G. Calo headed the community, which numbered 500 Jews. During WWII, a concentration camp was set up in M. and 58 members of the community perished in the war. After the war, the community numbered 200 and in 1969 about 150.

MARASESTI Moldavia dist., Rumania. Early in the 20th cent. a Jew established a chemical factory which employed many Jews. The J. pop. was 77 in 1930 (2% of the total). At the outbreak of the Russo-Rumanian war in 1941 the Jews were expelled to Focsani.

MARBURG Hesse–Nassau, Germany. Jews had a community there in 1317, but fell victim to the Black Death massacres of 1348–49 and were expelled before 1452. Descendants of theirs in Italy adopted the surname Morpurgo. Readmitted in 1532, the Jews founded a small community (numbering 80 in 1827) with a district rabbinate (1824) and an elementary school (1867–1940). Under Leo Munk (1876–1918), an exponent of Neo-Orthodoxy, they dedicated a new synagogue of Byzantine design in 1897 and numbered 512 (2% of the total) in 1905. By that time Otto Boeckel, founder of the antisemitic People's Party (1890), had turned M. and its Lutheran university into a hotbed of racial prejudice and agitation. The university conferred a medical degree on a Jew as early as 1758, but professing Jews—both students and teachers—were not welcome there. Although Hermann Cohen (1842–1918), who founded the M. School of neo-Kantian philosophy, became dean of the philosophy faculty in 1886, the rectorship was denied him. In the face of anti-J. hooliganism, Central Union (C.V.) and Zionist groups increased their activities during the Weimar Republic, when the community numbered 370 (in 1925). Avraham Halevi Fraenkel, who occupied the chair of mathematics at the university, emigrated to Palestine

and served as rector of the Hebrew University (1938–40). Moshe Silberg, a law graduate, settled in Tel Aviv and became a justice of the Israel Supreme Court (1950-70). Nazi persecution forced leading J. intellectuals to emigrate and reduced the community from 341 in 1933 to 149 in Nov. 1938. On *Kristallnacht* (9–10 Nov. 1938), the synagogue was burned down in a pogrom. Of the remaining Jews, 23 were deported to the Riga ghetto in 1941 and 54 to Theresienstadt and other camps in 1942; 18 Jews housed in a local psychiatric hospital were murdered in the Nazi "euthanasia" program in Oct. 1940. J. Displaced Persons organized a postwar community, numbering 234 in 1946, and young pioneers trained at a farm established nearby. Most of these Jews left for Israel and by 1961 the community had dwindled to 15.

MARCALI Somogy dist., Hungary. Jews settled in the early 18th cent., mostly as tradesmen, forming a Neologist congregation in 1869. A J. school was opened in 1850. The J. pop. was 279 in 1930 and 231 in 1941. Six Jews were killed in White Terror attacks (1919–21). In May 1944, those not sent to forced labor were brought to Kaposvar and at the beginning of July deported to Auschwitz, where 185 perished.

MARCKOLSHEIM (Ger. Markolsheim) Bas-Rhin dist., France. The J. community numbered 47 members in 1784. Its synagogue was inaugurated in 1835. By 1865, there were 156 Jews in M., dropping to 56 in 1936. During WWII, the Germans expelled all to the south of France. The local synagogue was damaged during the bombardments, and the cemetery was destroyed. Six local Jews were deported. In 1965, there were 39 Jews living in M.

MARCULESTI-COLONIE Bessarabia, Rumania, today Republic of Moldova. M. was established by migrants from the Ukraine in 1837 as one of the J. agricultural villages in Bessarabia. In 1898 land was purchased by the ICA for 158 of the 292 J. families (1,534 persons). The ICA also assisted in the purchase of cattle and seeds and in digging wells and provided loans for building. With the development of the railway, the Jews of M. engaged mainly in the export of farm produce to Odessa, Danzig (Gdansk), and Koenigsberg, Germany. During and after WWI, the cultivation of sunflower seeds and in the 1930s also of soya beans made M. one of the leading suppliers of oil products throughout Rumania. In 1918–21, thousands of J. families fleeing from the Ukraine passed through M. and the J. community provided assistance. A modern J. school was set up by ICA officials, becoming the center of J. cultural life under the influence of *maskilim* from the Ukraine. Manifestations of antisemitism were rife, mainly at times of pogroms and persecution in Russia. The J. pop. in 1930 was 2,319 (88% of the total). On 9 July 1941, local peasants plundered J. property, murdered Jews, and raped young women. Returning Rumanian soldiers rounded up the J. pop. and murdered all.

MARDORF (now part of Amoeneburg) Hesse–Nassau, Germany. The J. community had a synagogue in 1860 and numbered 47 (5% of the total) in 1885. On *Kristallnacht* (9–10 Nov. 1938), the synagogue's interior was destroyed. By 1938, 13 of the remaining 27 Jews had left; at least nine perished in Nazi camps.

MARENICENI Bukovina, Rumania, today Ukraine. The Jews belonged to the Vijnita community and had no independent institutions. The J. pop. in 1930 was 15–20 families. In June 1941, ten J. families were murdered by Ukrainians and the rest deported to Transnistria.

MARGANETS Dnepropetrovsk dist., Ukraine. Jews apparently settled in the 1920s, in the Soviet period, and numbered 139 (total 58,148) in 1939. Shortly after their arrival in Aug. 1941, the Germans murdered 500 Jews from the area, among them the Jews of M.

MARGHITA (Hung. Margita; Yid. Margareten) N. Transylvania dist., Rumania. An organized J. community existed in the mid-18th cent. In the early 19th cent. a yeshiva with up to 350 students was established. The J. pop. in 1920 was 1,647 (18% of the total). In May 1944, the community was transferred to the Oradea Mare ghetto and then deported to extermination camps.

MARIAMPOL Stanislawow dist., Poland, today Ukraine. Jews settled in the second half of the 17th cent., the J. pop. reaching 663 (50% of the total) in 1890. A great fire in 1912 along with the attacks of the Russians and the Petlyura gangs brought the pop. down to 241 in 1921. The community was most likely liquidated by the Germans in the fall of 1942.

MARIANSKE LAZNE (Ger. Marienbad) Bohemia (Sudetenland), Czechoslovakia. Jews settled from 1820, becoming active in the resort trade. Many Jews visited the spa from other countries and some settled in the town. The J. pop. was 405 (total 7,202) in 1930. The community maintained a J. school and the Zionists with their youth movements became active after WWI. Most Jews left during the Sudetenland crisis in fall 1938. The Nazis arrested those who stayed behind, later deporting them to the Theresienstadt ghetto. The Nazis also burned down the community's splendid synagogue, vandalized the J. cemetery, and used the tombstones as building materials.

MARIAPOCS Szabolcs dist., Hungary. Jews are mentioned in 1770. They sold religious articles to Catholic pilgrims to M., believed to be the site of a miracle by Mary, mother of Jesus. The Jews numbered 181 in 1880 and 84 in 1930. On 28 May 1944, they were deported to Auschwitz via Nyirbator.

MARIBOR (Ger. Marburg) Slovenia, Yugoslavia, today Republic of Slovenia. Jews lived in M. from the 12th cent. Many were moneylenders, but in the 15th cent., when local Christians began to compete with them, the Jews lost most of their clients and went bankrupt. Antisemitism rose and in 1497 the Jews were expelled. There were 257 Jews in 1490 (total 1,030). In 1869 Jews began to resettle and there were 100 in 1940 (total pop. in 1931: 33,131). In 1941 they were deported to Serbia and murdered. Only about a dozen survived the Holocaust.

MARIENBURG (Pol. Malbork) East Prussia, Germany, today Poland. Jews settled in 1815. The community established two synagogues in 1830 and 1898 and a cemetery in 1830. In 1880, the J. pop. stood at 306, declining to 180 towards the end of the cent. A Jew served on the city council from 1864, becoming chairman in 1886. In the early 20th cent., the Association of East Prussian Communities opened an office in M. to care for indigent J. immigrants from Eastern Europe. Under Nazi rule, the J. pop. declined from 170 in 1932 to 60 in June 1938 and only 33 in May 1939. No further information about the fate of the J. residents is available.

MARIENTHAL Palatinate, Germany. The J. pop.

was 110 (22 families, with 18 in trade) in 1848. It then dropped to 42 (total 395) in 1875 and two in 1930.

MARIENWERDER (Pol. Kwidzyn) East Prussia, Germany, today Poland. The first J. family settled in 1798. The J. pop. was 220 in 1846 and 295 in 1880. The community established a cemetery in 1815 and subsequently two synagogues in 1830 and in 1930. The J. pop. increased after WWI with the addition of Jews from the neighboring territories that now came under Polish rule. Paul Hirsch, who became minister-president of Prussia in the Weimar Republic was born in M. On the eve of the Nazi rise to power, about 200 Jews were living in M. Economic boycott measures intensified in 1934–35 and the economic status of the community declined. By 1937, only 13 Jews remained. On *Kristallnacht* (9–10 Nov. 1938), the synagogue was set on fire and several Jews were arrested. By May 1939, there were no Jews in M. It is not known how many managed to emigrate to safe countries and how many perished in the Holocaust.

MARIJAMPOLE (Yid. Mariampol) Marijampole dist., Lithuania Jews first settled in the 18th cent. The J. pop. in 1861 was 3,015 (81% of the total). In the 1890s M. provided fertile ground for the creation of the Hovevei Zion movement, because Bible and Hebrew were taught in its schools. While there was much Zionist activity prior to WWI, the Bund also was active in M. and openly challenged the Zionists. In the 1920 elections for the Lithuanian Sejm, M.'s rabbi was elected as a representative. In three elections for the municipal council, between 26 and 40% of those elected were Jews and a Jew served as deputy mayor. In the mid-1930s the economic situation of the Jews deteriorated, partly due to a boycott by Lithuanian businessmen. Many young Jews emigrated to the west and to Palestine. In 1919 one of the first Hebrew high school in the Diaspora was established. Most of the school's students emigrated to Palestine and many of its teachers and administrators were influential in the nascent education system of Palestine and Israel. Most Jews were Zionists, as indicated by their participation in Zionist Congress elections. Many joined preparatory groups and kibbutzim prior to their emigration to Palestine. Among the many illustrious natives of M. were Dr. Barukh Ben-Yehuda (Leibovitch), who served as the first director general of Israel's Ministry of Education. The J. pop. in 1940 was about 2,800 (18% of

the total). When the Soviets entered M. in 1940, all communal and economic life was disrupted. After the German invasion in June 1941, Jews were arrested and murdered. In July, the Lithuanian governor issued an edict to wear the yellow Star of David. After all the Jews were concentrated in the synagogues, they were abused, taken to forced labor, and some were killed. At the end of Aug. those remaining were taken to pits and shot by Lithuanians.

MARIKOVA Slovakia, Czechoslovakia, today Republic of Slovakia. The J. pop. was 150 in 1840 with a synagogue and cemetery in use. The remaining Jews were deported to the death camps in 1942.

MARINA GORKA Minsk dist., Belorussia. Jews apparently settled at the turn of the 19th cent. They numbered 271 in 1924 and 786 in 1939 (total 6,547). Under the Soviets, a few dozen Jews earned their livelihoods in agriculture. The Germans occupied M. on 1 July 1941. On 28 Sept., they murdered most of the town's Jews (700) and another 500 (996 according to another source) from the surrounding area at Popova Gorka.

MARITEI Bukovina, Rumania. The J. pop. in 1930 was 64, most engaged in agriculture and commerce. In 1941, the Jews were transferred to Suceava and then to Transnistria.

MARIUPOL (until 1780, Pavlovsk; from 1948, Zhdanov) Stalino dist., Ukraine. Jews arrived following the development of the local metal industry in the 19th cent. An organized community existed by the mid-19th cent., reaching a pop. of 1,378 in 1864 and 5,013 (total 31,116) in 1897. Seven J. farm settlements were also located in the dist. Most children were enrolled in the city's four J. schools. In 1899, in the wake of the fighting against the Turks in the Black Sea area, the community cared for 3,000 J. refugees. A J. hospital was opened in 1902. On 20–22 Oct. 1905, on the heels of the revolution, Jews were attacked in a pogrom that claimed seven J. lives, including that of Yitzhak Berkovitz, the head of J. self-defense. More J. refugees arrived in WWI and were assimilated with the assistance of the Joint Distribution Committee. In 1929, under the Soviets, an agricultural cooperative embracing 12 J. families was founded with funds from the Joint, ORT, and the ICA. In 1936, about

360 Jews were employed in the city's new steel plant. A J. newspaper, *Emes*, was published in M.; a J. elementary school continued to operate; and 650 volumes in Yiddish were housed in the city's central library. R. Yitzhak Kosovsky, who studied at the Telz yeshiva in Lithuania, was the community's rabbi in 1922–25. In 1939, the J. pop. was 10,444 (5% of the total). The Nazis captured the city on 8 Oct. 1941. Refugees from the western part of the Soviet Union, including Odessa, brought the J. pop. up to 18,000. On 9 Oct., the Jews were ordered to wear the Star of David on their arms, appoint a representative, and furnish neighborhood head counts. On 12 Oct., they were ordered to hand over their valuables, including gold dental fillings. On 16 Oct., they were ordered to report to the city's old army headquarters. From there they were taken to the Agrobaza area about 4 miles (6.5 km) outside the city in groups of 500–1,000 and shot beside antitank ditches. Over 20,000 were murdered there in two days, including refugees and Jews of mixed descent.

MARKELSHEIM Wuerttemberg, Germany. Jews fell victim to the Black Death persecutions of 1348–49 and in the 17th cent. maintained a small community which was attached to neighboring Igersheim in 1832 and never grew to much more than 50. Twenty Jews remained in 1933 (total 1,199). On *Kristallnacht* (9–10 Nov. 1938), a J. apartment was destroyed and Jews were taken to the Dachau concentration camp for a few weeks. Most emigrated by 1941; five were deported to the Theresienstadt ghetto in Aug. 1942 along with three from Igersheim.

MARKI-PUSTELNIK (Yid. Markes) Warsaw dist., Poland. The Jews in the two adjoining settlements formed a single community in the 19th cent., numbering 524 (total 4,485) in 1921. On the eve of their expulsion to the Warsaw ghetto on 6 April 1942, 170 J. men and women were shot down trying to save the Torah scrolls being burned by the Germans. The rest shared the fate of Warsaw's Jews.

MARKOEBEL (now part of Hammersbach) Hesse-Nassau, Germany. Numbering 33 in 1750, the J. community grew to 91 (8% of the total) in 1885 but thereafter declined to 46 in 1933. The Nazis destroyed the synagogue and by May 1939 all the Jews had left.

MARKOVKA Vinnitsa dist., Ukraine. Four Jews

were present in 1765. In 1897, the J. pop. was 257 (total 1,610), dropping to 124 in 1926, when many left because of economic hardship. The Germans arrived on 22 July 1941. Before the town was annexed to Transnistria, the Germans probably murdered those Jews who had neither escaped nor been evacuated.

MARKOWA Lwow dist., Poland. The J. pop. in 1921 was 126 (total 4,364). The Jews of M. were killed in the Holocaust either in the vicinity or in the Belzec death camp.

MARKT BEROLZHEIM Middle Franconia, Germany. A J. community is known from the early 17th cent. and numbered 174 (total 898) in 1812, declining to 65 by 1933. A J. school closed in 1924. An antisemitic atmosphere prevailed before the Nazi rise to power, with persecution growing after 1933. In 1936 Jews were attacked on local trains and on *Kristallnacht* (9–10 Nov. 1938), the synagogue was burned to the ground. In 1934–38, 23 Jews emigrated, including 18 to the U.S., and 16 left for other German cities (ten for Nuremberg). Twenty-one of the 24 Jews remaining after *Kristallnacht* were arrested, and after their release dispersed to other places in Germany.

MARKTBREIT (in J. sources, Bratt) Lower Franconia, Germany. Jews are first mentioned in 1487 and were expelled in 1553. They settled again from 1636 and in 1642 received a general letter of protection from the emperor granting them religious freedom and other rights which promoted the development of the community into one of the most important in the principality, with the seat of the chief rabbinate established there until 1806. From the late 17th cent., Court Jews were active. Among the prominent families were the Wertheimers, Oppenheimers, and Astruques. The Wertheimers built a synagogue in M. and Samson Wertheimer was the chief agent of the Viennese court. Also in the late 17th cent. Prince Ferdinand restricted J. residence to 14 families (which remained in force until 1862). From 1806, with annexation to Bavaria, the community was under the aegis of the Wuerzburg district rabbinate, serving as its seat for a time. The J. pop. reached a peak of 320 in 1890 (total 2,385) and then declined steadily to 127 in 1933, with the communities of Obernbreit, Marktsteft, and Gnodstadt attached to it. A J. public school was opened in 1920. Under Nazi rule, the economic boycott quickly undermined J. livelihoods. Nevertheless, between 1933 and 1939 the community was active in education, culture, and social welfare. On *Kristallnacht* (9–10 Nov. 1938), the J. public school and synagogue were vandalized, including 12 Torah scrolls, 11 J. apartments were destroyed, and six men were sent to the Dachau and Buchenwald concentration camps. Afterwards all the Jews were evicted from their homes and ghettoized in the community center. In 1933–42, 54 additional Jews moved to M. and a total of 146 left, 83 of them emigrating. Of the remaining Jews, 23 were deported to Izbica in the Lublin dist. (Poland) via Wuerzburg on 24 March 1942 and nine were sent to the Theresienstadt ghetto in Sept. 1942.

MARKT ERLBACH Middle Franconia, Germany. The community suffered in the Rindfleisch massacres of 1298. In 1533 and 1535 the Jews received letters of protection from the local burgrave and in the 17th cent. a J. quarter existed. In 1837 the community numbered 90 and ten in 1933 (total 1,071). All left for other German cities before the *Kristallnacht* disturbances (9–10 Nov. 1938).

MARKTSTEFT Lower Franconia, Germany. Jews are first mentioned in 1532. In 1837 the community numbered 75 (total 1,310), maintaining a synagogue and serving as the seat of the district rabbinate. In 1933 three Jews remained, attached to the Marktbreit community. They were deported to the Theresienstadt ghetto in 1942.

MARKUSOVCE Slovakia, Czechoslovakia, today Republic of Slovakia. The J. pop. was 114 in 1910 and the community maintained a synagogue, elementary school, and cemetery. In 1930, 41 Jews remained.

MARKUSZOW Lublin dist., Poland. An independent J. community existed by 1766, building a synagogue in 1799 and then another in 1855. R. Avraham Moshe Weintraub established a local hasidic dynasty and in 1916 the first Zionist group formed. The J. pop. grew from 340 in 1827 to 1,123 (total 1,739) in 1897. After WWI, the Jews lived under straitened economic circumstances and Zionist activity expanded. The Germans captured the town on 11 Sept. 1939, setting up a *Judenrat* and sending Jews to work at forced labor. In May 1941, a ghetto was established and in April 1942, 500 of the sick and old were deported to

the Sobibor death camp. Refugees from Slovakia brought the ghetto pop. up to 1,500. On 8 May 1942, as another *Aktion* commenced, many escaped from the town. Those found hiding or sick were immediately shot. The rest were deported to Sobibor the next day. A group of 50 young Jews formed three partisan units, augmented by escaped J. prisoners of war, but in the end they were hunted down and murdered by the Germans along with others who had fled to the forests.

MAROLDSWEISACH Lower Franconia, Germany. The community was founded no later than the first half of the 18th cent. and numbered 140 in 1837 (total 550) and 22 in 1933. Ten Jews are known to have emigrated and none remained by May 1939.

MARSEILLE (Lat. Massalia) Bouches-du-Rhone dist., France. The earliest evidence of a J. presence is from 574. In 591, Bishop Theodore of Marseille attempted to convert the Jews, but Pope Gregory I intervened. The Radanites, J. merchant-adventurers, sailed in the ninth cent. from M. to the Far East. During his visit to M. in the 12th cent., Benjamin of Tudela found 300 J. families. After 1492, Jews expelled from Spain settled here, comprising half the community. With the general expulsion order in 1500 for the Jews of Provence, many chose conversion in order to remain in M. The community revived for a brief time in the second half of the 17th cent. (until its expulsion in 1682) when several Jews from Leghorn (Livorno) were granted privileges because of their activities in maritime commerce. A new community established in 1760 owned a small synagogue and a cemetery. In 1804 the community numbered 300 members and 1,000 in 1821. A Sephardi synagogue was dedicated in 1864. At that time, the J. pop. was 2,500. Following the loss of Alsace-Lorraine in 1870, waves of immigration increased the J. pop. of M. The newcomers were joined by Jews from Central and Eastern Europe as well as from the Ottoman Empire. From 2,662 Jews in 1872, the pop. rose to almost 12,000 on the eve of WWI. Prior to the war, 80% were French and 20% were foreigners; on the eve of WWII, 60% were foreigners and 40% were French (36% local Jews). Following the occupation, M. was the only port from which departure from France was possible. Between 1940 and 1942, M. was in the Free Zone along with Lyon. It was the city in the southern zone where the greatest number of Jews and J. organizations and institutions found refuge. The J. pop. increased to 15,000. Jews were active in the underground movement. The hunt for Jews in M. was accompanied by arrests in Jan.–Feb. 1943. About 4,000 Jews were deported from M. After liberation, the community was rebuilt, mostly by Jews from North Africa. With 60,000 members in 1964, M. developed into the third largest J. community in Western Europe.

MARTONVASAR Fejer dist., Hungary. Jews are mentioned in 1778. They numbered 95 in 1880 and 79 in 1930. Most died during the Holocaust.

MARTYNOVKA (I) Mogilev dist., Belorussia. M. was founded as a J. colony on private land in 1847 and had a pop. of 54 in 1898. In the mid-1920s, under the Soviets, 25 J. families engaged in agriculture. A four-grade J. school was opened in 1927. In 1930, the settlement became a kolkhoz. The Germans arrived in Aug. 1941 and murdered the few remaining Jews.

MARTYNOVKA (II) Smolensk dist., Russia. M. was founded as a J. colony in 1849 and numbered 117 Jews in 1898. Thirty-five families were present in 1923, a number of them farming at nearby kolkhozes. After the German occupation in mid-July 1941, the few Jews in M. were expelled to the Khislavichi ghetto, where they shared the fate of local Jews (probably being murdered in March 1942).

MASSBACH Lower Franconia, Germany. The community was most likely founded in the early 18th cent., reaching a peak pop. of 180 in 1837 (total 1,172). In 1830–54, 23 young bachelors emigrated overseas. A synagogue was constructed in 1899 and a cemetery consecrated in 1904. In 1933, the J. pop. of 34 suffered from anti-J. agitation and the economic boycott, though J. cattle traders were still active in 1937. On *Kristallnacht* (9–10 Nov. 1938), the synagogue and J. homes were vandalized. Fourteen Jews emigrated in 1933–40; another seven moved to other German cities and eight were deported to Izbica in the Lublin dist. (Poland) and the Theresienstadt ghetto in 1942.

MASSENBACH Wuerttemberg, Germany. Jews are first recorded in 1556. A synagogue was dedicated in 1720 and the community grew to a peak of 85 in 1843, mostly living off the cattle trade and forming

close ties with the local pop., which resisted the excesses of the Nazi era. Of the 15 Jews in M. in 1933, ten emigrated to the U.S. and three were expelled to the east and perished.

MASSOW (Pol. Maszewo) Pomerania, Germany, today Poland. Jews are mentioned in M. from 1705. The small community numbered 82 in 1849 and maintained a synagogue from 1830 and a cemetery. By 1907, the community, now reduced to 20 members, became affiliated with the Naugard community. The synagogue, closed in 1900, was sold in 1930. When the Nazis came to power in 1933, there were 22 Jews in M. No further information is available about their fate. The J. cemetery was completely wrecked in 1938.

MATESZALKA Szatmar dist., Hungary. Jews settled in the mid-18th cent. and numbered 932 (20% of the total) in 1890 and 1,555 in 1941. The community maintained a J. public school and, in addition to the synagogue, a hasidic *shtibl*. After the German occupation in spring 1944, one of the largest concentration camps in Hungary was established here (17,000 inmates). All were deported from 19 May to 5 June to Auschwitz. Of the postwar community, 98 remained in 1959.

MATEUR Bizerte dist., Tunisia. According to tradition, the first Jews arrived in the 16th cent., but the community only began to grow from the early 19th cent., when Jews from Tunis and Bizerte arrived. The nationalistic ardor of local Arabs was the source of much friction with Jews and numerous anti-J. incidents, even in the period of the French Protectorate. The J. pop. was 496 in 1921 (11.2% of the total) and 332 in 1936. Rich, property-owning grain merchants formed the upper class of the J. community, followed by tradesmen, professionals, and white-collar workers, all receiving a French education and inhabiting the European quarter. At the bottom of the scale was a poorer class crowded into a J. quarter of two streets in the Arab part of the city, living in traditional houses (*oukala*). All children attended the French public school in addition to a *talmud torah* in the afternoons (frequented more by boys in the J. quarter). The community council, referred to as the J. Relief Fund (Caisse de Secours et de Bienfaisance or simply the Comite) since 1909, maintained the community's single synagogue and two cemeteries and provided charitable as-

Jewish bakery on Rue Massicaut, Mateur, Tunisia, early 20th cent. (Bernard Allali Collection, Paris/photo courtesy of Beth Hatefutsoth, Tel Aviv)

sistance to the needy. Its income was mainly derived from the meat tax and donations. M. was bound to Tunis as a satellite community and followed its social and cultural lead, including some Zionist activity through a Mevaseret Zion society founded in 1919. Despite a number of violent anti-J. incidents (in 1917, 1932, and 1934), relations with the Arabs until WWII were based on peaceful coexistence and generally quiet. During WWII the Jews suffered from food shortages and from the Vichy regime's racial laws. Under the German occupation from 9 Nov. 1942, Jews were forced to furnish supplies and property was confiscated. The Arab pop. welcomed the Germans and pillaged J. shops and homes. Many fled to outlying farms during the Allied bombings. The city was liberated on 3 May 1943. The French authorities, as well as the Joint Distribution Committee and the OZE, helped the community to recover from the war. Attempts to establish Zionist groups failed. The poorer Jews emigrated to Israel, mainly in 1948–56, while the wealthier left for France.

Eight forced labor camps under German command holding about 600 Jews were in operation around M. from 13 Dec. 1942. Most of the Jews came from Tunis and a few from M. The largest, Saf-Saf, held 200 in a big barn. The Jews were forced to work on fortifications and carry supplies to German positions from dawn to dusk in the freezing winter. The Jefna camp had the harshest conditions. Here about 120 Jews carried ammunition boxes up steep hills to frontline positions 18 hours a day. At the initiative of Morris Tayyib, a member of the Committee for Recruiting J. Manpower (the Tunisian version of the *Judenrat* and responsible for supplying forced laborers with food), many Jews were smuggled out of the camps under various pretenses. The last of the camps was liquidated on 25 April 1943.

MATMATA   Matmata dist., Tunisia. Jews are known from the 14th cent. but an organized community was only established in the early 19th cent. Most of the Jews came from Djerba and Gabes, at first trading mainly in the *alafa* plant, used in paper production and in cloth. Most were troglodytes, their homes carved out of the hills and sometimes including a second and third story. Toward the end of the 19th cent., Jews played a significant role in the economic development of M. Some grew dates and olives in partnership with local Arabs and between the World Wars, Jews operated six relatively large general stores in the town. Jews also engaged in moneylending and benefited economically from visitors seeking an asthma cure or coming as tourists to see the cave-dwelling community. The Najar family dominated the community council, until challenged by the rival Maimon family in the 1920s. A power-sharing modus vivendi was eventually established. The J. pop. was 165 in 1909 and 128 in 1936. All social and cultural activity revolved around the synagogue, which was partly built underground at the end of the 19th cent. and later above-ground. A *talmud torah* was established at the synagogue. During WWII, the Jews barely felt the Vichy laws. Many refugees ar-

rived from Gabes during the Allied bombings of early 1943 because the caves provided shelter. The German occupation was also quiet since the Germans found it difficult to distinguish the Jews in their traditional dress from the Arabs. Many of the Maimons left the town after WWII. Anti-J. agitation marked the period of Israeli statehood, with J. shops and stalls pillaged in the market and J. businesses boycotted. In 1952, 103 Jews were brought as a group to Israel, half belonging to the Najar family.

MATTERSDORF (until 1924, Mattersburg) Burgenland, Austria. The M. community formed one of the Seven Communities (*Sheva Kehillot*). Jews possibly settled here in 800 or 1222. By the middle of the 14th cent. there was a J. settlement and a synagogue was consecrated in 1354. In 1622 the community came under the protection of the House of Esterhazy. In the beginning of the 18th cent., a J. elementary school was opened, functioning until the 1920s.

Yeshiva students, Mattersdorf, Austria, 1932

There were 767 Jews in M. in 1785 and 1,500 in 1848, representing a third of the total. The J. pop. declined to 752 in 1902 and to 600 in 1934. Jews were engaged in trade and crafts. A Mizrachi youth group and a women's organization were active until the beginning of the 1930s. Immediately after the *Anschluss* (13 March 1938), J. property was confiscated. In May 1938, the remaining 500 Jews were expelled from M. By Oct. 1938, some had managed to emigrate or escape. Others were sent to Vienna and from there to the concentration camps in the east.

MAYEN   Rhineland, Germany. Jews first arrived in the 14th cent. During the Black Death persecutions of 1348-49, a number of Jews were murdered and the community came to an end, its property expropriated. Two J. families received letters of protection in 1570 but at the end of the cent., the Jews were again expelled. J. settlement was renewed in the 18th cent. In 1773, the J. pop. was 39. In 1847, M. became the seat of a regional congregation and a new cemetery was opened. A synagogue was consecrated in 1855 and a J. elementary school was founded in 1869, becoming a public institute in 1878. The community reached a peak pop. of 328 in 1905. In 1933, 225 Jews remained. On *Kristallnacht* (9–10 Nov. 1938), SA troops burned the synagogue and damaged J. homes and stores. The J. school closed down in 1939. By May 1939, 95 Jews remained. Some managed to emigrate from Germany but the last 77 were deported to the death camps of the east in the 1941-42 period.

MAYFELD   (until 1929, Khaklay) Crimea, Russia, today Ukraine. M. was founded as a J. agricultural settlement in 1923 by 100 Hehalutz members with the support of the Joint Distribution Committee. Its pop. grew to 362 (79 families) in the first year, with most working the land on 65 farm units. Thirty women worked at weaving in a local cooperative. A J. school for 136 children, aged 12–18, from 15 settlements in the Dzhankoy region, was opened in 1928. In 1941, the pop. of M. was 150 families, apparently including non-Jews. The Germans arrived around the end of Oct. 1941, murdering the dozens of J. families who remained there in Jan. 1942. In all, they murdered 1,512 Jews in the area, including those living in kolkhozes (Oktyiaber, Nay Veg, Spartak, Fray Leben). After the war, 61 families (172 people) returned, most appa-

rently Jews. The chairman of the local kolkhoz was a Jew. Most Jews subsequently left.

MAYIAKI   Odessa dist., Ukraine. Jews numbered 648 (total 4,575) in 1897 and 178 under the Soviets in 1926. In WWII, the Nazis presumably murdered the few Jews who had neither escaped nor been evacuated.

MAYKOP   Krasnodar territory, Russia. Jews probably settled in the late 19th cent., erecting a synagogue at the end of the cent. The Germans murdered 117 Jews after their arrival on 10 Aug. 1942. On 14 Aug., they murdered seven Jews from the nearby village of Khanskaya and in late Aug., at the village of Kuzhorskaya, 36 J. refugees from the western Soviet Union.

MAZEIKIAI   (Yid. Mazheik) Mazeikiai dist., Lithuania. Jews first settled in the 1870s. The Zionist Organization was active, with many contributing to settlement funds for Eretz Israel. The J. pop. in 1897 was 435 (21% of the total). Between the World Wars a J. community council established Hebrew elementary and high schools. After a period of prosperity, the situation worsened and many emigrated to America, South Africa, and Palestine. In 1934 three Jews were elected to the 12-member municipal council. Social welfare, and Zionist organizations operated. The J. pop. in 1940 was 900. After the German invasion in June 1941, a few Jews escaped to the USSR. Some were killed trying and others were forced to return. In July, all the Jews were rounded up and in Aug. murdered beside freshly dug pits next to the J. cemetery.

MECHETYNSKAYA   Rostov dist., Russia. The Germans occupied the village on 28 Aug. 1942. During their short occupation, they murdered 48 J. families, comprising local residents and refugees.

MECKENHEIM   Rhineland, Germany. First evidence of J. settlement dates back to 1598. In 1711, the Jews acquired a cemetery site and by 1804 there were 14 Jews in M. The community grew to 95 in 1869, reaching its peak in 1883 with 133 members. A synagogue was dedicated in 1870. At the time of the Nazi takeover in 1933, there were only 57 Jews in M. On *Kristallnacht* (9–10 Nov. 1938), the synagogue was desecrated but not set on fire because of

The Mazeikiai soccer team, Lithuania

the adjoining non-J. houses. J. stores and homes were wrecked. The community was forced to bear the cost of clearing the area of debris. In 1939 there were 21 Jews in M. Eighteen were deported, first to Endenich and then to the east.

MECKESHEIM Baden, Germany. Jews arrived in 1700 and numbered 63 in 1875 (total 1,261), taking an active part in local life. A synagogue was built in 1830 and a cemetery was opened in 1896. In 1933, 17 Jews remained. Ten left in 1934–38, half emigrating, and five more left for Holland after *Kristallnacht* (9–10 Nov. 1938). The last five Jews were deported to the Gurs concentration camp on 22 Oct. 1940, all perishing along with three deported to the camps from other places.

MEDDERSHEIM Rhineland, Germany. In 1855, the J. pop. reached a peak of 55, after which the community was attached to the Sobernheim congregation. In 1925, 16 Jews remained (total 714). Four were deported to the east in spring 1942.

MEDEBACH Westphalia, Germany. Fifty-one Jews were present in 1871 (2% of the total) and 32 in 1925. The community was affiliated to Brilon. On *Kristallnacht* (9–10 Nov. 1938), Nazi thugs vandalized J. property and destroyed the synagogue, though it had already been sold. All the Jews left before the outbreak of war, about half to the U.S. and South America.

MEDEMBLIK Noord-Holland dist., Holland. Small-scale J. settlement began in the 18th cent. and peaked at 65 Jews in 1854. The J. pop. in 1941 was seven (total 4,461). On 17 April 1942, the few Jews living in the area were sent to Amsterdam and from there to the death camps; four survived in hiding. Nearby in Meerpolder, a training farm was established in 1934 for young J. refugees from Germany preparing to emigrate oversees. The 287 Jews there in 1941 were sent by the Germans to the Mauthausen concentration camp and killed.

MEDENICE Lwow dist., Poland, today Ukraine.

The Jewish quarter, Medenine, Tunisia, 1910

The community never exceeded 200 (about 10% of the total), some engaged in farming. A great flood in 1927 left 90% homeless. The Germans took the city in July 1941 and the Ukrainians carried out a pogrom. Those who had not fled were deported to the Belzec death camp in August 1942.

MEDENINE Orgama dist., Tunisia. J. settlement commenced in the mid-19th cent. when itinerant peddlers from Djerba and Gabes struck roots there. More substantial emigration from Djerba commenced after the establishment of the French Protectorate in 1881. The Jews of M. resided in a separate, walled J. quarter. Jews traded in sugar, coffee, tea, and the *alafa* plant. They supplied the local French army base, the mainspring of economic development in the area, and thanks to the J. chief engineer there many were employed in public works. M. was a commercial center for the Jews of Zarzis, Ben Gardan, and Tataouine and was itself under the sway of Djerba and Gabes, the former in religious matters, the latter commercially. The J. pop. was 451 in 1921 and 708 (total 1,562) in 1936. The

community council was established in 1922 along the lines of the prevailing Caisse de Secours et de Bienfaisance. R. Humani Alush was the spiritual leader of the community from 1926 to 1950, when he came to Israel. Like the other satellite communities of Djerba, M. was barely touched by modern ways. Community life revolved around the J. quarter's single synagogue. Built at the end of the 19th cent. with a new section added in 1910, it contained 40 Torah scrolls. Children studied at a *talmud torah*. Relations with the Arab pop. were based on economic dependence with occasional social contact. In WWII the Vichy laws had little affect on the community. Under the German occupation of Nov. 1942–Feb. 1943, Jews were forced to furnish provisions and then fled to Djerba to escape the Allied bombardments. When they returned they found their homes and stores pillaged by local Arabs. The community recovered after the war with assistance from the Joint Distribution Committee and OZE. Zionist activity expressed itself in the establishment of a branch of Djerba's Ateret Zion movement, which emphasized the teaching of modern Hebrew. The movement was forced to go underground with the rise of Arab nationalism in 1947. The Jews of M. assisted 500 Libyan Jews who were smuggled out to Israel in 1947–52. With the economic and security situation in the region deteriorating further for the Jews, a Southern Rescue Committee began operating and in 1951–52, about half the Jews of M. left, most for Israel.

MEDGYESEGYHAZA Csanad dist., Hungary. Jews settled in the late 19th cent., trading mainly in grain. A synagogue was consecrated in 1870. The J. pop. was 60 in 1930. In WWII, 51 Jews were sent to Bekescsaba; 20 were deported on 26 June 1944 to Auschwitz and the rest to Austria, where most survived the war. Twenty–one survivors tried to reestablish the community but failed and in 1947 it was dissolved.

MEDIAS (Hung. Medgyes) S. Transylvania dist., Rumania. A J. community was founded in 1875 and a synagogue was built in 1895. The J. pop. in 1880 was 722. A *talmud torah* and yeshiva were opened in 1915. At the beginning of the 20th cent, M. was one of the wealthiest Orthodox communities in S. Transylvania. In 1943 almost half the J. pop. required aid. After the anti-Nazi revolt (23 Aug. 1944) Jews from neighboring villages streamed into M. as one of the main industrial centers in the region. In 1947, the pop. increased to about 1,000 but by 1964 dropped to 100, with more than half settling in Israel, the rest having left for the larger cities.

MEDIASUL AURIT (Hung. Aranyomeggyes) N. Transylvania dist., Rumania. Jews settled in the mid-18th cent. and most engaged in agriculture. In 1920 the J. pop. was 357 (10% of the total). In May 1944 the community was transferred to the Satu Mare ghetto and in June deported to Auschwitz.

MEDJEZ EL-BAB Medjez el-Bab dist., Tunisia. A J. community is known from the early days of the French Protectorate in the late 19th cent. In 1921, the J. pop. was 99 (7.5% of the total), dropping to 58 in 1946. In WWII the Jews fled as the town came under heavy bombardment. Arabs pillaged J. homes and stores. In 1956, 16 Jews remained.

MEDVEDOVKA Kirovograd dist., Ukraine. Jews probably settled in the early 19th cent. and numbered 1,453 (total 3,683) in 1897. Only 35 remained in

1926. The others were presumably murdered or fled during the pogroms of the civil war years (1918–21). After they occupied the town in Aug. 1941, the Germans apparently murdered the few remaining Jews.

MEDYKA Lwow dist., Poland, today Ukraine. The J. pop. in 1921 was 132. The Jews were probably executed locally or expelled to Przemsyl for liquidation in July–Aug. 1942.

MEDZHIBOZH Kamenets-Podolski dist., Ukraine. Jews are first mentioned in 1509. M. was the site of large fairs, attracting merchants from Podolia, Volhynia, Kiev, and the cities of Poland, Germany, and Italy. In the 16th and 17th cents. it was a center of tal-

Title page of Medzhibozh Mishna Society publication, Ukraine, 1860 (The Russian Ethnographic Museum, Petersburg/photo courtesy of Yad Vashem, The Holocaust Martyrs' and Heroes' Remembrance Authority, Jerusalem)

mudic scholarship. R. Yoel Sirkes, one of the greatest talmudic sages of Poland, is mentioned in connection with M. in 1611. The town suffered from Cossack attacks in 1651, 1664, and 1703. The Ba'al Shem Tov (Yisrael ben Eliezer) settled in M. in 1740, residing there until his death in 1760 and founding the first hasidic community there. A magnificent hasidic court continued after his death as well. The jester Hershele of Ostropol was active in the court of the *tzaddik* Barukh ben Yehiel of M. The J. pop. rose to 6,040 (74% of the total) in 1897. Russian army units bivouacking in the area were a source of income for the Jews. On 3–5 April 1882, J. self-defense units prevented a pogrom but one was successfully staged after the Oct. 1917 Revolution, on 18 Nov. In the Soviet period, a J. council (soviet) was active and a Yiddish newspaper appeared. A J. kolkhoz was founded in 1930. In 1939, the J. pop. was 2,347. The Germans captured M. on 8 July 1941. After setting up a ghetto, the Germans together with their Ukrainian collaborators executed 2,588 Jews on 22 Sept. 1942 (Yom Kippur). The killing continued until 31 Oct., when the last of the Jews were murdered.

MEDZILABORCE Slovakia, Czechoslovakia, today Republic of Slovakia. The Jews were apparently present in the early 18th cent, if not before. The J. pop. rose sharply in the late 19th cent., numbering 232 in 1869 and 347 (total 1,065) in 1880. A *beit midrash* and J. elementary school were opened and in the 1880s, M. became the seat of the regional rabbinate. With J. families arriving from neighboring villages, the J. pop. rose to 662 in 1919 and in the 1930s reached a peak pop. of about 900. Betar and Bnei Akiva were active among the Zionist youth groups and Agudat Israel operated a large branch. Jews served on the local

The Ba'al Shem Tov synagogue in Medzhibozh, Ukraine (The Russian Ethnographic Museum, Petersburg/photo courtesy of Yad Vashem, The Holocaust Martyrs' and Heroes' Remembrance Authority, Jerusalem)

council and owned 28 business establishments, seven workshops, and two banks. In 1941, under Slovakian rule, they were forced out of their businesses. On 25 March 1942, 100 J. girls from the area were deported to Auschwitz. On 28 March, young men were sent to the Majdanek concentration camp and on 20 May, 370 Jews (in a transport of 1,000 from the area) were deported to the Pulawy ghetto in the Lublin dist. of Poland. Another 170 were sent to the death camps on 2–6 June. Most of the remaining 100 or so Jews were evacuated to western Slovakia in May 1944.

MEERHOLZ (now part of Gelnhausen) Hesse–Nassau, Germany. Established in the 18th cent., the community numbered 117 (about 17% of the pop.) in 1835 but dwindled to 32 in 1933. After disposing of their synagogue in 1937, all the Jews left, 13 emigrating to the U.S.

MEERSSEN Limburg dist., Holland. A community was established at the end of the 18th cent. and reached a peak of 140 Jews in 1892. It then dwindled and only 22 were left by 1938. All but four, who survived in hiding, perished in the Holocaust.

MEGYASZO Zemplen dist., Hungary. Jews settled in the late 18th cent., numbering 151 in 1880 and 99 in 1930. In late May 1944, they were brought to Sataraljaujhely and from there deported to Auschwitz.

MEHLEM Rhineland, Germany. Jews were present in 1663. Their pop. reached a peak of 48 in 1875, when a synagogue was consecrated. In 1933 the J. pop. was 21, with the community attached to the Bad Godesberg congregation. Most Jews emigrated. The last two were deported on 23 Jan. 1942 to the ghettoes in Theresienstadt or Lodz via the Benedictine monastery in Bonn-Endenich.

MEHLINGEN Palatinate, Germany. The J. pop. was 73 (13 families) in 1848, dealing in cotton goods, old clothes, spices, fruit, flour, livestock, etc. Five Jews remained in 1900. One perished in Auschwitz in the Holocaust.

MEHRING Rhineland, Germany. A. J. community developed in the first half of the 19th cent., growing from two families in 1808 to 33 Jews in 1843 and 57 (total 1,606) in 1885. The community maintained a

synagogue and cemetery. The J. pop. then dropped to 36 in 1900 and 30 in 1932. All left before the *Kristallnacht* disturbances (9–10 Nov. 1938). At least one Jew perished in the Majdanek concentration camp. The Nazis destroyed the synagogue and desecrated the cemetery.

MEIMBRESSEN (now part of Calden) Hesse–Nassau, Germany. Survivors of the Chmielnicki massacres of 1648–49 reinforced the community, which adopted their Polish rite and customs. The community had a large burial ground and established a synagogue in 1842. It maintained an elementary school (1844–1934) and numbered 134 (18% of the total) in 1861. Affiliated with Kassel's rabbinate, it declined to 51 in 1933. The interior of the synagogue was destroyed on *Kristallnacht* (9–10 Nov. 1938), and by 1939 all the Jews had left, 33 emigrating. At least 15 perished in Nazi camps.

MEINERZHAGEN Westphalia, Germany. Jews are first mentioned in 1806. The J. pop. reached a peak of 51 (total 2,567) in 1885. In the early 1930s, most Jews were merchants (six out of the 11 dealing in cattle). In June 1933, about four months after the Nazi rise to power, there were 43 Jews in M. In 1935–41, 29 Jews left the city, including nine for the U.S., six for Argentina, and nine for other localities in Germany. Eleven Jews were deported to the east in April and July 1942.

MEININGEN Thuringia, Germany. The Jews of M. suffered various persecutions in the 13th and 14th cents., notably during the Black Death disturbances of 1348–49. In 1384, the empty synagogue was converted into a Christian chapel. There is evidence of J. settlement in M. and its environs at least until the first half of the 16th cent. and possibly later. In the wake of the Hep! Hep! riots in 1819 only one J. family remained. In 1831, Jews were officially allowed to trade in M. In 1844, the J. pop. was 44 and in the 1880s about 450. The community dedicated a synagogue in 1883 and opened its own cemetery in 1874. Jews became well integrated into the life of the city. The banker Gustav Strupp served as chairman of both the J. community and the chamber of commerce and was a member of the Landtag (1903–18). The J. community, numbering 235 in June 1933, remained on the whole relatively unmolested during the first two or three years of Nazi rule. As the situation deteriorated, many emigrated. On *Kristallnacht* (9–10 Nov. 1938), the synagogue was desecrated and later destroyed. The remaining Jews were concentrated in 1941 in a "J. house" in the center of the city until their deportation to the death camps.

MEISENHEIM Rhineland, Germany. The first Jew is mentioned in 1551 and Jews resided in the city without a break from the mid-17th cent. Their pop. reached a peak of 198 (total 1,882) in 1864. In 1836, the community started a J. elementary school, which operated intermittently until WWI. A splendid synagogue was consecrated in 1865 and a new cemetery was opened in 1880. The J. pop. dwindled to 38 by the eve of the Nazi era. The synagogue was partially burned on *Kristallnacht* (9–10 Nov. 1938), when 16 Jews were still living in M. One was taken to the Dachau concentration camp in the wake of the pogrom and perished there. About eight were deported to the death camps.

MEISSEN Saxony, Germany. There was a J. community with a synagogue in the last decade of the 12th cent. which came to an end in the Black Death persecutions of 1348–49. Individual Jews lived in M. in the 15th cent. A new settlement was started only in the second half of the 19th cent. It numbered 62 Jews in 1910 and 60 in 1925. The community was affiliated to the Dresden community and had no institutions of its own. Already in the first year of Nazi rule, about 25% of the Jews moved away. By 1937 there were 35 Jews in M. On *Kristallnacht* (9–10 Nov. 1938), J. businesses were looted and wrecked. In 1939, only seven Jews were still living in M. They were later deported to the east.

MEJSZAGOLA Vilna dist., Poland, today Lithuania. A J. community of 354 was present by 1865, most farming and living in straitened economic circumstances. After WWI the Jews numbered 55 families, the tradesmen among them undermined by Polish competition. Under Lithuanian rule in 1939 and again on the eve of the German occupation in June 1941, Lithuanian antisemites staged pogroms. The Germans set up a *Judenrat* and ghetto, instituting a regime of forced labor and extortion. On 28 Sept. 1941, the Jews were executed near the village of Wilnowo.

MEKHOVOE Vitebsk dist., Belorussia. M. was oc-

cupied by the Germans in Aug. 1941. The 150 Jews in the area were murdered in Feb. 1942 near Yezerishche.

MELITOPOL Zaporozhe dist., Ukraine. In 1897, the J. pop. was 6,563 with another 454 Karaites (total 15,489). On 18–19 April 1905, J. self-defense units stopped a pogrom but not before 40 stores were burned and 15 Jews injured. In April 1917 another attempted pogrom failed. Under the Soviets, a J. school was founded in 1923. In the 1930s, dozens of J. families earned their livelihoods in J. kolkhozes and many worked in factories. In 1939, the J. pop. was 6,040. The Germans arrived on 5 Oct. 1941, finding 1,800 Jews there. On 10 Oct., they executed 49 J. prisoners of war and the next day murdered 3,000 Jews from M. and the surrounding area at the villages of Vozneshenko and Konstantinovka. A final group of J. women, married to non-Jews, was executed on 9 Oct. 1942.

MELLRICHSTADT Lower Franconia, Germany. Jews are known from the late 13th cent. Four were burned in 1283 and others fell victim to the Rindfleisch massacres of 1298. Jews lived under letters of protection in the subsequent centuries. A cemetery was consecrated in 1869 and a synagogue in 1881, with the pop. growing to 165 in 1910 (total 2,176) and Jews owning most of the business establishments in the town. In 1933, 126 remained. The J. school remained open until 1938. On 30 Sept 1938, in wild anti-J. riots provoked by German refugees from the Sudetenland, the synagogue as well as J. homes and stores were wrecked and Jews were forced to sell their houses. In 1933–1942, 82 left, of whom 36 emigrated, including 31 to the U.S. Of those remaining in 1942, 24 were deported to Izbica in the Lublin dist. (Poland) via Wuerzburg on 25 April and nine to the Theresienstadt ghetto on 23 Sept.

MELNIK Bohemia, Czechoslovakia. Jews are mentioned in 1402 but through the mid-19th cent. few were permitted to reside there. A synagogue was consecrated in 1862 and the community reached a pop. of 194 in 1872, dropping to 84 (total 5,813) in 1930. In 1942, the Jews were deported to the Theresienstadt ghetto together with the Jews of Prague and from there transported to the death camps of Poland. Few survived.

MELSUNGEN Hesse–Nassau, Germany. Established around 1776, the community built a large synagogue in 1841 and operated an elementary school from 1854 to 1924. It numbered 188 (5% of the total) in 1880. Anti-J. riots and disputes with German cattle traders occurred in the 19th cent. Affiliated with Kassel's rabbinate, the community declined to 89 (2%) in 1925 and by Nov. 1938 it had shrunk to 28. On *Kristallnacht* (9–10 Nov. 1938), the synagogue's interior was vandalized and Jews were attacked, one detainee later dying in the Buchenwald concentration camp. After 1935, 42 Jews left (25 emigrating), ten were deported, and at least 18 perished in the Holocaust.

MELYKUT   Bacs–Bodrog dist., Hungary. The J. pop. was 113 in 1909 and 71 in 1930. The Jews were deported to Auschwitz via Bacsalmas in May 1944.

MEMEL   (Klaipeda) Memel dist., Lithuania. In 1567 the Jews of M. were expelled as a result of pressure from Church fundamentalists. In 1662 Jews were invited back to help develop M.'s economy. A Dutch

Jew, Moshe Yaakovzon de Junge, developed a salt business, employing other Jews. When he returned to Holland, Jews again were prohibited from living in M., though they were allowed to come for trade fairs. Jews were permitted to settle in M. in the beginning of the 19th cent. but their numbers only became significant in the mid-19th cent. There were two communities: German Jews and Russian-Polish Jews. Despite the Prussian government's demand that the two J. communities unite, each community saw to its own religious and educational needs. R. Dr. Yitzhak Rilf, the rabbi of the German community in the second half of the 19th cent., initiated educational, cultural, and social welfare activities for the whole J. community. He was a leader of the Hovevei Zion movement. R. Yisrael Salanter, founder of the Musar movement and a resident of M., initiated a Talmud study group and a magazine devoted to Torah subjects. The J. pop. in 1875 was 1,040. Between 1880 and 1886 many Jews without Prussian citizenship were expelled. Jews from Russia resided "temporarily" in M. to ply their trades. In 1905 the J. pop. was 488 (2.4% of the total). After WWI, the French governor appointed by the Allies abol-

"Ma'ale," an urban kibbutz in Memel, Lithuania, 1935

ished all restrictions on the Jews and granted them citizenship. When M. was annexed by independent Lithuania in 1923, Zionist activity increased. David Wolfsohn (1856–1914), Herzl's successor as president of the World Zionist Organization, was raised and educated in M. The J. pop. in 1939 was 7,000 (14% of the total). In March 1939, the German army captured the town and in April all the Jews fled to other places in Lithuania, where they were killed after the German invasion in June 1941. After WWII Jews again began to settle in the town. By 1967 there were 1,000 Jews in M., but no organized community.

MEMMELSDORF Lower Franconia, Germany. Jews first arrived during the Thirty Years War (1618–48). A synagogue was built in the first third of the 19th cent., a cemetery was consecrated in 1835, and a J. public school operated from 1819 to 1912. The J. pop. reached a peak of 97 in 1890 (total 596) and fell to 25 in 1933. On *Kristallnacht* (9–10 Nov. 1938), the synagogue was vandalized. In 1933–39, 24 Jews left for other German cities, 11 of them for Munich.

MEMMINGEN Swabia, Germany. Jews are first mentioned in the second half of the 13th cent. The community was destroyed in the Black Death persecutions of 1348–49 when the Jews were burned alive. Jews returned later in the cent. but by the end of the 15th cent. none remained. Only with the Bavarian annexation of 1802 were restrictions lifted on the presence of Jews for purposes of trade and only in 1862 was permanent residence permitted. Jews contributed significantly to the economic development of the city, opening factories (knitted goods, aluminum, cheese) and dominating the horse and cattle trade. The J. pop. grew to 203 (total 9,600) in 1890. In 1933, 161 Jews remained. In 1933–38, 47 Jews left, 25 of them emigrating. On *Kristallnacht* (9–10 Nov. 1938), the synagogue was wrecked with the participation of local schoolchildren and 23 J. homes were destroyed. A number of Jews were also sent to the Dachau concentration camp. In summer 1940, the remaining Jews were ghettoized in five houses (later reduced to two apartments). Another 57 left in 1939–41, with 42 emigrating from Germany. The community was liquidated in 1942: 22 Jews were deported to Piaski (Po-

Synagogue in Memmingen, Swabia, Germany

land) on 3 April after being held at the Milbertshofen camp near Munich and at least 12 others were sent to the Theresienstadt ghetto. By 1947, 125 Jews, mostly concentration camp survivors, had gathered in the city; most emigrated soon after.

MENA Chernigov dist., Ukraine. Jews settled in the 19th cent., their pop. growing to 1,659 (total 6,277) in 1897 after a train station was built there. In 1939, 586 Jews remained. The Germans captured M. on 8 Sept. 1941 and on 15 Oct., together with Ukrainian police, they murdered 124 Jews. A total of 752 Jews were murdered in the region.

MENDELDORF Nikolaiev dist., Ukraine. In late Aug. 1941, the Germans murdered 143 Jews in the two J. colonies of M. and neighboring Rottendorf.

MENDEN Westphalia, Germany. Jews are known from the mid-17th cent. By the late 17th cent., there were over 30 and they maintained a synagogue. During the 18th cent., the community numbered five to six families. In the 19th cent., the J. pop. was about 50 (total 2,000). A new synagogue was built in 1822 and a cemetery was opened in 1837. In 1848, the J. pop. reached a peak of 133, with several Jews prominent in the grain trade, the paper manufacturing industry, and banking. Five Jews were elected to the municipal council in 1861–78. The J. pop. dropped to 60 in 1880 and 32–36 at the outset of the Nazi era (total 15,000). On *Kristallnacht* (9–10 Nov. 1938), the synagogue was partially burned and the cemetery was desecrated. Thirteen Jews left M. and in April and July 1942, 13 were deported to the camps, where ten perished.

MENGERINGHAUSEN (now part of Arolsen) Hesse, Germany. Established around 1800, this small J. community numbered 21 in 1847 and 1925. Most of the Jews left (some emigrating) before 1938.

MENZEL BOU-ZELFA Grombalia dist., Tunisia. Jews from Nabeul and Tunis settled in the 19th cent, living traditional lives centered a around small synagogue. Between the World Wars they numbered 100–120 (about 2% of the total), living in relative harmony with the Arabs but for the riots of 1917. During WWII and the German occupation, the men were sent to forced labor. After the war, most of the community left for Nabeul and Tunis.

MENZHINSKOYE (until 1936, Ganshtakovka) Stavropol territory, Russia. M. was founded by Mountain Jews (Tats) as a farm settlement in 1928. A J. rural council (soviet) was established in the same year and in 1930 a J. school teaching in the Tat dialect was opened. During the period of collectivization, a J. kolkhoz named Kim was founded. The J. pop. comprised 93 families in 1930 and 70 (about 330 Jews) in 1933. In addition to farming, Jews engaged in crafts. On the eve of the German occupation of late Aug. or early Sept. 1942, a few families, including Ashkenazi Jews, left, leaving behind about 40 families of Mountain Jews and ten Judaizing Subbotniki families. Most were murdered on 19 Sept. at a brickyard in the village of Kurskaya.

MENZINGEN Baden, Germany. Jews were present in the 16th cent. and numbered 96 (total 1,555) in 1875. The last family emigrated to the U.S around the end of 1938.

MEPPEL Drenthe dist., Holland. Jews began to arrive in M. in the early 18th cent. Despite limitations on J. settlement throughout the cent. their numbers continued to increase. The community grew significantly in the first half of the 19th cent., peaking at 512 members in 1892. A number of social welfare organizations were established, as well as a J. school and a branch of the Alliance Israelite. M. was the seat of Drenthe's chief rabbinate from 1853 until 1905. The Jews of M. were engaged primarily in trade and industry. In the 1920s and 1930s the community's pop. declined. The J. pop. in 1941 was 256 (total 13,945). In Aug. 1942, J. men were sent to forced labor. Most of the Jews were deported to the Westerbork transit camp in Oct. Some 30 survived the Holocaust, most in hiding.

MEPPEN Hanover, Germany. A J. family lived in M. in the 18th century. By the mid-19th cent. the J. pop. had increased to more than 60, reaching its peak in 1871 with 95 Jews. The community maintained a cemetery and a J. elementary school, which operated from 1843 to 1918. A synagogue was dedicated in 1855. In June 1933, there were 49 Jews in M. On *Kristallnacht* (9–10 Nov. 1938), SA troops organized a regional pogrom, burning the synagogue in M. and others in neighboring towns. Jews were beaten and humiliated and the men were dispatched to the

Sachsenhausen concentration camp. Of the 49 Jews registered in 1933, 18 moved to other parts of Germany; 14 emigrated (six to England) and ten perished in the Holocaust.

MERANO Italy. The J. presence in M. dates from 1830, when merchants from Central Europe settled in the city. A J. cemetery was established in 1893 and the local synagogue was dedicated in 1901. M. was a summer resort and the site of a famous J. sanatorium. In 1918, M. passed from Austrian to Italian rule. The J. community in M. was recognized in 1921. The communities of Bolzano and Trento were included in its district. In the 1920s and 1930s, Dr. Yehoshua Grunwald was the spiritual leader of the community. In 1922, the community comprised 50 J. families and in 1924, 300 registered Jews, many earning their living as merchants or from the local hotels and medical facilities. When in 1930 the Fascist prefect of M. decreed that no J. inscriptions appear on the tombstones in the J. cemetery, the Jews of Italy protested. Community records indicate that in 1931, 168 J. families resided in M. (about 500 Jews) and that in 1936 there were 200 Jews registered. Prior to 1938, M. was a place of refuge for Jews who had escaped from Hitler's Germany. Community records show 600 Jews registered in M., but only 400 living in the city. The census of 22 Aug. 1938 listed 638 "foreigners" in M. and 133 Italians, altogether 771 Jews. With the promulgation of the 1938 racial laws, many foreigners who had acquired Italian citizenship after 1919 now lost their status and were required to leave. Nevertheless, there were still 359 foreigners in M. after 12 March 1939. In 1940, many local Jews were arrested, but released a few days later. Men and women were seized for forced labor. Others escaped and the J. pop. dropped to 60–80 Jews. On 8 Sept. 1943, the SS occupied M. and by 16 Sept. 1943, 25 local Jews had been taken to the Reichenau (Innsbruck) concentration camp. From there, several months later, some were taken to other death camps, probably to Auschwitz. Of the 25 deported, only one returned. There were 45 Jews in M. in 1945 and 30 in 1970.

MERCHINGEN Baden, Germany. The first Jews settled after the Thirty Years War (1618–48) and by 1740 they numbered 40 families. A synagogue was consecrated in 1737 and a cemetery opened in 1768. A J. elementary school was in operation from the

1830s. In 1850, the J. pop. reached a peak of 325. R. Dr. Y. Blumenstein served as one of the two J. chaplains in the Franco-Prussian War of 1870–71. With emigration and the exodus to the big cities, the J. pop. dropped to 101 in 1900 (total 967) and 39 in 1933. Under Nazi rule, 12 Jews emigrated by 1938 and six in 1939 after the synagogue was vandalized on *Kristallnacht* (9–10 Nov. 1938). Nine others left for other German cities. The last three Jews (and three living in other cities) were deported to the Gurs concentration camp on 22 Oct. 1940; five perished in Auschwitz.

MERCUREA CIUC (Hung. Csikszereda) N. Transylvania dist., Rumania. Jews settled in the late 18th cent. and were employed mainly in the lumber industry. The J. pop. in 1930 was 268 (7% of the total). Zionist activity began in 1925 and increased considerably during the 1930s. In 1941 the Hungarian authorities expelled the Jews, who dispersed throughout the country.

MERCUREA NIRAJULUI (Hung. Nyaradszereda) N. Transylvania dist., Rumania. Jews settled in the mid-19th cent. The J. pop. in 1930 was 225 (14% of the total). The Zionists were active between the World Wars. In May 1944 the community was transferred to the Targu-Mures ghetto and in June deported to Auschwitz.

MEREFA Kharhov dist., Ukraine. The J. pop. in 1939 was 124 (total 5,512). The few Jews who had neither fled nor been evacuated were murdered after the German occupation of 21 Oct. 1941.

MERGENTHEIM, BAD see BAD MERGENTHEIM.

MERK Szatmar dist., Hungary. Jews settled in the late 19th cent. and numbered 85 in 1930. In 1941, SS men murdered 18 Jews sent to forced labor in the Ukraine. In late May 1944, the rest were deported to Auschwitz via Mateszalka.

MERKINE (Yid. Meretch) Alytus dist., Lithuania. Jews first settled in the 15th cent. In the 19th cent. the community maintained *hadarim*, a *talmud torah*, and a J. elementary school. Prior to WWI a small yeshiva was established. The Zionist movements, including Mizrachi, were active despite objections by the community's rabbi. The usual social welfare organizations were maintained. Throughout this period Jews emigrated mainly to America but also to South Africa and Eretz Israel. The J. pop. in 1897 was 1,900 (74% of the total). Between the World Wars Jews survived economically only with outside help. There was much Zionist activity. The J. pop. in 1941 was about 800. During the German invasion in June 1941, the Germans shelled the city center, leaving many Jews homeless. Lithuanian nationalists arrested Jews, especially those connected to the Soviet regime (1940–41), and then murdered them. All the Jews were forced to live in a ghetto. The men were taken to forced labor and from time to time groups of men were killed. On 8 Sept. 1941, 854 Jews were murdered.

MERSEBURG Saxony, Germany. Jews were living in M. already in 973–74, making this one of Germany's oldest J. communities. After suffering during the Black Death persecutions of 1348–49, Jews were expelled in 1514 and 1565. It was not until 1773 that two Jews were again permitted to engage in commerce in M. In the 19th cent., a small community was set up, which was affiliated with the Weissenfels community. The first religious services in M. were only held in 1929. In 1933, there were 50 Jews in M., dropping to six in 1939. There were still four Jews in M. in Oct. 1942. No information about their fate is available.

MERTZWILLER (Ger. Merzweiler) Bas-Rhin dist., France. The J. community numbered 73 members in 1784. Its local synagogue was inaugurated in 1858. In 1865, the J. pop. was 226, dropping to 113 in 1936. During WWII, the Germans expelled all to the south of France with the rest of Alsace-Lorraine Jewry. Altogether 31 were deported. The synagogue was pillaged. In 1965, there were 17 Jews living in M.

MERXHEIM Rhineland, Germany. The J. settlement numbered 37 in the early 19th cent, 65 at mid-cent., and 43 (total 1,300) late in the cent. A synagogue was built in 1853 and later sold. The one built to replace it was closed in the 1920s. In 1933, the J. pop. was 24. Most Jews left before *Kristallnacht* (9–10 Nov. 1938) and the last two shortly after. Fourteen Jews managed to emigrate; five who remained in Germany perished.

MERZHAUSEN (now part of Willingshausen)

Hesse–Nassau, Germany. Jews from Willingshausen and Schrecksbach formed part of the community, which numbered 147 in 1861 and maintained an elementary school (1833–1933). Affiliated with the Marburg rabbinate, the J. pop. dwindled to 20 by 1933. The synagogue was vandalized on *Kristallnacht* (9–10 Nov. 1938) and at least two of the remaining Jews were deported.

MERZIG Saar, Germany. Evidence of J. settlement dates back to the 14th cent. The modern community began to develop in the 18th cent. and a cemetery was established in 1770. In 1808 there were 83 Jews living in M. and 277 by 1905. The community's synagogue was probably dedicated at the beginning of the 19th cent. From 1846 Jews served as town councilors. By 1933, the J. pop. was 159. The Saarland's annexation to the German Reich in 1935 caused many to emigrate and by 1936 there were only 14 Jews in M. The community was subsequently affiliated with Illingen and Neunkirchen. On *Kristallnacht* (9–10 Nov. 1938), the synagogue was burned down, the mortuary at the cemetery was desecrated, and J. businesses and homes were wrecked. On 22 Oct. 1940, at least seven Jews who had remained in M. were deported to the Gurs concentration camp.

MESCHEDE Westphalia, Germany. Six J. families are mentioned in 1802 and in 1829 there were 30 Jews. They engaged in petty trade with one butcher among them. A synagogue was consecrated in 1879. The J. pop. was 103 (total 2,982) in 1895. In 1933, when the Nazis came to power, the J. pop. numbered 45. On *Kristallnacht* (9–10 Nov. 1938), the synagogue and J. homes and stores were wrecked. Most Jews sold off their property and left by 1939. The last couple was deported to a concentration camp in late 1943.

MESERITZ (Pol. Miedzyrzecz) Posen–West Prussia, Germany, today Poland. The first documented reference to Jews dates from 1507, and there are reports in the 16th and 17th cents. of recurring expulsions. In 1656 (during the Swedish wars), Poles executed 100 Jews on trumped-up charges of collaborating with the enemy. A *beit midrash* was destroyed. In the 18th cent., the J. pop swelled, reaching a peak of 850 in 1847 (23% of the total). Jews worked as tailors, bookbinders, distillers, dealers in spirits, and innkeepers. By 1880, the J. pop. had declined to 377. The community maintained a synagogue and a cemetery. On the eve of the Nazi assumption of power in 1933, 105 Jews were living in M. On *Kristallnacht* (9–10 Nov. 1938), the synagogue was set on fire, J. stores were wrecked, and men were taken to the Sachsenhausen concentration camp. In March 1940, the remaining Jews were arrested and interned in the Buergergarten camp near Schneidemuehl and then deported to the east.

MESHCHOVSK Smolensk dist., Russia. Jews probably settled in the early 20th cent., numbering 48 in 1926 and 34 (total 3,629) in 1939. After their arrival in fall 1941, the Germans murdered the few remaining Jews.

MESSEL Hesse, Germany. Jews settled at the beginning of the 18th cent. According to popular tradition, a phenomenally high death rate among the local Jews was curtailed in 1800 when R. Seckel Wormser, the "Ba'al Shem of Michelstadt," urged them to repair their Torah scrolls. Numbering 84 in 1830, the community declined to 21 by 1933 and most of the remaining Jews emigrated before WWII.

MESSELHAUSEN Baden, Germany. The J. community was founded in the late 19th cent. and numbered 86 in 1871. Six Jews remained in 1933 (total 476). Two left for the U.S. in the Nazi era and three were deported to the Gurs concentration camp on 22 Oct. 1940.

MESSURATA (also Misrata) Tripolitania dist., Libya. A J. community was apparently reestablished immediately after the Almohad disturbances of the 12th cent. In the 14th and 15th cents., Jews arrived from Syrte and the community was active until the end of the 15th cent. in the flourishing caravan trade. The trans-Sahara trade revived only in the 17th cent. and Jews again achieved a measure of prosperity, dominating the city's commerce and occupying a J. quarter. Jews traded in farm produce, oil, wool, and spices. In the late 19th cent., the community maintained three synagogues. In 1886 the J. pop. (including the village of Yidder a mile away) was 610. In 1909, the Moslems founded a small school where many J. children studied and where Italian and French were taught. Despite a number of incidents of vandalism in the synagogues (in 1864, 1887, and 1897), relations with the Arabs were generally satisfactory and the

head of the J. community even sided with them against the Italians in the Arab Revolt of 1915–22. Most Jews, however, fled the city together with the Italians. After the suppression of the revolt, the Italians made the city into a dist. capital, bringing a hospital, hotel, movie theater, and high school to the city. Most Jews continued in traditional occupations, owning most of the stores in the market alleyways and engaging in crafts. In 1935, the Italian authorities appointed Yehuda Zanzuri president of the community. Together with the newly appointed chief rabbi of M., R. Yosef Tayyar (known as R. Sasi), he dominated public life in the community. Two of the synagogues were refurbished and a *talmud torah* was established. Together they promoted the founding of a youth club, modeled after the Ben-Yehuda Association, that became a focus of Zionist activity after WWII. Although the Italian racial laws were not felt as strongly in M. as elsewhere, the Jews were discriminated against. While the Arabs could supplement rationing with produce from their farms, the Jews were forced to engage in black market activity, leading to the arrest of many. With the Allied bombing of the city in 1940, the situation of the Jews worsened, forcing them to flee, mainly to Yidder. After the arrival of the British in Jan. 1943, Yehuda Zanzuri was arrested for alleged collaboration with the Italians. R. Moshe Balulu became chief rabbi and did much to revive the community. The Joint Distribution Committee and the OZE relief organization opened soup kitchens and clinics. In 1944, the J. pop. was 1,222. The Jews were untouched by the riots of 1945 and 1948 but anti-J. agitation increased in 1949 after Israel gained its independence. When a J. girl who had been abducted for conversion was found and taken to Israel, the Arabs demanded another 50. Young J. women began to flee to Tripoli and in retaliation J. stores were burned and pillaged. In Aug. 1949, a J. peddler trying to collect debts in an Arab village was murdered. Jews began making preparations for *aliya* and in 1951–52 most left for Israel.

METELIAI Alytus dist., Lithuania. The J. pop. in 1923 was 62 (11% of the total). All the Jews were murdered after the German occupation of 1941.

METTERNICH Rhineland, Germany. The J. pop. was 67 in 1858. Three Jews were deported to the east in 1942.

METZ   Moselle dist., France. The J. presence in M. dates back to the ninth cent. The great Rabbenu Gershom (Me'or ha-Golah; 960–1028) was born here. In 1096, during the First Crusade, 22 Jews were murdered in anti-J. persecutions. The rest of the Jews left. During the 13th cent. Jews are mentioned again in M. but it was only after M. was annexed with Toul and Verdun to France in 1552 that J. residence was officially permitted. By 1592, the community numbered 120 Jews. In 1657, Louis XIV granted privileges to the Jews of M., who by 1677 numbered 665 persons. The coexistence of the Jews in M. with their neighbors was threatened from time to time, such as in 1669–70 and in 1677, when false ritual murder accusations were brought before the courts. By 1718, the community included 480 families. Thirty years later, the community numbered 3,000 members and maintained a cemetery, a synagogue, and an almshouse. Among the illustrious rabbis were Moise Cohen Narol, Yona Teomin-Frankel, Gershon Oulif, and Gavriel Eskeles. In 1764, a Hebrew printing press was established by Moses May. The first rabbi from Alsace recognized by the authorities was Aharon Worms, a native of M. In 1808, a consistory was created in M. which included Moselle and Ardennes and served 6,517 Jews. The local Jews spoke Judeo-Alsacien. The yeshiva in M. became the Rabbinical Seminary of France in 1829. It was transferred to Paris in 1859. Among its graduates were illustrious rabbis, including chief rabbis of France, such as Marchand Ennery, Salomon Ullmann, Isidore Lazare, and Zadoc Kahn. The J. hospice in M., active already for two centuries, attained public recognition in 1833. A charitable society was established by Emmanuel Lambert in 1838. By 1867, the community numbered 2,000 members. After the German annexation in 1871, about 600 Jews left for France but immigrants from other parts of Germany soon replaced them. In 1885, the M. community included 1,446 Jews (with 6,687 in the dist.). In 1910, the J. pop. rose to 1,911, continuing to grow to 4,147 in 1931. A *mikve* (ritual bath) was built in 1929. Under the German occupation in WWII, M., like the rest of Moselle and Alsace, became "free of Jews" (*judenrein*) following the flight of the pop. and expulsion after the entry of the Germans. There were 150 J. refugees interned at the M. fortress. Following deportations, about 1,500 died, including R. Elie Bloch, a youth movement rabbi active in the Resistance. During the war, the Great Synagogue was looted and used as a military warehouse. After lib-

eration the community was reorganized, numbering 3,220 Jews in 1964.

MEUDT   Hesse–Nassau, Germany. Prohibitive taxation impoverished the Jews for almost a century (1750–1845). Numbering 113 (13% of the total) in 1885, the community dwindled to 43 by 1933. Its synagogue was burned down on *Kristallnacht* (9–10 Nov. 1938). Some Jews emigrated; 21 were deported in 1942.

MEZHA   Vitebsk dist., Belorussia. During the Soviet period, a Yiddish-language elementary school (four grades) was in operation. The Germans occupied the village in Oct. 1941 and in Sept. 1942 murdered the 100 Jews still there.

MEZHERICH   Zaporozhe dist., Ukraine. Jews from the Vitebsk and Mogilev regions founded M. as a J. colony in 1846. The J. pop. declined from 540 in 1858 to 448 (total 549) in 1897 and 289 in 1926. In the 1920s, new J. settlers from Podolia and the Vitebsk region founded a J. kolkhoz. A J. elementary school was still operating in the mid-1930s. Shortly after their arrival in Oct. 1941, the Germans murdered the few Jews remaining in M.

MEZHYROV   Vinnitsa dist., Ukraine. Jews settled in the mid-18th cent. and included 64 poll tax payers in 1784. In 1897, the J. pop. was 1,345 (total 2,268) and in 1926, under the Soviets, it was 1,015. Most Jews were members of artisan cooperatives or kolkhozes (70 families). A J. school was active. The occupying Germans murdered 279 Jews in the second half of April 1942. According to another source, 800 were brought to Brailow for execution.

MEZOBERENY   Bekes dist., Hungary. Jews settled in the mid-19th cent., founding a spinning mill with over 100 workers. A J. school was opened in 1879 and a synagogue in 1884. The J. pop. was 319 (2.5% of the total) in 1890. In 1941, 152 remained. All were deported to Auschwitz or Austria via Budapest and Bekescsaba on 26 June 1944.

MEZOCSAT   Borsod dist., Hungary. Jews were present in the mid-18th cent. In 1880, numbering 487, they built a new synagogue. They also operated a J. school and yeshiva. The poet Jozsef Kiss (1843–

Zionist youth group, Mezokovesd, Hungary, 1938

1921) was born here. In 1930, the J. pop. was 536. Zionist activity was carried out by Mizrachi. Many died in the Ukraine under forced labor from 1942. In early June 1944, the rest were deported to Auschwitz via Goromboly (near Miskolc). Eighty survivors reestablished the community but most left after 1956.

MEZOKERESZTES Borsod dist., Hungary. A community of 215 existed in 1880, growing to 257 in 1930 and operating an elementary school for 30 children. All were deported to Auschwitz via Miskolc on 12–15 June 1944.

MEZOKOVACSHAZA Csanad dist., Hungary. Jews were present in 1840. Their pop. rose from 92 in 1880 to 269 in 1920 and 382 in 1930. A synagogue was built in 1912 and a yeshiva was founded by R. Aharon David Rubinstein. The 1938 racial laws hurt J. livelihoods and in 1944 the local authorities implemented on their own initiative the full scope of the laws. On 15 May 1944, the Jews were brought to Bekescsaba and from there deported on 25–26 June to Auschwitz and Austria. Most of those sent to Austria survived the war. The postwar community of 108 dwindled to about ten families by 1963.

MEZOKOVESD Borsod dist., Hungary. The modern J. community was formed in the early 19th cent., numbering 275 in 1880, 862 in 1920 (4.6% of the total), and 798 in 1941. The community maintained a synagogue, yeshiva, and school. After WWI, M. was occupied by the Rumanian army, which persecuted the Jews. Later, the Hungarian White Terror gangs attacked the Jews for cooperating with the Rumanians. The Zionists, mainly Mizrachi, were active prior to WWI. The Jews were deported to Auschwitz via Miskolc on 12–15 June 1944.

MEZOLADANY   Szabolcs dist., Hungary. Jews settled in the early 19th cent., numbering 97 in 1880 and 133 in 1930. On 25–27 May 1944, they were deported to Auschwitz via Kisvarda.

MEZOSZILAS   (also Szilasbalhas) Veszprem dist., Hungary. A J. community of 151 existed in 1880, operating a beautiful synagogue and a J. school until 1928. Most J. families left following the White Terror attacks (1919–21). The few who remained were deported to Auschwitz via Veszprem at the beginning of July 1944.

MEZOTUR   Jasz–Nagykun–Szolnok dist., Hungary. Jews arrived in the first half of the 19th cent., reaching a peak pop. of 836 (3% of the total) in 1900 and then declining steadily to 406 in 1941. Jews operated brick and lumber yards and a weaving mill. They opened a school in 1859 and formed a Neologist community. In 1940, 150 men were taken to forced labor and then in 1942, another 30. At the end of June 1944, the remaining Jews were deported to Auschwitz and Austria via Nagykanizsa and Szolnok. The postwar community of 210 dwindled to 26 by 1961.

MGLIN   Oriol dist., Russia. Jews probably settled in the early 19th cent. Their pop. rose from 1,920 in 1847 to 2,674 (total 7,640) in 1897. Pogroms were staged in 1882 and late 1918. In the latter, Red Army soldiers killed 15 Jews, injured others, and looted numerous J. homes. In the Soviet period, the J. pop. dropped to 1,244 in 1926 and 726 in 1939. The Germans occupied the town on 18 Aug. 1941. On 21 Jan. 1942, all the Jews were imprisoned in the local jail, 60 soon dying of hunger, disease, and the cold. About 600 from M. and its environs were murdered on 2 March 1942.

MIADZIOL-NOVY   Vilna dist., Poland, today Belarus. Jews apparently settled in the first half of the 19th cent., their pop. reaching 436 (total 1,164) in 1895. After WWI, 60 J. families remained, 30 of them owning

stores and barely earning a living in the face of heavy taxes. J. artisans were even worse off because of local competition. The Germans arrived in June 1941, establishing a *Judenrat* and ghetto under a regime of forced labor and extortion. After 70–80 Jews escaped to the forest, 100 were executed, but a partisan attack in Oct. 1942 under J. command liberated the remaining 90 Jews, who safely reached the Soviet Union.

MIASTKOVKA   Vinnitsa dist., Ukraine. Jews numbered 604 in 1765 and 2,105 (total 7,996) in 1897. In the 1880s, most of the town's 30 store were in J. hands. After the Oct. 1917 Revolution, a number of pogroms were staged against the Jews (on 30 Oct. 1917 and in 1919) in which J. property was heavily damaged. In the 1920s, a J. council (soviet) and J. school were in operation. Jews belonged to artisan cooperatives and 120 (in the late 1920s) worked in a J. kolkhoz. In 1939, the J. pop. was 832. The Germans occupied M. on 21 July 1941. After it was annexed to Transnistria, a ghetto was established and Jews from Bukovina and Bessarabia were expelled there. Many died of starvation and disease.

MICHALANY   (Hung. Alsomihalyi) Slovakia, Czechoslovakia, today Republic of Slovakia. Jews are mentioned in 1746 and again in the early 19th cent. Their pop. rose from 60 in 1869 to 90 (total 712) in 1910 and stood at 77 in 1941. After WWI, Jews served on the local council and owned most of the business establishments in the town. A synagogue was erected in 1934. After the annexation to Hungary in Nov. 1938, Jews were mobilized for forced labor and their livelihoods undermined. On 21 May 1944, they were deported to Auschwitz via the Satoraljaujhely ghetto.

MICHALISZKI   Vilna dist., Poland, today Belarus. A community of 396 taxpaying Jews was present in 1765. They were permitted by the local nobility to purchase one-acre plots of land where they could set up auxiliary farms. The Jews were shopkeepers, artisans, and wholesalers dealing in lumber and flax. By 1897 their pop. had grown to 951 (total 1,224). Most lost their property in WWI, and required assistance from the relief agencies in the aftermath. However, recovery was stunted by stiff competition from the Polish cooperatives. Yiddish and Hebrew schools were founded between the World Wars and the Zionist youth movements became active. After two years of Soviet rule

(1939–41), the Germans arrived on 24 June 1941, instituting a regime of forced labor and persecution. In fall 1941 a ghetto was established for the town's 1,500 Jews. On 25 March 1943, after Jews from other ghettoes had been brought there, all were sent to Vilna and Kovno, but most were detoured within a few days to Ponary for execution.

MICHALOVCE (Hung. Nagymihaly) Slovakia, Czechoslovakia, today Republic of Slovakia. One J. family is mentioned in the census of 1726 and eight in 1746, most living on the estates of nobles. In the early 19th cent., Jews began arriving from neighboring villages and a 300-seat synagogue was built, subsequently becoming a hasidic *klaus*. A new synagogue in the Oriental style was built in 1888 as the J. pop. increased to 1,079 in 1880 and 1,492 (total 4,906) in 1900. A *beit midrash*, *heder*, and *talmud torah* were also built in this period. R. Shimon Ehrenfeld, who served in 1893–1932, ran a yeshiva with 80 students. The Zionists became active in the early 20th cent. and an Agudat Israel group began operating in 1913. After WWI, J. businesses were looted in riots and there was considerable damage to J. property. The J. pop. grew steadily, to 2,200 in 1910, 3,386 in 1930, and 4,197 in 1940, with J. refugees from Galicia arriving in WWI and joining the hasidic congregation. Jews served on the municipal and district councils and owned numerous stores and workshops. Zionist activity intensified between the World Wars, with WIZO and Mizrachi the first to open branches and the youth movements attracting most of the young (300 in Hashomer Hatzair; 250 in Bnei Akiva). A Beth Jacob school was opened in the 1930s but the first J. elementary school was only opened in 1939–40, expanding to include the junior high school grades after J. children were expelled from the public schools. The school eventually reached an enrollment of 500. In 1941, the authorities closed down 436 J. businesses and dozens of men were seized for forced labor. On 25 March 1942, 120 J. girls were deported to Auschwitz via Poprad and in early April, 100 young men were sent to the Majdanek concentration camp via Zilina. Several young men managed to escape from the deportations and joined up with the partisans. In early May, about 3,100 Jews were deported to the Lublin dist. of Poland, including nearly two-thirds to the Lukow ghetto where most perished. The remaining 1,000 Jews were sent to western Slovakia on 15 May 1944 as the fighting

neared the city. About half of the postwar community of 600 left for Israel in 1949. A few dozen Jews remained in 1995.

MICHALOWO-NIEZABUDKA Bialystok dist., Poland. Jews first settled in the mid-19th cent, entering the thriving cloth industry which German industrialists had established. Some bought up discarded hand looms and developed a home industry. Young Jews were in the forefront of the fight against the long hours and exploitation of child labor at the factories. With the decline of the industry after 1906, many Jews emigrated, their number dropping from 1,033 in 1897 to 887 (total 2,176) in 1921. During WWI, Jews worked abandoned farms to feed themselves. After the war, economic difficulties continued under heavy taxes and stiff competition. Mutual aid societies and a YEKOPO-sponsored bank offered relief. In the mid-1920s, a Bund-supported CYSHO Yiddish school joined the Hebrew school founded by the Zionists before the war. The leading Zionist party was Po'alei Zion and the most popular youth movement Hashomer Hatzair. An Orthodox anti-Zionist Neturei Karta group was also prominent. Afer two years of Soviet rule in 1939–41, the Germans captured the town on 29 June 1941, confining its 800 Jews to a ghetto. In Nov. 1942 they were brought to the old Polish cavalry barracks near Bialystok and from there deported to the Treblinka death camp. Most of the 50 young Jews who managed to escape were subsequently caught and murdered.

MICHAYLOVSKAYA Krasnodar territory, Russia. In 1917, there were four prayer houses in the village, mostly serving converts. There were also Karaites present. A Tarbut school founded by the Zionists was closed down shortly after the Soviets seized power. When the Germans arrived in summer 1942, they murdered those Jews who had neither fled nor been evacuated, most of them refugees.

MICHELBACH AN DER LUECKE Wuerttemberg, Germany. The first Jews were apparently refugees from Rothenburg (1519–20). The community grew rapidly in the 19th cent., numbering 216 (total 692) in 1869 but thereafter declining steadily through emigration. The first synagogue was built in 1755 and a J. school was founded in the 1830s. From the second half of the 19th cent., Jews were mainly engaged in the cattle and horse trade and were among the town's wealthier residents, fully involved in local life. The Gundelfinger family were social leaders and founders of large steel plants in Nuremberg and Ulm. In 1933, 33 Jews remained, suffering from the social and economic boycott imposed by the Nazis. Thirteen emigrated and of the 18 sent to ghettoes in Riga (1 Dec. 1941) and Theresienstadt (22 Aug. 1942), two survived.

MICHELFELD   Baden, Germany. A community existed from the late 16th cent., reaching a peak pop. of 242 in 1841 and operating a synagogue, cemetery, and elementary school. The two J. families present in 1933 dispersed in the Nazi era.

MICHELSTADT   Hesse, Germany. Established around 1740, the community rebuilt its synagogue in 1791, when it comprised 18 families. J. life flourished in the first half of the 19th cent., thanks largely to R. Seckel Loeb Wormser (1768–1847), the "Ba'al Shem of M." who opened a yeshiva attended by 70 students in 1805. He gained particular renown as a healer, devising treatments that combined herbal remedies with science and Kabbalah. Legends were woven around the "Ba'al Shem" and pilgrimages were made to his grave, non-Jews maintaining this practice in secret during the Nazi era. At its height, in 1871, the community numbered 194 (6% of the total). Its members, affiliated with the Orthodox rabbinate of Darmstadt, were sheltered from antisemitism until the 1930s. On *Kristallnacht* (9–10 Nov. 1938), however, the synagogue's interior was destroyed (although Torah scrolls had been rescued in advance), J. stores were looted, and Jews sent to the Buchenwald concentration camp. Of the 91 Jews living there in 1933, 48 emigrated (mostly to the U.S.) and 14 were deported in 1942–43. After WWII, the grave of the "Ba'al Shem" was restored and the newly repaired synagogue was transformed into a J. historical museum

MICHOW   Lublin dist., Poland. Jews are first mentioned in the second half of the 17th cent. In the mid-19th cent. they became prominent in the pottery industry. Their pop. grew to 1,643 (total 2,791) in 1897. After WWI, economic conditions deteriorated in the face of heavy taxes and tight credit and antisemitism was widespread. Although the community was tradition-oriented, young Jews were drawn to the Zionist youth movements. The Germans captured M. on 23

Sept. 1939 and soon confined the Jews to a ghetto in Lukow, which came to include 700 Jews from Lysobyki as well. The overcrowded conditions led to a typhoid epidemic. On 6 June 1942, all were expelled to Opole, the men subsequently removed to an unknown destination and the rest deported, apparently to the Sobibor death camp.

MICULA   (Hung. Mikola) N. Transylvania dist., Rumania. Jews settled in the late 18th cent. The J. pop. in 1920 was 132 (8% of the total). In May 1944 the community was transferred to the Satu Mare ghetto and in June deported to Auschwitz.

MIDDELBURG   Zeeland dist., Holland. Portuguese J. traders lived there in the early 17th cent. and a Sephardi community developed. Freedom of J. religious practice was granted in 1700. In the early 18th cent., many left for Amsterdam and The Hague, ending the Portuguese community. In 1725, the few remaining Portuguese Jews joined the Ashkenazi community established in the late 17th cent. This community grew significantly in the first half of the 19th cent. Early in the cent. a J. school was established. The community's numbers began to dwindle towards the end of the cent., however, as Jews from M. and the surrounding villages moved to larger towns. There were 429 Jews in 1850 but only 56 by 1941 (total 18,079). In March 1942, all were evacuated to Amsterdam and deported to camps from there.

MIDDELHARNIS   Zuid-Holland dist., Holland. A community was formed with neighboring villages in 1800 and 102 Jews lived there in 1892. The J. pop. in 1941 was 42 (total 4,780). All but one were deported and perished in the Holocaust.

MIECHOW   Kielce dist., Poland. Although Jews are not mentioned before 1862, M. being one of the 42 settlements in Poland with a *de non tolerandis Judaeis* privilege, there apparently were some present before then. The increase of the J. pop. to 1,436 (total 3,731) in 1897 was no doubt related to the creation of a rail link with Silesia and central Poland in the 1880s. In the late 19th cent., Jews were especially active in the salt trade as well as producing and selling alcoholic beverages and importing wines and spices from Hungary and the Ottoman Empire. Jews were also prominent in the tanning industry, operating five

Neighbors chatting, Miechow, Poland, 1932

major hide-processing plants and 40 smaller ones in the late 19th cent. With the decline of the salt industry, Jews became active in the lumber industry, exporting to the Austrian Empire and Danzig. Orthodox circles vehemently resisted first Haskala and later the socialists and Zionists, who began to organize in 1894. In the first decade of the 20th cent., boys' and girls' schools for supplementary Hebrew education were opened. A *talmud torah* was founded in 1911. In 1920, Jews suffered from rampaging Polish gangs and a typhoid epidemic. Between the World Wars, the J. pop. was around 2,500. Most Jews continued to earn their livelihoods in trade. Of the 367 J. artisans in 1920, nearly half were employed in the garment industry. The Zionists controlled the community council throughout most of the period and numerous youth movements were active. The Germans captured the city on 3 Sept. 1939. A *Judenrat* was soon set up. In April 1940, German soldiers broke into J. homes and stores, beating and robbing their owners and raping women. Large numbers of J. refugees arrived, including 1,000 from Cracow in summer 1940. In Sept.

1941, all were confined to a ghetto. On 28 Aug. 1942, 600 of the sick and old were transferred to Slomniki and many murdered there. On 4 Sept., after 800–900 of the able-bodied were dispatched to labor camps in Prokoczim and Plaszow, the rest of the Jews were deported to the Belzec death camp. A final 600 survivors from the province were concentrated in the ghetto in Nov. 1942 and then executed in the Chodow forest. Some 27 Poles from the area were executed by the Germans for helping to hide Jews.

MIEDZESZYNEK (Miedzeszyn) WILLE Warsaw dist., Poland. The J. community only began to develop after WWI and numbered about 100. In the 1920s, the Bund founded a convalescent home for children of the region. About 100 of its children were brought to the Falenica orphanage after the German occupation in Sept. 1939 and from there deported to their deaths in the Treblinka death camp on 18 Aug. 1942.

MIEDZNA Lublin dist., Poland. Jews probably settled in the late 17th cent. In 1897, their pop. was 150 (total 1,013). In 1920 they were attacked by Polish soldiers and peasants. In WWII, they were most likely deported by the Germans to the Treblinka death camp.

MIEDZNO Kielce dist., Poland. About 90 Jews were present in the village in 1880 and 30 families before WWII. Most were poor. After their arrival in Sept. 1939, the Germans murdered 12 young men, probably in the Buchenwald concentration camp. All but nine families were transferred to Brzuki Island in 1941. Some were selected for forced labor, but most were deported to Auschwitz-Birkenau on 22 June 1942 via Kuznicka.

MIEHLEN Hesse–Nassau, Germany. Jews lived there from 1780, numbering 63 (4% of the total) in 1871 and 47 in 1924. The interior of the synagogue built in 1873 was destroyed by SA troops in Sept. 1935. Most Jews left before Nov. 1938, some emigrating to Palestine.

MIELEC Cracow dist., Poland. The community began to develop in the 18th cent., soon forming a majority of the pop. despite repressive measures under Austrian rule. Economic conditions improved in the second half of the 19th cent., with all trade and crafts in J. hands and the pop. reaching 3,280 (total 6,135) in 1910. Noteworthy was the lively export trade in feathers. Economic crises at the turn of the cent. and a great fire in 1904 set the community back considerably. R. Yaakov Naftali Tzevi Horowitz founded a branch of the hasidic Ropshits dynasty there. The Zionists became active in 1894 and a Baron Hirsch school was founded in 1896. In WWI, Russian soldiers left a trail of rape and robbery, taking J. hostages when they withdrew in 1915. Three pogroms shook the community in 1918–19. Hundreds of Jews emigrated or were killed in the war, leaving the J. pop. at 2,807 in 1921. Between the World Wars, Zionist activity developed while Agudat Israel controlled the community council. The German occupation commenced on 8 Sept. 1939. In retaliation for J. violation of a ritual slaughter ban prior to Rosh Hashanah (14 Sept.), the Germans burned to death 150 Jews locked up in the building housing the synagogue and ritual bath. Forced labor ensued, with many sent to the Pustkow camp. In the *Aktion* of 9 March 1942, over 1,000 more of the refugee-swelled pop. were sent to the camp from the ghetto and 500

of the "unproductive" were murdered before the remaining 3,000 were dispersed to settlements in the Lublin dist. (Poland) to share the fate of local Jews.

MIELIGIANY Vilna dist., Poland, today Belarus. The first Jews apparently arrived in 1903, earning their livelihoods as shopkeepers, peddlers, and artisans while operating auxiliary farms. In 1931 they numbered 25 families. With the arrival of the Germans in June 1941, Lithuanian officials robbed and persecuted the Jews. On 27 Sept. 1941 the Jews were expelled to the Poligon transit camp (near Swienciany). They were murdered there on 7 Oct.

MIELNICA (I) Tarnopol dist., Poland, today Ukraine. Jews were present from the second half of the 18th cent. with the pop. growing to 1,429 (40% of the total) in 1880, subsequently declining through emigration, and then rising again between the World Wars to its previous level. A fire in 1935 added to the economic distress of J. tradesmen in the face of competition from the Ukrainian and Polish cooperatives. Soviet rule in 1939–41 brought confiscations of property and the closure of J. institutions. With the Soviet evacuation, the local Ukrainian pop. went on an anti-J. rampage that was only stopped short of a pogrom a few days later with the arrival of the Hungarian army on 8 July 1941. The German takeover in Aug. intensified the reign of terror, with Gestapo units and drunken border police making night raids on J. homes to pillage, murder, and rape. Despite the thinning out of the pop. through forced labor consignments and flight, the number of Jews grew to around 2,500 with the arrival of refugees. On 26 Sept. 1942, up to 2,000 were deported to the Belzec death camp after 100–300 were murdered in the town. The remaining few hundred were expelled to the Borszczow ghetto in Oct.; 28 survived in hiding and about 100 found refuge in the Soviet Union.

MIELNICA (II) Volhynia dist., Poland, today Ukraine. Jews probably settled after the granting of the municipal charter in 1569, numbering 1,599 (total 2,588) in 1897 and 875 (total 1,372) in 1921. The Germans took M. on 26 June 1941, first killing 60 Jews after alleging that their relatives had been Komsomol members during Soviet rule in 1939–1941. Another 280 J. males were murdered on 16 July. The rest were executed on 3 Sept. 1942.

MIELNICZNE   Lwow dist., Poland, today Ukraine. The J. pop. in 1921 was 110. The Jews were expelled to Turka for liquidation in July 1942.

MIELNIK   Bialystok dist., Poland, today Belarus. Jews arrived in the 16th cent. as tax collectors. An organized community was only formed in the 18th cent. A synagogue was built in the first half of the 19th cent. and the J. pop. grew to 460 (total 1,147) in 1878, most living in poverty. Many emigrated to the U.S. after WWI, the J. pop. dropping to 180 in 1937. A small factory for manufacturing oven bricks was set up in a rare J.-Polish partnership, but economic conditions remained difficult. Most children attended a CYSHO Yiddish school. After the German occupation of June 1941, the town's 260 Jews (including refugees) were expelled to the Siemiatycze ghetto and on 2 Nov. 1942 deported to the Treblinka death camp.

MIENDZYRZEC KORECKI   (Yid. Mezhirech) Volhynia dist., Poland, today Ukraine. Jews are recorded from 1569. The town suffered in the Chmielnicki massacres of 1648–49 and was destroyed in the early 18th cent. during the Swedish war but recovery was rapid. Dov Baer, the *Maggid* of Mezhirech, was active in the town in 1761–72, making it a hasidic center. The J. pop reached 2,107 in 1897 (total 3,131), falling to 1,743 in 1921. After the Feb. 1917 Revolution the Zionists began to operate openly, intensifying their activity between the World Wars through the youth movements with their pioneer training. There was a Hebrew school and kindergarten. With the occupation of M. on 6 July 1941 by the Germans, a *Judenrat* was established and a regime of forced labor and extortion followed; most of the 160 young Jews sent to Kiev in Oct. 1941 were killed or died under the harsh work conditions. On 22 May 1942, most of the Jews were rounded up and executed beside freshly dug pits. The remaining 950 were confined to a ghetto. Almost all were executed on 26 Sept. 1942.

MIENDZYRZEC PODLASKI   (Yid. Mezhirech, Mezrich) Lublin dist., Poland. Jews first settled in the 16th cent. M. was one of the first places in Poland where Hebrew books were printed, with a J. press operating in 1595. In the Chmielnicki massacres of 1648–49, 300 Jews were murdered. A synagogue was consecrated in 1700. In the 19th cent., Jews played a leading

role in the city's brush bristle industry. The J. pop. grew from 3,612 in 1827 to 9,042 (total 11,493) in 1897 and 9,455 in 1921. R. Yaacov Kranz, the Dubno *Maggid*, resided there and numerous hasidic groups maintained *shtiblekh*. R. Meir Shelomo Yehuda Rabinowicz established a court there and R. David Bleicher founded a Beit Yosef yeshiva as a branch of the Musar yeshiva in Nowogrodek. The Zionists became active in 1893, a group of 20 founding the farming village (*moshava*) of Yesod ha-Ma'ala in Eretz Israel. The J. labor movement was also active. After WWI, many J. orphans were brought to M. and eventually sent to families in Canada. The loss of the Russian and Austrian markets and the general economic crisis following the war reduced many Jews to petty trade and peddling, where they faced stiff competition from Polish merchants and cooperatives. In the late 1920s, Jews opened new factories (steel wire, batteries, light bulbs) and operated three flour mills. Many entered the professions, but economic conditions remained difficult. Hundreds of Jews joined mutual aid societies providing easy credit and the community operated extensive welfare services, including a soup kitchen, orphanage, hospital, and clinics. Zionist activity was also extensive. In the 1920s, Hashomer Hatzair had nearly 500 members and in the 1930s the Gordonia branch had 200–300. Tarbut, CYSHO, and Beth Jacob schools all operated. In the 1927 municipal elections, J. parties held 17 of 24 council seats. On the final retreat of the Red Army in late Sept. 1939, about 2,000 mostly young Jews fled east. The Germans captured M. permanently on 9 Oct. In Dec. a *Judenrat* was established and at the same time refugees began to arrive, the overcrowding leading to a typhoid epidemic. Thousands were sent to labor camps and others were employed in brush factories. On 25 May 1942, 800 Jews were deported to the Treblinka death camp. On 25–26 Aug., 12,000 Jews were herded into the city square. About 1,000 of the sick and old were shot and the rest sent to Treblinka. Those still working for the Germans were confined to a ghetto, soon joined by surviving Jews in the Radzin province. More were deported to Majdanek and Treblinka in Oct. 1942. In Dec., 550 brush factory workers and their families were brought to Trawniki; in Nov. 1943 they were all murdered in Treblinka. In new roundups starting in May 1943, another 3,000 were sent to Treblinka and hundreds more murdered locally. Of the last 1,000 Jews, 700 came out of hiding in despair and were sent to the Majdanek concentration camp; the other 300 were soon found and murdered.

MIHAILENI Moldavia dist., Rumania. Jews settled in the late 18th cent. and a community was organized in 1897, numbering 2,447 (66% of the total) in 1899. Jews manufactured wagons and supplied them to the entire area. M. was a center of Yiddish and Hebrew culture. In 1930, 300 of the 424 voters electing the municipal council voted for the J. party. After Bessarabia was annexed to the USSR in June 1940, Jews in M. were arrested by the Rumanian army and charged with planning to assist the Russians. On 21 June 1941 the Jews were taken through Bucecea to Dorohoi and on 8 Nov. they were deported to Mogilev in Transnistria. About half returned after the war.

MIHOVA Bukovina, Rumania, today Ukraine. Jews settled in the late 19th cent. and numbered 356 in 1880. Zionist activity began after WWI and many Jews emigrated to Palestine. The J. pop. in 1930 was 243. Antisemitism was rife in the 1930s. In June 1941 the J. pop. was deported to Transnistria. Many were killed in the Tarasiwca camp. The few survivors left for Palestine.

MIKASZEWICZE Polesie dist., Poland, today Belarus. The community dates from the late 19th cent. and numbered around 400 in the 1930s. All were executed by the Germans on 6 Aug. 1942.

MIKHALPOL (from 1944, Mikhailovka) Kamenets-Podolski dist., Ukraine. Jews settled in the first half of the 18th cent., numbering 356 in 1765 and 1,392 in 1897. A J. rural council and kolkhoz were active in the Soviet period. In 1939 the J. pop. was 728 (34% of the total). The Germans occupied M. on 11 July 1941, murdering 60 Jews inside the town. The rest were brought to Yarmolnitsy with other Jews from the area and executed in fall 1942. The Nazis also destroyed the local synagogue, a wooden structure with colorful decorations dating from the 18th cent.

MIKHAYLOVKA Zaporozhe dist., Ukraine. J residence was permitted from 1903. The J. pop. was 926 (total 23,568) in 1910 and 102 in 1939. The Germans captured M. on 4 Oct. 1941, murdering about 50 Jews in mid-Nov. and 120 J. children from M. and the surrounding area in the local children's home in March 1942.

MIKOLAJOW (I) Stanislawow dist., Poland, today Ukraine. Jews were present from the early 17th cent. but suffered from residence restrictions until the 19th. The J. pop. grew steadily to 632 in 1910 (total 3,448) but dropped by 20% in the wake of WWI and the violence instigated by General Denikin's White Army troops and the Petlyura gangs. The Germans took possession of the town on 3 July 1941, initiating a regime of extortion and forced labor. Most of the Jews were deported to the Belzec death camp in the summer of 1942. The rest were executed in the course of the following year.

MIKOLAJOW (II) Lwow dist., Poland, today Ukraine. Present from the late 19th cent., the community numbered 315 (total 938) in 1921 and was expelled by the Germans to the Bobrka ghetto in the second half of 1942.

MIKSTAT Poznan dist., Poland. The community was established after the reannexation to Prussia in 1815, growing to a peak of 152 (total 1,437) in 1871. In 1921, there were 61 Jews. The few dozen present when the Germans arrived in Sept. 1939 were expelled to General Gouvernement territory.

MIKULICZYN Stanislawow dist., Poland, today Ukraine. J. settlement began in the late 19th cent. and received a big economic boost when the town developed into a health and tourist resort. The permanent J. pop. reached 552 in 1921 (total 5,310) but most of the 4,000–5,000 tourists were also Jews. The Maccabi World Union sports organization set up its national center there between the World Wars and the Zionist groups ran summer camps. The Soviet occupation of 1939 brought nationalization. The arrival of the Hungarian army on 30 June 1941 led to widespread confiscations. With the Germans taking charge soon after, the J. pop. was murdered off in three separate *Aktions* at the end of 1941.

MIKULINCE Tarnopol dist., Poland, today Ukraine. Jews are first mentioned in the early 18th cent. and comprised two-thirds of the pop. in 1880 with 2,411 residents, providing the town with mayors and other leading figures. A fire in 1903 extensively damaged the community, hastening the emigration trend which depleted the pop. to 1,891 by 1921. Economic conditions deteriorated under Polish rule between the

World Wars. Zionist activity became extensive but was challenged politically by Agudat Israel, which drew support from the Hasidim (Ruzhin dynasty). The Germans entered the town on 5 July 1941 after a heavy bombardment, unleashing a Ukrainian pogrom that claimed J. lives. Arrests of leading Jews followed and Jews were systematically stripped of their possessions, including even food supplies, and put to forced labor. Confined to a special quarter, the Jews were rounded up on 31 Aug. 1942, with 1,200 deported to the Belzec death camp and 80–100 murdered in the town. The few dozen who escaped were expelled two months later and met a similar fate.

MIKULINO   Smolensk dist., Russia. M. was located in the J. Pale of Settlement. The J. pop. was 530 in 1847 and 1,171 (total 1,527) in 1897, dropping to 403 under the Soviets. After the German occupation in mid-July 1941, the Jews were expelled to Rudniya, where they were murdered on 24 Oct.

MIKULOV   (Yid. Nikolsburg) Moravia (Sudetenland), Czechoslovakia. Jews are mentioned as money-lenders in 1369 but the community was probably founded in 1420 by refugees from Vienna, joined in 1454 by refugees from Brno, Olomouc, and Znojmo. In 1591, the House of Dietrichstein granted a charter which gave the Jews a measure of autonomy. Additional refugees arrived in the wake of the Chmielnicki massacres of 1648–49 and 80 families expelled from Vienna settled in 1670. The Familiants Law of 1798 fixed the J. residence quota at 620 families, making the community the second largest in Bohemia and Moravia after Prague until emigration to Vienna and Hungary commenced after 1848, when the J. pop. reached a peak of 3,670 (total 10,000). M. was the seat of Moravia's chief rabbi (*Landesrabbiner*) from the 16th cent. to 1851. Among those who served were R. Menahem Mendel Krochmal (1648–61), who chaired the 1652 conference formulating the well-known "311 Regulations" that guided J. life in Moravia. The community maintained a famous yeshiva and a J. elementary school, as well as a school for deaf and dumb children, the only one in the state. In the mid-19th cent., at least 12 synagogues were in operation. By the 20th cent., only two remained open as the J. pop. dropped to 1,917 in 1869, 900 in 1900, and 437 in 1930. The J. cemetery probably dated to the 15th cent. M. was the largest J. community in Moravia with political

autonomy (*politische Gemeinden*), lasting from 1848 to 1919. Jews were prominent in the wine industry but most were peddlers and others artisans. The Zionists were active after WWI. Nearly all the Jews left the city the day after the signing of the Munich Agreement on 1 Oct. 1938. The remaining 30 left for Znojmo within the following weeks. Those who failed to emigrate from the country were deported to the Theresienstadt ghetto via Brno in late 1941–early 1942 and from there transported to the death camps of Poland. Only 40 survived.

MILAN   Lombardy, Italy. The presence of the Jews in M. is recorded in the Roman period. In 1320, the local Jews were expelled. In 1387, Duke Gian Galeazzo Visconti granted the Jews of Lombardy privileges, which were confirmed by Francesco Sforza and his successors. From time to time, though, they were expelled. A famous privilege was granted by Francesco II Sforza in 1533 to the Jews of the Duchy of Milan. In 1535, M. came under Spanish rule and Jews were not allowed to reside in M. until 1714, when it came under Austrian rule. In 1832, a piece of land was bought for the use of a J. cemetery. In 1840, a synagogue was built. Officially, the community was established in 1856. In 1859, M. became part of the new Italian kingdom and the local Jews were emancipated. In 1869, the community numbered 630 and in 1886, 1,100. A new synagogue was established in 1892. Alessandro da Fano served as the community's rabbi. In 1892, the beginnings of Hebrew schooling in M. began with the opening of a kindergarten; in 1910 three elementary school classes were added. More classes were opened over the next two decades and in 1935 the school was named after R. Da Fano. With the development of M. as a commercial and industrial center, the Jews prospered and the community grew. By 1900, the community numbered 2,000 members and in 1910, 4,500. Albert Einstein lived in M. with his parents between 1894 and 1900. In the mid-1920s, J. life in M. revived. There were various cultural and social activities and the Zionists became active. According to the 1930 law reforming the J. communities in Italy, M. was designated one of the 26 communities recognized by the government. The M. district comprised the communities of Como, Pavia, Monza (50 Jews in 1936), Voghera (20 Jews in 1936), Varese, Legano, Busto Arsizio, and Gallarate. In the 1930s, the community maintained a Hebrew school, several welfare organizations, a Zionist group, a women's association, etc. In 1933, a council was established in M. to assist refugees from Germany. In 1937, an old age home was inaugurated. In 1938, Prof. G. Castelbolognesi served as rabbi of the community. The Hebrew high school in Milan was established after the racial laws were promulgated and J. pupils were expelled from state schools. In 1936, in the M. district, 10,000 Jews were listed and 12,000 in 1938,. Between 1939 and 1941, about 5,000 escaped to Palestine and the U.S. On the eve of the German occupation there were 4,500 Jews in Milan itself. Between Sept. and Oct. 1943, at least 1,500 escaped to Switzerland. During WWII, Allied bombing destroyed the local synagogue. The Nazis deported 896 local Jews to the death camps. Only 50 survived. Many were captured in the towns and villages where they were hiding out. By 1948, the community numbered 2,885 Italian Jews and 1,665 foreign nationals. After 1949, immigrants from Egypt and from other Arab countries arrived. A new synagogue was built in 1953. By 1965, the community numbered 8,488 persons, mostly Sephardi Jews. After 1967, more immigrants arrived from Egypt and Libya. Besides the Central Synagogue practicing the Italian rite, seven other synagogues operate according to various rites. The community published various newspapers: *La Rassegna Mensile d'Israel, Il Bollettino della Comunita di Milano, Hed ha-Hinukh ha-Yehudi, Quaderni del Bollettino*. In 1993, the Contemporary Jewish Documentation Center (CDEC) in Milan inaugurated one of the largest J. videotheques in Europe. The collection includes 700 titles, among them Holocaust documentaries.

MILANOWICZE   Volhynia dist., Poland, today Ukraine. The J. pop. in 1921 was 91 (total 436). The Jews were probably brought to Maciejow for liquidation during the Holocaust.

MILATYN   Volhynia dist., Poland, today Ukraine. The J. pop. in 1921 was 82 (total 366). The Jews were probably liquidated at the Horochow ghetto in the Holocaust.

MILEJCZYCE   Bialystok dist., Poland. The first Jews arrived in the 16th cent. An organized community was formed in the early 19th cent. and a synagogue was built in 1857. Potters were particularly prominent among the J. artisans and Jews were also storekeepers.

The J. pop. was 814 (total 1,685) in 1897. After WWI, economic conditions deteriorated and many Jews left the town. The Germans arrived on 24 June 1941, setting up a *Judenrat* and ghetto. On 2 Nov. 1942 the town's 1,000 Jews were removed to the Kleszczele ghetto and from there to the Treblinka death camp.

MILEVSKO   Bohemia, Czechoslovakia. The first J. family settled around the mid-17th cent. A new synagogue was constructed during WWI, with the J. pop. reaching 103 in 1921. In 1930 the J. pop. was 81 (total 3,298). The remaining Jews were deported to the Theresienstadt ghetto via Tabor in Nov. 1942. In Jan., Sept., and Oct. 1943, most were transported from there to Auschwitz, none surviving.

MILIE   Bukovina, Rumania, today Ukraine. Jews settled in the late 19th cent. The J. pop. in 1930 was 197. In June 1941, Ukrainian gangs murdered all the Jews.

MILITSCH   (Pol. Milicz) Lower Silesia, Germany, today Poland. Individual Jews were present by the mid-17th cent. at the latest but the modern community was only founded in the early 19th cent. The J. pop. was 41 in 1811 and reached a peak of 197 in 1864. The community maintained a cemetery opened in 1818 and a synagogue established in 1827. There was a rabbi from 1845. In the 1830–32 period, Jews served on the municipal council. On the eve of the Nazi era, the J. pop. was 73, dropping to 56 in 1936. On *Kristallnacht* (9–10 Nov. 1938), the synagogue and six J. stores were destroyed. Five Jews remained in May 1939. The fate of the community in WWII is unknown. Those Jews who failed to emigrate were presumably deported and died.

MILLAU   (Millau en Rouergue) Aveyron dist., France. Around 1300, there was a J. community of about 30 Jews in M. Mostly engaged in moneylending, the Jews were forced to wear the yellow badge (*Rouelle*) in the shape of a wheel to distinguish them from the gentiles. With the expulsion of all Jews from France in 1394, the community ceased to exist. In 1940, the community consisted of about 250 members (100 families). Two-thirds were of Central European origin and one-third were Sephardi Jews. According to the 1941 census, there were about 40 families in M., including refugees from the Bas-Rhin region. Several community members succeeded in fleeing to Switzerland before German forces occupied the Southern Zone in Nov. 1942. On 27 Aug. 1942, 377 foreign Jews in the district were arrested by the French police and deported to Auschwitz through Drancy. Other Jews found refuge in the Catholic church in M. and were arrested later. In June 1942, a few months before the Germans arrived in M., the French police caught the remaining Jews, who were sent to the death camps. Only one survivor returned.

MILOSLAVICHI   Mogilev dist., Belorussia. The J. pop. was 410 in 1847 and 628 in 1897. Jews engaged in petty trade and crafts. In 1905 peasants from the neighboring villages tried to attack Jews but Christian townsmen chased them off. In 1919, during the civil war, a J. kolkhoz was founded nearby, supporting 32 J. families in 1930 and 45 on the eve of WWII. The J. pop. of M. was 571 in 1923 and 24 of the town's 25 artisans were Jews. The Germans occupied the region in early July 1941. Kolkhoz members smuggled their cattle eastward and soon followed. The Nazis and local police murdered the 30 J. families who remained behind.

MILOSNA   Warsaw, Poland. A few J. families settled at the turn of the 19th cent. The J. pop. grew to about 100 families in 1939, confined to a ghetto under a regime of forced labor after the arrival of the Germans. On 23 March 1942 they were expelled to the Warsaw ghetto, ultimately perishing in the Treblinka death camp.

MILOWKA   Cracow dist., Poland. The Jews numbered 116 (total 2,059) in 1890 and 163 in 1921. Periodic antisemitic disturbances occasionally reached violent dimensions. Between the World Wars the Jews lived off the Carpathian Mt. tourist trade and the Zionists expanded their activity. Most were expelled to Kalwaria Zebrzydowska by the Germans around the end of 1940.

MILTENBERG   Lower Franconia, Germany. Jews settled in the 14th cent. and were victims of the Armleder massacres of 1336–39 and the Black Death persecutions of 1348–49. At that time they had a synagogue and cemetery and lived in a J. quarter. In 1429 the synagogue was impounded and the Jews were apparently expelled. Those present in the early 17th cent. were ex-

pelled in 1647. Between 1661 and 1779, 15 meetings of the regional *Judenlandtag* were held in M. The J. pop. grew to 109 in 1880 (total 3,683) and maintained nearly that level until the Nazi era. Under the Nazis, J. tradesmen were banned from local fairs. In 1933–40, 43 emigrated, including 31 to the U.S., and 42 left for other German cities. Of the remaining Jews, eight were deported to Izbica in the Lublin dist. (Poland) via Wuerzburg on 25 April 1942 and one to the Theresienstadt ghetto on 10 Sept. 1942.

MINARALNYIE VODY   Stavropol territory, Russia. On 10 Sept. 1942, the Germans murdered the few Jews in this resort town who had neither fled nor been evacuated. At the same time, they also killed numerous J. refugees who arrived after the outbreak of war between the Soviet Union and Nazi Germany as well as Jews from the neighboring towns of Yessentuki, Kislovodsk, Piatigorsk, and others.

MINDEN   Westphalia, Germany. Jews are first mentioned in 1270, living under the protection of the local bishop as moneylenders with the right to own immovable property. In 1350, in the Black Death persecutions, the Jews were "slaughtered like cattle" according to a Christian witness. Jews returned later in the cent. but, until the 17th cent., were present only in small numbers. The permanent settlement with a synagogue and cemetery apparently began when five J. families received letters of protection in the early 17th cent. By the late 17th cent. the J. pop. was 69. By the early 19th cent., the community was, for the most part, exceptionally prosperous. The J. pop. reached a peak of 267 (total 17,867) in 1880. Jews entered banking, crafts, and the professions. Of the 44 children born in the 1822–38 period, 80% attended secondary schools. Although Jews were elected to the municipal council and were active in local life, the debate surrounding emancipation and the economic prominence of the Jews also provoked antisemitism, which persisted throughout the cent. Liberal religious tendencies were apparent from the 1820s and the new synagogue opened in 1865 was equipped with an organ and prayers were conducted in German. A J. elementary school operated until 1879. In June 1933, about four months after the Nazi rise to power, the J. pop. was 192. On *Kristallnacht* (9–10 Nov. 1938), the synagogue with its 14 Torah scrolls was set on fire and J. homes and stores were wrecked. Some Jews were beaten and 60 men were sent to the Buchenwald concentration camp. Subsequently, on 3 Dec. 1938, seven J. business establishments and 18 parcels of J.-owned land were "offered" for sale. Fifty-four Jews remained in Oct. 1939. On 10 Dec. 1941 and 30 March 1942, most were sent to Bielefeld preparatory to deportation to the Warsaw ghetto. The last Jews were sent east on 28 July 1942.

MINDSZENT Csongrad dist., Hungary. Jews are mentioned in 1727 and numbered 237 in 1880. Many left during the White Terror attacks (1919–21) and by 1940, the J. pop. stood at 90. At the end of June 1944, the Jews were deported to Auschwitz via Szeged.

MINGOLSHEIM, BAD see BAD MINGOLSHEIM.

MINKOVTSY Kamenets-Podolski dist., Ukraine. The J. pop. was 378 in 1765 and 2,196 in 1897. Jews earned their livelihoods from petty trade, the wood industry, oil pressing, and tanning. A Hovevei Zion group was founded in the late 19th cent., followed by branches of the Zionist Organization and the Bund. Hehalutz became active in 1921. In the Soviet period, the Jews founded a kolkhoz and two artisan cooperatives. A Jew headed the local council (soviet) and J. children attended a Yiddish school. The Germans occupied M. on 12 July 1941. A ghetto was established in early Aug. and on 31 Aug. the Nazis executed 1,840 Jews. Another 70 were discovered in hiding and put to forced labor until transferred to the Dunayevtsy ghetto and executed there on 18 Oct. 1942.

MINSK Minsk dist., Belorussia. J. settlement in M. commenced in the 15th cent. with the arrival of Jews expelled from Lithuania in 1495. In 1579, the Polish king, Stephen Bathory, granted the Jews a charter of privileges which was afterwards confirmed by King Sigismund III. In 1623, the community was under the jurisdiction of Brest-Litovsk but in 1631, because of its growth, the Lithuanian Council accorded it special regional status together with its Russian hinterland. In the period of the Chmielnicki massacres of 1648–49, the Jews were expelled from the city, returning only in 1658. Anti-J. riots broke out in 1671. After King John Sobieski III confirmed J. rights in 1679, the community enjoyed a long period of prosperity. The first M. yeshiva was founded in 1685. Among the

Jewish State Theater of Minsk, Belorussia, 1934. The building appears to be a former synagogue (YIVO Archive, New York/photo courtesy of Yad Vashem, The Holocaust Martyrs' and Heroes' Remembrance Authority, Jerusalem)

community's rabbis were some of the greatest in Poland and Lithuania, such as R. Yehiel Heilprin (serving in 1712–43). In 1766, the J. pop. was 1,322. In the Second Partition of Poland in 1793, M. was annexed to Russia. The J. pop. rose from 2,675 in 1802 to 47,662 (total 90,884) in 1897. As a railroad junction from the early 1870s, M. became a regional center for the lumber and grain trade. In the 1880s, 88% of commerce was in J. hands and Jews almost completely dominated certain trades, such as tailoring. In 1904, 6,600 Jews, almost half the J. breadwinners in the city, were artisans. However, though most factories were also in J. hands, few Jews worked there and the difficult economic conditions prevailing in the city were among the major causes of the emigration of thousands of Jews (estimated at as much as 20–25% of the J. pop.), mainly to the U.S. Hasidism exercised a limited influence. A number of *yeshivot* were founded, mostly by students of the Gaon of Vilna. In addition to the beautiful stone-built Great Synagogue, about 40 prayer houses were active in the 1880s and 1890s, their number rising to 83 in 1917 when thousands of J. refugees arrived from western Russia. In the late 19th cent., R. Yehuda Perelmann (known as "the Great [Scholar] of M.") officiated in the community. In the 1890s, the number of J. children attending state or private Russian-language schools grew considerably. In 1881–82, 140 J. boys (of a total 552 students) were enrolled at the classical high school and 22 girls (of 59) at the natural sciences high school. In addition, three two- and four-year state schools for J. children were in operation along with a *talmud torah* and numerous *hadarim*. Of J. welfare institutions, the 65-bed J. hospital was particularly prominent. In the late 19th cent., the J. labor movement under the leadership of the Bund came to the fore. The latter held its founding convention in M. in 1895 and in 1900 numbered about 1,000 members. Its leaders were among the organizers of J. self-defense in the face of local riots that officers and soldiers initiated during Easter of 1897 and 1905. In 1898, at the initiative of the Bund, the first convention of the All-Russian Social Democrat Party was held in M. As early as 1882 a Niddehei Yisrael association was founded which sought to purchase land in Eretz Israel. In the late 19th cent., the Zionist parties became active. In 1901, the founding convention of Po'alei Zion was held in M. and in 1902 the second convention of the Russian Zionists. In 1911, Tze'irei Tziyyon convened in M. The large number of J. refugees who arrived after the outbreak of WWI included students from the famous Volozhin yeshiva. The J. pop. rose to 67,000 in 1917. Under the German occupation, elections to the community council were held in 1918 with the Zionists gaining a majority of the seats. The Orthodox parties took second place and the Bund third. In Jan. 1920, a convention of J. community councils was held in M., with the Zionists again prevailing; their representatives were placed at the head of the National Council of Belorussian J. Communities. On the withdrawal of the Polish army from the city on 9–11 July 1920, Polish soldiers looted two-thirds of the city's stores (most under J. ownership) as well as a hide-processing plant and J. pharmacy. In addition to robbing thousands of residents (also mainly Jews), the soldiers raped and murdered and burned down a number of J. homes. Immediately after the arrival of the Soviet authorities in July 1920, the activities of the community council as well

as of the J. political parties were curtailed. Many activists were exiled. Only Po'alei Zion continued to operate within a Communist framework, until it too was closed down in 1928. A number of Zionists managed to leave for Palestine. During the Soviet period, the J. pop. rose from 53,686 in 1926 to 70,998 (total 238,970) in 1939. A J. law court which carried out its proceedings in Yiddish was opened in 1926. A J. teachers' college founded in 1922 was incorporated into the general teachers' college as a separate department in 1931 but closed down in the mid-1930s. A special department of Belorussian J. studies was also opened at M. University as well as a J. section in the Belorussian Academy of Sciences (in 1924). In the early 1930s, a J. section was included in the Institute of Belorussian Culture and in 1931 a department for Yiddish speakers was opened at the local transportation institute (closed in 1934). Over 6,470 J. children (of a total 10,300 J. children) were enrolled in J. schools in 1926–27. In 1931 there were still as many as ten J. schools in M., most of them for elementary education and some of which continued to operate until 1938. A number of clandestine *yeshivot* were active in the late 1920s (with 400 students in 1928). A clandestine *heder* was also active in one of the synagogues in 1929. The *Yevsektsiya* tried to promote (without much success) a "Red" community with a "Red" rabbi. In 1926, the Belorussian J. State Theater was founded as the successor of the J. Theater Studio operating since 1921. A J. library with 40,000 volumes was established at the Lenin Central Library in the 1920s. Three additional J. libraries with large collections were also operating during this period. In the late 1920s, J. artisans organized in a union (980 of whose 1,100 members were Jews) had their own club. The number of J. factory workers steadily increased. In the late 1930s, a third (10,000) of all factory workers in the city were Jews while over 83% of Jews still declared Yiddish to be their mother tongue at the end of the 1920s. Two Hebrew printing presses were operating in the early 19th cent. In the early 20th cent., Yiddish newspapers such as the *Minsker Vochenblat* were appearing, some clandestinely printed. After the Feb. 1917 Revolution, M. became a center of the J. press for all of Belorussia, especially in Yiddish. The daily *Veker*, the organ of the Bund in 1917–25, was succeeded by *Oktyabr* in 1925–41. *Der Yunger Arbeter* appeared twice a month from 1922 to at least the mid-1930s. In 1926–31, the J. section of the Belorussian

Academy of Sciences published five volumes of *Tsayt-shrift*, a journal devoted to J. literature, history, and social studies. The important daily newspaper *Der Shtern* (1918–1941), the literary monthly *Shtern* (1925–41), and numerous other political, professional, and scientific publications appeared in M. Among the well-known J. figures born in M. were the Yiddish-Russian writers Lev Osipovich Levanda (b. 1835) and Rivka Rovina (b. 1906); the historian of Russian Jewry Shaul Ginzburg (b. 1866); the director Yaakov Viktor Golovtchiner (b. 1905); the Zionist leader and first finance minister of Israel, Eliezer Kaplan (b. 1901); and the linguist and educator Avraham Even-Shoshan (b. 1906).

The Germans captured M. on 28 June 1941 following heavy bombardment on the outbreak of war with the Soviet Union. Because of the rapid German advance, few Jews managed to escape the city. A few days after the occupation, the Germans ordered all J. males aged 15–50 to report to military headquarters.

All were transferred to camps on Shirokaya Street near the Svisloch River in Staro-Razhevski, where they joined Jews from Borisov, Vitebsk, Vileike, and other places, making a total of 25,000. Another camp was established at Drozdy. Hundreds at both camps were murdered before being transferred back to the newly established M. ghetto. On 7 July, the Germans executed about 100 Jews for alleged Communist links. On 20 July, the Jews were ordered into the ghetto. They were also ordered to wear, in addition to a yellow badge on the front and back of their clothes, a white triangular patch with their addresses. The ghetto included 34 streets and alleys as well as the J. cemetery. In addition to local Jews and those returning from the camps, thousands of Jews were brought in from Dzerzhinsk, Uzda, Slutsk, etc. The exorbitant tributes the Germans exacted from the Jews were presumably earmarked for a ghetto wall but instead barbed wire was used. A *Judenrat* was established in July along with a J. police force. The first head of the *Judenrat* was El-

Communist Pioneer parade, Minsk, Belorussia

iyahu Mushkin (until March 1942). After he was hanged along with the head of the J. police, the Germans appointed Moshe Yaffe, a refugee lawyer from Vilna. An estimated 100,000 Jews were concentrated in the ghetto. Jews forced to work at the local jail were held nearby, outside the ghetto, to keep them from revealing what went on there. (They were also among the last to be executed in May 1943.) Almost from the outset of the occupation, the Germans regularly seized Jews and after murdering them, threw their bodies into freshly dug pits at the J. cemetery. Thus, on 14 Aug. a few hundred were executed; on 26 Aug. a few hundred men and women were removed to an unknown destination; and on 31 Aug., 916 were murdered. Another 600–700 were seized and murdered in Oct. Mass murder by *Einsatzkommando E. K. 8* units commenced in July 1941, with 1,100 Jews killed over a six-week period. The *Reichsfuehrer*, Heinrich Himmler, was present during one of the *Aktions*. On 1 Sept., 330 Jews were murdered. On 9 Oct., 142 Jews caught without the yellow badge were executed. The Germans set up a second ghetto near the first for German Jews (called the Hamburg ghetto). It, too, had a *Judenrat*, headed by Dr. Frank. During all of its existence (Nov. 1941–Sept. 43), this ghetto, which had almost no contact with the first ghetto, received 23,500 Jews from Germany, Vienna, and Czechoslovakia. Almost all were murdered soon or even immediately after their arrival. Thousands were forced to work long hours outside the ghetto in factories, workshops, army camps, and at the railroad station. In payment they received thin soup and a few slices of bread. To overcome their perpetual hunger, many Jews traded with their "Aryan" neighbors on the other side of the fence and with Jews in the Hamburg ghetto. The non-J. pop. responded to the suffering of the Jews with little humanity. Many took part in pillaging J. property from the outset of the occupation. Few tried to save Jews. The German officials responsible for the extermination of the Jews in the city were Wilhelm Kube, *Generalkommissar* of Belorussia with headquarters in M., and A. Strauch, chief of security police. Members of the Communist Party, some of them refugees from western Belorussia or Poland, established an underground in Aug. 1941. With the failure of resistance in the "Aryan" part of the city, the ghetto underground was in effect nearly the only one operating in M. It received substantial assistance from the *Judenrat*. The first large-scale *Aktion* took place on 7 Nov. 1941. Its aim was to "make room"

for thousands of Jews being brought in from the Reich. Thus, the *Einsatzkommando*, with the assistance of Lithuanian, Ukrainian, and Belorussian police executed 12,000 at Tuchinka. During the *Aktion*, J. homes were looted by local residents and peasants from the neighboring villages. Only three Jews escaped from the pits at the killing site and returned to the ghetto, including a child of ten and a woman. The second *Aktion* took place on 20 Nov., with 7,000 Jews massacred in the same place. After the *Aktion*, many Jews tried to find hiding places in the ghetto or escape to the forest. The third *Aktion* occurred on 2 March 1942 when the *Judenrat* was ordered to hand over thousands of Jews. On orders from the J. underground, the *Judenrat* refused and the Germans swooped down on convoys of J. workers, murdering over 5,000. The underground, which grew to 450 members, concentrated mainly on getting thousands of Jews out of the ghetto and into the forests, where they could join existing partisan units. It also set up seven of its own partisan units, such as Detachment 208 in the Mogilev area, Detachment 406 and the Budyonny Detachment in the Zaslavl area, and Detachment 106 under the command of S. Zorin. Following the *Aktion* of 2 March, the Germans carried out night *Aktions*, such as the one on 3 April, when 500 Jews were murdered. The next major *Aktion*, using gas vans, took place at the nearby village of Maly Trostenec on 28–31 July 1942 and claimed 30,000 J. victims. Nine thousand Jews now remained in the ghetto, which became a camp and was liquidated on 21 Oct. 1943. The *Judenrat* was dismantled and an administrative apparatus set up with a number of collaborators from among the prisoners. About 3,000 Jews were deported to Polish camps in summer 1943, including the Budzyn camp near Lublin. The remaining "essential" workers were murdered at Maly Trostenec on 21 Oct. There, in the fall, the Germans began burning the bodies of tens of thousands of victims. In all, 90,000–100,000 ghetto residents, including thousands from the Reich, were murdered by the Germans. About 5,000 Jews returned to the city from the forests. In 1945, the first memorial in Yiddish in the Soviet Union was dedicated: "To the Jews–Victims of Nazism." In Jan. 1948, Shelomo Mikhoels, chairman of the J. Anti-Fascist Committee and the leading actor in Moscow's J. State Theater, was killed in M. in a staged automobile accident. His murder marked the end of J. culture in the Soviet Union and the start of the Soviet Union's antisemitic campaign.

MINSK MAZOWIECKI Warsaw dist., Poland. The J. settlement probably dates from the early 19th cent. and in the absence of residence or trade restrictions grew to 3,655 (total 9,286) in 1897. Many J. laborers found work paving the new Warsaw–Brest-Litovsk–Moscow highway or in the construction of barracks for the Russian army, while other Jews acted as army suppliers. Numerous hasidic sects were represented, with the Karlin-Koidanov dynasty maintaining its seat there until WWI. R. Yaakov Perlov established his court there in 1873 and founded a yeshiva in 1896 with 200 students. The large J. proletariat encouraged the formation of such socialist groups as the Bund and Po'alei Zion. In the German occupation of WWI many Jews were reduced to penury by heavy taxes and property expropriations and in 1918 suffered the depredations of General Haller's Polish troops. Between the World Wars a traditional way of life continued to be maintained, with Agudat Israel the dominant political force despite growing Zionist influence. Many emigrated to Palestine in the period of the Fourth Aliya (1924–32), including a number of hasidic families. A Tarbut school was founded in 1921. Throughout the period, economic boycotts undermined J. livelihoods. In 1936, 60 J. homes and stores were looted and 50 Jews were injured in large-scale rioting. The Germans captured the city on 13 Sept. 1939, pillaging J. homes and seizing Jews for forced labor. Many fled but a large influx of refugees swelled the J. pop. to 5,246 when all were crowded into a ghetto in Oct. 1940. On 21 Aug. 1942, 3,500 were deported to the Treblinka death camp and another 1,000 who protested were murdered in the ghetto. Thirteen who escaped to the forest engaged in bold partisan operations before being killed a few months later. The few hundred who remained, mainly skilled workers, were mostly housed in a school building. A hundred were transferred to Kaluszyn in Nov. 1942 and 218 were executed at the J. cemetery on 24 Dec. When the liquidation of the last 300 Jews commenced on 10 Jan. 1943 it was met with spirited resistance, culminating in the murder of the Jews gathered in the school. About 100 survived, working for the Germans until they were killed on 5 June.

MIORY Vilna dist., Poland, today Belarus. Jews were officially accorded residence rights in 1903 under Czar Nicholas II but were probably present before that. Many earned their livelihoods in the flourishing flax industry. The Jews of M. identified with the *Mitnaggedim*. The J. pop. of 371 in 1921, recovering from the war, required assistance from the Joint Distribution Committee and relatives abroad. The flax industry revived and 35 Jews also ran farms. However, in the 1930s economic conditions again deteriorated in the face of the general crisis and competition from the new cooperatives. Betar and Hehalutz were active, sending a few pioneers to Palestine before WWII. The Germans arrived in late June 1941, establishing a *Judenrat* and a ghetto. On 3 June 1942 the town's 1,300 Jews (including refugees) were executed in a nearby forest.

MIR Nowogrodek dist., Poland, today Belarus. Jews probably settled in the early 17th cent. The Lithuanian Council met four times in M. (1687, 1697, 1702, 1751). Among the community's illustrious rabbis in the 18th cent. were Meir ben Yitzhak Eisenstadt and Tzevi Hirsch ha-Kohen Rappoport. In 1815, the famous Mir yeshiva was founded by R. Shemuel ben Hayyim Tiktinski, headed by his descendants until the eve of WWII. Students from around the world studied at the yeshiva, which reached an enrollment of 500. In 1897 the J. pop. stood at 3,319 (total 5,401). Particularly numerous were scribes of holy texts, of whom there were about 70 in M. The Zionists became active in the late 1890s. M. was the birthplace of the philosopher Shelomo Maimon (1753–1800) and Zalman Shazar (Rubashov; 1889–1974), third president of Israel. After WWI the J. economy revived with outside help. Already in 1917 a modern J. elementary school was founded, soon joining the CYSHO network. In 1921 the J. pop. was 2,074. Between the World Wars the full range of J. political organizations was active, from the Bund to the Revisionists. The Germans captured M. in late June 1941 in fighting that destroyed 75% of the town. Two weeks later, 25 J. community leaders were murdered. A ghetto was set up in Oct. 1941 and on 9 Nov. 1,300 Jews were murdered beside three mass graves. Among the remaining 800, an armed resistance movement was organized. Three hundred escaped to the forest and joined the partisans; the rest were murdered on 13 Aug. 1942.

MIRGOROD Poltava dist., Ukraine. Jews were leasing land in M. before the Chmielnicki massacres of 1648–49 but an organized community was only formed in the late 18th cent. In 1897 the J. pop. was

1,248 (total 10,037). Yaakov Gordin (1853–1909), author of over 100 Yiddish plays ("Mirele Efrat," "Hasya the Orphan Girl," "The J. King Lear"), was born in the town. A modernized *heder* was set up in 1920 and J. boys studied at a school of arts and crafts. In 1939, the J. pop. was 686. The Germans arrived on 14 Sept. 1941. In Oct. they murdered 22 Jews and on 3 Nov. the remaining 168.

MIRONOWKA Kiev dist., Ukraine. A few dozen Jews lived in M. during the 19th cent. On 24 Aug. 1919, they were attacked by General Denikin's White Army soldiers. In 1939, under the Soviets, the J. pop. was 159 (total 5,995). The Germans occupied the town on 22 July 1941 and murdered the Jews soon afterwards.

MIROPOL Zhitomir dist., Ukraine. Jews are first mentioned in 1721 but were probably present earlier. In 1897, they numbered 1,912 (total 4,194). Jews owned flour mills and a factory for felt blankets. The *tzaddik* R. Dovidl resided in the town. Jews were attacked in the 1905 disturbances and in the civil war (on 1 Dec. 1917). The J. pop. dropped to less than 1,000 between the World Wars. In the 1920s, most Jews were artisans or laborers. A J. school and J. kolkhoz were active through the 1930s. The Germans arrived on 6 July 1941, murdering 960 Jews in Oct.–Nov.

MIROSLAV Moravia (Sudetenland), Czechoslovakia. Jews expelled from Znojmo apparently arrived after 1454. Others arrived after the Chmielnicki massacres of 1648–49. In the mid-18th cent., many traded in cloth, hides, and flour or were tailors and peddlers. The J. school, opened in conformity with the edict of tolerance (*Toleranzpatent*) of 1782, had a peak of 138 students in 1873. A synagogue with a Reform service was consecrated in 1845. The J. pop. was 1,032 in 1857 but dropped to 528 in 1900 and 267 (total 1,736) in 1930. From 1867 to 1925, the community enjoyed political autonomy with its own mayor. The Zionists were also active. During the Sudetenland crisis in fall 1938, a few Jews managed to flee to Palestine or the U.S. Those who remained or moved to other localities in Bohemia and Moravia were deported to the death camps of Poland starting in 1942. A few were deported to the Theresienstadt ghetto in late 1942 and remained there until the end of the war.

MIROSLAVAS (Yid. Miraslov) Alytus dist., Lithuania. Jews lived here from the early 19th cent. and numbered some 60 families in 1897. Between the World Wars most of the youth emigrated to Palestine; the adults emigrated to America. The J. pop. in 1940 was about 20 families. All the Jews were murdered in Aug.–Sept. 1941, following the German occupation.

MISKHOR Crimea, Russia, today Ukraine. Jews received formal residence rights in 1903, but a few were present before that time. In 1939, the J. pop. was 61 (total 2,368). The Germans occupied M. on 8 Nov. 1941, murdering the few Jews still there in Dec.

MISKOLC Borsod dist., Hungary. Jews settled in the late 18th cent. and in the 19th cent. replaced Christians of Greek, Armenian, and German origin as the town's leading merchants, even founding a business school in 1848. J. manufacturers led the way in the town's industrialization, opening a textile factory, brickyard, flour mill, porcelain factory, and machinery plant. They also put in the town's telephone lines and founded all its banks. The community provided a wide range of social services and established a J. public school in 1784 which reached an enrollment of 800 in 1895. Three *yeshivot* and three *talmudei torah* were also in operation. Synagogues were consecrated in 1863 and 1901, the congregation splitting when a choir was introduced into the former synagogue and a Neologist outlook was adopted. The J. pop. rose from 1,096 in 1840 to 5,117 in 1880 and 11,300 (20% of the total) in 1920. After the depredations of the White Terror attacks in 1919–23, economic prosperity returned as Jews dominated commerce and industry as well as the legal and medical professions. Antisemitism, however, continued unabated and new boys' and girls' schools were founded to avoid exposing J. children to its manifestations. A teachers' college for women, founded in 1928, was the only one of its kind in Hungary. From 1942, Jews were subjected to forced labor and many were sent to the Ukraine, where they perished. Following the German occupation in 1944, the Jews were confined, in April, in a ghetto. Jews from neighboring settlements were concentrated separately in the brick factory. SS troops murdered a group of J. doctors from M. sent by the authorities to Pusztavam to form a J. Doctors Unit that would provide public medical services. On 15 June, the rest were deported to Auschwitz from M. and the neighboring settlements. Fourteen thousand Jews perished in the Holocaust. Four hundred survivors returned, forming the nucleus of a community that declared itself Orthodox Zionist and numbered 2,357 in 1946. In the 1970s about 300 remained, most having left for Israel.

MISTELBACH Lower Austria, Austria. Almost nothing is known about the medieval J. settlement, which ceased to exist in the beginning of the 14th cent. In the 17th cent., Jews were allowed to attend the local markets. Jews resettled in M. in the middle of the 19th cent. In 1880, a J. cemetery was consecrated and in 1890 the community was recognized as a religious association (*Kultusverein*) and maintained a synagogue. Jews were engaged in all kinds of trade. In 1934, the J. pop. stood at 225, declining to 130 in May 1938. In June, Jews were subjected to several antisemitic outbursts. In Aug., the synagogue was handed over to the municipality. In the beginning of Nov. 1938, Jews were deported to Vienna, their property confiscated before departure.

MITTELSINN Lower Franconia, Germany. The community was probably founded in the early 18th cent. and numbered 162 in 1869 (total 1,033), thereafter declining to 105 in 1933. The community maintained a synagogue and a J. public school. In riots following the Austrian *Anschluss* (13 March 1938), the synagogue and J. stores were damaged. Most of the Jews (88) left soon after, 61 of them moving to Frankfurt.

MIZOCZ Volhynia dist., Poland, today Ukraine. Jews settled in the 18th cent., numbering 1,175 (total 2,665) in 1897 and 845 (total 1,247) in 1921 after the disturbances of the WWI period. Most of the community identified with Turzysk Hasidism, effectively suppressing Zionist activity until after the Feb. 1917 Revolution. Light industry developed in the late 19th cent. with Jews operating factories for felt, oil, and sugar as well as sawmills and a flour mill. The economy expanded between the World Wars as Jews engaged in the marketing of hops and fruit. About 300 Jews left with the retreating Red Army in June 1941. On 29 June, the Ukrainians commenced a week-long pogrom. The Germans established a *Judenrat* and in March 1942 the Jews were confined to a ghetto. Those caught smuggling in food were publicly hanged.

With intimations of an *Aktion*, resistance was organized. Hundreds fled as the German and Ukrainian police began to close in on the ghetto on 13 Oct. 1942. The next day fighting broke out and houses were set ablaze to cover the mass escape. About 1,000 Jews were killed in the *Aktion*. Many who fled were also killed; the survivors took to the forests.

MIZUN STARY Stanislawow dist., Poland, today Ukraine. The J. pop. in 1921 was 182. The Jews were probably expelled by the Germans to Dolina or Bolechow for liquidation in spring–summer 1942.

MLADA BOLESLAV (in J. sources, Bumsla) Bohemia, Czechoslovakia. With Kolin, Roudnice, and Nachod, M. was one of the four important Bohemian J. communities known by the Hebrew acronym KRBN derived from the initials of the towns. M. is first mentioned in 1471. By 1687, Jews numbered 775 (about half the pop.). Many Jews died in the plagues of 1680 and 1691. After a 1697 fire, the J. quarter was closed off. Hostility and persecution, against a religious and economic background, marked relations with the Catholic pop. A new synagogue was built in 1785 after another fire struck the ghetto. In the 18th cent., Jews were peddlers and manufacturers of soap, flour, and cooking utensils. In 1858, a Jew was appointed mayor. The J. pop. rose to 845 (total 9,195) in 1880 and then declined steadily, to 402 in 1910 and 264 in 1930. For hundreds of years, M. was considered an important religious center, earning the sobriquet "Jerusalem of the Jizera River." On 4 June 1942 the Jews were registered for deportation after being confined in an ancient castle near the city. In mid-Jan. 1943, they were sent to the Theresienstadt ghetto. Most were dispatched to Auschwitz in the same month. In all, 184 of the 232 J. deportees perished. The rest of the Jews, mostly those in mixed marriages or economically influential, were deported in 1944.

MLADA VOZICE Bohemia, Czechoslovakia. The J. community dates from the early 18th cent. and numbered about 250 in 1921. The Nazis closed down the synagogue in Oct. 1941 and transported the Jews to the Theresienstadt ghetto via Tabor on 16 Nov. 1942. From there most were deported to Auschwitz in Jan. 1943. None survived.

MLAWA Warsaw dist., Poland. Small numbers of

Nidborska St., Mlawa, Poland (Wiesenthal Institute/photo courtesy of Yad Vashem, The Holocaust Martyrs' and Heroes' Remembrance Authority, Jerusalem)

Jews were present in the 16th and 17th cents. The community began to develop in the 19th, numbering 1,650 in 1857 and 4,854 (total 11,709) in 1897. Jews were active in the clothing and textile trade and many were stallkeepers or peddled in the neighboring villages. A new synagogue was completed in 1858. Most children studied in the *heder* system while a J. secondary school founded in 1917 developed into a high school with a peak of 290 students. The Zionists became active in 1904 and were soon represented by numerous groups. The Bund started operating in 1906. J. commerce came to a standstill in WWI and the community suffered from serious food shortages. In 1918 it also suffered from the depredations of General Haller's Polish troops. The postwar economic crisis affected J. tradesmen adversely, necessitating the establishment of loan societies and welfare agencies to support them. Agudat Israel contended with the Zionists for control of the community council, running its own youth movements and a Beth Jacob school for girls. A Beit Yosef yeshiva was founded in 1927. A

Yiddish biweekly (*Dos Mlawer Lebn*) appeared from 1932. The writers Joseph Opatoshu (1883–1954) and Yakir Warshavsky (1885–1943) were born there, as was Victor Alter (1890–1941), one of the outstanding leaders of the Polish Bund. Antisemitism intensified in the 1930s, with J. shops closing down in the face of the economic boycott. Most of the city's 6,400 Jews fled the German bombardment of 1 Sept. 1939, returning after the end of fighting in mid-Sept. to be caught up in a regime of forced labor and severe persecution under the German occupation. Largely through the efforts of the young, dynamic Eliezer Perlmutter, appointed head of the *Judenrat* at around the end of the year, the situation of the Jews improved somewhat. On 6 Dec., 3,000 Jews were deported to General Gouvernement territory, hundreds dying in the harsh winter and many others dispersing among the cities of the Lublin dist. Many made their way back to M., bringing the J. pop. up to about 5,000 together with the influx of 1,000 refugees from Szrensk, Radzanow, and Zielun, all packed into a ghetto. Perlmutter was mur-

Jewish soldiers from Mlawa, Poland, in the Russian army prior to WWI (Wiesenthal Institute/photo courtesy of Yad Vashem, The Holocaust Martyrs' and Heroes' Remembrance Authority, Jerusalem)

dered by the Germans in Jan. 1942. Public executions commenced on 18 Apr., when four Jews were hanged on the charge of smuggling food; 13 more were hanged on 4 June and 50 were arbitrarily murdered on 17 June. Mass deportations commenced on 10 Nov. 1942 when the sick and old were dispatched to the Treblinka death camp. Two more transports to Auschwitz (13 and 17 Nov.) virtually emptied the ghetto, which was immediately filled with 5,000 Jews from Makow Mazowiecki and 1,000 from Strzegowo. These too were deported to Auschwitz, the last transport with the remnants of M. Jewry leaving on 10 Dec. 1942.

MLIECNO   (Hung. Tejfalu) Slovakia, Czechoslovakia, today Republic of Slovakia. A few Jews were present in the late 17th cent. They engaged in peddling, operated concessions, and distilled liquor. In the latter half of the 18th cent., they erected a synagogue. In the 1840s, the J. pop. reached a peak of about 350, subsequently declining as many left for the cities. The J. pop. was 100 (total 752) in 1880 and 12 in 1940. The Jews

were deported to Auschwitz via Budnieske Starda on 16 June 1944.

MLYNOW   Volhynia dist., Poland. Jews settled from the late 18th cent., numbering 672 (total 1,105) in 1897. M. was the birthplace of Shelomo Mandelkern (1846–1902), author of the Bible concordance *Heikhal ha-Kodesh*, and the Hebrew poet Yitzhak Lamdan (1899–1954). Fire and plague struck the town in the 1890s. The 400 workers at a local steel plant provided an additional market for J. tradesmen from the early 20th cent. Between the World Wars, Polish competition increased. Most of the Jews were Hasidim (Olyka, Turzysk, Karlin-Stolin). The Zionists were active after WWI. The German occupation from 24 June 1941 was at first marked by sporadic killing. A *Judenrat* was established and on 22 May 1942 the Jews were confined to a ghetto together with 100 families from Murawica. All but the few who escaped were executed on 9 Oct.

MNISZEW   Kielce dist., Poland. The J. pop. was

164 (total 722) in 1921. In Feb. 1942, the Jews were expelled by the Germans to the Magnuszew ghetto and in Sept. 1942 to Kozienice before deportation to the Treblinka death camp on 29 Sept.

MOCENOK Slovakia, Czechoslovakia, today Republic of Slovakia. Jews settled in the mid-18th cent. They maintained a synagogue and cemetery and reached a peak pop. of 132 (total 2,515) in 1880, which subsequently dropped to 79 in 1940, with Jews owning about a dozen grocery stores and taverns. Under Slovakian rule, they were forced out of their businesses in 1941 and on 20 April 1942 deported via Nitra to the Rejowiec ghetto in Poland.

MOCIU (Hung. Mocs) S. Transylvania dist., Rumania. Jews first settled in the 1860s. M. was an ultra-Orthodox community and Zionist activity never took place there. The J. pop. in 1930 was 160 (6% of the total). At the end of June 1941 the Jews were transferred to Turda, Sarmas, and Ludus. After the war some Jews returned; in 1947 they numbered 70.

MODENA Emilia, Italy. The first Jew is recorded in Saliceto, a village near M., in 1025, but a J. community was established in M. only in 1393, when Alberto d'Este granted several Jews privileges to open banks. The first wave of immigrants arrived in the area from Spain and Portugal after the expulsion from the Iberian Peninsula at the end of the 15th cent. A second wave of immigrants arrived in the middle of the 17th cent. M. developed into a center of J. scholarship and Kabbalah. Among the leading scholars here were Avraham Yosef Shelomo Graziani, Aharon Berechiah of Modena, Avraham Rovigo, and Ishmael Cohen. In 1638, the Jews were confined to a ghetto, which was enlarged in 1783, and forced to wear a yellow badge, later altered to a red band on the hat. Boys under 12 and women were exempted. In 1766, the community numbered 1,262 members. By 1796, with the fall of the house of Este, and under the provisional government, the Jews acquired civil equality, but their status was not yet embodied in law. As soon as M. became part of the Cisalpine Republic, Jews were granted civil equality by the constitution. Moses Formiggini, who played an important role in the new political order, later entered the senate. In 1814, the house of Este returned to power under Francesco IV and the ghetto was reinstituted, but without gates. Some of the new rights were abol-

ished. Full equality was acquired in 1859 when M. became part of the Kingdom of Italy. Cesare Rovighi, a native of M., was a decorated hero of the Italian Risorgimento. In 1873, the community included 1,620 members and a new synagogue was built. In 1886, the community included 1,700 members. In 1900, Prof. Carlo Conegliano started the monthly *L'Idea Sionista* in M. According to the 1930 law reforming Italian J. communities, M. was declared one of the 26 communities legally recognized by the state. It included in its jurisdiction, the communities of Carpi (71 Jews in 1869; 15 in 1936), Finale (191 Jews in 1766; 15 in 1936), Reggio Emilia, and Scandiano (35 in 1873; five in 1936,). In 1931, the J. community of M. comprised 474 members. By 1936, 340 remained. In the mid-1930s, the community maintained a *talmud torah* and several local cultural and social associations. According to the census of Aug. 1938, there were 547 Jews in the province of M. During WWII, 13 local Jews perished in Auschwitz. After liberation, the community consisted of 185 members, dropping to 150 by 1969.

MODLIBORZYCE Lublin dist., Poland. Jews are first mentioned in the mid-17th cent. and numbered 312 in 1827 and 957 (total 1,913) in 1921. Between the World Wars, most lived in straitened economic circumstances. The Orthodox controlled the community council but in the 1936 elections the Zionists won a majority. Under the German occupation (from Sept. 1939), the J. pop. doubled with the arrival of 1,031 deportees from Vienna in March 1941. In Oct. 1942, all were expelled to the Krasnik ghetto and from there to the Belzec death camp in Nov.

MODRA (Hung. Modor) Slovakia, Czechoslovakia, today Republic of Slovakia. Jews were present in the 17th cent. and were organized as a community by 1787. Their pop. only began to grow significantly from the mid-19th cent., reaching a peak of 170 (total 5,230) in 1900. J. homes and stores were looted in riots in 1848. Later M. became the seat of the regional rabbinate with 12 settlements under its jurisdiction. In 1902 a synagogue in the Moorish style was consecrated. The J. pop. began to drop with the exodus of the young to the big cities from the early 20th cent. and numbered 116 in 1921 and 49 in 1940. The Zionists and Agudat Israel were active after WWI. In May 1941, the Slovakian authorities ordered the "Aryanization" of 15 J. stores and workshops. The young were deported to the Majdanek concentration camp in late March 1942. Most of the others were subsequently sent to the death camps. Thirty-five J. children from different places in Slovakia found refuge in the orphanage of the local evangelist church and were saved.

MODRY KAMEN (Hung. Kekko) Slovakia, Czechoslovakia, today Republic of Slovakia. Jews apparently settled in the 1860s, numbering 30–35 (2–3% of the total) from the 1880s until WWII and with the surrounding villages constituting a congregation of 200. In late March–early April 1942, young J. men and women were deported to the Majdanek concentration camp and Auschwitz, respectively. In June families were deported to the Lublin dist. (Poland), where most perished.

MODZELE WYGODA Bialystok dist., Poland. The J. pop. in 1921 was 173 (total 291). Most of the Jews were presumably murdered by the Germans after their occupation in 1941.

MOEDLING Lower Austria, Austria. Jews first settled in the beginning of the 14th cent. By 1380 they occupied a J. quarter. In 1421, during the Wiener Gesera persecutions, they were expelled. In 1833, the Jews resettled in M. In 1876 a J. cemetery was consecrated. The community was recognized as an independent religious corporation (*Kultusgemeinde*) in 1895 and maintained two synagogues, one from 1888 and a second from 1914. Jews owned shops and were represented in the professional class as lawyers and architects. They were active in public life. From 1918 to 1925 the famous composer Arnold Schoenberg (1874–1951) lived in M. In 1910, the J. pop. stood at 288 (total 17,800), rising to 302 in 1934. During the 1920s, various social, political, cultural, and sports associations were established. Antisemtism was rife in M. and on several occasions J. shops were damaged and the windows of the synagogue were broken. Before the *Anschluss* (13 March 1938), the well-known psychologist Viktor Frankl taught at the local high school. In April 1938, J. shops were marked and boycotted. In May the interior of the synagogue was damaged. During this time many Jews managed to emigrate. On *Kristallnacht* (9–10 Nov. 1938), community archives were confiscated and the synagogue was burned down completely. J. shops were looted and

afterwards destroyed. Several J. males were arrested and sent to the Dachau concentration camp. The community was taken over by the Vienna community. Most of the Jews still living in M. were forced to move to special houses in Vienna. Some were still able to emigrate. Others were sent to the east where they perished.

MOENCHENGLADBACH Rhineland, Germany. Jews are first mentioned in 1337 as moneylenders. A community with a synagogue inhabited a J. quarter in the 1340s. The community ended in 1349, either through massacre or flight during the upheavals accompanying the Black Death. Jews are again mentioned in 1413, living under the protection of the Duke of Juelich, but over the next 200 years there is no evidence of their presence in the city. Beginning in 1684 a new J. community began to develop, with four families in 1719 and eight in 1788. Until 1704, the Jews of M. were under the jurisdiction of the state rabbi of the Cologne archbishopric; from 1706 they were attached to the Duesseldorf state rabbinate. In 1818, the community became part of the Krefeld consistory. Until the mid-19th cent., most Jews were butchers (12 of 15 family heads in 1847; 18 of 23 adult males in 1853); others were cattle traders. In the second half of the 19th cent., the percentage of Jews engaged in trade grew from 41.8% (1865) to 61.4% (1888). About 5% were artisans. In 1888, 61 of the 218 gainfully employed Jews were women, including 24 assistants in business establishments and eight servants. With the development of the textile industry in the 1850s, making the city a European textile center, J. industrialists came to the fore. Newcomers were responsible for starting most J. textile plants. Avraham Gotthelf opened the first weaving mill in the city in 1855 and in the late 1860s became the wealthiest Jew in M. Between 1864 and 1913, Jews operated no fewer than 43 textile plants. Two J. weaving mills set up in this period employed 150 workers together; one of them was equipped with 55 mechanical looms. A J. knitting mill had 250 workers in 1899. J. merchants were also active in the textile industry and in the period between 1865 and 1907, 29 of the 38 newly opened J.-owned stores dealt in textiles. In 1898, a Jew founded a private business school. J. economic success led to membership, and sometimes leading positions, in local commercial and industrial associations. Jews were also prominent as members of the professional class and served as city assemblymen.

Three J. judges were appointed between 1888 and 1918 and four J. lawyers were also active in the period. The J. pop. grew from 91 in 1854 to 516 in 1885 and 840 (total 66,000) in 1910. From the 1870s, the community was the largest and most important in the regional congregation established in 1854 under Prussian law. In 1890, the regional congregation was dissolved and the M.-Rheydt congregation was formed with a number of independent satellite communities. A synagogue was consecrated in 1865. A new one was completed in 1883. The congregation's Liberal tendencies were curtailed somewhat in the second half of the 19th cent., owing largely to the efforts of Yonas Binyamin Yonas, the community's most prominent figure and its chairman from at least 1893 until WWI. Orthodox tendencies were bolstered by the arrival of Polish families in the early 1920s. A private J. elementary school was started in 1863, becoming a J. public school in 1888 after an enrollment of 73 children was reached. In the Weimar period, the J. textile industry continued to prosper. The Aschenburg factory (with a branch in Hungary) operated 204 looms and employed about 500 workers. In 1929, Jews owned (solely or in partnerships with non-Jews) 21 of the city's 98 clothing factories; 11 of its 90 weaving mills; six of 36 cloth-manufacturing factories; and three of 22 spinning mills. Jews also owned five of the city's 12 wholesale textile establishments and operated some of the largest retail outlets in the trade. In the 1920s, eight J. doctors were practicing locally. Jews were active in M.'s social and cultural life, supporting the arts, starting the city's only modern dance band, and joining sports clubs. The J. elementary school maintained an attendance of 50–60 throughout the 1920s. Zionist activity was limited, with just 17 members in the local branch in 1922. On the eve of the Nazi era, the community maintained a number of welfare and charity organizations and local branches of the Central Union (C.V.) and the J. War Veterans Association.

In 1933, the J. pop. was 907 (total 126,631). Persecution commenced immediately with Jews arrested on various allegations, including racial defilement (even before the publication of the Nuremberg Laws). In late July 1935, Jews were banned from local swimming pools, also earlier than in other places in Germany. Between Dec. 1933 and Dec. 1936, the J. pop. dropped by 16%. Arrivals (mostly relatives of local Jews) partially offset departures. Zionist support increased considerably in the Nazi period. Although a Maccabi sports club with 60 members was founded in 1933, the community leadership remained by and large anti-Zionist. Fifteen Jews with Polish citizenship were expelled in late Oct. 1938; at least ten remained behind. According to Gestapo lists, 57 J. business establishments were still in operation in Jan. 1938. The liquidation sale in the big Weinberg textile store was so successful that the Nazi administration in Duesseldorf banned further liquidation sales. Two large textile factories owned by the Meyer family and employing 790 workers were placed in German hands. From Dec. 1936 to Sept. 1938, the J. pop. dropped by a further 19% (140 Jews) to 609, while the number of J. students dropped from 82 to 51. On *Kristallnacht* (9–10 Nov. 1938), the synagogue was burned and J. homes and stores were destroyed. At least four Jews were beaten and at least 39 were arrested, some being detained in the Dachau concentration camp until mid-Dec. Another 120 Jews emigrated between Sept. 1938 and March 1939. Total emigration for the June 1933–May 1939 period was 443. The 58% drop in the J. pop. during this time was the average for Germany as a whole. According to municipal figures, 375 Jews remained in May 1939. Between Jan. and March 1939, another three large J. textile factories were transferred to German ownership and the last in Oct. Between *Kristallnacht* and Oct. 1940, 129 of 204 J.-owned buildings were sold. From early 1939, Jews were mobilized for forced labor on swamp reclamation and road building projects as well as quarry work, subterranean construction, debris clearance, and other physical labor. In 1940, Jews were moved to "J. houses." In May, 16 Jews were seized from their beds in the middle of the night and whipped. With the commencement of deportations via Duesseldorf in fall 1941, five Jews committed suicide. On 27 Oct., about 50 were deported to the Lodz ghetto; on 11 Dec., 130 to the Riga ghetto; on 21–22 April 1942, 80 to Izbica in the Lublin dist. (Poland); on 14 June, six to Izbica; on 24–25 July, 35 to the Theresienstadt ghetto. In all, 481 Jews were deported from M., Rheydt, and Wickrath. Others who had emigrated were deported from German-occupied Europe. At least 14 of the deportees survived. A community of 40–45 Jews was established after the war, growing to 100 in 1960 and 270 in 1993. A new community center with a prayer hall was dedicated in 1967.

MOENCHENGLADBACH-RHEYDT Rhineland,

Germany. A J. merchant is mentioned in 1571 and three to five families were present in the second half of the 18th cent. From 1819, Jews from the surrounding villages began to settle in the city. The J. pop. rose to 88 in 1846 and 263 (total 22,658) in 1885. The community was attached to the Krefeld consistory under French rule and then became part of the Moenchengladbach regional congregation in 1854 and an independent congregation in 1890 with three satellite communities (Odenkirchen, Giesenkirchen-Schelsen, and Rheindahlen). A synagogue was consecrated in 1876 with an attached *mikve*, indicative of the Orthodox leanings of the community. A private J. school was started in 1866, reaching an enrollment of 72 in 1884. With the development of the textile and shoe industries in the city in the late 19th cent., a number of Jews opened factories. Between 1860 and 1890, Jews founded four textile plants, including a weaving mill that became the largest J. enterprise in the city with 260 employees and 226 looms in 1896. Many Jews also became textile merchants. In 1887, 44.8% of J. breadwinners were merchants, 5% were industrialists, 25% were butchers, and 22% (13) were women, including four butchers. Jews also owned the largest department store in the city. Four J. doctors were practicing medicine in the late 19th cent. and a J. judge sat on the local bench in 1895–1902. Jews were active in social and economic societies. A local J. teacher, Clara Grunewald, founded the German Montessori Society. The J. pop. grew to a peak of 390 (total 78,227) in 1925 and in 1929 the city was united with Moenchengladbach. During the Weimar period, a number of J. enterprises continued to prosper. The Stern shoe factory employed 345 workers in 1928 and manufactured 36,000–38,000 pairs of shoes a week. In mid-1933, 351 Jews remained in the city. Anti-J. activity intensified in 1935. On 11 May, SA troops desecrated the J. cemetery, J. homes were vandalized, and windows were smashed. In July, Jews were banned from local swimming pools, preceding other German cities. Before the mid-1930s, few Jews left the city and according to Gestapo lists, 11 J. stores were still open in 1938. On *Kristallnacht* (9–10 Nov. 1938), the synagogue was destroyed with its Torah scrolls and religious articles. A number of Jews were sent to the Dachau concentration camp. On the night of 11 Nov., two J. apartments were destroyed. In Dec. 1938, the Stern shoe factory was transferred to German ownership. From early 1939, Jews were mobilized for forced labor, the men on swamp reclamation and road work, the women in textile plants, mostly mending army uniforms. In May 1939, 232 Jews remained, a pop. drop of a third since 1933 as opposed to the national average of 58% (possibly attributable in part to difficulties in raising cash for emigration). Deportations began in fall 1941. On 27 Oct., 20 or 21 Jews were deported to the Lodz ghetto; on 10 Dec., 40 or 48 were sent to the Riga ghetto; on 22 April 1942, 14 were deported to Izbica in the Lublin dist. (Poland) and on 15 June another seven; on 24 July, 65 or 71 were sent to the Theresienstadt ghetto.

Page from Mahzor (prayer book) dating from the turn of the 13th cent., Moenchsdeggingen, Germany

MOENCHSDEGGINGEN   Swabia, Germany. Jews are known from the 16th cent. A new community was founded in 1684 by Jews expelled from Hoechstaedt. The first synagogue was erected in 1733 and a cemetery was opened in 1833. The J. pop. was 226 (total 718) in 1811. Many subsequently left for the U.S.

and others were among the founders of Noerdlingen in 1860. No Jews remained in 1890.

MOENCHSROTH Middle Franconia, Germany. Jews were present in the late 16th cent. A synagogue was built in 1760 and the J. pop. reached 194 (total 848) in 1812. In 1933, 23 Jews were left. By April 1938, eight had emigrated and 12 had left for other German cities. On *Kristallnacht* (9–10 Nov. 1938), the synagogue was vandalized and by Jan. 1939 the remaining Jews had left the town.

MOERFELDEN Hesse, Germany. Jews first lived there in the 16th cent. The community numbered 80 (5% of the total) in 1861, declining to 35 (1%) by 1900. In 1936, the community disbanded and approximately half (19) of the remaining Jews left before *Kristallnacht* (9–10 Nov. 1938), when Nazis made an attempt to burn the synagogue, even though it had already been sold. Eight Jews emigrated, two committed suicide, and 12 were deported in 1942.

MOERS Rhineland, Germany. Although Jews were present from the early 17th cent., their numbers were limited by the few letters of protection that were issued – six in all the duchy and three in M. from 1678. Their quota was increased to 20 families in 1715 and they were allowed to engage in trade and moneylending. In the 18th cent., a number of J. students were accepted in local high schools and afterwards studied at the university in Duisburg. In 1808, nine of the ten J. breadwinners in M. were butchers but subsequently they moved gradually back to trade, mostly as horse and cattle dealers. In 1816, eight or nine of the 16 J. families in the city owned homes or land. From 1808 to 1848, the community was part of the Krefeld consistory. In 1854 it was attached to the Rheinberg regional congregation. A synagogue was consecrated in 1818 and a private J. school was opened in 1850. The J. pop. rose to 100 in 1826 and remained at around that level for the rest of the 19th cent. Jews were active in local life, serving as assemblymen and volunteer firemen and joining recreational clubs. However, they were excluded from the local racket club and J. high school students encountered antisemitism, which increased in the early 1930s. In the 1920s, the J. pop. included about nine families of Polish origin, representing a more Orthodox orientation. For the most part, J. stores remained open on the Sabbath but

a *minyan* was maintained and kosher butchering continued at the municipal slaughterhouse. The community maintained charitable organizations and in the 1920s founded two new organizations: a branch of the Central Union (C.V.) in 1920 and a youth group in 1928. In the March 1933 elections to the Reichstag and municipal council, the Nazis received 44% and 48% of the vote, respectively. In June 1933, the J. pop. was 191 (total 28,870). The rise of the Nazis led immediately to the social isolation of the Jews and their removal from public positions. After the publication of the Nuremberg Laws in 1935, most stores and taverns refused to serve Jews. Jews were also not allowed to sit on park benches. The economic situation of the Jews deteriorated as stores and homes were sold off. Zionist activity intensified with J. youth joining the Hehalutz organization in early 1933 and a Macabbi sports club starting to operate. The J. pop. dropped to about 90 by 1938 as 170 Jews left and 69 new J. residents arrived. On *Kristallnacht* (9–10 Nov. 1938), windows were smashed in J. homes and stores, the synagogue was vandalized, and a number of J. men were sent to the Dachau concentration camp. In 1939, the remaining Jews were moved to four "J. houses," which they seldom left. Some were put to forced labor. Between late 1938 and late 1941, another 51 Jews left the city and another 29 arrived. Of the total 221 who left, 112 emigrated, including 20 to Holland; 17 to Palestine; 17 to Argentina; 13 to the U.S.; and 11 to South Africa. On 10–11 Dec. 1941, 45 Jews were deported to the Riga ghetto and on 25 July 1942, 15 were deported to the Theresienstadt ghetto. In all, 97 Jews from M. perished in the Holocaust.

MOGENDORF Hesse–Nassau, Germany. Established around 1820 and numbering 114 (16% of the pop.) in 1871, the community dwindled to 20 in 1933. Most Jews emigrated before *Kristallnacht* (9–10 Nov. 1938), and by 1939 none remained.

MOGIELNICA Warsaw dist., Poland. The first Jews probably arrived in the late 18th cent. and by the mid-19th cent. constituted a majority of the pop. In 1828 R. Hayyim Meir Yehiel Shapira, grandson of the *Maggid* of Koznitz, established his dynastic court there, attracting hundreds of hasidic visitors and thereby boosting the town's economy. R. Shapira also founded a yeshiva and after his death in 1849 his sons established new branches of the Koznitz-M. dynasty in Bledow, Grodzisk, and Piaseczno. A wooden synagogue that was one of the most splendid of its kind in the region and remained standing until WWII was erected in the early 19th cent. Most of the town's tradesmen were Jews, introducing such crafts as tanning and the perforation of shoe uppers as well as supplying leather to hundreds of shoemakers. In WWI the Jews were expelled under the Russian occupation and subjected to property expropriations under the Germans (1915–18). In 1921 the J. pop. stood at 2,722 (total 5,316), up from 1,202 in 1857. Heavy taxes, the general economic crisis, and growing antisemitism undermined J. livelihoods between the World Wars. Zionist activity (commencing in the late 19th cent.) expanded to include almost all the existing parties, with the Bund and Agudat Israel active as well. Tarbut, Yavne, and Beth Jacob schools were active. The Germans took the town on 8 Sept. 1939, burning down the old wooden synagogue. A *Judenrat* was appointed in Oct. and charged with regulating the supply of forced labor. It also provided for the 1,500 J. refugees that flooded the town. All the Jews were soon confined to a ghetto. On 27–28 Feb. 1942 all 4,000 Jews there were transported to the Warsaw ghetto to share the common fate of its inhabitants.

MOGILEV Mogilev dist., Belorussia. In 1522, a Lithuanian Jew, Mikhail Ezofovich, leased taxes and inns in M. Local townsmen petitioned the Polish king in 1583 to ban J. residence but their expulsion was not implemented. An organized community existed in the 17th cent. King Sigismund III granted the Jews a charter of rights in 1626 which limited their residence to the street where the synagogue was located but in 1646 King Wladyslaw IV curtailed J. rights under local pressure. The Jews suffered grievously in the Polish-Russian war of 1654–55 and had to flee the city. Those who remained behind converted to save themselves but returned to their faith after the danger passed. A special prayer was composed in the wake of these events. Under King John Casimir in 1664, J. rental and trade rights were restricted under further local pressure. Despite the hostility of the local authorities and townsmen, a synagogue was erected in 1680 and meetings of the Lithuanian Council were occasionally convened. In 1847, the J. pop. was 7,897, rising to 21,539 (total 43,119) in 1897. Jews opened 219 small factories employing 667 workers. The city had 93 distilleries, all but one belonging

to Jews, and 460 small merchants and wholesalers. The majority of J. artisans were tailors (244 in number) and 132 Jews were carters. The community maintained 44 *hadarim*, a *talmud torah*, a three-year girls' school, a four-year coeducational school, and a one-year school for needy girls. M. was the birthplace of the writer David Pinski, the actor Aharon Meskin, and the writer and educator Eliezer Zweifel. The Zionists became active after the Feb. 1917 Revolution with Kadima becoming the most prominent group. In late 1917, Red Army soldiers staged a pogrom in the J. quarter. In 1923, under the Soviets, the J. pop. was 16,748. Five hundred Jews requested permission from the authorities to operate *hadarim* and a public debate on religion was held between the young rabbi M. Shulman and *Yevsektsiya* representatives. In 1924, 432 Jews were artisans. Many Jews worked the 2,000 acres of land allocated to them by the authorities at three locations near the city. In 1928, a kolkhoz was also set up nearby, joined by 22 J. families in 1930. Two seven-grade and one four-grade J. schools were in operation, as was a J. library. In 1927, a J. section was opened in the law courts and a third of the members of the municipal council were Jews as their pop. grew to 19,715 (total 99,428) in 1939. The Germans captured the city on 26 July 1941. In Aug., 80 Jews were shot. A ghetto and *Judenrat* were established and Jews from the area concentrated there. The Nazis shot another 337 Jews in late Sept. The ghetto was then relocated and 113 Jews who refused to move were also shot. On 2–3 Oct., 2,208 J. women, children, and old people were murdered in a major *Aktion*. Sixty-five Jews attempting to escape were also murdered. Another 3,600 were executed on 19 Oct. and in a final *Aktion* in Nov., a further 3,726 were massacred. A few hundred skilled workers were herded into a labor camp. The camp was liquidated in Dec. with 180 murdered on the spot; 135 caught escaping were also murdered. A small number succeeded in hiding. Those discovered were murdered in winter 1942. Those who were caught later were sent to the Shiroka camp in Minsk with the remnant of Minsk and Bobruisk Jewry (3,000 survivors in all). These were deported to various death camps in summer 1943.

MOGILEV-PODOLSKI Vinnitsa dist., Ukraine. Jews are first mentioned in 1713 and numbered 957 in 1765. In 1897, their pop. was 12,344 (total 22,315). Jews traded in grain, farm produce, and lum-

Synagogue in Mogilev-Podolski, Ukraine

ber, which they marketed via the Dniester River and the port of Odessa. The community maintained various welfare and charity organizations, including a J. hospital. In 1905 and Dec. 1919, Jews were attacked in pogroms. In the Soviet period, two Yiddish elementary schools were opened; a section of the law courts conducted business in Yiddish; and two J. kolkhozes were active. In 1939, the J. pop. was 8,703. The Germans captured the city on 19 July 1941. Some Jews fled, but about 1,000 were murdered before the city was transferred to Rumanian control in early Sept. The Rumanians established a ghetto under a *Judenrat* and J. police. In Dec. 1941 it held 3,700 local Jews and 15,000 expelled by the Rumanians from Bukovina and Bessarabia. Up to June 1942, 1,250 died of a typhoid epidemic, including hundreds of orphaned children. The thousands of Jews apparently expelled by the Rumanians to various localities in order to control the epidemic perished either en route or in their new places of residence. In April 1946, the J. pop. was about 3,000.

MOGILNO (I) Poznan dist., Poland. Jews first settled after the annexation to Prussia in 1772 and established a small community with a synagogue and elementary school. The J. pop. reached a peak of 200 (total 2,464) in 1881 and then declined through emigration to the big German cities. The London and Levin families were leading industrialists and philan-

thropists. Isidor London served on the municipal council 37 years until his death in 1918. A few dozen Jews remained after WWI. On 18 Sept. 1939 the Germans blew up the synagogue with ten Jews locked inside

MOGILNO (II) Minsk dist., Belorussia. J. settlement probably began at the turn of the 18th cent. Jews numbered 24 in 1808 and 305 (total 1,076) in 1897, their pop. dropping to 176 in 1923 under the Soviets. After the German occupation in late June 1941 the Jews were expelled to the Uzda ghetto, where 61 were murdered together with most of the Jews there in mid-Oct. 1941.

MOHACS Baranya dist., Hungary. Jews from Bonyhad arrived in 1840, forming a Neologist congregation in 1869 with a number of smaller communities under its jurisdiction. The J. pop. rose to a peak of 963 (.6% of the total) in 1910 and then declined to 707 in 1941. Between the World Wars, Jews ran a hide-processing plant, brickyard, soap factory, and other important industrial enterprises. In 1938, the community organized to teach farming and various industrial professions to young men who lost their livelihood because of the racial laws. In WWII, M. was a regional center for J. labor battalions earmarked for the Ukraine. In May 1944, a ghetto was established. Its pop., including neighboring Jews, numbered about 5,000. All were deported to Auschwitz via Pecs on 5 July.

MOHELNICE Moravia, Czechoslovakia. Jews probably settled only in the late 19th cent., affiliated with the Lostice congregation from 1890 and numbering 87 in 1921 and 59 (1.3% of the total) in 1930. They were apparently deported to the Theresienstadt ghetto together with the Jews of Brno in late 1941–early 1942 and from there transported to the death camps of the east.

MOINESTI Moldavia dist., Rumania. Jews first settled in the early 18th cent. and the community was organized in 1885. In summer 1881, 50 families founded the Palestine Settlement Movement of Rumania and in Aug. 1882, 22 families emigrated to Eretz Israel and established the village of Rosh Pinna. The J. pop. in 1899 was 2,398 (51% of the total). During WWI J. refugees from Bukovina were aided by the M. community. In 1930, a Jew served as deputy mayor and Jews were on the municipal council. On 15 July 1941, the Jews were ordered to move to Bacau. About 80 families returned after the war.

MOISEU   (Hung. Majszin; Yid. Mosif) N. Transylvania dist., Rumania. An organized J. community existed in the early 19th cent. and engaged in agriculture and the lumber industry. The J. pop. declined after WWI – from 1,356 in 1920 to 1,067 in 1941. In 1942 all J. males aged 20–42 were drafted into labor battalions in the Ukraine, where they died. In April 1944 the community was transferred to the Viseul de Sus ghetto and later deported to Auschwitz. The 180 survivors who returned after the war soon left.

MOKNINE   Sousse dist., Tunisia. According to tradition, Jews from Mahdia seeking refuge from the Spanish siege of 1550 settled in M. In the mid-19th cent., the J. pop. numbered 100 families, living in a separate quarter and trading in oil, wool, and hides while importing woven goods, metals, and spices. Others owned small neighborhood grocery stores. In the late 19th cent. Jews earned a countrywide reputation manufacturing the enamel-plated jewelry that became popular at the turn of the cent. The Jews were highly taxed and discriminated against by the legal system. Many Jews belonged to the middle class, with a quarter of the pop. requiring assistance. Between the World Wars, J. jewelers also produced the Byzantine-style jewelry that came into fashion. Another J. occupation was moneylending, with some Jews acting as representatives of banks in Mahdia and Sousse. The community identified closely with the kabbalist R. Pinhas Uzan, who spent most of his life in M., honoring his memory twice a year and believing his grave had the power to ward off evil. From 1913 the community was managed by a council referred to as the J. Relief Fund (Caisse de Secours et de Bienfaisance) as in the rest of Tunisia. The wealthy Yishai family held the presidency of the community from 1918 to 1945. Reuven Bitan and Shemuel Tayyib were the chief rabbis in this period, during which a Great Synagogue was built alongside the old one. Zionist sympathies manifested themselves early in the community, with 12 of a group of 24 local Jews remaining in Eretz Israel after a pilgrimage to the grave of Shimon bar Yohai in 1904. The first Zionist group, called Agudat Yisrael, was founded in 1918–19. A Betar group established in 1932 disbanded after two years. There were occasional

anti-J. outbursts, as in Aug. 1917 and in the drought of 1932–36. The J. pop. was 600–700 (5% of the total) through the first half of the 20th cent. During WWII, despite food shortages and the growing hostility of the Arabs, many Jews from Sousse sought refuge in M. from German persecution and the Allied bombardments. The J. pop. of M. thus tripled to 2,000. The racial laws of the Vichy regime imposed limitations on the rights of rich Jews to hold real estate or industrial assests. Required to supply 300 forced laborers, the Jews, under German supervision, were made to repair roads and to unload German ships at Sousse. The city was liberated on 12 April 1943. Zionist activity intensified, with Betar reopening its doors in the summer and its local leaders leaving for Israel in 1948–49. Most of the community arrived in Israel in 1948–52.

MOKOBODY   Lublin dist., Poland. Jews were present by the early 19th cent., earning sufficiently well as peddlers and merchants to maintain an orphanage and old age home. Their pop. dropped from 486 (total 1,482) in 1884 to 290 in 1921 as a result of anti-semitic harassment by Polish soldiers. After three years of German and Polish persecution the Jews were deported to the Treblinka death camp in Oct. 1942.

MOKRAJA KALAGIRKA   Kiev dist., Ukraine. The J. pop. was 1,677 (total 3,190) in 1897 and 537 under the Soviets in 1926. The Germans arrived on 30 July 1941 and murdered the Jews shortly afterwards.

MOKROWO-SIENKIEWICZE   Polesie dist., Poland. About 250 Jews lived in the two villages on opposite banks of the Lan River in the 1930s. The Germans arrived on 3 July 1941. In April 1942 the Jews were taken to the Lachwa ghetto where they were killed in the *Aktion* of 3 Sept. 1942.

MOL   Vojvodina dist., Yugoslavia. Jews settled there in the late 19th cent. The J. pop. in 1931 was 117 (total 11,715). All perished in the Holocaust.

MOLCZADZ   Nowogrodek dist., Poland, today Belarus. Jews settled in the first half of the 16th cent., building a synagogue in 1648 and becoming an independent community in 1691 after breaking away from Dworzec. In the 18th cent. Jews received permission from the town's proprietor to erect two flour mills.

Most of the Jews were Hasidim, their pop. growing to 1,188 (total 1,733) in 1897. After WWI the Joint Distribution Committee and HIAS helped the community get back on its feet, the latter financing land purchases for 13 J. farming families. Jews also lived off the tourist trade and many were artisans. However, heavy taxes undermined J. livelihoods. Most children attended Tarbut and Horev Hebrew schools and Zionist activity intensified after the publication of the Balfour Declaration in 1917. After two years of Soviet rule, the Germans entered the town on 29 June 1941, instituting a regime of forced labor and extortion. On 14 Feb. 1942, 22 Jews (including two women) were murdered by local police. On 15–18 July 1942, despite armed resistance and the successful flight of 60 young Jews to the forest to join the partisans, 3,300 Jews were executed outside the town. Another 200 were lured out of hiding in Aug. and murdered 20 days later.

MOLDAVA (Hung. Szepsi) Slovakia, Czechoslovakia, today Republic of Slovakia. Jews apparently arrived in the early 18th cent. but seem to have been expelled in the mid-1740s because of the town's proximity to the mining dist. They returned only in the 1820s. A synagogue was erected in 1853. The community also maintained a *talmud torah*. From 1880 to WWII, the J. pop. leveled off at about 200–220 (10% of the total). A new synagogue was built in 1931 after the old one burned down. Jews were active in public life, identifying with Hungarian culture but also supporting Agudat Israel and the Zionist movement. They owned 40 business establishments, 12 workshops, and a big flour mill. After the annexation to Hungary in Nov. 1938, dozens of Jews were seized for forced labor, some perishing in the Ukraine. The rest were deported to Auschwitz via Kosice on 15 May 1944.

MOLDOVITA Bukovina, Rumania. An independent community was founded in 1930 when 436 Jews lived there. In Nov. 1940, the J. pop. fled to Gura–Humorului and in fall 1941 was deported to Transnistria. About a third returned after the war.

MOLETAI (Yid. Maliat) Utena dist., Lithuania. Jews first settled in the 18th cent. In the 1880s many Jews emigrated to South Africa. The J. pop. in 1897 was 1,948 (81% of the total). During WWI the Jews were expelled by the Russian army and many were robbed, raped, and murdered. Two-thirds returned

after the war. Between the wars many Jews emigrated to the U.S., Uruguay, and South Africa. The J. pop. in 1940 was about 350 families. After the German invasion in June 1941, Lithuanian nationalists executed suspected Soviet sympathizers, especially Jews. Sixty young Jews were killed and buried in the Babulka swamps. Some were killed in Utena. The rest were murdered outside the town on 29 Aug. 1941.

MOLIATICHI Mogilev dist., Belorussia. The J. pop. was 139 in 1880 and 429 in 1923 under the Soviets. A J. kolkhoz with 27 families was founded in 1929 and a second one with 35 families in 1930. The Germans occupied M. in late Aug. 1941 and murdered the Jews in a Nov. *Aktion*. Another 11 were discovered in hiding the next day and also executed.

MOLOCHANSK (until 1915, Galbshath) Zaporozhe dist., Ukraine. The J. pop. in 1939 was 249 (total 11,676). The Germans captured M. on 5 Oct. 1941, murdering 32 local residents (probably all Jews) on 16 Oct. and another 36 on 15 Dec.

MOLODECZNO Vilna dist., Poland, today Belarus. Jews first settled in the early 18th cent. The coming of the railraod in the late 19th cent. stimulated J. commerce, particularly in the lumber and flax trade. In 1897 the J. pop. was 1,105 (total 2,393), dropping to 950 in 1925 after the dislocations of WWI. The YEKOPO relief organization helped get the community back on its feet. A Tarbut Hebrew school was opened and the Zionist youth movements became active. After two years of Soviet rule (1939–41), the German *Wehrmacht* entered the town in July 1941. Within a few days 50 J. men were removed to an unknown destination. Another 400–800 Jews were executed outside M. in Oct. 1941 after a selection. The remaining 350–600, including refugees, were housed in a barn and put to forced labor until herded into an unfinished building in Dec. and burned alive.

MOLOTOV Nikolaiev dist., Ukraine. M. was probably founded in the late 1920s by so-called "classless" elements of the J. pop. seeking livelihoods. Several of them set up the J. kolkhozes in the area (which numbered 160 former city dwellers in the early 1930s). A J. rural council (soviet) was active there as well as a J. elementary school. Council territory embraced 265 Jews in 1932, most living in M. The few who had neither fled nor been evacuated were murdered after the arrival of the Germans in Aug. 1941.

MOLSHEIM   Bas-Rhin dist., France. In 1308, Emperor Henry VII "gave" the Jews of M. to the Church of Strasbourg. Although in 1343 the Jews were permitted to hold prayer services, their chapel was destroyed in 1349 during the Black Death persecutions. Jews settled in M. after their expulsion from Strasbourg in 1369. In 1866 there were five Jews in M. and in 1900 there were 70. In 1936, only 55 Jews were listed as living in M. Like the rest of the Jews of Alsace-Lorraine, the Germans sent them to the south of France. During the occupation four were deported and the local synagogue was plundered. In 1956 there were 30 Jews living in M.

MOMMENHEIM   Bas-Rhin dist., France. The J. community numbered 167 in 1784 and 257 in 1865. In 1886, a Jew served on the city council. The local synagogue was inaugurated in 1904. R. Zadoc Kahn (1839–1905), chief rabbi of Paris, was born in M. In 1936, there were 125 Jews living in M. Like the rest of the Jews of Alsace-Lorraine, those from M. were expelled to the south of France during the occupation. Four were deported. The synagogue was completely destroyed during the occupation and restored in 1958. In the 1960s there were 25 Jews in M.

MONASTERZYSKA   Tarnopol dist., Poland, today Ukraine. Jews are recorded from 1625. Most of M.'s craftsmen were Jews; later some belonged to the professional class and others were employed in the home-based toy industry set up by the Viennese Relief Organization of German Jews (Hilfsverein) in 1902. In the second half of the 18th cent., the well-known Yaakov of Lissa (Lorbeerbaum) served as the community's rabbi for a number of years. Hasidism was widespread and the Zionists were active from the 1890s. In 1903 a fire destroyed the synagogue and left many Jews homeless, contributing to the emigration that together with the tribulations of WWI reduced the J. pop. by over 50% from an 1890 high of 2,450 (total 4,400). In the war, Russians, Ukrainians, and the Petlyura gangs successively terrorized the J. pop.; epidemics took a further toll. In its heyday, the affairs of the community were run by the well-to-do Safrin family, with a son-in-law serving as mayor. With the Soviet annexation of 1939–41, artisans were organized in cooperatives

and tradesmen put to work in factories. The Germans arrived on 4 July 1941, immediately inaugurating a regime of forced labor under Ukrainian supervision and widespread pillaging. In early Oct. 1942 a selection was made and 800 Jews were deported to the Belzec death camp while around 60 were murdered within the town. In the middle of the month those remaining were ordered to Buczacz, leaving behind only the handful employed by the *Wehrmacht*. Of the few hundred Jews escaping the net, most were hunted down and murdered, a fate shared by the remaining workers as well.

MONASTIR   (also Mnestir, Mestir) Sousse dist., Tunisia. Jews were present in the period when Islamic culture was at its height (8th–11th cent.) The community declined in the 12th cent., to be revived in the 16th cent. with the arrival of Spanish exiles. They were joined by Leghornian Jews in the 17th cent. The J. economy was boosted in the 19th cent. when European companies, particularly Italian, opened branches in the city, using J. translators and brokers. Jews were also active in the burgeoning olive oil industry. J. life was organized around the community's two synagogues. The grave of the 19th cent. kabbalist Pinhas Uzan, born in M. but buried in Moknine, became a place of pilgrimage for local Jews. Under the French Protectorate (from 1881) the community again declined as Sousse and Moknine became more attractive centers of J. settlement. The J. pop. dropped from 405 in 1909 to 142 (total 10,572) in 1936. Anti-J. outbursts in 1917 and 1934 led to an increase in Zionist activity. In WWII, Jews from Sousse fleeing the Allied bombardments found refuge in M. Under the German occupation, the Jews of M., together those from nearby Sousse and Moknine, were mobilized for forced labor. After the war the Joint Distribution Committee and OZE helped the community. The Zionists were represented by Hashomer Hatzair and Torah ve-Avodah. Only 33 Jews remained by 1956, most having left for the big cities in the early 1950s.

MONASTYRISHCHE   Vinnitsa dist., Ukraine. Jews numbered 107 in 1765 and 2,620 (total 9,404) in 1897. Three were murdered in a pogrom on 19 Nov. 1917. In the Soviet period, a J. council (soviet), school, and kolkhoz were active. The J. pop. was 1,398 in 1939. The Germans captured the town on 22 July 1941. Nearly 5,000 Jews from the M., Oratov, and Dashev regions were murdered in the Poperechni forest on 29 May 1942.

MONASTYRSCHINA Smolensk dist., Russia. M. was located in the J. Pale of Settlement. The J. pop. was 864 in 1847 and 2,179 (total 2,696) in 1897. Two private J. schools were open in 1910. In the Soviet period, the J. pop. dropped to 1,370 in 1926 and 856 in 1939. The Germans occupied the town in Aug. 1941. A ghetto established in Oct. held over 750 Jews from M. and the surrounding area. By Feb. 1942, hundreds had been murdered. Subsequently, about 50 others were flushed out of hiding and also killed.

MONCHOCICE Kielce dist., Poland. The J. pop was 113 (total 1,492) in 1921. The Jews were presumably deported by the Germans to the Treblinka death camp via Bodzentyn in fall 1942.

MONNIKENDAM Noord-Holland dist., Holland. A J. community was organized by 1787 and numbered 58 in 1850. The J. pop. in 1941, including the nearby villages of Edam and Broek in Waterland, was 69. In the Holocaust, 65 were transferred to Amsterdam and deported from there to death camps. One survived in hiding and the fate of three others is unknown.

MONOK Zemplen dist., Hungary. Jews are mentioned in 1735. The community began developing in the 1830s, reaching a pop. of 198 in 1880 before declining to 66 in 1941. In 1942, 15 young men were seized for forced labor. On 12–15 June 1944, the remaining Jews were deported to Auschwitz via Satoraljaujhely.

MONOR Pest–Pilis–Solt–Kiskun dist., Hungary. Jews settled in the first half of the 19th cent. and contributed significantly to the town's industrial development, founding a flour mill, sawmill, and cement factory. In 1869, the community formed a Neologist congregation and in 1885 became a regional center with jurisdiction over numerous smaller settlements. A synagogue was built in 1863 with a contribution from Emperor Francis Joseph I. A J. school was opened in 1886. The J. pop. reached a peak of 570 in 1910, declining to 344 in 1941. Jews suffered greatly in the White Terror attacks (1919–21) and again in the economic depression of the 1930s. Hungary's racial laws of 1938 further undermined the community. In 1942,

Jews were seized for forced labor. After the German occupation of 1944, they were held in a ghetto from 22 May until deported to Auschwitz on 7–9 July. Some 75 survivors reestablished the community, but it gradually declined over the years.

MONSHEIM Hesse, Germany. The community, numbering 46 (7% of the total) in 1861, underwent a process of decline and the last 12 Jews probably emigrated to the U.S. before WWII.

MONTABAUR Hesse–Nassau, Germany. Founded during the Crusades, M. took its name from Mount Tabor in the Holy Land. Jews lived there in the early 14th cent. but fell victim to the Armleder massacres of 1336–39 and the Black Death persecutions of 1348–49. A community was only established 400 years later, numbering 115 (3% of the pop.) in 1885. Its members built a synagogue in 1889 and was affiliated with the rabbinate of Bad Ems. SA units, joined by many townspeople, launched a pogrom on *Kristallnacht* (9–10 Nov. 1938), burning the synagogue and looting J. property. Of the 82 Jews registered there in 1933, 41 emigrated, mostly to the U.S., and 20 perished in the Holocaust.

MONTPELLIER Herault dist., France. Jews are first mentioned in 1121 and were active in commerce. The community was renowned for its distinguished scholars and physicians, including various members of the Ibn Tibbon family such as Yaakov ben Machir ibn Tibbon (1236–1307), an astronomer who played a leading role in defense of philosophy in a polemic between the supporters and opponents of philosophy in M. in the 14th cent. In the 13th cent. M. passed to the kings of Majorca, from whom it was purchased in 1349 by Philip VI of France. In 1359, Jews reestablished the community after being expelled. Final expulsion came in 1394. In the middle of the 16th cent. a community of Conversos emerged in the town, living mainly among the Prostestant pop. Jews from Comtat-Venaissin began to trade in the town. In 1714, nine Jews were permitted to settle. In 1805, the community numbered 105 persons. Its president, R. Moise Milhau, represented the department of Vaucluse at the Sanhedrin (1807) convened by Napoleon. Joseph Salvador (1796–1873), a trained physician who attained prominence as an historian of religions, was born in M. At the beginning of the 20th cent. there were 35 families in M. Prior to WWII, the community numbered 50 families (about 250 persons): two-thirds Ashkenazi and one-third Sephardi Jews. In 1941, there were 800 Jews in M. Since M. was in the unoccupied zone during the war, it became a center for J. refugees from the occupied part of France and abroad, as well as an important relay station for the J. partisans. About 3,500 J. refugees received aid here, including 1,700 French Jews and 1,800 Jews of foreign origin. Wealthy local Jews extended help and cooperation. R. H. Schilli, working with the OSE (Organisation de Secours aux Enfants), managed to save mainly children. ORT and the CAR (Comite d'Assistance aux Refugies) opened branches in M. and the J. Scouts (EIF) and the local Zionist organizations engaged in resistance activities. After liberation, the community was reorganized and in 1964, the J. pop. of M. was 2,300, primarily due to an influx of Jews from North Africa.

MONTREUIL-SOUS-BOIS Seine-Saint-Denis dist., France. Jews settled in M. in the 1880s. Local French Jews were joined by immigrants, mostly from Poland, but also from Russia and Rumania. The Amicale Israelite de Montreuil society (AIM) was established in 1922. A synagogue was constructed in 1932–33 at the initiative of the Foyer Israelite de Montreuil, an association created for the immigrants. Before WWII, the J. pop. numbered 1,757. On 14 May 1941, more than 50 Jews were arrested and sent to the Pithiviers and Beaune-la-Rolande concentration camps. There were further arrests in July, Sept., and Oct. 1942 and again in 1943. From Pithiviers and Drancy, the prisoners were deported to Auschwitz, the Majdanek concentration camp, and the Sobibor death camp. Altogether 501 Jews from M. were deported, including 304 foreign Jews. After liberation, in May 1945, the Commission Centrale de l'Enfance (CCE) established a children's home in M. In 1948, an ORT vocational school was opened.

MOR Fejer dist., Hungary. Jews are first mentioned in 1735. As winegrowers and beer brewers, as well as dealers in knitted goods and steel, they were considered the wealthiest in the district. In 1749, Naftali Rosenthal, a noted scientist and philanthropist with close links with Emperor Joseph II, founded the organized community. M. defined itself as Neologist in 1869. The J. pop. was 483 in 1869 and 150 in 1941.

On 18 June 1944, the Jews were deported via Szekesfehervar to Auschwitz, where 125 perished.

MORAVSKE BUDEJOVICE Moravia, Czechoslovakia. Jews are mentioned in 1386 and again in the 16th cent., when they were active as moneylenders and traded in grain, livestock, and clothing. In 1564 they were expelled, settling again only in the mid-19th cent., though others visited the local fairs before then. In the late 19th cent., Jews contributed to the town's economic development. Their pop. reached a peak of 127 in 1890 and then dropped to 77 (total 4,129) in 1930. The Nazis closed down the synagogue in Oct. 1941 and in May 1942 deported the Jews to the Theresienstadt ghetto via Trebic. About half were transported to the Lublin dist. (Poland) in the same month and others to the Treblinka death camp in Oct. 1942. Few survived.

MORAVSKE LIESKOVE Slovakia, Czechoslovakia, today Republic of Slovakia. Jews numbered 200 in the mid-19th cent., dwindling to 35 in 1920. They remained under the jurisdiction of the Nove Mesto rabbinate until the deportations of 1942. After WWII, a synagogue, cemetery, and school remained.

MORAVSKY KRUMLOV (Yid. Kromenoi) Moravia, Czechoslovakia. Jews are mentioned in 1402. A synagogue was erected in 1547. In 1830, the J. pop. was 356 but after 1848 and the lifting of residence restrictions, it declined steadily as Jews left for the big cities. In 1930, 34 Jews remained (total 2,304). In late 1941–early 1942 the Jews were deported to the Theresienstadt ghetto together with the Jews of Brno and from there sent to the death camps of the east.

MORAVSKY SVATY JAN Slovakia, Czechoslovakia, today Republic of Slovakia. The J. pop. was 190 in 1828 with a synagogue and cemetery in use. In the late 19th cent., many began to leave and by 1930, there were 24 Jews in M.

MORDY Lublin dist., Poland. Jews were probably present in the late 17th cent., organizing communal life around the *beit midrash* and synagogue and the hasidic *shtiblekh* (Gur, Ruzhin, Mezhirech). Their relations with their Polish neighbors were good. The J. pop. grew from 1,206 in 1857 to 1,746 (total 3,268) in 1921. In Sept. 1920 Polish soldiers staged a pogrom, looting J. property and murdering the Bund leader. Four others were accused of helping the Bolsheviks, tried, and executed. Zionist activity expanded after WWI. Most of the town was destroyed in the German bombardments of Sept. 1939. A *Judenrat* was soon established, with an open ghetto set up in summer 1941. Large numbers, including 500 Jews from Warsaw, were put to work in a local labor camp. On 22 Aug. 1942, the 3,500 Jews in M. including refugees were brought to Siedlce and deported to the Treblinka death camp. After liberation by the Red Army in 1945, about 20–25 survivors returned, but most left after 10 or 11 were murdered by Polish partisans in May 1945.

MORENI Walachia dist., Rumania. Jews first settled in the early 20th cent. The J. pop. in 1930 was 156 (3% of the total). On 4 Nov. 1940, the Jews were ordered to leave.

MORINGEN Hanover, Germany. Although some Jews lived there from the 16th cent., no community was established before 1750. Numbering 65 (3% of the total) in 1848, the Jews maintained an elementary school from 1854 to 1918. In June 1933, there were 21 Jews in M. Six left (three emigrating to Palestine) and the community disposed of its synagogue before *Kristallnacht* (9–10 Nov. 1938). The first women's concentration camp, established in M. (1933–38), had 12 J. detainees. Four Jews deported from the town perished in Nazi camps.

MOROZOVSK Rostov dist., Russia. Jews arrived in the late 1920s and numbered 25 (total 11,536) in 1939. The Germans occupied the town in mid-July 1942, later murdering 248 Jews from M. and its environs. On 1 Sept. they murdered 70 and in addition about 40 children brought to the town from the Ukraine as part of the Soviet evacuation.

MORTENI Latgale dist., Latvia. All 37 Jews in this mostly J. agricultural village were murdered under the Germans in the second half of 1941.

MOSBACH Baden, Germany. A J. community existed by the 13th cent. Fifty-five Jews were murdered in the Rindfleisch massacres of 1298. The community was again attacked in 1343 and wiped out in the Black Death persecutions of 1348–49. Few Jews lived there until the early 18th cent., when the community began

to grow despite residence restrictions. They numbered 16 families in 1775. In 1782, Jews obtained the salt monopoly for the entire Palatinate. After annexation to Baden in 1806, restrictions were gradually removed. In 1827, M. became the seat of the district rabbinate, with jurisdiction over 14 communities. A synagogue was built in 1860 and a J. elementary school was in operation in 1830–76. The outstanding rabbi in the period was the Conservative Leopold Loewenstein (1843–1924), who also published important historical works on the Jews of Baden. The J. pop. reached a peak of 229 in 1871 and then declined steadily to 134 (total 4,848) in 1933. At the outset of the Nazi era, Jews operated three factories and 14 business establishments. In all, 107 left in 1933–40, most emigrating from Germany. On *Kristallnacht* (9–10 Nov. 1938), the synagogue was burned down, J. homes were vandalized, and eight J. men were sent to the Dachau concentration camp. Sixteen Jews were deported to the Gurs concentration camp on 22 Oct. 1940. Another 26 were sent to the camps from their places of refuge after leaving M. Of those deported, 39 perished.

MOSCISKA Lwow dist., Poland, today Ukraine. The J. presence dates from the mid-16th cent., but the town was destroyed in the Chmielnicki massacres of 1648–49 and the community was only rehabilitated in the course of the 18th cent. By the end of the 19th cent., the J. pop. had reached 2,500 (60% of the total) with Jews dominating commerce and comprising the majority of the town's tailors, furriers, carpenters, glaziers, and butchers. Zanz Hasidism was the leading force in the community toward the end of the 19th cent., but Haskala and Zionism made early inroads, the latter dominating community life between the World Wars, when economic conditions worsened owing to stiff competition and anti-J. boycotts. The Soviet arrival in late Sept. 1939 quickly put an end to J. commercial and public life. The Germans took the town on 27 June 1941 and, with the J. pop. swelling to 3,500 after expulsions from the surrounding settlements, instituted a regime of forced labor, periodically rounding up Jews at random (500 in May 1942) and sending them to labor camps. In a mass *Aktion* on 10 Oct. (or 28 Nov.) 1942, up to 2,000 were murdered, deported, or sent to the Janowska camp in Lwow. The rest were expelled to the Jaworow ghetto in Dec.

MOSEDIS (Yid. Maisiad) Kretinga dist., Lithuania.

Jews first settled in the 17th cent. and their numbers increased after they received privileges in 1742. The J. pop. in 1897 was 363 (40% of the total). The Bible scholar M. H. Segal (1876–1978), professor at the Hebrew University, was a native of M. The J. pop. in 1940 was 130–150. After the German invasion in June 1941, Lithuanians confined and abused all the Jews in the synagogue for two weeks. In July most of the men were killed at Skuodas; the women and children were killed at Kretinga.

MOSHNY   Kiev dist., Ukraine. Jews numbered 130 in 1784 and 1,022 (total 8,049) in 1897. Most were Hasidim. In 1881, a fire destroyed 60 J. homes and in Aug. 1919 General Denikin's White Army soldiers attacked the Jews of M. In 1926, under the Soviets, 68 Jews remained. The Jews were murdered during the German occupation in WWII.

MOSKALOWKA   Stanislawow dist., Poland. The J. pop. in 1921 was 158. The Jews were executed locally in April 1942, or expelled to Kosow in Oct. 1942.

MOSONMAGYAROVAR   Gyor–Moson dist., Hungary. J. settlement commenced in the early 18th cent. In 1880, the J. pop. was 519, reaching a peak of 646 (5% of the total) in 1920 and then dropping to 466 in 1941. Most Jews were tradesmen and one employed 300 in his factory. After the German occupation of 1944, the Jews were confined in a ghetto in mid-May and on 11–17 June deported to Auschwitz. Thirty survivors returned to reestablish the community, but most left after 1956.

MOST   Bohemia (Sudetenland), Czechoslovakia. A Street of the Jews probably existed from 1356 with the Jews expelled in 1453. The modern community was established in 1861 and a synagogue consecrated in 1873. Jews at first traded in grain and livestock but then became prominent in the coal mining industry. The J. pop. rose to 868 in 1910, with Zionist activity already under way and WIZO, Maccabi, and Hehalutz opening branches after WWI. Jews were also active in public life, serving on the municipal council in 1937. Their pop. was 662 (total 28,212) in 1930. All left in Sept. 1938 with the signing of the Munich Agreement and annexation to Germany. On *Kristallnacht* (9–10 Nov. 1938), the synagogue was burned down and the cemetery desecrated.

MOSTAR   Bosnia-Hercegovina, Yugoslavia, today Republic of Bosnia. The first records of Jews date from the 16th cent. In the 18th cent. more Jews, of Sephardi origin, settled there. Under Austro-Hungarian rule (from 1878) Ashkenazi Jews joined them and a united community was established. Zionist activity began in 1912 and became a dominant part of community life. In 1920 the movement pioneered agricultural training for immigration to Palestine – a first in Yugoslavian Zionism. The J. pop. in 1940 was 142 (total 20,000). In 1941–42 hundreds of refugees arrived ino M. The Italians (ruling from April 1941) protected the Jews from the Germans and Croatians and in 1943 evacuated them to the Adriatic coast and islands in order to save them. After Italy's surrender (Sept. 1943), some Jews joined the partisans and others found a haven in Allied-controlled southern Italy. A small community existed after the war.

MOSTOVOE   Odessa dist., Ukraine. The J. pop. was 862 (total 1,607) in 1897 and 226 in 1939 under the Soviets. The Germans captured M. on 1 Sept. 1941 and murdered the Jews there in the fall. The Rumanians expelled about 4,000 Jews from Odessa and Bessarabia to M. after it was annexed to Transnistria. Many died of starvation and disease; others were shot and their bodies burned.

MOSTY   Bialystok dist., Poland. Jews settled after the nobility received proprietorship of the town, building a new prayer house in 1738. In the 19th cent., Jews were prominent in the lumber trade, floating logs down the Nieman River in summer and supporting themselves as artisans in winter. All had auxiliary farms. After WWI the J. pop. fell from an 1897 peak of 868 (total 2,633) to 171 in 1921, struggling under deteriorating economic conditions. The 350 Jews of M. were expelled by the Germans to Wolkowysk on 2 Nov. 1942 and kept in underground bunkers until deported to the Treblinka death camp at the end of the month.

MOSTY MALE   Lwow dist., Poland, today Ukraine. The J. pop. in 1921 was 147. The Jews were deported to the Belzec death camp in summer–fall 1942, directly or via Rawa Ruska.

MOSTY WIELKIE   Lwow dist., Poland, today Ukraine. Jews, mainly from Belz, were present from the mid-16th cent. with wide-ranging privileges accorded

Members of Agudat Israel's "Maharam of Lublin" pioneer group, Mosty Wielkie, Poland

to the community. However, the town was virtually destroyed in the Tartar invasion of 1662 and the J. settlement was only renewed in the 18th cent., reaching a peak pop. of 1,611 (total 4,454) in 1900. The Jews suffered grievously in WWI, stricken by hunger and then by fire as the retreating Russians burned the town. Ukrainian and Polish soldiers also contributed to the general devastation, which reduced the J. pop. to 1,142 in 1921 (total 3,795). From the early 19th cent., Belz Hasidism dominated communal life, suppressing the Haskala and retarding Zionist activity until after WWI, when it flourished despite depressed economic conditions. After the Soviet regime (1939–41) the Germans took the town in early summer of 1941. A month-long wave of murder and persecution by the Germans and Ukrainians followed. The Jews were allowed to settle into a routine of forced labor until Aug. 1942, when the majority of able-bodied men were confined to a labor camp. The rest of the J. pop. was ordered into a ghetto. The relatively tolerable conditions in the camp under a lenient *Wehrmacht* commander made it a much sought after destination for Jews in the area,

swelling its pop. to around 2,000. Deportations from the ghetto to other, nearby ghettoes commenced in Oct. 1942. Its liquidation occurred on 10 Feb. 1943, when the remaining Jews were taken to the forest and murdered along with about 1,000 of the labor camp inmates. By May the labor camp had been liquidated as well.

MOTOL   (Yid. Motele) Polesie dist., Poland, today Belarus. Jews settled in the first half of the 18th cent. and prospered in the lumber industry. Israel's first president, Chaim Weizmann (1874–1952), was born there and his father headed the community. Jews numbered 1,354 in 1897 and 1,140 (total 4,390) in 1921. The Germans arrived on 26 June 1941. On 2 Aug., 800 J. men were murdered at a local estate; the next day the women and children were executed by an SS cavalry unit.

MOZDOK   Stavropol territory, Russia. Jews settled in the late 19th cent., numbering 44 (total 10,500) in 1877. A wooden synagogue served the community.

During the civil war (1918–21), many Mountain Jews (Tats) fled to M. from their villages and in 1926 numbered 303 of the total 726 Jews in the town. In the late 1920s, most Jews engaged in crafts and trade and a few in agriculture. Over a quarter were unemployed. Some Mountain Jews left in the late 1920s and early 1930s within the framework of government-organized agricultural settlement, including the M. region. A four-year J. elementary school was set up for the Mountain Jews in 1929. After their arrival on 25 Aug. 1942, the Germans murdered all the Jews who had neither fled nor been evacuated.

MOZHAYSK   Moscow dist., Russia. Jews probably settled after the Oct. 1917 Revolution. They numbered 16 in 1926 and 244 (total 11,731) in 1939. After occupying the town in the second half of Oct. 1941, the Germans murdered the few Jews still there. On 20 Nov. they also murdered a number of Jews from the village of Oreshki.

MOZYR   Polesie dist., Belorussia. Jews are first mentioned in the 16th cent. Many were robbed and murdered in the Chmielnicki massacres of 1648–49. In 1766, the number of tax payers within the J. pop. came to 896. In 1897 the J. pop. stood at 5,631 (total 8,076). A Russian-language state J. school was opened in 1899. A yeshiva was also in operation at the time. The Zionists became active in the early 20th cent. In Nov. 1920, the Balakhovich brigade staged a pogrom against the Jews in which 44 were murdered. Many were also injured, women raped, and homes looted. In the early 1920s, under the Soviets, J. teachers were put on trial for continuing to teach the Torah despite a ban against doing so. Two J. elementary school operated until 1938. In 1939, the J. pop. was 6,307. The Germans occupied M. on 22 Aug. 1941. Some Jews managed to flee. A ghetto holding 1,500 Jews was set up in the fall. All were murdered near the village of Bobr during the week of 7 Jan. 1942. Another 700 Jews were drowned in the Pripet River.

MROZY   Warsaw dist., Poland. J. settlement apparently commenced in the late 19th cent. The J. pop. was 306 (total 508) in 1921. The Germans arrived on 12 Sept. 1939 and subjected the Jews to a regime of severe persecution with Polish participation. All were expelled to the Warsaw ghetto in Sept. 1942, perishing in the Treblinka death camp.

MSCIBOW   Bialystok dist., Poland. Jews appeared in the 16th cent. In 1897 the community numbered 389 (total 1,228). During WWI the Jews were able to ward off hunger by working abandoned farm land. After the war 13 families engaged in agriculture. The J. pop. in 1921 was 255. After two years of Soviet rule (1939–41) the Germans arrived in late June 1941. On 2 Nov. the Jews were transferred to the Wolkowysk transit camp and on 26 Nov. all 260 were deported to the Treblinka death camp.

MSELLATA   (also Qusbat), Tripolitania dist., Libya. The medieval J. community was destroyed in the Almohad persecutions of the 12th cent. The Jews fled to the island of Djerba in Tunisia and returned afterwards accompanied by Djerba Jews, who settled in M. In the 16th–19th cents., J merchants participated in the flourishing trans-Sahara trade but the pop. declined in number at the end of the Ottoman period when epidemics struck the area. In 1853, the J. pop. included about 150 families. The Jews excelled in winemaking at the time. In the early 20th cent., with the J. pop. at 700, many were reduced to penury under the burden of heavy taxes. Jews engaged in petty trade and crafts (jewelers, tailors, metalworkers, shoemakers) while the women did weaving, sewing, and embroidery work. The wealthier Jews also engaged in moneylending. During the Arab Revolt (1915–22) that followed the Italian occupation of 1911, Jews fled the city, afterwards returning to resume their former occupations under the same conditions of impoverishment. In 1931, the J. pop. was 342 (total 12,125). In 1930, the young, dynamic Bibi Shakir became president of the community, remaining in office until 1950 and doing much for the welfare of the community. Yosef Jerad and Makhluf Shakir served as rabbis and teachers between the World Wars. Boys studied at the Italian public school in the mornings and at the *talmud torah* in the afternoon. In 1940, Arabs attacked Jews, vandalized J. homes, and burned the synagogue after a foiled attempt to kidnap a J. girl. On 5 Nov. 1945, in the wake of the Tripoli riots, Jews were again attacked and robbed, with three murdered. Jews were then made to undergo mass conversion as a condition for stopping the riots. Only the arrival of the British army put a stop to the proceedings. Jews subsequently began leaving for Tripoli and Khoms and by 1949 the last had left, en route to Israel.

Synagogue in Mstislavl, Belorussia, built in the first half of the 17th cent. According to the Jewish community's record book, when Czar Peter the Great arrived in the town in Aug. 1708 his soldiers attempted to stage a pogrom. "And if God had not moved the Czar to personally visit our synagogue there would have been bloodshed. Only with the help of God did the Czar save us ... and the land quieted down." (YIVO Archive, New York/photo courtesy of Yad Vashem, The Holocaust Martyrs' and Heroes' Remembrance Authority, Jerusalem)

MSTISLAVL Mogilev dist., Belorussia. Jews first settled in the 16th cent. and formed an organized community by the beginning of the 17th. Peter the Great's soldiers staged a pogrom against the Jews in 1708. In 1765, the community included 552 poll tax payers. In 1808, a group of 271 Jews, from among the poorer class, left the town and settled in a J. agricultural colony in the Novorossyisk region. The J. pop. rose to 5,076 (total 8,514) in 1897. In the late 19th cent., M. was a commercial center owing to the activity of J. merchants. Of the town's 291 artisans, 194 were Jews. The well-known J. historian, Simon Dubnow (1860–1941), was born in M. as was Dr. Moshe Rachmilewitz (1899–1985) of Hadassah Hospital, one of the founders of the Hebrew University School of Medicine. In 1920, under the Soviets, a J. elementary school (four grades) was opened and in 1927 it had an attendance of 52 children. A J. kolkhoz was founded in 1924, accommodating 45 families in 1930. A second J. kolkhoz, established in 1925, had 64 families in 1930. J. shoemakers set up the first artisan cooperative in the town in 1928. In 1939, the J. pop. was 2,067. The Germans captured M. on 14 July 1941. Some Jews succeeded in fleeing. In early Oct. the Germans murdered 30 elderly Jews and on 15 Oct., with the aid of local police, they massacred 850 (other sources have 1,300) in the market square.

MSTIZH Minsk dist., Belorussia. Jews settled in the 19th cent. and numbered 28 families in 1926. In the mid-1920s, 20–25 J. children were still studying in *hadarim*. The few remaining Jews were murdered by the Germans after their arrival in late June 1941.

MSTOW (Yid. Emstow) Kielce dist., Poland. The few Jews probably present before the Third Partition of Poland in 1795 grew to 200 families by the end of WWI. Many earned their livings weaving coarse wool. In the 1930s, economic conditions deteriorated in the face of Polish competition. There were 532 Jews in M. on the eve of the German occupation in Sept.

1939. Their property was confiscated and they were subjected to forced labor. In Aug. 1942, about 600, including refugees, were brought to the Radomsk ghetto and in Oct. they were deported to the Treblinka death camp. Some young men succeeded in escaping the deportation only to be caught later and executed at the J. cemetery.

MSZANA DOLNA   Cracow dist., Poland. Jews are first mentioned in the late 19th cent., their pop. reaching 410 (total 3,016) in 1921. Anti-J. agitation and disturbances marked the period between the World Wars. The J. pop. in 1939 was 800. In the second half of 1941, the Germans set up a *Judenrat* along with a ghetto for the 900–1,000 Jews in M., including 200 refugees. Most were made to work in the local quarries. On 19 Aug. 1942, all but 120–130 young men were executed at a nearby cannery. The remnant was returned to forced labor and subsequently liquidated.

MSZCZONOW   (Yid. Amshinov) Warsaw dist., Poland. Jews probably settled in the late 17th cent. The J. pop. grew to 2,523 in 1897 (total 5,124), having recovered slowly from a fire that destroyed 100 homes and the synagogue in 1862. R. Yaakov David Kalish (d. 1878), a descendant of R. Yitzhak of Warka, founded the hasidic Amshinov dynasty, whose court was maintained until the Holocaust. After WWI, Agudat Israel was a strong influence in the community but the Zionists also made inroads. The Germans captured M. on 5 Sept. 1939, shooting 13 Jews and burning others alive in the synagogue. Most were expelled to the Warsaw ghetto on 6 Feb. 1941; the remainder on 8 July 1942.

MTZENSK   Oriol dist., Russia. J. settlement probably began in the late 19th cent. The J. pop. was 151 in 1926 and 115 (total 11,480) in 1939. The Germans occupied M. on 11 Oct. 1941 and apparently murdered the few remaining Jews towards the end of the year.

MUEHLHAUSEN (I)   Saxony, Germany. The first definite evidence of a J. presence in M. dates from 1278. The community, which had a synagogue in 1380 and a cemetery in 1407, suffered from intermittent persecution, including the Black Death disturbances of 1348–49. The Jews were finally expelled in 1561. In 1643, J. settlement was renewed. The medieval cemetery was in use up to 1860 and then replaced by a new one. A synagogue was built in the 1840s. Towards the end of the 19th cent., the Jews played an important role in the local textile industry, constituting at times as much as 30% of the textile manufacturers. From as early as 1848, up to 1926, Jews were elected to the city council. Between 1880 and 1925, the J. pop. of M. was about 190. In 1933, when the Nazis came to power, it was 170. Emigration began against a background of boycotts, attacks, and a show trial on charges of so-called racial defilement (*Rassenschande*). By Jan. 1938 the community numbered 110. On *Kristallnacht* (9–10 Nov. 1938), the synagogue and the cemetery were wrecked while businesses and homes were looted and destroyed. The community's teacher was shot and two elderly women were beaten up on the street, dying shortly afterwards either from their injuries or by suicide. Some 20–30 Jews were arrested and taken to the Buchenwald concentration camp. In 1942, 34 of the remaining Jews were deported to the east. In Oct., only 19 Jews were left in the city, most of them probably protected by marriage to non-Jews. In all, at least 59 Jews from M. perished under Nazi rule, including several who sought refuge in other cities or neighboring countries.

MUEHLHAUSEN (II)   (Pol. Mlynary) East Prussia, Germany, today Poland. Evidence of a J. presence dates from the early 19th cent. The community remained small, numbering 47 in 1880 and 33 in 1925. There was a cemetery and religious services were held in a private house. No information is available about the fate of the 31 Jews of M. after the Nazis assumed power in 1933.

MUEHLHEIM AM MAIN   Hesse, Germany. Jews settled there in 1815, but a community was not established until 1887, when they numbered around 60 (1% of the total). Jews in nearby Dietesheim formed part of the congregation. As late as March 1933, the Social Democrat vote in M. exceeded the Nazi vote. When the Nazis came to power, they imposed a rigorous anti-J. boycott. On *Kristallnacht* (9–10 Nov. 1938), they vandalized the synagogue. Altogether, 50 Jews emigrated from M. and Dietesheim (mainly to the U.S.); 19 of those who moved to other parts of Germany died in the Holocaust.

MUEHLHEIM AN DER RUHR   Rhineland, Germany. Jews are mentioned for the first time in 1620. Thereafter letters of protection granted to the Jews in the duchy of Broich allowed them to engage in trade, moneylending, and butchering. Despite a specific ban, they also seem to have dealt in hides and furs. In the 18th cent., Samuel Gumbel achieved prominence in sea transport and as court banker of Broich, becoming a member of the prestigious Societaet social club. A new synagogue was erected in the 1790s and a J. school was in operation by the end of French rule in 1815. In the first half of the 19th cent., most Jews were butchers; in the second half of the cent., trade became the leading occupation. Gustav Hanau, a grandson of Samuel Gumbel, served as a city assemblyman from 1849 to 1902 and other Jews fought in Germany's wars. The J. pop. reached 250 in 1852 and then grew to 643 (total 38,000) in 1900. M. became the seat of a regional congregation in 1855. Jews were active in local life, belonging to sports and music clubs and the War Veterans Association. They also did charity work. Jews entered new fields of employment, with one developing a method for producing margarine that dominated the industry. Among artists, Arthur Kaufmann (1888–1971) became famous as a founder of the Young Rhineland group in 1919. His painting "Our Generation – Duesseldorf of the Spirit, 1925" is considered the seminal work of the New Objectivism. A new synagogue was consecrated in 1907. In 1913, Meyer Kann became chairman of the community, serving until 1943. In the Weimar period, most Jews of the established class were members of the bourgeoisie while Jews of East European origin occupied a lower socio-economic rung with their own areas of trade and crafts (shoemakers, tailors, junk dealers, etc.). During the first quarter of the 20th cent., at least 100 East European Jews arrived in the city, partially offsetting the declining birthrate among local Jews that brought about a drop of 22% in the J. pop. between 1910 and 1933. Most East European Jews were Orthodox and some preferred to pray in the East European prayer house of Oberhausen, generally keeping their distance from the old community. After WWI, they also founded a local branch of the East European Cultural Society, a body with links to the Zionist movement. A number of J. youth groups were also active, such as the Juedischer Jugendbund. While Zionist affinities were in general weak, a sports club, affiliated with the Maccabi organization, was founded in 1925. Jews continued to be active in political life but antisemitism also continued to make inroads. In 1932, the J. cemetery was desecrated. In both the Reichstag and Landtag elections of March

1933, the Nazis received about 37% of the vote. In mid-1933, the J. pop. was 517 (total 133,279). Anti-J. boycott activities commenced even before 1 April, the official boycott day. Jews were subsequently dismissed from public employment and banned from local swimming pools. About 200 Jews, many of East European origin, emigrated in 1933–36. About a third of those who remained were on relief as economic conditions deteriorated. By early Nov. 1938, 250 Jews were left in the city. On *Kristallnacht* (9–10 Nov. 1938), J. homes and stores were destroyed, the synagogue was burned, and about 80 Jews were arrested and detained in the Dachau and Buchenwald concentration camps for up to a month and a half. At least 259 Jews managed to emigrate during the Nazi era, including 57 to Palestine, 48 to the U.S., and 65 to South America (39 to Argentina). The remaining Jews were moved to at least nine "J. houses" in Aug. 1939. In summer 1941, they were mobilized for forced labor, moving pipelines in the Broich forest. Deportations began on 27 Oct. 1941, when at least 22 Jews were sent to the Lodz ghetto. At least 21 were deported to the Riga ghetto on 10 Dec. and at least 55 to Auschwitz on 21 April 1942. Another 43 at least were transported to the Theresienstadt ghetto on 21 July 1942. A few more were deported on various occasions in 1942 and 1943. Jews were also deported from places of refuge in occupied Europe, including 20 from Holland. Of the 291 known deportees, 265 perished in the camps. The community was reestablished after the war, reaching a pop. of 76 in 1960. With the influx of Soviet Jews, the pop. rose to 700 in 1995 and 1,250 in late 1996. A community center with a synagogue was dedicated in 1960.

MUEHRINGEN Wuerttemberg, Germany. Jews arrived during the Reformation and the community enjoyed steady growth and economic prosperity from the mid-18th cent., reaching a peak pop. of 512 in 1854. M. was a center for the J. communities of southwest Germany, becoming the seat of the district rabbinate in 1832 while its ancient cemetery, the largest and most beautiful in Wuerttemberg, served Jews far and wide. A synagogue was dedicated in 1728 and a J. public school in 1825. Emigration reduced the J. pop. sharply in the second half of the 19th cent. In 1933, 45 Jews remained (total 608), mostly engaged in the cattle trade. Good relations prevailed with the local pop., which resisted Nazi measures. On *Kristallnacht*

(9–10 Nov. 1938), when the synagogue was set on fire by SA troops, it was saved by the local fire department. Sixteen Jews emigrated to the U.S. and 11 were expelled and perished.

MUELHAUSEN   Upper Franconia, Germany. The community suffered grievously during the Thirty Years War (1618–48), fleeing to Hochstadt in 1631. In the early 18th cent. it consecrated a cemetery and synagogue. The J. pop. reached 187 in 1812 (total 758), declining steadily to 43 in 1933. On *Kristallnacht* (9–10 Nov. 1938) the synagogue and 15 J. homes were vandalized. On 14 May 1939, nearly all the tombstones in the cemetery were smashed. In 1938–42, 16 Jews emigrated, including 11 to the U.S., and 12 left for other German cities. The last four Jews were deported to Izbica in the Lublin dist. (Poland) and to the Theresienstadt ghetto in 1942.

MUELHEIM   Rhineland, Germany. There is evidence of a "Jews' Alley" in 1456, indicating previous J. settlement. A community developed towards the end of the 18th cent., numbering 57 Jews in 1811. The community was formally constituted in 1863. There were 71 Jews in 1885 and 63 (1.5% of the total) in 1925 when a synagogue was consecrated. Prior to the Nazi takeover in 1933, a wave of cemetery and synagogue desecrations took place. On *Kristallnacht* (9–10 Nov. 1938), the synagogue was burned down. In March 1942, 27 Jews were deported directly from the town to the Nazi death camps; three more were deported on 1 July.

MUELLHEIM   Baden, Germany. Four J. families from Stuehlingen and Switzerland arrived in 1716. A synagogue was built in 1754 and a religious school was opened in 1790. The *beit midrash* founded in 1819 under Reform influence provided rabbis and leaders to communities throughout Germany. A J. elementary school was opened in 1828 and a new synagogue in the Neo-Romantic style was erected in 1830. Jews fled during the revolutionary disturbances of 1848, when their homes were attacked. They earned their livelihoods as cattle and horse traders, wine merchants, and shopkeepers. The J. pop. reached a peak of 422 in 1864 (total 2,997). With the trend of emigration setting in, the J. pop. fell steadily to 80 in 1933. On *Kristallnacht* (9–10 Nov. 1938), the synagogue, community center, and J. homes were vandalized and most J.

men were sent to the Dachau concentration camp. Afterwards, the last J. businesses closed and emigration was stepped up. In all, 51 Jews emigrated in the Nazi period, most to the U.S. and Switzerland. Fourteen of those who had left for other German cities or for subsequently occupied European cities perished in the camps, 11 of them at Auschwitz.

MUENCHEBERG   Brandenburg, Germany. Jews lived in M. from 1353 until the expulsion of all the Jews of Brandenburg in 1510. There is evidence of Jews living in M. from 1674. The J. community numbered three families in 1743 and 55 individuals in 1880. It maintained a synagogue and a cemetery from 1756. When the Nazis came to power in 1933, there were 34 Jews in M. On *Kristallnacht* (9–10 Nov. 1938), the synagogue went up in flames, windows in J. apartments were smashed, and J. men were arrested. It may be assumed that those who did not manage to emigrate were deported to the east. In Oct. 1942, only one Jew was still living in M., probably protected by marriage to a non-Jew.

MUENSTER (I)   Hesse, Germany. The community numbered 48 (3% of the total) in 1861 and 19 in 1933. Most of the remaining Jews left after *Kristallnacht* (9–10 Nov. 1938). Six emigrated, but eight were deported to Auschwitz and the Theresienstadt ghetto in 1942.

MUENSTER (II)   Westphalia, Germany. Two Jews arrived c. 1130 to collect a debt from the local bishop. Jews apparently began to settle later in the cent. and may have established a permanent settlement by the late 13th cent. In the first half of the 14th cent., the community was the largest and most important in the bishopric, maintaining a synagogue, cemetery, *mikve*, and kosher butchering facilities. The community ended in 1350, either through massacre or expulsion during the upheaval associated with the Black Death. Jews only returned to M. in the first half of the 16th cent. after ten J. families were granted protection by Bishop Franz von Waldeck in 1536. They earned their livelihoods as small-scale moneylenders and lived on the outskirts of the city. However, in 1554, after the Bishop's death, the municipal council expelled all the Jews. Jews again received letters of protection from the local bishops in the 17th and 18th cent. but the municipality denied them permanent residence rights. Nonetheless their number in the whole bishopric increased to 203 families in 1795. Most Jews engaged in peddling and petty trade. Only in 1810, under the French authorities as rulers of the Grand Duchy of Berg, were Jews allowed to settle permanently in the town for the first time since the 1554 expulsion. In 1852, the J pop. was 275, increasing to 567 (total 58,135) by 1895. During the 19th cent., the Jews began increasingly to regard themselves as Prussians "by blood and property" (*"mit Gut und Blut Preussen"*), though there are no recorded instances of conversion or intermarriage. By 1836, most J. children had German first names and integration into German society continued apace. Jews served in municipal government and other public positions. At the same time, from the late 19th cent., various antisemitic publications made their appearance in the city and in 1900 Jews were banned from a local commercial agents association. A new J. cemetery was opened in 1811 and a new synagogue was consecrated in 1880. In 1815, Dr. Abraham Sutro (1784–1869) became state rabbi (*Landrabbiner*) with his seat in M. from 1816. Though not acting as local rabbi, his influence on the community was great and he was a leader in the Orthodox struggle against the Reform movement as well as in the fight for J. equal rights. In 1861, after 50 years of service, Dr. Sutro became the first German rabbi to be awarded the Imperial Order of Excellence. The leader of the Reform movement in M. from the mid-1840s was Dr. Salomon Friedlaender, grandson of the Reform state rabbi of Westphalia and Wittgenstein, Yosef Avraham Friedlaender. Reform continued to make inroads and an organ was installed in the new synagogue. Under the influence of Dr. Friedlaender the spirit of Reform also spread to the J. Teachers and Artisans Seminary founded in 1827 by Alexander Heindorf. By 1848, 130 teachers and 250 student artisans had graduated from the seminary and by 1871, 244 and 346, respectively. Between 1895 and 1900, the seminary accommodated about 80 students a year. About 40 students attended the attached J. elementary school and about 20 (1% of the student body) were enrolled at the local university. The J. pop. reached a peak of 732 in 1919. In the Weimar period, Jews continued to engage mainly in commerce (60% of breadwinners), including the cattle and grain trade. About 30 Jews were in the trades (eight butchers, six seamstresses, four painters, etc.) and about 25 belonged to the professional class (five lawyers, five doctors and dentists, etc.). Six

were public servants and, in all, 51% were self-employed. Jews also continued to serve on the municipal council and in various local societies (sports, music, volunteer firemen, etc.). Other societies, including the student societies, still refused to allow J. membership. In general, Jews and Germans were not intimate to the extent of inviting one another to family celebrations and an undercurrent of antisemitism was always present. In 1919, Dr. Fritz Steinthal became district rabbi, the first since the retirement of Dr. Sutro. Also in 1919, the first Zionist group in the city was started. By 1925, 4% of the Jews were foreign nationals (mostly of East European origin). Between 1928 and 1931, 12 of 31 J. marriages involved a non-J. partner and in 1933, six of eight. Most of the children were raised as Christians.

The J. pop. in 1933 was 558 (total 122,210). In March 1933, the Nazis received 40.2% of the vote in the Reichstag elections. Already in Feb., members of the Nazi Students Union disrupted a lecture at the university by a J. professor. The boycott against J. stores also started earlier than in other places (at least five closed in 1933). On 29 March, two J. lawyers were ejected by Nazis from the regional court and J. professors were prevented from entering the university. Jews were subsequently dismissed from their jobs and from the public service. All J. lecturers were dismissed from the university by 1936, a total of 22 including those married to Jews. In Aug. 1935, Jews were banned from municipal swimming pools and libraries. Jews were also prohibited from sailing on the Werse and Ems rivers. SS forces vandalized J. stores and homes. By early Nov. 1938, 25 J. stores had been sold off. In Oct. 1938, 16 Jews with Polish citizenship were expelled to Poland. Despite emigration, the J. pop. was still above 550 in 1938 as Jews arrived from neighboring settlements. Among the emigrants was Dr. Steinthal, who moved to Argentina in 1938 and was replaced by Dr. Julius Voos. Zionist activity continued. In 1935 the local Zionist group numbered 63 members, WIZO 33, and a Hehalutz group 15. On *Kristallnacht* (9–10 Nov. 1938), the synagogue was burned and at least nine J. stores and 11 J. homes were destroyed. Jews were beaten and arrested. With emigration continuing, the J. pop. dropped to 350 in 1939, 200 in 1940, and 100 in 1941. At least 40 J. stores were sold between Dec. 1938 and March 1939, leaving none under J. ownership. In summer 1939, Jews began to move to 14 special "J. houses." In 1933–45, 264 (or 280) Jews emigrated, including 49 to the U.S., 48 to Holand, 45 to Palestine, and 36 to England. On 13 Dec. 1941, 104 local Jews were included in the first transport of 1,000 Westphalian Jews deported to the Riga ghetto. Another 11 were sent there on 27 Jan. 1942. On 30 or 31 March 1942, 11 Jews were deported to the Warsaw ghetto and in the last transport with Jews from M., 50 (the old, the sick, and children under the age of six) were sent to the Theresienstadt ghetto. Estimates of the number of local Jews who perished in the Holocaust vary between 247 and 288; 24 are known to have survived the concentration camps. A community of 28–35 Jews was established after the war. The congregation numbered 136 in 1960 (including 40 from neighboring settlements). A new synagogue was consecrated in 1961 and in 1993 the J. pop. reached 252, mostly from Russia, Poland, and Israel. Anti-J. incidents occurred throughout the postwar period.

MUENSTEREIFEL Rhineland, Germany. Jews were victimized in 1349 during the Black Death persecutions. They are mentioned again in the early 17th cent. Five J. families were present in the 1656–66 period, mainly trading in livestock and maintaining a synagogue in a residential building. At the turn of the 17th cent., encouraged by the authorities, a number of Jews converted to advance themselves economically. The J. pop. reached a peak of 133 (total 2,518) in 1868. A Jew was elected to the municipal council in 1857. After the passage of the Prussian "J. Law" of 1847, M. became part of the Rheinbach regional congregation. A private J. elementary school was opened in 1824 and operated intermittently. From 1859 it was housed in the synagogue building and attended by 30–34 children. In 1849, the first Jew graduated from the municipal high school. Jews considered themselves full citizens and were accepted as such in the town. Their pop. dropped to 100 in 1900 and 65 in 1933. In the Weimar period, their economic condition was generally good. In the early 1930s, ten were cattle dealers, four merchants, and three butchers. The Oskar Nathan textile and shoe store was the largest retail enterprise in M. Under the Nazis, J. merchants were targeted for persecution. On *Kristallnacht* (9–10 Nov. 1938), J. homes and stores were vandalized along with the synagogue and J. cemetery. The disturbances effectively ended J. commercial life in the town as Jews sold off their businesses and homes. Many left, going abroad or moving in with relatives in Cologne. By the end

of 1938, 15 Jews had emigrated, mainly to the U.S. Fifteen remained in early 1941. In summer 1941, they were confined with other Jews in a camp in the region and from there deported to the death camps. In all, 28 Jews perished in the Holocaust along with another 11 from the neighboring towns of Arloff and Kirspenich.

MUENSTERMAIFELD Rhineland, Germany. Ninety Jews were murdered in M. on 17 July 1287 in the wake of the Oberwesel blood libel. Jews were attacked again in 1337 and in the Black Death persecutions of 1348–49. They are mentioned again in 1410, maintaining a synagogue and school. The modern community had a pop. of 40–70 in the 19th cent. A synagogue was erected in 1887. Of the 60 Jews present when the Nazis came to power, 32 left before the outbreak of war in 1939. The synagogue was burned on *Kristallnacht* (9–10 Nov. 1938). Two Jews died in the Dachau concentration camp in 1941. In 1942, 15 were deported to the east, where they perished. In all, 25 natives of M. are known to have died in the Holocaust.

MUENZENBERG Hesse, Germany. Townsfolk instigated a blood libel against the medieval community in 1188, but Jews from Mainz, Worms, and Speyer found temporary shelter there during the Third Crusade (1189–92). Having become a regional Torah center, the community flourished until the Black Death persecutions of 1348–49, when the Jews were expelled. They returned about 100 years later and comprised a third of the pop. in 1700. Numbering 138 (14%) in 1861, they dwindled to 32 by 1914. Nazis organized a pogrom in advance of *Kristallnacht* (9–10 Nov. 1938) and destroyed the synagogue's interior. Most Jews had left by 1939; seven were deported in 1942.

MUENZESHEIM Baden, Germany. Jews were present from the 17th cent., reaching a peak pop. of 90 in 1801 but living in straitened economic circumstances. In 1933, 17 Jews remained. By 1938, five had emigrated to the U.S. and one to Holland. The synagogue, built in 1750, was sold in 1937 and the rest of the community was variously dispersed.

MUGGENSTURM Baden, Germany. The J. pop. in 1875 was 80. By 1939 the Jews of M. belonged to the Rastatt community. The last three Jews were deported by the Germans in WWII.

Doorway of Jewish home, Mukacevo, Czechoslovakia, 1938

MUKACEVO (Hung. Munkacs) Carpatho-Russia, Czechoslovakia, today Ukraine. Jews probably arrived in the latter half of the 17th cent. and comprised nine families in 1736. Their pop. rose to 651 in 1830 and 4,468 (total 9,644) in 1880. Before the mid-19th cent., M. had become one of the important centers of Hungarian Hasidism and later of Czechoslovakian Hasidism as well. The yeshiva founded in 1851 reached the peak of its activity when the hasidic leader

Performing tashlikh *("sin-casting") ceremony from bridge over a stream in Mukacevo, Czechoslovakia (Bildarchiv Abraham Pisarek, Berlin/photo courtesy of Yad Vashem, The Holocaust Martyrs' and Heroes' Remembrance Authority, Jerusalem)*

Hayyim Eleazar Shapira served as rabbi of the community (1914–37). At its height, the yeshiva had an enrollment of 250 students from various countries. In the period of the Czechoslovakian Republic, the J. pop. rose significantly, to 10,012 in 1921 and 13,488 (total 21,602) in 1941. The community maintained a number of *talmudei torah*, elementary schools, a Beth Jacob school for girls, an orphanage, and a few kindergartens. A Hebrew elementary school was opened in 1920, joined in 1925 by the first Hebrew secondary school to be opened in Czechoslovakia. Zionist as well as non-Zionist political parties were active in the community. Four newspapers and periodicals were published in Yiddish. Many Jews were professional people and the community included 20 doctors, 21 lawyers, five pharmacists, and a number of engineers and administrative officials. Hungary annexed M. in Nov. 1938. J. livelihoods were gradually undermined and in 1940–41, hundreds of Jews were drafted into labor battalions for forced labor or service on the eastern front, where many died. In late July and early Aug. 1941, dozens of families without Hungarian citizenship were expelled to Stanislawow in Eastern Galicia and to Kamenets-Podolski, many perishing. After the Germans occupied Hungary in March 1944, the Jews of M. as well as those from a number of settlements in the Berehovo dist. were concentrated in an improvised ghetto and a *Judenrat* was appointed. In the second half of May, several transports made their way to Auschwitz. After the war, about 2,500 Jews returned to the city, but after it was annexed by the Soviet Union many left for Czechoslovakia or emigrated to Palestine and other countries.

MULHOUSE (Muelhausen)   Haut-Rhin   dist., France. The earliest reference to Jews in M. dates from 1290. There was a massacre of Jews in 1337 and persecution during the Black Death disturbances of 1348–49. According to official documents from 1385, the Jews had to pay the treasury a sum equal to a third of their assets. In 1418, nine J. families were living in M. Though not expelled, there were no Jews in M. between 1512 and 1655. At the beginning of the 18th cent., the few J. families residing in M. engaged in commerce, which aroused the ire of Christian competitors. By 1784, 23 families (94 persons) resided in the town. Following riots in Alsace in 1789, the number of Jews in M. grew. The first small synagogue built in 1822 was replaced by a new one in

1849. The community founded a school in 1842 and an almshouse-hospital in 1863. Alfred Dreyfus (1859–1935) was born here. By 1885, the J. pop. was 3,839, decreasing to 3,506 in 1905 and 2,710 in 1926. From 1930, the *Kadima* bulletin provided information about the social activities of the local mutual aid societies. The Zionists were active, establishing a society with 60 members in 1935, as well as committees representing Keren Hayesod, Keren Kayemet (nine members), and Maccabi (30 members). On the eve of WWII, the community decreased to 2,240 members. Under the German occupation, M. was the site of a regional camp, mainly for female internees. On 16 July 1940, the Jews of M. were expelled by the Germans to the south of France, along with the other Jews of Alsace-Lorraine. The synagogue, partially damaged, was saved from total destruction. In 1964, the community numbered 1,920 members.

MUNICH (Muenchen) Upper Bavaria, Germany.

Jews were present in the early 13th cent., living in a J. quarter with a synagogue, cemetery, and other communal facilities. Most of the trade between east and west passing through the town was in the hands of Jews, who dealt in furs, jewelry, and spices. They also served the rulers of Bavaria as moneylenders. In 1285 the community was wiped out in a blood libel when 180 Jews, refusing to convert, were burned alive in the synagogue. Persecution continued throughout the 14th cent. alongside various ducal privileges. With the expulsion of the community in 1442, followed in 1450 by the expulsion of the rest of the Jews of Bavaria, J. property was impounded and the synagogue converted into a church. In 1489, the J. cemetery was plowed under and the tombstones used as building blocks. A small community was reestablished in the late 17th cent. but in 1715 it, too, was expelled. Later in the 18th cent. a number of Court Jews were allowed to settle in M. These included Wolf Wertheimer and the Bavarian army supplier Aron Elias Se-

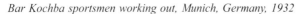

Bar Kochba sportsmen working out, Munich, Germany, 1932

ligmann. Jews continued to finance Bavaria's wars into the 19th cent., providing the state treasury with 80% of its budget in the Napoleonic era. Jews also acted as moneychangers, discounted promissory notes, and traded in salt and horses. The new community numbered 216 in 1798 and its first rabbi was appointed in 1802. In 1805 Jews were permitted to live in all parts of the city, engage in crafts, trade in certain goods, and conduct public prayer. A "Jew decree" in 1813 allowed 30 additional well-to-do families to settle in M. but limited the right to start new families in the city to eldest sons. Jews continued to play a leading role in banking and opened numerous factories, particularly in the food and clothing industries, helping to make M. an important commercial center. By 1848 the J. pop. stood at 842 (total 87,000), with about 20% engaged in farming and the crafts. In the first half of the 19th cent., a number of J. schools were established. The Wolfsheimer public school, opened in 1842, had 215 pupils in 1862–63 but was forced to close in 1872 under assimilationist pressure, leaving the community without a J. day school until after WWI while local children attended German schools. In the face of the restrictions of the 1813 "Jew decree," many disqualified from starting families left the city, mainly for the U.S. After it was rescinded in 1861 the J. pop. began to grow rapidly, reaching 4,144 in 1880, making the community the largest in Bavaria. After 1885 immigration from Eastern Europe, first mostly from Austro-Hungary and then from Russia, pushed the J. pop. up to its peak of 11,083 in 1910 (total 596,467). The community was economically well-off and strongly assimilationist, with intermarriage amounting to 24% in 1880 and 50% in 1915. The department store opened by Hermann Tietz in 1888 led to the spread of such stores throughout Germany. The Jews monopolized the textile industry as well as bank-related real estate brokerage. In 1907, 43% of M.'s Jews were engaged in trade, 14% in crafts, and 11% in the professions, including 118 doctors, 100 lawyers, and eight judges. The community operated a broad range of social services, including an old age home, summer camps, and welfare and employment agencies. With the secularization of J. life, the Reform movement grew stronger under the leadership of R. Dr. Josef Perles (1871–94), a noted Orientalist, and R. Dr. Cosman Werner (1895–1918), who was among those rejecting Theodor Herzl's proposal to hold the First Zionist Congress in M. in 1897. A mag-

nificent synagogue was completed in 1887, incorporating an organ and changing the prayer service. The Orthodox countered by forming their own Jeshurun congregation. The community also housed an important J. library with the largest collection of Hebrew manuscripts in the German-speaking world. Raphael Nathan Rabbinovicz published his *Dikdukei Soferim* there in 16 vols. (1867–97), an anthology of variant readings of the Babylonian Talmud that became one of the cornerstones of J. scholarship. Antisemitism, always rife in Bavaria, intensified during WWI and continued unabated in the Weimar Republic when M. became the cradle of the Nazi movement and Hitler's home, with the major Nazi organ, the *Voelkischer Beobachter*, published there. A particular hotbed of antisemitism was the university, where J. students (numbering 247 in 1928) were attacked and J. candidates for teaching positions rejected on racial grounds. In 1923, the year of Hitler's unsuccessful "beer hall putsch," Nazi thugs beat Jews in the streets and on public transportation facilities and 180 J. families of East European origin were expelled from the city. Between the World Wars a declining birthrate and increasing intermarriage (59% in 1931) continued to contribute to the drop in the J. pop. that had commenced in WWI. In 1924 a J. public school was opened, reaching an enrollment of 132 in 1932–33. A *talmud torah* provided supplementary J. education and WIZO operated a Hebrew kindergarten. Among the East European Jews, numbering 2,300 in 1931, or 25% of the community, and having little contact with the social institutions of the German Jews, most of the young were organized in Zionist youth movements. M. was also the center of many Bavarian and German J. organizations — 68 in 1932 — and the home of such figures as the young Albert Einstein (1877–1955), Nobel Prize chemist Richard Willstaetter (1872–1942), and the writers Arnold Zweig (1877–1968) and Lion Feuchtwanger (1884–1958).

In 1933 the J. pop. was 9,005 (total 735,388). Over 50% were engaged in commerce, industry, and crafts; 22% in banking and brokerage; and 20% in the professions. With the advent of Nazi rule a regime of severe persecution was instituted. Jews were arrested and sent to Dachau, the first of Germany's concentration camps. A strict economic boycott was enforced and Germans were kept away from J. stores while nearly half the city's J. lawyers were barred from appearing in court and J. civil servants were fired. In May 1935 J. store windows were smashed throughout the

Phot.:
Lamm

Münchener jüdisches Jugendheim
Kaffeetafel — Führerberatung — Zeitungslektüre — Unterricht — Schachspiel —
Orchester — Tischtennis.

At the Jewish Youth Center, Munich, Germany, 1932

city and the stores forcibly closed with Hitler Youth painting "Jews Not Wanted Here" signs on sidewalks. Windows were again smashed on 14 Aug. and the Nazi paper *Der Stuermer* started publishing lists of "Aryans" patronizing J. businesses. In Aug.–Oct. 50 Jews were tried for violating the racial defilement (*Rassenschande*) provision of the Nuremberg Laws. Despite Nazi actions, J. community life was maintained. The J. public school system was expanded to accommodate 407 children by 1935–36 and various vocational schools were in operation. A branch of the J. Cultural Association (Juedischer Kulturbund) supported the arts and invited such figures as Martin Buber to deliver lectures. During the 1933–38 period, 3,574 Jews left the city while another 803 died. Of the emigrants, 3,130 left Germany entirely, including 701 to Palestine and 637 to the U.S. In June 1938, the Great Synagogue was razed by the local authorities. Community institutions were transferred to an abandoned J. cigarette factory, with the production floor serving as a synagogue. On 9 Nov. 1938, Propaganda Minister Josef Goebbels delivered a virulent antisemitic speech in M. that sparked the *Kristallnacht* riots throughout Germany. In M., store windows were smashed, the interior of the Orthodox Ohel Yaakov synagogue was destroyed along with other communal property, and around 1,000 Jews were arrested. In May 1939 all Jews of Polish origin were expelled from the city while the Aryanization Office continued to press for the liquidation of J. businesses, bringing the total still open by March 1939 down to 27, most engaging in apartment rentals. Until fall 1941, Jews were evicted from 1,440 apartments, the best of them being handed over to "deserving" Nazis. Jews on the community's relief rolls were subjected to forced labor, many in the construction of the Milbertshofen ghetto about 4 miles from the city, where 450 Jews were sent to live in 1941. The ghetto also served as a transit camp for Jews being deported to the Riga and Theresienstadt ghettoes. Another 300 Jews, mostly sick and old, were sent to the Berg-am-Leim ghetto under a regime of hard labor. In all, ten labor and concentration camps were set up in the area, holding Jews as well as others, including 2,000 Jews at the Feldmoching branch of Dachau. Expulsions reduced the number of Jews in the city from 4,407 in June 1939 to 3,249 in Aug. 1941 and in the wake of further large-scale expulsions, to 645 in Dec. 1942. Only 146 of this latter group were defined as "full Jews."

Of the 2,991 Jews expelled between 20 Nov. 1941 and 23 Feb. 1945, 1,555 were sent to Theresienstadt, 980 to Riga, 343 to Piaski (Lublin dist. of Poland), and 113 to Auschwitz. At the end of the war, 400 Jews with non-J. spouses remained in M. These were joined by J. refugees and 796 former residents to bring the J. pop. up to 2,800 in March 1946. M. became the center for the J. organizations aiding survivors of the Holocaust, including the Joint Distribution Committee and the Jewish Agency. Between 1945 and 1951, 120,000 Jews passed through the city, many on the way to Palestine/Israel. In 1947, 57,731 Jews were in Displaced Persons camps and other localities in the area. In 1995 there were 5,000 Jews in M., making it the third largest J. community in West Germany after Berlin and Frankfurt am Main.

MURAFA Vinnitsa dist., Ukraine. Jews settled in the early 18th cent. In 1735, the Haidamaks murdered several and ten J. homes were burned. The J. pop. was 509 in 1765 and 1,350 (total 1,361) in 1897. In 1926, under the Soviets, the J. pop. was 1,421, with a J. council (soviet) and school in operation. The Nazis occupied M. on 22 July 1941. After it was annexed to Transnistria in early Sept., an open ghetto, *Judenrat*, and J. police force were established. Thousands of Jews from Bessarabia and Bukovina were expelled there, with 2,605 remaining on 1 Sept. 1943. Hundreds were sent to different camps and perished. In 1946 the J. pop. was 600.

MURAWICA Volhynia dist., Poland, today Ukraine. Jews were present from at least 1569, numbering 757 in 1897 (total 958). Half the J. artisans worked in the building trades. The town was destroyed in WWI and many Jews settled in neighboring Mlynow, leaving a J. pop. of 167 in M. (total 376). They were expelled to the Mlynow ghetto by the Germans on 24 May 1942, with all but 25 executed on 9 Oct.

MUROVANYE KURILOVTSY Vinnitsa dist., Ukraine. The J. pop. was 1,410 (total 4,340) in 1897. In the 1920s, a J. council (soviet) and J. elementary school (four grades) were active. A savings and loan society had 168 members in the early 1920s. In 1939, the J. pop. was 1,014. The Germans occupied the town on 17 July 1941. In Jan. or Feb. 1942 a ghetto and *Judenrat* were established. Jews from surrounding towns (Verbovtshe, Shnitkov) and from Bessarabia and

Bukovina were expelled there. On 21 Aug. 1942, the Germans executed 2,314 Jews in the Galeykovtshe forest – 978 from M. and the rest from the surrounding settlements. The 120 skilled workers left in the ghetto were murdered in late Oct. 1942.

MURSKA SOBOTA (Hung. Muraszombat; Ger. Delsnitz an der Mur) Slovenia, Yugoslavia, today Republic of Slovenia. A J. community was established in the early 19th cent. The J. pop. in 1930 was 156 (total 3,571), including many Jews from the surrounding villages. On 26 April 1944 the Germans deported the Jews to the local concentration camp in Najkanizha, and from there they were taken to Auschwitz on 17–20 May, where 212 died. In all, 41 survived the Holocaust.

MUSNINKAI Ukmerge dist., Lithuania. Jews first settled in the 18th cent. Prior to WWI, social and religious associations, a Hebrew library, and Zionist groups were active. Between the wars economic conditions forced many to leave. The J. pop. in 1938 was 220 (47% of the total). After the German invasion in June 1941, the Lithuanian commander of the Ukmerge dist. ordered Jews to wear yellow badges. On 5 Sept. all the Jews were murdered in the Pivonija grove.

MUSTVEE Estonia. Of the dozen J. artisans there in the latter 19th cent., six Jews remained in the 1930s, all but one perishing in the Holocaust.

MUSZYNA Cracow dist., Poland. Jews first settled in the second half of the 19th cent., mostly from Nowy Soncz and its environs, making Zanz Hasidism the dominant force in the community. The J. pop. reached 265 in 1890 (total 2,358) and 423 in 1921. Many earned their livelihoods from the town's health resort trade. Despite longstanding tensions, antisemitism only became virulent in the 1930s. The Jews were expelled by the Germans in Oct. 1940, mainly reaching Nowy Soncz, Stary Soncz, and Grybow, from where they were deported to Belzec and other death camps in 1942.

MUTTERSTADT Palatinate, Germany. Jews are first mentioned in 1719–22. They reached a peak pop. of 171 in 1860, declining steadily to 91 (total 6,024) in 1933. In 1838, the community built a synagogue. A new one was erected in 1905. In the Weimar period, most Jews were merchants and about half were livestock dealers. In 1934, under the Nazis, 16 J. peddlers lost their licenses. By early Nov. 1938, 30 Jews had left the town. On *Kristallnacht* (9–10 Nov. 1938), the synagogue was burned, J. homes and stores were destroyed, money and automobiles were stolen, and J. men were sent to the Dachau concentration camp. In Feb. 1940, Jews were mobilized for forced farm labor. Of the 48 who emigrated through 1940, 18 reached the U.S. Those remaining were moved to "J. houses" and on 22 Oct. 1940, 50 were deported to the Gurs concentration camp. In all, 39 perished in the Holocaust.

MUTZIG Bas-Rhin dist., France. The medieval J. community dates back to before the 14th cent. In 1328 Jews were accused of a ritual murder and forced to find refuge in Colmar. They later returned to M., where they were tolerated in a relatively more benevolent manner than elsewhere in the area. The Jews buried their dead in the nearby village of Rosenwiller. In 1784, the J. community consisted of 307 Jews. At that time, M. was the seat of the Union of Alsatian Jews and of the rabbinate of the Strasbourg bishopric. In 1895, the community numbered 154 members. In 1936, there were only 54 Jews living in M. During the German occupation, nine were deported. In 1965, there were 33 Jews in M.

MUZIJOVO (Hung. Nagymuzsaly) Carpatho-Russia, Czechoslovakia, today Ukraine. Jews apparently settled in the early 19th cent., numbering 50 in 1830 and 172 (total 959) in 1880. In 1921, under the Czechoslovakians, the J. pop. was 279 and in 1941 it was 358. Jews owned ten business establishments and five workshops and some farmed (as winegrowers). The Hungarians annexed the town in Nov. 1938 and in 1941 drafted dozens of Jews into labor battalions, some for forced labor, others for service on the eastern front, where most died. In late July 1941, a number of J. families without Hungarian citizenship were expelled to the German-occupied Ukraine and murdered. The remaining 300 were deported to Auschwitz on 18 May 1944.

MYJAVA Slovakia, Czechoslovakia, today Republic of Slovakia. Jews may have been present at the turn of the 17th cent. In the late 18th cent., most traded in the cloth used as flour sieves in the mills. A synagogue was erected in 1846 and a J. school was opened in the late 1840s. In 1848, rioting heavily damaged J. homes and stores. The J. pop. grew from 183 in 1828 to a peak of 430 (total 10,018) in 1880. R. Akiva ha-Kohen Strasser (1882–97) ran a yeshiva with a few dozen students; the last rabbi of the community, Yosef Broda, subsequently served for 47 years. The Zionists became active in 1900. The J. pop. dropped to 204 in 1919 and 111 in 1940. Betar, Bnei Akiva, the Maccabi sports club, and Agudat Israel all operated intensively between the World Wars. In March 1939, as part of the Slovakian state, M. was included in the German defense zone and German soldiers and the Slovakian Hlinka Guard severely abused the Jews. At the end of March 1942, dozens of young Jews were deported to Auschwitz via Patronka and to the Majdanek concentration camp via Sered. In the summer, most of the families were deported to the Lublin dist. in Poland and to Auschwitz. Some Jews succeeded in fleeing before the Germans occupied the town in Sept. 1944.

MYSLENICE Cracow dist., Poland. Jews began to settle with the end of residence restrictions in 1860, numbering 386 in 1880 (total 2,455) and 675 in 1921 (of 1,921). The pop. was distinctly hasidic with life centering around the *beit midrash* and various *minyanim*. There was little scope for Zionist activity. The community supported a yeshiva for 50 students and a *talmud torah* for 150 children. Among the J. tradesmen, hatmakers were particularly prominent. Antisemitism was widespread. Most Jews fled in the riots of 1898 and in late 1918 were caught up in the pogroms that raged through W. Galicia. In 1936, armed bands of the National Party under Adam Dowoshinski descended on M. with Jews as a special target. Damage was limited since the Polish army and police intervened. The German occupation of Sept. 1939 introduced a reign of terror, with a *Judenrat* set up to supply men for forced labor. About 100 Jews were sent to labor camps in Cracow and Dembice up through 1942 and other groups to Plas-

Walking home from the synagogue, Myslenice, Poland, 1920

zow. The rest were expelled to Skawina on 21 or 22 Aug. 1942. Seven hundred of M.'s Jews were exterminated in the Holocaust.

MYSLOWICE Silesia dist., Poland. Jews first arrived in the 17th cent. In the 18th they ran inns and sold mead and alcoholic beverages. They also held the tobacco monopoly. Others dealt in cattle and sheep and in rabbit pelts. Despite antisemitic incidents and a decline in status after the Katowice J. community removed itself from M.'s auspices in 1866, the community maintained its prosperity until WWI, with a peak pop. of 900 (total 14,000) in 1887. It also served as a way station for refugees fleeing the Russian pogroms of the 1880s en route to America. Most of the Jews abandoned the town for the interior of Germany during WWI and were replaced by Polish Jews in its aftermath. The J. pop. in 1931 stood at 463. In Nov. 1939 the Germans expelled the Jews to Chrzanow. Subsequently a labor camp for Jews was established in the town.

MYSZHKOW NOWY Kielce dist., Poland. Jews were present in the late 19th cent. as operators of sawmills and flour mills and as shopkeepers. In 1921, their pop. was 563 (total 1,774), with 30 J. business establishments employing 128 Jews. The Zionists were active and a Hashomer Hatzair branch was set up in the 1920s. The Germans arrived on 3 Sept. 1939, instituting a regime of forced labor and extortion. A ghetto was established in neighboring Miechow in late 1941. In June 1942, most of M.'s 1,200 Jews were transferred to Zawiercie and from there deported to Auschwitz. A group of 200, including many who had been in hiding, were subsequently rounded up and sent to Auschwitz on 28 Aug.

MYSZYNIEC Bialystok dist., Poland. A J. community is known from the early 19th cent., growing to 727 in 1857 and 912 (total 1,872) in 1921, with most living in poverty. The Zionists and Agudat Israel were active after WWI, the latter controlling the community council. Many of the Jews were murdered in the first days of the German occupation (Sept. 1939); the others were soon deported to ghettoes in the area to share the fate of the Jews there.

N

NABBURG Upper Palatinate, Germany. The J. pop. in 1933 was eight (total 2,437); six left for Leipzig in 1939.

NABEUL Grombalia dist., Tunisia. According to local tradition, the first Jews arrived in the early 18th cent., when security in the area improved under the Husseini dynasty and N. became an urban center attracting Europeans. The beginnings of the community are associated with the kabbalist R. Yaakov Salama of Tunis (d.1774), whose tomb in N. became a place of pilgrimage. An organized community of 100 families existed by the mid-19th cent. Most Jews were engaged, uncharacteristically, in agriculture until the early 20th cent. Jews of Leghornian origin were the primary economic beneficiaries of increased European influence in the late 19th cent. In the 1860s, 41 Jews were European subjects, most under the protection of the French consulate. In 1839, Arabs murdered a pregnant J. woman and her three small children. In 1864, anti-J. rioting broke out against the background of the bey's constitutional reform granting equal rights to the Jews and J. foreign nationals had to be evacuated on a French warship. Again in 1891 a Jew (R. Yom Tov Ghez) and his three sons were murdered and further violence occurred in 1909 and 1914. Under the French Protectorate (1881) Jews began to return to their traditional occupations in commerce and crafts. A few dominated the cloth and camel hair trade. Jews also benefited economically from the development of N. as a tourist center and from pilgrimages to R. Salama's tomb. The community was managed by a council (Caisse de Secours et de Bienfaisance) from 1905, under the presidency of the Carilla family until the eve of WWII. The community maintained seven synagogues, the largest seating nearly 400 and housing 40 Torah scrolls. In the 1930s there were four *talmudei torah*.

Most children also attended a French public school. From an early period, N. was a stronghold of Zionism in Tunisia. The periodic visits of fundraisers from the Holy Land cemented ties with Eretz Israel. A number

The tomb of the tzaddik *Yaakov Salama, Nabeul, Tunisia (Beth Hatefutsoth Photo Archive, Tel Aviv/courtesy of Charles Haddad, Marseilles)*

of the community's rabbis left for Eretz Israel toward the end of their lives to be buried there. In 1911, R. Yitzhak ben Yaakov Mamo was one of Tunisia's delegates to the Tenth Zionist Congress in Basel and within a few years representatives of 12 local families made *aliya*. A Bnei Zion society was founded in 1912. Another Zionist group, called Tikvat Zion, was set up in 1919, entering into spirited rivalry for control of the community council with Tipode Zion, founded at about the same time and dedicated to raising funds for the Keren Kayemet. In the 1930s, Betar and the UUJJ scout movement became active in N., the former soon becoming the dominant Zionist movement. The J. pop. reached 1,560 in 1909 and 1,912 (total 8,489) in 1936. Though there was an improvement in Arab-J. relations in the 1930s against the background of mutual economic interests, tensions still ran high, intensifying under the Vichy regime in 1940 and its anti-J. laws. Under Vichy rule, Jews were dismissed from the public service and banks and J. children were not allowed to attend school after the fourth grade. After the arrival of the Germans in Nov. 1942, J. property was confiscated and a regime of forced labor introduced. Jews also suffered from Allied bombardments. Many were able to escape as the German occupation reached its end. The city was liberated on 11 May 1943. After the war, the Zionists, especially Betar, renewed their activity. In the mid-1940s Betar was joined by Torah ve-Avodah and Tze'irei Tziyyon-Deror. A Gordonia-Maccabi Tza'ir group was started in 1949, soon becoming the largest Zionist youth group in Tunisia. Many movement members left for Israel in 1950. Mass emigration to Israel commenced after Tunisia gained its independence in 1956.

NACHOD Bohemia, Czechoslovakia. The community is first mentioned in 1455 as one of the four J. communities (together with Roudnice, Bumsla [Mlada-Boleslav] and Kolin) referred to by the Hebrew acronym "Karban." A synagogue, school, and cemetery were opened in the 16th cent. In 1663, the J. ghetto and the synagogue burned down in a general conflagration for which the Jews were blamed and consequently expelled. Later returning, their pop. reached 60 families in 1724. A new synagogue was built in 1777 but the Jews were forced to live again in a ghetto from 1753 until 1848. Jews were active in the textile industry. In 1899, J. property was looted in riots. The J. pop. was 504 in 1890 and 293 (total 13,538) in 1930. In

1939, the Nazis desecrated the synagogue and J. cemetery and in Dec. 1942 the Jews were deported to the Theresienstadt ghetto and from there to the death camps.

NACINA VES (Hung. Natafalva) Slovakia, Czechoslovakia, today Republic of Slovakia. Galician refugees settled in the first half of the 18th cent. The J. pop. was 163 (total 1,064) in 1880 and 89 in 1940. On 7 May 1942, the Jews were deported to the Lukow ghetto in the Lublin dist. (Poland) and perished.

NADARZYN Warsaw dist., Poland. Jews apparently settled in the first half of the 16th cent. Many left after a devastating fire in 1902. About 100 J. families lived there after WWI. Most fled to Warsaw on the approach of the Germans in Sept. 1939, returning a few days later to bury the 60 Jews murdered by the Germans and themselves expelled later to the Warsaw ghetto, perishing in the Treblinka death camp.

NADAS Slovakia, Czechoslovakia, today Republic of Slovakia. Moravian refugees settled in the 17th cent. A synagogue was erected c. 1732 and the J. pop. rose to about 150 in 1790 and a peak of about 230 in the 1830s. A J. school combined religious and secular studies. In April 1848, during Easter, anti-J. riots seriously damaged J. homes and stores. R. Avraham Rozink served the community for 45 years starting in 1894. There were 17 other settlements attached to the local rabbinate. The well-known Buechler family of rabbis and scholars came from N. A Zionist society was founded in 1899. In the early 20th cent., as the young left for the cities, the J. pop. began to drop, numbering 123 (total 1,604) in 1910 and 49 in 1940. Under Slovakian rule, Jews were forced out of their businesses and in April 1942 deported to the east.

NADEZHNAIA (Yid. Hofnung) Zaporozhe dist., Ukraine. Since Jews from the Vilna region founded N. as a J. colony in 1855, it was initially called Vilner. In 1858, the total pop. of N. was 532, mostly Jews. In the pogroms of May 1881, a J. self-defense group apprehended 12 rioters and turned them over to the police. The J. pop. was 634 in 1897 and 476 in 1926. A. J. school was active in 1910. In the civil war (1918–21), the Machno gangs murdered several Jews. Most of the 63 local residents murdered during the German occupation in WWII were also Jews.

NADLAC (Hung., Nagylak) S. Transylvania dist., Rumania. Jews settled here in the mid-18th cent. Prior to WWI, the J. pop. numbered 254 (1910), but afterwards many Jews left and in 1930 the J. pop. was 129 (1% of the total). In June 1941, the Jews were expelled to Arad. After the war, 80 Jews settled in N.

NADUDVAR Hajdu dist., Hungary. Jews are mentioned in 1770. Most were merchants dealing in farm produce, feathers, and leather, while others operated taverns. The J. pop. reached a peak of 505 (6% of the total) in 1900 and then declined to 210 in 1941 under unremitting antisemitism, including forced labor. In May 1944, the Jews were expelled to Debrecen and from there deported to Auschwitz on 12 June. A small group deported to Regensburg in Austria survived. After the war, the community was reestablished but by 1953, all Jews had left N.

NADWORNA Stanislawow dist., Poland, today Ukraine. The J. community developed from the late 18th cent. Jews traded in farm produce as well as operating oil wells and refineries, sawmills and flour mills. From the 20th cent., they became active in the tourist trade. The town was an important center of Hasidism and the Frankists too exercised a significant influence. A great fire in 1907 destroyed around 100 J. homes as well as some of the more than 20 synagogues in the town. In WWI, Cossacks, Ukrainians, and the Petlyura gangs successively terrorized the J. pop., which after the war stood at half its 1880 peak of 4,182 (two-thirds of the total). The depressed economic conditions were somewhat relieved by J. employment in the lumber industry. The Zionist organizations maintained youth and pioneer training groups in the area. All such activity was curtailed by the Soviets on their arrival in Sept. 1939. With the arrival of the Hungarian army on 1 July 1941, the Ukrainians staged a bloody pogrom claiming dozens of J. lives. In Sept., with the Germans taking control of N., about 1,000 J. refugees arrived from Carpathia, some being among the 2,000 Jews murdered in the Bukowinka forest in the *Aktion* of 6 Oct. 1941. Two ghettoes, one for the able-bodied and the other for the unemployable, were subsequently set up, with around 600 Jews working in a sawmill. Disease and starvation decimated the pop. along with random killing. In further *Aktions* in Sept. and on 24 Oct. 1942, the remaining Jews were sent to Stanislawow to meet their end.

NAGARTAV Nikolaiev dist., Ukraine. N. (for the Heb. *nahar tov* = "good river") was founded as a J. colony in 1807–09 by Jews from the Mogilev region and numbered 80 families in 1815. In the 1930s, N. became a J. settlement center for the Kherson region. The J. pop. rose to 1,571 (total 1,711) in 1897, most engaged in farming. In April 1899, the Christians of the neighboring town of Bereznegovatoye staged a pogrom against the Jews of N., causing much property damage but no loss of life. In 1905 and 1919, additional pogroms occurred and a number of Jews were killed. In 1926, in the Soviet period, the J. pop. was 1,748. A J. rural council (soviet) and J. elementary school were active and there were a number of J. kolkhozes nearby, such as the Kim kolkhoz with 98 members and the Naye Virtschaft kolkhoz with about 100 families (in 1932). The Germans captured N. on 18 Aug. 1941 and on 14 Sept. murdered 865 Jews.

NAGORZANKA Tarnopol dist., Poland, today Ukraine. The J. pop. in 1921 was 232. The Jews were probably deported to the Belzec death camp in the second half of 1942, directly or via Buczacz.

NAGOVO (Hung. Nyagova) Carpatho-Russia, Czechoslovakia, today Ukraine. Jews apparently abandoned the town after settling there in the 18th cent., returning in the early 19th. Their pop. was 28 in 1830 and 99 in 1880. In 1930, under the Czechoslovakians, it rose to 110 and in 1941 to 118 (total 1,460). After the Hungarian occupation of March 1939, 68 Jews were expelled to Kamenets-Podolski, where they were murdered. The rest were deported to Auschwitz in late May 1944.

NAGYATAD Somogy dist., Hungary. Jews are mentioned in 1746 and numbered 371 in 1880. The first synagogue was erected in 1840. The J. pop. was 256 in 1930. The Hungarian Zionist Organization set up a branch in N. in 1935. From 1942, Jews were subjected to forced labor, many perishing in the Ukraine. The rest were deported to Auschwitz via Nagykanizsa at the end of June–beginning of July 1944. Five families allowed to remain behind were subsequently slaughtered by Hungarian fascists.

NAGYBAJOM Somogy dist., Hungary. Jews are mentioned in 1746. They developed commerce in the area and ran a flour mill and bank. A J. school was opened in 1861 and a new synagogue in 1878. The J. pop. was 120 in 1900 and 112 in 1930. The Jews were deported to Auschwitz via Kaposvar on 1–2 July 1944.

NAGYDOBOS Szatmar dist., Hungary. Jews settled in the first half of the 19th cent. and numbered 241 in 1880 and 101 in 1930. They were deported to Auschwitz via Mateszalka in late May 1944.

NAGYDOROG Tolna dist., Hungary. Jews numbered 79 in 1880 and 87 in 1930. All were deported to Auschwitz via Dunafoldvar at the beginning of July 1944.

NAGYECSED Szatmar dist., Hungary. Jews settled in the late 18th cent., most trading in farm produce. A synagogue was consecrated in 1850 and the J. pop. grew to 117 in 1880 and 600 in 1941. Despite the racial law prohibitions, Jews in N. continued to farm their land, a rare occurrence at the time. In 1941, 120 were drafted into the labor battalions and sent to the

Ukraine, where most perished. The rest, about 600, were deported to Auschwitz via Mateszalka in late May 1944. After the war, survivors sold the community's buildings and used the money to finance their *aliya* to Israel.

NAGYHALASZ Szabolcs dist., Hungary. Jews are first mentioned in the mid-18th cent and were mostly merchants dealing in textiles, lumber, and grain. They numbered 182 in 1880 and 270 in 1944. In 1941, J. WWI refugees from Galicia who had settled in N. were expelled to Kamenets-Podolski and executed there. On 17 May 1944, the rest were deported to Auschwitz via Harangod-puszta. Survivors reestablished the community, but gradually most left for Israel.

NAGYKALLO Szabolcs dist., Hungary. Jews were present in the Middle Ages. In 1851, they numbered 693, mostly employed as artisans and farmers. A synagogue was founded in 1800 and in 1855 a J. school whose principal, Zigmond Kuthy, was the first to issue a children's newspaper in Hungarian. R. Yitzhak

Beit midrash *in Nagykallo, Hungary*

Taub, one of the leaders of Hungarian Hasidism, was active in N. in 1781–1821, establishing a yeshiva, *talmud torah*, and *heder*. The J. pop. reached 1,060 in 1920 and then dropped to 869 in 1941. The Jews were deported to Auschwitz via Nyiregyhaza on 17 May 1944. After the war, 98 survivors reestablished the community.

NAGYKANIZSA Zala dist., Hungary. Jews settled in the early 18th cent., engaging in the grain trade and manufacturing metal products and knitted goods as well as operating a brickyard, lumber yard, beer brewery, and printing press. In 1869, they formed a Neologist community with 20 smaller settlements under its jurisdiction. The J. pop. rose from 1,000 in 1840 to 3,573 (17% of the total) in 1890. A J. school was opened in 1786 and enrolled 588 children by 1886. The synagogue, consecrated in 1821, was the first in Hungary to introduce the use of an organ. Later, *Kol Nidrei* services were eliminated at the synagogue. Sir Moses Montefiore prayed there on his way to Eretz Israel in 1863. A J. hospital was founded in 1830. In 1941, the J. pop. was 2,091. In that year, young men were sent to forced labor in the Ukraine and in the Bor mines in Yugoslavia. Most perished. A concentration camp was set up in the city in 1942, mainly for Jews accused of so-called economic crimes. On 29 April 1944, J. males aged 16–60 were deported to Auschwitz. This was the first deportation from Hungary. The remaining Jews were sent there on 3–4 June. The postwar community numbered 279 in 1946 and 136 in 1960.

NAGYKATA Pest–Pilis–Solt–Kiskun dist., Hungary. Jews from Tapiobicske settled in N. after 1848, developing an international reputation as grape growers. They also dominated local commerce, establishing a bank and flour mill. By 1868, N. was the leading community in the district with many others affiliated to it. A synagogue and school were opened in 1904. The J. pop. was 269 in 1910 (3% of the total) and 214 in 1941. After WWI, the Jews suffered attacks from demobilized soldiers as well as from White Terror gangs. In 1938, the district head, the antisemite Endre Laszlo, strictly enforced Hungary's racial laws. In 1941–43, N. was a distribution center for J. forced labor, with 10,000 Jews channeled through it. The director of the camp, Lt. Col. Murai, was particularly cruel and was tried and executed after the war. At the beginning of June 1944, the local Jews were deported to Auschwitz via Kecskemet. Survivors reestablished the community, but soon left

NAGYKOROS Pest–Pilis–Solt–Kiskun dist., Hungary. Jews settled in the late 18th cent. and by the end of the 19th cent. were prominent as exporters of farm produce. In 1817, they established a synagogue with the assistance of Christian estate owners. The J. pop. reached a peak of 900 in 1890, dropping to 540 by 1930. After WWI, demobilized soldiers and White Terror gangs robbed and attacked the J. community, at one point murdering five Jews. In spring 1944, the Jews were confined to a ghetto and, at the end of June, deported to Auschwitz. Sixty survivors reestablished the community, but gradually it dwindled.

NAGYLETA Bihar dist., Hungary. Jews probably settled in the first half of the 19th cent. because of the town's proximity to Debrecen and its fairs. The Jews were shopkeepers (mostly grocers), but some were also merchants dealing in beef, chickens, and wine. One (Erno Letai) represented the district in the Hungarian parliament and others served on the municipal council. A synagogue was established in 1840. The J. pop. was 276 in 1930. In 1941, young men were mobilized for forced labor battalions. Most died as a result of the harsh conditions. On 7 May 1944, the Jews were brought to Nagyvarad and on 23 May those not selected for forced labor were deported to Auschwitz.

NAGYOROSZI Nograd–Hont dist., Hungary. Jews settled in the early 19th cent., maintaining a synagogue, cemetery, and yeshiva and numbering 68 in 1930. On 12–14 June 1944, they were deported to Auschwitz via Balassagyarmat and Nyirjes. In fall 1944, German soldiers killed 19 Jews working at the forced labor camp at N.

NAGYRABE Bihar dist., Hungary. Jews settled in the first half of the 19th cent. and numbered 83 in 1880 and 59 in 1930. In spring 1944 they were sent to Nagyvarad and on 3 June deported to Auschwitz.

NAGYSIMONYI Vas dist., Hungary. Jews settled in the early 18th cent. and numbered 101 in 1930, with a new synagogue consecrated in 1892. In July 1944, they were deported to Auschwitz via Szombathely.

Synagogue in Nagykoros, Hungary, before WWII

NAGYTETENY Pest dist., Hungary. The J. community was one of the oldest in the Budapest area, dating back to 1737 when Jews from Moravia arrived. N. was a place of residence for Jews trading in Budapest but not allowed to live there. The J. pop. numbered 498 in 1880 and 158 in 1930. In WWII, the Jews were brought to the Budafok ghetto and on 29 June 1944 deported to Auschwitz. In 1956, there were still ten Jews in N.

NAGYVAZSONY Veszprem dist., Hungary. Jews are first mentioned in 1722, reaching a peak pop. of 178 in 1840 and then declining to 42 in 1941. All were deported to Auschwitz via Veszprem at the end of June 1944.

NAHACZOW Lwow dist., Poland, today Ukraine. The J. pop. in 1921 was 123. The Jews were probably expelled to Jaworow or Krakowiec for liquidation in Nov.–Dec. 1942.

NAKLO Poznan dist., Poland. A small J. community with a synagogue existed in the 16th cent. It grew to a peak pop. of 982 (total 5,554) in 1871, with a community building erected in 1845, a spacious new synagogue completed in 1853, and Jews entering new crafts like metalworking and expanding into industry, large-scale trade, and the professions. In the late 19th cent. growing antisemitism led to emigration to the big German cities (Breslau, Berlin) as well as abroad to the U.S. and Canada, leaving 336 Jews in 1907. In the 1920s and 1930s Jews were attacked in the streets by Polish youths. The J. pop. in 1932 was 58. The few Jews remaining when the Germans arrived were expelled to General Gouvernement territory by the end of 1939.

NALBACH Saar, Germany. Jews were present by the early 18th cent. In 1808, their pop. was 16, reaching a peak of 68 in 1858 and then dwindling to 24 (total 2,735) in June 1933. A synagogue consecrated in 1854 and a cemetery were shared with the Jews of Diefflen. The synagogue was damaged on *Kristallnacht* (9–10 Nov. 1938) and afterwards razed. Sixteen Jews left in the Nazi era but only a few managed to find a haven. The rest were expelled or deported to

Regina Taub and her children, Nalenczow, Poland, c. 1934–1937

the Gurs concentration camp up to the end of 1940. Fourteen perished in the Holocaust.

NALCHIK   Kabardino-Balkar ASSR, Russia. J. settlement probably began in the early 19th cent. and comprised about 25 families of Mountain Jews (Tats), growing to a pop. of about 400 in 1867 and 1,354 (total 19,343) in 1897, of whom 1,041 were Mountain Jews and the rest Ashkenazi Jews. Most Jews engaged in trade and crafts (60% as hide processors). A few of the Mountain Jews were farmers (vineyards and orchards) and owned considerable amounts of land. Two synagogues and a *talmud torah* were open in the late 19th cent. In the early 20th cent., R. Hizkiyahu Amirov, rabbi of the Mountain Jews in N., founded a small yeshiva. J. political parties, like the Zionists, also became active. In late 1919 or early 1920, a few hundred Jews, organized for self-defense, thwarted an attempted pogrom. A few dozen Mountain Jews left for Palestine via Turkey in 1920–22. In 1927, the J. pop. was 1,783: 1,458 Mountain Jews and 325 Ashkenazi Jews. A J. council (soviet) with deliberations in the Tat dialect was set up in 1925 as was a

J. school, its attendance reaching 300 in 1926–27. Later it was expanded to include high school classes. Tat was taught as a foreign language while Russian remained the language of instruction. Cooperatives for hide processors and shoemakers were founded in 1927, employing dozens of J. families. Despite the trend from the late 1920s on to leave the town for farm settlements, especially among the Mountain Jews, the J. pop. grew to 3,007 in 1939 (total 47,959). The Germans occupied N. on 28 Oct. 1942. In early Nov., they murdered a number of Jews. The Jews were then confined to a J. area and the remaining Ashkenazi Jews were murdered. The Mountain Jews succeeded in convincing the Germans that they were not Jews and were liberated in early Jan. 1943, before the order to execute them finally arrived. N. was the birthplace of Isai Ilazorov, Hero of the Soviet Union, killed in 1944. After the war, N. remained a center for Mountain Jews.

NALENCZOW   Lublin dist., Poland. Jews settled in the 19th cent., becoming active in the tourist trade centered around the town's mineral springs. They numbered 268 (total 918) in 1921. In WWII, the town was a transit center en route to the death camps. The Jews of N. were deported to the Sobibor death camp by the Germans in May 1942.

NALIBOKI   Nowogrodek dist., Poland, today Belarus. Individual Jews were present by the 19th cent., their number growing to 95 (total 2,465) in 1885 and 185 in 1921. In the 1930s, half (22 families) were engaged in agriculture, working about 500 acres of land. Hashomer Hatzair and Betar were both active in the town. In Dec. 1941 the Jews were expelled by the Germans to Rubiezhowicze and Nowogrodek and the able-bodied sent to the Dworzec labor camp, where they were murdered in the course of 1942, as were the Jews in Rubiezhowicze. A group of 32 from Dworzec, including Jews from N., escaped to join the Bielski partisans.

NAMESTOVO   Slovakia, Czechoslovakia, today Republic of Slovakia. Jews apparently settled in the 1780s, opening a regional elementary school in 1850 as their pop. rose from 176 in 1828 to 286 (total 1,911) in 1880. After WWI, with the young leaving for the big cities, the J. pop. dropped to 135 in 1921 and to 114 in 1940. The Zionist movement was active, including WIZO and the youth organizations. Jews held public positions and owned 16 business establishments. In 1941, under Slovakian rule, J. businesses were shut down. In late March and early April 1942, young Jews were deported, the men to the Majdanek concentration camp and women to Auschwitz. Another 80 Jews were sent to the death camps of the Lublin dist. (Poland) on 2 June. The 20 or so who remained either fled or were rounded up for execution after the arrival of the Germans in Sept. 1944.

NAMSLAU   (Pol. Namyslow) Lower Silesia, Germany, today Poland. Jews inhabited a Street of the Jews no later than the early 14th cent., some engaged in moneylending. Though Jews were occasionally present in the 17th cent, the modern community was only founded in the late 18th cent. A cemetery was consecrated in 1794 and a synagogue in 1856. The J. pop. was 174 in 1840 and 239 in 1861, subsequently dropping to 81 in 1925. Antisemitic incidents occurred in 1930–32, such as an attack on a Jew by a Nazi and the desecration of the J. cemetery. In 1932, the J. pop. was 68. On *Kristallnacht* (9–10 Nov. 1938), the syna-

gogue and J. stores were destroyed. Only 25 Jews were living in N. at the time. No information is available about the fate of the community in WWII. Presumably those Jews who did not emigrate in time were deported and died.

NAMUR   (Flem. Namen) Belgium. A small community was established in the 19th cent. In 1808, there were only two J. families living in N. and 20 Jews in 1846 with some sources claiming 47 Jews. With only 68 members in 1865, the community never received a full-time rabbi. The community declined to two families in 1907 and the synagogue was closed down in 1908. According to the German census of 1 Oct. 1941, there were 50 Jews in N. at the time.

NANCY   Meurthe-et-Moselle dist., France. The dozen J. families residing in N. around 1470 were expelled in 1476. A few Jews were present in the 16th cent. Official authorization to reside in N. was granted in 1721. The community numbered twelve families in 1753. In 1784, Louis XVI granted them the right to build a synagogue, which was completed in 1788, when the community was also granted the right to open a cemetery. The synagogue, which was enlarged and renovated in 1841, 1861, and 1935, was one of the Seven Consistorial Synagogues of France. In 1860 the community comprised 1,386 members. Following the influx of immigrants from Alsace-Lorraine in 1865–75, local Jews constituted 57% of the J. pop. in the department of Meurthe-et-Moselle in 1890. By 1900, the J. community of N. numbered 1,860 Jews. In 1905, a religious association, the Association Cultuelle Israelite de Nancy (ACI), was founded. Immigrants from Eastern Europe settled in N. between the World Wars. The ACI had 545 members in 1933. The influx of Polish Jews led to a split within the community between the old French community and the newcomers. This was reflected in the development of separate religious and cultural organizations and in 1930 the Polish Jews set up their own synagogue. In 1933, the municipality named two streets after illustrious Jews, the painter Henri Levy and the prominent neurologist Prof. Hippolyte Bernheim (1840–1919). In 1939, the community included the 1,200 French Jews and 2,500 immigrants from Eastern Europe. The Germans entered N. on 16 June 1940. In 1940, the number of the Jews listed in N. was 2,625. On 8 May 1942, they were ordered to wear the yellow star. Many Jews had already left for

18th cent. Scroll of Esther, Nancy, France (Nancy Museum, France/photo courtesy of Beth Hatefutsoth, Tel Aviv)

the south of France, the unoccupied zone. The synagogue was used as a hospital supply depot. Many local Jews such as Jean Blum joined the resistance movement. Arrested in Dec. 1940, he was executed in 1941 to serve as an example. On 19 July 1942, the first arrests of foreign Jews began in N. Pierre Marie, head of the department for foreigners in the local police, warned the Jews of the forthcoming arrests and helped them to escape. There were further arrests on 9 Oct. 1942 and 23 Feb. 1943. During a major *Aktion* on 2 March 1944, 230 Jews of French origin were deported. The chief rabbi of N., Paul Hagenauer, was deported with 700 other Jews. The regional railroad which took Jews from other localities to the death camps passed through N. In 1964 there were 3,320 Jews living in the city.

NANTES   Loire-Atlantique dist., France. In the Middle Ages, N. was the center of the Jews of Brittany. An expulsion decree in 1240 followed a Crusader massacre in 1235. During the second half of the 16th cent., many Marrano Jews settled in N. By 1808 the comunity was composed of 25 families.

An organized community was established in 1834 and a synagogue was founded in 1870. In 1873 the consistory of N. was established. By 1898 the J. community comprised about 50 families. In 1904, there were antisemitic outbursts with calls to boycott J. and Masonic businesses. Between the World Wars, the Jews played an important economic role in the city. In 1939, there were 54 J. enterprises in N., of which 60% were prosperous shops or small industrial establishments. In 1940, of the 537 Jews in N., 357 were of French origin; the rest were immigrants. In a July 1942 *Aktion*, 98 Jews were arrested—28 from the N. region and 66 from the St. Nazaire region. By Sept. 1943, there were only 53 Jews in N. In 1960 there were about 25 families. With the influx of Jews from North Africa, the J. pop. increased and numbered over 320 in 1964.

NAOUSSA   (Nausa) Macedonia, Greece. In WWII, 30 of N.'s 50 Jews were deported to death camps; the rest went into hiding.

NAPKOR   Szabolcs dist., Hungary. Jews settled in

the first half of the 18th cent., trading mostly in farm produce from the region – potatoes, tobacco, fruit, sugar beet, and grapes. They numbered 87 in 1880 and 206 in 1930. In 1941, 30 men were sent to forced labor in the Ukraine. Eight survived. In spring 1944, the remaining Jews of N. were sent to Nyiregyhaza and Varjulapos and on 17 May to Auschwitz.

NAPLES   Italy. J. tombstones from the first cent. B.C.E. indicate the presence of Jews in N. from ancient times. In 536, local Jews helped the Goths defend the city when it was besieged by the Byzantines. In the second half of the 12th cent., Benjamin of Tudela found 500 Jews in N. Dominican preachers incited riots against the Jews and in 1290 the synagogue was converted into a church. In 1330, Robert of Anjou invited Jews from the Balearic Islands to settle in N., granting them privileges. Under Aragonese rule from 1442, conditions were favorable for the Jews and the community increased in number, absorbing many refugees from Spain, Sicily, and Sardinia after 1492. For many Iberian refugees, N. was only a temporary haven on their way to the east. A Hebrew press was established in N. no later than 1485. When Naples was conquered by Spain in 1495, a decree expelling the Jews was issued (in 1496), but it was not implemented until 1510; 200 wealthy J. families were exempted. A general expulsion took place in 1541. In 1738, Charles II of the House of Bourbon invited the Jews to relocate in N. and its vicinity in order to strengthen his kingdom economically. But seven years later, the Jews were once again expelled, to return only in 1830. By Sept. 1831, there were eight Jews in N. In 1860, when N. was annexed to the Kingdom of Italy, the J. community began to flourish and in 1863, a synagogue was consecrated. In 1864, Rabbi Prof. Benjamin Artom became the community's rabbi. In 1873, the community numbered 600 persons. In 1900, the community established a hospital and a J. school. According to the 1930 law reforming the J. communities in Italy, N. was declared one of the 26 communities legally recognized by the government. By 1936, the community, headed by Rabbi L. Laide Tedesco, consisted of 500 Jews. During WWII, 11 local Jews were deported to extermination camps. After the war, the reorganized community consisted of 534 Jews. Within the Italian secret police a unique J. unit for seeking out Nazis and Nazi collaborators is credited with having helped convict more than a thou-

sand war criminals and collaborators. By 1969, the community numbered 450 Jews.

NAPRASNOVKA   Mogilev dist., Belorussia. N. was founded as a J. colony in the 19th cent. In 1924, under the Soviets, 48 J. families were there, 45 of them engaged in agriculture. A four-year J. elementary school was attended by 48 children in 1924. In 1930, the J. pop. was 248. The Germans arrived in late June 1941. In March 1942, they executed 250 Jews.

NARAJOW   Tarnopol dist., Poland, today Ukraine. Jews were present in the late 18th cent., earning a livelihood mainly by farming, though diversifying their occupations between the World Wars. The J. pop. fell from its 1880 level of 1,088 (total 2,473) to 775 in 1921, partly through emigration to the U.S. The German occupation of 1 July 1941 brought a regime of forced labor. Swelled by refugees to around 1,400, the J. pop was rounded up on 22 Sept. 1942, the day after Yom Kippur, and deported to the Belzec death camp via Brzezany. The 500 or so who eluded the net met the same fate at the end of the year and those subsequently found hiding were murdered.

NAREV   Bialystok dist., Poland, today Belarus. A few Jews were present in the 16th cent. as tax farmers and liquor licensees. Local opposition to the Jews led to a blood libel in 1564 and the execution of an innocent Jew. The J. community began to grow only in the 19th cent., reaching a pop. of 601 in 1897 (total 1,434). The J. pop. dropped steadily in the absence of economic development after WWI, numbering 251 in 1939. In Oct. 1941, J. men were expelled to the Pruzhana ghetto; the rest were sent to Bielsk Podlaski on 2 Sept. 1942 and from there to Bialystok, where they were rounded up in the *Aktion* of 5–12 Feb. 1943 and deported to the Treblinka death camp

NAREWKA MALA   Bialystok dist., Poland. Jews settled in the late 18th cent., numbering 1,004 (total 1,263) in 1897 and 758 in 1921. Between the World Wars, many had to close their stores under the heavy tax burden; others tried to earn a living as factory workers. The Hehalutz organization was active among the young. On 15 July 1942 the Germans murdered all the J. men in the local labor camp and then sent the remaining women and children to the Kobryn ghetto where they perished in the *Aktion* of 27 July 1942.

NARODICHI Zhitomir dist., Ukraine. Four tax-paying J. householders were present in 1629. The community was reestablished after the Chmielnicki massacres of 1648–49. By 1765, it included 241 taxpayers. In 1897, the J. pop. was 2,054 (total 4,576). Jews engaged in hide processing, petty trade, and crafts. Two kolkhozes, with mostly J. members, were founded in the Soviet period. Other Jews joined shoemakers' and tailors' cooperatives. A J. school was started in 1921 and had an enrollment of 200 in the mid-1930s. In 1939, the J. pop. was 1,233. The Germans entered N. on 22 Aug. 1941. A week later they murdered 350 Jews outside the town and in Nov. they executed 370 at the J. cemetery.

NARO-FOMINSK Moscow dist., Russia. Jews probably settled after the Oct. 1917 Revolution. In 1939, they numbered 157 (total 31,400). During the short period of their occupation (from late Oct. to late Dec. 1941) the Germans murdered the few remaining Jews.

NAROL Lwow dist., Poland. A flourishing community developed in the 17th cent., but was wiped out in a Cossack massacre during the Chmielnicki disturbances of 1648–49, when the refugee-swollen J. pop. was said to have reached over 10,000. The community revived in the 18th cent. but stagnated under economic duress, with a pop. of 779 in 1880 (half the total). Belz Hasidism dominated the town, leaving little scope for Zionist activity until the period between the World Wars. The Germans entered N. on 9 Sept. 1939 and expelled the Jews to Rawa Ruska in the Soviet sector. About a hundred sent farther east survived the war.

NAROVLYA Polesie dist., Belorussia. The number of J. poll-tax payers in N. and its environs was 316 in 1765. In 1897, the J. pop. of N. was 1,060 (92% of the total). Many Jews traded in forest products and grain. In the Soviet period, the number of J. artisans increased. A J. elementary school was opened in 1922

Hebrew and Bible class, Narol, Poland, 1934 (Beth Hatefutsoth Photo Archive, Tel Aviv/courtesy of Helena Halpern, Petah Tikva)

and a J. council was established in 1926. There were three synagogues in the early 1920s. A J. kolkhoz founded near the town in 1925 supported 25 families in 1930. Two multinational kolkhozes were set up in 1930, with another 36 J. families working there. In 1939 the J. pop. was 1,167. The Germans occupied N. in Aug. 1941. In Nov., 100 Jews were packed into a single house and abused. On 23 Nov. all the Jews remaining in the town were murdered at the J. cemetery.

NARVA Estonia. The J. community was founded by Cantonists in the mid-19th cent. A synagogue was built in 1884 (closed by the authorities in 1890 and reopened in 1895). The J. pop. grew to 474 in 1897, with trade in forest products an important source of income. Zionist activity commenced in the early 20th cent. and expanded significantly after the Feb. 1917 Revolution. Almost all the community's leaders were Zionists. At the same time Yiddishist circles remained influential. In 1922 the J. pop. stood at 318 (total 26,912), declining to 182 in 1935 due to emigration. Most Jews were tradesmen living under satisfactory conditions, while a third required welfare assistance. Under Soviet rule (1940–41) all J. institutions were closed down and business establishments nationalized. Most Jews left for the Soviet Union on the approach of the Germans. The Germans took the city on 17 Aug. 1941. The 20 remaining Jews were executed by the Estonian *Omakaitse* ("self-defense" units) under German *Sonderkommando 1a* supervision. In fall 1943 a few hundred Jews from Vilna were brought to a concentration camp set up at a textile factory in N. and which came to be known for its brutality. Many died from hunger, disease, and beatings and the weak were murdered along with children. Among those imprisoned was Hirsh Glick (1922–44), the Yiddish poet who composed "The Song of the Partisans." Before the arrival of the Russians in Feb. 1944, the survivors were transferred to other camps. Most of the city was destroyed in the heavy fighting in its environs. Some Jews settled there in the 1960s and 1970s to work in the newly established power plants.

NARVA-JOESSU Estonia. Around 65 J. families lived here between the World Wars, with many more arriving in the summer tourist season. Most escaped

to the Soviet Union on the approach of the Germans in summer 1941.

NASAUD (Hung. Naszod) N. Transylvania dist., Rumania. Jews settled in the mid-19th cent., immigrants from Galicia at first setting up a separate community. They worked mainly in the lumber industry. The J. pop. in 1920 was 583 (12% of the total). Zionist activity began in the 1920s. In May 1944 the community was transferred to the Bistrita ghetto and in June deported to Auschwitz. An attempt was made to rehabilitate the community after the war but its 100 members left during the 1950s.

NASICE Croatia, Yugoslavia, today Republic of Croatia. Jews first settled in the 19th cent. The community, numbering 229 in 1940 in a total pop. of 5,000, was destroyed in the Holocaust.

NASIELSK Warsaw dist., Poland. Jews are first mentioned in the 17th cent., with a synagogue and cemetery consecrated in 1650. Most were craftsmen, founding a guild in the mid-18th cent. that was independent of the community council and maintained its own synagogue. By the 19th cent. the majority of tradesmen were peddlers and stallkeepers living in straitened economic circumstances. The J. pop. rose to 3,030 in 1897 (total 4,693). R. Avraham Bornstein, founder of the Sochaczew dynasty, served as rabbi in 1883–87. The Zionists became active in 1904, the Bund in 1905, and Agudat Israel in 1916. After the depredations of Russian and Polish soldiers and the severe food shortages of WWI, economic conditions remained difficult between the World Wars, with the Joint Distribution Committee supporting 200 J. families in the early 1920s. Of the Zionist groups, Mizrachi emerged as the most influential. Agudat Israel ran a Beth Jacob school for 100 girls. The Germans occupied the city in Sept. 1939, immediately initiating a reign of terror. On 3–4 Dec., all 3,000 Jews in the town were transported to Miendzyrzec Podlaski and Lukow in the Lublin dist. (Poland). Afterwards many made their way to Warsaw and other localities, sharing the fate of local Jews.

NASSAU Hesse–Nassau, Germany. Established in 1856, the community dedicated a synagogue in 1882 and numbered 65 (4% of the total) in 1885. The community was affiliated with the rabbinate of Bad Ems.

Synagogue in Nasielsk, Poland, 1879

The synagogue was vandalized on *Kristallnacht* (9–10 Nov. 1938). All 66 Jews registered there after 1933 left by Aug. 1939. Fourteen emigrated while 20 perished in the Holocaust.

NASTAETTEN Hesse–Nassau, Germany. Jews lived here from 1664 and established a community numbering 79 (5% of the total) in 1885 and 49 in 1933. The synagogue was destroyed on *Kristallnacht* (9–10 Nov. 1938), and at least 15 Jews emigrated.

NASTASHKA Kiev dist., Ukraine. A small number of Jews lived in N. during the 18th cent. In 1897, they numbered 535 (total 4,197) and in 1926, under the Soviets, 154. In Sept. 1941, the Germans probably murdered the Jews of N. together with the Jews of Vasilkov prov.

NAUEN Brandenburg, Germany. There is evidence of Jews in N. in 1315 and in 1509. A settlement developed towards the end of the 17th cent. The J. community numbered 53 in 1813 and 70 in 1880. It established a synagogue in 1800 and a cemetery in 1819. When the Nazis came to power in 1933, there were 34 Jews in N. On *Kristallnacht* (9–10 Nov. 1938), the synagogue was destroyed. The cemetery was probably desecrated at the same time. Several Jews managed to emigrate, but at least five families were deported to the east.

NAUGARD (Pol. Nowogard) Pomerania, Germany, today Poland. A Jew under a letter of protection (*Schutzbrief*) for N. is mentioned in 1692. In 1752, 54 Jews were living in N. and by 1871, the J. pop. numbered 147. The community maintained a synagogue, consecrated in 1865–66, and a cemetery established in 1817. When the Nazis came to power in 1933, there were 26 Jews in N. By May 1938, two J. businesses were still operating, an indication that only a few Jews had moved away. On *Kristallnacht* (9–10 Nov. 1938), the synagogue was burned down and the windows of the J. business premises were smashed.

Three families who did not manage to emigrate were later deported.

NAUHEIM Hesse, Germany. In 1861 the community numbered 34 (4% of the total). Eight Jews emigrated after 1933; the remaining 11 mostly perished in the Holocaust.

NAUHEIM, BAD see BAD NAUHEIM.

NAUMBURG Hesse–Nassau, Germany. Established in the 18th cent., the community dedicated a synagogue in 1795 and together with members in three local villages numbered 145 in 1847, but dwindled to 40 in 1925. The 30 Jews living there in Oct. 1938 received notice to leave and only two families remained on *Kristallnacht* (9–10 Nov. 1938), when the synagogue was destroyed. By Sept. 1939 they had also left. Few emigrated, most settling in Frankfurt and Kassel.

NAUTRENI Latgale dist., Latvia. The J. pop. in 1930 was 26. Those not fleeing to the Soviet Union were murdered after the German occupation of July 1941.

NAVLIA Oriol dist., Russia. Jews probably settled in the late 19th cent. In 1939 their pop. was 93 (total 5,207). After their arrival in early Oct. 1941, the Germans murdered over 400 people at the Lesokhim wood factory, including Jews who had remained in the town.

NAWARIA Lwow dist., Poland, today Ukraine. A community, never exceeding 40–50 families (around a third of the total), existed from the 17th cent. Belz rabbis had their hasidic court in N. from the end of the 19th cent. The Germans liquidated the community by the fall of 1942.

NAY BROYIT Crimea, Russia, today Ukraine. N. was founded in the 1920s as a J. farm settlement within the framework of J. agricultural settlement in the Crimea and was part of the J. county of Fraydorf. In 1932, its J. pop. was 175. The Germans occupied N. in late Oct. 1941 and murdered 26 Jews in the second half of Nov.

NAYLAND Odessa dist., Ukraine. N. was founded as a J. colony in 1924 by 24 J. families (144 individuals) coming mainly from the Kiev dist. Nearly all previously earned their livelihoods from trade and crafts. Most presumably perished in the Holocaust.

NEA (Orestias, Orestiada) Thrace, Greece. Jews settled in N. at the end of WWI as tailors, jewelers, and producers and purveyors of alcoholic beverages. The community maintained a synagogue and two social organizations. The J. pop. in 1940 was 197 (total 12,047). In WWII the Jews were deported to Auschwitz via Didimoticho and Salonika on 10 May 1943. Only three survived.

NECHAYEVKA Zaporozhe dist., Ukraine. Jews from the Kovno (Kaunas) region founded N. as a J. colony in 1853. Its pop. was 386 in 1853 (mostly Jews) and 239 in 1897. In a pogrom staged on 6 May 1881, villagers destroyed considerable J. property. In a pogrom on 24 Dec. 1918, 125 Jews were killed. The few Jews who had neither fled nor been evacuated were presumably murdered during the German occupation in WWII.

NECKARBISCHOFSHEIM Baden, Germany. Jews were present in the 17th cent., with a synagogue built in 1769 and the community growing to a peak pop. of 189 in 1859 (total 2,010). In 1848, a new synagogue was built on pillars because of the marshy ground. The J. pop. declined to 109 in 1900 and 37 in 1933. On *Kristallnacht* (9–10 Nov. 1938), the synagogue was vandalized, with 14 Torah scrolls destroyed or stolen. Twenty-five Jews emigrated; 14 were deported to the Gurs concentration camp on 22 Oct. 1940 and three were deported to the Sobibor death camp from their refuge in Holland. Seven of those deported survived the Holocaust.

NECKARSTEINACH Hesse, Germany. Established in the early 18th cent., the community numbered 59 (4% of the total) in 1861. The synagogue (rebuilt in 1889) was evidently sold before Nov. 1938, as it escaped damage on *Kristallnacht* (9–10 Nov. 1938). Most of the 30 Jews living there in 1933 had left by 1937, some emigrating to Palestine.

NECKARZIMMERN Baden, Germany. Jews are first mentioned in the mid-16th cent. and maintained a limited presence through the following centuries under the auspices of the Worms rabbinate. The J.

pop. reached a peak of 69 (total 566) in 1825 and fell to 27 in 1933. By Nov. 1938, ten had emigrated. On *Kristallnacht* (9–10 Nov. 1938), the contents of the synagogue were taken out and burned. Fourteen of the last 15 Jews were deported to the Gurs concentration camp on 22 Oct. 1940; three of the young survived.

NEDED (Hung. Negyed) Slovakia, Czechoslovakia, today Republic of Slovakia. Jews probably settled in the 1840s. Their pop. grew from 64 in 1869 to a peak of 140 (total 4,478) in 1910. In the 1930s, a yeshiva was attended by about 20 students. In 1941, 119 Jews remained. The ruling Hungarians seized dozens for forced labor in 1941. A J. school with 40 students was still serving the area when the Germans arrived in March 1944. On 15 June, the Jews were deported to Auschwitz via Nove Zamky.

NEDVEZHYNO Minsk dist., Belorussia. N. was founded in 1842 as a J. agricultural colony and had a pop. of 114 Jews in 1895. In addition to farming, Jews also worked in nearby Minsk. In 1925, the J. pop. was 252 (43 families), most still employed in agriculture. The settlement apparently became a suburb of Minsk shortly before the outbreak of WWII. The Germans arrived on 28 June 1941, the Jews of N. sharing the fate of the Jews of Minsk.

NEFTA Tozeur dist., Tunisia. A small community existed in the mid-19th cent., originating in the southern region of Tunisia and Algeria. Jews traded in dates, distilled the popular local date beverage, and worked as tailors and jewelers. J. women wove and knitted for the local market. The wealthy Touitou family owned numerous date orchards and headed the community. The J. pop. was 130–150 (1% of the total) between the World Wars. WWII passed in relative quiet but economic conditions and Arab-J. relations subsequently deteriorated and most of the Jews left for Israel, settling in various cooperataive farming villages (*moshavim*).

NEGRESTI (I) Moldavia dist., Rumania. Jews settled in the 1830s and in 1899 constituted a majority. During the 1907 peasant revolt, 173 J. families were left destitute. In June 1941 the 408 Jews were expelled to Vaslui. The J. pop. in 1947 was 195.

NEGRESTI (II) (Hung. Avasfelsofalu) N. Transylvania dist., Rumania. A J. community existed here in the early 19th cent. and engaged mainly in agriculture. The J. pop. in 1920 was 240 (9% of the total). By 1930 the J. pop. had more than doubled to 538. In May 1944 the community was transferred to the Satu Mare ghetto and then deported to Auschwitz.

NEGROVEC (Hung. Negroc) Carpatho-Russia, Czechoslovakia, today Ukraine. Jews probably settled in the latter part of the 18th cent., numbering 13 in 1830 and 68 (total 841) in 1880. In 1921, under Czechoslovakian rule, the J. pop. rose to 127 and in 1941 to 272. The Hungarians occupied N. in March 1939 and in Aug. 1941 expelled many Jews to Kamenets-Podolski, where they were murdered. The rest were deported to Auschwitz in the second half of May 1944.

NEGROVO (Hung. Maszarfalva) Carpatho-Russia, Czechoslovakia, today Ukraine. Jews probably settled in the early 19th cent. Their pop. was 20 in 1830 and 104 (total 689) in 1880. A few Jews were farmers and one owned a flour mill. In 1921, under the Czechoslovakians, the J. pop. rose to 168 and in 1941 to 272. The Hungarians occupied the town in March 1939 and in 1941 drafted a few dozen Jews into forced labor battalions, sending some to the eastern front. In Aug. 1941 a numbers of J. families without Hungarian citizenship were expelled to Kamenets-Podolski and murdered. The rest were deported to Auschwitz on 21 May 1944.

NEHEIM Westphalia, Germany. Jews are first mentioned in 1651. In 1722, four families were present under letters of protection. Until the Prussian period, most Jews were itinerant merchants. With the annexation to Prussia in 1815, they became businessmen and industrialists; cattle dealers opened butcher shops and textile manufacturers opened stores. A Jew opened a pin and needle factory in 1833 with 48 workers and a lamp factory in 1835 with progressive working conditions. A J. school operated from 1819. A new synagogue was built in 1875. In 1855, N. was attached to the Arnsberg regional congregation. The J. pop. reached a peak of 103 in 1910, dropping to 62 (total 13,500) in 1933. Under Nazi rule, Germans working for Jews were told to leave their jobs; J. girls were excluded from dances at the local hotel; and in 1938, J. students were expelled from the municipal high school. On *Kristallnacht* (9–10 Nov. 1938), the synagogue was vandalized. The last J. stores were closed or "Aryanized" in Dec. 1938. In 1941, the remaining

Jews were moved to a single building and mobilized for forced labor. In 1943, they were deported, most to Auschwitz. Eighteen Jews from N. and neighboring Huesten emigrated from Nov. 1935 to May 1939.

NEHOIU Walachia dist., Rumania. Jews first settled in the early 20th cent. and in 1920, 35–40 Jews from Maramures and Bukovina were brought in to work in the J.-owned lumber factory. Manifestations of anti-semitism were rife in the interwar period. On 22 June 1941 the last Jews were expelled to Buzau.

NEIDENBURG (Pol. Nidzica) East Prussia, Germany, today Poland. The first protected Jew (*Schutz-jude*) was allowed to live in N. in the second half of the 18th cent. In 1812, the J. pop. numbered ten families. In 1871, there were 241 Jews, declining to 132 in 1905. The community established a synagogue in 1884 and a cemetery in the first half of the 19th cent. Barukh Hirsch Strausberg (Bethel Henry Strousberg; 1823–84), a native of N., became one of the most important industrialists of his time. On the eve of the Nazi rise to power in 1933, the J. community numbered 125. Local Nazis went far beyond general boycott measures and by Aug. 1933, about 20 J. businessmen were facing financial ruin. Sixty-one Jews were left in Feb. 1938, 38 requiring financial assistance. On *Kristallnacht* (9–10 Nov. 1938), the synagogue, which the community had apparently abandoned by the end of Oct., was burned down and several Jews were murdered. By May 1939, only 23 Jews remained in the whole N. region. Several Jews who had moved to Berlin were deported from there. The subsequent fate of the others is unknown.

NEIDENSTEIN Baden, Germany. Jews were present from the 16th cent. A J. elementary school was opened in 1828 and the synagogue built in 1831 was among the most splendid in Baden's village communities. The J. pop. reached a peak of 281 in 1842 and then dropped to 125 in 1900 and 64 in 1933. Twenty-four Jews emigrated by Nov. 1938 (15 to the U.S. and seven to Palestine) and another four after *Kristallnacht* (9–10 Nov. 1938), when the synagogue was vandalized and Jews were taken to the Dachau concentration camp. The last 19 Jews were deported to the Gurs concentration camp on 22 Oct. 1940, joined by three who had previously left N. Five survived the Holocaust.

NEISSE (Pol. Nysa) Upper Silesia, Germany, today Poland. Jews arrived in the first half of the 14th cent. They had a cemetery in 1350 and a synagogue in 1410. During the Black Death persecutions of 1348-49, one Jew burned his house with all his family in it to avoid baptism. The Jews were expelled in 1468, and J. settlement was only renewed in the early 19th cent. The community grew rapidly to 278 in 1840 and a peak of 464 in 1861. Subsequently the J. pop. declined through emigration to the big cities, especially Breslau. Branches of the Central Union (C.V.), J. War Veterans Association, and Zionist youth movements were active in the 1920s. After the Nazi rise to power, Zionist and educational activity expanded and Hebrew classes were organized. On *Kristallnacht* (9-10 Nov. 1938), the synagogue, the community building, a warehouse, a pharmacy, a dental clinic, 11 stores, and 31 homes belonging to Jews were destroyed. In the aftermath, out of 220 Jews in 1933, 93 remained. Deportations to General Gouvernement territory commenced in July 1942.

NELIDOVO Kalinin dist., Russia. Jews probably settled in the late 19th cent., and numbered 194 (total 1,445) in 1926 and 124 in 1939. The few remaining Jews were murdered after the arrival of the German in Sept. 1941.

NELIPENO (Hung. Harsfalva) Carpatho-Russia, Czechoslovakia, today Ukraine. Jews probably settled in the late 18th cent. and numbered nine in 1830 and 209 (total 795) in 1880, growing to 496 in 1921 under the Czechoslovakians and 672 (total 2,765) in 1941. A few Jews were farmers. Many of the young were members of the Zionist youth movements. The Hungarians arrived in March 1939 and in 1941 drafted a number of Jews into forced labor battalions. In the second half of May 1944, the Jews were deported to Auschwitz.

NEMAKSCIAI (Yid. Nemoksht) Raseiniai dist., Lithuania. Jews first settled in the 17th cent. The community supported social welfare organizations. Zionist activities began in the 1890s. The J. pop. in 1897 was 954 (81% of the total). Many emigrated to Eretz Israel. The J. pop. in 1940 was about 70 families. After the German invasion in June 1941, J. males aged 15 and up were seized for forced labor and abused. On 24 July 1941 they were shot beside previously prepared pits. The women and children were murdered in Aug.

NEMESDED Somogy dist., Hungary. Jews settled c. 1780 at the encouragement of estate owners to market their produce. They numbered 101 in 1880 and 40 in 1930. A Neologist congregation was established in 1876. In May 1944, the Jews were deported to Auschwitz via the Marcali ghetto.

NEMESSZALOK Veszprem dist., Hungary. Jews settled in the first half of the 18th cent. From 1885, the community exercised jurisdiction over numerous smaller settlements. In 1930, its pop. was 73. In 1941, the young men were taken to forced labor in the Ukraine, where most perished. In early July 1944, the Jews were deported to Auschwitz after being detained in the Papa ghetto since May.

NEMIROV Vinnitsa dist., Ukraine. The J. community originated around the turn of the 16th cent. Chmielnicki's Cossacks massacred about 6,000 Jews in the area on 20 June 1648. In the 18th and 19th cents. Jews operated a large distillery, dyeing facilities, knitting mills, hide-processing plants, etc. The J. pop. was 602 in 1764 and 5,287 (total 8,920) in 1897. In the civil war (1918–21), Jews and Christians formed self-defense groups, stopping a pogrom on 19 Jan. 1918. In the 1920s, most Jews worked in cooperatives and a few dozen families in a kolkhoz. A. J. school and orphanage were in operation. In 1939, the J. pop. was 3,001. The Germans captured the town on 21 July 1941. On 7 Aug., the Jews were forced to pay a large fine. A ghetto was established and in Nov., about 2,000 were executed. Another 1,500 were murdered on 26 June 1942. About 1,000 Jews brought over from Transnistria were also murdered. The last Jews, mostly skilled workers, were murdered in April–Aug. 1943. In all the *Aktions*, 3,460 Jews from the ghetto were executed, most from N.

NEMUNAITIS (Yid. Nemoneitz) Alytus dist., Lithuania. The J. pop. in 1897 was 361 (49% of the total). By WWII this Orthodox J. community numbered 15 families. All were killed after the German occupation of 1941.

NEMUNELIO-RADVILISKIS (Yid. Nai-Radvilshok, Nemonelis-Radvilishkis), Birzai dist., Lithuania.

A secular J. community was established in the beginning of the 20th cent., though later it employed a rabbi. The J. pop. in 1923 was 205. All 70 remaining Jews were killed shortly after the Germans took over in 1941.

NENTERSHAUSEN Hesse–Nassau, Germany. Dating from the 18th cent., the community built a synagogue in 1810 and numbered 149 (14% of the total) in 1861 apart from members in Solz (32) and Imshausen (11). It dwindled to 37 in 1925 and 14 Jews emigrated during the Nazi period; the last 13 were deported in 1942.

NENZENHEIM Middle Franconia, Germany. The J. community dates from the late 18th cent. The J. pop. reached 94 in 1880 (total 715) and a synagogue was built in 1892. In 1933, 32 Jews remained; 14 left before Nov. 1938, including eight to the U.S. and five to Palestine, and the rest after *Kristallnacht* (9–10 Nov. 1938), when the synagogue was set on fire.

NERESNICE (Hung. Alsoneresznice) Carpatho-Russia, Czechoslovakia, today Ukraine. Jews probably settled at the turn of the 18th cent. The J. pop. was 69 in 1830 and 327 (total 976) in 1880. It then rose to 469 in 1921 under the Czechoslovakians and 664 in 1941. A *talmud torah* was opened in 1929 for children attending the Czech state school. Within the J. pop. there were 75 artisans and 40 were shopkeepers, petty traders, and peddlers. Such youth organizations as Tze'irei Mizrachi, Pirhei Agudat Israel, and Hehalutz were active in the 1920s and 1930s. After their arrival in March 1939, the Hungarians proceeded to undermine J. livelihoods and in 1941 drafted about 50 Jews into forced labor battalions. Six J. families lacking Hungarian citizenship were expelled to Kamenets-Podolski in Aug. 1941 and murdered there. The rest were deported to Auschwitz on 24 May 1944. A few survivors returned after the war but soon left for Czechoslovakia.

NERETA Zemgale (Courland) dist., Latvia. The J. pop. in 1935 was 54 (total 612). The Jews were murdered in July 1941 shortly after the arrival of the Germans.

NESSELROEDEN (now part of Herleshausen) Hesse–Nassau, Germany. Established around 1776, the community numbered 107 (23% of the total) in

1861. Having dwindled to 14 in 1933, it disbanded in 1937. The last Jews, three elderly sisters, were deported to the Theresienstadt ghetto in 1942.

NETRA (now part of Ringgau) Hesse–Nassau, Germany. Established around 1776, the community converted a farmhouse into its synagogue, numbered 110 (13% of the total) in 1861, and later had members in Datterode. By 1937 only 11 Jews remained; several perished in the Holocaust.

NETTESHEIM Rhineland, Germany. Jews were present in 1685 and a synagogue was in use in 1786. They numbered 80 in 1835 and 21 in 1932. They shared the fate of the Jews of neighboring Neuss in the Holocaust.

NEUBRANDENBURG Mecklenburg-Strelitz, Germany. Jews are first mentioned in N. in 1440. The settlement came to an end in 1492 when the Jews of Mecklenburg were accused of desecrating the Host and burned or expelled. Settlement in N. was renewed only in 1766. The J. pop. numbered 60 in 1868 and 98 in 1903. The J. community, which was constituted officially in 1864, included all the Jews in the Free State of Mecklenburg-Strelitz. In 1903, the community numbered 126 members. It maintained a synagogue, built in 1876–77, and a cemetery, opened in 1868. When the Nazis came to power in 1933, there were 182 Jews living in Mecklenburg-Strelitz with 34 Jews registered in N. On *Kristallnacht* (9-10 Nov. 1938), the synagogue and the mortuary at the cemetery were burned down. By May 1939, only 11 Jews remained in the city. Most were deported.

NEUBUKOW Mecklenburg-Schwerin, Germany. Jews apparently arrived in 1778, numbering 54 in 1819 and a peak of 107 in 1850. Their number then declined to 64 in 1880; 30–40 up to 1922; and 27 in 1933. Most engaged in trade, with 15 of the town's 46 workshops and business establishments in J. hands. A synagogue was built in the mid-19th cent. and became a residential building after being sold in the early 1930s. Most Jews left when the Nazis came to power. The few who remained left in 1936, mostly emigrating from Germany. Those local Jews who remained in Germany were deported to the Theresienstadt ghetto and Auschwitz, except for one women married to a non-Jew. The J. cemetery was destroyed

in 1934. The last Jew was clandestinely buried there in 1941. In 1942, the Nazi authorities officially declared N. to be "free of Jews" (*judenfrei*).

NEUDENAU Baden, Germany. Jews are mentioned from the mid-13th cent. and were victims of the Rindfleisch massacres of 1298 and the Black Death persecutions of 1348–49. In the 15th cent., the community dwindled and was only revived in the 18th cent. Throughout the 19th cent. the Jews maintained a pop. of around 40–50 (3–4% of the total). A small synagogue was erected in 1875. Of the ten Jews present in the Nazi era, nine left for other German cities; all were subsequently deported, six perishing in Auschwitz in 1942–43.

NEUENAHR, BAD see BAD NEUENAHR.

NEUENHAUS Hanover, Germany. The first recorded J. settlement dates back to 1685. The small community reached a peak pop. of 37 in 1812. The community had its own synagogue (built around the mid-19th century) but buried its dead in nearby Hilten. Only 26 Jews remained in 1933. After Hitler's assumption of power in 1933, most emigrated to Holland. During *Kristallnacht* (9-10 Nov. 1938), SA troops destroyed the synagogue and wrecked J. property. In July 1942, the last 14 Jews were deported to their death.

NEUHOF Hesse–Nassau, Germany. The Jews of N., Ellers, and Opperz established a rural community numbering 70 (3% of the total) in 1905. It disbanded in 1939: 18 of the 48 Jews emigrated; 17 were eventually deported.

NEUILLY-SUR-SEINE Seine dist., France. In 1866, a J. home for delinquent children called Foyer Le Refuge was established by Coralie Cahen. The synagogue was dedicated in 1878. In 1886, Isidore Lione, vice president of the J. community, was nominated as deputy mayor of N. In 1941, there were 1,115 Jews in N. In July 1942, 48 Jews were arrested. Under the German occupation, the fate of local Jews was similar to the fate of Parisian Jews.

NEU ISENBURG Hesse, Germany. Affiliated with neighboring Sprendlingen's community, the Jews numbered 40 (0.5% of the total) in 1900. Bertha Pappenheim (1859–1936), a pioneer social worker who founded Germany's League of J. Women, established a training school there for unmarried mothers and homeless (mainly illegitimate) girls in 1907. By 1933 it housed 150 trainees, but Pappenheim died after a Gestapo interrogation and on *Kristallnacht* (9–10 Nov. 1938), the children's home was burned down. Only younger girls (evacuated to Britain) survived the Holocaust. Of the 64 local Jews in 1933–35, 34 emigrated before WWII; the others dispersed throughout Germany, 15 of them dying in the Holocaust.

NEUKIRCHEN (now part of Haunetal) Hesse–Nassau, Germany. Jews lived in N. from the 17th cent., numbering 113 (7% of the total) in 1885 and 83 in 1933. Many left before *Kristallnacht* (9–10 Nov. 1938), when the synagogue was vandalized. About 50 perished in the Holocaust.

NEULEININGEN Palatinate, Germany. Jews are known from the early 17th cent. and numbered 138 in 1836, maintaining a synagogue. A J.-owned porcelain factory operated there. The community was officially dissolved in 1902. Two Jews perished in the Holocaust.

NEUMAGEN Rhineland, Germany. Jews are first mentioned in 1351. In 1699, four Jews were living there under letters of protection. A synagogue and J. school were in operation by the first quarter of the 19th cent. The J. pop. rose to a peak of 109 (including neighboring Niederemmel) in 1857 and then declined steadily. In 1889 a united congregation was formed with Niederemmel, Minheim, Rivenich, Sehlem, and Hetzerath and in 1909 N. and Niederemmel became a single community. In 1891, the J. school received public school status. The J. cemetery was desecrated in 1931. In 1933 the J. pop. of N.-Niederemmel was 74 (total 1,742). J. businesses were boycotted in 1933–34 with accompanying anti-J. agitation. The cemetery was again vandalized in 1935 and on *Kristallnacht* (9–10 Nov. 1938), the synagogue was wrecked. J. homes were also destroyed. In 1933–39, 33 Jews left the town, 18 of them to the U.S. On 16 Oct. 1941, two local Jews were among those deported from the county to their deaths in the east. The last two Jews were deported to the Minsk ghetto via Trier on 26 Feb. 1942. In all, four local Jews perished in the Holocaust.

NEUMARKT (I) Upper Palatinate, Germany. The 13th cent. community was destroyed in the Rindfleisch massacres of 1298. New communities were ended in the Black Death persecutions of 1348–49 and the general expulsion from the Palatinate in 1555. Through the Middle Ages the Jews dealt in livestock and wool products and from the mid-15th cent. in moneylending. The modern community commenced in the mid-19th cent. and grew to 148 (total 5,703) in 1890. A synagogue was dedicated in 1868 and a cemetery and J. public school were opened in the 1870s. In 1933, 105 Jews lived there; 30 left by March 1936. On *Kristallnacht* (9–10 Nov. 1938), men and women were arrested and beaten and the synagogue was vandalized along with J. homes. On 2 April 1942, 15 Jews were expelled to Piaski in the Lublin dist. (Poland).

NEUMARKT (II) (Pol. Sroda Slaska) Lower Silesia, Germany, today Poland. Jews in significant numbers were present by the early 14th cent. but their residence was banned in 1455 and only renewed in 1812. The J. pop. was 130 in 1845 with the community maintaining a cemetery from 1844 and establishing a synagogue in 1864. It became independent in 1860 after being under the jurisdiction of the Schweidnitz community. In 1925, the J. pop. was 47. When the Nazis came to power in 1933, it was 33. On *Kristallnacht* (9–10 Nov. 1938), the synagogue and two J. stores were destroyed. Four intermarried Jews remained in Nov. 1942. There is no additional information about the fate of the community under the Nazis. Presumably those who did not emigrate perished after deportation.

NEUMORSCHEN (now part of Morschen) Hesse–Nassau, Germany. Numbering 38 (6% of the total) in 1861, the J. community's membership dwindled to ten in 1933 and in nearby Malsfeld from 45 to nine. No Jews remained in 1940.

NEUMUENSTER Schleswig–Holstein, Germany. Jews were living there in 1842 and, though affiliated in 1913 with the Bad Segeberg community, often objected to its financial policies. As N. was a much larger town, with a J. pop. greater than that of Bad Segeberg (over 50 in 1932), it made efforts to gain communal autonomy. In 1935, a Jew from N. became head of the united community, which ceased to exist in 1938. Those who did not emigrate perished in the Holocaust.

NEUNKIRCHEN (I)   Saar, Germany. Jews are first mentioned in 1777. In 1790 their residence was limited to ten families. Their number grew to 188 in 1843. Among breadwinners, 23 were merchants, peddlers, and shopkeepers, eight artisans, and four butchers. A synagogue was consecrated in 1865. In the 1870s, after the Jews received equal rights, they played an active part in local life and fulfilled such obligations as military service. Among the leading J. business enterprises was the local branch of the Levi chain for industrial supplies, which became a large department store in 1901 and employed 300 workers in the 1920s. After WWI, N. came under French control and developed industrially. In 1927, the J. pop. reached 234 (total 41,031). There were few manifestations of antisemitism until the region was annexed to the Reich by plebiscite in Jan. 1935. Many Jews subsequently sold their businesses and left the city. In 1935, 142 Jews remained in N. and its attached communities (Elversberg, Spiesen, Schiffweiler, and Wiebelskirchen). Emigration intensified still further after the publication of the Nuremberg Laws. The local pop. and the Church did little to help the Jews in the face of mounting persecution. On *Kristallnacht* (9–10 Nov. 1938), the synagogue was burned and Jews were arrested and beaten. Seven Jews were deported to the Gurs and Drancy concentration camps. Of the vast majority who fled, 63 reached France, 20 Luxembourg, and 27 Palestine. The 59 who left for other German cities are presumed to have died in the Holocaust.

NEUNKIRCHEN (II)   Lower Austria, Austria. Jews were present in 1343. They were expelled by the Landtag of Bruck an der Mur in 1496, but resettled in 1504. Jews were engaged in trade. In 1893, a new synagogue was built. In 1894, the community was recognized as a religious corporation (*Kultusgemeinde*). By 1934, the J. pop. numbered 500, thereafter declining sharply to 140 in May 1938. Only a small number of Jews managed to emigrate or escape. The others were sent to Vienna and from there to the east.

NEURUPPIN   Brandenburg, Germany. The 14th cent. community here maintained a synagogue (first mentioned in 1362). The community ended with the two expulsions of the Jews from Brandenburg in 1510 and 1571. By 1790 there were again 40 Jews living in the town and in 1880 there were 146. The community subsequently established two synagogues and two cemeteries (1824 and 1885). The latter was desecrated in 1892. When the Nazis came to power in 1933, there were 96 Jews in N. By May 1939, there were still 76 Jews and 11 persons of partial J. origin (*Mischlinge*) in N. It may be assumed that those who did not manage to emigrate were deported to the east. In Oct. 1942, there were three Jews in N., probably protected by marriage to non-Jews.

NEUSALZ   (Pol. Nowa Sol) Lower Silesia, Germany, today Poland. The J. pop. was 71 in 1925 and together with the adjoining village about 60 (15 families) on the eve of the Nazi era. The community was not recognized by law as a congregation but only as a synagogue association (*Synagogenverein*). It maintained a cemetery (opened in 1870) and a prayer room in a residential building. After the Nazi rise to power in 1933, a rapid exodus of Jews took place. Those who were left behind, the aged and the poor, could not afford the maintenance of the prayer room and it was ceremoniously closed in 1935. The J. pop. was 17 at the time (total 10,700); two years later just nine Jews remained. No further information is available about the fate of the community under the Nazis. Presumably those Jews who did not emigrate were deported and perished.

NEUSS   Rhineland, Germany. Jews from Cologne fleeing the rampaging Crusaders arrived in 1096 but a number were massacred on St. John's Day in the same year by residents of the area and in 1097 others were brutally murdered or forcibly converted. Jews were again victimized in the wake of the Oberwesel blood libel of 1287 and during the Black Death persecutions of 1348–49, when they were expelled. They were present again in 1401, numbering a few families and including a Court Jew under the protection of King Sigismund. In 1425 they were once more expelled. A few returned but a final expulsion occurred in 1563. The modern community developed from the early 19th cent., its pop. growing from 12 in 1810 to 200 in 1861 and a peak of 366 (total 20,074) in 1885. Jews were active in the grain and livestock trade and opened a number of spinning and textile mills. The J.-owned Simons household oil refinery became the largest in Germany. Jews were involved in local life and active in the revolutionary events of 1848. During the same period there were also manifestations of antisemitism. In 1857 N. became the seat of a regional congregation including Zons, Dormagen, Rommer-skirchen, and Nettesheim. The congregation remained basically Orthodox until assimilationist tendencies brought on by the economic prosperity of the 1860s began to engender religious Liberalism as well. The synagogue, consecrated in 1867, was one of the largest and most beautiful in the Rhineland. The J. elementary school was recognized as a public school in 1890. The J. pop. dropped to 245 in 1900 and remained around that level until the Nazi era. Persecution commenced with the Nazi rise to power in 1933 and Jews soon began to liquidate their businesses and to prepare for emigration. The first to leave were the Zionists, who maintained a pioneer training farm in the vicinity of the nearby village of Buetgen. The Simons refinery was "Aryanized" in 1937; the Alsberg clothing factory in 1938. On *Kristallnacht* (9–10 Nov. 1938), the syna-gogue was burned down, J. homes were brutally van-dalized, and 33 J. men were sent to the Dachau concen-tration camp. In the wake of the disturbances, 63 Jews left the city, some for Holland, others for Cologne or Duesseldorf. In all, 120 Jews emigrated in the 1933–41 period, including 30 to the U.S., 21 to Palestine, 16 to England, and 14 to Argentina. Another 54 moved to other German cities. Deportations began on 13 Oct. 1941, when the first Jews from N. and the at-tached communities were sent to the Lodz ghetto; 24 followed on 27 Oct.; 25 were sent to the Riga ghetto in Dec.; and the last 11 to the Theresienstadt ghetto in 1942. A total of 177 Jews from N. and the attached communities were deported, either directly or from oc-cupied Europe; 119 perished in the camps.

NEUSTADT (I)   Palatinate, Germany. A J. presence in the 13th cent. is indicated by the remains of a syna-gogue found there. Jews are mentioned throughout the 14th cent. as moneylenders. Some were burned at the stake in 1343 following a blood libel. During the Black Death disturbances of 1348–49, they were perse-cuted. In 1390–91, Rupert II expelled them along with the rest of the Jews of the Palatinate. The modern com-munity grew from 112 in 1804 to 306 in 1871 and a peak of 397 (total 17,795) in 1900. Most engaged in trade. A J. elementary school was built in 1830 (29 stu-dents in 1910) and a synagogue was consecrated in 1866. An old age home was opened in 1914 (40 resi-dents in 1932). The Zionists organized in 1902. In the Weimar period, Jews remained active in the city's social and economic life, with over 80 businesses in operation.

In 1933, the J. pop. was 266. On *Kristallnacht* (9–10 Nov. 1938), the synagogue was set on fire and two Jews were burned alive when the old age home was burned down. J. men were sent to the Dachau concen-tration camp. Most Jews liquidated their businesses dur-ing the period and emigrated or moved to other German cities. Thirty-eight remained in Jan. 1940. On 22 Oct. 1940, 22 were deported to the Gurs concentration camp. A total of 33 perished in the Holocaust, including 13 in Auschwitz and eight in the Sobibor death camp.

NEUSTADT (II)   (Pol. Prudnik) Upper Silesia, Ger-many, today Poland. In 1534, the J. pop. was 25 (total 114). The community established a synagogue in 1540 and a cemetery in 1541. In 1570, the Jews were ex-pelled and banned from trading in N. and the neighbor-ing villages. The community was reestablished in the 19th cent. In 1840, the J. pop. was 147 (total 6,058). The community was constituted as a legal body in 1854. A new cemetery was consecrated in 1861 and a synagogue in 1877. Samuel Fraenkel, who also started the burgeoning local textile industry, financed the con-struction of the synagogue. In 1880, the J. pop. was 184 and in 1925 it was 110. The Nazi racial laws put into effect from 1933 were not extended to N. until July 1937 because of the League of Nations' minority rights convention. During this period, a pioneer training farm was set up near the city. On *Kristallnacht* (9–10 Nov. 1938), the synagogue was set on fire and in 1939, only 31 Jews remained. Many were expelled to General Gouvernement territory in July 1942. On 19 Nov., ten Jews were still in the city. Their fate is unknown.

NEUSTADT (III)   Hesse–Nassau, Germany. Jews lived there from 1646, established a community num-bering 160 (7% of the total) in 1885, and dedicated a new synagogue in 1887. After WWI, branches of the Central Union (C.V.) and J. War Veterans Association were active. Affiliated with the rabbinate of Marburg, the community numbered 101 (4%) in 1925 and 89 in 1933. Nazis destroyed the synagogue and looted J. homes in a three-day *Kristallnacht* pogrom (8–10 Nov. 1938). At least 28 perished in the Holocaust; 43 emigrated.

NEUSTADT, BAD   see BAD NEUSTADT.

NEUSTADT AM RUEBENBERGE   Hanover, Ger-many. Arriving there before 1700, Jews acquired a burial ground. They numbered 47 in 1828. A community, drawing members from Mandelsloh, Rodewald, and Wuelfelade was established and a regional synagogue opened. Reaching its peak in 1871 with 100 Jews, the community shrunk to 47 in 1928. In June 1933, there were 45 Jews living in N. On *Kristallnacht* (9–10 Nov. 1938), local SA troops vandalized the synagogue's interior and looted and destroyed J. homes. Most Jews left before the outbreak of war. The 25 Jews who did not make it to safe havens were deported to the east. Only three survived.

NEUSTADT AN DER AISCH   Middle Franconia, Germany. In the Rindfleisch massacres of 1298, 71 Jews were murdered and in the Black Death persecutions of 1348–49 the community was destroyed. In 1409, Jews received a charter of privileges permitting them to engage in moneylending and moneychanging. In 1499, refugees from the Nuremberg expulsion arrived and in 1515 the Jews of N. were themselves expelled, some finding shelter in Frankfurt and others in Prague. In 1803, the Jews were victims of a blood libel. Only in the mid-19th cent. did Jews again settle in significant numbers. A synagogue was built in 1883. The Jews numbered 210 (total 3,870) in 1900 and 74 in 1933. N. was one of the hotbeds of Nazism in Bavaria. Christian stores were forbidden to sell bread to Jews and J. stores were forbidden to sell bread at all. By Nov. 1938, 55 Jews had left the town, most for other German cities. The rest left immediately after the *Kristallnacht* riots (9–10 Nov. 1938).

NEUSTADT IM ODENWALD   Hesse, Germany. The community, numbering 93 (about 11% of the total) in 1871, dwindled to 20 in 1933. On *Kristallnacht* (9–10 Nov. 1938), the synagogue's interior was destroyed and by 1939 the Jews had mostly emigrated.

NEUSTETTIN   (Pol. Szczecinek) Pomerania, Germany, today Poland. In 1718 there were three J. families in N. and a cemetery had probably been established. The J. community numbered ten families in 1812 and 455 individuals in 1880. A synagogue was consecrated in 1829. The Jews of N. encountered fierce antisemitism and in 1863 antisemites broke into the synagogue and desecrated two Torah scrolls. In 1881, several days after an inflammatory speech by the antisemitic leader Dr. Ernst Henrici, antisemites burned down the synagogue. The J. community itself

was charged with the crime and several members were put on trial and only acquitted on appeal in 1884. The incident gave rise to outbreaks of violence against Jews throughout Pomerania and in West Prussia. In N., economic and social contacts between gentiles and Jews diminished and Jews were expelled from some local associations. Five months after the arson, J. houses and business premises were destroyed. In 1883, a new synagogue was consecrated but the J. pop. began to diminish drastically. When the Nazis came to power in 1933, the community numbered 124 members. Under the pressure of boycott measures, many Jews emigrated. By June 1934, there were only about 60 Jews in N. On *Kristallnacht* (9–10 Nov. 1938), the synagogue and the cemetery were probably desecrated. By May 1939, there were 52 Jews and 18 persons of partial J. origin (*Mischlinge*) in N. No further information about their fate is available.

NEU-ULM   Swabia, Germany. The community was attached to Ichenhausen for many years, numbering 109 in 1880 and 44 (total 12,741) in 1933. Fifteen left the city in 1939–40, 12 emigrating; seven were deported to Piaski (Poland) on 3 April 1942.

NEUWIED   Rhineland, Germany. Jews arrived in 1661. From 1691 to 1748, Moses Abraham Wolf served the local count as a Court Jew. Under the count, Jews were accorded freedom of trade and worship. A synagogue was consecrated in 1748 and the private J. school opened in 1818 moved to the enlarged and renovated synagogue in 1844. Liberal tendencies were seen in the community already about 1810 when most women ceased to use the *mikve*. Later in the cent., a mixed choir and organ were introduced into the synagogue. The J. pop. grew to 210 in 1816 and 400 in 1843, remaining at around that level until WWI though dropping from 5% to 2% of the total. In 1864, N. became the seat of a regional congregation, which included the communities of Heddesdorf, Irlich, Oberbieber, and Dierdorf. Most Jews engaged in trade, and in the Weimar period, over half the textile businesses and butcher shops in the city belonged to Jews. The livestock trade was entirely in J. hands and Jews also ran four insurance agencies, an x-ray institute, and a lottery. In 1933, the J. pop. was 281. Under the Nuremberg Laws of 1935, about 50 more who had converted were defined as Jews. On

Kristallnacht (9–10 Nov. 1938), the synagogue was blown up, its contents being burned outside; J. homes and stores were destroyed; and Jews were brutally beaten. By May 1939, 111 Jews were registered in N. In all, 194 Jews perished in the camps, including 45 in Auschwitz, 27 in the Theresienstadt ghetto, 21 in Izbica, and 16 in the Minsk ghetto.

NEVARENAI (Yid. Naveran) Telsai dist., Lithuania. The J. community became consolidated here in the late 19th cent. Many emigrated to the west. The J. pop. in 1923 was 95 (21% of the total). All the Jews were murdered shortly after the German occupation of 1941.

NEVEKLOV Bohemia, Czechoslovakia. An organized community existed by 1657, apparently founded by German J. refugees or their children who arrived during the Thirty Years War (1618–48). In 1870 the J. pop. was 116, dropping to 28 (total 1,050) in 1930. The Jews were apparently deported to the Theresienstadt ghetto together with the Jews of Benesov on 4 Sept. 1942. Subsequently they were sent to the death camps of Poland, mainly Treblinka and Maly Trostinec in Belorussia.

NEVEL Kalinin dist., Russia. J. settlement probably began in the mid-18th cent. In 1765, the number of J. poll-tax payers in N. and the attached communities was 388. In 1780, the J. pop. of the town was 123 (total 950). The J. pop. subsequently rose to 3,201 in 1847 and 5,836 (total 9,349) in 1897. Most Jews earned their living in petty trade and crafts (most of the town's 230 artisans and their apprentices being Jews). In all the province there were four J. landowners. In 1910 the community maintained a *talmud torah* and a boys' elementary school with a section for girls. In addition to the synagogue, there were 16 hasidic *shtiblekh*. Some J. workers were employed at a brush factory. Both the Zionists and the Bund were active. A pogrom was staged in 1905. In 1910, the J. pop. reached 12,333. In 1926, under the Soviets, a J. elementary school was opened and during the 1920s an annex of the local law courts conducted its deliberations in Yiddish. Dozens of J. families found employment in a multinational kolkhoz founded in 1929 and known throughout the district for its orchards, livestock, and gardens. In 1928, the authorities closed down the (clandestine) yeshiva and then, in the early 1930s, all the prayer houses that were still active.

The J. school continued to exist until 1939. In 1939, the J. pop. was 3,178. After a heavy bombardment, the Germans occupied N. on 16 July 1941. Although there was a mass flight from N., many returned as a result of misleading information in the Soviet media. After a short period of relative quiet, the Jews were made to wear armbands and badges and a ghetto was established which also held hundreds of Jews from the surrounding area. On 5 or 6 Sept., the Germans murdered about 2,000 Jews from N. and its environs at Goluboi Datcha and Petino. Another 13 were murdered near Klastysy in Dec.

NICE (Ital. Nizza) Alpes-Maritimes dist., France. The first reference to Jews in N. dates to the fourth cent. The Statutes of N., enacted in 1342, when it belonged to Provence, compelled the Jews to wear the distinguishing badge. By 1406, when N. belonged to Savoy, the community had a bailiff. From 1406 it owned a cemetery and at least from 1428, a synagogue. In 1499, Jews expelled from Rhodes were permitted to settle in N. At first, the community was affiliated to Turin, but from the beginning of the 17th cent., it was independent. Marranos from Italy and Holland were attracted to N. from 1648, receiving privileges through the free port edict. They were followed by newcomers from Oran (Algeria). The King of Sardinia forced the local Jews in 1732 to move to the ancient ghetto. By 1818, the community consisted of approximately 300 persons. They spoke Judeo-Nicois, a mixture of the local dialect and Hebrew. Temporary reunion of N. with France from 1796 to 1814 brought emancipation to the Jews, but it was rescinded with the restoration of Sardinian administration. The Jews returned to the ghetto between 1828 and 1848. After the plebiscite in 1860, N. was annexed to France. A new synagogue was inaugurated in 1886. In 1892, a sanatorium for J. tuberculosis patients was opened in Cimiez, a suburb of N. In addition, there were such philanthropic projects as hot lunches and clothes for needy J. children. By 1909, the community numbered 500 Jews (total pop. 95,000). Jeunesse Israelite de Nice, which had been active prior to WWI, resumed its activities aimed at promoting J. education. Funds were allocated to charity and the Zionists were active. Between the World Wars, the community absorbed a great number of Polish and Russian Jews. The community council represented Sephardi and Ashkenazi Jews. In 1940, the community consisted of about

1,000 families. After Nov. 1942, Axis troops entered free zones, while the Italians occupied eight departments in the southwest of France. Since N. was occupied by the Italians, thousands of Jews found refuge there. It was estimated that the total number of Jews in N. at this time was 25,000–30,000. N. also became a center for various J. organizations. At the end of Dec. 1942, following the intervention of the J. banker Angelo Donati with the Italian consul in N., the Italian foreign ministry informed the Vichy authorities that the Jews in their occupied zone were only subject to measures taken by the Italian government. After the Italians signed the armistice with the Allies, German troops invaded the former Italian zone (8 Sept. 1943) and initiated brutal raids. Many Jews joined the Resistance. Among the Jews in N., 809 were caught and deported. After liberation, several hundred Jews, including both former inhabitants of N. and refugees, reestablished the community. With the influx of Jews from North Africa in 1964, the J. community in N. and the vicinity numbered 20,000.

NIDDA   Hesse, Germany. Although Jews lived there in medieval times, a community was not established until the 18th cent., growing to 95 (5% of the total) in 1900. Affiliated with the Orthodox rabbinate of Giessen, it also had members in Geiss-Nidda. The Nazi boycott forced Jews to leave, disbanding the community (and disposing of the synagogue) before *Kristallnacht* (9–10 Nov. 1938). Many emigrated, the last Jew being stoned to death on 19 Oct. 1939.

NIEBYLEC   Lwow dist., Poland. Jews first settled around the end of the 17th cent., mostly engaged in farming. They attained a maximum pop. of 343 (50% of the total) in 1900. Pogroms in 1919, the ravages of WWI, and straitened economic circumstances caused a decline of the total to 283 in 1921. The Germans established an open ghetto around the end of 1941 and liquidated the community in June 1942, expelling the pop. to Rzeszow en route to the Belzec death camp.

NIEDENSTEIN   Hesse–Nassau, Germany. The founder of the community, Selig Heinemann, settled in N. at the end of the Thirty Years War (1618-48). His descendants constituted the wealthiest family in the community, holding the most important public offices. Numbering six protected Jews (*Schutzjuden*) in 1744, the J. pop. grew to 120 in 1834, reached a peak of 147 (total 643) in 1861, and declined to 87 in 1925. Most of the Jews earned their living as tradesmen or artisans. The community maintained a synagogue, endowed by Kalman Heinemann-Michaelis in 1816, and buried its dead in the regional J. cemetery at Obervorschuetz. A J. elementary school, opened in 1826, existed until 1928. In 1894, it was attended by 22 children, about half of all the J. schoolchildren in N. The longest-serving teacher was Heiser (1875–1914), who also served as a substitute teacher in the local public school. N's strictly Orthodox Jews kept aloof from local associations and shunned non-J. restaurants. They practiced ritual slaughter and maintained a *mikve*. Under the Nazis, many of the community's members left, emigrating to the U. S., South America, France, and Holland. Fifteen departed to other cities in Germany. The synagogue's interior was vandalized in 1938 and the building was subsequently sold and renovated. The last remaining Jews were evacuated to Kassel on 6 Sept. 1942 and from there deported to the death camps in the east. At least 15 perished in the Holocaust.

NIEDERAULA   Hesse–Nassau, Germany. Established in 1735, the community dedicated a synagogue in 1836 and ran an elementary school from 1868 to 1933. The community numbered 145 (14% of the total) in 1885 and 100 (8%) in 1925-33. Nazi persecution forced many Jews to leave before *Kristallnacht* (9–10 Nov. 1938), when the synagogue and J. property were vandalized. By 1941, 34 Jews had emigrated; nine were deported in 1942.

NIEDERBRONN-LES-BAINS   (Ger. Niederbronn) Bas-Rhin dist., France. In 1766, there were 26 Jews in N. The local synagogue was inaugurated in 1869. In 1936, the community numbered 82 members. During WWII, they were expelled to the south of France with the rest of Alsace-Lorraine Jews. The local synagogue was damaged. Nineteen Jews were deported. In 1965, there were 35 Jews in N.

NIEDER-FLORSTADT   Hesse, Germany. The community, numbering 148 (12% of the total) in 1861, dwindled to 28 by 1933. On *Kristallnacht* (9–10 Nov. 1938), the synagogue was burned down and most Jews left, some emigrating.

NIEDER-GEMUENDEN   Hesse, Germany. The

community, numbering 51 (10% of the total) in 1861, included Jews of Sephardi origin. All but one left (some emigrating) by 1939.

NIEDERHOCHSTADT Palatinate, Germany. Jews are mentioned in 1685. Seven protected families were living in N. in the early 18th cent. and by 1848 their pop. grew to a peak of 221. The community maintained a synagogue, cemetery (opened in 1856), and elementary school (1836–1924). Zachariah Frank, the great-grandfather of Anne Frank, was born in N. in 1811. The J. pop. dropped to 148 (total 1,382) in 1875 and 45 in 1932. In the Nazi era, 19 Jews emigrated and 12 moved to other places in Germany. Seven were deported to Gurs in Oct. 1940. Eight perished in the Holocaust. The synagogue was destroyed on *Kristallnacht* (9–10 Nov. 1938).

NIEDERKLEIN (now part of Stadtallendorf) Hesse–Nassau, Germany. Numbering 63 (6% of the total) in 1861, the community dwindled to 11 in 1933. Eight Jews emigrated to the U.S.; three perished in Nazi death camps.

NIEDERMARSBERG Westphalia, Germany. The J. community is first mentioned in 1844. In 1849, the synagogue was destroyed in a devastating fire. A new synagogue was consecrated in 1856 and a new cemetery was opened in 1885. In 1854, N. became the seat of a regional congregation with two sister communities (Obermarsberg and Heddinghausen) and others attached to it (Borntosten, Erlinghausen, Udorf, Leitmar, Canstein). A private J. school was started in 1863 to replace the one in the old synagogue. In 1894–95, attendance came to 36. The J. pop. reached a peak of 150 (total 3,337) in 1885. In the Weimar period, a number of leading families owned stores (glassware, women's fashions, textiles), a sawmill, and a carpentry shop. The community was not Orthodox and stores remained open on the Sabbath, but the High Holidays were observed. Close relations prevailed between Jews and Christians. In 1933, the J. pop. was 93. Though Jews continued to participate in local life for awhile under the Nazis, there were also antisemitic incidents. On *Kristallnacht* (9–10 Nov. 1938), SS troops from Arolsen destroyed the synagogue, effectively ending the community's religious and cultural life. About half the Jews emigrated before *Kristallnacht* and many more in 1939. Among them, 32 reached the U.S.; another 33 moved to other German cities. Twenty-four Jews from N. and its attached communities were deported to the east in 1942 and early 1943, most perishing there.

NIEDERMENDIG Rhineland, Germany. Jews are first mentioned in 1760. In the early 19th cent., they numbered 25 and in the late 19th cent., 54. A synagogue was consecrated in 1886 and a cemetery was opened in 1889–90, also serving the Jews of Obermendig. The J. pop. grew to 60–70 in the first decade of the 20th cent. and then dropped to 44 (total 3,352) in 1925 and 38 in 1933. Three Jews left for other places in Germany before the *Kristallnacht* disturbances (9–10 Nov. 1938) and 19 emigrated from Germany in their wake, five to Holland and the rest to North and South America. The seven remaining Jews were deported to the camps and at least ten perished in the Holocaust. The synagogue was destroyed on *Kristallnacht* (9–10 Nov. 1938).

NIEDER-MOCKSTADT Hesse, Germany. Numbering 89 (13% of the total) in 1861, the community declined to 35 in 1933. Most J. families were surnamed Halberstadt and evidently originated there. All but one of the Jews left after *Kristallnacht* (9–10 Nov. 1938), when the synagogue's interior was destroyed.

NIEDER-OHMEN Hesse, Germany. Established in the 18th cent., the community numbered 109 (9% of the total) in 1871 and was affiliated with Giessen's Orthodox rabbinate. Members observed a fast after the desecration of their Torah scrolls in 1935 and attended daily services until 1938, a year after the synagogue's forced sale. By Sept. 1940, 45 Jews had emigrated; almost as many perished in the Holocaust.

NIEDER-OLM Hesse, Germany. A Torah scroll dating from 1236 and written by Yosef ben Moshe of Olmin (or Ulmen) is preserved in Milan. The community, numbering 64 (4% of the total) in 1880, drew members from other villages. It disbanded in 1937 and by May 1939 only two Jews remained, several having emigrated.

NIEDER-SAULHEIM Hesse, Germany. Numbering 71 (4% of the total) in 1861 and 29 in 1933, the community suffered under the Nazis and dispersed in Nov. 1938.

NIEDERSTETTEN   Wuerttemberg, Germany. The medieval J. settlement was destroyed in the Rindfleisch massacres of 1298. In the 17th cent. Jews were living in N. under a letter of protection. Despite various disabilities, they were able to expand their economic activities, primarily in cattle, wool, wine, and hides. The J. pop. grew to 215 in 1854 (total 1,701), a subsequent decline being slowed when commerce was boosted by the coming of the railroad in 1869. A synagogue was dedicated in 1824 and a J. school founded in 1838. In the second half of the 19th cent. Jews owned some of the largest business establishments in the town, including a diamond-polishing factory. In the Weimar period Jews were active in public life but a strain of antisemitism also ran through the town. In 1933, 81 Jews remained, mostly leading a religious way of life. Persecution was severe from the outset of Nazi rule in 1933 and the last J. stores were closed after Nov. 1938. Most of the young left; in all, 37 emigrated, mostly to Palestine and the U.S. Of the 42 deported – to the Riga ghetto on 1 Dec. 1941 and to the Theresienstadt ghetto in Sept. 1942 – three survived.

NIEDERWEIDBACH   Hesse-Nassau,   Germany. Numbering 43 (10% of the total) in 1885, the community had a synagogue and members in nearby Hohensolms and Mudersbach. Of the 26 Jews registered there in 1933, 16 were deported in 1942.

NIEDER-WEISEL   Hesse, Germany. The community numbered 104 (6% of the total) in 1861 and 41 in 1939. It also had members in Ostheim and Fauerbach. As a result of the Nazi boycott, 32 Jews left by the end of 1938, 13 emigrating.

NIEDERWERRN   Lower Franconia, Germany. The community was established no later than the second half of the 17th cent. and was one of the oldest attached to the chief rabbinate at Wuerzburg. In 1796, French forces looted the J. ghetto. The J. pop. numbered around 300 in 1836 (40% of the total). Most of the Jews were craftsmen, particularly watchmakers. In 1850, there were 54 J. schoolchildren in N. In 1880, the J. pop. was 197 and in 1933 it was 39. On *Kristallnacht* (9–10 Nov. 1938), a gang of 50 SA troops, bolstered by local residents and armed with hammers and axes, destroyed 11 J. homes. One woman was raped and another, 70 years old, was thrown into a freezing lake. Afterwards the synagogue was vandalized and re-

ligious articles were burned. All the Jews were forced to sell their homes and land holdings. In 1934–40, 39 Jews left N., 21 emigrating (including 12 to the U.S.). The last nine were deported to Izbica in the Lublin dist. (Poland) and to the Theresienstadt ghetto in 1942.

NIEDER-WIESEN   Hesse, Germany. The community, established in the early 18th cent., numbered 124 (21% of the total) in 1861 but gradually declined. On *Kristallnacht* (9–10 Nov. 1938), the synagogue was demolished and seven of the 20 Jews living there in 1933 emigrated to the U.S.

NIEDER-WOELLSTADT   Hesse, Germany. Established around 1725, the community numbered 71 (8% of the total) in 1861 and then declined. The Jews mostly earned their livelihoods in the cattle trade and as storekeepers and butchers. On *Kristallnacht* (9–10 Nov. 1938), the Nazis organized a pogrom and demolished the synagogue. Twenty-three of the town's 40 Jews emigrated; three married to non-Jews survived the Holocaust.

NIEDERZISSEN   Rhineland, Germany. Jews are first mentioned in 1752. In 1808, the J. pop. was 53 and an organized community existed by 1830, reaching a peak pop. of 89 in 1854. N. became the seat of a regional congregation in 1863 with a number of attached communities (Oberzissen, Burgbrohl, Glees, Niederweiler, Wehr, Kempenich). A synagogue and school operating out of a private home are known from 1763. A new synagogue was completed in 1844. The community was Orthodox. In the Weimar period, most Jews were merchants, dealing mainly in livestock. In 1925, the J. pop. was 73 (total 1,258). By 1935, only two small butcher shops, a shoe store, and a few J. cattle traders were active. The synagogue was wrecked on *Kristallnacht* (9–10 Nov. 1938). Nine Jews emigrated in Jan.–Feb. 1939 and 44 remained in early 1942. Ten were deported in July 1942 along with 26 Jews, mostly women, brought to the town from Bad Neuenahr for forced labor. In all, 29 local Jews perished in the Holocaust.

NIEDZWIEDZICA   Nowogrodek dist., Poland, today Belarus. An organized community existed in the late 19th cent. with a pop. of 274 in 1897 and 116 (total 949) in 1921, with some engaged in agriculture. All were executed by the Germans near Siniawka in Aug. 1941.

NIEGORELOYE   Minsk dist., Belorussia. Jews probably settled in the late 19th cent. In 1939, their pop. was 80 (total 1,078). The Jews still there were murdered within a few days of the German occupation in late June 1941.

NIEHEIM   Westphalia, Germany. Jews are first mentioned after the Thirty Years War (1618–48). The community was struck by a number of natural disasters between 1698 and 1744. In the 18th cent., Jews earned their living by trading in a wide variety of items, from textiles to metals. A synagogue was completed in 1799 and a cemetery was opened in 1840. A J. elementary school was in operation in 1890. The J. pop. was at a peak of 150 in the 1870–85 period (about 9% of the total) and then declined steadily to 53 in 1933. The synagogue was destroyed on *Kristallnacht* (9–10 Nov. 1938), along with a J. home and store. Eleven Jews emigrated in 1933–39. Twenty-six were deported in late 1941–42. In all, 31 perished in the camps, including 11 in Auschwitz.

NIEHNIEWICZE   Nowogrodek dist., Poland, today Belarus. A J. settlement existed from around the late 18th cent., growing to a pop. of 276 in 1897 and dropping to 112 in 1921. All were expelled by the Germans to Nowogrodek in summer 1941, sharing the fate of the Jews there.

NIEMCE   (Yid. Nimches) Lublin dist., Poland. The J. pop. was 105 (total 1,579) in 1921. The Jews were presumably deported to Auschwitz by the Germans after being expelled to Bendzin or Sosnowiec in 1942.

NIEMENCZYN   Vilna dist., Poland, today Lithuania. Jews probably settled in the late 19th cent. Their pop. in 1885 was 340 (total 471). After the hardships of WWI the community was assisted significantly by J. relief organizations. Between the World Wars J. tradesmen faced less competition than in other places and were able to maintain their position. Most children studied in a Hebrew school. The Germans arrived in late June 1941. On 20 Sept. the Jews were led to the forest and murdered beside open pits. A small group escaped, some joining the Soviet partisans and later the Bielski group.

NIEMIROW (I)   Lwow dist., Poland, today Ukraine. Jews were among the town's first settlers in the late 16th cent., receiving various privileges. The development of N. as a health resort in the 19th cent. served to diversify J. occupations. Among the artisans Jews practiced such rare trades as the manufacture of wooden roof tiling and horsehair screens and strainers. Hasidism dominated and left little room for the development of J. political and social movements until relatively late. Many J. homes, along with the community's ancient stone synagogue, were destroyed in WWI, with many Jews fleeing never to return. The 1910 J. pop. of 1,962 declined to 1,298 (half the total pop.) by 1921. Economic conditions deteriorated in the 1930s against a background of increasing anti-semitism. Under Soviet rule (from late Sept. 1939) refugees swelled the J. pop. to 2,500. With the Soviet withdrawal the Ukrainians arrested and murdered 38 Jews, while the coming of the Germans on 27 June 1941 saw the introduction of a regime of extortion and forced labor. The first deportations to the Belzec death camp, via Rawa Ruska, occurred in July 1942 and included around 800 Jews. Almost all the rest were shot or deported in Sept.

NIEMIROW (II)   Bialystok dist., Poland, today Belarus. Jews numbered 107 in 1807 and 149 (total 777) in 1921, barely earning a living between the World Wars. They were apparently expelled by the Germans to Siemiatycze on 2 Nov. 1942 and from there deported to the Treblinka death camp.

NIEMOWICZE   Volhynia dist., Poland, today Ukraine. The J. pop. in 1921 was 94. In the Holocaust, the Jews were expelled to the Sarny ghetto for liquidation.

NIENBURG AN DER WESER   Hanover, Germany. In 1681, the first protected Jew (*Schutzjude*) was living in N. The J. community grew slowly, from 34 members in 1816 to 102 in 1861. A cemetery dated back to 1694 and a synagogue was dedicated in 1821. When the Nazis assumed power in 1933, there were 86 Jews living in N. On *Kristallnacht* (9–10 Nov. 1938), the synagogue was burned down, J. businesses were looted, and 22 J. men were arrested and detained for awhile in the Goettingen prison. Since the J. cemetery was the only one in the area not damaged, the Jews of the whole district used it. The 18 Jews who remained in N. were deported on 28 Mar. 1942. Those who had moved to bigger towns or to neighboring countries were also deported and perished.

NIEPOLOMICE Cracow dist., Poland. Jews are known from the mid-18th cent., reaching a pop. of 507 (total 4,692) in 1900, when Yosef Teitelbaum, son of R. Shemuel of Gorlice, was rabbi of the community. Armed bands terrorized the J. pop. in Nov. 1919. Between the World Wars the Zionists were active. The Germans burned down the synagogue on entering the town in Sept. 1939. Around 2,000 refugees, mainly from Cracow, arrived in 1940–42. On 20–22 Aug. 1942 all were expelled to Wieliczka and from there deported to the Belzec death camp on 27 Aug.

NIESUCHOJEZE (Yid. Neskhizh) Volhynia dist., Poland, today Ukraine. Jews are first mentioned in 1569. From the mid-18th cent. to the early 20th religious life was dominated by the Shapira branch of the Neskhizh hasidic dynasty. The J. pop. stood at 814 (total 1,862) in 1897 and 435 (total 469) in 1921. The Germans entered on 27 June 1941 and established a *Judenrat*, terrorizing the Jews with the aid of brutal Ukrainian police. In Aug. 1942, the Jews were taken to open pits outside the town and murdered.

NIESWIEZ Nowogrodek dist., Poland, today Belarus. The J. settlement commenced in the early 16th cent., developing under the auspices of the Radziwill family and maintaining jurisdiction over a number of smaller communities. In the 17th–18th cents. N. was an important community and frequently mentioned in the protocols of the Lithuanian Council. In 1897 the J. pop. was 4,687 (total 8,459), with 13 synagogues in operation, including two for the Hasidim (Habad, Koidanov) and others for artisan groups. Hovevei Zion became active in the 1880s. Hebrew and Yiddish schools were opened at the outset of Polish rule after WWI and the Zionist movements proliferated between the World Wars, with Hashomer Hatzair embracing 550 members in 1933. The J. pop. in 1931 was 3,364 (total 7,586). The Germans captured the city on 27 June 1941, appointing a *Judenrat* and instituting a regime of forced labor and extortion. On 29 Oct. 1941, 585 skilled workers and their families were confined to a ghetto and the remaining 4,000 Jews exe-

cuted in the vicinity. The German attempt to liquidate the ghetto on 17 July 1942 was met by armed resistance by a J. underground. The ghetto was set on fire and most of the Jews were killed after inflicting 40 casualties on the Nazis. About 25 fighters escaped and joined the Soviet partisans.

NIESZAWA Warsaw dist., Poland. J. communal life began in the mid-18th cent. Between 1826 and 1862 the Jews were forced to live in a special quarter. Between the World Wars, when there were 262 Jews (11% of the total), many emigrated to the U.S. and Mexico for economic reasons. When the Germans captured N. in Sept. 1939, a few Jews managed to escape to eastern Poland, which the USSR had annexed. On 14 Sept. (Rosh Hashanah) the Germans burned down the synagogue. In Oct. 1939, the Jews were expelled to Kutno, and from there to Vodzislav.

NIEUWESCHANS (Nieuwe Schans) Groningen dist., Holland. Jews lived there from the 17th cent. A community was established by the early 19th cent. and numbered 60 in 1860 (with 30 in neighboring Bellingwolde). In 1941, seven were left in N. and 15 in Bellingwolde. All but two who hid perished in the Holocaust.

NIEVERN Hesse–Nassau dist., Germany. Originally based in Fruecht, this community numbered fewer than 20 Jews (1843–1933) and also had members in Fachbach. By Feb. 1939 no Jews remained.

NIEZHIN Chernigov dist., Ukraine. Jews settled in the early 17th cent. The community was destroyed in the Chmielnicki massacres of 1648–49. Jews probably returned in the early 18th cent. In 1897, they numbered 7,631 (total 32,000). In 1828, N. became an important center of Habad Hasidim. Among its well-known *tzaddikim* was Yisrael Noah Schneersohn of the Lubavich dynasty. Much J. property was pillaged and destroyed in a pogrom on 20–22 July 1881. New pogroms occurred in late 1905. On 2 Sept. 1919, over 100 Jews were killed, with many raped and robbed. The Yiddish poet Mani-Leib (pseudonym of Mani-Leib Brahinsky, 1881–1953) was born in N. The J. pop. dropped between the World Wars, standing at 2,725 in 1939. The Germans captured the city on 13 Sept. 1941 after most Jews fled. The few dozen who remained were murdered by Oct.

NIJKERK Gelderland dist., Holland. Records of Jews in N. date back to the 17th cent. Italian Jews formed a Sephardi community by the 18th cent. Ashkenazi Jews began to settle there in the 18th cent. and organized a separate community by 1761. The two were united in 1810 and by 1844 followed the Ashkenazi rite only. The J. pop. in 1860 was 218. The community's pop. decreased in the 20th cent. In 1941 it was 60 (total 11,188) and ten in neighboring Barneveld. All the Jews were deported to the Vught transit camp in April 1943. From there they were sent to the east, via Westerbork; 12 survived the Holocaust. In Barneveld, hundreds of Jews received protection from the Dutch government, among them intellectuals and artists. However, all 680 were transferred to Westerbork in Sept. 1943. Twenty-two managed to escape and the rest were taken to the Theresienstadt ghetto in Sept. 1944. Many died there until the rest were liberated by the Soviets.

NIJMEGEN Gelderland dist., Holland. N. was the principal J. community in Holland in the Middle Ages. It came to an end in 1349 during the Black Death persecutions but settlement was renewed soon after and the community reorganized. It persevered until the late 15th cent. when the Jews were expelled. In the 17th cent. a new community was established. The community was subjected to a blood libel in 1715 and various restrictions were imposed on J. trade and residence throughout the cent. Nevertheless, a small number of Jews contributed to the economic development of N. through their banking and commercial activities. The community grew significantly in the 19th cent. N. was the seat of the regional chief rabbinate from 1804 until 1881. A J. school was opened in 1827 and social welfare organizations were established. The J. pop. in 1900 was 451 (total 44,000). The community continued to grow in the first decades of the 20th cent. and dozens of refugees arrived in N. in the 1930s. Following the German occupation in 1940 the number of refugees reached 133. The J. pop. in 1941 was 528 (total 96,324). The Jews were deported in 1942–43 and most perished. Only 50 survived, the majority in hiding.

NIKITOVKA Stalino dist., Ukraine. The J. pop. in 1939 was 375 (total 14,407). Those Jews who had neither fled nor been evacuated perished in the German occupation initiated on 19 Nov. 1941.

NIKOLAIEV Nikolaiev dist., Ukraine. Jews settled with the founding of the city in the late 18th cent. A Great Synagogue was erected in the 1820s. Jews were attacked in pogroms in May 1881 and April 1899. Their pop. was 20,109 (total 92,012) in 1897. In 1905, J. self-defense groups prevented a new pogrom. In the early 20th cent., the community maintained 15 different educational facilities. In the Soviet period, the J. pop. grew to 21,786 in 1926 and 25,280 (total 166,688) in 1939. A law court with deliberations in Yiddish was opened in 1926 and in the late 1920s, five J. elementary schools, a vocational school, and a high school were operating. Aside from crafts, many Jews were employed in factories (including a steel plant) and even the local shipyards (300 young Jews in the late 1920s). The Germans captured the city on 17 Aug. 1941 and commenced the mass murder of the Jews in Sept. On 21–23 Sept., about 7,000 were massacred between Kalinovka and Voskresenskoye as well as at the nearby village of Temvod.

NIKOLAIKEN (Pol. Mikolajki) East Prussia, Germany, today Poland. The J. community was apparently established in the 19th cent. The J. pop. was 66 in 1880, 75 in 1905, and 40 in 1925. The community maintained a synagogue and a cemetery. No information is available about the fate of the 43 Jews living in N. when the Nazis assumed power.

NIKOLAYEV Kamenets-Podolski dist., Ukraine. Jews were present from the late 16th cent. They were murdered in the Chmielnicki massacres of 1648–49. In commemoration of the event, the community observed, until the early 20th cent., a day of mourning and fasting including a special prayer service at the mass grave. The J. pop. was 1,087 in 1765 and 2,189 (60% of the total) in 1897. The Jews of N. were known for their expertise in processing sheep hides and sewing sheepskin coats. In the Soviet period, a J. rural council (soviet) was active. The J. pop. was 1,262 in 1926. The Germans occupied N. on 7 July 1941, instituting a regime of forced labor. On 5 March 1942, the Jews were brought to Proskurov, where 879 were executed on 1 Nov. 1942.

NIKOPOL Dnepropetrovsk dist., Ukraine. Jews are first mentioned in the 1780s. They numbered 322 in 1847 and 3,284 (total 17,097) in 1897. In 1905, they were attacked in a pogrom. Under the Soviets, in the late 1920s, N. was one of the organizational centers for the transfer of J. farm settlers to the Kryvoy Rog region. The J. pop. was 3,767 in 1939. The Germans took the city on 17 Aug. 1941 and on 5 Oct. murdered a number of Jews. On 28 Feb. 1942, about 20 Jews from neighboring Kamenka-Dnepropetrovskaya were murdered in N. Another few hundred Jews were murdered on 24-25 March.

NIMES (Nismes) Gard dist., France. A J. community was established during the second half of the tenth cent. At the beginning of the 13th cent., the community consisted of about 100 families. As with the rest of the Jews in France, they were expelled in 1306 and returned in 1359. The community ceased to exist in 1394 after the general expulsion of the Jews from France. From the 17th cent., some Jews from Comtat-Venaissin began to trade in N. Expelled again and again, some managed to obtain temporary residence rights. By the second half of the 18th cent., a small community was established. The restrictions on J. commerce and crafts were abolished in 1787. At that time, the community was affiliated to the consistory of Marseilles. After a split in the community in 1794, a synagogue was inaugurated in 1796. It was renovated in 1893. At the end of the 18th cent., the community numbered between 30 and 40 families. In the 19th cent., the J. pop. increased after an influx of Jews from the Balkans as well as from Poland. Adolphe Cremieux (1796–1880) was a native of N. As a young lawyer in 1827 he refused to take the *more judaico* oath in the court of N. He was president of the central consistory of France and the Alliance Israelite Universelle. Another native of N. was Bernard Lazare (1865–1903), who wrote several books in defense of Alfred Dreyfus. Among the prominent rabbis of the community was Solomon Kahn (1854–1931), historian of the Jews of southern France and rabbi for 40 years. From the close of the 19th cent., the J. pop. dropped, standing at about 300 in 1939. Approximately half were immigrants. From the end of May 1940 the community absorbed 1,200 J. refugees. In 1941, there were 1,022 Jews listed in N. N. became a center of relief. The CAR (Comite d'Assitance aux Refugies) as well as UGIF (Union Generale des Israelites en France) operated there. On 25–26 Aug. 1942, foreign Jews were rounded up. On 11 Nov. 1942, Germans forces occupied N. and on 13 Feb. 1943 the roundup of the Jews (aged 18–65) in the southern

zone began. In July 1943, the deportation of the first Jews from N. began. During the final months of Vichy rule, no exceptions were made concerning age, origin, and physical condition and 380 of 2,350 Jews in the Gard dist. were deported (16%). Only 12 deportees survived. Of the original community of N., 56 members were deported (19%). After liberation, with the influx of Jews from North Africa, the community reached a pop. of 1,040 (1964).

NIMIGEA DE JOS (Hung. Magyarnemegye; Yid. Nimizshe) N. Transylvania dist., Rumania. Jews, settled in the early 19th cent. The J. pop. in 1920 was 219 (15% of the total). In May 1944, the community was transferred to the Bistrita ghetto and in June deported to Auschwitz.

NIRZA Latgale dist., Latvia. The J. pop in 1925 was 45 (in the village and environs). Those remaining were murdered on 18 Aug. 1941 by the Nazis and their Latvian collaborators.

NIS Serbia, Yugoslavia. Sephardi Jews arrived in the 17th cent. In the 19th cent., the community experienced economic distress and an association was established to assist the needy while encouraging mutual assistance within the community. In 1878 the J. pop. reached a peak of 900 (total 12,817). Zionism was introduced in the first years of the 20th cent. A synagogue was built in 1801 and another in 1924. In 1939, Yugoslavia's prime minister, Dragishe Cvetkovic, a native of N., warned community leaders of difficult times ahead for the Jews. He recommended that they leave for Turkey and promised to procure entry visas. The Jews turned down the gesture. In 1940 there were 430 Jews in N. and in 1941 the number rose to 970, including 540 refugees from Germany, Austria, and Poland (total pop. 46,000). On 9 April 1941, the Germans entered N. The Jews were forced to wear the yellow badge, their property was plundered, and their movements were restricted. They were seized for forced labor and later concentrated in camps. By Feb. 1942, all had been murdered, most of them in nearby Bubanj together with the Jews of neighboring areas and refugees. A small community was reestablished after the war.

NISKO Lwow dist., Poland. Jews first settled in the late 18th cent., constituting less than 10% of the total

(273 in 1880; 409 in 1921). The Russians burned down most of the town at the outset of WWI. Deadly epidemics and rampant looting by the local pop. subsequently caused further distress. After WWII broke out, many of N.'s Jews escaped or were expelled to Soviet-controlled territory. Within the framework of the shortlived Nazi plan to turn the Lublin dist. into a J. reservation, some 95,000 refugees arrived in the area from Oct. 1939 to March 1940, at which time all were dispersed, presumably including the Jews of N.

NITRA Slovakia, Czechoslovakia, today Republic of Slovakia. The J. community dating back to the Middle Ages was one of the oldest, largest, and most important in Slovakia. In the early 18th cent., the Jews were probably expelled along with other Jews in the dist., establishing a new community in the 1740s. By 1793, the J. pop. was 450. A new and spacious synagogue was built in 1818 and in 1820 a J. school was opened. In 1831 a cholera epidemic claimed many J. victims. In the 1840s, the J. pop. was about 2,000. R. Yehezkel Baneth served the community in 1836–54 and founded its famous yeshiva. Jews suffered in the riots of 1848. In 1869 their pop. was 3,141 (total 10,893). The community then split into Orthodox (the majority) and Neologist congregations, each with its own institutions but with a joint school under Orthodox sway. The Neologists consecrated a new synagogue in 1911. Jews owned most of the business establishments in the city and were among the pioneers of its industry. A sawmill founded in 1867 employed 200 workers; a roofing factory employed 150; and a flour mill 100. Jews also owned a number of distilleries and two banks. Zionist activity commenced after the First Zionist Congress in 1897, under the leadership of Tzevi Neumann, one of the heads of Hungarian Zionism. Zionism spread between the World Wars, with

The Svarc family shoemaking shop, Nitra, Czechoslovakia, 1924 (Beth Hatefutsoth Photo Archive, Tel Aviv/courtesy of Gruenwald Family, Tel Aviv)

Hashomer Hatzair, Bnei Akiva, Betar, WIZO, and the Maccabi sports club all playing a role. The J. pop. continued to grow steadily, reaching a peak of 4,358 in 1940. In 1931, R. Shemuel David Halevi Unger, one of the outstanding rabbis in Slovakia, took over the yeshiva, seeing it reach an attendance of 250–300. The community's J. school also reached an enrollment of 250–300. In 1936, a modern J. hospital, the second in Slovakia after Bratislava's, was dedicated. Jews served on the municipal council and as judges in the district and magistrates courts. In 1921 they owned 458 of the city's 605 business establishments and 112 workshops in addition to the factories. After the establishment of the Slovakian state in March 1939, the local authorities and residents persecuted the Jews. In 1941, hundreds were consigned to forced labor and J. businesses were closed down. In late 1941, 1,018 refugees arrived from Bratislava, bringing the J. pop. up to 5,430. In March 1942, 250 young J. men and 300 girls were rounded up for deportation to the Majdanek concentration camp and Auschwitz, respectively. Another 3,120 from N. and its environs were sent to the Lubartow and Rejowiec ghettos in the Lublin dist. of Poland in April. Despite the deportations, the J. pop. grew to 1,500 in Sept. 1944, made up of those left behind: workers under "certificates of protection"; students at R. Unger's yeshiva (the last in Eastern and Central Europe to remain in operation); refugees; and other Jews who had evaded the deportations. In the course of suppressing the Slovakian rebellion, the Germans and the Hlinka Guard hunted these Jews down and deported them to Auschwitz. Most of the postwar community of 600 emigrated to Israel and the U.S., leaving behind 150 in 1950 and 60–70 in 1990.

NIWKA   Kielce dist., Poland. Sixty J. families settled in the late 19th cent. After WWI, newcomers leased mines and started an iron foundry. The J. pop. was 329 (total 5,308) in 1921. In late 1941, the Jews were expelled by the Germans to Dandowka and in March 1942 they were brought to Sosnowiec for deportation to Auschwitz

NIWKI   Vilna dist., Poland, today Belarus. N. was founded as a J. farm settlement for 15 families in 1848. One Jew also built a brick and whitewash factory. In 1921 the J. pop. was 76. In March 1942 the Jews of N. were among 350 burned alive by the Germans in an unfinished building near Molodeczno.

NIZANKOWICE   Lwow dist., Poland, today Ukraine. Jews are mentioned from 1602 but the community only developed in the 19th cent., reaching a pop. of 546 (total 2,009) in 1890. The Zionists were active between the World Wars. The community was probably liquidated by the Germans toward the end of July 1942 as part of their general *Aktion* in the area.

NIZHNEDNEPROVSK   (until 1917, Amur) Dnepropetrovsk dist., Ukraine. Jews settled in the latter half of the 19th cent. and numbered 1,235 (total 6,060) in 1897. The first synagogue was erected in the early 1880s. A. J. elementary school was still operating in 1936 and a J. drama circle started in the mid-1920s was performing in the late 1930s. In 1939, the J. pop. was 3,323 (total 49,419). With the German occupation of Aug. 1941, those Jews who had neither fled nor been evacuated shared the fate of the Jews of Dnepropetrovsk.

NIZNI APSA   (Hung. Alsoapsa; Yid. Unter Apsa) Carpatho-Russia, Czechoslovakia, today Ukraine. J. settlement probably commenced in the mid-18th cent. The J. pop. was 18 in 1768; 57 in 1830; and 409 (total 3,466) in 1880. It then rose to 867 in 1921 under the Czechoslovakians and to 978 in 1941. The Zionists and Agudat Israel were active in the 1920s and 1930s. The Hungarians arrived in March 1939 and proceeded to undermine J. livelihoods. In 1941, a few dozen Jews were drafted into forced labor battalions and dispatched to the eastern front, where many were killed. In Aug. 1941 another few dozen without Hungarian citizenship were expelled to Kamenets-Podolski and murdered. The rest were deported to Auschwitz in the second half of May 1944. A few survivors returned after the war but soon left for Czechoslovakia.

NIZNI BYSTRY   (Hung. Alsobisztra; Yid. Unter Bystra) Carpatho-Russia, Czechoslovakia, today Ukraine. Jews probably settled in the early 19th cent. Eight Jews were present in 1830 and 88 (total 1,214) in 1880. Their pop. rose to 213 in 1921 under the Czechoslovakians and to 446 in 1941. Many Jews worked at two J.-owned sawmills and in agriculture. The Hungarians annexed the town in March 1939. In 1941, they drafted a number of Jews into labor battalions for forced labor or service on the eastern front. In Aug. 1941, a few families without Hungarian citizenship were expelled to Kamenets-Podolski and murdered. The rest were deported to Auschwitz on 22 May 1944.

NIZNIOW (Yid. Nizhneve) Stanislawow dist., Poland, today Ukraine. Jews settled with the founding of the town in the 17th cent. but the community developed slowly with 40% of the total lost to emigration in the late 19th cent. (down from 711 of a total 3,859 residents in 1880 to 409 in 1900). Nonetheless, public life was spirited between the World Wars with marked Zionist activity. With the end of the Soviet rule of 1939–41, the Ukrainians staged a pogrom. When the Germans took over the town in Aug. 1941, persecution and forced labor were stepped up. The community was liquidated in May 1942 when around 300 Jews were sent to Stanislawow and killed there.

NIZNI SELISTE (Hung. Alsoszelistye) Carpatho-Russia, Czechoslovakia, today Ukraine. Jews probably settled in the mid-18th cent. Their pop. was 50 in 1830; 130 in 1880; and 195 in 1930. The Germans occupied the town in March 1944 and deported the Jews to Auschwitz in the second half of May.

NIZNI STUDENY (Hung. Alsohidegpatak) Carpatho-Russia, Czechoslovakia, today Ukraine. Jews probably settled in the late 18th cent. The J. pop. was 181 in 1830 and 124 in 1880 (total 846). It rose to 153 in 1921 under the Czechoslovakians and to 167 in 1941. Twelve Jews were merchants, eight were artisans, one operated a flour mill, and a few were farmers. The Hungarians occupied the town in March 1939 and in 1941 drafted a number of Jews into forced labor battalions. In Aug. 1941, they expelled about ten families without Hungarian citizenship to Eastern Galicia. The rest were deported to Auschwitz in early June 1944.

NIZNI VERECKY (Hung. Alsovereczke) Carpatho-Russia, Czechoslovakia, today Ukraine. Jews probably settled in the 18th cent. and numbered 169 in 1830 and 545 (total 1,276) in 1880. In 1921, under the Czechoslovakians, their pop. rose to 633 and then dropped to 582 in 1941. Jews owned 19 business establishments and 15 workshops. A few were farmers. There was also a J.-owned bank. Among the J. political parties, Agudat Israel was prominent. The Hungarians occupied N. in March 1939 and in 1940–41 drafted dozens of Jews into forced labor battalions, sending some to the eastern front, where most died. In late July and early Aug. 1941, 80 Jews lacking Hungarian citizenship were expelled to Kamenets-Podolski and murdered and in the second half of May 1944, the rest (about 500) were deported to Auschwitz. A few Jews joined the Czechoslovakian army created in the Soviet Union and fought against the Nazis. After the war a few survivors returned to the town but most then left for Czechoslovakia.

NIZNY KOMARNIK Slovakia, Czechoslovakia, today Republic of Slovakia. Jews numbered 121 in 1880 and 11 in 1940. In 1942 they were deported to the death camps.

NOERDLINGEN (in J. sources, Merlingen, Nerlgin) Swabia, Germany. Jews are known from the 12th cent. The medieval community ended in 1290 when hundreds of Jews were slaughtered by the local pop. The few who survived were murdered in the Rindfleisch massacres of 1298. A community with a synagogue and cemetery inhabited a J. quarter in the 14th cent. but it too was destroyed in the Black Death persecutions of 1348–49. A new community was wiped out in 1384 when 200 Jews were murdered. Jews were living under the protection of Emperor Sigismund in the early 15th cent. until the last 11 J. families were expelled in 1507. Despite restrictions, Jews continued trading in N. until permanent settlement was permitted in 1860. The J. pop. grew to a peak of 469 in 1890 (total 8,004), with a cemetery opened in 1876 and a synagogue in 1886. In 1933, 186 Jews remained. By Nov. 1938, 71 had left, 38 of them emigrating (including 22 to the U.S.). On *Kristallnacht* (9–10 Nov. 1938) the synagogue was vandalized. Nine Jews were sent to the Dachau concentration camp. Another 45 left by the end of 1941, 33 emigrating (18 to the U.S.). On 31 March 1942, 25 Jews were deported to Piaski (Poland) via Munich; the last 16, mostly aged, were sent to the Theresienstadt ghetto on 6–7 Aug.

NOERENBERG (Pol. Insko) Pomerania, Germany, today Poland. In 1717, there were three J. families in N. In 1871 the community numbered 68 Jews. It maintained a synagogue and a cemetery. When the Nazis came to power in 1933, there were 33 Jews in the town. It may be assumed that those who did not manage to emigrate were deported. By Oct. 1942, only two Jews remained in N., probably protected by marriage to non-Jews.

NOGAYSK Zaporozhe dist., Ukraine. Jews numbered 508 (total 3,963) in 1897 and 103 in 1939. The Germans captured N. on 6 Oct. 1941 and murdered about 200 Jews from B. and its environs in the first half of Nov. Forty-seven J. children at a children's home in nearby Preslav were murdered on 30 Oct. 1941.

NOMME Estonia. A few Jews were present in the early 20th cent. and 75 in 1934. In WWII, some escaped to the Soviet Union while the others were sent to Tallinn by an Estonian "self-defense" unit and murdered there by the Germans.

NONNENWEIER Baden, Germany. Jews helped resettle the town after it was destroyed in the War of the Spanish Succession (1701–1714). By 1744 Jews were among its property owners. The J. pop. rose to 249 in 1871, with the synagogue enlarged in 1865 and a cemetery opened in 1880. A J. elementary school operated from 1840. Throughout the 19th cent. there were frequent incidents of vandalism against J. property and full-scale riots in 1846 when the subject of J. civil rights was being debated in Baden's Landtag. By 1927, 15 young Jews from N. had graduated from Heidelberg University. The most prominent was the jurist Ludwig Frank (1874–1914), the first Reichstag member to volunteer in WWI, where he lost his life. In 1933, 65 Jews remained. On *Kristallnacht* (9–10 Nov. 1938), the synagogue was destroyed and all J. men sent to the Dachau concentration camp. At least 30 Jews managed to emigrate from Germany in the Nazi era; another 28 were deported to Gurs and other concentration camps.

NORDECK (now part of Stadtallendorf) Hesse–Nassau, Germany. Jews lived there from 1733, numbering 42 (7% of the total) in 1861 and 18 in 1925. The village head managed to prevent the synagogue's destruction on *Kristallnacht* (9–10 Nov. 1938). No Jews remained in 1941.

NORDEN Hanover, Germany. In 1569, Jews established a community under the local ruler's protection. They earned their living from trade in cattle, grain, and porcelain. By 1660, there were 22 J. families in N. and four in the outlying village of Hage. With a pop. growing from 193 in 1802 to 362 in 1878, this community was one of the largest in East Friesland.

It dedicated a new synagogue in 1804, employed a *hazzan-shohet*, and maintained a J. school until 1934. There were also philanthropic and burial societies, women's and youth groups, and a synagogue choir. In June 1933, 204 Jews were registered in N. On *Kristallnacht* (9–10 Nov. 1938), SA troops launched a pogrom, burning the synagogue and herding Jews into an abattoir. Most Jews left before WWII. Fifty emigrated (24 to Holland; 13 to England; and four to Palestine). The last 75 were expelled in 1940. At least 39 perished in Nazi concentration camps.

NORDENBURG (Rus. Krylovo) East Prussia, Germany, today Russia. Jews probably came to N. only after 1810. There were eight Jews there in 1831 and 70 in 1885. The community maintained a synagogue and a cemetery. By 1925, there were only 36 Jews in N. and religious services could be held only on the High Holidays. By Oct. 1942, only one Jew was still living in N., probably protected by marriage to a non-J. It may be assumed that those who did not emigrate to safe countries were deported by the Nazis.

NORDENHAM-BRAKE Oldenburg, Germany. N. and a number of neighboring communities formed a congregation which, until the early 20th cent., was centered in Ovelgoenne, where the synagogue and J. cemetery were located. However, the number of Jews there dropped and by 1913 only one Jew remained. The synagogue in Ovelgoenne was abandoned already in 1906. In Brake, the first Jews arrived in 1775 and by 1855, with a pop. of 35, outnumbered the Jews of Ovelgoenne. But by 1925, their number had also shrunk to five. Thus, N. with a pop. of about 20 became the congregational center. In 1933, the congregation numbered 40, 17 living in N. On *Kristallnacht* (9–10 Nov. 1938), J. men were arrested. One committed suicide and others were confined in the Sachsenhausen concentration camp for a few weeks. Most Jews left, with one remaining in May 1939, but not all who left survived the Holocaust. At least 15 were deported to concentration camps; only two are known to have survived.

NORDHAUSEN Saxony, Germany. The first definite evidence of Jews in N. dates from 1290. The community, which had a synagogue, a cemetery and a *mikve*, was attacked several times, as in the Black Death persecutions of 1348–49. The community was finally expelled in 1559. Uninterrupted settlement began only in 1808. A prayer room and a cemetery were set up in 1821 and a synagogue was consecrated in 1845. The J. pop. was 495 in 1880 and 438 in 1925. The community maintained a broad range of social and cultural associations. The Jews were also active in public life, several serving as members of the city council or engaged in promoting cultural activities. Antisemitic incidents occurred after WWI, including the 1922 desecration of the synagogue. In 1933, there were 394 Jews living in N. In the mid-1930s, an elderly J. businessman was accused of racial defilement (*Rassenschande*), dragged through the streets, and thrown into a well. In Oct. 1938, 43 Jews with non-German citizenship were deported to Poland. On *Kristallnacht* (9–10 Nov. 1938), the synagogue was set on fire, J. businesses and homes were looted and wrecked, and about 150 Jews were arrested. About 75 men were deported to the Buchenwald concentration camp, where three, including the community's cantor, died. By 1939, 180 Jews from N. had managed to flee abroad. The 128 remaining Jews were billeted in "J. houses." Most were deported by Oct 1942, when only 19 J. residents were reported to be living in N. Most were probably protected by marriage to non-Jews. A subterranean armaments factory was situated in nearby Dora-Nordhausen. Here, even as late as 1944–45, some 10,000 forced laborers brought in from Auschwitz were employed.

NORDHEIM V.D. RHOEN   Lower Franconia, Germany. Jews settled around the turn of the 19th cent. A new synagogue was erected in 1852. In 1890 the J. pop. was 86 (total 812) and in 1933 it was 25, soon reduced to penury under the Nazi economic boycott. The synagogue was vandalized on 2 Oct. 1938 and again on *Kristallnacht* (9–10 Nov. 1938) along with J. homes and stores. Twelve Jews emigrated in 1934–40; the last six were deported to Izbica in the Lublin dist. (Poland) and to the Theresienstadt ghetto in 1942.

NORDHORN   Hanover, Germany. Jews are recorded as living here from 1694, but a small community only began to develop in the 19th cent., numbering 23 in 1809 and 44 in 1925. The synagogue, dedicated in 1814, was rebuilt in 1875 after a fire devastated N. In June 1933, 50 Jews were registered in N. During *Kristallnacht* (9–10 Nov. 1938), the synagogue was destroyed and J. men were deported to the Sachsenhausen concentration camp. Altogether, 32 of the 50 Jews registered in 1933 (including some who fled to Holland)

perished in Auschwitz, Sobibor, and other Nazi camps. One Jew found safety in England; only two deportees survived the Holocaust.

NORDSTETTEN   (in J. sources, Narshalin) Wuerttemberg, Germany. The J. community began to develop in the 16th cent. Many died in a great fire in 1821 but the pop. grew from 175 in 1800 to 352 in 1854. A synagogue was built in 1721 and the J. elementary school founded in 1822 was the first in Wuerttemberg. Berthold Auerbach (1812–82), author and a leader of J. emancipation in Germany, was born and buried in N. In the Weimar period Jews operated a large cigarette factory. Just 12 Jews (affiliated to the Horb congregation) remained in 1933. Four emigrated; six perished in the Nazi era.

NORINSK   Zhitomir dist., Ukraine. Jews settled in the early 17th cent. The community was destroyed during the Chmielnicki massacres of 1648–49 and their aftermath. Jews returned in the early 18th cent.

Interior of Norinsk synagogue, Ukraine (The Central Archive for the History of the Jewish People, Jerusalem/photo courtesy of Yad Vashem, The Holocaust Martyrs' and Heroes' Remembrance Authority, Jerusalem)

and numbered 121 in 1765 and 584 (total 1,683) in 1897. Most were tanners or leased farm land. Internal migration reduced the J. pop. to 329 in 1923. The Germans arrived on 20 Aug. 1941. Some Jews fled and the rest were murdered.

NORTHEIM   Brunswick, Germany. The first mention of Jews is in 1305 and there is evidence from 1513 of the existence of a Street of Jews and a J. burial ground. However, the modern community only began to develop at the beginning of the 19th cent. with the settlement of two J. families from Sudheim in 1810. Despite the hostility of guildsmen, they were allowed to remain, but rival traders and the local authorities made it difficult for Jews to earn a livelihood. The J. pop. expanded slowly, increasing from 26 in 1867 to 64 in 1895, and reaching a peak of 117 in 1910. Services were held in a private home and part of the municipal cemetery was allocated as a J. burial ground. In June 1933, there were 113 Jews registered in N. By Nov. 1938, 32 had emigrated (13 to the U.S.; ten to Latin America; nine to Palestine). Of those who remained, 56 moved to other German cities (three eventually emigrating) after *Kristallnacht* (9–10 Nov. 1938), when the makeshift synagogue was destroyed. In all, 39 Jews perished in the Holocaust.

NOSOVICHI   Gomel dist., Belorussia. Jews numbered 382 in 1847 and 686 (total 2,721) in 1897. Their main sources of livelihood were petty trade and crafts. On 17 Oct. 1905, J. property was damaged in riots but without loss of life. In 1930, under the Soviets, 30 J. families were employed at a nearby kolkhoz. The Germans occupied N. in Aug. 1941. In Sept., the Jews were expelled to Uvarovichi together with all the Jews in the region and on 15 Nov. they were executed outside the town.

NOSOVKA   Chernigov dist., Ukraine. A few Jews were probably present in the first half of the 19th cent., increasing to a few hundred by the end of the cent. In 1917, the J. pop. was 542 (total 19,638). Only 116 Jews remained in 1939. The Germans arrived on 14 Sept. 1941. They killed 76 people, most of them apparently Jews.

NOUA-SULITA   Bessarabia, Rumania, today Republic of Moldova. Jews first settled at the end of the

18th cent. Two communities existed on either side of the Prut River. During the Russian occupation (1912-1918) Jews handled goods exported from northern Bessarabia passing through the Russo-Austrian border post at N. The economy flourished and Jews prospered. Jews also abetted the illegal movement of thousands of refugees from Russia to Austria. A strong hasidic (Sadagora) community existed and its members controlled communal affairs. The first synagogue was built in 1780 and the great synagogue in 1854. Until 1914, Zionist activity was clandestine, becoming legal after the Feb. 1917 Revolution in Russia. The Hebrew school was reopened and adult education classes were held. In 1917–18, J. self-defense units were set up to guard against gangs and Russian army deserters passing through the town who tried to attack Jews and plunder their property. The situation of the Jews improved under the Austrian regime in 1918 but declined again under Rumanian rule. Young Zionists trained for immigration to Palestine and on 24 Sept. 1921 the first group arrived in Haifa. The J. pop. in 1930 was 4,152 (86% of the total). About 100 Zionists were exiled to Siberia by the conquering Soviet army on 29 June 1940. Before the Holocaust, some 7,000 Jews were living in N. When Rumanian troops recaptured N. on 7 July 1941 a pogrom broke out: 975 Jews were murdered, half the J. houses were set on fire, and J. property was plundered. On 29 July the J. pop. was rounded up. On the forced march to Transnistria, many died of starvation and disease or were killed by the gendarmes. Few survived.

NOVA BANA   (Hung. Ujbanya) Slovakia, Czechoslovakia, today Republic of Slovakia. Jews arrived in the 1850s, reaching a peak pop. of 76 (total 4,813) in 1910 and numbering 54 in 1940. The Zionists became active in the 1920s. Under Slovakian rule, J. businesses were "Aryanized" and Jews were seized for forced labor. In late March 1942, the young were deported to Auschwitz and the Majdanek concentration camp. On 9 June, families were dispatched to the death camps of the Lublin dist. of Poland. A concentration point and subsequently a labor camp were maintained in the nearby resort town of Vyhne. About 350 Jews were released in the Slovakian uprising of Sept. 1944, the young joining the fighting against the Nazis.

NOVA CEREKEV   Bohemia, Czechoslovakia. Jews

were probably present before 1520 and a community with a synagogue and cemetery are known from the late 17th cent. The J. pop. was 160 in 1850 and 22 in 1942. The Nazis executed three Jews in June 1942. The rest were arrested on 13 Nov. 1942 and transferred to the Tabor assembly station for deportation to the Theresienstadt ghetto within a few days. Most were sent on to Auschwitz in late Jan. 1943. Only three survived.

NOVA CHARTORIYA   Zhitomir dist., Ukraine. The J. pop. was 49 in the mid-18th cent. and 502 (total 2,776) in the late 19th cent. Pogroms and internal migration produced a steady decline in the pop. The remaining Jews were presumably murdered after the arrival of the Germans in early July 1941.

NOVA GORICA   Slovenia, Yugoslavia, today Republic of Slovenia. Jews lived there from the 13th cent. From the 17th cent. they lived in a ghetto and suffered discrimination. They numbered 275 in 1890 (total 21,825) but only 45 by 1940. In 1943 the Germans deported all the Jews to death camps.

NOVA GRADISKA   Croatia, Yugoslavia, today Republic of Croatia. Jews settled there from the end of the 18th cent. The J. pop. in 1931 was 207 (total 4,218). In the Holocaust they were liquidated by the Ustase.

NOVAKY   Slovakia, Czechoslovakia, today Republic of Slovakia. Jews are thought to have arrived in the 1730s and were apparently expelled at mid-cent., returning only in the early 19th cent. Their pop. rose to 115 (total 503) in 1869 and then dropped steadily to 26 in 1940. In spring 1942, the Jews were deported to the death camps of Poland. The N. transit camp processed about 4,500 Slovakian Jews en route to the death camps in March–Sept. 1942. The 1,600 still there in Sept. were put to forced labor and released in the Slovakian national uprising of 1944 with about 250 men joining the fighting.

NOVAYA ODESSA   (until 1832, Fedorovka) Nikolaiev dist., Ukraine. Jews settled in the late 19th cent., reaching a pop. of 1,010 (total 5,504) in 1897. In 1939, 228 remained. The Germans arrived on 12 Aug. 1941 and in early Oct. murdered 249 Jews. Throughout the area, 282 were killed, most of them Jews and some of them J. refugees from Bessarabia.

NOVAYA PRAGA   Kirovograd dist., Ukraine. J. settlement probably commenced in the first half of the 19th cent. Jews traded in farm produce and fish products. On 4 April 1882, they were attacked in a pogrom. In the early 20th cent. the community maintained a *talmud torah* and a girls' school. In the Soviet period, the J. pop. declined, numbering 591 in 1926 and 113 (total 9,476) in 1939. A few months after their occupation of the town in Aug. 1941, the Germans murdered the few remaining Jews.

NOVAYA PRILUKA   Vinnitsa dist., Ukraine. Jews settled in the early 18th cent. and numbered 203 in 1765 and 2,011 (total 3,579) in 1897. A number of Jews were killed in a pogrom on 10 Jan. 1917. In 1926, under the Soviets, the J. pop. was 2,151. A J. school was still operating in the early 1930s. The Germans captured the town in mid-July 1941 and murdered 2,500 Jews in Nov., including some from the surrounding settlements.

NOVAYA USHITSA   (until 1829, Letnevtsy) Kamenets-Podolski dist., Ukraine. The J. pop. was 229 in 1765 and 2,213 (total 6,371) in 1897. In the Soviet period, a J. rural council (soviet) was active. In 1939 the J. pop. was 1,547. The Germans captured N. on 14 July 1941. In Sept., the Jews were confined in a ghetto surrounded by a barbed wire fence. They were subjected to a regime of forced labor, paving roads and moving rocks and earth. In spring 1942, Jews from the neighboring villages were brought to the ghetto and on 20 Aug., after a selection, 3,222 were executed. The able-bodied were later transferred to a labor camp at Letichev and continued to do roadwork. They all perished there. Another group in the ghetto was liquidated on the night of 16 Oct. 1942. The Nazis murdered a total of 2,620 Jews from N.

NOVE BAROVO   (Hung. Ujbard; Yid. Vybaryf) Carpatho-Russia, Czechoslovakia, today Ukraine. Jews probably arrived in the early 19th cent., numbering 35 in 1830 and 116 (total 633) in 1880. In 1921, under the Czechoslovakians, their pop. rose to 191 and in 1941 to 280. Many were farmers. The Hungarians occupied N. in March 1939 and in 1940–41 drafted dozens of Jews into labor battalions for forced labor or service on the eastern front. In late July 1941, a few J. families without Hungarian citizenship were expelled to the Ukraine and murdered. The rest were deported to Auschwitz in the second half of May 1944.

NOVE DAVIDKOVO   (Hung. Ujdavidhaza) Carpatho-Russia, Czechoslovakia, today Ukraine. J. settlement probably began in the late 19th cent., with one family present in 1868. In 1880, the J. pop. was 115 (total 1,305). A few were farmers. In 1921, under the Czechoslovakians, the J. pop. was 119, rising to 132 in 1941. The Hungarians occupied N. in March 1939 and in 1941 drafted a number of Jews into labor battalions. In Aug. 1941, they expelled a few families without Hungarian citizenship to Kamenets-Podolski, where they were murdered. The rest were deported to Auschwitz in the second half of May 1944.

NOVE MESTO NAD VAHOM   (Hung. Vagujhely) Slovakia, Czechoslovakia, today Republic of Slovakia. N. had one of the oldest and most important J. communities in Slovakia, with settlement commencing in the Middle Ages. The modern community was founded by refugees from Uhersky Brod fleeing the massacres of 1683. Additional Jews arrived in the 1720s and 1730s, following new disturbances in Moravia. A synagogue was opened in 1780 and in 1784 a J. school, combining religious and secular studies, one of the first of its kind in Slovakia. The J. pop. grew to 1,087 in 1787, making the community the second largest in Slovakia after Bratislava. The J. pop. then reached a peak of 2,459 (total 5,417) in 1828 but fell off following a period of economic hardship in the 1840s. It leveled off at about 1,500 in the second half of the 19th cent. In 1848, 5,000 rioting peasants looted nearly all J. homes, stores, and warehouses. One Jew was killed and many injured. In 1856, a devastating fire destroyed most J. homes and the community's two synagogues. The community gradually recovered and again achieved a measure of prosperity in the 1870s, building a magnificent 350-seat Great Synagogue. In 1860, the J. school became a secondary school emphasizing the natural sciences, the only J. school of the kind in Hungary until WWI. A girls' school including junior high school classes was also opened at the time. Jews owned most of the businesses in the town and were among the pioneers of its industry, opening a distillery in 1842 and a soap factory in 1850. Ignaz Einhorn (1825–75) was the first Jew to serve as a minister in the Hungarian government. In 1921, the J. pop. was 1,553. About 40 Orthodox families broke off from the

Status Quo congregation to maintain their own synagogue and *beit midrash*. Jews served on the local council and owned 135 business establishments, 35 workshops, and most of the town's factories. Zionist activity intensified, with Hashomer Hatzair, Bnei Akiva, WIZO, and the Maccabi sports club all active. In 1940, after Slovakian independence, J. children were expelled from the public schools and in 1941 J. businessmen were forced out of their businesses. The arrival of 706 refugees from Bratislava brought the J. pop. up to 2,215 in early 1942. On 30 March, 120 J. men were deported to the Majdanek concentration camp and on 1 April, 55 girls were sent to Auschwitz. Another 350 Jews (including 75 from neighboring settlements) were deported in two transports on 11 and 18 April. Six hundred with 400 more from Hlohovec and Piestany were dispatched to the Opole ghetto in the Lublin dist. (Poland) on 26 April. Deportations to the death camps continued in June–Aug. About 400 essential J. workers remained after the 1942 deportations, joined by 300 refugees in May 1944. Those who did not join the partisans or hide out in the villages with Slovakian peasants were rounded up and deported by the Germans in Sept.–Oct. Of the postwar community of 150, a third left for Israel in 1949. Community life continued into the 1970s.

NOVE SELO   (Hung. Ujfalu; Yid. Novoshelits) Carpatho-Russia, Czechoslovakia, today Ukraine. Jews probably settled in the early 19th cent., numbering 36 in 1830 and 117 in 1880 and earning their livelihoods in trade, crafts, and agriculture. Their pop. was 120 in 1921 and 205 in 1941. The Hungarians occupied the town in Nov. 1938 and in 1941 drafted a few dozen Jews into forced labor battalions. The rest were deported to Auschwitz on 17 May 1944.

NOVE ZAMKY   (Hung. Ersekujvar) Slovakia, Czechoslovakia, today Republic of Slovakia. Jews are known from the early 18th cent. but were apparently expelled in 1725. The community was probably only renewed in the 1840s when residence restrictions were lifted. A synagogue was erected in 1863 but in 1870 the community split into Neologist and Orthodox congregations, dividing up the cemetery between them and opening separate elementary schools. An Orthodox synagogue was built about 1880. Dr. Shemuel Klein, as Neologist rabbi from 1913, imbued the young with a Zionist spirit and later became a professor of geography at the Hebrew University of Jerusalem. The J. pop. grew from 1,205 in 1869 to 2,535 (total 22,457) in 1930, equally divided between the two congregations. A girls' secondary school, the only one of its kind in Slovakia, was opened in 1926. Many Jews identified with the minority Hungarian culture in the city, speaking Hungarian as a first language and founding such Hungarian-language periodicals as *Shabbat* (edited by Peter Ujvari) and the Zionist *Ha-Madrikh*. WIZO and Maccabi had hundreds of members and Hashomer Hatzair, Bnei Akiva, and Betar were active. Agudat Israel had one of its largest Slovakian youth groups in N. Jews served on the municipal council and owned 302 commercial establishments, 89 workshops, and nine factories (including a hide-processing plant with 300 workers and a shoe factory with 100). Anti-J. agitation accompanied annexation to Hungary in Nov. 1938. In 1941, 500 J. men (J. pop. 3,000) were seized for forced labor and on 7 May, 1944, 2,260 were herded into a ghetto. Another 430 families from the area were held at a J.-owned brickyard. On 10–12 June 1944, 4,830 Jews, including those from the area, were deported to Auschwitz. Half the postwar community of 521 left for Israel in 1949. About 70 remained in 1990.

NOVGOROD   Leningrad dist., Russia. Jews probably settled in the first half of the 19th cent. In 1870, they were permitted to erect a prayer house. In 1897, their pop. was 854 (total 25,000). In the Soviet period, it reached 926 in 1926 and then dropped to 639 in 1939. The Germans occupied N. on 19 Aug. 1941 and murdered the few Jews who had not fled or been evacuated.

NOVGOROD-SEVERSKI   Chernigov dist., Ukraine. Jews settled in the mid-16th cent. The community was destroyed in the Chmielnicki massacres of 1648–49, the Jews returning only in the late 18th cent. In 1897, the J. pop. was 2,956 (total 9,182). The Russian army, staging a pogrom before its retreat in April 1918, killed 88 Jews. The J. pop. dropped to 982 in 1939. When the Germans arrived on 26 Aug. 1941, about 200 Jews remained. They were subjected to a regime of forced labor and on 7 Nov., 174 were murdered beside an antitank ditch outside the city. Fifty more Jews were murdered there in the following days.

NOVI BECEJ   (Hung. Torok Becse) Vojvodina dist.,
Yugoslavia. A J. community was established in 1845. In June 1940 the J. pop. was 204 (total 7,000). Most Jews perished in the Holocaust.

NOVI KNEZEVAC   (Hung. Torok Kanyizsa) Vojvodina dist., Yugoslavia. Jews first settled in the early 18th cent. The community, which had been under the jurisdiction of Kikinda, was independent from 1935 until the Holocaust. The J. pop was 101 in 1940. In Aug. 1941 all the Jews were arrested; in Sept. they were taken to Belgrade and murdered.

NOVI PAZAR   Serbia, Yugoslavia. A J. community was established in the 18th cent. The J. pop. in 1931 was 250 (total 10,361). The Germans entered N. in April 1941. The Jews were harshly abused until March 1942, when they were taken to their deaths in a Belgrade camp.

NOVI SAD   (Ger. Neusatz; Hung. Ujvidek) Vojvodina dist., Yugoslavia. From the end of the 17th cent. Jews began to settle on the site that was to become N. In the early 1740s a community was established. The J. pop. in 1774 was 100 (total 4,620). During the 18th cent., the Jews were subjected to special taxes and restrictions in professional life, while residence rights were also limited. In the first years of the 19th cent. the community opened a medical clinic and school. From 1843 the Jews had to pay a "tolerance tax" as well as various other taxes. Nevertheless, the economy slowly opened up to the Jews. Concurrently, they began to identify with Hungarian culture (which also sparked some Hungarian antisemitism), and participated in the Hungarian revolt of 1848. Most J. homes, the synagogue, and the school were destroyed in this uprising. A welfare association was established in 1876 by 53 women and was maintained until WWII. The community numbered 1,507 in 1891 (total 22,224) and was well organized. However, there was constant tension in the community because the Jews as a minority found themselves caught between the rival Serbs and Hungarians in N. The community also experienced economic hardship at this time. The Jews developed various religious, social, cultural, and welfare organizations, most of which were active until the Holocaust. Following WWI, the economic situation of the Jews declined, but they were able to maintain reasonable standards of living. In the early 20th cent., the community built a new synagogue, administration building, and school. Zionism was introduced at the end of WWI. In 1927, the Zionists organized a J. party which obtained five seats (out of 80) in the town council. The appearance of Revisionism divided the Zionist movement in the town. The first youth movement was founded in 1919 and in the late 1930s there was tension between Hashomer Hatzair and Betar. Religiously, the congregation was primarily Neologist, but in the 1930s an Orthodox group was established. In 1935 a large J. administration building was opened, including offices for the various organizations (notably, the regional office of the Zionist Organization), a kosher restaurant, lecture halls, a gym, and a kindergarten. From the mid-1930s, local newspapers were increasingly hostile to the Jews. In 1938–39, J. refugees arrived from Austria, Czechoslovakia, and Germany. In 1940 the community, which numbered 4,300 (total 68,500), was subjected to discriminatory laws restricting education and trade. On 12 April 1941, Hungarian forces entered N. and immediately began terrorizing the J. and Serb inhabitants. Possessions were confiscated. Non-resident Jews were sent to areas under the rule of the Croatian Ustase, who killed all Jews falling into their hands. Men between the ages of 16 and 65 were drafted into labor battalions and were sent to the Ukraine, where most died. Some J. Zionist youths organized effective underground resistance to the Hungarian forces. On 21–23 Jan. 1942, Jews were taken from their homes, in the freezing cold, and murdered. Most were drowned in the Danube River. Over 800 Jews died in the massacre and other Jews fled to Budapest. The Zionist underground continued its sabotage activities, but many of the activists were arrested and killed by the Hungarians; others escaped and joined the partisans. In March 1943, some Jews were taken to forced labor in Serbia and were killed a few months later. The remaining Jews were able to continue living in N. until March 1944, when the Germans entered. In April, all the Jews (about 1,600) were taken to the Auschwitz death camp. Only a few youths, who had been sent to work in German factories, returned. About 1,000 Jews survived the Holocaust, of whom 700 emigrated to Israel. A small community continued to exist there.

NOVOARKHANGELSK Kirovograd dist., Ukraine. Jews probably settled in the late 19th cent. and numbered 943 (total 6,262) in 1897. In 1919, General Denikin's White Army staged a pogrom against the Jews. In the Soviet period, the J. pop. dropped to 636 in 1926 and 209 in 1939. Shortly after they entered the town on 30 July 1941, the Germans murdered the few remaining Jews.

NOVO BERISLAV Nikolaiev dist., Ukraine. N. was a J. colony founded in the latter 19th cent. The J. pop. was 452 in 1898 and 349 in 1922. It included many who had left farming and went over to trade and crafts. A J. council (soviet) and J. elementary school were operating in the 1920s and 1930s. The Germans captured N. on 23 Aug. 1941 and on 10 Sept. murdered 87 Jews (57 from N. and others expelled from Kremenchug and Bessarabia).

NOVOCHERKASK Rostov dist., Russia. Jews were only allowed to settle after the Feb. 1917 Revolution but did not begin to arrive until the early 1920s, when the city underwent accelerated industrial development and became a regional center for academic education. In 1939, the J. pop. was 673 (total 75,917). After their arrival on 23 July 1942, the Germans murdered the few remaining Jews.

NOVODAROVKA (until the 1920s, Bogodarovka) Zaporozhe dist., Ukraine. Jews from the Vilna region founded N. as a J. colony in 1855. The pop. was 608 in 1858 (most probably all Jews) and 503 in 1926. A. J. school probably including eight grades was still active in the late 1930s. After their arrival in Oct 1941, the Germans murdered the few remaining Jews.

NOVO-DEREVYAIANSKAYA Krasnodar territory, Russia. The Germans murdered about 40 Jews in the village on 23–24 Oct. 1942

NOVODUGINO Smolensk dist., Russia. The J. pop. in 1939 was 40 (total 1,654). After their arrival on 8 Oct. 1941, the Germans murdered the few remaining Jews.

NOVOGEORGIEVSK Kirovograd dist., Ukraine. J. settlement commenced in the mid-19th cent. In 1897, the J. pop. was 1,455 (total 11,594). In the mid-1920s, under the Soviets, the community maintained a J. elementary school. The J. pop. dropped to 381 in 1939. The Germans captured the city on 7 Aug. 1941 and in Jan. 1942 murdered about 470 Jews from N. and the surrounding area.

NOVOGRAD-VOLINSKII (Zwiahel) Zhitomir dist., Ukraine. Survivors of the Chmielnicki massacres of 1648–49 probably founded the J. settlement in the late 17th cent. In 1765, the J. pop. of N. and its environs was 577 (taxpayers). In 1897, the J. pop. was 9,378 (total 16,904). The writer Mordekhai Ze'ev Fayerberg lived in N. at the turn of the 19th cent. A Hebrew school operated at the time. Jews suffered grievously in the civil war (1918–21). In July–Aug. 1919, about 1,000 Jews were murdered, the city was burned to the ground, and the remaining Jews were dispersed. Between the World Wars, N. was an important military center and many Jews were employed in various trades. In 1939 their pop. was 6,839. The Germans captured the city on 8 July 1941. The Jews were moved to an open ghetto in the center of the city. A thousand were executed near a local tractor station in Aug. In Sept., 4,000 were executed outside the city, near the Kholodianka train station. The few hundred skilled J. workers still remaining were held in a labor camp. A mass escape took place in early Nov. 1942 and some joined partisan units beginning in Dec.

NOVO-KONSTANTINOV Kamenets-Podolski dist., Ukraine. The 17th cent. community was destroyed in the Chmielnicki massacres of 1648–49. The J. pop. was 694 in 1765 and 2,320 (59% of the total) in 1897. A pogrom was staged against the Jews on 18 July 1919. In the Soviet period, a J. elementary school was opened while the J. pop. dropped to 1,612 in 1926. The Germans captured the town in mid-July 1941. The Jews were brought to Medzhibozh around the end of Sept. 1942 and murdered there.

NOVO-MINSKAYA Krasnodar territory, Russia. The Germans murdered 42 Jews in the village (probably in late summer 1942).

NOVOMIRGOROG Kirovograd dist., Ukraine. Jews along with other residents were expelled in 1821 for military reasons. After they returned, they engaged in trade with the local garrison. A synagogue was in use by the 1880s. In 1897, the J. pop. was 1,622 (total 9,364). On 4–5 Feb. and 17 May 1919, the Jews were attacked in pogroms, with 105 losing their lives during the latter event. In the mid-1920s, under the Soviets, a rabbi was still serving the community. The J. pop. dropped to 315 in 1939. The Germans captured N. in early Aug. 1941. On the night of 6 Feb. 1942, Ukrainian police murdered 69 Jews. The remaining 250 in N. and its environs were murdered near the village of Martonosha, probably in 1942.

NOVOMOSKOVSK Dnepropetrovsk dist., Ukraine. Jews began settling in the late 18th cent. and numbered about 100 in 1803 and 1,436 (total 12,883) in 1897. A government school for J. children was operating in the 1860s. On 4 Sept. 1883, 200 Jews were killed in a pogrom and J. property suffered large-scale damage. Under Soviet rule, difficult economic conditions forced many Jews to leave the city during 1926 and become farmers. The J. pop. dropped to 757 in 1939. The Germans captured N. on 26 Sept. 1941. In late Dec. 1941, they murdered 136 Jews and on 3 March 1942 another 400 from N. and the surrounding area.

NOVOPAVLOVKA Odessa dist., Ukraine. The J. pop. was 953 (total 1,581) in 1897 and 971 in 1926. The Germans captured N. around early Aug. 1941 and murdered the Jews in Sept. The few who remained were sent to the Bolshaia Vradievka labor camp, where they shared the fate of the other prisoners.

NOVOPAVLOVSKOYE Krasnodar territory, Russia. The Germans murdered ten Jews after occupying the village on 4 Aug. 1942.

NOVOPODOLSK Dnepropetrovsk dist., Ukraine. N. was founded as a J. colony in 1849. Its pop. was 619 in 1858, most or all probably Jews, and 354 in 1926. In the late 19th cent., most were still farmers with some engaging in petty trade and crafts. The few Jews who had neither fled nor been evacuated when the Germans captured the city in Aug. 1941 were murdered together with the 450 Jews in the area in May 1942.

NOVO POLTAVKA Nikolaiev dist., Ukraine. Jews from the Latvian Courland dist. founded N. in 1840 as a J. farm settlement. The J. pop. was 1,959 (total 2,179) in 1897 and 1,877 in 1926. During the civil war (1918–21), marauding gangs murdered a few dozen Jews. In the Soviet period, a J. council (soviet) and J. elementary school were active. In 1924, the first J. agricultural college in the Ukraine was established. (It was transferred to Odessa in 1933.) Of 450 J. breadwinners, about 80 were engaged in crafts and 20 in trade. The Germans captured N. on 13 Aug. 1941 and on 10 Sept. murdered 870 people (apparently all Jews).

NOVOROSSYISK Krasnodar territory, Russia. Jews probably settled in the mid-19th cent., numbering 980 (total 13,120) in 1897. A J. school was functioning in 1910. The community also had a synagogue and rabbi. The J. pop. rose to 1,915 in 1926. On 10 Sept. 1942, the Germans captured most of the city. On 16 Oct. they murdered the 1,000 Jews of N. and its environs.

NOVORZHEV Kalinin dist., Russia. Jews probably settled in the mid-19th cent., numbering 295 (total 2,838) in 1897 and, under the Soviets, 204 in 1926 and 59 in 1939. The Jews who had neither fled nor been evacuated were murdered after the German occupation of 17 July 1941.

NOVOSELICE (Hung. Taracujfalu) Carpatho-Russia, Czechoslovakia, today Ukraine. Jews probably arrived in the early 19th cent. Their pop. was 36 in 1830 and 117 (total 805) in 1880. In 1921, under the Czechoslovakians, it was 334 and in 1941, 205. Most were engaged in trade and a few were artisans or farmers. Jews also owned a marble quarry and a flour mill. The Hungarians annexed the town in March 1939 and in 1941 drafted a number of young Jews into forced labor battalions. In late July or early Aug. 1941, a few J. families without Hungarian citizenship were expelled to Kamenets-Podolski and apparently murdered. The rest were deported to Auschwitz on 24 May 1944.

NOVOSOKOLNIKI Kalinin dist., Russia. Jews probably settled at the turn of the 19th cent., numbering 339 (total 4,676) in 1926 and 253 in 1939. The Germans captured the town on 25 July 1941. The few Jews who had neither fled nor been evacuated were murdered, among them 11 women burned alive in one of the houses.

NOVOUKRAINKA Kirovograd dist., Ukraine. Jews settled in the mid-19th cent. The J. pop. grew after the completion of the Odessa–Yelysavetgrad railway line in the late 1860s, reaching 2,909 (total 16,028) in 1897. A pogrom was staged in spring 1881. In the mid-1920s, under the Soviets, a J. school and *talmud torah* were still operating (apparently

closed by the authorities in 1926). The J. pop. dropped significantly in the 1930s, standing at 802 in 1939. The Germans captured N. on 2 Aug. 1941 and on 19 Aug. murdered a few hundred Jews, leaving just 82 alive for forced labor. They, too, were murdered, probably in Oct.

NOVOVITEBSK Dnepropetrovsk dist., Ukraine. N. was founded as a J. colony in the 1820s and numbered 849 Jews (of a total 980 inhabitants) in 1897. In the 1930s, N. was attached to the Stalindorf J. Autonomous Region. In 1932, the N. rural council (soviet) had jurisdiction over 4,310 Jews (total 5,323), including a J. kolkhoz with 700 inhabitants on 180 farm units and a mixed kolkhoz with 300 J. and Ukrainian families. A regional secondary school and an agricultural school were still open in 1939. The Germans arrived in mid-Aug. 1939 and in late May 1942 murdered 93 of the remaining 103 J. families.

NOVO VORONTSOVKA Nikolaiev dist., Ukraine. Jews numbered 1,685 (total 5,188) in 1897 and 703 in 1926. The Germans arrived on 18 Aug. 1941 and on 24 Sept. murdered 23 Jews.

NOVOYE KOVNO Dnepropetrovsk dist., Ukraine. N. was founded as a J. colony in 1849 and had a pop. of over 370 in 1858. In 1897, the J. pop. was 796 (total 928) and in 1926 it was 673. In the 1930s, N. was attached to the Stalindorf J. Autonomous Region. The N. rural council (soviet) had jurisdiction over 2,259 Jews and a total pop. of 4,731. The settlement had a J. elementary school. Almost all the Jews were farmers (95 farm units in 1930). The Germans captured N. in mid-Aug. 1941 and in May 1942 murdered the Jews who had neither fled nor been evacuated.

NOVOZHITOMIR Dnepropetrovsk dist., Ukraine. N. was a J. colony founded in the mid-19th cent. It numbered 423 Jews (total 551) in 1897 and 712 in 1926. In the 1930s, it was attached to the Stalindorf J. Autonomous Region. The N. rural council (soviet) had jurisdiction over 2,766 Jews and a total pop. of 3,046. A J. elementary school was still open in the 1930s. The Germans arrived in mid-Aug. 1941. The Jews of N. were among the 540 Jews in the area whom the Germans murdered near Zlatoustovka in late May 1942.

NOVOZHYBKOV Oriol dist., Russia. J. settlement probably dates from the early 18th cent. Despite a residence ban, the J. pop. reached 446 in 1847. Some Jews were employed manufacturing matches in J.-owned workshops. The J. pop. grew to 3,836 (total 15,362) in 1897. A pogrom was staged on 20 Oct. 1905. In 1910 a *talmud torah* was founded. In 1926, under the Soviets, the J. pop. rose to 4,825 but then declined to 3,129 in 1939. A J. school was in operation in the early 1920s. The Germans captured N. on 16 Aug. 1941. On 18 Feb. 1942, they murdered about 950 Jews in the Karkhovsk forest, near the local railroad station.

NOVO ZLATOPOL Zaporozhe dist., Ukraine. Jews from the Vitebsk region founded N. as a J. colony in the late 1840s. It had a J. pop. of 669 (total 817) in 1897. In the Soviet period, in July 1929, a J. autonomous region was established in the area, including 1,800 J. families in 28 J. farm settlements (total regional pop. 11,518) and organized into ten councils (soviets), nine of them J. In the early 1930s, a school for raising animals was established in N. and in 1936 the local elementary school was expanded to include higher grades. Other J. settlements with J. schools in the autonomous region were Ratendorf (eight grades) and Kobilna. During the 1930s, a Yiddish newspaper called *Der Kolvirt Shtern* appeared in N. The J. pop. was 1,109 in 1939. The Germans arrived on 9 Oct. 1941 and immediately murdered 800 Jews. Hundreds of Jews from the area were ghettoized in N. in Nov.-Dec. In an *Aktion* commencing on 20 Dec. 1941, a few thousand Jews from N. and the region were executed. Some were expelled to Stary-Kermencik and perished there.

NOVY BYDZOV Bohemia, Czechoslovakia. Jews are mentioned in 1432 and 1514. A synagogue was erected in 1559. In 1715 the Jews were expelled following an epidemic and in 1901 the ancient J. quarter, except for the synagogue, burned down. Jews then moved to other parts of the town. Their pop. reached a peak of 1,024 in 1868 but dropped steadily to 84 (total 7,727) in 1930. In late 1941, 98 Jews were present. In Dec. 1942 they were apparently deported to the Theresienstadt ghetto via Hradec Kralove. Nearly all were sent to Auschwitz in 1943. One returned.

NOVY BYKHOV Moligev dist., Belorussia. The J. pop. was 560 in 1847 and 490 in 1897. R. Hirsh Betlin officiated as community rabbi in 1903. In 1923, under the Soviets, the J. pop. was 343 (total 2,083). A Yiddish and Hebrew library was active in the town and, in 1923, 160 children were enrolled at a four-year J. elementary school. Seventy J. homes were destroyed in a fire on 25 May 1925, leaving 350 Jews homeless. The Germans occupied N. on 5 July 1941 and in Nov. (or Dec.) murdered all the Jews there.

NOVY FASTOV Vinnitsa dist., Ukraine. Eight Jews were present in 1775. The J. pop. was 451 (total 2,355) in 1897 and 289 in 1926. A pogrom was staged on 11 July 1919. In the fall of 1941, the Nazis murdered the few dozen families who failed to escape with the retreating Red Army along with the rest of the Jews in the area.

NOVYI BUG (Semenovka) Nikolaiev dist., Ukraine. Jews settled in the late 19th cent. and numbered 1,962 (total 13,391) in 1897. A pogrom was staged on 19 May 1919. The J. pop. fell to 269 during the Soviet period. The Germans captured N. in mid-Aug. 1941 and on 14 May 1942 murdered the 34 remaining Jews.

NOVY JICIN Moravia (Sudetenland), Czechoslovakia. Jews were apparently present in the 14th cent., possibly earlier. In 1562, they were expelled. The modern community was only established after the 1848 revolution, reaching a pop. of 275 in 1880 and consecrating a synagogue in 1908. Jews owned a big sawmill and developed a home hatmaking industry. In 1930, 206 remained (total 13,997). Various Zionist parties were active and a training farm, established in 1921 and the first in Moravia, prepared the young for immigration to Palestine. All left during the Sudetenland crisis of fall 1938.

NOWA MYSZ Nowogrodek dist., Poland, today Belarus. Jews probably settled in the mid-16th cent. They traded in grain and forest products and were active as shopkeepers and artisans. In 1897 they numbered 1,764 (total 2,995) but many abandoned the town after Baranowicze was founded as a railroad junction 3 miles (5 km) away. The J. pop. was 632 in 1921. The Germans entered N. on 27 June 1942 and executed the Jews outside the town in late summer 1942.

NOWE MIASTO (I) (Yid. Neishtat) Lodz dist., Poland. Jews first settled in the late 18th cent. The J. pop. in 1897 was 1,711 (52% of the total). Jews owned the water mill, a sawmill, and the town's only oil-processing factory. They ran textile home workshops, most of the bakeries, the smithy, and the bus line to Warsaw. A Ha-Po'el ha-Mizrachi training group worked at the sawmill. All Zionist groups were active. Between the World Wars, Agudat Israel dominated the community council. In the 1930s antisemitic manifestations were widespread. The Germans formed a *Judenrat* and set up a ghetto in 1940 which, with the influx of refugees, held 3,700 Jews by Nov. 1940. On 22 Oct. 1942 the ghetto inhabitants were transported to Opoczno and then to the Treblinka death camp.

NOWE MIASTO (II) (Yid. Neistat) Lwow dist., Poland, today Ukraine. The 17th cent. community was apparently wiped out in the Chmielnicki massacres of 1648–49, only reviving in the 19th cent. but never exceeding a few dozen families (about a third of the total). The Germans took the town on 28 June 1941 and the community was probably liquidated around the end of July 1942.

NOWE MIASTO (III) (Yid. Neishtat) Warsaw dist., Poland. Jews first arrived in the 16th cent. The community grew from 513 in 1808 to 1,667 (total 3,761) in 1897. Most supported themselves through petty trade and crafts. Some dealt in grain and lumber and in the late 19th cent. Jews opened a number of button factories. The Hasidim established themselves in the late 19th cent., Gur becoming the largest group. The Zionists were active from 1904. After WWI the Jews suffered from the general economic crisis as well as rising antisemitism, with boycott watches posted around J. stores. The Zionist youth groups undertook extensive cultural and educational activity, including pioneer training for *aliya*. The Germans captured the city on 5 Sept. 1939. On 23 Sept. (Yom Kippur) the entire J. pop. was gathered in the market square and sent to do roadwork after being tormented for hours. Five Jews were murdered. In Nov. 1941 a ghetto was set up, swelled by 1,200–1,500 refugees from Ciechanow and 700 from Drobin. About 170 died from a typhoid epidemic. On 18 Nov. 1942, all 1,800–2,400 Jews in the ghetto were transported to Plonsk and from there to Auschwitz.

NOWE SIOLO (I) Lwow dist., Poland. The J. pop.

in 1921 was 125. In 1939 some may have fled to Soviet-occupied territory, with the remaining Jews meeting their deaths in the Belzec death camp in 1942.

NOWE SIOLO (II) Tarnopol dist., Poland, today Ukraine. The J. pop. was 109 in 1921. The Jews were probably expelled to Zbaraz for liquidation in Sept.–Oct. 1942.

NOWINY POKARCZMISKA Lublin dist., Poland. The J. pop. stood at 113 (total 210) in 1921. The Jews were presumably deported by the Germans to the Treblinka death camp via Lukow in fall 1942.

NOWOGROD Bialystok dist., Poland. The J. settlement dates from the 15th cent., maintaining small numbers in the 16th and 17th cents. in the face of residence and trade restrictions. In the 19th cent., the community grew rapidly, constituting half the total pop. by midcent. and owning most of the town's factories as well as the Narev River ferry. All the Jews were expelled by the Russians at the outset of WWI. In 1921 only 514 were present as compared with a J. pop. of 1,542 in 1908. With much of the city destroyed in the German bombardment of Sept. 1939, the Jews fled to Lomza and were presumably deported to Auschwitz in Jan. 1943. Of the 300 J. families involved, not a trace remains.

NOWOGRODEK (Yid. Novaredok) Nowogrodek dist., Poland, today Belarus. Jews probably settled in the second half of the 15th cent. and in 1623 were placed under the jurisdiction of the Brest-Litovsk community by the Lithuanian Council. In 1847, the J. pop was 2,576 and in 1897 it was 5,015 (total 7,887). Many owned wagons and worked as carters to and from the distant railroad station. Jews were also known for their *matza* industry. The well-known Yiddish lexicographer Alexander Harkavy was born there in 1863 and the Petersburg branch of his family endowed the local hospital and old age home. Among the prominent 19th cent. rabbis were Yitzhak Elhanan Spektor and Yehiel Mikhal Epstein. In 1896 a Musar yeshiva was founded by Yosef Hurwitz, attracting hundreds of students from the area. The Zionists and the Bund became active at the turn of the 19th cent., the latter organizing strikes and J. self-defense. Emigration to the U.S. and the dislocations of WWI reduced the J. pop. to 3,405 in 1921. The principal J. educational institution was a Tarbut

Hebrew school founded in 1919. A CYSHO Yiddish school was established later. A wide range of Zionist groups was active between the World Wars. During the two years of Soviet rule (1939–41), all political and community life ceased, private enterprises were nationalized, and artisans were organized into cooperatives. German bombardments prior to the occupation of the city on 3 July 1941 caused heavy damage which left thousands homeless. The Jews were subjected to forced labor, extortion, and numerous restrictions. Dozens of Jews belonging to the educated class were murdered. After a ghetto for skilled workers was set up on 8 Dec. 1941, the remaining 4,500 Jews were executed near the village of Skridlewa. Refugees again swelled the ghetto pop. and on 7 Aug. another 2,500 were murdered, leaving 1,240, who were divided into two groups—700 skilled workers in one ghetto and 500 in another one. The latter were murdered on 4 Feb. 1943 and 298 of the former on 7 May. Another 200 who succeeded in escaping through a tunnel dug by a resistance group led by Berl Joselewicz and Natan Sucharski joined up with the Bielski partisan battalion and other fighting groups in the forests.

NOWOJELNIA Nowogrodek dist., Poland, today Belarus. Jews first settled in about 1903. The J. pop. in 1921 was 135 (total 373). The Jews were presumably murdered by the Germans after being expelled to Nowogrodek in WWII.

NOWO-SWIENCIANY Vilna dist., Poland, today Lithuania. J. settlement commenced in the 1850s. The existence of a large railroad station late in the cent. created subsidiary occupations for the Jews. J. merchants sold lumber, mushrooms, blackberries, crabs, and geese. In 1897 the J. pop was 540 (total 1,340), growing to 900 in 1925. The Jews were able to maintain their commerce throughout most of WWI. However, conditions deteriorated between the World Wars and many merchants went overseas, leaving their workers without jobs. The YEKOPO relief organization provided significant aid, enabling Jews to set up shops and stalls in the town's new market. In the 1930s, competition from a Polish railroad workers' cooperative undermined J. retail trade. In addition to the Yiddish school founded in 1919, a Tarbut Hebrew school was opened in 1928 and Zionist activity expanded, with small groups of pioneers leaving for Palestine. Most Jews accommodated themselves to the

Soviet regime of 1939–41. The Germans captured the town on 24 June 1941. They were joined by pro-Nazi Lithuanian "partisans" who celebrated with acts of rape and murder. Lithuanian police subsequently murdered another 43 Jews in a hunt for former Komsomol members. A *Judenrat* and ghetto were established and in Sept. 1941 most Jews were taken to the Poligon camp, where they were murdered in groups of 25, the men on 8 Oct., the women and children a day later.

NOWY DWOR (I) Nowogrodek dist., Poland, today Belarus. Jews probably settled in the early 19th cent., their pop. reaching 370 (total 655) in 1921. Most worked in crafts and petty trade. Haskala made inroads in the early 20th cent. when the influence of the revolutionary movements on the young was significant. Economic life came to a standstill during the German occupation in WWI. With the transition to Polish rule, Polish soldiers robbed and beat Jews. With aid from the YEKOPO relief organization, J. trade revived somewhat as merchants bought up farm produce and others opened stores. In the 1930s, Jews set up small industrial enterprises—pitch-making and hide-processing plants and a brickyard—but the general economic crisis again took its toll. Hehalutz was active in sending young pioneers to Palestine and a Tarbut Hebrew school was in operation from 1925. The J. pop. in 1939 was 500. The arrival of the Red Army in Sept. 1939 saw the introduction of a Soviet regime. The Germans captured the town in late June 1941. Fifty Jews were immediately taken off to an unknown destination. In Oct. 1941 the remaining 500 Jews were transferred to the Ostryna ghetto. In Oct. 1942 they were sent with the Jews there to the notorious Kelbasin transit camp near Grodno and then deported to Auschwitz.

NOWY DWOR (II) Bialystok dist., Wolkowysk county, Poland, today Belarus. Jews lived there in the 19th cent. and numbered 100 in 1886 (total 1,183). The J. pop. in 1921 was 146. The Jews were probably expelled to Wolkowysk by the Germans in Nov. 1942 and from there deported to the Treblinka death camp.

NOWY DWOR (III) (Yid. Neihof) Warsaw dist., Poland. Jews settled in the 18th cent. because of residence restrictions in neighboring Warsaw. N. became famous for its Hebrew printing press, founded in 1780 by a Christian from Warsaw, Johann Anton

Members of Zukunft youth organization demonstrating in Nowy Dwor, Poland

Kreiger, and employing 40 Jews. A lively book trade sprang up around it. In 1813 it was transferred to Warsaw under J. ownership. The proximity of the Modlin fort defending Warsaw also benefited the Jews since their stores and taverns served the local garrison and construction workers. The J. pop. rose from 1,305 in 1857 to 4,737 (total 7,292) in 1897. The Zionists and the Bund became active in the early 20th cent. Despite economic duress after WWI, community life flourished. The Zionists expanded their activities, with Mizrachi particularly influential. Yiddish and Hebrew schools were in operation. A Beth Jacob school enrolled 150 girls and in 1930 a Beit Yosef yeshiva was opened. Hundreds of the town's 4,500 Jews were killed in the heavy fighting of Sept. 1939. Under the German occupation, the Jews were subjected to a regime of persecution and forced labor. An expulsion order led many of the young to flee to the Soviet Union while most others went to Warsaw,

leaving about 1,000 Jews in N. In early 1941, the Piaski quarter was designated as a ghetto and a *Judenrat* appointed. Many died in a typhoid epidemic and on 14 May 1941, 400 of the sick and old were transferred to the Legionowo ghetto. With many returning from Warsaw, the ghetto pop. rose to 2,000 when it was sealed off in June 1941. In July, all but 600–750 of the able-bodied were deported to the Pomiechowek concentration camp. A new influx of refugees, including 1,200 from Wyszogrod, brought the ghetto pop. back up to 3,000. At least 200 more died of typhoid fever in the following winter. Public hangings commenced in May 1942 and 38 Jews escaping to N. from Legionowo after it was liquidated in early Oct. were taken to the General Gouvernement border and executed. On 28 Oct. 1942, 2,600 Jews from Cerwinsk were brought to the ghetto. Deportations to Auschwitz commenced on 20 Nov., the third and last transport leaving N. on 12 Dec. to empty the ghetto. A number of Jews from N. participated in the Warsaw ghetto uprising in spring 1943 as well as the Treblinka and Auschwitz *Sonderkommando* uprisings of 2 Aug. 1943 and 7 Oct. 1944. About 400–450 survived the Holocaust, mainly in the Soviet Union. An attempt to reestablish the community proved unsuccessful.

NOWY DWOR (IV) Bialystok dist., Sokolka county, Poland, today Belarus. Jews settled in the first half of the 16th cent. Their pop. reached 897 (total 1,452) in 1878, but declined to 490 in 1897. In late 1941, 250 were expelled by the Germans to Suchowola and on 2 Nov. 1942 they were sent to Kelbasin for subsequent deportation to the death camps. Those left behind in Kelbasin were subsequently transferred to the Grodno ghetto and then on 16 Nov. deported to Auschwitz.

NOWY KORCZYN Kielce dist., Poland. Jews are first mentioned in the 15th cent., when they were restricted to residence outside the town walls. In 1866, they completed one of the most magnificent synagogues in Poland. The J. pop. grew from 1,232 in 1827 to 2,781 (total 3,787) in 1897. After WWI, Jews opened new workshops (for hide-processing, tailoring, and work in wood and wicker). Zionist activity was extensive. The Germans arrived on 20 Sept. 1939. With the influx of refugees, the J. pop. rose from 2,400 to 3,700 in April 1941, all confined to a ghetto. Many artisans worked in "shops" organized by the *Judenrat*. On 2 Oct. 1942 they were marched to Slupia Nowa and deported to the Treblinka death camp after many, including children, the old, and the sick, were shot on the way. The 270 who afterwards came out of hiding were sent to labor camps.

NOWY POHOST Vilna dist., Poland, today Belarus. A community of 50 Jews existed by 1859, growing to 157 (total 625) in 1921. Between the World Wars, J. tradesmen barely earned a living and an attempt to farm by some in the 1930s was unsuccessful because of the poor soil. The Germans arrived on 12 July 1941, instituting a regime of forced labor and extortion. On 7 Nov. 1941 the town's 300 Jews were expelled to the Nowo-Swienciany ghetto with 1,600 Jews from other settlements. In anticipation of an *Aktion*, about 700 Jews broke out on 17 Aug. 1942. The next day the remaining 1,200 were slaughtered. Of those who escaped, some joined partisan units while others sought

refuge in the Glembokie ghetto and perished there in the *Aktion* of Aug. 1943.

NOWY SONCZ (Yid. Zanz) Cracow dist., Poland. Jews are recorded from the end of the 15th cent., living there in small numbers under various residence and trade restrictions until the second half of the 17th cent. Jews were then welcomed in the effort to rebuild the city after the mid-cent. invasions and epidemics destroyed its economy. Under a privilege granted in 1673, they laid the basis of an organized community. Jews dealt mainly in trade (honey, wine, copper, textiles, furs, and tobacco). They were also active as millers and distillers, craftsmen and moneylenders, the last particularly to the local nobility. A fire in 1769 allegedly spreading from the J. quarter and destroying the Franciscan church provoked anti-J. agitation cut short only by the Austrian annexation of 1772. Under Austrian rule, J. trade expanded into the Empire but heavy taxation and numerous restrictions affected the J. economy adversely. The J. grain trade was cut back and Jews were not allowed to purchase houses from Christians or employ Christian servants. The liberalization ushered in by the 1848 revolutions eliminated most J. disabilities and paved the way for increasing J. prominence in the city's economy. Almost all its merchants were Jews as well as most distillers and innkeepers as the J. pop. grew to nearly half the total in 1880 (5,163 out of 11,185). In the 1840s, R. Hayyim ben Leibush Halberstam established his court there, making the community one of Galicia's more important hasidic centers. The dominance of the Hasidim also retarded the advent of Zionism until the beginning of the 20th cent. Prosperity was cut short by fires in 1890 and 1894, the latter destroying nearly the entire J. quarter. This was followed by anti-J. riots in 1898 with further incidents in 1909 and 1914 as antisemitism intensified. By 1910 the J. pop. stood at 7,990 (total 25,004). Under the Russian occupation in WWI, the community suffered considerably, with recovery slow in its aftermath owing to the anti-J. policy of the Polish authorities and the competition of the Polish cooperatives. Over the next decade, the J. pop. remained at its 1921 level of around 9,000. Most J. tradesmen dealt in food and clothing with welfare agencies playing an increasing role in community life. Orthodox circles still controlled the community's institutions but the Zionists made increasing headway, operating a wide variety of youth organizations as well as numerous cul-

Bikkur Holim and Jewish school, Nowy Soncz, Poland

tural facilities. The Bund was also influential, particularly among salaried workers. A devastating flood in 1934 left 350 J. families homeless and destroyed many stores and workshops, adding to the economic distress of the community, which intensified with the upsurge of antisemitism in the 1930s. The Germans captured the city on 6 Sept. 1939 and immediately instituted a regime of persecution and forced labor. A *Judenrat* was set up in the same month and J. businesses were systematically impounded, mostly being handed over to local ethnic Germans (*Volksdeutsche*). From the end of the year and all through 1940, refugees kept arriving in the city and Jews were increasingly confined to labor camps, with around 1,000 in Roznow by Aug. 1940 and 600 sent to Lipie in the fall. By Nov. 1940 the JSS organization (Juedische Soziale Selbsthilfe), operating alongside the *Judenrat*, was extending assistance to 2,500 of the needy. The winter of 1940–41 brought disease as well as hunger and with the coming of spring the Germans carried out periodic executions

of designated groups of Jews (Hasidim, young street-vendors hawking cigarettes, leftist youth movement activists, etc.). In July 1941, the J. quarter was divided into two ghettoes, now containing around 12,000 people. Random killing continued through 1942. On 21 Aug. 1942 all Jews were ordered to one of the city's squares and from there, after a selection in which around 800 essential workers were spared but many others were left dead in the streets, the rest were deported to the Belzec death camp in three transports (25–28 Aug.). There were attempts at armed resistance in the ghetto. Those remaining were dispersed over the next year among various labor camps while those in hiding were hunted down and murdered.

NOWY TARG (Yid. Neimarkt) Cracow dist., Poland. Few Jews were present until the late 18th cent. With the end of residence restrictions, Jews began to settle in greater numbers in the 1860s, reaching a pop. of 773 in 1890 (total 5,878) and 1,342 in 1921

Jewish soccer team, Nowy Soncz, Poland, 1927

(total 8,071). A thriving souvenir industry, the lumber and building-material trade, and the tourist trade provided a livelihood. The abandonment of the traditional religious way of life was particularly noticeable in the community and the J. press singled it out for its public flouting of the Sabbath and "primitive backwoods" ways. In late 1918, gangs of Austrian army deserters attempting to attack Jews were stopped by a J. militia. The Zionists, active since 1898, expanded their presence between the World Wars, with 200 in the youth movements. Antisemitic agitation intensified in the 1930s, accompanied by economic boycotts and occasional violence. The Germans arrived in Sept. 1939 and immediately victimized the Jews, seizing men and women for forced labor, looting J. property, and transferring J. stores to "loyal Aryans." A *Judenrat* was set up around the end of 1940 to regulate the forced labor and exact "contributions." In May 1941 a refugee-swelled ghetto was established. On 29 Aug. its 3,000–4,000 inhabitants were gathered for a selec-

tion: about 80 of the sick and old were executed at the J. cemetery; those chosen for work were separated from their families and the rest were deported to the Belzec death camp. In a mopping-up action, 150 more Jews who had escaped the net were rounded up and murdered.

NUR   Bialystok dist., Poland. The J. community, dating from the early 19th cent., numbered 239 in 1857 and 400 in 1921 (33% of the total). In Sept. 1939, N. was annexed by the USSR. It was a transit point for Jews escaping from German-occupied territory to the USSR and its Jews assisted the refugees. In 1940, the Soviets transferred N.'s entire pop. to Ciechanowiec and when Ciechanowiec was captured by the Germans on 22 June 1941, all the Jews in the town were executed.

NUREMBERG   (Nuernberg) Middle Franconia, Germany. A J. community is first mentioned in the last third of the 12th cent. after the arrival in 1146 of Rhineland Jews seeking protection from the king during the disturbances arising from the Second Crusade. In the late 13th cent. the Jews achieved a solid economic position, engaging mainly in moneylending and moneychanging, but were excluded from various areas of commerce. The first synagogue was consecrated in 1280. In the Rindfleisch massacres of 1298, 740 Jews were murdered, including R. Mordekhai ben Hillel, author of the talmudic compendium known as the *Mordekhai*. Within a few years the community was revived by Jews from Frankfurt, reaching a pop. of around 2,000 in 1338 with the addition of Jews from the Upper Palatinate and Swabia as well as more distant regions. A well-known yeshiva operated under such distinguished rabbis as Yaakov Weil and Yaakov Pollack. The community was again destroyed in the Black Death persecutions when 562 Jews were murdered in 1349 by local residents. J. property was looted, the synagogue destroyed, and the cemetery plowed under. A small J. community was reestablished, never exceeding 200 but again achieving wealth. In 1416 the Jews received a letter of protection from King Sigismund. In 1451 they were ordered to wear special clothes to distinguish them from Christians and 18 were hanged in 1467 charged with murdering four Christians. After unrelenting pressure from local residents, the Jews were expelled by King Maximilian I in 1499. Most found refuge in Frankfurt. Thereafter Jews were not permitted to reside permanently in N. until the early 19th cent. and were only authorized to form a community in 1862. In 1867 the J. pop. reached 1,254 (total 77,895). A new synagogue, one of the most magnificent in Germany, with seating for 935 worshipers, was dedicated in 1874. The minority Orthodox Jews formed their own Adass Jisroel congregation in opposition to the community's majority Reform orientation, erecting a synagogue in 1902. A third synagogue, serving East European Jews, was built in 1917. Most J. children studied at municipal schools while the Orthodox maintained a *talmud torah* from 1908 and a J. public school from 1921. Adass Jisroel also ran a yeshiva. By 1900 the J. pop. had risen to 5,596 and in 1922 it reached a peak of 9,280. Antisemitism accompanied the development of the modern community from its beginnings. N. was from the outset one of the key Nazi centers. A leading role in anti-J. agitation was played by the Nazi organ *Der Stuerm-*

er, founded in N. in 1923 by Julius Streicher, whose declared aim was to make N. the first J.-free (*judenrein*) city in Germany. Attacks on Jews in public places became an everyday occurrence and efforts were made to enforce an economic boycott. Jews were a dominant commercial factor in the city, operating 676 business establishments and 40 factories in 1930, including 12 banks and branches of the Tietz and Schocken department stores. The community provided extensive welfare and cultural services. Among the organizations active in N. were the Central Union (C.V.), the Zionist Organization, with 200 members in the Habonim youth movement and 110 in WIZO, the Maccabi sports club, Mizrachi, and Agudat Israel. The J. library with 4,000 volumes was one of the first in Germany (founded in 1877). With the rise of the Nazis to power in 1933, the economic boycott was strictly enforced. SA forces together with Hitler Youth attacked Jews in the streets and with Streicher now *Gauleiter* of Franconia hundreds were arrested and many murdered at the Dachau concentration camp. The exodus that had commenced in the 1920s continued. By 1935–36, with the continuing expulsion of J. students from municipal schools, the enrollment at the J. public school was 550 with another 80 in vocational training. Of the 7,502 Jews in N in 1933 (total 410,400), 5,638 left the city through April 1939, 2,539 of them leaving Germany, including 1,030 to the U.S., 572 to England, and 226 to Palestine. On 10 Aug. 1938 the Great Synagogue was destroyed. On *Kristallnacht* (9–10 Nov. 1938), the Adass Jisroel synagogue was burned down and the East European synagogue destroyed along with numerous J. stores while Jews were beaten and thrown from windows. During the riots, 26 Jews died (of a total 91 in all of Germany): 16 were murdered and ten committed suicide. Beginning in May 1939, Jews were subjected to forced labor. By Nov. 1941, 1,800 Jews remained in the city. Their expulsion commenced on 29 Nov., when 535 were transported to Skirotawa-Jungfernhof near Riga, where they remained until March 1942, when 450 were sent to labor camps and the rest executed; 16 survived the war. Another 426 Jews, all those remaining in N. up to the age of 65, were deported to Izbica in the Lublin dist. (Poland) on 24 March; none survived. The final transport of 533 aged Jews left for the Theresienstadt ghetto on 10 Sept. 1942; 27 survived the war. The few dozen Jews remaining in N. were deported to the

Theresienstadt ghetto and Auschwitz. After the war a new community was formed by concentration camp survivors from Eastern Europe. It numbered about 200 in 1990.

NUSFALAU (Hung. Szilagynagyfalu) N. Transylvania dist., Rumania. Jews settled in the early 19th cent. and engaged in agriculture. The J. pop. in 1920 was 202 (10% of the total). In the 1920s many Jews were involved in the lumber industry. Zionist activity began in the 1930s. In May 1944 the community was transferred to the Simleul Silvaniei ghetto and in June the Jews were deported to Auschwitz.

NUSSLOCH Baden, Germany. The first three J. families arrived in 1743. Anti-J. riots broke out during the 1848 revolution. In 1866, Jews set up a cigarette factory that employed 300 by the end of the cent. The J. pop. numbered 65 in 1875 (total 2,766) but declined steadily thereafter to 21 in 1933. In the Nazi era, 11 emigrated and five left for other German cities. The last four Jews were deported to the Gurs concentration camp on 22 Oct. 1940.

NYEKLADHAZA Borsod dist., Hungary. Jews arrived in the first half of the 18th cent., mostly as tradesmen. They also opened a cement factory, distillery, and lumber yard. They numbered 121 in 1880 and 87 in 1930. During the White Terror attacks (1919–21), the rioting against the Jews was so severe that most J. families fled to Miskolc. In 1940, the men were taken to forced labor. Eight of 23 survived. In April 1944, the Jews were taken to Lenc and after six weeks to Diosgyor. On June 10, the remaining 67 Jews were deported to Auschwitz via Diosgyor.

NYIRABRANY Szabolcs dist., Hungary. Jews settled in the late 18th cent. They numbered 126 in 1880 and 167 in 1930. They suffered during the White Terror attacks (1919–21) after WWI, and their livelihoods were undermined under the 1938 racial laws. In June 1944, 200 including Jews from the surrounding area were deported to Auschwitz.

NYIRACSAD Szabolcs dist., Hungary. Jews settled in the 1730s, marketing farm produce from the area and supplying the farmers with goods. A synagogue was built in 1861. The J. pop. rose from 171 in 1880 to 210 in 1930. During the White Terror attacks

(1919–21), the Jews were attacked by local residents. The Zionists were not well received by the community. On 16 April 1944, the Jews were brought to Nyiregyhaza and from there sent to Harangod, where they were held under a reign of terror until final deportation to Auschwitz on 17 May. After the war, some J. women who had worked in Germany and 46 men who had been allowed to escape from forced labor camps by sympathetic commanders aware of SS plans to execute the remaining Jews reestablished the community but most eventually left, many for Israel.

NYIRADONY Szabolcs dist., Hungary. Jews arrived in the first half of the 19th cent. and numbered 199 in 1880 and 229 in 1930. J. livelihoods were undermined by Hungary's racial laws and in 1941 the young were subjected to forced labor. On 15 April 1944, the Jews were expelled to Nyiregyhaza and from there to Simapuszta. On 23 May, they were deported to Auschwitz. Thirty survivors reestablished the community after the war.

NYIRBATOR Szabolcs dist., Hungary. Jews settled in the late 18th cent. and controlled all the town's trade. The community was founded in 1816 by Shimon Mandel and his five sons, who also established a factory employing 400 workers. Mandel's grandson served in the Hungarian parliament. In 1869, the community split and the Orthodox created a separate congregation which gained control over smaller communities in the area. The J. pop. rose to 1,017 in 1900 and 1,899 (16% of the total) in 1941. Antisemitism was strongly felt throughout the community's existence. In 1922, bombs were placed in the Orthodox synagogue with the complicity of the police and in 1924, following an examination of citizenship papers, many J. family members were cruelly separated one from another. A regime of forced labor was instituted in the wake of Hungary's 1938 racial laws. On 22 April 1944, the Jews were expelled to Nyiregyhaza and on 17 May deported to Auschwitz. A postwar community of 500 helped many come to Israel. By 1958, there were no Jews left in N.

NYIRBELTEK Szabolcs dist., Hungary. Jews settled in the early 18th cent., numbering 108 in 1880 and 130 in 1930. In 1942, the young men were taken to forced labor. On 17 April 1944, the remaining 117 Jews, mainly women, children, and the elderly, were expelled to Nyiregyhaza and from there deported to Auschwitz on 17 May.

NYIRBOGAT Szabolcs dist., Hungary. Jews are first mentioned in 1747. Most were merchants dealing in grain, textiles, and food products. Their pop. grew to 278 in 1880 and 322 in 1930. In the early 1920s and late 1930s, they suffered from severe persecution, first during the White Terror attacks (1919–21) and later under the 1938 racial laws. On 17 May 1944, they were deported to Auschwitz via Nyiregyhaza.

NYIRBOGDANY Szabolcs dist., Hungary. Jews are first mentioned in 1770. They numbered 159 in 1880 and 130 in 1930. Twenty died under forced labor in WWII and the rest were deported to Auschwitz via Nyiregyhaza on 17 May 1944.

NYIRCSAHOLY Szatmar dist., Hungary. In the early 19th cent., estate owners encouraged the Jews to settle and promote trade in the area. A community was organized in 1832. A synagogue was built in 1849. In 1890, the J. pop. stood at 105, growing to 126 by 1941. Following WWI, demobilized soldiers attacked the Jews and J. property. The Zionists were active between the World Wars. In 1941, 32 men taken for forced labored perished in the Ukraine or at the Mauthausen and Gunskurchen concentration camps. On 30 May 1944, the Jews were deported to Auschwitz after being detained in Mateszalka from 23 April.

NYIRDERZS Szatmar dist., Hungary. Jews settled in the late 18th cent, numbering 105 in 1880 and 57 in 1930. At the end of May, they were deported to Auschwitz via Mateszalka.

NYIREGYHAZA Szabolcs dist., Hungary. Jews arrived c. 1840. From 17 June to 3 Aug. 1883, the Tiszaeszlar blood libel trial was held in N., leading to anti-J. agitation and the organization of J. defense groups After the 1869 split, Status Quo and Orthodox congregations existed side by side. A hasidic *shtibl* was opened in 1918 and a splendid synagogue designed by Lipot Baumhorn was consecrated in 1924. R. Bela Bernstein, who served in 1909–44, was one of the leading rabbis in Hungary. The J. pop. rose from 1,128 in 1869 (5% of the total) to 2,097 in 1880 (9% of the total) and around 5,000 between the World Wars (about 10% of the total). A J. school founded in 1865 reached an enrollment of 430 in 1940. The Zionists were active from the end of WWI with several youngsters arriving in Palestine in 1932–35. In April 1944, a ghetto was set up, where 11,000 Jews, many from the surrounding settlements, were confined. On 5 May, its inhabitants were dispersed in Nyirjes, Harangod, and Sima; a week later, deportations to Auschwitz commenced. A postwar community of 1,000 declined steadily, with many leaving for Israel after the 1956 revolt.

NYIRGALSA Szabolcs dist., Hungary. Jews settled in the mid-18th cent., mostly as tradesmen and farmers. They numbered 119 in 1880, dropping to 52 in 1930 as the young moved to the larger cities. Following the 1938 racial laws, young J. men were taken to forced labor battalions, where most died. The remaining Jews were deported to Auschwitz via Nyiregyhaza and Harangod in late May 1944.

NYIRGYULAJ Szabolcs dist., Hungary. Jews settled in the second half of the 18th cent., numbering 122 in 1880 and 89 in 1930. Most were small tradesmen. In 1942, the men were taken to forced labor. In late May 1944, the remaining Jews were deported to Auschwitz via Nyiregyhaza.

NYIRJAKO Szabolcs dist., Hungary. Jews are first mentioned in 1747 and numbered 74 in 1930. Following WWI, they suffered from anti-J. attacks by demobilized soldiers as well as from White Terror gangs. Several community leaders were sent to concentration camps and executed. The 1938 racial laws severely affected the economic status of the Jews. In 1940, the men were taken to forced labor, primarily within Hungary. In the beginning of May, the remaining Jews were transferred to Kisvarda and on 25–27 May deported to Auschwitz.

NYIRKARASZ Szabolcs dist., Hungary. Jews settled in the early 18th cent., numbering 220 in 1880 and 164 in 1930. Most were small storekeepers and peddlers. They suffered from the White Terror attacks (1919–21), the 1938 racial laws, and the general anti-semitic atmosphere between the World Wars. In late May 1944, they were deported to Auschwitz via Kisvarda.

NYIRLUGOS Szabolcs dist., Hungary. Jews arrived

in the first half of the 18th cent. and numbered 115 in 1880 and 145 in 1930. They were deported to Auschwitz via Nyiregyhaza on 22 May 1944.

NYIRMADA   Szabolcs dist., Hungary. J. settlement commenced in the mid-19th cent. Jews dominated the town's trade in lumber, leather, feathers, and agricultural produce and ran a number of factories manufacturing alcoholic beverages, vinegar, soap, and chemicals. The community maintained a kindergarten, *heder*, yeshiva, elementary school, and synagogue. In 1900, there were 200 Jews in N., rising to 532 in 1930. In 1941, 350 remained. On 23 April 1944, they were expelled to Kisvarda and on 25–27 May deported to Auschwitz and Birkenau, with the able-bodied transferred to the Dachau concentration camp. After the war, some 40 survivors reestablished the community, but by 1957 most Jews had left N.

NYIRMARTONFALVA   Szabolcs dist., Hungary. Jews settled in the late 19th cent and numbered 54 in 1930. They were deported to Auschwitz via Nyiregyhaza on 22 May 1944.

NYIRMEGGYES   Szatmar dist., Hungary. Jews settled in the first half of the 18th cent. and numbered 227 in 1880 and 139 in 1930. They were deported to Auschwitz via Mateszalka in late May 1944.

NYIRMIHALYDI   Szabolcs dist., Hungary. Jews settled in the first half of the 18th cent., numbering 137 in 1880 and 74 in 1930 as the young left for the larger cities. In 1942, the men were taken to forced labors and all J. stores and businesses forced to close down. On 22 May 1944, the remaining Jews were deported to Auschwitz via Nyiregyhaza.

NYIRTASS   Szabolcs dist., Hungary. Jews settled in the early 18th cent, under the protection of the Esterhazy family. The J. pop. rose from 150 in 1850 to 248 in 1930. Following WWI, the Jews responded to their increasing victimization by turning toward Hasidism. In 1941, 40 J. men seized for forced labor were sent to Poland and the Ukraine. Only nine survived. In late May 1944, the rest were deported to Auschwitz via Kisvarda.

NYMBURK   Bohemia, Czechoslovakia. A J. community was founded only in 1875 after a long-standing residence ban. A synagogue and J. school were opened as the J. pop. rose to 116 in 1891. In 1930, 83 Jews remained (total 11,892). Eight Jews were deported to the Theresienstadt ghetto on 16 April 1942.

NYRSKO   Bohemia, Czechoslovakia. Jews were probably present in the 15th cent. A small community existed in the 17th–18th cents. with Jews living in a special triangular-shaped quarter (*Judenwinkel*, or "Jew corner"). In the 18th cent., Jews were mostly peddlers and merchants. They subsequently became industrialists (glass polishing and optical lenses, textiles, matches), exported feathers, and operated a large flour mill and a sawmill. The J. pop. in 1930 was 139 (total 3,230). In 1942, the Jews were deported to the Theresienstadt ghetto together with the Jews of Prague and from there transported to the death camps of Poland. In spring 1945, 108 J. women were massacred nearby during a death march from Auschwitz.

O

OBBACH (in J. sources, Affikh) Lower Franconia, Germany. A J. community is known from the 18th cent. A synagogue was built in 1840 and a J. public school had 41 students in 1850. The J. pop. was 192 in 1867 (total 668) and 106 in 1933, with most owning homes and fields in the area of the synagogue and community center. On *Kristallnacht* (9–10 Nov. 1938), the synagogue was burned down and J. homes and stores were destroyed. In the 1937–41 period, 39 Jews emigrated, including 30 to the U.S. Of the 36 remaining in 1942, 30 were deported to Izbica in the Lublin dist. (Poland) via Wuerzburg in April and the last six, all aged, were sent to the Theresienstadt ghetto on 10 Sept. 1942.

OBCHUGA Minsk dist., Belorussia. J. settlement probably commenced in the first half of the 19th cent. The J. pop. was 412 (total 896) in 1897 and 272 in 1923 under the Soviets. The Germans occupied O. in early July 1941. The Jews still there were probably murdered in early Oct. with the rest of the Jews in the area.

OBELIAI (Yid. Avel) Rokiskis dist., Lithuania. Tombstones indicate that the J. community was over

Boating on the river, Obeliai, Lithuania, Oct. 1936

400 years old. It was split between Hasidim and *Mitnaggedim*, whose relations were acrimonious. There was no community organization to care for the needy. The J. pop. in 1897 was 652 (67% of the total). R. Eliezer Silver, from 1929 president of the Union of Orthodox Rabbis of the U.S. and Canada, was born here. In 1915 the Russians expelled the Jews. When Lithuania became independent the Jews returned, establishing a community in 1933. Growing antisemitism on the part of the Lithuanian government led to emigration to the U.S., South Africa, and Palestine. Intensive Zionist activities ended with the Soviet takeover in 1940. The Germans entered O. on 26 June 1941. Lithuanian nationalists arrested J. men, who were never seen again. J. men and women were taken by farmers for forced labor. On 25 Aug. 1941, armed Lithuanians rounded up 1,160 Jews from O. and neighboring towns, took them to nearby Antanose, and murdered them.

OBERALTERTHEIM Lower Franconia, Germany. The community probably began in the first half of the 17th cent. A cemetery was consecrated in 1792 and a new synagogue was built in 1827. The J. pop. was 90 in 1890 (total 751) and 22 in 1933. The synagogue was wrecked on *Kristallnacht* (9–10 Nov. 1938). In 1936–40, 16 Jews emigrated, 13 to the U.S. The last four were deported to Izbica in the Lublin dist. (Poland) via Wuerzburg on 24 April 1942.

OBERASPHE (now part of Muenchhausen) Hesse, Germany. The community numbered 41 (13% of the total) in 1871, but dwindled to 22 by 1933. Eleven Jews perished in the Holocaust.

OBERAULA Hesse–Nassau, Germany. Jews lived there from the 17th cent. and built a synagogue in 1837. They numbered 106 (11% of the total) in 1861 and 79 in 1933. Affiliated with the Marburg rabbinate, they were mostly cattle traders and farmers. Two nearby communities, Schwarzenborn (with 102 Jews in 1837) and Raboldshausen (144 in 1835), had practically vanished by 1925. On *Kristallnacht* (9–10 Nov. 1938), the synagogue in O. was destroyed; 61 Jews left (17 emigrating) and at least 16 perished in the Holocaust.

OBERDOLLENDORF Rhineland, Germany. An independent community existed around the turn of the 17th cent. A synagogue was in use in 1847, when the J. pop. was 42; it was burned on *Kristallnacht* (9–10 Nov. 1938). The community was eventually attached to the Bad Honnef congregation. Some Jews emigrated in the Nazi era. Seven perished.

OBERDORF Wuerttemberg, Germany. Jews first settled in 1510, living under protected status and a heavy tax burden. Their situation improved after 1810 with the transfer of rule to the Wuerttemberg principality, the J. pop. reaching a peak of 548 in 1854 (40% of the total) and Jews spearheading the prosperous economy with two big glue factories and other commercial activity. At mid-cent., Jews also began settling in the adjacent village of Bopfingen, from where they had been expelled in the 16th cent. In 1832, O. became the rabbinical seat for a number of surrounding settlements. The J. elementary school founded in the 1820s continued to operate until 1924. In 1933 there were 137 Jews in O. (including 50 in Bopfingen). They operated textile and chemical factories, engaged in the cattle trade, and owned stores. Despite good neighborly relations, Nazi pressure subsequently succeeded in isolating the Jews socially and economically. About 200 Jews arrived in O. from other settlements after 1933. Of the total J. pop., ten men were sent to the Dachau concentration camp and 230 managed to emigrate. The rest were deported and died in the Holocaust.

OBERELSBACH Lower Franconia, Germany. A J. community is known from the mid-18th cent. The J. pop. was 70 in 1837 (total 1,015). A new synagogue was built in 1899 after the first one burned down in 1895. In 1933, 28 Jews remained. On *Kristallnacht* (9–10 Nov. 1938), their homes were wrecked along with the synagogue. Subsequently 13 emigrated, 11 to the U.S. The last nine were deported in 1942, seven to Izbica in the Lublin dist. (Poland) and two to the Theresienstadt ghetto camp.

OBERGIMPERN Baden, Germany. Jews were expelled in the late 16th cent. and were present again in the 18th. A synagogue was built in 1820 and Jews were represented in the local council and the civil guard as their pop. grew to a peak of 70 in 1887 (around 5% of the total). In 1933, 17 remained; nine left in 1934–37 and four after *Kristallnacht* (9–10 Nov. 1938). Three perished in Auschwitz.

OBER-GLEEN   Hesse, Germany. The community numbered 58 (8% of the total) in 1880. All the Jews left by Oct. 1939, seven emigrating.

OBERGLOGAU   (Pol. Glogowek) Upper Silesia, Germany, today Poland. Jews probably arrived in the Middle Ages. However, a permanent settlement is known only from the early 19th cent. The community maintained a cemetery (possibly established in 1821). A synagogue was consecrated in 1864. The congregation was Progressive-Reform. In 1840, the J. pop. was 133 and in 1880 it reached a peak of 170. In 1933, 63 Jews remained. The Nazi racial laws instituted from 1933 were not applied to the Jews of O. until July 1937 because of the League of Nations' minority rights convention. Most Jews continued living in the city until that time. On *Kristallnacht* (9–10 Nov. 1938), the synagogue was set on fire and J. homes and stores were wrecked. Only six Jews remained on 19 Nov. 1942. Presumably those Jews who did not emigrate perished following deportation.

OBERGROMBACH   Baden, Germany. The J. community in 1825 numbered 43 and maintained a synagogue and cemetery dating from 1632. The last Jew was deported by the Germans to the Gurs concentration camp on 22 Oct. 1940.

OBERHAUSEN   Rhineland, Germany. Jews settled in the 1850s, most of them as merchants and butchers, opening shops in the center of the city. They were active in local life and when one was denied membership in a men's gymnastics club in 1890, all J. members demonstratively resigned. Until becoming independent in 1893, the community was part of the Muelheim regional congregation. A J. elementary school with 32 students was started in 1874 and a synagogue was consecrated in 1899. The J. pop. rose to 163 in 1890; 336 in 1905; and 686 (total 186,322) in 1925. Antisemitism rose from the mid-1920s but in the Weimar period, Jews continued to be active politically and socially in the city. They owned about 30 stores and altogether over 200 Jews in O. and the neighboring settlements of Sterkrade, Holten, and Osterfeld earned their livelihoods in trade. Their number included four doctors, four lawyers, three miners, and three musicians. Among the women, five were milliners. In 1932, 75 children attended public secondary schools. The Zionist movement started a local branch with 17

members in 1923. Both the Zionists and the East European Jews in the city were underrepresented in community bodies until the early 1930s, when Zionist support began to increase. The East Europeans conducted their own separate Orthodox prayer services. The local women's society started a kindergarten for needy children and the Bar Kokhba sports club was affiliated with the Maccabi organization. In the March 1933 elections, the Nazis received 31% of the vote for the Reichstag and 33% for the city assembly. In the same month, the J. pop. was 581. Persecution commenced immediately as J. lawyers were forced out of their practices and over 100 J. civil servants were dismissed from their jobs. In May, the first J. stores closed and during the year, six J. children were expelled from secondary schools. Other Jews were arrested. In 1935, German stores and restaurants stopped serving Jews. In Sept., Jews were prohibited from using public transportation facilities, a measure instituted in most other German cities only in the 1940s. The last Jews were expelled from secondary schools in summer 1938. On 28 Oct. 1938, 40 Jews with Polish citizenship were expelled (at least 11 perishing in the Holocaust). Efforts were made in the community to prepare members for emigration: 80–100 attended seven Hebrew courses and 60 studied English. Membership in the local Zionist group doubled and a Hehalutz group was also started. By late Oct. 1938, 263 Jews from O. and the three neighboring settlements had left. On *Kristallnacht* (9–10 Nov. 1938), the synagogue was burned, the J. cemetery was desecrated, J. homes and stores were destroyed, and about 30 Jews were sent to the Dachau concentration camp. Subsequently Jews were mobilized for forced labor. In May 1939, just 139 remained. These were moved to an abandoned furniture store designated a "J. house." Another 69 left up to 1941. Of those who emigrated throughout the period, 107 reached Palestine, 23 the U.S., 14 Argentina, 11 South Africa, and ten England. Of the 73 who left for Holland, 26 perished in camps in the east following deportations from there, as did two of the nine reaching Belgium and three of the 18 who fled to France. Deportations to the death camps from O. commenced in fall 1941.

OBERHAUSEN-WALLHALBEN   Palatinate, Germany. In 1804 a few Jews lived in O. and 65 in W.; in 1875, there were 42 in O. and 59 in W. The congregation was united but each village maintained its own J. cemetery. In 1900, the combined J. pop. was 43 and in June 1933 it was 31. Sixteen Jews emigrated in the Nazi era and 12 were deported to the Gurs concentration camp in 1940.

OBER-INGELHEIM   Hesse, Germany. Founded in the early 18th cent., the community numbered 166 (6% of the total) in 1871. Augmented by the Jews of Nieder-Ingelheim, O. began to develop. A synagogue in the Moorish style was constructed and a community center was established. Jews played a leading role in the twin township's affairs until the Nazi era. On *Kristallnacht* (9–10 Nov. 1938), stormtroopers destroyed the synagogue and looted J. homes. Of the 134 Jews living there and in Nieder-Ingelheim after 1933, at least 48 emigrated. Those who remained in Germany were mostly deported to the camps in 1942.

OBER-KLINGEN   Hesse, Germany. The community, numbering 62 (9% of the total) in 1861, dispersed after *Kristallnacht* (9–10 Nov. 1938), 14 Jews being deported to Nazi camps in 1942.

OBERLAHNSTEIN   (now part of Lahnstein) Hesse–Nassau, Germany. Jews living there in medieval times fell victim to a blood libel in 1287 and the Black Death persecutions of 1348–49. Established around 1700, the modern community opened a synagogue and numbered 64 (1% of the total) in 1885. During the Weimar Republic it was affiliated with the rabbinate of Bad Ems and had members in Braubach, Camp, and Niederlahnstein. As a result of the Nazi boycott, 22 Jews left before the *Kristallnacht* pogroms (9–10 Nov. 1938); at least 44 Jews from the area perished in the Holocaust.

OBERLAURINGEN   Lower Franconia, Germany. The J. community was founded by the early 18th cent. A cemetery was consecrated in 1832 and a new synagogue in 1864. In 1880 the J. pop. reached a peak of 177 (total 927), thereafter declining steadily to 47 in 1933. On *Kristallnacht* (9–10 Nov. 1938), rioters vandalized the synagogue and J. homes. All J. men were arrested and held at the Hofheim prison and forced to engage in hard labor. They were then sent to the Dachau concentration camp. Thirty Jews managed to leave O. in 1938–40, 20 of them emigrating from Germany. Of the last 17, 13 were deported to Izb-

ica in the Lublin dist. (Poland) via Wuerzburg on 25 April 1942.

OBERLUSTADT   Palatinate, Germany. The J. pop. was 188 in 1848 and 108 (total 1,370) in 1875. A cemetery was opened in 1824 (and desecrated in 1828) and a synagogue in 1851 (together with Niederlustadt). The two communities also operated a joint elementary school in 1836–1905. In 1932, the J. pop. was 26. Most Jews left in the Nazi era. From among the last ten deported to the Gurs concentration camp in Oct. 1940, seven perished. Three others from the community also died in the Holocaust. The synagogue was burned down on *Kristallnacht* (9–10 Nov. 1938).

OBER-MOCKSTADT   Hesse, Germany. The community numbered 43 (6% of the total) in 1861 and 27 in 1933. Thirteen Jews left before *Kristallnacht* (9–10 Nov. 1938) and by Feb. 1939 none remained.

OBERMOSCHEL   Palatinate, Germany. Four J. families were present in 1786 and 15 (64 Jews) in 1848. A cemetery was opened in 1819 and a synagogue in 1841. The J. pop. was 85 (total 1,347) in 1900 and 35 in 1932–33. No Jews remained by Sept. 1939. The local J. elementary school closed in 1926 and the synagogue was wrecked on *Kristallnacht* (9–10 Nov. 1938).

OBERNAI   (Ger. Oberehnheim) Bas-Rhin dist., France. The first evidence of the presence of Jews dates from 1215. They were persecuted in 1336 and massacred in 1349. Over the next two centuries, there were Jews in O., but they only received permission to settle on a permanent basis in 1647, when O. was annexed to France. In 1720, 21 J. families resided in O. A synagogue was built in 1749. By 1784 there were 196 Jews in O. and in 1883 there were 219. A synagogue was inaugurated in 1876 and a small cemetery was purchased at the beginning of the 20th cent. By 1936, the community consisted of 138 members. During WWII, they were expelled to the south of France with the rest of Alsace-Lorraine Jews and the synagogue was destroyed. In 1948, O. Jews restored their synagogue. In 1970, there were 70 Jews.

OBERNBREIT   Lower Franconia, Germany. Jews were present in the 16th cent. under letters of protection. They numbered 126 in 1867 (total 1,355) and nine in 1933, when they were attached to the Markt-breit community Under the Nazis, five left and four were deported to Izbica in the Lublin dist. (Poland) and to the Theresienstadt ghetto in 1942.

OBERNKIRCHEN Hesse–Nassau, Germany. The community numbered 91 (4% of the total) in 1861 and 57 in 1925. Several Jews died in Auschwitz and other Nazi camps.

OBER-OLM Hesse, Germany. The community, numbering 43 (3% of the total) in 1900, had members in Klein-Winternheim. During the Nazi era, 17 Jews emigrated to the U.S.; six were deported in 1942.

OBER-RAMSTADT Hesse, Germany. Numbering 95 (over 3% of the total) in 1871, the community had shrunk to 26 before *Kristallnacht* (9–10 Nov. 1938), when the synagogue and J. property were destroyed. By WWII, 48 Jews had emigrated (37 to the U.S.), others moving elsewhere. Two of the 15 Jews deported in 1942 to the Theresienstadt ghetto and Polish death camps survived the Holocaust.

OBERSEEMEN Hesse, Germany. Established in the 18th cent., the community grew to 151 (17% of the total) in 1861 and opened a new synagogue 40 years later. Nazi violence mounted from 1933 and early in 1938 the community disbanded, leaving only 13 Jews. On *Kristallnacht* (9–10 Nov. 1938) a pogrom was staged. Most younger Jews emigrated before WWII; others perished in the Holocaust.

OBERTHULBA Lower Franconia, Germany. The 19th cent. community reached a peak pop. of 64 in 1871 (total 849), dropping to 44 in 1933. Most Jews ran auxiliary farms, where a group of religious youth was sent in 1937 for pioneer training. On *Kristallnacht* (9–10 Nov. 1938), the synagogue and J. homes were vandalized. In the 1936–40 period, 16 Jews left O., 13 for the U.S. The last 11 Jews were expelled via Wuerzburg at the end of April 1942 and from there deported to Izbica in the Lublin dist. (Poland).

OBERTYN Stanislawow dist., Poland. The J. settlement probably dates from the late 17th cent. The J. pop. in 1900 was 2,070 (40% of the total). Between the World Wars, with the J. pop. declining to 1,131, the Zionist movement became very active. Red Army

units entered the town on 9 Sept. 1939 and closed down the community's institutions while continuing to allow freedom of worship. When the Red Army left at the end of June 1941, Ukrainian nationalists instituted a reign of terror in the region. The community enjoyed a short respite with the Hungarian occupation, but in Aug. the Germans gained control of the town and instituted a regime of repressive measures, including forced labor. On 14 April 1942 many Jews were expelled to Kolomyja. Five hundred who remained were deported on 7–10 Sept. 1942, most to the Belzec death camp via Horodenka. Seventy-five Jews survived (37 of whom had been in hiding in O.).

OBERURSEL Hesse–Nassau, Germany. Established in the 17th cent., the community opened a synagogue in 1803. It numbered 59 (2% of the total) in 1871 and 57 in 1925. Most of the 33 Jews who remained in 1933 left by 1939, 12 emigrating.

OBERWALDBEHRUNGEN Lower Franconia, Germany. Jews settled in the mid-18th cent. and operated a synagogue, cemetery, and J. school by the mid-19th cent. In 1837 the J. pop. was 130 (total 340) and in 1933, eight. The last Jew left in Oct. 1938.

OBERWARTH Burgenland, Austria. A J. settlement was founded only in 1868. In 1903 a synagogue was inaugurated and the community maintained a cemetery and a J. elementary school. During the 1910s and 1920s, Jews served on the city council. They were engaged in trade and were represented in the professional class as lawyers and bankers. In 1934, there were 236 Jews in O. After the *Anschluss* (13 March 1938), private and community property was liquidated immediately. Almost all Jews left for Vienna; others succeeded in escaping. The community came to an end in Oct. 1938.

OBERWEILERSBACH Upper Franconia, Germany. A J. community of 81 (total 425) existed in 1810 but was disbanded in 1876.

OBERWESEL Rhineland, Germany. A J. community was already in existence in the mid-13th cent. Forty Jews from O. and from neighboring Boppard were murdered in 1287 in riots brought on by a blood libel in which Jews were accused of murdering a Christian youth before Easter. The community was again victimized in 1337 in the Armleder massacres and in 1349 it was destroyed in the Black Death persecutions. Jews were again present in the early 19th cent., their pop. ranging from 30 to 55 until the Nazi period. In 1932, the J. pop. was 44. Eighteen Jews perished in the Holocaust. The synagogue built in 1886 was wrecked on *Kristallnacht* (9–10 Nov. 1938).

OBODOVKA Vinnitsa dist., Ukraine. Jews numbered 33 in 1865 and 1,676 (total 7,754) in 1897. Jews were attacked in a pogrom by the Zeleny gang in May 1919. In the mid-1920s, a J. elementary school (four grades) was opened and in 1924 a few dozen Jews set up an agricultural commune. In 1939, the J. pop. dropped to 535. When the Germans captured O. on 28 July 1941, they attached it to Transnistria and set up a closed ghetto which held 9,000 Jews whom the Rumanians expelled from Bukovina and Bessarabia. Five thousand Jews (according to the Soviets, 11,000) died of starvation and disease there. Throughout the region there were numerous camps and about 25,000 refugees probably perished in them.

OBOLTSY Vitebsk dist., Belorussia. The J. pop. was 421 in 1897 and 353 (total 382) in 1923 under the Soviets. Most Jews earned their livelihoods in agriculture. Thirty J. families worked at the Svoboda kolkhoz founded in 1928. The Germans occupied the town in July 1941. A ghetto for the remaining 150 Jews who had not fled or been evacuated was established on 14 Aug. Sixty Jews escaped to the forest and joined the partisans after learning of the execution of the Jews of neighboring Smoliany. The rest were murdered on 4 June 1942.

OBORNIKI Poznan dist., Poland. Jews first settled in the first half of the 16th cent. The wealthier among them were lumber merchants; others dealt in salt and pickled fish. They were joined by tradesmen (bakers, tailors, butchers, shoemakers) after the annexation to Prussia in 1793. From the mid-19th cent., friction between the Orthodox and Liberal camps became marked. In 1878, the community reached a peak pop. of 395 (total 2,379) and then declined steadily, with large numbers leaving for Germany after WWI. Sixty Jews remained in 1939. On 9 Dec. they were expelled by the Germans to General Gouvernement territory. Shortly afterwards a forced labor camp was set up in the town for Jews from various other places.

OBOYAN Kursk dist., Russia. J. settlement probably began in the early 20th cent. In 1926, the J. pop. was 118 (total 12,200). After their arrival in mid-Nov. 1941, the German murdered the few Jews who had neither fled nor been evacuated.

OBRZYCKO Poznan dist., Poland. A J. community of 476 existed at the time of the annexation to Prussia in 1793 and an organized community existed with a synagogue and elementary school from 1825. The merchant class prospered in the 19th cent., opening large stores, while the wealthier Jews set up factories later in the cent. The scholar Abraham Berliner (1833–1915) was born there. The first Zionist group was formed in 1906. The J. pop. reached a peak of 700 (total 1,700) in 1841 and then declined steadily through emigration, few remaining by 1939.

OBUDA Pest-Pilis-Solt-Kiskun dist., Hungary. Although there was a prosperous J. community in O. during the 15th cent., it ended with the Turkish conquest in 1526. Jews once again began settling there in 1712, subsequently arriving from Moravia, Czechoslovakia, Poland, Austria, and Italy. They enjoyed the patronage of Countess Zichy, who granted them freedom of worship and trade. Their rights and obligations, for which they were obliged to pay heavily, were set out in a document issued in 1746 and later extended in 1765. In 1746, they were joined by Jews from nearby Buda after their expulsion by Maria Theresa and in 1749 they were subjected to a tolerance tax by the empress. The J. pop. reached 1,647 in 1785 and 3,530 in 1840. The community's first synagogue was built in 1738. A Great Synagogue consecrated in 1820 was considered at the time to be the most beautiful in the Hapsburg Empire. A J. hospital with 16 beds was built in 1772 (closed in 1899). In 1783, a dist. school was housed in one of the community's buildings, but it aroused opposition because of the employment of Christian teachers. The community established a school with J. teachers in 1790 (closed in 1869). In 1793, Moshe Muenz (1750–1831) was named chief rabbi of the district with his seat in O., making it one of the great centers of Orthodox Jewry in Hungary. From the early 19th cent., J. weavers in O. were famous throughout the land, with J. tailors even manufacturing frocks for the clergy. Between the World Wars, the J. pop. was about 4,000, with some entering the professional class. A new J. school enrolled 150 students in 1927 and among the Zionists, Hashomer Hatzair and Betar were active. After the German occupation of 1944, the situation of the Jews deteriorated radically. On 15 Oct., members of Ferenc Szalasi's antisemitic Arrow Cross Party seized Jews and tortured them to death. In early Nov., the Jews were expelled to Pest and on the 10th sent on a death march to the Austrian border, where SS forces awaited them. Many escaped and returned to Pest, where the Zionist underground supplied them with food, money, documents, and guidance. About 3,000 Jews from O. died in the Holocaust. The postwar community amalgamated with Budapest in 1949.

OBUKHOW Kiev dist., Ukraine. Jews settled in the early 19th cent. In an 1881 pogrom, 186 J. families had their homes looted and destroyed. The J. pop. was 1,140 (total 8,596) in 1897. On 25 July 1919, the Zeleny gang pillaged and destroyed J. property and on 10 Sept. 1919 the Petlyura bands staged a similar pogrom. During the Soviet period, the J. pop. was around 100. The Germans captured O. on 30 July 1941 and murdered the Jews there shortly afterwards.

OCHAKOV Nikolaiev dist., Ukraine. Jews settled in the 18th cent. and numbered 1,480 (total 10,786) in 1897. A stone synagogue was erected in 1853. In the Soviet period, the J. pop. dropped to 377 in 1939. The Germans arrived on 21 Aug. 1941 and in Sept. and early Oct. murdered 97 Jews.

OCHOTNICA Cracow dist., Poland. The J. pop. in 1921 was 103 (total 3,018). The Germans deported the Jews to the Belzec death camp on 30 Aug. 1942 via Nowy Targ.

OCHTRUP Westphalia, Germany. One J. family was present in 1720. The community grew to eight families (31 Jews) by the mid-19th cent. Most were engaged in petty trade. A synagogue was opened in 1868. On the eve of the Nazi assumption of power, the J. pop. was about 41 (total 8,197). On *Kristallnacht* (9–10 Nov. 1938), the synagogue was vandalized. Most Jews left before the outbreak of war: four to South America and the rest to Holland (about 25) and Belgium (two). Eight moved to other localities in Germany. The last two Jews were deported, as were 19 who had remained in Germany or fled to Holland.

OCKENHEIM Hesse, Germany. Established around 1750, the community numbered 57 (over 4% of the total) in 1895 and 29 in 1933. No Jews remained after Sept. 1938.

OCNA SUGATAG (Hung. Aknasugatag) N. Transylvania dist., Rumania. Jews settled in the late 19th cent. The J. pop. in 1920 was 142 (7% of the total). In April 1944 the Jews were transferred to the Berbesti ghetto and then deported to Auschwitz.

OCSA Pest-Pilis-Solt-Kiskun dist., Hungary. The community was formed in 1904 and numbered 153 in 1941. On 8 July 1944 the Jews were deported to Auschwitz via Lajosmizse and Monor.

ODELSK Bialystok dist., Poland, today Belarus. Jews first settled in the late 17th cent. In the late 18th cent. Jews from western Poland began to arrive, expelled by the Prussian administration as "unproductive." In 1849, 26 of the poorest families settled on farm land in the area. The J. pop. reached 234 (total 1,462) in 1897 and maintained a level of about 100 families between the World Wars. The Germans took the town in June 1941 and in Nov. 1942 sent the Jews to the Kelbasin transit camp and shortly thereafter to Auschwitz.

ODENBACH Palatinate, Germany. The J. pop. was 25 in 1804 and 124 in 1848. In 1932 it was 27 (total 1,000). Most Jews left the village in the Nazi era. The last two were deported to the Gurs concentration camp on 22 Oct. 1940 and perished in the Holocaust along with another two Jews from the community. The synagogue (erected in 1752) survived the *Kristallnacht* riots (9–10 Nov. 1938). Owing to its wall paintings, it was declared a preserved site after the war and renovated.

ODENHEIM Baden, Germany. Jews are mentioned in 1548 and were living in straitened economic circumstances in the early 19th cent. Their situation improved later in the cent. with the development of the local tobacco industry. The J. pop. reached a peak of 125 in 1871 (around 5% of the total) and then dropped steadily through emigration and the exodus to the big cities, totaling 20 in 1933. Thirteen Jews emigrated in 1935–39. The last four were deported to the Gurs concentration camp on 22 Oct. 1940. Four who had earlier emigrated to France were deported after the German occupation. Only one survived.

ODENKIRCHEN Rhineland, Germany. Jews are first mentioned in 1346. In 1730, 12 Jews were present and in the second half of the 19th cent. their number ranged between 85 and 95. In 1854 the community became part of the Moenchengladbach regional congregation and in 1890 it became a satellite of Rheydt. A synagogue was erected in 1817 and a new one was consecrated in 1911. In the Weimar period, Jews were active mainly in commerce and industry. The J. pop. was 112 in 1924 and 90 in 1932. The synagogue was destroyed on *Kristallnacht* (9–10 Nov. 1938). In spring 1939, the remaining Jews were moved to two houses. Three were deported to the Riga ghetto on 11 Dec. 1942 and four to the Theresienstadt ghetto on 25 July.

ODESSA Odessa dist., Ukraine. Five Jews were present when the Russians captured the Turkish fortress of Khadzhibei in 1789. Jews from Volhynia, Podolia, Lithuania, and later Galicia streamed to the port built on the site in 1794 by Catherine II. In 1795 they numbered 246 (total 2,350). An organized community with a synagogue, cemetery, *talmud torah*, and charitable institutions existed by 1798. A hospital was built two years later. Until the mid-19th cent., Jews engaged mainly in the grain and textile trade. The development of the port and official encouragement of J. settlement served to stimulate the growth of the J. pop. and its economic prosperity. From the mid-19th cent., the Jews also dominated the trade in cattle and hides. By 1910, 80% of grain exports were in J. hands as well as half the city's wholesale trade and 70% of its banks. In the same period, 70% of the city's doctors were Jews as were half its lawyers and a third of its engineers, architects, and chemists. About two-thirds of the Jews were artisans and manual laborers. In the second half of the 19th cent., numerous educational institutions were established, including two public schools, one for boys and the other for girls, a *talmud torah*, 51 *hadarim*, a German-language school for Galician children, and a number of private schools. In 1860, there were 44 synagogues and prayer houses. Assimilationists and Haskala proponents dominated the community and shaped its institutions. By the early 20th cent., the community maintained 200 *hadarim* for 5,000 children while another 6,500 children attended 40 elementary

Cover of score of Avraham Goldfaden's musical "Shulamit," Odessa, Russia, 1883 (Beth Hatefutsoth Photo Archive, Tel Aviv/photo courtesy of Yad Vashem, The Holocaust Martyrs' and Heroes' Remembrance Authority, Jerusalem)

schools, including 13 supported by the Society for the Promotion of Culture among the Jews of Russia, which had one of its largest and most active branches in O. Half the children in state-run secondary schools were Jews and another 2,500 J. children studied in private secondary schools. A further 700 were enrolled in J. vocational schools and in 1906, 746 Jews were studying at the local university. A modern yeshiva was founded in 1866 and later headed by Rav Tza'ir (Hayyim Tchernowitz). Its teachers included Hayyim Nahman Bialik and Yosef Klausner, the literary critic and historian. The first Hebrew newspaper, *Ha-Melitz*, was published in O. in 1860–70 before moving to Petersburg. During 1860, the Russian-language weekly *Razsvet*, founded by Osip Rabinovich, was also published in O. *Kol Mevasser*, edited by Alexander Zederbaum, started appearing in 1863. In 1869 the Russian-language *Den*, edited by S. Orenstein, I. Orshanski, and M. Margulis, and *Zion*, edited by E. Soloveichik and L. Pinsker, began to appear. During this period, Vladimir Jabotinsky and his circle were active in O. In 1897, the J. pop. was 138,935 (total 403,815). In addition, an unknown number of unregistered Jews of the poorer class as well as 1,049 Karaites were living there. In effect, Jews comprised about 40% of the city's pop. In 1879, Avraham Goldfaden arrived in O. and set up a J. theater troupe, the first in Imperial Russia. The group appeared in the big cities until broken up by the authorities. Jews were attacked and their property pillaged in 1821, 1859, 1871, and 1881. The jobless and local thugs responsible for the attacks were stirred up by rival Christian merchants while the authorities turned a blind eye to the violence. The most violent outburst occurred in 1905, when 300 Jews were killed and thousands injured in a pogrom organized with the collusion of the authorities. Among the victims were members of the J. self-defense groups. After the Oct.

1917 Revolution, J. officers and soldiers in the Association of J. Combatants organized defense units that prevented further pogroms during the civil war (1918–21). O. was the chief center of the Hovevei Zion movement from where the call of Moshe Leib Lilienblum and the *Auto-Emancipation* (1882) of Pinsker, analyzing the roots of antisemitism, were issued. After the Kattowitz Conference, O. became the movement's headquarters. In 1889, Ahad Ha-Am (Asher Ginsberg) founded the Benei Moshe society, whose aim was to organize activists and intellectuals for movement work. In 1890, the O. Committee was established with government approval. It was known officially as the Society for the Support of Agricultural Workers and Craftsmen in Syria and Palestine. The first settlers left for Eretz Israel through the port of O., making it the "Gateway to Zion." The numerous writers and activists working for the Zionist movement and its institutions included Lilienblum, Ahah Ha-Am, M. Ussishkin, who headed the O. Committee for the last ten years of its existence, Meir Dizengoff (later Tel Aviv's first

Prominent Jewish writers and historians in Odessa, Ukraine, 1913 (r. to l.: Yehoshua Rawnitzki, Mendele Mokher Seforim, Simon Dubnow, Hayyim Nahman Bialik, Alter Druyanow) (YIVO Archive, New York/photo courtesy of Yad Vashem, The Holocaust Martyrs' and Heroes' Remembrance Authority, Jerusalem)

mayor), Zalman Epstein, Yom Tov Lewinsky, M. Ben-Ammi, Y. Rawnitzki, Bialik, Alter Druyanow, Tchernowitz, M. Gluecksohn, and Jabotinsky. A number of important literary publications were also founded at the time: *Kavveret* (1890), *Pardes* (1891–95), *Ha-Shilo'ah* (1897–1902), and *Haolam* (1907–12). The Devir publishing house founded by Bialik, Rawnitzki, S. Ben-Zion, and Lewinsky helped spread Hebrew literature. In the 1920s it moved to Palestine. Other writers participating in O.'s literary life were Mendele Mokher Soferim, S. Dubnow, S. Frug, Shaul Tchernichowsky, Y. Berkowitz, Y. Fichmann, Z. Shneour, A.A. Kabak, and E. Steinman. The Zionist leadership and the assimilationist Society for the Promotion of Culture engaged in an ongoing debate. Under the pressure of the *Yevsektsiya*, a group of Zionist writers and activists left for Palestine in June 1921. In the Soviet period, Kharkov and Kiev became the centers of Yiddish culture. A Yiddish faculty existed at the university, which also engaged in the study of J. history in southern Russia. Only 22% of J. children attended Yiddish-language schools. During the 1920s, various militia organizations and law courts conducted their business in Yid-

dish. In 1926, pedagogical courses were transferred from Kharkov to O. to create a J. department in the local teachers' college. There was also a department to train officials for the cooperatives and J. councils. A. J. vocational school funded by the Joint Distribution Committee was in operation and in 1927 a museum of J. culture was opened. The many J. libraries were amalgamated into a single one named after Mendele Mokher Seforim, where books were censored in the Soviet spirit. J. operetta and theater groups of indifferent quality also operated under state auspices. Isaac Babel, whose stories of life in O. were dramatized and are still popular, perished in Stalin's purges. In the late 1920s, numerous J. institutions were closed down in the drive to destroy J. culture. In 1939, the J. pop. was 200,961 (total 604,217).

German and Rumanian forces occupied O. on 16 Oct. 1941. The city was then full of J. refugees from Bukovina, Bessarabia, and the cities of the southern Ukraine. On 22 Oct., Soviet partisans blew up Rumanian military headquarters in the city, killing and wounding hundreds of officers and soldiers. In retaliation, 5,000 people were executed the next day and

Convocation of Jewish farmers, Odessa, Ukraine, 1926

large numbers of Jews were arrested. All the Jews were then ordered to appear for registration in the suburb of Dalnik. On 24 Oct., 5,000 were packed into four wooden buildings on the outskirts of the city and burned to death. Another two buildings filled with Jews were burned down the next day and a further 1,000 Jews were incinerated on 15 Nov. Those who reported for registration were taken to Bogdanovka. On 7 Dec., O. became the capital of Rumanian Transnistria. At the same time, it was decided to eliminate the remaining Jews. On 9–11 Jan. 1942, they were ordered into a ghetto in the Slobodka quarter. In the next month, 33,000 Jews were brought to the Berezovka region and murdered by local German "self-defense" units. One German unit from the village of Likhtenfeld murdered 1,200 Jews. Jews were also brought to the Ivanov, Voznesensk, and Mostovoi regions, where they were shot or died of exposure or starvation. About 70,000 Jews perished in the Nazi occupation. Many who had joined the Soviet urban underground like Robert Soifer and Prof. Tatiana Bragarenko-Friedman, or the catacomb fighting units and the local partisan units, fell in battle. After the liberation of the city on 10 April 1944, Jews began to return. The authorities frustrated efforts to mark the mass graves with a monument and eight Jews who had raised money for the purpose were sentenced to 8–10 years of imprisonment in the Soviet camps. According to the 1958 census, the J. pop. was 102,000, but the real figure was probably higher. By 1979, 86,000 remained.

ODOBESTI Moldavia dist., Rumania. Jews first settled in this vineyard area in 1820. The J. pop. in 1899 was 1,312 (28% of the total). In 1895 a modern J. school was set up and by 1899 it had 120 pupils. Zionist activity began in 1895. Jews suffered under the rule of the Iron Guard and J.-owned vineyards were confiscated in fall 1940. The J. pop. in 1941 was 522 (7% of the total). With the outbreak of the Soviet-Rumanian war, 60 J. males aged 18 and over were taken to Videle and in fall 1942 were sent to Vapniarca in Transnistria. The other males were sent to forced labor camps, but returned at the end of the war.

ODOREU (Hung. Szatmarudvari) N. Transylvania dist., Rumania. Jews from Galicia settled in the late 18th cent. The J. pop. in 1900 was 162 (9% of the total). They engaged in agriculture and were the first to introduce modern methods. In May 1944 the com-munity was transferred to the Satu Mare ghetto and in June deported to Auschwitz.

ODORHEI (Hung. Szekeluudvarhely) N. Transylvania dist., Rumania. Jews settled in the 1850s and in the 1880s were involved in the lumber industry. Between the World Wars skilled J. workers from Maramures settled. The J. pop. in 1930 was 313 (4% of the total). Zionist youth groups were formed in 1924. In summer 1941, Jews originating from Maramures were expelled and murdered by Hungarian soldiers in Kamenets-Podolski. In May 1944 the J. community was taken to the Sfantul Gheorghe ghetto and then deported to Auschwitz.

ODRZYWOL Lodz dist., Poland. The J. pop. was 342 in 1897 and 321 in 1939. In 1935 farmers incited by the Endecja attacked Jews and ransacked their market stands. In 1941 the Jews were ghettoized, on 20 Aug. 1942 transported to Nowe Miasto, and later executed in the Treblinka death camp.

OEDHEIM Wuerttemberg, Germany. The Teutonic Order, which controlled most of the village's land, opposed J. settlement, so that Jews arrived only after it was annexed in 1805 by the kingdom of Wuerttemberg. Their pop. reached a peak of 94 in 1828 but declined steadily thereafter. Most were engaged in the cattle trade. A synagogue was built in 1864. Fifteen Jews lived in N. in 1933, of whom nine emigrated. Those who remained were attacked on *Kristallnacht* (9–10 Nov. 1938) and eventually expelled to the Theresienstadt ghetto, where they died.

OEDT Rhineland, Germany. Jews were present by the 17th cent., numbering 54 in 1871 and 13 in 1925. Seven perished in the Holocaust, three after deportation to the Riga ghetto.

OEHRINGEN Wuerttemberg, Germany. Jews were already present in the mid-13th cent. All were murdered in the Black Death persecutions of 1348–49 and the J. settlement was only renewed in the mid-19th cent., with the Jews maintaining a pop. of 150–180 (4% of the total) until the Nazi era. Jews played a leading role in the town's economic life as retailers and wholesalers. Seventeen of the 24 Jews serving in WWI received the Iron Cross. The J. pop. in 1933 was 163. Under the Nazis, around three-quarters emigrated. Of the 36 expelled to the east, three survived the war.

OELDE Westphalia, Germany. Jews are known from the late 16th cent. A permanent settlement was apparently established around 1680. At least two families were present in 1730, four in 1795, and five in 1803. A synagogue was erected in 1742 and a cemetery was opened in 1775. Living under letters of protection, Jews primarily earned their living as merchants, peddlers, and butchers. A new synagogue was consecrated in 1829. In 1821 and 1831, a number of Jews converted to Catholicism. The J. pop. grew to a peak of 87 (total 2,556) in 1871. From 1853, O. was the seat of a regional congregation. Jews were active in local social clubs and one was head of the volunteer firemen. In 1932, the J. pop. was 41. Jews began to emigrate in small numbers from the onset of Nazi rule. Six left for the U.S. in 1937 and by late Oct. 1938 another five emigrated. On *Kristallnacht* (9–10 Nov. 1938), the synagogue was wrecked and at least eight J. homes and stores were destroyed. In early 1939, a J. family of eight emigrated to Argentina. From 30 April 1939, the remaining Jews were forced to reside in two special "J. houses." On 10 Dec. 1941, 13 Jews were deported to the Riga ghetto and Stutthof concentration camp via Muenster. Nine perished in the Holocaust.

OELS (Pol. Olesnica) Lower Silesia, Germany, today Poland. J. settlement commenced no later than 1329. In 1535, the Jews were expelled and the synagogue was converted into an armory. The community was reestablished only in the 18th cent. Its pop. in 1758 was 24. A synagogue was consecrated in 1817 and a cemetery was opened around the same time. In 1845, the J. pop. was 121, increasing to 335 in 1885. From the early 20th cent., O. became the seat of the regional rabbinate and numerous organizations were active within the community, such as the Central Union (C.V.) and the J. Youth League. The J. pop. nonetheless declined in this period, standing at 118 in 1925 and 114 in 1933. On *Kristallnacht* (9–10 Nov. 1938), the synagogue and a number of J. homes were set on fire and five J. stores were destroyed. Seventeen Jews remained in 1939 and only four Jews, married to non-Jews, in Nov. 1942. No further information is available about the fate of the community under the Nazis. Presumably those who did not leave on time were deported and died.

OESTRINGEN Baden, Germany. Jews probably settled in the early 18th cent. A synagogue was consecrated in 1834 and the J. pop. grew to a peak of 99 (4% of the total) in 1871 as their economic position improved. Jews opened four cigarette factories and most operated auxiliary farms. The J. pop. then dropped sharply through emigration to the big cities, leaving ten Jews in 1933. Three left and the rest were deported in 1940.

OETTINGEN Swabia, Germany. The community was virtually destroyed in the Rindfleisch massacres of 1298 and the Black Death persecutions of 1348–49. Jews were present again in the late 14th cent. under ducal protection. In the 17th cent. they were active as moneylenders and horse and cattle traders. With the city divided between two rival duchies, two J. communities arose in the second half of the 17th cent., each constituting the seat of a district rabbinate. In 1690 the Jews were saved from a pogrom in a blood libel and commemorated the event annually by a special fast until the 20th cent. A new synagogue was consecrated in 1853. In 1857, 88 children were enrolled in a J. public school. The J. pop. reached a peak of 430 in 1837 (total 3,210) and thereafter declined steadily to 66 in 1933. On *Kristallnacht* (9–10 Nov. 1938), the synagogue was vandalized and 13 Torah scrolls were destroyed; afterwards J. homes and stores were wrecked. Forty-five Jews left for other German cities in the Nazi era; another ten emigrated. Of the remaining Jews, eight were deported to Piaski (Poland) via Munich on 3 April 1942.

OFEHERTO Szabolcs dist., Hungary. Jews settled in the late 18th cent. and numbered 120 in 1930. About 80 perished in the Holocaust after deportation via Kisvarda to Auschwitz on 25–27 May 1944.

OFFENBACH A. GLAN Rhineland, Germany. The J. pop. was 50–100 in the first half of the 19th cent., mostly employed as merchants and cattle dealers, with a few butchers, brokers, and servants. In 1870–85, the community reached a peak pop. of 130 (16–17% of the total). It then dropped to 99 in 1900 and 32 in 1932. The community maintained a cemetery and a synagogue built in 1915 to replace the old one.

The J. elementary school operating in the late 19th cent. closed in 1909 for lack of students. Twenty Jews remained in 1933. Eight emigrated before the outbreak of war in 1939. The rest left for other German cities. The synagogue and four J. homes were vandalized on *Kristallnacht* (9–10 Nov. 1938)

OFFENBACH AM MAIN Hesse, Germany. After the Jews living there fell victim to the Black Death persecutions of 1348–49, no independent community was established until 1706, when it numbered about 100 families. During the 18th cent., Hebrew printing flourished and among the well-known Jews residing in O. were R. Yaakov Yehoshua Falk (d. 1756), a great halakhic authority, and the notorious Shabbatean pseudo-messiah Jakob Frank, whose luxurious court was visited by thousands of "Frankists" (1788–91) and maintained by his daughter Eva after he died (1791–1817). Wolf Breidenbach, the wealthiest and most influential German Jew of his time, succeeded in having the shameful "body tax" (*Leibzoll*) abolished in 1805. Numbering 1,078 (over 6% of the total) by 1861, the community maintained its ties with Frankfurt Jewry and members promoted the growth of local industries (textiles and footwear). While the noted J. thinker Solomon Formstecher was rabbi (1842–89), Liberal Judaism became predominant and 25 local families established an Orthodox congregation in 1862 without seceding from the community. A modern synagogue center was built in 1913–16. Prior to WWI, the number of East European Jews (*Ostjuden*) rose to 1,131 (48% of the J. pop.). Efforts were made to westernize the newcomers and provide their children with vocational training. Branches of the Alliance Israelite Universelle, Central Union (C.V.), German Zionist Organization, J. War Veterans Association, and other national bodies were founded during the Weimar Republic. Jews also made important contributions to civic and cultural life, journalism, and politics. Max Dienemann, a leading figure in the World Union for Progressive Judaism, served as the community's rabbi (1919–38). In 1927 a beautifully illustrated edition of the 18th-cent. *Offenbach Haggadah* was published by Siegfried Guggenheim. Most Orthodox Jews and many active Zionists were *Ostjuden*. In March 1933, the J. pop. still numbered 1,435. Immediately after Hitler's rise to power in 1933, Jews and anti-Nazis were dismissed from public employment. Boycott measures grew more severe and

the community was forced to open its own day school in 1934. Having lost their German citizenship, "foreign" Jews were driven across the Polish border and most J. business firms were "Aryanized" by May 1938. During the *Kristallnacht* pogrom (9–10 Nov. 1938), stormtroopers made a bonfire of Torah scrolls and prayer books. They then set fire to the main synagogue (causing only minor structural damage) and vandalized J. property. Over 140 Jews were imprisoned for a time in the Buchenwald and Dachau concentration camps. By 22 April 1941, 807 Jews had emigrated to the U.S., England, Palestine, and other countries. The 344 who still remained in Feb. 1942 were mostly deported to the Theresienstadt ghetto and Auschwitz. Altogether, 400 Jews are known to have perished in the Holocaust. Revived after WWII, the community numbered 662 in 1970.

OFFENBURG Baden, Germany. Jews are known from the early 13th cent. In 1243 they were victims of anti-J. riots. A substantial community existed by the early 14th cent. but ended in the Black Death persecutions of 1348–49 when the Jews burned themselves alive to avoid expulsion and certain death as a consequence of a well-poisoning libel. The few Jews who were present in the 17th cent. were expelled in 1689 owing to local hostility. The modern community was only founded in 1862 on the emancipation of Baden's Jews. In 1880 the J. pop. reached 387 (total 7,274), with 61 of the 74 J. families (in 1884) engaged in commerce (wine, cattle, hides). In 1875 the community inaugurated a synagogue. In 1893 the seat of the dist. rabbinate was transferred to O. from Schmieheim. By the end of WWI, many belonged to the professional class and the community continued to maintain a rich inner life. In 1933, 271 Jews lived in O. (total 17,976), with others subsequently joining the community. Jews were dismissed from public employment and banned from public places. In 1938 all J. children were expelled from the public schools. Many of the young emigrated to Palestine with the aid of the local Hehalutz office. By the end of 1938, 118 Jews had emigrated, among them many to the U.S.; 32 left for other German cities. On *Kristallnacht* (9–10 Nov. 1938), the interior of the synagogue was wrecked and all J. males over 16 were arrested and sent to the Dachau concentration camp for a few weeks after being abused and humiliated in the streets of the city. In all, 156 Jews managed to emigrate directly from

O. in 1933–40, with another 45 going to other German cities (and 23 emigrating from them). Of the 92 deported to the Gurs concentration camp on 22 Oct. 1940, 21 survived the Holocaust. The fate of the Jews in the eight communities attached to O. was similar. Durbach's 19th cent. community of around 100 was reduced to a single family in 1933. In Gengenbach, 30 remained, 16 emigrated, and nine were deported to Gurs. In Nordrach, where a sanatorium for pulmonary patients was founded by Adelaide Rothschild in the 19th cent., the last 26 patients along with the head doctor were sent to Auschwitz in Sept. 1942 and executed on arrival.

OGRE Vidzeme (Livonia) dist., Latvia. The J. pop. in 1935 was 50 (total 1,727). The Jews were murdered by the Germans after their occupation of Latvia in 1941.

OGULIN Croatia, Yugoslavia, today Republic of Croatia. In 1921 59 Jews lived in the province and 21 in the town. During the Holocaust they perished at the hands of the Ustase.

OHLAU (Pol. Olawa) Lower Silesia, Germany, today Poland. Jews settled no later than 1358 but were apparently expelled in 1363 and did not return until the 17th cent. Their number rose from 21 in 1800 to 210 in 1861. A synagogue was consecrated next to the church in 1831 and a cemetery was opened later. In 1930, the J. pop. was 50. On the eve of the Nazi rise to power in 1933 it was 40. On *Kristallnacht* (9–10 Nov. 1938), the prayer house and two J. stores were destroyed. Eighteen Jews remained in 1939. No further information is available about the fate of the community under the Nazis. Presumably those who did not emigrate were deported and perished.

OKANY Bihar dist., Hungary. Jews settled in the mid-19th cent. Accused of profiteering during WWI, they were attacked by demobilized soldiers and White Terror gangs. Under the 1938 racial laws, they lost their lands and business licenses. In April 1944, the 42 remaining Jews were transferred to Nagyszalonta and then deported to Auschwitz in late June.

OKRZEJA Lublin dist., Poland. The J. pop was 133 in 1921 with most Jews tradesmen peddling their wares in the neighboring villages. In WWII, the Jews were probably expelled by the Germans to Lukow and from there deported to the Treblinka death camp.

OKTIABER (until 1928, Tel Khai) Crimea, Russia, today Ukraine. A Hehalutz group founded O. in 1922 as an agricultural settlement. Most Jews farmed but some worked as tailors, shoemakers, carpenters, blacksmiths, and, in the beginning, in processing hides. In 1923, settlement members numbered 25. The number rose to about 200 in 1932 but apparently not all were Jews. In 1928, the name of the settlement was changed for a non-J. one following anti-Zionist agitation. Following their arrival in late Oct. 1941, the Germans destroyed the settlement. The remaining 33 J. families were murdered at the nearby J. agricultural settlement of Mayfeld. After WWII, a few surviving J. families returned and reestablished themselves at the kolkhoz there. Although a Jew became chairman in the mid-1940s, most Jews apparently left about this time.

OKTIABERFELD Zaporozhe dist., Ukraine. The J. colony of O. was attached to the Novo-Zlatopol J. Autonomous Region in 1929 and had a J. council (soviet). The J. Dzerzhinski kolkhoz was founded nearby. O. had a J. school and a clandestine Zionist group was still operating in 1940. The few Jews remaining in WWII were probably murdered together with the Jews of Roskoshnaya during the Nazi occupation. Sixteen people, presumably Jews, were murdered in the J. Oktiaber kolkhoz, which was under the jurisdiction of the J. rural council (soviet) of O. In the Petrovski kolkhoz, also in council territory, 61 people were executed on 20 Nov. 1941, also probably all Jews.

OKUNIEW Warsaw dist., Poland. Jews settled in the late 18th cent. and numbered 287 by 1897. By 1921, the J. pop. was 489 (total 1,891). In the 1930s many Jews emigrated, mainly to France and South America. Under German occupation (28 Sept. 1939), Jews were sent to forced labor, and in March 1942 all were expelled to Warsaw, and from there to the Treblinka death camp.

OLASZLISZKA Zemplen dist., Hungary. Jews settled in the first half of the 18th cent., attracted by the town's vineyards. Despite local hostility they became prominent wine merchants, even selling to Russia and Poland. Under R. Tzevi Hirsch Friedman (1840–

74), a student of R. Moshe Teitelbaum of Satoraljaujhely, O. became an important hasidic center. The J. pop. grew to 191 in 1850 and 227 in 1930. On 25 May 1944, the Jews were deported to Auschwitz via Satoraljaujhely.

OLDENBURG Oldenburg, Germany. After the Black Death persecutions of 1348–49, no Jews settled there for over 400 years. Down to the Napoleonic era, only one J. family was permitted to live and trade in O. The community then grew from 27 to 80 between 1807 and 1820. In 1827, a law regulating its affairs authorized the establishment of a district rabbinate. Nathan Marcus Adler, the first incumbent (1829–30), went on to serve as chief rabbi of the British Empire.

Shimshon Rafael Hirsch, Adler's successor (1830–41), laid the foundations of Neo-Orthodoxy. Heinrich Graetz (1817–91), the future J. historian, lived in O. in 1837–40 as a guest in Hirsch's home. Under Grand Duke Paul Friedrich August's tolerant rule, the community prospered, but the Neo-Orthodox religious direction was reversed after Hirsch was succeeded by Bernhard Wechsler (1841–74), a radical reformer who officiated at the first mixed marriage after J. emancipation (1849). While he was rabbi, the community built a new synagogue in 1855, installed an organ, and endeavored to enhance social integration. R. David Mannheim however, before assuming office in 1891, insisted on the restoration of Orthodox worship. Old Liberal families, objecting to his religious stand, left the com-

Petty bourgeois Jews in Oldenburg, Germany, 1900 (Leo Baeck Institute, New York/photo courtesy of Yad Vashem, The Holocaust Martyrs' and Heroes' Remembrance Authority, Jerusalem)

munity but without abandoning Judaism. Cattle traders from East Friesland and the Netherlands, retired couples, and immigrant Jews from Eastern Europe (*Ostjuden*) were absorbed by the community, which grew from 169 in 1876 to 265 in 1905 and 320 at its peak in 1925. During the Weimar Republic, most Jews continued to trade in cattle, meat, and farm produce or owned stores; J. professionals were rare. Antisemitism was combated by the Central Union (C.V.) and the J. War Veterans Association. O. was the first state in Germany to elect a Nazi administration in 1932. From April 1933, boycott measures succeeded in ruining or "Aryanizing" local J. firms. By the end of 1935, 100 persons were receiving aid from the community's Winter Relief Fund. New Zionist and cultural groups were founded in 1934–36 as violence, persecution, and racial discrimination drove many Jews from the city. On *Kristallnacht* (9–10 Nov. 1938), SA units burned the synagogue and school, demolished stores, and conducted mass arrests throughout the region (including Rastede and Wardenburg). Over 30 J. residents were transported to the Sachsenhausen concentration camp. Of the 279 Jews registered in 1933, 70 emigrated to Holland and 120 to Latin America; others left for Palestine (25), the U.S. and Canada (24), England (22), and South Africa (11). Those who arrived in Palestine and England were mostly children rescued by Youth Aliya and the *Kindertransport*. Leo Trepp, the community's last rabbi (1936–38), also reached England. Those who moved to Bremen, Hamburg, and Berlin (and some who fled to Holland) as well as the remaining Jews were finally deported to Nazi concentration camps or ghettoes in 1941–42. Twenty-seven perished in Auschwitz alone. The postwar J. community numbered 150 in 1997, two-thirds from the Soviet Union.

OLDENZAAL Overijssel dist., Holland. Jews were present in the 14th cent. and then from the 17th cent. During the 19th cent., the community was particularly influential in religious affairs. In 1892, uncharacteristically for Holland, Jews were attacked following a blood libel. The authorities quickly intervened. The community had 212 members in 1892 and 122 in 1938. In Sept. 1941, J. youths were sent to the Mauthausen concentration camp (Austria) and in 1942 the remaining Jews were sent to Poland; 13 survived in hiding.

OLESKO Tarnopol dist., Poland, today Ukraine. The beginnings of J. life can be traced to the early

16th cent. Despite being the seat of a hasidic court connected to the Belz dynasty, the J. pop. remained stagnant, reaching a maximum of 832 (approx. 20% of the total) in 1910. Economic hardship and the removal of the court to Lwow led to further decline between the World Wars. Only 472 Jews remained in the town at the time of the German occupation in Jan. 1942. Most were deported to the Belzec death camp on 28 Aug. 1942 or the Zloczow ghetto in Nov.; others were imprisoned in a forced labor camp and murdered in June 1943.

OLESZNO Kielce dist., Poland. Jews first settled at the end of the 19th cent. In 1921, the J. pop. was 114. The Jews were expelled by the Germans to Wloszczowa on 19 Sept. 1942 and from there to the Treblinka death camp.

OLESZYCE (Yid. Halshitz) Lwow dist., Poland, today Ukraine. Jews are recorded from the founding of the town in 1576, coming under the protection of its proprietor. Until the mid-18th cent. the Jews earned their livelihood as leaseholders under the *arenda* system, as innkeepers, and as traders in wines and spices, but afterwards they engaged mainly in petty trade and the crafts. Their number reached 1,514 (total 2,917) in 1900 but declined after WWI. The community was always strongly hasidic under the influence of the Belz dynasty, which retarded Zionist activity until after WWI. The Russian occupation of 1914–15 was for the Jews a time of plunder and rape. The German occupation of the town in June 1941 brought with it severe anti-J. measures: fines, confiscations, and forced labor. In Nov. the Jews were expelled, mostly to the Lobaczow ghetto. No more than 50 survived the war.

OLEVSK Zhitomir dist., Ukraine. Jews are first mentioned in 1750 in a jurisdictional dispute between Pinsk and Volhynia. By 1872 the Jews constituted a significant part of the local pop. and in 1897 numbered 1,187 (total 2,070). Jews became prominent in the lumber industry that developed in O. after the completion of the Brisk (Brest-Litovsk)–Kiev railway line. In a two-day pogrom in late Dec. 1918, the Petlyura gangs beat and robbed Jews as well as exacting a large tribute. The pogrom has been described by the Hebrew writer Yosef Arikha (Dolgin; 1907–72), a native of O. Many Jews left during the Soviet period, when O. became a border town. The Germans arrived on 5 Aug. 1941, accompanied by the Ukrainian militia commanded by Taras Borovets. In Oct., the Jews were ordered to wear a yellow badge, pay a large tribute, and enter a ghetto. The Ukrainians robbed and abused the Jews continuously and on 19 Nov. 1941 murdered about 580 at a pit outside the city. In 1959, there were 1,300 Jews in O.

OLGOPOL   Vinnitsa dist., Ukraine. Jews are first mentioned in 1799 and numbered 2,473 (total 8,134) in 1897. A mixed J.-Ukrainian school with 600 students was active in the 1930s. A kolkhoz with 100 members (mostly Jews) was operating in the first half of the 1930s. The rural council (soviet) was also mixed, serving the local pop. in its own languages (Ukrainian and Yiddish). In 1939 the J. pop. was 660. The Germans and Rumanians captured O. on 26 July 1941. The Rumanian authorities attached the city to Transnistria and set up a closed ghetto which held hundreds of Jews expelled from Bukovina and Bessarabia. The ghetto also held a few dozen local J. families who had not managed to escape with the Red Army. On 1 Sept. 1943 and until liberation on 22 March 1944, 191 Jews were still living in the ghetto (164 from Bessarabia and 27 from Bukovina)

OLIZARKA   Volhynia dist., Poland, today Ukraine. Founded as a J. farm settlement in 1849, O. numbered 321 Jews in 1921 working 375 acres of land but mainly employed in the building trade. A Ukrainian-staged pogrom preceded the German occupation of July 1941. The Jews were transferred to the Rafalowka ghetto on 1 May 1942 and murdered beside open pits on 29 Aug.

OLKIENIKI   Vilna dist., Poland, today Belarus. Jews are thought to have settled in the second half of the 16th cent. The community's importance is indicated by the convening of the Lithuanian Council there in 1695. By the late 18th cent. O. was known for its J. merchants. The beautiful synagogue built there in 1802 aroused the admiration of Napoleon when he passed through the town. The construction of the railroad in the mid-19th cent. boosted the local economy. Jews monopolized the trade in forest products (tar, charcoal, medicinal plants, wild berries) while others, mainly Cantonists, founded three farming villages in the neighborhood. Jews also benefited from the summer resort trade. A hasidic *shtibl* and a small

yeshiva operated in the late 19th cent., when the J. pop. stood at 1,126 (total 2,619). The first Hebrew elementary school was opened in 1912 and in 1920, following the food shortages and forced labor of WWI under the German occupation, a first group of pioneers left for Palestine, settling in Kibbutz Ein Harod. Economic hardship was marked after WWI, exacerbated by heavy taxes, with the J. pop. falling to 798 in 1925. The wealthier Jews traded in grain, flour, lumber, and meat and a prewar J. carton factory grew to employ 300. The Germans arrived on 23 June 1941 after a two-year Soviet presence. Within a few days a group of young educated and activist Jews was murdered. A conceivably errant bomb destroyed much of the J. quarter on 25 July. Many sought shelter among friends and relatives in neighboring villages. On 20–21 Sept. all were brought to Ejszyszki and imprisoned in stables and the local *beit midrash*. After being held for 60 hours without food or water they were taken to freshly dug pits and executed. Nearly 800 perished in the Holocaust.

OLKUSZ   (Yid. Elkish) Kielce dist., Poland. Despite a residence ban officially in force until 1862, Jews were leasing mines in the area in the 14th cent. and were active economically as distillers and innkeepers as well as in the mineral-refining industry. In 1897, their pop. reached 1,835 (total 3,433). A synagogue and cemetery were consecrated in the 1890s. In 1916, after R. Yehoshua Heschel Horvitz-Sternfeld settled in O., it became one of the largest hasidic centers in Poland. The Zionists became active in the late 19th cent. A Hebrew school was opened in 1909. In addition to dominating the mining industry, J. merchants traded in grain, cattle, and eggs. Many kept shops and stalls in the market or peddled in the villages. Among J. artisans, tailors producing cheap readymade wear were particularly numerous. In WWI, the J. pop. suffered under the Russian and Austrian occupations, with economic activity coming to a standstill. In the first years after the war, the J. pop. continued to grow (reaching 2,700 in 1921) but economic conditions remained difficult, necessitating assistance from the Joint Distribution Committee. In the course of their slow recovery, the Jews opened 34 workshops and small factories. Most earned their livelihood in the retail trade (food and clothing), which they dominated in the town. In 1933, 300 families still required assistance to get through the Passover holidays. Zionist activity intensified in the face of growing antisemitism, with Hehalutz sending young pioneers to Palestine. In 1929, a Tarbut Hebrew school was opened. A third of city council members were Jews and one served as deputy mayor. The arrival of the Germans in Sept. 1939 inaugurated a period of severe persecution, including forced labor, property confiscation, and "contributions." A *Judenrat* was soon established as the J. pop. rose to 2,983 with the arrival of refugees. From fall 1940, groups of Jews were dispatched to distant labor camps, mostly in Silesia, never to return. In Sept. 1941 the Jews were confined to a ghetto. On 13 June 1942, after a few hundred were selected for the labor camps, the rest were deported to Auschwitz. All but 150 perished. Several survivors returned to O. in 1945–46 with the intention of regaining their property, but after the murder of a young J. girl, all left.

OLNHAUSEN   Wuerttemberg, Germany. Jews settled in the mid-17th cent. after the Thirty Years War (1618–48), reaching a peak pop. of 158 (total 638) in 1854 and thereafter dwindling steadily through emigration. Jews were active in the cattle trade. The first synagogue was built in 1736–37 and a J. school was opened in the 1830s. Both were burned on *Kristallnacht* (9–10 Nov. 1938). Of the 26 Jews left in 1933, seven managed to emigrate while 12 were expelled to the Riga ghetto in Dec. 1941 and to the Theresienstadt ghetto in Aug. 1942 to meet their end.

OLOMOUC   (Yid. Olmitze, Olmuntz) Moravia, Czechoslovakia. Jews are mentioned in 906. In 1060 they were confined to a special quarter and forced to wear a yellow badge. In 1454 they were expelled by King Ladislaus Posthumus at the instigation of the priest John of Capistrano. Although the expulsion order was only rescinded after the 1848 revolution, Franz Josef Neumann founded a Hebrew printing press in the city in 1753. A large synagogue was consecrated in 1897 as the J. pop. rose from 747 in 1869 to 1,676 (total 21,707) in 1900. Jews were active in industry, owning ten malt-manufacturing plants. They traded in grain and textiles and comprised 70% of the city's professional class. The composer Gustav Mahler and Sigmund Freud lived in O. for awhile. The Zionists were active from the late 19th cent. The J. pop. was 2,077 in 1921 and 4,015 in 1941. Eight hundred J. men were arrested on 15 March 1939. Some were beaten in the local jail while others were

sent to the Dachau concentration camp. The invading Germans and their Czech Fascist collaborators burned down the synagogue. In June and July 1942, 3,445 Jews were deported to the Theresienstadt ghetto in four transports and from there to death camps in Poland where 3,213 perished. There were 285 survivors.

OLPINY   Cracow dist., Poland. The J. pop. in 1921 was 185 (total 2,674). On their arrival in Sept. 1939 the Germans instituted a reign of terror with a *Judenrat* supplying forced labor. In July 1942 around 40 J. men were sent to the Plaszow concentration camp and on 9 Aug. 120 men, women, and children were taken to the forest and executed.

OLSHANA   Kiev dist., Ukraine. Jews numbered 26 in 1765 and 1,233 in 1897. They engaged in petty trade, lumber wholesaling, leasing, and crafts. During the civil war (1918–21), J. homes and property were looted and destroyed in riots. In 1924, under the Soviets, the 150 J. artisans in O. organized various cooperatives. Many Jews moved to the nearby kolkhoz. In 1939, the J. pop. was 195. The Germans captured O. on 25 July 1941. In Oct., they murdered a large number of Jews in a first *Aktion*. Afterwards the survivors were herded into a ghetto. On 2 May 1942, the ghetto residents were expelled to Zvenigorodka. From there, the men and children were sent to a labor camp in Niemorozh and then on to other concentration camps. On 2 Nov. 1942 all the Jews still alive were executed.

OLSZTYN   Kielce dist., Poland. Jews are first mentioned in 1764 and numbered 141 (total 631) in 1859. A Zionist group was active after WWI. Anti-J. riots broke out in 1935 and 1937. On the eve of WWII, the J. pop. was 135. The Germans expelled all the Jews, 200 including a few dozen refugees, to Koniecepol in Aug. 1942 and from there to the Treblinka death camp on 7 Oct.

OLTENITA   Walachia dist., Rumania. The first ten Jews settled in 1860. The J. pop. in 1899 was 126. The community gradually declined and only 52 remained in 1930.

OLYKA   Volhynia dist., Poland, today Ukraine. Jews were present from the mid-16th cent. During the sack of the town by Chmielnicki in 1648 they found refuge in the local fortress. The community became inde-

Synagogue in Olyka, Poland

pendent in the late 17th cent. and was one of the largest in Volhynia. It recovered quickly from fires in 1805 and 1833 as well as from one in 1855 that reduced the J. pop. by 75% to 547. By 1897 the J. pop. stood at 2,606 (total 4,210). An important source of income were the visitors at the hasidic court founded by Hirsch Leib ben Avraham Landau. During WWI the Jews suffered from the Cossacks and Russians. Further depredations were suffered at the hands of roaming local gangs during the Russian civil war (1918–21) and the Polish army in 1920. The Feb. 1917 Revolution in Russia brought about a great awakening among the Jews with the founding of many Zionist parties and organizations. Between the World Wars the Zionists exercised political control of the community. A Hebrew school and kindergarten were maintained. Soviet rule from Sept. 1939 to June 1941 brought J. public life to an end. A heavy aerial bombardment by the Germans on 1 July 1941 destroyed 70% of the town's houses and claimed 100 J. lives. On occupying the town the Germans immediately instituted a regime of forced labor and extortion and appointed a *Judenrat*. In Aug. 1941 they mur-

dered 700 Jews at the J. cemetery. A ghetto swollen to a pop. of 3,500 after the arrival of refugees was set up in March 1942. Most were murdered on 29 Aug. beside open pits near the old Radziwill castle. Around 130 artisans were spared, meeting their end in early 1944. A group of 23 youngsters escaped to the forest and engaged in effective partisan action for awhile.

OMMEN Overijssel dist., Holland. Jews settled in the early 18th cent. and numbered 72 in 1860. In Nov. 1942 the 30 Jews there were transferred to Westerbork. All perished, most in the Sobibor death camp.

ONESTI Moldavia dist., Rumania. Jews settled in the 1890s. The J. pop. in 1899 was 110. In 1907 Jews were expelled, returning after WWI. Under Antonescu, goods were confiscated from J. shops and Jews were persecuted and fled. In June 1941 the few left were transferred to Targu-Ocna and Bacau.

ONGA Abauj-Torna dist., Hungary. Jews settled in the first half of the 19th cent. and numbered 62 in

1930. In mid-May 1944 they were deported to Auschwitz via Kassa.

ONOD   Borsod dist., Hungary. A J. community existed by the mid-18th cent., mostly trading in grain. By 1880, its pop. was 159, rising to 183 in 1930. A splendid synagogue was built in 1883. Jews suffered from White Terror attacks in 1919 and the racial laws of 1938. On 10 June 1944, they were deported to Auschwitz via Diosgyor.

ONOK   (Hung. Ilonokujfalu; Yid. Alyne) Carpatho-Russia, Czechoslovakia, today Ukraine. J. settlement probably began at the turn of the 18th cent. The J. pop. was 135 (total 1,040) in 1880, rising in the period of the Czechoslovakian Republic to 189 in 1921 and to 238 in 1941 under the Hungarians. After the annexation to Hungary in March 1939, a number of Jews were drafted into labor battalions and sent to the eastern front where most perished. In July 1941, a few dozen Jews without Hungarian citizenship were expelled to Kamenets-Podolski, where they were murdered. The rest were deported to Auschwitz in the second half of May 1944.

ONUSKIS (I)   (Yid. Anushishak) Troki dist., Lithuania. The J. pop. in 1897 was 217 (38% of the total). In the 1922 elections to the Lithuanian Sejm almost all J. votes in O. went to the Zionists. On 23 June 1941, after the German invasion of Lithuania, Lithuanian nationalists robbed, tortured, and murdered Jews. Weapons were planted in J. houses and the owners were executed. On 21 Sept. 1941, Rosh Hashanah eve, J. houses were raided and the occupants forced into the synagogue while their homes were looted. On 30 Sept. 1941 (Yom Kippur eve), all 1,446 Jews were murdered at the Varnikai forest.

ONUSKIS (II)   (Yid. Anushishak) Rokiskis dist., Lithuania. J. settlement began in the mid-18th cent. By the beginning of the 19th cent. Jews comprised the majority of O.'s pop. Prior to WWI, 80–90 J. families lived in O. WWI caused many Jews to flee to Russia, most of whom did not return. The J. pop. declined to 25 families, mainly elderly and supported by their children who had emigrated. In 1941, the Germans and Lithuanians murdered the town's Jews.

OPALIN   Volhynia dist., Poland, today Ukraine.

Jews were present from the 17th cent. with extensive privileges and numbered 769 (total 1,612) in 1897. The Germans captured the town in late June 1941. On 2 Oct. 1942, 582 Jews were led to the J. cemetery and murdered.

OPALYI   Szatmar dist., Hungary. Jews settled in the late 18th cent, numbering 197 in 1900 and 160 in 1930. In late May 1944, they were deported to Auschwitz via Mateszalka.

OPATIJA   (Ital. Abbazra) Croatia, Yugoslavia, today Republic of Croatia. Jews first settled in the late 19th cent. and were closely linked with the community of nearby Fiume. The J. pop. in 1930 was 100. The Germans entered in 1943, persecuted the Jews, plundered their property, and expelled them to a concentration camp. Over 50 of O.'s Jews died in the Holocaust.

OPATOW   (Yid. Apta) Kielce dist., Poland. Jews settled in the 16th cent., living in their own quarter and engaging in extensive trade, mainly with Danzig (Gdansk) but also as far afield as Breslau in the west. The J. settlement grew with an influx of German and Polish Jews. The Swedish war of the mid-17th cent. curtailed the community's development. The J. quarter was burned and looted and many Jews were massacred by Stefan Czarniecki's irregular Polish troops. In 1657, King John Casimir authorized them to rebuild their homes and resume trade, but a fire in 1680 again gutted the J. quarter. Many also died in an epidemic. The community grew considerably in the 18th cent., particularly under Austrian rule in 1793–1807, when Jews were permitted to live outside the J. quarter. Jews controlled the wholesale trade in farm produce and lumber and contributed to local industry, opening two hide-processing plants, a sugar-refining factory, and a dyeing facility. O. was the birthplace of R. Yisrael of Kozienice (b. 1733), one of the founders of Hasidism. In the late 18th cent. R. Moshe Leib of Sasow established his seat in O., making it an important hasidic center. Other prominent hasidic figures were R. Yaakov Yitzhak of Przysucha ("the Holy Jew") and Avraham Yehoshua Heschel ("the Rabbi of Apta"). The provision of services to the Hasidim was an important source of income. The J. pop. grew from 1,377 in 1827 to 4,138 (total 6,603) in 1897. Zionist activity commenced in the early 20th cent. After WWI, most factories and workshops were in J. hands, over half (146) in the garment industry. Most Jews, however, engaged in petty trade and barely made a living. The J. pop. rose to 5,462 in 1921. Orthodox circles controlled community institutions, with a branch of Agudat Israel opened in 1921 and a Beth Jacob school for girls operating from 1925. Most of the Zionist organizations were also active. Hehalutz ran a pioneer training farm and a Tarbut Hebrew school was founded in 1934. Many of the young fled eastward to Soviet-controlled territory on the approach of the Germans in Sept. 1939. However, 200 were seized in O. by the Germans. They were removed to an unknown destination and never heard from again. In early 1941, a *Judenrat* was set up and in spring a ghetto was established, its pop. swelled by refugees from Warsaw and Lodz. The overcrowing let to typhoid. The TOZ health organization operated infirmaries and a 30–40-bed hospital. Soup kitchens were opened as well as a school and brush workshop. Many of the able-bodied were sent to labor camps, mainly in Skarzysko-Kamienna and Starachovice, their places in the ghetto taken by refugees from Silesia. In winter 1942, with information from informers, the Germans tortured and murdered young people in the ghetto who had been trying to acquire arms and organize an underground. On 20–22 Oct. 1942, after another 500 were sent to the Sandomierz labor camp, the last 6,000 Jews were deported to the Treblinka death camp. Of the 1,500 still in the labor camps, nearly 300 survived the war.

OPATOWIEC Kielce dist., Poland. A J. community of a few dozen existed by 1827, mostly engaged in farming. Its pop. was 166 (total 762) in 1921 and 120 on the eve of the German occupation in Sept. 1939. With the arrival of refugees, the pop. doubled over the next two years.. All were confined to a ghetto. In anticipation of an *Aktion* on 9 Nov. 1942, many fled and the Germans found only the sick and old. As the Germans hunted down and murdered those who had escaped to the forests, one group of 36 offered armed resistance. In the end, they too were murdered.

OPAVA Silesia (Sudetenland), Czechoslovakia. Jews are first mentioned in 1281 and were expelled a final time in 1523, returning only in the first half of the 19th cent. Their pop. was 134 in 1867; 1,127 in 1921; and 971 (total 11,627) in 1930. Zionist activity was extensive from the late 19th cent. Most left before the annexation to Germany in Sept. 1938 and suffered

the fate of the Jews of Bohemia and Moravia. Of those who remained, 80 were deported to the Theresienstadt ghetto in 1942, 57 of them on 18 Nov.

OPOCHKA Kalinin dist., Russia. Jews probably settled in the mid-19th cent. Fifty-three J. families were present in 1879. In the late 19th cent., the Jews received permission to build a prayer house, which was apparently erected in the early 20th cent. The J. pop. was 521 (total 5,735) in 1897 and 577 in 1926 under the Soviets. In 1939, the J. pop. was 289. A few days after the German occupation of 8 July 1941, a number of Jews were murdered at the J. cemetery. In Aug., the Jews were transferred to a military facility and between Nov. 1941 and March 1942 they were executed in groups near the villages of Maslovo and Pukhli. In fall 1943, the Germans disinterred and burned the bodies of their victims, 200 in all.

OPOCZNO Lodz dist., Poland. A legend claims that the J. "Esterke," mistress of King Casimir the Great, lived here (14th cent.) In 1588 Sigismund III authorized the municipality to expel all Jews from the city but in 1646 Jews were permitted to purchase plots of land for housing, a synagogue, and a cemetery. By 1765 the majority of artisans were Jews. Early in the 19th cent. the community grew following an influx of Jews deported from the surrounding villages. The J. pop. in 1897 was 2,425 (38% of the total). The synagogue built at the end of the 17th cent. was considered one of the finest in Poland. At the end of the 18th cent. the renowned rabbi Yehuda Leib Lipschitz served the community. The Gur Hasidim reached O. in the late 19th cent. The situation of the Jews declined rapidly in the 1930s following attacks in the markets and the boycott of their shops. Communal bodies were dominated by Agudat Yisrael up to 1929 but afterwards by the Zionist parties (mainly left wing). During WWII, refugees increased the J. pop. from 2,954 in 1939 to 4,231 in April 1942. The ghetto was set up at the end of 1940. The men were sent to work in the peat bogs, limestone quarries, and labor camps. In Oct. 1942 the Germans began rounding up the Jews and deporting them to the Treblinka death camp. Some managed to escape and form partisan units, one under the command of Julian Eisenman that successfully carried out sabotage actions. In Jan. 1943, the last 500 Jews were transported to Treblinka.

OPOLE (Yid. Apla) Lublin dist., Poland. J. settlement commenced in the late 16th cent. In the Chmielnicki massacres of 1648–49, most J. homes were burned and many Jews murdered. The community recovered with the help of new trade and property rights granted by the town's proprietors. In the late 18th cent., the Jews formed an organized community with a synagogue and cemetery. In the 19th cent. Jews were instrumental in O.'s industrial development. The J. pop. reached 3,328 in 1897. Between the World Wars, J. political life flourished, with widespread Zionist activity. The residence of R. Yermiyahu Kalish made O. an important hasidic center. At the outset of the Nazi invasion of Sept. 1939, the J. pop. was 4,300, rising to 10,200 in 1942 with the arrival of refugees from Pulawy, Jozefow, and Vienna. A ghetto was set up in March 1941, with a typhoid epidemic claiming 500 J. lives the following winter. Another 2,000 refugees arrived from Kazimierz Dolny; 800 from Wonwolnica; and 1,350 more from Jozefow. Deportations commenced in March 1942: 1,950 to the Belzec death camp on 31 March and 2,000 to the Sobibor death camp At this point there were 7,600 refugees in the ghetto, including refugees from Slovakia and France. On 24 Oct. 1942, most were deported, after a selection, to Sobibor. Those left behind were soon murdered or sent to labor camps.

OPPELN (Pol. Opole) Upper Silesia, Germany, today Poland. A number of J. families were present in 1396 but there were apparently Jews here before that. They were evidently murdered by their neighbors in the Black Death persecutions of 1348–49 as the supposed cause of the plague. In 1427 the Jews received a privilege from the local duke enabling them to build a synagogue and houses. Eight families (70 Jews together with servants) were living in O. in 1532. They lived on their own street and were subjected to heavy taxes. All were expelled in 1563. J. settlement was only renewed in 1746, four years after the beginning of Prussian rule. By 1812, the J. pop. reached 48. A cemetery was consecrated in 1822 and a new synagogue was completed in 1842. The dedication ceremony was conducted by R. Abraham Geiger, one of the leaders of the Reform movement. The J. pop. reached a peak of 718 in 1895. In this period the community founded various welfare organizations as well as a library, an historical and literary society, and a branch of the Kameraden youth

movement. Leo Baeck served as rabbi in 1897–1907, later becoming one of the outstanding J. leaders in Germany. During his stay he opened another synagogue and married a local woman. The Zionists, Central Union (C.V.), and B'nai B'rith were active between the World Wars. In 1930, the J. pop. was 607. Right-wing nationalists and antisemites were particularly active in O. by this time. Despite protection from the Nazi racial laws until 16 July 1937 by the League of Nations' minority rights convention, the Jews were nonetheless subjected to persecution and economic boycott. In 1936, Jews numbered 453. On *Kristallnacht* (9–10 Nov. 1938), the synagogue was burned down, 13 J. stores were destroyed along with the building housing the J. organizations, and 13 Jews were arrested. Emigration was subsequently stepped up and by 1939 only 280 Jews remained. Deportations commenced on 13 Nov. 1942, with additional transports on 20 Nov. and 11 Dec. as well as during 1942 and early 1944.

OPPENHEIM Hesse, Germany. In the 13th cent., local Jews were part of the group headed by R. Meir ben Barukh (the "Maharam") of Rothenburg that tried to reach Eretz Israel (1286). Many preferred martyrdom to forced conversion during the Black Death persecutions of 1348–49. The large number of J. families retaining Oppenheim or Oppenheimer, etc., as their surname indicates the medieval community's importance. Around 1720, a new community was established. It grew prosperous, embraced Liberal Judaism (installing an organ and a mixed choir in the synagogue), and numbered 257 (about 8% of the total) in 1871. A sudden outbreak of Nazi violence on Yom Kippur eve in 1928 provided a foretaste of *Kristallnacht* (9–10 Nov. 1938), when the synagogue was destroyed. By then, 25 of the 56 remaining Jews had left; three others survived the Holocaust.

OPSA Vilna dist., Poland, today Belarus. Jews are first mentioned in 1790. In 1921 they numbered 334 (total 714). Between the World Wars, Hehalutz and Betar groups were active with many of their pioneers leaving for Palestine. Under Soviet rule (Sept. 1939–June 1941) J. stores were nationalized and J. artisans organized into cooperatives. With the German arrival, a large number of young Jews were executed. In Dec. 1941 all but 60 skilled workers were expelled to Widze and Braslaw and subsequently murdered.

The remaining 60 were also brought to Braslaw, in late 1942, similarly meeting their end.

OR   Szabolcs dist., Hungary. Jews are first mentioned in 1770 and numbered 158 in 1880 and 70 in 1930. On 25–27 May 1944, they were deported to Auschwitz via Kisvarda.

ORADEA MARE   (Hung. Nagyvarad; Ger. Grosswardein) N. Transylvania, Rumania. A J. community probably existed here in the 15th–16th cents. Jews settled again at the end of the 17th cent. In the 1720s they inhabited four quarters: Varad, the city's commercial center; Velence, the center of religious and communal activity; Olaszi, a few families only; Varal-ja, where Jews were permitted to set up stands to sell their wares outside the fortress and later to build houses in the military area, and which by 1740 had the largest J. pop. in O. The focus of communal activity shifted from Velence to Varalja and a synagogue was built there in 1787. In the early 19th cent., Jews began to play an important role in the town's economic life and by mid-cent. they became involved in the social and intellectual life of the city. The community was reorganized during the 1880s and 1890s under the leadership of Yisrael Ullman, who headed it for 19 years. The J. pop. in 1930 was 10,115 (26% of the total). A group of 200 Jews set up a Neologist (Reform) community which by 1899 had its own religious facilities. The yeshiva in O., one of the larg-

Class of 1926–27 at the Neologist Jewish Lyceum, Oradea Mare, Rumania (The Museum of the Federation of Jewish Communities in Rumania, Bucharest/photo courtesy of Beth Hatefutsoth, Tel Aviv)

est in Hungary, was authorized to train rabbis. A J. school was opened in 1786 at the order of Emperor Joseph II, but the majority of J. children continued to attend government schools and later private schools, including that of the Neologist community. In 1877 the community educational system was reorganized by Yaacov Yehiel Gabel and by 1894–95, 427 of the 1,576 children attended the community's school. At the end of the 19th cent. the Jews set up factories that made O. an important industrial center. They also controlled its major financial institutions. Jews were integrated into cultural life and in 1896, 97% spoke Hungarian. Some held official positions and many were prominent in literature, medicine, law, and politics. A Hebrew periodical appeared here in 1875 and Jews founded daily newspapers. De-

spite the liberal policies of the government, there were manifestations of antisemitism in the late 19th cent. By the beginning of the 20th cent., the community became the largest in the area annexed to Rumania. Jews joined the revolutionary organizations active following the fall of the Austro-Hungarian monarchy. After the conquest of O. by the Rumanian army in 1919, the J. pop. suffered from restrictions in many areas of life. J. children were no longer permitted to attend schools in which the language of instruction was Hungarian and both the Orthodox and Neologist communities opened high schools. All the Zionist organizations established branches in O. The Zionists helped the J. Party gain a significant number of votes in the parliamentary elections between the World Wars. Hasidim from Bukovina and Galicia settled after WWI. The

Jewish wedding, Oradea Mare, Rumania, 1936

first to set up court was R. Yisrael Hagar of Vijnita, followed by the Zydaczow rabbi. Both courts attracted Hasidim from Eastern Europe and did their utmost to curb the spread of Zionism. On 4–6 Dec. 1927, university students attending their national convention in O. set off a pogrom. They attacked Jews in the streets, pillaged J. shops, plundered J. homes, and devastated the synagogues. This was the worst manifestation of antisemitism in Rumania up to the Holocaust and had repercussions in the Western world. After the initial shock, the Jews of O. increased their Zionist activity and many emigrated to Palestine. A J. hospital was opened with some famous specialists practicing there. A B'nai B'rith lodge was active. Students refused entrance to Rumanian universities studied in Italy and Germany. With the return of O. to Hungarian rule in Sept. 1940, the situation of the Jews deteriorated radically and they were accused of disloyalty because of their Zionist leanings. The Jews organized to deal with the situation: the Orthodox and Neologist communities joined forces; factory owners took on non-J. partners. In Dec. 1940, J. youth were drafted into the armed forces, but shortly after were placed in special labor units. The J. pop. in 1941 was 21,337 (23% of the total). In 1941, Jews whose citizenship was "doubtful" were expelled to German-occupied Poland where the majority died. In 1942, 500 young men were drafted into labor battalions and sent to the conquered territories of the USSR where most died. The Germans occupied O. on 19 March 1944, and on 3 May the J. pop. was ghettoized. From 20 May to 3 June, the Jews were deported to Auschwitz. After the war some survivors returned and established a community but the majority soon left for Palestine or the West.

ORASTIE (Hung. Szaszvaros) S. Transylvania dist., Rumania. A community existed here in 1852 and joined the Neologist association in 1868. A synagogue was built in 1891. The J. pop. stood at 211 in 1930 (1% of the total). Antisemitic manifestations were widespread between the World Wars. At the outbreak of the Soviet-Rumanian war (June 1941), J. men were sent to forced labor to Pancota and then to Focsani. After the liberation in 1944 they returned.

ORASUL NOU (Hung. Avasujvaros) N. Transylvania dist., Rumania. Jews first settled in late 18th cent. The J. pop. in 1920 was 237 (12% of the total). In May

1944 all the Jews in the town were transferred to the Satu Mare ghetto and in June they were deported to Auschwitz.

ORATOV Vinnitsa dist., Ukraine. Jews numbered nine in 1765 and 529 (total 2,439) in 1897. Most engaged in petty trade and crafts. Under the Soviets, the J. pop. fell to 114 in 1939. The Germans arrived on 27 July 1941 and on 15 Oct. 1941, they murdered those Jews who had neither escaped nor been evacuated.

ORAVITA (Hung. Oravicabanya; Ger. Orawitza) S. Transylvania dist., Rumania. A J. community was founded in 1860 and joined the Neologist association. The J. pop. was 140 in 1930 (2% of the total). After the outbreak of WWII, 306 Jews from the Caras dist. were transferred to O. About half remained after the war.

ORB, BAD see BAD ORB.

ORDZHONIKIDZE (until 1937, Rikov; from 1943, Yenakievo) Stalino dist., Ukraine. J. residence was banned until the 20th cent. In the Soviet period, with the development of the Rikov steel plant, J. laborers began to arrive. In 1923, the J. pop. was 2,141. In addition to the J. steelworkers, about 500 Jews worked as factory hands in other plants and as coalminers. These latter suffered from antisemitism at work. A J. school operated in 1926–35 and a J. kolkhoz numbering ten families was started in 1939. In 1939, the J. pop. was 3,293 (total 88,566). The Germans captured O. on 1 Nov. 1941. A *Judenrat* was set up and in Feb. 1942, the 750 registered Jews in O. were transferred to the Krasni Gorodok ghetto. Under prevailing conditions, ten Jews a day died there. In April 1942, 500 Jews were taken to Gorlovka and murdered. Another 55 were murdered on other occasions.

ORDZHONIKIDZEGRAD Oriol dist., Russia. The settlement was founded in 1870 under the name of Bezhitsa. During the Soviet period, the town was called O. From 1944, the original name was used. The J. pop. was 768 in 1926 and 1,712 (total 82,334) in 1939. The few Jews who had neither fled nor been evacuated were murdered by the Germans after their arrival on 7 Oct. 1941.

OREKHI VYDRITSA Vitebsk dist., Belorussia.

The J. pop. in 1939 was 123. The Germans took the town in July 1941 and in April 1942 murdered the 53 remaining Jews.

OREKHOV Zaporozhe dist., Ukraine. J. property was seriously damaged in a May 1881 pogrom. In 1897, the J. pop. was 971 (total 5,996), dropping in the Soviet period to 358 in 1939. The Germans captured O. on 4 Oct. 1941 and in mid-Oct. murdered 122 people, apparently all Jews, at the local brickyard.

ORHEI Bessarabia, Rumania, today Republic of Moldova. Records of Jews living here in the 16th cent. exist in rabbinical literature. Jews came in the wake of the Russian army in 1812 and enjoyed special privileges granted to settlers. The Great Synagogue was built in the early 18th cent. A J. hospital and an old age home were opened in 1886. The community had a policy of vocational training for youths and in 1898 a J. agricultural school was opened that functioned until 1905. The J. pop. in 1902 was 6,000 (47% of the total). After WWI there was an influx of J. refugees from the Ukraine. Zionist activity began in 1894 and in 1919 a pioneer training farm was opened. In the 1930s, branches of the major Zionist youth organizations were active and Hebrew was taught in many of the schools. In 1927, ORT opened a vocational school training boys in woodwork and girls in tailoring. There were manifestations of antisemitism between the World Wars. The J. pop. in 1930 was 6,302. Under Soviet rule in 1940, many of the community's leaders were exiled to Siberia and disappeared. When the Germans took O. at the end of June 1941, many Jews fled with the retreating Soviet forces. Those who survived reached Uzbekistan and Central Asia. In 1941, the Jews remaining in O. were ghettoized. On 6 Aug. 1941, soldiers of the 23rd Rumanian regiment murdered 200 Jews and threw their bodies into the Dniester River. In 1942, the J. pop. was expelled to Tiraspol; many died on the way, others in camps in Transnistria. Few survived.

ORININ Kamenets-Podolski dist., Ukraine. Jews were first present in 1582 and in 1765 they numbered 386. In 1897, their pop. was 2,142 (total 5,727). In the Soviet period, the town had a J. council (soviet), kolkhoz, tailors union, and a school with a library. The J. pop. was 1,797 in 1926 and 1,508 in 1939. In late June 1942, the Nazis and their Ukrainian collaborators surrounded the J. quarter and selected 250 skilled workers for transfer to Kamenets-Podolski, where they later perished. The remaining 1,745 Jews were led a mile outside the town towards the village of Zherdya and executed. Among the victims were 530 children and 40 infants.

ORIOL Oriol dist., Russia. Jews probably settled in the mid-19th cent. and were allowed to open a prayer house in 1876. They were also provided with a government-appointed rabbi. In 1897, the J. pop. was 1,765 (total 20,800). Some of the Jews traded in grain through the port of Rostov-on-Don. A number of Jews were injured and J. businesses looted in a pogrom staged on 31 Oct. 1905. In 1939, under the Soviets, the J. pop. was 3,143 (total 110,564). The Germans captured the city on 3 Oct. 1941 and ordered the Jews to wear a yellow Star of David. They appointed a community member as responsible for J. affairs. Most of the remaining Jews were murdered between Aug.–Dec. 1942. In Aug., 185 were murdered at the village of Malaya Gat and in Dec. a few dozen more. About 120 were murdered in the Feb.–July 1943 period, the majority on 10 July in the Streleckyi forest.

ORKENY Pest–Pilis–Solt–Kiskun dist., Hungary. Jews settled in the first half of the 19th cent., building a synagogue in 1890 and numbering 108 in 1930. Jews enjoyed a respected position in O., with some holding public office. Their situation deteriorated following the 1938 racial laws. The Germans unleashed a murderous reign of terror on their arrival in April 1944. The remaining 78 Jews were deported to Auschwitz via Lajosmisze and Monor on 8 July 1944.

ORLA (I) Bialystok dist., Poland, today Belarus. Jews are first mentioned in the early 17th cent., working the land and engaging in the grain trade. In the mid-cent. Swedish war, many lost their homes and property but recovery was rapid. By 1766, all 15 of the town's wholesalers were Jews. Jews also ran flour mills, sawmills, and distilleries. Most, however, were shopkeepers, peddlers, and petty traders. The J. pop. grew to 2,310 (total 3,003) in 1897 and then dropped to 1,167 in 1921. The Germans captured the town on 26 June 1941 after a two-year Soviet occupation. A *Judenrat* was appointed to regulate the supply of forced labor and in Aug. 1942 the J. quarter was closed off as a ghetto. In Nov. 1942 all 1,450 Jews, excluding a group of skilled workers, were deported to the Treblinka death camp. Most of those who remained died in Auschwitz in early 1943 after working for awhile in the Bielsk Podlaski ghetto.

ORLA (II) (Yid. Orlova) Novogrodek dist., Poland, today Belarus. Jews are first mentioned in 1657. Their pop. grew to 354 (total 804) in 1897, dropping through emigration to 195 in 1921. The community operated a synagogue, *beit midrash*, and *mikve* and most lived in straitened economic circumstances. The Germans arrived in late June 1941. On 2 Nov. all the Jews were expelled to the Zholudek ghetto. Most were murdered there in the *Aktion* of 8 May 1942.

ORLEANS Loiret dist., France. Jews lived here before 585. The second (533) and third (538) Councils of O. protested against mixed marriages between Jews and Christians and the Synod of O. (541) initiated restrictive measures against J. slave owners. After the expulsion of the Jews from the French kingdom in 1182, the local synagogue was converted into a church. The Jews returned in 1198 and the community became famous for J. learning, the most renowned scholar being Yosef ben Yitzhak Bekhor Shor. The end of the community came with the expulsions of the Jews of France in 1306 and in 1394. Between the World Wars, there were Jews living in O. The community was reconstructed in 1940. During WWII, O. served as the regional headquarters of the Commissariat General aux Questions Juives (CGQJ). The railroad station here served as deportation point to the death camps. In 1964 there were about 600 Jews in O., mostly from North Africa.

ORLOVA Silesia, Czechoslovakia. The late-19th cent. community erected Orthodox and Reform synagogues and was well integrated in local economic and social life. The Zionists were active after WWI. In 1930, the J. pop. was 394. In the wake of the Munich Agreement, O. was annexed to Poland in Sept. 1938 and Jews of Czech origin were expelled. The rest were deported to the ghettoes and death camps and the Nazis destroyed the two synagogues.

OROS Szabolcs dist., Hungary. Jews were apparently present in the 16th cent. and numbered 159 in 1880. Most were petty tradesmen and a few engaged in farming. Children studied in the J. school in Nyire-

gyhaza and came under Zionist influence there. In 1930, the Jews numbered 113. On 14 April 1944, they were taken to the Nyiregyhaza ghetto and then deported to Auschwitz on 17 May 1944.

OROSHAZA Bekes dist., Hungary. Jews probably settled in the early 19th cent., building a splendid synagogue in the Neologist style in 1890. A J. school founded in 1852 had 176 students in 1886 and the community reached a peak pop. of 938 in 1900 (4% of the total). Many earmarked for deportation to Auschwitz on 26 June 1944 arrived in Austria by mistake. After the war, 300 returned to renew the community, most of the young people subsequently leaving for Israel.

OROSZVAR Zichy estate, Hungary. An organized community existed by 1725, reaching a peak pop. of 460 in 1848 but declining to nine in 1930. In 1944, the remaining Jews were deported to Auschwitz via Magyarovar.

OROW Lwow dist., Poland, today Ukraine. The J. pop. in 1921 was 101. The Jews were murdered locally by the Ukrainians or deported to the Belzec death camp via Boryslaw in Aug. 1942.

ORSHA Vitebsk dist., Belorussia. Jews are first mentioned in the 16th cent. Their pop. was 368 in 1765 and 7,383 (total 13,061) in 1897. Most of the town's artisans were Jews (383 of a total 464). In a pogrom staged against the Jews in Oct. 1905, 30 were murdered, many injured, and homes and stores pillaged. In the first decade of the 20th cent., the community maintained four J. schools, a *talmud torah*, and numerous *hadarim*. Under the Soviets two J. elementary schools operated until the authorities closed them down in the mid-1930s. Among the J. artisans, 95% were organized in cooperatives and in 1930, 47 J. families were employed in agriculture. In 1939, the J. pop. was 7,992 (total 37,578). The Germans captured the city on 16 July 1941. Some Jews managed to escape. A *Judenrat* was appointed and charged with collecting various tributes for the Germans. In Sept., two ghettoes were set up with 2,000 Jews in each. On 26 Nov. 1941, over 5,000 Jews were murdered at the J. cemetery.

ORSOVA S. Transylvania dist., Rumania. Jews from Slovakia first settled in the early 19th cent. and in 1876 the community joined the Neologist association. The majority supported Zionism and many emigrated to Palestine prior to WWII. The J. pop. was 192 in 1930 (2% of the total). In Sept. 1940, J. property was confiscated and most males were taken to the Targu-Jiu camp for forced labor. Others were exiled to Transnistria. After the war, the majority moved to larger towns.

ORTELSBURG (Pol. Szczytno) East Prussia, Germany, today Poland. The first Jews were allowed to settle in O. in 1768. The J. pop. grew to 110 in 1848 and to 199 in 1871. A cemetery was established in 1815 and a synagogue was consecrated in 1864. It was destroyed by the Russians at the beginning of WWI together with many other city buildings. A new synagogue was dedicated in 1924. In the early 1930s, stones and even a fire bomb were thrown at J. homes and Nazis attacked Jews in the street. About 120 Jews were living in O. when the Nazis came to power. Intensive boycott measures, including the smashing of shop windows and the harassment of non-J. customers of J. stores, began in March 1933, prior to the 1 April boycott. At the same time, several Jews were arrested. On *Kristallnacht* (9–10 Nov. 1938), the synagogue was burned down. By May 1939, only 27 Jews remained in O. No further information about their fate is available.

ORTENBERG Hesse, Germany. Although Jews lived there in medieval times, no organized community was established until the 17th cent. It numbered 102 (9% of the total) in 1861 and dedicated its third synagogue in 1877. Jews played a leading role in the town's social, cultural, and sporting life, and some were even members of the church choir. As a result of the Nazi boycott, however, Jews hastened to leave (44 emigrating) and the community disbanded in 1936.

ORZECHOVNO Vilna dist., Poland, today Belarus. The J. pop. in 1921 was 101 (total 301). The Jews were probably deported by the Germans to the death camps in June 1942.

OSANN Rhineland, Germany. The J. pop. was 77 in 1833 (13% of the total) and 106 in 1843. There was a synagogue in use at this time. In 1899, a new one was consecrated. In 1933, 17 Jews remained. In 1935, Jews owned only a grocery and butcher shop. The town had 24 Jews in 1936; three emigrated over the next two years. On *Kristallnacht* (9–10 Nov. 1938), the synagogue and the homes of the four remaining families were destroyed. Between Dec. 1938 and April 1939, six more Jews emigrated and six left for Trier. In May 1939 none were left.

OSCHERSLEBEN Saxony, Germany. Jews settled in O. about 1650. The J. pop. in 1900 was 100. There were two synagogues, established in 1718 and 1856, and two cemeteries (1678 and 1905). When the Nazis assumed power in 1933, there were only 40–50 Jews in the city. The community was forced to sell both the synagogue and the cemetery in Sept. 1938, which was probably the reason they were not damaged on *Kristallnacht* (9–10 Nov. 1938). After *Kristallnacht* most Jews fled abroad. The last five Jews moved to Berlin and Halberstadt. No further information about their fate is available.

OSIAKOW (Osjakow) Lodz dist., Poland. A community was established here in the second half of the 18th cent. and by 1897 numbered 759. In Oct. 1939, 600 Jews were concentrated in a ghetto, and in Aug. 1942 were sent to Wielun and then deported to the Lodz ghetto and Chelmno death camp.

OSIECK Lublin dist., Poland. A small community existed in the early 19th cent., reaching a pop. of 324 (total 1,568) in 1921. Anti-J. riots and agitation occasionally erupted. The Zionists were active in the 1920s and 1930s. In WWII the Jews were probably transferred to larger settlements by the Nazis and deported to the Treblinka death camp in fall 1942.

OSIEK (I) Cracow dist., Poland. An organized J. community of around 50 families (a quarter of the total) existed through the second half of the 19th cent., with 10–20 families subsequently emigrating to larger towns or fleeing in WWI. The Germans expelled the ghettoized Jews to Staszow on 17 Oct. 1942 and from there most of them were sent to the Treblinka death camp.

OSIEK (II) Lublin dist., Poland. Jews settled in the first half of the 19th cent. and numbered 154 by 1857, mainly engaged in agriculture but later active also as tradesmen. Between the World Wars their number reached 500, with the Zionists active. Antisemitism intensified in the 1930s as J. property was vandalized and

Jews were attacked physically. The Germans arrived in Sept. 1939, appointing a *Judenrat* in Oct. and instituting a regime of forced labor. A ghetto was established in April 1942, bringing hunger and disease. On 15 Oct. 1942 all were deported to the Treblinka death camp after the sick and old were murdered in the streets.

OSIENCINY   Warsaw dist., Poland. J. settlement began in the late 1700s. The J. pop. in 1921 was 436 (total 820). Agudat Israel maintained leadership of the community. Under the German occupation (10 Sept. 1939), a *Judenrat* was appointed, mainly to supply forced labor. The ghetto, set up in 1940, was liquidated in April 1942 and its Jews sent to the Chelmno death camp.

OSIJEK   Croatia, Yugoslavia, today Republic of Croatia. The J. community was organized in the mid-19th cent. O. became a regional center of Zionism and of J. youth rallies in the early 1900s. The first Yugoslavian Zionist weekly was published in O. in 1909. The Jews at first worked in trade and as clerks and later went into commerce, management, and academic professions. The J. pop. in 1931 was 3,020 (total 40,337). Antisemitism was rare until the Germans entered O. with their Croatian collaborators in April 1941. The Jews were persecuted and arrested and their property plundered. They were soon sent to camps around O. and concentrated in Jasenovac, where they perished.

OSIPENKO   (until 1929 and from 1959, Berdiansk) Zaporozhe dist., Ukraine. J. settlement commenced shortly after the founding of this important Azov Sea port city. In 1864, the J. pop. was 703. The region's first *talmud torah* was opened in 1860 and the city's first J. private school was founded in 1882, with three operating by the 1890s. The J. pop. rose to 3,048 including 258 Karaites in 1897 (total 26,496) but dropped to 2,393 in 1939 (total 51,681) under Soviet rule. The Germans captured the city on 7 Oct. 1941 and murdered about 1,000 Jews on 19 Oct. In 1942, J. women in mixed marriages were murdered along with their children.

OSIPOVICHI   Mogilev dist., Belorussia. Jews settled in the 1880s after the local railway station on the Romny line was completed. At first Jews were employed carting building materials for the new railroad; later they entered the lumber trade. An organized community was already in existence by the late 19th cent. Most Jews were *Mitnaggedim*. The hasidic minority were followers of Lubavich and Koidanov. The Zionists and the Bund were both active during this period. In 1905, the Jews organized for self-defense. In 1910, their pop. was 755 (total 1,695). In 1919, during the civil war, the Poles staged a pogrom against the Jews, pillaging and raping and also hanging one Jew. Tze'irei Tziyyon and Hehalutz groups were founded in 1920. In 1925, under the Soviets, the Hehalutz group had 40 members. In the mid-1920s, 37.5% of the Jews were blue- and white-collar workers and 42% artisans. A J. school operated throughout the period. The J. pop. in 1939 was 1,694. The Germans captured the city on 30 June 1941. In Jan 1942, the Germans stopped the 3.5 ounce daily bread ration for all Jews except those put to hard labor. All Jews were forced to wear the yellow badge. In May 1942, the Germans murdered 3,000 Jews from O. and the surrounding area.

OSLANY   Slovakia, Czechoslovakia, today Republic of Slovakia. J. settlement is noted in the 1830s and in 1851 a community was constituted with a cemetery, prayer house, and *mikve* from 1855. A J. elementary school was opened in 1860 as the J. pop. rose to 74 in 1869 and 125 (total 1,577) in 1900. After WWI, rioting peasants and demobilized soldiers attacked Jews, who fought them off in an organized and armed defense effort. The Zionists were active. Jews owned 13 business establishments, two workshops, a sawmill, and a brickyard. Overall economic conditions were generally satisfactory. The local rabbinate served Jews in numerous smaller settlements and communities. In 1940, the J. pop. was 85. With the creation of the Slovakian state in March 1939, the Jews were subjected to severe persecution and their businesses "Aryanized." Young men were sent to the Novaky transit camp in March 1942 and young women to Auschwitz via Patronka in April. In June, families were deported to death camps in the Lublin dist. and thus O. became one of the first settlements in western Slovakia where all the Jews were deported and perished.

OSLAW BIALY   Stanislawow dist., Poland, today Ukraine. The J. pop. in 1921 was 187. The Jews were apparently expelled to Nadworna for liquidation in summer 1942.

OSLO capital of Norway. During the 17th and 18th cents., when Denmark and Norway were united, most regulations concerning the Jews of Denmark applied to those of Norway. According to the Norwegian Legal Code of 1687, a clear distinction was made between Sephardi and other Jews. Since the latter required special authorization to stay in the country, very few did. The Constitution of 1814, when Norway broke away from the Danish crown, specifically barred Jews and Jesuits from entering the kingdom. It was not until 1851 that the ban on J. immigration was lifted. Its repeal was largely due to the vigorous efforts of Henrik Wergeland, Norway's national poet, who devoted years of his life to this goal. In 1866, there were 14 Jews in O. A cemetery was opened in 1876. After 1880, immigration increased, with Jews arriving from Eastern Europe. Formally, the community, designated a "Mosaic Congregation," was established in 1892 by the 136 Jews residing in the city. The community grew to 343 in 1900; 688 in 1910; and 852 in 1930. A synagogue was consecrated in 1920 and a second one in 1921. In 1930, the J. pop. of Norway was 1,359 and in 1940, prior to the German occupation, 1,500–1,600, including about 200 refugees from Central Europe. A J. relief committee was organized in O. With the Norwegians surrendering on 9 June, Hitler appointed Joseph Terboven as Reich Commissioner in occupied Norway. In Oct. 1940, all Jews were barred from academic and other professions. In June 1941, about 60 Jews, all Russian citizens, were arrested and tortured before being released three weeks later. On 1 Feb. 1942, a national government was formed under Vidkun Quisling. In June, the J. community of O., numbering 800, was forced to register. In the face of the government's collaboration with the Nazis, the rescue of almost half of Norway's J. pop., smuggled to Sweden by the Norwegian resistance, takes on added significance. It is estimated that in 1940–45, 925 Jews were among the 50,000 Norwegians who escaped to Sweden. Of all the J. communities in Scandinavia, Norway's J. community had the highest level of loss (45%) during the Holocaust. By Oct., all J. property had been officially confiscated. On 26–27 Oct., Norwegian police arrested all J. males over the age of 16 and on 25–26 Nov., women and children. Concentration camps were established at Bredvedt near O. and at Berg near Tonsberg. On 27 Nov., 532 J. prisoners were put on board the *Donau* sailing for Stettin, from where they were transported to Auschwitz. Another ship with J. prisoners

was the *Monte Rosa* The persecution of the Jews did not end with the Nov. deportations. Another major deportation took place on 25 Feb. 1943, when 158 Norwegian Jews were put on board the *Gotenland* and transported to Auschwitz via Stettin. In all, 740 Jews were deported from Norway during the Holocaust, 471 of whom were Norwegian citizens. Only 24 survived. Twenty-two lost their lives through other war-related actions. In 1968, there were 650 Jews in O.

OSNABRUECK Hanover, Germany. Jews settled in the late Middle Ages. A J. moneylender is mentioned in 1267 and others joined him later in the cent. In 1309, Bishop Engelbert II granted letters of protection to ten J. families. Twelve new families received letters of protection in 1327. Jews lived in their own quarter and maintained a synagogue and cemetery. In 1350, during the Black Death persecutions, Jews were accused by townsmen of spreading the plague and consequently massacred. But the community survived the blow and continued to grow until renewed local pressure brought about their expulsion. From 1431 until the early 19th cent., there were no Jews in O. J. settlement was renewed under French rule, with the Jews receiving equal rights in 1808 under the Westphalian constitution. In 1810, eight J. families were living in the town. The position of the Jews was subsequently undermined in the Kingdom of Hanover when old discriminatory measures were invoked, causing the community to stagnate at a pop. level of 30–50 until the annexation to Prussia in 1866 and the general emancipation in 1871. The J. pop. then grew from 138 in the latter year to a peak of 480 (total 59,580) in 1905. Jews played a leading economic role in the city. A Jew was the chief local army supplier in the last quarter of the 19th cent. and the Wertheim and Alsberg families established large retail outlets for household goods and textiles. Emancipation opened the doors to the city's professional, social, and cultural life but at the same time saw the rise of antisemitic forces. In religious affairs, the community had no rabbi of its own and remained under the jurisdiction of Emden. In 1906, a synagogue was completed. The local J. school had a peak enrollment of 40 children in 1901. The Relief Organization of German Jews (Hilfsverein), the Central Union (C.V.), and the Zionists were active in O., though the latter only became influential in the Nazi era. In the Weimar period, Jews were also active in public life, sitting in the municipal assembly. In

1933, the J. pop. maintained a stable level of 403. In the general boycott of 1 April, over 40 J. stores were affected as well as J. doctors and lawyers. Anti-J. legislation led to the subsequent dismissal of Jews from the public service. In 1935, the Wertheim and Alsberg establishments were "Aryanized." Those among the local residents not actively participating in the persecution of the Jews were at best indifferent to their plight. By 1938, 200 Jews had left the city and 427 by 1943. Of these, 238 emigrated, including 83 to Holland, 44 to Palestine, 43 to the U.S., 19 to England, and 17 to South America. The remaining 189 moved to other cities in Germany, with at least 82 later emigrating as well. On the eve of *Kristallnacht* (9–10 Nov. 1938), 17 or 18 J. businesses were still operating in the city. On 9 Nov. 1938, SA troops carried out mass arrests and burned down the synagogue. About 80–90 Jews were sent to the Buchenwald concentration camp. Three were murdered there and the rest released in the following months after undergoing severe abuse. In May 1939, the remaining Jews were moved to "J. houses" and placed under a regime of forced labor. They could no longer use public transportation facilities freely, leave their houses in the evening, receive guests, keep pets, own radios, etc. Their food rations included no meat, fish, or fruit. Of the 69 Jews remaining in 1941, 35 were deported to the Riga ghetto on 13 Dec. In late July 1942, 27 of the more elderly were deported to the Theresienstadt ghetto. The last seven Jews in O. were sent to Auschwitz on 1 March 1943. In addition, at least 38 Jews who had moved to other German cities and 40 who reached Holland were also deported. In all, 134 Jews perished in the Holocaust. A nearby prisoner-of-war camp held 400 Jews from Yugoslavia. These were transferred to Strasbourg in Aug. 1944. A J. community of 69 was present in 1969, when a new synagogue was consecrated.

OSOJ (Hung. Szajkofalva) Carpatho-Russia, Czechoslovakia, today Ukraine. J. settlement probably commenced in the mid-19th cent. In 1880, the J. pop. was 95 (total 1,530). With the establishment of the Czechoslovakian Republic, the J. pop. rose to 149 in 1921 and then to 163 in 1941 under the Hungarians. A number of J. families engaged in agriculture. The Hungarians occupied O. in March 1939 and in 1941 drafted a number of Jews into labor battalions for forced labor. In late July 1941, a number of families without Hungarian citizenship were expelled to Ger-

man-occupied territory in the Ukraine and murdered there. The rest were deported to Auschwitz in mid-May 1944.

OSOWA WYSZKA Volhynia dist., Poland, today Ukraine. O. was founded as a J. farm settlement in 1836 when 137 Jews purchased around 7,000 acres of land from a local estate. The community grew to 577 in 1898 but in the course of the years fewer and fewer relied on agriculture to earn a living. The Germans captured O. in July 1941. In Oct. 1942, after the harvest, the Germans transported the Jews to Kostopol, where they were murdered. About 30 youngsters escaped to the forest and formed a partisan unit.

OSS Noord-Brabant dist., Holland. Jews lived in O. in the Middle Ages and again in the early 18th cent. The J. pop. in 1899 was 226. In the 19th–20th cents. the Jews played a major role in the development of industry: Jews founded the Organon pharmaceutical company, whose best-known product was insulin, and the company which developed into the giant Unilever concern. There were over 370 Jews in 1941 (including 61 refugees). Between Aug. 1942 and June 1944, 282 were deported to Poland; 26 survived. A community was reestablished after the war.

OSTEND (Flem. Oostende) West Flanders prov., Belgium. In the second half of the 18th cent., Jews settled in O. They were mostly English and Dutch merchants involved in international commerce. Some municipal officials opposed granting them citizenship, fearing they would set up businesses in the town. Nevertheless, Salomon Mendes, a Portuguese J. businessman who settled in O. in 1781, received permission in 1788 to open a J. cemetery. The community ceased to exist in the first half of the 19th cent. In the middle of the 19th cent. Jews settled permanently in O. but only received permission to establish a synagogue in 1904. The synagogue was consecrated in 1911. According to a 1941 census, 93 Jews were residing in O. On 29 Aug. 1941, Jews were forbidden to reside there. In summer 1942, the deportations of the Jews of Belgium began, including the Jews of O. After liberation, the small O. community was reestablished as one of the 14 J. communities officially recognized in Belgium.

OSTER Chernigov dist., Ukraine. J. lessees appeared in the 17th cent. and a J. community is known from the 19th cent. In 1897, the J. pop. was 1,596 (total 5,370). General Denikin's White Army staged a pogrom against the Jews in Aug. 1919. By 1939, the J. pop. had dropped to 841. The Germans captured the town on 9 Sept. 1941, with some of the Jews fleeing. About 250 were murdered around the end of Oct. 1941.

OSTERBERG Swabia, Germany. Jews are mentioned in the mid-16th cent. The modern community was constituted when 30 J. families were settled by a local baron in 1802 and granted freedom of trade and worship. The community was dismantled in 1896 and by 1920 no Jews remained.

OSTERODE (Pol. Ostroda) East Prussia, Germany, today Poland. Jews settled in O. at the beginning of the 18th cent. and by 1735 had a cemetery and a synagogue. The J. pop. in 1880 was 222 and in 1893 a larger synagogue was inaugurated. In the early 20th cent., the J. pop. was 240–250. A bomb was placed in front of a J. store in 1932, but failed to explode. When the Nazis came to power, there were 156 Jews in O. Boycott measures reached a peak in July 1935 when J. businessmen were marched through the streets and J. shops were compelled to close for a time. By 1937, the J. pop. had declined to 75. Although at the beginning of Nov. 1938, the synagogue had been sold, it was destroyed on *Kristallnacht* (9–10 Nov. 1938). The cemetery was desecrated and J. shops were vandalized. By May 1939, the J. community had ceased to exist. Only one Jew remained. It is not known how many local Jews managed to emigrate to safe countries and how many perished in the Holocaust.

OSTERODE AM HARZ Hanover, Germany. Seven protected Jews (*Schutzjuden*) established the community in 1697, which, despite local opposition, grew to 16 families by 1754. During the 18th cent., it hired a teacher and a cantor (*hazzan*) and in 1788 built a larger synagogue. At its height between 1833 and 1843, the community numbered 104 but declined to 62 (less than 1% of the total) in 1909. On the eve of the Nazi rise to power in 1933, the community numbered just 42. Several Jews emigrated (three to Palestine) and on 19 June 1938, the community disbanded. On *Kristallnacht* (9–10 Nov. 1938), SA and SS units destroyed the synagogue's interior and looted the few remaining

J. homes. At least ten Jews from O. perished in the Holocaust.

OSTHOFEN Hesse, Germany. Established in 1722, the community numbered 129 (4% of the total) in 1880, with Jews from Abendheim and Rheinduerkheim augmenting its membership. The community adopted a Liberal form of worship in 1897. It gradually declined, numbering 62 in 1933. The district's first Nazi concentration camp was set up there (May 1933–Dec. 1934) and by 1939 all the Jews had left.

OSTRAVA (until 1929, Moravska Ostrava) Moravia, Czechoslovakia. With few exceptions, J. residence was banned until the 19th cent. The first *minyan* was formed in 1832. A decree issued by Francis Joseph I led to full rights only in 1860. The J. pop. began to grow after the discovery of coal deposits in the region and the founding of steel works by the Rothschild family (sold to the Gutmann brothers in 1873). The first synagogue was consecrated in 1857 and a Great Synagogue seating 700 men was opened in 1879 as the Silesian and Moravian communities of the city reunited after years of conflict. With the J. pop. reaching 3,000 in the 1890s, at least six additional synagogues were opened through the 1920s. The community also maintained an orphanage and old age home. A B'nai B'rith lodge was active. A J. elementary school was opened in 1863, reaching an enrollment of 303 in 1899 but then declining in attendance as assimilation took its toll. Zionist influence reestablished the school's prominence. In the 1920s, the Zionist Organization and Hehalutz opened their national offices in O. The city was also the center of most of the youth movements and the community was the first large one in the country with a Zionist majority. The Second Czechoslovakian Maccabiah was held in O. in 1929, with 2,000 J. athletes participating. The community was the third largest in Czechoslovakia after Prague and Brno with a 1930 pop. of 6,895 (total 125,304). Among the 1,889 Jewish breadwinners, 1,088 engaged in trade, especially in food and clothing; 272 were laborers; and 164 belonged to the professional class. Teddy Kollek, future mayor of Jerusalem, was born in O. in 1911. With the situation of the Jews deteriorating even before the German occupation of March 1939, Jews began emigrating, some to Palestine. The last group of 2,400 from O. and the surrounding area left on 15 Oct. 1939 with the approval of the Gestapo. Meanwhile, Jews were being arrested and their businesses "Aryanized." In spring 1939, Jews were seized for forced labor and between 5 and 14 June the Nazis burned down two synagogues. Local Jews were made to supply building materials for the construction of the Nisko labor camp in the Lublin dist. in Poland, where 1,300 Jews from O. were directed. In April 1940, some 600 Jews were forced at gunpoint to enter Soviet territory, an action which saved the lives of some; 400 were returned to O. In 1941 the J. pop. of O. was 3,903. Deportations to Auschwitz via the Theresienstadt ghetto began in Sept. 1942, when 2,582 Jews were dispatched in three transports. In all, 3,567 Jews were deported from O.; 253 survived.

OSTROG (Heb. Ostraha) Volhynia dist., Poland, today Ukraine. Jews began to settle in the late 14th cent., becoming prominent in the cloth and cattle trade with Walachia and by 1563, when the J. pop. reached 1,000, paying the highest head tax of any J. community in Volhynia. The community occupied a leading position on the Council of the Four Lands and with its great rabbis became a spiritual center for all of Poland. It was famous for its yeshiva and among its prominent rabbis were Shelomo Luria (the "Maharshal"), Yeshayahu Horowitz (the "Shelah"), Shemuel Edels (the "Maharsha"), and David Halevi Segal (the "Taz"). The community was destroyed in the Chmielnicki massacres with 600 Jews murdered in 1648 by the Cossacks with the aid of Christian townsmen and another 300 a year later when some of those who had fled returned. By the 18th cent. the community had regained its prominence, extending its jurisdiction over 23 J. settlements. Yaakov Yosef of O. brought Hasidism and his grandson Yaakov Yosef II established a hasidic dynasty. Under Russian rule in the 19th cent. the community tripled in size, numbering 9,208 (total 14,749) in 1897, though Jews remained unrepresented in local government. Jews were especially active in the lumber, cattle, and farm produce trade. They operated sawmills, hide-processing plants, candle and furniture factories, and two banks. In 1889 a great fire devastated the community and economic development was adversely affected when O. was bypassed by the Rovno–Kiev railroad. Zionist and Bund activity commenced in the early 20th cent. During WWI the community extended aid to J. refugees arriving mainly from Galicia and in 1918 organized for self-defense to ward off a Bolshevik pogrom. The new Polish-Soviet border cut the city off from 250 settlements in its eastern hinterland, leading to economic retrenchment. Between the World Wars, the Zionists increased their activity and cultural life revolved around two libraries (Hebrew and Yiddish). A Hebrew school, kindergarten, and junior high school flourished. After two years of Soviet rule (1939–41) the Germans captured the city in heavy fighting that claimed 500 J. lives (28 June–3 July 1941). Around 1,000 Jews were able to escape with the Russians. A *Judenrat* was immediately established. SS units conducting mopping-up operations against Red Army forces seized the opportunity to execute 2,000 Jews, mainly women, the sick, and the old. Another 2,500 J. men were murdered in the forest on 1 Sept. The remaining 3,000 Jews were herded into a ghetto, sealed off in June 1942, and subjected to forced labor. On 15 Oct. 1942 they were led into the forest and murdered. Most of the 800 who had escaped were soon rounded up and likewise murdered.

OSTROGOZHSK Voronezh dist., Russia. Jews probably settled in the late 19th cent. and numbered 221 (total 22,990) in 1926. After the Germans captured the city on 5 July 1942, they murdered the remaining Jews in the area at the local prisoner-of-war camp.

OSTROH (Uhersky; Yid. Shtaynitz) Moravia, Czechoslovakia. Organized J. life is attested from the 14th cent. with a synagogue and cemetery apparently opened by the 16th cent. R. David ben Shemuel ha-Levi, author of the *Turei Zahav* commentary on the *Shulhan Arukh* was active in O. in 1658. The J. pop. rose to 478 in 1848 and was 123 (total 3,497) in 1930. After WWI, the Zionists were active. The Jews were probably deported to the Theresienstadt ghetto together with the Jews of Brno in late 1941–early 1942. From there they were transported to the death camps. The Nazis destroyed the ancient synagogue.

OSTROLENKA Bialystok dist., Poland. Towards the end of the 18th cent. Jews established a community and from 1826 to 1862 were restricted to a special quarter. By 1897 the J. pop. numbered 3,600. Apart from their traditional occupations, the Jews developed the timber industry and ran flour mills. In the spring of 1914, most of the homes belonging to the Jews were burned down and they were expelled under the subsequent German occupation. Some returned after the war but the community (4,291 in 1931; total 13,341) suf-

Main street of Ostrolenka, Poland

fered from economic and physical oppression due to growing antisemitism. The community was led by Agudat Israel but the J. representation on the city council was mostly Zionist. The Germans occupied O. on 10 Sept. 1939, persecuting those Jews who had not fled. On 6 Oct. 1939 the Jews were expelled to Soviet-held territory, living until the spring of 1941 in Bialystok, Brisk (Brest-Litovsk), Slonim, Lomzha,

Synagogue in Ostropol, Ukraine (The Russian Ethnographic Museum, Petersburg/photo courtesy of Yad Vashem, The Holocaust Martyrs' and Heroes' Remembrance Authority, Jerusalem)

and Szczuczyn. They shared the fate of the Jews of those communities.

OSTROPOL Kamenets-Podolski dist., Ukraine. The community was destroyed in the Chmielnicki massacres of 1648–49. In 1765, the J. pop. was 58; in 1897 it stood at 2,714 (36% of the total). The late 18th cent. Yiddish jester Hershele Ostropoler was born here. In the Soviet period, the J. pop. dropped to 1,325 in 1926 and 1,063 in 1939. A J. rural council (soviet) and elementary school were active between the World Wars. The Germans captured the town on 10 July 1941. On 23 June 1942 they executed 581 Jews from O. at Staro-Konstantinov. Another 17 families (73 Jews) were murdered in Lubar in the Zhitomir dist.

OSTROSHITSKI GORODOK Minsk dist., Belorussia. Jews probably settled in the first half of the 19th cent. In 1897, their pop. was 760 (total 1,115), remaining stable through the beginning of the Soviet period. Many Jews worked in agriculture (323, or 46 families, in 1924–25 and 17 families in a kolkhoz in the early 1930s). The Germans occupied O. in late June 1941 and murdered the few remaining Jews there in late summer 1941.

OSTROV Leningrad dist., Russia. Jews probably settled in the mid-19th cent. They were permitted to erect a prayer house in 1869 and in 1897 reached a pop. of 749 (total 1,869). In the Soviet period, the J. pop. declined, to 442 in 1926 and 174 (total 12,849) in 1939. Following the German occupation of the town on 6 July 1941, about 200 Jews and gypsies were taken to Pskov and executed.

OSTROVNO Vitebsk dist., Belorussia. Jews settled in the late 17th cent., numbering 167 in 1765 and 514 (total 848) in 1897. In 1923, under the Soviets, their pop. dropped to 410. In 1930, 35 J. families were employed at a nearby kolkhoz. A J. elementary school was in operation during the period. The Germans arrived on 9 July 1941, establishing an open ghetto on 19 July. On 30 Sept., the 169 Jews there were murdered.

Water carrier in Ostrow, Poland, Sept. 1939 (Bundesarchiv/photo courtesy of Yad Vashem, The Holocaust Martyrs' and Heroes' Remembrance Authority, Jerusalem)

OSTROW Lublin dist., Poland. Jews settled in the late 17th cent. and were instrumental in the town's industrialization towards the end of the 19th cent., establishing a flour mill and hide-processing plant. Most, however, eked out a living as tradesmen on market and fair days and circulating through the villages with their wares the rest of the year. The J. pop. grew from 885 in 1857 to 1,267 (total 3,813) in 1921. Between the World Wars, the Zionist movements, the Bund, and Agudat Israel were active. The Germans arrived in Sept. 1939 and set up a *Judenrat* and a ghetto whose pop. rose from 2,110 to 3,333 in May 1940 with the influx of refugees. Another 1,700 refugees arrived in 1941. In Oct. 1942, the sick and old were murdered and the rest deported to the Belzec death camp. Many who fled joined the Polish Armia Ludowa partisans. Yehiel Grynszpan, a native of O., established a J. partisan group which operated in the Parczew forest and cooperated with Soviet units.

OSTROWIEC (Yid. Ostrovtsa) Kielce dist., Poland. Jews were present in small numbers in the late 16th cent. In the 1640s, they built one of the most beautiful synagogues in Poland as well as consecrating a cemetery. Most fled during the Chmielnicki massacres of 1648–49 and those remaining suffered grievously during the first Swedish war in the 1650s. Recovery was relatively rapid. The community had a permanent representative on the Council of the Four Lands and was considered one of the most important in the region. Among its illustrious rabbis was Azriel Meisels (d. 1786), who brought Hasidism to Central Poland. At the turn of the 19th cent., R. Meir Yehiel Halstok established his court in O. and made it a hasidic center. A branch of the Nowogrodek yeshiva was also set up. The Jews enjoyed a period of prosperity in the 19th cent. The city underwent industrialization and Jews initiated the opening of cement, soap, and soft drink factories. Many entered the building trades when army barracks were constructed for the Russian garrison. Others operated taverns and restaurants. Great fires struck the community in 1895 and 1910, but the J. pop. continued to grow, rising from 2,720 in 1857 and 6,146 in 1899 to 10,095 (total 19,765) in 1921. The Zionists became active in 1904, joined by the Bund and Po'alei Zion in 1906, and a few years later by Mizrachi. Community life continued to flourish during WWI despite Russian and Polish depredations, but in its aftermath economic conditions deteriorated.

Most J. workshops and small factories (283 in the clothing industry, 76 in food) operated seasonally and J. tradesmen had to compete with the new Polish cooperatives, forcing many J. establishments out of business. The Joint Distribution Committee offered financial assistance and the TOZ organization provided health care from 1935. The Zionists and the Bund promoted cultural life, respectively sponsoring Tarbut and CYSHO schools, while Agudat Israel, operating since 1918, ran a Beth Jacob school for about 150 girls. The Maccabi sports organization had nearly 150 members and included a drama circle and orchestra. The Zionists also played an important role in the public life of O., gaining nearly a third of municipal council seats in the 1928 elections and a majority in the community council. Before the occupation of the city by the Germans on 7 Sept. 1939, there were about 10,000 Jews in O. Many fled with the Polish army. In late Sept., a *Judenrat* was set up and about 3,000 Jews were put to work in German war factories. An exorbitant "contribution" was then exacted from the community and families were relieved of their household possessions. A ghetto was set up in April 1941, its pop. swelling to 15,000 by the end of the year with the influx of refugees, including Jews from Warsaw, Lodz, and Vienna. In May 1942, 3,000 Jews were deported to the death camps. Calls for resistance by J. activists from Warsaw were dismissed by the *Judenrat*. Thousands more were murdered locally or deported to the Treblinka death camp in Oct. On 10 Jan. 1943, 2,000 more were sent to Treblinka in a new *Aktion*. The remaining 1,000 Jews continued to work in the German plants. Groups of young people succeeded in escaping and joining up with Polish partisans, who, in several instances, betrayed or murdered them. The ghetto and its remaining inhabitants were finally liquidated in April 1943.

OSTROWIEC-LOSZY   Vilna dist., Poland, today Belarus. A few Jews were present by 1886 and about 100 by 1913, mostly engaging in petty trade, with a few prominent merchants dealing in lumber and farm produce and others running a flour mill and beer brewery. Most were impoverished between the World Wars. After two years of Russian rule the Germans arrived in June 1941 and in fall 1941 confined the Jews, including refugees, to a ghetto. Almost all were executed at the end of the year. The few who remained were joined by Jews sent there from other villages and the ghetto

became a labor camp. All its inhabitants were killed either in April 1942 or April 1943.

OSTROW-MAZOWIECKA   Bialystok dist., Poland. Jews in small numbers settled in the 18th cent. despite a residence ban. The community grew to 2,412 in 1857 and 6,595 (total 7,914) in 1897. Most Jews were tradesmen but a few were active in light industry and as army suppliers. Tensions ran high between the *Mitnaggedim* and the many hasidic groups (Gur, Warka, etc.). Among the rabbis, David Shelomo Margolioth served in 1883–86, replaced, after being rejected by the Hasidim, by Gershon Hanokh Leiner of Radzyn. Subsequently R. Yehuda Leib Gordin, whose Russian-language book on the Talmud was used by the defense in the Beilis trial (1913), was installed as acceptable to both sides. After WWI the Jews lived in straitened economic circumstances but community life was well developed. Most of the Zionist groups were represented as was Agudat Israel and the Bund. In addition to the traditional *heder* system, where 200 children studied, there was a J. public school and kindergarten with 160 pupils sponsored by the Tarbut organization, a Yavne (Mizrachi) school founded in 1934, and Agudat Israel schools for boys and girls (Beth Jacob) teaching in Yiddish. A Musar yeshiva attracted dozens of local and outside students. The Germans captured the city on 8 Sept. 1939. Four hundred Jews were shot in Nov. in retaliation for a local fire. Most of the others fled to Soviet territory, most concentrating in Slonim and Stolin in eastern Poland and perishing after the Germans arrived in Sept. 1941.

OSTROW WIELKOPOLSKI   Poznan dist., Poland. Twelve Jews were granted residence and trade rights in 1724 and the community was permitted to consecrate a synagogue and cemetery. In the 19th cent. many ran large workshops in the clothing and fur industry or large stores while descendants of the community's founding families became leading merchants. With the spread of education, a professional class emerged, accompanied by a process of Germanization and emigration to the big German cities. The J. pop. reached a peak of 1,919 (total 7,220) in 1861 before a steady decline set in. A. J. elementary school was opened in 1835, enrolling 136 children, and a *talmud torah* for 362 children was founded in 1860. Also in 1860 a synagogue with a domed roof in the Moorish style was completed. A fire during Yom Kippur prayers in 1872 killed 14 women and 21 children. The Zionists became active in 1905. After WWI, emigration was stepped up, with some reaching North and South America and Palestine. All the remaining 17 Jews managed to flee the city in Dec. 1939 after the German invasion.

OSTROZEC   Volhynia dist., Poland, today Ukraine. Jews were present with various privileges from the 16th cent. and numbered 636 (total 1,464) in 1897. The town was captured by the Germans on 26 July 1941. In Aug., 40 J. men were murdered and in Sept. another 100. A ghetto was set up in April 1942, swelled by refugees to 1,700 people. On 9 Oct. they were led out of the town and murdered beside open pits.

OSTRYNA   Nowogrodek dist., Poland, today Belarus. Jews were probably present in the late 16th cent. The community dwindled with the wars of the 17th–18th cents. but by 1897 reached a pop. of 1,440 (total 2,410). J. tradesmen based their livelihoods on weekly market days. The J. pop. in 1921 was 1,067. A Yiddish school was founded in 1921 and a Hebrew Tarbut school in 1923 which became the center of the community's cultural life, housing a band, choir, and drama circle. The Germans captured the town on 25 June 1941. Executions commenced within two weeks, including teachers and those providing religious services. A ghetto was set up in Oct. 1941. The arrival of 500 J. refugees from Nowy Dwor brought the pop. up to 1,200, subjected to a regime of forced labor. In Oct. 1942 all were sent to the Kelbasin transit camp near Grodno and a month later deported to Auschwitz.

OSTRZESZOW   Poznan dist., Poland. Jews were probably present by the mid-17th cent. Most engaged in crafts and petty trade, with a few big wholesalers dealing in grain. During the 19th cent. a professional class educated in German universities also emerged. The J. pop reached a peak of 422 (total 2,979) in 1885 and then declined steadily through emigration. Fourteen remained on the eve of WWII; 11 fled and three were expelled by the Germans to the Lodz ghetto in late 1939.

OSVEYA   Vitebsk dist., Belorussia. The J. pop. was 316 in 1765 and 1,660 (60% of the total) in 1897. In 1926, under the Soviets, it was 700. A J. council was established in 1924 and a J. elementary school was active. In the 1920s, 45% of the Jews were artisans, most organized in cooperatives. In 1930, 22 J. families were employed in two nearby kolkhozes. The J. pop. in 1939 was 350. The Germans occupied the town on 1 July 1941. In early March 1942, they executed 650 Jews in the municipal park, apparently including Jews from the surrounding area.

OSWIENCIM   (Ger. Auschwitz; Yid. Ushpizin) Cracow dist., Poland. Jews arrived before the town's annexation to the Polish kingdom in 1564 and were soon saddled with residence restrictions. The community suffered grievously in the Swedish invasion of 1655–56, recovering slowly. Under Austrian rule from 1772 the town's cattle market became a mainstay of J. trade. Development accelerated in the late 19th cent. when O. became an important railroad and highway junction. Jews were among the pioneers of light industry, setting up food, tanning, and building-material plants, as well as dominating trade and the crafts. The J. pop. reached 2,535 in 1880 (total 4,754) and more than doubled in the next 30 years despite two great fires that left many homeless. During this period, Zanz Hasidism was the dominant force in the community, while R. Shelomo Halberstam, the founder of the Bobow dynasty, established his court there. Nonetheless, Zionism was able to make early inroads and between the World Wars the two camps operated vigorously side by side, the Hasidim controlling the community council and the Zionists winning a majority of J. votes for the Sejm. At the end of WWI, local Poles abetted by militiamen and garrison troops pillaged and persecuted the Jews despite the resistance of self-defense groups, leaving the community on the brink of starvation. Anti-J. agitation continued to cut into J. livelihoods and endanger J. lives. The Germans entered O. on 9 Sept. 1939. Many Jews fled after the German bombardment a week earlier. Immediately Jews were terrorized with the active participation of the populace. The synagogue was burned down within a few days. In Dec. 1939, a *Judenrat* was set up. In Feb. 1940, 200–500 Jews per day (builders, glaziers, carpenters, painters) were put to work at the old Polish barracks next to a major railroad terminal just outside the town. This was to become the first Auschwitz camp. In the course of 1940 the Jews were concentrated in a special quarter. In Oct., 600 were sent to

Railroad tracks leading into Birkenau (Auschwitz II), Oswienecim, Poland

the Annaberg labor camp in Germany and at the end of the year another few hundred were sent to Silesian camps. Those remaining were expelled in April 1941, mostly to Sosnowiec and Bendzin, and were caught up in the wave of deportations to the Belzec death camp in the summer and fall of 1942. The complex of concentration and extermination camps outside the city became operative in June 1940 with Auschwitz I and in Oct. 1941 with Birkenau (Auschwitz II). The camps played a central role in implementing the Nazi "Final Solution," claiming 1.5–2 million J. lives before the camps were liberated by the Soviet army on 27 Jan. 1945.

OSZMIANA Vilna dist., Poland, today Belarus. Jews are first mentioned in 1765, mostly engaging in the lumber trade and leasing concessions. In the early 19th cent. they were joined by artisans and village peddlers as their pop. grew to 1,460 in 1847 and 3,803 (total 7,214) in 1897 after many expelled from the neighboring villages by Czar Alexander III settled in

O. Most Jews dealt in farm produce and petty trade with the more substantial merchants trading in grain, livestock, lumber, and hides. Various artisan groups operated their own prayer houses in addition to the Great Synagogue and the hasidic *shtibl*. R. Yehuda Leib Fein (1906–14) headed the local yeshiva and was considered one of the outstanding rabbis of Poland. WWI left many Jews without an income as the J. pop. dropped to 3,300 in 1925. Between the World Wars many Jews were artisans while 26 J. families ran farms. In this period most of the Jews identified with Zionism, though an anti-Zionist coalition of Yiddishists and Agudat Israel controlled the community council. Children studied at a Hebrew Tarbut school (190 students), a Mizrachi Yavne school, and a Yiddish CYSHO school. The Germans captured the city on 26 June 1941. J. homes were looted by *Wehrmacht* troops guided by young Poles. A *Judenrat* was appointed to supply goods to the Germans while the able-bodied were seized for forced labor. In mid-July, hundreds of Jews accused of being pro-Soviet were transported out of the city and never seen again. On 25 July, 700 J. males were taken to the village of Bartel and executed beside freshly dug pits. The widows and orphans were confined to a ghetto on 2 Oct. 1941, its pop. swelling to 1,800 with the arrival of refugees. On 19 Oct. 1942, 406 of the sick and old were executed at Oglyovo. The rest, around 2,500 Jews, were divided in spring 1943 between the Vilna and Kovno ghettoes and the labor camps, with 713 murdered at Ponary while in transit and the rest sharing the fate of local Jews.

OTRADNAYA Krasnodar territory, Russia. The Germans occupied the village in summer 1942, murdering 64 Jews at Bezyminnyi. Another group of 40 J. refugees was murdered at Armavir. In all, about 500 Jews from the area were murdered, most of them refugees from the western Soviet Union.

OTTENSOOS Middle Franconia, Germany. The J. community dates from the 15th cent. Heavy taxation and looting during the Thirty Years War (1618–1648) undermined its economic position. In 1698 the town was annexed to Bavaria and despite local opposition the community continued to grow. With the abrogation of the state rabbinate in 1808, it became independent. In 1837 the J. pop. reached 133 (total 570). A new synagogue was erected in 1872. In 1933, 25 Jews remained. The synagogue was wrecked on *Kristallnacht* (9–10 Nov. 1938). By 1939 all the Jews had left.

OTTERSTADT Palatinate, Germany. Jews settled in the 18th cent. and numbered 57 in 1848. In 1856 they formed with the Jews of Waldsee a congregation independent of Speyer. Twenty-two Jews remained in 1900 and two in 1939. At least one perished in the Holocaust.

OTTRAU Hesse–Nassau, Germany. Established in the 18th cent., the community numbered 52 in 1835, dwindling to 18 in 1933. The undamaged synagogue was sold after *Kristallnacht* (9–10 Nov. 1938) and all the Jews left, seven emigrating.

OTTWEILER Saar, Germany. Jews are first mentioned in the late 18th cent. Many dealt in livestock. In 1815, a synagogue was consecrated, with the community under the jurisdiction of the Liberal R. Yosef Cahan of Trier from 1840. A private J. elementary school was started in 1825. The J. pop. rose to a peak of 170 (total 2,963) in 1843, including 70 children up to the age of 14. With the inauguration of a railway station in St. Johann in 1852, promoting the industrial development of the Saar, Jews began to leave O. for the industrial towns, their pop. dropping to 55 in 1895. In the late 19th cent. antisemitism flared up under the influence of a local doctor. With the defeat of the Center Party in the 1907 Reichstag elections, Catholic elements began agitating against Liberals and Jews. In mid-1933, the J. pop. was 81. With the Nazi rise to power and the annexation of the Saar to the Reich by plebiscite in 1935, most Jews left, including 19 to Palestine, 12 to the U.S., 13 to France, and 19 to other German cities. On the morning after *Kristallnacht* (9–10 Nov. 1938), the synagogue was wrecked, the J. cemetery was desecrated, J. homes were vandalized, and Jews beaten and arrested. After the disturbances, the community ceased to function. On 22 Oct. 1940, 13 Jews were deported to the Gurs concentration camp. In all, 20 Jews perished in the Holocaust, including 11 in Auschwitz.

OTTYNIA Stanislawow dist., Poland, today Ukraine. Jews are first mentioned in 1635, but the community only began to grow significantly toward the end of the 19th cent., reaching a pop. of 2,081 in 1900 (total 4,940). The hasidic Vishnitz dynasty had an influential court there which generated additional sources of income along with an iron foundry. The economic prosperity of the community came to an abrupt end with the Russian occupation in 1914–17, which was also marked by anti-J. acts. After the war, the number of Jews declined and many were on welfare. Antisemitism increased in the 1930s. In Aug 1941, a pogrom by Germans and Ukrainians caused the death of many Jews. Around 1,800 were expelled on 25 Sept. 1942 to Stanislawow and from there to the Belzec death camp.

OTWOCK Warsaw dist., Poland. The J. community grew with the development of the city as a health resort in the early 20th cent., numbering 3,356 in 1909 and 5,408 (total 8,560) in 1921. Jews ran hotels and kosher restaurants for the large J. clientele, worked as musicians and waiters, and owned most of the stores in the city. On the eve of WWI, the first J. clinics were opened for children and for the mentally ill, followed in 1928 by a tuberculosis sanatorium. A luxurious new synagogue with 650 seats also dated from 1928.

Purim performance, Otwock, Poland

O. was the seat of a number of hasidic courts, including the Lubavitch Rebbe's (Yosef Yitzhak Schneersohn) from 1936. He also founded a yeshiva there. The largest group were the Gur Hasidim, who found political expression in Agudat Israel, which controlled the community council throughout the 1930s. There were two separate Orthodox schools for boys and girls, a Yavne religious school, and, until 1928, a Tarbut Hebrew school. Almost all the Zionist parties were represented in O. as well as the youth movements. The Germans captured O. on 29 Sept. 1939. Jews were seized for forced labor and a number were murdered. A *Judenrat* was appointed in Oct. and in Dec. about 15,000 were crowded into a ghetto, where a semblance of normal life was maintained in the face of severe want. In Jan. 1942, 150 young Jews were deported to the Treblinka death camp to be among the first executed there. On 19 Aug. 1942, about 8,000 Jews were sent to Treblinka and Auschwitz and most of the 4,000 who evaded deportation were sought out and murdered in the ghetto or the forests.

OUD-BEIJERLAND Zuid-Holland dist., Holland. J. settlement began in the mid-18th cent. and 205 Jews were living there in 1852. In 1941 there were 30 Jews (total 6,410). Most were sent to the Sobibor death camp and Auschwitz in 1942. Only eight survived the Holocaust.

OVENHAUSEN Westphalia, Germany. Jews are first mentioned in 1702 and numbered 48 (total 955) in 1871 and 14 in 1925. Twelve were deported by the Nazis to concentration camps in 1941–42.

OVIDIOPOL Odessa dist., Ukraine. The J. pop. was 394 (total 5,187) in 1897 and 78 in 1926. Jews were attacked in a pogrom in 1905. The Germans captured O. in WWII and on 16 Oct. 1941, it was annexed to Transnistria. A total of 150 Jews from the area were murdered.

OVRUCH Zhitomir dist., Ukraine. Three J. families were present in 1629. In 1750, O. Jews are mentioned in a dispute over taxes between Pinsk (Council of Lithuania) and Volhynia (Council of the Four Lands). In 1897, the J. pop. was 3,445 (total 7,393). Jews were particularly active in the lumber and tanning industries. Most were Habad Hasidim. After the Oct. 1917 Revo-

Synagogue in Ozarintsy, Ukraine, 1928 (Historical Museum, Ukraine/photo courtesy of Yad Vashem, The Holocaust Martyrs' and Heroes' Remembrance Authority, Jerusalem)

lution, the Jews were attacked in a number of pogroms, the bloodiest of them in late 1918–early 1919, when the Petlyura gangs killed 80 in a 17-day period and pillaged and burned all J. homes. In the mid-1930s, under the Soviets, 26% of the Jews were factory workers, 33% white-collar workers, and 30% artisans. Most (80%) belonged to cooperatives, where the majority of members were Jews. The J. pop. was 3,862 in 1939. The Germans entered the town on 22 Aug. 1941. In Sept., in "cleansing" operations, the 1st Infantry Regiment of the SS liquidated the Jews in the area, murdering 516 and later small groups. Presumably many Jews fled. In 1957 the J. pop. of O. was 2,200.

OZARICHI Polesie dist., Belorussia. Jews numbered 93 in 1811 and 1,308 (total 1,356) in 1897. In the Soviet period, a J. school was active, attended by 85 children in 1928. A J. council (soviet) was established in 1925. In the late 1920s, many Jews were organized in artisan cooperatives (as shoemakers, tailors, etc.). In 1939, the J. pop. was 1,059. The Germans oc-

cupied the town in late Aug. 1941, establishing a ghetto and ordering the Jews to wear the yellow badge. All the Jews were murdered on 3 March 1942.

OZARINTSY Vinnitsa dist., Ukraine. The J. pop. was 148 in 1784 and 994 (total 3,954) in 1897. After the Oct. 1917 Revolution, the J. pop. fell to 600. A J. elementary school (four grades) was founded in the mid-1920s and attended by about 40 children until 1937. A few dozen J. families lived in a J. kolkhoz. Following the German occupation of 21 July 1941, the local pop looted J. property. On 25 July, 71 Jews were murdered and immediately afterwards hundreds of Jews from Bukovina and Bessarabia were expelled to O., some perishing there.

OZAROW Kielce dist., Poland. The first Jews arrived in the 18th cent. and soon dominated trade and crafts. In the late 19th cent., they also ran a glass factory, sawmill, and flour mill. A synagogue and cemetery were consecrated around 1860. R. Yehuda Aryeh

Leib Epstein (d. 1837) founded a hasidic dynasty. The J. pop. rose from 1,264 in 1857 to 2,258 in 1921 (total 3,456). In WWI, the Jews were subjected to forced labor and heavy taxes under the Austrian occupation but community life flourished. The first of many Zionist groups was established at this time. The German occupation of Sept. 1939 was followed by the establishment of a *Judenrat* and ghetto under a regime of forced labor, tributes, and property confiscation. The ghetto pop. was doubled to around 6,000 with the arrival of refugees (from Wloclawek, Kielce, and the Radom dist.) through summer 1942, when large groups began to be sent to labor camps. In late Oct. 1942, 4,648 Jews were deported to the Treblinka and Majdanek camps, after which O. was declared "free of Jews" (*judenrein*). Sixty of O.'s 3,000 Jews survived the war.

OZD Borsod dist., Hungary. The J. settlement developed around a large J.-owned metal factory founded in the late 19th cent. and employing many Jews. In 1900, with a pop. of 384 (4% of the total), the community became independent. The community maintained a J. elementary school. In 1941, the J. pop. was 721. The young were seized for forced labor and some Jews of Polish origin were expelled and murdered. After the Germans arrived in spring 1944, the rest were deported on 12–15 June to Auschwitz via Miskolc.

OZDZIUTYCZE Volhynia dist., Poland, today Ukraine. A small community existed after the Chmielnicki massacres of 1648–49. By the late 19th cent all of the town's 701 residents were Jews. In 1921, their pop. was 739 (total 1,015). In Jan. 1942, the Germans expelled the Jews to Torczyn. They were murdered at the J. cemetery there on 23 Aug.

OZLYIANY Minsk dist., Belorussia. Jews probably settled in the late 18th cent., numbering 51 in 1794 and 658 (total 690) in 1897. The community possessed one of the most beautiful wooden synagogues in the dist. In 1923, under the Soviets, the J. pop. fell to 541. In 1924–25, 220 Jews earned their livings farming and in 1930, 12 families worked in a kolkhoz. The Germans occupied U. in late June 1941. The Jews were apparently murdered in Oct. together with those of Rudensk.

OZORA Tolna dist., Hungary. Jews settled in the early 18th cent. and numbered 72 in 1930. They were deported by the Germans to Auschwitz via Bonyhad and Pecs on 5 July 1944.

OZORKOW Lodz dist., Poland. A leading textile manufacturer, Avraham Livrach, opened his factory here in the 1830s and Jews became prominent in the cotton industry as owners and workers. The J. pop. in 1897 was 5,837 (50% of the total). Export of textiles to Russia declined when Poland regained its independence after WWI and the economic situation of the Jews, most of whom worked in this field, declined drastically. In the 1930s, representatives of J. political parties held a third of the seats in the municipal council. In the 1930s, Jews were attacked, some fatally, and their shops boycotted. A strike in 1937 produced antisemitic slogans aimed at J. factory owners. Soon after the outbreak of war, the community's 5,000–5,500 Jews were confined in a ghetto where workshops were opened for the manufacture of goods for Germany. In 1940, over 1,000 Jews were working in a German factory outside the ghetto. From 1941, Jews were rounded up by the Nazis and sent to labor camps in Poznan and the surrounding areas. On 21–23 May 1942, between 1,700 and 2,000 Jews were deported to Chelmno and the remaining 790 were sent to Lodz. The last 1,027 were transported to the Lodz ghetto in Aug. 1942. After the war 30 Jews lived in O. for a time.

P

PABIANICE Lodz dist., Poland. Jews settled in the early 19th cent. and played a leading role in the production and sale of cotton goods. In the early 20th cent., they owned nine of the largest factories in the city. The community was stricken by a cholera epidemic in 1848–52. The J. pop. in 1897 was 5,017 (19% of the total). Jews were active in the Polish Socialist Party (P.P.S.), in the Bund, and in the Zionist parties. Agudat Israel also had a large branch. A Polish-Hebrew high school was founded after WWI with 150 pupils, but had to close down in 1925. Agudat Israel's *talmud torah* had 500 pupils. Between the World Wars, P. became a center for several hasidic courts and many of their rabbis remained in P. with their followers until meeting their death in the Holocaust. In the 1930s, two Yiddish weeklies appeared in P. When the Germans entered P. on 8 Sept. 1939, they forced the Jews to destroy the interior of the synagogue and turned it into a stable. Jews caught praying, especially on the High Holidays, were humiliated and forced to perform menial tasks. Factories and looms belonging to Jews were confiscated. The first *Judenrat* was set up in Sept. 1939, headed by three representatives of the political parties and workers' unions, but they were expelled to Lodz and perished in the Dachau concentration camp. In Oct., a nine-member *Judenrat* was set up and in Feb. 1940 a ghetto was erected. One of the first in occupied Poland, it housed 8,000–9,000 Jews including refugees. About 1,200 J. craftsmen were put to work in confiscated textile factories and in home workshops, mainly producing uniforms for German airmen, as well as army tents. About 20,000 meals a month and other forms of community aid were provided for the poor, mainly refugees, and special arrangements were made for their children. From May 1941 to Jan. 1942, 800 men and 280 women were sent to forced labor camps. On 16 May 1942,

the Germans rounded up all the Jews. The ill and the children were packed into railway cars and transported to Chelmno. The able-bodied (about 3,600) were sent to the Lodz ghetto and then to forced labor camps; in the end, they shared the fate of the inmates of the ghetto. The 150–190 Jews remaining in P., mainly tailors, were made to complete orders for goods and in Aug. 1942 were transferred to Lodz. In Oct. 1945, 148 survivors set up a J. committee, but eventually all left.

PACANOW Kielce dist., Poland. Jews settled in the mid-16th cent. The community was decimated in the Swedish war of the mid-17th cent. and did not recover until the early 19th cent. It grew to a pop. of 1,689 (total 2,598) in 1921. Since the German occupation of Sept. 1939 was relatively mild, P. attracted many refugees. A ghetto was established in Sept. 1942, reaching a pop. of 2,000 including refugees. Hundreds were sent to the Skarzysko-Kamienna labor camp in Oct. 1942 and the rest were deported to the Treblinka death camp shortly thereafter.

PACKANOVO (Hung. Patakos; Yid. Peckenyf) Carpatho-Russia, Czechoslovakia, today Ukraine. Jews probably settled in the early 19th cent., numbering eight in 1830 and 47 (total 1,054) in 1880. Jews farmed their own small plots of land and also operated two flour mills and a few inns. In 1921 their pop. was 129, dropping to 106 in 1941. The Hungarians occupied the town in March 1939. Most of the Jews were deported to Auschwitz in the second half of May 1944.

PACOV Bohemia, Czechoslovakia. Jews apparently arrived in the mid-16th cent. In the late 18th cent. most traded in wool, cloth, hides, grain, and spices. Their pop. rose to 164 in 1910 and then dropped to 101 (total 2,673) in 1930. Only four declared themselves to be of J. nationality. In 1942 the Jews were deported to the Theresienstadt ghetto together with the Jews of Prague and from there to the death camps of Poland.

PACSA Zala dist., Hungary. Jews settled in the mid-18th cent., forming a Neologist congregation in 1869, when they numbered 201. A synagogue was built in 1840 and a J. school opened in 1856. In 1941, young men were seized for forced labor. The 63 remaining Jews were expelled to the Zalaegerszeg ghetto in May 1944 and on 4 July all but the able-bodied were deported to Auschwitz.

PADERBORN Westphalia, Germany. Jews are first mentioned as moneylenders in 1285. Most were apparently massacred in 1350 during the disturbances accompanying the Black Death. In 1624, the community celebrated the 60th anniversary of the presence of its oldest members in the town. In this period, J. livelihoods were restricted to moneylending and money-changing and trade in precious stones and jewelry. In 1661, with the J. pop. growing to 11 families, Jews were also allowed to trade in grain and malt. Under new regulations published in 1719, their residence was restricted and they were prohibited from purchasing farm land, learning crafts, dealing in alcoholic beverages, or baking bread. Religious affairs were placed under the jurisdiction of the state rabbi. A synagogue is mentioned for the first time in 1764. During the 17th and 18th cents., there were a number of antisemitic incidents. In 1808, under the French, the Jews became full citizens but in 1835 the measure was rescinded. Nonetheless, by the time full emancipation was achieved in 1871, Jews were fully integrated in local life. They belonged to the prestigious Harmony Club and in 1875 one was elected to the municipal council. At the same time, P., as one of the main centers of Catholic antisemitism in Germany, especially during the *Kulturkampf* of the 1870s and 1880s, maintained an active antisemitic press. The J. pop rose from 175 in 1802 to 359 in 1855 and 421 (total 24,380) in 1901. While many Jews were peddlers, some became prominent as bankers and owners of flour mills, oil presses, metalworking plants, and other major business establishments. P. became the seat of a regional congregation in 1853. A new synagogue with an organ and seating 290 was consecrated in 1882. Two classrooms were allocated to the J. school, which had oper-

ated intermittently from 1811. A girls' boarding school for secondary studies was opened in 1832 and attended by 20 girls in 1854. An orphanage was founded in 1856, housing 46 boys and girls in 1904-05. In the Weimar period, Jews were mostly self-employed and belonged to the middle class. Most of the local pop. distanced itself from antisemitic manifestations but radical right-wing and Catholic circles rekindled antisemitic agitation. Anti-J. demonstrations were held in 1919 and the J. cemetery was desecrated in 1925. The Nazi Party started a local branch in 1929. Deteriorating economic conditions and emigration weakened the community in the late 1920s. In 1933, 273 Jews remained. In May, J. businesses were removed from the list of municipal suppliers. The J. cemetery was again vandalized in 1934; in 1935, J. merchants were excluded from the grain market. Eight Polish Jews, including five orphans, were expelled from the city in early Nov. 1938. By the end of the year, 170 more Jews had emigrated. The last J. businesses were "Aryanized" by 1 Jan. 1939. On *Kristallnacht* (9-10 Nov. 1938), the synagogue was burned and 41 J. men were sent to the Dachau concentration camp, two dying from the beatings there. The rest were detained for a few weeks to a few months. Subsequently the orphanage became the center of community life, with all J. students in P. and the immediate vicinity transferred there for their schooling. The eight community organizations operating in 1935, including the Kulturbund and Central Union (C.V.), all closed down in 1938 and 1939. In 1942 and 1943, the orphans were dispersed, to perish in Auschwitz and the Theresienstadt ghetto. Local Jews were moved to six "J. houses" in May 1939. An agricultural training camp supposedly intended to prepare Jews throughout Germany for emigration was set up in the city in June 1939 but in effect was exploited for forced labor; its 99 residents were deported to Auschwitz on 1 March 1943. Seventeen local Jews (and 12 from the neighboring villages of Bad Lippespringe, Neuhaus, and Altenbeken) were deported to Minsk on 13 Dec. 1941; 14 more were deported on 31 March 1942 and the last 36 were sent to the Theresienstadt ghetto on 31 July 1942. Five survived the camps.

PADUA Padua province, Italy. The J. presence in P. dates back to the 13th cent. The Carraras ruled P. and Jews were tolerated and enjoyed exceptional liberties there, earning their livelihoods as bankers and traders.

In 1405, P. was annexed to the Venetian Republic. In 1456, the J. bankers were expelled from P., but returned in 1468. R. Yohanan Treves founded the Italian Congregation synagogue in 1548. Communal life was highly developed in P., which in the 16th –17th cents. became a center of J. learning under the guidance of eminent rabbis such as Yehuda and Aharon Minz, Meir Katzenellenbogen, Meir ben Yehezkel ibn Gabbai, Menahem Delmedigo, Yehuda ben Moshe Fano, Shemuel de Archivolti, Hayyim Moshe Cantarini, and Aharon Romanin. Mutual aid societies operated and Hebrew books were printed there as well. J. physicians graduated from the local university, one of the most important in Europe. Among them was Elyahu ben Moshe Abba Delmedigo. Hebrew books and the Talmud were burned in 1556 and in 1601 Jews were confined to a ghetto. By 1616, the J. community numbered 665 members, most engaged in the silk industry. In the plague of 1630–31, 421 of the 721 Jews in P. perished. On 20 Aug. 1684, local residents attacked the ghetto, accusing the Jews of treason during the siege by the Austrian and Venetian armies on Buda. The community's salvation was commemorated by a special Purim festival, celebrated every year. From the early 17th cent., synagogues practicing German and Spanish rites operated in P. One of the most distinguished rabbis of the 18th cent. was Moshe Hayyim Luzzatto. French troops entering the city in 1792 emancipated the Jews. The gates of the ghetto were taken down and in 1805–14, P. was part of Napoleon's Kingdom of Italy. R. Yitzhak Rafael ben Elisha Finzi represented the J. community in the Paris Sanhedrin. After the Treaty of Vienna in 1815, when P. was again under Austrian rule, Jews lost some of their rights. Full emancipation was attained in 1866, when P. was again part of the Kingdom of Italy. The J. community numbered 850 in 1873, increasing to 950 in 1886. (Other sources indicate a pop. of 1,378 in 1881.) In 1897, all the charity organizations were combined. Among the rabbis and prominent figures of the 19th cent. were Mordekhai Shemuel ben Benzion Aryeh Ghirondi, Giuseppe Basevi, and Giuseppe Almanzi. In the 20th cent., Gustavo Castelbolognesi, Paulo Nissim, and Dante Lattes were noteworthy. By 1910, the community consisted of 875 members and its spiritual leader was Dr. Zammatto. The synagogue of the Italian Congregation became the sole synagogue of the community in 1910. Prior to WWI, a cultural club was active in P. During the war its activities ceased, but were resumed in 1921. Under Fascist rule, there were episodes of violence and on 1–2, Nov. 1926, the synagogue was vandalized. According to the 1930 law reforming the J. communities in Italy, P. became one of 26 communities legally recognized by the government. The P. district included Rovigo, which numbered 430 Jews in 1873 and 49 in 1936. In 1936, the community's spiritual leader was Gustavo Castelbolognesi. In that year it consisted of 560 members. With the promulgation of the racial laws in Italy, many local Jews abandoned the city, some emigrating to Palestine. In 1938, the community was headed by R. Prof. Eugenio Cohen Sacerdoti. In 1943–45, over 85 Jews from P. were deported to death camps, including R. Sacerdoti. In 1948, only 269 Jews remained in P., their number decreasing to 220 in 1970.

PAGIRIAI (Yid. Pagir) Ukmerge dist., Lithuania. The J. community was formed in the beginning of the 19th cent. and maintained a synagogue. Towards the end of the 19th cent. many emigrated to larger Lithuanian towns and overseas. The J. pop. in 1940 was about 40. All the Jews were murdered by the Germans and Lithuanians in fall 1941.

PAIDE (Ger. Weissenstein) Estonia. The J. pop. in 1934 was 18 (total 3,000). Those who failed to escape to the Soviet Union were murdered in the Holocaust by the Germans and their Estonian collaborators.

PAJENCZNO Lodz dist., Poland. Jews lived there from the 18th cent. and numbered 594 in 1897 (28% of the total). The community's economic situation declined during the 1930s as a result of antisemitic agitations and a quarter of the J. pop. left the town. Over half lived on welfare and requests for aid were sent to J. communities overseas. The Germans entered P. on 4 Sept. 1939 and together with peasants from neighboring villages plundered J. property. A *Judenrat* was set up in Sept. or Oct. 1939 and over 2,000 refugees arrived, mainly from Dzialoshyn after its destruction and from Brzeznice in 1941. Jews were mobilized for labor in nearby quarries and in the German settlement near Konstantynow, and later sent to labor camps near Poznan. The ghetto was created at the end of 1941. On 19 Aug. 1942, 1,800 Jews were herded into the church, where they were kept for several days without food or water. On 21 Aug. the Germans

Betar members, Pajenczno, Poland, 1938

shot elderly men and women in the churchyard and on the following day the remaining 1,300–1,400 Jews were deported to Chelmno.

PAJURIS (Yid. Payure) Taurage dist., Lithuania. Prior to WWI, about 50 J. families lived in P. under Russian rule. The children studied at a Hebrew school. On the eve of WWII, many emigrated to South Africa. In 1940 there were about 30 families in P. With the German invasion in June 1941, several families fled to the village of Teneniai, where two J. families lived. All were murdered on 29 June. Those who remained in P. were brought to Silale and executed with the local Jews on 16 Sept. 1941.

PAKRAC Croatia, Yugoslavia, today Republic of Croatia. In 1875, when a synagogue was opened, there were 63 J. families in P. The Jews numbered 99 in 1940 (total 3,500). All perished in the Holocaust.

PAKRUOJUS (Yid. Pokroi) Siauliai dist., Lithuania. Jews first settled in the beginning of the 16th cent. The oldest of the town's four synagogues was known for its beauty. Relations between Jews and non-Jews were correct, while those with the town's proprietors, the Von Ropp family, were especially good. Fires in 1879 and 1886 contributed to a deterioration in economic conditions, causing many to emigrate, mainly to South Africa. In 1810, the community's rabbi, Hayyim Katz, was among the first of the followers of the Gaon of Vilna to immigrate to Eretz Israel. The J. pop. in 1897 was 1,093 (71% of the total), dropping in 1939 to 454 (30%) because of persisting economic difficulties. Between the World Wars, three of the 12 town council members were Jews. The Zionist movement enjoyed widespread support. After the German invasion in June 1941, Lithuanian nationalists took control of the town, abusing, robbing, and murdering Jews. On 10 or 31 July, the J. men were brought to nearby Morkakalnis and murdered. The women and children suffered the same fate there on 5 Aug. 1941. The town's J. doctor and his family were spared, until April 1942, when they were murdered together with 20 other Jews who had been in hiding.

PAKS Tolna dist., Hungary. Jews were present under the Turks in the mid-16th cent. In 1735, about 80 Jews were encouraged to settle in P. by estate owners in order to provide supplies to residents. The J. peddlers gradually became merchants, artisans, and industrialists in the 19th cent. In 1781, they were granted a charter of rights and in 1788 a school was opened which soon closed because the Jews preferred to send their children to a *heder*. The community grew to 1,404 (11% of the total) by 1880 and then dropped to 730 in 1941 owing to emigration to the big cities and a declining birthrate. A Hebrew printing press operating in 1884–1921 published 183 rabbinical works. Anti-J. agitation and repressive racial laws preceded the arrival of the Germans in spring 1944. A ghetto was set up in May where 1,000 Jews were confined. On 4–6 July all were deported to Auschwitz. A postwar community of 180 dwindled to 20 by 1961.

PALANGA (Yid. Palongen) Kretinga dist., Lithuania. Jews first settled in the 15th cent. Until WWI, the community was well off economically. The main occupations were the harvesting and processing of amber and tourist services. J. children studied in a *talmud torah* and in a regional school serving both Christians and Jews. The Great Synagogue, which burned down in the 1850s and was rebuilt in 1880, was striking in its beauty. Many joined the Hovevei Zion movement and contributed to the community in Eretz Israel. The J. pop. in 1897 was 925 (43% of the total). Between the World Wars, Jews were active in local politics, serving on the municipal council and as mayor and deputy mayor. The economic situation, exacerbated by increasing antisemitism and an anti-J. boycott, caused many to emigrate to South Africa, the U.S., and Palestine. The Zionist movement enjoyed widespread support. The J. pop. in 1940 amounted to only 50–70 families. After the German invasion in June 1941, all the Jews, together with J. children from other localities attending summer camp in P., were brought to the bus station. J. males aged 13 and above were taken to a grove outside the town, forced into pits which they had been made to dig, and then shot. The women and children, after being incarcerated in the synagogue

under inhuman conditions, were taken to the Kunigiskiai forest and murdered.

PALERMO Sicily, Italy. The presence of Jews in P. goes back to the Roman period. The first documented evidence dates from the sixth cent. Under Saracen rule, the Jews enjoyed the same privileges as Christians. Under Norman rule from 1072, the Jews were allowed to own real estate. They earned their living from fishing and from the silk and dyeing industry. Benjamin of Tudela mentions 1,500 Jews in P. around 1172. The Jews of P. were restricted to a ghetto outside the city walls and obliged to wear the J. badge. In 1339, incitement by fanatical preachers against the Jews resulted in bloodshed. According to Ovadiah Bertinoro, the famous Mishna commentator, the community in 1487–88 consisted of 850 families, mainly coppersmiths, ironworkers, laborers, and porters. He also mentioned their impressive synagogue. Among the J. communities of Sicily, P. was the most important. With the expulsion of the Jews from Spain in 1492, the Jews of P. were also expelled. According to the 1911 census there were 1,159 Jews in Sicily (total 50,000). They lived scattered in various communities. In 1909, several German Jews settled in P., establishing a factory for producing sulfuric acid. Other immigrants engaged in wine production, furniture manufacturing, and upholstery. In accordance with the 1930 law reforming the J. communities in Italy, P. was designated as one of the 26 legally recognized communities of Italy. In 1936, 96 Jews resided in P., but there was no J. communal life. Racial laws were strictly enforced by the local police. Of the Italian Jews who perished in the death camps, two were born in P. In 1970, there were seven J. families living in P.

PANCEVO Serbia, Yugoslavia. Jews first settled in P. at the end of the 18th cent. An official community was established in 1870. In 1900 there were 751 Jews (total 19,044) and in 1940 they numbered 548. In Aug.–Oct. 1941 the Germans deported the Jews to death camps in the vicinity, to Belgrade, and to Auschwitz. Only a few survived.

PANCIU Moldavia dist., Rumania. Jews first settled in the early 19th cent. Most owned vineyards and were vintners. A J. school opened in 1893. In 1902 a synagogue was consecrated and a school for girls opened. Zionist activity began at the turn of the century. In

1907, peasants destroyed J. property in 72 places. A servant in a J. home spread a blood libel in 1913 and in 1919 an antisemitic newspaper called *Prefacerea* appeared. During WWI, all the inhabitants of P. were evacuated. The returning Jews found their homes destroyed but gradually their economic situation improved. The J. pop. was 1,509 in 1910 (52% of the total) and 677 in 1930 (10% of the total). In Nov. 1940, P. was destroyed by an earthquake and the Jews were evacuated to Focsani, Odobesti, and Bucharest. P. was declared a "Rumanian-Christian" city and Jews were not permitted to return.

PANCOTA (Hung., Pankota) S. Transylvania dist., Rumania. A J. community was founded in 1860. The J. pop. in 1930 was 131 (2% of the total). In 1941, the Jews were expelled to Arad.

PANDELYS (Yid. Ponedel) Rokiskis dist., Lithuania. Jews first settled at the end of the 17th cent. The J. pop. numbered 1,131 (95% of the total) in 1897. Most earned their living as tradesmen and artisans. After WWI, Jews returning from exile in Russia found their homes destroyed. With aid from the Joint

Distribution Committee and American relatives, the Jews rebuilt their community. In the 1920s and 1930s, town planners destroyed J.-owned stores and the Lithuanian merchants association boycotted J. businesses. The deteriorating situation led many to emigrate to South Africa, South America, and Palestine. Although the community was primarily hasidic and ultra-Orthodox, many of the young knew Hebrew and were involved in Zionist activities. Menahem Gilutz, one of the founders of Tel Aviv, came from P. The J. pop. in 1939 was about 300 (30%). After Germany's invasion in June 1941, the Jews fled to the Latvian border but the Soviets only allowed those with the appropriate permits to cross. The others returned to find most of their homes destroyed. Except for the few who managed to escape to Soviet Russia, all the Jews of P. died in the Holocaust, although exact details are unknown.

PANEMUNELIS (Yid. Panemunek) Rokiskis dist., Lithuania. Jews first settled in the 19th cent. following the construction of a railroad station there. They used the railway to sell grain and fruit throughout Lithuania. In 1914, the J. pop. numbered about 200. Most were

Members of Jewish soccer team on way to game with friends, Pandelys, Latvia, Aug. 1932

Hasidim. The J. pop. in 1940 consisted of 25 families. P.'s Jews together with those of Rokiskis were murdered in Aug. 1941.

PANEMUNIS (Yid. Panemun) Rokiskis dist., Lithuania. The J. pop. in 1923 was 387 (62% of the total). Most were small tradesmen or farmers. All the Jews were killed after the German occupation, probably in Aug. 1941.

PANEVEZYS (Yid. Ponivezh, Ponevezh) Penevezys dist. Lithuania. From the end of the 14th cent. until the period between the World Wars, a Karaite community originating in the Crimean peninsula was present. From a peak of 153 families, the community declined to a few dozen. Rabbanite Jews first settled in the 18th cent. In the late 19th cent., fires and forced relocation from neighboring villages left many Jews destitute, leading many to emigrate to South Africa. Most were educated in *hadarim* and *talmudei torah*. Many adhered to Haskala, including the poet Y. Gordon, who taught at a J. government school in P. in 1853–60. Of the 15 synagogues, the most magnificent

was built in the 18th cent The J. pop. in 1897 stood at 6,627 (51% of the total). A yeshiva nicknamed the "P. kibbutz" was founded in 1912. It was funded by benefactors from Moscow, admitted only top students, produced leading rabbis, and closed down in 1919. At the turn of the 19th cent., 80% of P.'s J. youth emigrated to South Africa and the U.S. because of the political and economic situation. In 1915, the Russians expelled the Jews to Russia; they returned after WWI. In 1919, Lithuanians robbed and murdered Jews, accusing them of pro-Bolshevik sympathies. The Jews contributed considerably to the economic life of P. They controlled the trade and export of linen and wheat and owned the largest flour mills in the city. Between the World Wars, community affairs were run by a community council for six years and then by the Knesset Yisrael society. Jews served on the municipal council; one was the deputy mayor for many years. The J. community maintained an extensive educational system, as well as a hospital and an orphanage. P. was the second largest bastion of ultra-Orthodoxy in Lithuania. In 1919, one of the most important *yeshivot* in the country was founded. R. Yosef Shelomo Kahaneman served

Pioneer woodcutters, Panevezys, Lithuania, March 1934

Students and teachers from the Panevezys (Ponivezh) yeshiva, Lithuania

as chief rabbi of P. in 1919–40, after which he immigrated to Palestine and founded the P. Yeshiva in Benai Berak. The Zionist movement won widespread support, with all Zionist parties represented. The J. pop. in 1939 was 6,000 (22% of the total). When Lithuania was annexed by the Soviet Union in 1940, businesses were nationalized, adversely affecting the middle-class majority of the J. pop. The three school systems — Hebrew-Zionist, Hebrew religious, and Yiddish — were combined into one Yiddish system. The yeshiva building was confiscated. J. Communists played a prominent role in municipal government. After the German invasion in June 1941, Lithuanian nationalists set up "headquarters" in the city and began abusing, humiliating, and injuring Jews. Many Jews seized for forced labor never returned. Others were jailed and tortured and then murdered in the nearby Kaizerlingas forest. On 11 July 1941, P.'s Jews, together with those from other towns, were crowded into a ghetto. Seventy of the community's leaders were

taken hostage, after which they were killed at Pajuoste. According to a German report, between 24 July and 26 Aug. 1941, 8,745 J. men, women, and children were executed at Pajuoste. After the war, some Jews returned to P., but by 1989, only 66 remained.

PANOSISKES (also Zydkaimis; Yid. Panasishok, Zhidkaimis) Troki dist., Lithuania. Jews first settled and formed an organized agricultural settlement in 1849. Local residents called P. the "Jew village." The J. pop. in 1898 was 158, dropping to 50 by 1938. After the German invasion in June 1941, Lithuanian police surrounded the synagogue on 21 Sept. 1941 (Rosh Hashanah eve) and took the Jews to Troki, where they were shot on 30 Sept. (Yom Kippur eve). Several managed to escape and hide in the forests, with some joining the Soviet partisans.

PAPA Veszprem dist., Hungary. Jews are first mentioned in 1698 and by 1736 constituted the largest J. community in the district. In the first half of the 19th cent., over 100 families earned their livelihoods in the tanning industry. Others produced textiles, paper, bricks, and smoking pipes. A synagogue was consecrated in 1846. R. Leopold Loew officiated in 1846–50 and was active in the Hungarian revolt of 1848, afterwards serving in Szeged and achieving widespread fame. The private J. school founded in 1818 was one of the first in Hungary, attaining an enrollment of 510 students in 1859. A famous yeshiva also operated in P., which was known as a center of Torah learning. The J. pop. grew to 3,550 (24% of the total) in 1880. Zionist activity commenced in 1904 with the founding of a Hovevei Zion society. The rabbi of P., Moshe Aryeh Roth, was an enthusiastic Zionist and later helped found the Mizrachi movement. Zionist activity intensified in the 1930s. In 1941, the J. pop. was 2,613 as P. became a mobilization center for forced labor. In May 1944, the Jews were confined to a ghetto with another 2,800 from neighboring villages. In the beginning of July, they were all sent to Auschwitz. A postwar community of 500 dwindled to just 50 by 1972.

PAPENBURG Hanover, Germany. During the 18th cent., Jews settled in P. and nearby Aschendorf, where they numbered 27 (3% of the total) in 1816. When the two groups established one district community in 1842, the 40 Aschendorf Jews already had a synagogue and a burial ground. Owing to economic changes, the J. pop. of Aschendorf declined whereas that of P. rose to 73 in 1877 and 130 (about 2% of the total) in 1890. David Wolffsohn, a close associate of Theodor Herzl and his successor as president of the World Zionist Organization, lived in P. for three years (1884–87). During the Weimar Republic, many Jews still engaged in the cattle trade and a few were elected to public office. The repeated desecration of J. graves preceded the Nazi rise to power. In June 1933, there were 71 Jews registered in P. and Aschendorf. Fifteen moved to other German cities before Nov. 1938 and 36 emigrated to safe havens (especially Latin America). During the *Kristallnacht* pogrom (9–10 Nov. 1938), SA troops burned and demolished the synagogue, looted J. property, and dispatched J. householders to the Sachsenhausen concentration camp. In all, 22 Jews from P. and ten from the immediate surroundings perished in the Holocaust.

PAPILE (Yid. Popelian) Siauliai dist., Lithuania. Jews first settled in the mid-18th cent. In the 19th cent. the community prospered and in 1897 the J. pop. stood at 965 (51% of the total). The Zionist movement enjoyed widespread support. Some Jews expelled to Russia in 1915 did not return after WWI. In the 1930s, many emigrated to South Africa and Palestine as a result of an anti-J. boycott. The J. pop. in 1923 was 257 (18%). During the 1930s, there was a J. school in P. After the German invasion in June 1941, Lithuanian nationalists robbed and humiliated the Jews, murdering the men on 18 July 1941 and the women and children on 2 Oct.

PAPPENHEIM Middle Franconia, Germany. The J. community dates from at least the early 14th cent., with the Jews living under various letters of protection. A new synagogue was erected in 1811. The J. pop. reached 259 in 1832 (total 2,080), declining thereafter to 101 in 1867 and seven in 1933. All the Jews left for other places in Germany in 1936. The J. cemetery was destroyed by local rioters in Nov. 1938.

PARABUC Vojvodina dist., Yugoslavia. Jews first settled there in the early 19th cent. They numbered 73 in 1940; most perished in the Holocaust.

PARADYZ Lodz dist., Poland. The J. pop. was 177 in 1921 (37% of the total), 151 in 1939, and 400 by 21

Oct. 1942 including refugees. The Jews were expelled to Opoczno and then to the Treblinka death camp.

PARAFIANOW Vilna dist., Poland, today Belarus. In 1866, 24 J. farming families lived in P. and seven neighboring villages. All were expelled under the 1882 May Laws and allowed to return only in 1903. In 1931 their pop. was 230. The Jews were mainly employed in the lumber industry, including two J.-owned sawmills. In 1929 they were forced out of the industry by the Polish government. A Tarbut Hebrew school was in operation and numerous pioneers from the Zionist youth movements left for Palestine. The Germans arrived in late June 1941, setting up a ghetto in Oct. under a regime of forced labor and frequent "contributions." On 31 May 1942, 500 Jews from P. and the surrounding villages were murdered in the Odokowski forest.

PARAMYTHIA Epirus, Greece. Excavations indicate a J. presence in the Byzantine period as well as in the 12th cent. and again in the early 19th cent. Active in the textile trade, they played a vital role in P.'s economy. The J. pop. in 1928 was 15 (total 15,688). All but two perished in the Holocaust, together with the Jews of Janina.

PARANESTION (Paranesti, Pravishte) Thrace, Greece. P. came under Bulgarian rule in WWII and in March 1943, 19 Jews were deported to death camps together with Jews from Thrace and Macedonia.

PARCHIM Mecklenburg-Schwerin, Germany. A J. community is known to have existed between the early 14th and late 15th cents. Jews returned in 1754 and slowly gained a foothold in the city. A J. cemetery was opened in 1765 and a synagogue in 1823, with the J. pop. reaching 88 in 1810 and remaining at a level of 80–100 up to the end of the cent. On the eve of the Nazi assumption of power in 1933, the J. pop. was 50. In summer 1935, the Germans arrested most of the Jews. Their stores were then pillaged and they were forced to sell them at a fraction of their value after being released. Many then left the city. On *Kristallnacht* (9–10 Nov. 1938), the synagogue was destroyed and many J. men were arrested. The five families who remained in May 1939 were confined in a single house. Those Jews who failed to emigrate were deported to the death camps with the exception of a J. woman married to a non-Jew.

PARCZEW Lublin dist., Poland. Jews are first mentioned in 1494. They suffered in the Swedish invasion of the mid-17th cent. and were massacred in 1656 by the irregular Polish troops of Stefan Czarniecki. The re-established community grew from 1,079 in 1827 to 3,392 (total 6,660) in 1897. The newly constructed army barracks were a source of livelihood to suppliers and building workers. Most craftsmen in the city were Jews and Jews ran sugar-refining and soap factories as well as a brickyard and flour mill. R. Avraham Bornstein, son-in-law of R. Menahem Mendel Morgenstern of Kotsk, served as rabbi for 20 years in the late 19th cent. and later established a hasidic dynasty. The Zionists became active in the early 20th cent. In the aftermath of WWI, Polish troops pillaged J. property. In 1921, the J. pop. was 4,005. The economic distress of the Jews continued between the World Wars. Many J. merchants closed their businesses and left the city while others were reduced to peddling. To alleviate the situation, the Jews organized mutual aid and credit societies. Most of the J. political parties were active. Agudat Israel derived most of its strength from the Gur Hasidim while the Bund was active in the trade unions and promoted Yiddish culture. Hashomer Hatzair and Hehalutz operated a pioneer training facility from 1929. The Germans entered P. on 5 Oct. 1939, confiscating J. businesses and exacting tributes from the community. In late 1939, a *Judenrat* was set up under a regime of forced labor. On 16 Aug. 1942, 4,000 Jews including refugees were deported to the Treblinka death camp and another 400 in hiding were shot when caught. A ghetto was established in Sept. Another 2,000 refugees were brought in and then 2,500 Jews were sent to Treblinka. The last 1,000 were expelled to Miendzyrzec Podlaski (Mezrich). A J. partisan unit operating in the forests of P. joined forces with Yehiel Grynszpan's command and engaged in bold guerilla action in the area. By liberation, there were only 100 survivors from among the Jews of P.

PARDUBICE Bohemia, Czechoslovakia. Jews are mentioned in 1492. In 1662, Emperor Leopold expelled all Jews who had settled after 1618. In 1744, Maria Theresa expelled the Jews of P. together with the rest of the Jews in the country. The hostility of the local pop., mostly against an economic back-

ground, continued into the late 19th cent. A synagogue was consecrated in 1880 and a new cemetery in 1883 with the J. pop. growing steadily from 378 in 1880 to 553 in 1910. The Schuetz family owned a large factory producing the city's famous honey cake (*perniky*). In 1930, 518 Jews remained (total 28,846). The Nazis closed down the synagogue in Oct. 1942. On 9 June 1942 they executed the J. journalist Ota Kafka and on 5 Dec. 1942 they deported 650 Jews from P. and its environs to the Theresienstadt ghetto together with Jews from Trutnov assembled in the city. Another 606 were deported on 9 Dec. Nearly all were sent to Auschwitz in 1943.

PARGA (Pargas) Epirus, Greece. Jews lived in P. from the 15th. There were Karaite and Rabbanite communities here. Most Jews traded in *etrogim* (citron), which were highly valued by J. communities in Europe and North Africa.

PARICHI Polesie dist., Belorussia. Jews are first mentioned in the 18th cent. Their pop. was 65 in 1789 and 3,132 (81% of the total) in 1897. Most Jews engaged in trade and crafts. During the civil war (1918–21), Jews set up self-defense groups in response to attacks from various gangs. A J. elementary school was attended by 220 children in 1925 and a J. council (soviet) was established in 1927. Two Hehalutz youth groups, only one legal, operated in the mid-1920s. During the 1920s, most J. artisans were shoemakers, tailors, and building workers. A J. kolkhoz for 35 families was founded near the town in 1930. In 1939, the J. pop. was 1,881. The Germans occupied P. on 5 July 1941, murdering about 140 Jews in Aug. Subsequently a ghetto was established and on 18 Oct., 1,700 were murdered at the nearby village of Vysokii Polk.

PARINCEA Moldavia dist., Rumania. The J. pop. in 1899 was 336 and a J. community was organized between the World Wars. In 1930, the J. pop. numbered 148 (18% of the total). When the Soviet-Rumanian war broke out in June 1941, women and children were expelled to Bacau. Some men were sent to forced labor in camps while others were deported to Transnistria.

PARIS capital of France. Jews lived along the banks of the Seine from Roman times. Their first synagogue was built in 582. During the Crusader era, they were

"I accuse!" – *Emile Zola's open letter to the president of France on the front page of* L'Aurore, Paris, 13 Jan. 1898. *The letter proclaims the innocence of the French-Jewish army officer Alfred Dreyfus and accuses his denouncers of libel*

accused of ritual murders. Pogroms, massacres, and expulsion decrees followed. Between periods of persecution the Jews of P. achieved intermittent fame and their talmudic academies were known throughout Europe. When expelled in 1182, their synagogue was converted into the St. Madeleine Church. In 1269, they were forced to wear the distinctive badge (the *rouelle*). With the general expulsion of Jews from France in 1394, the community ceased to exist for 300 years, though traveling Jews received temporary residence certificates. From the beginning of the 18th cent., Jews resettled in P., numbering 500 in 1789, including 50 Portuguese Jews, former Marranos from Bordeaux and Bayonne, mainly doctors, professors, and traders in silk, jewelry, and chocolate; 100 Jews from Avignon, mostly merchants; and 350 German Jews, mostly

peddlers dealing in old clothes and hardware. The French Revolution brought emancipation to the Jews of France. By 1815, there were 6,000 Jews in P. and after Germany occupied Alsace-Lorraine (1871), the community rapidly expanded, numbering 40,000 in 1880 (2% of the total), of which 1,000 were Sephardi Jews. In 1808, the P. Consistory – the Association Consistoriale Israelite de Paris (ACIP) – was established and became the primary organization of the J. community in P. With its growth, communal institutions began developing: in 1809 the Comite de Bienfaisance Israelite de Paris was founded and from 1850 the Fondation de Rothschild began operating, building a hospital, an orphanage, and other welfare institutions. In 1858, the rabbinical school of Metz moved to P. In 1860, the Alliance Israelite Universelle was founded

Alfred Dreyfus returns to the army after his successful appeal, 1906 (Roger Violett, Paris/photo courtesy of Yad Vashem, The Holocaust Martyrs' and Heroes' Remembrance Authority, Jerusalem)

with its headquarters located in P. The synagogue on Notre Dame de Nazareth Street and later the Rothschild Synagogue (from 1874) were the seat of the chief rabbi of France and the chief rabbi of P. The second largest synagogue in P., the Temple Tournelles, was built before the Franco-Prussian war of 1870 and burned down during the Commune, but was reconstructed in 1876. In 1877 a Portuguese synagogue was established. The two last decades of the 19th century marked an increase in antisemitism in France, primarily centered around the Dreyfus affair. From 1880 to 1939, 110,000 immigrants joined the J. community of P. and in 1930 the J. pop. was about 150,000 (including 90,000 from Eastern Europe and 15,000 Sephardi Jews). During the 1930s, P. was the largest J.

community in Western Europe and the third largest in the world after New York and Warsaw. The East European Jews arrived in waves from Russia in 1881, 1905, and 1914. The Federation des Societes Juives de Paris was created to assist the newcomers as well as to build new synagogues. The Le Medem Farband club, the Nomberg Bibliotheque library, and various organizations operated, some of which published periodicals like *Der Morgenstern* and *Unsere Stimme*. In 1918–39, about 70,000 Jews arrived from Eastern Europe, 5,000 from Central Europe, 5,000 from North Africa, and 10,000 from Greece, Turkey, and the Balkans. They settled mostly in the western part of P. Most, about 60%, worked in the garment industry; 10% were in the liberal professions; 10% worked as vendors and peddlers and in secondhand stores and banks; 5% were in furniture; 5% in metalwork; and 10% earned their livelihoods in various other occupations. German Jews immigrating to P. after 1933 constituted a highly skilled and cultivated segment of the J. pop. In 1936, the Comite d'Assistance aux Refugies (CAR) was established under Robert de Rothschild. The P. Consistory, traditionally presided over by a member of the Rothschild family, officially provided for all religious needs. Since 1905, it was the representative organ of French Jewry, and consulted by the public authorities whenever a legislative or administrative measure affected the J. community. At its height, in 1932, only 7,114 families were registered as belonging to the consistory. Outside this framework, J. life flourished in a wide variety of social, cultural, and religious institutions and associations. By the 1920s, the Federation des Societes Juives de France included 95 charitable societies operating side by side with many other political, social, cultural, and sports organizations. The Yiddish press, became increasingly important, although many weeklies and periodicals in Yiddish were short-lived because of rapid language assimilation. Leon Algazi ran a radio station called La Voix d'Israel which broadcast every Tuesday from 1928. The Sephardi Jews founded such organizations as the Association Amicale des Israelites Saloniciens, Ozer Dalim, Bene Mizrah (Jeunesses d'Orient), and the Fraternite (Association de la Jeunesse Sephardite de Paris). Among the numerous organizations of the Ashkenazi majority were the Union Liberale Israelite (members coming from among wealthier and more assimilated Jews), Communaute Israelite de la stricte Observance, Chema Israel, La Terre Promise, the local Po'alei Zion branch, Union Patriotique des Francais Israelites (which promoted J. service in the French army in WWI), etc. In 1939 there were 113 J. organizations in P. and the J. pop. was 150,000–200,000 (7% of the city's pop. and about 60% of all Jews in France). It is estimated that 25% belonged to the "old" community, 50% were immigrants, and 25% naturalized.

On 14 June 1940, the *Wehrmacht* entered P. and on 25 June an armistice was proclaimed in which France was divided into occupied and free zones, with P. in the former. Many Parisians left the city, including Jews. The economic position of the 150,000 Jews who remained in P. was undermined by the Statut des Juifs of 1940. The German census of Nov. 1940 recorded 149,734 Jews, 7,737 private J. businesses, and 3,456 J. companies. Many P. Jews remained in the south of France, in unoccupied French territory. From the southern zone there was the possibility of leaving for Algiers and Switzerland. In Aug. 1940, French Nazis, protected by the Germans, stoned a number of J. shops on the Champs Elysees. The anti-J. measures which followed affected P. Jews and J. shopkeepers began closing their stores to avoid the confiscation of goods. P. Jews were active in the resistance movement from the very first. Resistance sprang from the J. working class, among the immigrants. Such Jews as Francis Cohen, Suzanne Djian, and Bernard Kirschen were among those who organized the march of high school and university students to the Etoile on 11 Nov. 1940, the first major manifestation of resistance. The Amelot Comite was organized in June 1940, largely by J. immigrant groups. In 1942 the Organisation Juive de Combat (OJC) was established. Most of the J. organizations dissolved for lack of manpower and money. The remaining groups were forced to form a unified Comite de Coordination de Oeuvres de Bienfaisance de Paris on 31 Jan. 1941. This developed into the Comite de Bienfaisance Israelite de Paris, which after three months had more than 7,000 members. Jacques See was president of the P. Consistory during the occupation period. On 21 Nov. 1941 the Union Generale des Israelites de France (UGIF) was created, taking over from the Comite. All other groups dissolved and membership in the UGIF became mandatory. In 1942, with the economic decline of the J. community, the UGIF opened canteens and provided free meals to 20% of P.'s J. pop. Its *Bulletin de UGIF* replaced *Informations Juives*, appearing since April 1941. By July 1941, 139,979 Jews remained in P. The first major roundups of P. Jews of foreign nationality took place in 1941. The French police arrested 3,710 Jews on 14 May. They were interned in Pithiviers and Beaume-la-Rolande. Then on 20 Aug. 1941, 3,477 Jews were arrested and interned in Drancy. During the night of 2–3 Oct. 1941, French Fascists attacked seven synagogues in P. at the instigation of the German security police. On 12 Dec., about 1,000 J. intellectuals were arrested and two days later a fine of one billion francs was imposed on P. Jews. On 1 June 1942, an order to wear the yellow badge was announced. On 16 July 1942, mass arrests of Jews began. On 20 July, 13,152 Jews between the ages of 2 and 55 were arrested and put in the Velodrom d'Hiver. Between 27 July and 31 Aug., 592 more Jews were caught. The Swiss *Journal de Geneve* reported on 31 July 1942 that 24,014 J. businesses had been seized and handed over to non-J. directors. Most P. Jews were sent to camps near P. – Drancy, Compiegne, Pithiviers, and Beaume-la-Rolande. From these camps they were deported to Auschwitz. In P., there was a camp near the Austerlitz station where 400 Jews sorted the plundered contents of J. homes intended for Germans. In another camp located in P. 200 Jews oversaw the transport of J. goods and furniture to Germany. After the roundups in July 1942, there were 80,000 Jews left in P. In March 1943, three convoys left for Majdanek (Poland) and one transport in May 1944 went to Kovno (Lithuania). In 1943–44, half the J. pop. had left P., either by deportation or in flight. Altogether 37,661 Jews were arrested in P. and sent to camps in France.

Most were deported to death camps in Poland. After the Liberation, recovery and reconstruction was slow. The Joint Distribution Committee assisted. Between 1945 and 1950, the J. pop. of Greater P. grew from 125,000 to 150,000, doubling in 1964 to stand at 300,000. Destroyed synagogues were reconstructed and new ones were built.

PARIZHSKAYA KOMMUNA   Voroshilovgrad dist., Ukraine. The J. pop. in 1939 was 109 (total 21,071). The Germans occupied P. on 12 July 1942 and in Feb.–Sept. 1943, they murdered 1,100 people, including Jews.

PARKAN   Slovakia, Czechoslovakia, today Republic of Slovakia. Jews are thought to have been present in

Rue des Hopitaliers in the Jewish quarter of Paris, France

the late Middle Ages, fleeing during the Turkish invasion. They then returned in the late 17th cent. but apparently were forced to leave in the late 18th cent., only reestablishing the community in the 1820s. In the 1870s, the Jews established a Status Quo congregation. Their pop. grew rapidly from 84 in 1880 to 365 (total 2,836) in 1900. Jews traded mainly in grain and lumber and were active in public life. In the 1920s, seven served on the municipal council. The community maintained a *beit midrash* and elementary school and a large synagogue was consecrated in 1926. WIZO and the Zionist youth movements were active. Dozens of Jews were seized for forced labor after the annexation to Hungary and on 15 June 1944, 336 local Jews were deported to Auschwitz via Komarno. About 220 perished.

PARLITA (Yid. Perlitz) Bessarabia, Rumania, today Republic of Moldova. The settlement was founded mainly by Jews in the late 19th cent. The J. pop. in 1930 was 1,064. The majority traded in furs and grain. On 7 July 1941 P. was captured from the Soviets by German and Rumanian forces and on the same day 300 Jews were killed and their houses plundered. Those who remained alive were deported to Transnistria. All J. houses were destroyed.

PARMA Emilia Romagna, Italy. There are indications of a J. presence in P. from the 14th cent. In 1348, Jews were persecuted for supposedly causing the Black Death. In the 15th cent., there were several famous physicians living in P., among them Elias (1440), the doctor of the Duke of P. and lecturer at the medical school of Pavia. In the middle of the 15th cent., under the rule of Sforza, the Jews enjoyed various privileges. In the second half of the cent., they were permitted to open loan banks. With the establishment of a Christian loan bank, Monte de Pieta, in 1488, J. moneylending declined and J. bankers gradually began leaving P. to settle in nearby cities, primarily in Piacenza. After 1555, Jews were no longer permitted to reside in P., but seven years later they returned and reopened loan banks. In 1570, the Jews were forced to wear the yellow badge. Few Jews remained in P. itself, but Jews settled in nearby towns such as Borgo S. Donino, Busseto, Colorno, Corte Maggiore, Fiorenzuola, and Monticelli. In accordance with a decree issued in 1749, Jews were no longer permitted to remain in P. for more than 24 hours without

authorization. In 1805, the Duchess Maria Luisa allowed Jews to resettle in P. In 1840, there were 510 Jews in P. In 1845, *Rivista Israelitica*, the first Hebrew periodical in Italy, was published in P. It ran three years. The Jews of P. were emancipated in 1859. In 1866, the revived community drew up a constitution and built a synagogue. There were 684 Jews in P. in 1881, dropping to 415 in 1911. In accordance with the 1930 law reforming the J. communities in Italy, P. was declared one of the 26 communities legally recognized by the Italian government. The P. district included such communities as Busseto (70 Jews in 1873, ten in 1936); Corte Maggiore (60 in 1873, ten in 1936); Fidenza (ten in 1936); Fiorenzuola (90 in 1873, 70 in 1886, 15 in 1936); Monticelli (140 in 1873, ten in 1936); and Soragna (80 in 1873, 85 in 1886, five in 1936). In 1931, the district included 100 Jews, dropping to 80 in 1936. The officiating rabbi was E. della Pergola. During WWII, the first concentration camp in the province of P. was established in 1940, followed by others in Montechiarugolo, Scipione di Salsomaggiore, and Monticelli. Of the 80 Jews present in 1943, 18 were deported to death camps. Most Jews escaped to mountain villages with some fleeing to Switzerland. Jews were active in the resistance. After liberation, the community consisted of 86 Jews; in 1969, 60.

PARTENHEIM Hesse, Germany. Numbering 165 at its height in 1855, the community dwindled to 36 (3% of the total) in 1900 and 12 in 1933. P. was a Nazi stronghold from 1930 and the Jews disposed of their synagogue before *Kristallnacht* (9–10 Nov. 1938). By the end of 1939, there were no Jews in P.

PARYSOW Lublin dist., Poland. A few Jews were present around the turn of the 18th cent. In the mid-19th cent., R. Yehoshua Asher Rabinowicz of Zelechow founded an opulent hasidic court in P. which attracted many followers and stimulated the local economy. R. Yehoshua initiated the founding of a synagogue and cemetery before his death in 1862. The J. pop. reached 2,014 (total 3,140) in 1897. The hasidic majority blocked Zionist activity until WWI, when Mizrachi and Tze'irei Tziyyon opened their doors. Alongside the Zionist parties, the Bund and Agudat Israel also became active. During the war, the Jews suffered from the depredations of Russian and Polish troops. J. economic distress increased in the 1930s in the face of anti-J. agitation and boycotts. The Germans captured P. on 17 Sept. 1939 and established a *Judenrat* a month later, charged with organizing forced labor and extortionate "contributions." A ghetto was set up in Nov. 1940. Cooperation between J. and Polish artisans, the former producing goods, the latter selling them, enabled the Jews to support themselves. The ghetto was liquidated on 27 Sept. 1942, when its 3,500 inhabitants, including 2,000 refugees, were deported to the Treblinka death camp.

PARZENCZEW (Yid. Parenchav) Lodz dist., Poland. Jews settled here in the 18th cent. The J. pop. in 1857 was 545 (46% of the total). The wooden synagogue built in the early 19th cent. was considered one of the most beautiful in Poland. The J. community, numbering only 30 in 1939, ceased to exist with the German conquest in WWII.

PASCANI Moldavia dist., Rumania. The 86 Jews living here in 1859 were probably among the founders of P. In 1882, four synagogues and six *hadarim* were functioning; J. elementary schools opened in 1900 and 1911. A 1914 fire left 300 Jews homeless. P. was a hasidic center in Rumania. Antisemitism increased between the World Wars. The J. pop. was 1,862 in 1899 and 1,481 in 1930 (13% of the total). On 12 June 1942, all J. males were transported to Falticeni; 240 were taken to Bessarabia to work on roads. In spring 1944, the local non-J. residents were allowed to leave P. in the face of the advancing Soviet army but the Jews were forced to remain and consequently 100 were killed in Soviet air raids. When the Jews were eventually permitted to leave, they fled to Falticeni. In April 1944, they were moved to Botosani. About half the J. pop. returned after the war.

PASEWALK Pomerania, Germany. Evidence of a J. presence in P. dates from the first half of the 14th cent. and from 1466. In modern times, Jews are first mentioned in 1782. The J. pop. numbered 286 in 1855, dropping to 160 by the end of the cent. The community established a synagogue in 1834 and a cemetery. At the beginning of the 20th cent., the community became Liberal, introducing a harmonium for services. This led several members of the affiliated Loecknitz community to leave the congregation. When the Nazis came to power in 1933, there were 47 Jews in P. In 1937 there were 36. On *Kristallnacht* (9–10 Nov.

1938), the synagogue was burned down, J. shops were wrecked, and the cemetery was desecrated. Of the 26 Jews and ten of partial J. origin (*Mischlinge*) who had remained in P., nine were deported on 12–13 Feb. 1940, together with the Jews of Stettin, to the Lublin dist., where they perished. No further information about the fate of the others is available.

PASIECZNA Stanislawow dist., Poland, today Ukraine. The J. pop. in 1921 was 135. The Jews were possibly executed locally in Oct. 1941 with 15 remaining families expelled to Nadworna on 4 May 1942.

PASSAU (in J. sources, Poysin, Passy) Lower Bavaria, Germany. J. merchants possibly arrived in P. with the Romans and the J. quarter dates from at least the 11th cent. Most of the Jews were killed in the wake of the massacre of the Jews of Deggendorf in 1338 and in the Black Death persecutions of 1348–49. In 1478, ten were executed in a blood libel, 40 were forced to convert, and the rest were expelled. The 19th cent. community was attached to Straubing. The Jews traded in knitted goods, readymade wear, shoes, and lumber. In 1933 they numbered 40 (total 25,151). Most Jews left for other German cities.

PASUSVYS (Yid. Pashushve) Kedainiai dist., Lithuania. The J. pop. in 1923 was 100 (39% of the total). All the Jews were murdered shortly after the German occupation of June 1941.

PASVALYS (Yid. Posvol) Birzai dist., Lithuania. A Karaite community existing in 1643 gradually disappeared over the years. Rabbanite Jews first settled in the mid-18th cent. At the end of the 19th cent., many emigrated to South Africa and the U.S.. The Hovevei Zion movement enjoyed widespread support. The J. pop. in 1897 was 1,590 (52% of the total). In WWI the Jews were exiled to Russia, some returning after the war to independent Lithuania. Despite objections from religious circles, boys and girls studied together at a Hebrew-Zionist school. There were occasional incidents of antisemitic vandalism. The J. pop. in 1939 was 700 (25%). After the German invasion in June 1941, Lithuanian nationalists took control of the town, robbing and abusing Jews to such an extent that the Jews appealed to the Germans for help. Those who attempted to flee to Russia were caught and murdered in the Simbeline forest. In July, 150

Jews were incarcerated, transferred to Siauliai, and executed. The Jews were forced into a ghetto, joined by others from nearby towns. On 26 Aug. 1941, the town council decided to liquidate the ghetto's residents. All were brought to the Zadeikiai forest and brutally murdered.

PASVITINYS (Yid. Pashvitin) Siauliai dist., Lithuania. Jews first settled at the end of the 18th cent., establishing a synagogue in the 1860s. The J. pop. in 1897 was 435 (57% of the total). In 1900, a blood libel led to riots and attacks on Jews. The Zionist movement won widespread support in the 1920s and Hashomer Hatzair opened a branch in P. In the 1930s the economic situation deteriorated, partly due to an anti-J. boycott, resulting in emigration to South Africa, the U.S., and Palestine. By 1940, there were only 20 J. families in P. After the German invasion in June 1941, Lithuanian nationalists took over the town and dispatched the Jews to Zagare, where they were murdered on 2 Oct. 1941.

PASZTO Heves dist., Hungary. Jews were present in the early 15th cent. A synagogue was erected in 1840. The J. pop. reached a peak of 502 in 1909 and numbered 414 in 1930. Most Jews were small artisans or tradesmen. In May 1944, they were expelled to the Hatvan ghetto and on 12 July deported to Auschwitz. Twenty survivors returned to P. but soon left for Israel.

PATRAS (Patre, Patrai, Palea Patra, Balyabadra) Peloponnesus, Greece. The first Jews to settle in P. arrived from Syria between 323 and 281 B.C.E. In the 12th cent., Benjamin of Tudela recorded the presence of a Romaniot community of 50 Jews (dating from the Byzantine period). In 1500, the Ottoman Turks conquered P. and some Jews were exiled to Istanbul, where they formed their own congregation. The community in P. continued to grow, however, especially after absorbing Jews from Spain and Sicily. It peaked in 1569–70 with about 2,500 Jews. It was then the largest and most important community in the region. Throughout the 16th cent., P. was the site of a number of battles between the Ottoman Empire and the Venetian rulers. This led a large number of Jews to flee to Naupaktos (Central Greece), while many others were taken captive by the Venetians. Many J. communities in Europe were active in ransoming the captives. In the 16th and early 17th cents., the community was divided into Romaniot, Sicilian, and Sephardi congrega-

tions. During this period P. was home to a number of well-known rabbis. The Jews were active in local and international trade (and were known for their wide-ranging travels), as well as in the free professions, such as medicine. The Sephardi congregation disappeared in the early 17th cent.; in 1616 there was a Romaniot congregation and three Sicilian congregations. Heavy taxes, political instability, and lack of security led many to leave P. In 1647 and again in 1684, the Venetians took over and destroyed the community. Many fled to other towns (especially Larissa) and others were taken captive; Italian and Dutch Jews were active in ransoming them. In the early 18th cent., the Turks regained P. and many Jews returned and reestablished the community. During the Turkish-Russian war (1768–74), P. was burned down and the community practically destroyed. Towards the end of the cent., a small community was revived. With the outbreak of the Greek revolt in 1821, most Jews fled to Larissa, Chalkis, and Corfu; by 1829, none remained. When the Greek state was declared in 1832, Jews returned, but left again during the 1881 Greek revolt. In 1917, J. families from Corfu reestablished the community, inaugurating a new synagogue in 1920 and organizing Zionist activity. The J. pop. in 1928 was 170 (total 64,838). On the eve of WWII (1940), there were 337 Jews in P. Warned of the Nazi plans for the Jews, most had gone into hiding by March 1944 or joined the partisans in the surrounding hills. The partisans called upon villagers to assist the Jews and warned them that those informing on Jews would be put to death. Nevertheless, the Germans caught 12 families, who were sent to the death camps. After the war, many survivors left for Athens, Palestine, and the U. S. In 1946, 122 Jews lived in P. and by 1978 there were only five.

PATROHA Szabolcs dist., Hungary. Jews arrived in the mid-18th cent. and numbered 181 in 1880 and 137 in 1930. In 1941, the young men were seized for forced labor and in late May 1944, the remaining Jews were deported to Auschwitz via Kisvarda.

PATTENSEN Hanover, Germany. There is evidence of the presence of Jews in P. in the 14th cent., but the modern community only began in the first half of the 19th cent. The small community, numbering 49 Jews (3% of the total) in 1845 and 82 (5%) in 1885, dedicated a synagogue in 1858 and maintained an elementary school until 1930. In June 1933, the number of Jews shrank to 19 (43 in 1932). SA men wrecked the synagogue on *Kristallnacht* (9–10 Nov. 1938). Those who had not managed to reach safe havens before the outbreak of war were deported to the east.

PAU Basses Pyrenees dist., France. The J. community dates from the beginning of the 19th cent. The local J. cemetery was created in accordance with a royal decree in 1822. The synagogue was inaugurated in 1880. In accordance with a 1905 law, the P. community came under the jurisdiction of the Bayonne community. The community declined after WWI. In 1939–40, with the arrival of refugees fleeing the Nazis, the J. pop. increased, so that in June 1941 there were 1,300 Jews listed in P. This included 600 locals and 700 foreign nationals. The local Jews were deported to the Gurs concentration camp. The community regained its independence from Bayonne in 1959. In 1964 there were 600 Jews in P., mostly immigrants from North Africa. A memorial was dedicated to the 1,070 Jews who died in the Gurs camp.

PAVILOSTA (also Saka) Kurzeme (Courland) dist., Latvia. The J. settlement antedated WWI and numbered 61 in 1935 (total 791). Most of the Jews were murdered by the Germans with Latvian assistance in summer 1941.

PAVLOGRAD Dnepropetrovsk dist., Ukraine. Jews probably settled in the late 18th cent. and numbered 160 in 1803 and 4,382 (total 15,775) in 1897. In the early 20th cent., a few private J. schools and a *talmud torah* were operating. A. J. school was still open in the late 1920s under the Soviets. A J. kolkhoz was located near the city. In 1939, the J. pop. was 2,510. The Germans captured P. on 10 Oct. 1941. The Jews were concentrated in a labor camp at the former Soviet army base and from there taken to the nearby village of Mavrino, where they were murdered beside ditches between Nov. 1941 and Jan. 1942. The Germans murdered, 3,700 inhabitants of P. and the surrounding area, most of them probably Jews. The labor camp was liquidated in June 1942.

PAVLOVCE NAD UHOM (Hung. Paloc) Slovakia, Czechoslovakia, today Republic of Slovakia. Jews apparently settled in the early 18th cent., trading in the nearby Uzhorod markets. Later Galician Jews settled and in the late 19th cent. a synagogue modeled on the Polish *beit midrash* was opened with certain hasidic customs preserved. The J. pop. rose from 50 in 1828 to 162 (total 1,857) in 1880 and 189 in 1921. Jews earned their living from trade and as artisans and farmers. In 1940, 108 Jews remained. These were deprived of their livelihoods in 1941. In spring 1942, the young people were deported and on 6 May 1942, families were transported to the Lukow ghetto in Poland.

PAVOLOCH Zhitomir dist., Ukraine. J. taxpayers are mentioned in 1629. In the 18th cent. Haidamak revolt, about 35 Jews were murdered and property losses were enormous. In 1897, the J. pop. was 3,391 (total 8,053). The J. pop. declined in the Soviet period, reaching 630 in 1939. When the Germans arrived in late July 1941, they murdered 156 Jews. Some succeeded in fleeing.

PAWLOWO (Odynowszczyzna) Polesie dist., Poland, today Belarus. P. was a J. farm settlement founded in 1850 by 30 families; 11 emigrated to Eretz Israel in 1884. The J. pop. in 1921 was 292. In the Holocaust the Jews were expelled to the Rozhana ghetto for liquidation.

PECEL Pest–Pilis–Solt–Kiskun dist., Hungary. Jews settled in the first half of the 18th cent. The J. pop. was 230 in 1848 and 157 in 1941. A synagogue was established in 1828 and a school opened in 1850. The young men were sent to forced labor in 1942, with most never returning. Following the German occupation in spring 1944, the Jews were brought to neighboring Rakoskeresztur and in mid-June all but those mobilized for forced labor were deported to Auschwitz via Hatvan.

PECHERA Vinnitsa dist., Ukraine. Jews numbered 135 in 1765 and 896 (total 2,455) in 1897. On 20 July 1919, the Petlyura gangs attacked the Jews. Only 62 remained in 1926 and even fewer when the Germans occupied the town in July 1941. On 1 Dec., after annexation to Transnistria, the Rumanians set up a dist. concentration camp there, also bringing in a few dozen Jews from Bessarabia and Bukovina. Mortality from starvation, disease, and sporadic shootings was high. Of the 6,500–11,000 Jews brought to the camp, 2,500–4,000 perished.

PECHISHCHE Polesie dist., Belorussia. P. was founded in 1862 as a J. colony. In the mid-1920s, about 400 Jews were living there, over 300 employed in agriculture. In 1930, the settlement became a kol-khoz where 36 J. families were employed. A J. elementary school was attended by 48 children in 1926. The Germans arrived in early July 1941. In Feb.–March they murdered the 82 Jews still there.

PECOVSKA NOVA VES (Hung. Pecsujfalu; Yid. Petcheneydorf) Slovakia, Czechoslovakia, today Republic of Slovakia. Jews were apparently present in the early 18th cent., with nine families, mostly from Galicia, mentioned in 1768. A wooden synagogue was constructed in the 1770s and a new one in 1868. The J. pop. rose from 141 in 1787 to 254 (total 1,316) in 1880. In the 1890s, P. was the seat of the rabbinate for 21 surrounding settlements. Emigration reduced the J. pop. to 76 in 1940. In late March 1942, young Jews were deported, the men to the Majdanek concentration camp and the women to Auschwitz. Most of the others were sent to the Rejowiec ghetto in the Lublin dist. of Poland on 23 May.

PECS Baranya dist., Hungary. Jews settled in the late 18th cent. in the face of local opposition, but only obtained unrestricted residence rights after 1840. A J. school was founded in 1854, reaching an enrollment of 390 in 1902. A magnificent synagogue was consecrated in 1869, when the community formed a Status Quo congregation which became Neologist in 1923. The J. pop. grew from 1,263 in 1869 and 3,124 in 1890 to 4,292 (9% of the total) in 1920. In 1930, J. breadwinners included 600 merchants and shopkeepers, 128 artisans, and 257 clerical workers. The well-known mathematician Prof. Lipot Fejer was born in P. in 1880 and Lajos Lenkel founded the Hungarian daily *Pecsi Naplo* in 1900. Jews had a significant enrollment at the local university and in some cases comprised nearly 50% of the faculty. J. defense groups, together with members of the Christian Socialist Workers Party, stopped the attacks of White Terror gangs against Jews in P. Zionist activity was intense, with Hashomer Hatzair, Ha-No'ar ha-Tziyyoni, and WIZO represented and many leaving for Palestine under the auspices of Youth Aliya. When the racial laws left many without jobs, the community began organizing retraining courses. In 1941, 3,486 Jews remained, dropping to 2,952 in 1944. On 21 May 1944, the Jews were confined in a ghetto and from 4–8 July held at the Laktis barracks until deported to Auschwitz. Those surviving forced labor returned after the war to constitute a community that numbered 267 in 1947.

PECSVARAD Baranya dist., Hungary. The J. pop. stood at 126 in 1930. In May 1944, the Jews were transferred to Mohacs and Pecs and then on 3–4 July deported to Auschwitz.

PECZENIZYN Stanislawow dist., Poland, today Ukraine. Jews were present in the 18th cent. After the discovery of oil in 1878, the J. pop. doubled to 2,024 between 1860 and 1890 (over a third of the total) with about 500 Jews employed in the oil industry. With the wells running dry on the eve of WWI a decline set in, leaving the J. pop. impoverished (reduced to 1,413 in 1921). The community was liquidated by the Germans in the course of 1942 when the Jews were expelled to Kolomyja.

PEINE Hanover, Germany. The nucleus of a community was established in 1603 by Jews from Hildesheim who settled on the outskirts of P. Their number grew to 140 in 1694 and a peak of 300 (58 families) in 1762. They opened a synagogue, acquired a burial ground, and were allowed to hire their own rabbis as well as *hazzanim* and teachers. Jews first moved into the town during the period of French rule (1807–13). The community provided up to 40 children with religious instruction. Merchants, bankers, and jurists acted as community leaders and also played a notable role in the town's cultural life and industrial development. From 180 (about 7% of the total) in 1830, the community declined to 101 in 1880, but soon recovered, numbering 150 (1% of the total) in 1900. Its new synagogue, built near the town center, was dedicated in 1907. After WWI, antisemitism revived, targeting J. Liberals and Social Democrats. At the outset of Nazi rule in 1933, the community numbered 103. Though no longer in J. hands, the synagogue and burial ground were devastated on *Kristallnacht* (9–10 Nov. 1938). SS troops also murdered a J. teenager and dispatched 16 other Jews to the Sachsenhausen concentration camp. Two-thirds of the Jews registered in 1933 left by Aug. 1939, with 20 emigrating and three committing suicide. The remainder (including refugees in Holland) were deported to the Warsaw and Theresienstadt ghettoes and to various Nazi camps. Only a handful survived.

PEISKRETSCHAM (Pol. Pyskowice) Upper Silesia, Germany, today Poland. J. settlement began in the 14th cent. under the protection of the Prince of Teschen. Jews earned their livelihoods as moneylenders, leaseholders, and petty traders. A synagogue and cemetery were opened in the late 14th cent. In 1787, the J. pop. was 104, rising to 256 in 1840. At the outset of the Nazi era, the J. pop. was 94, dropping to 43 in 1936. Nazi racial laws were not applied until 16 July 1937 since the Jews were protected by the League of Nations' minority rights convention. On *Kristallnacht* (9–10 Nov. 1938), the synagogue was set afire, all J. stores were seriously damaged, and most J. men were arrested. A few J. families subsequently emigrated. In Nov. 1941, the 17 remaining Jews were ordered into "J. houses." The mayor, who objected to their presence under any circumstances, consented to having them housed in the mortuary at the J. cemetery. Most were expelled to General Gouvernement territory on 8 and 23 June 1942. By 19 Nov. 1942, only five remained in P.

PEKELA, OUDE EN NIEUWE Groningen dist., Holland. Jews first lived there in the late 17th cent. A community was established by the end of the 18th cent. and developed throughout the 19th cent., numbering 373 in 1883. A J. school operated there. The J. pop. in 1941 was 153. In 1942, over 130 Jews were deported, some to Auschwitz. One survived the camps while 11 survived in hiding.

PELHRIMOV Bohemia, Czechoslovakia. The modern community was founded in the late 19th cent. with a synagogue consecrated c. 1890 and the J. pop. numbering 309 in 1901. In 1930, 105 Jews remained (total 6,511). The synagogue was closed down in Oct. 1941 and on 16 Nov. 1942 the Jews were deported to the Theresienstadt ghetto via Tabor.

PENESZLAK Szatmar dist., Hungary. Jews settled in the first half of the 19th cent., numbering 98 in 1880 and 55 in 1930. In late May 1944, they were deported to Auschwitz via Malteszalka.

PERBENIK Slovakia, Czechoslovakia, today Republic of Slovakia. Jews may have been present in

the 18th cent. Their number grew to 82 in 1880 and 164 (total 1,340) in 1919 and then dropped to 74 in 1941. In mid-May 1944 they were deported to Auschwitz after short stays in Kralovsky Chlumec and the Satoraljaujhely ghetto.

PERED Slovakia, Czechoslovakia, today Republic of Slovakia. J. settlement probably commenced at the turn of the 18th cent. The J. pop. reached 159 (total 1,893) in 1828 and a J. elementary school was opened in the 1880s. In 1941, the J. pop. was 100. Under the Hungarians, the Jews endured a regime of forced labor. The Germans deported them to Auschwitz in June 1944 after holding them in the Nove Zamky ghetto for awhile.

PEREHINSKO Stanislawow dist., Poland, today Ukraine. The Jews numbered 612 in 1921 (10% of the total), employed largely in the lumber industry. The Soviets took over P. on 20 Sept. 1939 and with their withdrawal on 30 June 1941 the Ukrainians took the opportunity to rob and beat the Jews, restrained somewhat by the appearance of the Hungarian army. With the arrival of the Germans in Sept., persecution was stepped up and forced labor instituted. The community was expelled to Bolechow in Aug. 1942 and from there deported to the Belzec death camp.

PEREKOP Crimea, Russia, today Ukraine. Three Jews were present in 1803, their pop. growing to 154 in 1847 and 680 (total 5,279) in 1897. A synagogue was operating in the early 20th cent, with local Jews attached to the Kakhovka community. Only a few dozen Jews remained in the 1930s under the Soviets. Those still there after the German occupation of late Oct. 1941, were probably murdered at the village of Voyenka in Feb. 1942.

PERETZ FELD Crimea, Russia, today Ukraine. Founded in the 1920s as a J. agricultural settlement by settlers from the western parts of the Soviet Union, P. was included in the J. county of Fraydorf. In 1932, its J. pop. was about 470. The Germans occupied P. in late Oct. 1941 and murdered the 103 Jews there on 15 Nov.

PERIGUEUX Dordogne dist., France. In the Middle Ages there was a small J. community. The Jews were expelled from the city in 1302. A new community was created only when the J. community of Strasbourg was evacuated to Dordogne during WWII. After liberation, when the Jews of Alsace returned to their homes, a few remained in P. The community grew with the influx of Jews from North Africa. A synagogue and community center were dedicated in 1967.

PERNU Estonia. The permanent J. settlement was founded in 1859 by four Cantonists, joined in subsequent years by numerous J. artisans to bring the J. pop. up to 505 (total 13,000) in 1881. A Russian high school known for its positive attitude to Jews attracted students from the Russian Pale of Settlement. The students were active purveyors of J. culture, setting up a drama circle, library, lectures, and public debates. A Zionist society was founded in 1901. Between the World Wars the J. pop. maintained a level of around 250, under conditions of relative prosperity that aroused antisemitic reactions. Most local Jews were tradesman, clerks, and teachers and boasted an uncharacteristically high level of education (34% graduated high school and 9% were academics). Under the Soviet occupation (1940–41) J. institutions were closed down and businesses nationalized. About 20 J. families joined the Soviet evacuation in June 1941, almost all of the men subsequently serving in the Estonian Corps of the Red Army. The rest of the town's Jews were trapped in the German occupation of 8 July. They were held in the local jail and in a special camp mainly for women. The men were sent to work on farms and the peat bogs, while young girls were raped and murdered by their Estonian guards. On 11 Sept. 1941, 92 J. men were executed outside the city and shortly afterwards 30 women were murdered in the forest. Their 50 children were killed a month later with poisoned cocoa. After the war a community was reestablished, numbering around 100 Jews in 1980.

PERUGIA Umbria, Italy. Decrees expelling local Jews in 1279 indicate the presence of a prior J. settlement. By 1310 five families were registered in the town, primarily engaged in moneylending. With the founding of a Christian loan bank, Monti di Pieta, in 1462, the economic situation of the Jews deteriorated. The violent preaching of the Franciscans aroused antisemitism and the Jews were expelled in 1485. They later returned, to be expelled in 1569 and then banished by Pope Clement VIII in the general expulsion of

1593. Jews studied at the medical school of the University of P. Among the graduates was David de Pomis (1525–93), a famous linguist, physician, and philosopher. In 1901, there were 101 Jews in P., decreasing to 60 in 1910. According to the 1930 law reforming the J. communities in Italy, P. was included in the district of Rome. By 1931, the number of Jews living in P. was 76; in 1938 it was 80. In 1948, only 37 Jews remained in P.

PERVOMAYSK (I) (Tokarovka) Zhitomir dist., Ukraine. The town was founded in 1933 and had a J. pop. of 279 (total 3,580) in 1939. The Germans captured P. on 10 July 1941. On 5 Jan. 1942, they brought the Jews to Baranovka, murdering them the next day with the rest of the local J. pop.

PERVOMAYSK (II) (Petro-Marievka) Voroshilovgrad dist., Ukraine. Jews probably settled in the early 20th cent. after the development of the local coal mines. In 1939, they numbered 214 (total 30,131). The Germans captured the city on 10 July 1942, murdering those Jews who had neither escaped nor been evacuated.

PERVOMAYSK (III) Odessa dist., Ukraine. P. was created in 1920 from the towns of Bogopol, Golta, and Olviopol. In 1799, 253 Jews were present in two of the towns. A pogrom was staged in Golta and Olviopol on 17–18 April 1881. In another pogrom, initiated on 22 Oct. 1905, nine Jews were injured in Bogopol and J. property was pillaged and destroyed. The J. pop. was 8,636 (total 21,172) in 1897. In the Soviet period, dozens of J. families earned their livelihoods in two J. kolkhozes. J. children attended two J. schools (one with high school classes). In 1939, the J. pop. was 6,087. The Germans captured the city on 2 Aug. 1941. Golta was annexed to Rumania (Transnistria) while the other two towns, on the opposite bank of the Bug River, remained under German control. After hundreds of Jews were murdered in Bogopol on 17 Sept., a ghetto was set up. In Oct., another 120 Jews were murdered at the local brickyard and in Dec., 3,600 were massacred at the Fray Leben kolkhoz. In Feb.–March 1942, 1,600 Jews expelled from Rumania were executed near the city. In Olviopol, Jews were locked into a local clubhouse and burned alive. In late 1942, Jews in the Golta ghetto were transferred to a number of concentration camps in the area (Bogdanovka and Akmechetka). In all, the Nazis murdered 5,469 people during the occupation, mostly Jews.

PESCHANAYA   (also Peschanka) Vinnitsa dist., Ukraine. J. settlement commenced in the early 19th cent. and reached a pop. of 3,682 (total 7,506) in 1897. A *talmud torah* was operating in the 1880s and later on a private J. school for boys. In the late 1920s, under the Soviets, about 120 J. families earned their livelihoods in agriculture. A J. elementary school operated until the 1930s. In 1939 the J. pop. was 1,602. The Germans occupied P. on 23 July 1941. On 3 Aug. an *Einsatzkommando 10a* unit murdered ten Jews. Presumably the same unit murdered most of the town's Jews in the same month.

PESCHANNAYA   Moldavia, today Republic of Moldova. Jews settled in the early 19th cent. The J. pop. was 870 (total 4,439) in 1897. During the Soviet period, the J. pop. stood at 915 in 1926 and 466 in

Facade of Peschannaya synagogue, Moldavia, 18th–19th cent.

1939. German and Rumanian forces captured P. on 23 July 1941. A ghetto containing 50 Jews was set up during the occupation.

PESTSZENTERZSEBET   Pest–Pilis–Solt–Kiskun dist., Hungary. Jews arrived in the late 19th cent. and helped make the city an important industrial center through their production of knitted goods, matches,

socks, soap, and alcoholic beverages. The J. pop. was 1,513 in 1900 and 4,522 (7% of the total) in 1930. The community defined itself as Neologist and built a synagogue in 1901, established a *talmud torah* in 1903, and opened a school in 1922. In 1942, J. males were seized for forced labor in the Ukraine. On 31 May 1944, the remaining 3,000 Jews were crowded into a ghetto. In late June they were brought to Monor and from there deported to Auschwitz on 8 July. Survivors reestablished the community, but most soon came to Israel.

PESTSZENTLORINC   Pest–Pilis–Solt–Kiskun dist., Hungary. Jews settled in the late 19th cent., many finding employment as factory and clerical workers. In 1930, they numbered 986 and in 1943, 879. In spring 1944, the Germans set up the first ghetto in the Budapest area at P. The Jews were confined there until the end of May and then transferred to the Monor ghetto on 30 June. On 8 July, they were deported to Auschwitz. Three hundred survivors returned after the war, but most soon left.

PESTUJHELY   Pest–Pilis–Solt–Kiskun dist., Hungary. Jews arrived in the early 20th cent., most working in nearby Budapest as sales clerks and factory workers. As P. grew and local prices rose, the Jews were held responsible and after WWI they were attacked by local mobs. Many fled to Budapest. Jews numbered 668 in 1930 and 584 in 1941. In April 1944, they were expelled to Rakospalota and in early June most were deported to Auschwitz. A small group was brought to the Sachsenhausen and Oranienburg concentration camps to counterfeit Allied currency. Survivors reestablished the community but most soon left for Israel.

PETERGOF   (also Petrodvorets) Leningrad dist., Russia. Jews probably settled around the turn of the 19th cent., numbering 81 (total 11,504) in 1926. The Germans arrived on 23 Sept. 1941, murdering the few Jews who had neither fled nor been evacuated and a small number from the neighboring villages (Novaya Niva, etc.).

PETERSHAGEN   Westphalia, Germany. A J. family was present in 1551 under the local bishop's protection. Nine families lived there in 1714. The J. pop. reached a peak of 82 (total 1,876) in 1871 with several dozen living in five attached village communities (Quetzen, Frille, Ovenstaedt, Windheim, Bierde). A synagogue and cemetery were operating in the late 19th cent. In 1933, the J. pop. was 35. On *Kristallnacht* (9–10 Nov. 1938), the synagogue was burned and two J. stores and five J. homes were destroyed. Ten Jews remained in Oct. 1939. Most apparently left for other German settlements, 20 perishing in the camps along with at least eight from the attached communities.

PETERVASARA   Heves dist., Hungary. Jews settled in the early 19th cent. Numerous communities were affiliated to the congregation. The J. pop. was 95 in 1880 and 57 in 1930. On 9 May 1944, the Jews were brought to Egercsehi, where 2,000 Jews from the Heves dist. were being held. On 11 June they were transferred to Kerecsend prior to deportation to Auschwitz.

PETNEHAZA   Szabolcs dist., Hungary. Jews are mentioned in 1770 and maintained two cemeteries and a synagogue. The J. pop. was 125 in 1880 and 85 in 1930. After Passover 1944, the Jews were brought to Nyiregyhaza and then deported to Auschwitz at the end of May. Survivors reestablished the community but soon left for Israel.

PETRAUTI   (Ger. Petrautz), Bukovina, Rumania. A J. community existed in 1916. The J. pop. in 1930 was 56 families. The majority left in the 1930s because of antisemitism and in late 1941 the few remaining Jews were deported to Transnistria.

PETRIKOV   Polesie dist., Belorussia. The J. pop., which included 282 tax payers in 1765, numbered 2,515 (total 5,538) in 1897. In a pogrom staged by the Balakhovich brigade in 1920, 45 Jews were murdered, many women raped, and J. homes looted. A Hehalutz youth group was active in the mid-1920s along with a J. elementary school with an enrollment of 200 in 1929. In the late 1920s, 35% of J. breadwinners were artisans, 20% blue-collar workers, and 6% merchants. In 1939, the J. pop. was 1,074. The Germans captured the town on 29 July 1941. On 22 Sept. they murdered about 300 Jews on the banks of the Pripet River. The next day they continued to murder Jews inside the town. In late Feb. 1942, 200 Jews discovered in hiding were executed at the village of Belki. The 50 or so remaining Jews were held in three houses until

they were murdered on the outskirts of the town in late April 1942.

PETRILA   (Hung. Petrilla) S. Transylvania dist., Rumania. Jews first settled in the late 19th cent. and were attached to the Petrosani community. The J. pop. was 282 in 1930 (3% of the total). At the outbreak of the Soviet-Rumanian war (June 1941) the J. pop. was transferred to Deva and neighboring villages. About half returned after the war.

PETROSANI   (Hung. Petrozseny) S. Transylvania dist., Rumania. The J. community began to develop in the 1870s around the coal mines. After the community joined the Neologist association, the Orthodox split off, but then the two joined together in 1904. There was also a community of Vizhnitz Hasidim. R. Asher Anschel Mueller, a rabbinical scholar, served the community for 50 years (1905-55). The Jews were active in local politics, culture, and the professions. Zionist activity developed between the World Wars. The J. pop. was 1,071 in 1930 (7% of the total). In 1940, the Iron Guard Legionnaires closed J. shops and forced their owners to sell at undervalued prices. In July 1941, the J. pop. was transferred to Deva, Hateg, Paclisa, and Ilia. They returned after the war.

PETROVA   N. Transylvania dist., Rumania. Jews settled in the early 19th cent. R. Shemuel Dov Chadrov set up his hasidic court at the end of the 19th cent.; after his death in 1928, he was succeeded by his widow. The J. pop. declined – mainly for economic reasons – from 1,103 in 1920 to 658 in 1930 (15% of the total). The rival Rumanian and Ruthenian communities often elected a Jew as head of the local council. In 1942, Jews were drafted into labor battalions in the Ukraine, where most died. In April 1944, the community was transferred to the Viseul de Sus ghetto and then deported to Auschwitz. About 100 returned after the war and tried to reestablish the community but soon left for Israel.

PETROVICHI   Smolensk dist., Russia. Jews probably settled at the turn of the 17th cent. In 1765, the J. pop. included 88 poll tax payers. The J. pop. increased to 570 in 1847 and 1,065 (total 1,435) in 1897. In 1926, under the Soviets, the J. pop. was 925. P. was the birthplace of the American-J. science fiction writer Isaac Asimov. The Germans occupied the town on 2 Aug. 1941, confining the Jews in a ghetto. They were forced to wear a badge bearing the word "*Jude.*" A similar sign was placed on their houses. On 22 July 1942, the Germans murdered them along with Jews from the surrounding area.

PETRZALKA (Hung. Ligetfalu) Slovakia, Czechoslovakia, today Republic of Slovakia. Jews arrived from nearby Kittsee in the late 19th cent. The J. pop. increased from 42 in 1919 to 241 (total 14,164) in 1930. Most fled to Bratislava in Oct. 1938 before the Germans arrived. The Germans murdered hundreds of Hungarian Jews in a nearby camp toward the end of the war.

PETSERI (Ger. Petchuz) Estonia. The single remaining J. family of four was murdered at the J. cemetery after the German occupation in summer 1941 by a local policeman who was afterwards one of the heads of the Estonian Fishing and Hunting Association in Toronto, Canada.

PEZINOK (Hung. Bazin) Slovakia, Czechoslovakia, today Republic of Slovakia. Jews were apparently present in the 13th cent., making the community one of the oldest in Slovakia. In the 15th cent., there were a few dozen families living on a Street of the Jews and maintaining a full range of community services, but constantly harassed by local German residents. The community ended in 1529 when 30 Jews were burned alive in the aftermath of a blood libel and the rest expelled. Jews settled again in the late 17th cent. and numbered 304 by 1787, constituting one of the largest and most important J. communities in Slovakia. In 1848, they were attacked in riots, fleeing the city as their homes and stores were looted. In 1857, the J. pop. reached a peak of 540 (over 10% of the total). A J. elementary school was opened in 1843 and a new synagogue was built in 1872. Jews were prominent as wine wholesalers and owned a brick and concrete plant employing 358 workers. New riots erupted in 1918 and 1919. After WWI, the community again flourished. The Zionists played a leading role in the community's social life with most of the young joining their youth movements. Most businesses were in J. hands. Antisemitism intensified in the late 1930s and led to vandalism and beatings and the institution of anti-J. measures even before they were officially introduced in the Slovakian state. About a quarter of the

Jews left in early 1940, leaving 235. In late 1941, only 175 remained. The young were deported to Auschwitz and the Majdanek death camp in March 1942. Subsequently, families were sent to the death camps in the Lublin dist. (Poland). Dozens of J. patients at the local mental institution were deported to Auschwitz on 20 Oct. In 1944, the Germans murdered 21 more and dispatched 32 Jews to Auschwitz.

PFAFFEN-BEERFURTH Hesse, Germany. The community played a major role in the livestock trade and numbered 59 (12% of the total) in 1900 and 25 in 1933. It disbanded in Oct. 1937 and only 12 Jews remained on *Kristallnacht* (9–10 Nov. 1938), when a pogrom occurred. At least ten Jews emigrated during the Nazi era.

PFAFFENHOFFEN Bas-Rhin dist., France. The J. presence here dates from the beginning of the 14th cent. In 1626, the Hanau-Lichtenberg family granted Jews the right of residence and in 1791 a synagogue was inaugurated. In 1808, the community numbered 136 Jews, dropping to 69 in 1936. The Germans expelled the Jews to the south of France together with the rest of Alsace-Lorraine Jews. During a bombardment, the synagogue was damaged. Eleven local Jews were deported. In 1954 the J. pop. was 34.

PFEDDERSHEIM Hesse, Germany. Jews lived here from the 16th cent. and by 1861 the community had grown to 72 (3.5% of the total). Most Jews emigrated before or soon after the Nazis came to power in 1933.

PFLAUMLOCH Wuerttemberg, Germany. The 17th cent. community grew to 255 in 1854 but in the wake of emigration no Jews were left by 1910. The cemetery was desecrated in 1976.

PFORZHEIM Baden, Germany. The 13th cent. J. community was victimized in a blood libel in 1267, with Jews tortured on the rack and hanged. The Jews also suffered in the Black Death persecutions of 1348–49. Few Jews were present in P. until the 17th cent. In 1614, they were expelled together with all the Jews of Baden-Durlach and only began to settle again in 1670. After the destruction of the city by the French in 1689 (in the Nine Years War) Jews were invited back under a letter of protection to help rebuild it.

In the late 1760s, Jews were among the founders of the gold and jewelry industry that brought prosperity to the city. However, all through the 19th cent. the Jews were subjected to local agitation aimed at curtailing their economic activity. In the early 19th cent., a number of special taxes and disabilities were discontinued and Jews were permitted to purchase farm land. Toward the end of the 19th cent. most of the Jews were well off, owning banks and department stores as well as factories. A new synagogue in the Gothic style was built in 1892, equipped with an organ and choir in keeping with the community's Reform and assimilationist tendencies. By 1910 the community had grown to 766 (total 69,066) and by 1927 to a peak of 1,000. After WWI, community life expanded, with the Zionists becoming active. An Adass Jeshurun congregation of 20 families was formed by Orthodox Jews of East European origin, with a separate synagogue erected in 1926. From the 1920s on, antisemitism became rampant. At the outset of the Nazi era, the J. pop. was 770. Persecution and the economic boycott were soon intensified. In March 1933, 18 J. families of Polish origin were expelled to the Polish border. Jews were dismissed from the public service and in 1935 a number of Jews were arrested for "racial defilement." The remaining East European Jews were expelled on 28 Oct. 1938 and on *Kristallnacht* (9–10 Nov. 1938), Jews were beaten, J. stores were looted, and the synagogue was set on fire. Twenty-three J. men were sent to the Dachau concentration camp. Of the 514 Jews allowed to emigrate, 175 went to the U.S., 102 to Palestine, and 87 to Latin America. On 22 Oct. 1940, 183 were deported to the Gurs concentration camp where 20 died; 50 perished in Auschwitz and 66 in other camps; 46 survived the Holocaust. The 51 Jews remaining in P. were deported mainly to Izbica (Poland) and to the Theresienstadt ghetto; 17 survived. The community formed after the war numbered 120 in 1976.

PFUNGSTADT   Hesse, Germany. Established in the 18th cent., the community built a synagogue in 1820. During the 19th cent. P. became an industrial town attracting affluent Jews and the community grew to 260 (6% of the total) in 1871. After a struggle between Liberals and traditionalists, it affiliated with the Orthodox rabbinate of Darmstadt in 1895. The religious high school founded by David Joel in 1857 gained an international reputation. Chaim Weizmann taught there

when he was a student at Darmstadt's Polytechnic in 1892. Jews were prominent in trade and industry under the Weimar Republic, when they numbered 77 (1% of the total), but many left (20 emigrating) after the Nazis came to power in 1933. On *Kristallnacht* (9–10 Nov. 1938), the synagogue's interior was destroyed and J. property vandalized. The last 18 Jews were deported in 1942.

PHILIPPSBURG   Baden, Germany. The 14th cent. J. community was destroyed in the Black Death persecutions of 1348–49. Jews were again present in the first half of the 17th cent. but most left when the seat of the bishopric was transferred to Bruchsal in 1723. Many again left in the second half of the 18th cent. The community revived in the 19th cent., reaching a pop. of 94 in 1842. In 1933, 45 Jews remained. Among their businesses were a big wholesale firm for farm produce, a cigarette factory, and a printing press. Most J. businesses closed and by Nov. 1938, 11 Jews had left Germany. Another eight left after *Kristallnacht* (9–10 Nov. 1938), when the synagogue was set on fire. On 22 Oct. 1940, the last 21 Jews were deported to the Gurs concentration camp, where 15 perished.

PHILLIPE THOMAS   Gafsa dist., Tunisia. A small J. community of merchants arose with the discovery of phosphates in 1886 by the geologist after whom the town was named. The J. pop. was 66 (9% of the total) in 1936 and 48 (5% of the total) in 1946. In WWII, the Jews suffered from the fighting in the area. Afterwards their numbers dwindled; most Jews left after Tunisian independence in 1956.

PIASECZNO (I)   Volhynia dist., Poland, today Ukraine. The J. pop. was 101 in 1921 (total 874). In the Holocaust, the Jews were probably liquidated with those of Powursk.

PIASECZNO (II)   Warsaw dist., Poland. Jews were permitted to settle in P. in 1689. Expulsion orders (1837, 1839, and 1847) were not implemented and in 1897 the community numbered 1,106 (total 2,760). Unusual among the J. occupations was stone quarrying. Though hasidic influence grew from the mid-19th cent., Jews on the municipal council of 1934 included four Zionists compared with one from Agudat Israel and one non-partisan. In 1921, the 2,256 Jews of P. represented 40% of the total pop. The Nazis occupied P. in Sept. 1939 and appointed a *Judenrat*. In Jan.–Feb. 1942, the Germans expelled P.'s Jews to Warsaw, from where they were sent to the Treblinka death camp.

PIASKI Bialystok dist., Poland, today Belarus. Jews may have been present in the 16th cent. By 1847 they numbered 622, mainly engaged in the lumber, grain, and cattle trade. The community had two architecturally distinctive synagogues, one of wood dating from the 18th cent., the other of red brick built in the 19th cent. Among the community's rabbis was Aryeh Leib Epstein (1705–75), author of *Sefer ha-Pardes*, and Moshe bar Yisrael Palya, founder of the hasidic Kobrin dynasty. The J. pop. rose to 1,615 (total 2,396) in 1897 but dropped to 1,162 in 1921 as a result of economic decline and the depredations of WWI. After the war the position of the Jews deteriorated further under heavy taxes, competition from the Polish cooperatives, and the exclusion of Jews from the tobacco industry. After the Balfour Declaration of 1917, Zionist influence grew, with a Tarbut Hebrew school founded and the youth movements sending pioneers to Palestine. The Germans arrived in late June 1941, confiscating J. property and setting up a *Judenrat* and ghetto. On 2 Nov. 1942, children and the old were taken to the J. cemetery and murdered while the remaining 1,600 Jews were marched to the Wolkowysk transit camp and soon after deported to Treblinka. Some who escaped joined the partisans.

PIASKI LUTERSKIE Lublin dist., Poland. Jews are first mentioned in 1699. Their pop. grew from 571 in 1827 to 1,836 in 1857 and 2,674 (total 3,974) in 1921. Between the World Wars, the Jews suffered economically from Polish competition and increasing antisemitism but J. public life flourished and Zionist activity was extensive. In 1939, the J. pop. was 4,165. As the Jews of P. fled east on the approach of the Germans in Sept. 1939, J. refugees from western Poland began arriving. In the interlude between Soviet and German rule, local Poles murdered and robbed Jews. In early 1940, a *Judenrat* and ghetto were established. Hundreds of Jews were sent to forced labor camps and with the arrival of refugees, the ghetto pop. rose to 5,000. A second ghetto, crowding 20 people into a room, was set up in June 1941. In March 1942, 3,500 Jews were deported to the Belzec death camp to make room for 4,200 Jews from Germany,

1,000 from Czechoslovakia, and others from Kalisz. The ghetto pop. at this time stood at about 6,500. In Sept. there were deportations to Belzec and in Oct. 4,000 were deported to the Sobibor death camp via Trawniki. Subsequently, 6,000 surviving Jews from the region were brought there. The ghetto was liquidated in Feb. or March 1943. The men were brought to Trawniki, but all traces of them have been lost. The fate of the children and women is unknown. Of the 35 survivors, most were young people who joined partisan units.

PIASKOVKA Kiev dist., Ukraine. A small number of Jews were present in the 18th cent. In 1939, the J. pop. was 186 (total 477). After their arrival on 22 Aug. 1941, the Germans murdered the Jews.

PIATEK Lodz dist., Poland. Jews settled here from the mid-18th cent. The J. pop. was 1,090 in 1897 (47% of the total) and 1,275 in 1939. The Germans arrived on 9 Sept. and established a ghetto. It was destroyed in April 1942 and the inhabitants were deported to Chelmno.

PIATIGORSK Stavropol territory, Russia. Jews probably settled in the mid-19th cent., reaching a pop. of 469 (total 12,836) in 1877. Mountain Jews (Tats) arrived during the civil war (1918–21) after being expelled from their villages during a pogrom. In 1926, the J. pop. rose to 1,500, including 52 Mountain Jews. The Germans arrived on 9 Aug. 1942, murdering all the Jews on 10 Sept. at Mineralnyie Vody.

PIATIGORY Kiev dist., Ukraine. Jews numbered 138 in 1765. In 1768, the Haidamaks beat and robbed Jews and murdered several. The J. pop. was 1,385 (total 4,383) in 1897 and 532 under the Soviets in 1926. Most Jews were Hasidim. In 1919, General Denikin's White Army troops attacked the Jews. The Germans occupied P. on 16 July 1941. On 31 July, three Jews were arrested and shot. On 28 Aug., 17 J. males were murdered. Jews were ordered to wear the Star of David and on 26 April 1942, the young and couples without children were sent to the Buki labor camp. Ukrainian police murdered all the rest on 14 Nov. 1942.

PIATKA Zhitomir dist., Ukraine. The J. pop. was 78 in the mid-18th cent. and 833 (total 2,703) in 1897. It dropped to several hundred on the eve of WWII. Many Jews were furniture makers, exporting to the larger cities of Russia. A. J. elementary school operated in the 1920s. The Germans captured P. on 7 July 1941, immediately murdering 11 Jews after taking them to Chudnov. The rest were held in the synagogue under a ghetto regimen. On 24 Oct., 200 were murdered outside the town with the active participation of Ukrainian police, who afterwards pillaged the victims' property.

PIATKOWA Lwow dist., Poland, today Ukraine. The J. pop. was 108 in 1921. The Jews were probably executed locally or expelled to their deaths in summer–fall 1942.

PIATNICA Bialystok dist., Poland. J. settlement began in the 16th cent., increasing in the second half of the 16th cent. when Lomza's Jews moved there following expulsion. From 1863, many Jews provided services and goods, particularly meat, to the Russian army. In WWI, the J. community dwindled, dropping from 1,239 (52% of the total) in 1897 to 520 (31%)

in 1921. The local Hehalutz branch founded in 1929 organized self-defense groups in the mid-1930s. J. livelihoods suffered before WWII as antisemitic attacks increased and J. businesses were boycotted. In 1941, the majority of Jews were expelled by the Germans to the Lomza ghetto and many were executed in the Galczyn forest.

PIATRA-NEAMT Moldavia dist., Rumania. Documentary evidence of J. settlement first appears in the late 18th cent. In 1841, 48 Jews from nearby villages were brought to P. after being accused in a blood libel and were freed only after the intervention of Moses Montefiore. In the late 19th cent., the authorities persecuted Jews and local professional and welfare organizations refused to accept J. members. In addition to the Great Synagogue built in 1776, members of various trades maintained 16 prayer houses. A *talmud torah* operating from 1770 was closed by the police in 1868. In 1882, B'nai B'rith opened an elementary school but it was closed in 1885. The J. community established a boys' school in 1896 and one for girls in

Dance group in Jewish girls' school, Piatra-Neamt, Rumania, 1920s (Beth Hatefutsoth Photo Archive, Tel Aviv/photo courtesy of Yad Vashem, The Holocaust Martyrs' and Heroes' Remembrance Authority, Jerusalem)

1899 with the support of the ICA. Of the town's 376 artisans, 267 were Jews. Industrialists founded factories and dominated the commerce in the town and district. Toward the end of the 19th cent., the economic situation of the J. pop. declined as a result of antisemitism and in 1900 several hundred Jews left the town, mainly on foot. The J. pop. in 1907 was 8,000 (about 50% of the total). Zionist activity began at the turn of the 19th cent. Zionist periodicals appeared in Yiddish and Hebrew. Between the World Wars, P. was a center of antisemitic agitation, and in 1925 Rumanian students looted the synagogue, the J. school, the Zionist clubrooms, and the J. library. In 1926, A. C. Cuza incited the local pop. to attack Jews. In 1931 the local branch of the Iron Guard advocated the eviction of Jews as part of their parliamentary election campaign. J. lawyers were ousted from the lawyers association in 1937 and prevented from practicing or appearing in court. A vocational school for girls was opened in 1927 as well as a Hebrew-speaking nursery school. In 1936–37, 400 J. pupils attended the schools. The Zionist movement with 700 members in 1919 was deeply involved in community leadership and in 1929 became the majority party. During 1940–41, Iron Guard Legionnaires persecuted Jews, seizing their shops and goods. A few days prior to the outbreak of the Soviet-Rumanian war, 1,500 Jews aged 16–60 were interned in camps and 21 were later deported to Transnistria. In May 1941, 500 Jews aged 16–66 were drafted into labor battalions and sent to Focsani, Girov, and Ramnicu-Sarat; another 500 were put to work in the town and its environs. During this period, the J. elementary schools with over 500 pupils and a high school with over 200 pupils continued to function. The J. pop. in 1941 was 7,267 (21% of the total), including 600 refugees from the villages. An orphanage was opened for children brought back from Transnistria. After the war, many of those expelled returned and settled there. In 1947 the J. pop. was 8,000.

PIATYKHATKA Dnepropetrovsk dist., Ukraine. J. settlement commenced at the turn of the 19th cent. The J. pop. was 304 (total 5,766) in 1926 and 210 in 1939. The Germans arrived on 13 Aug. 1941. Those Jews who had neither fled nor been evacuated from P. were among the 550 inhabitants of the area who were murdered shortly thereafter at a local coal mine.

PIEDRUJA (Yid. Fridroisk) Latgale dist., Latvia.

Jews were probably present in the mid-18th cent. and numbered 706 (total 1,017) in 1906, living mainly from trade and owning all the stores in P. Anti-J. peasant attacks struck the community in 1881 and 1882. After WWI, with the tightening of border controls in independent Latvia, the J. economic position deteriorated and many Jews left, leaving a J. pop. of 145 in 1935. After the German occupation in summer 1941 the Jews were marched to the forest and murdered.

PIENIONZKI Bialystok dist., Poland, today Belarus. The J. pop. was 108 in 1921 (total 278). The Jews were apparently expelled by the Germans to the Bogosha transit camp on 2 Nov. 1942 and from there sent to Treblinka and Auschwitz in Jan. 1943.

PIEREJASLAV Kiev dist., Ukraine. J. settlement commenced in the early 17th cent. Most Jews were murdered in the Chmielnicki massacres of 1648–49. They numbered 66 in 1801 and 5,754 in 1897. The last rabbi of the community was Yehoshua Zalman Diskin. In an 1881 pogrom, J. homes and stores were considerably damaged. A new pogrom broke out in Oct. 1905. After the Oct. 1917 Revolution, Po'alei Zion and the Bund became active. In another pogrom, in 1919, General Denikin's White Army soldiers killed several Jews and looted J. homes and stores. In the Soviet period, many Jews worked in a barrel factory and in tanneries. In the late 1920s, several families moved to Birobidzhan and the Crimea. In the 1920s, a museum was opened in the former home of Shalom Aleichem (1859–1916), who was born in P. The J. pop. was 937 in 1939. The Germans occupied P. on 17 Sept. 1941 and on 6 Oct. executed 600 Jews. Another 200 were murdered after being discovered in hiding. Converted J. women married to Ukrainians were murdered in May 1942.

PIERZCHNICA Kielce dist., Poland. The J. pop. was 180 in 1921 (total 1,070). The Jews were presumably expelled by the Germans to a nearby ghetto in fall 1942 and subsequently deported to the Treblinka death camp.

PIESOCHIN Kharkov dist., Ukraine. The J. pop. in 1939 was 551 (total 9,917). Most Jews presumably left before the German occupation of 20 Oct. 1941.

PIESTANY (Hung. Posteny) Slovakia, Czechoslovakia, today Republic of Slovakia. Jews probably settled in the early 18th cent., with 12 families enjoying the patronage of Count Forgacs and living on his estate in 1736. An independent community of 50 families was constituted in 1795. In 1848, J. homes and stores were looted in peasant riots. A J. elementary school was opened in the 1870s. The J. pop. grew to 732 in 1900 and 1,254 (total 9,321) in 1921. A large synagogue was built in 1904. Jews contributed to the development of the town as a health resort. In 1922, they owned 112 business establishments, many catering to tourists, 43 workshops, and six factories, including one of the biggest flour mills in the state. Following WWI, an organized defense effort by the Jews succeeded in fending off a new wave of riots. In 1926, about 140 Jews split off to form a Liberal congregation, building a synagogue in 1928 and opening a Hebrew school in 1933. The Zionists became active in 1919 and Agudat Israel in 1920. In the 1930s, 100 children attended the J. elementary school as the J. pop grew to 1,559 in 1940. After the establishment of the Slovakian state in 1939, the authorities closed down J. businesses and seized men for forced labor. Forty J. girls were deported to Auschwitz on 1 April 1942. On 27 April, about 330 Jews were sent to the Opole ghetto in the Lublin dist. of Poland. Another 369 were dispatched to the Sered transit camp on 8 May. In all, 90% of the Jews were sent to the death camps in 1942. Of the remaining Jews, those still in P. when the Germans arrived in Sept. 1944 were deported to Auschwitz. The postwar community numbered 250; most emigrated to Israel or overseas in 1949.

PIKELIAI (Yid. Pikeln) Mazeikiai dist., Lithuania. Jews first settled at the end of the 18th cent. and maintained two synagogues and a yeshiva. The J. pop. in 1897 was 1,206 (68% of the total). Many emigrated prior to WWI. The Zionists were active. In 1940 the J. pop. amounted to about 20 families. After the German invasion in June 1941, the Jews were taken out of the town and shot on 9 Aug. 1941.

PIKOV Vinnitsa dist., Ukraine. Jews are first mentioned in 1713 in connection with a Cossack raid. In 1765 they numbered 585 and in 1897, 1,479. In 1926, under the Soviets, the J. pop. was 1,644 (total 3,449). Jews belonged to artisan cooperatives and a few dozen families worked on a J. kolkhoz. A J. council (soviet) was active and about 300 children attended a J. el-

ementary school. The Germans captured P. in early July 1941, immediately concentrating the Jews from the smaller settlements in a ghetto together with the local Jews. Most (960) were murdered at the J. cemetery in late May 1942. Another 76 were murdered on 6 June. A few of the young tried to organize a revolt.

PILAWA Lublin dist., Poland. Few J. families were present before WWI. The J. pop. was 179 in 1921 (total 1,208). Most earned their living by supplying vegetables to Russian army units garrisoned in the area. Between the World Wars, the area's resorts provided a livelihood for many. After the German occupation of Sept. 1939, the Jews were expelled to neighboring settlements and in Oct. 1942 deported to the Treblinka death camp.

PILDA Latgale dist., Latvia. A few dozen J. families lived there in the 19th cent. and just seven Jews in 1930. All were murdered after the German occupation of July 1941.

PILICA (Yid. Piltz) Kielce dist., Poland. A small J. settlement existed in the early 17th cent., but in 1662 Christians took over the J. synagogue and turned it into a church. In 1781, the Jews were granted a privilege allowing them free trade and in the 19th cent. they were prominent in the town's industrial development, employing 300 workers in their factories (paper, wool, yeast, and starch). They also owned most of the town's saloons. In 1892, the J. pop. reached 2,688 (total 3,975). Among the community's rabbis was Yehiel Danziger (d. 1894), future founder of Aleksandrow Hasidism. The first Zionist group was organized in 1894. Antisemitism increased in the early 20th cent. Following the ravages of WWI, the economically distressed J. pop. dropped to 1,877 in 1921. The Zionists were active in culture and education and Agudat Israel opened a Beth Jacob school for 120 girls in 1926. In the late 1930s, there were instances of anti-J. violence. When the Germans arrived on 5 Sept. 1939, there were 1,500 Jews present. The *Judenrat* was probably established in late 1939. German police periodically looted J. property. In fall 1941, the J. pop. rose to 2,000 after an influx of refugees. In spring 1942, a large group of young Jews was sent to labor camps in Plaszow and Bochnia. On 6 Sept. 1942, 1,060 Jews were deported to the Belzec death camp after most of the young were sent to labor camps. As many as half the J. pop. of 3,000 succeeded in escaping at this time. The last of the few hundred left in the ghetto, including new refugees, were murdered, probably in Nov. A J. underground including about 60 youth movement members from P. and Zarki failed in its attempt to organize local resistance. Some hid out in bunkers outside the town after the deportation; most were killed fighting when discovered by the Germans.

PILIS   Pest dist., Hungary. Jews are mentioned in 1784. In 1930, they numbered 136. They were probably deported to Auschwitz via Monor in the beginning of July 1944.

PILISVOROSVAR   Pest–Pilis–Solt–Kiskun dist., Hungary. Three J. families were present in the early 18th cent., later augmented by Jews from Moravia and Czechoslovakia. R. Engel Mozes (1779–1819) established a yeshiva which attracted students from all over Hungary. The J. pop. reached a peak of 310 in 1840 and declined sharply late in the cent. as many left for Budapest. Jews were violently attacked in the White Terror after WWI. They numbered 177 in 1930 and 78 in 1941 after many died in the Ukraine under forced labor. At the end of May 1944, the Jews were transferred to Budafok and Budakalasz before final deportation to Auschwitz in early July.

PILSEN   Bohemia, Czechoslovakia. Dozens of J. families, with a small synagogue and cemetery at their disposal, were present by 1315. In 1505 they were expelled in a Host desecration libel, only returning in the mid-19th cent. In 1850, P. became the seat of the dist. rabbinate. A cemetery was consecrated in 1856 and a synagogue in 1859. A new synagogue with 2,800 seats was completed in 1893, the second largest in Europe after the one in Budapest. Jews helped make P. an important industrial center – the Skoda armaments factory was located here – and the community became one of the five largest and richest in Bohemia by the early 20th cent., its pop. reaching a peak of 3,517 in 1910. Between the World Wars, the Zionists were active. In 1930, the J. pop. was 2,738 (total 89,374). The German occupation of March 1939 brought persecution and arrests. Fifty-one Jews in an underground anti-Nazi group were arrested in 1940 and ultimately deported to the Mauthausen concentration camp. In Jan. 1942, 2,604 Jews from P. and western Moravia were deported to the Theresien-

stadt ghetto in three transports and from there to death camps in Poland where 2,400 perished.

PILTENE   Kurzeme (Courland) dist., Latvia. The J. settlement was one of the earliest in Courland, perhaps going back to the 16th–17th cent. A synagogue is mentioned from 1708 and was probably the oldest in Courland. The town was destroyed in the Swedish wars of the early 18th cent. but was rebuilt and continued to be one of the few in Courland where J. residence was allowed. In 1881 the J. pop. reached a peak of 721 (total 1,830). The Jews lived mainly from trade (grain, fruit, alcoholic beverages) and also operated distilleries and inns and worked as tailors. In the late 19th cent. many Jews left for the burgeoning port town of Ventspils (Windau) nearby, contributing significantly to its development and causing the J. pop. of P. to drop to 359 on the eve of WWI. During WWI the Jews were expelled from the town, with only a few dozen returning. The community was presumably wiped out by the Germans in the second half of 1941.

PILVISKIAI   (Yid. Pilvishok) Vilkaviskis dist., Lithuania. Jews first settled in the second half of the 18th cent. The community maintained a *heder*, yeshiva, and two synagogues. Zionist youth groups were active. The J. pop. in 1897 was 1,242 (53% of the total). Between the World Wars the deteriorating economic situation led many to emigrate. Others subsisted with help from American relatives. There was considerable Zionist activity between the World Wars. The J. pop. in 1939 was 700 (24% of the total). After the German invasion in June 1941, Lithuanian nationalists took over the town, imposing harsh and humiliating measures upon the J. pop. Ironically, it was a German officer who restrained the Lithuanians. After a few days he was replaced and the abuses resumed. On 28 Aug. 1941, J. men were shot and thrown into the pit they had dug. On 15 Sept. the women, children, and few remaining men were brought to a second pit, forced to strip, and shot. Children were thrown alive into the pit.

PILYAVA   Kamenets-Podolski dist., Ukraine. Fifty Jews resided in P. in the 1780s and 752 (total 3,701) in 1897. In 1923, under the Soviets, the J. pop. was 619. The Germans occupied P. in mid-July 1941 and on 19 Aug., they murdered 211 Jews. Another 180 were executed near the village of Alexeyevka in the fall.

Firemen's brigade, Pilviskiai, Lithuania

PILZNO Cracow dist., Poland. Few Jews settled in P. until the residence ban was lifted in 1860 under the Austrians. The J. pop. grew to 551 in 1880 (total 2,128). The local hasidic *rebbe* was a member of the Ropshits dynasty. In 1905–06 the community extended aid to J. refugees from Russia passing through en route to the U.S. In the ensuing years of economic distress and the Russian occupation of 1914–15 many joined the exodus. The community also aided the 12,000 J. refugees caught in the area after the Russian withdrawal in May 1915, with the Joint Distribution Committee and Alliance Israelite offering support. Anti-J. disturbances erupted in 1918 and 1919. In 1921, the J. pop. stood at 752. The Zionists, active since 1894, expanded their activities between the World Wars. Antisemitism intensified in the 1930s. Under the Germans in WWII a *Judenrat* was established and forced labor imposed. In Nov. 1940, the Jews were expelled, mainly to Nowy Soncz, meeting their end in the Belzec death camp in 1942.

PINCZOW Kielce dist. Poland. Jews are first mentioned in the early 16th cent. and formed one of the most important communities in Lesser Poland, with representation on the Council of the Four Lands. The first of its three synagogues was built in the 17th cent. and remained standing until WWII. The great Talmud scholar Yonatan Eybeschuetz was born in P. in 1690 or 1695 (d. 1764). Later rabbi of Metz, Hamburg, and Prague, he became embroiled in the famous dispute with Yaakov Emden when accused of Shabbateanism. In the 18th cent., J. merchants traded in grain, furs, and hides, traveling as far as Leipzig, Danzig, and Breslau. Jews were also prominent in the book trade, exporting and importing to and from communities in Poland and abroad. In the late 19th cent., they were active in industry, opening factories for building materials, wool processing, knitting, and dyeing. The J. pop. grew from 2,883 in 1857 to 5,176 (total 8,199) in 1897 but dropped to 4,324 in 1921 as economic conditions worsened with the closing of the Russian market and the rise of state-assisted Polish competition. Zionist activity, which commenced under the Austrian occupation in WWI, expanded considerably, with Hashomer Hatzair the most prominent youth movement and Mizrachi opening a Hebrew school. In 1924, the Zionists won control of the community council from Agudat Israel. Antisemitism intensified in the 1930s, causing accelerated emigration. The Germans found 3,500 Jews in the city when they occupied it on 10 Sept. 1939. A *Judenrat* was appointed to supply forced labor and in May 1941 a ghetto was set up, accommodating refugees as well but not growing in pop. owing to the high deathrate due to illness and deportations to distant labor camps. In Oct. 1942, the Jews were expelled to Sandomierz with many of the old and weak shot along the way. From there they were deported to the Treblinka death camp. A few groups escaping to the forest joined the Polish Armia Ludowa. In addition to helping fellow

Jews who had escaped to the forests, they engaged in effective partisan action.

PINIAVA (Yid. Piniave) Panevezys dist., Lithuania. The J. pop. in 1923 was 58 (46% of the total). After the German invasion of 1941, the Jews were deported to Panevezys and then murdered in the Pajuoste forest on 24 Aug. 1941 together with the Jews of Panevezys.

PINSK Polesie dist., Poland, today Belarus. In 1506, as part of Prince Feodor Yaroslavski's efforts to develop the city, about a dozen J. families from among those expelled from Lithuania were granted a charter based on Prince Vitold's 1388 Brest-Litovsk charter,. They were accordingly granted freedom of trade and worship and the right to reside on a Street of the Jews near the

Pinczow town council, Poland, 1927–30. Half were Jewish

Heavy Jewish work, Pinsk, Poland

fortress and marketplace, where they could enjoy protection and easy access to the city's commercial center. The community grew steadily with economic activity focusing on land purchases, moneylending, and trade, including the leasing of the state salt and distillation monopolies. Among the leading commercial figures in the early period were Nahum and Yisrael Pesahovich. In the mid-16th cent., Jews expanded into the river trade in grain and lumber and continued to prosper despite efforts by the local pop. to impose trade and residence restrictions on them. By the 1640s, the J. pop. was around 1,000, with Jews settling in the surrounding villages as well and founding communities under the auspices of P. J. merchants exported hides and furs, wax and tallow, and imported metal and textile products, fruit, wine, and spices. From 1632 Jews were allowed to engage freely in crafts. P. also became an important center of Torah learning, with a yeshiva founded in the late 16th cent. achieving renown. The Jews suffered greatly in the wars of the mid-17th cent. and many fled to escape the Cossack invaders. In the aftermath, they recovered more quickly than the non-J. pop., which left in large numbers for the vil-

lages to take up agriculture, leaving 200 homes at the disposal of the Jews, who became a majority in the city from the late 17th cent. Nonetheless, the economic situation remained difficult and more and more Jews tended toward petty trade, with some large-scale leasing. The community's rabbinical seat remained one of the choicest in Lithuania. Outstanding among its rabbis was the *maggid* Yehuda Leib Pukhovitser (c. 1630–1700). After the capture of the city by the Swedes in 1706 in the Northern War, many Jews fled to the neighboring settlement of Karlin, where a rival community developed which was constantly embroiled with P. in its efforts to achieve independence, like many other communities under the aegis of P. Under the influence of R. Aharon ben Yaakov (1736–1772), a student of Dov Baer, "the *Maggid* of Mezhirech," Karlin became a stronghold of Hasidism from the 1760s, from where it spread throughout Lithuania and to Rzeszow. Despite the sympathies of the community P. itself only joined the Gaon of Vilna's ban on Hasidism in 1781. In 1793 Hasidism revived in P. after the Second Partition of Poland left P. under Russian rule and deprived the *Mitnaggedim* of Polish government support. Karlin,

Floating market on Pina River, Pinsk, Poland

on the other hand, gradually became a refuge for the *Mitnaggedim*. The hasidic rabbi Levi Yitzhak of Berdichev served here for ten years but was dismissed in 1785 and succeeded by Avigdor ben Yosef Hayyim, an opponent of Hasidism who denounced Shneur Zalman of Lyady to the authorities. In the late 18th cent. J. trade was further boosted by the improvement of the canal system. The leading figure in J. commercial life in the early 19th cent. was Shaul Levin, who with his daughter Hayya Luria operated extensive holdings and accumulated extraordinary wealth. J. foreign trade focused on export of the Ukraine's agricultural surpluses and import from the West. Local business was also dominated by Jews, who owned 244 of the city's 250 stores in 1860. Moshe Luria was a pioneer of modern industry, opening a table oil factory and flour mill powered by steam engines in 1860. A new economic crisis descended on the city in the 1860s when it was bypassed by the railroad, causing many Jews to move to the Ukraine. However, the J. pop. of P. continued to grow, reaching 21,065 (total 28,368) in 1897. Haskala began to make inroads in the 1830s and as the cent. progressed the movement contributed to the

decline of Hasidism and to the growth of modern education. In 1862, two *talmud torah* schools which attempted to incorporate academic studies were opened in P. and Karlin. Each had about 200 students toward the end of the cent. The traditional *heder* system enrolled about 1,000 while a modernized *heder* founded in 1895 introduced the "Hebrew through Hebrew" system. A Hovevei Zion society became active in 1882. Yaakov Shertok, father of Israel's future foreign minister Moshe Sharett, joined the Bilu and emigrated to Eretz Israel, as did Aharon Eisenberg, one of the founders of Rehovot. Zionist groups proliferated in the following decades and the Bund opened its offices in 1897 and became a leading force in the revolutionary movement of 1905. With the revival of the city's economy and the growth of industry through J. initiative after the establishment of a railway link in 1887, a J. proletariat began to take shape, encompassing about 2,000 workers in 27 factories in 1902. The Lurias set up a factory for wooden pegs along with a big sawmill and there were also match and plywood factories. Another 2,000 Jews practiced a large variety of trades. Some were porters and carters, while others were employed in printing and book production. Many J. wholesalers took advantage of the new railway link to expand the transit trade. Under German occupation in WWI almost all commerce ground to a halt and the army seized food and farm produce. About 9,000 Jews were transferred to Poland in 1916; a similar number remained behind. In 1918, thousands began to return, reduced to penury and suffering further as the city changed hands repeatedly in the anarchy that ensued. On 5 April 1919, the Polish army executed 35 young Jews for allegedly holding a Communist meeting when they were in fact discussing the disposition of aid from the Joint Distribution Committee. The incident had international repercussions and forced the Polish authorities to relax their persecution of the J. community for awhile, but on 26 Sept. 1920 another 11 Jews were murdered when General Balakhovich's forces entered P. In all, around 1,000 Jews in the region were murdered by his men, with 2,000 J. survivors fleeing to P. A period of economic and demographic stagnation set in between the World Wars. Many Jews emigrated to the U.S. and Palestine and the pop. leveled off at about 21,000 in the 1930s. Many J. factories closed and the industrial work force dropped by 50% while trade with the Ukraine was curtailed within Poland's new borders. All the J. ideological movements attempted to maintain educational facilities, the most successful being the Tarbut high school founded in 1922 on Zionist initiative and considered one of the best among the seven in Poland. The Red Army arrived on 16 Sept. 1939, nationalizing J. businesses and closing down J. institutions while introducing a Soviet curriculum into the schools along with Yiddish as the language of instruction. "Undesirables" were expelled or exiled to Siberia. Many others fled with the Soviets on the approach of the Germans, who entered the city on 4 July 1941. Within a few days they murdered 16 young Jews pulled off the streets. A regime of severe persecution and extortion ensued. A *Judenrat* was set up late in the same month, organizing the supply of 4,000–5,000 Jews for forced labor. The first *Aktion* commenced on 4 Aug. 1941, when 300 J. men were seized from their homes as hostages to assure that 8,000 Jews reported to the railway station. All were led to the village of Iwaniki and executed after being chased naked to the edge of open pits. Another 2,500–3,000 Jews were rounded up on 7 Aug. and murdered in the Kozliakovich forest. About 10,000 Jews remained in the city, mostly women and children, as the Germans continued to despoil J. homes and extort "contributions." In April 1942, refugees began arriving from neighboring towns and a ghetto was ordered to be set up, allotting 13 sq. ft. of living space per person. Disease claimed 30–40 lives a day while the *Judenrat* organized a hospital, pharmacy, orphanage, and soup kitchen. Two large sewing and shoemaking shops within the ghetto provided services to the Germans and city residents for a bit of money or food and thousands of others continued to work outside the ghetto. Attempts to organize resistance or join the partisans never came to fruition as a final *Aktion* commenced before dawn on 14 Oct. 1942. About 1,200 trying to escape were machinegunned down alongside the ghetto fences. After another 200 were murdered at the hospital, all the others were brought to Dobrovolia in groups of 200–300 and murdered beside open pits. The death toll reached 10,000. Those in hiding were afterwards flushed out and also executed there. Of those spared in the previous selection, all but 134 were shot on 1 Nov. The survivors were kept in a small ghetto in Karlin until they too were executed on 23 Dec. 1942.

PIOTRKOWICE Kielce dist., Poland. The J. pop. in 1921 was 248 (total 782). The Jews were apparently expelled to a nearby ghetto by the Germans in fall 1942 and subsequently deported to the Treblinka death camp.

PIOTRKOW KUJAWSKI Warsaw dist., Poland. Founded in the 1760s, the community numbered 742 (82% of the total) in 1921. The Germans established a ghetto early in WWII. In 1942 the Jews were expelled to Chelmno.

PIOTRKOW TRYBUNALSKI Lodz dist., Poland. Jews first settled in the early 16th cent. but in 1657 the 50 families living there were massacred by soldiers and the synagogue was destroyed. Permission to organize as a J. community was granted by King John Sobieski on 16 Sept. 1679. The synagogue built in 1689 was destroyed in 1740 and rebuilt in 1791 as one of the most beautiful in Poland. The Jews were attacked by local inhabitants several times during the 17th cent. and defended themselves with only a few losses. In 1801, a school for J. children was opened where German and mathematics were taught. Jews engaged in trade and crafts and when P. became the seat of the district gov-

Jewish-inhabited Old City of Piotrkow Trybunalski, Poland (Zydowski Instytut Historyczny/photo courtesy of Yad Vashem, The Holocaust Martyrs' and Heroes' Remembrance Authority, Jerusalem)

ernment, they found employment in government offices and institutions. The majority of the factories opened in the 1880s were owned by Jews. In the 1870s, the first Hebrew press was established and printed religious works. Further presses opened in the early 20th cent., employing Jews only. Among the rabbis serving the community during the early period was R. Eliezer Waks (1884–89), who openly supported J. settlement in Eretz Israel. A number of hasidic rabbis set up courts in P., including Dr. Hayyim David Bernard, who also headed the J. hospital (founded in 1804) and was renowned as a miracle worker. After his death in 1858 and up to the Holocaust, Hasidim from all over Poland visited his grave. Another colorful figure was R. Brokman (called the "Stonemason Rabbi" because of his employment prior to taking up rabbinical studies). He arrived in P. during the 1840s and also became well known for his miracle healing, attracting Jews from throughout the world. Jews were prominent in local politics and already in 1867 J. rep-

resentatives were elected to the district council. A branch of Hovevei Zion was founded in 1886 and these early Zionists established a synagogue. The J. pop. in 1897 was 9,370 (32% of the total). The Bund began its activities in 1902. A J. secular school was opened in 1858 and in 1902 the authorities opened two elementary schools for Jews (*szabasowka*). A high school was established on the eve of WWI. The Zamir society founded in 1908 was a center for dramatic presentations, with a choir and an orchestra. A J. orphanage was opened after WWI and provided for children until WWII. Of the 50 representatives on the municipal council elected in 1916, 14 were Jews. Between the World Wars J. artisans organized in unions and J. merchants established their own association. The J. pop. in 1931 was 11,400 (22% of the total). The Ha-No'ar ha-Tziyyoni youth movement was founded in 1931 with 300 members, but in 1934 its members joined Betar. The largest youth movement, Hashomer Hatzair (founded in 1921), constantly struggled against the J. Communists, who endeavored to penetrate its ranks. The Bund organized 600 J. workers in 1936 in 12 unions. Agudat Israel, founded at the end of WWI, controlled the community council until 1936. In the 1937 elections the Bund gained a majority. R. Yehuda Meir Shapira, one of the leading sages in Poland and a member of the Sejm, served as rabbi from 1924. From 1936, R. Moshe Hayyim Lau, one of the founders of the Beth Jacob school system for girls in Poland, was the community's rabbi. In 1924, the Zionists published a Yiddish weekly and were followed by the Bund and Agudat Israel with their own weeklies. Antisemitism was rife between the World Wars; Jews were attacked, their shops were boycotted, and J. coachmen were prevented from transporting non-J. travelers.

German troops entered P. on 5 Sept. 1939. Surrounding the J. quarter, they tossed grenades into homes, fired shots through the windows, and set the houses on fire. Many were killed. German soldiers plundered J. property and raw materials were confiscated. Religious practice was forbidden. On 14 Oct. 1939, a 12-member *Judenrat* was set up with the J. council chairman at its head. The *Judenrat* was regarded positively by the community, mainly because its members (later 24) had previous political experience. It looked after the needs of the J. pop. in the ghetto and was involved in underground activities. All the members were murdered by the Nazis in July 1941. The second *Judenrat* was severely criticized for its actions. Jews were rounded up for labor gangs and in spring and summer 1940, males aged 16–45 were taken to labor camps in the Lublin area, mainly to improve fortifications on the frontier with the USSR. Most died in the camps or from illness upon their return. The ghetto was created in Oct. 1939, and in April 1942 numbered 16,500 (including 8,000 refugees), 2,000 living there illegally. Up to summer 1940, the Jews were allowed to move in and out of the ghetto freely and many were employed outside the ghetto manufacturing goods for the Germans. The *Judenrat* set up workshops inside the ghetto. Food was brought into the ghetto by returning work gangs and "professional" smugglers. The *Judenrat* supported ever-increasing numbers of destitute Jews, providing food and clothing and medical services. Soup kitchens were opened for children and adults, eventually providing 2,100 meals a day. An orphanage was set up for up to 500 children. In winter 1940–41, a typhus epidemic broke out but despite the lack of medication and facilities it was overcome. A second epidemic in winter 1941–42 was quickly suppressed with the improved pest control facilities available. Orthodox educational institutions continued to function within the ghetto, but there were no schools for the children of secular families. A drama group put on plays and held literary readings. The political parties, especially the Bund, continued to function clandestinely within the ghetto. In April 1942, the ghetto was closed and all non-Jews were made to vacate it. On 14 Oct. 1942, German troops, SS units, Ukrainians, Lithuanians, and Latvians surrounded the ghetto. From 15 Oct., over a period of eight days, 22,000 Jews (including those brought in from surrounding villages) were deported to the Treblinka extermination camp. About 2,400 Jews employed in factories and workshops remained. Jews were frequently taken out and shot in the nearby forests and in July 1943 the majority of the remaining Jews were deported to death camps. Those who were employed in factories and lived in labor camps survived until 25 Nov. 1944, when they were deported to Buchenwald and Ravensbrueck in Germany. A few hundred survivors returned to P. after the war (372 in 1945) but the majority left.

PIR (Hung. Szilagyper) N. Transylvania dist., Rumania. Jews settled in the 1770s. In 1791, a J. innkeeper charged with slaying a Christian child was proved innocent. The J. pop. in 1930 was 106 (5% of the total). In 1934–35 Hashomer Hatzair and Betar set up

a training farm. In 1942–44, 20 J. men were drafted into labor battalions in the Ukraine, where most died. In May 1944, the community was transferred to the Simleul Silvaniei ghetto and in June deported to Auschwitz. Survivors returned after the war but soon immigrated to Israel.

PIRIATIN Poltava dist., Ukraine. Jews were present in the first half of the 17th cent. and were murdered in the Chmielnicki massacres of 1648–49. They returned only in the late 18th cent. In 1897, their pop. was 3,166 (total 8,022). A J. elementary school with separate classes for boys and girls operated in addition to the *heder* system. On 4–5 Feb. 1919, General Denikin's troops staged a pogrom against the Jews. A J. kolkhoz was founded in 1929, with 100 families working 750 acres of land within two years. In 1939, the J. pop. was 1,747. The Germans arrived on 18 Sept. 1941 and murdered 1,600 Jews on 6 April 1942. Later they murdered 1,400 Jews from neighboring settlements and from among the refugees.

PIRICSE Szabolcs dist., Hungary. Jews are mentioned in the census of 1747 and were mainly grain merchants. The community organized in the mid-18th cent. The Jews numbered 171 in 1880 and 73 in 1930. They were deported to Auschwitz via Nyiregyhaza and Nyirjespuszta on 25 May 1944.

PIRMASENS Palatinate, Germany. A Jew was granted a letter of protection in 1767 and five J. families were present in 1772. Their pop. rose to 140 in 1800 and 209 in 1848. A cemetery was opened in 1813, a J. elementary school in 1828 (attended by 50 children in 1834), and a new synagogue in 1884. In 1863, a Jew was elected to the municipal council. J. breadwinners in 1879 included a vinegar manufacturer, butcher, lumber merchant, livestock dealer, dyer, and ragpicker. The J. pop. continued to expand, reaching 528 (total 30,195) in 1900 and a peak of 800 in 1924. In 1933, the J. pop. was 574. With the start of Nazi rule, the bank accounts of Jews of East European origin were closed and the large J.-owned Ehape department store was seriously vandalized. Nazi pressure gradually curtailed social and business relations with the local pop. The J. hide-processing industry and cattle trade were ended altogether. Between Jan. 1933 and Jan. 1936, 67 Jews left the city, including 19 for the U.S., 14 for France, and 12 for Palestine. In Oct.

1938, Jews with Polish citizenship were expelled from the country and in Nov. 1938 numerous J. businesses were "sold" to "Aryans." On *Kristallnacht* (9–10 Nov. 1938), the synagogue was burned, J. stores were vandalized, and 82 Jews were sent to the Dachau concentration camp. In all, 19 Jews died in concentration camps. Fifteen Jews returned after the war.

PIRNA Saxony, Germany. There is evidence of the occasional presence of Jews in P. from the mid-16th century, but a permanent settlement started only in 1870. The community was affiliated to the Dresden community and from 1908 religious instruction was given by teachers from Dresden. The J. pop. in 1890 was 45 individuals and 23 in 1933. In the latter year, two Jews were arrested as Communists. In 1938, a Jew was sentenced to three years in prison on charges of "racial defilement" (*Rassenschande*). On *Kristallnacht* (9–10 Nov. 1938), J. stores were looted and wrecked and five Jews were taken to the Buchenwald concentration camp. By May 1939, most Jews had moved away, some later deported from the cities and countries where they had sought refuge. Only two Jews and ten persons of partial J. origin (*Mischlinge*) were still living in P. No further information about their fate is available.

PIROT (Yid. Sharkoi) Serbia, Yugoslavia. A J. community was active in the late 16th cent. Many fled when P. was annexed to Serbia in 1878. The Jews were victims of libels from time to time. The J. pop. was 284 in 1900 (total 10,421). In 1915, the Bulgarians captured P. and a number of community leaders were exiled. The community dwindled over the following years and by 1939 numbered only 100 (total 11,600). The Germans handed P. over to the Bulgarians in April 1941 and the latter ostracized the Jews, who were denied citizenship, forced to pay high taxes, and had their property confiscated. Many Jews joined the partisan fighters and underground activists. In May 1942, all J. men were sent to forced labor in Bulgaria. On 12 March 1943, the Jews were assembled in a school, where young women were raped and personal possessions confiscated. On 19 March, hospitalized Jews were taken to the school where the rest of the Jews were held. From there the Bulgarians deported all the Jews to the Treblinka death camp. Only a few managed to escape and survive the Holocaust.

PISA Tuscany, Italy. The first information about the Jews of P. comes from Benjamin of Tudela, who visited the city around 1160 and mentioned 20 J. families as residing there. From the end of the 13th cent. to the beginning of the 14th cent., the J. community. became a center of moneylending activity. In 1322, the Jews were forced to wear the J. badge. In the 15th–16th cents., J. banking families dominated bank activity throughout Italy. Chief among these families was the one founded by Vitale (Yehiel) ben Matassia da Pisa. Although originally of Roman origin, he commenced his banking activities first in P. After 1492, Jews from Spain settled in P. The war between P. and Florence in 1494–1509 adversely affected the local community, reducing it in size. In 1547, the Duke of Tuscany, Cosimo I de Medici, and in 1593 Ferdinand I de Medici invited Jews and Marranos to settle, granting them extensive privileges, including jurisdiction over their internal affairs. In 1552, the J. community numbered 50, rising to 450 in 1613 and to 500 three years later (total 15,157). The synagogue, built in 1595, was renovated in the 19th cent. Towards the end of the 18th cent., Shemuel Foa established a Hebrew printing house in P. Local Jews were also involved in various industries, such as cotton. The J. pop. in 1873 was 460, increasing to 640 in 1886 and dropping to 600 in 1900. In 1910, the community consisted of 520 Jews, decreasing to 333 in 1927. In 1905, the senator Alessandro d'Ancona was elected mayor. The 1930 law reforming the J. communities recognized P. as one of the 26 communities of Italy, including in its district the communities of Lucca (35 Jews in 1936), Pietrasanta (ten Jews in 1936), and Viareggio (160 Jews in 1936). The J. pop of P. was 280 in 1936, 400 in 1938, and again 280 in 1939. The community's spiritual leader was R. Augusto Hasda. During WWII, 20 Jews from P., including R. Hasda, were deported. On 1 Aug. 1944, SS troops broke into the home of the president of the community, Giuseppe Pardo Roques, and murdered him together with six Jews and five Christian citizens of P. who had taken refuge there. In 1948, the J. community of P. numbered 120 Jews.

PISCOLT N. Transylvania dist., Rumania. Jews settled in the late 18th cent. The J. pop. in 1930 was 121 (4% of the total). In May 1944 the community was transferred to the Valea lui Mihai ghetto and in June deported to Auschwitz.

PISEK Bohemia, Czechoslovakia. Jews were in the area in the 12th or 13th cent. and are mentioned in P. in the late 14th cent. In 1610, they were subjected to sumptuary laws and in 1742 soldiers looted J. homes and stores with the participation of local residents. The J. school opened in the 1860s became Bohemia's first J.-Czech school in 1893. A synagogue was consecrated in 1872. and the J. pop. reached a peak of 408 (total 10,886) in 1898, dropping to 256 in 1930. The Nazis closed the synagogue in Oct. 1941 and in 1942 deported the Jews to the Theresienstadt ghetto together with the Jews of Prague. From there they were transported to the death camps of Poland, where most perished.

PISTYN Stanislawow dist., Poland, today Ukraine. Jews arrived with the founding of the town in the 18th cent. and constituted its urban element, reaching a pop. of nearly 900 (a quarter of the total) toward the end of the 19th cent. Declining economic conditions in the absence of a railroad link and the tribulations of WWI served to reduce the J. pop. to 525 in 1921. The arrival of the Germans in June 1941 brought forced labor and on 9 April 1942 a killing spree claimed hundreds of lives with others escaping to the forests. Those remaining were transferred to Kolomyja.

PISZCZAC Lublin dist., Poland. Jews are first mentioned in the late 18th cent., numbering 495 in 1857 and 394 (total 1,088) in 1921 after many were expelled by the Russians in WWI because of the area's proximity to the front. The Zionists and Agudat Israel were active between the World Wars. About 500 Jews, including refugees, fled with the Red Army in Sept. 1939, leaving 200 when the Germans arrived, augmented by new refugees from the neighboring villages. A *Judenrat* was charged with supplying forced labor. In Oct. 1942, after a selection which sent a small group to labor camps, most were deported to the Sobibor death camp.

PITESTI Walachia dist., Rumania. Jews first settled in the early 19th cent. and mainly engaged in commerce. In 1876, there were elementary schools for boys and girls with a registration of 150 by 1883. Zionist activity began in 1896. The J. pop. in 1899 was 899, dropping in 1930 to 615 (3% of the total). In 1940, Jews were persecuted by the Iron Guard and their shops boycotted. In the second half of 1941, some were drafted into forced labor battalions in Gaiesti and others sent to Transnistria. In 1944, Jews were forced to repair roads in the Covurlui and Braila districts. After the war, the J. community was renewed.

PITIGLIANO Tuscany, Italy. In 1576, the community comprised 50 Jews (total 4,000). In 1672, there were 180 Jews in P. and a synagogue was built in 1746 (renovated in 1931). Because of the rich cultural life of the community it was referred to as "Little Jerusalem" or "Little Sister." In 1773, the community included 200 Jews; in 1858, 420. The community maintained various mutual aid societies and the pop. included 18 merchants, six shopkeepers, and six artisans. In 1920–24, Gustavo Calo served as rabbi, followed by Azeglio Servi. P. is the birthplace of Flaminio Servi (Italian rabbi and publicist; 1841–1904); Samuele Colombo (rabbi and scholar; 1868–1923), and Dante Lattes (writer and educator; 1876–1965). Following the 1930 law reforming the J. communities, P. was included in the district community of Leghorn (Livorno). In 1936, the community consisted of 70 Jews. Many abandoned the community, moving to other J. centers, especially Florence and Rome. By 1938, 50 Jews remained (15 families). In April 1940, the rabbi left and the synagogue was closed. P. was liberated on 14 June 1944. In 1948, there were only 40 Jews there.

PITSCHEN (Pol. Byczyna) Upper Silesia, Germany, today Poland. The J. pop. was 13 in 1787 and reached a peak of 105 in 1852. The community maintained a prayer house, cemetery, and J. educational facilities. In 1932, the J. pop. was 31. In the same year, a handgrenade thrown into a J. home caused considerable damage. The Nazi racial laws were not applied to the Jews until 16 July 1937 owing to the extension of the League of Nations' minority rights convention to the area. Only 18 Jews remained in 1936. With the introduction of the racial laws, anti-J. disturbances commenced. On *Kristallnacht* (9–10 Nov. 1938), the prayer house was set on fire. Subsequently a number of Jews emigrated to various countries in Europe. The fate of the six left behind is unknown.

PIWNICZNA Cracow dist., Poland. Jews lived there from the mid-18th cent. The community averaged around 250 residents (approximately 7% of the total) from the second half of the 19th cent. An additional source of income for the Jews between the World

Wars developed when the town became a vacation site for hasidic courts and their followers. Zionist activity also commenced then. After enduring a regime of forced labor and extortion under the Germans, the community was expelled mainly to Nowy Soncz in Nov. 1942 and from there to the Belzec death camp.

PLATELIAI   (Yid. Plotel) Kretinga dist., Lithuania. Jews first settled at the end of the 18th cent. In the late 19th cent., many emigrated to the U.S. and South Africa. The J. pop. in 1897 was 171 (28% of the total), dropping to 120 (14%) in 1940. Between the World Wars, the Zionist movement won widespread support. Shortly after the German occupation in June 1941, the Germans and Lithuanians murdered all the Jews.

PLATTLING   Lower Bavaria, Germany. Around a dozen Jews attached to the Straubing community lived here in the 20th cent. (total pop. 4,000–6,000). All left by March 1938. A branch of the Flossenburg concentration camp for 400 J. prisoners operated from Feb. 1945.

PLATZ   Lower Franconia, Germany. Jews were present in the late 17th cent. and numbered 64 in 1816 (total 404) and eight in 1933. Six left for the U.S. in 1938 and two were deported to Izbica in the Lublin dist. (Poland) on 25 April 1942.

PLAUEN   Saxony, Germany. Evidence of a J. presence is found between 1308 and 1484–85, when the Jews were expelled. A settlement was reestablished in 1870. Services were held in rented rooms and in 1899 a cemetery was consecrated. The town's geographic proximity to Eastern Europe and the flourishing textile industry attracted East European Jews. By 1913, the community numbered 553 and in 1928 its pop. was 836. East European immigrants had their own Orthodox prayer room (before 1904) and a *talmud torah* school. The German J. majority set up Liberal associations such as a branch of the Central Union (C.V.) and a B'nei B'rith lodge. There were also a branch of the German Zionist Organization and several youth associations. A synagogue was consecrated in 1930. From the mid-1920s, P. became a Nazi stronghold. The cemetery and synagogue were desecrated and J. houses were marked in red. Growing hostility led many J. pupils to leave the local high school. When the Nazis came

to power in 1933, the J. pop. was 652. In spring 1933, two J. Communists and a J. member of the German Democratic Party (DDP) were arrested. On 1 April, boycott day, a Jew was murdered. By 1934, the number of Jews living in P. had shrunk to 360 and by 1 Jan. 1938 to 297. In Oct. 1938, 57 Jews without German citizenship were deported to Poland. On *Kristallnacht* (9–10 Nov. 1938), the synagogue was set on fire, J. homes and businesses were looted and wrecked, and J. men were taken to the Buchenwald concentration camp. By 1939, there were 134 Jews in P. Those who had not managed to leave were forced to move to "J. houses" and in 1942 were deported to the east with the exception of nine Jews married to non-Jews.

PLAVINASI   Livonia dist., Latvia. The J. pop. in 1935 was 35 (total 1,496). In the Holocaust the community shared the fate of the Jews in neighboring Gostini.

PLAWNO   Lodz dist., Poland. A small J. community existed here in the 18th cent. The J. pop. in 1897 was 752 (53% of the total). The community was reduced to about 400 in 1939. R. Yitzhak Mordekhai Hacohen Rabinowitz set up a yeshiva prior to WWI and was among the first Jews murdered by the Germans on 4 Sept. 1939. On 10-12 Oct. 1942 all the Jews were deported to the Treblinka death camp.

PLESHCHENITSY   Minsk dist., Belorussia. Jews probably settled in the late 18th cent., numbering 124 in 1765 and 884 (total 1,086) in 1897. In the 1930s, a few dozen J. families worked in a number of kolkhozes. A. J. school (founded in 1925) was still open in 1931 and a local council (soviet) had a J. majority (seven of nine members) in the late 1920s. In 1939, the J. pop. was 827. The Germans occupied P. on 27 June 1941, establishing a ghetto for 1,000 Jews from the town and its environs. Most were executed beside freshly dug pits on the outskirts of the town in early Nov.

PLESIVEC   (Hung. Pelsoc) Slovakia, Czechoslovakia, today Republic of Slovakia. Jews settled in the mid-19th cent. after residence restrictions in the mining region of central Slovakia were lifted. Their pop. rose from 70 in 1880 to 205 (total 2,393) in 1910. A synagogue was erected in the early 20th cent.; a J. elementary school was also opened. The Zionists became active after WWI. In 1941, 157 Jews remained. After the annexation to Hungary in Nov. 1938, J. livelihoods were undermined and dozens of Jews were mobilized for forced labor. In May 1944, the remaining Jews in P. were confined in a ghetto and on 13 June they were deported to Auschwitz.

PLESZEW Poznan dist., Poland. Though Jews settled in the environs of P. from the 16th cent. they were kept out of the city itself until the beginning of Prussian rule in 1793. During the interval of the Grand Duchy of Warsaw (1807–15), about 100 Jews lived there. A synagogue was completed in 1843. The situation of the Jews improved in the second half of the 19th cent., with the community reaching a peak pop. of 1,039 (total 5,929) in 1871. The well-to-do sent their children to the universities, producing a growing professional class that sought better opportunities in the big cities and across the sea. Continuing emigration caused the J. pop. to drop sharply to 550 in 1895 and 116 in 1921. The Relief Organization of German Jews (Hilfsverein) opened an office in 1903 and the Zionists became active in 1905. The few Jews who may still have been present at the outset of WWII were presumably expelled by the Germans to General Gouvernement territory by Feb. 1940.

PLETTENBERG Westphalia, Germany. The J. community numbered 25–35 in 1834–50, growing to 45–60 in the later 19th cent. By June 1933, the J. pop. had dropped to 36. The community maintained a cemetery and a synagogue was established in 1898. It was closed a few months before the disturbances of Nov. 1938. On *Kristallnacht* (9–10 Nov. 1938), 20 J. men were arrested and subsequently most Jews left the city. The last eight Jews were deported to the east in April and July 1942.

PLISKOV Vinnitsa dist., Ukraine. Jews settled in the late 18th cent. Six were present in 1765 and their pop. was 1,828 (total 3,890) in 1897. In May and Aug. 1918, Jews were attacked in pogroms. In the 1920s, a J. council (soviet) was active and from 1922 a J. school (four grades) was attended by 150 children. In 1939, the J. pop. was 793. The Germans occupied P. on 22 July 1941. On 22 Oct., an *Einsatzkommando* unit murdered 513 Jews in the Proznakovsk forest. In 1942, a group of Jews from Dziunkov was murdered. Over 700 Jews were murdered in the region.

PLISSA Vilna dist., Poland, today Belarus. Jews were presumably present by the 19th cent. Most Jews left during WWI when fighting raged in and around the town. On their return they were assisted by the YEKO-PO relief organization. The J. pop. in 1925 was 578 (total 1,358). The Zionists were active between the World Wars and a Tarbut Hebrew school operated. The Germans arrived in late June 1941. In June 1942, they executed P.'s 459 Jews outside the town.

PLOCK (Plotsk) Warsaw dist., Poland. Jews are first mentioned in 1237 and formed one of the earliest J. communities in Poland, drawn by the town's position as an international trade center linking Kiev, Novogrod, and the Baltic ports via the Vistula River. In the early 14th cent. the Jews were forced out of trade and confined to moneylending for 150 years by the ruling Order of Teutonic Knights. As a result the pop. diminished but in the 15th and 16th cents. it again grew with the influx of Jews from Germany, despite efforts of the local pop. to restrict J. trade and periodic anti-J. rioting. In the early 17th cent. J. merchants imported textile and metal products, oils and spices, while exporters dealt in grain, cattle, lumber, and hides. J. craftsmen were active in a wide range of trades. The prosperity of the community was cut short by the Swedish war of the mid-17th cent. and the depredations of the Polish commander Stefan Czarniecki's troops in its aftermath. Fire and plague in the late 17th cent. undermined J. efforts to rehabilitate the community and left it riddled with debt in the face of renewed anti-J. agitation by the Church in the 18th cent. The J. pop. doubled to 1,793 under Prussian rule (1793–1807) despite efforts to curtail traditional J. means of livelihood in order to make the Jews "useful" (many in fact became building workers), while in the Grand Duchy of Warsaw (1807–15) the tax burden became even greater. In this period Haskala made its first inroads, with R. Yehuda Leib Margolioth (1747–1811) one of its early proponents. R. Aryeh Leib Zunz (d. 1833), one of the outstanding scholars of the time and later rabbi of Warsaw, also served the community. As a provincial capital in Congress Poland, P. atttracted Jews despited the necessity of living in a special quarter and contending with compulsory military service (1840) and legislation banning traditional J. dress (1846). Some moved to Kuchary and other villages under Zalman Posner's scheme to turn Jews into farm and factory workers (in his weaving mill). Posner also led the fight against local Hasidism.

"Street of the Jews," Plock, Poland

The J. pop. grew to 5,259 in 1857 and 10,500 (total 24,871) in 1887 but then dropped to 7,480 in 1897 as hundreds of families emigrated across the sea. One factor in the exodus was the crisis in the grain trade with Danzig, which occupied 30% of J. merchants (196 of the 656 J. families who were engaged in trade in 1897); the others dealt in textiles or owned small stores or stalls or were peddlers. Another 1,053 Jews were employed in crafts and light industry. Tax records from the period indicate that about a third of the community was destitute. Community activity was broad and bolstered by the participation of the wealthy class. A new synagogue was completed in 1868 and a modern hospital was opened in 1872. In 1891 an old age home and children's shelter were opened. In 1888 a J. elementary school for 100 children was started by government order. In the late 1890s the *maskil*-inspired *talmud torah*, inaugurated in 1868, introduced secular studies and in 1903 a reformed *heder* teaching Hebrew through Hebrew was founded. In 1896 the community's first public library was opened. Hovevei Zion became active in 1891 with 200 members. Bundists and Zionist Socialists soon became active as well, participating in the strikes and demonstrations of the 1905 revolution. Such Zionist leaders as Nahum Sokolow (1829–1936) and Yitzhak Gruenbaum (1879–1970) were active in P. Public life continued to flourish through WWI under the German occupation and a J. high school was opened in 1917 under Zionist influence. In the aftermath of WWI, the Jews suffered from the depredations of General Haller's Polish troops. The hasidic leader R. Hayyim Shapira was publicly executed for supposedly signaling to Bolshevik forces when he went out to pray on his balcony. The J. economy suffered with the closing of traditional Russian and Prussian markets after WWI and from the general economic crisis. Many J. tradesmen were forced out of business. A large proportion of the Jews were employed in the clothing industry and in most shops work was seasonal. Between the World Wars, Zionist activity expanded. The most influential group was Po'alei Zion while the leading youth movement was Hashomer Hatzair (300 members). Many of the young received pioneer training at Hehalutz facilities. Agudat Israel was active from 1919, concentrating on community affairs and religious education, while the Bund operated within the trade unions and sought to promote Yiddish culture. Most children studied at state-run J. elementary schools with after-school classes in the *heder* and *talmud torah* system. The J. pop. in 1931 was 6,571. Antisemitism intensified in the 1930s, with boycott calls and occasional outbursts of violence.

The Germans captured the city on 8 Sept. 1939, instituting a reign of terror. Hundreds of men were made to stand naked and tormented in the street while others were buried up to their necks near a neighboring village. All J. businesses were taken over by the Nazis and religious practice was outlawed. In Dec. a *Judenrat* was appointed and charged with supplying forced labor. In Sept. 1940 a ghetto was established, crowding together 7,600 local Jews (after hundreds fled to Warsaw) and 3,000 refugees. Residents of the old age home were murdered at the Dzialdowo penal camp and periodic killings continued until the liquidation of the ghetto in Feb. 1941. Throughout the period the *Judenrat* tried to organize relief, supplying food and firewood to the needy and organizing cooperatives for artisans to supply German needs. On 21 Feb., about 4,000 Jews were transported to Dzialdowo and subjected to brutal beatings. Another 3,000 were deported on 1 March. Torture and beatings continued after their arrival, with Jews deprived even of their clothes. Most were afterwards sent on to the Radom dist. and dispersed among smaller localities, ultimately meeting their end in the Treblinka death camp, as did the 1,000 or so Jews who had fled to Warsaw. After the war about 300 Jews gathered in the city but attempts to revive the community failed and only a few remained in the late 1950s.

PLOIESTI Walachia dist., Rumania. Jews first settled in the late 17th cent., to be joined by Sephardi Jews from the Balkans in 1806 and Ashkenazi Jews from Russia and Poland in 1848–56. A J. community was established in 1840 to serve both Sepharadi and Ashkenazi members, the only one in Rumania at the time. The Great Synagogue built of wood was rebuilt in stone in 1840; the Sepharadi congregation constructed its own synagogue in 1807. J. schools functioned from 1875 when the Luca Moise boys' school

opened, followed by a girls' school in 1896. The renowned Rumanian J. linguist and historian Lazar Schein-Saineanu (1859–1934) and the leading mathematician David Emanuel (1854–1941) were born in P. A branch of Hovevei Zion opened in 1894. The J. pop. in 1899 was 2,478 (6% of the total). Between the World Wars, a J. Party was organized and its members were active in municipal affairs and in the community council. A Hebrew-speaking nursery school opened in 1926. A J. cultural institute established in 1939 offered courses in J. history, Hebrew, and others related subjects. In 1940, a large German military force garrisoned in P. to guard oil installations persecuted Jews. On 17 Nov., Iron Guard Legionnaires destroyed synagogues, the J. school, and other communal institutions. On 27–28 Nov., the Iron Guard executed 11 Jews of a group of a 30 they had been holding and torturing for two weeks. In Dec. and Jan. 1941, J. property was plundered and most J.-owned factories were taken over by Legionnaires. The J. pop. in 1941 stood at 3,596. On 14 July 1941, all J. males aged 18–60 were sent to the Teis camp and then transferred to other forced labor camps in Rumania. Although the J. pop. was impoverished and lacked means of livelihood, a J. high school with 50 pupils was opened during the war. After the war Jews returned and reestablished the community.

PLOKSCIAI (Yid. Plokshtsh) Sakiai dist., Lithuania. The J. pop. in 1923 was 39 (9% of the total). All the Jews were murdered after the German occupation of June 1941.

PLONSK Warsaw dist., Poland. Jews are first mentioned in 1446. They engaged in moneylending, traded at the fairs in Poznan, Gniezno, and Sochaczew, and maintained commercial ties with Plock (Plotsk). The community was virtually destroyed by the Polish commander Stefan Czarniecki's troops in the Swedish war of the mid-17th cent. It was revived under royal authorization and a new synagogue was built and a cemetery concentrated. In the 18th cent., J. trade expanded, with Jews dealing in lumber and agricultural produce. In the early 19th cent., Jews settled in the surrounding villages as farm and factory workers in a unique program initiated by Shelomo Zalman Posner. In 1831, 298 of the 502 Jews in the village of Kuchary were employed in Posner's weav-

Hehalutz pioneer training farm, Ploiesti, Rumania, 1929 (Beth Hatefutsoth Photo Archive, Tel Aviv/photo courtesy of Yad Vashem, The Holocaust Martyrs' and Heroes' Remembrance Authority, Jerusalem)

ing mill, but subsequently the project failed and the Jews returned to the towns. Among the prominent rabbis of P. were Barukh Harif (d. 1792), Avraham Yekutiel Lichtenstein (d. 1810), Tzevi Yehezkel Michaelson (1894–1922), and Yisrael Bronstein (from 1922). The J. pop. rose to 2,630 in 1857 and 4,447 (total 7,897) in 1897. *Maskilim* were active from the 1840s, embodying assimilationist tendencies that expressed themselves in political involvement and use of the Polish language. Hasidism spread in the late 19th cent. under the influence of R. Yehiel Meir of Gostynin, with Gur, Aleksandrow, and Ciechanow Hasidism also represented. Most children received a traditional education in the *heder* and *talmud torah* system. The Zionists became active in the 1880s. Avigdor Green, the father of David Ben-Gurion (born in P. in 1886), was one of its earliest proponents. The Jews were victims of a typhoid epidemic in the aftermath of WWI and suffered from deteriorating economic conditions as the Polish farm sector col-

lapsed and J. tradesmen were left without their traditional customers. Joint Distribution Committee aid supported the community while most cultural and social services were under Zionist control. A Hehalutz office was opened in 1928, operating a pioneer training facility. Most children transferred to the Tarbut Hebrew school opened in the same year. Agudat Israel operated its own Beth Jacob school for 150 girls. The J. pop. in 1931 was 4,913. Polish antisemitism intensified in the late 1930s, including an economic boycott and occasional outbursts of violence. The Germans captured P. on 5 Sept. 1939, instituting a regime of forced labor and extortion. Jews were put to work on roads, farms, and peat bogs and sent to labor camps in the vicinity. The relief committee organized by the Jews was designated a *Judenrat* by the Germans in July 1940. An influx of refugees brought the J. pop. up to 7,000–8,000. All were confined to a ghetto in May 1941, with three or four families crowded into a room. Others were forced to live in stables and barns. Jews caught smuggling in food were murdered. A typhoid epidemic immediately broke out, only brought under control in April 1942. In July 1941, 1,200 nonresident Jews were deported to the Pomiechowek concentration camp. On 28 Oct. 1942, 2,000 of the old and sick were deported to Auschwitz. Three more transports went out at approximately two-week intervals, each with another 2,000 Jews. The second, on 30 Nov., included the Jews of the Nowe Miasto ghetto. The last, on 16 Dec., included the members of the *Judenrat* and 340 children from the children's shelter. A number of Jews formed an underground group affiliated with the Polish Workers Party and a few were able to escape and join their military arm in partisan action. They either fell in battle or were murdered by the Gestapo after capture.

PLOPANA Moldavia dist., Rumania. Jews settled with the establishment of P. in 1844. They became renowned for their meat products. The J. pop. in 1930 stood at 176 (25% of the total). At the outbreak of the Soviet-Rumanian war in June 1941, the J. pop

was transferred to Barlad and suffered the fate of the Jews there. The Jews never returned to P.

PLOSCA Bukovina, Rumania, today Ukraine. Jews settled in the late 19th cent. The J. pop. in 1930 was 99. In fall 1941, the J. pop. was deported to Transnistria, where most perished.

PLOTNICA Polesie dist., Poland, today Belarus. Jews settled in the early 20th cent. and before WWII numbered 130–150 families (of a total 700 families), mostly Stolin Hasidim. In the Holocaust, presumably all were expelled to the Stolin ghetto for liquidation.

PLUNGE (Yid. Plungian) Telsiai dist., Lithuania. Jews first settled in the 16th cent. establishing the first synagogue in 1719. In the 1880s many emigrated, mainly to South Africa, some to the U.S.. A conflagration in 1894 destroyed community property and left some 2,500 Jews homeless. The estate owner M. Oginski played a significant role in assisting the community to reestablish itself. The community maintained a

Jewish firemen, Plunge, Lithuania, before WWII

heder and later a modernized *heder* which was forced to close owing to ultra-Orthodox opposition. The J. pop. in 1897 was 2,502 (56% of the total). Around the turn of the cent. the Zionist movement won widespread support. Between the World Wars, in three elections for the municipal council, Jews won a high percentage of the seats; a Jew served as mayor and another later served as deputy mayor. After antisemitic riots, the mayor and local judge signed a statement condemning such incidents. In the 1930s, an anti-J boycott contributed to the deteriorating economic situation. The community maintained two schools, Hebrew and Yiddish, which were subsequently united; a *talmud torah*; a Hebrew high school; and a Hebrew-Yiddish library. Many participated in Zionist activities, including elections to the Zionist Congresses. There were five synagogues and social welfare organizations. When Germany annexed Memel (Klaipeda) in 1939, P.'s J. community cared for its refugees. The J. pop. in 1940 was about 1,700 (28% of the total). After the German invasion in June 1941, some Jews fled. The Lithuanian nationalists who took over the town incarcerated most of the Jews under unbearable conditions and instituted a regime of forced labor, abuse, and humiliation. Young people who were sent to work on nearby estates were murdered at the village of Milosaiciai. The others, including a group of young women who were convinced to convert to Catholicism in order to save themselves, were herded into pits near the village of Kausenai and shot on 13–14 July 1941. Only 221 Jews from P. survived the war. Following liberation, 30 J. families returned. They encountered considerable hostility, leading to murder, and by 1989 only 15 Jews remain there.

PLUSY (Yid. Palush) Vilna dist., Poland, today Belarus. Jew were present in the 19th cent. as fishermen, brokers, shopkeepers, artisans, and lumber merchants, many leaving for nearby Ignalin after a railway station was built there in 1862. After the German occupation in WWII, the few remaining Jews were expelled to Ignalin as well.

PLUZHNOYE Kamenets-Podolski dist., Ukraine. The J. pop. was 145 in 1939 (total 4,141). The Nazis arrived on 3 July 1941 and in an *Aktion* on 28–30 July murdered 1,685 Jews from the region. Another 1,643 Jews were executed in a second *Aktion* on 1 Aug. In June–July 1943 a further 150 Jews were murdered.

PNIEWNO Volhynia dist., Poland, today Ukraine. The J. pop. was 143 in 1921 and 650 in 1941. The German occupation of mid-1941 was marked by Ukrainian pillage and rape. The community was expelled to the Kamien Koszyrski ghetto in spring 1942 and liquidated in two *Aktions* on 10 Aug. and 2 Nov.

PNIEWY Poznan dist., Poland. A J. settlement with a cemetery existed from the 14th cent. but only began to develop in the 16th cent. under a charter of privileges granted by the town's proprietors. A fire in 1767 left many Jews destitute. Most were peddlers and artisans. There was an especially high number of tailors with their own guild. Some were employed in a sewing shop set up by the proprietory family of nobles. Annexation to Prussia in 1793 led to a gradual improvement of economic conditions. In the second half of the 19th cent., many J. workshops were converted into small factories employing 10–15 workers; peddlers became merchants and shopkeepers. The J. pop. rose to 707 (total 1,851) in 1837. A new synagogue was built in 1826 and remained standing until WWII. In 1836, a J. hospital was founded and a school for religious education was opened. Expanding education and university studies in Germany produced a growing professional class as well as an identification with German culture that exacerbated anti-J. feelings among the local Polish pop. In the revolutionary fervor of 1848, anti-J. rioting broke out in the city, causing many to flee temporarily. Continuing emigration reduced the J. pop. to 225 on the eve of WWI. Fourteen Jews remained when the Germans captured the city in Sept. 1939. All were expelled to the Buk transit camp on 7 Nov. and on 9 Dec. sent to General Gouvernement territory.

PNIOW Stanislawow dist., Poland, today Ukraine. The J. pop. was 286 in 1921. The Jews were possibly executed locally in Oct. 1941 with the remnant expelled to Nadworna in summer 1942.

POBEREZE Stanislawow dist., Poland. The J. pop. was 144 in 1921. The Jews were possibly expelled to the Rodolf Mill camp in Stanislawow for liquidation in Sept.–Oct. 1942.

POBEZOVICE (also Ronsperk) Bohemia (Sudetenland), Czechoslovakia. Jews settled in the 16th cent, erecting a synagogue in 1816 and reaching a pop. of

240 in the second half of the 19th cent. In 1930, 41 remained. The Jews left for other places in Bohemia after the annexation of the Sudetenland to the German Reich in Sept. 1938. Most subsequently emigrated, mainly to England and Palestine. The Nazis destroyed the synagogue and cemetery.

POBOLOVO   Gomel dist., Belorussia. In 1826 there were 82 J. poll tax payers in P. In 1929, under the Soviets, the J. pop. comprised 78 families. Fifty-seven J. families worked in a kolkhoz founded the same year. The Germans occupied P. in July 1941. In Aug., they murdered three Jews after tormenting them and kept up sporadic abuse and killings until the remaining Jews were executed in a field outside the town in Oct.

POCHEP   Oriol dist., Russia. Jews were present in the 17th cent. Most were massacred when Chmielnicki's Cossacks attacked the town in 1648. In 1882, about 100 houses and 120 stalls belonging to Jews burned down. The J. pop. reached 3,172 (total 9,714) in 1897 and in the Soviet period increased to 3,616 in 1926 before dropping to 2,314 in 1939. The Soviet-J. composer Blanter Matvey (1903–90), who wrote the well-known Soviet song "*Katiusha,*" was born in P. The town was captured by the Germans on 22 Aug. 1941. Hundreds of local Jews were among the 2,200 murdered in the area. After the war a monument, with an inscription in Hebrew was erected over the mass grave of the Jews who had been murdered.

POCHINOK   Smolensk dist., Russia. Jews probably settled at the turn of the 18th cent. Their pop. was 528 (total 1,356) in 1926 and 283 in 1939. The Germans occupied the town on 17 July 1941 and after confining the Jews to a few houses murdered them on 21 April 1942.

POCSAJ   Bihar dist., Hungary. Jews settled in the first half of the 19th cent. and numbered 69 in 1930. They were deported to Auschwitz via Nagyvarad in early June 1944.

POCZAJOW   Volhynia dist., Poland, today Ukraine. Jews only settled after 1763 as P. was considered a holy site sanctified by the Russian Orthodox Church. In 1897, the J. pop. numbered 1,377 (total 1,921), living mainly from the pilgrim trade (renting rooms, selling religious articles, etc.). The local monastery was a source of anti-J. agitation. The Jews were evacuated by the Austrians in WWI, returning in 1918 to find the town half in ruins. The J. pop. in 1921 was 1,083. Others emigrated as economic conditions worsened, with half the J. pop. on relief. The Germans arrived on 30 June 1941, established a *Judenrat*, and executed 119 Jews in two *Aktions*. In Jan. 1942 the Jews were confined to a ghetto and on 7 Sept. 1942 they were brought outside the town and murdered.

PODBORANY   Bohemia (Sudetenland), Czechoslovakia. The P.-Letov community was formally established in 1890 with the synagogue transferred from the latter town already in 1874. In 1930, the J. pop. was 108 (total 3,730). Most Jews left for other places in Bohemia and Moravia after the signing of the Munich Agreement in Sept. 1938. Some emigrated but most were deported to the death camps of Poland in 1942. Some remained in the Theresienstadt ghetto until the end of the war.

PODBRODZIE   Vilna dist., Poland, today Lithuania. Jews arrived in the early 19th cent. and lived there in small numbers until officially granted residence rights in 1903. Many earned their livings from the summer resort trade and until WWI from the nearby army camp. From the early 20th cent. the Bund was influential among the young. After WWI the Jews recovered slowly with the aid of J. credit facilities but their livelihoods were undermined by the competition of a Polish cooperative and many were sustained only by their auxiliary farms. Children attended Yiddish and Hebrew (Tarbut) schools and the Zionist youth movements engaged in intensive activity, sending groups of pioneers to Palestine. The J. pop. in 1939 was 850. After two years of Soviet and Lithuanian rule in 1939–1941, the Germans arrived on 29 June 1941. On 15 July their Lithuanian collaborators murdered 60 Jews on German orders. The Jews were then confined to a ghetto under a regime of forced labor and a *Judenrat* was appointed. Some fled on the eve of an anticipated *Aktion* in late Sept. 1941. The rest were taken to the Poligon camp and murdered on 28 Sept. 1941. Few Jews from P. survived.

PODBUZ   Lwow dist., Poland. The 19th cent. community did not exceed 200 (10–15% of the total) from the 1880s on. Almost all were affiliated with the Zionist movement between the World Wars. All were expelled by the Germans to the Boryslaw ghetto in Aug. 1942.

PODDEMBICE   Lodz dist., Poland. Jews first settled here in the 1770s and in 1821 were permitted to buy land and engage in weaving. The J. pop. in 1897 was 1,266 (46.5% of the total). Between the World Wars, Jews developed the transportation system between P. and Lodz. The Germans occupied the town on 14 Sept. 1939. In Nov. 1940, 1,500 Jews, including refugees, were ghettoized in the most dilapidated quarter of P. and in early 1941 some 600 refugees from Lenczyca were brought there. On 17 March 1942, all the Jews were forced to watch the hanging of five Jews in the marketplace. From 10 April 1942, Jews were deported to the Lodz ghetto, to labor camps, and finally to Chelmno.

PODDOBRIANKA   Gomel dist., Belorussia. The J. pop. was 481 in 1847 and 1,486 (total 1,535) in 1897. Jews owned all 19 stores in the town as well as a small hide-processing plant and two sawmills. In 1926, under the Soviets, the town's 1,127 Jews comprised 92% of the total and were accordingly represented on the local council (soviet) established in 1925. Most Jews were artisans and were organized in cooperatives. A kolkhoz founded in 1929 provided employment to 15 J. families in 1930. A J. elementary school (four grades) was active from the early 1920s and had about 100 students in 1928. A number of illegal *hadarim* were also in operation. Two prayer houses were open on the Sabbath and J. holidays. The Germans occupied P. in Aug. 1941. In late Sept. 1941 they executed 50 Jews and in late Nov. another 40. The remaining 105 Jews were murdered at the local cemetery on 24 Jan. 1942 with the aid of local police.

PODEBRADY   Bohemia, Czechoslovakia. There is evidence of a J. presence in the early 15th cent. A community with a synagogue and school was established after the 1848 revolution, its pop. reaching 120 in 1921. Jews were active as distillers, brewers, grain merchants, and manufacturers of vegetable oil. In 1930, 49 remained (total 7,244). In 1942, they were deported together with the Jews of Prague to the Theresienstadt ghetto and from there sent to the death camps of Poland. The postwar community numbered 171 in 1946 and also opened an old age home accommodating 65 Jews.

PODHAJCE   Tarnopol dist., Poland, today Ukraine. Jews were present in the early 15th cent. and constituted an important community with many illustrious rabbis until the First Partition of Poland in 1772. Shabbateanism exerted a significant influence and Jakob Frank prosyletized there. Hasidism became the leading spiritual force with the Strettin, Belz, and Ruzhany dynasties all represented. Under the Austrians the Jews were burdened by heavy taxation. With the abrogation of special taxes in 1848, the community began to flourish, with a peak pop. of 4,012 (two-thirds of the total) in 1880. It then began to diminish through emigration. Under the Russian occupation of WWI, most Jews fled the town. On their return, they were caught between rampaging gangs. By 1921 the J. pop. had dropped to 2,872, supported by aid from the Joint Distribution Committee and American relatives as the economic situation continued to decline through the 1930s. Soviet rule in 1939–41 suppressed J. public life under a regime of economic nationalization. The Germans arrived on 4 July 1941 and persecution was stepped up and forced labor instituted. In the first mass *Aktion*, on Yom Kippur (21 Sept.) 1942, over 1,000 Jews were deported to Belzec. A ghetto crowding over 4,000 people into a few alleys was then set up along with a local labor camp. The second *Aktion* took place on 30 Oct. 1942 with another 1,200 Jews sent to Belzec. Hunger and disease took their toll during the winter. The liquidation of the ghetto and labor camp commenced on 6 June 1943. All those caught were led to the J. cemetery and executed there. Hundreds escaped to the forests, but most were hunted down and murdered by the Ukrainians.

PODHORANY   (Hung. Orhegyalja; Yid. Pitharn) Carpatho-Russia, Czechoslovakia, today Ukraine. A few J families were present in the 18th cent. In 1880, the J. pop. was 117 (total 675). In 1921, under the Czechoslovakians, the number rose to 191 and in 1941 to 210. The J. pop. included 12 artisans, 11 tradesmen, and a few farmers. The Hungarians arrived in March 1939, drafting a number of Jews into labor battalions and dispatching them to forced labor camps. In July 1941, a few J. families without Hungarian citizenship were expelled to Kamenets-Podolski and murdered. The rest were transferred to the Mukachevo ghetto on 17 April 1944, en route to Auschwitz.

PODHORODYSZCZE   Lwow dist., Poland, today

The family of the famous hasidic rabbi Bursztyn, Podhajce, Poland 1938

Ukraine. The J. pop. in 1921 was 186. The Jews were expelled to Bobrka for liquidation in the second half of 1942.

PODIVIN   Moravia, Czechoslovakia. Four J. families were present during the Thirty Years War (1618–48). A synagogue was constructed c. 1630. In the 17th and 18th cents., Jews traded in salt, tobacco, wine, wool, goose liver and fat. A J. school was opened in the early 1860s, with an attendance of 130 in 1890. The J. pop. reached a peak of 684 in 1857 and then declined steadily to 143 in 1938. The Zionists were active after WWI. The Jews were apparently deported to the Theresienstadt ghetto together with the Jews of Brno in late 1941–early 1942. From there they were transported to the death camps of the east.

PODKAMIEN (I)   Tarnopol dist., Poland, today Ukraine. Jews settled in P. in the 17th cent. and re-

mained under the aegis of the Lwow community until becoming independent in the second half of the 18th cent. Economic life was boosted by yearly trade fairs and the J. pop. grew to 1,552 (half the total) by 1880. Irreversible decline set in with the depredations of Russian soldiers in WWI, the pop. dropping to 822 in 1921. There was intensive Zionist activity between the World Wars. The Germans arrived on 2 July 1941 and in Aug. and Sept. 1942 apparently deported most of the Jews to the Belzec death camp, the remainder being sent to the Brody ghetto.

PODKAMIEN (II)   Stanislawow dist., Poland, today Ukraine. The J. pop. in 1921 was 104. The Jews were expelled to Rohatyn for liquidation in July 1942.

PODOLINEC   Slovakia, Czechoslovakia, today Republic of Slovakia. Jews probably settled in the mid-19th cent. Their pop. grew to 138 (total 1,755) in

Members of Bnei Akiva, Podkamien, Poland

1900 and about 170 between the World Wars. The Zionists were active and most Jews earned their livelihoods in trade. In the Slovakian state, Jews were attacked by the German minority and pushed out of their businesses by the authorities while J. children were expelled from the public schools. In spring 1942, most were deported to the death camps in the east.

PODRAVSKA SLATINA Croatia, Yugoslavia, today Republic of Croatia. Jews first settled in the 18th cent. and enjoyed an active communal life in the 20th cent. In 1940, the J. pop. was 136; all perished in the Holocaust.

PODUL-ILOAEI (Podul Leloaei) Moldavia dist., Rumania. P. derives its name from a J. woman, Lea, who owned the local inn during the early 17th cent. Jews engaged in trade, crafts, and some fishing. Children attended a J. school from 1899 and in 1928 a Hebrew nursery school was opened. A branch of Hovevei

Zion began operating in 1894. The J. pop. was 1,962 in 1899 (68% of the total). In 1907, 700 peasants attacked P. and 50 J. stores were plundered. During WWI, Jews were seized for forced labor and tortured. Two subsequently died. The J. pop. in 1930 was 1,601 (40% of the total). On 30 June 1941, the J. survivors of the massacre in Iasi arrived in P. after 1,194 died on the way, leaving only 700 survivors. Gypsies and peasants robbed the corpses. In April 1942, 1,500 Jews were transferred to Iasi. After the war, 300 survivors returned.

PODUL-TURCULUI Moldavia dist., Rumania. The Jews first arrived in the early 19th cent., organizing a community in 1835. Jews traded at the eight annual fairs which drew 10,000–15,000 participants on each occasion. A J. school opened in 1898. The J. pop. in 1899 was 1,085, or 50% of the total. It dropped to 502 in 1930 (30% of the total). At the outbreak of WWII, three synagogues were active. The J. pop. was expelled on 21 June 1941 to Tecuci. The men were transferred to the Targu-Jiu camp for political internees and then to labor battalions in Piatra-Olt and finally to forced labor in the Romanati district. Prior to deportation, the district governor begged the Jews for forgiveness, explaining that he was only obeying orders. About a quarter of the J. inhabitants returned after the war.

PODVYSOKOE Kirovograd dist., Ukraine. A few dozen Jews were present in the late 18th cent. and just ten in 1887. In 1939, the J. pop. was 96 (total 4,124). After their arrival on 7 Aug. 1941, the Germans murdered those Jews who had neither fled nor been evacuated.

PODWOLOCZYSKA Tarnopol dist., Poland, today Ukraine. Jews were among the founders of the town in the 1860s and constituted as much as 70% of the pop., numbering 3,779 in 1900 and 2,275 in 1921. Most were exiled to Skalat by the Russians during WWI, effectively curtailing the community's prosperity under the insufferable conditions. Between the World Wars some 60% of the pop. had no source of livelihood. Nonetheless public and cultural activity under the auspices of the Zionists, active from early in the cent., was maintained. The German occupation commenced on 7 July 1941 after a two-year Soviet presence. The ghetto they set up was liquidated in Sept. 1942 when the inhabitants were expelled to Zborow to await their fate. Those who managed to evade the net were absorbed into the local labor camp; most were among the 600 shot there on 28–29 June 1943 by the SS. About 200 survived the war, in hiding, in the labor camps, and in the Soviet Union.

POEMBSEN Westphalia, Germany. A J. family is mentioned in 1704. By the early 19th cent., there was a small community with a synagogue, which grew to about 45 individuals (8% of the total) in 1843–71. The J. pop. dropped to 28 in 1905 and 21–24 on the eve of the Nazi era. On *Kristallnacht* (9–10 Nov. 1938), the synagogue was set on fire and J. homes and stores were vandalized. On the eve of the deportations nearly all Jews had left. No information is available about their fate.

POGAR Oriol dist., Russia. Jews probably settled in the late 18th cent., numbering 261 in 1847 and 1,159

(total 4,965) in 1897. In the Soviet period, their pop. dropped to 628 in 1926 and 276 in 1939. The Germans arrived in mid-Aug. 1941, murdering about 220 Jews from P. and its environs on 22 Nov. 1942.

POGOST (I) Minsk dist., Belorussia. J. settlement apparently commenced in the mid-18th cent., reaching a pop. of 193 in 1765 and 685 (total 863) in 1897. In the Soviet period, many Jews engaged in agriculture—29 families in 1924–25 and 36 families in 1930 (employed at a multinational kolkhoz). In 1930, the J. pop. numbered 158 families (total 235). In the mid-1920s, some J. children still attended *hadarim*. A J. elementary school (four grades) was also in operation. In the early 1930s, two illegally operated *battei midrash* were closed down. The Germans occupied the town in late June 1941 and set up a ghetto. Soon afterwards executions commenced. In Aug., 150 Jews were murdered, followed by another 35 (or 80 according to another source). In all, 440 Jews from the ghetto and from the surrounding area were murdered. A few escaped to the forests and joined the partisans.

POGOST (II) Mogilev dist., Belorussia. Jews numbered 215 in 1794 and 704 in 1897. In the Soviet period, a J. kolkhoz was started nearby, employing 20 families in 1930. The Germans captured P. in July 1941 and murdered 200 Jews outside the town in early 1942.

POGREBISHCHE Vinnitsa dist., Ukraine. Jews are first mentioned in the early 17th cent. All were killed in the Chmielnicki massacres of 1648–49. The J. pop. was 664 in 1765 and 2,494 in 1897 (total 6,284). On 18–21 Aug. 1919, the Zeleny gang murdered 400 Jews and injured hundreds more in a pogrom. In the 1920s, under the Soviets, a J. elementary school was founded and a J. council (soviet) was active. In the two cooperatives where J. artisans formed the majority, no work was done on the J. Sabbath. In 1939, the J. pop. was 1,445. The Germans captured P. on 21 July 1941. Forty J. refugees were murdered in late July. A ghetto was established and starting on 18 Oct. over 1,750 Jews were murdered in a nearby forest around the village of Borshchagovka. A few dozen artisans were murdered soon after. A Soviet source identifies graves with 2,000 bodies.

POHL-GOENS Hesse, Germany. Numbering 48

(8% of the total) in 1900, the community also had members in neighboring Kirch-Goens. By 1940 all the Jews had left.

POHORELICE Moravia (Sudetenland), Czechoslovakia. The community was perhaps the oldest in Moravia. According to legend, it began with three Jews following the conquering Romans. The community was most probably established by the early tenth cent. In the 17th cent. the Jews owned 43 houses and were engaged in moneylending, horse trading, and the beverage trade. In the modern community, a German-language J. elementary school was started in 1847. It was known as one of the best in the country. A synagogue was erected in 1855. The J. pop. reached a peak of 769 in 1857. From 1849 to 1919, the community enjoyed political autonomy with its own mayor. Most Jews traded in farm produce and some owned large farms. After WWI, Zionist activity was extensive. In 1930, the J. pop. was 234 (total 4,290). Most Jews left after the signing of the Munich Agreement in Sept. 1938, either moving to other localities in Bohemia and Moravia or going overseas. The Nazis destroyed the synagogue. A transit camp for Hungarian Jews en route to Bergen-Belsen and the Theresienstadt ghetto was maintained in the city in 1944–45. Most of P.'s Jews perished in the Holocaust.

POHOST ZAHORODZKI Polesie dist., Poland, today Belarus. The J. settlement dates from the early 19th cent. and numbered 593 (total 846) in 1897, mostly farming and attached to Stolin Hasidism. A devastating fire struck the community in 1929. The Germans arrived in late June 1941 and established an open ghetto. They murdered 120 J. men on 10 Aug. 1941 the rest were murdered on 15 Aug. 1942.

POHOST ZARZECZNY Polesie dist., Poland, today Belarus. The J. pop. in 1921 was 264 (total 721). The Jews were probably murdered by the Germans in early Sept. 1942.

POIENILE DE SUB MUNTE (Hung. Havasmezo; previously Ruszpolyana) N. Transylvania dist., Rumania. Galician Jews settled in the early 18th cent. The J. pop. in 1930 was 726 (13% of the total). A number of distinguished rabbis served there, including R. Barukh Hager of the Vizhnitz dynasty. There were manifesta-

tions of antisemitism in the 1930s. In April 1944, the Jews were transferred to the Viseul de Sus ghetto and then deported to Auschwitz.

POKOTILOVKA Kharkov dist., Ukraine. The J. pop. in 1939 was 184 (total 4,978). The few Jews who had neither fled nor been evacuated were murdered after the German occupation of 20 Oct. 1943.

POKOTILOVO Kirovograd dist., Ukraine. Jews probably settled at the turn of the 18th cent., numbering 1,670 (total 3,030) in 1897 and 1,426 in 1926. A fire left hundreds homeless in 1901. In the Soviet period, 260 children in 1927 and 160 in 1934 attended a J. elementary school. The Germans arrived on 8 Aug. 1941 and in Feb. 1942 murdered nearly 500 residents of the town, almost all of them Jews.

POLANIEC Kielce dist., Poland. According to tradition, a J. settlement existed in the 14th cent. In the 17th cent. the Jews were living under a royal privilege allowing trade and residence. In the 18th and 19th cents. they enjoyed relative prosperity. The J. pop. was 753 in 1857 and 1,025 (total 2,561) in 1921. Between the World Wars, the Jews suffered from economic hardship and increasing antisemitism. Zionist activity was widespread. The Germans arrived in Sept. 1939, finding 864 Jews there and immediately instituting a regime of forced labor and extortion. In Oct. 1939, the Jews were ordered to set up a *Judenrat* and in April 1942 a ghetto was established. In Oct. 1942, its 2,000 inhabitants including refugees were transferred to Sandomierz and on 29 Oct. deported to the Belzec death camp. Five days after the liberation of P., 40 J. survivors were murdered by Polish Armia Krajowa partisans.

POLCH Rhineland, Germany. The J. pop was about 20 in the first quarter of the 19th cent., growing to 192 in 1843. However, most left, with only 39 remaining in 1858. At the turn of the 19th cent., the J. pop. was 60–70 and in 1933 it was 44. Twenty-four Jews emigrated by 1941 and 15 moved to other localities in Germany. The last five Jews were deported to the east in 1942. At least seven perished in the Holocaust. The synagogue (built in the mid-19th cent.) was vandalized on *Kristallnacht* (9–10 Nov. 1938).

POLGAR Szabolcs dist., Hungary. Jews settled in

the mid-19th cent. and maintained two synagogues, two *yeshivot*, and a school as their pop. grew to 317 in 1867 (5% of the total) and 488 in 1941 (3% of the total). The Zionists were active from 1935. In 1941, 60 Jews were seized for forced labor in the Ukrainian minefields, only six surviving. In 1942, following a fire in a flour mill, several members of the community were tortured and 13 were sent to the Nagyikanizsa concentration camp. From 17 May 1944, the Jews were deported to Auschwitz via Nyiregyhaza. In 1949, 42 survivors in P. gradually began to leave.

POLGARDI Fejer dist., Hungary. The J. pop. was 56 in 1930. The Jews were deported to Auschwitz via Kapolnasnyek on 18 June 1944.

POLNA Bohemia, Czechoslovakia. Jews are mentioned in the area in 1415 and in the city itself in 1532. A ghetto was established in 1676 and a synagogue was erected in 1684. In the first half of the 18th cent., three fires devastated the community and a cholera epidemic killed 450 people in the city in 1866, many in the ghetto. Many Jews afterwards left the city, reducing their pop. from 430 in 1869 to 238 in 1890 (total 5,000). In 1899, the trial and conviction for murder of a local Jew, Leopold Hilsner, developed into a blood libel and sparked anti-J. riots throughout Bohemia and Moravia, leading to the liquidation of many small J. communities. In 1930, 51 Jews remained in P. In May 1942, the Jews were deported to the Theresienstadt ghetto via Trebic. Half were sent to the Lublin dist. (Poland) in the same month and others to the Treblinka death camp in Oct. The rest were deported to Auschwitz in 1943–44.

POLOGI (in 1928–37, Tchubarovka) Zaporozhe dist., Ukraine. Jews probably settled in the early 20th cent. In the Soviet period, their pop. dropped from 706 in 1926 to 416 (total 12,944) in 1939. The Germans captured the town on 5 Oct. 1941. Most of the Jews still there were murdered in Dec. On 4 Feb 1942, the Germans executed another 100 Jews from P. and its environs. In all, 700 inhabitants of the area were murdered during the German occupation, including 165 children (most of them Jews).

POLONKA Nowogrodek dist., Poland, today Belarus. Jews probably arrived in the second half of the 16th cent. They numbered 549 in 1897 (total 645)

and 206 in 1921. Between the World Wars, J. carpenters won a reputation for their fine furniture. Jews also owned two flour mills. In the first months of the German occupation (from 26 June 1941), J. homes were looted and vandalized and a number of the town's 350 Jews were murdered. Eighty of the elderly were executed on 18 April 1942 and the rest on 12 Aug. 1942.

POLONNOYE Kamenets-Podolski dist., Ukraine. Jews are first mentioned in 1601. By the mid-17th cent., a large community was in existence. In 1648, during Chmielnicki's siege of the city, 12,000 Jews found refuge within its walls. Jews were also among the city's defenders. With the fall of the fortress after three days, nearly 10,000 Jews were massacred, including the well-known kabbalist Shimshon of Ostropol. In 1684, the community was permitted to build new homes but in the early 18th cent., it suffered from attacks by the Haidamaks as well as by Polish and Swedish soldiers. In 1765, the J. pop. was 1,241. In the first half of the 18th cent., R. Yaakov Yosef Kohen, one of the first students of the Ba'al Shem Tov and author of the first hasidic work (*Toledot Yaakov-Yosef*), was active in the city. In 1783, a J. printing press was founded, producing mainly hasidic works. In 1897, the J. pop. rose to 7,910 (total 16,288). A specialty of J. artisans here was the manufacture of parquet flooring. Jews also operated a porcelain factory and other workshops. In Dec. 1905, Jews were attacked in a pogrom and on 24–25 Sept. 1917 a unit of infantry reservists injured 98 Jews in another pogrom,. The unit returned on 15–17 Oct. and again attacked Jews. In the Soviet period, a J. school (founded in 1917) and culture club (with a Yiddish drama circle) were active. The J. pop. was 5,337 in 1926 and 4,171 in 1939. The Germans captured the city on 6 July 1941. In early Aug., 19 Jews were executed as alleged Communist agents. On 23 Aug., German police murdered 113. Another 1,270 Jews were executed in June 1942. In all, 2,000 Jews were murdered during the German occupation. The killing site was a forest about a mile outside the city. Another 15 families (nearly 50 Jews) were executed at Lubar in the Zhitomir dist.

POLOTSK Vitebsk dist., Belorussia. Jews are first mentioned in 1551, when the town was part of the Kingdom of Poland. In 1563, during the Livonian war, the Russian czar, Ivan the Terrible, ordered 300

Jews who refused to convert to be drowned in the Dvina River. The Jews returned in 1579, when the Poles recaptured P., but in 1580 they were forbidden to engage in trade and build or buy houses within city limits. In 1654, during the Russo-Polish war, the J. settlement was again destroyed in a Cossack raid. In 1765, the J. pop. was 1,003, with the city becoming a hasidic center during the 18th cent. The preacher R. Yisrael ben Peretz of P. was a student of Dov Baer, the "*Maggid* of Mezhirech." After the First Partition of Poland in 1772, the city was annexed by Russia. The J. pop. rose to 12,481 (61.5% of the total) in 1897. In the early 20th cent., the community maintained 23 synagogues, a *talmud torah*, and a state J. secondary school. In Oct. 1905, the Jews were attacked in a pogrom. In the mid-1920s, under the Soviets, 340 children attended two Yiddish-language elementary schools. A J. orphanage and kindergarten were also in operation. Of the city's 237 artisans organized in cooperatives, 220 were Jews. In 1939, the J. pop. was 6,464 (total

29,577). The Germans captured the city on 16 July 1941. A ghetto was established in Aug. but in Sept. all the Jews were transferred to a closed camp near the village of Lozovka. Cold and hunger prevailed there and many died of disease. In Dec., 7,000 Jews from P. and the surrounding area were executed at a local brickyard.

POLTAVA Poltava dist., Ukraine. Jews were probably present in the first half of the 17th cent. when the town was under the proprietorship of Prince Vishnieviecki. The community ended in the Chmielnicki massacres of 1648–49 and was only reestablished in the late 18th cent. In 1803, the J. pop. was 350, rising to 11,046 (total 53,703) in 1897. By the late 19th cent., Jews owned four large flour mills, a number of lumber warehouses, most of the city's distilleries and liquor warehouses, and two substantial printing presses. A savings and loan fund was founded in 1906 and the community maintained a society for the relief of the

Jewish schoolchildren in their vegetable garden, Poltava, Ukraine, 1917 (The Central Archive for the History of the Jewish People, Jerusalem/ photo courtesy of Yad Vashem, The Holocaust Martyrs' and Heroes' Remembrance Authority, Jerusalem)

poor, a free hospital and clinic for the poor, and a society for the relief of needy students. In addition to *hadarim*, the J. educational system included a *talmud torah* for 300 boys, an ICA vocational school for girls, a small yeshiva, and a J. public library with thousands of volumes. Many Jews attended state schools. In 1915, the Mir yeshiva and part of the Lubavich yeshiva were transferred to P. Among those born and active in P. were Yitzhak Ben-Zvi (Shimshelevich; 1884–1963), second president of Israel, and Yaakov Zarubavel (Vitkin; 1886–1967), both founders and leaders of the Zionist Socialists and Po'alei Zion. Po'alei Zion was founded in P. in 1906 and its journal *Yevreyskaya Rabochaya Khronika* was published there. The Orthodox weekly *Ha-Modi'a* appeared in P. in 1912. The Russian author Vladimir Korolenko prevented the outbreak of pogroms in 1905 and March 1918 and also assisted the Maccabi Fighting Group in its government-recognized self-defense efforts. The J. pop. grew to 19,580 in 1923, dropping to 12,860 (total 130,487) in 1939. A children's home operated from 1921, housing 586 children up to 1936. Two J. schools, each attended by hundreds of children, operated from 1926. Also established were a J. section in the local railroad workers school, a J. law court, and a J. section in the militia where Yiddish was spoken. Among 9,000 J. breadwinners in 1926, 2,415 were white-collar workers, 1,862 artisans, 1,676 blue-collar workers, and 995 tradesmen. Jews constituted an 80% majority in the artisans union and a majority of the workers in the local textile factory. In the 1920s, the Joint Distribution Committee and ORT furnished machines and wool to hundreds of declassed Jews to enable them to work. Many Jews were subsequently employed at the government sock factory which supplied the entire Soviet Union. The Germans captured the city on 19 Sept. 1941, ordering the Jews to wear the Star of David and to put it on their doors and windows. A *Judenrat* was established and in late Sept. Jews were registered. On 16 Sept., 5,000 were executed. In a second *Aktion*, on 23 Nov., 3,000 were murdered following a new registration. Those failing to register were hunted down and murdered singly or in groups.

POLZIN, BAD   see BAD POLZIN.

POMAZ   Pest-Pilis-Solt-Kiskun dist., Hungary. Jews arrived in the early 19th cent. from Moravia, erecting a synagogue in 1910 and numbering 142 in 1930. They established factories for producing alcoholic beverages, vinegar, and sports equipment. J. men were seized for forced labor in 1940. From May 1944, the remaining Jews were held at Csillaghegy and then transferred to Monor on 30 June en route to Auschwitz.

POMIECHOWEK   (Yid. Ponikhove) Warsaw dist., Poland. Jews settled there in the 19th cent. and numbered 202 (30% of the total) in 1921. After J. residents fled or were deported by the Nazis (Oct. 1939), the town's "Third Fort" served as a concentration camp for 3,000 Jews from other ghettoes (July–Aug. 1941). Many were killed and the remainder transported to the Warsaw ghetto. A monument was erected in P. in 1972.

POMORZANY   (Yid. Pomarin) Tarnopol dist., Poland, today Ukraine. Jews are first mentioned in 1605, receiving extensive privileges and from the Austrian period constituting the town's sole urban element. The J. pop. stood at 1,910 (total 4,476) in 1880 but declined steadily thereafter to 799 in 1921 with most J. homes burned to the ground in WWI. The Zionists were active from early in the cent. and controlled the community council between the World Wars. The community was expelled to the Zborow ghetto in Oct. 1942.

POMOSCHNAYA   Kirovograd dist., Ukraine. The J. pop. in 1939 was 175 (total 5,209). A few months after their arrival in Aug. 1941, the Germans probably murdered the few Jews who had neither fled nor been evacuated.

PONINKA   Kamenets-Podolski dist., Ukraine. The J. community grew with the opening of a paper factory in 1870. In 1897, the J. pop. was 206 (total 1,025). In the Soviet period, a J. elementary school (four grades) operated. In 1939, the J. pop. was 675. The Germans captured the town on 5 July 1941. In the fall of 1941, 485 Jews were murdered. During their occupation they murdered 4,000 Jews from P. and the neighboring settlements.

POPELNIA   Zhitomir dist., Ukraine. J. residence was banned until the early 20th cent. In 1939, the J. pop. was 129 with another few dozen Jews in the kolkhozes in the area. The Germans arrived on 14 July

1941, murdering 297 people during the occupation, most of them Jews.

POPOVTSY Vinnitsa dist., Ukraine. The J. pop. included 57 poll tax payers in 1784 and numbered 511 (total 3,454) in 1897. In 1926, under the Soviets, the J. pop. fell to 348. The Germans captured P. on 20 July 1941. After it was annexed to Transnistria in early Sept. 1941, about 1,000 Jews were brought there from Bessarabia and Bukovina, most perishing together with the local Jews.

POPOWO KOSCIELNE Warsaw dist., Poland. The first synagogue of this very old community was probably built before the 17th cent. Between the World Wars the J. pop numbered 109 (total 324). All the Jews were expelled by the Germans to the Makow Mazowiecki ghetto in late 1940; at least 133 perished in the Holocaust

POPPENLAUER Lower Franconia, Germany. A J. community existed in the mid-18th cent. In 1830–54, 27 Jews emigrated overseas. A new synagogue was dedicated in 1867 and a J. public school operated until 1924. The J. pop. was 111 in 1880 (total 1,553) and 45 in 1933. Nineteen Jews left P. in 1934–38, 15 of them emigrating (13 to the U.S.). On *Kristallnacht* (9–10 Nov. 1938), the synagogue and all nine J. homes were vandalized. Six more Jews left for the U.S. in 1941 and of those remaining 14 were deported to Izbica in the Lublin dist. (Poland) via Wuerzburg on 25 April 1942 and seven to the Theresienstadt ghetto on 23 Sept. 1942.

POPRAD Slovakia, Czechoslovakia, today Republic of Slovakia. After residence restrictions were lifted in 1840, Jews from neighboring Huncovce began to settle. The community grew slowly in the face of local hostility, reaching a pop. of 108 on 1890 and 202 (total 1,530) in 1900. A synagogue was consecrated in 1906 and a J. elementary school was opened in 1908. The J. pop. was 618 in 1930, with Jews owning (in 1921) 42 commercial establishments, 13 workshops, and a number of factories, including a sawmill employing 150 workers. Jews served on the municipal council and one was deputy mayor. Most of the young belonged to the Zionist youth movements and a few left for kibbutzim and moshavim in Palestine. After the creation of the Slovakian state in March 1939, the German minority and

Hlinka Guard attacked Jews and vandalized their property. In 1941, the authorities closed down about 100 J. businesses while seizing Jews for forced labor. On 25 March 1942, 63 J. girls were deported to Auschwitz. Dozens of young men were then sent to the Majdanek concentration camp. Families were deported to Auschwitz and the Lublin dist. of Poland on 23 April and 31 May. In all, 420 Jews (80% of the total) were deported in 1942 and perished. Those left behind either fled in 1944 during the Slovakian national uprising or were subsequently rounded up by the Germans for execution. In March–Oct. 1942, about 10,000 Jews passed through the P. transit camp en route to the death camps.

PORCSALMA Szatmar dist., Hungary. Jews settled in the early 19th cent., numbering 147 in 1900 and 244 in 1941. Good relations existed with fellow residents until late April 1944, when the Jews were expelled to Mateszalka and then deported to Auschwitz at the end of May.

POREMBA-KOTSEMBY and **POREMBA SHREDNYA** Warsaw dist., Poland. These twin communities (numbering 251 in 1921) suffered from antisemitic violence during the 1930s. Under Nazi rule they presumably shared the fate of the other communities in the region.

PORKHOV Leningrad dist., Russia. J. settlement probably began around the turn of the 19th cent. A prayer house was also erected at the time. The J. pop. was 264 in 1926 and 175 (total 12,681) in 1939. The Germans occupied P. on 11 July 1941. In 1943 they murdered about 40 local Jews.

POROHY Stanislawow dist., Poland, today Ukraine. The J. pop. in 1921 was 150. The Jews were expelled to Stanislowow for liquidation in Sept. 1942.

POROMBKA Kielce dist., Poland. Jews settled in the mid-19th cent. and maintained a pop. of 30 families (about 120 people) from the late 19th cent. until WWII. In 1940, J. males were sent by the Germans to labor camps in Upper Silesia. The remaining Jews were dispatched to the Bendzin and Sosnowiec ghettoes and then to Auschwitz.

POROSZLO Heves dist., Hungary. Jews arrived in the early 19th cent. under the patronage of the Catholic

Church, interested in advancing the economic prosperity of its estates. The Jews engaged in trade (grain, lumber) and some light industry (bricks, brushes, flour, woodworking). They numbered 182 in 1880 and 154 in 1930. In the 1930s, a blood libel led to the arrest of many community members. In mid-June 1944, the Jews were deported to Auschwitz via Tiszafured.

POROZORKI Vilna dist., Poland, today Belarus. Jews probably settled in 1882 after being expelled from nearby villages by the May Laws. In 1921 they numbered 134 (total 255), opening stores and returning to work as artisans and farmers with the restoration of stability. The Germans arrived in late June 1941. On 5 Dec. they executed the 250 Jews of P. and the neighboring villages at the J. cemetery, burying infants alive.

POROZOW Bialystok dist., Poland, today Belarus. Jews are believed to have arrived in the late 16th cent. In the 19th cent. most were engaged in agriculture, entering petty trade and opening shops at the turn of the cent. when their pop. reached 931 (total 2,028). Under the German occupation in WWI, they suffered from food shortages and were subjected to forced labor. After the war, with their pop. dropping to 567 (1921), they suffered economically from heavy taxes and the competition of the Polish cooperatives. Zionist influence grew in the 1920s and Hehalutz pioneers left for Palestine. The Germans captured P. on 26 June 1941. In fall 1942 a ghetto was set up, and residents suffered from hunger and disease. On 2 Nov., 600 were brought to the Wolkowysk bunker camp and from there deported to the Treblinka death camp. The 220 left behind were murdered in the Porozow forest.

PORUMBESTI (Hung. Kokenyesd) N. Transylvania dist., Rumania. Jews settled in the late 18th cent. The J. pop in 1930 was 92 (7% of the total). The few remaining families were transferred to the Nagyszollos ghetto in May 1944 and in June deported to Auschwitz.

PORYCK Volhynia dist., Poland, today Ukraine. Jews are first mentioned in 1569 and numbered 1,316 (total 2,264) in 1897. With the outbreak of WWI, they were subjected to a pogrom. As the fighting grew near, 150 families temporarily fled while peasants and Russian soldiers pillaged J. property. The J. pop.

grew to 3,000 as refugees poured in after the German occupation of 23 June 1941. A *Judenrat* and an open ghetto were established. On 1 Sept. 1942, after the old and sick were murdered, the Jews were kept under the open sky without food or water for three days before being executed by Ukrainian police

PORZECZE Bialystok dist., Poland, today Belarus. Jews settled in the 19th cent. after a railroad station on the Petersburg–Warsaw line was built in the town. In 1921 their number was 181 (total 1,098) and in 1939, 400. Between the World Wars the Hehalutz organization was active in the community. After two years of Soviet rule (1939–41) the Germans arrived on 23 June 1941, randomly murdering a few dozen Jews before herding the community into a ghetto of 20 rickety shacks under a regime of forced labor and extortion. A *Judenrat* was appointed. On 2 Nov. 1942, the Jews were brought to the Kelbasin transit camp near Grodno and a month later deported to Auschwitz.

POSTAWY Vilna dist., Poland, today Belarus. A few dozen Jews were living in the village in the early 19th cent. Their number reached 1,310 (total 2,397) in 1897. After fleeing in WWI, about 850 returned in 1925 to ruined homes. They recovered with the help of the YEKOPO relief organization, but in the 1930s their livelihoods were again undermined by competition from Polish and Belorussian cooperatives. In the 1920s, most children attended a Tarbut Hebrew school, which promoted the activities of the Zionist youth movements. A Bund-oriented Yiddish school also operated later on. The German occupation of late June 1941 brought with it random killing and forced labor. A ghetto and *Judenrat* were soon set up and on 25 Dec. 1942 the town's 2,000 Jews were taken to nearby pits and murdered. A group of young Jews escaped to join up with the Soviet partisans in the forest.

POSTOLOPRTY Bohemia (Sudetenland) Czechoslovakia. Jews are first mentioned in 1671, when Count Sinzendorf granted a letter of protection to 20 families. The J. quarter burned down in 1781 and another devastating fire struck the community in 1810. A J. school was opened in 1817. In 1930, the J. pop. was 114 (total 3,311). After the annexation of the Sudetenland to the German Reich in fall 1938, the Jews

Synagogue in Poryck, Poland

left the city. Those subsequently caught were sent to the death camps via the Theresienstadt ghetto.

POTOK ZLOTY Tarnopol dist., Poland, today Ukraine. Jews are first mentioned in 1635 and organized themselves into an independent commmunity in the 18th cent., with many notable rabbis and a peak pop. of 1,247 (40% of the total) in 1880. Emigration as well as Cossack and Ukrainian violence in WWI depleted the pop. to 895 in 1921 with dire poverty the lot of many. Zionist youth movements were active between the World Wars. The German occupation of 10 July 1941 brought a regime of forced labor and in the fall of 1942 expulsion to Buczacz in time for the *Aktions* there.

POTSDAM Brandenburg, Germany. The first evidence of a J. family dates from 1691. In the 18th cent., a J. community developed along with the emerg-

ing textile industry. In 1731, David Hirsch received the monopoly to manufacture velvet for the entire kingdom. By 1769, there were 19 J. manufacturers. In 1814 the Jew pop. was 70 families and in 1895, 477 individuals. The community set up a cemetery in 1743 and established three synagogues (1767, 1802, and 1903). The first was erected with the aid of Frederick II of Prussia, with members of the royal family present at the consecration. From 1851, rabbis were engaged and reforms were introduced. In the Weimar years, a home for J. girls was established in 1929 and in 1932 a home in nearby Caputh for J. children whose parents had divorced or emigrated. Jews served on the city council and occupied official positions. When the Nazis came to power in 1933, there were 365 Jews in P. In 1933 the children's home in Caputh was converted into a boarding school. On *Kristallnacht* (9–10 Nov. 1938), the synagogue was wrecked and the mortuary in the cemetery gutted by fire; stores were

Learning mathematics with Dr. Ising, Potsdam, Germany (Juedisches Museum im Stadtmuseum, Berlin/photo courtesy of Yad Vashem, The Holocaust Martyrs' and Heroes' Remembrance Authority, Jerusalem)

vandalized and J. men were arrested and taken to the Sachsenhausen concentration camp. On 11 Nov., the boarding school in Caputh was wrecked. By May 1939, there were 255 Jews in P. About 40 persons were deported on 11 Jan. 1942 to the Riga ghetto. By Oct. 1942, only the residents of the J. old age home were still living in P. They were probably deported to the Theresienstadt ghetto.

POTYLICZ Lwow dist., Poland, today Ukraine. Jews are known from the late 15th cent. and were subsequently granted trade privileges. The J. pop. in 1900 was 335 (10% of the total). The community was expelled by the Germans to the Rawa Ruska ghetto in Sept. 1942.

POVAZSKA BYSTRICA (Hung. Vagbeszterce) Slovakia, Czechoslovakia, today Republic of Slovakia. Jews were present in the mid-17th cent., augmented by refugees from Moravia late in the cent. and under the protection of Count Szapary. A synagogue was built in 1823 and a Neologist congregation was formed after 1869. A J. elementary school was opened in 1870 and a new synagogue was erected in 1898. The J. pop. reached a peak of 402 (total 2,307) in 1880 and then declined steadily to 324 in 1900 and 260 in 1940 as the young left for the big cities. In the post-WWI Czechoslovakian Republic, Jews were active in public and economic life. They owned 21 businesses (including 12 groceries) and ten workshops. Most of the young belonged to the Zionist youth movements. In the Slovakian state, J. businesses were closed down and the synagogue and J. school were seriously damaged in riots on 4 Nov. 1941. Subsequently, Jews were sent to forced labor camps. In late March–early April 1942, young J. men and women were deported to Majdanek and Auschwitz, respectively. Deportations continued in April–June, increasing the total sent to the death camps in 1942 to 85% of the community.

POWURSK Volhynia dist., Poland, today Ukraine.

The J. pop. numbered over 200 in the 1930s. The Germans entered on 26 June 1941 and brought Jews from the environs to the open ghetto in P. The Jews were expelled by the Germans to Mielnica on 4 Sept. 1942 and murdered there. An organized group of 12 young Jews escaped to the forest and joined the partisans.

POZDISOVCE (Hung. Pazdics) Slovakia, Czechoslovakia, today Republic of Slovakia. Jews probably arrived in the late 17th cent. In the 18th cent., many families from Galicia settled here. The J. pop. reached a peak of 101 (total 1,184) in 1900 and numbered 52 in 1940. On 7 May 1942, after the deportation of the young, J. families were dispatched to the Lukow ghetto in the Lublin dist. of Poland, where they perished.

POZNAN (Ger. Posen) Poznan dist., Poland. J. refugees may have arrived from Germany after such upheavals as the Rhineland massacres of the First Crusade, the peasant riots of 1248, and the Black Death persecutions of 1348–49. A J. settlement was in existence in the second half of the 14th cent., with Jews engaging in moneylending and moneychanging, mostly on a small scale under charters guaranteeing religious freedom and internal autonomy. In 1399 Jews were murdered and their account books destroyed in one of the recurring anti-J. incidents that accompanied the community over the centuries. Epidemics and fires also plagued the community during its early existence. In the 15th and 16th cents. Jews increasingly went over to trade and crafts. Although there were residence and trade restrictions at this time, by the mid-16th cent. Jews comprised half the city's pop. There was a general atmosphere of prosperity and the community was one of the most important in Greater Poland, with a much coveted rabbinical seat and a renowned yeshiva. Among the yeshiva heads were R. Shemuel Edels ("Maharsha"), R. David ha-Levi (the "Taz"), author of the well-known *Turei Zahav* on the *Shulhan Arukh*, and R. Moshe Lipschitz. A Hebrew printing press was founded in the late 16th cent. A period of crisis commenced in the mid-17th cent. Just 300 of the city's 2,000 J. families survived the Swedish invasion of 1656. In the Northern War of the early 18th cent. the Jews again suffered grievously. Many Jews left the city during a plague in 1709; the J. quarter was destroyed in 1716 by invaders from the so-called Tarnograd Confederation and a year later a great fire destroyed more J. homes along with the synagogue. In 1736 Jews were

The New Synagogue in Poznan, Poland

arrested in a blood libel and held in prison for four years. Throughout the cent. the process of economic decline continued unabated. With the establishment of Prussian rule in 1793, interrupted in 1807–15 when P. was included in the Grand Duchy of Warsaw and J. rights were suspended, Jews gradually achieved a measure of equality and with increasing education underwent a process of cultural and political Germanization. Active among the *maskilim* was the Hebrew writer and educator David Caro (1782–1839), who opened the first modern J. school there in 1816. The J. pop. grew to a peak of 7,255 in 1871 (total 56,240) but thereafter emigration substantially depleted the community, particularly among the educated class, while J. tradesmen continued to face strong competition from the city's Germans and Poles. In the late 19th cent., the community was split in two between adherents of Haskala and religiously conservative elements. A Hovevei Zion group was formed in 1895. WWI accelerated the decline in the pop. as many settled in the interior of Germany, leaving 2,088 Jews in 1921. The community operated a hospital (founded in 1887), public health services, an old age home and orphanage, and summer camps. Most children studied in public schools. Prominent among the Zionist youth movements was Hashomer Hatzair, which sent many of its pioneers to Palestine in the 1930s, when the Jews were subjected to violent outbursts of antisemitism along with economic boycotts. In 1933, 277 J. breadwinners were engaged in trade, 66 in crafts, 53 in the professions, and 28 were laborers. The Germans captured the city on 1 Sept. 1939, finding 1,500 Jews there. Persecution with the participation of the local *Volksdeutsche* ensued immediately, with Jews seized for forced labor, evicted from their homes, and their shops pillaged. On 12 Dec. 1939 all were expelled to General Gouvernement territory, mostly to Ostrow in the Lublin area, later ending their days in the death camps. A labor camp operated in P. from Nov. 1939 to Aug. 1943. After the war a community numbering 200 in 1946 existed for awhile but most left over the next 20 years.

PRAGUE (Praha) capital of Czechoslovakia. P. is the oldest community in Bohemia. Jews first settled there in the tenth cent. During the Crusades, Jews were murdered and others forced to convert. Under the reign of Przemysl Ottokar (1254–68), Jews were allowed to established a J. quarter. Toward the end of the 13th cent., the famous Altneuschul was inaugurated. Jews were engaged in moneylending. They suffered from persecution during the years 1298 and 1338. The great kabbalist Avigdor Kara (d. 1439), who served as a rabbi in P., described the murder of 3,000 Jews in 1389 in an elegy which was incorporated subsequently into prayers recited by P. Jews on Yom Kippur. In the 15th cent. the J. quarter was looted several times. Despite the fact that Jews were expelled on several occasions during the 16th cent., their numbers increased rapidly. In 1522 there were about 600 Jews in P. and in 1541 about 1,200. P. became a center of J. learning in Europe and in 1512, Gershom ben Shelomo Kohen opened the first Hebrew press north of the Alps. Under Rudolf II (1576–1611) and Matthias (1611–19) the status of the Jews improved. During this time, regarded as the Golden Age of the Jews of Prague, R. Yehuda Loew (1525–1609), the "Maharal" of P., created the *golem* according to legend. Yom Tov Lippman Heller (1579–1609) became chief rabbi of Prague and wrote the *Tosafot Yom Tov*. David Gans (1541–1613), an astronomer and scientist, also lived here at this

time. In 1627, Jews from all over Bohemia settled in Prague. In order to stop the influx, several restrictions were imposed in 1650. In 1680, about 3,000 Jews died of the plague and three years later nearly all of the J. quarter, including 11 synagogues, burned down. In 1726, Charles VI imposed the Familiants Laws, which stipulated that only the eldest son could marry and establish a family, the other males in the family having no alternative but to remain single or leave Bohemia. In 1744, Maria Theresa expelled the Jews from P., but four years later, promising to pay high taxes, they were allowed to resettle. In 1754 a second fire caused serious damage to the J. quarter. Despite all difficulties and disabilities, the community remained a center of J. learning. In 1718, David Oppenheim (1664–1736), the well-known bibliophile, presided in P. as chief rabbi of Bohemia. Yonatan Eybeschuetz (1690–1767), the kabbalist, became head of one of several flourishing *yeshivot* in P. Another yeshiva was headed by Chief Rabbi Yehezkel Landau (1755–93). During the reign of Joseph II, the Jews won emancipation but were forced to attend regular schools and serve in the army. With the 1848 revolution, they were given equal rights. In 1852 the ghetto was opened and named Josefstaedt. During the second half of the 19th cent. the majority of Jews tended to adopt the German language

The novelist Franz Kafka, Prague, Czechoslovakia (Jewish National and University Library, Jerusalem/photo courtesy of Beth Hatefutsoth, Tel Aviv)

Josefstaedterstrasse in the Prague ghetto, Czechoslovakia, early 20th cent. (The Hulton Picture Company/photo courtesy of Yad Vashem, The Holocaust Martyrs' and Heroes' Remembrance Authority, Jerusalem)

and German culture. As antisemitism grew in the 1880s and 1890s, a Czech assimilationist movement (Cechu Zidu Svaz) developed. In 1896, the J. quarter was restored and many houses were torn down. Only the Altneuschul, the quarter's cemetery with over 15,000 tombstones, and the J. city hall from 1560 were left untouched. In 1880, the J. pop. was 20,508, increasing to 27,289 in 1900 and to 35,463 in 1930 and representing 46% of all Bohemian Jews. During these years, almost half the Jews were engaged in trade, about 22% were lawyers, and 8% doctors. In 1906, the J. Museum of Prague was founded. Before WWI, the Bar Kochba students organization under the leadership of Samuel Hugo Bergman became a center of cultural Zionism. In 1911–12, Albert Einstein taught at the German University of Prague. The Prague circle (*Prager Kreis*), produced writers like Franz Kafka (1883–1924), Max Brod (1884–1968), and Franz Werfel (1890–1945) who gained international recognition. The conductor/composer Gustav Mahler (1860–1911)

lived several years in P. The community maintained various women's and welfare organizations and several J. schools. Some synagogues modernized their liturgy, but not necessarily in accordance with the Reform movement. After WWI and the foundation of the Czechoslovak Republic, the process of secularization became intense and P. had one of the highest percentages of mixed marriages in Europe – 24% in 1927 and 30% in 1930. Jews supported the Realist Party of T.G. Masaryk. In Aug. 1933 the 18th Zionist Congress was held in P. From 1935, two years after Hitler's rise to power in Germany, there was a constant influx of refugees from Germany and in 1938 also from Austria and the Sudetenland. In March 1939, after the Nazi occupation of parts of Czechoslovakia, mainly Bohemia and Moravia, the number of Jews in P. was about 56,000. In July 1939, the *Reichsprotektor* Constantin von Neurath founded a Central Office for J. Emigration (Zentralstelle fuer Juedische Auswanderung) headed by Adolf Eichmann. With the outbreak of war in

Jewish doctor, Prague, Czechoslovakia. Below: *Permit to practice medicine issued by Emperor Joseph II*

Sept. 1939 several prominent P. Jews, among them Marie Schmolka and Hanna Steiner, both engaging in rescue work for the refugees, were arrested and deported as hostages to the Buchenwald concentration camp. J. organizations increasingly devoted their activities to social welfare and emigration. By the end of 1939, the Palestine Office of P., headed by Yaakov Edelstein, who subsequently became J. Elder (*Judenaeltester*) in the Theresienstadt ghetto, succeeded in bringing about the emigration of 19,000 Jews. The Palestine Office continued its work until April 1941. In Feb. 1940, the authority of the Central Office for J. Emigration was extended over the entire Protectorate. Consequently the J. community became officially the central organization of the Jews in the Protectorate and responsible for implementing various Nazi measures. It was forced to provide the Nazis with lists of candidates for deportation and to ensure that they arrived at the assembly point. From Oct. 1941 until March 1945, 46,067 Jews were deported from P., mostly to Theresienstadt, but also directly to the east. The Nazis set up a Trustee's Office (Treuhandstelle) responsible for the abandoned apartments, furniture, and other possessions. Since the goods were stored in 11 synagogues as well as 54 warehouses all over Prague, these synagogues were not destroyed. Some of the goods were also sold to the German Winter Aid (Winterhilfe). As deportations got under way, J. scholars made efforts to save the artifacts and archives of the abandoned J. communities. From 1942–43, about 5,400 religious objects, 24,500 prayer books, and 6,070 historical artifacts as well as over 300,000 documents were collected and catalogued. The Nazis meant to use the collection for a "Central Museum of the Extinguished J. Race," but after the war it became one of the richest collections of J. art in the world. About 4,980 Jews returned from the concentration camps; 227 had been living underground. In 1948–49 many of the survivors settled in Israel or emigrated overseas.

PRAID (Hung. Parajd) N. Transylvania dist., Rumania. Jews settled in the 1850s and the community was organized in the 1880s. The J. pop. in 1930 was 123 (4% of the total). In May 1944 the community was transferred to the Sfantul Gheorghe ghetto and in June deported to Auschwitz.

PRASZKA Lodz dist., Poland. J. merchants trading with towns in Silesia first settled in the early 17th

cent. The J. pop. was 1,878 in 1897 (60% of the total) and about 1,000 in 1939. The Zionists set up a training farm in 1922. Agudat Israel and the Bund were also active. The 1930s was marked by antisemitic agitation, especially in the city council. P. was occupied by the Germans in Sept. 1939. A *Judenrat* was set up and the Jews were ghettoized in 1940. In addition to the 840 inhabitants of P., the ghetto housed 121 refugees and a further 700 transferred by the Germans from Wielun and Wieruszow. In winter 1941, 500 Jews were taken to a forced labor camp in nearby Przedmoscie, and in Aug. 1942 the remaining Jews were deported to Chelmno.

PRAVIENISKES (Yid. Pravenishok) Kaunas dist., Lithuania. P. was the site of a prison camp where local Jews and Jews from Kaunas (Kovno) were executed during the Holocaust by Germans and Lithuanians. On 4 Sept. 1941, 241 men and eight women, all Jews, were shot following an abortive uprising.

PREILI (Yid. Preil) Latgale dist., Latvia. Jews were present from the beginnings of the town in the early 19th cent. and came to constitute one of the largest J. communities in Latgale in the second half of the cent., numbering 1,375 (total 2,104) in 1897. Many fled to Russia in WWI but dozens of J. refugees from Lithuania and W. Galicia took their place. The community suffered considerably under the Bolshevik occupation in 1918. Between the World Wars the Zionists with their youth movements were highly influential, sending settlers to Palestine, and the Yiddish-language elementary school went over to Hebrew. In 1935 the J. pop. was 847. Under Soviet rule, J. businesses were nationalized and community life was ended. The Germans arrived on 28 June 1941 and instituted a regime of severe persecution. The Jews were murdered in the area of the J. cemetery in two groups, on 28 July and 8 Aug. 1941, after being forced to dig their own graves.

PRENZLAU Brandenburg, Germany. Evidence of Jews dates from 1309. There was a J. community in the 14th. and 15th cents. A settlement developed again in the 1670s. In 1751 the J. pop. included 17 families; in 1890, 423 indivuals. The community established two synagogues (1752, 1832) and two cemeteries (1716, 1881) and engaged a rabbi from 1850. Jews served on the city council. Paul Hirsch, minister-president of Prussia (1918-20), was born in P.

When the Nazis came to power in 1933, the J. pop. dropped to 174, many having emigrated or moved to Berlin owing to the pressure of the Nazi boycott measures. On *Kristallnacht* (9–10 Nov. 1938), the synagogue was set on fire and the town's cemeteries were desecrated. J. men were interned in the Sachsenhausen concentration camp. By May 1940, there were 40 Jews in P. Most were deported, the last five to the Treblinka death camp on 10 April 1942. At least two Jews, married to non-Jews, managed to survive in P.

PREROV   (Yid. Prera) Moravia, Czechoslovakia. Jews are known from the first half of the 14th cent. The community was probably augmented by refugees from Olomouc in 1454 and was economically stable in the 15th–16th cents. In the 1590s, it suffered from natural disasters and in the 17th–19th cents. from numerous fires. In the plague of 1771, all but 82 of the city's residents died. A new synagogue was erected in 1860 and the J. pop. rose to a peak of 717 (total 17,000) in 1901 before declining to 336 in 1921. In 1938 the J. pop. was 316. The Jews were probably deported to the Theresienstadt ghetto together with the

Jews of Brno in late 1941–early 1942. From there they were transported to the death camps of Poland.

PRESOV   (Hung. Eperjes) Slovakia, Czechoslovakia, today Republic of Slovakia. The first Jew to settle was the wealthy Galician-born merchant Mordekhai Hollaender in 1785. A *beit midrash* was opened in the Hollaender household in 1831 and a J. school was founded in 1843. The community's first rabbi, Dr. Shelomo Menahem Schiller-Szinessy, was appointed in 1844 but forced to flee to England after supporting the Hungarians in the 1848–49 revolution. He subsequently become rabbi of Manchester and a professor at Cambridge University. The first synagogue was consecrated in 1849 and a Neologist congregation was formed under the influence of R. Meir Austerlitz, who served the community for 53 years until his death in 1913. A new synagogue in the Moorish style was erected after the first one burned down in 1887. In 1871, 46 Orthodox families formed their own congregation, building a new synagogue in 1898. The Orthodox school, which opened in 1873, reached an attendance of 200 on the eve of WWI; the well-known Etz

Agudat Israel, Presov, Czechoslovakia, 1930s (Beth Hatefutsoth Photo Archive, Tel Aviv/courtesy of Sarah Golan, Ramat Gan)

Hayyim *talmud torah* (founded in 1891) had 60 students. In 1912, 26 hasidic families in the Orthodox community organized a third congregation. The J. pop. rose to 1,010 in 1869 and 2,106 (total 13,098) in 1900. Jews engaged mainly in trade but many also belonged to the professional class and served as public officials. Zionist activity commenced in the late 19th cent., mainly under the leadership of Dr. Hayyim Farbstein. J. property was heavily damaged in general riots in 1918. In 1921, the J. pop. was 3,477. A new Orthodox synagogue was built in 1930 and the Hasidim opened a *shtibl* in 1935 with a *beit midrash* and *talmud torah* alongside it. In 1928, R. Moshe Hayyim Lau opened the Torat Ahim yeshiva, attracting students from many countries and reaching a peak attendance of 150. Jews published two newspapers – the Orthodox *Juedische Nachrichten* and the Hungarian-language *Uj vilag*. Jews comprised 31 of the city's 44 lawyers and 14 of its 22 doctors along with 338 merchants and 124 artisans. Zionist activity expanded and the Zionist branch in P. was the third largest in Slovakia. Most of the young belonged to the Zionist youth movements. With the establishment of the Slovakian state in March 1939, anti-J. riots broke out, marked by looting and vandalism. When German soldiers entered the city after the invasion of Poland, they too looted and vandalized J. property. In Jan. 1941, local rioters burned down the Orthodox synagogue. Jews were fired from the public service and the Slovakian authorities closed down or "Aryanized" their businesses. The Jews of P. were the first in Slovakia required to wear a special badge. About 400 Jews were seized for forced labor. The arrival of 826 refugees from Bratislava in Dec. 1942 increased the J. pop. to 5,134. In late March and early April 1942, about 1,000 young J. men and women were deported to the Majdanek concentration camp and Auschwitz, respectively. Family deportations commenced in mid-April, with hundreds of Jews sent to Auschwitz on 23 April and about 2,100 dispatched to the Demblin ghetto in the Lublin dist. of Poland on 13–14 May. In all, 4,000 Jews from P. and its environs were deported in 1942. Hundreds more were evacuated to central and western Slovakia in May 1944; dozens joined the partisans and the Czechoslovakian army and another few hundred were murdered by the Germans in the city. The affiliated postwar community dwindled from 716 in 1945 to about 100 in 1990.

PRESTICE Bohemia, Czechoslovakia. Jews were present before 1685. In the late 19th cent., P. was a regional center for Jews in the area and in 1862 the J. pop. was 750, dropping to 430 in 1900. In 1930, the J. pop. in P. was 54 (1% of the total). A synagogue was erected in 1910. Jews were especially active in textiles. In Jan. 1942, the Jews were deported to the Theresienstadt ghetto. A few weeks later most were sent to the death camps of the east.

PRETZFELD Upper Franconia, Germany. Jews are mentioned in the 14th cent. and in the 16th and 17th cents. resided on estates belonging to the nobility. In 1719 they were restricted to the cattle trade and in the late 18th cent. most of their letters of protection were canceled and they left. The community numbered 75 in 1812 (total 779) and ended in 1866 when it was attached to Hagenbach.

PREUSSISCH-FRIEDLAND (Pol. Debrzno) Posen–West Prussia, Germany, today Poland. At the beginning of the 19th cent., 14 J. families were living in the town. By 1831, the J. pop. had grown to 141 and in 1880 to 287. In the early 20th cent., there were about 150 Jews living in P. By the end of the 19th century a synagogue and a cemetery were established. After the Nazi assumption of power in 1933, the economic situation changed very rapidly for the 118 Jews living in P. Up to 1935, J. property was continually attacked, the windows of the synagogue and private homes were frequently broken, and tombstones were overturned. On *Kristallnacht* (9–10 Nov. 1938), the synagogue was destroyed, J. business premises were demolished, and J. men were taken to the Sachsenhausen concentration camp. In 1940, the remaining Jews were arrested, interned in the Buergergarten camp near Schneidemuehl, and then deported to the east.

PREUSSISCH-HOLLAND (Pol. Paslek) East Prussia, Germany, today Poland. Jews settled in P. towards the end of the 17th cent. The community grew to 175 in 1880, but soon afterwards began to decline. A synagogue was built in the early 1860s. The cemetery was desecrated in 1930 and in 1931 Nazis attacked a Jew, who subsequently died of his injuries. About 60 Jews were living in P. when the Nazis came to power. By 1938, only about 15 remained and the community was dissolved. Although the synagogue had been sold, it was set on fire on *Kristallnacht* (9–10 Nov. 1938). By May 1939, there were only eight Jews in

P. It may be assumed that those who did not emigrate were deported, with the exception of one still living in P. in Oct. 1942, probably protected by marriage to a non-J. partner.

PREVEZA (Preveze) Prevezis dist., Greece. Jews were present in P. in the 16th cent. but then disappeared from the town until the mid-19th cent., when Jews arrived from Janina, Arta, and Corfu. The community organized in 1903. In 1904, the J. pop. was 200. From 1908, a J. school was supported by the Alliance Israelite. Zionist activity began in 1913. The J. pop. in 1940 was 250. With the outbreak of WWII and heavy Italian bombing in the region, many fled to the surrounding villages. German occupation followed and more fled, some joining the partisans. On 25 March 1944, the Germans assembled 245 local Jews and transferred them to Arta. They were then transported with 352 Jews from Arta to Agrinion, where they were held for two days in a tobacco factory. On 2 April, they were sent to Auschwitz, part of the first transport of Jews from Athens. After the war, 17 Jews returned to P. from hiding, but their number dwindled in the following years.

PRIBETA Slovakia, Czechoslovakia, today Republic of Slovakia. Jews probably arrived in the 1820s, numbering 133 (total 3,072) in 1880 and 92 in 1941. In June 1944, they were deported to Auschwitz via Nove Zamky.

PRIBOR Moravia, Czechoslovakia. A few J. families were present in the first half of the 19th cent. Sigmund Freud was born in P. in 1856. The J. pop. was 157 in 1890 and 48 (1% of the total) in 1930. In Sept. 1942, the Jews were deported to the Theresienstadt ghetto via Ostrava. From there nearly all were immediately transported to Maly Trostinec, where they perished.

PRIBRAM Bohemia, Czechoslovakia. Jews were probably present in the 14th–15th cents. A synagogue was erected in 1874 and the J. pop. numbered 300 in 1921 and 235 (total 10,469) in 1930. In 1942 the Jews were deported to the Theresienstadt ghetto together with the Jews of Prague and from there sent to death camps in the east.

PRICHSENSTADT Lower Franconia, Germany.

Jews were present in 1462 and were living under various letters of protection from 1528. They numbered 74 in 1880 (total 761) and 53 in 1933. Sixteen left up to early 1938. On *Kristallnacht* (9–10 Nov. 1938), the synagogue was vandalized and religious articles set on fire in the street. The Jews were then forced to sell their homes and reside in a single house. By 1941 another 17 had left. Of the remaining ten, seven were deported to Izbica in the Lublin dist. (Poland) via Wuerzburg on 25 April 1942 and three to the Theresienstadt ghetto on 23 Sept.

PRIEKOPA Slovakia, Czechoslovakia, today Republic of Slovakia. J. settlement probably began in the 18th cent. After the arrival of refugees from Galicia in the mid-19th cent., the community grew steadily, numbering 115 (total 381) in 1880. In 1941, under Hungarian rule, the J. pop. was 89. The Jews were deported to Auschwitz in May 1944.

PRIEKULE Kurzeme (Courland) dist., Latvia. A few dozen Jews lived there after WWI; 23 were executed by the Germans around 1 Nov. 1941.

PRIENAI (Yid. Pren) Marijampole dist., Lithuania. Jews first settled in the 15th cent. In antisemitic riots on 15 Aug. 1882, many Jews were injured, as was the local priest, who tried to defend them. The community maintained four synagogues. In 1883, 30 families founded an association for settlement in Eretz Israel. The J. pop. in 1897 stood at 1,190 (48% of the total). The Russians expelled P.'s Jews in WWI. Some returned after the war to find their homes and institutions ransacked and destroyed. Between the World Wars, a third of municipal council members were Jews. Many Jews emigrated overseas after their economic situation deteriorated as a result of an anti-J. boycott. The Zionist movement won widespread support. During the 1930s a Hebrew school was established. The J. pop. in 1940 was 650 (16% of the total). After the German invasion in June 1941, Lithuanian nationalists took control of the town and executed J. intellectuals. On 26 Aug., all Jews were taken to an animal cemetery, where pits had been dug, and shot.

PRIEVIDZA (Hung. Privigye) Slovakia, Czechoslovakia, today Republic of Slovakia. Jews first settled in 1808, with a community constituted at mid-cent. and the J. pop. reaching 308 (total 2,858) in 1880. A prayer house was consecrated in 1860 and a J. elementary school was opened in 1863. The congregation defined itself as Status Quo after the split of 1869 and built a synagogue in the late 19th cent. J. homes and stores were looted in post-WWI riots. The Zionists were influential in the community. Jews served on the municipal council and in 1921 owned 45 business establishments, nine workshops, and several factories. After the establishment of the Slovakian state in March 1939, Jews were pushed out of their businesses and seized for forced labor. In 1940, their pop. was 403. On 31 March 1942, 145 young J. men and women were deported to Majdanek and Auschwitz, respectively. On 5 June, another 267 Jews were deported to the ghettoes and death camps of the Lublin dist. in Poland. Most of the remaining few dozen Jews managed to escape before the arrival of the Germans in 1944.

PRIJEDOR Bosnia-Hercegovina, Yugoslavia, today Republic of Bosnia. Jews first settled there in the late 19th cent. There were 43 in 1940. Nearly all perished in 1941 when the Ustase expelled them to Banja Luka and from there to the Jasenovac death camp.

PRILUKI Chernigov dist., Ukraine. Jews were present in the 16th cent. but the community ended in the Chmielnicki massacres of 1648–49. It was renewed at the end of the cent. but its pop. only grew significantly from the early 19th cent., reaching a figure of 5,722 (total 18,532) in 1897. Jews owned two tobacco factories, two flour mills, and a few small oil presses. Jews were prominent in the manufacture of readymade wear and their sale in distant markets and fairs. In addition to *hadarim*, the community maintained schools for boys and girls and from the early 20th cent., a Hebrew-language school and kindergarten. The J. political parties, primarily the Zionists, were active and also continued to operate after the Oct. 1917 Revolution. A pioneer group left for Palestine in 1921 and helped found Kibbutz Kiryat Anavim. Pogroms broke out during the civil war, on 23 Oct. 1917, on 4–14 June 1919 (with fatalities), and in Sept. 1919. During the 1920s, a J. law court operated and Yiddish was used in the municipal council. In 1927, most Jews (65%) were employed as factory hands and artisans and 165 Jews were members of a J. kolkhoz. In the late 1920s, 80 J. families moved to Birobidzhan and dozens more to J. kolkhozes in Kherson, Krivoi Rog, and the Crimea. In 1930, the

J. pop. was 6,140. The Germans captured the city on 18 Sept. 1941. Some of the Jews managed to flee. On 15 Jan. 1942, a few hundred were shot. On 20 May 1942, another 1,290 were executed and hundreds more on 10 July and 10 Sept. In all, about 3,000 Jews perished in the Holocaust. In 1959, the J. pop. was about 2,000.

PRISLOP (Hung. Nagypriszlog) Carpatho-Russia, Czechoslovakia, today Ukraine. Jews probably arrived in the late 18th cent., numbering 100 in 1830 and 164 (total 934) in 1880. A few were farmers. In 1921, the J. pop. was 199; in 1941, 163. Following the Hungarian occupation in March 1939, Jews were drafted into forced labor battalions. In summer 1941 a number of Jews without Hungarian citizenship were expelled to the German-occupied Ukraine and murdered. The rest were deported to Auschwitz in late May 1944.

PRISTINA Serbia, Yugoslavia. In 1897 a synagogue was built and by 1913 the J. pop. was 452 (total 10,000). The Zionist movement was active in the 1920s and 1930s. Prior to the Holocaust some 50 refugees arrived from Germany, Austria, and Czechoslovakia and the community saw to their needs. In 1940 there were 385 Jews in P. In April–June 1941 the Germans occupied P. and the Jews suffered degradation and forced labor. From June 1941, under Italian rule, Jews who had not joined the partisans or gone into hiding were sent to Albania. The Germans took over again in Sept. 1943 and in May 1944 arrested the few Jews who had returned from Albania. They were taken to a camp

Purim party, Pristina, Yugoslavia (Beth Hatefutsoth Photo Archive, Tel Aviv/courtesy of Jenny Lebel, Tel Aviv)

and tortured and then sent to Bergen-Belsen. Most of these Jews survived the Holocaust and the great majority of them moved to Israel at the end of 1948.

PRIUTNOYE Zaporozhe dist., Ukraine. Jews from the Vitebsk region founded P. as a J. colony in 1848. It had a pop. of 616 (mostly Jews) in 1858. In 1897, the J. pop. was 292 (55 families). A J. kolkhoz with a few dozen new J. settlers from Podolia was attached to the colony in 1924 and in 1929 P. was included in the Novo-Zlatopol J. Autonomous Region. A J. rural council (soviet) had its seat in the colony and a J. elementary school was active. P. was captured by the Germans in Oct. 1941. In Feb. 1942, Ukrainian police murdered 19 or 20 Jews. Another eight Jews were discovered dead shortly afterwards.

PROBUZNA Tarnopol dist., Poland, today Ukraine. Jews were present from the late 18th cent., with an organized community from the 1830s or 1840s. The J. pop. climbed from 978 in 1880 to 1,226 in 1921 (40% of the total). Between the World Wars the economic position of the Jews deteriorated in the face of competition from the Ukrainian cooperatives and anti-J. agitation while the Zionist groups increased their influence. Most of the Jews, together with refugees arriving from Husyatin, were deported by the Germans to the Belzec death camp on 30 Sept. 1942; the rest to Kopyczynce in Oct.

PROLETARSK Voroshilovgrad dist., Ukraine. The J. pop. in 1939 was 109 (total 21,071). After their arrival on 10 July 1942, the Germans murdered the remaining Jews.

PROLETARSKOYE (until 1925, Grafskaya) Zaporozhe dist., Ukraine. Jews from the Vitebsk and Mogilev regions founded P. as a J. colony in 1848. In 1858 its pop. was 450, mostly Jews. Neighboring villagers staged a pogrom on 6 May 1881 in which J. property was looted. The J. pop. in 1922 was 249. The Germans captured P. in Oct. 1941 and apparently murdered the Jews still there shortly afterwards.

PROPOISK (Slavgorod) Mogilev dist., Belorussia. Jew settled in the 16th cent., numbering 148 in 1766 and 2,304 (total 4,351) in 1897. A synagogue and four *battei midrash* were erected in the early 19th cent. In 1926, under the Soviets, the J. pop. was 1,513. Artisan cooperatives were opened in the late 1920s, with Jews representing 44% of the town's craftsmen in 1929. In 1930, 50 J. families worked in a nearby kolkhoz. Some Jews were faithful to religious tradition and until 1935 several J. cooperatives did not work on the J. Sabbath and on J. holidays. A J. elementary school was active in the town. In 1939, the J. pop. was 1,038. The Germans captured P. in Aug. 1941. Some Jews succeeded in escaping. A ghetto was established immediately after the occupation. The Jews were shot in Nov. 1941 and the children drowned in a lake.

PROSKUROV (from 1954, Khmelnitski) Kamenets-Podolski dist., Ukraine. Jews are first mentioned in 1629, when the town was called Ploskirov. They were pillaged by Chmielnicki's Cossacks in the mid-17th cent. In 1765 there were 750 Jews in P., with many artisans earning their living as shoemakers, weavers, tailors, furriers, blacksmiths, and coopers. By 1847, the J. pop. was 3,107. When the town was linked to the Zhmerinka–Volochisk railway line, this accelerated economic development and boosted J. wholesale trade, particularly in lumber, grain, and textiles. Jews also owned a number of factories (sugar, bricks and roof tiles, ceramics, tobacco, candles). In 1897, the J. pop. was 11,411 (total 22,855). The community maintained nine synagogues and a J. hospital. Educational facilities included 18 *hadarim* and a *talmud torah*, augmented by a J. library, reading room, and theater. After the Feb. 1917 Revolution, 24 of the municipal council's 50 members were Jews. On 15 Feb. 1919, during the civil war, the Petlyura gangs massacred over 1,600 Jews and crippled many for life. In the Soviet period, many documents in the municipality and law courts were drawn up in Yiddish. A J. school was also operating at this time. In 1939, the J. pop. was 14,518. The Germans captured the city on 7 July 1941, executing over 800 Jews towards the end of Aug. Jews from the surrounding area were transferred to labor camps in the city. About 8,000 Jews were murdered in Aug. 1942, including 2,700 from P. Another 7,000 were executed on 30 Nov. 1942. Nearly 18,000 Jews were murdered in P.

PROSTEJOV (Yid. Prostich) Moravia, Czechoslovakia. Jews are mentioned in 1445 with the community most likely founded in 1454 by Jews expelled from Olomouc and other royal cities. Jews traded in livestock, grain, wool, feathers, cloth, and silk. The J.

Street scene, Proskurov, Ukraine

pop. grew with the arrival of refugees after the Chmiel-nicki massacres of 1648–49 and the expulsion from Vienna in 1670. A second synagogue was opened in 1676. J. commercial success led to riots in the 1670s, with J. stores destroyed in the ghetto. Two Jews were hanged in 1683. Persecution continued into the 18th cent. A big fire destroyed many J. homes in 1697 and fires in 1823 and 1847 caused further damage. In the 17th–19th cents. the community was the second largest in Moravia after Mikulov and was known as the "Jerusalem of the Hana Valley" for its religious scholarship. Moravia's first Hebrew printing press operated in P. From the early 19th cent to WWII, the J. pop. ranged from 1,500 to 1,800. The first modern J. textile plant was founded in P. in 1831 and the first in Europe for readymade wear in 1859. The community enjoyed political autonomy in 1849–1919. After WWI, the J. cultural center was the first to offer courses in modern Hebrew and Zionist activity was extensive. Of 140 textile establishments in the city, over 100 belonged to Jews and the local Sborowitz family owned a countrywide chain of 108 stores. The philosopher Edmund Husserl (1859–1938) was born in P. In fall 1938, J. refugees from the Sudetenland flooded the city and anti-J. agitation commenced almost immediately. After the German occupation of Bohemia and Moravia in March 1939,

the Gestapo constantly harassed the Jews with searches, arrests, and various forms of abuse. The synagogue was vandalized in June 1939 and closed by the Nazis in 1940. Many Jews managed to emigrate in 1940. By late 1941, the J. working pop. (aged 16–60) numbered 903. Young men were sent to Zarovice as farm laborers. In early 1942, J. family heads without Czech citizenship papers were sent to concentration camps. In June and July 1942, the rest were assembled in Olomouc and from there deported to the Theresienstadt ghetto. Within a few weeks they were sent on to Maly Trostinec and Baranovici and to the Treblinka death camp, where they perished. Jews who were married to non-Jews were deported to Theresienstadt in 1943–45. Over 1,200 local Jews perished in the Holocaust.

PROSTKEN   (Pol. Prostki) East Prussia, Germany, today Poland. In 1905, the J. pop. of P. was 82. The community maintained a cemetery and held religious services in a private house. Since P. was an important border crossing point in the early 20th cent., the Association of East Prussian Communities established an office to care for needy J. immigrants from Eastern Europe. No information is available about the fate of the 56 Jews who were living in P. when the Nazis came to power.

PROSTYN Lublin dist., Poland. Jews probably arrived in the late 19th cent. In 1921 they numbered 136 (total 669). After the German occupation in Sept. 1939, they were sent to Backi for forced labor. In Sept. 1942, they were deported to the Treblinka death camp.

PROSZOWICE Kielce dist., Poland. Jews may have been present by the 16th cent. but are first mentioned only in the early 19th cent. Their pop. grew to 639 in 1897 and 1,307 (total 3,297) in 1921. Most Jews owned small stores or were peddlers. The more substantial merchants dealt in grain, livestock, and lumber, while J. artisans were mainly tailors, carpenters, and shoemakers. Between the World Wars a *matza* (unleavened bread) factory was known throughout Poland. With the intensification of antisemitism in the late 1930s, the Zionists won control of the community council from Agudat Israel. Both opened schools in the 1930s (Tarbut and Beth Jacob). Occupying the town in Sept. 1939, the Germans systematically looted J. property and soon after confiscated their businesses. Jews were subjected to forced labor and during periodic visits by the Germans, who did not maintain a permanent presence in P., beaten, robbed, and sometimes murdered. A ghetto was never established in P. and Jews continued to live in their houses and to practice their professions as before. A thousand refugees joined the 2,000 Jews of P. in 1939–40. They were housed with local Jews and fed from a soup kitchen. On 29 Aug. 1942, 2,000 Jews were transferred to the Slomniki transit camp. From there most were deported to the Belzec death camp. Although many fled, 100–200 Jews remained in P. after the *Aktion*. Others were murdered by peasants. The last Jews were sent to Belzec in Nov. 1942. Sixty survivors returned but left when two were murdered by Polish nationalists.

PRUCHNIK Lwow dist., Poland. Jews are first recorded in 1563 but only formed an organized community in the 1860s, attaining a pop. of 800 (total 1,796) in 1900. Many emigrated after WWI, to Vienna, Berlin, and the U.S., in the face of economic hardship. Between the World Wars, heavy taxes, competition from the cooperatives, and anti-J. agitation added to the distress of the community. Various Zionist groups were active from 1919. The Germans arrived in Sept. 1939 and commenced a regime of persecution. On the initiative of the Polish mayor, the town's 150 J. families were assembled for expulsion across the San River in

Nov., but left stranded in a freezing field for two weeks when the Soviets refused to receive them. Most managed to return, some after being transported to Cracow, and were forced to inhabit the J. poor quarter after finding their homes destroyed. All were sent to the Pelkinia transit camp in Aug. 1942, where some were murdered. The rest were deported to the Belzec death camp.

PRUDNOYE Tula dist., Russia. The Germans arrived in Oct. 1941 and on 19 Nov. assembled a few dozen Jews from P. and the neighboring villages and burned about 20 alive in a warehouse in one of the nearby kolkhozes.

PRUNDUL BARGAULUI (Hung. Borgoprund) N. Transylvania dist., Rumania. Jews settled in the mid-19th cent. The J. pop. in 1930 was 325 (10% of the total). P served as a center for other communities: Aldorf with a J. pop. of 37; Bistrita-Bargaului with 33; Budus (41); Lad (30); Mijloceni Bargaului (43); Mureseni Bargaului (82); Suseni Bargaului (49); Tiha Bargaului (37). Most Jews were Sighet Hasidim. A Zionist organization functioned from the 1920s. In May 1944 the community and those of the neighboring villages were transferred to the Bistrita ghetto and in June deported to Auschwitz.

PRUSKE Slovakia, Czechoslovakia, today Republic of Slovakia. Jews from Moravia apparently settled in the early 18th cent. The community reached a peak pop. of about 125 (10% of the total) in the 1870s, forming a Status Quo congregation and building a synagogue in 1874. Jews enjoyed favorable economic conditions, owning a number of stores, a sawmill, and a brickyard. Forty remained in 1940. In spring 1942, they were deported either to Auschwitz or to the death camps in the Lublin dist. (Poland).

PRUSZKOW Warsaw dist., Poland. J. settlement began in the second half of the 19th cent., with an organized community formed in 1904. The basis of the community was laid when land was donated for a synagogue and cemetery by two of its wealthier members, Mordekhai Gottovitch and Yaakov Teichfeld. The latter owned a porcelain factory. Other J. factories produced printers' inks, glassware, and chemical products, their proprietors forming the community's well-to-do class along with a number of merchants. Numerous additional prayer houses served the Hasidim, with the Skiernie-wice sect particularly prominent. The J. pop. stood at 971 (total 15,132) in 1921. After WWI, dozens of Jews helped support their families while working in Warsaw. The Zionist movement, which became active under the German occupation in WWI, was dominated in its first years by the General Zionists. Poa'lei Zion gained influence in the late 1920s and Hehalutz undertook pioneer training. Antisemitism intensified in the 1930s as Polish gangs attacked Jews and an economic boycott was introduced. The Germans entered the city on 7 Sept. 1939. A *Judenrat* was set up in Oct. and at least 1,000 Jews were confined to a small ghetto area behind the porcelain factory where up to eight families were crowded into each apartment. Epidemics immediately broke out. The Jews tried to lead a normal life, operating a clandestine school, library, and drama circle. In Feb. 1941, all but 180 workers were transferred to Warsaw, suffering the fate of the Jews there with some fighting in the ghetto uprising. Of those left behind, most were deported to the Treblinka death camp in summer 1942 while others were murdered on the spot.

PRUZHANA   Polesie dist., Poland, today Belarus. Jews began to settle around the mid-15th cent. In 1623 the community was under the aegis of Brzesc and from 1644 enjoyed extensive residence and trade privileges. The community grew significantly in the second half of the 19th cent, reaching a pop. of 5,080 in 1897 (total 7,633). Trade centered on cattle, farm produce, and wooden utensils and most of P.'s 99 stores were in J. hands, with weekly market days and four yearly trade fairs constituting major sources of income. A fire in 1863 destroyed 300 homes and the three largest of P.'s nine synagogues; a cholera epidemic in 1871–72 claimed many lives. Zionist activity commenced at the turn of the cent. and a Bund group was founded in 1904. J. tradesmen prospered at the outset of WWI supplying the Russian army, but under the Austro-German occupation of 1915–17 the Jews were put to forced labor and restricted in their movements. They all suffered from a typhoid epidemic. In the void created by the German withdrawal a J. self-defense group with 100 armed members helped keep order. Under Polish rule the J. pop. stood at somewhat above 4,000, living in straitened economic circumstances. The community operated an orphanage and old age home. There was a Hebrew school and a Yiddish

school, each with over 200 students, and rival weekly journals were published in the two languages. There was also a yeshiva in the town. The Soviets arrived in Sept. 1939, annexing P. to the Belorussian Republic and soon closing down commerce and J. schools. The Germans took the town on 23 June 1941. A *Judenrat* was set up and 18 alleged J. Communists were executed. On 10 Aug. the Jews were ordered into a ghetto. Thousands of refugees from Bialystok and the neighboring towns began to arrive in Sept., pushing the ghetto pop. up to 18,000 and considerably reducing living space. Starvation was avoided by smuggling food into the ghetto as well as medicines and Jews were placed under a regime of forced labor, working in construction, logging, and peat gathering. The liquidation of the ghetto commenced on 28 Jan. 1943 when three transports took the Jews to Auschwitz-Birkenau. In Birkenau, 2,000 men and women were selected for labor (only 200 of the latter surviving the war). Of the 2,700 Jews who fled during the *Aktion*, most were caught and murdered. Many of those reaching the forests joined the partisans.

PRZASNYSZ   (Yid. Proshnitz) Warsaw dist., Poland. Jews first settled in the 16th cent. At the end of the 18th cent. a synagogue and cemetery were established. A J. quarter existed in 1822–62. Some Jews dealt in lumber, but most were tradesmen or artisans. In the 19th cent. Hasidism spread and P.'s first Zionist group was organized in the 1890s. Eventually the entire range of Zionist youth groups and the Bund were active. Early in WWI the Russians expelled the Jews. After the Germans captured the town in July 1915, Jews returned, reduced to dire poverty. The J. pop. in 1897 was 3,554 (total 7,771) declining to 2,158 (36%) in 1921. Antisemitism increased from the mid-1930s and J. goods were boycotted. When the Germans took the town in the first days of the war, the Jews fled, but soon returned. Expelled at the end of Sept. 1939, some again returned but were sent to Makow Mazowiecki in 1940. Jews in a local labor camp paved roads until their deportation in 1943 to the Stutthof concentration camp.

PRZECLAW   Cracow dist., Poland. Jews first arrived in the early 18th cent. but only formed an organized community in the late 19th. The J. pop. reached 299 (total 1,026) in 1880, dropping to 158 in 1921 through emigration. The Zionists were active between

Synagogue in Przedborz, Poland

the World Wars. In spring 1941, the Germans dispersed the Jews to larger settlements to await their end.

PRZEDBORZ Lodz dist., Poland. J. settlement began in the late 16th cent. A wooden synagogue, considered to be one of the most beautiful buildings in central Poland, was built in the mid-18th cent. Many distinguished rabbis served in P., including R. Yeshayahu Weltfreid (d. 1831), the founder of the P. hasidic dynasty. The J. pop. was 4,089 in 1897 (69% of the total) and 4,500 in 1939. Nearly all the J. parties were active, except the Bund, Mizrachi being the strongest Zionist party. A large group of J. Communists was active in cultural life. The J. quarter, including the ancient synagogue, was destroyed in the opening battles of WWII. A *Judenrat* was set up, and 2,800 Jews were ghettoized in 1940; by April 1942, with the influx of refugees, they numbered 4,300. On 9 Oct. 1942, P.'s Jews were expelled to Radomsko and on 10–12 Oct.

they were deported to the Treblinka death camp. In 1945, nine survivors were murdered by members of the Polish rightist movement.

PRZEDECZ Warsaw dist., Poland. Jews apparently settled in P. in the 14th cent. The J. pop. numbered 606 (31% of the total) in 1857 and 840 in 1921. The Zionists were influential in the community. The Germans took the town early in WWII and burned the synagogue, blaming the Jews. Half the Jews were sent to forced labor camps in the Poznan dist. in 1940. The others were kept in a ghetto until it was demolished in 1942. Those remaining were expelled to Chelmno after being held without water for three days.

PRZEMYSL Lwow dist., Poland. J. traders may have been active in P. from the tenth cent. and a permanent J. settlement probably existed under Ruthenian rule before the annexation to Poland in 1340 by King

Synagogue in Przemysl, Poland (Sammlony Franz Haberman/photo courtesy of Yad Vashem, The Holocaust Martyrs' and Heroes' Remembrance Authority, Jerusalem)

Casimir the Great. In 1559, under King Sigismund Augustus, the Jews were granted extensive residence and trade privileges and the J. pop. increased from 13 families in 1565 to 300 in 1671. Throughout the period, local townsmen attempted to undermine the position of the Jews, resorting to periodic outbursts of violence. Jews nonetheless continued to expand their trade and from the late 15th cent. maintained commercial relations with Hungarian Jews, importing wine, metals, oil, and furs and exporting salt and cattle. Jews also operated a beer brewery and flour mill and engaged in tax farming. Despite fierce opposition, J. tradesmen, such as butchers, tailors, and bakers, were active, though many had to pursue their livelihoods clandestinely. Though the Jews were spared bodily harm in the wars of the 17th and 18th cents., wartime conditions took a heavy economic toll, compounded by discriminatory taxation and continuing anti-J. agitation, with rampaging Jesuit students staging a virtual pogrom in 1746. The community nevertheless remained one of the largest and most important in the Rzeszow province and with the decline of Lwow's influence it had 100 smaller communities attached to it in 1765. The onset of Austrian rule in 1772 with its punitive fiscal measures further debilitated the community. The Christian guilds continued their efforts to restrict J. craftsmen but most merchants (137 of 143 in 1820) were Jews. With the coming of the railroad and the large-scale fortification of the city in the second half of the 19th cent. an era of economic prosperity set in. Jews supplied steel, grain, and foodstuffs, set up flour mills, sawmills, and brickyards, and acted as building contractors. However, most remained petty traders operating stalls in the markets or peddling their wares in the surrounding villages. Many emigrated to the U.S. in the 1880s. The J. pop. grew from 2,298 in 1830 to 10,998 in 1890 and 16,062 (total 54,078) in 1910. In the second half of the 19th cent., Hasidism began to spread, with the Blazowa (Dynow), Belz, and Sadagora sects predominating. Their political rivals in the community were the assimilationists, organized in the Shomer Israel society and known as "*Deutschen*" for their modern clothes and clean-shaven appearance. Their center was the Scientific Literature Reading Room, which built up a collection of 30,000 volumes. A Temple for "enlightened" worshipers and J. soldiers in the local garrison accustomed to a modern service was completed in 1890. The Zionists became active in the 1890s and the Polish Socialist Party attracted many Jews at around the turn

of the cent. when modern cultural frameworks began to arise for the first time among the Jews, including drama, sports, and social clubs. However, most Jews in P. preserved a traditional outlook, with the *heder, beit midrash*, and *klaus* the predominating educational institutes. Among the leading rabbis was Yitzhak Yehuda Schmelkes, who headed the rabbinical court in 1869–93 and wrote the well-known *Beit Yitzhak* on the *Shulhan Arukh*. His nephew R. Gedalya Schmelkes served as rabbi from 1905 and worked to unify the community, even attending Zionist Congresses in 1909 and 1911. The community operated extensive welfare services, building a new hospital in 1904–05 and an old age home in 1907 as well as operating a ward for the terminally ill, an orphanage, and a soup kitchen. With the approach of the Russian army in Sept. 1914, some 8,000 Jews fled the city. The Russians entered P. after a four-month siege that left the city ravaged. In May 1915 all the remaining Jews were expelled, returning two months later with the arrival of the Austrians to find their homes destroyed and belongings gone. After the Poles gained control of the city in Nov. 1918, the Jews were subjected to a pogrom in which 67 homes and 76 stores were looted by soldiers. Between the World Wars the Jews remained in dire economic straits, struck hard by the general economic crisis as well as anti-J. agitation and the competition of the Polish and Ukrainian cooperatives. About half the J. pop. engaged in petty trade and there were about 100 J. doctors and 100 J. lawyers in the city. The Zionist youth movements intensified their activities, with Hashomer Hatzair having 500 members in the early 1920s and Gordonia 300 in the 1930s. Agudat Israel also became active, founding the Etz Hayyim yeshiva (enrollment 200) and a Beth Jacob school for girls. A second yeshiva also enrolled 200 and ordained rabbis. J. elementary, secondary, and vocational schools were also opened between the wars. In 1931 there were 17,300 Jews in the city. Antisemitism intensified in the 1930s, with physical attacks increasing between 1936 and 1938. The city was captured by the Germans on 14 Sept. 1939. Within a few days 600 Jews were executed. Before withdrawing in the face of the Soviet advance, the Germans burned down a number of synagogues, including the Temple, and looted J. stores. The Red Army arrived on 28 Sept. and immediately closed down all J. institutions. A number of community leaders were exiled to the Soviet Union, as were about 7,000 Jews, mainly refugees, in

Members of Tze'irei Tziyyon and Herzl Society, Przemysl, Poland

April–June 1940. The Germans retook the city on 28 June 1941. In July a *Judenrat* was set up and made responsible for supplying forced labor. Through the summer Jews were arrested and murdered at the city jail. In Nov., about 1,000 were sent to labor camps as the killing of supposed collaborators continued. Extortionate "contributions" were exacted from the community and furs confiscated. During the winter many died of starvation and disease. In the spring another 1,000 young Jews were sent to the Janowska Road labor camp in Lwow. In July 1942, the city's 22,000 Jews were crowded into a ghetto and work permits withheld from all but 5,000. On 27 July, 7,000 Jews without work permits were deported to the Belzec death camp. The sick and old were murdered in the streets, as were those who attempted to escape. Three days later the *Aktion* was renewed and another 3,000 were sent to Belzec. On 3 Aug. patients in the J. hospital were murdered and after a selection among permit holders, an additional 3,000 were deported, leaving behind essential workers in German factories and those in hiding. About 100 of the latter were lured out of their

hiding places with a promise of clemency and murdered at the J. cemetery. After a new selection on 18 Nov. 1942, a further 4,000 Jews were deported to Belzec, including all the children in the J. orphanage. The ghetto was now divided into two sections: Ghetto A for about 800 essential workers and Ghetto B for those now classified as unfit for work (about 4,000 Jews) but nonetheless sent out to forced labor each day. On 2 Sept. 1943, 3,500 Jews in Ghetto B were sent to Auschwitz and a day later 600 Jews were removed from Ghetto A and sent to the Szebnie labor camp. Jews in hiding continued to be rounded up and on 10–11 Sept., 1,200 were executed. The 200 or so remaining were sent to labor camps or to Auschwitz in the following months. In 1943 there were cases of resistance in the ghetto by groups and by individuals and attempts to make contact with partisans in the forests. About 250 survivors appeared in the city when it was liberated by the Soviets on 27 July 1944.

PRZEMYSLANY Tarnopol dist., Poland, today Ukraine. Jews are first mentioned in the late 16th cent. A local hasidic dynasty founded in the 18th cent. was prominent for many years. Zionist activity was marked from the early 20th cent. The J. pop. in 1900 was 2,934 (total 4,743). A fire in 1910 left 200 J. families homeless and the town was burned again by the Russian garrison in WWI. These events, combined with Cossack depredations and a cholera epidemic, reduced the postwar pop. to 2,051. There was extensive Zionist activity between the World Wars. The German occupation of 1 July 1941 inaugurated a reign of terror with the active partnership of the Ukrainians. The synagogue was burned on 15 July and around ten Jews thrown into the flames. On 5 Nov., 450 men aged 18–60 were murdered in the forest after a selection. In May 1942 dozens of hospital patients were murdered and in the summer and fall hundreds were deported to Belzec. In Oct. 1942 the Jews were packed into a ghetto and from there around 3,000 were sent to the Belzec death camp on 5 Dec. Most of those remaining in the ghetto were killed off on 22 May 1943 while those in the local labor camp were executed on 28 June.

PRZEROSL Bialystok dist., Poland. Jews first settled in P. in the 18th cent. They numbered 690 (36% of the total) in 1857 and 185 (25%) in 1921. Almost all the Jews were expelled when the Germans took the city in Oct. 1939 and died in the Holocaust.

PRZEWORSK Lwow dist., Poland. Jews settled in the early 16th cent. and despite residence and trade restrictions the community grew, living mainly off the grain and cattle trade but also operating as moneylenders and tax farmers. Throughout the 19th cent. a traditional-hasidic atmosphere prevailed, with Zionist influence making itself felt in the early 20th cent. The J. pop. stood at 1,224 (total 2,926) in 1880 and reached a peak of 1,477 in 1910 after the economy was boosted by the opening of a big sugar refinery in 1895. Between the World Wars, anti-J. feeling persisted but when a big fire in 1930 leveled J. homes the Christian pop. offered assistance. The Germans took the town on 14 Sept. 1939 and around 28 Sept. (Sukkot) expelled almost the entire J. community of 2,000 across the San River into Soviet-held territory. At the end of 1940, 35 Jews remained; they were murdered in Aug. 1942. Many survived the war in the Soviet Union.

PRZYBOROWICE GORNE Warsaw dist., Poland. The J. pop. was 130 in 1915 (total 323). In summer

17th cent. synagogue in Przeworsk, Poland

1941 those with German papers were transferred to the Plonsk ghetto and the others to the Pomiechowek concentration camp.

PRZYBYSZEW Warsaw dist., Poland. The J. pop. was 104 in 1921 (total 1,089). The Jews were probably expelled to the Germans to the Warsaw ghetto in Feb. 1941.

PRZYGLOW Lodz dist., Poland. The J. pop. of this summer resort was 50 (58% of the total) in 1921. The Germans arrived on 6 Sept. 1939. In June 1940, the Jews numbered 450, mainly refugees, and in April 1942, 2,251. The *Judenrat* was unable to prevent deaths from starvation and unsanitary conditions. On 13–21 Oct. 1942, 2,000 Jews were deported to the Treblinka death camp.

PRZYROW Kielce dist., Poland. Jews are first mentioned in the late 18th cent. and numbered 954 (total 2,206) in 1857. At the turn of the cent., they formed an organized community with a synagogue and cemetery. The depredations of WWI caused many to leave. Despite unremitting economic hardship between the World Wars, Zionist activity continued unabated. The Germans found 715 Jews there when they captured P. in Sept. 1939. Many were sent to a local labor camp in 1940 and on 18 Sept. 1942 all were expelled to Koniecepol and from there deported on 7 Oct. to the Treblinka death camp.

PRZYSUCHA (Yid. Pshischa) Lodz dist., Poland. The increase in the J. pop. from 1,658 in 1827 to 2,168 (75% of the total) in 1897 was due to P.'s position as a center of Hasidism led by R. Yaacov Yitzhak, known as "the Holy Jew" (d. 1814 or 1815), and his successor, R. Simha Bunem (d. 1827). A source of income was the sale of metal and leather goods fashioned by local artisans. J. political parties including most Zionist groups and the Bund were active here only after WWI. The community was governed mainly by trade union representatives. Between the World Wars there were manifestations of antisemitism and Poles opened shops to compete with J. businesses. When the Germans entered P. on 8 Sept. 1939, the J. pop. was about 2,500. By 1942, the *Judenrat* was forced to find accommodations for an additional 1,500 refugees and displaced persons whose residential quarters had been sequestered for military training. One hundred and eight J. families from Przytyk were transferred here. The ghetto was set up in 1941 or early 1942 and in summer 1942 all members of the *Judenrat* and the J. police were murdered. On 27–31 Oct. 1942 all the Jews were transported to the Treblinka death camp.

PRZYTYK Kielce dist., Poland. Jews first settled in the mid-15th cent., constituting a large group of artisans and merchants (dealing in mead, lumber, hides, and grain). By the early 19th cent., Jews comprised 85% of the total pop. and in 1897 they numbered 1,504 (total pop. 1,802). P. was known for its Hasidism. R. Yitzhak Dov Baer, prominent among the Kotsk Hasidim, settled there. In the late 19th cent., rabid antisemitism made itself felt, encouraged by the Endecja Party. During WWI, the Jews were expelled by the Russians in 1915 and returned only in 1917. Although Agudat Israel controlled communal institutions, the Zionists and Bundists were active between the World Wars. In the late 1920s, a process of economic decline set in, exacerbated by extreme anti-J. agitation again led by the Endecja Party. Violent rioting erupted in the market on 4 March 1936, as the police stood idly by. Jews organized self-defense groups, but on 9 March a pogrom was staged during which J. market stalls were overturned and Jews beaten and robbed. A Jew fired shots at the rioters and the attacks spread to J. homes, where three Jews were beaten to death and many injured. In the court proceedings that followed, the severest punishments were meted out to the Jews who had tried to defend themselves. Subsequently, 30 J. families left the city for Radom. The traumatic effect of the pogrom was echoed in Mordekhai Gebirtig's famous song *"Undzer Shtetl Brent"*

("Our Town is Burning"). In 1939, there were 2,309 Jews in P. The German occupation of Sept. 1939 introduced a regime of forced labor and extortion. The synagogue and *beit midrash* were burned down and a *Judenrat* was established in early 1940. Refugees increased the J. pop. to 3,500 by Feb. 1941. In April, the Jews were dispersed among other settlements. Most, together with the local Jews, were deported to the death camps, mainly to Treblinka in fall 1942.

PSKOV Leningrad dist., Russia. Jews probably settled in the mid-19th cent. A prayer house was opened in 1867 and a synagogue was erected in 1880. Most Jews were demobilized soldiers and artisans. In 1897, the J. pop. was 1,444 (total 30,000), remaining stable throughout most of the Soviet period but dropping to 1,068 in 1939. A J. elementary school (four grades) operated in the 1920s. The Germans captured the city on 9 July 1941, establishing a ghetto and forcing the Jews to wear a yellow patch on their clothes. In Feb. 1942, 1,000 Jews from P. and the surrounding area were murdered at the nearby village of Vasilevo. A concentration camp was set up near the village of Moglino where over 100 Jews from the area were also murdered. In Sept. 1943, the Germans began burning their victims' bodies to obliterate all traces of their crimes.

PSZCZYNA (Yid. Pels) Silesia dist., Poland. Jews from Bohemia first settled in the 17th cent. The community reached a peak pop. of 331 (total 3,154) in 1861 but dropped to around 20 families in 1918. The Germans captured P. in Sept. 1939, annexing it to the Third Reich. The 15 J. families who remained were put to forced labor, mostly as streetcleaners. All were expelled to Trzebinia in May 1940 to share the fate of the local Jews.

PTICH Polesie dist., Belorussia. Jews were only permitted to settle in 1903 and numbered 230 in the mid-1920s. Some owned private farms. The Germans occupied P. in late May 1941. In Dec. 1941, they murdered 28 Jews and a few days later another 25.

PTYCZA Volhynia dist., Poland. Five Jews lived in P. in 1921 (total 1,163).

PUCHOV (Hung. Pucho) Slovakia, Czechoslovakia, today Republic of Slovakia. Jews are first mentioned in the 17th cent., numbering 87 in 1768 after an influx of

Jews from Moravia. A synagogue was built in 1806. The community reached a peak pop. of 472 (total 1,466) in 1840, subsequently dropping steadily as the young left for the big cities. A J. school was opened in the 1850s and a splendid new synagogue was built in 1868 after a fire destroyed the old one in 1860. After the split of 1869, the community defined itself as Status Quo and in 1912, 17 settlements were under the jurisdiction of its rabbinate. In the Czechoslovakian Republic, Jews were active in public life and owned 40 business establishments, 12 workshops, and a number of factories. The Zionist clubroom was a focus of community activity. In 1940, 215 Jews remained. In the Slovakian state, the authorities liquidated or "Aryanized" J. businesses. In spring 1942, young men and women were deported to Majdanek and Auschwitz, respectively. Families followed them to the death camps of the east. In all, 80% of the Jews were deported in 1942.

PUDERBACH Rhineland, Germany. The J. pop. was 22 (total 272) in 1817 and 71 in 1843. It then dropped to about 20 in the late 19th cent. and rose again to 36–38 in 1925–32. Forty-two Jews from Ur-

bach and Steimel also belonged to the congregation. The synagogue built in 1911 was burned on *Kristallnacht* (9–10 Nov. 1938).

PUESTI Moldavia dist., Rumania. Jews first settled in the mid-19th cent. The J. pop. in 1930 stood at 187 (21% of the total). At the outbreak of the Soviet-Rumanian war in June 1941, the J. pop. was expelled to Barlad. After the war, the Jews did not return to P.

PUKHOVICHI Minsk dist., Belorussia. Jews are first mentioned in the late 16th cent. Their pop. grew from 154 in 1811 to 1,761 (total 1,910) in 1897. In 1926, under the Soviets, it dropped to 929. In June 1921, one of the gangs operating in the area raided the town and murdered three Jews. Another 20 Jews were carried away to the forest, never to be heard from again. A four-year J. school was founded in 1924, its enrollment reaching 100 in 1927. Many Jews worked at two nearby kolkhozes, one J. and the other mixed. The Germans captured P. in early July 1941. On 28 Sept., they murdered about 500 of P.'s Jews at Popova Gorka near the town of Marina Gorka.

Funeral of Zionist activist, Pulawy, Poland

PULA Yugoslavia. Jews lived in P. in the 15th–19th cents.

PULAWY Lublin dist., Poland. Jews arrived shortly after the Third Partition of Poland in 1795. In the late 19th cent., they owned two flour mills, two sawmills, a distillery, and a beer brewery. Their pop. reached 3,883 in 1897 and 6,111 (total 10,031) in 1910. R. Hayyim Yisrael Morgenstern (d. 1905), the grandson of Menahem Mendel of Kotsk, settled there in 1882, turning P. into a hasidic center and stimulating the local economy. The Zionists and the Bund became active in the early 20th cent. In 1917, a Yiddish weekly, *Shprozungen*, appeared, the first of its kind in provincial Poland. The J. pop. dropped to 3,221 in 1921 as economic distress riddled the community, necessitating assistance from the Joint Distribution Committee and relatives abroad. Zionist activity continued, while Agudat Israel, supported by the Hasidim, controlled the community council. Tarbut, CYSHO, and Beth Jacob schools were in operation. The Germans arrived in mid-Sept, 1939, setting up a *Judenrat* and transferring the city's remaining 2,000 Jews to a ghetto by 4 Nov. On 28 Dec. all were expelled to Opole, remaining there until the mass deportations on 24 Oct. 1942 to the Sobibor death camp.

PULTUSK Warsaw dist., Poland. A community developed from the late 18th cent., when the city came under Prussian rule and Jews were allowed to become residents. One of the area's most important communities, it numbered 5,308 (5% of the pop.) in 1897. The first communal rabbi (1853–61) was Yisrael Yehoshua Trunk, a leading halakhist and supporter of the Hovevei Zion movement. An economic decline before WWI threatened J. tailors, shoemakers, and other artisans. With the help of the Joint Distribution Committee, two credit banks reopened after the war, saving many from impoverishment and bankruptcy. Between the World Wars, Jews faced growing antisemitism, which ranged from plunder by the Polish volunteer army (Haller's Army) in 1919 to trade boycotts and riots in 1931 and 1936. Jews sat on the municipal council and most J. parties were represented on the community council, which was first dominated by Agudat Israel (1924–31) and later by a General Zionist, Mizrachi, and artisan alliance. Education and culture in P. flourished, with new schools, reading rooms, and sports activities. Immediately after the German occupation (7 Sept.

1939), P. was annexed to the Greater Reich and a typical Nazi pogrom occurred four days later when more than a dozen Jews were shot by the SS and another 300 expelled. On 26 Sept. nearly 7,000 Jews were robbed of their possessions, beaten mercilessly, and driven across the Narew River toward Bialystok (in the Soviet-occupied zone of Poland). Most found temporary refuge in the USSR, where some joined local partisan units. Others eventually escaped to Palestine or the U.S., but two-thirds perished in the Holocaust.

PUMPENAI (Yid. Pumpian) Birzai dist., Lithuania. Jews first settled in the 17th cent. In the first half of the 18th cent. there was a Karaite community in the town. In the 19th cent., a local Jew took responsibility for a blood libel in order to save the community and was burned alive. Towards the end of the cent., the economic situation led many to leave for South Africa. The J. pop. in 1897 was 1,017 (69% of the total). After WWI, emigration to the U.S. and South Africa continued. The Zionists were active among J. youth in Z. The J. pop. in 1941 was 300. After Germany's invasion in June 1941, the community's rabbi was tortured to death by Lithuanians. On 26 Aug. 1941 all the Jews were taken to the Pajuoste forest and shot.

PUNGESTI Moldavia dist., Rumania. At the end of the 19th cent., over 500 Jews were living here, dropping to 255 in 1930 (21% of the total). In July 1941, the J. pop. was expelled to Vaslui. Only part of the community returned after the war.

PUNSK Bialystok dist., Poland. Jews numbered 228 (51% of the pop.) in 1921. Those who escaped to Lithuania in 1939 perished there after the German invasion in 1941.

PUSALOTAS (Yid. Pushalot) Panevezys dist., Lithuania. A Karaite community predated the Rabbanite Jews who first settled at the beginning of the 19th cent. The J. pop. in 1897 was 920 (69% of the total). After WWI, many emigrated to Palestine, South Africa, and the U.S. The Zionists were active. The J. pop. in 1939 was 120 (15%). The Germans and Lithuanians probably killed all the Jews of P. in July 1941.

PUSHKIN (until 1930, Tsarskoye Selo; in 1930–37, Detskoye Selo) Leningrad dist., Russia. J. settlement probably began in the first half of the 19th cent.

Tarbut Hebrew school, Pumpenai, Lithuania, March 1929

when demobilized J. soldiers arrived there. A synagogue was constructed and the Jews were given a plot of land for burials next to the local cemetery. In 1897, the J. pop. was 910 (total 22,000) with another 80 in neighboring villages. In 1926, under the Soviets, the J. pop. dropped to 537. The Germans arrived on 18 Sept. 1941 and immediately executed about 800 Jews from P. and its environs in Yekaterinovsk Park.

PUSPOKLADANY Hajdu dist., Hungary. Jews settled in the early 19th cent., mostly as artisans living in straitened economic circumstances. The J. pop. reached 741 (9% of the total) in 1880, augmented after WWI by Hasidim from the Maramaros dist. fleeing the czar's armies. The latter were expelled to Kamenets-Podolski at the outset of WWII and murdered there. In mid-June 1944, the 552 who had not been taken in 1940-41 to forced labor were sent to the Debrecen ghetto and from there deported on 1 July 1944 to Auschwitz and Austria. All members of the postwar community of 185 left by 1960.

PUSTOSHKA Kalinin dist., Russia. Jews probably settled in the latter half of the 19th cent. after officially receiving residence rights. J. artisans were especially prominent as leatherworkers, carpenters, and blacksmiths. The J. pop. was 931 (total 1,643) in 1926 and 308 in 1939. A J. school remained open until 1937. The Germans occupied the town on 16 July 1941 and after confining the Jews to a single building murdered 60–70 outside the town on 3–4 Feb. 1942. They murdered another 15–20 around the end of Feb. In all, about 100 were killed.

PUSZTADOBOC Szabolcs dist., Hungary. Jews settled in the late 19th cent. and numbered 93 in 1880 and 100 in 1940. In April 1944, they were expelled to Kisvarda and on 22 May deported to Auschwitz.

PUTILA Bukovina, Rumania, today Ukraine. Jews settled in the late 19th cent. Zionist activity began in 1920. The J. pop. in 1930 was 379. In June 1941, Ukrainians set fire to J. houses and synagogues and Jews fled to nearby villages. The rest were marched to Edineti and from there deported to Transnistria. About 75% perished.

PUTIVL   Sumy dist., Ukraine. Jews numbered 341 in 1926 and 152 in 1939. Most Jews probably fled before the arrival of the Germans on 11 Sept. 1941. One Jew is known to have joined Sidor Kovpak's partisan group.

PUTNOK   Borsod–Gomor dist., Hungary. Jews are mentioned in 1746 but the community only began to grow after 1848, reaching a pop. of 508 in 1880 and 783 in 1930. Most Jews were in trade, mainly marketing wines and grain. A synagogue was built in 1865–66 and a J. elementary school was opened in 1875. R. Yaakov Tannenbaum (served 1873–95) founded a yeshiva. The historian Yehuda Aryeh Blau (1861–1936), rector of the Budapest rabbinical seminary, was born in P. Following WWI, Jews successfully prevented the economic decline of P. by initiating a railroad line between the city and the Hungarian interior. Between the World Wars, the community supported Zionist activities financially and socially. In 1942, J. males were seized for forced labor, 60 perishing on the Ukrainian front. In 1944, 60 were deported to Auschwitz via Garany in early May and 564 via Miskolc on 12–15 June. In all, 509 Jews perished.

PYRITZ   (Pol. Pyrzyce) Pomerania, Germany, today Poland. Jews are first mentioned in P. in 1481. In the modern period a J. settlement of seven families existed in 1705. A cemetery was opened c. 1735, the first synagogue in 1794, and a second, larger one in 1870. The community numbered 327 in 1871. When the Nazis came to power in 1933, there were about 100 Jews in P. By Aug. 1935, J. businessman were suffering considerably from boycott measures. At this time, the influence of the Zionists had grown and a branch of the German Zionist Organization was founded. On *Kristallnacht* (9–10 Nov. 1938), the synagogue, which had already been damaged in 1935, was burned down. By May 1939, there were 30 Jews and 20 persons of partial J. origin (*Mischlinge*) in P. No further information about their fate is available.

PYRMONT, BAD   see BAD PYRMONT.

PYSZNICA   Lwow dist., Poland. The J. pop. in 1921 was 191 (total 2,380). The Jews were probably expelled to Soviet-held territory in 1939 and murdered there by the Germans after 1941.

PYZDRY   (Yid. Pyzer) Lodz dist., Poland. Jews were living in P. in 1387. The J. pop. was 890 in 1857 (29% of the total) and 500 in 1939. The Germans took the town in Sept. 1939 and set up a *Judenrat*. On 17–18 July 1940 the Jews were expelled to Rzgow, Grodziec, and Zagorow and deported with the Jews of the Konin region to death camps.

Q

QUAKENBRUECK Hanover, Germany. This community originated in the town of Badbergen, where three J. families had a prayer house in 1816 that eventually served a membership of 96, including the Jews of Alfhausen, Berge, Bersenbrueck, and Menslage. By 1895, however, there were 37 J. residents (over 1% of the total) in Q., which became the center of communal activity. Following the construction of a new synagogue in 1897, the community, affiliated with Emden's rabbinate, then acquired a burial ground in 1900. In 1897–1924, the community maintained an elementary school. On *Kristallnacht* (9–10 Nov. 1938), SA men looted J. homes after burning the synagogue to the ground. Jews were driven through the streets and one was later murdered at the Buchenwald concentration camp. Most of the 46 Jews registered in 1933 left by Feb. 1940, 33 emigrating chiefly to Holland and Belgium, South Africa, and Palestine. Eleven other Jews from Q. and ten from nearby towns perished in the Holocaust.

QUATZENHEIM Bas-Rhin dist., France. A small J. community was established in the village during the 19th cent. In 1807 the community consisted of 151 Jews. A synagogue was founded in 1819. By 1844, the community numbered 267; in 1861, 305. By 1885, the J. pop. had dwindled to 234 and by 1931 to 87. By 1936, there were only 60 Jews listed in Q. During WWII, the local Jews were expelled to the south of France with the rest of the Jews from Alsace-Lorraine and the synagogue was desecrated and the furnishings stolen. In the 1960s there were only 20 Jews in Q.

QUEDLINBURG Saxony, Germany. There is evidence of Jews from the 13th cent. up to 1482 and then again in 1685. With French rule at the beginning of the 19th cent., the J. pop. grew, numbering 47 in 1810 and 112 in 1905. The community established a cemetery in 1814 and a synagogue about 1820. In 1903, the community abandoned the dilapidated synagogue for a rented prayer room. When the Nazis came to power in 1933, only 44 Jews were living in Q. On *Kristallnacht* (9–10 Nov. 1938), the cemetery as well as J. businesses and homes were wrecked. By 1939, the community numbered 16 individuals. Those who were no longer able to escape were deported to the east, probably in April 1942. In Oct. 1942, there were still two Jews in Q., protected by marriage to non-Jews.

R

RAALTE Overijssel dist., Holland. The J. community dates back to the 18th cent. and numbered 56 in 1911. The J. pop. in 1941 was 44 (total 11,154). A total of 37 perished in the Holocaust; two survived in hiding and one returned from the camps.

RABKA Cracow dist., Poland. Jews arrived in the second half of the 19th cent. and numbered 172 (total 1,747) in 1921, trading primarily in yarn and knitwear and working at the town's health and resort facilities. The General Zionists with their Akiva youth movement were active among the local Jews and vacationers. Arriving in Sept. 1939, the Germans set up a *Judenrat*. They established a training school for security personnel which "practiced" its techniques of torture and murder on the Jews. In 1941 the Jews were ghettoized. On around 20 May 1942, 40 Jews were executed after a selection and 160 on 26 June. In a final *Aktion* on 28–31 Aug., 200 were sent to labor camps and the rest to the Belzec death camp.

The Rapaport, Friedman, Engelrad, and Weiss families vacationing in Rabka, Poland, 1927 (Beth Hatefutsoth Photo Archive, Tel Aviv/ courtesy of Devora Handfeld, Israel)

RACACIUNI Moldavia dist., Rumania. Jews first settled in the second half of the 19th cent. Antisemitic outbursts and a peasant revolt in 1907 forced the Jews to leave. They returned after a time and built a synagogue and a J. school. A branch of Hovevei Zion was founded in 1901. The J. pop. stood at 208 in 1899 and 176 in 1930 (9% of total). In Sept. 1940, the Green Shirts began persecuting the Jews and destroyed the synagogue. On 11 Jan. 1941 the J. pop. was expelled to Bacau and suffered the fate of the Jews there. No Jews returned to the village after the war.

RACALMAS Fejer dist., Hungary. Jews settled in the early 18th cent. The Status Quo congregation maintained a synagogue and school. It numbered 165 in 1880 and 33 in 1944. During the White Terror attacks of 1919–21, a J. teacher was murdered by rioters and many Jews fled to Budapest. On 16 May 1944, the Jews were brought to Dunapentele and on 12 June to Szekesfehervar en route to Auschwitz.

RACHMANOWO Volhynia dist., Poland, today Ukraine. In 1921, 62 Jews remained of a pre-WWI total of 465. In the Holocaust, the community was expelled to the Szumsk ghetto for liquidation.

RACIONZH Warsaw dist., Poland. A J. settlement existed by the 1740s and an organized community from the 1820s. Jews were innkeepers and leaseholders and later expanded into trade and crafts as well as light industry. The community grew from 216 in 1827 to 2,179 (total 4,656) in 1897. A new synagogue was completed in 1891 and there were also a number of hasidic *shtiblekh*. The burning of J. homes in 1918 by rampaging Poles led to emigration among the young. A fire in 1932 destroyed more J. homes. Between the World Wars, J. political activity was widespread. Agudat Israel derived its strength from the Gur Hasidim and controlled the community council, though Zionist influence continued to grow. Many Jews were forced to liquidate their businesses following the economic boycott of the 1930s. The German occupation of Sept 1939 brought forced labor and unremitting persecution. All the Jews were expelled on 10 Nov., most reaching Warsaw to share the fate of the Jews there.

RACISTORF (Hung. Recse) Slovakia, Czechoslo-vakia, today Republic of Slovakia. Jews probably founded a community in the early 19th cent. after maintaining a token presence until then. Their pop. reached 96 in 1828 and 52 (total 6,967) in 1940. Under Slovakian rule, J. businesses were liquidated and in spring 1942 the Jews were deported to Auschwitz and the Lublin dist. via Patronka.

RACKEVE Pest–Pilis–Solt–Kiskun dist., Hungary. Jews arrived in the early 19th cent. and the community organized in 1879. The J. pop. was 95 in 1885 and 146 in 1930. After enduring a reign of terror under Hungary's racial laws, the Jews were deported to Auschwitz via Csepel on 8 July 1944.

RACZKI Bialystok dist., Poland. The J. settlement began in the late 17th cent., numbering 1,758 (total 2,093) in 1857. Jews operated candle and porcelain factories, a brickyard, and two hide-processing plants. Half left by the end of WWI. Those remaining engaged in crafts and petty trade, buying up farm produce to market in the cities. After a brief Soviet occupation, many Jews left with the Red Army in late Sept. 1939. The rest were expelled by the Germans around a month later.

RADAUTI (Yid. Radewitz) Bukovina, Rumania. Jews settled in the late 18th cent. and became known throughout Austria for the production of alcoholic beverages and beer. In 1880 the J. pop. was 3,452. During the 19th cent. the Hasidim and the Orthodox struggled for power within the community. By the end of the cent. the struggle was between the Zionists and the Orthodox and leftist groups, especially the Bund. During his visit to R. in 1880, Emperor Francis Joseph granted the Jews a plot of land in the center of the city on which to build a large synagogue, which was consecrated on 18 Aug. 1883. R. Yitzhak Kunstadt, who served as rabbi until 1909, was one of the founders of the first Zionist association in 1892. A Hebrew school was opened in 1907 and by 1939 it had 200 pupils. In 1919–26, a high school operated in which the language of instruction was Hebrew. After WWI, R. became an important center of Zionist activity. An immigration movement sent hundreds of pioneer youth to Palestine between the World Wars. The Bund was active in culture and sports. In 1930 the J. pop. was 5,647 (34% of the total). On the eve of WWII, 250 business enterprises in R. were owned by Jews. Jews owned

90% of the shops, banks, hotels, restaurants, and bars and comprised a majority of the professional class. Jews were persecuted under the Goga-Cuza regime from 1937. Their situation worsened under Soviet rule in June 1940 and under the Iron Guard in Sept. On 24 Jan. 1941, 12 Jews were killed in a pogrom and on 12–13 Oct. the city's 10,000 Jews (including refugees) were deported to Transnistria. In 1945, about 1,500 survivors returned to R. After the war, in 1945–46, over 30,000 Jews passed through R., the majority of whom went to Palestine. In 1950–51, 2,000 R. Jews left for Israel. In 1962, 800 Jews remained but their number soon dwindled.

RADEBEUL   Saxony, Germany. The small J. community was affiliated to the Dresden community and numbered 65 individuals in 1925. In Aug. 1935, residents of R. staged a demonstration against their J. neighbors. By 1939, most Jews had moved to Dresden or abroad and in Oct. 1941, there were only 12 Jews in R. Most were probably deported. The only remaining Jew in Oct. 1942 was probably protected by marriage to a non-Jew.

RADGOSZCZ   Cracow dist., Poland. Jews numbered 363 in 1875 and 188 in 1921 (total 3,322). They were probably expelled to the Zabno or Dabrowa Tarnowska ghetto in July 1942 and from there deported to the Belzec death camp.

RADLOW   Cracow dist., Poland. Jews numbered 174 in 1921 (total about 2,000). The German occupation of Sept. 1939 brought a regime of forced labor, extortion, and restricted movement, though J. farmers were able to work their land until Sept. 1941. The community was expelled to Bochnia and Tarnow in Aug. 1942, sharing the fate of the local Jews.

RADOM   Kielce dist., Poland. Jews are first mentioned in 1568 but were excluded from residence by a *de non tolerandis Judaeis* privilege granted to the town in 1633 by King Wladyslaw IV. Subsequently Jews frequented the town for trade purposes. During Sejm sessions, they were permitted temporary residence. Some remained in the city illegally. Most were again expelled in 1746. In 1789, they were again permitted to reside in the city, though in 1814 they were re-

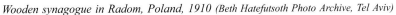

Wooden synagogue in Radom, Poland, 1910 (Beth Hatefutsoth Photo Archive, Tel Aviv)

Jewish family outside its home in Radom, Poland, after looting by Russian soldiers in 1917 (Beth Hatefutsoth Photo Archive, Tel Aviv/ courtesy of Polska Akademia, Nauk Warsaw)

stricted to a special quarter. J. trade was also restricted, but by 1838, with the J. pop. nearing 1,650, there were 20 J. merchants in the city dealing mainly in alcoholic beverages, knitted goods, and perfume, 14 food manufacturers, and 15 storekeepers. Jews subsequently pioneered the local textile industry and in 1841 all restrictions were lifted. The Beckerman family built up an industrial concern manufacturing building materials; other J. factories produced farm implements, candles, and soap. By 1902, Jews owned 41% of the town's real estate, with the J. pop. growing from 11,277 in 1897 to 16,976 (total 39,981) in 1909. Among the community's prominent rabbis was Shemuel Mohilewer (1868–83), a leader of Hovevei Zion, which began operating in R. in the 1880s under his influence. From the mid-19th cent., the Hasidim also exerted an influence (Gur, Aleksandrow, Kozienice, etc.) as did the *maskilim*, who opened secular schools and a modern *talmud torah*. The Bund became active in 1903 and together with the Zionist Socialists, participated in the revolutionary events of 1905. The community opened a hospital in 1859 and an old age home in 1882. In

WWI, the Jews suffered from pillaging by Russian soldiers and three were murdered. Under the Austrian occupation of 1915–18, the community cared for hundreds of refugees and public life revived, with Po'alei Zion and Mizrachi founding a cultural society and Hehalutz beginning to operate. In 1921, the J. pop. was 24,246 (total 61,599). Jews owned 1,174 workshops and factories, mostly in the garment industry. J. workers, under Bund influence, were active in the fight for better conditions, 700 of them striking in 1922. Throughout the postwar period the Endecja Party spearheaded local antisemitism, with increasing violence in the 1930s. Community life nonetheless continued to flourish. An orphanage was opened and in 1924 the TOZ public health organization started a local branch, caring for hundreds of J. children. Yavne and Horev schools were founded and ORT offered vocational training. The Yiddish daily *Radomer Tzaytung* appeared in the mid-1920s and the pro-Zionist weekly *Radomer Lebn* was published from 1924 to 1939. Throughout the 1920s the Zionists shared power with Agudat Israel in the community council.

The Germans captured R. on 8 Sept. 1939, seizing Jews for forced labor and exacting an exorbitant tribute from the community. The *Judenrat*, established in Dec. 1939 under the chairmanship of Yosef Diamant, also served as the district *Judenrat* responsible for 280,000 Jews. The JSS (a J. self-help organization) opened soup kitchens, distributing thousands of meals a day. In summer 1940, large numbers of Jews were sent to labor camps in the Lublin area, including 1,000 on 20 Aug. On 18 Dec. 1940, 1,840 Jews were expelled to various settlements in the area, but at the same time 2,000 refugees arrived from Cracow. They were followed by other refugees. On 7 April 1941, two ghettoes were sealed off, the larger one in the city's old quarter housing 27,000 Jews and the smaller one in the Glinica suburb accommodating 5,000. In Feb. 1942, the Germans carried out their first *Aktion*, when 40 mainly left-wing activists were deported to Auschwitz. On 28 April, community leaders were rounded up; some were shot and others, including Diamant, were also sent to Auschwitz. On 4 Aug. 1942 the smaller ghetto was liquidated: 1,000 Jews with work permits were transferred to the larger ghetto; 60 were murdered; and 4,000 were deported to the Treblinka death camp together with 2,000 from the larger ghetto. New deportations from the larger ghetto commenced on 16 Aug. About 20,000 were deported, 400 murdered, and 1,800 selected for labor. Those spared were confined in the smaller ghetto. About 1,000 worked in the local Witbornia munitions factory together with 3,200 Poles; others worked at the Korona warehouses sorting the belongings of the deportation victims. A number of small workshops were also opened, mainly to repair abandoned property, and another 300 Jews were sent to other labor camps in the area. On 3 Dec. 1942, about 800 of the Jews were transferred to the Szydlowiec ghetto and on 13 Jan. 1943, all those who had applied for visas to Palestine or were in possession of immigration certificates were deported to the Treblinka death camp. Subsequently a concentration camp holding 3,000 Jews in 20 shanties was erected. On 26 June 1944 they were deported to Auschwitz via Tomaszow Lubelski.

RADOMSKO (previously Novo-Radomsko) Lodz dist., Poland. A J. community existed here from 1822. Jews owned and worked in the city's furniture factories. The court of the Radomsk hasidic rabbi, R. Shelomo ha-Kohen Rabinowich, was visited by numerous Hasidim from Poland and western Galicia and was the third largest court in Poland (after Gur and Aleksandrow). The rabbis of this dynasty set up a yeshiva with branches throughout Poland. The J. pop. in 1897 was 11,767 (43% of the total). Jews built the barracks for the Russian forces encamped in R. in 1905–15. The first synagogue was built in the 1830s and a second at the end of the cent. Zionist activity began in 1898 and the Bund in 1905. A self-defense group for protection against rioters was set up in 1904. Members of the J. labor parties were actively involved in strikes during the 1904–05 revolution. During the economic crisis in the 1930s, the J. pop. declined by almost half, with artisans constituting the majority of breadwinners. The Zionist parties were involved in local politics and in 1926, Po'alei Zion had two representatives in the municipal council, one of whom was elected mayor. Agudat Israel was established in 1918 and dominated the J. community council. It was involved in Zionist activities and many of its members immigrated to Palestine and were among the founders of Kefar Hasidim. The Bund, which had ceased operating in 1910, was reactivated in 1921 and a tailors union was organized. Between the World Wars, two government elementary schools for J. children and a high school with eight classes were opened. On 12 Sept. 1939, shortly after they entered the city, the Germans rounded up the Jews, abused them physically, and put them to work at menial tasks. One of the first tasks of the *Judenrat* was to provide up to 3,000 J. workers daily for forced labor. Jews were forced to vacate their homes and provide funds for the relief of Polish refugees from the areas annexed by the Reich. The ghetto set up on 20 Dec. 1939 was one of the first in Poland. By May 1940 it housed 7,000 Jews (including refugees) in overcrowded conditions. In winter 1939–40, and again in late 1941, typhus epidemics killed many. Hundreds of young Jews were sent to forced labor camps and the few who returned were physically broken. On 9 Oct. 1942, the Germans rounded up the J. pop. and deported 5,000 to the Treblinka death camp. The remaining 9,000 Jews (including refugees from the surrounding towns and villages) were deported to Treblinka on 12 Oct. A group of 321 Jews was kept back, but on 26 Oct. 175 were transferred to the labor camp at Skarzysko-Kamienna. The remaining 150 Jews cleaned out the houses in the ghetto and eventually suffered the fate of the R. Jews. The ghetto was opened again on 14 Nov. for 4,500 Jews from the surrounding towns who were deported to the Treblinka death camp on 6 Jan. 1943.

Another 600 Jews who gave themselves up to the Germans were murdered at the J. cemetery, where they were buried in mass graves. Young Jews in the ghetto tried to make contact with the Polish underground and join the partisans but most of these attempts failed. After the war, in early 1945, 200–300 Jews returned but only three families remained in 1947.

RADOMYSL Zhitomir dist., Ukraine. Jews are first mentioned in 1764 and by 1792 numbered 1,424. In 1897, their pop. was 7,502 (total 10,906). Of the town's 198 self-employed artisans, 161 were Jews. In the early 20th cent., the community had a *talmud torah* and three private J. schools. In March 1918, the local militia head exacted an exorbitant tribute from the community. Hundreds of Jews were killed in pogroms in 1919 (400 in May alone). In 1939, the J. pop. was 2,348. The Germans arrived on 9 July 1941. The Jews were crowded into an open ghetto, 15 to a room. In Aug., 389 Jews were murdered in two *Aktions*. In another *Aktion* on 6 Sept. 1941, a *Sonderkommando 4a* unit murdered 1,107 J. adults outside the city while Ukrainian police murdered 561 children.

RADOMYSL NAD SANEM Cracow dist., Poland. Jews are first recorded in 1765, with the pop. averaging around 400 (nearly a quarter of the total) from the second half of the 19th cent. All, including 400 refugees, were deported by the Germans to the Belzec death camp in fall 1942.

RADOMYSL WIELKI Cracow dist., Poland. Jews were at first restricted to the outskirts of the town and worked the land, but later came to constitute the town's urban element, forming an independent community in the 18th cent. Straitened economic circumstances and a fire destroying most J. homes at the beginning of the 20th cent. promoted emigration as the J. pop. fell from a peak of 1,920 (total 3,332) in 1890 to 1,422 in 1921. In the wake of WWI and a pogrom staged by Polish soldiers and the local rabble in Nov. 1918, half the J. pop. was on welfare. The situation improved slightly in the late 1920s when trade, hatmaking in particular, expanded, but many remained unemployed and some emigrated, including a group of youngsters to Germany. Most of the Jews were Hasidim. Zionism was introduced in the late 19th cent., with the General Zionists becoming prominent between the World Wars. Agudat Israel ran a Beth Jacob school. The German occupation

in Sept. 1939 brought a regime of forced labor and restrictions. Starvation and disease beset the community through the winter of 1940–41. The difficult situation was compounded in 1942 by a steady stream of refugees. On 19 July 1942, all were expelled to Dembica after the old and sick were murdered; more were murdered in the *Aktion* there and the rest deported to the Majdanek concentration camp. Of a group of 60 armed Jews, most from R., 35 were able to break through to Soviet territory in 1944 after fighting a pitched battle with the Germans in the Dolcza forest.

RADOSINA Slovakia, Czechoslovakia, today Republic of Slovakia. Jews were present in the early 18th cent., forming an independent community in the early 19th cent. and constructing a synagogue at mid-cent. The J. pop. reached a peak of 84 (total 1,242) in 1900 and then declined to 30 in 1919 and 14 in 1940. The Jews were deported to the Lublin dist. in Poland in March–April 1942.

RADOSOVCE Slovakia, Czechoslovakia, today Republic of Slovakia. Jews numbered about 150 in 1840, maintaining a synagogue and cemetery. In 1930, 22 remained.

RADOSZKOWICZE Vilna dist., Poland, today Belarus. Jews probably arrived in the late 18th cent, the merchants among them exporting grain and lumber to Germany and Hungary. A fire in 1891 destroyed many J. homes along with the synagogue. Many never recovered from the blow. The J. pop. was 1,519 (total 2,614) in 1897. Some were Habad or Koidanov Hasidim. During the 19th cent., numerous community welfare agencies were created. The Hebrew poet Mordekhai Tzevi Manne was born in R. in 1857. Haskala and Zionism made inroads at the turn of the 19th cent. After WWI the Jews found themselves cut off from the agricultural hinterland by the new borders and suffered from heavy taxes. The YEKOPO relief organization helped 50 J. families start farms; others left for Palestine and the English-speaking countries. Zionist activity was extensive and a Hebrew Tarbut school was opened, despite the opposition of the strictly Orthodox, who opened their own Horev religious school. The J. pop. in 1925 was 1,215. Under Soviet rule in 1939–41, the Jews joined the cooperatives and the young took advantage of new educational opportunities. The Germans captured R. in early July 1941, immediately appointing a *Judenrat* to regulate forced labor and demanding exorbitant "contributions." On 11 March 1943, the town was surrounded by a chain of German soldiers and local police. About 800 Jews were executed in groups of four in a nearby barn and their bodies burned; 200 escaped the slaughter while 50 were shot down attempting to flee; another 110 were left alive as skilled workers, crowded into two houses. Their number grew to 300 after being joined by Jews coming out of hiding. On 8 March 1943, 260 were taken to a barn in a nearby village and burned alive; about 50 escaped to the forest.

RADOSZYCE Lodz dist., Poland. The J. pop. in 1897 was 1,728 (49% of the total). R. was the center of an outstanding Hasidic dynasty founded by R. Yissakhar Dov Baer in the 1820s. The economic situation of the J. community deteriorated between the World Wars due to the decline of Hasidism and the boycott by Poles. The Revisionists were the strongest of the Zionist movements founded after WWI. The majority of the Jews evacuated the bombed town in 1939, but during 1940–41 the influx of refugees increased the J. pop. from 549 to 2,400. On 3 Nov. 1942, all 4,000 Jews now there were deported to the Treblinka death camp.

RADUCANENI Moldavia dist., Rumania. Jews settled in the early 19th cent. and constituted the majority up to the beginning of the 20th cent. In 1908, the city council attempted but failed to expel the Jews. In 1910, a J. school was opened with 264 pupils. The Zionists were active between the World Wars. The J. pop. in 1930 was 656 (22% of the total). At the outbreak of WWII, five synagogues were open. In summer 1940, the Iron Guard force-marched the J. pop. to Vaslui and Bacau. The Jews returned to find their property plundered and by June 1941, the beginning of the Soviet-Rumanian war, all the Jews had left.

RADUN (Radin) Grodno dist., Poland, today Belarus. Little is known about the J. community until the 19th cent. The J. pop. in 1897 was 896 (total 1,621). Its pride was the yeshiva founded by Hafetz Hayyim

A Jew and his wagon, Radun, Poland, 1909 (The Russian Ethnographic Museum, Petersburg/photo courtesy of Yad Vashem, The Holocaust Martyrs' and Heroes' Remembrance Authority, Jerusalem)

(R. Yisrael Meir ha-Kohen; 1838–1933), who lived there after his marriage supported by his wife's grocery store and producing ethical and talmudic writings. Between the World Wars, 300 students studied there, and in 1940 the yeshiva with most of its students and teachers was transferred to the U.S. via Japan. The J. pop. in 1925 was about 900. The Germans captured R. on 30 June 1941. A ghetto was set up in Oct., swelling to 1,700 residents with the arrival of refugees from Dowgieliszki, Zablocie, Zirmun, and Nacza. On 10 May 1942, 1,000 of them were murdered; 300 escaped to the forest, some joining the partisans. The remaining 300 skilled workers were sent to Szczuczyn and from there to their death at an unknown destination.

RADVAN   Slovakia, Czechoslovakia, today Republic of Slovakia. Jews settled on the Radvanski estate in the 1830s and traded in the market towns. A community was founded in the 1880s, with the J. pop. maintaining a level of around 80 (5% of the total) through WWII. Under Slovakian rule, most Jews were deported to the death camps of the Lublin dist. of Poland in April 1942.

RADVILISKIS   (Yid. Radvilishok) Siauliai dist., Lithuania. Jews first settled in the beginning of the 19th cent. The J. pop. in 1897 was 676 (17% of the total). During WWI, the Jews were expelled to Russia; most returned after the war. The J. pop. grew when the Germans brought in Jews from Vilna as forced laborers. Between the World Wars, Jews were elected to the town council. The economic situation and an anti-J. boycott in the mid-1930s led many to leave. Most children studied in a Tarbut Hebrew school. The Zionist movement won widespread support and all parties had branches in R. In 1940 there were about 250 J. families living in R. After the German invasion in June 1941, Lithuanian nationalists introduced a regime of forced labor, abuse, and humiliation. In July, the Jews were confined to an abandoned army barracks and on 12 July all males 16 years old and above were shot. In Aug. 1941, about 400 of the remaining Jews, mostly women and children, were transferred to Zargare where they were murdered on 2 Oct. with other Jews from the area. Some were also murdered in Siauliai. A few were sent to a concentration camp in Germany and survived the war.

The first Hehalutz group in Radviliskis, Lithuania, 1924 (Beth Hatefutsoth Photo Archive, Tel Aviv/courtesy of Eliezer Nachomov, Israel)

RADYANSKOYE (until 1929, Kniazevo, Kniaze, or Kniaze-Timanovka) Vinnitsa dist., Ukraine. Jews numbered 1,040 (total 1,094) in 1897 and 421 in 1926 under the Soviets. In 1929, a kolkhoz was founded where most J. families (46) found employment. In 1936, the J. pop. amounted to 63 families (of a total 127). A. J. council (soviet) was active for awhile. The Germans arrived on 22 July 1941, murdering those Jews who had neither fled nor been evacuated.

RADYMNO (Yid. Redem) Lwow dist., Poland. The few Jews allowed to settle in the town were expelled in 1711, with settlement renewed only when the Austrians lifted residence restrictions in 1772. The J. pop. reached 898 (half the total) in 1880 and grew to over 1,300 before WWI and its aftermath reduced it to its earlier level. Almost all the town's trade was in J. hands, including the marketing of yarn and knitted woolen goods, produced by the local home industry, and the area's fine fruit. Zanz and the dominant Dynow-Belz Hasidim maintained a fierce rivalry with separate ritual slaughter. The Zionists became active in the early 20th cent. and increased their influence between the World Wars. The Germans arrived in the second week of Sept. 1939. On 22 Sept. (Yom Kippur eve) the Jews were expelled on two hours' notice across the San River and into Soviet-held territory. Those who remained or returned were sent to the Pelkinia transit camp in Aug. 1942 to be killed or deported to the Belzec death camp.

RADZANOW Warsaw dist., Poland. Jews appeared in the early 18th cent., engaging mostly in petty trade. Many emigrated in the late 19th cent., reducing the J. pop. from 532 in 1897 to 303 (total 1,336) in 1921. The Zionist groups were active between the World Wars. The Germans captured the city in early Sept. 1939, subjecting the Jews to a regime of forced labor. The 200 who remained were expelled to the Mlawa ghetto on 28 Nov. 1941 and confined to a single house, with 25-30 crowded into a room. Almost all of R.'s 300 Jews perished in the Holocaust.

RADZIECHOW Tarnopol dist., Poland, today Ukraine. Jews were present when the town was founded in the 18th cent. The J. pop. stood at around 1,800 from the 1880s (a little less than half the total). Jews operated a sawmill and distillery and a dozen estates were in the hands of the more wealthy, while tailors,

furriers, and hatmakers predominated among the J. artisans. Between the World Wars, all the Zionist groups were active. Under the Soviet regime in 1939-41, the J. estates were broken up and the artisans formed into cooperatives. Hunger and disease racked the refugee-swollen J. pop. through the spring of 1942 under the German occupation. On 15 Sept., 1,400 were deported to Belz. On the 21st, 500 men were sent to the Kamionka Strumilowa forced labor camp, where they soon met their deaths. A final 1,000 were deported to the Belzec death camp on 7 Oct.

RADZIEJOW Warsaw dist., Poland. Jews are first mentioned in the mid-18th cent. as innkeepers and leaseholders, later branching into trades and crafts. Their pop. reached 599 (total 3,164) in 1921. The Germans entered R. early in Sept. 1939. All the Jews were deported to the Chelmno death camp on 10-14 April 1942.

RADZILOW Bialystok dist., Poland. A small J. settlement existed in the 17th cent. with most Jews engaging in crafts and a few trading in grain. A wooden synagogue built at the time remained standing until WWII. The J. pop. grew from 225 in 1827 to 639 (total 1,495) in 1857. During WWI the Zionists became active, founding a Hebrew school in 1917 which was later incorporated into the Tarbut system and became the community's cultural center. Between the World Wars, most Jews barely eked out a living. Anti-J. riots broke out in 1935 and 1938. Under Russian rule in 1939-41, J. commercial life was curtailed and many were exiled to Siberia. The Germans arrived on 23 June 1941 and gave Polish mobs free reign to "deal" with the Jews. On 7 July, most were locked into a barn that was then set on fire. Others, including infants and small children, were rounded up and brutally murdered or thrown into the flames. In all, 800-1,000 perished in the Holocaust.

RADZIWILOW Volhynia dist., Poland, today Ukraine. Jews are first mentioned in 1578. Development was promoted by the border trade with Austrian Galicia after the partition of Poland in the late 18th cent. In 1882 a great fire destroyed 150 houses and all but one synagogue but recovery was rapid. In 1897 the J. pop. numbered 4,322 (total 7,313) with Olyka and Turzysk Hasidism prominent. Jews operated small factories; a J. hospital was founded; and a halfway house sheltered emigres fleeing to the west after the Russian pogroms. Many Jews fled to Kremieniec when R. was in the frontline during WWI and others emigrated in the face of economic duress. The J. pop. in 1921 was 2,036. Between the World Wars, Jews dominated the grain trade. The Zionists resumed their prewar activities and a Tarbut Hebrew school enrolled 300 children. The Soviet annexation of Sept. 1939 put an end to J. communal life. With the arrival of the Germans on 27 June 1941, Jews were systematically attacked with Ukrainian assistance and 28 were murdered on 15 July. A *Judenrat* was established and a regime of forced labor instituted. On 9 April 1942, 2,600 Jews were crowded into a ghetto. On 29 May, 1,500 were murdered outside the town. The execution of those classified as "useful" was delayed to 6 Oct.; 300 tried to escape, mostly to Brody, but few survived.

RADZYMIN Warsaw dist., Poland. Jews probably settled with the founding of the town in 1475, engaging in trade and crafts as well as moneylending and lease-holding. The J. pop. rose from 432 in 1827 to 2,133 (total 3,991) in 1897. In the second half of the 19th cent. R. Yaakov Aryeh Guterman established a hasidic dynasty in R. and the many visitors to his court boosted the local economy significantly as Jews opened restaurants and boarding houses. The Zionists became active in 1904. Nobel Prize winner Isaac Bashevis Singer (1904–91), whose father was a *dayyan* and yeshiva head in R., commemorated his childhood years there in the book *In My Father's Court*. Economic conditions deteriorated in WWI and its aftermath. Many were unemployed, requiring support from relatives abroad and from the Joint Distribution Committee. An additional 150 Jews from 16 neighboring settlements were affiliated with the R. congregation. Almost all the J. political parties and youth movements in Poland were active in the town. On the approach of the Germans in Sept. 1939, many Jews fled to Soviet-held territory. In Nov. the Germans executed 14 community leaders. A ghetto was established in Dec., crowding together 2,800 Jews including refugees under conditions of starvation and disease. The ghetto was liquidated on 2–3 Oct. 1942; those who resisted were killed on the spot and the others were deported to the Treblinka death camp. About 200 of the young escaped to the forests but were eventually killed. Seventy were sent to the Izabelin labor camp near Warsaw and were subsequently murdered there.

RADZYN Lublin dist., Poland. Jews are first mentioned in the 16th cent. The community grew steadily, reaching a pop. of 875 in 1827 and 2,853 (total 5,332) in 1897. In the 19th cent., Jews played a leading role in the town's economic development, opening two factories for steel products, a sawmill, and a flour mill. They also ran inns, farmed taxes, and kept stalls and shops in the market. R. is known for the hasidic dynasty established by R. Yaakov Leiner in 1867. His son and successor, R. Gershon Hanokh Leiner, re-introduced the manufacture of the blue dye derived from snails found in the Italian Mediterranean and used for *tzitzit* thread. The large court also boosted the local economy but retarded the development of secular community life. The Zionists only became active from 1916, expanding their activities between the World Wars. Agudat Israel and the Bund were also influential. A Hebrew Tarbut school and a Beth Jacob school for girls were established. Economic circumstances remained difficult throughout the period in the face of the general crisis and the anti-J. boycott. The Germans captured R. in mid-Oct. 1939. Many of the young fled eastward with the retreating Red Army. The Jews were immediately subjected to a regime of forced labor and tributes and on 6 Dec. 1939, most were expelled to nearby Slawatycze. They were only allowed to return in April 1940. In late 1940, a ghetto was set up. By May 1942, it contained 2,071 Jews. On 22 Sept. 1942, 200 Jews were murdered by the Gestapo outside the city. In early Oct., 800 were deported to the Treblinka death camp; subsequently, 1,000 were rounded up and sent to Treblinka on 27 Oct. via the Miendzyrzec Podlaski ghetto. There were several partisan groups operating in the area, acting boldly against the Germans and managing to kill high-level officers and informers.

RAESFELD Westphalia, Germany. Jews were present in 1575. In 1683, the two J. families there were expelled for failing to obtain residence permits from the Muenster authorities. In the 18th cent., Jews filtered in without authorization, forming a small permanent community. In 1740, all were imprisoned for 33 weeks for disregarding an expulsion order. In 1750, Yisrael Jost was granted residence rights. When he died in 1807, his six children with their families constituted the J. community. Under French rule, additional Jews arrived, setting up a prayer house and study hall in a rented barn. In 1849, the J. pop. was 43.

Main Street on the Sabbath, Radzyn, Poland

In 1854, the community was attached to the Borken dist. congregation and in 1863 a synagogue was consecrated. Only 20 Jews remained in 1872 after many left for the industrial towns of the Ruhr. The pop. climbed back to 53 in 1907. The community was Orthodox and active in local life. In 1932, 22 Jews remained. On *Kristallnacht* (9–10 Nov. 1938), the synagogue was destroyed along with J. homes and stores and the cemetery was desecrated. Thirteen Jews remained in 1941. The last eight were deported to the Theresienstadt ghetto in July 1942. In all, 32 perished in the Holocaust, including 21 who emigrated before the deportations (ten to Holland and others to other German settlements).

RAFALOWKA   Volhynia dist., Poland, today Ukraine. An organized J. community existed in Old R. in the first half of the 17th cent. The J. pop. grew to 1,054 (half the total) in 1897 as Jews, mainly from Wlodzimierz, flocked to New R. (about 8 miles away), settling around the new railroad station. By the 1920s, the J. pop. had declined by 50% and Jews were active in the burgeoning lumber industry. Zionist activity was extensive and a Tarbut Hebrew school enrolled 200 children. Under the Soviets (1939–41) many J. refugees settled in R. Between the Soviet withdrawal and the German occupation in July 1941, the Ukrainians staged a pogrom. A *Judenrat* was established and a ghetto filled with refugees was set up on 1 May 1942. On 29 Aug., 2,250 Jews were murdered outside the town. Of the dozens who fled, some fought as partisans.

RAGELIAI   (Yid. Ragole) Rokiskis dist., Lithuania. The J. pop. in 1923 was about 70 (30% of the total). Following the German occupation, all were killed in fall 1941.

RAGUVA   (Yid. Rogeve) Panevezys dist., Lithuania. Jews first settled in the 17th cent. The J. pop. in 1897 was 1,223 (69% of total). In WWI the Jews were exiled to Russia; only half returned after the war. Between the World Wars, antisemitic attacks and an anti-J. boycott led many to emigrate to Palestine, the U.S., and South Africa. There was a Hebrew school and the

Old wooden synagogue, Raguva, Lithuania

Zionist movement enjoyed widespread support. The J. pop. in 1940 was about 500. After the German invasion in June 1941, the entire J. community was transferred to Panevezys. On 24–26 Aug., the Jews of Panevezys together with those of R. were killed in the Pajuoste forest.

RAHDEN Westphalia, Germany. It is unclear when J. settlement started. In 1821, the J. pop. was 217. A synagogue was erected in 1852 and a J. elementary school operated from 1890. In 1933, the J. pop. was 67 (total 11,645). The synagogue was burned on *Kristallnacht* (9–10 Nov. 1938), and three J. homes were destroyed. Twenty-six Jews left R. before *Kristallnacht*. Another 34 left by March 1942, 32 to other places in Germany. The last three were deported on 28 July 1942. Most apparently perished in the Holocaust.

RAIGORODOK Zhitomir dist., Ukraine. Jews arrived in the early 18th cent. and numbered about 100 in the mid-18th cent. In 1897 their pop. was 946 (total 2,058), dropping by at least 50% between the

World Wars. The Germans captured R. on 5 July 1941, murdering 125 local Jews in various *Aktions* and another 47 from other settlements.

RAIPOLE Latgale dist., Latvia. On the eve of WWII, eight Jews remained of a pre-WWI community of 220. All were murdered by the Germans after their arrival in July 1941.

RAJCZA Cracow dist., Poland. The Jews lived there from the mid-19th cent. and numbered 132 in 1921 (total 2,790). Antisemitic disturbances were a periodic occurrence. The General Zionists and Bnei Akiva youth movement were active from 1933. All the Jews were expelled by the Germans to General Gouvernement territory in fall 1939.

RAJEC Slovakia, Czechoslovakia, today Republic of Slovakia. Jews were present in the early 1720s. They reached a peak pop. of about 300 (10–11% of the total) in the mid-19th cent. After the split in 1869, they formed a Neologist congregation with 31

neighboring settlements attached to it. Most Jews were well established economically, including a number of wealthy lumber merchants. The community maintained a synagogue, cemetery, community center, and classroom for religious instruction. The Zionists were active. In 1940, 55 Jews remained, down from 218 in 1900 and 123 in 1919. Most were deported to the death camps in the east in spring 1942.

RAJGROD   Bialystok dist., Poland. Jews are known from 1587. The community had a synagogue and cemetery by the early 18th cent. and reached a pop. of 1,659 (total 1,907) in 1857. Jews traded in grain and manufactured table oil and alcoholic beverages. The Zionists were active from the early 20th cent. After WWI the J. pop. dropped to 745. After two years of Soviet rule (1939–41) the Germans took the town on 22 June 1941. Within a few days, 100 Jews were led to the Choinki forest and murdered. The rest were put to forced labor and a *Judenrat* was appointed. In Oct. 1942, all 600 remaining Jews were sent to Grajewo and from there deported to the Treblinka death camp and Auschwitz.

RAJKA   Gyor-Moson dist., Hungary. Jews settled in 1706. They numbered 253 in 1840 and 136 in 1930. In June 1944 they were deported to Auschwitz via the Mosonmagyarovar ghetto and Gyor. Survivors renewed the community, but in the face of local hostility most left for Israel.

RAKAMAZ   Szabolcs dist., Hungary. Jews from Maramarossziget and Galicia arrived in the late 18th cent. The community organized in 1840. The Jews played a prominent role in the economic life of the region. In 1930, they numbered 170. All were deported to Auschwitz via Satoraljaujhely on 16, 22, and 26 May 1944.

RAKHOV   (Hung. Raho) Carpatho-Russia, Czechoslovakia, today Ukraine. J. refugees from Galicia probably settled in the late 1840s. The J. pop. was 288 (total 4,716) in 1880, with the community becoming independent in the late 1880s. Its second rabbi, Shelomo Zalman Friedman, founded a yeshiva for about 100 students after WWI. The J. pop. rose to 912 in 1921 and 1,707 (total 12,455) in 1941. During this period, the community maintained an elementary school, a *talmud torah*, and a number of traditional *hadarim*. Some

Jews farmed or practiced various professions (among them two doctors and three lawyers). J. involvement in public life was extensive. Jews sat on the municipal council, providing a secretary, and on the bench in magistrate's court. The Zionist and religious parties were active among the young, a number of whom emigrated to Palestine prior to WWII after receiving pioneer training. Following the Hungarian occupation in March 1939, some young Jews succeeded in fleeing to the Soviet Union, being among the first to join the Czechoslovakian brigade that fought against the Nazis on the eastern front. In 1941, the Hungarians drafted many young people into labor battalions and sent them east for forced labor. In summer 1941, dozens of J. refugee families were expelled to Kamenets-Podolski, where they were murdered. The remaining 950 were deported to Auschwitz in the second half of May 1944, most perishing there. In all, about 1,220 local Jews died in the Holocaust. A few hundred survivors from R. and its environs returned after the war. Most left for Israel in the 1970s

RAKOSCSABA   Pest–Pilis–Solt–Kiskun dist., Hungary. Jews settled in the first half of the 19th cent. The community organized in 1868. The J. pop. numbered 225 in 1910 and 406 (3% of the total) in 1941. On 20 July 1944, the remaining Jews were deported to Auschwitz via Monor.

RAKOSKERESZTUR   suburb of Budapest, Hungary. Jews were present by 1784 and numbered 229 in 1930. They were deported in mid-June 1944 to Auschwitz via Budakeszi.

RAKOSLIGET   Pest–Pilis–Solt–Kiskun dist., Hungary. From the beginning of the 20th cent., Budapest Jews settled in R. because of its cheap housing. They numbered 268 in 1930 and 195 in 1940. In 1941, the men were taken to forced labor and most perished. The remaining Jews were transferred to Rakoscsaba and then to Auschwitz on 10 July 1944.

RAKOSPALOTA   Pest–Pilis–Solt–Kiskun   dist., Hungary. Jews settled in the late 19th cent. The community organized in 1869. A school was opened in in 1890. With growing industrialization underway in nearby Budapest, the J. pop. increased from 242 in 1890 to 1,552 in 1910 and 2,240 (5% of the total) in 1941. Zionist activity intensified in the 1930s under

Mizrachi. J. males aged 18–48 were seized for forced labor in 1942. Two J. families were taken from the ghetto under the protection of the Swiss consul; the remaining Jews were deported on 5 July 1944 to Auschwitz after being detained at Budakalasz and Bekesmegyer. The postwar community of 300 dispersed by 1957, many leaving for Israel.

RAKOSSZENTMIHALY Pest–Pilis–Solt–Kiskun dist., Hungary. Jews settled in the late 19th cent., attracted by the proximity of Budapest. The Neologist community, organized in 1900, maintained a synagogue, school, and old age home. In 1932, a J. cultural center serving the whole area was opened. The J. pop. numbered 787 in 1941. Most of the men perished under forced labor in WWII and the rest of the Jews were deported to Auschwitz via Hatvan from 12 June 1944.

RAKOVNIK Bohemia, Czechoslovakia. Jews are mentioned in 1441. A community was probably established in the 17th cent. and by 1900 the J. pop. was 329. In 1930 it was 153 (total 11,078). In 1942 the Jews were deported to the Theresienstadt ghetto together with the Jews of Prague and from there to the death camps of Poland.

RAKOW (I) Vilna dist., Poland. The J. community was one of the oldest in the Minsk region and received a sizable contribution from the Lithuanian Council in 1628 to construct a synagogue. In 1771 the community, up to then under the aegis of the Minsk community, became independent. Its pop. stood at 2,168 (total 3,641) in 1897. Jews opened factories manufacturing farm machinery and pottery, which became the mainstays of the J. economy. In the early 20th cent. the Bund sought to improve working conditions in the factories. The Zionist influence was extensive, with a Hebrew school founded in 1919 and Hehalutz active from 1924. In 1925 the J. pop. was 2,400, receiving assistance from J. relief organizations. Under Soviet rule (1939–41), J. businesses were nationalized and a cooperative was organized for craftsmen. Following the arrival of the Germans on 26 June 1941, 49 young Jews were executed as alleged Communists and a week later another 14 were murdered. A *Judenrat* was appointed and in Oct., 112 Jews were executed at the J. cemetery. A ghetto was then established, crowding together 950 Jews. All but ten were shot down at the entrance to the

synagogue or burned inside after being brought there in groups on 2 Feb. 1942. The ten fled to other ghettoes, a few later joining a Soviet partisan unit.

RAKOW (II) Kielce dist., Poland. Jews are first mentioned in the early 17th cent. In 1705, Eleazar Roke'ah became rabbi of the community, later serving as head of the rabbinical court of Amsterdam. In his honor, the Dutch authorities struck a coin bearing his portrait. In the late 18th cent., most Jews were artisans. In the early 20th cent., Jews operated a beer brewery and flour mill and a few supplied a nearby army garrison. The J. pop. was 1,263 (total 2,090) in 1897. The Zionists became active in the early 20th cent. and reached the peak of their influence between the World Wars, while Agudat Israel ran a Beth Jacob school for 100 girls. After WWI, Jews kept stores and stalls in the market, with some earning their living from the resort business in the area. In the 1930s, boycotts undermined J. livelihoods. When the Germans arrived in Sept. 1939, they found about 1,000 Jews in R. All were confined to a ghetto in 1940 and on 28 Aug. 1942, they were transferred to Jendrzejow for deportation to the Treblinka death camp on 16 Sept.

RAKVERE Estonia. The first J. settlers were Cantonists arriving in the 1850s, joined in 1865 by a number of J. artisans. The J. pop. grew to around 100 families in the 1880s but various disturbances and restrictions at the end of the cent. led many to emigrate while others were expelled, leaving ten families on the eve of WWI. The arrival of J. refugees and soldiers during the war revived J. public life but the J. pop. never exceeded the level of 100 (1% of the total) between the World Wars. They lived under satisfactory economic conditions. Most cultural activity had a Yiddish orientation. Some Jews escaped to the Soviet Union shortly before the arrival of the Germans in summer 1941; the rest were murdered.

RAMNICU-SARAT Moldavia dist., Rumania. A J. community existed in 1710. The first synagogue was erected in 1830 and three more were subsequently built. In 1875, a J. school was opened and in 1896, 96 pupils attended. In 1880, a branch of the Settlement in Eretz Israel movement was founded, headed by R. Avner Casvan, who served in R. from 1861 to 1898. In 1899, Dr. Moshe Gaster, community chairman, represented the community at the Third Zionist Congress

Jewish women in national dress, Ramnicu-Sarat, Rum'ania

in Basle and headed the J. Colonial Bank. In 1899, the J. pop. was 1,599, dropping to 1,040 in 1930 (7% of the total) as many left for Bucharest or emigrated overseas. From fall 1940, the Green Shirts and Iron Guard persecuted the Jews and looted their property. At the outbreak of the Soviet-Rumanian war (June 1941) J. men were incarcerated in a concentration camp in the city and the community became impoverished. After the war, the community renewed its activities.

RAMNICU-VALCEA Oltenia dist., Rumania. Jews lived here in the 14th cent., but a J. community developed only at the end of the 19th cent. Antisemitism was widespread between the World Wars. The J. pop. was 245 in 1899 and 197 in 1930 (1% of the total). In 1940, the Green Shirts persecuted the Jews and forced them to close their stores. In June 1941, at the outbreak of the Soviet-Rumanian war, 83 Jews from surrounding towns and villages were brought to R.

RAMYGALA (Yid. Remigole) Panevezys dist., Lithuania. Jews first settled at the end of the 16th

cent. The J. pop. in 1897 was 650 (49% of the total). During WWI, the Russian army expelled the Jews to Russia; two-thirds returned after the war. In 1929, a fire destroyed many J. homes and institutions. An anti-J. boycott in the mid-1930s led many to emigrate. The Zionist movement won widespread support. The J. pop. in 1940 was about 350 (27%). After the German occupation, the sick and elderly were buried alive at the *beit midrash* in R. while the rest where shot by Lithuanians in the Pajuste forest on 24–25 Aug. 1941 on the way to Panevezys.

RANDEGG Baden, Germany. The first six J. families settled in 1656 and an organized community was established in the 18th cent. In the early 19th cent., Michael Levi Neumann, court agent for the Austrian emperor, purchased the local castle and village lands and became the benefactor and head of the community. A new synagogue was erected in 1800 and in 1849 the J. pop. reached a peak of 351. A yeshiva attracting students from far and wide was opened around the mid-19th cent. In 1933, 62 Jews remained (total 721).

Anti-J. agitation intensified in the Nazi era, with Jews sometimes beaten in the streets at night by German border police. By 1938, all J. businesses had been liquidated and 22 Jews had emigrated. On *Kristall-nacht* (9–10 Nov. 1938), the synagogue was blown up. Another eight Jews subsequently emigrated and nine moved to other German cities in 1935–40. The last 17 Jews were deported to the Gurs concentration camp on 22 Oct. 1940 and another ten were deported after leaving the village. A total of 22 perished in the Holocaust.

RANIZOW (Yid. Raisnov) Lwow dist., Poland. The J. pop. stood at around 350 until WWI, dropping to 278 (total 1,561) in the wake of wartime tribulations and the peasant rioting in Nov. 1918 and May 1919. The Germans expelled the Jews to Sokolow and Glogow in July 1941.

RAPPENAU, BAD see BAD RAPPENAU.

RASEINIAI (Yid. Rasayn) Raseiniai dist., Lithuania. Jews first settled in the 17th cent. By 1857, the J. pop. stood at about 5,000 (59% of the total). In the 1880s, although the Jews controlled most of the commerce in R., the harsh edicts of the czar and three fires led to a failing economy and many Jews emigrated abroad, mainly to South Africa. Many Jews in the community were Haskala adherents who spoke Hebrew. Zionist fund raising and educational activities began in the 1880s and several community members emigrated to Eretz Israel. In 1897, the J. pop. was 3,484 (47%). The Jews were active in local politics. The 12-member city council included five Jews after WWI and a Jew served as deputy mayor for several years. In the mid-1930s, the economic situation deteriorated, in part because of an anti-J. boycott. Many emigrated to the U.S., South Africa, and Mexico, with some younger Jews emigrating to Palestine. The community maintained a synagogue and Hebrew educational institutions from kindergarten to high school. One of the teachers was the poetess Lea Goldberg (1911–70). The Zionist movement won widespread support and most parties and movements had branches in R. Among the rabbis who served R. was Moshe Soloveitchik (from 1908). In 1931 he became head of the R. Isaac Elhanan Seminary in New York, one of the constituent bodies of Yeshiva University. In 1940 the J. pop. was about 2,000 (about 32%). After the German invasion in June 1941, most Jews fled to the countryside. The bombings as well as acts by individual Lithuanians destroyed many J. houses and community institutions. The Lithuanian police seized Jews for forced labor and in July 1941 most of R.'s Jews were transferred in stages to a monastery outside the town. Over the next few weeks they were taken to prepared pits and shot. On 29 Aug. 1941, the last group of Jews, mainly women and children who had been transferred to a nearby estate, were shot.

RASHKOV Moldavia, today Republic of Moldova. Jews settled in the early 18th cent. After a Haidamak pogrom in 1738, the community recovered and numbered 103 in 1765 and 634 in 1790. The hasidic dynasty founded by R. Shabbetai in the early 19th cent. was famous throughout Bessarabia. The J. pop. was 3,201 (total 5,823) in 1897 and 2,031 under Soviet rule in 1926. In 1910, a *talmud torah* and two private girls' schools were operating. A pogrom occurred in 1918. In 1924, a J. kolkhoz was set up. German and Rumanian troops captured R. in July 1941. Dozens of Jews were immediately executed. In May 1942, Rumanian gendarmes drowned two J. families in the Dniester River. Most of the 109 people killed in the town were Jews.

RASLAVICE (Hung. Totraszlavica) Slovakia, Czechoslovakia, today Republic of Slovakia. Jews settled in the first half of the 18th cent. and formed an independent community in the mid-19th cent., maintaining a yeshiva, *beit midrash*, and *talmud torah*. There were 21 surrounding settlements under the community's religious jurisdiction. A synagogue was erected late in the cent. as the J. pop. rose to a peak of 132 (total 689) in 1880. In 1940, 85 Jews remained, forced out of their businesses in 1941 by the Slovakian authorities. On 20 March 1942, young J. men were sent to the Majdanek concentration camp via Zilina; on 25 March, 20 young J. girls were deported to Auschwitz via Poprad; and on 17 May, 150 Jews from R. and environs were deported to the Pulawy ghetto in the Lublin dist. of Poland.

RASTATT (in J. sources, Rechstett) Baden, Germany. Jews are recorded in 1560 and following expulsions in 1584 and 1615 established a new community after 1683. Towards the end of the 17th cent., the

The New Synagogue in Rastatt, Germany

Court Jew Mattityahu Schweitzer was active on behalf of the community and his sons served as heads of the community. A Hebrew printing press operated in the 1770s and 1780s. In 1829 a synagogue was completed. The J. pop. grew to 230 in 1875 (total 12,219) and remained stable until emigration, mostly of the young, accelerated after WWI. Jews were regularly elected to the municipal council. A new syna-

gogue was consecrated in 1906 and the Central Union (C.V.) and Zionist Organization opened offices in 1918 and 1924, respectively. Anti-J. agitation intensified in the early 1930s. In 1933, 155 Jews remained, operating 19 business establishments and two factories. After the economic boycott of 1 April 1933, Jews were banned from public places. On *Kristall-nacht* (9–10 Nov. 1938), the synagogue was set on fire (with its ruins subsequently blown up), J. homes and businesses were heavily damaged, and Jews were sent to the Dachau concentration camp after being viciously beaten and tormented. In 1933-40, at least 38 Jews emigrated from Germany, mostly to the U.S., France, and Palestine, and another 19 left for other German cities. In Oct. 1940, 29 Jews were deported to the Gurs concentration camp; another ten were sent to the camps after leaving R. Twelve deportees survived the Holocaust.

RASTENBURG (Pol. Ketrzyn) East Prussia, Germany, today Poland. Jews settled in R. in the early 19th cent. and by 1880 the J. pop. had grown to 141. A new building constructed in 1916 replaced the first

Consecration of synagogue in Rastenburg, Germany, 1916 (Beth Hatefutsoth Photo Archive, Tel Aviv/courtesy of George Fogelson, U.S.A.)

synagogue. In Jan. 1933, shortly before the Nazi take-over, a pro-Nazi newspaper accused the Jews of R. of ritual murder. By June 1933, the J. pop. was 117. The community still maintained a wide range of activities and new youth associations were founded. By Aug. 1938, the J. pop. had declined to 62. A month later the synagogue was sold. By May 1939, only 29 Jews were registered in R. No further information about their fate under Nazi rule is available.

RASTOACE (Ukr. Rostocki) Bukovina, Rumania, today Ukraine. Jews first settled in the late 19th cent. In 1930 the J. pop. was 71. After war broke out between the USSR and Rumania in June 1941, many Jews from the vicinity fled to Russia. On 25 June 1941, 320 Jews were murdered by Ukrainian gangs from eastern Galicia and Rumanian soldiers.

RATHENOW Brandenburg, Germany. Jews were probably living in R. from the first half of the 14th cent. until the expulsion of the Jews of Brandenburg in 1571. A new settlement developed c. 1700. Its pop. was eight families in the 1770s and 68 individuals in 1880. The community maintained a prayer room and two cemeteries. By 1925 the J. pop. was 112 individuals and in 1926 a synagogue was dedicated. In 1927, there was an arson attack on the synagogue and in 1930 a local SA leader abused the community's teacher. When the Nazis came to power in 1933, there were 100 Jews in R. Four Jews were arrested in June 1933 and held for several months and maltreated. On *Kristallnacht* (9–10 Nov. 1938), the synagogue was vandalized, Torah scrolls were destroyed, J. apartments were wrecked, and J. men were taken to the Sachsenhausen concentration camp. By Dec. 1941, there were 29 Jews in R. They were forced to move to three "J. houses." Most were deported in 1942–43. In 1934, the Association of J. Religious Pioneers (Bahad) set up an agricultural training farm on the Steckelsdorf estate near R. From 1940, the trainees were required to do forced labor. In May 1942, most were deported.

RATIBOR (Pol. Raciborz) Upper Silesia, Germany. Jews are first mentioned in 1367. They lived on their own street where a synagogue was located and earned their livelihoods from petty trade. They also engaged in moneylending, crafts, and the cattle trade. Although in 1510 the city received a *de non tolerandis Judaeis*

privilege, renewed by Charles VI in 1736, nonetheless there is evidence that Jews continued to live there at least until the mid-16th cent. and afterwards well into the late 17th cent. In 1831, the J. pop. was 478. It rose to 1,500 in 1881 and then began to drop, to 948 in 1900 and 770 in 1910. The community established a cemetery in 1813 and a synagogue in 1887 and maintained a school, welfare agencies, and various social organizations. Also active were a literary and historical society, the Society for Liberal Judaism, and branches of the Central Union (C.V.) and the Zionist movement. The J. pop. was 640 at the beginning of the Nazi era. The Nazi racial laws were not applied until July 1937 owing to the existence of the League of Nations' minority rights convention. Emigration was nonetheless stepped up, with the J. pop. dropping to 563 in 1933, the first year of Nazi rule. After the implementation of the racial laws, the local J. school served J. children from neighboring communities expelled from their own schools. On *Kristallnacht* (9–10 Nov. 1938), the synagogue was set on fire and almost all J. stores were destroyed along with J.-owned distillation facilities. In 1939, 282 Jews remained. Deportations to the death camps in General Gouvernement territory began in July 1942. On 19 Nov. 1942, one Jew remained, apparently married to a non-Jew.

RATKOVA Slovakia, Czechoslovakia, today Republic of Slovakia. The small community maintained a synagogue and cemetery and numbered 44 in 1940. Most of the Jews were deported to the death camps in 1942.

RATNO Volhynia dist., Poland, today Ukraine. Jews are first recorded in 1516. The community began to develop in the 19th cent., numbering 2,219 in 1897 (total 3,089). Zionism had its beginnings in the early 20th cent. Neskhizh Hasidim were prominent in the town. The hardships of WWI reduced the J. pop. to 1,554. Between the World Wars the Zionist youth movements became active and a Tarbut school enrolled 200 youngsters. Jews served as deputy mayors and owned a few small factories as well as marketing farm produce. The Soviets took over in fall 1939 and after the withdrawal of the Red Army in June 1941 the Ukrainians staged two pogroms. The Germans set up a *Judenrat* in July. After partisans took the town temporarily in June 1942, the SS retaliated by murdering 120 Jews.

On 25 Aug., 1,300 were brought to the town's quarry and executed. Of the hundreds who fled, many were shot and only a few survived.

RATZEBUHR (Pol. Okonek) Pomerania, Germany, today Poland. In 1737, there were three J. families living in R. In the 19th cent., the J. community numbered around 100 members and maintained a synagogue and a cemetery. When the Nazis came to power in 1933, there were 22 Jews in R. By 1935, their economic situation had seriously deteriorated and in summer 1935, the town put up a sign warning that Jews entered R. at their own risk. Although the community sold the synagogue to the town in Sept. 1938, the building was burned down on *Kristallnacht* (9–10 Nov. 1938). The community chairman was arrested and compelled to pay for the demolition of the synagogue's ruins. No further information about the fate of the remaining Jews is available.

RAUDONE Raseiniai dist., Luithuania. In 1923 there were 80 Jews in R. and in 1940 ten J. families. Most were killed after the German occupation of 1941. Some managed to escape to the nearby forest. They survived until Oct. 1944 when they were ambushed by a German unit.

RAUSCHENBERG Hesse–Nassau, Germany. Established around 1810, the community opened a synagogue in 1858, and numbered 78 (7% of the total) in 1905. It was affiliated with the Marburg rabbinate. Of the 31 Jews living there in 1933, 22 emigrated to the U.S.

RAVENSBURG Wuerttemberg, Germany. The Jews of the 14th cent. community were burned alive in the Black Death persecutions of 1348–49. The community was reestablished in 1835, numbering 40 in 1900 and under the aegis of the neighboring Bad Buchau rabbinate. Twenty-seven Jews remained in 1933, 20 subsequently emigrating and six dying in the camps.

RAWA MAZOWIECKA Lodz dist., Poland. The Jews were victims of a blood libel in 1547 and left the town soon after. In 1775 the village of Zamkowa Wola with its predominantly J. pop. was integrated into R. and the J. community flourished during the early 19th cent. with the development of the textile industry. The J. pop. in 1897 was 2,774 (49% of the total). The economic boycott between the World Wars hit the community hard, and on 4 Sept. 1934 a pogrom broke out. When the Germans arrived on 8 Sept. 1939, hundreds of Jews fled to Skierniewice. In early 1941 the Jews were ghettoized. In Oct. 1940, the J. pop. was 2,700; in 1942, it was 4,000, including refugees. On 26 Oct. 1942, 4,000 refugees were brought in from Biala Rawska and deported together with the other Jews in R. to the Treblinka death camp.

RAWA RUSKA Lwow dist., Poland, today Ukraine. The first Jews arrived with the founding of the town in 1624. In the 18th cent. they were subjected to restrictions and to heavy taxes under the Austrians from 1772. Most Jews identified with Belz Hasidism. The town developed as a stopover on the Lwow–Warsaw railway line, the J. pop. growing from 3,878 in 1880 to 6,112 in 1910 (total 10,775). J. trade centered on the marketing of eggs abroad. Jews were also prominent as furriers and hatmakers and ran a stoneware factory which declined with the advent of porcelain utensils. Another factory produced table and cooking oil. In 1884 a fire destroyed 234 J. homes. Late in the cent. emigration overseas commenced. A Baron Hirsch school was founded in 1892, reaching an enrollment of 200 within six years. The J. Socialist Party became active in 1908 and the Zionists in 1910. In the wake of WWI the J. pop. was reduced by about 1,000 and 70%, including 1,800 children, received assistance from the Joint Distribution Committee. Devastating fires struck the community again in 1923 and 1932. Between the World Wars the J. fur trade developed considerably with markets throughout Poland. The Soviet annexation (Sept 1939–June 1941) curtailed J. communal and commercial life. The Germans took the town on 28 June 1941. The Ukrainian militia immediately executed 100 Jews and the Germans instituted a regime of forced labor and extortion. A *Judenrat* was established in July 1941 and in spring 1942 Jews were concentrated in a crowded ghetto. The first mass *Aktion* took place on 20 March 1942, when 1,500 Jews were deported to the Belzec death camp; a second *Aktion* took place on 29 July with many murdered on the spot. Many Jews who were being transported to the Belzec death camp succeeded in jumping from the trains and reaching R. but eventually they shared the fate of the local Jews. The ghetto was liquidated in early Dec. 1942 when the remaining old and

The Rawa Ruska market, Poland, 1910 (Roger Violett, Paris/photo courtesy of Yad Vashem, The Holocaust Martyrs' and Heroes' Remembrance Authority, Jerusalem)

sick were deported to the Belzec death camp or murdered in the forest. Those in hiding were flushed out and also murdered. Most of the others met their end in labor camps.

RAWICZ Poznan dist., Poland. Two J. families settled in the first half of the 17th cent. and another dozen, under various disabilities, in the early 18th. The community began to develop after annexation to Prussia in 1793 and the lifting of residence restrictions. Peddlers and petty tradesmen became shopkeepers, proprietors of bakeries, booksellers, and printers and small factories were opened (for cigarettes, hats, gloves, furniture). Several merchants traded in hides, wool, and metals while others were brokers dealing in real estate and farm produce. An increasing number of Jews became doctors, lawyers, and teachers. Most J. children studied in public schools, with a dispropor-

tionate number attending the local high school (54 in 1887, representing 27% of the student body). The J. pop. rose to 1,780 in 1840 but dropped through emigration to 1,077 in 1885 (8% of the total). A new synagogue was completed in the 1880s. A branch of the Hilfsverein, supporting settlement in Eretz Israel as well as J. education, was opened in 1902 while the Zionists became active in 1905. Arthur Ruppin (1876–1943), future head of the Palestine Office of the Zionist Organization, was born in R. in 1876. Under Polish rule with its growing antisemitism, emigration continued as the J. pop. fell to 139 in 1921. With municipal authorities attempting to gain control of J. communal property, valuable religious articles were transferred from the synagogue to Benei Berak in Palestine. On the eve of WWII, only seven Jews remained, all of whom fled on the approach of the Germans.

Synagogue in Rawicz, Poland

RAYGOROD   Vinnitsa dist., Ukraine. Jews numbered 211 in 1765 and 995 (total 2,240) in 1897. A pogrom was staged against the Jews on 20 May 1919 and in 1926 the J. pop. dropped to 497. The Germans captured R. on 22 July 1941, concentrating the Jews of the area in a ghetto. In late Aug., 106 were murdered. A labor camp was set up, mainly for the Jews of Teplik, who were afterwards executed like the Jews of R.

RAZDELNOYE   Odessa dist., Ukraine. The J. pop. was 139 in 1926 and 283 (total 5,925) in 1939. A J. kolkhoz (Ivanovo) was located nearby with an elementary school (apparently four grades) where some children from R. studied. The Germans captured the town on 9 Aug. 1941. Most Jews in the area perished in the Holocaust.

RECA   (Hung. Rete) Slovakia, Czechoslovakia, today

Republic of Slovakia. J. refugees from Moravia arrived in the early 18th cent., if not before. They built the first synagogue in the late 18th cent. The J. pop. was 97 (total 1,070) in 1880 and 30 in 1941. In mid-May 1944, the Jews were brought to Senec and then moved to the Nove Zamky ghetto on 12 June and from there deported to Auschwitz on 15 June.

RECHITSA   Gomel dist., Belorussia. Jews settled in the late 16th cent. They were murdered in the Chmielnicki massacres of 1648–49. In 1765, 133 Jews were living in the town. Their pop. rose to 5,334 (total 9,280) in 1897. Most engaged in petty trade and crafts with a few wholesalers and a match factory operator among them. The community maintained a small yeshiva, headed by R. Hayyim Shelomo Kumm, who later founded a Mizrachi branch in the town. The Zionists and the Bund became active in the late 19th cent. A J. self-defense group was organized following a pogrom on 23 Oct. 1905 in which six Jews were killed and 12 seriously injured resisting the rioters. In 1927, under the Soviets, a J. section was opened in the local law courts. Two J. elementary schools were active. In 1939, the J. pop. was 7,237 (24% of the total). Many Jews succeeded in fleeing prior to the German occupation of R. on 23 Aug. 1941. In Nov. the remaining 3,000 Jews (785 families) were moved to a ghetto. All were executed on 25 Nov.

RECHNITZ   Burgenland, Austria. Jews first settled in 1527. By 1649 they maintained a small synagogue, inaugurating a larger one in 1718 with the help of the well-known Court Jew and Chief Rabbi of Burgenland, Samson Wertheimer. In the 19th cent., Jews earned their livelihood as tailors, butchers, furriers, and businessmen. A J. elementary school was functioning from 1847 until after WWI. In 1713, the J. pop. stood at 400, rising to 850 in 1850 and then declining to 145 in 1934. Jews served on the city council. By June 1938 only 43 Jews remained. Some were rounded up, severely beaten, and then deported to the Yugoslavian border without passports. Others were sent to Vienna and from there to the east. By July 1938, there were no Jews in R.

RECKENDORF   Lower Franconia, Germany. Jews began settling in the abandoned village as the first to return after the Thirty Years War (1618–48). They suffered from riots in 1696 and a blood libel in 1746. The

J. pop. was around 300 (a third of the total) in 1814 but declined from mid-cent. through emigration to other Bavarian cities and to the U.S. In 1933, 20 Jews remained. J. homes were vandalized by SA troops on *Kristallnacht* (9–10 Nov. 1938), along with the synagogue. Thirteen Jews emigrated in 1936–41, ten to the U.S. Four were deported to Izbica in the Lublin dist. (Poland) via Wuerzburg on 25 April 1942.

RECKLINGHAUSEN Westphalia, Germany. Jews were present in R. from at least the early 14th cent. They apparently perished in the Black Death persecutions of 1348–49. They were again present by 1418 and apparently left the town after 1512. The small number of Jews who passed through R. in subsequent years did not allow for the creation of an organized community. There is no mention of Jews after 1671, until two J. butchers were permitted to settle in 1816 to improve the local meat supply. A J. cemetery was opened in 1823 and in 1824, public prayer services were held for the first time in a private home. The community was formally established in 1827 and in 1846 numbered nine families. In 1853, R. became the seat of a regional congregation that included the communities of Ahsen, Datteln, Herten, Horneburg, and Waltrop. A synagogue was consecrated in 1880 and a J. school was opened in 1885. The accelerated economic development of R. and the Ruhr led to a sharp rise in the J. pop. in the last quarter of the 19th cent., to 120 in 1890 and 220 in 1900, necessitating the erection of a new synagogue in 1904. The assimilationist tendencies of the community can be seen in the addition to the building of a churchlike belfry even though it served no practical purpose. Nonetheless, R. joined the Westphalian Association for the Defense of Orthodoxy and the Association's rabbi, Moshe Marx, made R. his seat in 1903. In the Weimar period, the friction between the Liberals, who controlled the management of community institutions, and the Zionist and Orthodox opposition intensified. The East European Jews in effect held the balance of power in the city, with the Zionists and Orthodox wooing them and the Liberals attempting to neutralize them in community elections. While satisfactory relations prevailed with the local pop., antisemitic incidents occasionally occurred and a certain distance from the Jews was maintained. The J. pop. grew to a peak of 451 (total 84,609) in 1925. In 1930, among 152 J. breadwinners, 111 were engaged in trade (70 of them self-employed), 16 had academic

professions, 15 were artisans or laborers, and ten were butchers. The leading youth group was the Jugendverein, supported by the community leadership. In 1933, the J. pop. was 411. J. ritual slaughter was banned in the municipal slaughterhouse on 20 March, a month before the measure was instituted in the rest of Germany. In late 1933, two East European J. families lost their German citizenship and in Sept. 1934, the municipality banned J. students from the public schools. Vandalism against J. property was stepped up in 1935 and the social and economic isolation of the Jews continued apace. Many German stores refused to serve Jews. Community life was maintained and the Zionist Organization, the Central Union (C.V.), and the J. Cultural Association (Kulturbund) continued to operate. A *mikve*, *shohet*, and regular prayer services attest to the strength of the Orthodox presence. On *Kristallnacht* (9–10 Nov. 1938), the synagogue was partially burned (later razed). The J. school was also attacked and the teacher thrown out the window. J. stores were vandalized and about 40 J. men were arrested and detained for two weeks. In late Nov. 1938, 22 Jews with Polish citizenship were expelled to Poland and another ten or 11 in early 1939. Between 1933 and 1941, 161 Jews emigrated, including 63 to other European countries (25 to Holland and 14 to England), 33 to Palestine, 19 to South America, and 13 to North America 175 left for other German cities. From early 1939, Jews were transferred to "J. houses." In Oct. 1941, 91 lived in five such houses. On 24 Jan. and 3 Feb. 1942, 95 Jews were deported to ghettoes and camps in the east. Ten survived the war. The postwar community numbered 60 in 1974.

REDKI Polesie dist., Belorussia. R. was founded in 1849 as a J. farm settlement and had a pop. of 152 in 1898. In the late 1920s, under the Soviets, it became a J. kolkhoz where 28 families were employed. The Germans arrived in late Aug. 1941 and murdered the few remaining Jews.

REES Rhineland, Germany. Jews were intermittently present in the 14th–15th cents. A permanent settlement was established in the 18th cent., reaching a peak pop. of 119 (total 3,520) in 1871. The J. pop. then dropped to 79 in 1885, 55 in 1905, and 41 in 1932. The J. elementary school was closed before WWI. The synagogue, built in 1810, was set on fire on *Kristallnacht* (9–10 Nov. 1938) and both cemeteries (dating back to the mid-18th cent. and 1872, respectively) were desecrated in 1938.

REGENSBURG (in J. sources, Gushpurk, Rushpruk) Upper Palatinate, Germany. Jews may have arrived in Roman times but are first mentioned in 981 and formed an organized community in the early 11th cent. It was the first community in Germany, housed from the late 12th cent. in a special quarter surrounded by walls for its protection. In 1096, during the First Crusade, the Jews were forcibly baptized in the Danube River, but allowed to return to their faith a year later. Many were again forced to convert in 1137. In the early 12th cent. the Jews were accorded wide-ranging trade privileges, dealing in salt, horses, and slaves, gold, silver, and other metals, and engaging in moneylending. With R. an international center of commerce, local J. merchants reached Russia and western Asia and in many places helped found J. communities. From the 11th cent., R. was a great center of Torah learning and its scholars, known as "the sages of R.," included talmudic commentators (tosafists) like Rabbenu Tam and liturgical poets (*paytanim*). Among its illustrious rabbis was Yehuda ben Shemuel he-Hasid (1130–1217), who founded a yeshiva there and was one of the formative influences on German Judaism in the Middle Ages. He was one of the key figures in the Hasidei Ashkenaz movement of which R. was a major center. In the early 13th cent. a magnificent synagogue was erected. Jews continued to be valued for their economic contribution to the city's economy, with king, nobles, and townsmen vying to accord "protection" in return for substantial taxes. Thus the Jews of R. escaped the Rindfleisch (1298), Deggendorf (1336, 1338), and Black Death (1348–49) massacres. However, the decline of the city's commercial standing brought on an era of persecution and restrictive measures. In the 14th cent., Jews were confined to pawnbroking, which gave rise to the J. trade in used clothing and other secondhand articles. They were subjected to particularly heavy taxation and in 1393 they were forbidden to employ Christian servant women under the age of 50. In 1452 they were forced to wear a distinctive badge. During Lent, young townsmen made it a practice to attack and beat Jews and monks from the religious orders agitated vitriolically against them. In 1475, 17 Jews were imprisoned in a blood libel and in 1519 all 500 J. residents and another 80 studying at the yeshiva were expelled from the city. From

their places of refuge, the yeshiva students developed a special style of casuistic Talmud study (*pilpul*) which spread to Eastern Europe. In R. the synagogue was destroyed, 5,000 tombstones were removed from the J. cemetery to be used in building, and the ghetto was razed. The modern J. community commenced in the second half of the 17th cent. but was restricted to a few families until the second half of the 18th cent. when Jews again became active in trade (coffee, sugar, wine, knitted goods). The *Matrikel* laws of 1813 limited the number of J. families to the 17 present at the time. A new cemetery was inaugurated in 1822 and a J. public school was opened in 1832. In 1841 a new synagogue was dedicated. An era of rapid growth commenced in the 1860s, with Jews arriving from other settlements. In 1881 the J. pop. reached a peak of 675 (total 34,516). In religion, the Reform movement gained a firm foothold in the community. A new synagogue was consecrated in 1912 after the former building was pulled down in 1907 for fear of collapse. J. merchants and bankers played a leading role in the city's commerce at the turn of the cent. In 1933 the J. pop. stood at 427 (total 81,106). The era of Nazi rule was marked by virulent antisemitic agitation and a strict economic boycott. Throughout the period, community life continued with extensive cultural activity and welfare services. The J. Cultural Association (Juedischer Kulturbund) with 200 members put on concerts and other performances; the Maccabi sports club had 125 members; and the community offered vocational training and foreign language courses for those contemplating emigration. The Zionists, whose membership rose to 60 after the publication of the Nuremberg Laws in 1935, provided Hebrew instruction. Between 1933 and 1938, 268 Jews left R. – 101 to other German cities and 167 going abroad, including 93 to Palestine. On *Kristallnacht* (9–10 Nov. 1938), the synagogue and community center were burned to the ground, J. apartments were destroyed. and J. men, women, and children were arrested and humiliated. About 30 were sent to the Dachau concentration camp. Of the remaining Jews, including many who arrived after 1938, 76 more managed to leave the city by summer 1942, 66 of them emigrating abroad (including 17 to Palestine and 21 to the U.S.); another 103 were expelled to Munich on 2 April 1942 and from there transported to Piaski near Lublin (Poland) and 117 mostly elderly people were deported to the Theresienstadt ghetto in Sept. 1942. The last 14 Jews, living in mixed mar-

Älte Regensburger Synagoge,
erbaut im 14. Jahrhundert im fog. Übergangsstile (vom Romanischen
zum Gotischen), zerstört 1519.

**Innenanficht der alten
Regensburger Synagoge.**

**Portikus der alten Regens=
burger Synagoge,** im gotischen
Stile erbaut im 15. Jahrhundert.

Nach Radierungen des Regensburger Malers Älbrecht Altdorfer (1480–153).

Woodcuts of 14th cent. Regensburg synagogue, Germany

riages, were also deported to the Theresienstadt ghetto, on 14 Feb. 1945. Between March 1944 and April 1945, about 150 Jews were kept in a forced labor camp set up in R. as a branch of the Flossenbuerg concentration camp. They were subsequently transferred to the Landshut concentration camp. After the war, tens of thousands of J. Displaced Persons were housed and cared for in the area. In 1970 the renewed J. community numbered 140.

REGENWALDE (Pol. Resko) Pomerania, Germany, today Poland. There is evidence from 1692 of a Jew receiving a letter of proctection (*Schutzbrief*) for R. By 1728, four J. families were living in the town and 15 in 1812. In 1840, the community numbered 119 individuals and maintained a synagogue and a cemetery. When the Nazis came to power in 1933, there were 53 Jews in R. J. businesses suffered severely from boycott measures. By Oct 1942, most Jews had emigrated or been deported. Only five Jews remained, probably protected by marriage to non-Jews.

REGGIO EMILIA Emilia, Italy. The presence of Jews in R. is first recorded in 1413. Under the House of Este, the local Jews prospered, engaging mainly in moneylending. The community grew following the expulsion of the Jews from Spain and Portugal at the end of the 15th cent. Another wave of immigration developed after the Duchy of Ferrara came under papal rule in 1597. The local Jews, numbering 885, were restricted to a ghetto in 1669. When the old synagogue outside the ghetto was destroyed, a new one was built inside. There was a famous yeshiva in R. and among its renowned rabbis were Binyamin ben Eliezer ha-Kohen Vitale and Yeshayahu Bassano. In 1735, plague struck the town and a charitable society, Hesed ve-Emet, was founded to supply needy members of the community with shrouds. Emancipation came in 1796 and the ghetto was abolished as R. became part of the Cisalpine Republic. In 1806, R. Yaakov Yisrael Carmi represented the community in the Paris Sanhedrin. In 1814, with the Restoration, all the privileges were abrogated. Equality was gained in 1859, when R. became part of the Kingdom of Italy. A new synagogue was inaugurated in 1858. By 1873, the community consisted of 630 Jews, dropping to 545 in 1886. According to the 1930 law reforming the Jewish communities in Italy, R. was in-

cluded in the district of Modena. In 1936, the J. pop. of R. was 70. In 1969, the community numbered fewer than 100.

REGHIN (Hung. Szaszregen) N. Transylvania dist., Rumania. A J. community was founded in the 1840s and in the early 20th cent. a synagogue seating several hundred was built. A J. school was founded in 1874, closed, and then reopened in 1910 with up to 160 pupils. After the war, R. Yisrael Yeshurun Rubin set up a hasidic court. The J. pop. in 1930 was 1,587 (16% of the total). Jews were involved in the wine industry and the lumber trade. R. was a center of Zionist activity, which began prior to WWI, and in the 1920s some of the young immigrated to Palestine. A branch of Agudat Israel was established. R. served as a center for other communities: Deda (170 Jews, in 1930); Filea (106); Iernuteni (143); Alunis (44); Apalina (26); Brancovenesti (20); Gurghiu (72); Ibanesti (49); Porcesti (24); and Rusii Munti (31). After the annexation of N. Transylvania to Hungary in Aug. 1940, the economic situation of the J. pop. declined. In summer 1941, ten J. families were expelled and murdered in Kamenets-Podolski. In 1942, Jews were drafted into labor battalions in the Ukraine, where they died. On 4 May 1944, 6,000 Jews (including those from the Toplita and Ciuc districts) were ghettoized. On 4 and 10 June they were deported to Auschwitz. After the war the community was reconstituted but declined from 1948 with the majority emigrating to Israel.

REICHELSHEIM Hesse, Germany. Established in the 18th cent., the community numbered 260 (about 16% of the total) in 1871, thereafter declining. Its synagogue was dedicated in 1817. Anti-J. riots broke out during the 1848 revolution and many Jews had to take refuge in the forests. Nazi boycott measures were rigorously applied after March 1933. SS men from Bensheim organized a pogrom on *Kristallnacht* (9–10 Nov. 1938) and destroyed the synagogue's interior. Jews were compelled to dance around blazing Torah scrolls, their homes were looted and destroyed, and J. men were sent to the Buchenwald concentration camp. Of the 109 Jews living there in 1933, at least 66 emigrated (mostly to the U.S.); others were deported in 1942.

REICHENBACH (I) Hesse, Germany. The community, established by 1829 and numbering 76 (7%

of the total) in 1861, also had members in Elmshausen, Schoenberg, and Zell. Most of the 34 Jews remaining there in 1933 left by 1939; six were deported in 1942.

REICHENBACH (II) (Pol. Dzierzoniow) Lower Silesia, Germany. Jews settled no later than 1367 but were expelled in 1453-54. The community was reestablished only in the 19th cent., numbering 59 in 1840 and maintaining a synagogue and a cemetery (from 1826). A new synagogue was erected in 1875 and the community reached a peak pop. of 155 in 1880. Its pop. began to decline late in the cent., dropping to 52 in 1930. On *Kristallnacht* (9–10 Nov. 1938), the synagogue, three J. stores, and four J. homes were destroyed. In 1939, 19 Jews remained and in Nov. 1942 two Jews with non-J. spouses. Toward the end of the year, one Jew was sent to the nearby Tormersdorf camp. No further information is available as to the fate of the community under Nazi rule. Presumably those Jews who did not emigrate perished following deportation.

REICHENBERG Lower Franconia, Germany. The J. community was founded no later than the mid-18th cent. A synagogue was built in 1796 and the J. pop. stood at 133 in 1814 (total 428), subsequently declining steadily to 35 in 1933. On *Kristallnacht* (9–10 Nov. 1938), J. men were sent to the Buchenwald concentration camp. Fourteen Jews left in 1937–40, ten for the U.S. Of the 20 remaining in 1942, 12 were deported to Izbica in the Lublin dist. (Poland) via Wuerzburg on 25 April; three to the Theresienstadt ghetto on 23 Sept.; and two to Auschwitz on 17 June 1943.

REICHENSACHSEN (now part of Wehretal) Hesse–Nassau, Germany. Established before 1730, the J. community was the region's largest after Eschwege, numbering 236 (14% of the total) in 1861. It maintained an elementary school from 1835 to 1934 and opened a new synagogue in 1803. It was affiliated with Kassel's rabbinate. Most Jews left after *Kristallnacht* (9–10 Nov. 1938), when the synagogue's interior was vandalized. Over 30 perished in the Holocaust.

REICHMANNSDORF Upper Franconia, Germany. Jews are mentioned in 1779 and numbered 60 in 1867 (total 616). Just two remained in 1933.

REICHSHOFEN Bas-Rhin dist., France. A small community was established during the 19th cent. inaugurating a synagogue in 1852. In 1936, the community consisted of 59 Jews. During WWII, they were expelled to the south of France together with the rest of Alsace-Lorraine Jews. During the war, the synagogue was looted.

REILINGEN Baden, Germany. The first Jews settled in the 18th cent., erecting a synagogue in 1840. The community reached a peak pop. of 112 in 1871, dropping to 42 in 1900 (total 2,349) after the exodus of the young. In 1933, the J. pop was 11, with Jews owning two textile stores and a cigarette factory. Four perished in the camps after 1940; a few managed to reached the U.S.

REIMS (Rheims) Marne dist., France. The J. presence dates from the 12th cent. with Jews living in a *Vicus Judaeorum* (J. quarter) subsequently referred to as Rue de Gie (Jews) and Rue des Elus. The Jews were expelled from R. in 1306 and under the pressure of conversion the community disappeared entirely around 1394. In 1820, individual Jews began to settle, but a community was established only after the arrival of Jews from Alsace-Lorraine in 1870. The local synagogue was inaugurated in 1879 by a community numbering 120 families (640 members). In 1905 a local Association Cultuelle was founded. In 1939, the community consisted of 100 J. families (600 members). Several J. families left R. in 1940, but most were still in the city when the Germans arrived. In March 1942, J. males of foreign nationality began to leave R. anticipating arrests, which in fact began on 6 March and continued throughout the summer. The prisoners were brought to Drancy and then deported in 1942–43 to Auschwitz. On 7 June 1942, all Jews. were obliged to wear the yellow star. Signs with the words "*Interdit aux Juifs*" ("Forbidden to Jews") were placed in front of various establishments and places of entertainment. Arrests of foreign-born women and children started in July 1942 and deportations began in Sept. 1942. The Nazis rounded up the remaining 52 Jews (locals and foreigners) on 27 Jan. 1944. Those who were sent to Drancy were mainly directed to Auschwitz. Jews from R. were deported also to Majdanek and Sobibor as well as in the direction of Kaunas (Lithuania) and Reval (Estonia). Only one of the deported J. families survived. It was joined by survivors from other towns. American J. soldiers stationed in R. cared for the survivors, numbering 48 families (109 people) in 1945. With new arrivals, first from Egypt in 1956 and then from North Africa after 1958, the community grew to 600 Jews in 1964 and 650 (150 families) in 1970.

REINHEIM   Hesse, Germany. The community numbered 86 (4% of the total) in 1900 and was affiliated with the Orthodox rabbinate of Darmstadt. Jews attending Sabbath eve services in March 1933 were brutally assaulted and 42 left before *Kristallnacht* (9–10 Nov. 1938), when the synagogue (already sold to a non-Jew) was spared total destruction. Of the 64 Jews living there in 1933, at least 24 emigrated (mostly to the U.S.). The local SS officer responsible for the 1933 pogrom was hanged by inmates of the Buchenwald concentration camp prior to their liberation in April 1945.

REISKIRCHEN   Hesse, Germany. Numbering 42 (4% of the total) at its height in 1925, the community lost its synagogue on *Kristallnacht* (9–10 Nov. 1938) and dwindled to 12 by 1939. The last nine Jews were deported in 1942.

REJOWIEC   (Yid. Reyvitch) Lublin dist., Poland. Jews settled in the mid-16th cent. and by 1857 numbered 824 (80% of the total). At the turn of the 19th cent., J. factories employed many Jews in a general atmosphere of prosperity. The Bund organized a J. self-defense group when anti-J. riots broke out in Nov. 1904. The Zionists became active between the World Wars as the J. pop. dropped to 361 following the dislocations of WWI. Anti-J. riots were renewed in 1919 and towards the end of the 1930s. The Germans captured R. in Sept. 1939, closing down J. businesses and instituting a regime of severe persecution. A ghetto was established in 1941, reaching a pop. of 2,380 in late 1941 with the influx of refugees (1,300 from Lublin and Cracow). In April 1942, 2,000 Jews were deported to the Sobibor death camp. Of the remaining 500, some were killed trying to escape and 300 were sent to the Krichow labor camp attached to Sobibor. In April–May 1942, 3,300 Czechoslovakian Jews were brought to the ghetto. They were deported to Majdanek and Auschwitz between 7 April and 2 July 1943. After the war, the Polish government presented awards to a group of young J. men and women who fought

bravely with the partisans. Survivors who returned to the village soon left in the face of Polish hostility.

REMAGEN   Rhineland, Germany. The medieval J. community was destroyed in the Black Death persecutions of 1348–49. The modern community numbered 20–35 in the early 19th cent., growing to 67 (total 2,847) in 1871 and then dropping to 42 in 1900 and 25 in 1932. A society for promoting crafts among the Jews operated from 1837, teaching trades to needy children and numbering 240 members from R. and other communities in the 1890s. The community maintained two cemeteries. A synagogue founded in 1869 was set on fire on *Kristallnacht* (9–10 Nov. 1938). Most Jews left by May 1939. The nine who remained were deported to the camps in April 1942. Twelve Jews perished in the Holocaust.

REMBERTOW   Warsaw dist., Poland. The J. settlement began to grow after WWI with the development of the town as a resort. Jews provided services to the vacationers while J. butchers supplied the army and sent kosher meat to Warsaw. The Zionists were widely represented and the Bund and Agudat Israel were active, with most J. children receiving a traditional education. The Germans captured the city on 12 Sept. 1939. Many Jews fled, leaving about half the 2,000 there before the war. Refugees from Kalisz, Sieradz, and Lodz brought the number up to 1,800, all confined to the ghetto established in late 1939. On 20 Aug. 1942, all were deported to the Treblinka death camp. Another 1,000 Jews at a local labor camp were murdered in June 1943.

REMETI   (Hung. Palosremete; Yid. Remit) N. Transylvania dist., Rumania. A J. community existed in the mid-19th cent. The J. pop. in 1930 was 399 (25% of the total). In April 1944 the J. pop. was transferred to the Berbesti ghetto and then deported to Auschwitz.

REMSCHEID   Rhineland, Germany. Nine J. residents are mentioned in 1864. R. was attached to the Elberfeld regional congregation together with the neighboring settlements of Lennep and Luetringhausen, which were united with the city in 1929. The J. pop. of R. grew to 88 in 1895 and 167 (total 71,990) in 1910. Of 48 taxpayers in 1894, 14 owned clothing and shoe stores, 15 were traveling salesmen, and nine were sales clerks. In 1900–15, Jews from Russia, Gali-

Henric Kushmider (center) and his officer friends, Rembertow, Poland

cia, and Austria-Hungary began to arrive seeking employment. In 1915, the East European Jews in the community numbered 45, constituting a middle and lower class vis-a-vis the more established J. pop. East European Jews came to comprise over 50% of the permanent J. pop. and a large proportion of the transient J. pop. (75 of the 167 Jews who resided temporarily in the town in 1919–32). While Liberal Jews continued to attend services in Elberfeld, Orthodox Jews used three local prayer houses according to their country of origin. They also comprised most of the members in the local Zionist organization as well as of the Zionist Bar Kokhba sports club. Relations with the local pop. were confined to business dealings. In the 1920s there were manifestations of antisemitism. In the July 1932 Reichstag elections, the Nazis received 39.5% of the vote. In 1933, the J. pop. was 273 including Lennep and Luetringhausen. Half the J. pop. was self-employed, with 80% engaged in trade (furniture, clothing, shoes, raw materials, and metals). In March 1933, two J. doctors were dismissed from the public health services and in April, the munic-

ipality decided not to renew supply contracts with J. businesses, directing its employees not to patronize J. establishments. In 1935, the Nazi Party listed 57 J. breadwinners, including 36 shopkeepers. Ten J. businesses were liquidated by April 1938 and between April and Nov. the eight largest J. business establishments were "Aryanized." The smaller J. shops conducted business clandestinely with the German pop. during the night. In the municipal elementary school, J. students were ostracized. Eleven Jews emigrated in the second half of 1933 and another 52 by late 1937. A Hehalutz branch was opened in 1938 to prepare young Jews for immigration to Palestine and a few groups managed to leave via Holland within the framework of Youth Aliya. Jews with Polish citizenship were expelled to Poland in late 1938 and early 1939. On *Kristallnacht* (9–10 Nov. 1938), J. homes and businesses were vandalized and five Jews were sent to the Dachau concentration camp. The last J. businesses ceased to operate in Dec. 1938. (One belonging to a Rumanian J. national stayed open until late 1939.) In 1939, the Jews were forced to sell their homes to "Aryans" and moved to a few designated houses. In all, 159 Jews emigrated in 1933–41 while 40 left for other German cities in the May–Dec. 1939 period. Ten were deported on 24 Oct. 1941; 23 on 25 Oct.; and 11 on 21–24 Nov. In all, at least 63 Jews were deported to the concentration camps directly from R. and another 23 from occupied Europe. All perished: 20 are assumed to have died in the Lodz ghetto, 17 in the Minsk ghetto, and 13 in Auschwitz.

RENDSBURG   Schleswig–Holstein, Germany. Incentives offered by Christian V of Denmark led to the establishment of a community there in 1695. By 1835, the community had grown to 292 (3% of the total) and ten years later, Jacob Ettlinger, chief rabbi of Schleswig–Holstein, dedicated its elegant new synagogue. In the last decades of the 19th century and the early 20th century, the community declined sharply, shrinking to just 30 Jews on the eve of the Nazi takeover in 1933. Its property, including the synagogue, was "Aryanized" in 1938 and after *Kristallnacht* (9–10 Nov. 1938), the community disbanded. Those who did not manage to emigrate to safety died in Nazi camps and ghettoes.

RENI   Bessarabia, Rumania, today Republic of Moldova. It is not known when Jews began to settle in R. In 1847 there were 22 J. families living in R., and by 1897 the J. pop. was 730 (total 7,000). The Jews of R. were active in trade, especially of farm produce. The city was under Rumanian rule from 1918 to 1940 and was later annexed by the Soviet Union. In 1930, the J. pop. was 1,201. The Germans occupied R. on 19 July 1941. In Aug. 1941 they murdered 19 inhabitants, 18 of them Jews. Most of the J. pop. of R. presumably did not survive the Holocaust.

REPINE   (Hung. Repenye) Carpatho-Russia, Czechoslovakia, today Ukraine. Jews probably settled in the early 19th cent., numbering 79 in 1830 and 121 in 1880. Most engaged in trade, crafts, and agriculture. Jews owned five grocery stores, three inns, and three butcher shops as well as a flour mill and sawmill. The Hungarians occupied R. in March 1939 and proceeded to undermine J. livelihoods. A number of Jews were drafted into forced labor battalions. In Aug. 1941, a few J. families without Hungarian citizenship were expelled to Kamenets-Podolski, where they were murdered. The rest were deported to Auschwitz in late May 1944.

REPKI   Chernigov dist., Ukraine. Jews numbered 3,049 (total 3,336) in 1897 and only 79 in 1939. After their arrival in the area on 30 Aug. 1941, the Germans murdered 161, including the few remaining Jews of R.

RESITA   (Hung., Resicabanya) S. Transylvania dist., Rumania. The J. community was founded in 1871 and joined the Neologist association. Zionist activity began at the end of the 19th cent. The J. pop. in 1930 was 348 (2% of the total). In Sept. 1940, Iron Guard Legionnaires plundered J. property and the Jews were forced to sell their shops at undervalued prices. On 7 July 1941, the majority of the J. pop. was expelled to Oravita.

RETEAG   (Hung. Retteg) N. Transylvania dist., Rumania. A J. community existed in the mid-18th cent. The Hebrew author Yehuda Leopold Winkler settled in R. in 1847 and his contacts with local officials enabled him to rescue Jews during the 1848–49 revolution. The J. pop. in 1930 was 473 (18% of the total). In the 1930 census, all community members defined Yiddish as their language. Jews exported cattle, eggs, and fruit. Zionist activity began in the 1920s. After the annexation of N. Transylvania to Hungary (Aug. 1940) the economic situation of the Jews declined. In June 1942 some J. males were drafted into a labor battalion and sent to the Ukraine, where most died. On 6 May 1944 the J. pop. was transferred to the Dej ghetto and then deported to Auschwitz. After the war about 8% of those deported to Auschwitz returned. During the 1950s all left, mainly for Israel.

REUTLINGEN   Wuerttemberg, Germany. A J. settlement existed in the 13th cent. The Jews were attacked in the Black Death persecutions of 1348–49 and expelled in 1495. The settlement was renewed in the 19th cent. and numbered 60 in 1890 (total 18,542). It was attached to the Tuebingen community in the early 20th cent. Of the 54 Jews in the city in 1933, at least 31 left. Of the 12 who were expelled, two survived.

REVUCA   (Hung. Nagyrocze) Slovakia, Czechoslovakia, today Republic of Slovakia. Jews apparently arrived in the 1850s after the mining districts of central Slovakia were opened to J. settlement. A synagogue was consecrated in 1889 and the J. pop. rose to a peak of 129 (total 1,921) in 1910. The Zionists became active in the early 1930s and the J. National Party gained seats on the municipal council. When the town was annexed to Hungary in Nov. 1939, it became the seat of a dist. rabbinate with 13 attached settlements. A J. school for the area was opened in 1940–41. J. businesses were soon liquidated or "Aryanized" and in March and April 1942, with 83 Jews left in the town and 213 in the county, 48 young Jews were deported, the men to Majdanek and the women to Auschwitz. Most of the others were deported via Novaky to the death camps of the Lublin dist. of Poland on 6 June. The remaining 26 Jews from R. and 54 from the surrounding area reorganized the community. In Oct. 1944, prior to the German suppression of the Slovakian uprising, the Jews managed to escape. Some found refuge in the forests or with Slovakian peasants; others joined the partisans and fought the Nazis. Others were caught by the Germans and either killed immediately or sent to concentration camps.

REXINGEN   Wuerttemberg, Germany. The first permanent J. settlers were refugees from Eastern Europe fleeing the Chmielnicki massacres of 1648–49. They received residence rights but were heavily taxed by the relatively tolerant Order of St. John. Under Wuerttemberg rule from 1805, the Jews traded mainly in cattle but also purchased farm land to qualify for citizenship under the J. Law of 1828. The J. pop. reached a peak of 427 in 1854 (around a third of the total) and remained fairly stable in the subsequent period of marked emigration. An especially high proportion of young people followed in the footsteps of their elders in preserving the Orthodox character of the community. The first synagogue was dedicated in 1710 and the cemetery in 1760. A J. elementary school was opened in 1824. Relations with the local pop. were marked by mutual respect and Jews participated in the town's public life. With the return of J. soldiers after WWI a new spirit imbued the community and in 1924 a Zionist group was formed. In 1933, there were 262 Jews in R., steadily isolated under Nazi rule, but at the same time community life intensified. A youth hostel was opened in winter 1933–34 and Hebrew and English lessons were offered for potential emigrants. In 1938 a group of 38 young people left

for Palestine and founded the *moshav shittufi* Shavei Zion. On *Kristallnacht* (9–10 Nov. 1938), the synagogue was vandalized and burned. Of the 380 Jews in R. (including another 118 added to the community in the intervening years), 174 emigrated; 128 were expelled to the east in late 1941 and 1942, mainly to the Riga and Theresienstadt ghettoes; four survived. Of the 23 Jews in the attached community of neighboring Tuttlingen, 14 emigrated and eight were expelled, five of whom perished. The community is commemorated by a local monument and by a memorial hall in Shavei Zion, where a damaged Torah scroll from R. is preserved.

REZEKNE   (Yid. Rezhitze) Latgale dist., Latvia. Jews expelled from neighboring Makasan settled in R. in the late 18th cent. The community grew to 6,478 (total 10,795) in 1897 and about 11,000 on the eve of WWI (50% of the total). Most traded in farm produce, mainly grain and flax. The rapid growth of the J. pop. and its economic distress in the 1880s outstripped the ability of J. welfare agencies to serve the community adequately until the situation was rectified in the 1890s. A *talmud torah* accommodated 100 children. Hovevei Zion became active in the 1890s and the Bund with its 100 members led strikes among the town's workers in 1905. The Bund also played a leading role in J. self-defense and the anti-czarist underground. Many Jews left for Russia during WWI, while large numbers of refugees from Courland and Lithuania arrived in the town. In 1920, demobilized soldiers pillaged J. stores three times in the month of June. With the refugees moving on and many of the repatriated Jews not returning to R., the J. pop. stood at 3,911 (total 12,620) in 1925 and continued to decline. Though J. tradesmen faced stiff competition from the government-backed Latvian local pop., Jews still owned 299 of the town's 398 larger business establishments in 1935. Together with the Bund, the J. Folkspartei, backing Diaspora autonomy with one of the largest and strongest branches in Latvia, and the Independent Socialists formed an anti-Zionist front. The community had 11 synagogues. The Russian-language J. elementary school went over to Yiddish and enrolled 448 children in 1923. After a long struggle a Hebrew-language school was also opened but was combined with the Yiddish one under the Ulmanis regime in 1934–40. The J. high school founded in 1922 graduated 349 pupils until WWII. The J. pop in 1935 was

3,342. J. community life was phased out under Soviet rule in 1940–41. Hundreds of Jews managed to flee to the Soviet Union on the approach of the Germans in June 1941. The Germans captured R. on 3 July 1941. On 4 July, dozens of J. men were murdered by the Latvian auxiliary police and at least another 140 under the supervision of German security forces during the week of 10 July. The systematic liquidation of the community now commenced. The men were murdered in groups through the month of Aug. and the women raped and tormented before their execution. According to German sources, 3,219 Jews were murdered in R. After the war a community of a few hundred Jews was reestablished in the town; most left for Riga in the course of time.

RHAUNEN Rhineland, Germany. The J. pop. was 80–100 (10% of the total) down through the 19th cent. (In the attached village communities of Stipshausen and Hottenbach, the J. pop. was 36 and 140, respectively, in 1843 and together 44 in 1925.) The community was under the jurisdiction of the Trier dist. rabbinate in 1827. Children studied in local public schools and religious services were apparently held in rented prayer rooms. A cemetery was opened c. 1885. Jews earned their livelihoods mostly as livestock and hide dealers, butchers, and petty traders. Until the Nazi era, satisfactory business and social relations were maintained with the local pop. In 1933, the J. pop. was 60. With living conditions deteriorating, most of the young left the town by 1938, emigrating (to the U.S., Sweden, Palestine) or moving to the larger cities of the Rhineland. On *Kristallnacht* (9–10 Nov. 1938), the synagogue was vandalized (and razed a few days later) and J. homes and stores were seriously damaged. The last 17 Jews were deported to the concentration camps of Eastern Europe on 15 Oct. 1941.

RHEDA Westphalia, Germany. Jews were present from 1576 until their expulsion in 1689. They returned in 1711, numbering eight families by 1735. Jakob Moises acted as court agent and supplier and eventually became a member of the local chamber of commerce in 1779 despite the opposition of the municipal authorities. The community consecrated a cemetery in 1772 and a synagogue in 1802. It maintained a J. school until 1924. The J. pop. reached a peak of 116 in 1912. In June 1933, 92 Jews remained. The synagogue and school building were vandalized on *Kristallnacht*

(9–10 Nov. 1938) and J. men were sent to the Buchenwald concentration camp. All but one of the local Jews emigrated or left for other German cities by Sept. 1939, but several were deported from the places where they had hoped to find shelter.

RHEINBACH Rhineland, Germany. The first Jew is mentioned in 1345, while records of a J. community date only from the mid-17th cent. The J. pop. was 26 in 1813 and reached a peak of 113 in 1901. A synagogue was consecrated in 1872 and a new cemetery was opened in 1893. In 1933, only 27 Jews were still living in the town. The synagogue was burned on *Kristallnacht* (9–10 Nov. 1938), the Torah scrolls and ritual objects were confiscated, and five men were arrested and sent to a concentration camp. The 19 Jews left in R. on the outbreak of WWII were sent to the Bonn-Endenich transit camp in Feb. 1942 and from there deported to the east.

RHEINBISCHOFSHEIM Baden, Germany. The first Jews settled in the mid-17th cent. with the privilege of operating shops and stalls. In the 19th cent. many ran auxiliary farms. The J. pop. reached a peak of 155 in 1875 (total 1,600) and then dropped sharply. In 1933, 57 remained. During the Nazi era, 39 emigrated and five moved to other German cities (two of them also emigrating). On *Kristallnacht* (9–10 Nov. 1938), the synagogue was vandalized. The last seven Jews were deported to the Gurs concentration camp on 22 Oct. 1940. Three others were deported after leaving R. All perished, seven of them in Auschwitz in 1942.

RHEINDAHLEN Rhineland, Germany. Jews are first mentioned in 1637 and maintained a pop. of somewhat over 50 from the 1840s until emigration commenced in the 1890s. R. was attached to the Moenchengladbach regional congregation in 1854 and became a satellite of Moenchengladbach-Rheydt in 1890. Twenty Jews remained in 1933. Six left the town in the Nazi era and another six were deported to Izbica in the Lublin dist. (Poland) and the Theresienstadt ghetto.

RHEINE Westphalia, Germany. Jews are first mentioned in 1343 and were victimized in the disturbances associated with Black Death in 1350. They were again present for a short while in the 16th cent. and expelled in 1560. One J. family was present in 1678. A small synagogue was erected in 1768. In 1856, the community, together with the Jews from Emsdetten and Neuenkirchen, was attached to the Burgsteinfurt regional congregation. In 1884, it became independent. A J. elementary school, also teaching such secular subjects as mathematics and German, was opened in 1850. A new synagogue was consecrated in 1887. The J. pop. rose to 112 in 1871 and 139 (total 13,415) in 1913. In 1933, the J. pop. was 126. Of 51 breadwinners, 25 were merchants and ten livestock dealers. Eight were forced to sell their businesses in 1937. On *Kristallnacht* (9–10 Nov. 1938), J. homes and stores were heavily damaged and the synagogue was burned. Most Jews were moved to two houses in 1939. In all, 56 emigrated by 1941, including 14 to Holland and 23 to the U.S. On 10 Oct. 1941, 13 were bussed to Muenster for deportation to the Riga ghetto; on 26 Jan. 1942, another three were sent to the Riga ghetto; and on 1 Oct. 1942, seven were sent to the Theresienstadt ghetto. At least 26 perished in the Holocaust.

RHEINHAUSEN   Rhineland, Germany. The J. pop. in 1933 was 65 (0.2% of the total). In the Nazi era, 39 Jews left the city, 16 for other German towns. Ten were deported to the Riga ghetto on 10 Dec. 1941, perishing together with six others deported from their places of refuge.

RHINA   (now part of Haunetal) Hesse–Nassau, Germany. Encouraged to settle there around 1650, J. immigrants from Bavaria established a community in 1682 but only acquired a permanent synagogue 100 years later. They maintained a *talmud torah* and an elementary school (1782–1938), but could not afford to build a new synagogue and had the old one renovated in 1834. A J. civil guard was organized in R. during the 1848 revolution. By 1885 these strictly Orthodox Jews numbered 314 (56% of the total). Affiliated with the rabbinate of Fulda, the community shrank from 225 (43%) in 1925 to 87 (22%) in Oct 1938. Nazis burned the synagogue on *Kristallnacht* (9–10 Nov. 1938) and by 1 March 1939, R. was officially "free of Jews" (*judenrein*). A total of 76 Jews emigrated (50 to the U.S.) and about the same number perished in the Holocaust.

RHODEN   (now part of Diemelstadt), Hesse–Nassau, Germany. Numbering 70 in 1847, the community was affiliated with Kassel's rabbinate. The synagogue was burned down on *Kristallnacht* (9–10 Nov. 1938) and most of the 34 Jews registered there in 1933 left. Nine from R. and two from nearby Wrexen were deported in 1942.

RHODES   (Gr. Rhodos, Rodos) Dodecanese Islands, Greece. Romaniot, Greek-speaking Jews are mentioned as residing in R. in the second cent. B.C.E. The 12th cent. traveler Benjamin of Tudela recorded a J. community of about 400 Jews. The Jews built a synagogue during the rule of the Knights of St. John (1309–1522). An earthquake in 1481–82 destroyed the J. quarter and many left the island. Towards the end of the 15th cent., at the time of the Spanish and Portuguese expulsions, anti-J. sentiment mounted in R. The Jews were expelled in 1502, but some remained and newcomers arrived. R. was under Ottoman rule from 1522 to 1912. Refugees from Spain and Portugal, as well as 40 families imported from Salonika by the Turkish Sultan, formed a predominant Sephardi community that became known for its rabbis, its numerous rabbinical institutions, and its rabbinical court. The Jews enjoyed religious autonomy, but did not receive equal civil rights. Many worked in the textile industry and traded in silk, coffee, and other products. Jews dominated wine production in R. A second synagogue was built in 1577. A number of associations were established, dealing with various aspects of the community's life (e.g., burial, hospitality, welfare, redemption of captives, and education). In 1714–36, R. Moshe Israel held the position of chief rabbi of R. During his tenure the island gained renown as a center of Torah study. The Jews' financial standing was undermined in the 19th cent. During the ten-year Greek revolt (1821–31) in the Peleponnesus, anti-J. disturbances prompted some Jews to flee the island. A severe epidemic broke out in 1837 and killed ten Jews. A blood libel in 1840 was terminated with the assistance of Moses Montefiore. Earthquakes in 1851 and 1863–64, an explosion in 1855, and fires in 1865 and 1876 caused severe material damage and financial losses to the J. community. Funds to assist the community were raised abroad. The J. pop. in 1884 was 2,401. Numerous *yeshivot* operated in the 19th cent. and two more houses of prayer were opened. In 1899, a boys' school that included the study of French was opened and received support from the Alliance Israelite. In 1902. a J. girls' school was founded. Emigration from R. increased in the early 20th cent. and the community's financial position

Funeral of R. Reuven Eliyahu Israel, chief rabbi of Rhodes, Greece, 1933 (Beth Hatefutsoth Photo Archive, Tel Aviv)

continued to decline. R. came under Italian rule in 1912, when the Jews numbered 4,500 (total 14,100). During WWI the Jews experienced increased hardship and many suffered severe hunger. Additional J. welfare organizations were established during the period, as well as a branch of B'nai B'rith (1913). Italian influence made its way into the community, with Italian replacing French in the schools. In the 1920s, Zionist groups were active. An illustrious rabbinical seminary was established in 1928, when the Fascist Party in Italy sought ways to increase Italy's influence in the Middle East. The seminary attracted the support of wealthy Jews in R., Italy, and the Middle East, thus underscoring Italy's influence in the region. However, when Italy cemented its ties with Nazi Germany in 1936 and adopted racist policies, the seminary lost the support of many influential communities. Foreign nationals were soon expelled from the island, accounting for a significant decrease in the seminary's students and faculty, and the institute was eventually closed down on 27 Aug. 1938. A few days later, Italy's racial laws were applied in R., involving the restriction of J. movement, business activities, and welfare and cultural activities. The J. pop. in 1938 was 4,000. Many were deprived of their Italian citizenship. All "foreign" Jews, who numbered about 480, were then ordered to leave

R. A large J. exodus subsequently took place, primarily to Rhodesia and the Belgian Congo (Zaire) The J. pop. in 1940 was 2,200 (total 55,181). In May 1940 a ship sponsored by the Betar movement and carrying 500 Jews from Bratislava to Palestine sank. The passengers survived and were brought by the Italians to R., where they were held for 500 days before being transferred to Italy. Three remained and shared the fate of R.'s Jews. On 15 Sept. 1943, with the J. pop. standing at 1,900, the Germans occupied R. and the Jews were soon seized for forced labor. In Feb.–April 1944, 36 Jews were killed when the British bombed the island. The Germans confiscated all radios and correspondence from abroad, so that the Jews were unaware of the deportations and death camps. On 12 July, the Jews were ordered to assemble in villages on the northern coast of R., supposedly to protect them from Allied bombings. On 19 July, all the J. men there were ordered to report for defense work. On the following day, all the women and children were likewise ordered to report, for transfer. By 21 July, all the Jews had been arrested and their possessions confiscated. The Turkish consul managed to save 40 Jews who were subjects of Turkey. He was subsequently named one of the Righteous among the Nations in 1990. The Jews were held until 23 July

Interior of Rhodes synagogue, Greece

under harsh conditions and were then boarded on fishing boats. They were taken via Leros and Samos to a camp near Athens (five died along the way), where the men were separated from the women and children. Their number in Athens reached 1,769. On 3 Aug., the Jews were deported to Auschwitz, arriving there on 16 Aug. On the way, 22 died and a few managed to escape. Some were later sent to the Mauthausen concentration camp. Survivors of the Holocaust returned to R. after the war and numbered 200 in 1947, when R. was annexed to Greece. The community decreased thereafter and only 50 remained by 1959.

RIASNA   Mogilev dist., Belorussia. The J. pop. was 551 in 1847 and 918 (71% of the total) in 1897. In 1926, under the Soviets, the J. pop. was 739. A J. kolkhoz was founded nearby in 1929, employing 30 families in 1930. A J. council was established in 1930 and a J. school (four grades) was active. The Germans occupied R. in July 1941. On 3 March 1942, the Nazis and local police murdered the 600 Jews of R. on the outskirts of the town. Many of the children were thrown alive into the burial pits.

RIBEAUVILLE   Haut-Rhin dist., France. In 1689 there were over ten J. families. The synagogue was inaugurated in 1830. In 1885, there were 580 Jews in R., dwindling to 339 in 1910 and 169 in 1931. During WWII they were expelled to the south of France with the rest of Alsace-Lorraine Jews.

RICHELSDORF   (now part of Wildeck) Hesse–Nassau, Germany. Numbering 63 (11% of the total) in 1871 and 40 in 1933, the community disbanded after

Kristallnacht (9–10 Nov. 1938). Most of the remaining Jews emigrated; two were deported in 1941.

RICHEN   Baden, Germany. J. settlers are first mentioned in 1722. In the early 19th cent. they traded in cattle, wool, and hides. Anti-J. rioting broke out during the revolutionary disturbances of 1848. The J. pop. reached a peak of 103 in 1875 (total 915) but then fell to 34 in 1900 through emigration and the move to the big cities. In 1933, 15 remained, all but one leaving by 1936.

RICKA   (Hung. Kispatak) Carpatho-Russia, Czechoslovakia, today Ukraine. Jews probably settled in the early 19th cent. and numbered 37 in 1830 and 92 in 1880. Most engaged in trade and agriculture. They owned three grocery stores, five inns, and two butcher shops. The J. pop. rose to 135 in 1921 and then dropped slightly to 127 (total 1,109) in 1941. The Hungarians occupied the town in March 1939. In late May 1944, the Jews were deported to Auschwitz.

RICSE   Zemplen dist., Hungary. Jews were present by 1811 and in 1918 became a congregational center for 12 surrounding settlements. Adolph Zukor, founder of Hollywood's Paramount Pictures, was born in R. The J. pop. was 122 in 1880 and 171 in 1930. The Jews were deported to Auschwitz via Satoraljaujhely on 6 June 1944.

RIEBENI   (Silajani; Yid. Riebinishki) Latgale dist., Latvia. A few dozen Jews settled on estate lands in the early 19th cent. and were reduced to working as day laborers there in the 1890s to meet their tenancy payments. After dropping from a peak of 533 (total 584) in 1897, the community maintained a pop. of 300–400 between the World Wars, living under primitive conditions. The J. elementary school opened in 1921 only went up to the fifth grade and lacked all basic equipment. Social life revolved around the Tze'irei Tziyyon clubhouse. Many left with the Soviets on the approach of the Germans in June 1941. The Latvians immediately commenced torturing and murdering Jews. Between 23 and 26 Aug. 1941, the Latvian police brought the remaining 200–300 Jews to the forest and executed them.

RIENECK   Lower Franconia, Germany. Jews suffered during the Rindfleisch massacres of 1298 and were expelled at around the beginning of the Thirty Years War (1618–48). Jews were present again in 1699 and numbered 96 (total 1,542) in 1837, with 18 emigrating to the U.S. in 1830–54. A new school was built in 1873. Nineteen Jews remained in 1933. The last 13 left for Frankfurt in March 1939 after being forced to sell their homes.

RIESENBURG (Pol. Prabuty) East Prussia, Germany, today Poland. Individual Jews lived in R. already around 1700, but a community only came into being at a later time. The J. pop. was 69 in 1831, 148 in 1895, and 70 in 1925. A synagogue was built about 1870. A cemetery dates back to the 18th cent. By May 1937, many Jews had left and the J. pop. dropped to 65. No further information is available about the fate of the R.'s Jews under Nazi rule.

RIETAVAS (Yid. Riteve) Telsiai dist., Lithuania. Jews first settled in the 16th cent. The J. pop. in 1897 was 1,397 (80% of the total). Many emigrated to South Africa, a few to Palestine. The community maintained two synagogues, a traditional *heder*, and a modern Zionist *heder*. During WWI, under the German occupation, young men were taken to forced labor. Be-

tween the World Wars, many joined relatives in South Africa, with a few going to the U.S. and Palestine. In 1919, a religious Hebrew school was established. In the mid-1930s an anti-J. boycott led to a further deterioration of the Jews' economic situation. In the 1930s Zionism took hold, mainly among the young, and a training kibbutz operated in R. The J. pop. in 1940 was 500. After the German invasion in June 1941, a regime of forced labor, abuse, and murder was instituted. The Jews were marched to the Rainiai camp outside Telsiai and on 15 July 1941, all males aged 13 and over were murdered in the adjacent grove. On 29 Aug. 1941 the remaining women and children were transferred to Geruiliai and later executed there.

RIGA Vidzeme (Livonia) dist., Latvia. J. merchants began to appear in the city in the 16th cent. and carried out their trade without being allowed to take up permanent residence, though some managed to filter through and strike roots. Under the Swedish occupation from 1621, residence restrictions were reinforced and Jews were only permitted to reside in a special J. inn outside the walls of the city. After the Russian conquest in 1710 a number of J. commercial agents representing the czar's court were permitted to settle in the city

Street in Rietavas, Lithuania

Celebrating historian Simon Dubnow's 70th birthday, Riga, Latvia, 1935

with their families. A J. cemetery was opened in 1725, marking the establishment of the community. In 1743, the Jews of R. were expelled as part of the general expulsion of the Jews from Russia under Empress Elizabeth. In addition to a few J. merchants allowed to settle in 1764 under letters of protection, there were others who again took up residence over the years in the refurbished inn. In 1766 Catherine II canceled the residence ban and additional J. merchants were now allowed to stay in the city as tolerated foreigners without permanent residence rights. When the nearby town of Sloka came under her rule, still other J. merchants interested in trading in R. settled there. By 1811 the J. pop. numbered 736, just 77 living within the city and the rest in Sloka, the inn, and the suburbs outside the city walls. Half the Jews were merchants and brokers and a third artisans. When the walls of the city were torn down in 1857 restrictions were lifted and Jews were allowed to purchase property and settle in the city as well as to join guilds. The J. community was divided into a Yiddish-speaking majority originally from Belorussia, Poland, and Lithuania and a minority from Courland and Germany with a German cultural orientation. Friction between the two carried over from the days when the community was divided between "protected" Jews and temporary residents. Rivalry between the two focused at first on the struggle over control of the synagogue opened by the "protected" Jews in 1767. The community's first rabbi, Moshe Yehezkel Metz, was appointed in the early 19th cent. A *talmud torah* for needy children and a *heder* also operated from that time, reaching an enrollment of 43 in 1835. A modern J. school was founded in 1840, the fourth of its kind in all Russia, differing from the others in that German was the language of instruction. Its first principal was Dr. Max Lilienthal, followed by Reuven Wunderbar, future historian of the Jews of Livonia and Courland. By 1866 it had 500 students in nine grades, with twice as many girls as boys. The community grew rapidly in the second half of the 19th cent. as did the city. The J. pop. rose from 2,641 in 1864 to 14,222 in 1881 and 22,115 in 1897 (total 282,230), owing mainly to the right accorded to various categories of Jews from the 1860s to reside outside the Pale of Settlement. Jews played a leading role in the dynamic commercial and industrial development of the city in the last third of the century. About a third of the city's trade was in J. hands. They controlled a substantial part of the export trade in grain, flax, hides, and eggs. As operators of ten sawmills and as lumber merchants, the Jews helped make R. one of the great lumber-exporting ports in the world. Among the leading J. lumber dealers and industrialists were Leib and Shelomo Shalit and Shelomo-Zalman and Yeshayahu Berlin, the latter the great-grandfather of the British philosopher Sir Isaiah Berlin, who was born and raised in R. Jews were also among the city's leading financiers, operating ten banks by the end of the cent. Most textile and clothing stores in R. were owned by Jews and Jews remained well represented in the crafts, with a large number of tailors and about 500 in 50 workshops stitching shoes. Another few hundred labored in light industry (paper, candy, flour, cigarettes, printing) and most of the city's 100–120 dentists and 20% of its doctors were Jews. Though the friction between the Russo-Polish and German-Courland elements in the community lessened in time, there remained an economic division between the two. The former was to be found at both ends of the spectrum, as merchants and industrialists and as the poorer class crowded into a slumlike "Moscow" quarter. The latter comprised the professional and skilled-artisan class. Numerous welfare agencies existed to aid the needy. From the second half of the 19th cent., a number of synagogues were built, including one founded by a group of 135 Cantonists in 1873. From 1886 to 1911, Moshe Shapira served as the community's rabbi. Afterwards two rabbis officiated, one for the Moscow quarter and the other for the rest of the city. The Hasidim were led by R. Leib Schneersohn until 1915. At the same time the historian and poet Aharon Eliyahu Pomiansky (1873–93) and Yehuda Leib Kantor (1909–15), founder of the first Hebrew daily, *Ha-Yom*, served as official (state-appointed) rabbis. From the 1880s to the pre-WWI period, a large number of J. schools were added to the one founded in 1840: two for boys and two for girls with Russian as the language of instruction; 6–7 modernized *heder* schools teaching Hebrew through Hebrew and enrolling 270 children in 1911; two night schools; and a vocational school. The first J. high school in R. grew out of the 1840 school and in the 1870s, 750–800 were studying in the local polytechnic institute, though their number dropped to 200 in the decade before WWI. The chief organization promoting J. education and culture was the Society for the Promotion of Culture, founded by Leib Shalit and Dr. Paul Mintz in 1898 and the third of its kind to be established in Russia. The Society was responsible for setting up a 7,000-volume public library. Zionist activity commenced in the 1880s, with Ze'ev (Wolf) Luntz and Leib Shalit representing R. at the Kattowitz Hovevei Zion Conference in 1884. In 1890 an Eretz Israel settlement society was founded and Shalit was instrumental in the purchase of 1,000 acres of land around Hadera, where ten local families settled in 1891. Shalit also represented R. at the First Zionist Congress in Basle in 1897. In the aftermath, Zionist groups began to proliferate. The Bund was also active, leading strikes, organizing J. self-defense after the 1903 Kishinev pogrom, and participating in the revolutionary events of 1905, when a number of its members were shot down. The J. pop. rose to 33,651 in 1913. The period before WWI was marked by economic crisis, with the lumber industry affected by competition with the port of Windau in Courland, leaving many Jews unemployed. In 1915, 40,000–45,000 J. refugees received assistance from the community. By the end of 1916 about a third of R.'s Jews had left as well. After the Feb. 1917 Revolution J. public life began to revive and under the provisional Latvian government set up in Nov. 1918, the Bund and other Yiddishists gained control of the J. educational system. The shortlived Bolshevik government of 1919 introduced a regime of nationalization and antisemitic persecution but J. institutions continued to function and became active in the rehabilitation of the community when the Latvians returned to power. Once again the community extended aid to J. refugees, now fleeing the Soviet Union on their way west. Most of the aid, along with assistance to the community, was financed by the Joint Distribution Committee. With the return of local Jews after the war and the influx of foreign refugees and other Latvian Jews, the J. pop. rose rapidly to 39,459 in 1925 (total 337,699) and came to represent about half the number of Jews in all Latvia. Jews were largely responsible for the revival of the city's economy after WWI. About 35% were engaged in trade, 30% in crafts (a third tailors), 20% in sales and clerical work, and 12% in the professions (many of them teachers). Jews were again active in the wood industry as well as in textiles, food, and tanning. The Frumchenko family ran a chocolate factory and later founded Israel's well-known Elite firm. Others were leading producers

The main synagogue in Gogol St., Riga, Latvia

of tobacco, beer, and liqueurs. In the 1922–24 period Jews also founded five banks and ran a roof organization for 25 credit societies serving Jews in Latvia's provincial towns. In the 1930s, despite the ongoing economic crisis and the decline of the local wood industry and the trade in grain and flax, Jews were able to maintain a measure of their economic strength, aided by German-J. capital seeking outlets after the Nazi rise to power. A substantial part of the city's bigger businesses remained in J. hands and the J. professional class remained prominent. The J. educational system was reorganized under the Latvian cultural and educational autonomy law for minorities. In addition to the three city-supported Yiddish schools opened in 1919, the Zionists founded two Hebrew public schools with Joint and community aid. The two systems enrolled 2,600 children or 50–60% of the J. school-age pop. in the early 1920s and two-thirds by the early 1930s. By that time, three kindergartens, a Hebrew high school, and an open university teaching sociology and the natural sciences were operating. Under the Ul-

manis regime from 1934, the system was forced to take on a more religious coloration under Agudat Israel influence. In 1924 a six-story building was erected to house the J. hospital, including a dental clinic, X-ray department, and pharmacy. In 1931, 1,434 patients were treated there, a third of them non-J. The well-known surgeon Prof. Vladimir Mintz headed the hospital. Mintz had worked in Moscow and saved Lenin's life after the assassination attempt in 1918, earning him the gratitude of the Soviet leadership and a special dispensation to return to Latvia. His brother, Prof. Paul Mintz, was one of Europe's leading authorities on criminal law and chairman of the National Democratic Party. A maternity ward and nursing school operated in a second medical facility. The community also ran preventive medical services, including psychological counseling, infant care stations, and a tuberculosis clinic treating nearly 4,000 people in 1931. The J. health insurance fund was the second largest in Latvia, covering 13,000 members. The old age home was housed in a new four-story building from 1932, with 150 beds, and an orphanage accommodated 80 children. From 1915 until his murder by the Nazis in 1941, Menahem Mendel Sack, strongly identified with Agudat Israel, was chief rabbi of the community, founding its first yeshiva in 1921 and educating a generation of rabbis and scholars. About 40 prayer houses were in operation. Among the Hasidim, the Lubavich followers had the largest *minyan*, also founding a yeshiva in the 1930s. The unification of the Tze'irei Tziyyon Party with the Zionist Socialists in 1931 made it a leading force in the Zionist camp, contending with the Revisionists for primacy in the community. Among its leaders was Prof. Mattityahu (Max) Laserson, an expert in international law who helped draft the Latvian constitution and was later active in founding the Tel Aviv School of Law and Economics (subsequently becoming Tel Aviv University). The Revisionist movement was born in R. and with it Betar, inspired by a visit by Vladimir Jabotinsky in 1923 and under the leadership of Dr. Yaakov Hoffmann. The religious Zionists were led by R. Mordekhai Nurock, a founder of Mizrachi, whose personality left a mark on the community far beyond the limited strength of the movement there. He and his brother Aharon were elected to the Sejm and later he served in the Israeli government. The Bund continued to be influential among the intelligentsia as well as the poorer classes, its strength concentrated in the trade unions and the Yiddish educational institutes. The influence of Agudat Israel derived mainly from the forceful personality of R. Mordekhai Dubin, who was close to Prime Minister Ulmanis and served four consecutive terms in the Sejm. In 1927 he arranged for the Lubavich Rebbe, Yosef Yitzhak Schneersohn, to be let out of the Soviet Union and come to R. and in 1929 he was received by President Hoover in the U.S. Under Ulmanis, he was licensed to publish the Yiddish daily *Haynt*, which was the only J. newspaper to appear in Latvia in 1934–40. Among the Zionist youth movements, Hehalutz operated pioneer training farms for hundreds of its members throughout Latvia. Hashomer Hatzair, reaching a membership of 350–400, was led by Barukh Bag, one of the founders of the Maccabi organization and later of the Wingate Institute in Israel. In addition to sports, Maccabi promoted cultural activities in the city, founding a drama circle, choir, and orchestra. Betar too operated a pioneer training farm and sent its members to Palestine while the local branch headed Betar's world organization from 1926. It also operated

a unique naval school whose graduates would one day serve in the Israeli fleet.

The Red Army entered the city on 17 June 1940. All J. political and cultural organizations were immediately closed down and such leaders as Mordekhai Dubin were exiled to the Soviet Union. The educational network was converted into a Soviet system with Yiddish imposed as the language of instruction. On the other hand, higher education was opened to J. students, their percentage at R. University climbing to 21%. J. businesses underwent nationalization, though former owners continued to serve as advisors and experts in their factories. The possibilities for work and study in R. brought many young Jews there from all over Latvia, pushing the J. pop. up to 50,000. On the eve of the Nazi invasion, thousands of Jews classified as "elements hostile to the Soviet regime" were exiled to Siberia. These included Zionist, Bund, and Agudat Israel leaders and big businessmen. Five thousand more fled to the Soviet Union on the evacuation of the city at the end of June 1941. The Germans arrived on 1 July. Latvian "self-defense" groups, drawing their members from such nationalist and fascist organizations as the Aizsargs and Perkonkrust and led by Voldemars Veiss and Victors Arajs, immediately staged a pogrom, encouraged by the Germans. Mass arrests and imprisonment under nightmarish conditions and sadistic guards followed together with forced labor where beatings and murder occurred daily. Organized executions commenced in the same month when at least 5,000 detainees were led to the Bikernieki forest and shot down. At the same time Latvian volunteers burned down synagogues and J. homes were systematically emptied of their contents while Jews were evicted from the better apartments. Among the many anti-J. measures instituted were a night curfew, impoundment of radios and cameras, restrictions on food purchases, and bans on ritual slaughter, the use of public transportation, and presence in public places. J. professionals were not allowed to practice their trades and a work force of around 20,000 able-bodied Jews was placed at the disposal of the Germans for backbreaking labor repairing war damages, emptying J. apartments, and wielding spades in peat bogs. In Aug. the Jews were ordered into a ghetto in the Moscow quarter with a council of elders (*Aeltestenrat*) set up commensurately and bolstered by a J. police force. J. women in mixed marriages were allowed to remain with their husbands outside the ghetto if they underwent sterilization. On 25

Oct. 1941, the ghetto was officially sealed off, surrounded by a 6-foot-high barbed wire fence patrolled by Latvian police. The area of the ghetto was 2 1/4 acres and it contained about 30,000 Jews under primitive sanitary conditions, the able-bodied continuing to be employed in forced labor, mainly at army facilities. In the night Germans and Latvians broke into J. homes in the ghetto, robbing, beating, and murdering the inhabitants. On 26 Nov. 1941 the ghettto was divided in two. Working men were separated from their families and confined to a "small ghetto" while the rest remained in the "big ghetto." On the night of 29 Nov. the western section of the big ghetto was emptied of its residents. Women, children, the old and the sick were led in the morning to the Rumbuli forest 5 miles outside the city, stripped naked, laid face down in deep pits, layer upon layer of the dead and dying, and executed by German and Latvian firing squads. The process was repeated in the eastern section of the big ghetto on 7–9 Dec. Among those murdered was the historian Simon Dubnow, who had been living in R. since 1933. The two *Aktions* claimed 25,000–28,000 J. lives. The big ghetto was now filled by 15,000–16,000 German Jews from a group of 25,000 brought to Riga from the larger cities, including Prague and Vienna. The rest were sent to concentration camps in the area (Salaspils, Jungfernhof, Strazdenhof) or murdered on arrival. Soon afterwards, thousands more were pulled out of the German ghetto and murdered in the nearby forests. Nonetheless, the German Jews tried to maintain a semblance of community life, with public synagogue services, concerts, and lectures. The pop. of the small ghetto reached 4,000, including 200–300 seamstresses who were spared in the big *Aktions*. In 1942 around 700 Jews from Kaunas (Kovno) were brought to the small ghetto, a number of them setting up a clandestine bakery and grocery store to ease food shortages. Underground activity in the ghetto commenced in late 1941 and was organized in secret cells comprising 250–300 mostly young Jews, who managed to stockpile a large quantity of weapons. On 28 Oct. 1942, ten attempting to link up with partisan groups clashed with the Germans, with just one escaping. In retaliation, 108 Jews in the ghetto were executed and 42 J. police, most also in the underground, were shot. On 11 June 1943 the main arms cache was discovered

The poet Hayyim Nahman Bialik with students of the Hashahar school in Riga, Latvia

by the Germans and mass arrests followed, effectively ending underground activity. On 1 Nov. 1942, the two ghettoes were combined and in summer 1943 the liquidation of the ghetto commenced, with inmates transferred to the big labor camps or to the Kaiserwald concentration camp. At the same time, survivors from other ghettoes (Vilna, Liepaja, Dvinsk) were brought to the city. In Nov. large-scale *Aktions* were carried out, with children sent separately to Auschwitz for extermination. The ghetto area was then transferred to the R. municipality and the remnant of Latvia's Jews was henceforth sent to Kaiserwald and its branches, which held over 10,000 prisoners. In 1944 thousands of J. women from Hungary were also brought there. Before the German evacuation of Latvia in 1944, an effort was made to obliterate the traces of executions by opening the mass graves and burning the bodies. Thousands more Jews were also murdered. The able-bodied were evacuated and mostly brought to concentration camps within Germany. R. was liberated by the Red Army on 13 Oct. 1944. Few Latvians helped Jews trying to escape during the war. An outstanding exception was Janis Lipke, a former stevedore and smuggler who took advantage of his experience to save 40 Jews and was honored by Yad Vashem as one of the Righteous among the Nations. In all, over 100 Jews managed to evade the Germans. After the war, many former residents returned from the Soviet Union along with survivors from the concentration camps. With new Soviet-J. families settling in R., the J. pop. reached 30,267 in 1947, maintaining that level through 1970, after which the emigration that followed Israel's Six-Day War reduced the J. pop. to about 20,000. Organized community activity with Zionist overtones continued unabated in the following period until the doors were finally opened in the late 1980s. An estimated 11,000 Jews were living there in 1995.

RIJEKA (Ital. Fiume) Croatia, Yugoslavia, today Republic of Croatia. A J. community was established in the late 18th cent. By 1900 it included 2,000 Jews, but prior to the Holocaust, in 1940, they numbered only 136. From April 1941 to Sept. 1943, R. was in Italian hands and some Jews were sent to Italy, where they survived the Holocaust. The Germans then occupied the city and sent the remaining Jews to death camps. The beautiful synagogue was destroyed by *Wehrmacht* sappers on 25 Jan. 1944. The community was reconstituted after the war.

RIJSSEN Overijssel dist., Holland. J. settlement began in the 18th cent. A community was organized after 1813 and numbered 107 in 1901. Some dealt in textiles. The J. pop. in 1941 was 122 (total 10,924). Most were deported in 1942. About 14 survived in hiding and six survived the camps.

RIMAVSKA SEC (Hung. Rimaszecz) Slovakia, Czechoslovakia, today Republic of Slovakia. Jews settled in the 1850s after residence restrictions in the mining regions were lifted. They erected a synagogue in the early 20th cent. After WWI, riots damaged J. property. The J. pop. rose from 73 in 1880 to 143 (total 1,625) in 1930. Most Jews earned their livelihood from trade but a few were artisans and farmers. After annexation to Hungary in Nov. 1938, they were persecuted and seized for forced labor. When the Germans arrived in March 1944, 129 Jews remained. After being confined in a ghetto they were deported to Auschwitz via Salgotarjan on 13 June.

RIMAVSKA SOBOTA (Hung. Rimaszombat) Slovakia, Czechoslovakia, today Republic of Slovakia. Jews settled in the mid-19th cent. A large synagogue was built in 1886 and a *talmud torah* was opened in the late 19th cent., accommodating (in separate classes) boys and girls who received their general education in public schools. The J. pop. grew from 278 in 1869 to 595 in 1900 and a peak of 816 (total 8,044) in 1930. Jews were active in public life before and after WWI. Samuel Hazay (b. 1851) was appointed Hungarian defense minister in 1910 and others served on the municipal council. In 1918 Jews fought off rioting peasants and townsmen intent on looting their property. Jews owned 76 business establishments, 14 workshops, and four factories. The young joined Hashomer Hatzair and Betar while Tze'irei Mizrachi ran a pioneer training farm. In 1941, the J. pop. was 635. After annexation to Hungary in Nov. 1938, J. businesses were forced to close and Jews were seized for forced labor. In April 1944, they were herded into a ghetto and in June they were sent to Miskolc and from there to Auschwitz. In all, 624 Jews perished in the Holocaust. Most of the postwar community of 200 left in 1949.

RIMBACH Hesse, Germany. The community, established in 1774, dedicated its new synagogue in 1840 and numbered 232 (13% of the total) in 1861.

Originally prominent in the livestock trade, Jews opened stores and business firms. The J. pop. declined to 100 (5%) by 1910. During the Weimar Republic era, the community was affiliated with Darmstadt's Liberal rabbinate and a branch of the Central Union (C.V.) was established. On 1 April 1933 Jews arrested by the Gestapo were sent to the Osthofen concentration camp and by Nov. 1938 the Nazi boycott campaign had forced 51 Jews to leave R. On *Kristallnacht* (9–10 Nov. 1938), a pogrom was organized. Jews were attacked and their property destroyed, but the anti-Nazi pastor foiled an attempt to burn down the synagogue. Of the 82 Jews living in R. after 1933, 47 emigrated (mainly to the U.S. and Argentina) and 24 perished in the Holocaust.

RIMBECK-SCHERFEDE Westphalia, Germany. The J. community numbered 26 in 1843 and reached a peak pop. of 72 in 1885. It maintained a synagogue from 1853 and a cemetery from 1875. In June 1933, 36 Jews remained. The synagogue was vandalized on *Kristallnacht* (9–10 Nov. 1938) and afterwards razed while J. homes and stores were looted and J. men sent to the Buchenwald concentration camp. The last Jews were deported to the Riga ghetto in Dec. 1941 and July 1942.

RIMPAR Lower Franconia, Germany. The J. settlement dates from no later than the first half of the 18th cent. The J. pop. grew to 142 in 1867 (total 2,152). R. was the birthplace (1878) of Herbert Lehman, governor of New York in 1932–42 and U.S. senator in 1949–57. In 1933, 54 Jews remained; 37 left in 1936–40, 22 emigrating to the U.S. On *Kristallnacht* (9–10 Nov. 1938) the synagogue was vandalized and Jews were beaten. Of the nine Jews remaining in 1942, six were deported to Izbica in the Lublin dist. (Poland) on 24 April and three to the Theresienstadt ghetto on 23 Sept. 1942.

RINTELN Hesse–Nassau, Germany. Founded in the 19th cent., the community numbered 80 (1% of the total) in 1905 and 73 in 1933. Although many of the remaining Jews had left by 1939, at least 32 perished in the Holocaust.

RIPICENI Moldavia dist., Rumania. Jews first settled in the late 19th cent. The majority of the J. pop. worked as clerks in the local sugar refinery or in other J. factories. Attached to the Stefanesti and Saveni communities, the Jews of R. had no independent institutions. The J. pop. in 1930 was 274 (12% of the total). Between the World Wars, 180 Zionist pioneers trained in R. In summer 1940, the Iron Guard seized J. factories. At the outbreak of the Soviet-Rumanian war in June 1941, the J. pop. was deported to Botosani, with many dying along the way. Only 65 Jews returned after the war.

ROANNE Loire dist., France. The J. community developed between 1919 and 1939. At the end of WWI, there were three families of French origin there. The community grew to include ten J. families, most working in the local cloth and hat factory. They established an independent Association Cultuelle Juive de Roanne. Jews of Polish origin built a synagogue and community center in 1933. After 1933, German J. refugees began to arrive. A Hebrew school was founded in 1933. By 1938, there were 50 J. families in R. and the community was officially constituted on 23 Feb. 1939. On the eve of WWII, there were 282 Jews (92 families) in R. (176 from Poland, 14 from France, and seven from Germany). After July 1942, there was an influx of refugees and the J. pop. rose to 750. The French pop. helped some Jews hide, but almost all were arrested in April 1943 and deported to Drancy. J. property was confiscated and 41 Jews were killed. After the war, communal life was revived and by the mid-1960s the community numbered about 500 members, many from Egypt and Tunisia.

ROCKENHAUSEN Palatinate, Germany. Jews were present in the latter half of the 13th cent. Some were beaten and forcibly converted in the aftermath of the Oberwesel blood libel of 1287. All were expelled during the Black Death persecutions of 1348–49. In 1802, the J. pop. was 39, reaching a peak of 140 in 1836 but dropping to 86 in 1857. A J. school was functioning in 1864. The communities of Marienthal and Dielkirchen were attached to the local congregation. In Jan. 1933, the J. pop. was 82 (total 2,209). During the Nazi era, 37 moved to other German cities and 17 emigrated to the U.S. On *Kristallnacht* (9–10 Nov. 1938), Jews were sent to the Dachau concentration camp and in Oct. 1940, nine Jews were deported to Gurs. In all, 14 perished in the Holocaust.

RODALBEN Palatinate, Germany. The J. pop. was 100 in 1802 and reached a peak of 148 (total 1,436) in 1836. Jews were active in local life and served on the municipal council. A synagogue was opened in a rented apartment in 1838 and in 1882 authorization was received to erect a synagogue. A J. school was opened in 1869 (26 students in 1886). In 1933, the J. pop. was 75. Most local residents ignored the Nazi economic boycott at first but anti-J. agitation intensified through the years. On *Kristallnacht* (9–10 Nov. 1938), J. stores were vandalized and J. men were sent to the Dachau concentration camp. The last Jews left the town in 1939. Four Jews perished in the Holocaust.

RODENBERG Hesse–Nassau, Germany. The J. community, numbering 93 (5% of the total) by 1861, dwindled to 11 (1925–33), and disbanded in 1937.

RODHEIM VOR DER HOEHE Hesse, Germany. Numbering 88 (6% of the total) in 1900, the community also drew members from six neighboring villages. The synagogue was burned down on *Kristallnacht* (9–10 Nov. 1938). Of the 51 Jews living there after 1933, 29 emigrated to South Africa or the U.S. and six to Holland; the rest moved to other parts of Germany.

RODNA (Hung. Oradna; Yid. Rogne) N. Transylvania dist., Rumania. Jews first settled in the 1820s. The community consisted mainly of Hasidim and the ultra-Orthodox. Its first rabbi, Avraham Yehoshua Freind (1855–1932), was one of the most extreme in Transylvania. The J. pop. in 1930 was 299 (6% of the total). Antisemitism was widespread in this hotbed of Rumanian nationalism, especially between the World Wars. In May 1944, the J. pop. was transferred to the Bistrita ghetto and in June deported to Auschwitz.

RODNIA Mogilev dist., Belorussia. Jews numbered 305 in 1847 and 367 under the Soviets in 1923. A kolkhoz was started in 1929, with 27 J. families employed there in 1930. The Germans arrived in Aug. 1941 and on 10 Dec. murdered 56 Jews at the J. cemetery.

ROEDELHEIM Hesse–Nassau, Germany. Established around 1680, the community built its first synagogue in 1730. From 1798, Wolf Heidenheim and Barukh Baschwitz operated a Hebrew printing press that made R. famous throughout Europe. Their prayer books and Pentateuch went through numerous editions and are still reproduced. The community ran an ele-

mentary school, built a new synagogue in 1838, and numbered 421 (18% of the total) in 1845. R. became part of Frankfurt am Main in 1910, but the community was obliged to remain independent under the jurisdiction of the city's (Orthodox) rabbinate. It dwindled to 113 (1%) in 1927. On *Kristallnacht* (9–10 Nov. 1938), Nazis vandalized the synagogue, which was sold in 1939. Most of the Jews remained in Frankfurt; two committed suicide and at least 12 perished in the Holocaust.

ROEDELSEE Lower Franconia, Germany. A J. cemetery is known from before the 15th cent. and the community grew significantly under the House of Hessberg from the first half of the 16th cent. with a renowned yeshiva accommodating 80 students in 1560. A new synagogue was built in 1851, but the J. pop. declined rapidly from a peak of 122 in 1830 (about 15% of the total). The J. public school was closed in 1874 and after 1910 only the cemetery caretaker's family remained. Four Jews were living there in 1933. Whatever communal property remained in the Nazi era was vandalized on *Kristallnacht* (9–10 Nov. 1938).

ROERMOND Limburg dist., Holland. Jews were present in the Middle Ages, until the mid-16th cent. Settlement was renewed in the early 19th cent. The community grew rapidly from 1822; social welfare organizations were established and a J. school was opened. The J. pop. in 1883 was 128. Its numbers decreased towards the end of the cent. Many refugees arrived in the 1930s, numbering 76 by 1941, when the J. pop. stood at 117 (total 18,947). Deportations took place in Aug. 1942, Nov. 1942, and April 1943. A few hid on nearby farms and were saved, but 70 perished in the camps.

ROESSEL (Pol. Reszel) East Prussia, Germany, today Poland. There is evidence of a J. community from the early 19th cent. By 1880 it had grown to 133 members, declining to 72 by 1905. The community maintained a synagogue and a cemetery. In June 1933, four months after the Nazis came to power, the J. pop. had shrunk to 20 individuals. By May 1939, ten Jews remained. No further information about their fate is available.

ROGACHEV (I) Gomel dist., Belorussia. There were 200 J. poll tax payers in 1766 and a J. pop. of

1,305 in 1847 and 5,047 (total 9,038) in 1897. Of the ten small factories operating in the town, five manufacturing ship cable were in J. hands. Most Jews engaged in petty trade, wholesaling, and crafts (156 artisans). Zionist activity was extensive. R. was the birthplace of R. Yosef Rozin (1858–1936), known as "the Rogachover" and author of commentaries on the Babylonian and Jerusalem Talmuds and Maimonides' *Mishneh Torah*. The painter Tanhum Kaplan was also born there. In 1923, under the Soviets, the J. pop. reached 6,320. A J. artisan association with 150 members and Yiddish as its official language was founded in the same year. During the 1920s, two J. agricultural cooperatives were set up near the city and in 1927–30 three J. kolkhozes supporting 74 families were also started in the vicinity. In 1928, 320 children attended a J. elementary school. In 1939, the J. pop. stood at 4,601 (30% of the total). The Germans captured R. on 3 July 1941. Soon afterwards the Jews were ordered into a ghetto where they suffered from hunger and overcrowding. From Nov. 1941 to March 1942, 3,500 were murdered.

ROGACHEV (II) Zhitomir dist., Ukraine. The J. pop. was 404 in 1847 and 1,303 (total 1,381) in 1897. As a result of attacks during the civil war (1918–21) and internal migration, their pop. dropped to 265 in 1926. The Germans captured R. in early July 1941 and ordered the Jews to wear the yellow badge. Ukrainian police beat and robbed the Jews and on 10 Oct. 1941 (Yom Kippur) they seized and murdered young Jews when their ransom demands were not met. Afterwards the rest of the Jews were brought to the municipal park and also murdered.

ROGATICA Bosnia-Hercegovina, Yugoslavia, today Republic of Bosnia. The Jews of this community, numbering 47 in 1931 (total 10,024), were all murdered in the Holocaust.

ROGOZNO (Yid. Rogozhin) Poznan dist., Poland. J. settlement probably dates from the 14th cent. An organized community with a synagogue and cemetery is known from the late 16th cent. In the Swedish war of the mid-17th cent., the Jews suffered from Stefan Czarniecki's irregular troops. The Jews afterwards helped rebuild the city. A new synagogue was erected in 1792 and a new cemetery was opened in 1808. By the time of the Prussian annexation in 1793, the J. pop.

stood at 1,044, growing to 1,500 (total 3,950) in 1829. A J. elementary school for 200 children was opened in 1838. In the 19th cent. J. peddlers opened stores and J. artisans enlarged their workshops and in the 1870s and 1880s the Jews developed the local clothing industry. The bookdealer Alexander Yunis started a printing press and published the German weekly *Oborniker Kreis*. Many of the young attended German universities, subsequently entering the professions and moving to the cities. Jews also became active in public life, with seven elected to the municipal council in 1860. Emigration reduced the J. pop. to 834 in 1898 and 250 in 1921. Fewer than 50 remained on the eve of WWII. The last 20 were expelled by the Germans on 7 Nov. 1939 to General Gouvernement territory and from there to the death camps.

ROHATYN Stanislawow dist., Poland, today Ukraine. The J. community dates from the mid-16th cent., receiving various privileges from the Polish kings in the 17th cent. Shabbateanism won many followers in R. as did the Frankist movement, with 49 Jews converting to Christianity in 1759 under the influence of the latter sect. Under Austrian rule from 1772 the Jews suffered many disabilities, including the abrogation of autonomy and heavy taxation. Hasidism began to spread in the early 19th cent. under the domination of the Stretyn dynasty. From 1886, after the town was linked up with the railroad, economic conditions improved. Small factories were set up, almost all owned by Jews. Zionism first made its appearance in the 1890s when the J. pop. reached 3,503 (half the total). Many fled in WWI; the remaining heads of families were exiled till the end of 1917, 150 of them dying in epidemics. Persecution continued under the Ukrainian and Polish regimes with the J. pop. dropping to 2,223 in 1921, most on relief. The competition of the Ukrainian cooperatives and depressed economic conditions brought further hardship between the World Wars. The Germans arrived on 2 July 1941. A *Judenrat* was set up at the end of the month to supply forced labor and satisfy extortionist demands. In the fall an overcrowded ghetto was established and a typhoid epidemic was soon claiming dozens of victims a day. Refugees from the surrounding settlements were directed there at the end of the year. On 20 March 1942, over 2,000 Jews, including 500 children, were brought to open pits near the railroad station and shot. On 2 Sept. another 1,000 were deported to the Belzec

Klezmer *musicians, most from the Faust family, Rohatyn, Poland, 1912 (YIVO Archive, New York/photo courtesy of Yad Vashem, The Holocaust Martyrs' and Heroes' Remembrance Authority, Jerusalem)*

death camp. More refugees were packed into the ghetto in Oct.–Nov. 1942 and on 8 Dec. another 1,500 were deported to the Belzec death camp. Sporadic killing followed, stepped up in the spring. An effort at resistance with the participation of J. police was brutally suppressed when the latter were seized and publicly hanged on 6 June. A few hours later ghetto houses were set on fire, handgrenades thrown inside, and the survivors led away to execution.

ROHRBACH Hesse, Germany. The community numbered 86 (22% of the total) in 1880 and 37 in 1933. On *Kristallnacht* (9–10 Nov. 1938), the synagogue's interior was destroyed and by Dec. 1939 no Jews remained, at least 31 having emigrated (chiefly to the U.S.).

ROKISKIS (Yid. Rakishok) Rokiskis dist., Lithuania. Jews first settled in the late 18th cent., at the invitation of the local proprietor's business manager. The J. pop. in 1897 was 2,067 (75% of the total). During WWI many left for Russia. Those who remained were seized for forced labor by the Germans. After the war, some Jews returned and others from sur-

rounding areas moved there, leading to a short period of development. Economic conditions deteriorated partly because of the nationalization of trade in linen and grain and the establishment of a Catholic bank which helped Lithuanians undercut the prices of J. merchants. In 1925 many Jews went bankrupt, resulting in emigration to South Africa, the U.S., and Palestine. Jews were active in municipal politics and filled such positions as mayor and deputy mayor at different periods. The J. pop. in 1923 was 2,013 (46.5%). The community maintained two *yeshivot* and four Hebrew schools. Most of the Jews were Habad Hasidim. In 1939 the J. pop. was about 3,500 (40%). Among the noted natives was Yaacov Shmushkevich, who became the commander of the Soviet air force and was executed for alleged "treason" in 1941. Y. Harmatz, a Vilna ghetto activist, was the director of World ORT. After the German invasion in June 1941, J. men were separated from the women and children; both groups were taken to forced labor. Between 15 and 25 Aug. 1941 all were herded into pits outside the town and shot.

ROKITNO Volhynia dist., Poland, today Ukraine.

In 1901 there were 105 Jews in R. The inauguration of a railroad station, glass factory, and some sawmills boosted the economy and the J. pop. grew to 663 (total 3,403) in 1921. With the outbreak of WWII, 400 Jews left for the east on 10 July 1941. A *Judenrat* was established and a ghetto set up on 15 April 1942. On 26 Aug., 1,631 Jews were assembled in the market square and surrounded by Germans and Ukrainian police. At the sound of a woman's cry to flee for their lives they began to run; 100 were shot down. The 800 who remained were sent to the Poleska camp in Sarny for liquidation. Of the 700 who made it to the forests most were turned in by Ukrainian peasants. After liberation (4 Jan. 1944) there were attempts to renew J. life locally, but the Jews soon left.

ROKITNOYE Kiev dist., Ukraine. Jews numbered 2,073 (total 5,818) in 1897. Most were Hasidim. A private boys' school was opened in 1910. In 1905, rioting railroad workers attacked Jews but were driven off by local peasants, known for their friendly relations with the Jews. However, in 1917, peasants from a distant village murdered three Jews in a pillaging spree. In 1919, the peasants staged a pogrom, murdering 25 Jews, raping women, and looting and burning homes. In the Soviet period, a J. council was established. Numerous families moved to kolkhozes: 15 in the Crimea; 25 near the Fastow railroad; 30 in the vicinity of R.; and another 50 founding one nearby. In 1939, the J. pop. was 711. The Germans entered R. in July 1941 and murdered the Jews there in the first days of the occupation.

ROKOSOV (Hung. Rakasz) Carpatho-Russia, Czechoslovakia, today Ukraine. Three J. families were present in 1768 for a short period of time. Jews returned in the mid-19th cent. and numbered 41 (total 1,637) by 1880. In 1921, their number was 159 and in 1941 it was 192. A few were farmers. The Hungarians occupied R. in March 1939 and in 1941 drafted a number of young Jews into forced labor battalions. In July 1941, a few J. families were expelled to the Ukraine, where they perished. The rest of the Jews were deported to Auschwitz in May 1944.

ROKYCANY Bohemia, Czechoslovakia. Jews settled in the late 19th cent. Their pop. rose to 206 in 1890 and then declined steadily to 59 (total 7,741) in 1930. In Jan. 1942, the Jews were deported to the

Theresienstadt ghetto via Pilsen. A few weeks later most were sent to the death camps of the east.

ROMADAN Poltava dist., Ukraine. A few dozen Jews resided here in the early 20th cent. Two were murdered in a pogrom in March 1918. In 1939, the J. pop. was 155 (total 3,529). After their arrival on 14 Sept. 1941, the Germans murdered the few remaining Jews.

ROMAN Moldavia dist., Rumania. Jews first settled in the early 18th cent. In 1714 the Jews were subjected to a blood libel. When the city council desecrated and destroyed the J. cemetery in 1867, it led to an international outcry. The council was dissolved and a new cemetery consecrated. The community minted its own coins, called the "*pruta*" and given to the poor. The longest-serving rabbi (1839–1907), R. David Isaacson, was followed by his grandson R. Shelomo (1910–47). A *talmud torah* was opened at the beginning of the 19th cent. and in 1865, 20 *hadarim* were functioning, but in 1929 only four were left. In 1886 the J. community was ordered to open a school for boys; a school for girls was opened in 1899 with the aid of the ICA. During the 1907 peasant revolt, 98 J. houses were destroyed. Zionist activity began at the end of the 19th cent. The J. pop. was 6,432 in 1899, dropping in 1930 to 5,963 (28% of the total) as a result of economic discrimination. On the eve of WWII, the community had 18 synagogues, two elementary schools, a nursery school, a hospital, and an old age home. A yeshiva existed from 1918 to 1920. The Zionist movement was most active between the World Wars and published a biweekly. In 1934, a Jew was elected deputy mayor. Manifestations of antisemitism abounded immediately after WWI. From Aug. 1941, Jews were persecuted and forced to pay huge sums to the authorities. At the outbreak of the Soviet-Rumanian war on 21 June 1941, 800 J. refugees expelled from small towns in the vincinity were added to the community. In July, 100 Jews were imprisoned in the synagogue for 20 days, after which 38 were expelled to Transnistria; another 80, accused of Communism, were transferred to the Vapniarca camp. Almost all returned in 1943–44. About 1,000 Jews were sent to forced labor battalions and J. doctors were sent to camps in Transnistria. In April 1944, 1,400 J. refugees from Targu-Frumos and 1,000 from Pascani were brought to R. and cared for by the community. Between May and Aug. 1944, J. men and women aged 15–55 were designated for forced labor, such as construction work for the men and laundering for the women. In spring 1944, 132 returning orphans were brought to R. and cared for by members of the community. Some of those expelled from Bukovina returned to R. in spring 1944 and settled there.

ROMANOV (Dzerzhinsk) Zhitomir dist., Ukraine. Jews are first mentioned in 1787 and numbered 2,599 (total 5,645) in 1897. In the mid-1920s, a Yiddish-language elementary school was operating. About 180 Jews worked in the town's 22 hide-processing plants. The J. pop. was 1,720 in 1939. The Germans captured the town on 10 July 1941 and murdered 2,198 people, including most of the Jews of R. and the neighboring villages.

ROMANOVKA (I) Nikolaiev dist., Ukraine. Jews from the Vitebsk region founded R. as a J. colony in the 1840s. Twenty new J. families arrived in the 1860s and established an adjacent settlement. (The two settlements were subsequently called Greater and Lesser R.). In 1898, the combined J. pop. was 1,283 (total 1,302) and 1,563 in 1926, under the Soviets. A J. council and J. elementary school were active. The Germans arrived in mid-Aug. 1941 and murdered the Jews in mid-Sept. About 1,000 Jews were murdered in the area during the German occupation.

ROMANOVKA (II) Zhitomir dist., Ukraine. R. was founded as a J. farm settlement on leased land in 1830 and reached a pop. of 379 (69 families) who were farming 1,600 acres in 1897. By the mid-1920s, their number was reduced to 41 families on 1,100 acres, growing mainly fruit and vegetables. In the late 1920s, the colony became a kolkhoz. The Jews were murdered after the arrival of the Germans on 7 July 1941.

ROMANSWILLER Bas-Rhin dist., France. A small J. community was established in the 18th cent., numbering 26 families in 1716 and 41 families (206 individuals) in 1784. The local synagogue was inaugurated in 1849. By 1936, there were only 43 Jews. During WWII all were expelled to the south of France, with the rest of Alsace-Lorraine Jews and the synagogue was looted. No Jews lived there subsequently.

ROME Lazio, Italy. The J. community in Rome is the oldest in Europe with an uninterrupted J. presence in the city of over two 2,000 years, since the first cent. B.C.E. The original nucleus of mostly merchants and manumitted slaves grew with the arrival of prisoners after Pompey's campaigns in Judea. Following the destruction of the Second Temple in 70 C.E. many freed prisoners flooded the capital. There were about 40,000 Jews in ancient Rome, enjoying certain civil and religious rights. They were divided into at least 13 "*Sinagogai*" (communities) of various denominations, according to place of origin or residential quarter. Following Constantine's conversion to Christianity in 312 and the Edict of Milan, making Christianity the official religion of the empire, the condition of the Jews in R. deteriorated. With the growing prestige and influence of the papacy, the character of each individual pope was a determining factor in the history of the Jews. The Jews were subjected to various restrictions and to heavy taxes. Cultural life developed and J. scholars from R. became widely known. The Jews dealt mainly in cloth and silk, carpets and precious objects, and moneylending. The medieval J. traveler Benjamin of Tudela found 200 Jews (heads of households) in R. Among them were craftsmen, tradesmen, scholars, poets, and physicians. In 1215, the Fourth Lateran Council

Entrance to Jewish Soldiers Club, Rome, Italy, after WWII

Jews baking matzot *in the Rome ghetto, Italy, at the turn of the 19th cent. (The Nahon Museum of Italian Jewry, Jerusalem/photo courtesy of Beth Hatefutsoth, Tel Aviv)*

under Pope Innocent III obliged Jews to wear the J. badge on their clothes. They were also banned from holding public office. Like the rest of the pop., a plague in 1348 diminished and impoverished the J. community of R. After 1492, following the expulsions of the Jews from Spain, Navarre, Portugal, and Sicily, large numbers settled in R. In 1526, out of a total pop. of 54,000 in R., there were 373 J. families (1,772 individuals). There were frequent conflicts between the original J. nucleus and the newcomers. Following the burning of the Talmud in 1553, antisemitism reached its peak in 1555 when Pope Paul IV issued a bull which led to the establishment of a ghetto in R. and such anti-J. measures as forcing the Jews to sell their land holdings, to trade only in secondhand goods, and to wear a yellow cap. They were allowed only one synagogue, but the Jews evaded the restriction by creating five synagogues practicing different rites under a single roof. When Pope Pius V forced the Jews to concentrate in R. and Ancona in 1566 and 1596, the ghetto of R. became overcrowded, since by the end of the 16th cent., the J. pop. had almost doubled in 50 years to around 1,750. In 1682, the authorities closed the J. banks. Most ghetto inhabitants subsisted on allowances from J. welfare societies. Over the next two cents., the Jews of R. suffered severely from oppression and poverty. The 6,000 Jews living in the ghetto in the 18th cent., earned their living from peddling, tailoring, and selling secondhand goods. The French Revolution reached R. in 1798, but it was a brief interlude, since the Jews again suffered oppression and plunder during the First Roman Republic. The restoration of papal rule in 1814 renewed the previous restrictions. In 1848, Pius

IX ordered the gates and walls of the ghetto to be removed. A year later, with the establishment of the short-lived Second Roman Republic, the Jews received equality of rights, but the return of the Pope again brought back certain restrictions. Complete freedom was achieved only in 1870, after the Italian army liberated R. and Italy was unified. The Jews of R. began to play an active part in the social and cultural life of the country, contributing to political life, literature, and science. Under the leadership of Samuel Alatri, the community was reorganized. In 1873, the J. pop. was 4,880, increasing to 5,600 in 1886. In 1904, the Great Synagogue was established. Alatri and Settimo Piperno were elected to the Rome city council. In 1910, the community, numbering 10,000, was headed by R. Prof. Hayyim (Vittorio) Castigioni. Six years later, the J. pop. increased to 11,000 and its officiating rabbi was Dr. Angelo Sacerdoti. According to the 1930 law reforming the Italian J. communities, R. was one of 26 legally recognized communities. The R. district included Albano Laziale (30 Jews in 1936); Prascati (40 Jews in 1936); Perugia (80 Jews in 1936); and Terni (20 Jews in 1936).

In 1936, the J. pop. was 13,000. In 1938, the Laws for the Defense of the Race introduced by the Fascist regime caught the community unprepared. Excluded from work, schools, and public office, the Jews were second-class citizens by 1941 and compelled to engage in forced labor. With Mussolini's overthrow on 25 July 1943, the Germans entered R. on 9–10 Sept. 1943. H. Kappler, the SS commanding officer, demanded 50 kilos of gold from the J. community. It was collected in 36 hours. Over the next few days, the SS occupied

Jewish store in the Rome ghetto, Italy, at the turn of the 19th cent. (Association of Jewish Women in Italy, Rome. Photographer: Count Giuseppe Primoli/photo courtesy of Beth Hatefutsoth Photo Archive, Tel Aviv)

community offices, confiscated registers and documents and plundered the old library of the community and the rabbinical seminary. The roundup of Jews in R. began during the night of 15–16 Oct. 1943. In less than 24 hours, 1,259 Jews were seized and deported two days later to Auschwitz. During the nine months the Germans occupied R., 2,091 Jews were deported to the death camps. Only 73 men and 28 women returned. Many local Jews were saved by fellow citizens who hid them. Jews were very active in the resistance in the city and surrounding area. In 1948, the community numbered 11,000 members. By 1965 the J. pop. increased to 12,928.

ROMMERSKIRCHEN   Rhineland, Germany. The local synagogue dates back to 1696. The J. pop. was 46 in 1861 and 33 in 1932. Five Jews from a single family perished in the camps of the east in the Holocaust.

ROMNY   Sumy dist., Ukraine. Jews settled in the

late 18th cent. and numbered 6,378 (total 22,510) in 1897. J. property was destroyed in a pogrom on 3 May 1881. In another pogrom on 19–20 Oct. 1905, eight Jews were killed and 30 injured. J. stores were also damaged. Among those born in R. were Hayyim Arlosoroff (1899–1933), a leader of the Zionist labor movement; Pinhas Rutenberg (1879–1942), founder of the Palestine Electric Co. and one of the heads of the Hagana and Va'ad Le'ummi; and Prof. Avraham Yoffe, one of the Soviet Union's greatest physicists. A group of local pioneers left for Eretz Israel in 1905 and were among the founders of Kibbutz Deganya. In the early 20th cent., a *talmud torah* and J. hospital were opened. Most tobacco factories and all the flour and grist mills in R. were in J. hands. In 1919, General Anton Denikin's White Army captured R., causing the loss of J. lives and damage to J. property. The J. occupational structure began to change in the 1920s; many Jews went to work in local textile factories as well as for the railroad as clerks and in other similar capacities. The J. pop. dropped to 3,834 in 1939. The Germans captured R. on 10 Sept. 1941. In early Nov. 1941, the Jews were concentrated at the local army barracks and on 19 Nov. 3,000 were brought outside the city and murdered. Another 700 Jews were executed by Jan. 1942.

ROMROD   Hesse, Germany. The community, numbering 74 in 1871, disbanded in 1935. By Sept. 1938 all the Jews had left.

ROMSTHAL-ECKARDROTH   (now part of Bad Soden-Salmuenster) Hesse–Nassau, Germany. With a membership drawn from two adjoining villages, the community had a synagogue in E. and a combined pop. of 162 in 1861. Most of the 24 Jews who remained there in 1933 left before WWII.

ROMULI   (previously Romuli Stramba; Hung. Romoly; Yid. Strimba) N. Transylvania dist., Rumania. A J. community existed in the mid-19th cent. The J. pop. in 1930 was 333 (21% of the total). In May 1944, the J. pop. was transferred to the Bistrita ghetto and in June deported to Auschwitz.

RONA DE JOS   (Hung. Alsorona; Yid. Unterrine) N. Transylvania dist., Rumania. Jews first settled in the early 18th cent. and some engaged in agriculture. In 1930 the J. pop. was 477 (17% of the total). In

April 1944, the J. pop. was transferred to the Sighet ghetto and then deported to Auschwitz.

RONA DE SUS (Hung. Felsorona; Yid. Oiberrine) N. Transylvania dist., Rumania. Jews first settled in the early 18th cent. In 1930 the J. pop. was 410 (14% of the total). In 1941, dozens of Jews were expelled by the Hungarians to Galicia and most were murdered in Kamenets-Podolski. In Oct. 1942, males aged 21-42 were drafted into labor battalions in the Ukraine, where most perished. In April 1944, the J. pop. was transferred to the Sighet ghetto and then deported to Auschwitz.

RONDORF Rhineland, Germany. The local community was affiliated to the Cologne community. From 54 members in 1871 it dwindled to 20 in 1885, but grew to 60 in 1925. By May 1939 there were only 24 community members left. Those who failed to leave shared the fate of the Cologne Jews.

ROPCZYCE (Yid. Ropshits) Lwow dist., Poland, today Ukraine. Jews are recorded from the late 16th cent., enjoying full residence and trade rights from the time of King John Casimir (1648–68). R. was the seat of the famous hasidic dynasty established by R. Naftali Tzevi Ropshitser (1760–1827), a disciple of Elimelekh of Lyzhansk and Yaakov Yitzhak, the "Seer of Lublin." The thousands of visitors streaming to the court provided local Jews with additional sources of income. Despite opposition, Zionism began to develop in the late 19th cent., when the J. pop. stood at around 1,050 (30% of the total). Antisemitism also intensified from the end of the cent. After the ravages of WWI and its aftermath the J. pop. stood at 840 and many required assistance from the Joint Distribution Committee. The Germans entered the town in Sept. 1939, torturing and killing the rabbi and burning religious books. Hundreds of Jews, including refugees, were sent to the Pustkow labor camp; 23 were murdered in June 1942. On 23 July the ghetto set up in June was liquidated: children and the old were murdered and the rest brought to Sedziszow Malopolski en route to the Belzec death camp.

ROS Bialystok dist., Poland. Jews were present in the first half of the 17th cent. Their pop. grew to 500 by 1897. In 1921 the J. pop. fell to 389 (total 822), living under straitened economic circumstances. The Ger-

mans entered R. in late June 1941. On 2 Nov. 1942 the Jews were brought to the Wolkowysk transit camp and on 26 Nov. deported to the Treblinka death camp.

ROSASNA Vitebsk dist., Belorussia. Twenty-eight J. families were living in R. in the mid-1920s. The Germans captured the town in July 1941. The few remaining Jews were taken to nearby Lyady on 2 April 1942 and murdered along with the local Jews.

ROSBACH A. D. SIEG Rhineland, Germany. A few J. cattle dealers and butchers settled in the latter half of 19th cent., with the J. pop. reaching 45–50 at the turn of the cent and then dropping to 31 (total 4,464) in 1932. The community buried its dead in the Hamm J. cemetery. The synagogue built in the 1870s was destroyed on *Kristallnacht* (9–10 Nov. 1938). Over 20 Jews were still living in the town in 1939–41. Most were deported to the east in June 1942. At least 15 Jews perished in the Holocaust.

ROSENBERG (I) (Pol. Olesno) Upper Silesia, Germany, today Poland. The J. pop. was 112 in 1787, 213 in 1832, and 244 in 1880. The community maintained a synagogue and cemetery. In 1925, the J. pop. was 180. In 1932, Nazis threw a handgrenade into a J.-owned hotel, causing much property damage. In 1933, the J. pop. was 112. The Nazi racial laws were not applied until July 1937 owing to the extension of the League of Nations' minority rights convention to the area. In this period, the Yom Tov pioneer training kibbutz was functioning with 30 members along with a Zionist group organized in 1934. The J. pop. dropped to 83 in 1936 and 58 in 1938. On *Kristallnacht* (9–10 Nov. 1938), the synagogue was burned. Subsequently many Jews emigrated, leaving 34 in 1939. Their fate is unknown.

ROSENBERG (II) (Pol. Susz) East Prussia, Germany, today Poland. Jews were present from 1811. The J. pop. was 72 in 1831 and 145 by 1880. The community maintained a synagogue and a cemetery. When the Nazis came to power in 1933, 54 Jews were still living in R., dropping to 48 according to the May 1939 census. No information about their subsequent fate under Nazi rule is available.

ROSENHEIM Upper Bavaria, Germany. The community, attached to Munich, numbered 56 in 1910 and 38 in 1933 (total 19,060). By 1938, 29 Jews had left R., including 14 to other countries and eight to Munich.

ROSENTHAL Hesse–Nassau, Germany. Jews lived there from the 17th cent., numbering 63 (5% of the total) in 1861 and 27 in 1933. The community disbanded in 1938 and 14 Jews were eventually deported.

ROSHEIM Bas-Rhin dist. France. Jews were living in R. at least from the 13th cent. They suffered during the Black Death persecutions of 1348–49. In the 15th cent. there were very few J. families in R. The *shtadlan* Josel Loans, also known as Josselman de Rosheim, lived here until his death in 1554. He was named by the Emperor Maximilian head of the Jews of Germany. In 1696 the community consisted of only 18 families. In the 19th cent. the community revived, numbering 265 members. The synagogue was built in 1835 and renovated in 1882. By 1936 there were 69 Jews in R. During WWII, all were expelled to the south of France with the rest of Alsace-Lorraine Jewry; the synagogue was desecrated and the furniture stolen and a total of 35 Jews were deported. In the 1960s, there were only 14 Jews in R.

ROSIORI-DE-VEDE Walachia dist., Rumania. A J. community of mainly Sephardi Jews was founded in 1880, earning its living from the grain trade. The J. pop. was 132 in 1899 and 53 in 1930. Persecution of Jews began in 1937 under the Goga-Cuza regime. From Sept. 1940, the Green Shirts plundered J. property and Jews left the town.

ROSITSA Vitebsk dist., Belorussia. The J. pop. was 529 (total 755) in 1897 and 412 in 1923 under the Soviets. Of 75 J. breadwinners, 35 were artisans, 11 farmers, and the rest merchants. The Jews still there when the Germans occupied R. in 1941 were murdered.

ROSKOSHNAYA Zaporozhe dist., Ukraine. Jews from the Vitebsk region founded R. as J. colony in 1855. It had 616 inhabitants in 1858, mostly Jews. It was included in the Novo-Zlatopol J. Autonomous Region in 1929. The 90 J. families there after the German occupation of Oct. 1941 were murdered.

ROSLAVL Smolensk dist., Russia. The first J. settlers, in the mid-19th cent., were demobilized soldiers,

well-to-do merchants, and a few artisans. In 1897, the J. pop. was 1,145 (total 4,773) and permission was granted to erect a synagogue. During WWI, many J. refugees arrived from the war zone in western Russia and the J. pop. rose to 3,254 (total 25,992) under the Soviets in 1926. In the 1920s, about 100 artisans belonged to a J. cooperative and another 150 were in the civil service. Many were unemployed since they were defined as "classless." A J. club with a drama circle started after the Oct. 1917 Revolution. A J. school and orphanage also operated. In 1939, the J. pop. was 2,935. The Germans captured the city on 3 Aug. 1941, moving the Jews to a ghetto in Sept. In Nov., about 600 were murdered at the J. cemetery.

ROSSDORF Hesse, Germany. The community numbered 62 (2% of the total) in 1900 and 47 in 1933 but dispersed in 1938. Most Jews emigrated to the U.S. before *Kristallnacht* (9–10 Nov. 1938).

ROSSONY Vitebsk dist., Belorussia. The J. pop. was 327 (total 1,060) in 1897 and 47 in 1939. The Germans occupied R. in July 1941. A ghetto was set up in Sept. to confine the 500 or so Jews in the district (from Yukhovichi, Albrekhtovo, Kliastits, and Gorbachevo). Many died of starvation and the cold. In Jan. 1942, they were murdered outside the town but only buried in April.

ROSSOSH Voronezh dist., Russia. Jews apparently settled after the Oct. 1917 Revolution. They numbered just 20 in 1926. The Germans occupied the town on 7 July 1942 and in July–Nov. 1942 murdered the Jews who had not fled or been evacuated from the area.

ROSSOSZ Lublin dist., Poland. A few J. families were probably present in the late 18th cent., with the J. pop. reaching 279 in 1857 and 364 (total 1,391) in 1921. At the end of the 19th cent., Jews established a flour mill and sawmill and a factory for producing bleach. In the wake of the postwar economic crisis, increasing antisemitism during the 1930s, and the German occupation of Nov. 1939, fewer than 200 Jews remained during WWII. It is believed that they were deported to the Sobibor death camp in summer 1942.

ROSTOCK Mecklenburg-Schwerin, Germany. Evidence of J. settlement exists from the late 13th cent. but Jews apparently did not return after the Black

Death persecutions of 1348–49. In any event, they were banned from Mecklenburg after the 15th cent. and were only allowed to settle from 1868 following special legislation. Within a year, their pop. grew to about 20 families, mainly merchants. Later the Jews entered all areas of local life, becoming doctors, lawyers, public figures, and well-known scholars at the local university. The J. pop. grew from 118 in 1871 to a peak of 321 (22% of the total) in 1910. The community maintained a synagogue, consecrated in 1902, and a cemetery, opened in 1873 and expanded in 1897. In 1932, the J. pop. was about 350. Persecution commenced almost immediately after the Nazis came to power in 1933. On Boycott Day (1 April 1933) a number of Jews were taken into "protective" custody and only released a few weeks later. Dr. Gustav Posner, who was among the J. officials dismissed from their positions, committed suicide in April 1933. Dr. Friedrich Rubensohn, an attorney active in the struggle against antisemitism before the Nazi rise to power, was expelled from the city. On *Kristallnacht* (9–10 Nov. 1938), the synagogue was burned and J. property looted. Sixty-four Jews were placed under "protective" custody in the Altstrelitz jail. By Sept. 1939, only about 70 Jews remained, the rest having emigrated or moved to other places in Germany. Those who remained were deported: 24 local Jews and another 67 from the rest of Mecklenburg in a first transport to the Theresienstadt ghetto on 11 July 1942; 14 (and another 36 from the dist.) on 11 Nov.; and a few small contingents, including Jews in mixed marriages, later on. Another seven local Jews were deported from Hamburg. Altogether, just two Jews returned after the war.

ROSTOV-ON-DON Rostov dist., Russia. Jews probably settled in the early 19th cent., reaching a pop. of about 5,000 (total 100,000) in 1880. The community maintained a number of prayer houses and a *talmud torah*. Residence restrictions went into force in 1888 and in 1893 a pogrom was staged against the Jews. J. settlement accelerated with the development of R. as a transport center, to which Jews contributed substantially (especially the Poliakov brothers). Some Jews dealt in grain and a few of the city's banks were in J. hands. Many were professionals and about 80% of the city's doctors were Jews. Most, however, engaged in crafts and petty trade. In 1897, the J. pop. was 11,838 (total 119,000). In fall 1905, rioting mobs and a Cossack army unit in particular staged another

Jewish doctors, Rostov, Russia, 1917 (Beth Hatefutsoth Photo Archive, Tel Aviv/courtesy of Zehava German, Israel)

pogrom which claimed about 150 J. lives in three days. Hovevei Zion became active in the 1880s and the first Zionist party circles were founded in the late 1890s. In 1910, the community supported three *talmudei torah*, a general J. school for girls, and another school at the main synagogue. During WWI hundreds of J. refugees from western Russia arrived, including followers of the Lubavich Rebbe, R. Shalom Dov Schneersohn. In the Soviet period, the J. pop. grew to 26,323 in 1926 and 27,039 (total 502,928) in 1939. In the mid-1920s, a third of J. workers were employed in the state bureaucracy; many were unemployed. In 1921 (a year after the Rebbe died) government authorities brought Habad followers to trial; they subsequently moved to Leningrad in 1924. In the same period, many members of the semi-legal Hehalutz organization were also arrested. The Soviets closed down independent J. institutions and opened a Yiddish-language school and J. club. These, too, were shut down in the 1930s. The Germans occupied R. twice, from 21 to 29 Nov. 1941 and from 24 July

1942. The murder of the city's Jews commenced a short time after the second occupation. In an *Aktion* carried out on 11 Aug., the Germans executed about 13,000 Jews near the village of Zmiyevka 2, about 3 miles (5 km) from R. Those discovered afterwards in hiding were murdered at the J. cemetery. In all, 15,000–18,000 Jews from R. and its environs were murdered during the Nazi occupation. Among the city's native sons was Ceasar Kunikov (b. 1909), naval commander and Hero of the Soviet Union.

ROSULNA Stanislawow dist., Poland, today Ukraine. The J. pop. was 154 in 1921. The Jews were probably expelled to the Rodolf Mill camp in Stanislawow for liquidation in Sept. 1942.

ROTENBURG AN DER FULDA Hesse–Nassau, Germany. Jews lived in the town from its foundation (c. 1200). After the Black Death massacres of 1348–49, however, no community was established for 350 years. Numbering 133 in 1731, its members built a synagogue in 1738 and maintained an elementary school from 1826 to 1913. Moses Gans invented a "Sabbath oven" which found a market in England as well as in Germany. The community, which grew to 390 (12% of the total) in 1880 and dedicated a larger synagogue in 1924, was affiliated with the rabbinate of Kassel. In 1933, there were 97 Jews still in R. Shortly before *Kristallnacht* (9–10 Nov. 1938), SA men destroyed the synagogue and vandalized J. property. Most Jews left within a year, 16 emigrating. At least 13 perished in the Holocaust.

ROTH Hesse–Nassau, Germany. Jews from R., Lohra, and Fronhausen established a united community in 1823, building a new synagogue in 1860, after which Lohra and Fronhausen became independent (1881). Affiliated with Marburg's rabbinate, the Jews of R. numbered 43 (8% of the total) in 1861 and 31 in 1933. Their synagogue was vandalized on *Kristallnacht* (9–10 Nov. 1938) and the last nine Jews perished in the Theresienstadt ghetto.

ROTH BEI NUERNBERG Middle Franconia, Germany. Jews are mentioned in 1414 and lived under various letters of protection. A synagogue was built in 1737. In 1837 the J. pop. reached 200 (total 2,440) with a considerable number of artisans among them, but declined thereafter as many departed for nearby

Nuremberg and Fuerth. In 1933, 19 Jews remained. All left by Dec. 1935 and the Germans wrecked the interior of the abandoned synagogue.

ROTHENBURG OB DER TAUBER Middle Franconia, Germany. Jews were present in the early 12th cent., occupying a J. quarter with a synagogue and cemetery and restricted to the occupation of money-lending. Under R. Meir ben Barukh (the "Maharam"; 1220–93), the outstanding scholarly authority of the age and head of the local yeshiva, the community became a religious center for Bavarian Jewry and beyond. Persecution in the 1280s led many Jews in Germany to leave for Eretz Israel with R. Barukh at their head. He was arrested on the way by Emperor Rudolf and imprisoned at Ensisheim in Alsace, where he died, refusing to be ransomed so as not to create a precedent. In the Rindfleisch massacres of 1298 the entire com-

Jewish wedding hall, Rothenburg ob der Tauber, Germany, 1925 (Tim Gidal Collection, Jerusalem/photo courtesy of Beth Hatefutsoth, Tel Aviv)

munity of over 450 was slaughtered. The renewed community was again wiped out in the Black Death persecutions of 1348–49. A third community was expelled in 1397 on the charge of well poisoning and for the last time in 1519–20 at the instigation of a local cleric. The modern community was founded in the 1870s and grew to 115 in 1900 (total 7,923). The 45 Jews remaining in 1933 left by 1938, most for other German cities.

ROTMISTROVKA Kiev dist., Ukraine. The J. pop. was 1,785 (total 4,823) in 1897. In a pogrom on 13–14 May 1919, 45 Jews were murdered, many injured, and 60 J. homes burned. In 1926, under the Soviets, the J. pop. was 125. The Germans occupied R. on 1 Aug. 1941 and within a few days murdered all the Jews.

ROTTENDORF Nikolaiev dist., Ukraine. R. was a J. colony apparently founded in the 1920s. After the German occupation of Aug. 1941, 143 Jews from R. and the neighboring J. colony of Mendeldorf were murdered.

ROTTERDAM Zuid-Holland dist., Holland. Portuguese J. traders settled in R. in 1610 and Marranos in 1647. An affluent community was formed, but declined in the early 18th cent. and came to an end in 1736. The remaining few Portuguese Jews joined the Ashkenazi community that had been organized in the 1660s. In the 18th cent. J. trade and business were severely restricted, leading to widespread poverty. Nevertheless, a grandiose synagogue was built for the community in 1725. The community leaders were intimately involved in the day-to-day life of the Jews, from setting time limits on wedding celebrations to taking steps against married women who did not cover their hair. The community grew rapidly, numbering about 2,500 by 1797 and constituting the second largest J. community in Holland. Discriminatory restrictions were lifted in 1796, but poverty continued. An outstanding member of the community in this period was Dr. Leonard Davids, who spearheaded the struggle for smallpox immunization, which was instituted in 1800. Davids was also active in the community, fighting for the acceptance of J. children in R.'s general schools for the poor. He eventually succeeded and in 1812, 60 J. children were enrolled in general schools. In the course of the 19th cent. the J. pop. increased fourfold, reaching 9,490 in 1900 (total 319,866). The

seat of the region's chief rabbi was established in R. in 1815. A J. school was opened in 1822. The economic situation among the Jews improved from the second half of the 19th cent., although a large percentage was still needy. A number of refugees from the Russian pogroms arrived in the 1880s, forming a separate community and conducting services in a synagogue of their own. Alongside formal emancipation and economic betterment, the Jews became more involved in R.'s politics, economy, education, and culture. Since the larger community was now spread throughout R. and no longer surrounded the Great Synagogue, a number of smaller synagogues were established. In 1891 a new Central Synagogue was dedicated and the old synagogue ceased to be used. By 1899, 32 J. religious, social, and cultural organizations had been founded, including a branch of the Alliance Israelite. The Montefiore Association, established in 1883, assisted refugees arriving in R., continuing to do so in the 1930s for refugees from the Nazi regime. Other associations focused on welfare for the poor and J. awareness. A J. weekly, *Weekblad voor Israelitische Huisgezinnen*, was published from 1869 until 1940. The community's growth continued until the mid-1920s, when some moved to the suburbs and others to Amsterdam. Zionist activity began in 1900 and R. played an important role in the Dutch Zionist Organization from the 1920s. Three Zionist youth groups were founded in the 1920s and 1930s. In the early 1920s a branch of Agudat Israel was opened. New synagogues continued to be established and in 1929 there were four J. schools in which 450 pupils were enrolled. More organizations were also founded, totaling 75 in 1936 and including political, religious, social, and cultural bodies. A large number of journals were published over the years. Many refugees arrived in R. in the 1930s, numbering 454 by 1938.

The J. pop. in 1938 was 10,357. German bombing in May 1940 destroyed R.'s old synagogue, which had been preserved for its architectural value. Many J. homes and institutions were also destroyed, forcing thousands of Jews to seek shelter in other towns, while 700 refugees were ordered to leave. Thus, the number of Jews in R. dropped radically in the very first days of German occupation. At the same time the Zionist youth groups united to defend the community. The community continued to function and even maintained social welfare, cultural, educational, and religious activities. As the economic situation declined in 1941, a commit-

Ketubbah (marriage contract) of Yitzhak Pereira and Rahel da Pinto, married in Rotterdam, Holland, 1648 (Ministry of Education and Culture/photo courtesy of Yad Vashem, The Holocaust Martyrs' and Heroes' Remembrance Authority, Jerusalem)

tee organized the distribution of meals to the community. J. students were expelled from the general schools in Sept. 1941 and most grades were taught in J. schools. Some of the community's basic services were organized by the J. Council from Oct. 1941. The J. pop. in 1941 was 8,368 (total 588,999). Deportations to the death camps began in July 1942. While many local inhabitants assisted the Germans, others sympathized with the Jews, hiding hundreds in their homes and publicly protesting the deportations. Of the first 1,000 Jews to report for deportation, about 150 were sent home, as they were J. Council workers. This led the J. Council to increase its staff from 200 to 400, in the hope of saving more Jews from deportation. From Aug. 1942, a few J. men were sent to Dutch labor camps. They were eventually sent to Auschwitz, via the Westerbork transit camp. Arrests and deportations continued in waves until April 1943, when the last Jews were ordered to report to the Vught camp. Only two J. Council representatives and the cemetery's watchman were permitted to stay, but they too were finally deported in June. Those who remained were Jews in hiding and in mixed marriages. Fewer than 1,400 Jews from R. and its immediate surroundings survived the camps or were saved by hiding, while an estimated 10,000 perished. The R. community was revived after the Holocaust.

ROTTWEIL Wuerttemberg, Germany. Jews were living in a J. quarter in the early 14th cent., engaged in moneylending and trade and without civil rights. In the Black Death persecutions of 1348–49, Jews were massacred and all J. property was confiscated. Severe restrictions prevailed through the 16th cent. as the community dwindled. Development commenced in the 19th cent. with the number of Jews growing to 136 in 1880 (total 6,047). A synagogue was built in 1861 and Jews were active in local life. On the eve of the Nazi era, 96 remained, operating six factories and business establishments, mainly in the clothing and shoe trade, a printing press, and a successful daily newspaper. The economic boycott of 1933 was strictly enforced. The newspaper closed down in 1934 and by the end of 1938 all J. businesses had been "Aryanized." On *Kristallnacht* (9–10 Nov. 1938), the synagogue was vandalized. In all, 75 Jews emigrated, mostly to the U.S. and Palestine; eight perished after expulsion. Another 17 Jews from neighboring Oberndorf, Schwaningen, and Schramberg also emigrated.

ROUBAIX Nord dist., France. On the eve of WWII, there was a small J. pop. of local Jews and immigrants, but there was no communal life. During WWII, the Nord and Pas-de-Calais departments were under the jurisdiction of the military commander of Belgium. According to the 1942 census, there were 68 Jews in R. In several instances Jews were able to hide, receiving false documents from the municipality and assistance from the local Protestant minister, who obtained information about Nazi intentions from a German officer. On 27 Oct. 1943, a J. family was arrested, and later deported to Auschwitz via Malines (Mechelen).

ROUDNICE NAD LABEM Bohemia, Czechoslovakia. Jews are first mentioned in 1541. With Kolin, Bumsla, and Nachod the community was one of the four known by the acronym KRBN. In the early 17th cent., the Jews established themselves in a new quarter, building a synagogue there in 1619. Most Jews traded in grain and wine, raised cattle, or worked as artisans and peddlers. About a third succumbed to the plague in 1713 and many were murdered after the expulsion from Prague in 1744. A J. elementary school was opened in 1841 and a new synagogue was erected in 1853. The J. pop. included 176 families in 1851 but by 1930, only 166 Jews remained. The Germans closed the synagogue in Oct. 1941 and deported most of the Jews to the Theresienstadt ghetto in 1942. From there they were sent to the death camps of Poland.

ROUEN Seine Inferieure dist., France. The J. record dates back to the Roman era. In the Middle Ages, the Jews of England regarded R. as a center of J. learning. An Avenue des Juifs marks the site of the medieval community, which was first persecuted in 1066. At the end of the 12th cent., a member of the community, Calot of R., was made Procureur des Juifs du Royaume (representative of the Jews of the kingdom). After the expulsion of the Jews from France in the 14th cent., no Jews were present in R. for two centuries. Then several Marrano families settled there, afterwards leaving for Amsterdam, Antwerp, Hamburg, and London. During the 18th cent., this Marrano community almost entirely disappeared. The modern J. community, formed by Jews from Alsace, emerged only after the French Revolution. The synagogue was inaugurated in 1864. During WWI, the synagogue was heavily damaged. In 1940 there were 1,080 Jews (717 of them of French origin) in the Seine Inferieure department. During the occupation, R. was the seat of the regional delegation of the UGIF (Union Generale des Israelites de France) as well as the CQJ (Commissariat General aux Questions Juives). In 1942, R. became a deportation center to the death camps. In Jan. 1943, the Germans arrested 222 Jews near R. in retaliation for the killing of a German officer. During the occupation, the synagogue was confiscated for the use of the Red Cross (May 1944). It was heavily damaged in bombardments and subsequently reconstructed in 1950. In 1964 the community consisted of 800 Jews.

ROUSINOV Moravia, Czechoslovakia. Jews expelled from Brno and other royal cities in 1454 were most likely the first J. settlers. A synagogue was erected in 1591 and a J. school was opened in the late 18th cent. The J. pop. was somewhat over 1,000 (half the total) through the first half of the 19th cent. but then dropped to 199 in 1900 and 31 in 1930. In late 1941–early 1942 the Jews were deported to the Theresienstadt ghetto together with the Jews of Brno. From there they were sent to the death camps of Poland. The Nazis vandalized the synagogue.

ROVENKI Voroshilovgrad dist., Ukraine. Jews probably settled at the turn of the 19th cent. and numbered 152 (total 20,944) in 1939. The Germans captured the city on 18 July 1942, executing 315 people, including 60 Jews, in a nearby forest.

ROVINE-PECICA (Hung. Vilaagos-Pecska) S. Transylvania dist., Rumania. A J. community founded in 1810 maintained a synagogue and a J. school. The J. pop. in 1930 was 118 in R. and 93 in P. In June 1941, the J. pop. was expelled to Arad. A few returned after the war.

ROVNOPOL Stalino dist., Ukraine. R. was founded as a J. colony in 1855 by emigrants from Vilna, Mogilev, and Kovno (Kaunas). It included 42 families in 1857. The J. pop. was 447 in 1897 and 285 (total 381) in 1926. The Germans captured R. in fall 1941. All the Jews there perished during the occupation.

ROVNOYE Kirovograd dist., Ukraine. Jews numbered 470 in 1923 and 106 (total 7,775) in 1939. Those remaining perished under the German occupation instituted in Aug. 1941.

ROWNE (Rovno) Volhynia dist., Poland, today Ukraine. A J. community apparently existed by the mid-16th cent. Only six J. houses were left standing after the Chmielnicki massacres of 1648-49 but recovery was rapid. Until the first half of the 18th cent., the community was bound to Ostrog, only achieving independence after a long struggle. For a number of years, R. was the seat of the hasidic leader Dov Baer, the "*Maggid* of Mezhirech," and many of his followers flocked there after the "Gaon of Vilna" placed a ban on Hasidim in 1772. In the 19th cent. J. merchants expanded into the lumber and farm produce trade and became importers of cloth, shoes, porcelain, and glass. With the start of the construction of barracks for the Russian army in the 1870s, many Jews began working in the building trades. The J. pop. in 1897 was 13,780 (total 24,573), up from 4,850 in 1885. In the early 20th cent., industrial development accelerated and Jews operated the largest beer brewery in Volhynia, soap and match factories, flour mills, and brickyards. The community itself employed 100 public workers and maintained six synagogues, a hospital, and an old age home. Zionist activity began in 1884 with a Hovevei Zion group. The Jews suffered economically in WWI and in the anarchy after the Oct. 1917 Revolution they were attacked by the Petlyura gangs, who staged a pogrom in 1919 that left dozens of Jews dead and injured. In 1921, the J. pop. reached 21,702. Recovery was slow, but the Jews reestablished their economic preeminence, dominating industry, trade, and the crafts, where 75% of the Jews were employed. Jews also comprised three-quarters of the city's doctors, lawyers, and engineers. An extensive J. educational system was developed under the aegis of the Tarbut organization, including a high school that attracted students from all over Volhynia, three elementary schools, and three kindergartens. A business school had an enrollment of 200. The *talmud torah* was converted into J. public school with religious instruction and another 200 studied at the Etz Hayyim yeshiva. The Zionists were the leading force in the community's political life, controlling the community council and sending a representative to the Sejm. The Red Army arrived on 17 Sept. 1939, sovietizing economic life and closing down J. institutions. German aerial bombardments in June 1941 took a heavy toll on the Jews and about 2,000 fled with the Soviets as the Germans entered the city on 28 June. The regime of forced labor and extortion instituted by the Germans was accompanied by the indis-

Sabbath eve, Rowne (Rovno), Poland

criminate killing, of thousands of Jews by the end of Aug. A *Judenrat* was then set up. With R. becoming the administrative center of Nazi activity in the Ukraine, a decision was reached to eliminate the J. pop., to make room for the Nazi bureaucratic apparatus. On 6 Nov. 1941, about 21,000 Jews were led to a pine grove in nearby Sosenki and massacred. The remaining 5,000 were packed into a ghetto the following month. On 13 July 1942 they were transported toward Kostopol and murdered in the forest. After the liberation of R. by the Red Army on 5 Feb. 1944, 1,200 J. survivors from all over Volhynia gathered in the city, most leaving for the west in 1945–46.

ROZALIMAS   (Yid. Rozalye) Panevezys dist., Lithuania. The Jews first settled in the 19th cent. In 1897, the J. pop. was 265 (49% of the total), dropping to 110 in 1938. In WWI, the Jews were expelled by the Russian army; half returned later. After the German occupation of 1941, those not killed by Lithuanian nationalists were sent to Pakruojus, where they were murdered together with the Jews of Pakruojus on 4 Aug. 1941.

ROZAN   Warsaw dist., Poland. A J. settlement is known from the early 18th cent. Jews mainly traded with the surrounding farm villages and in the 19th

cent. ran a number of small factories and most of the town's stores. The J. pop. grew from 310 in 1827 to 1,159 in 1884 and 2,229 (total 3,855) in 1908. With the collapse of the rural economy after WWI, J. livelihoods suffered. Most of the J. political parties were active, with Agudat Israel controlling the community council. Eight of 18 municipal council members were Jews, including the deputy mayor. In 1936 and 1937, J. property was damaged in violent riots. The J. pop. in 1931 was 1,800. Many Jews fled in the first days of WWII. The Germans expelled the rest to the east on 8 Oct. 1939. In all, over 1,400 perished in the Holocaust.

ROZAVLEA   (Hung. Rozalia) N. Transylvania dist., Rumania. A J. community existed in the mid-19th cent.. In 1930 the J. pop was 723 (23% of the total). In April 1944, the J. pop. was transferred to the Viseul de Sus ghetto and deported to Auschwitz.

ROZDOL   (Yid. Razleh) Stanislawow dist., Poland. Jews were present in the early 17th cent., reaching a peak pop. of 2,465 (total 4,542) in 1880. In that year a major fire caused many to emigrate, a trend that was stepped up in WWI. The J. pop. in 1921 was 1,725. Jews were active in trade fairs throughout the area, selling in particular the decorative beads that were part of Ukrainian traditional dress. The hasidic courts (Zhidachov-Komarno, Zanz) provided another source of income. Zionism made inroads early in the cent., increasing its influence between the World Wars in the face of economic depression. The Germans occupied R. in June 1941. Most of the community was deported to the Belzec death camp on 4–5 Sept. 1942.

ROZHANA   (Rozhinoi) Polesie dist., Poland, today Belarus. A community existed in the early 17th cent. Under Russian rule from the late 18th cent., many Jews were employed in textile and tanning plants. In two big fires, in 1875 and 1895, most of the town's homes along with the ancient synagogue, the *talmud torah*, and the J. hospital as well as three factories were destroyed. By the end of the cent., the J. pop. was 3,599 (total 5,016). The restored *talmud torah* had an enrollment of 300 students with another 200 at the yeshiva. Among the religious Zionists, Yehiel Mikhael Pines (1843–1913) was an early leader of Hovevei Zion and a future leader of the *Yishuv*. With the burning of the town's knitting plants in WWI and other tribulations, the economy declined and the J. pop. fell to 2,400 (total 3,622) in 1921. The Zionists were active and a Hebrew Tarbut school was founded in 1922. Under Soviet rule (1939–41) the school was closed down and J. trade curtailed, with artisans organized in a cooperative. The Germans arrived in late June 1941, instituting a regime of forced labor and periodic executions. In Aug. the Jews were moved to an open ghetto. On 2 Nov. 1942, they were marched 28 miles (45 km) to Wolkowysk. Around 500 stragglers were shot on the way, including many children. At Wolkowysk they were crowded into underground bunkers where 20,000 Jews were being confined. On 28 Nov. they were all deported to the Treblinka death camp.

ROZHANKA   Nowogrodek dist., Poland, today Belarus. In 1847, there were 202 Jews in R., increasing to 543 (total 777) in 1897. After WWI, the J. relief organizations assisted the community to recover but a fire in 1927 destroyed most J. homes and economic conditions remained difficult. Traditional community life revolved around the *beit midrash* while the young congregated around the J. library, where a drama circle and Hehalutz group were formed. The Germans entered the town on 28 June 1941, immediately executing 70 J. men and putting the rest to forced labor. In Oct. 1942 the Jews were expelled to the Szczuczyn ghetto,

some being sent on to labor camps. The remaining Jews were murdered in the ghetto on 9 May 1943.

ROZHANOVCE   (Hung. Rozgony) Slovakia, Czechoslovakia, today Republic of Slovakia. Jews settled in the early 18th cent, building a small synagogue in the early 19th cent. and reaching a peak pop. of 230 (total 819) in 1840. Thereafter the J. pop. declined steadily as many left for nearby Kosice. The synagogue burned down in 1930. In 1941, the J. pop. was 31; most farmed. Under Slovakian rule, the Jews were deported via Presov to Demblin in the Lublin dist. of Poland in mid-May 1942.

ROZHEV   Kiev dist., Ukraine. Jews numbered 25 in 1787 and 610 (total 2,065) in 1897. In July 1919, they were attacked in a pogrom. In 1926, under the Soviets, only 19 remained. Those still there during the German occupation in WWII were murdered together with the Jews of the neighboring villages.

ROZNAVA   (Hung. Rozsnyo) Slovakia, Czechoslovakia, today Republic of Slovakia. Jews settled in the mid-19th cent., forming a Status Quo congregation in 1869 and erecting a splendid synagogue in the Moorish style in 1893 as their pop. rose from 104 in 1869 to a peak of 500 on the eve of WWI. Under Czechoslovakian rule, Jews served on the municipal council while J. doctors occupied important positions in the public health service. Most Jews identified with Hungarian culture but in the 1930s an awakening of J. national tendencies was discernible. Among the Zionists, Hashomer Hatzair was the largest youth movement with about 40 members. Jews owned 50 business establishments, 15 workshops, and three factories (a distillery, sawmill, and wood-processing plant). In 1941, the J. pop. was 388 (total 6,835). After the annexation to Hungary in Nov. 1938, ten J. families with Czechoslovakian citizenship were expelled and in 1939, J. business licenses were revoked. In April 1944, after the German occupation, the Jews were confined to a ghetto, its pop. swelling to 800 with the arrival of Jews from neighboring settlements. All were brought to Miskolc in mid-June and from there deported to Auschwitz.

ROZNIATOW   Stanislawow dist., Poland, today Ukraine. The J. community grew throughout the 18th and 19th cents., reaching a peak pop. of 1,589 in

1890 (50% of the total). The pop. then dropped in 1900 by a third because of emigration before rising again through an influx of Jews from the surrounding villages. The first Zionist group was founded in 1900 by the growing professional and educated class. Between the World Wars, the community suffered from Ukrainian pillaging and violence. Under the Germans the Jews were persecuted and compelled to work as forced laborers. On 1 Sept. 1942 they were dispersed in a mass expulsion, most arriving in Dolina and Bolechow after being hounded by the Ukrainians along the way. There they shared the fate of the local Jews.

ROZNOV   Moldavia dist., Rumania. Jews settled in the mid-19th cent. on a J.-owned estate. Attached to the Piatra-Neamt community, the Jews had no independent institutions. During the 1907 peasant revolt, Jews left R., but returned in 1910 and erected four lumber mills and an oil refinery. The J. pop. was 109 in 1899 and 141 in 1930 (10% of total). In 1940, the Iron Guard confiscated J. property and sent the Jews to forced labor. In Jan 1941, the J. pop. fled to Piatra-Neamt and Buhusi, never to return to R.

ROZNOW   Stanislawow dist., Poland, today Ukraine. The J. pop., growing mainly in the early 20th cent., stood at 418 (total 6,426) in 1921. The community ended in Oct. 1941 when the Jews were expelled by the Germans to nearby Kosow to await their end.

ROZOVKA   Zaporozhe dist., Ukraine. The J. pop. in 1939 was 238 (total 2,675). The Germans captured R. on 10 Oct. 1941 and shortly afterwards murdered the few Jews who had not fled nor been evacuated. Surviving members reestablished the neighboring J. kolkhoz after the war.

ROZPRZA   Lodz dist., Poland. Jews first settled here in the 17th cent. In the 1760s they traded with Danzig and other towns. The J. pop. in 1857 was 246 (58% of the total). During WWI, the community flourished because of its location on the Warsaw–Vien-

Jewish merchants in Rozniatow, Poland

na railway line. Zionist activity began between the World Wars with the left-wing parties dominant. The J. pop. of 600 in 1940 increased to 800 in July 1942. All were deported to the Treblinka death camp.

ROZWADOW Lwow dist., Poland. Few Jews settled until the 18th cent. The community grew to 1,678 (total 2,153) in 1880 and 3,373 in 1910, with Jews controlling the growing lumber trade. Most fled or were expelled in WWI, returning to find their homes destroyed by the Russians. In 1918, Polish soldiers and the local rabble again victimized the Jews, whose pop. dropped to 1,790 in 1921. The Hurwic dynasty dominated local Hasidism and Agudat Israel exerted much influence. A Baron Hirsch school founded in the late 19th cent. enrolled 177 children in 1911 and a supplementary Hebrew school served 97 in 1923. The *talmud torah* founded in 1922 had 317 pupils. Zionist activity was extensive between the World Wars. In the 1930s, antisemitism intensified with periodic outbreaks of violence and the economic situation of the community deteriorated. On their arrival on 14 Sept. 1939, the Germans emptied J. stores and starting on 28 Sept. expelled the community across the San River to Soviet-held territory, where it was dispersed. The few hundred who remained or succeeded in returning faced a regime of forced labor. On 21 July 1942, most were expelled to Dembica after a few dozen were murdered in the town. There they faced execution, labor camps, or deportation to the Belzec death camp.

ROZYSZCZE Volhynia dist., Poland, today Ukraine. Jews settled in the late 18th cent. and with the coming of the railroad their pop. grew to 3,169 (total 3,860) in 1897. Most Jews fled in the turbulence of WWI, returning afterwards to rebuild their lives with the support of the Joint Distribution Committee. In 1921 the J. pop. stood at 2,686. Between the World Wars, the Jews owned most of the town's factories (weaving, brewing, milling) and 270 of its 320 stores. They also dominated the trade in farm produce. All the Zionist parties and most of the youth movements were active and cultural activity centered around a Tarbut school. After a Ukrainian pogrom following the German occupation (completed on 28 June 1941), the Germans staged two *Aktions* in July, murdering 430 Jews. Forced labor ensued and a *Judenrat* was established. A ghetto crowding 25–30 Jews to a room was set up in Feb. 1942. On 23 Aug. 1942, the Jews were taken to

waiting pits and murdered; 80 found shelter with Czech and Polish families.

RUBENE Courland dist., Latvia. The J. pop. in 1935 was 12. The Jews were murdered by the Germans in fall 1941.

RUBEZHNOYE Voroshilovgrad dist., Ukraine. Jews settled in the Soviet period and numbered 355 (total 21,995) in 1939. Many were executed after the Germans occupied the city on 10 July 1942.

RUBIEL Polesie dist., Poland, today Belarus. A settlement of 100 J. families is known from the 1880s, dropping to 60 between the World Wars (over 10% of the total). In WWII, 53 J. men were murdered by the local pop. The others were expelled, mostly reaching Stolin to die in the *Aktion* of 11 Sept. 1942.

RUBIEZHOWICZE Nowogrodek dist., Poland, today Belarus. Jews apparently began to settle in the late 18th cent., trading in farm produce and also working the land. The J. pop. was 912 (total 1,482) in 1889. A pogrom was foiled in 1905 by J. self-defense forces and a few years later a blood libel was discredited. After WWI the Jews lost their eastern markets and the economic situation deteriorated still further in the 1930s. The Zionists became active after the publication of the Balfour Declaration in 1917. The J. pop. in 1921 was 903. The Germans arrived on 30 June 1941. On 1 Dec. the Jews were confined to a ghetto. In the first half of 1942 most were sent to Iwieniec and executed in a nearby forest on 8 June.

RUDAMINA (Yid. Rudamin) Seini dist., Lithuania. Jews first settled in the 18th cent. In 1899, a Jew bought most of the arable land, ushering in a short period of prosperity for this farming community which numbered 50 families. Between the World Wars, the economic situation led many to emigrate overseas, so that the J. pop. in 1940 amounted to about 20 families. After the German invasion in June 1941, the Jews were transferred to the Katkiskes ghetto and murdered in a nearby forest on 3 Nov. 1941.

RUDA PABIANICKA Lodz dist., Poland. The J. pop. in 1921 was 237 (5% of the total). On 19 Dec. 1939, the Jews were expelled to General Gouvernement territory.

RUDA SLĄSKA Silesia dist., Poland. Jews numbered fewer than a dozen families throughout the community's existence from the mid-19th cent. In 1942–45 a labor camp in nearby Stara Kuznia held 500 prisoners, mostly Jews. In Sept. 1944–Jan. 1945 another 500 were confined there in a branch of Auschwitz. They were subsequently transferred to camps in Germany.

RUDENSK Minsk dist., Belorussia. In the 1920s, under the Soviets, 12 J. families (70 Jews) were employed in agriculture. In 1939, the J. pop. was 176 (total 1,128). The Germans arrived in late June 1941 and in Oct. murdered about 150 people (most apparently Jews) on the outskirts of the town, burying them in three graves.

RUDKA Lublin dist., Poland. The J. pop. was 600 in 1921. No reliable information is available but it is believed that most of the Jews present after the German occupation in WWII were murdered in fall 1941; the rest in April 1942.

RUDKI (Yid. Ridik) Lwow dist., Poland, today Ukraine. Jews settled from the early 18th cent. Under the Austrians, Jews were active in the lumber, cattle, and liquor trade and with the coming of the railroad in the late 19th cent. as contractors and suppliers to the builders. In the trades they worked as butchers, bakers, tailors, glaziers, and locksmiths. The J. pop. was 1,352 in 1880 (half the total) and 1,824 in 1921 after flight, persecution, and economic hardship during WWI. Half the Jews engaged in commerce between the World Wars, while 30% were artisans. Relations with the Polish pop. were satisfactory in a common bond against the surrounding Ukrainians. The Soviet rule of 1939–41 brought community and commercial life to an end. The Germans arrived on 29 June 1941 and almost immediately executed 39 Jews. In Nov. 1942, 800 Jews were deported to the Belzec death camp. After a grievous winter in the ghetto, 1,700 were murdered in a nearby forest on 9 April 1943 while 300 taken to the Janowska Road camp.

RUDNIK Lwow dist., Poland. The J. community dates from the second half of the 17th cent., maintaining a pop. of 1,100–1,200 (35–40% of the total) from the late 19th cent. to WWI. A flourishing wickerwork industry was an important source of livelihood, as

were the local hasidic courts of the Halberstam dynasty. Many fled in WWI to the interior of the Austrian Empire never to return. Rampaging Cossacks pillaged and burned J. homes. The J. pop. dropped to 805 in 1921 and the Joint Distribution Committee was called on for support. Zionist activity was widespread between the World Wars. Those who did not reach Soviet territory in the beginning of WWII were deported to the Belzec death camp in 1942.

RUDNIYA Smolensk dist., Russia. The 18th cent. community had its own rabbi and numbered 589 in 1847. After the paving of a highway and the laying of a railway line through R. in the mid-19th cent., the J. pop. grew and reached a figure of 2,122 (total 2,958) in 1897. Two private J. schools were operating in the early 20th cent. In 1926, under Soviet rule, the J. pop. rose to 2,235. In 1925, 34 J. families worked at three J. kolkhozes. A J. school was still open in the early 1930s. In 1939, the J. pop. was 1,640. The Germans captured the town on 14 July 1941. About 1,200 Jews were confined in 20 houses on a single street. In Aug., about 20 young Jews were murdered and another 100 were shot to death soon after. On 21 Oct., the Germans murdered 1,000 Jews. Another 150 skilled workers were executed in Nov. 1941 and Feb. 1942.

RUECKINGEN (now part of Erlensee) Hesse–Nassau, Germany. The community, dating from the 17th cent., built a synagogue in 1765. The Jews numbered 46 (4% of the total) in 1871. Most who remained there (26) and in neighboring Niederrodenbach (25) after 1933 perished in the Holocaust.

RUEDESHEIM AM RHEIN Hesse–Nassau, Germany. After their evacuation to R., 60 Jews from Mainz chose martyrdom or were slaughtered during the First Crusade (1096). Expelled in 1470, Jews only returned some 230 years later, engaging in the wine trade. They built a district synagogue in 1843. The J. pop. was 58 (1% of the total) in 1885 and the community was affiliated with the Wiesbaden rabbinate. By 1933 the J. pop. had declined to 29. When the Nazis demolished the synagogue in a *Kristallnacht* pogrom (9–10 Nov. 1938) that spread to Geisenheim, the remaining Jews fled.

RUEGENWALDE (Pol. Darlowo) Pomerania, Germany, today Poland. The first evidence of a Jew allowed to settle in R. dates from 1701. A J. community developed slowly, numbering 36 members in 1752 and 124 in 1849. It maintained a synagogue and a cemetery. From the turn of the cent. to the 1920s, the J. pop. dropped sharply to about 45 members. In 1933, there were 36 Jews in R. The synagogue was sold in 1935–36 and the cemetery was desecrated in 1938, probably during *Kristallnacht* (9–10 Nov.). No further information about the fate of the Jews of R. is available.

RUELZHEIM   Palatinate, Germany. Jews numbered eight families in 1750 and reached a pop. of 179 in 1800 (the second largest in the Speyer bishopric) and 484 (total 2,975) in 1857, with their number dwindling steadily thereafter. Most were in trade and the Jews played an important part in the local tobacco industry, owning three cigarette factories. A synagogue was erected in 1832–33 and the community was one of the few in the Palatinate to have a *mohel*. On Passover, two bakeries prepared *matzot* for other communities as well as R. A J. elementary school was opened in 1830–31, reaching an enrollment of 104 in 1856. Relations with the local pop. were generally good. In 1933, 172 Jews remained. On *Kristallnacht* (9–10 Nov. 1938), the synagogue was wrecked along with J. homes and stores, the cemetery was desecrated, and J. men were sent to the Dachau concentration camp. Of the 198 Jews present in 1930, 88 left for other German cities by 1940 (75 in 1938–39), 49 emigrated to the U.S., and 26 went to other European countries. During the Holocaust, 56 perished in the concentration camps, deported either from other German cities or from occupied Europe.

RUESSELSHEIM   Hesse, Germany. Established in the early 18th cent., the community numbered 147 (6% of the total) in 1871. Its synagogue, built in 1844, housed 125 Torah scrolls. During the Weimar Republic, a branch of the J. War Veterans Association was established. The community changed its affiliation from the Orthodox to the Liberal rabbinate of Darmstadt and the synagogue's renovation in 1929 was generously funded by the Opel automobile manufacturing family. In 1933 the J. pop. had declined to 47. SA men destroyed the synagogue's interior and burned the Torah scrolls on *Kristallnacht* (9–10 Nov. 1938). The remaining Jews mostly emigrated or left by 1939; seven were deported during WWII.

RUETHEN   Westphalia, Germany. Jews are mentioned from the 13th cent. Three protected families were present in the early 17th cent., growing to five by mid-cent. and nine in the early 18th cent. In the mid-19th cent., the community reached a peak pop. of 60–80, subsequently dropping to 30–43 (total 1,700–2,300) in the latter half of the 19th cent. In June 1933, there were 26 Jews. The community maintained a cemetery from 1624 and a synagogue in 1810–90, afterwards using a prayer house that was destroyed on *Kristallnacht* (9–10 Nov. 1938). Some time before *Kristallnacht*, the Jews began leaving R., four emigrating and 11 moving to other places in Germany. Five were deported in July 1942.

RUGAJI   Latgale dist., Latvia. Jews settled from early in the 20th cent. and numbered 85 in 1935 (total 275). All were murdered after the German occupation of July 1941.

RUJIENA   Vidzeme (Livonia) dist., Latvia. Jews settled in the late 19th cent. and maintained a pop. of 60–70 (2% of the total) after WWI. Those not escaping to the Soviet Union were murdered after the German occupation of July 1941.

RUMA   Vojvodina dist., Yugoslavia. Jews settled in the 18th cent. and a community was organized towards the end of the 19th cent. In 1931 the J. pop. was 261 (total 13,403). In 1942 the Jews were murdered in Auschwitz; only one survived.

RUMBURK   Bohemia (Sudetenland) Czechoslovakia. J. settlement dates from the late 18th cent. Jews were active in the textile industry and most were German-speaking. In 1930, they numbered 109 (total 10,466), leaving the city after the annexation of the Sudetenland to the Third Reich in fall 1938. Most of those who failed to emigrate were deported to the death camps via the Theresienstadt ghetto.

RUMMELSBURG   (Pol. Miastko) Pomerania, Germany, today Poland. A J. family in R. is first mentioned in 1728. By 1752, there were three families; in 1895, the Jews in R. numbered 240. The community set up two synagogues in 1818 and 1848 and a cemetery in 1820. The antisemitic riots which broke out in Pomerania when the Neustettin synagogue was burned down in 1881 spread to R. In 1900, there were also riots in which J. property was attacked. When the Nazis came to power in 1933, the J. pop. was 60. By Sept. 1935, J. businessmen had sold their businesses or were facing financial ruin as a result of the Nazi boycott measures. The synagogue was sold in 1937. In 1939, there were only seven Jews in R. No further information about their fate is available.

RUMSISKES (Yid. Rumshishok) Kaunas dist., Lithuania. Jews first settled in the 19th cent. During WWI, the Russian army expelled the Jews. About half (50 families, or 42% of the total) returned. R. was a summer resort, mainly for yeshiva students and teachers. There was a Hebrew school, part of the Tarbut network, and the Zionist movement won widespread support. Relations with non–Jews were good until 1940 when the Soviet occupation brought out latent antisemitism. The J. pop. in 1938 consisted of 50 families. After the German invasion in June 1941, Lithuanian

nationalists took over the town. All able-bodied J. men were sent to forced labor in nearby Pravieniskes, where they were murdered on 4 Sept. The women and children were shot outside R. on 2 Sept. 1941.

RUNDENI Latgale dist., Latvia. The J. pop. in 1935 was five (total 288). All were murdered by the Germans and Latvians in summer or fall 1941.

RUSCOVA (Hung. Visooroszi) N. Transylvania dist., Rumania. Jews first settled in the early 18th cent. The community's rabbi, R. Avraham Shelomo Katz, ran a yeshiva with 75 students in the 1930s. Zionist activity began after WWI and members of the youth movements immigrated to Palestine. The J. pop. in 1930 was 1,034 (32% of the total). In June 1942, Jews aged 20–42 were drafted into labor battalions in the Ukraine, where most died. On 18 April 1944, the J. pop. was transferred to the Viseul de Sus

Jewish blacksmith in Ruscova, Rumania, 1930s. (YIVO Archive, New York/photo courtesy of Beth Hatefutsoth, Tel Aviv)

ghetto and then deported to Auschwitz. After the war, about 120 survivors returned, but all left, mostly for Israel.

RUSKE POLE (Hung. Urmezo; Yid. Vermezhayf) Carpatho-Russia, Czechoslovakia, today Ukraine. Jews settled in the first half of the 18th cent., numbering 32 in 1768, 113 in 1830, and 292 (total 1,274) in 1880. A few Jews were farmers. The J. pop. continued to grow in the 20th cent., reaching 317 in 1921 and 395 in 1941. The Zionist and religious youth movements were active. The Hungarians arrived in March 1939 and in 1941 drafted dozens of Jews into forced labor battalions. In Aug. 1941, they expelled some of the town's Jews to Kamenets-Podolski, where they were murdered. The rest were deported to Auschwitz in late May 1944. A few joined the Czechoslovakian brigade and fought against the Nazis on the eastern front.

RUSSKA MOKRA (Hung. Oroszmokra) Carpatho-Russia, Czechoslovakia, today Ukraine. Jews probably settled in the mid-19th cent. after residence bans were lifted in the mining districts. Their pop. was 41 (total 498) in 1880 with many employed at the mineral baths that were opened in the latter part of the 19th cent. The J. pop. then increased to 109 in 1921 and 180 in 1941. The Hungarians occupied the town in March 1939 and in 1941 drafted a number of young Jews into forced labor battalions and sent them east. They also expelled a few J. families without Hungarian citizenship to Kamenets-Podolski, where most were murdered. The rest were deported to Auschwitz on 24 May 1944.

RUST Baden, Germany. Jews were apparently present during the Thirty Years War (1618–1648). The community reached a pop. of 211 in 1842. A J. elementary school was opened in 1835 and a synagogue was built in 1895. In 1933, 26 Jews remained, over half emigrating by 1938. On *Kristallnacht* (9–10 Nov. 1938), the synagogue and J. homes were vandalized. On 22 Oct. 1940, the last nine Jews were deported to the Gurs concentration camp; seven were subsequently released and allowed to emigrate from Germany.

RUTKA Warsaw dist., Poland. The J. pop. in 1921 was 141 (total 180). The Jews were expelled by the Germans to the Warsaw ghetto in Jan. 1941, sharing the fate of the other J. refugees there.

RUTKI-KOSSAKI Bialystok dist., Poland. A J. community existed in the 19th cent. and numbered 713 (total 1,368) in 1921. Most of the Jews were murdered by the Germans after they captured the town in June 1941.

RUZA Moscow dist., Russia. In 1939 there were 165 Jews in the Mozhaisk prov., most in R. The 40 remaining Jews were murdered during the short German occupation of 25 Oct. 1941–17 Jan. 1942, including 16–18 at the outset.

RUZHIN Zhitomir dist., Ukraine. Jews probably settled in the early 18th cent. In 1897, their pop. was 3,599 (total 5,016). R. Yisrael of R. founded a local hasidic dynasty that spread to Bukovina and Galicia. In a 1919 pogrom, Jews were robbed and beaten and a large tribute was exacted from the community. The J. pop. dropped to 1,108 in 1939. The Germans captured the town on 16 July 1941. On 10 Sept. 1941, 750 Jews were taken to Mt. Karchev and executed with the participation of Ukrainian police; 250 skilled J. workers were left behind. Valuables were stolen and a large tribute was extorted from the community towards the end of the year. On 1 May 1942 another 300 Jews were murdered.

RUZOMBEROK (Hung. Rozsahegy) Slovakia, Czechoslovakia, today Republic of Slovakia. Jews first settled in the 1820s. A cemetery was opened in 1865 and a beautiful 300-seat synagogue in the Moorish style was consecrated in 1870 as the community formed a Neologist congregation. A J. elementary school was established in 1871. In the 1880s Yaakov (Koppel) Klein became chairman of the community and was one of its chief benefactors. He opened a cellulose and paper plant in 1895, the only one of its kind in the state, and was mayor of R. in 1906–07. The actor Peter Lorre (*Casablanca*, *The Maltese Falcon*) was born in R. in 1904. The J. pop. rose from 398 in 1869 to a peak of 1,063 (total 12,249) in 1910. After WWI, the Zionists enjoyed widespread support. The town's Maccabi society was one of the first J. sports clubs in Slovakia. Jews owned 110 business establishments, 36 workshops, and 11 factories, including a textile plant employing 2,700 workers. In 1940, the J. pop. was 804. Persecution began with the establishment of the Slovakian state in Oct. 1938. J. children were expelled from the public schools in 1940 and the authorities closed down or "Aryanized" J. businesses in 1941. In late March 1942, 55 young J. men were deported to the Majdanek concentration camp. J. girls succeeded in escaping thanks to a timely warning by Dr. Ferdinand Klinovsky, head of the county and largely responsible for the fact that barely half the Jews were deported. Most of the 350 who remained were able to evade the Nazis, some joining the partisans. A small community persevered into the 1980s.

RYBNIK (I)   Lwow dist., Poland, today Ukraine. The J. pop. in 1921 was 103. Many Jews were murdered or fled in the Ukrainian pogrom of summer 1941 with the Germans killing or deporting the rest in Aug.–fall 1942.

RYBNIK (II)   Silesia dist., Poland. The J. settlement began to develop in the 19th cent., numbering 380 in 1913 (total 11,656). About 30% left between the World Wars as R. passed to Polish rule. The J. pop. of 262 in 1931 was a target of unrelenting antisemitism on the part of both the Poles and the German minority in the town. Zionism now tended to replace Germanization as a cultural focus. At the outset of WWII, some fled but the Nazis expelled most or compelled them to work as forced laborers. In March 1940, all J. males were mobilized to dismantle the J. cemetery. On 22 May, the last 100 Jews were expelled to Trzebinia to share the fate of the local Jews.

RYBNITSA   Moldavia, today Republic of Moldova. The J. pop. was 1,574 (total 4,029) in 1897. A J. girls' school operated in 1910. In 1917, Jews were attacked in a pogrom. Their pop. rose to 3,216 in 1939. Many fled when German and Rumanian forces occupied R. on 5 Aug. 1941. Approximately 1,500 Jews remained behind. They were joined by another 1,500 J. refugees from Rumania en route to Transnistria. Under the Rumanian administration, a ghetto was established with a J. pop. of over 3,000, half of them deportees from the Vertyuzhani and Marculesti camps. Between Nov. 1941 and Feb. 1942, most of the ghetto residents were murdered in mass *Aktions* or died of starvation or typhoid fever. In Oct. 1943, 54 J. Communists were imprisoned in R. when the Vapnyarka camp was closed. A group of 650 Jews from the Regat was brought to R. in May 1943 for forced labor. Some managed to return to Rumania when the fighting neared R.

RYBOTYCZE   Lwow dist., Poland, today Ukraine. Jews are first mentioned in 1630 and numbered 459 (total 1,437) in 1880. Many supplied leather to local shoemakers and marketed their products. The uncompromisingly hasidic character of the community kept out Haskala and Zionism. The Germans most likely expelled the Jews around the end of July 1942 via Przemysl or Dobromil to the Belzec death camp.

RYCHNOV NAD KNEZNOU   Bohemia, Czechoslovakia. Jews were present in the first half of the 16th cent. The synagogue and most J. homes went up in flames in 1782. The J. pop. was 216 in 1890 and 71 (total 4,706) in 1930. Most of the Jews were deported to the Theresienstadt ghetto via Hradec Kralove in Dec. 1942 and then to Auschwitz in 1943. In all, 124 perished.

RYCHWAL   Lodz dist., Poland. Jews lived there from the 18th cent. and in 1897 numbered 151 (16% of total). The Germans took R. on 3 Sept. 1939. In Nov.–Dec. 1939 the majority of the Jews were transported to Grodziec and in Oct. 1941 shot in the Kazimierz Biskupi forest.

RYCZYWOL   Poznan dist., Poland. Jews probably arrived in the 16th cent, reaching a peak pop. of 348 in 1840 and contributing significantly to the local spinning and weaving industries. Emigration to the big German cities reduced the J. pop. to 168 in 1895 and 79 in 1921. The 31 Jews remaining in 1939 were expelled by the Germans to General Gouvernement territory on 7 Nov.

RYGLICE   Cracow dist., Poland. Jews settled in the second half of the 18th cent., numbering 372 (total 2,587) in 1880 and 282 in 1921 under deteriorating economic conditions. The German occupation in WWII brought forced labor, extortion, and restricted movement. Some of the young were taken to the Szebnie labor camp. In summer 1942 the community was expelled to Tuchow for deportation to the Belzec death camp.

RYIASNOPOL   Odessa dist., Ukraine. Most Jews in R. received land after the Oct. 1917 Revolution and engaged in farming. In 1927, the Jews numbered about 40 families (150 people). In the late 1920s, most of the 200 children in the coeducational elementary school were Jews. Nearly all the Jews remaining during the German occupation were presumably murdered.

RYKI Lublin dist., Poland. Jews are first mentioned in the late 16th cent. Toward the end of the 18th cent., J. residence was restricted to the town's periphery, but the J. pop. continued to grow, reaching 2,077 (90% of the total) in 1908. J. tradesmen ran shops and stalls and others engaged in light industry (producing lace and processing hides). The community's first rabbi, Barukh ben Meir, officiated for 30 years and was a leading hasidic figure. The Zionists became active in 1904 and in 1918 wrested control of the community council from the Hasidim. Afterwards Agudat Israel came into power, also opening a Beth Jacob school for 70–80 girls and a Yesodei Torah school for boys. After WWI, with the J. pop. at 2,419 in 1921, Jews sold fish and developed a home weaving industry. They owned all but one of the town's bakeries and most carters and porters were also Jews. Most, however, barely eked out a living. The town fell to the Germans on 17 Sept. 1939. In mid-Oct., a *Judenrat* was established. Hundreds of the able-bodied were sent to labor camps. A ghetto was set up in late 1940, crowding together 1,800 Jews. A typhoid epidemic killed 50 in winter 1941. On 7 May 1942, the Jews were marched 9 miles (15 km) to Demblin. Along the way, 130 were murdered; 200 were selected for labor and the rest were deported to the Sobibor death camp. After the war, 30 survivors returned to R. but left in 1945 when several were murdered.

RYLSK Kursk dist., Russia. Jews probably settled at the turn of the 19th cent. and numbered 245 (total 11,011) in 1926. The few Jews who had neither fled nor been evacuated were murdered after the arrival of the Germans on 5 Oct. 1941.

RYMANOW Lwow dist., Poland. Jews are known from the late 16th cent. An important factor in the development of the community was the dynastic court founded in the late 18th cent. by R. Menahem Mendel

Jewish merchants selling hats, Ryki, Poland

(Rymanower), a disciple of Elimelekh of Lyzhansk and one of the outstanding hasidic figures of the time. His house and the synagogues were the finest buildings in the town. Another source of income was the tourist trade generated by the mineral baths operating from the late 19th cent., when the J. pop. stood at around 1,750 (almost 50% of the total). WWI and its aftermath reduced the J. pop. to 1,412. The Zionists were active from the turn of the cent. while antisemitism intensified in the 1930s. The Germans arrived on 8 Sept. 1939. Despite mass expulsion across the San River to Soviet-controlled territory, only 300 failed to return. Refugees swelled the J. pop. to 3,000. Those not earmarked for the Plaszow labor camp were expelled to Barwinek on 13 Aug. 1942 and from there deported to the Belzec death camp.

RYMSZANY Vilna dist., Poland, today Belarus. The J. pop. in 1921 was 151 (total 290). After the German occupation of June 1941, the Lithuanian police massacred the entire J. pop. on 27 Aug. 1941 in the Dgoczai forest together with the Jews of Zarasai and Dukszty.

RYNDINO Tula dist., Russia. The Germans occupied R. in Oct. 1941. On 11 Jan. 1942, they murdered 18 Jews from the neighboring villages in the town.

RYPIN Warsaw dist., Poland. Jews are known from the 16th cent. and an organized community was formed in the mid-18th cent. By the end of the 19th cent., most ran shops or market stalls. About a quarter were craftsmen, a few were grain wholesalers, a number of families owned large estates, forest land, and sawmills while others leased lakes and orchards for their fish and fruit. The J. pop. grew to 1,706 (total 4,735) in 1897. In addition to a Great Synagogue completed before WWI, the Gur and Aleksandrow Hasidim ran their own *shtiblekh* and *yeshivot*. About 500 J. refugees crowded the town during WWI. The arrival of

Sewing class, Rypin, Poland, 1922 (Beth Hatefutsoth Photo Archive, Tel Aviv/courtesy of Eliezer Nachomov, Israel)

General Haller's Polish troops in 1918 initiated an era of antisemitic persecution that continued unabated between the World Wars. During WWI, modern Hebrew education commenced and the Peretz library became a common meeting place for both Zionist and Bund youth. In 1921 the J. pop. reached 2,791. Hehalutz operated pioneer training farms, with one of its groups joining the Labor Brigade in Palestine. The Zionists controlled the community council and supplied most of the community's representatives on the municipal council. The local Tarbut school enrolled hundreds of children. The Germans captured R. on 8 Sept. 1939, instituting a regime of forced labor and extortion. Many Jews fled east. On 15 Oct. about 150 Jews were murdered in the nearby forest. All but 100 of those remaining were expelled on 15 Nov., dispersed to various towns. The rest fled in early 1940. About 280 survived the Holocaust, mostly in the Soviet Union.

RYZHNOVKA Kiev dist., Ukraine. In 1897, the J. pop. was 1,374 (total 4,132). In 1918, a Ukrainian gang looted J. homes and stores and murdered a number of Jews. In 1926, under the Soviets, the J. pop. was 753. The Germans murdered the Jews in the Chalzhivy forest immediately after occupying the town in WWII.

RZECZYCA Lwow dist., Poland, today Ukraine. The J. pop. in 1921 was 120. The Jews were probably deported to the Belzec death camp in summer–fall 1942, directly or via Rawa Ruska.

RZEPIENNIK-STRZYZEWSKI Cracow dist., Poland. The J. pop. numbered 224 (total 1,802) after WWI and a pogrom in Nov. 1918 caused some to leave. In WWII the Germans murdered all but 30 (sent to Plaszow) in the Dombrie forest.

RZESZOW (Yid. Raishe) Lwow dist., Poland. Jews may have been present before the annexation of the city to Poland in 1340. In 1589 there were 20 J. families, engaged in a constant struggle for residence and trade rights, with tensions leading to occasional outbursts of violence, particularly among local students. Jews nonetheless maintained a prominent position in the city's economic life, operating as moneylenders, leaseholders, wholesalers, retailers, and peddlers and trading prominently at the city's fairs (in grain, cattle, hides, silk, wine, etc.). In the late 17th cent., the Jews

expanded their commercial relations with Breslau and Danzig, also visiting their fairs regularly. As artisans, the Jews were organized in guilds (furriers, jewelers, tailors). Until the second half of the 17th cent., while one of the largest and most important communities in the province, it remained under the aegis of Lwow, afterwards breaking away and associating itself with the Przemysl community until a dispute led it to declare its independence under R. Yehezkel Yehoshua Feivel Fraenkel-Teomim. A magnificent synagogue said to have been built in the late 16th cent. served in the defense of the city and remained standing until WWII. Another fortress-synagogue was built of brick in the baroque style in the late 17th cent. The community also maintained a yeshiva. In 1772 the city came under Austrian rule and heavy taxes were imposed on the Jews. Economic restrictions excluded them from leasing land and mills and dealing in alcoholic beverages as well as other traditional occupations. Despite these disabilities, the Jews were able to expand their commercial life, trading in tobacco, salt, and grain. Though Jews were active in the revolutionary events of 1848 and allied themselves with liberal Polish patriots, antisemitism intensified during the period. In the second half of the 19th cent. Zanz Hasidism became influential, later challenged by followers of the Sadagora-Ruzhin sect, with the two camps fighting over possession of the local *klaus*. The Zionists made their appearance in the 1890s with the founding of a Hovevei Zion society. Haskala adherents were also prominent in the community. Most children studied in the *heder* system. A new yeshiva was founded in 1897 and a school for supplementary Hebrew instruction was opened in 1898. In 1893 a Baron Hirsch vocational school was inaugurated. The J. pop. rose steadily, from 3,375 in 1800 to 5,820 in 1880 and 8,785 (total 23,688) in 1910. Many Jews abandoned the city during WWI, with some of the more well-to-do Jews remaining afterwards in Vienna and other big cities. Those who returned found their homes pillaged. In the anarchy of 1918–19, Jews were attacked by the Polish General Haller's soldiers and local mobs. In 1921 the J. pop. stood at 11,361. Between the World Wars, economic distress continued. Many J. artisans were without work while J. peddlers and stallkeepers were exposed to attacks in the streets. After initial assistance by the Joint Distribution Committee, the Jews organized mutual aid societies and welfare agencies. Zionist activity expanded, with Hashomer Hatzair representing the left and religious Zionists grouped around the Mizrachi synagogue. Agudat Israel became active in 1927, opening a Beth Jacob school for girls. Most children studied in Polish public schools. A modernized *heder* was set up by Mizrachi in 1920 and a Hebrew school was opened in 1928 as well as an open university sponsored by the Tarbut organization. Antisemitism intensified in the late 1930s, including economic boycotts and increasing acts of violence. The Germans entered the city in Sept. 1939 after a heavy bombardment, immediately instituting a regime of forced labor and persecution. The two synagogues were wrecked and Jews were evicted from choice apartments. Subsequently J. businesses were "Aryanized" and various "contributions" were exacted from the community. A *Judenrat* was set up in Oct. 1939. In Dec., thousands of J. refugees from western Poland began to arrive in the city, lacking all means of subsistence and crowded into public buildings. In the winter,

a dysentery epidemic struck the community. Through the summer and fall of 1941, Jews were moved into a special quarter and in Jan. 1942 a ghetto was sealed off, holding a J. pop. of 12,500. Jews were put to work in German industry and army facilities. Workshops that provided the Germans with essential services were set up in the ghetto as a hedge against expulsion and forced labor. Two soup kitchens were opened along with an elementary school. At around the end of April 1942, alleged J. Communists were executed in an *Aktion*. In June 1942, an additional 10,000–12,000 refugees from the surrounding settlements were brought to the ghetto. Mass deportations commenced on 7 July. In three waves, lasting through 18 July, most of the Jews were sent to the Belzec death camp. The sick and weak were murdered, about 1,000 in the Rudna forest and 250–300 within the city. Sporadic killing continued in the reduced area of the ghetto. On 7 Aug., 1,000 young mothers with their children

The Jewish Street in Rzeszow, Poland

were loaded onto trains for extermination and on 15 Nov. more of the sick and weak along with children were executed in the Rudna forest while others were deported to the Belzec death camp. The ghetto was now divided in two, one part as a labor camp and the other for workers' families and other survivors. Within a month, about 1,500 labor camp inmates, half the total, were deported to the Belzec death camp. Around 200 managed to jump from the trains and sneak back to the camp. The two ghettoes, containing 2,500–3,000 Jews, were liquidated around the end of Aug. 1942 when the able-bodied were sent to the Szebnia labor camp and the rest were deported to Auschwitz after patients in the J. hospital were murdered. Another labor camp, at the airplane engine factory in the nearby village of Lysia Gora, held 500–600 Jews from the area who were transferred to the Plaszow camp in 1944. Thirty-five Jews hiding in the cellar of a pharmacy were discovered and publicly executed in Feb. 1944.

Some Jews organized themselves into partisan groups in the forests and carried out attacks against German targets. After the liberation, about 600 survivors gathered in the city, most soon leaving.

RZHEV   Kalinin dist., Russia. Jews settled in the late 19th cent., numbering 780 in 1926 and 457 in 1939. The Germans occupied R. on 14 Oct. 1941 and murdered the few Jews still there (38 in summer 1942).

RZHISHCHEV   Kiev dist., Ukraine. Jews numbered 94 in 1784 and 6,008 (total 11,629) in 1897. Many Jews were employed in a J.-owned sugar refinery and iron foundry. A private boys' school was opened in 1910. A private school for girls was also opened. In July 1919 the Petlyura gangs attacked the Jews of R. In 1939, under the Soviets, the J. pop. was 366. The Germans arrived on 28 Aug. 1941 and shortly afterwards murdered the Jews.

S

SAALFELD (I) (Pol. Zalewo) East Prussia, Germany, today Poland. The J. community dates back to the early 19th cent. The J. pop. was 78 in 1880 and 40–50 in the 1920s. The community maintained a synagogue and a cemetery. When the Nazis came to power in 1933, the J. pop. was 44. The boycott measures of summer 1935 were particularly severe in S. with Jews abused. By May 1938, only five Jews were left and the synagogue was put up for sale. No further information about the fate of the local Jews under Nazi rule is available.

SAALFELD (II) Thuringia, Germany. There were Jews living in S. at the beginning of the 14th cent. The J. pop. was 60 in 1910 and 33 in 1932. On *Kristallnacht* (9–10 Nov. 1938), nine J. men were arrested. In 1939, 14 Jews remained. Two families were able to emigrate and four families were deported. No further information is available on the fate of the other Jews in S.

SAARBRUECKEN Saar, Germany. Jews are mentioned in neighboring St. Johann in 1321. Significant J. movement to S. commenced in 1760 and in the 1770s the municipality passed laws to encourage Jews to settle in order to stimulate economic growth. Jews were permitted to purchase homes and fields and received pasture and water rights for their cattle. In about 1776, the Jews were expelled following vehement opposition of local merchants to the competition they posed. Almost none were present in 1789. In 1808, under the French, the J. pop. reached 61. A wealthy merchant, Yirmeyahu Hirsch, was among the founders of the Assembly of J. Notables and the consistory of the Saar and served as the secretary of the former. With the inauguration of a railway station in St. Johann in 1852, S. became a center of the coal and steel industries in the Saar, but the Jews preferred to continue in trade. Most were peddlers. J. cemeteries were opened in 1840 and 1845 and a new synagogue was erected in 1890. In the second half of the 19th cent., most Jews belonged to the middle and lower classes. They also ran a few large businesses, like the Lyon department store in St. Johann (founded in 1857) with branches in Luxembourg and other countries, the Bamberger & Herz textile house, and the E. Weil Soehne firm with over 400 employees. In 1916, there were 74 J. business establishments in the city, including 13 selling textiles and 14 dealing in leather and shoes. In 1910, four of the city's 44 doctors were Jews and in 1919, seven of its 40 lawyers. The J. pop. was 1,000 in 1905, making the community the largest in the Saar. In 1909, St. Johann became part of the city. In accordance with the Treaty of Versailles, the Saar came under League of Nations administration in the aftermath of WWI. The decision produced a general strike and rioting that targeted J. and French businesses. Jews were elected to the municipal council from the late 19th cent. and were prominent in politics during the Weimar period. Dr. Walter Sender headed the Social-Democrat faction in the Saar state council in 1922–25 and served together with the Social-Democrat Eduard Lehmann on the city council. Twenty J. artists and administrative personnel were employed in the municipal theater in addition to its J. orchestra members. The J. pop. increased to 2,214 (about 2% of the total) in 1925 in an atmosphere of economic prosperity. By 1931, 136 J. firms and business establishments were operating in the city (about 8% of the total). Jews operated chemical and tobacco factories, two hotels and a pharmacy, and a wide variety of stores. The growth of the J. pop. derived from an influx of Jews from Eastern Europe as well as from Alsace-Lorraine after the Germans were forced to leave. The

East European Jews maintained their Orthodox traditions, opening their own synagogue and keeping their distance from the established Reform community. The East European presence also engendered Zionist activity after WWI. The Central Union (C.V.) had a major branch in the city. To accommodate the overflow crowds on the High Holidays, an additional synagogue was opened in a hall placed at the community's disposal by the municipality. Religious classes were attended after school by 200–300 children. A kindergarten was started in 1927, later becoming a day care center. ORT founded a branch in 1930, teaching crafts and agriculture to prepare Jews for emigration, especially to Palestine.

Though relations with the German pop. were generally good, there were also a number of antisemitic incidents in the post-WWI period. In 1933, when the Nazis came to power, S. was one of 18 J. communities in the Saar, with a pop. of about 2,400. The Nazi Party initiated anti-J. boycotts and persecution just as in the Reich. Jews were dismissed from jobs and banned from local swimming pools. Doctors were reduced to receiving non-J. patients clandestinely at night. J. schoolchildren were abused and physically attacked. Consequently a J. school for 200 children was opened in 1934. The economic position of the Jews quickly deteriorated and many liquidated their businesses. The day care center became a focus of J. organizational activity and from 1934 the J. Cultural Association of S. organized cultural affairs for all the J. communities of the Saar. With the annexation of the Saar to the Reich under the Jan. 1935 plebiscite, J. emigration increased. By June 1936, 36% of the city's Jews had left and by 1939 only 175 remained (total pop. 130,772). In 1935–36, 69 J. businesses were sold. Under Nazi rule, anti-J. agitation intensified. The community was the only one in the Saar still active in 1936. The J. school had 145 students in 1936, 20% from other communities. However, only 33 attended the following year. The Maccabi sports club was active; the Zionists opened an information office; and welfare services for all the communities in the Saar were coordinated in S. On *Kristallnacht* (9–10 Nov. 1938), the synagogue was burned and 130–150 J. men were led through the streets and abused before being sent to the Dachau concentration camp. With the outbreak of war in Sept. 1939, the city was temporarily evacuated. The Jews were sent to forced labor camps and not permitted to return. Six are known to have been deported to the

Gurs concentration camp in southern France on 22 Oct. 1940. At least 100 Jews perished in the Holocaust, including 73 in Auschwitz. After the war, 180 Jews returned to the city, some afterwards emigrating. In 1960 the J. pop. was about 700.

SAARLOUIS Saar, Germany. Jews from Wallerfangen settled when Louis XIV built S. as a border fortress town in 1680. They were expelled in 1710 at the instigation of the guilds but returned in 1715 and established themselves as butchers. Fifteen J. families were present in 1788. There was little friction with the local pop. other than business disputes which intensified in the 1840s when the economic situation of Christian merchants deteriorated. Most Jews engaged in trade in the mid-19th cent., many as shopkeepers. They were also active in local life. A Jew served in the municipal police force in the early 19th cent and the first Jew was elected to the municipal council in 1847 with others following. In the consistory period, the community was under the jurisdiction of the chief rabbi of Trier and in 1853, as the third largest in the Prussian Rhineland, it became the seat of a regional congregation. Most Jews were Reform in outlook. A prayer house was opened in a private home in 1820 and a synagogue was consecrated in 1828. A J. elementary school was started in the same year but closed after three years because of disputes between Orthodox and Liberal circles over educational principles. By the 1860s, all J. children were attending Christian schools. The J. pop. rose to 254 in 1833 but then dropped over the next few decades when many left for economic reasons. The J. pop. rose again to 307 (total 15,364) in 1910. In 1912, 60 Jews (75%) were engaged in trade, mostly in textiles, shoes, and clothing. The riots accompanying the decision in 1919 to place the Saar under League of Nations auspices caused much damage to J. businesses. In 1928, Jews owned a cigarette factory and a manufacturing plant for packaging materials. In 1933, the J. pop. was 364 (including Roden). Though the 1 April Boycott Day instituted in the German Reich was not observed in S., the social isolation of the Jews intensified from mid-1934 and their economic situation began to deteriorate as well. With the annexation of the Saar to the Reich in 1935 by plebiscite, J. emigration increased, mostly to France (Lorraine) and Luxembourg. Only 95 Jews remained by late 1935 and much fewer by March 1936. By 1938, only five J. businesses were still open. On *Kristall-*

nacht (9–10 Nov. 1938), the synagogue was wrecked along with J. homes. Forty-one Jews remained in May 1939. The last 18 were evacuated on the outbreak of war, 15 of them emigrating. The other three were deported to the Gurs concentration camp after returning to the city. In all, 45 Jews perished in the concentration camps, including 26 in Auschwitz.

SAARWELLINGEN   Saar, Germany. Jews are first mentioned in 1750 and engaged in moneylending down through the 19th cent. Their pop. rose to 191 (total 3,195) in 1895 but with the industrialization of the Saar many young left for the big cities. The community separated itself from the jurisdiction of the Trier rabbinate in 1879 and appointed its own rabbi. The private J. elementary school operating in the community received public school status in 1891. In 1933, the J. pop. was 134. When the Saar was annexed to the German Reich in 1935, most Jews left, either emigrating (36 to France, 27 to Luxembourg) or moving to other German cities (54). On *Kristallnacht* (9–10 Nov. 1938), the synagogue was vandalized and J. homes were destroyed. Subsequently the Jews were moved to a single house until deportation to the Gurs concentration camp in southern France (eight Jews on 22 Oct. 1940). In all, 32 perished in the Holocaust, including 22 in Auschwitz.

SABAC   Serbia, Yugoslavia. Jews settled in the first half of the 19th cent., encountering strong opposition from local Serb tradesmen. In the 1860s, in the wake of deteriorating economic conditions, a group of 20 families organized for settlement in Eretz Israel but the scheme did not come to fruition. In 1865 a branch of the Alliance Israelite was opened. When two J. tradesmen were killed that year, there was a strong J. reaction throughout Europe and foreign diplomats even intervened to protest against Serbian anti-J. policies. By 1900 the J. pop. was 232 (total 8,894). In Sept.–Oct. 1941 the Germans murdered the Jews of S. (who numbered 83 in 1940), along with some 700 Austrian refugees, in nearby Zasavica.

SABILE   Kurzeme (Courland) dist., Latvia. Jews were present from the early 19th cent. and an organized community was established in 1840. The J. pop. reached a peak of 873 (total 1,400) in 1881 and thereafter declined. In 1915 all were expelled by the Russians. About half returned (totaling 325 in 1925), sup-

Post office of Sabac, Yugoslavia

ported by the Joint Distribution Committee and American funds as one of the poorest J. communities in Courland. Dozens left in the following years and with the exodus of the young the Zionist movement barely gained a foothold. The Jews had two synagogues and in 1935 owned 37 of the town's 71 larger business establishments. More left for the big cities under the Soviet policy of nationalization in 1940–41. The Germans arrived on 1 July 1941. Shortly thereafter the Jews were led out of the town and murdered by a special unit of the Latvian police.

SABINKA   Lublin dist., Poland. The J. pop. stood at 139 (total 239) in 1921. The Jews were expelled by the Germans to Siedlce in Aug. 1942 and from there deported to the Treblinka death camp.

SABINOV   (Hung. Kisszeben) Slovakia, Czechoslovakia, today Republic of Slovakia. Jews probably settled in the early 1780s. Most were peddlers and petty tradesmen. A synagogue was erected in 1864 and a cemetery was opened in 1870 as the community grew to 239 in 1869 and 392 (total 2,954) in 1900. A *talmud torah* was founded c. 1890 and a yeshiva operated intermittently. In the post-WWI period, with the J. pop. rising above 500, Jews held public positions and served on the municipal council. The Zionist movement made inroads and WIZO opened a branch. Hashomer Hatzair and Bnei Akiva were active among the young and the Maccabi sports club had dozens of members. Jews owned 40 business establishments and ten workshops, paper and vinegar factories, and two banks. In 1941, under Slovakian rule, Jews were forced out of their businesses. In late March 1942, dozens of young Jews were deported, the men to the Majdanek concentration camp and the women to Auschwitz. The Hlinka Guard brutally rounded up families and deported them to the east, including 300 Jews to the Rejowiec ghetto in the Lublin dist. of Poland on 23 May. Most of the remaining 163 Jews were evacuated to western Slovakia before the Germans arrived in Sept. 1944.

SACEL (Hung. Izaszacsal) N. Transylvania dist., Rumania. Jews settled in the mid-19th cent. The J. pop. in 1930 was 666 (21% of the total). In 1941 restrictive regulations were imposed on the Jews. On 15 Dec. 1942 Jews were drafted into labor battalions in the Ukraine, where most died. In April 1944 the community was transferred to the Viseul de Sus ghetto and later deported to Auschwitz.

SACHSENHAGEN Hesse–Nassau, Germany. Jews lived there from the 18th cent. and were noted for their religious orthodoxy. Numbering 58 (7% of the pop.) in 1885, the community then dwindled; 17 Jews perished in the Holocaust.

SADAGURA (Yid. Sadigora; Ger. Sadagora) Bukovina, Rumania, today Ukraine. In 1770, Jews working in the Russian coin minting plant were among the founders of S. In 1774 the Austrians called on Jews to build barracks for the soldiers, but later forced J. families to leave. In 1842, R. Yisrael Friedmann of Ruzhin set up his court in S. and was followed by adherents to his hasidic sect. He built a luxurious synagogue for his followers seating 1,000 worshipers. The ostentatious manner in which he and his son R. Avraham Yaakov lived set off a controversy between the Sadagora and Zanz sects. From 1863 to 1914, a Jew served as mayor. Artisans with a particular trade lived on separate streets and had their own synagogues. The J. pop. in 1880 was 3,888 (80% of the

Synagogue in Sadagura, Rumania

total). Up to WWI, Jews were able to trade with Russia because of the proximity to the border and the wave of Hasidim visiting the court. In 1914, the Russian conquerors persecuted the Jews, destroyed J. homes, and exiled many to Siberia. The J. pop. dwindled from 5,060 in 1914 to 900 in 1919. Zionist activity began at the turn of the century, and pioneer training farms were set up after WWI. The J. pop. was 1,459 in 1930 and 654 in 1941 after the Soviets exiled many J. tradesmen and artisans to Siberia. On 7 July 1941, Ukrainians murdered 73 Jews in the nearby forest and in fall 1941 the rest of the community was deported under cruel conditions to Transnistria, where many perished.

SADOWA WISZNIA Lwow dist., Poland, today Ukraine. Jews were present from the mid-16th cent., at first earning a livelihood mainly as innkeepers. The community grew to around 1,300 (30% of the total) in the late 19th cent. but declined through emigration to about 1,000 in 1921. The Zionists became active in 1902 despite strong opposition from traditional circles. The community was liquidated by the Germans in three separate *Aktions* in 1942: 450 Jews were sent to the Janowska camp on 15 April, most of the others to Janowska and the Belzec death camp in Oct., and the remnant to the Jaworow ghetto in Dec.

SADOWNE Lublin dist., Poland. Jews probably settled in the late 19th cent. and numbered 245 (total 970) in 1921. On the eve of WWII, there were 380 Jews in S. In Dec. 1941, the Germans expelled them to Lukow and other places, from where they were deported to the Treblinka death camp in Sept. 1942.

SADZAWKA Stanislawow dist., Poland. The J. pop. was 100 in 1921. The Jews were possibly executed locally in Oct. 1941 with the remnant expelled to Nadworna for liquidation in summer 1942.

SAFOV Moravia (Sudetenland), Czechoslovakia. Jews are mentioned in 1670. A new synagogue was consecrated in 1822 after a fire destroyed the J. quarter a year earlier. The J. pop. was 135 in 1921 and 76 (total 772) in 1930. Most Jews fled to other localities in Bohemia after the annexation of the Sudetenland to the German Reich in fall 1938. Some subsequently emigrated and the rest were deported to the Theresienstadt ghetto and the death camps of Poland.

SAGAN (Pol. Zagan) Lower Silesia, Germany, today Poland. The Jews were expelled in 1462, only establishing a modern community in the early 19th cent., which numbered 170 in 1880. The community maintained a cemetery (opened in 1831) and a synagogue (from 1857). When the Nazis came to power in 1933, the J. pop. had dropped to 78, dwindling further to 30 in 1937 and seven in 1939. On *Kristallnacht* (9–10 Nov. 1938), the synagogue was burned and J. stores were destroyed. No further information is available on the fate of the community under the Nazis. Presumably those unable to emigrate perished following deportation.

SAGAYDAK Kirovograd dist., Ukraine. Jews probably settled in the first half of the 19th cent. A synagogue was built by 1853 and the J. pop. reached 770 (total 801) in 1897, subsequently dropping to 579 in 1926. In the Soviet period, a J. council (soviet) was operating. After they occupied the town in Aug. 1941, the Germans murdered the few Jews who had neither fled nor been evacuated.

SAHY (Hung. Ipolysag) Slovakia, Czechoslovakia, today Republic of Slovakia. After sporadic settlement in the 18th cent., Jews came in increasing numbers after 1840, opening stores and founding a community within a short time. A handsome synagogue was erected in 1852 and after the split in 1869, the congregation declared itself Status Quo with Yehuda (Julius) Grossman serving as rabbi for 50 years (from 1872). An Orthodox group split off in 1876 and formed its own congregation with its own community institutions. The two congregations shared a common elementary school. An Orthodox synagogue was built in 1893 and a new one in 1929. The J. pop. grew from 311 in 1869 to 660 in 1910 and a peak of 848 (total 5,804) in 1930. Jews spoke Hungarian among themselves and identified with Hungarian culture. Some served on the local and dist. councils and a number of J. physicians held senior positions in the public health service. Jews also owned 88 business establishments, 24 workshops, and two factories. The Zionists were active from the 1920s. After the annexation to Hungary in Nov. 1938, Jews were increasingly persecuted, with many seized for forced labor and sent to the eastern front, where most perished. In May 1944, after the German occupation, the Jews were moved to a ghetto, two families to a room. As more arrived from the surrounding area, the ghetto pop. rose to 1,205. Hungarian police tortured many in their search for valuables. Eighty Jews were sent to the Garany concentration camps and from there deported to Auschwitz. The rest were deported to Auschwitz via Balassagyarmat on 12–14 June. About 200 Jews returned to the town after the war.

SAINT-AVOLD (Ger. Sankt Avold) Moselle dist., France. A synagogue was built in 1860 and newly consecrated in 1923. During WWII, local Jews were expelled from their homes to the south of France with the rest of Alsace-Lorraine Jews. From 1940 until 1944, there was a concentration camp in S. where 46 victims are believed to have perished. In 1940, during the war, the local synagogue was completely destroyed by bombing, and the cemetery was desecrated. In the 1960s, the J. community consisted of 100 members.

SAINT-DENIS Seine dist., France. The J. presence dates to the Middle Ages when a royal decree enabled five J. families to settle in 1353, under the control of the local monastery. There was no communal life in S. in the modern era, although there were Jews in S. between the World Wars. During WWII, a concentration camp for British citizens was located in S. and J. prisoners of war from Palestine were also interned there. According to the 1941 census, there were 325 Jews in S. In July 1942, 63 Jews were arrested and J. property was confiscated.

SAINT-DIE Vosges dist., France. A small J. community was formed in the 19th cent. and a synagogue was built in 1862. During WWII, the local bishop secretly converted J. children. They were later interned at Ecrouves and deported.

SAINT-ETIENNE Loire dist., France. Jews from Alsace established the community after the Franco-Prussian war of 1870–71, building a synagogue in 1880. After WWI, immigrants from Russia and Poland joined the community. On the eve of WWII, the community consisted of about 80 families, mostly old local families. In 1939–40, 40 families from Alsace were evacuated to S. More refugees arrived from the north. There were about 200 families (600 persons) registered, but many families lived in hiding. In 1941, there were 500 Jews in the town with 62 receiving aid as refugees from the CAR (Comite d'Assistance

aux Refugies). Deportations first affected foreign Jews. In Aug. 1942, they were sent to Lyon for classification. First only men were arrested, but later women and children as well. Only some returned. The Germans entered S. on 11 Nov, 1942 and anti-J. regulations issued by the Vichy government were immediately implemented. J. enterprises were "Aryanized." In March 1943, 120 hostages, including 12 Jews, were arrested after an attack on a group of German officers. A third of the J. pop., about 280–300 Jews of French origin, were arrested. The apartments of the deportees were plundered and their property confiscated. Many members of the community chose to leave town, permanently or temporarily. In 1964 there were 800 Jews in S., many from North Africa.

SAJOKAZA Borsod dist., Hungary. Jews arrived in the mid-18th cent., numbering 65 in 1851 and 98 in 1930. Their position was severely undermined by the racial laws of 1938. In 1940, 40 young men were sent to forced labor in the Ukraine, where most perished. The remaining Jews were deported to Auschwitz via Diosgyor and Miskolc on 10 June 1944. Twenty-eight survivors reestablished the community but soon left.

SAJOKAZINC Borsod dist., Hungary. The first Jews settled in 1747. Organizing in 1806, they erected a synagogue in 1813 and formed a Status Quo congregation in 1869 with many smaller settlements affiliated to it. The J. pop. was 130 in 1840 and 70 in 1941. In 1942, the young men were sent to forced labor, where most died. On 10 June 1944, the remaining Jews were deported to Auschwitz via Sajoszentpeter and Miskolc.

SAJOSZENTPETER Borsod–Gomor dist., Hungary. Jews settled in the late 18th cent. The pop. declined when Jews were allowed to settle in the larger cities. They numbered 736 in 1840 and 597 in 1930. On 15 April 1944, they were concentrated in a ghetto and on 10 June brought to Miskolc. A week later they were deported to Auschwitz.

SAKI Crimea, Russia, today Ukraine. With the establishment of J. kolkhozes in the area in the 1920s, a large J. kolkhoz was set up in S. which employed many of its Jews. In 1926, nine J. families from Polesie founded the Horepashnik kolkhoz nearby. A regional J. agricultural school was opened in the village of Tschebotarka. In 1932, there were 240 J. families in the entire S. farm belt. In 1939, the regional J. pop. was 1,854, with 416 Jews (total 7,779) in S. itself. The Germans occupied S. in late Oct. 1941, murdering those Jews who had neither fled nor been evacuated in late Nov. Another 42 Jews (probably from the area) were murdered at the village of Novyi Karagurt in May 1942.

Door-to-door peddler, Sakiai, Lithuania, before WWII

SAKIAI (Yid. Shaki) Sikiai dist., Lithuania. Jews first settled in the 18th cent. and by 1897 the J. pop. was 1,638 (74% of the total). S. never succeeded economically and in the 19th and 20th cents. there was a steady stream of emigrants to the U.S., England, and South Africa and later to Palestine. The community maintained a synagogue and one of the leading rabbis of S. (1854–60) was R. Shemuel Mohilewer, a founder of the Hovevei Zion movement. The community's educational system consisted of a *heder, talmud torah*, and later in the 20th cent. a modernized *heder* and a Hebrew school established by the Tarbut network. During WWI most Jews left, but returned after the the war. Between the World Wars, Jews held the majority of municipal council seats and the chairman of a Zionist party was elected mayor. The Zionist movement enjoyed widespread support and an urban training kibbutz operated in S. By 1939, there were only 600 Jews in S. After the German invasion in June 1941,

Lithuanian nationalists took control of the town. On 5 July, all J. men 15 years and older were forced into the trenches they had dug on the outskirts of town and then shot. Forty of the wealthier J. women were then executed. A ghetto was established for the remaining Jews, and on 13 Sept. 1941, they were also murdered at the same site where their brethren had been murdered earlier.

SAKSAGAN Dnepropetrovsk dist., Ukraine. Jews settled in the 1880s and numbered 355 in 1897 and 158 (total 5,146) under the Soviets in 1926. After the German occupation of 12 Aug. 1941, those Jews who had neither fled nor been evacuated were murdered, probably at the Piatyhatka coal mines.

SALA (Hung. Vagsellye) Slovakia, Czechoslovakia, today Republic of Slovakia. Jews probably settled at the turn of the 18th cent., their number growing slowly in the face of residence restrictions. In 1880 their pop. was 153 (total 3,053). A splendid synagogue was built in 1896 with the J. pop. increasing to 272 in 1900. After WWI, the community maintained an elementary school for 70 children as well as a yeshiva, *beit midrash*, and *talmud torah*. Agudat Israel was the leading movement. Jews dominated the economy, owning 39 business establishments, 14 workshops, and two factories in 1921. Their pop. increased to 450 in 1941. After the annexation to Hungary in 1938, the J. economy was gradually undermined and dozens of Jews were seized for forced labor. After the German occupation of March 1944, Jews from nearby settlements were brought to the local ghetto and in mid-June deported together with local Jews to Auschwitz via Nove Zamky. Nearly half the postwar community of 109 emigrated to Israel and other countries in 1949. A few Jews remained in the 1990s.

SALAKAS (Yid. Salok) Zarasai dist., Lithuania. S. was one of the first J. settlements in Lithuania. Despite several devastating fires in the 19th cent., the J. community's economic situation was good until WWI, when new borders cut S. off from Vilna and the railroad. As a result, many emigrated to South Africa, Cuba, and Palestine. The community supported several synagogues, social welfare organizations, and Zionist groups. In 1897 the J. pop. was 1,582 (66% of the total), dropping to about 300 families in 1941. After Germany's invasion in June 1941, various antisemitic

Synagogue in Sala, Czechoslovakia, 1900 (Gross Family Collection, Tel Aviv/photo courtesy of Beth Hatefutsoth, Tel Aviv)

The Jews of Salakas, Lithuania, before WWII

measures were introduced and Jews were forced to work for Lithuanians. A *Judenrat* was appointed. On 2 Aug. 1941, all the Jews were taken to the Sungardas forest. From there 150 men were taken to the village of Paezere and murdered. After returning the remaining Jews to a ghetto in S., the Lithuanian nationalists, overseen by Germans, murdered all the Jews at the Pazhmis forest towards the end of Aug.

SALANKI (Hung Salank; Yid. Salanyie) Carpatho-Russia, Czechoslovakia, today Ukraine. J. settlement began in the early 18th cent. Two families were present in 1728. The Jews apparently abandoned the town and then returned in the latter part of the 19th cent., reaching a pop. of 80 (total 1,525) in 1880. In 1921, under the Czechoslovakians, their pop. rose to 145 and in 1941 to 152. The Hungarians occupied the town in March 1939, drafting dozens of Jews into forced labor battalions and sending them to labor camps. In Aug. 1941, a number of J. families without Hungarian citizenship were expelled to Kamenets-Podolski and murdered. The rest were deported to Auschwitz on 22 May 1944.

SALANTAI (Yid. Salant) Kretinga dist., Lithuania. Jews first settled in the 17th cent. The most famous of S.'s rabbis was Yisrael Lipkin (1810–83), named the "Salanter" and known for his ethical teachings. A noted native of S. was Beinush Salant, one of the seven founders of Jerusalem's Nahalat Shiva ("Settlement of Seven") neighborhood. The Zionist movement had widespread support prior to and after WWI. The J. pop. in 1897 stood at 1,106 (45% of the total). A fire in 1926 and a boycott of J. businesses in the 1930s by Lithuanians caused many to emigrate to South Africa, the U.S., and Palestine, the J. pop. dropping to about 500 in 1940. After Germany's invasion in June 1941, the Jews were abused and robbed. On 1 July all the Jews were congregated in the synagogue and forced to relinquish their money and valuables. Each night, groups of ten men were taken out and shot; 150 young women were forced to work for Lithuanian farmers, and then shot. The men were shot on the banks of the local stream. The remaining women and children were taken to the village of Sateikiai on 20 July 1941 and buried in a mass grave after execution. It is estimated that about 440 Jews were murdered.

SALDOBOS (Hung. Szaldobos) Carpatho-Russia, Czechoslovakia, today Ukraine. Individual Jews are

mentioned in the 18th cent. but it was only in the latter part of the 19th cent. that the community grew, numbering 35 in 1880. In 1921, under the Czechoslovakians, its number reached 104 and in 1941, 119 (total 2,147). Jews engaged in trade, crafts, and agriculture and owned a flour mill. The Hungarians arrived in March 1939 and in 1941 drafted a number of Jews into forced labor battalions. A few families without Hungarian citizenship were expelled to Kamenets-Podolski and murdered. The rest were deported to Auschwitz in the second half of May 1944.

SALDUS (Yid. Froienburg) Kurzeme (Courland) dist., Latvia. The J. settlement dates from the second half of the 19th cent., growing to a peak pop. of 1,159 (total 3,585) in 1897. The Jews were expelled from S. in WWI and after repatriation numbered 300–400 until WWII. They lived in straitened economic circumstances mostly as artisans seeking work in the neighboring villages and supported by the Joint Disribution Committee and relatives from the U.S. and South Africa. A Hebrew elementary school with a Zionist orientation was founded in the 1920s and a number of Zionist groups were active. Under Soviet rule (1940–41) J. commercial and communal life ended. After the Germans entered S. on 1 July 1941, the Latvian police held the Jews in the police building until they were all executed toward the end of summer.

SALGOTARJAN Nograd dist., Hungary. Jews settled in the early 19th cent. and the community built a luxurious synagogue in the latter part of the cent. The J. pop. rose to 489 in 1880 and 1,023 (7% of the total) in 1910. Jews ran the nearby coal mine. A J. school was founded in 1883 and a yeshiva enrolling 100 students operated until WWI. During the 1930s, a Zionist training farm was set up nearby. In 1941 the J. pop. was 1,255. The young were seized for forced labor in 1942. In spring 1944, a ghetto was set up for 3,200 Jews including those from nearby villages. Able-bodied men were sent to forced labor and the rest were deported to Auschwitz on 12–13 June. The postwar community numbered 244 in 1949 but gradually dispersed.

SALISTEA DE SUS (Hung. Felsoszeliste; Yid. Selisht) N. Transylvania dist., Rumania. A J. community was organized in the late 18th cent. and the majority barely made a living. The J. pop. was 437 in 1920

Yeshiva students, Salgotarjan, Hungary

(13% of the total). In April 1944 the community was transferred to the Dragomiresti ghetto and later deported to Auschwitz.

SALMUENSTER (now part of Bad Soden-Salmuenster) Hesse-Nassau, Germany. Jews lived there in 1384, but the community was founded centuries later, opening a synagogue in 1865 and numbering 56 (4% of the total) in 1905. By 1937 all the Jews had left, ten emigrating.

SALNITSA Vinnitsa dist., Ukraine. Jews probably settled after the Chmielnicki massacres of 1648–49. They numbered 903 in 1897 (total 3,699) and 567 in 1926 under the Soviets. The Germans captured S. in mid-July 1941. In Dec., German and local police expelled about 300 Jews to the Ulanov ghetto. The remaining 150 were sent there in spring 1942. All were murdered, together with the local Jews, on 12 June 1942.

SALOCIAI (Yid. Salat) Birzai dist., Lithuania. Between the 17th and 19th cents. there was a Karaite community here. Jews settled in the 19th cent. During WWI the Jews were expelled. Some returned later. The community sponsored a school and synagogue. The Zionist movement won widespread support. The J. pop. in 1940 stood at 100 (13% of the total). In Aug. 1941, the Jews were transported to Posvol (Pasvalys). On 26 Aug. 1941 they and the Posvol Jews, altogether 1,349, were murdered in the Zadeikiai forest

SALONIKA (Salonica, Thessaloniki) Macedonia, Greece. The record of J. settlement in S., which was to become the largest and most famous J. community in Greece, begins around 140 B.C.E. Most of the first settlers were from Alexandria and engaged in international trade. At the end of the Byzantine period, S. was home to 500 Jews. At the beginning of the Ottoman period (1453–1821), the Romaniot Jews were exiled to Istanbul, where they formed their own congregation.

R. Yaakov Meir, chief rabbi of Salonika, Greece, 1909

From the early 16th cent., waves of immigration from the west, especially from Spain and Portugal, formed a new J. pop., primarily Sephardi. The immigrants established separate congregations, synagogues, and institutions that bore the names and rites of their homelands, while the "community" constituted an umbrella organization uniting them all. Between the 16th and 18th cents., S. developed into the largest J. community in Greece and a center of Torah learning. The spiritual leaders of S. Jewry were frequently approached by communities all over Greece to settle disputes and issue halakhic decrees. In 1520–25 the J. pop. was 13,225 (total 24,315). The J. domination of the wool industry brought prosperity to the community. The port was closed on the Sabbath and J. festivals, as the Jews practically monopolized the harbor economy. Moshe Almosnino, a revered 16th cent. rabbi, played a leading role in achieving the community's autonomy from Turkish authority in 1567. In the 16th and 17th cents., the community was renowned for its efforts to redeem Jews fallen into captivity as a result of war

or sea travel. The messianic movement of Shabbetai Zvi (who resided in S. in 1651–54 after his expulsion from Izmir) swept up Jews from all walks of life. The large-scale voluntary conversion to Islam of some 300 families (called *Donme*), including influential and affluent Jews, prefigured the deep crisis that was to engulf the city's J. community in the 18th cent. following the collapse of the textile trade and the political chaos in the region. During this period, the Jews were subject to anti-J. allegations and abuse, poverty dominated the community, and the rabbinate's influence dwindled. During the 18th cent., epidemics also pushed the community's numbers down by thousands while devastating fires destroyed most of S.'s synagogues. The J. pop. dropped from 30,000 in 1714–15 to 23,000 in 1788. During the Greek revolt in the Peleponnesus region (1821–29), anti-J. disturbances prompted Jews to flee, many reaching areas still under Turkish rule, such as S. Although the Jews suffered damages and losses in a number of epidemics and fires in the first half of the 19th cent., nevertheless

No.15   9mé Aiihee (3eme Serie)   Prix D

למען ישראל

PRO ISRAEI

REVUE SIONISTE HEBDOMADAIRE
Eondée en 1917

Vendredi
20
TAMOUZ 5686
2 JUILLET
1926

REDACTION ET ADMINISTATION
Comninon 34 — Boite Postale No 126 — SALONIQUE

ABONNEMENTS PAR AN
Salonique Drs. 50. Intérieur Drs. 75. Extérieur Francs

LE REPOS DOMINICAL OBLIGATOIRI

La population juive demande à Mr. Pangl as la réparation de l'iniquité

Une pétition couverte de 7.000 signatures

Front page of Pro Israel, *written in French and published in Salonika, Greece, 1926 (Jacqueline Ben-Atar/photo courtesy of Yad Vashem, The Holocaust Martyrs' and Heroes' Remembrance Authority, Jerusalem)*

the community of S. grew during this period. In 1828 there were 36 synagogues, a large J. school, and a number of smaller schools. Greek hostility towards the Jews increased once Greece declared its independence in 1830. This found expression in anti-J. libels and allegations with occasional outbursts of violence. Although they no longer controlled the wool industry, Jews were active in trade, banking, and industry, operated flour mills and breweries, and entered municipal services. Growing modernization left its imprint on internal J. life: a modern educational system was established, based on linguistic, scientific, and technical studies; a network of schools run by the Alliance Israelite (from 1873) also engaged in vocational training; and many newspapers, libraries, clubs, and associations sprang up. The J. pop. reached 40,000–50,000 in 1876–70. In the second half of the 19th cent. and in the early 20th cent., numerous social welfare organizations were established to assist the poor and sick. A fire broke out in 1890, destroying most of S.'s syna-

gogues, a number of educational institutions, and important libraries. However, J. life was soon rehabilitated with assistance from England and Paris. In 1903, a J. hospital (named after Baron Maurice de Hirsch) was inaugurated. By 1910, there were some 60 institutes of religious studies. Following the Balkan wars (1912–13), S. was annexed to Greece. As a result of the country's territorial expansion, the general Greek pop. grew significantly and the percentage of Jews in S. dropped to 16%. This, in turn, led to a gradual decline in the J. predominance in the city. Violent Greek antisemitism increased but was denounced by the authorities. The first Zionist organization in S. was established secretly in 1908 but the general Zionist movement in Greece entered its golden era after the incorporation of S. into Greece. Vigorous and dynamic from the outset, Zionist activities encompassed fundraising for the J. National Fund, Hebrew lessons, public lectures, special events such as "Shekel Day" and "Hebrew Day," as well as diverse political activities,

R. Tzevi Koretz, Galician-born chief rabbi of Salonika from 1933, escorting the King of Greece (presumably at a synagogue ceremony)

including election to parliament, city hall, and the community's governing bodies. Zionists were dominant in the latter. After the Balfour Declaration in 1917, all Zionist associations in S. joined forces and united into a single club name after Theodor Herzl. A gathering of some 30,000 Jews celebrated the first anniversary of the Balfour Declaration in S. In 1919, in a speech by Foreign Minister Nicolas Politis, the Greek government expressed its sympathy for the movement. On 10 June 1919, an assembly of all Zionist associations in the country established the Greek Zionist Federation, headed by Dr. Moshe Cofinas. Several prominent Zionist leaders (David Ben-Gurion, Ze'ev Jabotinsky, and Menaham Ussishkin, among others) visited S. and spoke to enthusiastic audiences of thousands. A fire in 1917 devastated a significant part of the city, including 34 (out of 37) synagogues

and hundreds of J. homes, libraries, and institutions. The community received assistance from all over the world and was rehabilitated, but the J. character of S. was lost from this point on. Many Jews decided to emigrate (mostly to France and the U.S.) and emigration continued until WWII. Nevertheless, by 1928 the overwhelming majority of Greek Jews were living in S. (83.5%, or 55,250). The affluent J. community included bankers, jewelers, physicians, lawyers, merchants and traders, insurance and shipping agents. The J. proletariat worked in the tobacco and silk industries, the harbor and the shipyards. Over all, however, the economic situation of the Jews in the city was not particularly sound and in the mid-1930s, J. welfare authorities reported that nearly 60% of the community sufered from serious economic distress. Between the World Wars the Sephardi communities in S. maintained an extensive network of institutions, organizations, and associations in every sphere of public life. There were many welfare organizations assisting thousands of the poor and sick, homeless victims of the 1917 fire, as well as orphans and students. In 1923 there were ten community schools. Religious life also thrived, with nearly 40 active synagogues on the eve of WWII. A small congregation of Italian-speaking Jews (descendants of refugees from Sicily and southern Italy) also existed. Alongside the flourishing religious literature that was continually published and reprinted, S. was a publishing center for secular J. literature produced in Greece in Judeo-Spanish (Ladino), French, Greek, and Hebrew. Between the World Wars there was also an unprecedented flowering of the J. press, principally in Ladino, but also in French and Greek, while some newspapers were bilingual. Between 1900 and 1936, five dailies in French were published in S.; nearly all the other Greek J. dailies and periodicals also originated there. Although some were published irregularly and reached only a limited circulation, the publications ranged from ideological organs of political movements to community-oriented, cultural, and humorist papers covering a wide range of subjects of J. public interest. Antisemitism in the pre-WWII period was mainly of an economic nature in S., which had recently absorbed numerous Greek refugees from Turkey and where Jews held key positions in the city's economy. Anti-J. riots in the Campbell section of the city broke out in 1931, with the active instigation of the nationalist and antisemitic movement known as the "Triple Epsilon" or EEE (Greek National Union). The J. neighborhood was set on fire and 54 families were left homeless. Following these disturbances, thousands emigrated to Palestine and played vital roles in the development of its ports, towns, and settlements. During the last years before the occupation of Greece by the Germans, the Zionist movement by and large ground to a halt and the attempts to unite the various organizations within a single federation failed.

Immediately after the German occupation of S. in WWII (April 1941), anti-J. measures were introduced. J.-owned apartments were confiscated, prominent J. figures were arrested, communal and public organizations and institutions were liquidated, and J. cultural treasures—especially valuable Hebrew manuscripts—were looted. Jews began to flee from S. from the time of Germany's advance on the city and by July 1942, 1,200 had left, mostly for Athens. Thereafter the Germans executed fleeing Jews and their numbers decreased. A small number joined the Greek underground movement. In July 1942, in what later came to be called "Black Saturday," all J. men were assembled in one of the city's squares and sent to forced labor. More were taken in the following weeks. Men who attempted to escape the labor camps (in Katerini, Litochoron, Leptokaria, Dexamenes, Sedes, Nares, Olympias, Vavados, Methoni, Chalkis, Ghida, Agios Dimitrios, and others) were shot. The agony of forced labor stimulated efforts in the community to release the men, and the Germans agreed to a ransom of 2.5 million (old) drachmas. Later that year, J.-owned businesses and factories, as well as the ancient J. cemetery, were confiscated. Adolf Eichmann's deputy Rolf Gunther and Heinrich Himmler's assistant Dieter Wisliceny arrived in S. in Jan. 1943 to oversee the implementation of the "final solution." There were then 56,000 Jews in S. in Feb. 1943. Racial measures were introduced and the restriction of S. Jews to three designated sections of the city soon followed. Despite warnings from the J. underground of impending deportations, only 3,000 Jews fled to Athens. The Baron Hirsch ghetto near

"Black Saturday," Salonika, Greece, 11 July 1942 (Jacqueline Ben-Atar/photo courtesy of Yad Vashem, The Holocaust Martyrs' and Heroes' Remembrance Authority, Jerusalem)

Typical local Jewish dress, Salonika, Greece

the railroad station was the transit point. On 13 March 1943, the Jews were ordered to hand over all their possessions to the Germans. Following warnings that young single people would be taken to labor camps and that married couples would enjoy better conditions in Cracow, Poland, hundreds of Jews married within a few days. The first transport of deportees left for Auschwitz-Birkenau on 15 March and passed through Belgrade, Zagreb, and Vienna, reaching its destination on 20 March. On 24 March over 1,000 J. men were taken to forced labor. A total of 48,533 Jews were deported to the death camps in Poland in 19 transports. More than 37,000 of these deportees were gassed immediately upon arrival, the rest being sent to forced labor. The final, 19th transport (10 Aug. 1943) consisted of 1,800 starving J. forced laborers. On 2 Aug., 367 Jews of Spanish nationality and 74 Jews who held community positions were deported to Bergen-Belsen; most survived the Holocaust. Only a few Jews from S. were saved with the assistance of Greek inhabitants.

However, hundreds were helped by the Italian consulate, which granted Italian citizenship and assisted them to escape to the Italian zone (primarily Athens). A few subsequently fell into German hands. By the end of the war this great center of Sephardi Jewry in Europe had ceased to exist. After the war (Oct. 1944) about 400 Jews returned to S. from hiding and from the camps. Their numbers rose to about 600 by Jan. 1945 and to 1,950 by the end of the year. The community was revived and became the second largest J. community in Greece, after Athens.

SALONTA (also Salonta Mare; Hung. Nagyszalonta; Yid: Salanta) N. Transylvania dist., Rumania. A J. school was founded in 1872 and functioned until 1933. In 1886 the community concecrated a synagogue. In 1920 the J. pop. numbered 792 (5% of the total). The majority were merchants and tradesmen with some members of the free professions. Zionist activity was marked from the mid-1920s, especially among the young, some of whom arrrived in Palestine. During the 1930s, local Jews were active politically. The Hungarian regime from Sept. 1940 provoked manifestations of antisemitism and personal and economic restrictions were imposed on the Jews. In 1942–43 young J. males were drafted into labor battalions, where most perished. In June 1944 the community was transferred to the Oradea Mare ghetto and later deported to Auschwitz.

SALSK Rostov dist., Russia. Jews were only allowed to settle after the Feb. 1917 Revolution. In 1939, their pop. was 37 (total 11,365), with 94 in the entire region (including 31 in nearby Gigant). When the Germans arrived in late July 1942, they murdered the few Jews who had neither fled nor been evacuated.

SALUZZO Piedmont, Italy. The first Jews arrived in S. in 1484. In 1590, a small number of Jews, mainly engaged in moneylending, purchased a piece of land for a cemetery. In 1548, S. passed to France and in 1631 to Savoy. In 1724, the Jews were confined to a ghetto. According to the census of 1761, the community consisted of 13 families (68 individuals). In 1795, a new area was designated for ghetto and communal life was reorganized. A new cemetery was established and a *talmud torah* was founded in 1795, followed in 1802 by a charity society called "Confraternita di Misercordia." The local Jews were bankers, businessmen,

Max Reinhardt (fifth from left) conversing with Richard Strauss at theater party, Salzburg, Austria, 1926 (Bildarchiv der Oester. Nationalbibliothek, Wien/photo courtesy of Yad Vashem, The Holocaust Martyrs' and Heroes' Remembrance Authority, Jerusalem)

and artisans. In 1806, there were 140 Jews in S.; a year later, 210. In 1860, the J. community numbered 320 members, dropping to 150 in 1886 and to 70 in 1923. According to the 1930 law reforming the J. communities, S. was included in the district of Turin. By 1936, there were only 50 Jews residing in the town. Between 1939 and 1943, the number of Jews in S. increased. In spring 1942, J. men between the ages of 18 and 55 were sent to forced labor. On 11 and 12 Sept. 1943, the Germans occupied S. Several Jews succeeded in escaping but two-thirds of the J. pop. was deported and 29 local Jews perished in the Holocaust. In 1948, 12 Jews remained in S.

SALY Borsod dist., Hungary. Jews arrived in the first half of the 18th cent., numbering about 100 families in 1850 and 47 individuals in 1930. The community maintained a synagogue, yeshiva, school, and *heder*. The Jews were transferred to Mezoker-

esztes and Miskolc en route to Auschwitz in mid-June 1944.

SALZBURG Austria. Jews are first recorded in the beginning of the ninth cent. In the 13th cent. the J. community flourished with members engaged in moneylending and banking. During the Black Death persecutions of 1348–49, over 1,200 Jews were murdered in S. and nearby areas. In 1404, Jews were accused of desecrating the Host and almost all Jews except for 25 children and some pregnant women were burned alive. Jews resettled in 1439 and a synagogue was consecrated. Following false accusations Jews were expelled from S. in 1498. The community was reestablished in 1867 and in 1890 it was recognized as a religious association (*Kultusverein*) but under the jurisdiction of the community in Linz. In 1893, the community inaugurated a new synagogue and founded a burial society. In 1869, there were 47 Jews in S.; 115 in 1880;

199 in 1900; and 239 in 1934. From 1907 to 1914 and again in 1919–20 the well-known historian and rabbi Adolf Altmann (1879–1944) was chief rabbi of S. Owing to his efforts, the community gained independence in 1911. Jews contributed significantly to the rich cultural life of S. In 1884–85, Theodor Herzl practiced law in the local courts. After WWI, Stefan Zweig lived in S. and his home became a magnet for international literary figures. During the 1920s, local Zionists were active. Jews were engaged in trade and were represented in the professional class as doctors, lawyers, and artists. Throughout this period antisemitism was strong and in 1931, kosher slaughter was forbidden. On 1 April 1933, J. shops were boycotted. In 1937, Jews were not allowed to attend local recreation centers. Immediately after the *Anschluss* (13 March 1938), several Jews were arrested and J. shops were confiscated. At the end of April 1938, private property was confiscated. Several men were arrested and sent to the Dachau concentration camp. In Jan. 1939, the J. community ceased to exist. Most of its members emigrated and the 17 Jews who were still living in S. escaped or left for Vienna in May 1939.

SALZELMEN, BAD   see BAD SALZELMEN.

SALZKOTTEN   Westphalia, Germany. Jews settled in the late 18th cent. and numbered 18 families by 1808. A synagogue was consecrated in 1825 and a cemetery in 1837. The community reached a peak pop. of 138 in 1871, dropping to 50 in 1933. On *Kristallnacht* (9–10 Nov. 1938), the synagogue was burned down and 15 J. men were sent to the Buchenwald concentration camp with one elderly man dying after being severely beaten. Many Jews left before the deportations of late 1941. The rest were dispatched to the east, where most perished.

SALZSCHLIRF, BAD   see BAD SALZSCHLIRF.

SALZUFLEN, BAD   see BAD SALZUFLEN.

SALZWEDEL   Saxony, Germany. Jews are first mentioned at the beginning of the 14th cent. The community suffered in the Black Death persecutions of 1348–49. The Jews of S. were expelled in 1510 together with those from Brandenburg following the Host desecration trial in Berlin. A settlement was reestablished in 1800. The community numbered 103 in

1834 and 64 in 1925, with ten living in the area surrounding S. The community maintained a synagogue and subsequently set up two cemeteries in 1800 and 1850. On *Kristallnacht* (9–10 Nov. 1938), the synagogue was completely wrecked. Most Jews moved to other towns or emigrated abroad By 1939, only 20 Jews were still living in S. Most had to move into the community house in Jan. 1942 and shortly afterwards were deported. In Oct. 1942, there were four Jews still living in the city, probably protected by marriage to non-Jews.

SAMBOR   Lwow dist., Poland, today Ukraine. The J. settlement is first mentioned in 1447, but the Jews lost their residence rights in 1542 under a royal privilege granted to the Christian townsmen. Jews nevertheless continued to reside and trade in S., with formal rights accorded by the Polish king in 1735. In 1763 the Jews were allowed to commence construction work on a magnificent synagogue that remained standing until WWII. Under the Austrians, the Jews were confined to a special quarter until 1864. With the coming of the railroad in the 1870s, J.-owned factories multiplied, manufacturing furniture, textiles, glass, and porcelain. In 1880 the J. pop. reached 4,427 (total 13,586). Prominent among its spiritual leaders was the progressive-minded R. Aharon Levin, who served as community rabbi in 1904–27 and was elected to the Polish Sejm. S. was also a center of Hasidism. The Zionists became active in 1894. During WWI two orphanages were set up for 108 children as well as a modern *talmud torah* and a Hebrew day school accommodating 500 pupils. After the war, when the J. pop. stood at 6,068 (total 19,417), economic circumstances remained difficult, with a quarter of the J. pop. receiving assistance from American relatives. J. welfare services sent 200 needy children to summer camps with 100 receiving food and clothing from WIZO. The Zionists, bitterly opposed by Agudat Israel, were the leading political force in the community and the youth movements were particularly active. Under Soviet rule (Sept. 1939–June 1941), when thousands of refugees reached the town, J. commercial life was shut down and community activity curtailed. The Germans took the town on 30 June 1941. The next day the Ukrainians, assisted by the Germans, staged a pogrom, murdering 150 Jews. A *Judenrat* was set up in 1942 and a regime of forced labor instituted. In March 1942 the Jews were confined to an open ghetto. The

Group of Jewish girls, Sambor, Poland

first mass *Aktion* occurred on 4–6 Aug. 1942, when 4,000 were deported to the Belzec death camp after all J. hospital patients were murdered. On 4 Sept., 100 of the aged were executed and on 17–22 Oct. a further 4,000 Jews were sent to Belzec. The ghetto was sealed off on 1 Dec. Hunger and disease plagued the community through the winter. On 10 Apr. 1943, another 1,000 Jews were brought to the J. cemetery where children were first herded into a circle and murdered before their mothers' eyes. Another 900 Jews were murdered there four days later and on 22–23 May, 1,200 were dispatched to Belzec. Final liquidation of the ghetto came on 9 June 1943 when those remaining were murdered in the forest by the Germans and Ukrainians. Those in hiding were rounded up and murdered at the cemetery over the next few weeks. Around 150 appeared in the town on its liberation on 8 Aug. 1944, most emigrating to Palestine and the U.S.

SAMEZHEVO   Minsk dist., Belorussia. In 1897, the J. pop. was 288 (total 2,538). In 1931, under the Soviets, a J. school was still operating (probably two

grades). The few remaining Jews were murdered by the Germans after they occupied the town in late June 1941.

SAMHORODOK   Vinnitsa dist., Ukraine. The J. pop. was 1,334 (total 3,605) in 1897 and 1,243 in 1926. A pogrom was staged in 1919. The Germans arrived on 22 July 1941 and ordered the Jews to wear the yellow badge. A ghetto was established on 16 May 1942 and on 4 June, 492 Jews, including 245 children, were executed near the village of Gremnovka. A few dozen young skilled workers were spared.

SAMOKHVALOVICHI   Minsk dist., Belorussia. Jews apparently settled at the turn of the 18th cent., reaching a pop. of 160 in 1811 and 401 (total 567) in 1897. Jews engaged in petty trade, horticulture, and crafts. In 1925, a J. school was opened. After the German occupation in late June 1941, the Jews were expelled to the Minsk ghetto, where they perished.

SAMORIN   (Hung. Samorja) Slovakia, Czechoslovakia, today Republic of Slovakia. Jews, mainly from

Mliecno, settled after residence restrictions were lifted in 1840 but continued for many years their affiliation with their former congregation. A J. elementary school was opened in the late 19th cent., with the J. pop. growing steadily from 147 in 1880 to 318 (total 3,474) in 1930. A large synagogue was consecrated in 1912. Between the World Wars, Jews owned 35 business establishments, eight workshops, and a few farms. Both the Zionists and Agudat Israel were active. Persecution of the Jews began after the annexation to Hungary in Nov. 1938, with dozens seized for the labor battalions in 1940–41 and dispatched to the eastern front where most perished. After the outbreak of WWII, the town served as an important way station for Polish and Slovakian J. refugees heading for Budapest. In April 1944 the J. pop. was 284. The Jews were deported to Auschwitz on 15 June 1944 via Velky Mager and Dunieska Starda.

SAMOTEVICHI Mogilev dist., Belorussia. The J. pop. was 96 in 1880 and 263 (total 544) in 1897, dropping to 378 in 1926 under the Soviets. A four-year J. elementary school was opened in the early 1920s. In 1924–25, 58 J. families earned their livelihoods in agriculture and in 1930 a kolkhoz was founded nearby where 47 J. families worked as part of a mixed pop. The Germans captured the town in Aug. 1941. Some Jews managed to escape to the east. On 18 Dec. 1942, the Nazis executed 178 Jews, children under five being thrown into the burial pit alive.

SAMOTHRAKI North Aegean Islands, Greece. A J. settlement existed in the 12th–13th cents. S. came under Bulgarian rule during WWII. Three Jews were deported in March 1943 from the island and perished, together with Jews from Thrace, in the death camps.

SANDHAUSEN Baden, Germany. The first J. family settled in 1743 but a community was only formed in the 19th cent., reaching a pop. of 100 in 1875 (total 2,583). In 1933, 17 Jews remained. By fall 1938, four had emigrated to the U.S. and five to other German cities. On *Kristallnacht* (9–10 Nov. 1938), J. homes were destroyed and the men sent to the Dachau concentration camp. The last seven Jews were deported to the Gurs concentration camp on 22 Oct. 1940; all perished.

SANDOMIERZ (Yid. Tsuzmir) Kielce dist., Po-

land. The medieval community, one of the oldest in Poland, joined the Cracow and Lwow communities in 1367 in petitioning King Casimir the Great to confirm J. privileges. Throughout its history, the community faced the unremitting hostility of local townsmen, who sought to abrogate J. rights, sometimes successfully. In 1656, Stefan Czarniecki's irregular Polish troops massacred many Jews. The rest were expelled from S. for two years. In 1698, the head of the J. community, Aharon Berek, was executed in a blood libel instigated by the Church and Jews were beaten and pillaged in its aftermath. In 1889, 100 J. families were left homeless after a fire. The J. pop. numbered 2,164 (total 6,360) in 1897 and 2,641 in 1921. Between the World Wars, most Jews were shopkeepers but a few of the bigger merchants sold lumber, grain, and eggs in the big cities. J. workshops employed 124 Jews in 1921. Economic conditions declined in the 1930s, necessitating support from the J. credit and loan organizations. Political life continued unabated. The Zionist parties and youth movements were active and the Maccabi sports club, opened in 1928, numbered 100 members. In 1934, Jews were injured in antisemitic riots. The Germans captured the city on 12 Sept. 1939, setting up a *Judenrat* in Nov. and exacting an exorbitant "contribution" from the community in Dec. J. property was confiscated and Jews were seized for forced labor as 1,200 refugees arrived from Kalisz and Siedlce. In June 1942, all were confined to a ghetto, which became one of the last in the Radom region to be liquidated. On 29 Oct. 1942, 3,229 Jews were packed into railway cars and dispatched to the gas chambers of the Belzec death camp. Another 200 in hiding were murdered and over the next two weeks 480 more were flushed out and shot. Survivors in the district, suffering from cold and hunger, were lured to a new ghetto in S. by promises of immunity. Of the 9,000 Jews gathering there, 3,000 fled on the spread of rumors of an impending *Aktion* and the rest were deported to the Treblinka death camp on 10 Oct. 1943 after 400 of the able-bodied were selected for the Skarzysko-Kamienna labor camp, where most soon perished.

SANDROVO (Hung. Osandorfalva; Yid. Shandrif) Carpatho-Russia, Czechoslovakia, today Ukraine. Jews probably settled at the turn of the 18th cent. Their pop. was 41 in 1830 and 183 in 1880, rising to 358 in 1921 under the Czechoslovakians and to

City hall, Sandomierz, Poland

418 (total 1,738) in 1941. Among J. breadwinners were four grocers, two meat wholesalers, two butchers, and three innkeepers. Many were farmers. The Hungarians occupied the town in March 1939. In 1941, they drafted dozens of Jews into labor battalions. In Aug. 1941, they expelled a number of J. families without Hungarian citizenship to Kamenets-Podolski, where they were murdered. The remaining 400 Jews were deported to Auschwitz in the second half of May 1944.

SANGEORGIUL DE PADURE   (Hung. Erdoszentgyorgy) N. Transylvania dist., Rumania. Jews settled in the late 18th cent., constituting one of the first J. communities in the Szekelyfold region of Transylvania. The J. pop. in 1920 was 212 (8% of the total). In May 1944 the community was transferred to the Targu-Mures ghetto and in June deported to Auschwitz.

SANGEORZ-BAI   (Hung. Olahszentgyorg) N. Transylvania dist., Rumania. An organized J. community existed from the late 19th cent. providing services to those visiting the mineral baths. The J. pop. in 1920 was 103 (3% of the total). In May 1944 the community was transferred to the Bistrita ghetto and in June deported to Auschwitz.

SANISLAU   (Hung. Szaniszlo) N. Transylvania dist., Rumania. A. J. community was organized in the mid-19th cent. The J. pop. in 1920 was 184 (4% of the total). In May 1944, the Jews were transferred to the Satu Mare ghetto and then deported to Auschwitz.

SANKT GOAR   Rhineland, Germany. Jews are first mentioned in 1383 and lived in the town intermittently and in small numbers through the late 17th cent. A community of seven families existed in the 18th cent. Later in the cent. the town served as the seat of the chief rabbi of the Katzenellenbogen earldom. In the late 19th cent., the community was accredited as a dist. congregation for the Jews of the county. A synagogue was erected in 1844. Burial facilities were located in Bornich under the auspices of a *hevra kaddisha* which operated from 1763 up to 1942. The J. pop. declined from 35 (total 1,250) in the early 19th cent. to 16 at mid-cent. In 1932 there were 28 Jews in S. All left before the outbreak of war, most emigrating and a few moving to other localities in Germany. The synagogue was vandalized on *Kristallnacht* (9–10 Nov. 1938).

SANKT GOARSHAUSEN   Hesse–Nassau, Germany. A permanent settlement of one to two J. families dates from the 17th cent. By 1905 the J. population was 29. Services were held with the Jews of Botnich and Wellmich. Emigration began in 1936, and by 1938 all Jews had left.

SANKT INGBERT   Palatinate, Germany. The first Jew arrived in 1811, acquiring 12 parcels of land by 1845. In 1848, the J. pop. was 17 (three families) and in 1875 it was 74 (total 9,220). In 1867, Jews founded a credit society, the first of its kind in the Saar dist. It contributed significantly to economic development in the region. Wolfgang Kahn, chairman of the community, was a member of the municipal council for 20 years until his death in 1888. He also operated a soap factory that became one of the most important in southern German, employing 70 workers and supplying the German army in WWI. The community became independent in 1852, opening a synagogue in 1876. A private J. elementary school operated from 1861 until 1882 and again in 1919–22. A private J. kindergarten was started in 1926–27. In Dec. 1931, swastikas were painted on J. homes and stores but the League of Nations administration regularly suppressed anti-J. activity. Such activities increased in 1933–35 under the impact of Nazi rule in the Reich. In 1933, the J. pop. was 75, down from 90 in 1925. In June 1935, 46 Jews remained. With the annexation of the Saar dist. to the Reich in March 1935, the economic and social isolation of the Jews intensified. Most J. businesses were sold before Oct. 1936. In March 1936, the community lost its legal standing as a public body and in effect, community life all but ceased to exist and the synagogue was sold. Of the Jews who emigrated, 50 left for the U.S. and 16 for Luxembourg. On *Kristallnacht* (9–10 Nov. 1938), the J. cemetery

was desecrated and a Jew was arrested. J. children were expelled from the public schools in Nov. 1938 and the last two Jews were deported to the Gurs concentration camp in Oct. 1940. In all, 16 Jews perished in the Holocaust, including eight in Auschwitz and five in the Theresienstadt ghetto.

SANKT POELTEN   Lower Austria, Austria. A few Jews were present in S. in 1299. They were engaged in moneylending. In 1306, J. houses were looted and some Jews were murdered, but Duke Albrecht I suppressed the riots. Jews settled permanently at the end of the 18th cent. In 1851, a small synagogue was opened and in 1859 a J. cemetery was consecrated. The community gained acknowledgment as a religious corporation (*Kultusgemeinde*) in 1863. Jews were active as horse traders and in different handicrafts connected to the textile industry. They were represented in the professional class as doctors and lawyers. In 1913 a splendid synagogue – today serving as a museum – was inaugurated. By 1937, about 14 different J. organizations and groups were active in S., some of them with Zionist affiliations. The J. pop. stood at 242 in 1860, rising sharply to 1,600 in 1934 and then declining to 765 in May 1938. Immediately after the *Anschluss* (13 March 1938), J. houses and shops were confiscated. On *Kristallnacht* (9–10 Nov. 1938), Jews were thrown out of their houses and the men sent to the Dachau concentration camp. Emigration accelerated and most managed to leave Austria in time. In March 1940, the remaining 40 Jews were sent to Vienna and from there to the east.

SANKT TOENIS   Rhineland, Germany. Jews may have arrived in the first half of the 18th cent., making S. the last settlement in Viersen county where Jews settled. A community was in existence by 1735. The Jews were moneylenders and butchers, expanding into trade in the 19th cent., particularly as livestock dealers. In 1854, the community was attached to the Kempen regional congregation. From 1875 through the Weimar period, the J. pop. was stable at around 60 (1% of the total). A synagogue was consecrated in 1907. In the 1920s, a Jew served as a city assemblyman. In 1928, the community received independent status. In 1931 the J. pop. was 45. The Nazis received 44% of the local vote in the March 1933 Reichstag elections. Between Jan. 1933 and Oct. 1938, at least 13 Jews emigrated and 12 moved to other German cities. The evening after *Kristallnacht* (9–10 Nov. 1938), the synagogue was burned and at least four J. homes and stores were destroyed. A number of Jews were beaten. Another 13 Jews subsequently emigrated while others arrived in the town. Those remaining were moved to "J. houses." On 11 Dec. 1941, nine were deported to the Riga ghetto and on 25 July 1942, another 13 were sent to the Theresienstadt ghetto. Eleven were deported to unknown destinations. In all, at least 32 Jews perished in the Holocaust.

SANKT WENDEL Saar, Germany. Jews were present in the 14th cent. and apparently fell victim to the Black Death persecutions of 1348–49. After returning in 1358, they were again expelled in 1418 as part of the general expulsion from the bishopric. In this period the Jews were active as moneylenders. In 1862 Jews once again settled in S. with four families present in 1869. With the onset of industrial development in the region, the J. pop. rose to 90 in 1895 and 134 (total 6,857) in 1910. The Jews worked as retailers, livestock dealers, and butchers. A synagogue was consecrated in 1902 with the local pop. participating in the festivities to an extent rare in Germany. Nonetheless there were also antisemitic incidents throughout the period and the synagogue windows were smashed with rocks in 1916 and 1918. When S. came under League of Nations auspices in 1919 in accordance with the Treaty of Versailles, the ensuing riots and general strike had antisemitic undertones. After WWI, Jews from Eastern Europe and Alsace-Lorraine arrived as the J. pop. reached a peak of 143 in 1923. A J. merchant, Eugen Berl, served on the municipal council between 1920 and 1932. The community was Liberal in religious outlook, with an organ in the synagogue. Anti-J. agitation intensified in the 1933–35 period, following the lead of the Reich. Nazi activists promoted the boycott movement and J. children encountered physical violence in the schools. With the annexation of the Saar to the Reich in 1935, most Jews left, either emigrating or moving to other German cities. Those who remained were subjected to greater abuse. The synagogue was burned on the night following *Kristallnacht* (9–10 Nov. 1938). The last four Jews were deported to the Gurs concentration camp on 22 Oct. 1940 and subsequently to Auschwitz in Aug. 1942, where they perished. Of those who had left the city previously, at least 22 also died in the Holocaust.

SAN-NICOLAUL-MARE (Hung., Nagy-Szentmiklos; Ger. Gross-Sannikolaus) S. Transylvania dist., Rumania. Jews first settled in the mid-18th cent. A synagogue was built in 1794 and in 1911 a new, ornate synagogue was erected. In 1869, the community joined the Neologist association and in 1871 an Orthodox community was organized with a yeshiva. Jews were members of the free professions, particularly as doctors, and prominent as industrial leaders. A large, J.-owned press printed the district newspaper. Most of the young belonged to the Zionist movements. The J. pop. in 1930 was 369 (4% of the total). On 3 July 1941, the J. pop. was transferred to Timisoara. After the war many Jews returned and renewed communal activities on a reduced scale.

SANNIKI Warsaw dist., Poland. Jews settled here from the mid-19th cent. and by 1921 numbered 315 (22% of the total). The Germans bombed S. in Sept. 1939, causing many to flee. After the Germans captured S., they forced Jews to dismantle the local church, photographed them, and used the incident to incite antisemitism. Some Jews were sent to a forced labor camp and in summer 1942 the rest were sent to the Chelmno death camp.

SANOK Lwow dist., Poland. Jews settled in the early 16th cent., barely eking out a living as tradesmen. Austrian rule brought further hardship, but with the development of commercial links with Cracow and Lwow the economy improved and Jews gained control of the wholesale trade in steel, grain, flour, food products, and lumber. They also were among the pioneers of light industry, operating factories for rubber products, concrete piping, vinegar, and natural juices along with a brickyard, sawmill, brewery, mines, and two printing presses. J. doctors and lawyers were respected members of their professions. Hasidism became influential in S. as it spread through Galicia, with Zanz and Ruzhin Hasidim maintaining a *klaus* and the Dynow dynasty a court. The Zionists became active in the late 19th cent. when antisemitic agitation also began to intensify and the J. pop. stood at around 3,000 (50% of the total). At the beginning of WWI, Russian soldiers pillaged J. property while at the end of the war Polish soldiers unleashed a reign of terror lasting a few months. In 1921 the J. pop. reached 4,067. Between the World Wars, Jews were prominent in the textile and haberdashery trade as well as in businesses connected with the build-

Jewish dignitaries with visiting philanthropists, Sanok, Poland, July 1925

ing trade. Heavy taxes and economic boycotts cut into J. livelihoods. The Germans arrived on 9 Sept. 1939, inaugurating a regime of persecution and burning down the synagogues. On 28 Sept. (Sukkot) all those not selected for work were driven across the San River into Soviet-held territory; many were subsequently exiled into the interior of the Soviet Union. A *Judenrat* was established at the end of 1939. Those Jews remaining in S. were concentrated in an open ghetto in summer 1941. On 22 Sept. (Rosh Hashanah) a group of Jews caught praying was deported to Auschwitz, while Gestapo agents continued to carry out random killings. With refugees pouring in, the now closed ghetto was packed with 10,000–13,000 Jews. All but 1,500 were sent to the Zaslawie concentration camp in Sept. 1942 and afterwards deported to the Belzec death camp along with the last of those remaining in S. in Feb. 1943.

SAN REMO   Genoa dist., Italy. In 1936, there were 60 Jews registered in the town. In 1937, a small J. community was established in S. (also in Spezia). In 1948, only eight Jews were left in town.

SANSKI MOST   Bosnia-Hercegovina, Yugoslavia, today Republic of Bosnia. The community had 63 members in 1931 and 94 in 1940. All the Jews were murdered in the Holocaust.

SAPANTA   (Hung. Szaplonca; Yid. Spinka) N. Transylvania dist., Rumania. Jews settled in the early 18th cent. The majority were tradesmen; some owned land and others traded in cattle, mainly horses. R. Yitzhak Meir Weiss (1838–1909) founded a hasidic court which attracted followers from throughout the country. He was considered one of the greatest Kabbalah scholars of his generation. His son R. Yitzhak Eizik Weiss, also an erudite scholar, moved his court from S. during WWI, and this led to the decline of the J. community's economic situation between the World Wars. In April 1944, the Jews were transferred to the Tecso ghetto and then deported to Auschwitz. About 50 survivors returned after the war but none remained.

SAPEZHNIKI   Mogilev dist., Belorussia. S. was founded as a J. agricultural colony on state land in

Attias liquor store, Sarajevo, Yugoslavia, before WWII

1851 and in 1898 had a J. pop. of 264 (33 families). In 1925, under the Soviets, 25 J. families were engaged in farming and in 1930 the settlement became a kolkhoz with 33 J. families. The Germans arrived in July 1941 and in the fall probably murdered the Jews together with the Jews of the Bykhov region.

SARAJEVO Bosnia-Hercegovina, Yugoslavia, today Republic of Bosnia. Jews lived in S. from the 16th cent. In 1581 they resided in a special quarter and built a synagogue. The community was a leading spiritual center and a number of noted rabbis served there. In 1686–89, R. Tzevi Ashkenazi ("Hakham Tzevi"), known for his active opposition to the Shabbatean messianic movement, led the community. The Jews contributed greatly to the intellectual life of S., while many held respectable positions in the free professions, especially medicine. The Jews played a leading role in the development of continental and intercontinental trade during the Ottoman period (until 1878), although their civil rights were restricted during this era. From 1867, a branch of the Alliance Israelite was active in

S. An Ashkenazi community was established in 1879–80, soon after Austria-Hungary took over Bosnia-Hercegovina. By 1895, the J. pop. had grown to 4,058 (total 38,083). J. journalism began to develop in 1900 and various publications dealt with numerous subjects, including Judaism, culture, the economy, and politics. An Ashkenazi synagogue was inaugurated in 1902. During the Austro-Hungarian period (1878–1918) the Jews received equal rights and were active in modernizing S.'s economy. Many Ashkenazi Jews became industrialists and founded large companies; the Sephardi Jews focused on trade, crafts, and banking. Differences between the two communities were bridged in the first decade of the 20th cent., notably in their full cooperation within the Zionist movement. The first Zionist society was established in 1904. Formal activity began in 1918, when the local Zionist branch joined the Yugoslavian Zionist Organization. The Jews continued to play a major role in the economy throughout the Yugoslavian period (1918–41). There were tensions between the Sephardi and Ashkenazi communities after WWI, but the antagonism ended in 1928 when their differences were played down through joint youth movements and the publication of a joint Zionist journal, *Ha-Kol ha-Yehudi*. After WWI there were 9,000 Jews in S. (15% of the total of 60,000). By then about 30 J. welfare organizations had been founded. One of the main organizations was La Benevolencia (founded in 1892) which was operational until the Holocaust. Initially, it funded academic and professional studies for J. students all over Bosnia-Hercegovina. The organization's activities were extended in 1923 to include J. publications, a library, and a J. museum. The Zionist youth movements were active in the 1920s and many of their members immigrated to Palestine. Cultural and social activities were organized by an association called "Matetyah," in which many of S.'s J. intellectuals were involved. The association was founded in 1924 and prior to WWII it had 1,000 members (90% Sephardi, 10% Ashkenazi, reflectiong the ratio between the sectors). The community built a J. school and kindergarten, and two sports associations functioned in the 1920s and 1930s. A J. Religious Theological Seminary was opened in 1928 to train youth for religious functions in J. communities. (Of special J. interest is the Sarajevo Haggada – a 14th-cent. Spanish illuminated manuscript of great beauty, which has been in the State Museum, formerly the Landes Museum, since the end of the 19th cent.) With the increasing influence of Nazism in Yugoslavia in the 1930s, verbal and violent antisemitism grew in S. The Germans entered on 15 April 1941. The following day they plundered and wrecked the Sephardi synagogue (considered the most beautiful in the Balkans) and burned the J. library, archives, and museum. The Jews were forced to wear the yellow badge and their movements were restricted. The first deportation took place on 3 Sept. By early 1942 most of the Jews were in concentration camps (Kruscica, Djakovo, Jasenovac, and Lobograd) and at the end of Aug. only 120 Jews remained in S. At least 9,000 Jews from S. were murdered in the camps; only 40 survived. Others joined the partisan fighters, escaped to Italian areas, or were among those arrested in Germany as Yugoslavian hostages. Three of S.'s Jews who fought against the Nazi invaders were declared Yugoslavian national heroes after WWII. A few of the survivors returned in 1945 and reestablished a community in which about 300 Jews were living in the mid-1990s. The Benevolencia Society was refounded after the war and played an important role in assisting Jews and non-Jews during the civil wars of the 1990s.

Jewish soccer team, Sarajevo, Yugoslavia, 1933

SARASAU (Hung. Szarvaszo) N. Transylvania dist., Rumania. Jews settled in the early 18th cent. The J. pop. was 298 in 1920 (24% of the total). The majority left between the World Wars. Those who remained probably perished in Auschwitz.

SARBI (Hung. Szerfalva) N. Transylvania dist., Rumania. A J. community existed here from the early 18th cent. The J. pop. in 1930 was 95 (9% of the total). In April 1944 the Jews were transferred to the Berbesti ghetto and later deported to Auschwitz.

SARBOGARD Fejer dist., Hungary. Jews are first mentioned in 1753. They established a school in 1865 and a synagogue in 1879. Yehoshua Stampfer, one of Petah Tivka's founders, was born here. In 1880, the J. pop. reached 376; in 1941 it was 305. Most of the young perished under forced labor in the Ukraine and the rest were deported to Auschwitz via Kaposvar on 1-2 July 1944. After the war, survivors reestablished a Neologist community, but gradually most left.

SARGHIENI Bukovina, Rumania, today Ukraine. Jews settled in the late 19th cent. and belonged to the Putila community. The J. pop. in 1930 was 204. In fall 1941, the J. pop. was deported to Transnistria. Only 18 families returned after the war.

SARISSKE LUKY (Hung. Sebeskellemes) Slovakia, Czechoslovakia, today Republic of Slovakia. J. merchants from Galicia, trading in Presov and engaging in the transit trade between Poland and Hungary, settled in the early 18th cent. Under the protection and favorable treatment of Count Haller, the community became the largest in the Saris dist., providing hostel facilities for the many peddlers and merchants passing through on their way to the big fairs and markets and also serving as the seat of the dist. rabbinate. The first non-Jews settled only in the 1780s. R. Moshe Fraenkel served from 1792 to 1842, starting a yeshiva and producing a history of the Jews of Saris. A new synagogue was consecrated in 1833 and an elementary school was opened c. 1840. The J. pop. reached a peak of 783 in 1850 and then declined steadily as the young left for Presov and other cities. In 1940, the J. pop. was 321 (total 741). WIZO, Hashomer Hatzair, and Bnei Akiva were active between the World Wars. In the Slovakian state founded in March 1939, the Jews were first persecuted and then deported. About 50 young Jews were sent to Auschwitz and the Majdanek concentration camp in late March 1942 and about 200 Jews to Auschwitz on 20 April, the rest being sent to Demblin in the Lublin dist. (Poland) in mid-May.

SARKAD Bihar dist., Hungary. Jews from Gyulavar arrived in the first half of the 19th cent., marketing farm produce and working in a local sugar refinery. The community organized in 1840, establishing a Great Synagogue in 1862 and a school in 1864. The J. pop. was 329 in 1869 (4% of the total) and 245 in 1930. The Jews were deported to Auschwitz from 19 May to 1 June 1944. Survivors reestablished the community.

SARMAS (Hung. Nagysarmas) S. Transylvania dist., Rumania. Jews first settled in the 1880s. The community split in the 1930s over the appointment of a rabbi, which led to the creation of separate religious facilities. The majority of the Jews engaged in the sale of agricultural produce. The J. pop. in 1930 was 122 (4% of the total). At the beginning of the Antonescu regime (Sept. 1940), J. property was confiscated and the Jews force-marched to Ludus; 12 days later they were marched to a camp near Turda. The men were mobilized for forced labor in Canepesti. In June 1942 they were all permitted to return. In Sept. 1944, the Hungarian army ghettoized the J. pop. On 18 Sept 1944, 126 Jews were marched down the road to Cluj. On the edge of the forest, soldiers shot them and threw them into pits they had been made to dig. The Hungarian officer in charge of the operation was sentenced to death in 1946.

SARMASELUL (Hung. Kissarmas) S. Transylvania dist., Rumania. The Jews of S. were attached to the Sarmas community and had no independent institutions. In 1930 the J. pop. was 76 (6% of the total). In June 1941, the Jews were expelled to Turda. In 1942, they were moved to Sarmas and in Sept. 1944 the Hungarians murdered them together with the local Jews.

SARNAKI Lublin dist., Poland. Jews are first mentioned in the late 18th cent. In the 19th cent. J. businessmen established two windmills, a facility for producing edible oil, and a plant for dyeing local woven goods. A

Hebrew school was opened in 1917 and the J. pop. rose to 1,198 (total 1,588) in 1921 and 2,000 in 1939. S. was hasidic in orientation, but between the World Wars, the Zionists, the Bund, and Agudat Israel became active. Most fled with the Red Army, but 70 of the wealthier J. families remained when the Germans arrived in Sept. 1939. A *Judenrat* was established in Jan. 1940 as 1,000 J. refugees from Kalisz and Blaszki arrived. All were sealed into a ghetto in Jan. 1942 and in May expelled to Losice and Mordy. Those in Losice were executed locally on 21 July while those from Mordy were deported to the Treblinka death camp and to the Majdanek concentration camp on 27 Nov. 1942.

SARNY (I)   Volhynia dist., Poland, today Ukraine. Official J. settlement was permitted by ministerial decree in 1903 after S. became an important railroad junction. The J. pop. reached 2,808 in 1921 and 4,950 in 1937 (total 11,000). During the Russian civil war of 1918–21 the Jews suffered from the Petlyura gangs and afterwards from General Haller's Polish soldiers as well as from a typhoid epidemic. Between the World Wars the Jews continued their activities in the lumber industry, exporting timber to England, Holland, and Belgium and finished wood to Poland. They also exported hides and furs to Germany, Austria, and Poland. Most of the Zionist parties and youth movements were active in S. as were Berezne, Stolin, and Stepan Hasidim. A Tarbut school operated successfully between the World Wars. The Germans took the town on 5 July 1941 with the Ukrainians immediately staging a three-day pogrom. A *Judenrat* was established and on 2–4 April 1942, 6,000 Jews were packed into a ghetto. All were shortly thereafter brought to the Poleska camp and liquidated on 27–28 Aug. 1942. A few hundred were able to flee to the forest in an organized escape effort as the executions began; few survived the war.

SARNY (II)   Vinnitsa dist., Ukraine. Jews were permitted to settle from 1845 and numbered 1,555 (total 3,220) in 1897, dropping to 563 in 1926 under the Soviets. A J. school (four grades) was operating in the mid-1920s. Under the German occupation, 150 Jews were murdered, most in late May 1942

SAROSPATAK   Zemplen dist., Hungary. Jews settled in the early 18th cent. A J. school was opened in 1885. The J. pop. rose from 801 in 1869 to 1,096 (10% of the total) in 1930. In 1941, Jews without Hungarian citizenship were sent to Kamenets-Podolski in the Ukraine, where they were executed. In WWII, S. was a mobilization center for J. forced labor, with thousands employed in its environs. The local Jews were deported to Auschwitz from Satoraljaujhely between 15 May and 2 June 1944. A hundred survivors reestablished the community but gradually dispersed.

SAROWO   Polesie dist., Poland, today Belarus. S. was a J. farm settlement founded by 24 families in 1850, and numbering 47 Jews in 1921. In the Holocaust, they were brought to the Kamieniec Litewski ghetto for liquidation.

SARREBOURG   Moselle dist., France. The J. community was established in the 19th cent. A synagogue, built in 1858, replaced an older and smaller one located on the same site. In 1885 there were 1,243 Jews in S. On two occasions there were J. mayors and Jews served on the city council. By 1895, the number of Jews decreased to 1,017; by 1910 to 803; and by 1931, to 541. During WWII, all the Jews were expelled to the south of France together with the rest of Alsace-Lorraine Jews. The community lost 75 members through deportation; 68 died in Auschwitz. The synagogue, used as a warehouse, was damaged. In the 1960s the community numbered 200 members.

SARREGUEMINES   Moselle dist., France. The J. community was established in the 19th cent. and a synagogue was inaugurated in 1862. In 1885 the community numbered 883 members; in 1926, 718 members; and in 1931, 639. In 1919, the community's president, the banker Felix Coblentz, was nominated as a member of the Assembly of Lorraine. During WWII, all the Jews were expelled to the south of France along with the other Jews of Alsace-Lorraine. Bombing damaged the cemetery and the synagogue was destroyed. In the 1960s, the community consisted of 300 members.

SARRETUDVARI   Bihar dist., Hungary. Jews settled in the early 19th cent., dealing mostly in grain. The community maintained a synagogue, established in 1880, a yeshiva, *heder*, and *talmud torah*. The pop. reached 99 in 1880 and 115 in 1930. Young men were sent to forced labor in 1941, where six died. In late June 1944, the Jews were deported to Auschwitz via Nagyvarad.

SARRE-UNION   Bas-Rhin dist., France. A small J. community was established in the 18th cent. with 343 members in 1805. The local synagogue was inaugurated in 1840. In 1936, there were 81 Jews in S. During WWII, all the Jews were expelled to the south of France with the rest of Alsace-Lorraine Jews. During the war, the synagogue was badly damaged. In the 1960s there were 45 Jews in S.

SARVAR   Vas dist., Hungary. Jews are mentioned in 1656. The J. pop. was 560 in 1880 and 780 (7% of the total) in 1941. The community organized in 1805, splitting into Neologist and Orthodox congregations in 1882. The disappearance of a Christian girl in 1840 led to a blood libel and attacks on Jews. Jews owned a sugar refinery employing 1,000 workers, a large dairy, and a brickyard. The Jews were subjected to a reign of terror in 1918–19. The Zionists became active in the 1930s. On 7 May 1944, the Jews were confined to a ghetto and on 19 May, 875 from the entire area were deported to Auschwitz. The postwar community of 169 gradually dispersed, most emigrating to Israel.

SARZHABAN   (Hirsofolo, Chrysupolis) Thrace, Greece. Under Bulgarian rule in WWII, the 12 Jews of S. were arrested on 4 March 1943. They were transported to Ksanthi and Dofnitza and then deported to the Treblinka death camp on 19 March. Only one survived.

SASCUT   Moldavia dist., Rumania. There were a few Jews in the early 19th cent. and 178 in 1899. A community was founded in 1918. Between the Would Wars the Jews were active in local politics and a Jew served as deputy mayor. Zionist activity included the training of 120 young pioneers. On 21 June 1941, the J. pop. of 72 was deported to Foscani, where it suffered the fate of the J. community there.

SASD   Baranya dist., Hungary. Jews settled in the late 18th cent. In 1930 they numbered 92. In WWII, most of the young perished in Ukrainian minefields under forced labor. The rest were deported to Auschwitz on 29 June 1944 after being detained at Mohacs and Pecs.

SASHALOM   Pest–Pilis–Solt–Kiskun dist., Hungary. J. settlement commenced in the early 20th cent. as S.

developed as a vacation site with many Jews building and managing resort facilities. They numbered 407 in 1920 (4% of the total) and 515 in 1941. On 30 June 1944, they were deported to Auschwitz via Monor. The community was renewed after the war.

SASOW   Tarnopol dist., Poland, today Ukraine. Jews were apparently among the first settlers in the early 17th cent. In the 19th and 20th cents., J. artisans were particularly noted for their embroidered ritual objects, marketing their goods as far away as Warsaw, Berlin, and New York. The Hasid Moshe Leib of Sasow founded a dynasty here and S. became an important hasidic center. A Baron Hirsch school was set up in 1901 and Po'alei Zion became the first J. political group in the town in 1906. Emigration to the U.S. and the tribulations of WWI reduced the J. pop. from an 1880 high of 1,906 (60% of the total) to 1,096 in 1921. Between the World Wars, many received support from American relatives. Soviet rule in 1939–41 closed down commerce and J. public life. The Germans entered the town on 2 July 1941, murdering 22 community leaders within two weeks on charges of Communism. The Germans introduced a regime of forced labor and murder which became more systematic in July 1942, when 66 Jews were executed in three separate killing sprees. On around 12 Sept. (Rosh Hashanah), 100 were deported to the Belzec death camp while the disabled were murdered on the spot. At the end of Nov. the last 400 Jews were expelled to the Zloczow ghetto.

SASTIN   (Hung. Sasvar) Slovakia, Czechoslovakia, today Republic of Slovakia. There is evidence of J. settlement in the 16th cent., including a synagogue built perhaps in 1564. The community was under the protection of the Ctibor family of nobles. With a pop. of 181 in 1738, it was one of the largest in western Slovakia. Floods and a devastating fire in the 1760s destroyed many J. homes and claimed a number of lives, causing the community to decline until further growth commenced in the 1780s. A synagogue with a school building in the courtyard was consecrated in 1852. In 1869, the J. pop. reached a peak of 680 (total 2,635), thereafter dropping steadily as the young left for the big cities. It stood at 262 in 1919 and 156 in 1940. The Zionists became active after WWI, with WIZO and the Maccabi sports club opening branches. In the Slovakian state, Jews were forced out of their businesses and in spring 1942 they were deported to Auschwitz and to the Lublin dist. of Poland. Most of the remaining families were deported to Auschwitz after the Germans arrived in late Aug. 1944.

SASUOLIAI (Sesuoliai; Yid. Sheshol) Ukmerge dist., Lithuania. The pop. of S. in 1897 included 29 Jews, whose number increased to 160 prior to WWI. At the outbreak of WWII there were eight J. families in S. After the German conquest of 1941, the Jews of S. were murdered toward the end of summer.

SATANOV Kamenets-Podolski dist., Ukraine. Jews are first mentioned in 1532 and formed a community that was well known throughout Poland by the early 17th cent. Its development was curtailed in the Chmielnicki period when the Cossacks captured the town in 1651. Among the victims of the ensuing massacre was R. Shelomo Spiro (b. 1618), author of the kabbalistic work *Megaleh Amukot*. In the Haidamak revolt of 1703, Jews were again attacked. The J. pop. was 1,369 in 1765 and 2,848 (65% of the total) in 1897. In June 1915, the Jews were expelled from the town. When they returned a year later, they found their homes had been pillaged. In the Soviet period, a J. rural council (soviet) was active. In 1939, the J. pop. was 1,516. The Germans captured the town on 6 July 1941. On the night of 14 May 1942, they locked 240 Jews into a cellar, suffocating them to death. During 1942, another 210 Jews were shot. Of the 800 people murdered in S., most were Jews.

SATORALJAUJHELY Zemplen dist., Hungary. Jews are mentioned in the early 18th cent. and became prominent as tradesmen and industrialists. The community organized in 1760 and in the course of time three separate congregations, two Orthodox and one Status Quo, were formed. The first J. school was started in 1785 and new ones were opened in 1836 and 1887. A hospital with 200 beds was founded in 1862. R. Moshe Teitelbaum, who served in 1809–41 and was the author of *Yismah Moshe*, helped spread Hasidism throughout northwest Hungary and attracted followers from Galicia, Poland, and Russia. The J. pop. grew from 1,217 in 1825 to 3,253 (33% of the total) in 1869 and 6,446 in 1920. In 1941, 4,160 Jews remained. After the German occupation of Hungary on 19 March 1944, the Jews were confined to a ghetto. From 15 April, Jews from the surrounding settlements

Jewish tombstones, Satanov, Ukraine, 1832

began to be transferred there, swelling the pop. to about 15,000, with 20–25 people living in a room. Deportations commenced on 16 May, when 3,500 Jews were sent to Auschwitz, followed by 3,500 on 22 May, 4,000 on 25 May, and the remainder on 3 June. About 400 Jews returned after the war.

SATU MARE (Hung. Szatbarnemeti; Yid. Satmar, Sakmer) N. Transylvania, Rumania. A J. community was organized in 1842 and a synagogue seating 846 was built in 1892. In 1898, one of the leading rabbis in Hungary, Yehuda Greenwald, was appointed to serve the community (d. 1920). He opened what became one of the largest *yeshivot* in the country with over 400 students, many of whom served as rabbis in communities throughout Hungary. His appointment caused 210 of the wealthier community members to break away and set up their own facilities, including

a synagogue built in 1902. A J. school was opened in 1864–65 and when it was restricted only to boys, a girls' school was opened in 1890. Jews made a major contribution to the economic development of S. and in the 1880s opened the first banks, established factories, and bought land and forests in the area which they developed with modern machinery. Jews were prominent in the town's commerce and in the free professions. The J. pop. in 1890 was 3,472 (16% of the total). At the beginning of the 20th cent., S. was one of the largest J. communities in Transylvania. R. Yissakhar Dov Leifer set up a center for his hasidic followers and the Vizhnitz Hasidim also built a large court. Zionist activity began in earnest only after WWI. By 1930 the J. pop. was 11,533 (23% of the total). A factory producing *matzot* (unleavened bread) supplied most of the J. communities in Transylvania. In 1927 a large J. hospital with modern facilities was

Jewish children at day camp, Satu Mare, Rumania, 1920s (YIVO Archive, New York/photo courtesy of Beth Hatefutsoth, Tel Aviv)

opened. Jews controlled textile manufacture, the railway factory employing several hundred workers, and enterprises in other areas of the economy. Journalists writing in Hungarian were almost all Jews. R. Yoel Teitelbaum was appointed community rabbi in 1929 and set up a yeshiva for 300 students. He was saved from the Holocaust on the Kasztner refugee train in 1944. From 1947 until his death in 1979, he lived in New York as the Satmar Rabbi, head of one of the largest hasidic communities, noted for its zealous observance of traditional Judaism and its anti-Zionism. A number of Hebrew publications mainly devoted to J. studies appeared in S. from the beginning of the 20th cent. A Hebrew printer's shop was opened in 1903 and a modern printing press was opened by Meir Leib Hirsch in 1925. Over the next 20 years it printed 170 Hebrew works. Zionist activity began in 1924 and from the 1930s the religious Zionist youth groups predominated among the youth movements. In May 1934, 17 families immigrated to Palestine. After the entry of General Horthy's troops in 1940, the Jews were persecuted, physically and economically. In June 1941, about 1,000 Jews without Hungarian citizenship were expelled, the majority murdered by Hungarian soldiers and SS troops in Kamenets-Podolski. Between 1942 and 1944, most J. men aged 21–45 were drafted into labor battalions in the Ukraine, where they died. At the end of April 1944, 20,000 J. inhabitants of S. and refugees from the district were ghettoized. The J. pop. was deported to Auschwitz from 20 May to 3 June 1944. After the war, the majority of the survivors returned to S. and by 1947 numbered 7,500. During the 1950s most emigrated to Israel.

SAUKENAI (Yid. Shukian) Siauliai dist., Lithuania. Jews first settled and built a beautiful synagogue in the 18th cent., Among the community's rabbis (1867–69) was Yitzhak Reines, one of the founders of Mizrachi. The J. pop. in 1897 was 624 (63% of the total). Between the World Wars, a religious Hebrew school

Synagogue in Saukenai, Lithuania

was established. Many emigrated to South Africa, the U.S., and Palestine. The Zionist movement enjoyed widespread support. The J. pop. in 1940 was about 300 (43%). After the German invasion in June 1941, most Jews were killed in the Dulkiskis forest on 30 July. The rest were taken to Zagare on 29 Aug. and murdered on 2 Oct. together with the Jews of Zagare. Eight J. youngsters found in a church were murdered by the Lithuanians after being baptized.

SAUKOTAS   (Yid. Shakot) Kedainiai dist., Lithuania. The J. pop. in 1929 numbered 30 families (66% of the total). All the Jews were killed after the German conquest of 1941.

SAVENI   Moldavia dist., Rumania. Jews settled in 1816, building a synagogue in 1843, and opening a community school in 1901. The J. pop. in 1899 was 1,803 (50% of the total). From 1921 to 1937, Jews voted in the municipal elections and a Jew served as deputy mayor. Zionist activity began after 1917 and pioneers from S. immigrated to Palestine. On 20 June 1941, all males aged 16–60 were exiled to the Targu-Jiu internment camp. The remaining J. pop. was transferred to Dorohoi, and in Aug. the males were released and joined their families. On 8 Nov., the 2,000 Jews of S. were deported to Transnistria. About half the community returned after the war. In 1947, there were 1,200 Jews living in S..

SAVERNE   Bas-Rhin dist., France. S. is one of the ancient communities in Alsace-Lorraine. For three centuries after the Black Death persecutions of 1348–49, Jews were not admitted into the town. In the 17th cent., they established a small settlement. Between 1414 and 1789 the bishops of Strasbourg resided in S. In Bishop Leopold's edict of 1613, 26 articles dealt with the rights and obligations of the local J. residents. In 1622, several J. families from the countryside were granted refuge in the town. This was the origin of the J. street in S. In 1774 the community built a synagogue, which was renovated in 1837. In 1784, the community numbered 100 members; in 1808, 250; in 1900, 310; in 1936, 244. In the dist. of S. there were 1,048 Jews in 1931. During WWII, all were expelled to the south of France together with the rest of Alsace-Lorraine Jews. Thirty Jews from S. died in the Holocaust. In 1953, the community. consisted of 175 members, dropping to 100 in the 1960s.

SAVRAN   Odessa dist., Ukraine. The J. pop. was 150 in 1765 and 3,198 (total 5,887) in 1897. Local peasants staged a pogrom in which two members of a J. self-defense group were killed in spring 1918. General Denikin's White Army soldiers initiated another pogrom in early 1920. In the Soviet period, dozens of J. families earned their livelihoods working in a J. kolkhoz. A J. elementary school was attended by 300 children and a J. council (soviet) was active from the late 1920s. The J. pop. in 1939 was 1,101. The Germans captured the town on 30 July 1941 and expelled the Jews to Obodovka (Vinnitsa dist.) in Sept., where many died of starvation, disease, and the cold.

SAWIN   Lublin dist., Poland. In the late 19th cent., a J.-owned glassware factory provided employment for Jews in S. and neighboring Ruda. In 1921, the J. pop. in the two villages was 236 (total 583). The Germans set up a *Judenrat* on their arrival in Sept. 1939. In May 1942, all the Jews of S. and Ruda, together with 1,700 Jews from Cracow who had been sent there in 1940–42, were deported to the Sobibor death camp.

SBETLA   Kasserine dist., Tunisia. Jews from Gabes settled in the early 20th cent., numbering 18 in 1909. Most were tradesmen and artisans. Their customers were the workers at the local copper and tin mines, soldiers in the French garrison, and tourists attracted to the archeological finds in the area. A few wealthy merchants dealt in the *alafa* plant. A committee composed of the wealthier and better-educated members directed community affairs. The J. pop. was 81 in 1926 and 146 (total 1,366) in 1936. A large synagogue was built in 1933, accommodating a *talmud torah* which J. boys attended in addition to the coeducational French public school. Relations with the French were friendly, and contact with the Arabs was mainly confined to business. In WWII, the Jews suffered from food shortages and from Allied bombing after the arrival of the Germans in Nov. 1942. Most Jews fled to an Arab farm where they safely remained until the end of the German occupation in May 1943. Four Jews who remained behind in the town were killed in the bombings, which also destroyed the synagogue. The returning Jews found their shops and homes pillaged. Arab-J. relations deteriorated after the war with the growth of Arab nationalism and the J. economy never fully recovered. Most Jews left individually and openly for Israel in 1948–49, settling in the south.

SCHAAFHEIM Hesse, Germany. Established in the early 19th cent., the J. community numbered 94 (about 6% of the pop.) in 1871, but dwindled to 14 in 1933. Most Jews left before WWII, 11 emigrating.

SCHALBACH Moselle dist., France. There was a small J. community during the 19th cent. The local synagogue was inaugurated around 1802 and renovated in 1884. During WWII, the synagogue was slightly damaged. The mayor helped preserve the various holy objects.

SCHARMBECK-OSTERHOLZ Hanover, Germany. Jews settled in S. in the 1730s and in 1768 numbered 23 including neighboring Osterholz. A cemetery was consecrated in 1756–57 and a synagogue was erected in S. in 1830. The synagogue burned down in 1863 and a new one was built in S. in 1865–66 after a dispute with O. over its location. The J. pop. reached 127 in 1871, thereafter declining steadily. In June 1933, under Nazi rule, the J. pop. of the now united town of S.-O. was 59. In fall 1934, calls to boycott J. businesses increased, windows were smashed in a number of J. establishments, and a J. proprietor was beaten and arrested for 20 days. The synagogue building was rented out in Nov. 1938 with the community no longer able to afford its upkeep. A few days later, on *Kristallnacht* (9–10 Nov. 1938), it was burned. In May 1942, 42 Jews remained. All were apparently deported, mainly to the east.

SCHEINFELD Middle Franconia, Germany. The community began with the expulsion of the Jews of Nuremberg in 1499. The Jews received various privileges, including citizenship in 1629, from the counts of the House of Schwarzenberg. Jews helped defend the town in the Thirty Years War (1618–48) and erected a synagogue in 1651. A J. public school was opened in 1833. In 1871 the J. pop. reached a peak of 125 (total 1,166), dropping to 49 in 1933. Most of the Jews traded in cattle. The majority left up to Nov. 1938 in the face of persecution and the economic boycott; the last 18 after *Kristallnacht* (9–10 Nov. 1938).

SCHENKLENGSFELD Hesse–Nassau, Germany. Established by 1673, the community was subject to various restrictions and only developed in the 19th cent. Commercial success enabled the Jews to maintain an elementary school from 1843 to 1933. A new syn-

agogue was built in 1883, and the pop. grew from 65 (8% of the total) in 1819 to 188 (17%) in 1885. The Jews paid one-third of the local tax bill and provided the village with seven of its 12 councilmen (1898), but their prominence and prosperity aroused Christian resentment. After WWI, branches of the Central Union (C.V.) and the J. War Veterans Association were active and the community became affiliated with the rabbinate of Fulda. From March 1933 there was recurrent Nazi violence. Though temporarily spared on *Kristallnacht* (9–10 Nov. 1938), the synagogue was demolished three months later. By Sept. 1940 all the Jews had left. Of the 127 (14%) registered there in 1933, 84 emigrated (mostly to the U.S.); at least 23 perished in the Holocaust.

SCHERMEISEL (Pol. Trzemeszno Lubuskie) Brandenburg, Germany, today Poland. The J. pop. in 1840 was 231, dropping to 180 in 1858 (20% of the total) and 24 in 1910. The community maintained a synagogue and a cemetery. When the Nazis came to power in 1933, there were 27 Jews in S. It may be assumed that those who did not manage to emigrate to safe countries were deported to the east. By Oct. 1942, there was only one Jew in the town, probably protected by marriage to a non-Jew.

SCHESSLITZ Upper Franconia, Germany. Jews are known from the 14th cent. From the late 19th cent. they numbered around 30 (2.5% of the total pop.). Twelve emigrated in the Nazi era, including ten to the U.S. The last 13 were expelled to Bamberg on 22 March 1942 and from there deported to Izbica in the Lublin dist. (Poland) and to the Theresienstadt ghetto.

SCHIERSTEIN (now part of Wiesbaden) Hesse-Nassau, Germany. The community, which had members in nearby Frauenstein, engaged J. teachers and numbered 70 (2% of the pop.) in 1895. Its synagogue was burned down on *Kristallnacht* (9–10 Nov. 1938), and those who remained shared the fate of the Jews of Wiesbaden.

SCHIFFERSTADT Palatinate, Germany. Jews were present intermittently in the 18th cent. In the 19th cent., there was a permanent J. settlement which grew from a pop. of 12 in 1815 to 50 (total 6,075) in 1900. A synagogue was opened in 1830 and a new one consecrated in 1892 after the former burned down. A cemetery was opened in 1897. In 1932, the J. pop. was 39, dropping to 11 in May 1939 and three in late 1940. At least 18 Jews managed to emigrate. Ten who remained in S. or went to other localities in Germany were deported to the Gurs concentration camp on 22 Oct. 1940. Six perished there. The synagogue was burned on *Kristallnacht* (9–10 Nov. 1938) and the cemetery was desecrated also in 1938.

SCHIPPENBEIL   (Pol. Sepopol) East Prussia, Germany, today Poland. In 1880, there were 58 Jews in S. This number remained stable until WWI. S. was affiliated to the Bartenstein community. In 1868, a J. orphanage was opened; it eventually moved to Koenigsberg. A cemetery was established in 1860. The synagogue, which was destroyed in a fire around 1870, was never rebuilt. Instead, the community hired prayer rooms until 1923. When the Nazis came to power in 1933, there were 25 Jews living in S. By Oct. 1942, one Jew remained, probably protected by marriage to a non-J. partner. It may be assumed that those who did not manage to emigrate to safe countries were deported.

SCHIVELBEIN   (Pol. Swidwin) Pomerania, Germany, today Poland. Mention of the first J. family in S. occurs after 1700. By 1787, there were five J. families and probably a cemetery. During the 19th cent., the community grew steadily, numbering about 400 members in the 1890s. Two synagogues were established in 1821 and 1880. The antisemitic riots which broke out in Pomerania when the Neustettin synagogue was burned down in 1881 spread to S. Jews were attacked and their businesses wrecked and looted. During the 1890s, two Jews were elected to the city council and two to the district council at the beginning of the 20th cent. Although in 1933, when the Nazis came to power, the community only numbered 148 individuals, it was still one of the largest communities in the region. By 1934 it had become the seat of a district rabbinate for about 15 communities with a J. pop. of about 1,000. By Aug. 1935, J. businessmen had sold their businesses or were facing financial ruin as a result of the Nazi boycott measures. On *Kristallnacht* (9–10 Nov. 1938), Jews were abused and arrested, the synagogue was burned down, and the cemetery was desecrated. On 12–13 Feb. 1940, the Jews who had remained in S. were deported to Lublin together with the Jews of Stettin.

SCHLANGEN   Lippe, Germany. In 1756, four protected Jews (*Schutzjuden*) were living in S., a number which remained stable until 1810. By 1867, the small community had grown to six families. It established a cemetery (about 1830) and a synagogue in 1867. When the Nazis came to power in 1933, there were 25 Jews living in S. Although the synagogue was no longer used for worship, the windows were repeatedly smashed and the cemetery was desecrated. At least ten Jews from S. were murdered under Nazi rule.

SCHLAWE   (Pol. Slawno) Pomerania, Germany, today Poland. The first Jew settled in S. about 1718. In 1752 there were two J. families and 17 in 1812. In 1899, the community had 265 members and maintained a synagogue and a cemetery. When the Nazis came to power in 1933, the J. pop. was about 80. Some made their way to the U.S. and Latin America or to Berlin; 25 emigrated to Palestine. On *Kristallnacht* (9–10 Nov. 1938), the synagogue was destroyed and several Jews were arrested and deported to the Sachsenhausen concentration camp. In summer 1942, the remaining Jews were deported with the exception of one person, who was probably protected by marriage to a non-Jew.

SCHLEUSINGEN   Saxony, Germany. Jews in S. were murdered in 1298 and suffered in the Black Death persecutions of 1349–49. They were expelled in 1563, and only returned in 1660. In 1762, King Augustus II appointed two Jews from S. as "factors to the court and militia." In 1871, the community numbered 89 (3% of the total) and maintained a synagogue and a cemetery. When the Nazis assumed power in 1933, there were still 30 Jews living in S. On *Kristallnacht* (9–10 Nov. 1938), the synagogue was vandalized and its furnishings burned. The cemetery was desecrated. In 1939, only 18 Jews remained in S. Those who did not manage to escape were subsequently deported.

SCHLITZ   Hesse, Germany. Established in 1880, when it numbered 24 (1% of the pop.), the community grew to 64 (2%) in 1910 and was affiliated with the Orthodox rabbinate of Darmstadt. By Oct. 1938 most of the 43 Jews had left, and a year after *Kristallnacht* (9–10 Nov. 1938), none remained.

SCHLOCHAU   (Pol. Czluchow) Posen–West Prussia, Germany, today Poland. In 1831, 364 Jews were living in S. (22% of the total pop.). In 1880 the J. pop. was 495. The community established a synagogue in the second half of the 19th cent. and a cemetery. In 1900, local antisemites called for a boycott of J. businesses. In 1925, the synagogue was desecrated. On the eve of the Nazi assumption of power in 1933, 125 Jews were living in S. By May 1938, most J. businesses had been "Aryanized." On *Kristallnacht* (9–10 Nov. 1938), the synagogue was set on fire and J. men were taken to the Sachsenhausen concentration camp. The remaining Jews were interned in March 1940 in the Buergergarten camp near Schneidemuehl and from there deported to the east.

SCHLOPPE (Pol. Czlopa) Posen–West Prussia, Germany, today Poland. There is documentary evidence of 28 Jews living in S. in 1674. By 1774, their number had risen to about 250, peaking at 311 in 1839. About 1840, a synagogue and cemetery were established. The J. pop. declined throughout the 19th cent. In 1871 there were about 195 Jews in S. and about 100 on the eve of the Nazi assumption of power in 1933. By the beginning of 1938, most J. businesses had been "Aryanized," and in Oct., the community sold the town its property, including the synagogue and communal and adjacent buildings. In return, it received living accommodations and a room for religious services. In May 1939, the town evicted the J. residents from the same accommodations, and in March 1940, the remaining Jews were interned in the Buergergarten camp near Schneidemuehl, from where they were later deported.

SCHLUCHTERN Baden, Germany. The first J. family settled in 1722 and the community reached a peak. pop. of 96 in 1871. At the turn of the cent. half the Jews were cattle traders. In 1933, 28 remained (total pop. 1,062), with Jews operating a cigarette factory and small soap factory which they were forced to sell under the economic boycott. During the Nazi era, eight Jews emigrated directly from S. and others after leaving S. Twelve were deported to the Gurs concentration camp on 22 Oct. 1940 and two were deported after leaving S.; 12 perished in the camps.

SCHLUECHTERN Hesse–Nassau, Germany. Jews were encouraged to settle there by patrons of Suesskind von Trimberg (1250–1300), the only J. minnesinger, while others found refuge in S. during the Black

Old synagogue at Obertorstrasse, Schluechtern, Germany

Death persecutions of 1348–49. The community later absorbed refugees from Hungary and Spain in the 17th cent., building a synagogue in 1670. The community numbered 105 in 1776. Abandoning their former trades, some Jews became industrialists. This strictly Orthodox community, affiliated with the rabbinate of Hanau, dedicated an imposing new synagogue in the Byzantine style in 1898. The J. pop. grew to 395 (13% of the total) in 1905 and more than 80 children attended the J. elementary school (opened in 1903). After WWI, a branch of the Central Union (C.V.) was established and communal life flourished. Nazi boycott measures and violence heralded *Kristallnacht* (9–10 Nov. 1938), during which SA troops vandalized the synagogue's interior and Hitler Youth participated in the looting and destruction of J. homes. By May 1939, 362 Jews had left S., many emigrating to the U.S., Britain, and Palestine. In 1942, 26 were eventually sent to the Theresienstadt ghetto and over 100 perished in the Holocaust.

SCHMALKALDEN Hesse–Nassau, Germany. Accused of poisoning wells, 18 Jews were murdered in S. during the Black Death persecutions of 1348–49. The later community, dating from 1622, numbered 120 (1% of the total) in 1905. By *Kristallnacht* (9–10 Nov. 1938), when the synagogue was destroyed, half of the remaining 80 Jews had left. The last survivors were deported to the east in 1942–44.

SCHMALLENBERG Westphalia, Germany. Residence rights were granted to a protected Jew in 1685. Two J. families were present in the 18th cent., with the J. pop. subsequently growing from about 20 in the early 19th cent. to 40 in 1871 and a peak of 58 (total 1,603) in 1890. A cemetery was established in 1842 and a synagogue in 1857. In 1933, 51 Jews remained. Ten emigrated in the Nazi period, half to the U.S., half to Holland. All the rest were arrested on *Kristallnacht* (9–10 Nov. 1938). The women and children were released soon afterwards but the men remained in custody. The synagogue was burned during the disturbances. Most of the remaining Jews, including those who reached Holland, perished in the Holocaust.

SCHMALNAU (now part of Ebersberg) Hesse–Nassau, Germany. Numbering 72 (over 10% of the pop.) in 1871, the community affliated with the rabbinate of Fulda and also had members in Hettenhausen and Weyhers (where a regional cemetery was located). All the Jews left by 1937, 17 emigrating.

SCHMIEHEIM Baden, Germany. Jews are mentioned in 1709 and numbered 80 by 1747. The nearby cemetery, opened in 1703, was one of the most beautiful in south Baden and served many communities. The prosperous 19th cent. community developed into one of the largest in Baden, with 486 Jews (total 1,074) in 1875. In 1812, a new synagogue was built and in 1827, S. became the seat of the district rabbinate. Its last district rabbi was the Reform-minded Dr. Viktor Meyer Rawicz, who translated part of the Talmud into German and transferred the district rabbinate to Laufenburg in 1893. A J. elementary school was opened in the 1830s, numbering 120 students in 1855. At the turn of the cent. Jews continued to trade in cattle and opened a number of factories (cigarettes, liquor, metal screening). Many of the young acquired a higher education and left the village. In 1933, 121 Jews remained. Most left after the distur-

bances of *Kristallnacht* (9–10 Nov. 1938), when the synagogue and J. homes were heavily damaged, the cemetery was desecrated, and 28 men were taken to the Dachau concentration camp. In all, 32 emigrated while 61 moved to other German cities, 20 of them being deported to the Gurs concentration camp along with 14 directly from S. on 22 Oct. 1940. Half of them perished in Auschwitz. Altogether 44 Jews from S. died in the camps.

SCHNAITTACH Middle Franconia, Germany. Jews arrived from Nuremberg after the 1499 expulsion but may have been present earlier. From the late 16th cent. S. was the seat of an association of four communities (including Ottensoos, Huettenbach, and Forth). Many left after suffering greatly in the Thirty Years War (1618–48). Until the 1660s the community was under the auspices of the margrave of Rothenberg and thereafter under Bavarian rule. R. Shemuel Baermann of the well-known Fraenkel family served as rabbi of the community and chief rabbi of the Ansbach principality in the late 17th cent. In the 18th cent., Court Jews like Seligman Loew and Anschel Levi were active there. In 1837 the J. pop. stood at 262 (total 1,490), thereafter declining steadily to 42 in 1933. Under the Nazi regime, Jews continued to deal in cattle and beer hops, trading with local farmers despite the economic boycott. By Nov. 1938, 17 had left, including 11 to the U.S. On *Kristallnacht* (9–10 Nov. 1938), the contents of the synagogue were piled up and burned. The last 18 Jews left by the end of the year.

SCHNEIDEMUEHL (Pol. Pila) Posen–West Prussia, Germany, today Poland. A J. community existed in the 16th cent., its members playing an important role in the town's development by virtue of their financial activities. After a fire which broke out in a Jew's house destroyed the town in 1626, Jews had to settle in a separate quarter. When the Swedes attacked the town in 1656, they murdered 33 Jews and destroyed Torah scrolls. The community was slow to recover, but by 1816 it numbered 408 members. Reaching 805 in 1880, the J. pop. dropped to 653 in 1905. The community maintained a synagogue and cemetery. Antisemitic riots in 1900 damaged the synagogue. In 1925, the local J. community cared for some 100 J. inmates of a nearby Polish refugee camp. When the Nazis assumed power in 1933, about 600 Jews were living in S. Some of the deportations of Polish Jews from Germany in Oct. 1938 took place at the S. border crossing. On *Kristallnacht* (9–10 Nov. 1938), the synagogue was burned down and 63 J. businesses and 23 homes were plundered and demolished. By May 1939, only 116 Jews were left in the S. area. Those who failed to emigrate in time were interned in March 1940 in the Buergergarten camp and shortly afterwards deported to the east.

SCHODNICA Lwow dist., Poland. Jews pioneered the town's oil industry in the late 19th cent., their pop. growing from 122 (total 988) in 1880 to 689 (total 2,726) in 1921. Antisemitism rose in the 1930s, the Soviet arrival in Sept. 1939 forestalling a Ukrainian pogrom. With the Soviet withdrawal at the end of June 1941 the local pop. went on a rampage, murdering 200 Jews. Starvation, disease, and more killings under the Germans further decimated the pop., the last Jews being expelled or deported in summer and fall 1942.

SCHOELLKRIPPEN Lower Franconia, Germany. A J. community is known from the late 18th cent. A synagogue was built in 1826. The J. pop. reached a peak of 110 (total 851) in 1880 and then declined steadily to 48 in 1933. After *Kristallnacht* (9–10 Nov. 1938), all 44 remaining Jews moved to Frankfurt.

SCHOENEBECK Saxony, Germany. Evidence of Jews in S. in the Middle Ages relates to a Jew engaged in the salt trade about 1230. In 1750, a J. family was allowed to settle in the city. After being under French rule at the beginning of the 19th cent., the J. pop. grew to 92 in 1840. The community established a synagogue in 1877, a school for religious instruction in 1875, and a cemetery. In 1925, there were only 50 Jews in S. and 79 in 1933. On *Kristallnacht* (9–10 Nov. 1938), the synagogue's furnishings and ritual objects were wrecked. Jews were maltreated and their houses and businesses looted and vandalized. By 1939, there were 38 Jews in S. In 1941 the Jews were forced to live in the synagogue's upstairs rooms and in the "J. house" located in the affiliated community of Bad Salzelmen. Most were deported, but in 1942 there were still 13 Jews living in the town, probably protected by intermarriage. In all, 25 Jews from S. perished under Nazi rule.

SCHOENINGEN Brunswick, Germany. A community briefly existed between 1520 and 1582. It was reestablished by five J. families in 1797. Numbering 35 in 1880, the community adopted a Liberal form of worship from 1890 and services only took place on the High Holidays. The J. pop. grew to 55 in 1920. Only one of the 30 Jews registered in 1933 succeeded in emigrating (to Italy); 25 perished in Nazi concentration camps and ghettoes.

SCHOENLANKE (Pol. Trzcianka) Posen–West Prussia, Germany, today Poland. Jews first settled in S. in 1730. The first synagogue was built in 1740, but burned down in 1779. A second synagogue was used until 1820 and additional synagogue buildings were built in 1823 and in 1883. A *beit midrash* existed already in 1772 and the first rabbi was appointed in 1799. The J. pop. was about 300 in the 1780s and 750 in 1817 (23% of the total). Numbers dropped from the 1830s, so that the J. pop. was 584 in 1880 and 590 in 1902. On the eve of the Nazi assumption of power in 1933, there were 380 Jews in S. Boycott measures led to the economic ruin of the community. The Zionists played an important role in community life from 1936 on. On *Kristallnacht* (9–10 Nov. 1938), the synagogue was destroyed, a number of J. businesses were demolished, and J. men were interned in the Sachsenhausen concentration camp. In March 1940, the remaining Jews were interned in the Buergergarten camp near Schneidemuehl and later deported to the east.

SCHOETMAR Lippe, Germany. The first J. settlement, which is mentioned at the beginning of the 17th century, ended in 1614, when all the Jews were expelled from Lippe. By 1756, seven J. families were living in S. and by 1890 the community had grown to 74 individuals. It was affiliated to the Bad Salzuflen community, but maintained its own synagogue from the second half of the 18th cent. and a cemetery from 1877. In June 1933, about four months after the Nazis assumed power, 53 Jews were living in S. On *Kristallnacht* (9–10 Nov. 1938), the synagogue was burned down, J. businesses and homes were wrecked, and nine Jews were arrested and taken to the Buchenwald concentration camp. By May 1939, 38 Jews remained in S. Some probably managed to escape abroad. Twenty Jews were deported in Dec. 1941 and July 1942.

SCHOONHOVEN Zuid-Holland dist., Holland. The community dates from the mid-18th cent., numbered 108 in 1860, but dwindled from the end of the cent. All but two of its Jews (14 in 1941; total 4,617) perished in the Holocaust.

SCHOPFLOCH Middle Franconia, Germany. The community was probably founded by Jews expelled from Dinkelsbuehl in 1400. Its cemetery served 14 neighboring communities in the 16th–17th cents. After the town was annexed to Bavaria in 1608, the Jews were under the authority of the counts of Brandenburg and the rulers of Oettlingen. The J. pop. reached a peak of 393 in 1867 (total 1,788) and a new synagogue was built in 1877. In 1880 the J. pop. was 147 and in 1933, 37. In the Nazi era, few Jews left until mid-1938, but with anti-J. agitation intensifying, the last 27 left for other German cities.

SCHORNSHEIM Hesse, Germany. Numbering 103 (9% of the total) in 1880, the J. community disbanded in Feb. 1933. Most of the remaining 28 Jews emigrated or left before WWII.

SCHOTTEN Hesse, Germany. Jews lived there from the 17th cent. and the community, which numbered 153 (about 8% of the pop.) in 1880, was affiliated with the Orthodox rabbinate of Darmstadt. Jews played a leading role in the town's public, musical, and social life. The Nazi boycott imposed from April 1933 caused at least 40 of the 73 Jews to leave before *Kristallnacht* (9–10 Nov. 1938), when SA and SS troops organized a pogrom, destroying the synagogue's interior, Torah scrolls, and J. homes. Twelve Jews were deported in 1942.

SCHRIESHEIM Baden, Germany. Most of the 14th cent. community was massacred in the Black Death persecutions of 1348–49 and the survivors were expelled. Jews were again present in the 15th cent. and following the Thirty Years War (1618–48) the Marx and Oppenheimer families constituted the backbone of the community for the next 300 years. The community reached a peak pop. of 132 in 1865 and opened a cemetery in 1874. In 1933, 38 Jews remained. Most left by 1938, with 26 emigrating. Of the nine moving to other German cities, seven were deported to the Gurs concentration camp on 22 Oct. 1940 and five perished.

SCHUPBACH (now part of Beselich) Hesse–Nassau, Germany. This district community established by Jews from Gaudernbach, Heckholzhausen, Obertiefenbach, and Wirbelau numbered around 180 in 1864 and was affiliated with the rabbinate of Bad Ems. The synagogue in S. was renovated in 1877 but the community dwindled. After *Kristallnacht* (9–10 Nov. 1938), none of the nine Jews who had lived there in 1933 remained.

SCHWABACH Middle Franconia, Germany. The 14th cent. community was destroyed in local riots in 1384. In the 16th cent. the Jews were expelled at least twice (1560, 1585). Their situation improved in the 17th cent. under the collective privilege accorded by the counts of Brandenburg to the *Landjudenschaft* organization of the Ansbach principality. S. was the seat of the chief rabbinate of the principality for 80 years, starting in 1709. In 1713, the first chief rabbi, Tzevi Hirsch Fraenkel, was charged with witchcraft and defaming Christianity and imprisoned for 24 years. Riots followed a libel in 1729 that Jews had desecrated Christian holy objects. In 1744 the community's religious books were impounded as in other important Bavarian communities on charges of anti-Christian teachings. Despite persecution the community flourished, dealing mainly in jewelry and horse trading. In the 19th cent. Jews found themselves reduced to petty trade, totally excluded from the crafts. In 1823 the Bavarian government reduced the legal number of resident J. families from 41 to 20. Nonetheless, the J. pop. reached 250 in 1837 (total 7,160). A yeshiva and *talmud torah* were opened during the cent. In 1880 the J. pop. stood at 143; in 1933, it was 38. After 1933 many Jews were arrested on various pretexts. All left by 1938, ten for Palestine and the last 13 after *Kristallnacht* (9–10 Nov. 1938).

SCHWAEBISCH GMUEND (among Jews, Gmunda) Wuerttemberg, Germany. Jews are first mentioned in 1241 and in 1258 were living in a J. quarter (preserved until 1936) that included a synagogue, *mikve*, and school. Many were murdered in the Rindfleisch massacres of 1298 and the settlement was destroyed in the Black Death persecutions of 1348–49. It was re-established in 1392 but ended when the Jews were expelled in 1501. It was officially renewed only in 1861 when sons of J. businessmen in nearby settlements came there to set up factories and other enterprises, including the town's first private bank. The prosperous community numbered 97 in 1890 (total 16,817), with a synagogue dedicated in 1926. Among J. businesses were a department store, movie theater, bus company, and toy factory. Though Jews were prominent in the life of the city despite their small numbers, there was also a measure of social ostracism. Under Nazi rule the situation of the Jews gradually worsened. Most of the Jews had to sell their businesses and on *Kristallnacht* (9–10 Nov. 1938), the synagogue was vandalized. Of the 90 Jews in the town in 1933, 60–65 emigrated, mostly to the U.S. and Palestine; around 20 were expelled to the east, only one surviving.

SCHWAEBISCH HALL (among Jews, Hall) Wuerttemberg, Germany. A J. quarter is known from the 13th cent. Jews were victims of the Black Death persecutions of 1348–49 and were expelled in 1379. Although reestablished in 1401 numerous restrictions kept the community down to a handful of Jews until the 19th cent. A synagogue decorated with wooden engravings was built in 1738–39. Under Wuerttemberg rule from the early 19th cent., the community grew to 263 in 1880 (total 9,222), absorbing Jews from neighboring Unterlimpurg and Steinbach. In 1933, there were 115 Jews in S. J. businesses included a cigarette factory. Virulent anti-J. agitation commenced at the outset of Nazi rule. On *Kristallnacht* (9–10 Nov. 1938), the local prayer house along with J. stores and residences were vandalized and the Steinbach synagogue was burned. About 90 Jews managed to emigrate; 22 perished after expulsion to the east in late 1941 and 1942. Late in the war, 800 mostly J. detainees were kept in a labor camp branch of the Dachau concentration camp at the local airfield. After the war a mass grave was discovered in the vicinity. Sixteen hundred J. Displaced Persons were held from late 1946 until 1948 in three transit camps on the outskirts of the city and during their stay there they organized a community. Most left for Israel in 1948.

SCHWALBACH, BAD see BAD SCHWALBACH.

SCHWANDORF Upper Palatinate, Germany. The J. pop. in 1933 was 23 (total 9,808). In 1937–42, 20 left the city, 13 emigrating to the U.S. and Argentina and seven moving to other German cities. Many Displaced Persons gathered in S. after the war. Numbering 470 in 1946, they dispersed in 1949 with the closing of the DP camps.

SCHWANENBERG Rhineland, Germany. Jews numbered 61 (total 1,133) in 1871 and 24 in 1925. The community maintained a cemetery and a small synagogue which was destroyed on *Kristallnacht* (9–10 Nov. 1938) along with J. homes and stores. Some Jews were subsequently deported to the Buchenwald and Sachsenhausen concentration camps.

SCHWANFELD Lower Franconia, Germany. Jews are mentioned in 1298 in connection with the Rindfleisch massacres. The J. cemetery served numerous communities in the 17th–18th cents. A synagogue was built in 1786 and 32 children were enrolled in the J. public school in 1850. The J. pop. numbered 230 in 1816 and declined steadily to 58 in 1933. Thirty-eight Jews left in 1936–40, 25 of them for the U.S. On *Kristallnacht* (9–10 Nov. 1938), the synagogue was vandalized and on 25 April 1942 eight Jews were deported to Izbica in the Lublin dist. (Poland). Three Jews were later sent to the Theresienstadt ghetto.

SCHWEDT AN DER ODER Brandenburg, Germany. In 1671, a protected Jew (*Schutzjude*) is mentioned. The J. pop. was 95 in 1812 and 235 in 1880. A cemetery was established in the 17th cent., a synagogue in 1789, followed by a new building in 1862. The first rabbi was engaged in 1841. The Jews played an important role in the town's economic life. Nearly exclusively, Jews traded in horses, and in 1911, Jews owned eight of the 20 tobacco-processing plants in S. When the Nazis came to power in 1933, the community numbered 111. On *Kristallnacht* (9–10 Nov. 1938), the synagogue was destroyed, J. apartments and businesses were wrecked and looted, and J. men were arrested. By May 1939, there were 27 Jews and 11 persons of partial J. origin (*Mischlinge*) in S. Until 1941, six Jews managed to emigrate and nine moved to Berlin and Stettin, from where they probably were deported as were those who stayed in S. The last Jew died in 1942.

SCHWEGENHEIM Palatinate, Germany. A synagogue was built in 1834 and in 1848 there were 12 families (44 Jews) in S. In 1932, the J. pop. was 25 (total 1,500). On *Kristallnacht* (9–10 Nov. 1938), the synagogue was vandalized and in Oct. 1940 the last six Jews were deported to the Gurs concentration camp. Four perished in the Holocaust.

SCHWEICH   Rhineland, Germany. There are indication of a protected Jew (*Schutzjude*) living in S. in 1639. A small community slowly developed, numbering 90 in 1843 and 95 in 1895. It maintained a cemetery, a synagogue concecrated in 1862, and a school. In June 1933, about four months after the Nazis assumed power, there were 91 Jews living in S. On *Kristallnacht* (9–10 Nov. 1938), the synagogue was looted and seriously damaged. By May 1939, only 14 Jews remained. Five were deported in Oct. 1941. Many who had hoped to find shelter in other German towns were also deported. In all, at least 52 Jews from S. lost their lives under the Nazis.

SCHWEIDNITZ   (Pol. Swidnica) Lower Silesia, Germany, today Poland. Jews were present no later than 1285 and had the use of a cemetery. In 1372, a Street of the Jews and synagogue were in existence. The Jews were accused of "desecration" in 1453 and a few were burned at the stake; the rest were expelled from the city. The community was only reestablished in the 19th cent., numbering 174 in 1849 and attaining a peak pop. of 339 in 1880. A new synagogue was consecrated in 1877. The J. pop. declined in the 20th cent., standing at 100 on the eve of the Nazi era. On *Kristallnacht* (9–10 Nov. 1938), rioters burned the synagogue and destroyed six J. homes and many J. stores as well as a J.-owned factory. The J. pop. was 49 in 1938, dropping to 23 in 1939. No further information is available on the fate of the community in WWII. Presumably those Jews unable to emigrate perished following deportation.

SCHWEINFURT   Lower Franconia, Germany. Jews are known from the early 13th cent. and suffered greatly in the Rindfleisch massacres of 1298 and the Black Death persecutions of 1348–49. Under King Sigismund in 1420 the Jews were granted various rights but were forced to pay exorbitant taxes to the town. Conditions worsened under Emperor Ferdinand in the 16th cent. In 1544 the municipality shut down the synagogue and in 1555 the Jews were expelled. The modern community began to develop significantly in the 1860s, reaching a pop. of 490 (total 12,601) in 1880. S. became the seat of the district rabbinate in 1864. Antisemitism intensified under the Weimar Republic. In 1933 there were 363 Jews in S. Many others from the surrounding villages settled there in the Nazi era. The community had local

branches of the Central Union (C.V.) and Zionist Organization. A J. public school was also in operation. By 1937 many J. cattle traders had to liquidate their businesses in the wake of the economic boycott. On *Kristallnacht* (9–10 Nov. 1938), Jews were attacked and their homes and shops damaged along with the synagogue. About 30 were sent to the Dachau concentration camp. In 1933–42, 225 Jews left Germany, including 110 for the U.S. Another 221 left for other German cities. Of those remaining in 1942, 30 were deported to Izbica in the Lublin dist. (Poland) via Wuerzburg on 24 Apr. and 60 to the Theresienstadt ghetto in Sept. 1942.

SCHWEINSBERG   (now part of Stadtallendorf) Hesse–Nassau, Germany. Jews lived there from the 17th cent., opened a synagogue in 1822, and numbered 52 (6% of the total) in 1871, dwindling to 27 in 1933. The synagogue was destroyed on *Kristallnacht* (9–10 Nov. 1938), and by 1939 most of the Jews had left; 13 perished in the Holocaust.

SCHWEINSHAUPTEN   Lower Franconia, Germany. The J. settlement commenced no later than the first half of the 18th cent. and reached a pop. of 200 (total 715) in 1837, declining to 13 in 1933. The synagogue was sold in 1937. Six emigrated (five to the U.S.) and five left for other German cities by 1940.

SCHWELM   Westphalia, Germany. Jews are mentioned in 1593–95 and maintained a community without interruption from the early 18th cent. A synagogue was erected in 1819 and a cemetery opened. For most of the 19th cent., a J. elementary school was in operation. In 1895, the J. pop. was 100, dropping to 54 in 1933. On *Kristallnacht* (9–10 Nov. 1938), the synagogue was wrecked and the J. cemetery desecrated. Most Jews left S. by late 1939, about a dozen going abroad. The few who remained were deported to the death camps.

SCHWERIN   Mecklenburg-Schwerin,   Germany. Jews are mentioned in S. from the mid-14th cent. A permanent J. settlement began to develop at the end of the 17th cent. The J. pop. was 284 in 1794, 324 in 1830 (3% of the total), and 391 in 1876. From its outset, the community had a prayer room and a cemetery. New synagogues were established in the 1770s as well as in 1819 and 1841, and additional cemeteries in

1717 and 1882. Tensions between the Liberal majority and the Orthodox minority culminated in the secession of the Orthodox in 1850. By the beginning of the 20th cent. the local J. pop. was less than 300, then dropping to 218 in 1910 and 175 in 1925. In the wake of this decline, the seat of the district rabbi (*Landrabbiner*), which had been in S. since 1763, was moved in 1926 to Rostock. When the Nazis came to power in 1933, there were 151 Jews in S. In 1936 there were 71 and a year later 54. The anti-J. hate campaign was particularly intensive in S. On *Kristallnacht* (9–10 Nov. 1938), the synagogue and J. stores were destroyed. The 16 J. men who were left in S. were arrested and detained in Neustrelitz, only being released in March 1939. In that year, only 38 Jews remained in S. and the Jews were moved to "J. houses." Three deportations were carried out in 1942, in the beginning of July and in Nov. Only seven Jews subsequently remained, married to non-Jews. In 1944, three were deported. After the war, a small J. community with 46 members in 1946 was established.

SCHWERIN AN DER WARTHE (Pol. Skwierzyna) Posen–West Prussia, Germany, today Poland. Jews are first mentioned in 1507. By 1631, Jews owned 12% of the town's houses and in 1674 the J. pop. stood at 110. In the 17th cent., a cemetery and a synagogue were established, the latter burning down in 1784 and being replaced by a new building only in 1841. The community numbered 906 in 1800 and 1,543 in 1838, at which point J. representation on the town council was restricted to one–third. By 1871, the J. pop. had shrunk to 640. On the eve of the Nazi assumption of power in 1933, the number of Jews was 80. On *Kristallnacht* (9–10 Nov. 1938), the synagogue was burned down. The end of the community came with the arrest of the remaining Jews and their internment in the Buergergarten camp near Schneidemuehl in March 1940. From there they were later deported to the east.

SCHWERTE Westphalia, Germany. Jews are first mentioned in 1448. The modern community, which began to develop in the 17th cent., maintained a synagogue that was built in 1854 and a cemetery. In 1890, the J. pop. reached a peak of 142. Seven Jews served on the city council between 1900 and 1932. In June 1933, 60 Jews remained in S. The synagogue was vandalized on *Kristallnacht* (9–10 Nov. 1938). Nineteen

Jews remained in May 1939; 14 of them were deported to the east in 1942–43.

SCHWETZINGEN Baden, Germany. The first Jews settled under the letter of protection given by Count Johann Wilhelm in 1698 to 125 J. families in the Palatinate. In 1795, the Court Jew and army supplier Raphael Lazarus Traumann, representing the well-known Kaulla family, settled in S. and became active in the local economy, with his descendants remaining a dominant force in community and commercial life up through the 20th cent. The J. pop. grew to 119 in 1880 (total 4,640). In 1867, Karl Traumann served as commissioner of police. Antisemitism intensified in the Weimar period, with the J. cemetery (opened in 1893) desecrated many times, but a liberal reaction was also felt. In 1933, 79 Jews remained, with others subsequently arriving. Under the Nazis, the J. prayer hall was immediately impounded and J. communal prayer was thereafter confined to private homes. Most children were sent to Mannheim and Heidelberg for their schooling in the face of severe persecution in local schools. Throughout the period, 34 Jews emigrated and 53 left for other German cities. On *Kristallnacht* (9–10 Nov. 1938), J. homes were heavily damaged and J. men were sent to the Dachau concentration camp and forced to sell their homes at token prices. Twenty-one Jews were left at the end of 1938. The last five Jews were deported to the Gurs concentration camp on 22 Oct. 1940. Another 15 were deported after leaving S. In all, 18 perished in the camps.

SCHWIEBUS (Pol. Swiedbodzin) Brandenburg, Germany, today Poland. The J. pop. was ten in 1849 and 80 in the 1880s and 1890s. The community established a cemetery in 1892 and a synagogue in 1922–23. When the Nazis came to power in 1933, there were about 90 Jews in the town. The pressure of Nazi rule and emigration compelled the community to sell the synagogue in Oct. 1938. By May 1939, only 15 Jews and eight persons of partial J. origin (*Mischlinge*) remained. It may be assumed that those who failed to emigrate were deported to the east. In Oct. 1942 there was one Jew in S., probably protected by marriage to a non-Jew.

SCULENI Moldavia dist., Rumania, today Republic of Moldova. Jews first settled in the early 19th cent. The J. pop. in 1899 was 416, dropping in 1930 to

150 (26% of the total). The Jews controlled virtually all the grain and cattle trade with Bessarabia. In June 1940, the local pop. expelled the Jews to Iasi, where many were murdered in June 1941.

SEBEZH   Kalinin dist., Russia. J. settlement probably began in the early 18th cent. The J. pop. in 1766 was 243, increasing to 2,561 (total 4,326) in 1897. A state J. elementary school was functioning in the early 20th cent. In the Soviet period, the J. pop. dropped to 1,813 in 1926 and 845 in 1939. A J. school and club were opened in 1926. A few days after occupying the town on 9 July 1941, the Germans murdered two Jews for alleged agitation. In March 1942 they murdered 96.

SEBIS   (Hung. Szaszsebes) S. Transylvania dist., Rumania. A J. community was established in 1800. In 1868 it defined itself as Neologist. The J. pop. was 65 in 1930 (3% of the total). In June 1941, the Jews were expelled to Arad and the men drafted for forced labor.

SECEMIN   Kielce dist., Poland. Jews are mentioned in 1763 and numbered 224 in 1921 (total 1,611). The 180 remaining in 1939 were deported by the Germans to the Treblinka death camp in Sept. 1942 along with 20 refugees.

SECOVCE   (Hung. Galszecs) Slovakia, Czechoslovakia, today Republic of Slovakia. Jews are mentioned in the first half of the 18th cent. In 1820, 60 families were present and by 1828 the community had a synagogue and other community institutions. A cholera epidemic devastated the community in 1831 but with an influx of Jews from neighboring settlements and Hasidim from Galicia it grew to over 1,000 by 1880. A Great Synagogue built in 1873 burned down twice. A new synagogue in the Moorish style was built in 1904 with a school in its courtyard. Jews were among the town's important merchants, dealing in grain, lumber, and alcoholic beverages. Following WWI, J. homes and businesses were looted in riots. In 1928, 156 children attended the J. elementary school. Jews were elected to the municipal council and among the Zionists, the Revisionists and Mizrachi were prominent. Most breadwinners (96) continued to engage in trade, with 28 practicing crafts. In 1940, the J. pop. was 1,138 (total 4,274). J. children were expelled from the public schools and the authorities closed down J. businesses. J. girls were deported to Auschwitz on 2 April 1942 and on 5 May, 300 Jews from S. and 250 from the neighborhood were transported to ghettoes and death camps in the Lublin dist. (Poland). In all, 85% of the local Jews were deported in 1942. Virtually all perished in the Holocaust. The other 15% were evacuated to western Slovakia in May 1944.

SECURENI   Bessarabia, Rumania, today Republic of Moldova. Jews first settled in the early 19th cent. Each J. artisans' union had its own synagogue and in 1922 the main synagogue was built alongside the Zionist clubhouse. During 1918–20, the number of J. refugees from the pogroms in the Ukraine arriving in S. equaled that of the indigenous pop. but the majority soon moved on to Palestine or the U.S. and other countries. In the early 20th cent. a J. elementary school and a high school opened in which the language of instruction was Hebrew. A Hebrew kindergarten also functioned. At first the Jews traded with communities across the Dniester River but when the border was closed by the Russians this source of income ended. Jews were in the forefront of the growing lambskin trade when S. became the major center in Bessarabia. Zionist activity existed even before the Balfour Declaration of 1917 and an organized movement began in 1922 and developed rapidly during the 1930s. The J. pop. in 1930 was 4,200 (73% of the total). When German and Rumanian troops entered S. on 6 July 1941, they were followed by peasants from the surrounding villages, and during the next three days 90 Jews were murdered, J. property was ransacked and goods pillaged. A short time later, the J. pop. was marched from S. to Briceni and from there moved in large groups through the country until the majority died off or were killed. After the expulsion of the Jews, S. became a camp for 30,000 Jews of the dist. until they were deported to Transnistria on 3 Oct. 1941. The 500 survivors who returned to S. after the war soon left.

SEDA   (Yid. Shad) Mazeikiai dist., Lithuania. Jews first settled here in the mid-18th cent., earning their living as merchants and artisans and from agriculture. In the 19th cent., J. communal life centered around the synagogues. Though most Jews were ultra-Orthodox, some were devotees of Haskala. A fire in 1886, at Passover, left more than 1,000 Jews homeless, causing many to emigrate overseas. The J. pop. in 1897 stood at 1,384 (69% of the total). Among the noted natives of S. was Yaakov Moshe Geri (Herring), who served as Israel's minister of commerce and industry. Between the World Wars emigration continued. In elections for the Lithuanian Sejm, most of S.'s Jews voted for the Zionist list. The J. pop. in 1940 was 400 (19%). After Germany's invasion in June 1941, Lithuanian nationalists began killing Jews. All the Jews were concentrated outside the town, the men being killed on 3 July 1941 and the women and children on 9 Aug.

SEDAN   (Charleville) Ardennes dist., France. The J. presence in S. dates from 1609. In 1630 the Jews were granted plots to build a synagogue and to open a cemetery. Jews were expelled in 1633 but a new community was founded in 1651. The community reorganized in the second half of the 19th cent. and built a synagogue in 1880. During WWII there was a labor camp in S. for Jews. In 1964 there were 240 Jews living in S.

SEDLCANY   Bohemia, Czechoslovakia. The J. settlement developed in the late 19th cent. Many Jews died in an 1866 cholera epidemic. In 1890 the J.

pop. was 175, dropping to 50 (total 2,431) in 1930. Most of the Jews were deported to the Theresienstadt ghetto together with the Jews of Prague in 1942 and from there to the death camps of Poland.

SEDUVA   (Yid. Shadeve) Panevezys dist., Lithuania. Jews first settled in the 15th cent. Many Jews came in the beginning of the 18th cent. at the invitation of Lithuania's vice chancellor. During the 1831 Polish rebellion, Jews suffered at the hands of both the rebels and the Cossacks. The main synagogue was dedicated in 1866. The J. pop. in 1897 was 2,513 (56% of the total), dropping sharply after WWI, when S. was almost totally destroyed. Between the World Wars, a J. community council ran community affairs. In the 1931 municipal elections, Jews won two of nine council seats. The deteriorating economic situation, verbal and physical attacks on Jews, a blood libel in 1931, and a boycott of J. businesses led many to emigrate to the U.S., South Africa, and Palestine. The young knew Hebrew and the Zionist movement won widespread support. In 1940 the J. pop. was about 800 (21%). After the German invasion in June 1941, Lithuanian nationalists abused, robbed, and murdered Jews and they were

Wedding in Seda, Lithuania, 1927

also seized for forced labor. All the Jews were killed during Aug. 1941, most in the Liaudiskiai forest on 25 Aug.

SĘDZISZOW Cracow dist., Poland. Few Jews were present until the late 17th cent. After a period of stagnation, economic conditions improved from 1860 with the coming of the railroad but again declined from 1882 when a large sugar refinery in the town was relocated. The J. pop. stood at 1,433 (half the total) in 1890. All but 12 Jews fled the town in WWI. Of these, ten were murdered by the Cossacks, and anti-J. riots took a further toll in Nov. 1918. The J. pop. in 1921 was 861. Though the community failed to recover economically between the World Wars, public life was spirited with the Zionists active. Under the German occupation a ghetto was set up around the end of June 1942, crowding together 1,900 Jews including refugees from the surrounding settlements. At the end of July, 400 children and old or disabled Jews were executed and the rest deported to the Belzec death camp.

SEEHEIM Hesse, Germany. Jews lived there from 1700, established a community in 1850, and numbered 78 (7% of the total) in 1861. Most Jews left, ten emigrating to the U.S. after 1933; five perished in the Holocaust.

SEESEN Brunswick, Germany. Although Jews lived there from 1456, no community was organized until 1801 when Israel Jacobson (1768-1828), who had succeeded his late father-in-law as district rabbi of the Weser region and court agent to the Duke of Brunswick, established a vocational school for poor J. children. Services held in an adjoining prayer room were attended by the seven J. families living in S. Thanks to its educational reforms, the school had 46 pupils in 1805 and numbered almost 100 (after 20 non-Jews were admitted) a year later. As first principal (1806-38), Bendet Schott (Schottlaender) introduced prayers in German and confirmation exercises instead of the traditional bar mitzva for boys. While serving as head of the Westphalian J. consistory, Jacobson built a new synagogue in 1810, designed like a church. The community grew from 54 in 1819 to 178 (over 5% of the total) in 1871 and 209 in 1895. Jacobson's heirs founded a nonsectarian orphanage in 1852 which continued to operate until 1923. Intermarriage

and apostasy increased. The community also had a few members in Gandersheim, but dwindled to 30 in 1933. On *Kristallnacht* (9-10 Nov. 1938) Nazis burned the synagogue, killed one Jew, and dispatched two others to the Buchenwald concentration camp. No more than six Jews emigrated; at least seven perished in the Holocaust.

SEGEBERG, BAD see BAD SEGEBERG.

SEIDLISZCZE Lublin dist., Poland. Most of the town's residents were Jews, with an organized community existing by 1780. In the 19th cent., it maintained two synagogues and a number of hasidic *shtiblekh*. The J. pop. increased to 1,331 in 1897, but dropped to 724 in 1921 following the Cossack depredations of WWI. Community life recovered under the aegis of Chelm, which initiated Zionist activity in S. The Bund became influential in the trade unions while Agudat Israel ran a Beth Jacob school for girls. In the 1930s, increasing antisemitism undermined J. livelihoods. The Germans captured S. on 15 Sept. 1939, finding 1,360 Jews there. Local Poles and *Volksdeutsche* robbed, beat, and humiliated Jews while the Germans introduced a regime of forced labor and extortion. In Dec. 1939, the synagogue was blown up. A few hundred refugees arrived from Lublin and Cracow and many died in a typhoid epidemic. On 18 May 1942 all but the able-bodied were deported to the Sobibor death camp; the latter were sent there on 22 Oct.

SEINI (Hung. Szinervaralja) N. Transylvania dist., Rumania. Jews from Galicia settled in the 1760s. Many owned land and vineyards. A Hebrew press founded in 1905 by Yaakov Weider printed 130 books and eight magazines up to the Holocaust. The J. pop. in 1930 was 673 (13%). Between the World Wars the economic situation of the Jews declined and over 200 left. Zionist activity began in 1924. In May 1944 the community was transferred to the Satu Mare ghetto and later deported to Auschwitz.

SEIRIJAI (Yid. Serhai, Serai) Alytus dist., Lithuania. Jews first settled in the 18th cent., building a synagogue in 1726. In the 1890s many Jews emigrated to the west. The community had a *talmud torah* and a reformed *heder* which taught mathematics and Russian as well as religious subjects. The Zionist movement became entrenched in the 1880s with the Hovevei Zion organization active and contributions made for the settlement of Eretz Israel. The J. pop. in 1897 stood at 1,614 (60% of the total). During WWI the Jews were exiled; half returned later. Between the World Wars, a J. community council imposed taxes and administered all areas of J. life. The community maintained a J. elementary school and a number of welfare institutions. David Gordon, the editor of the first Hebrew journal, *Ha-Maggid*, resided here for six years. In the 1924 municipal elections four Jews were elected to the town council. Many Jews emigrated to the U.S., Mexico, South Africa, and Palestine following a boycott by the Lithuanian merchants association. In 1934, an urban kibbutz was established in S. The J. pop. in 1940 stood at about 800 (40% of the total). After Germany's invasion in June 1941, many young Jews were killed. The remaining 953 were murdered on 10–11 Sept. 1941 in the Avreisak woods.

SEJNY Bialystok dist., Poland. Jews settled in the 17th cent., conducting a flourishing trade with the cities of Lithuania. They operated as grain wholesalers and lumber merchants and owned a flour mill, sawmill, and distillery. The synagogue consecrated in 1778 was an oustanding example of wooden synagogue construction in Poland. In the early 19th cent. the community was served by R. Yehuda Bacharach, one of the leading rabbis of the time. The community reached a peak pop. of 2,368 (total 3,283) in 1857, dropping to 1,918 in 1897 and 661 in 1921 as a process of proletarianization and economic decline set in. The Zionists became active in 1898, founding a Hebrew elementary school and kindergarten immediately after WWI. In Oct. 1939, the Germans expelled the town's 573 Jews toward the Lithuanian border, holding them in an open field for over two weeks when the Lithuanians refused to permit their passage. Most ultimately managed to cross the border and suffered the fate of Lithuanian Jewry.

SELESTAT Bas-Rhin dist., France. The first Jews settled here in the second half of the 12th cent. The community had a yeshiva headed by R. Shemuel of Selestat. The local Jews were mainly engaged in moneylending. During the Black Death persecutions of 1348–49, the Jews were expelled, but some returned after obtaining various privileges. The community was renewed in the 19th cent., and in 1846 there were 200 Jews in S. A synagogue was inaugurated in 1890. By

1885, there were 1,635 Jews in the S. dist., dropping to 1,417 in 1895 and then to 1,030 in 1910 and 716 in 1931. In S. itself, there were 375 community members in 1900. On the eve of WWII the 213 Jews in S. were expelled during the occupation to the south of France with the rest of the Jews of Alsace-Lorraine. The Nazis deported 64 of them. The synagogue was destroyed during the war and then rebuilt in 1960, when the community consisted of about 180 members.

SELETIN Bukovina, Rumania, today Ukraine. Jews settled in the mid-19th cent. The J. pop. in 1930 was 736 (18% of the total). Antisemitism was widespread in the 1930s. In June 1940, Jews were exiled by the Soviets to Siberia and none returned. After the Rumanian and German conquest in 1941, the J. pop. was marched to Radauti and a month later deported to Transnistria. Only a tenth survived.

SELETS Mogilev dist., Belorussia. S. was founded as an agricultural colony on leased land in 1836 and reached a J. pop. of 561 (total 604) in 1897. In 1924–25, under the Soviets, 80 J. families (448 Jews) were engaged in farming. A J. rural council (soviet) was established in 1927 and a J. elementary school (four grades) was active. The Germans occupied S. in July 1941 and presumably murdered the Jews in the fall, together with the Jews of the Bykhov region.

SELIBA Mogilev dist., Belorussia. S. was founded as a J. rural settlement in the late 19th cent. and reached a pop. of 893 in 1897. Most Jews farmed. In 1919, during the civil war, rioting Polish soldiers murdered 17 Jews and looted their property. In 1923, under the Soviets, a rampaging gang attacked the settlement and caused heavy damage to J. property. The marauders burned houses and crops, but were chased off before they could take any lives. At this time, the J. pop. embraced 40 families working 500 acres of land. In 1924–25, 34 families (209 Jews) were farming and in 1930 the settlement became a kolkhoz supporting 11 J. families. A four-year J. elementary school was in existence from 1920. The Germans arrived in July 1941 and probably murdered the Jews in the fall.

SELIBA-YAKSHITSKAYA Mogilev dist., Belorussia. S. was founded as a J. colony on J.-owned land in 1846 and reached a pop. of 46 families (265 Jews) working 1,850 acres in 1898. In 1925, under the Soviets, the J. pop. was 496, including 97 families engaged in agriculture. In 1930 the settlement was converted into a kolkhoz that accommodated 40 J. families. The Germans occupied the area in July 1941 and presumably murdered the Jews in Dec. together with the Jews of Berezino.

SELICE   Slovakia, Czechoslovakia, today Republic of Slovakia. Jews probably settled in first half of the 18th cent. Their pop. rose to 124 in 1828 and 140 (total 1,480) in 1869 and then declined steadily to 15 in 1930. After the annexation to Hungary, J. men were mobilized for forced labor. In mid-June 1944, the Jews were deported to Auschwitz via Nove Zamky.

SELIGENSTADT   Hesse, Germany. Nominally protected by the Archbishop of Mainz, Jews fell victim to the Black Death persecutions of 1348–49. The Jews were banished in 1470 and only returned after the Thirty Years War (1618–48). Though no longer confined to the J. quarter (*Judengasse*) during the 18th cent., they met with civil and commercial discrimination. Numbering 121 (over 4% of the total) in 1828, the community dedicated a new synagogue in 1872. The community was affiliated with the Offenbach rabbinate and grew to 289 (8%) in 1880. By then Jews had entered the professions and were taking an interest in civic affairs and developing their own cultural life. Moses Hamburger, their veteran religious leader (1868–1930), was a noted musician and choir director. The J. pop. had shrunk to 146 when Nazi persecution began in April 1933. The synagogue was burned down on *Kristallnacht* (9–10 Nov. 1938) and Karl Nover, the former burgomaster, later risked his own life by smuggling food to "non-Aryans." By 1942, 90 Jews had left S., 47 emigrating (mostly to the U.S.); at least 56 perished in the Holocaust.

SELLYE   Baranya dist., Hungary. A community of 92 existed in 1880, dropping to 54 in 1930. At the end of May 1944, the Jews were transferred to Siklos en route to Auschwitz.

SELO-SLATINA   (Hung. Faluszlatina; Yid. Slaptina) Carpatho-Russia, Czechoslovakia, today Ukraine. J. settlement probably commenced in the early 18th cent. with the arrival of a few families from Galicia. In 1830, the J. pop. was 218, rising to 674 (total 3,642) in 1880. An organized community was appa-

Synagogue in Seligenstadt, Germany

rently established in the early 19th cent., maintaining various welfare and charity institutions. In the Czechoslovakian period, a yeshiva founded by the community's rabbi, Hayyim Yitzhak Halberstam, was active with an enrollment of 150 students. The J. pop. reached 1,785 in 1921 and 2,537 in 1941. Jews owned 62 business establishments, 35 workshops, and four factories. A few were white-collar workers and professionals. The Zionist and religious political parties were especially active. The Hungarians occupied the town in March 1939, undermining J. livelihoods and in 1940 drafting many Jews into forced labor battalions and sending some to the eastern front. In late July 1941, a number of J. families without Hungarian citizenship were expelled to Kamenets-Podolski, where they were murdered. Following the German occupation of March 1944, 2,044 Jews from S. and another 3,000 from the surrounding area were transferred to an improvised ghetto. In the second half of May, they were deported to Auschwitz in two transports. A few dozen surviving families returned after the war but most left for Czechoslovakia.

SELTERS (now part of Loehnberg) Hesse–Nassau, Germany. Established after 1800, the community drew members from neighboring villages, numbered 101 (8% of the pop.) in 1905, and was affiliated with the Bad Ems rabbinate before WWI. It had J. youth and women's organizations as well as a library. On *Kristallnacht* (9–10 Nov. 1938), the synagogue was burned down and most Jews left the district, 27 emigrating by 1939.

SELTSO Oriol dist., Russia. Jews probably settled in the late 19th cent. In 1939, they numbered 107 (total 8,462). The Germans arrived in early Oct. 1941 and murdered the few Jews who had neither fled nor been evacuated.

SEMELISKES (Yid. Semilishok) Troki dist., Lithuania. Jews first settled in the 18th cent. Communal activity centered around the synagogue and study groups. The Zionist movement won widespread support. In 1897, the Jews numbered 300 (31% of the total). They earned their living as merchants and artisans. In 1940, the J. pop. included 60 families and 200 Polish refugees. After Germany's invasion in June 1941, all the Jews were put in a crowded ghetto. The men were taken to forced labor. By 6 Oct. 1941, the Lithuanians had killed all the Jews. Several Jews whom Lithuanian peasants assisted to escape later joined the Soviet partisans.

SEMIONOVKA (I) Chernigov dist., Ukraine. Fewer than 500 Jews were present in the late 19th cent. Pogroms occurred in 1905 and in 1919. A yeshiva with 100 students and providing all the religious services was maintained clandestinely in the first half of the 1920s. A kolkhoz was founded by about 45 J. families and a J. school was also opened. The J. pop. was 852 in 1926 and 402 (total 7,465) in 1939. The Germans captured S. on 25 Aug. 1941 after some of the Jews fled. Those remaining were confined in a ghetto. In Dec., 58 were murdered outside the town.

SEMIONOVKA (II) Poltava dist., Ukraine. The J. pop. was 319 (total 1,487) in 1897. A J. kolkhoz was founded between the World Wars. In 1939 the J. pop. was 143. After their arrival on 12 Sept. 1941, the Germans murdered the Jews who had neither fled nor been evacuated.

SEMPOLNO Pomerania dist., Poland. Jews first settled in 1644 under broad residence and trade rights accorded by the town's proprietor to promote its development. Most of the Jews were petty traders and shopkeepers. Full equality was only achieved in the second half of the 19th cent. In 1808 a new synagogue was erected which remained standing until WWII. The J. pop. reached a peak of 1,218 (total 3,187) in 1853, thereafter declining through emigration to the big cities and across the sea. In 1921, 183 Jews remained. Anti-J. agitation intensified in the 1930s. The remaining Jews were probably expelled by the Germans to General Gouvernement territory by the end of 1939.

SENA Slovakia, Czechoslovakia, today Republic of Slovakia. Jews probably settled in the first half of the 18th cent., erecting a synagogue in the 1780s and reaching a peak pop. of nearly 300 in the late 19th cent. The community also maintained a J. elementary school for a few dozen children. From the early 20th cent., the J. pop. began to decline through emigration to the big cities. The J. pop. was 136 in 1919 (total 1,538) and 85 in 1941. The annexation to Hungary in Nov. 1938 brought persecution and on 16 May 1944 the remaining Jews were deported to Auschwitz.

SENDZISZOW Kielce dist., Poland. Jews hired from nearby settlements and from Russia in the 1880s to build a new railway line subsequently settled in S. An egg-packing plant, the crab-fishing industry, and the summer tourist trade provided work. In the early 1890s, the village was bought from its proprietor by a Jew, who contributed much to the community's development before selling it to Polish businessmen in the 1920s. In 1918, the J. pop. was 300. All suffered grievously from outbreaks of Polish antisemitism in 1918–19, followed by the collapse of their businesses under heavy taxes and Polish competition in the postwar economic crisis. Zionist activity was extensive between the World Wars. The Germans arrived in Sept. 1939, setting up a *Judenrat*. Three labor camps set up near the railway station held 300 Jews who were later sent to the Skarzysko-Kamienna labor camp. In Sept. 1942, most of S.'s 400 Jews were deported to the Treblinka death camp.

SENEC (Hung. Szempc) Slovakia, Czechoslovakia, today Republic of Slovakia. Jews were present in the

Jews wishing to leave for Palestine demonstrating in the town square of Sempolno, Poland

16th cent. and returned after 1686 when the invading Turks withdrew. They apparently again abandoned the town in the mid-18th cent. In the 1830s, the Jews formed an organized community, which grew significantly in the late 19th cent., from a pop. of 168 in 1869 to 416 (total 3,135) in 1880. A J. elementary school was also opened in this period and late in the cent. a splendid synagogue was erected. In the post-WWI Czechoslovakian Republic, Jews were active in public life and owned 45 business establishments, 17 workshops, and three factories. Both the Zionists and Agudat Israel were active. In 1940 the J. pop. was 450. In 1940–41, the Hungarian authorities seized dozens of Jews for forced labor. On 15 June 1944, the remaining Jews were deported to Auschwitz via Nove Zamky.

SENICA   (Yid. Semnitz) Slovakia, Czechoslovakia, today Republic of Slovakia. Jews settled in the early 17th cent., possibly before, and came to constitute one of the largest J. communities in Slovakia with a pop. of 104 in 1727, most coming from Moravia.

Jews were peddlers and shopkeepers. In 1739, three Jews falsely accused of theft were executed. The community grew to 550 in 1787 and 1,128 (total 2,713) in 1869, making it the second largest in the Nitra dist. after Nove Mesto. J. property was looted in the Easter riots of 1848. A J. elementary school was opened in 1846 with 120 students and 100 studied in a yeshiva. In 1866, a new synagogue was consecrated. The Zionists became active in the early 20th cent. After WWI, Mizrachi and WIZO were active. Agudat Israel was also influential. With the exodus of the young to the big cities, the J. pop. dropped to 304 in 1940. Between the World Wars, Jews served on the municipal council and owned 63 business establishments, 20 workshops, and seven factories (building materials, malt, candy, and a distillery). In the Slovakian state, J. children were expelled from the public schools and the authorities closed down or "Aryanized" J. businesses. In late March 1942, young J. men were deported to the Majdanek concentration camp and the women to Auschwitz. Families were deported to the death camps of Poland via Sered in April and June. Most of the 62 still in the town before the Germans arrived in Sept. 1944 managed to escape.

SENNFELD Baden, Germany. Jews first settled in the 17th cent. A synagogue was built in 1836 and the J. pop. rose to 121 in 1875 (total 1,253). In 1933, the J. pop. stood at 56. From 1936, a pioneer training farm was operated, preparing Zionist youth for *aliya*. On *Kristallnacht* (9–10 Nov. 1938), while the synagogue was being vandalized, the farm was attacked and Jews there were severely beaten. Including the pioneer youth, 143 Jews were present in S. in the Nazi period; 30 emigrated and 80 left for other German cities, most of them also emigrating. Another 22 perished in the camps, most being deported to the Gurs concentration camp on 22 Oct. 1940.

SENNO Vitebsk dist., Belorussia. Jews settled in the mid-17th cent. Their pop. was 480 in 1803 and 2,471 (total 4,000) in 1897. In this period, six synagogues were operating in the community, including one belonging to the followers of the Lubavich Rebbe. In 1924, under the Soviets, a J. council (soviet) was established. A J. elementary school attended by 160 children was also active. Thirty-seven J. families worked at nearby kolkhozes in 1930. In 1939, the J. pop. was 1,056. The Germans captured the town in late July 1941 and in Aug. set up a ghetto and *Judenrat* under a regime of starvation and forced labor. In Dec., all 965 Jews there were murdered near the village of Kozlovka. Children of mixed marriages were murdered afterwards.

SENSBURG (Pol. Mragowo) East Prussia, Germany, today Poland. The J. pop. was 78 in 1839, 171 in 1871, and 106 in 1905. A cemetery was established about 1820. The synagogue burned down about 1890 and was replaced by a new building. It was desecrated in 1930. Of the 66 Jews who were living in S. when the Nazis took over in 1933, not one was left in the town by May 1939. No information about their fate under Nazi rule is available.

SENTA Vojvodina dist., Yugoslavia. The first records of Jews and a J. community date back to the late 18th cent. Jews were killed during the Hungarian revolt of 1848. In 1867 the Jews received full civil rights from the Hungarian government. In the early 20th cent. the community was split between the moderately religious and smaller ultra-Orthodox sector. Between the World Wars the community thrived and enjoyed complete freedom in all branches of the economy. In 1931 it numbered 1,374 (total 31,969). Zionist groups were active during the period and a small number emigrated to Palestine in the 1920s and 1930s. The Hungarians arrived in 1941 and inaugurated a regime of persecution. Some Jews were taken to forced labor and five youths were executed. In 1942, all men under 50 were drafted into labor battalions; only a few survived. In 1944, with the German invasion, the remaining Jews were taken to Auschwitz. A few managed to reach Austria and survived. The community was reestablished after the war.

SERED Slovakia, Czechoslovakia, today Republic of Slovakia. Moravian refugees apparently founded the community after the Uhersky Brod massacre in 1683. In the 18th cent., most Jews were itinerant peddlers. A synagogue and school were opened late in the cent. In 1848, 3,000 rioting peasants looted J. homes and vandalized the synagogue, pillaging the Esterhazy castle and the Catholic church as well. The J. pop. grew from 333 in 1828 to a peak of 1,354 (total 5,004) in 1880 as Jews entered an era of economic prosperity as merchants, estate owners, and industrialists. In 1918, Jews fought off riots directed against them. From 1920, R. Moshe Asher Eckstein, one of the outstanding spiritual leaders of Czechoslovakian Jewry, served as rabbi, also running a highly esteemed yeshiva with 80 students. Agudat Israel was influential, with Orthodox girls attending its Beth Jacob school. Among the Zionists, Mizrachi and WIZO were especially active as were the youth movements. Jews served on the municipal council. In 1940, 726 Jews remained in S. In the Slovakian state, they were subjected to a regime of severe persecution and forced labor. In March and April 1942, dozens of young Jews were deported to the Majdanek concentration camp and Auschwitz. On 12 April, there was a deportation of about 350 in which the men were sent to Majdanek and the rest to Lubartow, Poland; on 7 June another 60 were sent to the Sobibor death camp; and in Aug. 50 to Auschwitz. A local concentration camp processed thousands of Jews for deportation to the east in 1942. In Sept. 1944–March 1945, another 13,000 Jews passed through en route to Auschwitz and other death camps.